3   *584.4 ALR*

LEARNING.
services

01209 722146

Duchy College Rosewarne
Learning Centre

This resource is to be returned on or before the last date stamped below. To renew items please contact the Centre

Three Week Loan

D1321151

THE MARIE SELBY
BOTANICAL GARDENS

ILLUSTRATED
DICTIONARY

OF ORCHID GENERA

Published in Association with

Selby Botanical Gardens Press
811 South Palm Avenue, Sarasota, Florida 34236
Phone: 941-955-7553, ext. 315 • Fax: 941-951-1474
www.selby.org

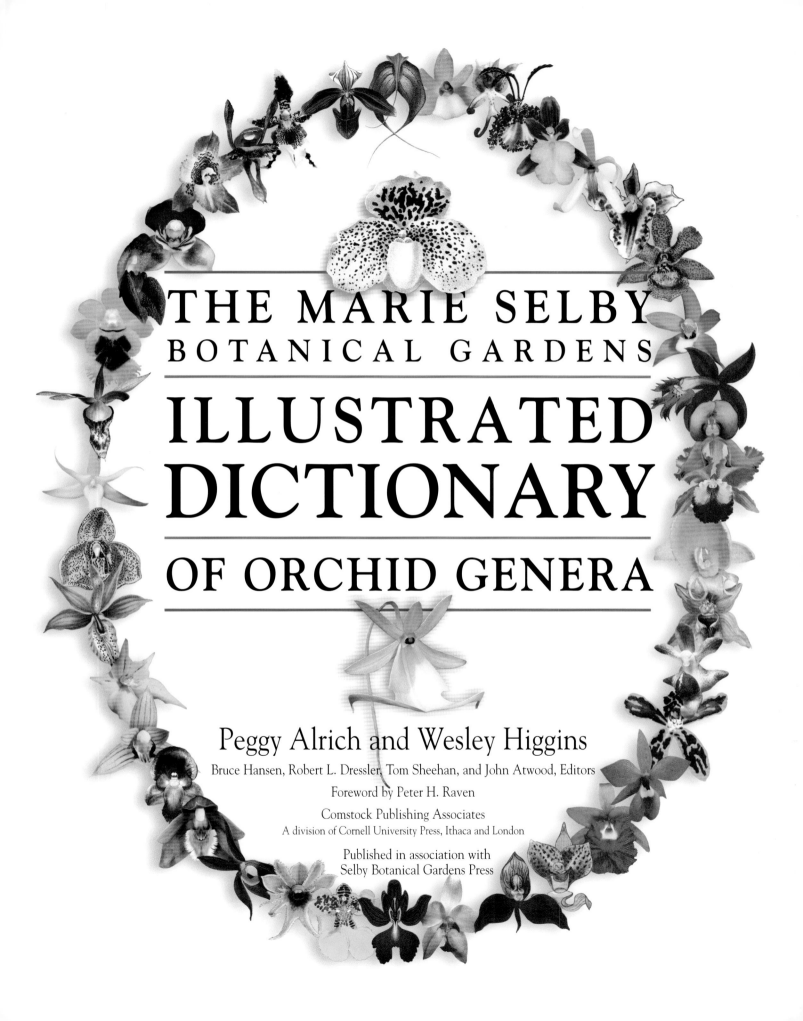

THE MARIE SELBY
BOTANICAL GARDENS

ILLUSTRATED
DICTIONARY
OF ORCHID GENERA

Peggy Alrich and Wesley Higgins

Bruce Hansen, Robert L. Dressler, Tom Sheehan, and John Atwood, Editors

Foreword by Peter H. Raven

Comstock Publishing Associates
A division of Cornell University Press, Ithaca and London

Published in association with
Selby Botanical Gardens Press

Copyright © 2008 by Selby Botanical Gardens Press

All rights reserved. Except for brief quotations in a review, this book, or parts thereof, must not be reproduced in any form without permission in writing from the publisher. For information, address Cornell University Press, Sage House, 512 East State Street, Ithaca, New York 14850.

Published in association with Selby Botanical Gardens Press, 811 South Palm Avenue, Sarasota, Florida 34236; www.selby.org

First published 2008 by Cornell University Press
Text and illustrations © Selby Botanical Gardens Press
Title page illustration by Peggy Alrich

Printed in China

Library of Congress Cataloging-in-Publication Data

Alrich, Peggy.
    The Marie Selby Botanical Gardens illustrated dictionary of orchid genera / Peggy Alrich and Wesley Higgins; edited by Bruce Hansen ... [et al.]; foreword by Peter H. Raven.
        p. cm.
    Includes bibliographical references.
    ISBN 978-0-8014-4737-2 (cloth : alk. paper)
    1. Orchids—Dictionaries. 2. Orchids—Classification. I. Higgins, Wesley E. II. Hansen, Bruce F.
III. Marie Selby Botanical Gardens. IV. Title.
    QK495.O64A446 2008
    584'.4—dc22
                                        2008011625

Cornell University Press strives to use environmentally responsible suppliers and materials to the fullest extent possible in the publishing of its books. Such materials include vegetable-based, low-VOC inks and acid-free papers that are recycled, totally chlorine-free, or partly composed of nonwood fibers. For further information, visit our website at www.cornellpress.cornell.edu.

Cloth printing   10 9 8 7 6 5 4 3 2 1

Dedicated to
Don and Sandy Coate
without whose love, care and support
this book would not have happened

F. Sanders *Reichenbachia* series 1, plate 10 (1888).

ORCHID GENERA

TABLE OF CONTENTS

❧

Van Standelcruyt. Cap. CCLXX.

Den naem.

A   Standelcruyt wordt in Griecx gheheeten Satyrion Triphyllon / ende in Latijn Satyrion trifolium. Bij onsen tijden heetment Testiculus vulpis oft sacerdotis / en dat niet sonder redene.

Faetsoen.

Standelcruyt en heeft ghemeynlick niet meer dan drij bladeren / die ghelijcken den bladeren van witte Lelien / maer si sijn cleynder ende wat rooder. Het heeft eenen naeckten steel / die is ontrent een elle lanck. Ende int sop van desen steel wassen witte bloemen / die sijn den witte Lelien bij na ghelijck / maer sij sijn veel cleynder. De wortelen sijn ghefaetsoeneert ghelijck twee ronde nootkens / ende die sijn buyten lijfverwich / ende binnen wit / ende sij hebben eenen sueten

B   lieflijcken smaeck / en sij en hebben niet veel veeselinghen / ende deen is grooter dan dander.

Plaetse sijnder wassinghe.

Men vindet dit Standelcruyt in beemden die aen berghen liggen / ende op plaetsen daer de sonne veel schijnt.

Den tijt.

Standelcruyt bloeyt meest in Junio.

Natuer ende complexie.

Ghemerct dat Standelcruyt eene suete smaec heeft / so moetet ooc werm ende vochtich sijn.

C   ### Cracht ende operatie.

De wortel van dit ghewas in rooden wijn ghedroncken / maect lust ende begeerte om bijslapen. In deser manieren wordet oock ghebruyckt / en tis goet voor den cramp die achterwaert trect. Plinius scrijft / datmen eenen sone sal crijgen / alsmen de onderste wortel inneempt die oock grooter is. Ende ist datmen de opperste wortel inneempt / die oock de cleynste is / soo salt een dochter sijn.

Satyrium trifolium.
Standelcruyt.

Van Cruys=

ORCHID GENERA

FOREWORD

The hundreds of orchid genera and thousands of species can seem unbelievably complex, but they are beautiful, mysterious, and alluring. Therefore we want reliable ways in which to refer to them — ways that will be understood by those who hear us or read our written communications about these fascinating plants. Though the practice of naming organisms began before we had written works, we can be sure that our ancestors who lived in areas where there were many kinds of orchids had names for only a few of them. They were not good to eat, not useful as building materials, nor, except for a very few, sources of medicine. But they must have been dazzling and perplexing for everyone who came into contact with them! A few hundred years ago, people began seriously to try to sort out the orchids that they found and to which they wanted to refer, and they began giving them names. In Victorian times, keeping orchids in heated green-houses became very fashionable, and having dependable names for them became important.

The exploration of the tropics over the past two centuries has led to an explosive growth in the number of known species of orchids, and dozens more are found each year in the cloud forests of Latin America, the slopes and treetops of Southeast Asia, and the hidden forested places of New Guinea. No one knows how many species of orchids may eventually be found, but the 850 or so accepted genera described in this useful book are unlikely to be increased greatly by further exploration. Thus the set of genera provide a kind of stable base around which the extraordinary diversity of this most numerous group of plants can be grouped, and provide a key to the patterns of variation that have been shaped by evolution over the tens of millions of years that the family has existed. Today, comparisons of sequences of bases in the plants' DNA have made it possible to deduce the outlines of that evolutionary explosion, to group genera with confidence, and to find some instances in which basically unrelated kinds of plants have been traditionally grouped together because of some evident shared features.

An understanding of the genera of orchids, their morphological features, species and names provides a vital key, by virtue of which it is possible to communicate clearly about these remarkable plants. To the extent possible, all of the names that have been applied to orchid genera are included here; and for the recognized genera, descriptive material about their features and their distribution have been added. The orchid enthusiast will appreciate having this volume always available for ready reference, since the framework it presents is an indispensable guide to the seemingly endless variety exhibited by the plants of this family. Furthermore, the useful profile of the family, written by David Benzing, makes it possible to understand the relationships among the genera as they are set forth and to appreciate the principal features that are used in their classification.

In 2007, we celebrated the 300th anniversary of the birth of the great Swedish naturalist Carl Linnaeus, whose encyclopedic work on all of the kinds of plants known at that time, the *Species Plantarum* of 1753, provides the starting point for all botanical names. For his genera, Linnaeus utilized names that had most often been used by other earlier scientists, which were in many instances the standard Latin or Latinized Greek names of the plants that had been used in older classical literature. Like a number of botanists who preceded him, Linnaeus found that no existing names were available for many kinds of plants, and for these he coined names; he tried to select distinctive ones that would be memorable because they reflected the characteristics by which these plants could be distinguished from others, or had some connection with people, geographical areas, or other features of their history or present occurrence. To Linnaeus, genera remained the fundamental unit of classification and communication, and so they still are today. He gave descriptive epithets to each of the species that he distinguished within these. Combined with the genera, the binomials formed by the combination of the generic name with the specific epithet, such as *Corallorhiza maculata*, became through general agreement the accepted names for species from 1753 onward. It was, however, the genera that formed the main point of communication about plants (and other organisms), and it is the genera that are featured in this convenient reference book.

In summary, Peggy and Wesley have written a book that will become a convenient reference for those many people who are fascinated by orchids. By referring to this guide, one can find a secure mooring for any species of orchid, one that makes it possible to understand its relatives and its place in the galaxy of orchid variation. They have performed a real service by bringing this material together for our use. This book has lasting value and will be consulted often and usefully over the decades to come.

Peter A. Raven

Peter Hamilton Raven
President, Missouri Botanical Garden and
George Engelmann Professor of Botany,
Washington University in St. Louis

ORCHID GENERA

PREFACE

Little did we know when deciding to produce this dictionary how much information would have to be assembled to make it exhaustive. Our task required recording every genus name published through 2007, both those done validly and invalidly and for fossil and pre-Linnaean taxa; no less important were the many orthographic variants on original spellings. Approximately 850 orchid genera are recognized today, but the number described in this volume is more than three times greater.

Preceding the dictionary is an introductory chapter that describes the plant features that botanists use to distinguish orchid genera. It also explains why Orchidaceae is the most species-rich, and in many ways, the most specialized family within Division Magnoliophyta. Particularly germane to deeper understanding of the orchids is familiarity with current thinking about why the flowers of these plants exhibit such diversity and intricacy compared with those displayed by the memberships of most of the other families of flowering plants.

Another point worth comment at the outset is the presently unstable state of orchid taxonomy. Despite the immense amount of effort already devoted to inquiries about orchid phylogeny, a subject that in turn influences orchid nomenclature, much ambiguity remains. More DNA must be sequenced and more morphological characters must be assessed before a definitive, that is, stable, classification is possible. In the meantime, the assignments in this volume of the recognized orchid genera to specific subtribes, tribes, and subfamily's must be considered tentative. A significant number of these decisions will prove incorrect as the relationships among the orchids become better resolved.

Our claim comes down to this: The material presented in this volume constitutes early 21st-century thinking on orchid systematics and a pre-2008 record of orchid nomenclature at the level of the genus. On point two, this volume presents the most complete listing of published orchid genus names available to date. This is so because the current taxonomic databases (ING, IPNI, IK, APNI, Harvard Grey Cards) do not always agree and have omissions and citation errors. Where possible, we compared citations with the original literature or indicated as "cited by."

Finally, we believe that the information provided herein can serve as a starting point for beginners as well as a definitive reference for seasoned professionals. It is our hope that users who fit the first definition will find this dictionary inspiring enough to pursue their interests further. Orchids are for everyone whether the consumer is a hobbyist captivated by botanical beauty or a biologist seeking subjects well-suited for investigating natural phenomena as disparate as pollinator-driven speciation and the physiology of drought tolerance.

ORCHID GENERA

A PROFILE OF THE FAMILY

by David H. Benzing

ew authorities would challenge the supposition that Orchidaceæ not only exceeds all of the other flowering plant families for species richness but also sets the record for adaptive variety and novelty. To appreciate this reality is to recognize that the modern orchids constitute the products of one of the most spectacular of all botanical radiations. Indeed, this single family, probably more than any other among the 400 or so that constitute the flowering plants, explains why Division Magnoliophyta exceeds the rest of the land flora combined for structural and functional sophistication.

This opening chapter profiles Orchidaceæ in three subject areas. Most useful for the nonspecialist are the treatments of the family's characteristic vegetative and reproductive morphology, biogeography, ecology, geologic history, and evolution and systematics. Included in these first order discussions are definitions of many of the technical terms, such as saprophyte, pseudobulb, and sympodial architecture, that botanists, including the authors of this dictionary, use to describe orchids.

Familiarity with the second, more technical subject area is less essential to make good use of the descriptions of the genera provided in this dictionary. These discussions detail how the orchids reproduce and conduct photosynthesis, and how they obtain mineral nutrients and mediate water balance by means of highly specialized flowers and seeds and roots and shoots, respectively. Likewise, subject area three is of less importance to most dictionary users because it concerns current thinking about why Orchidaceæ is so species-rich. It also suggests strategies for further inquiry aimed at fuller understandings of why the orchids have become so numerous, and how so many of them so successfully exploit extreme habitats and engage in such extraordinary lifestyles.

This introductory chapter also illustrates why Orchidaceæ is one of the best sources among the families of flowering plants for candidates on which to study plant adaptation and speciation. Growers will find this information on vegetative structure and function and growing conditions to be useful for practical applications.

Vital statistics and defining characteristics

The statistic most often mentioned in the literature is the family's immense numerical size, which comprises 17,000 to 35,000 species depending on the authority. Moreover, a stream of new discoveries continues to expand Orchidaceæ's lead over its closest contenders, the most impressive of which is undoubtedly Asteraceæ.

More interesting than family size are the reasons for this impressive record. One of them appears to be extreme seed reduction made possible by reliance on fungi for germination and seedling nutrition (Figure 1 I-J). Equally significant is the hyper-ovulate ovary with its matching pollen delivery device called a pollinarium (Figure 1 C, E). Readers need only peruse a few pages of this dictionary to appreciate still another contributing feature, namely the unparalleled complexity of the orchid flower.

Still another impressive statistic concerns ecology. Orchidaceæ account for at least half of the vascular epiphytes, with approximately 75 percent of its membership native to forest canopy habitats (Kress 1986). The remaining species exploit disparate terrestrial substrates distributed from the equator to the Arctic Circle and south to Tierra del Fuego. But diversity peaks in tropical highlands, with the densest concentrations of species occurring in the Andes of northern South America and in Australasia, particularly the mountains of New Guinea. The life zones are fragmented by elevation, geography, or climate, creating a dissected topography that helps to explain the pronounced insularity exhibited by so many of the tropical orchids.

Orchids lack woody tissue, or more fundamentally, the vascular cambium needed to produce it, as do almost all of the members of Class Liliopsida (the monocots). All Orchidaceæ live potentially extended lives as perennials that produce new sets of organs, growing in modular fashion, as the older ones die (Figure 2A-D, F) — a predominant feature among the monocots. Similarly, all orchids flower repeatedly, although how they accomplish this feat varies according to body plan, as described below.

About as legendary as family size are the relationships between orchids and their pollinators. Floral mimicry reaches its zenith here with the species having the most specialized arrangements dependent on one or a few kinds of insects, and sometimes only the males of specific species. Pollinators have driven much orchid speciation, although by no means have they done so without novel accommodations by their botanical partners.

Orchid systematics and taxonomy

Orchidaceæ fits the monocot stereotype by having three-parted flowers and fruits, leaves equipped with usually sheathing bases, and parallel rather than the net-like venation typical for dicots (Figures 1A-B, F, 3C). Stems viewed in cross section display their vasculature as collections of seemingly scattered bundles rather than discrete rings. The greatest deviation from the monocot pattern, however, involves the embryo, which, in its currently much reduced state, cannot be described as having either one or two cotyledons (Figure 3A).

More subtle aspects of flowers, certain vegetative organs, and diagnostic DNA sequences indicate membership in Order Asparagales within Class Liliopsida, which in turn falls under Division Magnoliophyta (Chase et al. 2003).

Every plant known to science bears a Latin name consisting of two words, the first one being the genus to which the species belongs and the second one identifying that species as a specific one among what are usually at least two species

ORCHID FLOWER PARTS

Dorsal Sepal

Petal

Petal

Column

Lip

Lateral Sepal

Lateral Sepal

Cattleya dowiana var. *aurea*

within the same genus. Genera and species, along with all of the higher taxonomic categories (*taxa*, singular = *taxon*) that make up the Linnaean system of classification, are spelled according to rules set down in the International Code of Botanical Nomenclature.

The International Code of Nomenclature of Cultivated Plants governs the naming of hybrids, which for Orchidaceæ with its marked sexual compatibilities among species, can be unusually challenging (Dressler 1981). Offspring produced by multiple crossings involving parents from more than two genera often bear names that reflect these complicated origins (e.g., *Brassolaeliocattleya*). Increasingly complex genealogies have prompted a recent rule change that allows simpler, more arbitrary names in special cases.

Orchid taxonomy remains fluid despite the family's being one of the most intensively studied; the magnitude of the challenge exceeds all efforts made so far to fully reconstruct its phylogeny. Recently identified markers based on DNA structure accord with some of the intra-familial boundaries inferred when using classic morphological characters, especially stamen number and structure (e.g., subfamilies Apostasioideæ and Cypripedioideæ). Other molecular data contradict long-presumed affinities elsewhere in Orchidaceæ. Supported by gross morphology and DNA, Orchidaceæ is a family divided into five taxonomically equivalent subgroups that differ by size of membership, geologic age, and degree of evolutionary specialization as described below (Chase et al. 2003, Figure 4).

Apostasioideæ. Members of this small group of the most primitive orchids inhabit moist tropical forests as soil-rooted herbs equipped with thin, broad, often plicate foliage. Flowers of Apostasioideæ bear three stamens that release powdery pollen rather than the aggregated form (pollinia) characteristic of most of the rest of the family. Quite likely this clade (the entire array of species derived from a common ancestor) has ancient origins. Its current modest membership of only two genera (*Apostasia* and *Neuwiedia*) and a handful of species suggests relic status, just a remnant of what was probably a more diverse collection of closely related lineages in earlier times.

Vanillioideæ. *Vanilla* and its relatives retain only one anther, but otherwise they exhibit features consistent with more basal status within Orchidaceæ. Pollinia are poorly organized, and seeds, like those of Apostasioideæ, are larger and harder-coated than the more specialized dust-type microsperms described below (Figure 11). Vining habits and unusual leaf venation constitute more specialized features among members of this group, as do the sometimes fleshy or leathery fruits.

Cypripedioideæ. These are the familiar slipper orchids. Molecular data confirm the long-held assumption that this clade is more primitive than much of the rest of Orchidaceæ. A pair of anthers and loosely consolidated pollen are characteristic, as are mostly terrestrial habits and affinities for humid substrates. Plicate, flat, or conduplicate, often mottled foliage that is frequently borne in two ranks rather than in the more primitive spiral leaf arrangement (phyllotaxis) further describe many of the members of the five genera that make up this subfamily.

Orchidoideæ. Most of the terrestrial orchids reside in this large assemblage of species. Despite continuing exploitation of ancestral substrates, more advanced features such as well-defined pollinia and dust-type seeds prevail here. Pollination syndromes as specialized as any based on deception in the family also occur in this group (e.g., *Ophrys*, *Pterostylis*). Relationships among members of Orchidoideæ have not been fully resolved, and the validity of leaving certain taxa outside and others within its boundaries remains controversial (Chase et al. 2003).

Epidendroideæ. By far, this subfamily accounts for the most species—about 80% of the total—and accordingly it presents the largest number of taxonomic challenges. Epiphytism predominates through much of Epidendroideæ, especially among its largest genera, suggesting that

---

Hierarchical Plant Classification

Kingdom - Chlorobionta
Division - Embryophyta
Class - Angiospermsida
Order - Asparagales
Family - Orchidaceæ

- -

Subfamily - Orchidioideæ
Tribe - Epidendreæ
Subtribe - Laeliinæ
Genus - *Cattleya*
Species - *dowiana*
Variety - *aurea*

this way of life has encouraged extensive speciation. Specialized lifestyles of many descriptions, such as myco-heterotrophy, twig epiphytism, and roots that also function like foliage (e.g., "shootless" *Campylocentrum*, *Taeniophyllum*; Figures 2E, 5), manifest themselves most extremely here. A large majority of the orchids that bear a male apparatus (androecium) reduced to a single anther belong to Epidendroideæ, as do species that engage in some of the most spectacular relationships with pollinators.

The same data that support the above inferences about intra-familial relationships identify Orchidaceæ as a mixed clade consisting of ancient as well as much more youthful elements (Figure 4). On the one hand, it is quite likely the characteristics that mark members of Apostasioideæ as orchids (e.g., family-typical association with fungi, male and female sexual organs partially fused) emerged long ago (Dressler 1981, Chase et al. 2003, Ramírez et al. 2007). On the other hand, low levels of DNA sequence divergence; specialized reproductive biology; and high concentrations of co-occurring, closely related, inter-compatible species suggest numerous, still-radiating clades, mostly within Epidendroideæ (e.g., Dendrobiinæ, Maxillariinæ, Pleurothallidinæ). High geographic insularity also accords with much on-going speciation.

Fossils and biogeography

It would be perfectly reasonable to expect lots of orchids in the plant fossil record, but this is not the case. All but a single discovery made so far consist of poorly preserved compressions of leafy shoots and fruits, none of which indisputably represents Orchidaceæ (Schmidt and Schmidt 1977). And none of these findings is more than 55 million years old, which is only about half the ages recorded for the oldest water lilies, and oak and walnut relatives, among many others. So when and where did the orchids come from?

Herbaceous plants are not particularly well disposed to yield identifiable macrofossils unless they produce durable, diagnostic organs such as the hooked fruits of *Ceratophyllum* or the similarly unique megaspores of the water fern genus *Azolla* do, both of which document origins deep in the Cretaceous Period. Being predominately epiphytic no doubt further militated against the preservation of orchids in sedimentary rocks. Thin-walled pollen grains massed in pollinia and tiny seeds lacking durable walls don't lend themselves to record-making either. Pollen most often fossilized is dispersed by wind, as happens for the grasses and many temperate zone trees, a condition alien to the orchids.

Nevertheless, one truly spectacular, recent find defies the odds and has allowed calibration of the molecular phylogeny of Orchidaceæ depicted in Figure 4 (Ramírez et al. 2007). This 15–20-million-year-old fossil consists of a solitary specimen of an extinct stingless bee (genus *Proplebeia*) bearing multiple pollinia attributable to *Meliorchis*, a genus assigned to subtribe Goodyerinæ, subfamily Orchidoideæ, found embedded in amber. Using its Oligocene age and the dates for some additional non-orchid monocots, Ramírez et al. calculated that Orchidaceæ shared its most recent common ancestor during the late Cretaceous Period some 76–84 million years ago. The massive radiations experienced by subfamilies Orchidoideæ and Epidendroideæ began later, at least by the beginning of the Eocene Epoch. The Eocene epoch is part of the Tertiary Period in the Cenozoic Era. And lasted from about 54.8–33.7 million years ago. Chase et al. (2003) used molecular clocks and cladograms based on DNA structure to place family origin between 90 and 100 million years ago.

It seems unlikely that the early history of Orchidaceæ will ever be known as well as that for some of the other prominent monocot clades. The palms, for example, have left a robust fossil record well back into the Cretaceous Period, thanks in large measure to early emergences of relatively large bodies featuring durable stem tissue and tough, distinctive foliage. Perhaps the orchids did otherwise, and for some time only remotely resembled any of their surviving descendents. If equipped with ordinary plicate foliage and rhizomatous habits much like relic Apostasioideæ still are to this day, any surviving remains of even more primitive orchids may be unrecognizable to the family.

If the compression fossils attributed to Orchidaceæ are indeed correctly assigned, then the family had colonized North America and Europe by at least mid to late Eocene times (Schmidt and Schmidt 1977). But whether or not these records have been read correctly, today, the family ranges across almost the entire planet, just as it does across broad gradients of moisture, substrate fertility, and soil pH, texture, and composition.

Considerable insularity within modern Orchidaceæ indicates either poor dispersability despite tiny wind-borne seeds, or, as mentioned above, vigorous, recent and independent radiations in different floristic provinces. For example, only a few tropical genera (e.g., *Polystachya*) span

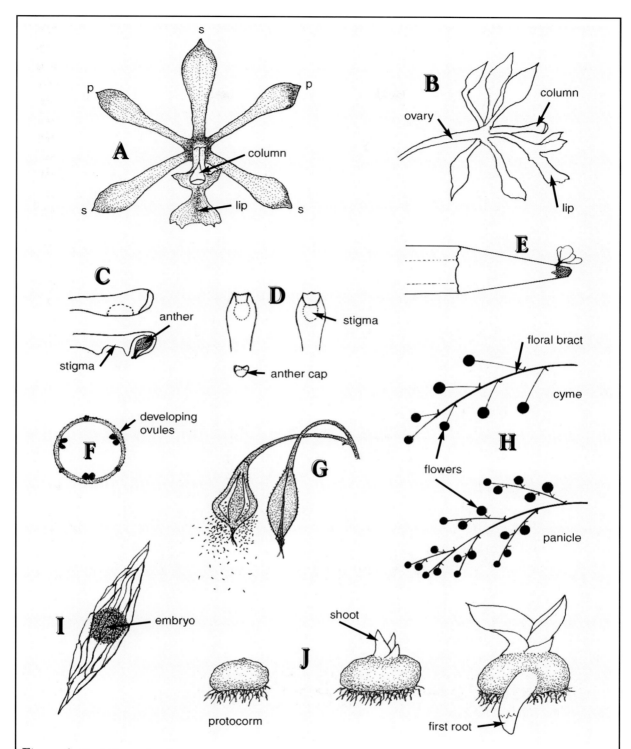

Figure 1. *Orchid reproduction.* **A.** An orchid flower (*Encyclia*) in face view. **B.** The same flower in side view. **C.** The column in side view (whole and in longitudinal sections) showing the stigma, pollinarium and anther. **D.** The same column in ventral view before and after removal of the anther cap. **E.** A pollinarum following removal with the tip of a pencil. **F.** Ovary in cross section. **G.** Intact and dehiscing capsules. **H.** Cyme and panicle type inflorescences. **I.** A dust-type seed (microsperm). **J.** Development from the protocorm stage including emergence of the first root and shoot.

the Atlantic or occur even more widely (e.g., *Bulbophyllum*). Circumboreal ranges are more common (e.g., *Cypripedium, Habenaria, Goodyera*), perhaps reflecting more recent land connections between the New and Old Worlds at higher latitudes. Distributions of the surviving, most primitive genera suggest an Old World, probably

East Laurasian origin for the family (Dressler 1981).

The vegetative body: the body plans

As authors so frequently point out, orchid flowers exhibit stunning combinations of color, shape, and chemistry to foster relationships with pollinators. These relationships are unequaled for intricacy and specificity. But to claim that the vegetative portion of these plants is far more consistent in form and function than the reproductive apparatus understates an important fact about orchid diversity. Modifications of leaves, stems, and roots and wholesale reorganizations of the entire soma parallel the orchid flower for adaptive variety and outright novelty.

Figure 2A-F illustrates the most common body plans displayed by the orchids. Ancestral to the others and widespread within Class Liliopsida is the sympodial arrangement whereby the mature plant consists of a series of joined, abbreviated shoots called ramets. Each of these modular shoots is developmentally determinate in the sense that it ceases growth when it flowers. Flowering in turn is preceded by the production of a more or less specific number of leaf or bract-bearing nodes, some of which also generate adventitious roots. Around flowering time, one or more buds inserted in the axils of leaves or bracts flush to become replacement ramets, whereupon the process repeats itself potentially without end. Orchids that share this regularly branched, modular architecture differ from one another depending on whether or not they produce pseudobulbs, consist of few to many nodes per ramet, flower terminally or laterally, and many other factors (Figures 2A, 3B).

Members of another large assemblage of orchids exhibit monopodial construction; their shoots grow in a more open-ended fashion than those of the sympodial types by producing many leaf-bearing modes from the same long-lived embryonic tips known as apical meristems (Figure 2B, D). Flowering occurs from axillary buds located at more or less consistent distances below the apex of the shoot that bears them. Monopodial types with long internodes and exceptionally indeterminate shoots qualify as vines (e.g., most vanillas), or if shorter, assume the more leaf-congested habit illustrated by *Vanda* and its relatives (Figure 2B).

Two additional, much less common, body plans serve orchids with distinctly different lifestyles. Architecture is derivative of the monopodial condition in both instances. Reduced root systems and foliage account for the abbreviated arrangement that serves the so-called saprophytes (Figures 2E, 6). Reliance on fungi for carbon/energy and mineral nutrition (mycoheterotrophy) may explain the diminished nature of the root system, whereas leaves no longer needed for photosynthesis definitely qualify as vestigial (Figure 2E).

The modest number of orchids that constitute the so-called shootless category possess greatly telescoped, nearly leafless shoots (Figures 2F, 5). These fully autotrophic (self-feeding by virtue of photosynthesis) species grow on bark or rocks where their unusually deep green and sometimes flattened aerial roots bearing only thin velamenta (described below) manage to intercept enough sunlight to allow them to replace what has become essentially non-functional foliage (Figure 5). In fact, all that remains of the leaves are minute, bract-like appendages. The proportions of the inflorescence, including its flowers and fruits, remain unaffected by the evolutionary transfer of foliar functions to roots.

Mention is also due the many terrestrial orchids that annually lapse into dormancy, forced to do so either by drought or by frost. Whether monopodial or sympodial, survival depends on the shoot dying back to a subterranean, condensed, tuber-like stem (corm) or to a reiterative series of similar organs (the sympodial types) equipped with buds to renew growth after favorable weather returns (Figure 2G). Some of the tuber-like structures produced by these species consist of both stem and root tissues. That portion of the root system still devoted to absorption may be perennial or renewed seasonally.

Leaves

Orchid leaves remain fairly conservative in the sense that none of them has assumed unconventional functions such as protection, as exemplified by the spines of *cacti*. Neither do they support prey capture as occurs among the botanical carnivores, or effect holdfast as illustrated by the tendrils of certain legumes. What the orchid leaf does exhibit is just about every known condition for operation in arid, hyper-humid, sunny, or deeply shaded environments. Thin, flat to plicate foliage mark the species native to ever-wet habitats such as rain forests, as well as those that regularly shed their leaves at sites featuring pronounced dry seasons (e.g., deciduous *Catasetum*, some *Dendrobium*).

Particularly attractive are the ornamentations of some of the softest leafed species, especially the jewel orchids. Natives of especially dark terrestrial habitats exhibit the most elaborate of these patterns. Leaf undersides are often deep red while other taxa display top-side variegations

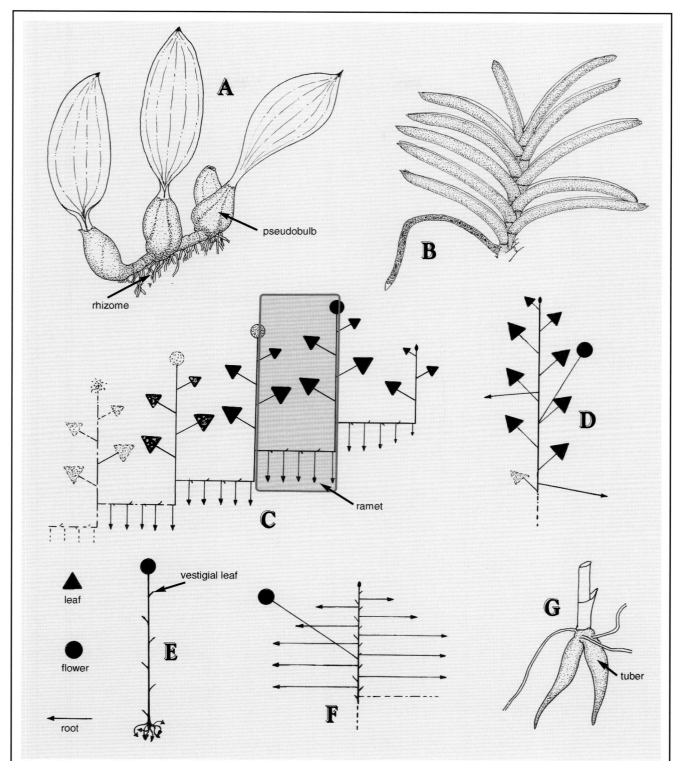

Figure 2. *The orchid vegetative body.* **A.** A sympodial orchid equipped with pseudobulbs. **B.** A monopodial orchid. **C-F.** Diagrammatic representations of the body plans of ... **C.** the sympodial orchids. **D.** the monopodial orchids. **E.** the so-called saprophytic orchids. **F.** the shootless orchids. **G.** a tuber of terrestrial *Orchis* (after Dressler 1981).

based on species-specific, intricate interspersions of red-purple, anthocyanin-rich, and chlorophyll-free zones (tessellations). Venation is often highlighted, suggesting differentiated function across individual blades. Other representatives of this exceptionally shade-tolerant group feature velvety leaves due to the presence of minute light-integrating spheres atop the cells of the upper epidermis (e.g., *Ludisia*). Foliage displayed by the epiphytes tends to be smooth (glabrous), while that of the terrestrials may be quite pubescent (e.g., some *Cypripedium, Calanthe*).

Many thousands of orchids display uniformly green, long-lived, robust CAM-type (crassulacean acid metabolism) leaves either to accommodate arid climates, or as epiphytes and lithophytes (rock dwellers) at wetter sites, to tolerate stress in what are drought-prone microsites (Figure 3C). CAM metabolism with its accompanying high water-use efficiency (described below in the Physiology section) is particularly well documented among the epiphytes. Capacities to store abundant moisture and to use it sparingly during photosynthesis also describe many arid-land terrestrial Orchidaceæ and most of the lithophytes.

Leaf form has taken myriad directions during orchid evolution. Terete (round) blades reduce organ surface to volume ratios, hence vulnerability to desiccation (e.g., *Brassavola*). Elsewhere, succulence is accomplished with thickened leaves still faithful to the lanceolate shape typical of the monocots (Figure 3C). Texture varies from brittle to leathery, and for no obvious purpose.

Internally, the thick, evergreen leaves characteristic of the most xerophytic (dry-growing) orchids exhibit divisions of labor into water storage and photosynthetic regions. Less-challenged species exhibit less differentiation, the interiors of their leaves being more uniformly occupied by what are still quite large cells containing relatively few chloroplasts (Figure 3C). Some variation is evident even here, however; most of the chloroplasts that lend green organs their color reside in the cells located close below the leaf surfaces, especially the upper, more exposed surface.

When drought causes the succulent foliage of a xerophytic orchid to desiccate, shrinkage occurs unevenly and to plant advantage. Most of the lost bulk reflects the partial collapse of the water storage tissues—those provisioned with the fewest chloroplasts. Specialization for either photosynthesis or water storage effectively helps the orchid faced with unfavorable weather maintain adequate hydration in the most desiccation-sensitive green parts of its leaves. Eventually, reserves become so seriously depleted that the ultimate defense comes into play. At this point, the stomata that most leaves bear, at least on their lower surfaces, close to minimize additional water loss until wet weather returns (Figure 3C).

Mention has already been made of the vestigial condition of the leaves of the mycoheterotrophic and shootless orchids (Figures 2E-F, 5, 6). Investments in foliage have declined in both instances because plants, just like human enterprises, must deploy available resources in a cost-effective manner to succeed. Simple economic principles explain why factories thrive or fail. Similarly, natural selection assures that resources no longer needed by plants for one purpose will increase Darwinian fitness, that is, promote reproductive success, when reallocated to satisfy other continuing needs. For both the mycoheterotrophic and shootless orchids, resources formerly used to produce leaf tissue are now available to make more seeds, or perhaps something else even more important for the survival of the individual plant and its species.

Stems

Orchid stems, like foliage, exhibit diverse architectures to meet diverse performance requirements imposed by different kinds of environments. Many of the epiphytic species and quite a few of the terrestrials produce pseudobulbs (Figures 2A, 3B). Unlike true bulbs that consist of tightly packed, fleshy scale-like leaves, the orchid pseudobulb is nothing more than a swollen stem, and not a particularly succulent one at that. Only the sympodial species possess these structures, and the number of nodes (points along stems where leaves and axillary buds insert) present ranges from one (e.g., *Bulbophyllum, Encyclia*) to many (e.g., *Catasetum, Myrmecophila*; Figures 2A, 3B).

Sympodial orchids that feature relatively elongated and slender ramets are described as cane-producers (e.g., many *Dendrobium*). Lengthy *internodes* separate successive leaves that are often arrayed in two ranks. Stems of the monopodial orchids tend to be obscured by congested foliage (e.g., *Vanda*; Figure 2B), or if their successive nodes are more widely separated, a vine-like arrangement prevails. Propensity to generate roots varies from wholly restricted to the basal few nodes of each ramet for most of the sympodial types, to every node for the vanillas that scramble through forest canopies as hemi-epiphytes.

Benefits imparted by pseudobulbs probably relate more to nutrition than to water economy. The deciduous orchids best demonstrate how nutrients stored in these organs can fuel seasonally renewed growth. Developing ramets in such species have nothing other than the attached, older and leafless ramets, in addition to their own developing foliage from which to draw sustenance. Conversely, the green tissues in pseudobulbs probably contribute little to plant energy budgets except for those rare species in which this organ is especially chlorophyll-rich but lacks accompanying foliage (e.g., *Bulbophyllum minutissimum*). A few

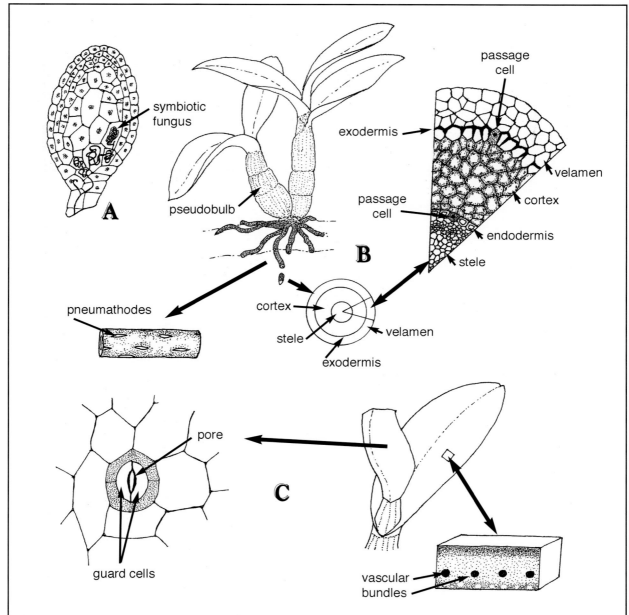

Figure 3. *The orchid vegetative body and orchid mycotrophy.* **A.** An embryo removed from a seed showing fungal hyphae infecting several of its cells (after Burgeff 1932). **B.** The anatomy of the aerial root. **C.** The anatomy of the leaf of an evergreen, drought-tolerant orchid (*Myrmecophila* sp).

evergreen Orchids house colonies of plant-feeding ants in their hollow pseudobulbs (e.g., *Caularthron*).

Pseudobulbous orchids exhibit the greatest degrees of shoot differentiation (Figures 2A, 3B). Progressing from the base to the apex of a single ramet, at least the first few nodes remain narrow, telescoped, and equipped with bracts rather than expanded leaves. These same nodes often grow roots unless elongated enough to qualify as *stolons*, in which case the roots are more likely to emerge around the base of the attached pseudobulb. Axillary buds in the same general region bring about the characteristic sympodial branching by becoming next generation ramets. Stimulus to flower either redirects the shoot meristem from the production of vegetative to reproductive organs or it truncates its growth while simultaneously releasing an axillary bud to effect lateral flowering.

Roots

Because lives spent clinging to rocks as lithophytes and to naked bark as epiphytes describe so much of the family, it should come as no surprise that the roots of many orchids exhibit elaborate modifications for survival under what for most plants would be hostile growing conditions. Modification in this instance includes multifunction. Not only does the typical orchid root absorb moisture and mineral nutrients, it also conducts photosynthesis; but just how much photosynthesis depends on additional circumstances.

Compared with the roots of a more conventionally structured herb, those of the orchids are generally thicker, branch less profusely, and bear a special absorptive and insulating, usually multilayered epidermis called the velamen (Figure 3B). Velamen thickness varies from one to about ten layers of cells, all of which upon maturing die to contribute to a sponge-like root mantle.

Immediately below the velamen lies a prominent, single-layered tissue known as the exodermis. All but a few of its component cells feature robust outer walls largely impermeable to liquid moisture and gasses (Figure 3B). The exceptions belong primarily to a category known as passage cells. Cells of this thin-walled type mediate the exchange of water and nutrients between the root interior and the velamen. More specifically, they represent portals between the living tissues that make up the root core and the adjacent physical environment that alternately delivers moisture and promotes evaporation (Figure 3B).

The living portion of the orchid root, which is delimited by the exodermis, includes a cylindrical cortex of photosynthetic cells that in turn surrounds the vascular center or stele (Figure 3B). An endodermis structured much like the exodermis and representing the outer layer of the stele also regulates moisture and nutrient transport, but in this case, to the water-conducting xylem tissue preparatory to export upward into the attached shoot.

The aerial orchid root functions in the following manner. Upon contact with precipitation, moisture quickly engorges what had previously been its air-filled velamen. No longer light-scattering, hence white in appearance, the root turns green. It becomes green because light, now reflected from what had previously been shielded chlorophyll below, traverses a velamen rendered transparent by being filled with water.

Following flux into the velamen, water moves by osmosis through the exodermis by way of its passage cells on its way to points still deeper into the root interior. Osmotic flow is slow, however, much slower than the step just described, which is the almost instantaneous flooding of a dry velamen.

Moisture continues to flow into the root's living core as long as deficits prevail there and the velamen remains engorged with water. By sequestering precipitation for a time after the adjacent medium—usually air or relatively unwettable bark or rock—has dried out, the orchid magnifies the benefits of brief showers. In effect, it extends its access to moisture longer than would be the case were it served by more conventionally constructed roots operating under identical conditions.

A second service comes into play after the velamen empties and conditions once again favor root desiccation. While empty, which is most of the time, the velamen holds a layer of humid air between the exodermis and the drying atmosphere. This allows the root to retain moisture more efficiently than it could were a simple, single-layered epidermis present. Without a velamen, the distance that diffusing water molecules would have to travel from the exodermis to the atmosphere would be significantly shorter. Viewed mechanically, the velamen and exodermis operate in tandem as a hydraulic rectifier, alternately promoting the flow of liquid water into the root core while rain is falling and for an interval thereafter, and then slowing its escape as vapor during subsequent dry weather.

Having a velamen is not always advantageous, however. Should a root so equipped, whether suspended in air or buried, remain water-saturated too long, death by suffocation follows. Special ventilating regions of the velamen called pneumathodes provide some protection by remaining air-filled while adjacent regions flood, but they cannot fully counter the effects of over-watering (Figure 3B). In short, root specialization under arid conditions has been a one-way adaptation for the orchids.

Quite a few of the terrestrial orchids produce root sprouts that account for their clone-forming habits. As a group the terrestrials also tend to maintain long-term associations with root-dwelling fungi, something that the epiphytes do less consistently. Species that engage in lifelong mycotrophy (feeding by fungi) produce far less root as well as less leaf mass than their green relatives, depending instead on fungi to deliver the nutrients and probably the moisture that other orchids obtain with better developed systems of roots and leafy shoots (Figures 2E, 6).

Physiology

Orchid physiology, or more precisely orchid ecophysiology, warrants inclusion in this profile if only to underscore the extraordinary range of conditions under which members of this family grow. Rooting media can be quite infertile for many of the epiphytes and lithophytes, and probably equally so for numerous of the terrestrials that also thrive even if the rooting system media lacks nutrients. The bog dwellers

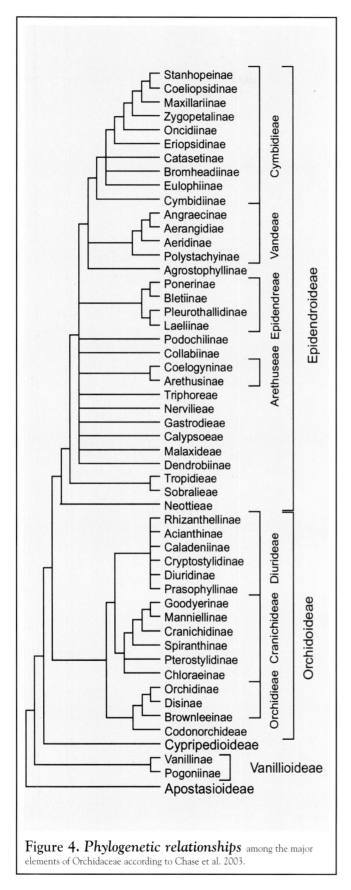

Figure 4. *Phylogenetic relationships* among the major elements of Orchidaceae according to Chase et al. 2003.

experience high acidity, and another subset of species relegated to chalky soils accommodate pronounced alkalinity, both of which can reduce access to key nutrients such as iron and nitrogen. Drought is an even more pervasive threat among orchids, as is deep shade for those species that root beneath the canopies of dense evergreen tropical forests.

One of the least understood, and sometimes misunderstood, aspects of orchid physiology is their so-called mycorrhizal association with certain fungi. If the orchids were indeed mycorrhizal, as the literature so often reports, they and their microbial partners would exchange nutrients, the plants receiving water and phosphorus and some of the other required minerals and the fungi, in turn, benefiting from the products of photosynthesis. The orchid version of this arrangement often involves only the earliest life stages (Figures 1J, 3A), but more important, rather than meeting the definition of mutualism, the relationship more closely resembles predation. Strange as it may sound, it is the orchid rather than the microbe that prevails, despite the fact that many of the subjugated fungi are pathogens elsewhere in the Plant Kingdom.

Green orchids require nutrients extracted from fungi to fuel the growth of their seedlings until they become competent to conduct photosynthesis, that is, develop chlorophyll and the rest of the apparatus for making food (Figures 1J, 3A). By some mechanism an appropriate fungus is encouraged to attack the poorly provisioned embryo, whereupon what ordinarily would be a victim defends itself and more. The infected cells of the young orchid literally digest the intruding *hyphae*, recovering released nutrients for its own use. Whether this one-sided arrangement continues beyond the protocorm stage varies (Figure 1J). But either way, the fungus appears to receive no reward for its contribution to orchid welfare.

That said, it is quite possible that unilateral benefits do accrue to some of the free-living fungi that infiltrate the otherwise empty cells that make up the orchid velamen (pers. obs.). Colonization of such a well-insulated and humidified living space—in effect, occupancy of what constitutes an internalized rhizosphere—may be especially important for species that require refuges to survive dry weather (Smith and Read 1997). Additionally, any saprophytes present stand to gain as well if the same metabolites that routinely leak from the more conventionally structured roots of nonorchids experience the same fate here. Finally, imagine how even more accommodating a velamen would be for its resident microbes should one or more of the members of that community practice biological nitrogen fixation.

Relationships between plants and fungi that likely benefit solely the botanical player occur in several additional families (e.g., Monotropaceæ of Ericales). What is unique to the orchids is the way in which most of them use their microbial associates predominately or exclusively to germinate and fuel just their earliest seedling stages. Only for the totally chlorophyll-free species is the arrangement lifelong and obligate (e.g., *Corallorhiza*, *Galeola*). Mycotrophy, or more specifically mycoheterotrophy, developed to this extent even allows members of Australian *Rhizanthella* to spend entire lives underground. Two questions remain: How should these intricate relationships with fungi be identified and how did they evolve?

If the fungus harnessed by an achlorophyllous (chlorophyll-free) orchid is a feeder on dead organic material rather than a parasite, then that orchid qualifies as an epi-saprophyte. If an orchid depends on fungi that extract nutrients from green hosts, then the label should be epi-parasite. Many of the fungi that induce green orchids to germinate are saprophytes, whereas at least some of those that provide lifelong support parasitize non-orchids from which they obtain the products of photosynthesis, some of which the orchids co-opt. All of these conditions constitute mycoheterotrophy if the orchid is totally dependent on fungi for its carbon and energy needs throughout its entire life cycle, or during the orchid life stage considered.

Certain herbs, including some orchids, that as mature plants lack sufficient amounts of leaf area to account for their overall size, practice a type of nutrition called mixotrophy. Leaf areas in these cases are indeed inadequate, and the resulting shortfalls are made up by contributions from root-dwelling fungi like those that support mycoheterotrophy. Discovery that achlorophyllous mutants of certain typically green terrestrial orchids belonging to genus *Cephalanthera* survive if infected with appropriate fungi suggests how mycoheterotrophy may have originated (Selosse et al. 2006). How widely mixotrophy pervades Orchidaceæ remains to be seen.

Plants that engage in long-term mycoheterotrophy receive everything they need from subjugated fungi, specifically, mineral nutrients in addition to the organic substances that only green plants can manufacture. This is not to say that capacity to perform photosynthesis equals nutritional uniformity. The ways in which the green orchids obtain mineral nutrients are more diverse than those practiced by the members of most of the other families of flowering plants.

Testimony to the power of naked bark and rocky substrates to promote adaptive novelty across evolving generations are the many ways that the epiphytes and lithophytes obtain mineral nutrients from sources other than their rooting media. Orchids that employ hollow stems to lure colonies of plant-feeding ants were mentioned already. Nutrients gained through carnivory is another possibility given the impoverished nature of many of the soils utilized by terrestrial orchids and the prey-capturing species in other families that sometimes share the same habitats.

Another group of mostly epiphytic orchids use "trash basket" systems of roots to impound litter and accommodate the biota necessary to release for plant use the nitrogen, phosphorus, and such that is contained in litter (e.g., *Cyrtopodium*). While root-based impoundments may be relatively ineffective for mineralizing shed plant material as compared with the water-impounding leafy tanks of bromeliads, the orchids equipped with trash baskets generally exceed for vigor their epiphytic relatives that lack them (Benzing 1990).

More fully investigated than orchid mycotrophy or mineral nutrition are the mechanisms these plants use to avoid injury caused by drought. Dry-growing members of Orchidaceæ far outnumber those native to wetlands, and the most extreme of the xerophytes easily match their non-orchid counterparts for drought tolerance. Not so the species modified for life in hyper-humid spaces. The most flood tolerant of the orchids colonize saturated soils and *Sphagnum* mats in bogs and fens; a few of them even anchor in patches of floating vegetation. But not one exhibits the delicately constructed foliage and other extreme anatomical modifications displayed by the truly aquatic members of many other families (e.g., *Elodea*).

Except for the small minority of evergreen types (e.g., *Goodyera*, *Tipularia*), the temperate zone terrestrials die back seasonally, employing a stress-avoidance strategy that has a tropical equivalent. Ecologists use the term drought-deciduous to describe these warm-growing orchids (e.g., *Catasetum*, *Cyrtopodium*). Deciduousness is sometimes facilitated by conspicuous abscission zones that foster clean separations of spent leaves from longer-lived stems.

Most of the orchids from frost-free, arid habitats possess evergreen foliage, that is, they operate as drought-tolerators rather than drought-avoiding deciduous types. Drought is tolerated by deploying a coordinated suite of structural and physiological features that allow the plant to rapidly hydrate during even brief bouts of wet weather (recall how the velamen-exodermis combination works), after which it sparingly expends what can be substantial reserves to conduct photosynthesis through subsequent dryer times. Such high water-use efficiency is accomplished in part by absorbing CO_2 from relatively humid air at night for temporary storage as malic acid, while simultaneously reducing daytime transpiration by way of a mechanism known as crassulacean acid metabolism (CAM). The requisite storage capacity to support this kind of lifestyle is provided by succulent tissues located in foliage and less commonly in stems or roots.

Nocturnal fixation of CO_2 for reprocessing to sugars using the energy of light the following day occurs in several types, taking place in leaves, green stems, and roots depending on an orchid's identity. Despite considerable research, no small part of it performed on orchids, CAM remains incompletely understood, especially its benefits under certain environmental conditions, not all of which include aridity. In addition to enhancing water-use efficiency, it definitely helps to protect overexposed foliage from photo-injury. Heightened nitrogen-use efficiency may be another reason for its occurrence among the orchids and other plants native to harsh environments.

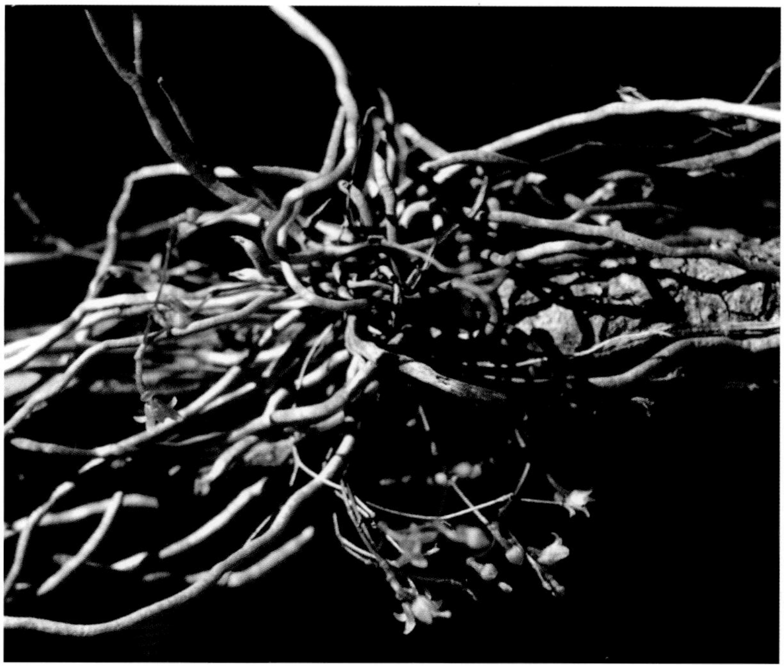

The shootless species raise an intriguing question about orchid photosynthesis and water management. The roots of these plants exhibit CAM-type activity despite the absence of the stomata that on the surfaces of leaves allow employment of the same process to reduce daytime water loss (Figure 5). Quite likely these unconventionally proportioned orchids gain less in water economy by performing CAM than they benefit in some other as yet unrecognized way.

The flower, fruit, and seed

The most distinctive feature of Orchidaceæ is its flower,

Figure 5. *Harrisella porrecta*
a shootless orchid from south Florida.

and among the parts of the flower, it is the consolidated male/female apparatus known as the column that most clearly signifies the family (Figure 1C-D). Only the few species characterized by single-gender flowers (e.g., *Cycnoches*) deviate from this pattern. At the tip of a typical column, or just under it, lies the anther cap and the pollinaria that it protects until removed by a pollinator. Each pollinarium consists of a terminal pollen-containing pollinium plus an attached stalk (caudicle) bearing a sticky *viscidium* that fastens the entire device to a flower-visiting animal (Figure 1E).

Lower down on the ventral side of the column, usually just below the anther, resides the concave *stigma* into which pollen must be deposited to achieve fruit set (Figure 1C). A *perianth*, consisting of six appendages organized as two whorls of three sepals or petals each, inserts around the base of the column (Figure 1A-B). The more uniform sepals alternate with the petals, one of which, the labellum or lip, is usually larger and more colorful than the other two. Insects seeking floral rewards generally land on the labellum, whereupon its shape and location relative to the column and other parts of the flower tend to guide their movements in ways that promote pollination.

Most orchid flowers are distinctly bilateral, meaning that two mirror halves result, should they be vertically bisected (Figure 1A). Below the points of insertion where the sepals and petals appear to join the column is the three-parted, inferior-positioned ovary (Figure 1B). Flower development usually includes a late-stage 180° twisting (resupination) of the *pedicel*, effectively reversing what initially were the dorsal and ventral positions of the labellum and column.

Orchid ovaries contain exceptionally numerous *ovules* (hyper-ovulate ovaries), which following fertilization become "dust" type seeds or microsperms within dry-walled, tri-dehiscent fruits technically known as capsules (Figure 1F, G, I). Softer-walled fruits with the same three-part organization and containing somewhat more robust seeds characterize the most primitive orchids.

Although many kinds of animals serve Orchidaceæ, some of its self-fertile species set their own seeds unassisted by pollinators, meaning, they exhibit autogamy. More common is allogamy (outcrossing), enforced either by genetically based self-incompatibility or by strategically juxtaposed stigmas and anthers if the plant is self-compatible.

The inflorescence

Orchids, like the rest of Magnoliophyta, produce flowers on shoots devoted exclusively to this purpose or on parts of shoots that also display foliage. Either way the flower-bearing apparatus is called an inflorescence. Minute to sizable homologs of leaves called floral bracts also adorn the inflorescences of most of the orchids, as for many other flowering plants (Figure 1G).

Inflorescences that terminate the apices of the individual ramets of the sympodial species probably demonstrate the ancestral condition within Orchidaceæ. Axillary buds perform this function for the monopodial types and for those sympodial species that flower laterally rather than apically.

Orchids display one to many flowers on each inflorescence, the most common multi-flowered arrangement being the raceme (Figure 1H). Each flower making up a raceme is equipped with a *pedicel* that attaches it to a main axis (peduncle). Should flowers be arrayed in the same, usually spiral fashion, but instead insert directly on the peduncle, the resultant inflorescence type is a spike. Multiply branched systems called *panicles* (e.g., *Renanthera*, *Oncidium*) are less common, as are those that display flowers crowded at the ends of peduncles (e.g., *Bulbophyllum lepidum*).

Orientation is another variable. Upright inflorescences predominate among the terrestrial species, whereas pendent types characterize many of the epiphytes and lithophytes. The racemose inflorescences of some of the stanhopeas exhibit positive geotropism even though this behavior often requires penetrating rooting media. Effective display of such species in cultivation requires suspended containers lined with sphagnum or some similarly loose material.

If large enough, the floral bracts enclose the flower buds that originate in their axils, and if the inflorescence is a panicle or another of the multiply branched types, each of its major subdivisions is similarly protected by first-order bracts during early development. A second, unrelated function sometimes follows the protective one. Both orders of bracts of *Cyrtopodium punctatum* heighten appeal to pollinators by being unusually large and colored to match the associated brown and yellow flowers.

Flowering within an inflorescence may be simultaneous or sequential, the latter arrangement extending the time available for fruit set. Simultaneous opening strengthens the plant's signal to pollinators while also shortening the time available for pollination. The order of flowering also varies among the species that follow the sequential pattern, with bottom to top of the inflorescence being the most common arrangement. Some orchids produce exceptionally long-lived flowers, especially those that practice floral mimicry.

Flower biology and speciation

One notion about orchid evolution has recruited more adherents than perhaps it should. It goes something like this. Orchidaceæ owes its exceptional size to a flower that is at once highly specialized and sufficiently plastic in the evolutionary sense to have engaged the services of diverse, often exclusive pollinators. These animals in turn have directed gene flow in patterns conducive to exceptionally rapid speciation (Benzing 1987).

Despite its intuitive appeal, this scenario has not inspired much hypothesis testing, perhaps because it is too vague. Progress on this issue requires that the attributes of orchid flowers and any of the other plant-based factors supposedly responsible for accelerating orchid radiation be specified (Benzing 1987). To be testable, it must also identify aspects of the environment, including characteristics of pollinators, that could have contributed to what undeniably has been an immense proliferation of plant species. Three propositions come to mind that help flesh out the pollinator-driven orchid speciation scenario.

First, the genetic program responsible for the development of the orchid flower was flexible enough to permit frequent shifts among the options for pollinator service. Second, tolerances for the ratio of flowers visited to fruits set was lower than usual among the antecedents of modern Orchidaceæ. Third, habitats were available that could accommodate dense concentrations of closely related orchid species, many of which lacked, and presumably still lack, substantial ecological differentiation.

What evidence suggests that any or all of these three conditions prevailed in the past? And do any of these conditions continue within and for taxa that show signs of recent, vigorous speciation? What features of the reproductive apparatus, and not just the flower, could render the orchids exceptionally amenable to pollinator-mediated speciation?

Having pollen delivery and reception sites fixed on the same rigid organ and this organ juxtaposed to, and often partially enclosed within, a relatively stiff perianth is central to the hypothesis (Figure 1A, D). The more precisely a flower can manipulate the movements of its visitors, the greater its capacity to specify pollinator identity, hence influence parentage, that is, direct gene flow. Tight control of visitors could also allow minor shifts in floral phenotype to alter who is attracted to a particular plant and who can set its fruits.

Fecundity is another crucial variable. How is it kept adequate while new floral phenotypes are being fine-tuned prior to fixation as components of sustainable reproductive strategies for emerging populations (new species)?

Pollen packaged in sufficient numbers in a pollinium to fertilize in a single pollination ovules housed by the thousands to millions in a single ovary is crucial to the proposed mechanism for orchid speciation. Acting together, these two devices can relax the quality of service required from pollinators. Co-opting an animal that does not ordinarily visit flowers, or is not well adapted to collect floral rewards as a fair number of orchids do, probably requires more than the usual fine-tuning before that animal and an emerging orchid population can become effective partners. Somehow, reproduction must succeed during this process. Once the relationship is established, its continuance discourages gene flow among diverging species should they remain sexually compatible.

Orchids are exceptionally well equipped to maintain populations even if their flowers attract inept or rare visitors. Either way, the few fruits ripened still yield high returns. High returns mean many, necessarily small seeds per capsule. And to be small enough to render viable the populations of orchids dependent on such low-quality service requires that the embryos inside these seeds rely on fungi rather than maternal parents for nutrients.

Existing support for the pollinator-driven orchid speciation hypothesis comes from what is already known about orchid reproduction. One particularly revealing phenomenon is the frequent low fruit set, often below one percent, experienced by many of the more advanced species. Also consistent with the hypothesis is the absence of physiologically based barriers to gene flow among many groups of closely related orchids, especially within predominantly epiphytic Epidendroideæ. Served by distinct and exclusive pollinators, the factors that favor the establishment of genetically based reproductive barriers elsewhere may have had less effect here.

How might the animal-mediated orchid speciation hypothesis be further supported? Discovery that spontaneous mutations cause streams of altered floral phenotypes upon which Darwinian selection can act would help; but thus far, sufficient research has not been conducted to prove this hypothesis. Should changes of this sort occur, they would have to be demonstrably powerful enough to modify flowers in ways that foster shifts among the kinds of pollinators that can fragment formerly coherent gene pools.

Determinations of the spatial and other tolerances required for orchid flowers and their pollinators to set

Figure 6. A totally fungus-dependent orchid
(*Hexalectris nitida*) showing the reduction of leaves.

capsules should be another priority for study. Measurements of the naturally occurring and perhaps inducible variations of flowers would also be useful. Groups of orchids suitable for study are those that exhibit evidence of ongoing rapid speciation, dependence on known, relatively exclusive pollinators, and flowers narrowly specialized to match these pollinators.

Final remarks

So there you have it: Orchidaceæ profiled as arguably the most adaptively diverse family of higher plants, and certainly one of the most intriguing in terms of its still poorly understood evolutionary history.

Many of the current ambiguities about orchid systematics and taxonomy will likely be resolved during the next decade or two. Likewise, more will be learned about the workings of the mislabeled orchid mycorrhizal association,

about the ways that orchids conduct photosynthesis, and about how they obtain and use water and mineral nutrients. Should investigators who possess the diverse skills required to take up this challenge succeed, we will also learn how Orchidaceæ has expanded to include so many species.

Armed with the information provided in this introductory chapter, dictionary users will know what is meant when members of a genus of orchids are described as sympodial or monopodial, mycoheterotrophic or shootless, and so on. The hypothesis offered about how flowers and pollinators have fostered vigorous orchid speciation should heighten appreciation for the immense floral variety evident in this illustrated dictionary. Finally, information about body plans and the ecological correlates of certain aspects of leaf, stem, and root anatomy should prove useful for developing well-informed strategies for orchid culture.

Literature cited and suggested readings

BENZING, D.H. 1987. Major patterns and processes in orchid evolution: a critical synthesis. In *Orchid Biology, reviews and perspectives IV*. Ed. J. Arditti, Cornell University Press, Ithaca, NY. pp 33–78.

BENZING, D.H. 1990. *Vascular epiphytes*. Cambridge University Press, New York, NY. 354 pp.

BURGEFF, H. 1932. *Saprophytismus und Symbiose: Studien an tropischen Orchideen*. Gustav Fischer, Jena.

CHASE, M.W., CAMERON, K.M., BARRETT, R.L., and FREUDENSTEIN, J.V. 2003. DNA data and Orchidaceae Systematics: a new phylogenetic classification. In *Orchid conservation*. Ed., K.W. Dixon, S.P. Kell, R.L. Barrett, P.J. Cribb, Natural History Publications (Borneo), Kota Kinabalu, Sabah. pp 69–89.

DRESSLER, R.L. 1981. *The orchids: natural history and classification*. Harvard University Press, Cambridge, Mass.

KRESS, W.J. 1986. A symposium: the biology of tropical epiphytes. *Selbyana* **9**: 1–22.

RAMÍREZ, S.R., GRAVENDEEL, B., SINGER, R.B., MARSHALL, C.R., and PIERCE, N.E. 2007. Dating the origin of the Orchidaceae from a fossil orchid with its pollinator. *Nature* **448**: 1042–1045.

SELOSSE, M.A., RICHARD, F., XINHUA, H., and SIMARD, S.W. 2006. Mycorrhizal networks: des liaisons dangereuses? *Trends in Ecology and Evolution* **21**: 621–628.

SCHMIDT, R., and SCHMIDT, M.J. 1977. Fossil history of the Orchidaceae. In *Orchid biology: reviews and perspectives I*. Ed. J. Arditti, Cornell University Press, Ithaca, NY. pp 27–45.

SMITH, S.E., and READ, D.J. 1997. *Mycorrhizal symbiosis*. Second edition. Academic Press, London.

ORCHID GENERA

SELECTED REFERENCES

These references are provided to give the reader a brief insight into some available orchid reference materials.
The array of reference books and materials used to research for this dictionary
are simply too numerous to list here but are included in the abbreviation section starting on page 443.

AMES, Oakes and CORRELL, D.S., 1952-1953
  Orchids of Guatemala, 2 vols. plus supplements
  In *Fieldiana* **26**: (1, 2) and **31**: (7)

BECHTEL, H., CRIBB, P.J. and LAUNERT, E., 1986
  Manual of Cultivated Orchid Species, 2nd ed.
  MIT Press, Cambridge, Massachusetts

CULLEN, James J., 1992
  The Orchid Book
  Cambridge University Press, New York

DAVIES, Paul & Jenne and HUXLEY, A., 1988
  Wild Orchids of Britain and Europe
  Chatto & Windus, London

DRESSLER, Robert L., 1981
  The Orchids: Natural History and Classification
  Harvard University Press, Cambridge
  —————, 1993
  Phylogeny and Classification of the Orchid Family
  Dioscorides Press, Portland, Oregon

DUNSTERVILLE, G.C.K. and GARAY, L.A.,
  1959-1976
  Venezuela Orchids Illustrated, 6 vols.
  André Deutsch, London

FANFANI, Alberto and ROSSI, Walter, 1989
  Simon & Schuster's Guide to Orchids
  Simon & Schuster, New York

HAWKES, Alex D., 1965
  Encyclopaedia of Cultivated Orchids
  Faber & Faber, London

INTERNATIONAL ORCHID COMMISSION, 1993
  Handbook on Orchid Nomenclature & Registration
  Royal Horticultural Society, London

LUER, Caryle A., 1972
  The Native Orchids of Florida
  New York Botanical Garden, New York
  —————, 1975

  The Native Orchids of the United States and Canada
  New York Botanical Garden, New York

MAYR, Hubert, 1998
  Orchid Names and Their Meanings
  A.R.G. Gantner Verlag, Vaduz

NICHOLLS, William Henry, 1969
  Orchids of Australia
  T. Nelson, Melbourne

PRIDGEON, Alec, 1992
  Illustrated Encyclopedia of Orchids
  Timber Press, Portland, Oregon

PRIDGEON, Alec and et al. 1999, 2001, 2003 & 2006
  Genera Orchidacearum
  Oxford University Press, Oxford, New York

SCHULTES, Richard E. and PEASE, Arthur S., 1963
  Generic Names of Orchids: Their Origin and Meaning
  Academic Press, New York & London

SHEEHAN, Tom and Marion, 1979
  Orchid Genera Illustrated
  Van Nostrand Reinhold, New York
  —————, 1994
  An Illustrated Survey of Orchid Genera
  Timber Press, Portland, Oregon

STEWART, Joyce, 1992
  Manual of Orchids
  Timber Press, Portland, Oregon

VEITCH, James and Sons, 1887-1894
  A Manual of Orchidaeous Plants, 2 vols.
  A. Asher & Co., Amsterdam

WITHNER, Carl L., 1959
  The Orchids: A Scientific Survey
  Ronald, New York
  —————, 1974
  The Orchids: Scientific Studies
  Wiley-Interscience, New York

Classis XX.

GYNANDRIA.

DIANDRIA

ORCHIS.

Bulbis indivisis.

1. ORCHIS bulbis indivisis, nectarii alis amplioribus ciliatis. *susannæ.*
Orchis amboinensis, floribus albis fimbriatis. *Herm. parad.* 209. *t.* 209.
Habitat in Amboina.

2. ORCHIS bulbis indivisis, nectarii labio lanceolato ciliato: cornu longissimo. *Act. ups.* 1741. *p.* 6. *ciliaris.*
Orchis nectarii labio lanceolato ciliato, seta germine intorto longiore. *Roy. lugdb.* 15. *Gron. virg.* 183.
Orchis palmata elegans lutea americana, cum longis calcaribus luteis. *Moris. hist.* 3. *p.* 499.
Orchis marilandica grandis & procera, floribus luteis, calcari longissimo: lobulo fimbriato. *Raj. suppl.* 588.
Habitat in Virginia, Canada. ♃

3. ORCHIS bulbis indivisis, nectarii labio lanceolato integerrimo: cornu longissimo petalis patentibus. *Act. ups.* 1740. *p.* 5. *Fl. suec.* 723. *Dalib. paris.* 273. *Mat. med.* 411. *bifolia.*
Orchis alba bifolia minor, calcari oblongo. *Bauh. pin.* 83. *Vaill. paris.* 151. *t.* 30. *f.* 7. *Segu. ver. t.* 15. *f.* 10.
Testiculi species V. *Cam. epit.* 625.
β. Orchis trifolia minor. *Bauh. pin.* 83.
γ. Orchis bifolia altera. *Bauh. pin.* 82.
Orchis bifolia latissima. *Bauh. pin.* 82.
Habitat in Europæ *pascuis asperis.* ♃

4. ORCHIS bulbis indivisis, nectarii labio trifido, petalis confluentibus, caule nudo. *cucullata.*
Orchis radice rotunda, cucullo tridentato: *Gmel. sib.* 1. *p.* 16. *t.* 3. *f.* 2.
Habitat in Sibiria. ♃
Folia *radicalia ovata, bina*

5. OR-

Linnaeus *Species Plantarum* 2: page 939 (1753).

ORCHID GENERA

BOTANICAL DESCRIPTIONS

An alphabetical listing of all currently known orchid names through 2007.

ORCHID GENERA

GUIDE TO DICTIONARY USE

The classification system used here is based on *Orchidaceæ systematics: A new phylogenetic classification* (M.W. Chase et al., 2003) with modifications for more recent publications.

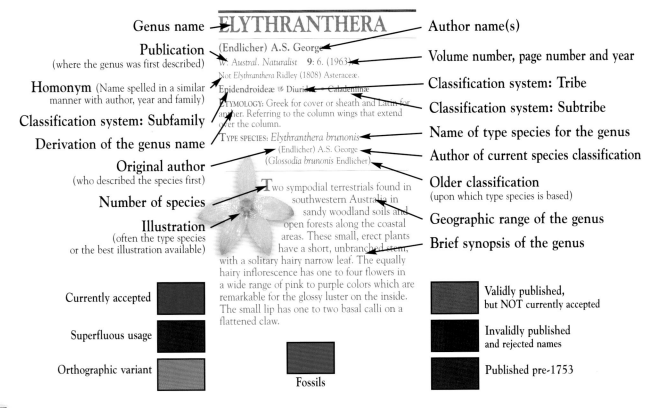

Genus name → **ELYTHRANTHERA** ← Author name(s)

Publication (where the genus was first described) → (Endlicher) A.S. George

W. Austral. Naturalist **9**: 6. (1963) ← Volume number, page number and year

Not *Elythranthera* Ridley (1808) Asteraceæ. ← Homonym (Name spelled in a similar manner with author, year and family)

Epidendroideæ ⚺ Diurideæ • Caladeniinæ ← Classification system: Tribe / Classification system: Subtribe

Classification system: Subfamily

ETYMOLOGY: Greek for cover or sheath and Latin for anther. Referring to the column wings that extend over the column. ← Derivation of the genus name

TYPE SPECIES: *Elythranthera brunonis* ← Name of type species for the genus

Original author (who described the species first) → (Endlicher) A.S. George ← Author of current species classification

(*Glossodia brunonis* Endlicher) ← Older classification (upon which type species is based)

Number of species →

Illustration (often the type species or the best illustration available) →

Two sympodial terrestrials found in southwestern Australia in sandy woodland soils and open forests along the coastal areas. These small, erect plants have a short, unbranched stem, with a solitary hairy narrow leaf. The equally hairy inflorescence has one to four flowers in a wide range of pink to purple colors which are remarkable for the glossy luster on the inside. The small lip has one to two basal calli on a flattened claw. ← Brief synopsis of the genus

← Geographic range of the genus

Currently accepted

Superfluous usage

Orthographic variant

Fossils

Validly published, but NOT currently accepted

Invalidly published and rejected names

Published pre-1753

---

*T*he genera listed in this dictionary are arranged in alphabetical order to serve as a guide to the vast array of orchids. Each listed plant has a two-part or binomial name representing a unique species. The name consists of the genus name (for example, *Elythranthera*) and the specific epithet (for example, *brunonis*). While the complete name of a genus is *Elythranthera*, the name for the species is incomplete without the genus name before the specific epithet (*Elythranthera brunonis*). The reason is that the same specific epithet must be used repeatedly with other genera. The name *skinneri* as a species has no meaning without the genus name *Cattleya* or *Lycaste* before it to separate the vastly different and unrelated *Cattleya skinneri* from *Lycaste skinneri*. Once a species has been named, the specific epithet is generally retained, even if it is formally recombined into a new genus. As an example, *Epidendrum amabile* Linnaeus has been changed to *Phalaenopsis amabilis* (Linnaeus) Blume. Note the authorship of this name includes the original author of the species (Linnaeus) and the recombining author, Blume. The rules for naming plants from the wild are published in the International Code of Botanical Nomenclature

(ICBN), which is revised periodically. The starting date for legitimate names has been set at 1753, which coincides with the publication of *Species Plantarum* by Carl von Linné (Linnaeus). Some genera have a single species; others, such as *Pleurothallis*, may have several. Unfortunately, controversy often exists among botanists regarding which and how many species belong to a particular genus; this can be a major problem with large genera. A well-known example is the broad, all-inclusive circumscription of *Bulbophyllum* (2000 species) versus a narrower circumscription (1852 species) and the acceptance of a second genus *Cirrhopetalum* (148 species), which many botanists would accept under the broad definition of *Bulbophyllum*. Volumes of new data on the relationships of orchids are appearing as the result of DNA testing. Many of the genus names of species will need to change, a process that will never end. This dictionary attempts to provide a base for genus names accepted by most orchid authors. Many of the generic names covered here are actually misspellings, formally designated as orthographic variants, and are so indicated, while other names are widely accepted as synonyms of other usually earlier published names.

AA

Reichenbach *filius*

Xenia Orchid. **1**: 18 (1854)[1858].

Orchidoideæ 🌿 **Cranichideæ** • **Cranichidinæ**

ETYMOLOGY: It was Reichenbach's desire that one of his genera would always be on top of the alphabetic list. He chose the first and final letters of *Altensteinia* from which this genus was separated.

Or possibly, in honor of Pieter van der Aa (1659-1733), a Dutch publisher, mapmaker and printer of Paul Herman's *Paradisus Batavus.*

LECTOTYPE: *Aa paleacea* (Kunth) Reichenbach f.
(*Ophrys paleacea* Kunth)

About twenty-seven sympodial terrestrials ranging in upper elevation, montane woodlands, open grasslands and river gravel from Costa Rica to Peru and northwestern Argentina. These erect plants have unbranched stems, each with several, narrow leaves often in a basal rosette. The tall, densely packed, few to numerous-flowered, cylindrical inflorescence, borne from the plant base, is often subtended by tubular sheaths and appears long before the leaves are mature. The small, white to green flowers (surrounded by papery bracts) have tiny petals, and an odd fragrance. The hood-shaped, entire lip has an inrolled entrance often marginally fringed. The flowers have a short, footless column.

ABAXIANTHUS

M.A. Clements & **D.L. Jones**

Orchadian **13**(11): 485 (2002).

ETYMOLOGY: Latin for away from, axis and anther. Referring to the flower that is borne from the leaf axil.

TYPE SPECIES: *Abaxianthus convexus*
(Blume) M.A. Clements & D.L. Jones
(*Desmotrichium convexum* Blume)

Recognized as belonging to the genus *Flickingeria*, *Abaxianthus* was proposed to include one epiphyte found in hot to steamy, low elevation, rain forests, swamps and mangroves from Malaysia, Indonesia, New Guinea and northeastern Australia to the Solomon Islands. This small plant has brittle rhizomes producing roots along a slender portion of the stem, often forming a mat of stems. The slender pseudo-bulb has a solitary leaf almost as long as the little pseudobulb. The short, solitary-flowered inflorescence, borne from a bract at the leaf axil, has a green-white flower with a white, curved column. The trilobed lip has a pale green hypochile, a bilobed, pale orange epichile, and the rather broad mesochile has a red disk with three large keels.

ABDOMINEA

J.J. Smith

Bull. Jard. Bot. Buitenzorg, sér. 2 **14**: 52 (1914).

Epidendroideæ 🌿 **Vandeæ** • **Aeridinæ**

ETYMOLOGY: Latin for an abdomen. Referring to the rostellum that is shaped like the abdomen of an insect.

TYPE SPECIES: *Abdominea micrantha* J.J. Smith

This type name is now considered a synonym of *Abdominea minimiflora* (Hooker f.) J.J. Smith; basionym *Saccolabium minimiflorum* Hooker f.

One uncommon dwarf, monopodial epiphyte is found in low elevation, hill forests of Thailand, Malaysia, Indonesia and the Philippines. This plant, vegetatively resembling a small *Phalaenopsis*, has short stems, each with several, broad, basal leaves. The several, long, numerous-flowered inflorescences have well-spaced, tiny, pale green-yellow or cinnamon-orange flowers sprinkled with black spots and do not open widely. The white, sac-shaped, trilobed lip has small side lobes, and the midlobe has a pointed, green tip. The broad, cone-like spur has an upward pointing tip, and a transverse callus with an incurved flap that closes the entrance to the spur. The flowers have a short or obscure, footless column.

ABERRANTIA

(Luer) Luer

Monogr. Syst. Bot. Missouri Bot. Gard. **95**: 253 (2004). Validated: *Monogr. Syst. Bot. Missouri Bot. Gard.* **103**: 310 (2005).

ETYMOLOGY: Latin for deviating or different and flower. An allusion to the combination of the unusual morphological characters.

TYPE SPECIES: *Aberrantia aberrans* (Luer) Luer
(*Pleurothallis aberrans* Luer)

Recognized as belonging to the genus *Pleurothallis*, *Aberrantia* was proposed to include one epiphyte found in humid, low elevation, hill forests from Costa Rica to Ecuador. This erect plant has stout stems, each with a solitary, broad, leathery leaf. The short, few-flowered inflorescence, borne from the base of the leaf, has green flowers with minute hairs. The long, narrow lateral sepals are united, with a thick, long, narrow, erect dorsal sepal and tiny, blunt petals. The dark green, shortly clawed, entire lip has a broad, roundish tip and a disc with a pair of roundish calli. The flowers have a small, slender column.

ABOLA

Lindley

Fol. Orchid. **4**: Abola, 30 (1853).
Not *Abola* Adanson (1763) Poaceæ.

ETYMOLOGY: There is no information available about the origin and meaning of this name. However, "A" is Greek for without and *bola* is Greek for shaft.

TYPE SPECIES: *Abola radiata* Lindley

Not validly published because of a prior use of the name, this homonym was replaced by *Caucaea.*

ABORCHIS

An orthographic variant cited in *Nomencl. Bot.* (*Steudel*), ed. 2, **1**: 2 (1840). The correct spelling is *Abrochis*.

ABROCHIS

Necker

Elem. Bot. (*Necker*) **3**: 130 (1790).

ETYMOLOGY: Greek for dry, unwetted or waterless. Probably an allusion to its exposed, sunny habitat.

TYPE SPECIES: *None designated*

Not validly published, this name is referred to *Platanthera*. *Abrochis* originally included ten species of Linnaeus' *Orchis* species. But the description Necker used was so vague that when Rafinesque (*Fl. Tellur.*, **4**: 36 (1836)[1838]) reviewed the genus description, he could only conclude that some of the species must belong to *Habenaria*. But Govaerts (*World Checkl. Seed Pl.*, **1**(2): 1 (1995)) suggests that the species belong to *Disa*.

ACACALIS

An orthographic variant introduced in *Orchid.-Buch*, 66 (1892). The correct spelling is *Acacallis*.

ACACALLIS

Lindley

Fol. Orchid. **4**: *Acacallis*, 30 (1853).

ETYMOLOGY: Greek Mythology. Dedicated to the nymph *Akakallis*, the daughter of King Minos of Crete. She bore a child named Miletus to Apollo, god of the sun, prophecy, music, medicine, and poetry. Afraid of her father, however, she later abandoned the child who was tended by wolves.

TYPE SPECIES: *Acacallis cyanea* Lindley

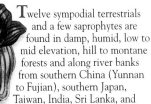

Now recognized as belonging to the genus *Aganisia*, *Acacallis* was previously considered to include three epiphytes found in low to mid elevation, along the Amazon River basin of Peru, Brazil, Venezuela, Colombia and Trinidad. These small plants have slender, egg-shaped pseudobulbs spaced at intervals along a creeping rhizome, each with one to two, leathery, short stalked leaves. The long, arching, few-flowered inflorescence, borne from the base of new pseudobulbs, has large, fragrant, showy flowers with sepals and petals that are a pristine white or blue-mauve on the outer surface and pink suffused inside. The clawed, red-brown to purple, entire lip has a blue-mauve center with an orange-pink callus, a roundish tip and a wavy margin. The flowers have an erect column with a long, slender foot.

ACAMPE

Lindley

Fol. Orchid. **4**: *Acampe*, 1 (1853).
Name ICBN conserved vs. *Sarcanthus* Lindley (1824) Orchidaceæ.

Epidendroideæ ◊ Vandeæ • Aeridinæ

ETYMOLOGY: Greek for rigid, not to bend or to turn. Refers to the small, brittle flowers in which there is no flexibility.

TYPE SPECIES: *Acampe multiflora* (Lindley) Lindley (*Vanda multiflora* Lindley)

This type name is now considered a synonym of *Acampe rigida* (Buchanan-Hamilton ex Smith) P.F. Hunt; basionym replaced with *Aerides rigida* Buchanan-Hamilton ex Smith

Seven monopodial epiphytes or occasional lithophytes are widely dispersed in low to mid elevation, hill to montane deciduous forests, coastal scrub and along river banks from Madagascar to Seychelles, India (Kashmir to Assam), southern China (Guangdong, Guangxi, Guizhou, Hainan and Yunnan), Thailand, Myanmar to Vietnam and eastern Africa (Kenya, Tanzania, Angola, Zimbabwe to Mozambique). These slow growing plants, often forming large masses, have long, simple or branched, short stems, subtended by distichous leaves, each with several, deeply channeled, thick, obliquely bilobed leaves arranged in two ranks along the stem. The stout, often branched, few-flowered inflorescence bears tight clusters of fragrant, waxy, small, fragrant, yellow flowers, often brittle to the touch, and blotched or spotted brown. The white, entire or trilobed lip, firmly attached to the column base, has erect side lobes with a basal splash of magenta, and the midlobe has a ragged margin. It often has raised calli or hairs descending into the short or swollen, bag-like spur. The flowers have a short, erect, fleshy, wingless, footless column.

ACANTHAPHIPPIUM

An orthographic variant introduced in *Syn. Pl. (D. Dietrich)*, **5**: 9 (1852). The correct spelling is *Acanthophippium*.

ACANTHEPHIPPIUM

An orthographic variant introduced in *Fl. Javæ*, **1**: Praef. vi (1828). The correct spelling is *Acanthophippium*.

ACANTHEPPHIPPIUM

An orthographic variant introduced in *Entwurf Anordn. Orch.*, 102 (1887). The correct spelling is *Acanthophippium*.

ACANTHOGLOSSA

An orthographic variant introduced in *Cat. Pl. Hort. Bot. Bogor.*, 43 (1844). The correct spelling is *Acanthoglossum*.

ACANTHOGLOSSUM

Blume

Bijdr. Fl. Ned. Ind. **8**: 381, *t.* 6 (1825).

ETYMOLOGY: Greek for prickle or thorn and tongue. A possible description of the hanging inflorescence that is covered by prominent thin, dry bracts.

TYPE SPECIES: *Acanthoglossum nervosum* Blume

Now recognized as belonging to the genus *Pholidota*, *Acanthoglossum* was previously considered to include one uncommon epiphyte found in low elevation, hill woodlands of western Indonesia (Sumatra and western Java). This plant has tightly packed, ovoid pseudo-bulbs, each with two dark green leaves that have prominent veins on the undersides. The short, numerous-flowered inflorescence has green flowers with a black fluff on the outer surfaces. The broad, trilobed lip has a cup-like base and small side lobes, and the midlobe has a flat or recurved, bilobed tip.

ACANTHOHIPPIUM

An orthographic variant introduced in *Hamburger Garten- Blumenzeitung*, **4**: 184 (1858). The correct spelling is *Acanthophippium*.

ACANTHOPHIPPIUM

Blume

Bijdr. Fl. Ned. Ind. **7**: 353, *t.* 47 (1825).

Epidendroideæ ◊ Collabiinæ • Currently unplaced

ETYMOLOGY: Greek for spur or thorn and saddle. Referring to the shape of the lip that with its two, parallel-toothed crests, bears a fanciful resemblance to a riding saddle.

TYPE SPECIES: *Acanthophippium javanicum* Blume

Twelve sympodial terrestrials and a few saprophytes are found in damp, humid, low to mid elevation, hill to montane forests and along river banks from southern China (Yunnan to Fujian), southern Japan, Taiwan, India, Sri Lanka, and Myanmar to Vietnam, the Philippines, Indonesia and New Guinea to southwestern Pacific Archipelago. These plants have large, ovoid or cone-shaped pseudobulbs, subtended by sheaths when young, each with two to three, large, pleated leaves borne at the tip. The short, stumpy, few-flowered inflorescence has rather large, heavily fragrant, bottle-shaped flowers in various shades from yellow to pink, and some species have spots or stripes. The united sepals form a swollen sepaline (urn-shaped) tube enclosing the petals and the lip. The saddle-shaped, mobile, deeply trilobed (almost obscured by the sepals) lip, hinged to the column foot, has erect side lobes; the midlobe is triangular to oblong, and the spur can be present or absent. The flowers have a broad, straight column.

NOTE: The spelling of this genus varies. The spelling **Acanthophippium** using the letter O first appeared in the 1825 publication *Bijdr. Fl. Ned. Ind.*, page 353. The letter O spelling was also used in *Tab. Pl. Jav. Orchid.* (Table 1 and illustration *t.* 47) 1825. The current popular spelling with the letter E first appeared in the preface (page vi) portion of the first volume of *Fl. Javæ Nov. Ser.* in 1829. And the spelling **Acanthephippium** was again later used by Blume in *Fl. Javæ*, 132 (1858). Neither of the spellings have been conserved.

ACANTHOPHIPPUM

An orthographic variant introduced in *Syn. Pl. (D. Dietrich)*, **5**: 91 (1852). The correct spelling is *Acanthophippium*.

ACANTHOPPHIPPIUM

An orthographic variant introduced in *Contr. Bot. Dept. Nebraska Univ.*, **3**(1): 53 (1902). The correct spelling is *Acanthephippium*.

Currently Accepted   Validly Published   Invalidly Published   Published Pre-1753   Superfluous Usage   Orthographic Variant   Fossil

Orchid Genera • 4

ACANTOPHIPPIUM

An orthographic variant introduced in *Hamburger Garten- Blumenzeitung*, **9**: 279 (1853). The correct spelling is *Acanthophippium*.

ACCRAS

An orthographic variant introduced in *Orchids Burma*, 322 (1895). The correct spelling is *Aceras*.

ACCROPERA

An orthographic variant introduced in *Neue Allg. Garten- Blumenzeitung*, **1**: 325 (1845-46). The correct spelling is *Acropera*.

ACERAS

R. Brown
Hortus Kew., ed. 2 **5**: 191 (1813).

ETYMOLOGY: Greek for without or lacking and horn or spur. Refers to the lack of a spur-like projection as seen in other related genera.

TYPE SPECIES: *Aceras anthropophorum*
(Linnaeus) R. Brown
(*Ophrys anthropophora* Linnaeus)

Now recognized as belonging to the genus *Orchis*, *Aceras* was originally considered to include one interesting terrestrial found in low to mid elevation, grasslands and woodland margins over much of Europe (Germany to Spain, Belgium to Albania, Greece and Turkey, certain Mediterranean islands (Balearic Islands, Corsica, Sardinia, Sicily, Crete) and northern Africa (Morocco to Tunisia). This small, erect plant has stout, unbranched stems, subtended by several leaf sheaths, each with basal rosette-like, deciduous leaves. The thick, tall, numerous-flowered inflorescence arising from an easily overlooked, grass-like plant has small, green-yellow flowers with varying tints of brown-red. The sepals and somewhat shorter petals converge, forming a hood over the small column. The deeply trilobed lip has long, narrow side lobes, and the long midlobe has a narrow, bilobed tip and a small tooth.

NOTE: Current DNA testing of this genus shows that *Aceras* is clearly nested within *Orchis*.

ACERATORCHIS

Schlechter
Repert. Spec. Nov. Regni Veg. Beih. **12**: 328 (1922).
Orchidoideæ • Orchideæ • Orchidinæ

ETYMOLOGY: Greek for without a horn and orchid. Referring to the spurless, entire lip.

TYPE SPECIES: *None designated*

Two uninteresting, sympodial terrestrials are found in mid to upper elevation, montane meadows and wooded slopes, facing south, and are native to west central and southern China (Hebei, Shanxi, Shaanxi, Qinghai, Xizang, Yunnan and Sichuan). These small plants have erect, unbranched stems, subtended by two leaf-like, sheathing bracts, each with a solitary (or rarely two) basal leaf. The erect, few-flowered inflorescence has dull purple-red, pale purple or white flowers not opening widely. The broad, concave dorsal sepal and petals converge, forming a hood over the short column and the flower has spreading lateral sepals. The spreading, strap-shaped, slightly concave, entire lip has a white blotch at the base and a slightly wavy or entire margin with a blunt or roundish tip.

ACHLYDOSA

M.A. Clements & D.L. Jones
Orchadian **13**(10): 439 (2002).

ETYMOLOGY: Greek for obscurity, darkness or trouble and embellishment, decoration or ornament. Refers to the plain, unadorned lip callus.

TYPE SPECIES: *Achlydosa glandulosa*
(Schlechter) M.A. Clements & D.L. Jones
(*Lyperanthus glandulosa* Schlechter)

Recognized as belonging to the genus *Megastylis*, *Achlydosa* was proposed to include one terrestrial found in New Caledonia. This small, erect plant has several, fleshy, lime-green leaves spaced up the hairy, brown stem. The equally hairy, solitary-flowered inflorescence has a green flower. The dorsal sepal and petals converge, forming a hood over the green column. The narrow lateral sepals spread outward, and then curve inward. The broad, spoon-shaped, entire lip tapers to a sharp point and the whole lip slightly folds inwards.

ACHROANTES

An orthographic variant cited in *Nomencl. Bot. (Steudel)*, ed. 2, **1**: 15 (1840). The correct spelling is *Achroanthes*.

ACHROANTHES

Rafinesque
Med. Repos., ser. 2 **5**: 352 (1808).

Name published without a description. Today this name is most often referred to *Malaxis* Lindley.

ACHROANTHES

Rafinesque
J. Phys. Chim. Hist. Nat. Arts **89**: 261 (1819), and *Amer. Monthly Mag. & Crit. Rev.* **4**: 195 (1819).
Name ICBN rejected vs. *Microstylis* Nuttall ex Eaton (1822) Orchidaceæ.

ETYMOLOGY: Greek for uncolored and flower. Descriptive of the dull color found in most of the species.

TYPE SPECIES: *None designated*

Although validly published this rejected name is now referred to *Malaxis*. *Achroanthes* was considered to include seventeen terrestrials ranging from northern Canada, United States, Mexico to Costa Rica, Cuba, Hispaniola and Jamaica. These erect, usually large plants have a solitary, softly textured, heart-shaped leaf, and the slender stem is usually swollen at the base into a pseudobulb. The numerous-flowered inflorescence, has small flowers with thin, thread-like petals. The heart-shaped, entire or obscurely trilobed lip is highly variable in its shape.

ACHROANTHUS

An orthographic variant introduced in *Rep. Geol. Surv. Ohio*, **7**(2): 193 (1893). The correct spelling is *Achroanthes*.

ACHROCAENE

An orthographic variant introduced in *J. Roy. Hort. Soc.*, **7**(1): 96 (1886). The correct spelling is *Acrochaene*.

ACHROCHAENE

An orthographic variant introduced in *Sander's Orchid Guide*, ed. 4, 34 (1927). The correct spelling is *Acrochaene*.

ACHROSANTHES

An orthographic variant introduced in *Taxon. Vasc. Plants*, 436 (1951). The correct spelling is *Achroanthes*.

ACIANTHELLA

D.L. Jones & M.A. Clements
Orchadian   **14**(7): 330 (2004).

ETYMOLOGY: *Acianthus*, a genus of orchids and Latin for diminutive.

TYPE SPECIES: *Acianthella amplexicaulis*
(F.M. Bailey) D.L. Jones & M.A. Clements
(*Microstylis amplexicaulis* F.M. Bailey)

Recognized as belonging to the genus *Acianthus*, *Acianthella* was proposed to include seven terrestrials with most species found in low elevation, coastal woodlands of New Caledonia and with a single species found in northeastern Australia. These plants have well developed aerial stems, each with a variably shaped, lobed leaf. The erect, branched inflorescence has ascending, small, pale green to green-white flowers suffused red-purple. The dorsal sepal is only slightly broader than the lateral sepals. The broad, entire or trilobed lip is apron-shaped and has a sharp point.

ACIANTHERA

Scheidweiler
Allg. Gartenzeitung   **10**(37): 292 (1842).
Not *Acianthera* T. Post & Kuntze (1903) Melastomataceæ.

Epidendroideæ ᛃ Epidendreæ • Pleurothallidinæ

ETYMOLOGY: Greek for point, sharp or barbed and anther. Descriptive of the anther's shape according to the original type species.

LECTOTYPE: *Acianthera punctata* Scheidweiler
designated by Luer, *Monogr. Syst. Bot. Missouri Bot. Gard.*,
20: 12 (1986).

This type name is now considered a synonym of
Acianthera recurva (Lindley) Pridgeon & M.W. Chase;
basionym
(*Pleurothallis recurva* Lindley)

One hundred thirty-one sympodial epiphytes, lithophytes or rare terrestrials are found in low to upper elevation, hill and montane forests with a wide range of habitats from Cuba to Trinidad, the Guianas, Venezuela, Mexico to Argentina, Paraguay and Uruguay with the largest concentration found in Brazil. These plants' stems are pencil-like or laterally compressed with two or three edges, each with a shiny, bright green, leathery leaf that is sometimes decurrent on the stem. The several, arching, solitary to few-flowered inflorescences is borne from tip of the stem or rarely directly from the rhizome. The pale brown flowers are suffused maroon with the fleshy sepals often hairy on the outer surfaces. The small petals sometimes have serrated or notched margins. The small, thick, entire or trilobed lip has some various colored tinges and the base often narrows into a claw and bilobed. The flowers have a short, thick, hooded, occasionally winged column.

ACIANTHOPSIS

Szlachetko
Polish Bot. J.   **46**(2): 143 (2001).

ETYMOLOGY: *Acianthus*, a genus of orchids and Greek for appearance or likeness.

TYPE SPECIES: *Acianthopsis elegans*
(Reichenbach f.) Szlachetko
(*Acianthus elegans* Reichenbach f.)

Not validly published, this name is referred to *Acianthus*. *Acianthopsis* was considered to include fourteen terrestrials with most species found in New Caledonia (Île de Pins) and northeastern Australia (Queensland).

ACIANTHOPSIS

M.A. Clements & D.L. Jones
Orchadian   **13**(11): 440 (2002).

Not validly published, this name is most often referred to *Acianthus*.

ACIANTHUS

R. Brown
Prodr. Fl. Nov. Holland.   321 (1810).

Orchidoideæ ᛃ Diurideæ • Acianthinæ

ETYMOLOGY: Greek for barb, point or needle and flower. Referring to the slender, tapering floral tips.

LECTOTYPE: *Acianthus fornicatus* R. Brown
designated by M.A. Clements, *Austral. Orchid Res.*,
1: 9 (1989).

LECTOTYPE: *Acianthus exsertus* R. Brown
designated by N. Hallé, *Fl. Nouv.-Caléd.*, **8**: 418 (1977).

Twenty-six unusual, interesting, sympodial terrestrials are found in humid, low to mid elevation, thick scrub, coastal slopes, gullies and open forests of eastern Australia (Queensland to South Australia), Tasmania, New Guinea, northern New Zealand and New Caledonia. These dwarf, colony-forming plants have erect stems, subtended by leaf-like sheathing bracts at each node, each with a solitary, heart-shaped leaf. These are held horizontally above the ground or sometimes are located midway up the stem and with or without veins. After flowering, the whole plant dies back. The solitary to few-flowered inflorescence has rather spidery, pink-green to red-purple flowers with an elf-like appearance. The short to long, narrow lateral sepals are with or without tails, and the dissimilar, large dorsal sepal forms a hood over the slender, club-shaped, footless column. The conspicuous, heart-shaped, often darker colored, entire lip is dissimilar in size and shape to that of the sepals and small petals and is not lobed, but has a flat or backward rolled margin. The flowers have a long column that is strongly incurved at the tip.

ACINETA

Lindley
Edwards's Bot. Reg.
29(Misc.): 67, section no. 100 (1843).

Epidendroideæ ᛃ Cymbidieæ • Stanhopeinæ

ETYMOLOGY: Greek for immovable. Descriptive of the flower's rigid jointless lip that is strongly incurved at the tip.

TYPE SPECIES: *None designated*

Fifteen robust, sympodial epiphytes, occasional lithophytes or terrestrials are found in wet, low to mid elevation, hill and montane forests on steep embankments from southern Mexico to Panama, Venezuela and Colombia to Peru. These plants have clustered, ovoid, often compressed, deeply furrowed pseudobulbs, each with several, pleated leaves at the tip. The hanging or erect inflorescence has large, thick, waxy, egg-shaped flowers heavily spotted with strange colors, and a few of the species have exotic fragrances. The fleshy, trilobed lip has a midlobe with variously shaped appendages, and the basal claw of the hypochile is narrow and united to form an indistinct column foot. The broad epichile has triangular side lobes each with a small, concave or flat, sharp point. The flowers have a stout, erect column with or without wings and with or without a foot.

ACINOPETALA

Luer
Monogr. Syst. Bot. Missouri Bot. Gard.
105: 3 (2006).

ETYMOLOGY: Latin for point and petal. Referring to the callus on the petals.

TYPE SPECIES: *Acinopetala minuta* (Lindley) Luer
(*Masdevallia minuta* Lindley)

Recognized as belonging to the genus *Masdevallia*, *Acinopetala* was proposed to include eighteen epiphytes or lithophytes found in low to mid elevation, hill scrub to montane cloud forests from Costa Rica to Panama and Ecuador. These plants have erect stems, each with a solitary, narrow, bright green leaf. The solitary-flowered inflorescence has a bell-shaped, waxy, long-lasting, green-white flower with the sepals forming a sepaline tube sometimes streaked red. Each sepal has long, orange-yellow tails and the lateral sepals are united basally for a short distance. The oblong petals are edged green. The small, tongue-shaped, orange, entire lip has a recurved tip. The flowers have an elongate, more or less club-shaped column.

Currently Accepted   Validly Published   Invalidly Published   Published Pre-1753   Superfluous Usage   Orthographic Variant   Fossil

Orchid Genera • 6

ACKERMANIA

Dodson & R. Escobar

Orquideologia **18**(3): 202 (1993).

Not *Ackermannia* Patouillard (1902) Fungi.

ETYMOLOGY: In honor of James David Ackerman (1950-), an American professor of botany and curator of the herbarium at the University of Puerto Rico-Rio Piedras.

TYPE SPECIES: *Ackermania caudata*
    (Ackerman) Dodson & R. Escobar
    (*Chondrorhyncha caudata* Ackerman)

Not validly published because of a prior use of the name, this homonym was replaced by *Benzingia*.

ACLINIA

Griffith

Not. Pl. Asiat. **3**: 320 (1851).

ETYMOLOGY: Greek for a bed, couch on which one lies, bending to neither side, without inclination, or persistent.

TYPE SPECIES: *None designated*

Now recognized as belonging to the genus *Dendrobium*, *Aclinia* was previously considered to include four epiphytes found in mid elevation, montane forests of Malaysia, Thailand and Myanmar usually with a distinct dry season. These plants have elongate, clustered pseudobulbous stems, each with several, thinly textured, narrow leaves borne at the tip. The several, few-flowered inflorescences have small, green-yellow to white flowers not opening widely. The rather narrow, entire lip has a wavy margin along the upper portion, and tapers to a point. The base of the lip is united with the column foot and forms a small spur or a chin-like projection.

ACOEOLODES

An orthographic variant introduced in *Séance Publique Soc. Argic.*, 194 (1852). The correct spelling is *Oeceoclades*.

ACOIDIUM

Lindley

Edwards's Bot. Reg. **33**: sub 1951 (1837).

ETYMOLOGY: Greek for ear. An allusion to the two ear-like structures located on the column.

TYPE SPECIES: *Acoidium fuscum* Lindley

Not validly published, this name is referred to *Trichocentrum*. *Acoidium* was considered to include one epiphyte found in Brazil, Peru and Bolivia.

ACORIDIUM

Nees von Esenbeck & Meyen

Nov. Act. Nat. Cur. **19**(Suppl. 1): 131 (1843).

ETYMOLOGY: Diminutive of *Acorus* (Araceæ), because the shape of the leaves somewhat resembles that of *Acorus calamus* (Sweet flag) leaves.

TYPE SPECIES: *Acoridium tenellum* Nees & Meyen

Now recognized as belonging to the genus *Dendrochilum*, as section *Acoridium* (Pfitzer & Kraenzlin), it was previously considered to include sixty-five epiphytes with most of the species found on Luzon island in the Philippines, but a few species were included from Indonesia (Borneo). These clump-forming plants have narrow, spindle-shaped or ovoid pseudobulbs, each with a solitary, grass-like, leathery, dark green leaf. The slender to wiry, erect, hanging or arching, numerous-flowered inflorescence, borne near the leaf tip (flowers arranged in twisted ranks), has small to tiny, generally short-lived, fragrant, white, pale yellow to creamy white flowers with widespreading segments. The lateral sepals are united to the base of the short, wingless column. The tiny, suffused yellow or green-yellow, trilobed lip, joined to the column foot, has small side lobes, and a slightly larger midlobe.

NOTE: This widely placed genus was originally described by Nees & Meyen in Philydraceæ (a small family of wetland plants). In 1843 Endlicher (*Grundzüge der Botanik*, 59) placed it in Burmanniaceæ; in 1862 Bentham & Hooker (*Genera Plantarum*, **2**: 123) placed the genus in Cyperaceæ; and in 1893 the original species, *Acoridium tenellum*, was placed in Orchidaceæ by B.D. Jackson (*Index Kew.*, **1**: 31, 488) as a synonym of *Ceratostylis gracilis*. Rolfe (1904) moved the type species to the orchid genus *Platyclinis* (*Orchid Review*, **12**: 219). In 1905 Ames reestablished *Acoridium* adding many more species (*Orchidaceæ*, **1**: 3) and he listed the type species as *Acoridium sphacelatum*. Today this genus is considered a synonym of *Dendrochilum* as placed by Ames in 1907 (*Philippine Journal of Science*, **2**: 318).

ACOSTAEA

Schlechter

Repert. Spec. Nov. Regni Veg. Beih. **19**: 22, 283 (1923).

Epidendroideæ • Epidendreæ • Pleurothallidinæ

ETYMOLOGY: In commemoration of Guillermo Acosta y Pieper (1878-1955), a Costa Rican businessman and amateur botanist from San Ramón, who sent orchid materials to both Alberto Brenes (1870-1948) in Costa Rica and Rudolf Schlechter (1872-1925) in Germany.

LECTOTYPE: *Acostaea costaricensis* Schlechter

Four remarkably interesting, tufted, sympodial epiphytes are found in cool, very wet, low to upper elevation, hill scrub to montane cloud forests from Costa Rica to Peru. These dwarf plants have short stems often subtended by several, tubular, overlapping sheaths, each with a solitary, narrow, leathery leaf. The several, slender, few-flowered inflorescences have tiny flowers borne in succession and vary in color from red-purple to yellow-green. The dorsal sepal is deeply hooded. The curious shape of the mobile lip varies within the genus. The lip, hinged to the column foot, is under tension and quickly snaps upward, causing the pollinating insect to be trapped, then after awhile the lip returns to the receptive position and releases the insect. The flowers have a small, arched, distinctly winged column.

ACRAEA

Lindley

Pl. Hartw. 155 (1845).

ETYMOLOGY: Greek for dwelling on high. An allusion to the plant's montane habitat.

TYPE SPECIES: *Acraea parvifolia* Lindley

Now recognized as belonging to the genus *Pterichis*, *Acraea* was previously considered to include five terrestrials found from Colombia, Ecuador, Peru and Brazil to northern Argentina. These erect, hairy plants have unbranched stems, each with a solitary, ground-hugging leaf. The numerous-flowered inflorescence has intricate, small, usually white to pink flowers with a minute, heart-shaped, entire lip that is uppermost.

ACRANTHUS

An orthographic variant introduced in *Bot. Mag.*, t. 6034 (1873). The correct spelling is *Aeranthes*.

ACREA

An orthographic variant introduced in *Venez. Orchid. Ill.*, **4**: 256 (1966). The correct spelling is *Acraea*.

ACRIDES

An orthographic variant introduced in *Schriften Ges. Beförd. Gesammten Nauturwiss. Marburg*, **2**: 126 (1831). The correct spelling is *Aerides*.

ACRIOPSIS

Reinwardt ex **Blume**

Cat. Gew. Buitenzorg   97 (1823), and
Bijdr. Fl. Ned. Ind.   **8**: 376, t. 71 (1825).

Epidendroideæ ❧ Cymbidieæ • Eulophiinæ

ETYMOLOGY: Greek for locust-like or grasshopper and appearance. Refers to the supposed resemblance of the column shape to that of a locust.

TYPE SPECIES: *Acriopsis javanica* Reinwardt ex Blume
    This type name is now considered a synonym of
    Acriopsis liliifolia (J. König) Seidenfaden;
              basionym
         Epidendrum liliifolium J. König

Seven mostly dwarf, sympodial epiphytes or occasionally terrestrials are found in low to mid elevation, moss laden hill forests from Thailand to Vietnam, Malaysia, Indonesia, the Philippines to the Solomons and northeastern Australia (Queensland). These unattractive plants have small, densely clustered, ovoid pseudobulbs, subtended at the base by thinly textured, silvery bracts, each with two tapering leaves at the tip. The simple to long-branched, arching, numerous-flowered inflorescences can reach up to a foot (30 cm) or more in length. The small to minute, widespreading flowers are usually cream or green-white, with a pink-purple or yellow stripe along the midline. The oblong dorsal sepal is hood-like, the lateral sepals are fused their whole length, and the flowers turn yellow just before they fall off. The entire or trilobed lip forms a tube along with the footless column base, and the lateral sepals are fused behind the lip.

ACROANTHES

An orthographic variant introduced in *J. Phys. Chim. Hist. Nat. Arts*, **89**: 261 (1819). The correct spelling is *Achroanthes*.

ACROBION

An orthographic variant introduced in *Kultuur Orchid.*, 54 (1856). The correct spelling is *Aerobion*.

ACROBIUM

Sprengel

Summarium   **1**: 68 (1830).

ETYMOLOGY: Greek for gland and column. Refers to the column that is swollen on both sides.

TYPE SPECIES: *Acrobium fragrans* Sprengel

Not validly published, this name is referred to *Jumellea*. *Acrobium* was considered to include one epiphyte found in the Mascarenes and Réunion Islands.

ACROCAENE

An orthographic variant introduced in *Orchids India*, ed. 2, 79 (1999). The correct spelling is *Achrochaene*.

ACROCHAENE

Lindley

Fol. Orchid.   **2**: Acrochaene (1853).

Epidendroideæ ❧ Dendrobiinæ • Currently unplaced

ETYMOLOGY: Greek for point, summit, terminal or tip and to gape. Descriptive of the open, laxly flowered inflorescence.

TYPE SPECIES: *Acrochaene punctata* Lindley

One sympodial epiphyte is found in cool, upper elevation, montane forests of north eastern India (Assam), Bhutan and Myanmar to northern Thailand. This plant has small, ovoid, dark brown pseudobulbs, each with a solitary, oblong, erect leaf that is strongly keeled below. The few-flowered inflorescence has attractive, small, but intricate, pale olive-green flowers covered with red dots and blotches. The shortly clawed, trilobed lip, attached to the tip of the column foot, has short, erect side lobes, and an oblong, deeply grooved midlobe with a blunt tip. The flowers have a long, slender column.

ACROCLAENE

An orthographic variant introduced in *Beitr. Morph. Biol. Orchid.*, 39 (1863). The correct spelling is *Acrochaene*.

ACROLOPHIA

Pfitzer

Entwurf Anordn. Orch.   59, 101 (1887), and
Nat. Pflanzenfam.   **2**(6): 132 (1888).

Epidendroideæ ❧ Cymbidieæ • Eulophiinæ

ETYMOLOGY: Greek for mountain ridge or summit and a crest. Alluding to the large keels located on the lip.

TYPE SPECIES: *None designated*

Seven sympodial terrestrials are found in low elevation, sandy coastal scrub and dry woodlands of southern South Africa. These erect plants have short stems, each with a few distichous, fleshy, long, narrow, rigid, overlapping leaves that appear after the flowering begins. The tall, stout, simple or often laxly branched, numerous-flowered inflorescence has small, generally dull brown-yellow, green-yellow, white or green flowers that often resemble *Eulophia*. The white to yellow, variously trilobed lip has red

or green markings, a wavy margin, several, large crests arranged down the center, and a minute spur. The flowers have an erect, short, stout, wingless column.

ACRONIA

C. Presl

Reliq. Haenk.   **1**: 103 (1827).

ETYMOLOGY: Greek for mutilation. Refers to its long, tapering, thread-like petals and sepals giving the multi-flowered inflorescence the appearance of being cut or mutilated.

TYPE SPECIES: *Acronia phalangifera* C. Presl

Now recognized as belonging to the genus *Pleurothallis*, *Acronia* was previously considered to include one epiphyte or terrestrial distributed in mid to upper elevation, montane forests of Venezuela, Colombia, Ecuador and Peru. This large, slender-stemmed plant, subtended by several, spotted, tubular sheaths, each have a solitary, thinly textured, but fairly stiff leaf. The several, arching, solitary to few-flowered inflorescences have fragile, pale yellow to purple-brown, spidery flowers opening simultaneously. The lateral sepals are united to the tips, and the small, narrow petals have ragged or notched margins. The thick, broad, trilobed lip is reflexed in the middle and has small, erect side lobes, and the midlobe has a sharp point. The flowers have a small, stout column with a bright yellow anther cap.

ACROPERA

Lindley

Gen. Sp. Orchid. Pl.   172 (1833).

ETYMOLOGY: Greek for end, summit or terminal and pouch. Descriptive of the conspicuous swelling at the basal end of the column.

TYPE SPECIES: *Acropera loddigesii* Lindley nom. illeg.
       Gongora galeata (Lindley) Reichenbach f.
             (*Maxillaria galeata* Lindley)

Now recognized as belonging to the genus *Gongora*, *Acropera* was previously considered to include eleven epiphytes found in low to mid elevation, hill scrub to montane cloud forests from southern Mexico to Nicaragua. These plants have clustered, ovoid to pear-shaped pseudobulbs, each with one to two, narrow leaves borne at the tip. The downward arching, numerous to few-flowered, various length inflorescence has large, long-lived, waxy, fragrant, brown-yellow, yellow to orange flowers that are highly variable in their floral structure. The trilobed lip, continuous to the column foot, has large side lobes, and a sac-like midlobe. The flowers have a slender, slightly curved column.

| Currently Accepted | Validly Published | Invalidly Published | Published Pre-1753 | Superfluous Usage | Orthographic Variant | Fossil |

Orchid Genera • **8**

ACRORCHIS

Dressler

Orquidea (Mexico City), n.s. **12**(1): 14 (1990).

Epidendroideæ ⚘ Epidendreæ • Laeliinæ

ETYMOLOGY: Greek for peak, summit or mountain top and orchid. Referring to this plant's normal, montane habitat.

TYPE SPECIES: *Acrorchis roseola* Dressler

One sympodial epiphyte or terrestrial is found in wet, low to mid elevation, hill scrub to montane forests on open rocky slopes from Costa Rica to Panama. This clump-forming, small plant has reed-like stems, subtended by slender, dull red leaf sheaths that are covered with wart-like projections, each with several, distichous, dark green leaves that have a dark vein underneath. The few-flowered inflorescence has thinly textured, white flowers with only one to two open at a time. The similar sepals and small petals are streaked or blotched pink. The white, obscurely trilobed lip has a yellow-orange basal splash and is sac-like at the base. The flowers have a straight, wingless, footless column.

ACROSTYLIA

Frappier ex Cordemoy

Fl. Reunion 227 (1895).

ETYMOLOGY: Greek for terminal, at the end or tip and column or style. From the remarkably elevated column.

TYPE SPECIES: *Acrostylia paradoxa*
　　　　　　　Frappier ex Cordemoy

Now recognized as belonging to the genus *Cynorkis*, *Acrostylia* was previously considered to include one terrestrial found in Réunion. This small, erect plant has glossy, bright green leaves that decrease in size up the unbranched stem. The few-flowered, red-brown inflorescence produces red or violet flowers from the upper bracts. The sepals and petals converge, forming a hood over the white, erect, but slightly curved column. The darker colored, uppermost lip has a short spur. The flowers have a short, broad column.

ACROSTYLIS

An orthographic variant cited in *Lex. Gen. Phan.*, 7 (1904). The correct spelling is *Acrostylia*.

ACTINIA

An orthographic variant introduced in *Fl. Brit. Ind.*, **5**: 718 (1890). The correct spelling is *Aclinia*.

ADA

Lindley

Fol. Orchid. **5**: *Ada*, 1 (1853).

Epidendroideæ ⚘ Cymbidieæ • Oncidiinæ

ETYMOLOGY: Turkish Mythology. Named for Ada, a sister of Artemisia (x-351 BC), who was the sister, wife, and successor of Mausolus of Caria. And later she would be the ruler of the whole region with the help of Alexander the Great.
Or possibly Hebrew for beauty.

TYPE SPECIES: *Ada aurantiaca* Lindley

Some sixteen sympodial epiphytes or occasional lithophytes are found in cool, wet, mid to upper elevation, montane cloud forests from Costa Rica to Panama, Guyana, Venezuela and Colombia to Bolivia. These plants have reduced or compressed, closely packed, pear-shaped, dark green pseudobulbs or even none at all (usually hidden by leaf-bearing sheaths), each with one to two, distichous leaves at the tip. The several, gracefully arching, long to short, numerous to few-flowered inflorescences are subtended by a large, papery leaf. The green, brown, yellow-brown or red-orange flowers do not open widely, but are quite showy. The oblong, narrow or fiddle-shaped, entire lip has two parallel calli often terminating in tooth-like mounds. The flowers have a short, stout, inflated column with a depression containing the base of the callus.

NOTE: Some of these species have been treated as members of *Brassia*, but most of the species were transferred from *Brassia* to *Ada* because of certain distinguishing differences.

ADACTYLUS

(Endlicher) Rolfe

Orchid Rev. **4**(47): 329 (1896).

ETYMOLOGY: Greek for lacking or without, and finger. Referring to the dorsal stamen that is entirely suppressed.

TYPE SPECIES: *Adactylus nudus* (R. Brown) Rolfe
　　　　　　　(*Apostasia nuda* R. Brown)

Now recognized as belonging to the genus *Apostasia*, *Adactylus* was previously considered to include four terrestrials found in damp (rich humus), shady, low elevation, evergreen forests and woodlands from India and Sri Lanka to Indonesia (Borneo). These erect, slender plants have well-spaced leaves (variable in size) on a tall stem and the base of each branch is covered with numerous, overlapping, narrow bracts. The several, branched, few-flowered inflorescences emerge from the leaf base and are either erect or hang downward. The small, white or yellow flowers are without a staminode.

ADAMANTHUS

Szlachetko

Richardiana **7**(1): 30 (2007).

ETYMOLOGY: Named in honor of Adam Zając (1940-), a Polish botanist and professor with the Institute of Botany, Jagiellonian University in Kraków. And Greek for flower.

TYPE SPECIES: *Adamanthus dendrobioides*
　　　　　　　(Schlechter) Szlachetko
　　　　　　　(*Camaridium dendrobioides* Schlechter)

Recognized as belonging to the genus *Maxillaria*, *Adamanthus* was proposed to include twelve epiphytes found in mid to upper elevation, montane forests from Costa Rica to Panama. The small, erect plant has long, stout, sometimes branching stems, each with well-spaced, narrow, fleshy, bilobed, densely distichous leaves. The several, short, solitary-flowered inflorescences, borne from the leaf axils, have a small, yellow-pink flower not opening fully. The long, orange-red, entire lip is tongue-shaped.

ADAMANTINIA

Van den Berg & C.N. Gonçalves

Orchid Digest **68**(4): 230 (2004).

Epidendroideæ ⚘ Epidendreæ • Laeliinæ

ETYMOLOGY: Latin for made of steel. Named for the area Chapada Diamantina (Portuguese for diamond plateau) in the Brazilian state of Bahia where the species is found.

TYPE SPECIES: *Adamantinia miltonioides*
　　　　　　　Van den Berg & C.N. Gonçalves

One sympodial epiphyte is found in low to mid elevation, hill woodlands and montane forests of east central Brazil (Bahia) usually growing in full sunlight. This plant has green, spindle-shaped pseudobulbs suffused dark pink-brown, each with a solitary (rarely two), dark olive-green, ovate, leathery to fleshy leaf. The long, few-flowered inflorescence, borne from the pseudobulb tip, has bright pink or purple flowers with narrow sepals and large, roundish petals. The trilobed lip, attached to the stout, footless column for a short distance, has small, spreading side lobes, and a large, broad midlobe with a shallowly notched tip that has a yellow splash at the base. The flower is similar to *Broughtonia* in appearance.

ADDA

An orthographic variant introduced in *Belgique Hort.*, **24**: 106 (1874). The correct spelling is *Ada*.

ADELEUTHEROPHORA

An orthographic variant introduced in *Orchideen (Schlechter)*, ed. 3, **13**: 792 (1983). The correct spelling is *Adeneleuterophora*.

ADELOPETALUM

Fitzgerald

J.Bot. **29**: 152 (1891).

ETYMOLOGY: Greek for unclear or obscure and petal or leaf. Refers to the petals that are reputedly absent.

TYPE SPECIES: *Adelopetalum bracteatum* Fitzgerald

Now recognized as belonging to the genus *Bulbophyllum*, *Adelopetalum* was previously considered to include eleven epiphytes and lithophytes found in low elevation, coastal scrub and woodlands of eastern Australia often forming, large dense mats on rocks and trees. These small, clustered plants have glossy, depressed, wrinkled, ribbed pseudobulbs each with a solitary, deep green, thinly textured leaf. The erect to hanging, numerous-flowered inflorescence, subtended by large bracts, has tiny, cream or yellow flowers heavily mottled purple or red, which open widely. The thick, bright red to yellow, tongue-shaped, entire lip is buff on the upper surface and purple on the underside. The flowers have a very short column.

ADENELEUTEROPHORA

Barbosa Rodrigues

Gen. Sp. Orchid. **2**: 170, *t.* 797 (1881).

ETYMOLOGY: Greek for gland, free and bearing. Alluding to the two, pollinia-like grains, found at the sack-like base of the lip, that are free from the lip.

TYPE SPECIES: *Adeneleuterophora graminifolia* Barbosa Rodrigues

Now recognized as belonging to the genus *Elleanthus*, *Adeneleuterophora* was previously considered to include one epiphyte or terrestrial found in wet, mid elevation, montane forests from Guatemala to Peru, Venezuela and the Guianas to northern Brazil. This small plant has erect, cane-like, often branched stems forming neat clumps, each with several, narrow, pleated, veined leaves. The flattened, numerous-flowered inflorescence has overlapping, distichous, brown bracts subtending the tiny, white, thinly textured flowers. The tubular-shaped, entire lip has a margin of slender processes. The flowers have a pale green, erect, footless column.

ADENELEUTHERA

An orthographic variant cited in *Lex. Gen. Phan.*, 9 (1904). The correct spelling is *Adeneleuterophora*.

ADENELEUTHEROPHORA

An orthographic variant introduced in *Nat. Pflanzenfam. Nachtr.*, **1**: 107 (1897). The correct spelling is *Adeneleuterophora*.

ADENOCHILUS

Hooker *filius*

Fl. Nov.-Zel. **1**: 246, *t.* 56 (1853).

Orchidoideæ ◊ Diurideæ • Caladeniinæ

ETYMOLOGY: Greek for gland and lip. Refers to the midlobe of the lip that is usually covered with calli.

TYPE SPECIES: *Adenochilus gracilis* Hooker f.

Two showy, sympodial terrestrials are found in low elevation, sphagnum mossy scrub, rocky crevices and sandstone cliffs of New Zealand and a small area in southeastern Australia (New South Wales). These short, erect plants have slender, unbranched stems, each with a solitary, flat, shallowly grooved leaf. The erect, solitary-flowered inflorescence has a dull green or white flower, whose outer surfaces are covered with red, glandular hairs. When opened it measures almost two inches (5 cm) across, and the broad dorsal sepal forms a hood over the stout, slightly upcurved, winged, red spotted column. The distinctly trilobed lip, attached to the column base by a short claw, has a narrow band of calli extending from the base to the tip.

ADENOCOS

An orthographic variant cited in *Dict. Gen. Names Seed Pl.*, 444 (1995). The correct spelling is *Adenoncos*.

ADENONCOS

Blume

Bijdr. Fl. Ned. Ind. **8**: 381, *t.* 17 (1825).

Epidendroideæ ◊ Vandeæ • Aeridinæ

ETYMOLOGY: Greek for gland and mass or tumor. Refers to the glandular callus on the base of the lip.

TYPE SPECIES: *Adenoncos virens* Blume

Sixteen monopodial epiphytes or rare lithophytes are found in low to mid elevation, deciduous hill to montane rain forests of Thailand, Malaysia, Indonesia and New Guinea to the Philippines. These small to tiny, inconspicuous plants usually have short, unbranched stems, each with thick, rather narrow leaves that have a distinctively grooved upper surface, and are arranged in two rows. The short, solitary to few-flowered inflorescence has small, green to yellow flowers. The short, wingless, footless column is attached to the broad, concave, somewhat sac-like, yellow-green, entire lip which turns orange as it ages.

ADENOSTYLES

Not *Adenostyles* Cassini (1816) Asteraceæ.

An orthographic variant introduced in *Gen. Pl. (Bentham & Hooker f.)*, **3**(2): 599 (1883). The correct spelling is *Adenostylis*.

ADENOSTYLIM

An orthographic variant introduced in *Coll. Orchid.*, 68 (1859). The correct spelling is *Adenostylis*.

ADENOSTYLIS

Blume

Bijdr. Fl. Ned. Ind. **8**: 414 (1825).

Not *Adenostyles* Cassini (1816) Asteraceæ.

ETYMOLOGY: Greek for gland and column. Refers to the column that is swollen on both sides.

TYPE SPECIES: *None designated*

Not validly published because of a prior use of the name, this homonym was replaced by *Zeuxine*.

ADIPE

Rafinesque

Fl. Tellur. **2**: 101 (1836)[1837].

ETYMOLOGY: Latin for of fat. Referring possibly to the fleshy texture of the flower.

TYPE SPECIES: *Adipe racemosa* (Hooker) Rafinesque (*Maxillaria racemosa* Hooker)

Now recognized as belonging to the genus *Bifrenaria*, *Adipe* was previously considered to include eleven epiphytes or terrestrials found in Brazil (Rio de Janeiro, São Paulo, Espírito Santo and Minas Gerais). These plants have compressed, egg-shaped, often mottled, dull brown, slightly four-angled pseudobulbs, each with a solitary, leathery, glossy, green leaf. The erect, few-flowered inflorescence has showy, fragrant, yellow to rich yellow, fragrant flowers. The densely hairy, clawed, trilobed lip, attached to the column foot, has red veins, a wavy margin, and a small spur. The flowers have an erect, curved column.

Currently Accepted | Validly Published | Invalidly Published | Published Pre-1753 | Superfluous Usage | Orthographic Variant | Fossil

ADNULA

Rafinesque

Fl. Tellur. **2**: 87 (1836)[1837].

ETYMOLOGY: A name composed by Rafinesque from the Latin *adnatus*, to swim together, that has come to mean congenitally jointed together. Referring to the fusion of the spur to the ovary.

TYPE SPECIES: *Adnula petiolaris*
(Swartz) Rafinesque nom. illeg.
(*Satyrium adnatum* Swartz)

Pelexia adnata (Swartz) Poiteau ex Richard
(*Satyrium adnatum* Swartz)

Now recognized as belonging to the genus *Pelexia*, *Adnula* was previously considered to include one terrestrial found in low elevation, hill scrub and meadows from the Bahamas to Jamaica and Mexico to Colombia and Venezuela. This tall plant has short, erect, unbranched stems, each with a basal rosette. The leaves' upper surface is shiny green, but the backside is rather dull. The erect, hairy, few-flowered inflorescence has dark green flowers. The concave dorsal sepal and narrow petals converge, forming a hood over the small, stout column. The bright white, fleshy, spear-shaped, trilobed lip has a recurved tip.

ADROHIZON

An orthographic variant cited in *Orchideen (Schlechter): Liter. Reg. Band I/A, B, and C*, 162 (2003). The correct spelling is *Adrorhizon*.

ADRORHIZON

Hooker *filius*

Handb. Fl. Ceylon **4**: 161 (1898).

Epidendroideæ ◊ Agrostophyllinæ • Currently unplaced

ETYMOLOGY: Greek for stout, thick or strong and root. Refers to the long, stout roots that are very thick for the size of the plant.

TYPE SPECIES: *Adrorhizon purpurascens*
(Thwaites) Hooker f.
(*Dendrobium purpurascens* Thwaites)

One sympodial epiphyte or lithophyte is found in wet, mid elevation, evergreen forests of Sri Lanka. This erect plant has stout stems, each with a solitary, leathery leaf that is purple underneath. They are borne from the stem base or tiny pseudobulb that is strongly suffused purple. The two-flowered inflorescence, subtended by sheathing bracts, has tiny, white to brown-red flowers with oblong sepals and smaller, narrow petals. The yellow, spatula-shaped, entire lip is shallowly notched and attached to the rather delicate, small column.

ADRORRHIZON

An orthographic variant introduced in *Nat. Pflanzenfam. Nachtr.*, **2/3**: 85 (1908). The correct spelling is *Adrorhizon*.

AECEOCEADUS

An orthographic variant introduced in *Fl. Brit. Ind.*, **6**: 37 (1890). The correct spelling is *Oeceoclades*.

AECEOCLADES

An orthographic variant introduced in *Dict. Univ. Hist. Nat.*, **9**: 170 (1849). The correct spelling is *Oeceoclades*.

AECEOLADES

An orthographic variant introduced in *Icon. Pl. Ind. Orient. (Wight)*, **5**(1): 10 (1851). The correct spelling is *Oeceoclades*.

AEERIDIUM

An orthographic variant cited in *Lex. Gen. Phan.*, 11 (1904). The correct spelling is *Aeridium*.

AEIROPSIS

An orthographic variant introduced in *Dict. Class. Hist. Nat.*, **12**: 310 (1827). The correct spelling is *Acriopsis*.

AENHENRYA

Gopalan

J. Bombay Nat. Hist. Soc. **90**(2): 270 (1993)[1994].

Orchidoideæ ◊ Cranichideæ • Goodyerinæ

ETYMOLOGY: Dedicated to Ambrose Nathaniel Henry (1936-), an Indian botanist who helped with the floral conservation of the Agastyamalai region of southwestern India.

TYPE SPECIES: *Aenhenrya agastyamalayana* Gopalan
This type name is now considered a synonym of
Aenhenrya rotundifolia
(Blatter) Sathish Kumar & F.N. Rasmussen;
basionym
Odontochilus rotundifolius Blatter

One sympodial terrestrial is found in damp, low to mid elevation, coastal forests of southwestern India (Kerala and Tamil Nadu). Although similar to the genus *Anoectochilus*, this erect plant has unbranched stems, each with two fleshy, five-nerved, mottled leaves. The short, hairy, one-to two-flowered inflorescence has white flowers that are densely hairy on the outside. The concave dorsal sepal and petals converge, forming a hood over the long, thick, grooved column. The sword-like, trilobed lip has small side lobes with fringed margins, and the midlobe has a long, thick, forked appendage at the tip, and two rows of fleshy appendages. The flowers have a long, incurved column.

AEONIA

Lindley

Bot. Reg. **10**: sub 817 (1824).

Name ICBN rejected vs. *Oeonia* Lindley (1824) Orchidaceæ.

ETYMOLOGY: Greek for everlasting. Referring perhaps to the extended flowering period.

TYPE SPECIES: *Aeonia aubertii* (Thouars) Lindley
(*Epidendrum volucre* Thouars)

Although validly published this rejected name is now referred to *Oeonia*. *Aeonia* was considered to include eight epiphytes found in the rain forests of Madagascar, the Comoros and Mascarene Islands. These climbing plants have ovate leaves spaced along thin, branching or hanging stems. The numerous-flowered inflorescence has small flowers. The trilobed lip has small side lobes, and the large midlobe is deeply notched or bilobed, and has a small, tapered spur. The above type name is now considered a synonym of *Oeonia volucris* (Thouars) Sprengel.

AERANGIS

Reichenbach *filius*

Flora **48**(12): 190 (1865).

Epidendroideæ ◊ Vandeæ • Aerangidinæ

ETYMOLOGY: Greek for air and a vessel or cup. Refers to the foot long spur of the lip in the type species that is slightly swollen toward the tip.

TYPE SPECIES: *Aerangis flabellifolia* Reichenbach f.
This type name is now considered a synonym of
Aerangis brachycarpa (A. Richard) Durand & Schinz;
basionym
Dendrobium brachycarpum A. Richard

Forty-nine exceptionally graceful, monopodial epiphytes or rare lithophytes comprise this unusual genus. Most species are found in low to mid elevation, hill to montane evergreen forests, savannas or along river banks of Ethiopia, Ivory Coast to Tanzania and Zambia, Madagascar and the Comoros Islands with one species in Sri Lanka. These mostly small, erect to hanging, fan-shaped plants have flat, leathery to rarely fleshy, channeled, unequally bilobed leaves arranged in two rows. The long or short, often zig-zagged, solitary to few-flowered inflorescence usually has white to cream, star-shaped, waxy flowers suffused pink or green. They are remarkably nocturnally fragrant and have widespreading or bent downward sepals and petals. The entire lip, often similar to the petals, has a slender, green or pink suffused, nectar-filled spur of various lengths. The flowers have a short and stout or long and slender, footless column.

AERANTHES

Lindley

Bot. Reg. **10**: *t. 817* (1824).

Epidendroideæ ⚘ Vandeæ • Angraecinæ

ETYMOLOGY: Greek for air or mist and flower. Refers to the damp, delicate habitats where this genus usually grows.

TYPE SPECIES: *Aeranthes grandiflora* Lindley

Some forty-five striking, monopodial epiphytes or lithophytes are mostly confined to Madagascar and the adjacent islands with one species found in Zimbabwe. They range in shady, humid, low to upper elevation, hill woodlands to montane rain forests. These plants have short stems or are stemless, each with several, distichous, leathery leaves forming a fan shape. The wiry, hanging, simple or branched, solitary to numerous-flowered inflorescence, borne from the stem base, will often reflower over long periods of time. The small to large, somewhat translucent flowers are either a brilliant green, yellow or green-white, and some of the species are fragrant. The lateral sepals are attached to the column foot forming a chin-like projection, and the similar petals are smaller. The oblong, entire lip tapers to a sharp point, and is set in front of the mouth of the usually short, club-shaped, cylindrical spur. The flowers have a short or fairly long column.

AERANTHUS

An orthographic variant introduced in *Syst. Veg. (Sprengel)*, ed. 16, 718 (1826). The correct spelling is *Aeranthes*.

AERANTHUS

Reichenbach *filius*

Ann. Bot. Syst. **6**: 899 (1861).

ETYMOLOGY: Greek for air and flower. Referring to the epiphytic habit of this genus.

TYPE SPECIES: *None designated*

Not validly published, this name is referred to various genera that include *Angraecum, Campylocentrum, Jumellea, Oeonia, Polyradicion* and *Rangaeris. Aeranthus* was considered to include eighty-six epiphytes found from Africa and Madagascar with a few species found from the southeastern United States (Florida) to Brazil.

NOTE: This genus, though invalidly published by Reichenbach f., was used as a valid genus by many authors for years.

AERIDES

Loureiro

Fl. Cochinch. **2**: 516, 525 (1790).

Epidendroideæ ⚘ Vandeæ • Aeridinæ

ETYMOLOGY: Greek for air. Alluding to the plants' epiphytic habit and the name is usually given as "daughters of the air."

TYPE SPECIES: *Aerides odoratum* Loureiro

An attractive genus with about twenty-five often spectacular, monopodial epiphytes or lithophytes usually known as foxtail orchids. They are found in tropical, low to mid elevation, hill scrub to montane evergreen forests ranging from southern China (Yunnan to Guangdong), northern India (Kashmir to Assam), Nepal, Bhutan, Sri Lanka, Myanmar to Vietnam, Indonesia and New Guinea to the Philippines. These coarse plants have short or long, erect or climbing, often stout stems, each with several, leathery leaves. The several, long, arching to hanging, densely packed, numerous to few-flowered inflorescences are sometimes up to two feet (61 cm) long. The spectacular, white, yellow, deep pink, purple to lilac, waxy flowers, opening all at once, are suffused rose or purple and have a wonderful, strong fragrance. The mobile or immobile, rose-colored, entire or trilobed lip has overlapping, often erect side lobes, and has a small or large, forward pointing midlobe, and a small, forward curved spur. The flowers have a short, thick, wingless column.

AERIDESIDES

An orthographic variant introduced in *Itin. Pl. Khasyah Mts.*, 203 (1848). The correct spelling is *Aerides*.

AERIDIS

An orthographic variant introduced in *Tab. Pl. Jav. Orchid.*, *t. 24* (1825). The correct spelling is *Aerides*.

AERIDIUM

Salisbury

Trans. Hort. Soc. London **1**: 295 (1812).

ETYMOLOGY: Greek for air. Refers to the epiphytic growth habit of the genus.

TYPE SPECIES: *Aeridium odorum* Salisbury

Now recognized as belonging to the genus *Aerides, Aeridium* was previously considered to include one epiphyte found in tropical forests from northern India (Sikkim), Nepal, Bhutan, southern

China, Myanmar to Vietnam, Malaysia and Indonesia to the Philippines. This highly variable plant has stout, drooping, branching stems, each with fleshy, incurved, oblong, pale green leaves with lobed tips. The several, hanging, stout, numerous-flowered inflorescences have small, sweetly fragrant, purple or nearly white flowers often spotted purple. The immobile or mobile, entire or trilobed lip almost encloses the short column, and has erect side lobes with entire or toothed margins and a short, incurved midlobe. The large, horn-like spur has a green or yellow recurved tip.

AERIDOSTACHYA

(Hooker *filius*) Brieger

Orchideen (Schlechter), ed. 3 **1**(11-12): 714 (1981).

ETYMOLOGY: Greek for air, spike and cluster. Refers to the long inflorescence that looks like a long shaft of grain.

TYPE SPECIES: *Aeridostachya robusta* (Blume) Brieger nom. illeg.
(*Dendrolirium robustum* Blume)
Eria robusta (Blume) Lindley

Now recognized as belonging to the genus *Eria, Aeridostachya* was previously considered to include twenty-two epiphytes found in mid elevation, montane forests from Taiwan, Myanmar, Thailand to Indonesia and the Philippines to the south-western Pacific Archipelago. These plants have short, stout stems, each with relatively long, tough, leathery leaves. The erect, few-flowered inflorescences are densely covered with short, scurfy brown hairs. The small, cream-colored to orange flowers are covered with numerous, short, red-brown hairs on the outside of the sepals. The clawed, boat-shaped to oblong, entire to trilobed lip has a rounded tip and erect, basal keels. The flowers have a long to short, stout column.

AERIOPSIS

An orthographic variant introduced in *Prakt. Stud. Orchid.*, 46, 185 (1854). The correct spelling is *Acriopsis*.

AEROBION

Kaempfer ex Sprengel

Syst. Veg. (Sprengel), ed. 16 **3**: 679, 716 (1826).

ETYMOLOGY: Greek for air and life. Referring to the epiphytic habit of the plants.

TYPE SPECIES: *None designated*

Now recognized as belonging to genus *Angraecum, Aerobion* was previously considered to include twenty-four epiphytes found in Madagascar and the Mascarene Islands. These plants have short to long stems, each with several, narrow, leathery, bilobed leaves that give off a strong, pungent odor when dried. The several, usually solitary-flowered inflorescences have a waxy, fragrant, long-lasting, white to green-yellow flower with a shell-shaped, entire lip, and a long, slender, green spur. The flowers have a footless column.

AEROBIUM

An orthographic variant introduced in *Nat. Syst. Bot.*, ed. 2, 340 (1836). The correct spelling is *Aerobion*.

AEROBTON

An orthographic variant cited in *World Checkl. Seed Pl.* (Govaerts), **1**(2): 3 (1995). The correct spelling is *Aerobion*.

AERONIA

An orthographic variant cited in *Lex. Gen. Phan.*, 12 (1904). The correct spelling is *Oeonia*.

AEROPERA

An orthographic variant introduced in *Cat. Pl.* (Warszewicz), 67 (1864). The correct spelling is *Acropera*.

AETHEORHYNCHA

Dressler

Lankesteriana **5**(2): 94 (2005).

Epidendroideæ ▨ **Cymbidieæ** • **Zygopetalinæ**

ETYMOLOGY: Greek for strange or different and snout or muzzle. Refers to the two-lobed, basal callus.

TYPE SPECIES: *Aetheorhyncha andreettae*
(Jenny) Dressler
(*Chondrorhyncha andreettae* Jenny)

One sympodial epiphyte is found in wet, mid elevation, montane forests of eastern Ecuador. This fan-shaped plant has short stems, each with several, distichous, over-lapping, narrow, thinly textured leaves. The erect, solitary-flowered inflorescence has a small, pale yellow to white flower with long, narrow, yellow sepals and the small, roundish, white petals are ear-like. The hairy, white, tubular, entire lip, sprinkled with red spots, has a variably notched margin, and a strong, bright yellow, basal callus to a bilobed, basal callus and is suffused with orange at the base. The flowers have a short, stout, club-shaped column that is hairy on the underside.

AETHERIA

An orthographic variant introduced in *Gen. Pl.* (*Endlicher*), 214 (1837). The correct spelling is *Hetaeria*.

AETTIERIA

An orthographic variant introduced in *Enum. Philipp. Fl. Pl.*, **1**: 278 (1925). The correct spelling is *Hetaeria*.

AFRORCHIS

(Schlechter) Szlachetko

Richardiana **6**(2): 82 (2006).

ETYMOLOGY: Abbreviation for Africa and Greek for Orchid. Referring to place of the plant's origins.

TYPE SPECIES: *Afrorchis angolensis*
(Schlechter) Szlachetko
(*Platanthera angolensis* Schlechter)

Recognized as belonging to the genus *Platanthera*, *Afrorchis* was proposed to include three terrestrials found in mid to upper elevation, swampy grasslands and woodlands of Cameroon, Angola, Zaire and Tanzania. These erect plants have slender, unbranched stems, each with a few well-spaced, narrow leaves along the stem. The erect, numerous-flowered inflorescence has white or mauve flowers. The trilobed lip has large, rounded side lobes and a small, spotted midlobe and the hypochile forms a sac-like spur. The flowers have a long, slender column. These were formerly included in *Brachycorythis*.

AGAISIA

An orthographic variant cited in *Dict. Fl. Pl.*, ed. 8, 30 (1973). The correct spelling is *Aganisia*.

AGANISIA

Lindley

Edwards's Bot. Reg.
25(Misc.): 46, section no. 65 (1839).

Epidendroideæ ▨ **Cymbidieæ** • **Zygopetalinæ**

ETYMOLOGY: Greek for mild, gentle or loving. Alluding to the pretty, neat appearance of the plant.

TYPE SPECIES: *Aganisia pulchella* Lindley

Three small, creeping sympodial epiphytes are found in humid, low to mid elevation, hill scrub, along river banks and montane forests from the Guianas, Venezuela, Trinidad, Colombia to Peru and northern Brazil. These often climbing plants have spindle-shaped pseudobulbs, subtended by papery sheaths, each with pleated, prominently nerved leaves. The several, few-flowered

inflorescences, borne from the base of the pseudobulb, have showy, large, blue-mauve, white or yellow, sometimes fragrant flowers with similar, spreading sepals and petals. The white to orange, trilobed, bilobed or entire lip has erect side lobes, and a spreading midlobe with a basal, yellow callus marked with purple. The flowers have a short, footless column.

AGGEIANTHUS

Wight

Icon. Pl. Ind. Orient. (Wight) **5**(1): 18, *t.* 1737 (1851).

ETYMOLOGY: Greek for a vessel or cup and flower. Referring to the tubular shape of the flowers.

TYPE SPECIES: *Aggeianthus marchantioides* Wight

Now recognized as belonging to the genus *Porpax*, *Aggeianthus* was previously considered to include one epiphyte or sometime lithophyte ranging from southern India (Maharashtra, Karnataka, Kerala and Tamil Nadu), Laos, Thailand and Vietnam. This tiny, clump-forming plant has flattened pseudobulbs, each with several, minute, oblong leaves. The minute, solitary, dull brown flower has its united sepals forming a sepaline tube in which the narrow petals and tiny, obscurely trilobed lip are borne. The above type name is now considered a synonym of *Porpax reticulata* Lindley.

AGGERANTHUS

An orthographic variant cited in *Lex. Gen. Phan.*, 14 (1904). The correct spelling is *Aggeianthus*.

AGLOSSORHYNCHA

An orthographic variant introduced in *Repert. Spec. Nov. Regni Veg. Beih.*, **1**(4): 320 (1912). The correct spelling is *Aglossorrhyncha*.

AGLOSSORRHYNCHA

Schlechter

Nachtr. Fl. Schutzgeb. Südsee 133 (1905).

Epidendroideæ ▨ **Agrostophyllinæ** • **Currently unplaced**

ETYMOLOGY: Greek for without or not, tongue and horn, beak or snout. Refers to a difference from *Glossorhyncha*, a genus of orchids, with the lack of a spur or for the sack-like projection at the base of the lip.

TYPE SPECIES: *Aglossorrhyncha aurea* Schlechter

Thirteen uncommon, sympodial epiphytes or terrestrials are found in misty, low to upper elevation, hill scrub to montane forest canopies covered with thick mosses from eastern Indonesia (Maluku) and New Guinea to the south-western Pacific Archipelago. These often colonizing plants have slender, leafy (toward the tips), usually branched stems. The usually spread out, distichous, leathery leaves are arranged in two opposite ranks. The narrow or strap-shaped leaves have either a sharp point or a sharp but not rigid, pointed tip. The solitary-flowered (or in pairs) inflorescence has a relatively small, white, green or bright to dull yellow flower, borne at the tip of the stem, which often deepens in color as it ages. The sepals are hood-like. The more or less hood-shaped, entire lip has inrolled margins. The flowers have a perfectly bare, slender, club shaped, footless column.

AGROSTAPHYLLUM

An orthographic variant introduced in *Beitr. Morph. Biol. Orchid.*, 39 (1863). The correct spelling is *Agrostophyllum*.

AGROSTIPHYLLUM

An orthographic variant introduced in *Cat. Pl. Hort. Bot. Bogor.*, 46 (1844). The correct spelling is *Agrostophyllum*.

AGROSTOPHYLLUM

Blume

Bijdr. Fl. Ned. Ind. **8**: 368, *t.* 53 (1825).

Epidendroideæ ◊ Agrostophyllinæ • Currently unplaced

ETYMOLOGY: *Agrostis*, a genus of grasses and Greek for leaf. Refers to the appearance of the grass-like, even reedy leaves of some, but not all of the species.

TYPE SPECIES: *Agrostophyllum javanicum* Blume

Ninety-one sympodial epiphytes or occasionally terrestrials are found in low to upper elevation, hill scrub and montane forests extending from the Seychelles to Malaysia, and Indonesia to Samoa with the largest group found in New Guinea. These tufted plants (easily overlooked by the casual observer because of their small size) have long, clustered, frequently hanging stems, each with numerous, distichous, thinly textured leaves arranged in two rows. The leaf sheaths have black or brown margins. The small, white, yellow or pale red flowers, borne on a short, tightly bracted, ball-like, numerous-flowered inflorescence, last for only a few days, and are self-pollinating in most of the species. The entire to trilobed lip is sac-like. The flowers have a long or short, winged column.

AGROSTOPOPHYLLUM

An orthographic variant introduced in *Bot. Jahrb. Syst.*, **45**(104): 22 (1911). The correct spelling is *Agrostophyllum*.

AILOGRAPHIS

An orthographic variant introduced in *Revis. Gen. Pl.*, **2**: 649 (1891). The correct spelling is *Aiolographis*.

AINIA

An orthographic variant introduced in *Intr. Orchids*, 290 (1981). The correct spelling is *Tainia*.

AIOLOGRAPHIS

Thouars

Hist. Orchid. Table 2, sub 3n, *tt.* 46-47 (1822).

Name published without a description. Today this name is most often referred to *Eulophia*.

AIRIDIUM

Not *Airidium* Steudel (1855) Poaceæ.

An orthographic variant cited in *Lex. Gen. Phan.*, 15 (1904). The correct spelling is *Aeridium*.

ALA

Szlachetko

Fragm. Florist. Geobot. **3**(Suppl.): 113 (1995).

Not validly published, this name is most often referred to *Alinorchis*.

ALAMANIA

Lexarza

Ann. Sci. Nat. (Paris) **3**: 452 (1824), and *Nov. Veg. Descr.* **2**(Orch. Opusc.): 31 (1825).

Epidendroideæ ◊ Epidendreæ • Laeliinæ

ETYMOLOGY: Honoring Lucas Ignacio José Alamán y Escalada (1792-1853), a prominent Mexican public official, who founded both the Museum of Antiquities and the Natural History Museum located in Mexico City, and who contributed many plant specimens sent to Augustin Pyramus de Candolle (1778-1841) in France.

TYPE SPECIES: *Alamania punicea* Lexarza

One dwarf, sympodial epiphyte or rare lithophyte is found in mid to upper elevation, open oak-pine forests, woodlands, pastures and lava flows of central and southern Mexico. This plant has short, inconspicuous, clustered, ovoid pseudobulbous stems, each with one to three, oblong, leathery leaves borne at the tip. The terminal, few-flowered inflorescence, borne from a leafless, dried sheath-covered pseudobulb, has fairly showy flowers that vary in color from vivid vermilion to scarlet. They have a white to yellow area around the lip that is similar in shape to other narrow segments. The bright red, wingless, erect column forms a tube with the claw of the entire lip. The long lip is obscurely angled on each side in the middle and has a basal callus of low, rounded ridges.

ALAMANNIA

An orthographic variant introduced in *Orchid. Scelet.*, 14 (1826). The correct spelling is *Alamania*.

ALAMARIA

An orthographic variant introduced in *Dict. Sci. Nat.*, **36**: 304 (1825). The correct spelling is *Alamania*.

ALATICAULIA

Luer

Monogr. Syst. Bot. Missouri Bot. Gard. **105**: 4 (2006).

ETYMOLOGY: Latin for ever and stem. Referring to the triangular (in cross section) shape of the inflorescence.

TYPE SPECIES: *Alaticaulia melanoxantha*
(Linden & Reichenbach f.) Luer
(*Masdevallia melanoxantha* Linden & Reichenbach f.)

Recognized as belonging to the genus *Masdevallia*, *Alaticaulia* was proposed to include one hundred ten epiphytes or lithophytes found mostly in mid to upper elevation, montane forests of the western Andes from northeastern Colombia to Bolivia. These small to large plants have erect stems, subtended by tubular sheaths, each with a solitary, thick, leathery leaf. The few to solitary-flowered inflorescence has yellow to dark maroon flowers. The sepals taper into blunt tips and the united lateral sepals form a tube or cup shape. The small petals are usually hard and thick textured with a rounded callus at the base. The tiny, bilobed lip has an epichile and hypochile section. The flowers have an elongate, more or less club-shaped column.

Currently Accepted   Validly Published   Invalidly Published   Published Pre-1753   Superfluous Usage   Orthographic Variant   Fossil

Orchid Genera • 14

ALATIGLOSSUM

Baptista

Colet. Orquídeas Brasil. **3**: 87 (2006).

ETYMOLOGY: Latin for winged and tongue or lip. Refers to the unusual, large side lobes that are like the wings of a bird.

TYPE SPECIES: *Alatiglossum barbatum*
(Lindley) D.H. Baptista
(*Oncidium barbatum* Lindley)

Recognized as belonging to the genus *Oncidium*, *Alatiglossum* was proposed to include sixteen epiphytes found in mid elevation, montane forests ranging from Ecuador to Bolivia, southern Venezuela, the Guianas, and Brazil to northern Argentina. These plants have clustered, ovate, yellow-green, compressed, furrowed with age pseudobulbs, each with a solitary, narrow, glossy leaf. The slender, erect or arching, slightly branched, few-flowered inflorescence, borne from the pseudobulb base, has waxy, yellow flowers heavily blotched or spotted chestnut-brown. The bright yellow, trilobed lip has large, ear-like side lobes and the small, yellow midlobe has a large, toothed callus sprinkled with red spots. These flowers have a long column with tiny, roundish to almost square wings.

ALATILIPARIS

Margońska & Szlachetko

Ann. Bot. Fenn. **38**(2): 78 (2001).

Epidendroideæ ⚘ **Malaxideæ**

ETYMOLOGY: Latin for winged (seed) and *Liparis*, a genus of orchids. Referring to the prominently winged column.

TYPE SPECIES: *Alatiliparis filicornes*
Margońska & Szlachetko

Two sympodial terrestrials or epiphytes are found in mid elevation, montane forests of western Indonesia (Sumatra and Java) usually growing on moss laden dead twigs. These species are known only from the type specimens, one is located at Kew's Herbarium (Britain) and the other is found at Rijksherbarium in Leiden (Belgium). These small plants have clustered, ovate pseudobulbs, subtended by a few sheaths, each with a few narrow, thinly textured leaves. The spirally arranged leaves have a prominent vein on the undersides. The flattened or winged, few-flowered inflorescence, slightly zig-zagged, has salmon-red to yellow flowers opening widely. The unusual entire (squared to trilobed near the base) lip is not stalked but has a cone-like structure just above the base with a small cavity located at the top. The flowers have a short, stout, slightly curved, strongly winged, footless column.

ALEMANIA

An orthographic variant introduced in *Syn. Pl. (D. Dietrich)*, **5**: 8 (1852). The correct spelling is *Alamania*.

ALEMANNIA

An orthographic variant introduced in *Syn. Pl. (D. Dietrich)*, **5**: 83 (1852). The correct spelling is *Alamania*.

ALINORCHIS

Szlachetko

Polish Bot. J. **46**(2): 129 (2001).

ETYMOLOGY: Dedicated to Alina Szlachetko née Jusis (1961-), wife of Polish botanist, taxonomist, and author Dariusz Szlachetko. And Greek for orchid.

TYPE SPECIES: *Alinorchis decorata*
(Hochstetter ex A. Richard) Szlachetko
(*Habenaria decorata* Hochstetter ex A. Richard)

Now recognized as belonging to the genus *Habenaria*. *Alinorchis* was previously considered to include three terrestrials found in low elevation, rocky woodlands and grasslands of Eritrea, Ethiopia, Uganda and Kenya. These short, stout plants have several leaves decreasing in size as they proceed up the erect, unbranched stem. The pale green flowers have white, erect petals. The white, distinctly trilobed lip has a massive, triangular midlobe that projects forward and has short, thick, side lobes that are also turned back and upward.

ALIPSA

Hoffmannsegg

Verz. Orchid. 20 (1842).

ETYMOLOGY: Greek for to anoint or polish. Refers to the texture of the smooth column.

Or possibly for a near-anagram attempt for *Liparis*, a genus of orchids, indicating a relationship to *Liparis*.

TYPE SPECIES: *Alipsa foliosa* (Lindley) Hoffmannsegg
(*Liparis foliosa* Lindley)
This type name is now considered a synonym of
Liparis reflexa (R. Brown) Lindley;
basionym replaced with
Cymbidium reflexum R. Brown

Now recognized as belonging to the genus *Liparis*, *Alipsa* was previously considered to include one terrestrial or epiphyte found growing in low to mid elevation, dense clumps from coastal plains to inland scrub of southwestern Australia (New South Wales). This plant has pear-shaped pseudobulbs, each with several, thick, long leaves. The erect, numerous to few-flowered inflorescence has small, pale green-white or yellow-green flowers with narrow sepals and petals and gives off a most unpleasant fragrance. The broad, entire lip is strongly recurved above the

middle. The flowers have a slender, slightly curved column.

NOTE: Today, there is no copy of Hoffmannsegg's publication available; this name is based on a secondary report published in *Linnaea*, **16**(Litt.): 228 (1842).

ALIPSEA

An orthographic variant cited in *Dict. Fl. Pl.*, ed. 8, 41 (1973). The correct spelling is *Alipsa*.

ALISMA

Gerard

Herb. Gen. Hist. Pl. 443 (1633).

Pre-1753, a name cited by Gerard in his text that is an early improper use for referring to *Cypripedium*.

ALISMA

Linnaeus

Sp. Pl. (Linnaeus), ed. 1 **1**: 342 (1753).

ETYMOLOGY: An ancient Greek word for this water plant that was used by Pedanius Dioscorides (AD c. 40-90), a Cilicia-born Greek soldier, herbalist and author of *De Materia Medica*.

TYPE SPECIES: *Not Orchidaceæ*

Linnaeus did not include this genus in Orchidaceæ. However in 1561, there was one species placed in this originally pre-Linnaeus named genus by Cordus. This single species is now recognized as belonging to *Cephalanthera*. It is found in open woodlands and grassy margins throughout Europe, the Mediterranean, Morocco to Tunisia, Turkey, Israel, Jordan and the Caucasian Mountains. This erect plant has unbranched stems, each with several, scale-like, basal leaves and several, narrow leaves ascending up the stem. The few-flowered inflorescence has white, narrow segmented flowers that do not open widely. The species (*Alisma quorundam* Cordus, *Hist. Stirp.*, 150 (1561)), was originally mistakenly included in the water-plantain family, but the name should now be correctly identified as a synonym of *Cephalanthera longifolia* (Linnaeus) Fritsch.

ALISMATIS

Thal

Sylva Hercynia 13 (1588).

Pre-1753, therefore not validly published in fulfillment of nomenclatural rules; this name is most often referred to *Epipactis*.

ALISMOGRAPHIS

Thouars

Hist. Orchid. Table 2, sub 3n, *tt. 41-42* (1822).

ETYMOLOGY: Greek for water-plantain and writing. The meaning is obscure.

TYPE SPECIES: *None designated*

Not validly published, this name is referred to the genus *Calanthe*. *Alismographis* was considered to include one epiphyte found from Malaysia to Japan and Taiwan.

NOTE: This name was attributed to Kuntze in error by Ames in *Orchidaceæ (Ames)*, **2**: 156 (1908). But Govaerts in *World Checkl. Seed Pl.*, **1**(2): 5 (1995) attributes the name to *Eulophia plantaginea* (Thouars) Rolfe ex Hochreutiner.

ALISMORCHIS

An orthographic variant introduced in *Hist. Orchid.*, Table 1, sub 2l, *t. 35* (1822). The correct spelling is *Alismorkis*.

ALISMORKIS

Thouars

Nouv. Bull. Sci. Soc. Philom. Paris **1**(19): 318 (1809).

Name ICBN rejected vs. *Calanthe* R. Brown (1821) Orchidaceæ.

ETYMOLOGY: Greek for water-plantain and orchid. Refers to the plant's preference for occupying or growing in a damp habitat.

TYPE SPECIES: *None designated*

Although validly published this rejected name is now referred to *Calanthe*. *Alismorkis* was considered to include sixty-three terrestrials found from tropical Africa and Madagascar to the Philippines. These highly variable plants have distinctly pleated, green to silvery colored leaves that are slightly hairy on the underside. The numerous-flowered inflorescence has dark flowers with an equally dark hued lip sprinkled with warts.

ALLOCHILUS

Gagnepain

Bull. Mus. Natl. Hist. Nat., sér. 2 **4**(5): 591 (1932).

ETYMOLOGY: Greek for different or diverse and lip. Referring to the difference of the lip between this genus and its nearest ally, the genus *Haemaria*.

TYPE SPECIES: *Allochilus eberhardtii* Gagnepain

Now recognized as belonging to the genus *Goodyera*, *Allochilus* was previously considered to include one terrestrial found in dark, mid elevation, evergreen forests from India to Sri Lanka, Malaysia, southern China (Yunnan to Hainan), Myanmar to Vietnam, Taiwan, southern Japan (Ryukyu Islands), Indonesia (Java) and the Philippines. This large plant has suberect stems, each with several, tapering leaves that are minutely hairy on the top and hairy on the underside. The erect, numerous-flowered inflorescence has small, fragrant, yellow-green or brown-green flowers. The veined dorsal sepal and petals converge, forming a hood over the small column. The pale brown, tongue-shaped, entire lip has a concave base and a green-yellow spur. The above type name is now considered a synonym of *Goodyera fumata* Thwaites.

ALOISIA

An orthographic variant introduced in *Revis. Gen. Pl.*, **2**: 678 (1891). The correct spelling is *Alvisia*.

ALTENSTEINIA

Kunth

Nov. Gen. Sp. **1**: 332, *tt. 72-73* (1815).

Orchidoideæ • Cranichideæ • Cranichidinæ

ETYMOLOGY: Dedicated to Karl Siegmund Franz, Freiherr von Stein zum Altenstein (1770-1840), a Prussian baron, lawyer, minister of education and culture, statesman, historian and botanical research enthusiast.

TYPE SPECIES: *None designated*

Seven unusual but interesting sympodial terrestrials are dispersed in wet, mid to upper elevation, montane forests, scrub or rocky slopes from Venezuela and Colombia to Bolivia. These small, erect plants have thick stems, each with overlapping leaves (when present) forming a basal rosette, then changing to subtending, spirally arranged sheaths upward. The tall, densely packed, numerous-flowered inflorescence has intricate, small, green-white to yellow flowers often not opening fully. Both the narrow, tapering to curled petals and the spurred lip are separate from the column. These attractive flowers tend to diminish in size from the base to the tip of the rachis. The large, broad, concave, entire lip is finely notched along the margin. The flowers have an erect, flat, lip-like, footless column that extends beyond the anther.

ALTISATIS

Thouars

Hist. Orchid. Table 1, sub 1c, *t. 11, t. 12e* (1822).

Name published without a description. Today this name is most often referred to *Habenaria*.

ALVISIA

Lindley

Fol. Orchid. 8: *Alvisia*, 1 (1859).

Not *Alvisia* Thwaites ex Lindley (1858) Orchidaceæ.

ETYMOLOGY: A substitute name derived from *Alwisia*, a genus of orchids.

TYPE SPECIES: *Alvisia tenuis* Lindley

Now recognized as belonging to the genus *Conchidium*, *Alvisia* was previously considered to include one epiphyte found in wet, low elevation, evergreen forests of Sri Lanka. This small plant has oval pseudobulbs, each with a solitary, thinly textured, narrow leaf. The long, few-flowered, zig-zagged inflorescence has well-spaced, small, orange flowers with tiny petals and blunt, concave sepals. The unusual U-shaped, long-clawed lip is obscurely trilobed at the tip. The above type name is now considered a synonym of *Conchidium articulatum* (Lindley) Rauschert.

ALWISIA

Thwaites ex Lindley

J. Proc. Linn. Soc., Bot. **3**: 42 (1858).

Not *Alwisia* Berkeley & Broome (1873) Myxomycetes-Tubiferaceæ.

ETYMOLOGY: Dedicated to Mudliyar Harmanis de Alwis (1791-1892), a native Sri Lankan, world-renowned botanical illustrator and draftsman at Peradeniya Botanic Gardens which is located in the Sri Lankan capital city of Colombo.

TYPE SPECIES: *Alwisia minuta* Thwaites ex Lindley

Now recognized as belonging to the genus *Taeniophyllum*. *Alwisia* was previously considered to include one epiphyte found in wet, low elevation, evergreen woodlands of Sri Lanka. This minute, leafless plant has a tangled mass of flattened roots. The slender, white-green, tiny, short-lived flowers, borne in succession from a slowly elongating inflorescence, have veined petals and sepals and a short, swollen spur. The sac-like, entire lip has its tip curved into a harpoon-like barb. The flowers have a short, cup-shaped column. The above type name is now considered a synonym of *Taeniophyllum alwisii* Lindley.

ALYPSA

An orthographic variant introduced in *Revis. Gen. Pl*, **2**: 670 (1891). The correct spelling is *Alipsa*.

ALYSIA

An orthographic variant introduced in *J. Linn. Soc., Bot.*, **18**(110): 294 (1881). The correct spelling is *Alipsa*.

Currently Accepted   Validly Published   Invalidly Published   Published Pre-1753   Superfluous Usage   Orthographic Variant   Fossil

O r c h i d   G e n e r a · 16

AMALIA

Reichenbach

Deut. Bot. Herb.-Buch 52 (1841).

Not *Amalia* Endlicher (1837) Bromeliaceæ, and not *Amalia* De Toni f. (1932) Cyanophyceæ-Oscillatoriaceæ.

ETYMOLOGY: Dedicated to Maria Amalia Friederike Augusta Karolina Ludovica Josepha Aloysia Anna Nepomucena Philippina Vincentia Franziska de Paula Franziska de Chantal (1794-1870), Princess of Saxony, and daughter of Maximillian (1759-1838), King of Saxony.

LECTOTYPE: *Bletia grandiflora* La Llave

    This type name is now considered a synonym of
Laelia speciosa (Kunth) Schlechter
basionym
Bletia speciosa Kunth

Not validly published because of a prior use of the name, this homonym was replaced by *Laelia* or *Sophronitis*.

AMALIAS

An orthographic variant introduced in *Verz. Orchid.*, 20 (1842). The correct spelling is *Amalia*.

AMARIDIUM

An orthographic variant introduced in *Hort. Donat.*, 15 (1880). The correct spelling is *Camaridium*.

AMATZAUHTLI

An orthographic variant introduced in *Nov. Veg. Descr.*, **2**: 24 (1825). The correct spelling is *Amazauhtli*.

AMAZAUHTLI

Hernández

Rerum Med. Nov. Hisp. Thes. **1**: 349 (1651).

ETYMOLOGY: A Nahuatl word (a language spoken by the peoples that inhabited the central valley of Mexico, whose speakers included the Aztecs).

TYPE SPECIES: *Amazauhtli* Hernández

Pre-1753, therefore not validly published in fulfillment of nomenclatural rules; this name is most often referred to *Prosthechea* (fide Hagsater). *Amazauhtli* was previously considered to include one epiphyte found in western coastal, pine-oak forests and occasionally on rocks of central Mexico. This name may be a synonym of *Prosthechea concolor* (Lexarza) W.E. Higgins.

AMAZAUTHTLI

An orthographic variant introduced in *Parad. Batav.*, 208 (1698). The correct spelling is *Amazauhtli*.

AMBLOSTOMA

Scheidweiler

Allg. Gartenzeitung **6**(48): 383 (1838).

ETYMOLOGY: Greek for blunt or obtuse and mouth. An allusion to the flat appearance of the flower due to the lip and the column forming an open throat.

TYPE SPECIES: *Amblostoma cernuum* Scheidweiler

Now recognized as belonging to the genus *Epidendrum*, *Amblostoma* was previously considered to include nine epiphytes or lithophytes found in mid elevation, on steep, damp, rocky slopes from Mexico to Bolivia, Peru and northwestern Brazil. This interesting group of plants has narrow, spindle-shaped, clustered pseudobulbs, each with several, thinly textured, narrow leaves. The nodding, numerous-flowered inflorescence bears small, rather pretty, fleshy, pale yellow to yellow-green flowers with concave sepals and narrow, recurved petals. The wedge-shaped, trilobed lip has a blunt midlobe smaller than the narrow, incurved side lobes. The flowers have a short, thick, green, footless column. The above type name is now considered a synonym of *Epidendrum tridactylum* Lindley.

AMBLYANTHE

Rauschert

Feddes Repert. **94**(7-8): 436 (1983).

ETYMOLOGY: Greek for blunt or obtuse and flower. Refers to the blunt edges of the flower.

TYPE SPECIES: *Amblyanthe melanosticta*
(Schlechter) Rauschert
(*Dendrobium melanostictum* Schlechter)

A superfluous name proposed as a substitute for *Amblyanthus*.

AMBLYANTHUS

(Schlechter) Brieger

Orchideen (Schlechter), ed. 3 **1**(11-12): 686 (1981).

Not *Amblyanthus* A.P. de Candolle (1841) Myrsinaceæ.

ETYMOLOGY: Greek for blunt and flower. Referring to the blunt edges of the flower.

TYPE SPECIES: *Amblyanthus melanostictus*
(Schlechter) Brieger
(*Dendrobium melanostictum* Schlechter)

Not validly published because of a prior use of the name, this homonym was replaced by *Dendrobium*.

AMBLYGLOTTIS

Blume

Bijdr. Fl. Ned. Ind. **8**: 369, t. 64 (1825).

ETYMOLOGY: Greek for around and tongue or lip. Referring to the way the lip is fused to the base of the column.

TYPE SPECIES: *None designated*

Now recognized as belonging to the genus *Calanthe*, *Amblyglottis* was previously considered to include eight terrestrials found in mixed forests from tropical Africa (Guinea to Nigeria, Tanzania to Zimbabwe), and Madagascar to Indonesia to southern China (Hainan) and the Philippines. These plants have ovoid to cone-shaped pseudobulbs, each with several, narrow leaves, subtended by sheathing leaf bases. The erect, few-flowered inflorescence has large, showy, dark mauve, white-pink or orange flowers. The pale colored, trilobed lip, attached to the short, stout, fleshy column base, has a purple-red to orange callus, erect, rounded side lobes with low keels between the lobes, a narrow to oblong, shortly pointed midlobe, and a slender, curved spur often with a strongly hooked tip.

AMBLYOGLOTTIS

An orthographic variant introduced in *Ann. Hort. Bot.*, **5**: 138 (1862). The correct spelling is *Amblyglottis*.

AMBLYSTOMA

An orthographic variant cited in *Lex. Gen. Phan.*, 23 (1904). The correct spelling is *Amblostoma*.

AMBRELLA

H. Perrier

Bull. Soc. Bot. France **81**: 655 (1934).

Epidendroideæ ◊ Vandeæ • Angraecinæ

ETYMOLOGY: Named for Montagne d'Ambre, a prominent volcanic massif (4,460 ft./1,360 m), located on the northwestern tip of Madagascar, where the type species was collected and what is now a national park filled with biological treasures. And Latin for diminutive.

TYPE SPECIES: *Ambrella longituba* H. Perrier

One uncommon, monopodial epiphyte is found in humid, low elevation, hill scrub of northern Madagascar usually on *Calliandra alternans* branches. This small plant has short stems, each with several, oblong, leathery leaves that have blunt tips. The erect, solitary-flowered inflorescence, borne from the leaf sheath, has a disproportionately large, tubular, green-white flower not opening fully that has long, narrow sepals and petals. The narrow, trilobed lip surrounds the entire length of the long, slender column, and then is rolled into a narrow, straight, tube-like structure.

AMBYGLOTTIS

An orthographic variant introduced in *Paxton's Mag. Bot.*, **2**: 152 (1836). The correct spelling is *Amblyglottis*.

AMENIPPIS

Thouars

Hist. Orchid. Table 1, sub 1f, *tt. 21-22* (1822).

Name published without a description. Today this name is most often referred to *Satyrium*.

AMERORCHIS

Hultén

Ark. Bot., ser. 2 **7**(1): 34 (1968), and *Arq. Bot. Estado São Paulo*, n.s., f.m. **7**: 34 (1968).

ETYMOLOGY: Shortened form of America and Greek for orchid. Referring to the geographical location of this close relative of Eurasian *Orchis*.

TYPE SPECIES: *Amerorchis rotundifolia*
(Banks ex Pursh) Hultén
(*Orchis rotundifolia* Banks ex Pursh)

Now recognized as belonging to the genus *Platanthera*, *Amerorchis* was previously considered to include one terrestrial dispersed in wet, low elevation, moss laden woodlands, thickets, fens, muskeg regions and river banks of far the northwestern United States (Alaska), Wisconsin to Michigan, across Canada (Yukon Territory to Newfoundland) and southern Greenland. This dwarf plant has erect, unbranched stems, each with a solitary, basal leaf and subtending sheaths that proceed up the stem. The erect, few-flowered inflorescence has showy flowers. The white dorsal sepal and the pink to pink-white petals converge, forming a hood over the short, erect column and the lateral sepals are wide-spreading. The white, deeply trilobed lip has spreading side lobes, a broad, notched midlobe variously spotted or sprinkled deep magenta and a small, slender, decurved spur.

AMESIA

A. Nelson & J.F. Macbride

Bot. Gaz. **56**: 472 (1913).

ETYMOLOGY: In honor of Oakes Ames (1874-1950), an American orchidologist, professor of economic botany at Harvard University and founder of the Orchid Herbarium of Oakes Ames at the Harvard Botanical Museum.

TYPE SPECIES: *None designated*

Now recognized as belonging to the genus *Epipactis*, *Amesia* was previously considered to include twenty-nine usually large-sized terrestrials found in northern temperate wetlands, marshes and dunes of Europe (southern Scandinavia to Ukraine, Turkey to Kazakhstan, Bulgaria to far eastern Russia), Korea, Japan, Pakistan to Vietnam, Indonesia to northern Australia, western Canada, the western United States and Africa (Morocco to Tunisia and Ethiopia to Malawi). These erect plants have smooth to hairy stems, each with several, ovate leaves. The numerous to few-flowered inflorescence has dull yellow, green-yellow or brown flowers heavily suffused and veined purple, with slightly similar, spreading sepals and petals. The concave, trilobed lip has raised, basal swellings or calli. The flowers have a small column.

AMESIELLA

Schlechter

Notizbl. Bot. Gart. Berlin-Dahlem **9**(88): 591 (1926).

Name published without a description. Today this name is most often referred to *Amesiella* Garay.

AMESIELLA

Schlechter ex Garay

Bot. Mus. Leafl. **23**(4): 159 (1972).

Epidendroideæ ⚘ Vandeæ • Aeridinæ

ETYMOLOGY: Commemorating Oakes Ames (1874-1950). And Latin for diminutive.

TYPE SPECIES: *Amesiella philippinensis* (Ames) Garay
(*Angraecum philippinense* Ames)

Three monopodial epiphytes are found in wet, low to mid elevation, mossy hill to montane rain forests of the northern Philippines (Luzon and Mindoro) on forested slopes. These small plants have short stems, each with several, oblong, distichous, leathery to fleshy leaves arranged in two ranks. The short, few-flowered inflorescence has disproportionately large, showy, pristine white, fragrant flowers with similar, rounded sepals

(lateral sepals are united to the column foot) and petals. The entire or trilobed lip, inserted at the tip of the distinct column foot, has a yellow basal stain, and erect, oblong side lobes, and the midlobe is rounded at the tip and has a long, slender spur. The flowers have a rather stout to slender, erect column.

AMITOSTIGMA

Schlechter

Repert. Spec. Nov. Regni Veg. Beih. **4**: 91 (1919).

Orchidoideæ ⚘ Orchideæ • Orchidinæ

ETYMOLOGY: Greek for without, web, thread or string and stigma. Does not have a thread-like stigma as originally thought.

TYPE SPECIES: *Amitostigma gracile* (Blume) Schlechter
(*Mitostigma gracile* Blume)

Twenty-eight slender, dwarf, sympodial terrestrials are found in low to upper elevation, shaded cliffs, valleys, along river banks and bogs of Thailand, Vietnam, eastern Russia (Kuril Islands) and Japan to Taiwan with the vast majority occurring in China (Huebi to Guangxi). These plants have slender, erect or ascending, unbranched stems, subtended by two leaf-like, sheathing bracts, each with a solitary, oblong or narrow leaf. The solitary to few-flowered inflorescence has showy, usually rosy-purple, pink, white or rarely yellow flowers. The long, slightly broader petals and sepals converge, forming a hood over the short column. The spreading, variously trilobed or bilobed lip often has deep purple markings of spots or lines on the disc and has a short or long, cylindrical to cone-like spur.

AMOENIPPIS

An orthographic variant introduced in *Revis. Gen. Pl.*, 649 (1891). The correct spelling is *Amenippis*.

| Currently Accepted | Validly Published | Invalidly Published | Published Pre-1753 | Superfluous Usage | Orthographic Variant | Fossil |

Orchid Genera • **18**

AMPAROA

Schlechter

Repert. Spec. Nov. Regni Veg. Beih.   **19**: 64 (1923).

Epidendroideæ ⚲ **Cymbidieæ** • **Oncidiinæ**

ETYMOLOGY: In honor of Amparo de Zeledón née López-Calleja (1863-1957), the Cuban-born wife of José Cástulo Zeledón (1846-1923), a Costa Rican scientist, businessman and ornithologist. She provided herbarium shipments to Schlechter and also sponsored many collecting excursions by Adolphe Tonduz (1862-1921) and Karl Wercklé (1860-1924) thus accumulating over 20,000 specimens for Costa Rica's herbarium.

TYPE SPECIES: *Amparoa costaricensis* Schlechter

This type name is now considered a synonym of *Amparoa beloglossa* (Reichenbach f.) Schlechter; basionym *Odontoglossum beloglossum* Reichenbach f.

One uncommon, sympodial epiphyte is found in moist, low to mid elevation, oak-pine forests from southern Mexico (Oaxaca) to southern Costa Rica. This plant has congested, flattened, oval, sharp-edged pseudobulbs, partially subtended by several, distichous, leaf sheaths, each with a solitary, thinly textured, narrow, deeply ridged leaf. The arching, few-flowered inflorescence has small, yellow to olive-green flowers with tiny, narrow petals and a yellow, wedge-shaped entire lip. The flowers have a bright yellow, slender, club-shaped, wingless, footless column.

AMPHIGENA

Rolfe

Fl. Cap. (Harvey)   **5**(3): 197 (1913).

ETYMOLOGY: Greek for both, on both sides, around and to generate. Refers to classification problems; resemblance in habit to *Herschelia* and floral structure of *Monadenia*; however, it is distinct from both and does not agree with any member of the related genus *Disa*.

LECTOTYPE: *Amphigena leptostachya* (Sonder) Rolfe (*Disa leptostachya* Sonder)

Now recognized as belonging to the genus *Disa*, *Amphigena* was previously considered to include two slender, reed-like terrestrials found in low elevation, grasslands of the southwestern Cape province of South Africa. These robust, small, erect plants have unbranched stems, each with several, grass-like leaves that appear just before the flowers and soon wither. The long, few-flowered inflorescence has small, rather variable, green flowers arranged in a loose or dense fashion. The spurred, concave dorsal sepal and small petals converge, forming a hood over the short, footless column, and the large, spreading lateral sepals are often variously spotted dark purple. The above type name is now considered a synonym of *Disa tenuis* Lindley.

AMPHIGLOTTIS

Salisbury

Trans. Hort. Soc. London   **1**: 294 (1812).

ETYMOLOGY: Greek for around or both sides and tongue. Referring to the attachment of the lip at the base of the column.

TYPE SPECIES: *Amphiglottis secunda* (Jacquin) Salisbury (*Epidendrum secundum* Jacquin)

Now recognized as belonging to the genus *Epidendrum*, *Amphiglottis* was previously considered to include five epiphytes found in low to mid elevation, hill to montane forests from the southeastern United States (Florida), Mexico to Panama, Cuba to Trinidad, Venezuela, Colombia to Peru and northern Brazil. These erect plants, often forming dense mats or clusters, have slender, erect stems, each with several, rigid, leathery leaves often suffused purple. The simple, few to numerous-flowered, sometimes ball-shaped inflorescence has fragrant, variably-sized flowers ranging from white, yellow, orange and rose to magenta. The flowers have oblong sepals and distinctly pointed petals. The deeply trilobed lip shows a wide variation in the degree of fringes of the slender processes or notches and has yellow-white basal markings.

AMPHIGLOTTIUM

Lindley ex **Wittstein**

Etym.-Bot.-Handw.-Buch, ed. 1   40 (1852).

Name published without a description. Today this name is most often referred to *Amphiglottis*.

AMPHORCHIS

An orthographic variant introduced in *Hist. Orchid.*, Table 1, sub 1b, *tt. 4-5* (1822). The name is now referred to *Amphorkis*.

AMPHORKIS

Thouars

Nouv. Bull. Sci. Soc. Philom. Paris **1**(19): 316 (1809).

ETYMOLOGY: Greek for both or double and orchid. Referring to the number of tubers these species have.

TYPE SPECIES: *None designated*

Now recognized as belonging to the genus *Cynorkis*, *Amphorkis* was previously considered to include twelve terrestrials found in low elevation, hill forests of Madagascar and the Comoros Islands. These small, erect plants have unbranched stems, each with a solitary, narrow leaf. The short, few-flowered inflorescence has

small, inverted, purple or rosy flowers with ovate to oblong sepals and petals. The small, wedge-shaped, trilobed lip has short side lobes with blunt or roundish tips, the roundish midlobe has a scalloped margin and a small, slightly curved to straight, thin spur.

AMPHYGLOTTIS

Blume

Bijdr. Fl. Ned. Ind.   **7**: 369 (1825).

ETYMOLOGY: Greek for blunt or obtuse and tongue. An allusion to the shape of the broad lip.

TYPE SPECIES: *None designated*

Now recognized as belonging to the genus *Calanthe*, *Amphyglottis* was previously considered to include seven terrestrials found in humid, low to mid elevation, hill scrub, woodlands to shady montane forests widespread from Africa to India, Sri Lanka, Thailand to Vietnam, Japan, Indonesia and Australia to Fiji. These highly variable plants have ovoid pseudobulbs, each with several, deep green or silvery, ribbed leaves that are hairy on the underside. The numerous-flowered inflorescence has showy, white to pale purple flowers with pale green tips. The trilobed lip has narrow to oblong side lobes, a broad, deeply divided midlobe, a crested, bright yellow or red callus, and a slender, curved spur.

AMPLECTRUM

An orthographic variant introduced in *Fl. Bor.-Amer. (Hooker)*, **2**: 194 (1840). The correct spelling is *Aplectrum*.

AMPLIGLOSSUM

Campacci

Colet. Orquídeas Brasil.   **3**: 83 (2006).

ETYMOLOGY: Latin for wide or extended and tongue or lip. Refers to the wide, broad lip when compared to the other segments.

TYPE SPECIES: *Ampliglossum varicosum* (Lindley & Paxton) Campacci (*Oncidium varicosum* Lindley & Paxton)

Recognized as belonging to the genus *Oncidium*, *Ampliglossum* was proposed to include thirty epiphytes found in cool to warm, low to mid elevation, hill to montane forests from Peru to Bolivia, southern Venezuela, the Guianas, Brazil to northern Argentina and Paraguay. These plants have clustered, oblong, yellow-green, slightly compressed, furrowed with age pseudobulbs, each with two (rarely three), narrow, leathery leaves. The erect or arching, multibranched, numerous-flowered inflorescence, borne from the pseudobulb base, has small, inconspicuous, dull yellow flowers barred pale red-brown. The large, bright yellow, trilobed lip has small, roundish side lobes and the two to three lobed midlobe has a large callus with a series of teeth standing in a row down the center. These flowers have a long, broadly winged column.

ANACAMPTIS

Richard

De Orchid. Eur. 19, 25 (1817), and
Mém. Mus. Hist. Nat. **4**: 47, 55 (1818).

Orchidoideæ ◊ Orchideæ ● Orchidinæ

ETYMOLOGY: From Greek to bend back. A possible reference to the shape of the slender spur located at the base of the lip or to its reflexed pollinia.

TYPE SPECIES: *Anacamptis pyramidalis*
(Linnaeus) Richard
(*Orchis pyramidalis* Linnaeus)

Thirteen cool-growing, sympodial terrestrials are found in dry, low to upper elevation, meadows, nutrient-poor grasslands, limestone to chalk deposits or seaside dunes from Scandinavia to Spain, Belgium to Greece, western Russia, Tunisia to Algeria, Turkey to Syria, Saudia Arabia, Iraq and Iran. These erect, plants have leafy, unbranched stems, each with a basal rosette of smooth, narrow leaves. The erect, thick, numerous-flowered inflorescence has a distinct shape with its pyramid spike of delightful, small, pink, rose, mauve or rare white flowers that have a sweet to musky fragrance. The concave dorsal sepal and small petals converge, forming a hood over the short column. The flowering buds at the tip of the pyramidal are strikingly dark colored. The shallowly or distinctly trilobed lip has an entire or bilobed midlobe and a short or long, cylindrical, broad or thread-like, downward pointing, slightly incurved spur.

ANACAMTIS

An orthographic variant introduced in *Ann. Hort. Bot.*, **5**: 176 (1862). The correct spelling is *Anacamptis*.

ANACAPTIS

An orthographic variant introduced in *Syn. Pl. (D. Dietrich)*, **5**: 14, 129 (1852). The correct spelling is *Anacamptis*.

ANACHASTE

Warszewicz

Allg. Gartenzeitung **21**(24): 192 (1853).

Lindley & **T. Moore**

Treas. Bot. **1**: 58 (1866).

ETYMOLOGY: Greek for upper and throat. Refers to the mouth found at the base of the lip.

TYPE SPECIES: *Anachaste sanguinea* Warszewicz

Not validly published, this name is referred to *Odontoglossum*. *Anachaste* was previously considered to include one epiphyte found from Ecuador to Peru.

ANACHEILIUM

Reichenbach ex **Hoffmannsegg**

Verz. Orchid. 21 (1842).

ETYMOLOGY: Greek for up or above and lip. Alluding to the apparent position of the lip.

TYPE SPECIES: *Anacheilium cochleatum*
(Linnaeus) Hoffmannsegg
(*Epidendrum cochleatum* Linnaeus)

Now recognized as belonging to the genus *Prosthechea*, *Anacheilium* was previously considered to include twenty-six epiphytes found in low to mid elevation, seasonally dry to tropical evergreen forests from southeastern United States (Florida), the Bahamas, Cuba to Puerto Rico, Mexico to Colombia and the Guianas to Venezuela. These variable plants have smooth, ovoid to oblong, slightly compressed, sometimes stalked pseudobulbs, partially subtended by overlapping, thin, dry sheaths, each with several, narrow leaves. The erect, numerous to few-flowered inflorescence has faintly fragrant, variable, green-yellow to lime-green flowers suffused purple. The cockleshell shaped, deep purple to black, entire lip is basally joined to the stout, wingless, footless column that has a three toothed tip.

NOTE: Today, there is no copy of Hoffmannsegg's publication available; this name is based on a secondary report published in *Linnaea*, **16**(Litt.): 229 (1842).

ANACHEILUM

An orthographic variant cited in *Etym.-Bot.-Handw.-Buch*, ed. 1, 42 (1852). The correct spelling is *Anacheilium*.

ANACHILIUM

An orthographic variant cited in *Lex. Gen. Phan.*, 26 (1904). The correct spelling is *Anacheilium*.

ANACOCHILUS

An orthographic variant introduced in *Gart.-Zeitung (Berlin)*, **2**: 155 (1883). The correct spelling is *Anoectochilus*.

ANACYLIA

An orthographic variant cited in *Lex. Gen. Phan.*, 26 (1904). The correct spelling is *Encyclia*.

ANAECTOCHILUS

An orthographic variant introduced in *Paxton's Mag. Bot.*, **5**: 16 (1838). The correct spelling is *Anoectochilus*.

ANAECTOCHYLUS

An orthographic variant introduced in *Coll. Orchid.*, 81 (1858). The correct spelling is *Anoectochilus*.

ANAGRAECUM

An orthographic variant introduced in *Fl. Analítica Fitogeogr. Estado São Paulo*, **6**: 1306 (1973). The correct spelling is *Angraecum*.

ANAJELI-MARAVARA

An orthographic variant introduced in *Bot. Mag.*, **70**: sub 4108 (1844). The correct spelling is *Ansjeli*.

ANANTALI

An orthographic variant introduced in *Summa Pl.*, **5**: 239 (1791). The correct spelling is *Anantaly*.

ANANTALY

Rheede

Hort. Malab. **12**: 15-16, *t. 7* (1693).

ETYMOLOGY: The meaning of this Malayalam word is not very clear. Aana is elephant (in the form of something big) and thaali is shampoo or soapy.

TYPE SPECIES: *Anantaly maravara* Rheede

Pre-1753, therefore not validly published in fulfillment of nomenclatural rules; this name is most often referred to *Dendrobium*. *Anantali* was previously considered to include one epiphyte found in low elevation, open forests of southwestern India (Karnataka). This plant has several, hanging, long, woody stems, each with small, leathery leaves, but are usually leafless when the plant is not in flower. The several, hanging, few-flowered inflorescence,

Currently Accepted   Validly Published   Invalidly Published   Published Pre-1753   Superfluous Usage   Orthographic Variant   Fossil

borne from the upper nodes, has small, pale white flowers. The pale olive-green or creamy-yellow, trilobed lip has a small, rounded midlobe. This name is usually considered as a synonym of *Dendrobium ovatum* (Linnaeus) Kraenzlin.

ANAPHORA

Gagnepain

Bull. Mus. Natl. Hist. Nat., sér. 2 **4**(5): 592 (1932).

ETYMOLOGY: Greek for rising up or above and vessel. Refers to the lip that is united for half the length of the column.

TYPE SPECIES: *Anaphora liparioides* Gagnepain

This type name is now considered a synonym of *Dienia ophrydis* (J. König) Seidenfadenia; basionym *Epidendrum ophrydis* J. König

Now recognized as belonging to the genus *Dienia*, *Anaphora* was previously considered to include one terrestrial found in low to mid elevation, mixed forests of Vietnam and Cambodia. This insignificant, deciduous plant has thick, erect secondary stems, subtended by leaf sheaths, each with several, thinly textured, tufted, bright green leaves. The erect, few-flowered inflorescence has tiny, long-lasting, white to yellow-green flowers suffused purple. The wide, trilobed lip has broad, blunt side lobes and a long, narrow midlobe.

ANATHALLIS

Barbosa Rodrigues

Gen. Sp. Orchid. **1**: 23, *t. 470* (1877).

Epidendroideæ ◊ Epidendreæ • Pleurothallidinæ

ETYMOLOGY: Greek for up or back again and to flower sprout or bloom. Refers to disposition of the flowers.

LECTOTYPE: *Anathallis fasciculata* Barbosa Rodrigues

Eighty-nine sympodial epiphytes, lithophytes or terrestrials are widespread in humid, low to upper elevation, hill scrub and montane cloud forests from Cuba to Puerto Rico, southern Mexico to Brazil and northern Argentina with the most species found from Colombia to Bolivia. These often small to tiny plants have rigid stems, subtended by a few tubular sheaths, each with a solitary, elliptical to ovate, thick, fleshy to leathery leaf. The several, erect, few-flowered inflorescences, borne at the leaf axils, have small, translucent, fleshy, yellow-green to pale yellow flowers. The sepals are hairy or papillose on the inner surfaces and the narrow to ovate, rounded to thread-like petals often have either toothed or fringed margins. The oblong, elliptical or ovate, entire lip, hinged to the column foot, tapers to a recurved point and has a pair of thin, fin-like growths. The flowers have a small, variously winged column often hooded in many species.

ANCIPITIA

(Luer) Luer

Monogr. Syst. Bot. Missouri Bot. Gard. **95**: 254 (2004).

ETYMOLOGY: Latin for flattened and two edged. Refers to the sharply, laterally compressed ramicauls that are two-edged.

TYPE SPECIES: *Ancipitia anceps* (Luer) Luer (*Pleurothallis anceps* Luer)

Recognized as belonging to the genus *Pleurothallis*, *Ancipitia* was proposed to include twenty-seven epiphytes found in mid to upper elevation, montane forests from southern Mexico to Ecuador. These erect plants have erect stems, subtended by a leaf-like basal sheath, each with a solitary, heart-shaped leaf. The short, solitary-flowered inflorescence, borne at the base of the leaf, has a small, red-orange to white flower. The thinly textured, lateral sepals are united with the petals that thicken toward the tips. The diversely shaped, entire, trilobed or five-lobed lip has various shapes resembling bizarre insects or heads of animals with ears or horns. The flowers have a short or long, stout or slender, wingless column that is either with or without a column foot.

ANCISTROCHILUS

Rolfe

Fl. Trop. Afr. **7**: 44 (1897).

Epidendroideæ ◊ Collabiinæ • Currently unplaced

ETYMOLOGY: Greek for fish-hook or barbed and lip. Refers to the long, recurved, hook-shaped midlobe of the lip.

TYPE SPECIES: *Ancistrochilus thomsonianus* (Reichenbach f.) Rolfe (*Pachystoma thomsonianum* Reichenbach f.)

Two showy, sympodial semi-terrestrials or epiphytes are found in low to mid elevation, coastal and hill rain forests of Guinea to Central African Republic, Equatorial Guinea to the Congo and Uganda to Tanzania. These plants have small, clustered, ovoid to pear-shaped pseudobulbs, each with several, thinly to softly textured, narrow leaves that will fall off before the appearance of the arching, hairy, few-flowered, green inflorescence that is borne from the base of a mature pseudobulb. The showy, long-lasting, fragrant, pale green, white, pink, mauve or rosy flowers have widespreading sepals and petals that are hairy underneath. The purple, trilobed lip has green and brown tints, with erect, rounded, green side lobes. The rich purple midlobe is somewhat triangularly shaped and strongly recurved like a long hook, and tapers to a yellow tip. The flowers have a slender, green-brown, slightly curved, hairy, winged column that is almost as long as the lip.

ANCISTRORHYNCHUS

Finet

Bull. Soc. Bot. France **54**(9): 44 (1907).

Epidendroideæ ◊ Vandeæ • Aerangidinæ

ETYMOLOGY: Greek for fish-hook and snout or horn. Refers to the shape of the flat rostellum that is folded back on itself to form an upward-hooked portion.

LECTOTYPE: *Ancistrorhynchus recurvus* Finet

Sixteen uncommon, monopodial epiphytes are found in low to mid elevation, evergreen hill and river forests from southern Ethiopia, Liberia, Congo to Uganda, Tanzania and Malawi. These small to large-sized plants have short or long stems, each with several, overlapping, leathery to fleshy, distichous leaves that have bilobed or notched tips. The usually short, few-flowered, almost spherical inflorescence has clustered masses of tiny, usually white, fragrant flowers with green or white markings. They are borne in the leaf axils or from the stem between the leaves. The rather large, entire or obscurely trilobed lip is much larger than the similar sepals and petals. The straight to S-shaped or abruptly bent spur has a wide mouth that is constricted in the middle and has a swollen tip. The flowers have a short, erect, fleshy column with an inconspicuous foot and a pointed downward rostellum that sharply, recurves upward.

ANCKENBAELLE

An orthographic variant introduced in *Opera Bot.*, **2**: 18 (1759). The correct spelling is *Anckenballen.*.

ANCKENBALLEN

Aretius

Stocc Hornii et Nessi 235a (1561).

ETYMOLOGY: An old german word from the alpine region meaning butter and ball. Butter made from the alpine regions is usually brighter yellow than that of the valley areas. Refers to the bright yellow, ball-like pouch of the *Cypripedium* flower.

TYPE SPECIES: *None designated*

Pre-1753, therefore not validly published in fulfillment of nomenclatural rules; this name is most often referred to *Cypripedium*. *Anckenballen* was previously considered to include one terrestrial found in woodland scrub of northern Europe, Scandinavia, Baltic states and northeastern Russia. This erect plant has unbranched stems, each with several, ovoid to elliptical leaves. The solitary-flowered inflorescence has red-brown, twisted dorsal sepals and petals. The pouch or slipper-shaped lip is bright yellow.

ANDINIA

(Luer) Luer

Monogr. Syst. Bot. Missouri Bot. Gard. **79**: 5 (2000).

Epidendroideæ ⚘ Epidendreæ • Pleurothallidinæ

ETYMOLOGY: Named for the Andes, a range of mountains stretching along the 4,000 mile (6,400 km) length of western South America.

TYPE SPECIES: *Andinia dielsii* (Mansfeld) Luer
(*Lepanthes dielsii* Mansfeld)

Twenty-four sympodial epiphytes are found in cool, mid to upper elevation, montane cloud forests and woodlands of Colombia to Bolivia. These unusual, colony-forming, creeping plants have erect stems, subtended by a few tubular sheaths, each with a solitary, well-spaced, narrow, leathery leaf. The erect, solitary to few-flowered inflorescence has fleshy to thinly textured flowers whose color varies through many shades and combinations of yellow, orange, red, brown and purple. The tiny (rarely minute), narrow petals are shorter than the lateral sepals which are united for a portion of their length. The broad, ovate or triangular lateral sepals have tail-like tips. The tiny, entire, deeply trilobed to five-lobed lip has ovate, ear-like side lobes surrounding the short, club-shaped, wingless, footless column, and a small, broadly rounded midlobe.

ANDINORCHIS

Szlachetko, Mytnik & Górniak

Polish Bot. J. **51**(1): 31 (2006)[2007].

ETYMOLOGY: Named for the Andes, a long range of mountains in western South America and Greek for orchid.

TYPE SPECIES: *Andinorchis klugii*
(C. Schweinfurth) Szlachetko, Mytnik & Górniak
(*Zygopetalum klugii* C. Schweinfurth)

Recognized as belonging to the genera *Chaubardia* and *Huntleya*, *Andinorchis* was proposed to include two epiphytes found in low elevation, woodlands and along river banks of Peru and Ecuador. These plants have small, compressed, ovoid pseudobulbs, subtended by leaf-bearing sheaths, each with a solitary, thinly leathery, narrow leaf. The solitary-flowered inflorescence has a small to large, dull yellow, pale green to white flower with narrow sepals and petals suffused violet to pink along the margins. The shortly clawed, entire lip has a raised, fleshy callus and a toothed front. The flowers have a long to short, hairy (beneath) column.

ANDRACHNITIS

Lobel ex Ray

Hist. Pl. (Ray) **2**: 1222 (1688).

Pre-1753, therefore not validly published in fulfillment of nomenclatural rules; this name is most often referred to *Orchis*.

ANDREETTAEA

Luer

Selbyana **2**(2-3): 183 (1978).

ETYMOLOGY: Honoring Father Ángel M. Andreetta (1920-), an Italian-born Ecuadorian priest of the S.D.B. Salesian order, from Paute, Ecuador and an amateur botanist who collects the local flora.

TYPE SPECIES: *Andreettaea ocellus* Luer

Now recognized as belonging to the genus *Pleurothallis*, *Andreettaea* was proposed to include one lithophyte found in mid elevation, moss laden vertical rock cliffs of eastern Ecuador. This minute, tufted plant has several, short stems, subtended by thinly textured, ribbed sheaths, each with a solitary, thick, leathery leaf. The erect, two to three-flowered inflorescence has equally tiny, deep maroon flowers borne successively. The united sepals form a tube shape with only the tip of the dorsal sepal free. The minutely notched, purple petals are translucent. The thick, deeply concave, bowl-shaped, oblong, trilobed lip contains long, purple hairs and is shortly united to the column foot. The flowers have a small column.

ANDROCHILUS

Liebmann ex Hartman

Bot. Not. **1844**: 101 (1844), and
Förh. Skand. Naturf. Möte **4**: 197 (1847).

ETYMOLOGY: Greek for man or anther and lip. Descriptive of the union of the lower part of the lip with the anther.

TYPE SPECIES: *Androchilus campestris* Liebmann

Now recognized as belonging to the genus *Ponthieva*, *Androchilus* was previously considered to include one terrestrial found in the cool, deep shade of western Mexico (Veracruz and Campeche). This plant has short, unbranched stems, each with several, basal leaves. The erect, long, few-flowered, hairy inflorescence has tiny, white flowers. The distinctly clawed, triangular petals have wavy margins. The trilobed lip, joined to the sides of the short, massive, footless column has wing-like side lobes with long tapering tips.

ANDROCORYS

Schlechter

Repert. Spec. Nov. Regni Veg. Beih. **4**: 52 (1919), and
Orchid. Sino-Jap. Prodr. 52 (1919).

Orchidoideæ ⚘ Orchideæ • Orchidinæ

ETYMOLOGY: Latin for male or man and helmet. An allusion to the hood-shaped anthers.

TYPE SPECIES: *Androcorys ophioglossoides* Schlechter

Ten relatively small, insignificant, sympodial terrestrials are found in upper elevation, montane forests and meadows of northeastern India (Kashmir), Nepal, Japan (Honshu) and Taiwan with the largest number of species found in China (Yunnan to Henan and Qinghai to Shaanxi). These erect plants have slender stems, subtended by tubular sheaths, each with one to two, ovate to oblong, green leaves. The erect, few-flowered inflorescence has minute, pale green to yellow-green flowers. The concave dorsal sepal and broad petals usually converge, forming a hood over the short, erect column. The lateral sepals are similar in shape to the dorsal sepal. The small, oblong or strap-shaped, entire lip is obscurely sac-like to concave at the base with a blunt, narrow tip that abruptly turns downward.

ANDROGYNA

An orthographic variant cited in *Lex. Gen. Phan.*, 29, 415 (1904). The correct spelling is *Androgyne*.

ANDROGYNE

Griffith

Not. Pl. Asiat. **3**: 279 (1851).

Name ICBN rejected vs. *Panisea* (Lindley) Lindley (1854) Orchidaceæ.

ETYMOLOGY: Greek for man and woman. Refers to the bisexual characteristics of the flower.

TYPE SPECIES: *None designated*

Although validly published this rejected name is now referred to *Panisea*. *Androgyne* was considered to include two species.

ANECOCHILUS

Blume

Bijdr. Fl. Ned. Ind. **8**: 411, *t.* 15 (1825), and
Tab. Pl. Jav. Orchid. *t.* 1 (1825).

Name ICBN rejected vs. *Anoectochilus* Blume (1828).

ETYMOLOGY: Greek for open and lip. Referring to the lip that is united to the column but has its blades spreading to give the appearance of openness.

TYPE SPECIES: *None designated*

Although validly published this rejected name is now referred to *Anoectochilus*.

| Currently Accepted | Validly Published | Invalidly Published | Published Pre-1753 | Superfluous Usage | Orthographic Variant | Fossil |

O r c h i d   G e n e r a • **22**

ANECOCHYLUS

An orthographic variant introduced in *Gartenflora*, **15**: 251 (1866). The correct spelling is *Anoectochilus*.

ANECTOCHILUS

An orthographic variant introduced in *Floric. Cab. & Florist's Mag.*, **24**(10): 198 (1856). The correct spelling is *Anoectochilus*.

ANETTEA

Szlachetko & Mytnik

Polish Bot. J. **51**(1): 49 (2006)[2007].

ETYMOLOGY: Dedicated to Anette Mülbaier, née Fehr (1961-), a German horticulturist and curator of the Orchid Living Collection at Heidelberg University.

TYPE SPECIES: *Anettea crispa*
(Loddiges ex Lindley) Szlachetko
(*Oncidium crispum* Loddiges ex Lindley)

Recognized as belonging to the genus *Oncidium*, *Anettea* was proposed to include thirteen epiphytes found in low to mid elevation, hill scrub to montane rain forests of southeastern Brazil (Minas Gerais to Paraná). These plants have large, oblong or ovoid, clustered, compressed, wrinkled, dark brown pseudobulbs, partially subtended by dry, thin bracts, each with one to three, oblong to narrow, slightly leathery to leathery leaves. The hanging to erect, strongly branched, numerous-flowered inflorescences have large, showy, slightly fragrant (musty), chestnut-brown or copper-brown flowers with all margin segments strongly wavy. The broad, shortly clawed, entire lip has a wavy margin and a yellow, basal callus with short protuberances. The flowers have a short, fleshy column.

ANGEIANTHUS

An orthographic variant introduced in *Nat. Pflanzenfam.*, **2**(6): 176 (1889). The correct spelling is *Aggeianthus*.

ANGELI

An orthographic variant introduced in *Hist. Pl. (Ray)*, **3**: 588 (1704). The correct spelling is *Ansjeli*.

ANGGREK

An orthographic variant introduced in *Malay. Penins.*, 523 (1834). The correct spelling is *Angrec*.

ANGIANTHUS

Not *Angianthus* J.C. Wendland (1809) Asteraceæ.

An orthographic variant cited in *Lex. Gen. Phan.*, 14 (1904). The correct spelling is *Aggeianthus*.

ANGIDIUM

Lindley

Nat. Syst. Bot. 340 (1836).

ETYMOLOGY: *Angraecum*, a genus of orchids, an abbreviated spelling. Implying a similarity.

TYPE SPECIES: *None designated*

Name published without a description. Today this name is most often referred to *Cymbidium*.

ANGLAECUM

An orthographic variant introduced in *Useful Pl. Japan*, 204 (1895). The correct spelling is *Angraecum*.

ANGORCHIS

An orthographic variant introduced in *Hist. Orchid.*, Table 2, sub 3o, *t.* 48 (1822). The name is now referred to *Angorkis*.

ANGORKIS

Thouars

Nouv. Bull. Sci. Soc. Philom. Paris **1**(19): 318 (1809).

ETYMOLOGY: *Angraecum*, a genus of orchids and Greek for orchid. Formed from the first syllable of *Angraecum*, thus implying a relationship.

TYPE SPECIES: *None designated*

Now recognized as belonging to the genera *Aerangis* and *Angraecum*, *Angorkis* was previously considered to include seventy-three epiphytes found primarily across tropical Africa (Ghana to northern South Africa), Madagascar and the Comoros Islands. These dwarf to large, robust plants are highly diverse in their vegetative appearance, with short or long stems, and the narrow leaves are almost always leathery and have bilobed tips. The solitary to numerous-flowered inflorescence has small to large, waxy, nocturnally fragrant, showy to spectacular flowers colored in various shades of white and green. The boat-shaped, entire lip is usually quite concave, and the spur alone may reach lengths of twelve or more inches (30 cm). The flowers have a small, footless column.

ANGRACUM

An orthographic variant introduced in *Encycl. (Lamarck) Suppl.*, **1**: 378 (1810). The correct spelling is *Angraecum*.

ANGRAECOPIS

An orthographic variant cited in *Orchideen (Schlechter): Liter. Reg. Band I/A, B, and C*, 162 (2003). The correct spelling is *Angraecopsis*.

ANGRAECOPSIS

Kraenzlin

Bot. Jahrb. Syst. **28**: 171 (1900).

Epidendroideæ ◊ Vandeæ • Aerangidinæ

ETYMOLOGY: *Angraecum*, a genus of orchids and Greek for appearance. Referring to a similarity to *Angraecum*.

TYPE SPECIES: *Angraecopsis tenerrima* Kraenzlin

Twenty-one monopodial epiphytes or rare lithophytes are found in low to mid elevation, deeply shady woodlands to montane evergreen forests often near or along river banks from Ethiopia to Uganda and Ivory Coast to Zambia, with a few species found in Madagascar and the Mascarene and Comoros Islands. These mostly dwarf, short-stemmed plants appear almost leafless with their gray-green roots often more conspicuous than the distichous, narrow or scythe-shaped, leathery or somewhat fleshy, unequally bilobed leaves. The several, long, hanging, numerous to few-flowered inflorescences have small to tiny, spidery, sweetly fragrant, long-lived, heavily waxy, white, yellow or green flowers, with widespreading lateral sepals and arranged in two ranks along the rachis. The usually smaller, triangular petals are often united to lateral sepals at the base. The deeply trilobed or rare entire lip has a long, mostly cylindrical, slender, curved spur that is often longer than the lip. The flowers have a short to long, footless column.

ANGRAECUM

Rumphius

Herb. Amboin. (Rumphius) **6**: 95-109 (1750).

Pre-1753, therefore not validly published in fulfillment of nomenclatural rules; this name is most often referred to *Dendrobium* and *Liparis*.

ANGRAECUM

Bory

Voy. Iles Afrique **1**: 359, *t. 19* (1804).

Epidendroideæ 〰 **Vandeæ** • **Angraecinæ**

ETYMOLOGY: Latinized form of the Malayan word (*Angrek* or *Anggrek*) for the epiphytic orchids that resemble *Aerides* and *Vanda* in habit. The name *Angraecum* seems to have originated with Rumphius, who formed it from the word *Angrec*, a name or title given by the Malayans to parasitical Epidendra plants, the meaning of which has not been discovered. From Kaempfer we learn that *Angurèk* or *Anggrèk* is also the name used by the Javanese for these plants.

TYPE SPECIES: *Angraecum eburneum* Bory

More than two-hundred nineteen showy, monopodial epiphytes and lithophytes have a wide distribution in low to mid elevation, hill scrub and woodlands to montane evergreen forests from eastern tropical Africa (Kenya to South Africa) and Madagascar, although one species is found as far away as Sri Lanka. These miniature to large, clump-forming to rambling, warm to cool growing plants are vegetatively and florally quite diverse. The short to long stems, subtended by leaf bases, are leafy throughout with their channeled, fleshy to leathery, unequally bilobed leaves arranged in two rows. The one to several, short to long, solitary to few-flowered inflorescences have small to large flowers typically in shades of white, ivory or green. The flowers are noted for their spurs of widely varying lengths from quite long to short, and this spur usually has a wide mouth. The flowers have a thick, almost leathery texture, an exceptionally long flowering period, and an extraordinarily heavy nocturnal fragrance and the lip is larger than the other segments. The entire or obscurely lobed lip is shell or boat-shaped, usually quite concave, its base more or less encircles the column, and it has a central callus. The flowers have a short, footless column with deeply divided lobes.

ANGREC

Rumphius

Herb. Amboin. (Rumphius) **6**: 95-109 (1750).

Pre-1753, therefore not validly published in fulfillment of nomenclatural rules; this name is most often referred to *Dendrobium* and *Liparis*.

ANGRECUM

An orthographic variant introduced in *Ann. Sci. Nat., Bot.*, ser. 2, **1**: 167 (1834). The correct spelling is *Angraecum*.

ANGREK

An orthographic variant introduced in *Herb. Amboin. (Rumphius)*, **6**: 95 (1750). The correct spelling is *Angrec*.

ANGROCEUM

An orthographic variant introduced in *Rev. Hort. Belge Étrangère*, **30**: 163 (1904). The correct spelling is *Angraecum*.

ANGROSTOPHYLLUM

An orthographic variant introduced in *Orchid. Nepal*, 43 (1978). The correct spelling is *Agrostophyllum*.

ANGULOA

Ruiz & Pavón

Fl. Peruv. Prodr. 118, *t. 26* (1794).

Epidendroideæ 〰 **Cymbidieæ** • **Maxillariinæ**

ETYMOLOGY: In honor of Francisco de Angulo (x-1815), a Spanish appointed director-general of mines (1788-1815) for the King of Spain (Carlos IV), especially to ensure the continued production of mercury at Almadén in Spain, a student of botany and a friend of Ruiz and Pavón.

Not for Francisco de Angulo who as mayor of the mercury mines founded the city of Huancavelica, Peru in 1571.

LECTOTYPE: *Anguloa uniflora* Ruiz & Pavón

Eleven fabulous, sympodial terrestrials or sometimes epiphytes make up this genus of tulip-shaped orchids found in low to upper elevation, hill scrub and montane forests of Venezuela and Colombia to Peru. These plants have fleshy, dark green, ovoid to spindle-shaped, lightly compressed, deeply furrowed pseudobulbs, each with several, large, broad, soft-ribbed, deciduous, pleated leaves that are shed during winter. A slender to stout, solitary to two-flowered inflorescence arises from the base of each new leafless pseudobulb as the new growth begins. Usually there are several scapes per pseudobulb which are subtended by overlapping sheaths. The typically large, waxy, cup-shaped, long-lived, fragrant flowers' color varies considerably from one species to another, and the broad lateral sepals are hood-shaped at the base. The erect, trilobed lip is parallel to the column, and it has large side lobes often rounded in the front, and the small midlobe has a central callus. The flowers have an erect, stout footed, wingless column that has a pair of fang-like appendages at the front.

ANGURECK

An orthographic variant introduced in *Def. Gen. Pl.*, ed. 3, 359 (1760). The correct spelling is *Angurek*.

ANGUREK

Kaempfer

Am. Exot. 866, 867, 869 (1712).

Pre-1753, therefore not validly published in fulfillment of nomenclatural rules; this name is most often referred to *Arachnis* and *Vanilla*.

ANIA

Lindley

Gen. Sp. Orchid. Pl. 129 (1831), and *Numer. List* 131, no. 3740-3741 (1831).

ETYMOLOGY: Greek for trouble or sorrow. Alluding to the uncertain taxonomical position of this genus at the time of its establishment to the genus *Tainia*.

LECTOTYPE: *Ania angustifolia* Lindley

Now recognized as belonging to the genus *Tainia*, *Ania* was previously considered to include sixteen terrestrials found from the Himalayas to Indonesia and New Guinea. These plants have shiny, purple-brown, cylindrical to cone-shaped pseudobulbs, usually with one internode, each with rather fragile, deciduous, pleated leaves. The long, wand-like, few-flowered inflorescence has large, pale yellow, thinly textured flowers covered with brown to purple stripes. The lateral sepals, attached to the column foot, form a chin-like protuberance or spur. The white, yellow tinged, entire or obscurely trilobed lip has tiny, red specks at the base of the raised keel, and a wavy margin. The flowers have a slender, slightly curved, winged column.

ANISOPETALA

(Kraenzlin) M.A. Clements

Telopea **10**(1): 283 (2003).

ETYMOLOGY: Greek for unequal or different shapes and petal. Descriptive of the vast disparity in the size and shape of the petals.

TYPE SPECIES: *Anisopetala mutabilis* (Blume) M.A. Clements (*Onychium mutabile* Blume)

Recognized as belonging to the genus *Dendrobium*, *Anisopetala* was proposed to include sixteen epiphytes or lithophytes found in humid, low elevation, shady forests and woodlands from Thailand to Malaysia, Indonesia, New

Currently Accepted | Validly Published | Invalidly Published | Published Pre-1753 | Superfluous Usage | Orthographic Variant | Fossil

O r c h i d   G e n e r a • **24**

Guinea, northern Australia, southern Japan (Ryukyu Islands) and the Philippines. These large, scrambling to frequently small plants have long, erect to drooping, narrow stems (turning red when exposed to full sun) with narrow leaves spaced along the entire length when young, and wither prior to flowering. The usually hanging, few-flowered inflorescence, borne near the tip of the stem, has showy, white flowers sometimes suffused rose to violet. The flowers have a distinct fusion of the basal portion of the lateral sepals which are always held away from the ovary, and the free portions of the petals and sepals are spreading. The broad, clawed, trilobed lip, without or with a small, bright yellow projection of the upper surface near the base, has small side lobes and a bilobed tip.

ANISOPETALON

Hooker
Exot. Fl. **2**(20): *t. 149* (1825).
ETYMOLOGY: Greek for unequal and petal or leaf. Descriptive of the vast disparity in the size of the inner and outer petals.
TYPE SPECIES: *Anisopetalon careyanum* Hooker

Now recognized as belonging to the genus *Bulbophyllum*, *Anisopetalon* was previously considered to include two epiphytes found in mid elevation, montane deciduous forests from Nepal, northern India (Assam) and Myanmar to Vietnam. These plants have roundish, lightly grooved pseudobulbs, each with a solitary, tongue-shaped, leathery leaf. The short-stalked, numerous-flowered inflorescence has numerous bracts and is packed with small flowers. The sour-smelling, green-yellow, ochre-yellow or coppery-brown flowers are often densely spotted purple-brown and have a small, entire lip.

ANISOPETALUM

An orthographic variant introduced in *Gard. Dict.*, ed. 9, **1**: 449 (1835). The correct spelling is *Anisopetalon*.

ANISTYLIS

Rafinesque
Neogenyton 4 (1825).
ETYMOLOGY: Greek for uneven or unequal and little pillar or style. Referring to the shape of the column.
TYPE SPECIES: *None designated*

Now recognized as belonging to the genus *Liparis*, *Anistylis* was previously considered to include two terrestrials found in mid elevation, open woodlands, fens, marshes and along river banks from Canada (Manitoba to Nova

Scotia), the eastern United States (Minnesota to Maine, Kansas to western North Carolina), southern Scandinavia, Britain, Germany to central Russia (West Siberia) and Kazakhstan. These short, delicate plants have the pseudobulbs subtended at their base by two fleshy, glossy green leaves. These plants are difficult to spot even when in bloom. The erect, few-flowered inflorescence has minute, yellow-green to purple flowers with narrow petals that are almost thread-like and similar, narrow, green sepals. The pale purple to green, sickle-shaped, recurved, entire lip has purple veining and a wavy, notched margin. Both species are now synonyms of *Liparis liliifolia* (Linnaeus) Richard ex Lindley and *Liparis loeselii* (Linnaeus) Richard.

ANKENBALLEN

An orthographic variant introduced in *Enum. Meth. Stirp. Helv.*, 276 (1742). The correct spelling is *Anckenballen*.

ANKENBULLEN

An orthographic variant introduced in *Vall. Apl.*, 130b (1633). The correct spelling is *Anckenballen*.

ANJELI

An orthographic variant introduced in *Hort. Donat.*, 210 (1858). The correct spelling is *Ansjeli*.

ANKYLOCHEILOS

Summerhayes
Bot. Mus. Leafl. **11**: 168 (1943).
ETYMOLOGY: Greek for crooked and lip. Referring to the shape of the incurved lip that forms a sharp slender hook shape.
TYPE SPECIES: *Ankylocheilos coxii* Summerhayes

Now recognized as belonging to the genus *Taeniophyllum*, *Ankylocheilos* was previously considered to include one epiphyte that is found in mid elevation, river forests from Ghana to Zimbabwe and Mauritius. Though leafless, this small plant is often concealed by the low mound of pale gray-green roots. The inflorescence has just a few tiny but complexly structured, orange-yellow, tubular flowers that open singly but have a long gap between appearances.

ANNELIESIA

Brieger & Lückel
Orchidee (Hamburg) **34**(4): 129 (1983).
ETYMOLOGY: In honor of Annelise Brieger, née Kaiser (1901-1995), the German-born wife of botanist, geneticist, professor, and noted author Fredrich Gustav Brieger (1900-1985).
TYPE SPECIES: *Anneliesia candida*
(Lindley) Brieger & Lückel
(*Miltonia candida* Lindley)

Now recognized as belonging to the genus *Miltonia*, *Anneliesia* was originally considered to include one epiphyte found in low elevation, woodlands of southeastern Brazil (Minas Gerais, São Paulo, Rio de Janeiro and Espírito Santo). This plant has ovoid (somewhat compressed), pseudobulbous stems, subtended by leaf-bearing sheaths, each with two strap-like, leathery leaves borne at the tip. The erect, few-flowered inflorescence has large, showy, waxy, fragrant, long-lasting, yellow or green-yellow flowers opening widely. The yellow tipped sepals and petals are heavily blotched purple-brown. The white, tubular or funnel-shaped, entire lip has a wavy margin, five to seven callus ridges at the base, then clasps, and is set at a 45° angle to the base of the short column.

ANOCHEILE

Hoffmannsegg ex Reichenbach
Nom. Bot. Hort. **2**: 235 (1846).
ETYMOLOGY: Greek for upward and lip. From the uppermost position of the lip.
TYPE SPECIES: *None designated*

Name published without a description. Today this name is most often referred to *Epidendrum*.

ANOCHILUS

(Schlechter) Rolfe
Fl. Cap. (Harvey) **5**(3): 280 (1913).
ETYMOLOGY: Greek for upward and lip. From the uppermost position of the lip.
LECTOTYPE: *Anochilus inversus* (Thunberg) Rolfe
(*Ophrys inversa* Thunberg)

Now recognized as belonging to the genus *Pterygodium*, *Anochilus* was previously considered to include two terrestrials distributed in dry, mid elevation, open scrublands of western and northwestern Cape areas of South Africa. These robust plants have erect, unbranched stems, each with several, wide, flat leaves spirally arranged. The numerous-flowered inflorescence has tiny, shallowly shaped, green-yellow or pale green flowers with narrow bracts. The shortly clawed, ovate, entire lip has a flat, wide, hairy and long appendage.

ROSEWARNE LEARNING CENTRE

ANOECOCHILUS

An orthographic variant introduced in *Wochenschr. Gartnerei Pflanzenk.*, **1**(18): 142 (1858). The correct spelling is *Anoectochilus*.

ANOECOCHYLUS

An orthographic variant introduced in *Gartenflora*, **15**: 250 (1866). The correct spelling is *Anoectochilus*.

ANOECTOCHILUS

Blume

Fl. Javæ Nov. Ser. 38 (1828), and
Fl. Javæ **1**: Praef. vi (1828).
Name ICBN conserved vs. *Anecochilus* Blume 1825 Orchidaceæ.

Orchidoideæ 🌿 **Cranichideæ** • **Goodyerinæ**

ETYMOLOGY: Greek for opened and lip. Refers to the lip that is attached to the column, which through a sharp bend in the narrow claw has widespreading blades giving the appearance of openness.

TYPE SPECIES: *Anoectochilus setaceus* (Blume) Blume (*Anecochilus setaceus* Blume)

There are forty-five of these scarce, taxonomically difficult sympodial terrestrials, lithophytes or rare epiphytes, also known as jewel orchids, which are found in low to upper elevation, undisturbed evergreen to deeply shady, hill and montane deciduous forests from southern China to the southwestern Pacific Archipelago and Hawaii (United States), but the greatest concentration is found in Indonesia. The small plants are not cultivated for their white, pink suffused flowers, but rather for their variegated, silvery to golden veined, metallic, velvety foliage. Some species form small, basal rosettes and others have ascending stems with alternating pairs of leaves. The erect to slightly hanging, few-flowered inflorescence has widely-spaced flowers whose petals and dorsal sepal converge, forming a hood over the short to obscure, footless column. The trilobed lip has a spurred or sac-like hypochile that is broadly cone-shaped, and extends beyond the spreading lateral sepals. The channeled, clawed mesochile is densely fringed to toothed, and the epichile has a broad-spreading, bilobed blade.

NOTE: There are several of these species used by the local people to treat certain health disorders.

ANOECHTOCHYLUS

An orthographic variant introduced in *Voy. Bonite, Bot.*, 92 (1866). The correct spelling is *Anoectochilus*.

ANOECTOCHYLUS

An orthographic variant introduced in *Prakt. Stud. Orchid.*, 192 (1854). The correct spelling is *Anoectochilus*.

ANOPLA

An orthographic variant introduced in *Ann. erd, Völk. Staat.*, **10**(1): 37 (1840). The correct spelling is *Aopla*.

ANOTA

(Lindley) Schlechter

Orchideen (Schlechter), ed. 1 587 (1914).

ETYMOLOGY: Greek for without and ear. Descriptive of the column that is without auricles or ear-like lobes.

TYPE SPECIES: *Anota densiflora* (Lindley) Schlechter (*Vanda densiflora* Lindley)
This type name is now considered a synonym of *Rhynchostylis gigantea* (Lindley) Ridley; basionym replaced with *Saccolabium giganteum* Lindley

Now recognized as belonging to the genus *Rhynchostylis*, *Anota* was previously considered to include five, short-stemmed epiphytes found in hot, low elevation, deciduous forests and savannas of Malaysia, Thailand and eastward to the Philippines. These plants have thick stems with leathery, strap-shaped leaves that basally overlap. The numerous-flowered inflorescence has highly fragrant, long-lived, waxy, pure white or pale blue flowers that are more or less spotted magenta. The entire or trilobed lip is a bright magenta, and has a small, sac-like or bent downward, hairy spur. The flowers have a short, stout column with an obscure foot.

ANSELIA

An orthographic variant introduced in *Bot. Zeitung (Berlin)*, **4**(48): 824 (1846). The correct spelling is *Ansellia*.

ANSELLA

An orthographic variant introduced in *Hamburger Garten- Blumenzeitung*, **11**: 223 (1855). The correct spelling is *Ansellia*.

ANSELLIA

Lindley

Edwards's Bot. Reg. **30**: sub 12 (1844).

Epidendroideæ 🌿 **Cymbidieæ** • **Eulophiinæ**

ETYMOLOGY: Honoring John Ansell (x-1847), a British gardener who collected the type species from Fernando Póo Island (now called Bioko) of Equatorial Guinea, when he was an assistant botanist on an 1841 expedition to the Niger River.

TYPE SPECIES: *Ansellia africana* Lindley

One highly variable, sympodial epiphyte or lithophyte that is quite common in low to mid elevation, dry, deciduous woodlands from Ghana to Rwanda and Kenya to South Africa. The widely varied, blotched markings of the large, long-lasting flowers lead to its common name of leopard orchid. This clump-forming plant has large dimensions ranging to about 5¹/₂ feet (1.8 m) tall and is difficult to raise in a small greenhouse and the root system can often be quite massive. The tall, cane-like pseudobulbs have fairly thinly textured, strap-shaped, ribbed, dark green leaves borne from the tip. The long, simple or branched, arching, numerous-flowered inflorescence has green-yellow, delicately scented flowers with dark red to brown-red markings varying considerably in their intensity. The trilobed lip has erect, oblong side lobes, and the oblong midlobe has two or three keels along the disc. The flowers have a slender, slightly curved, almost wingless column.

ANSICII

An orthographic variant introduced in *Summa Pl.*, **5**: 241 (1791). The correct spelling is *Ansjeli*.

ANSILIA

An orthographic variant introduced in *Jorn. Sci. Math. Phys. Nat.*, **4**(14): 184 (1873). The correct spelling is *Ansellia*.

ANSJELI

Rheede

Hort. Malab. **12**: 1-4, *t. 1* (1693).

ETYMOLOGY: This Malayalam word refers to *Artocarpus hirsutus*, a local species of trees, used to make canoes, upon which this species of orchid was found growing.

TYPE SPECIES: *Ansjeli maravara* Rheede

Pre-1753, therefore not validly published in fulfillment of nomenclatural rules; this name is most often referred to

Currently Accepted   Validly Published   Invalidly Published   Published Pre-1753   Superfluous Usage   Orthographic Variant   Fossil

Orchid Genera • 26

Rhynchostylis. Ansjeli was previously considered to include one epiphyte found in low elevation, deciduous forests and savannas of Sri Lanka, southern India, Myanmar and Thailand. This robust, semi-erect plant has short, thick stems, each with leathery, green-gray leaves. The hanging, numerous-flowered, cylindrical inflorescence has fragrant, pink-white flowers speckled or blotched purple. The concave, wedge-shaped, entire lip has an entire or notched tip, and a backward pointing, sac-like spur. The flowers have a short, stout, wingless column. This name is usually now considered as a synonym of *Rhynchostylis retusa* (Linnaeus) Blume.

ANTERIORCHIS

E. Klein & Strack

Phytochemistry **28**(8): 2136 (1989).

ETYMOLOGY: Latin for before or foremost and Greek for orchid. Alluding to the supposedly primitive flower structure of this species.

TYPE SPECIES: *Anteriorchis coriophora*
(Linnaeus) E. Klein & Strack
(*Orchis coriophora* Linnaeus)

Now recognized as belonging to the genus *Anacamptis*, *Anteriorchis* was proposed to include two terrestrials distributed in nutrient-poor meadows, open woodlands and scrub of Europe (France to central Russia), northern Africa (Morocco to Tunisia), most of the Mediterranean islands and Turkey to Israel. These erect plants have unbranched stems, each with several, narrow leaves located at the base. The numerous-flowered inflorescence has brown, red, pink or green flowers that range in fragrance from sour to sweet like vanilla. The sepals and petals converge, forming a beaked hood over the short column. The trilobed lip has long, toothed side lobes, and the midlobe widely varies in size and length and bears a long, cone-shaped spur.

ANTHEREON

Pridgeon & M.W. Chase

Lindleyana **16**(4): 252 (2001).

ETYMOLOGY: Greek for chin or anther. In reference to the thin projection formed by the attachment of the sepals to the column foot.

TYPE SPECIES: *Anthereon tripteranthus*
(Reichenbach f.) Pridgeon & M.W. Chase
(*Pleurothallis triperantha* Reichenbach f.)

Not validly published, this name is referred to *Pabstiella*. *Anthereon* was proposed to include six epiphytes distributed from Costa Rica to Bolivia, the Guianas, Venezuela and Brazil to Argentina (Misiones).

ANTHERIA

An orthographic variant introduced in *Syn. Pl. (D. Dietrich)*, **5**: 164 (1852). The correct spelling is *Aetheria*.

ANTHERICLIS

Rafinesque

Amer. Monthly Mag. & Crit. Rev. **4**: 195 (1819), and *J. Phys. Chim. Hist. Nat. Arts* **89**: 261 (1819).

ETYMOLOGY: Greek for anther and bending. In reference to the leaning anther.

TYPE SPECIES: *None designated*

Now recognized as belonging to the genus *Tipularia*, *Anthericlis* was previously considered to include three terrestrials found in the eastern United States (New York, Georgia to eastern Texas), Japan, southern China, Nepal and Myanmar. These inconspicuous plants have a solitary, mottled pale brown, strongly nerved, ovoid leaf that is produced in the fall. The erect, numerous-flowered, pale red inflorescence produced the following summer has small, nodding flowers varying from green-white and lemon-yellow to bronze. The trilobed lip has small, rounded side lobes, a narrow, spreading midlobe, and a long, slender, curved spur.

ANTHOGAYAS

An orthographic variant cited in *Index Raf.*, 100 (1949). The correct spelling is *Anthogyas*.

ANTHOGONICUM

An orthographic variant introduced in *Orchid. Icon. Index*, **1**: 21 (1931). The correct spelling is *Anthogonium*.

ANTHOGONIUM

Wallich ex Lindley

Nat. Syst. Bot., ed. 2 341 (1836), and *Numer. List* 247, no. 7398 (1789).

Epidendroideæ 🌿 Arethuseæ • Arethusinæ

ETYMOLOGY: Greek for flower and angle. Referring to the curious angle at which the tubular flower is joined to the ovary.

TYPE SPECIES: *Anthogonium gracile* Wallich ex Lindley

One sympodial terrestrial is found in low to upper elevation, hill and montane semi-deciduous to deciduous forests and scrub of southern China (Yunnan, Guangxi, Guizhou and Xizang), northern India (Sikkim, Assam and Arunachal Pradesh), Nepal, Myanmar, Laos, Thailand and northern Vietnam. This plant

has small, ovoid, partly subterranean (corm) pseudobulbs, each with one to three deciduous, narrow, pleated leaves. The erect, simple or branched, loosely arranged, white, tan to pale green. few-flowered inflorescence is borne from the tip of the pseudobulb. These flowers do not open widely but do open in succession. The mainly white to pink flowers have long, slender petals and sepals (lower portion) which are united, forming a distinct, tube-like structure with an extremely odd appearance. The petals are hidden in the sepaline tube below the middle with the upper part slightly curved outwards. The entire lip, joined to the column base, has an obscurely trilobed, notched tip and has red to purple lines and spotting. The flowers have a slender, pink or white, wingless, footless column with an abruptly bent tip.

ANTHOGYAS

Rafinesque

Fl. Tellur. **4**: 44 (1836)[1837].

ETYMOLOGY: Greek for flower and giant.

Or possibly Greek Mythology. The name of two mythical personages mentioned by Virgil: one was a Trojan and a companion of Aeneas, and the other a Latin, who was slain by Aeneas.

TYPE SPECIES: *None designated*

Name published without a description. Today this name is most often referred to *Bletia*.

ANTHOGYMAS

An orthographic variant cited in *World Checkl. Seed Pl. (Govaerts)*, **1**(2): 8 (1995). The correct spelling is *Anthogyas*.

ANTHOLIPARIS

Foerster

Fl. Excurs. Aachen 351 (1878).

ETYMOLOGY: Greek for flower and *Liparis*, a genus of orchids.

TYPE SPECIES: *None designated*

Name published without a description. Today this name is most often referred to *Liparis*.

ANTHOLITHES

Cockerell

Bot. Gaz. **59**: 332, f. 1 (1915).

ETYMOLOGY: Greek for flower and stone. Referring to the flower shape embedded in the stone.

TYPE SPECIES: *Antholithes pediloides* Cockerell

One fossil orchid based on a resemblance to the lip of a *Cypripedium* from the Lower Oligocene epoch (36 million years ago). The specimen was found at Florissant, Colorado in fresh-water limestone beds. The specimen is based on superficial resemblances, lacks significant details and is not validly accepted.

ANTHOSIPHON

Schlechter

Repert. Spec. Nov. Regni Veg. Beih. **7**: 182 (1920).

Epidendroideæ ⁄ Cymbidieæ • Maxillariinæ

ETYMOLOGY: Greek for flower and tube. Descriptive of the sepals, that are partially united into a tube.

TYPE SPECIES: *Anthosiphon roseans* Schlechter

One miniature, sympodial epiphyte is found in upper elevation, montane forests of Panama and Colombia. These creeping plants have compressed, oblong pseudobulbs, well-spaced along the rhizome, each with a solitary, leathery leaf. The short, solitary-flowered inflorescence has numerous, overlapping, leaf-like bracts. The tubular, bright white or pale pink nerved, white flower, not open fully, has narrow, similar sepals and petals. The narrow, sharply pointed, entire lip is extended at the base into a long, hollow spur. The flowers have a short, wingless, footless column.

ANTICHEIROSTYLIS

Fitzgerald

Austral. Orch. **2**(4): Backcover (1888).

ETYMOLOGY: Greek for against or in place of and *Cheirostylis*, a genus of orchids. Indicating a comparison to be made with *Cheirostylis*.

TYPE SPECIES: *Corunastylis apostasioides* Fitzgerald

A superfluous name proposed as a substitute for *Genoplesium*.

ANTICHIROSTYLIS

An orthographic variant cited in *Lex. Gen. Phan.*, 36 (1904). The correct spelling is *Anticheirostylis*.

ANTICHIROSTYLUS

An orthographic variant cited in *Lex. Gen. Phan.*, 144 (1904). The correct spelling is *Anticheirostylis*.

ANTIDRIS

Thouars

Hist. Orchid. Table 1, sub 1a, *t. 1* (1822).

Name published without a description. Today this name is most often referred to *Disperis*.

ANTILLA

(Luer) Luer

Monogr. Syst. Bot. Missouri Bot. Gard. **95**: 255 (2004).

ETYMOLOGY: Latin for Antilles, a collective name used for a group of Caribbean islands also known as the West Indies. These widely spaced islands, spanning some 1,300 miles (2,000 km), separate the Caribbean Sea from the Atlantic Ocean.

TYPE SPECIES: *Antilla trichophora* (Lindley) Luer (*Pleurothallis trichophora* Lindley)

Recognized as belonging to the genus *Pleurothallis*, *Antilla* was proposed to include twelve epiphytes found in low elevation, dense scrub and woodlands from Cuba and Hispaniola to Trinidad. These erect to hanging plants have short stems, each with a solitary, long, narrow leaf that has notched margins. The long, wiry, arching to hanging, few-flowered inflorescence, borne from the leaf base, has tiny, dark red flowers not opening widely. The lateral sepals are united, and have small, sometimes minutely serrated petals. The minute, entire lip is often conspicuously clawed. The flowers have a large column.

ANTILLANORCHIS

Garay

Bradea **1**(40): 423 (1974).

Epidendroideæ ⁄ Cymbidieæ • Oncidiinæ

ETYMOLOGY: Latin for Antilles, a collective name used for a group of Caribbean islands also known as the West Indies. These widely spaced islands, spanning some 1,300 miles (2,000 km), separate the Caribbean Sea from the Atlantic Ocean. And Greek for orchid.

TYPE SPECIES: *Antillanorchis gundlachii* (C.H. Wright ex Grisebach) Garay (*Oncidium gundlachii* C.H. Wright ex Grisebach)

One sympodial epiphyte is found on the islands of Hispaniola and Cuba in low elevation, hill forests. This small, fan-shaped plant has a few rigid leaves with serrated margins and covered with red blotches. The solitary-flowered inflorescence has a tiny, delicate yellow to white flower with narrow, olive-green sepals and petals. The white, deeply-lobed, trilobed lip has margins of golden yellow and a yellow callus. The lip is fused to the face of the short, broadly winged column, while the passageway beneath the column is filled with long, thin hairs. The whole flower gives an impression of motion as if it is reaching for an insect.

ANZYBAS

D.L. Jones & M.A. Clements

Orchadian **13**(10): 442 (2002).

ETYMOLOGY: From an acronym for Australia and New Zealand (ANZ) and Latin for basal on the ground. Refers to the area where the species are found.

TYPE SPECIES: *Anzybas unguiculatus* (R. Brown) D.L. Jones & M.A. Clements (*Corysanthes unguiculata* R. Brown)

Recognized as belonging to the genus *Corybas*, *Anzybas* was proposed to include six terrestrials found in low elevation, bogs, tree litter and damp, moss laden areas of southern Australia (Victoria), Tasmania and New Zealand. These small to minute plants have short, unbranched stems, each with a solitary, ovate leaf that is sometimes trilobed and strongly ribbed, its underside usually suffused purple. The short, solitary-flowered inflorescence has a deep red-purple flower recurved against the ovary. The large dorsal sepal is contracted into a narrow claw, that is about the same length as the leaf. The thread-like lateral sepals are often shaped like crab claws, and the tiny petals are also thread-like. The tubular lip is inflated in the middle, and has margins with minute hairs and two open slits.

AOPLA

Lindley

Edwards's Bot. Reg. **20**: sub 1701, no. 30 (1835).

ETYMOLOGY: Greek for unarmed or without heavy armor on. Referring to the lack of a spur on the lip.

TYPE SPECIES: *Aopla reniformis* (D. Don) Lindley (*Listera reniformis* D. Don)

Now recognized as belonging to the genus *Habenaria*, *Aopla* was previously considered to include one terrestrial found in low elevation, grassy forests of northern India, southern China (Guangdong and Hainan), Hong Kong, Cambodia and Vietnam. This small, wiry plant has erect, unbranched, slender stems, each with several, ovate to heart-shaped leaves at the base. The long, few-flowered inflorescence has small, green flowers, subtended by bracts, with narrow to ovate segments. The kidney-shaped, trilobed lip has curly, thread-like side lobes, a long, hanging, thin midlobe, and a tiny, club-shaped spur.

Currently Accepted   Validly Published   Invalidly Published   Published Pre-1753   Superfluous Usage   Orthographic Variant   Fossil

O r c h i d   G e n e r a • 28

AORCHIS

P. Vermeulen

Jahresber. Naturwiss. Vereins Wuppertal
25: 32 (1972).

Orchidoideæ ᔒ Orchideæ • Orchidinæ

ETYMOLOGY: Greek for not and *Orchis*, a genus of orchids. Referring to the similarities of *Orchis*, while supposably not generally fitting the description for that genus.

TYPE SPECIES: *Aorchis spathulata*
(Lindley) P. Vermeulen
(*Gymnadenia spathulata* Lindley)

Two terrestrials are found in upper elevation, montane meadows and scrub of northern India (Assam), Nepal, Myanmar, central China (Qinghai to Yunnan, Xizang to Shaanxi), Korea, Japan and eastern Russia (Kamchatka and Primorye). These erect, often colony forming plants have unbranched, smooth stems, each with one or two, spatula-shaped leaves. The erect, few-flowered inflorescence has long, leaf-like spreading floral bracts. The rose-purple to deep purple flowers have a veined dorsal sepal and oblong petals that converge, forming a hood over the very short column. The rachis, separate from the main stalk, has all the flowers twisted to one side. The spoon-shaped, spotted, shortly clawed, entire lip has a minutely scalloped or entire margin with a dark colored patch located at the mouth of the short, blunt spur.

APATALES

Blume ex Ridley

J. Linn. Soc., Bot. **22**(145): 245, 279 (1887).

ETYMOLOGY: Latin for illusion or deceit. Refers to the unusually small size of the thread-like petals.

TYPE SPECIES: *Apatales purpurascens* Blume ex Ridley
This type name is now considered a synonym of
Liparis montana (Blume) Lindley;
basionym
Malaxis montana Blume

Not validly published, this name is referred to *Liparis*. *Apatales* was considered to include one terrestrial found in the Mascarene Islands and Indonesia (Java and Borneo) to Thailand.

APATHURIA

An orthographic variant introduced in *Numer. List*, 131 (1789). The correct spelling is *Apaturia*.

APATION

An orthographic variant cited in *Lex. Gen. Phan.*, 37 (1904). The correct spelling is *Apatales*.

APATOSELIS

An orthographic variant introduced in *Bot. Mus. Leafl.*, **27**(7-9): 185 (1980). The correct spelling is *Apatostelis*.

APATOSTELIS

Garay

Bot. Mus. Leafl. **27**(7-9): 185 (1979).

ETYMOLOGY: Greek for illusion, deceit or fraud and *Stelis*, a genus of orchids. Referring to the separation of this genus from *Stelis*.

TYPE SPECIES: *Apatostelis hylophila*
(Reichenbach f.) Garay
(*Stelis hylophila* Reichenbach f.)

Not validly published, this name is referred to *Stelis*. *Apatostelis* was considered to include thirty-three epiphytes widespread from Mexico to Colombia and Brazil.

APATURA

An orthographic variant introduced in *Revis. Fl. Malay.*, ed. 2, **1**: 147 (1953). The correct spelling is *Apaturia*.

APATURIA

Lindley

Gen. Sp. Orchid. Pl. 130 (1831), and
Numer. List 131, no. 3737-3739 (1789).

ETYMOLOGY: Apaturia was an ancient annual religious festival held in nearly all the Ionian (Greek) towns and lasted three days, on which occasion the various clans met to discuss their affairs. The word probably means the festival of "common relationship."

TYPE SPECIES: *None designated*

Now recognized as belonging to the genus *Pachystoma*, *Apaturia* was previously considered to include four terrestrials found in low elevation, grasslands and hilly slopes extending from northern India (Kashmir to Assam), Nepal, southern China (Yunnan to Hainan) to Taiwan, Myanmar to Vietnam, Indonesia, the Philippines, New Guinea and northern Australia to the southwestern Pacific Archipelago. These erect plants have unbranched stems, each with a solitary, grass-like, papery leaf usually withered by flowering time. The erect, tall, few-flowered inflorescence, borne on a separate shoot, has rather small but attractive, shortly hairy, pink to yellow-green flowers that do not open widely. The trilobed lip is slightly sac-like at the base and has erect, large side lobes, and the shortly pointed to rounded midlobe is recurved and has longitudinal keeps. The flowers have a slender column with a short foot.

APETALON

Wight

Icon. Pl. Ind. Orient. (Wight)
5(1): 22, t. 1758, f. 1 (1851).

ETYMOLOGY: Greek for negative or lacking and petals. Refers to the apparent absence of petals that are actually combined with the posterior sepal to form one unusually large lobe.

TYPE SPECIES: *Apetalon minutum* Wight

Now recognized as belonging to the genus *Didymoplexis*, *Apetalon* was previously considered to include one saprophyte ranging from India to Indonesia and the Philippines. This small, leafless plant has erect, unbranched stems and the few-flowered inflorescence has small, pale olive-brown or pink flowers. The yellow-white, entire lip has a row of yellow warts down the center. The above type name is now considered a synonym of *Didymoplexis pallens* Griffith.

APETALUM

An orthographic variant cited in *Lex. Gen. Phan.*, 37 (1904). The correct spelling is *Apetalon*.

APHYLLANGIS

Thouars

Hist. Orchid. Table 2, sub 3o, t. 73 (1822).

Name published without a description. Today this name is most often referred to *Solenangis*.

APHYLLORCHIS

Blume

Tab. Pl. Jav. Orchid. t. 77 (1825), and
Coll. Orchid. 51 (1858).

Epidendroideæ ᔒ Neottieæ

ETYMOLOGY: Greek for without, leafless and orchid. Referring to the leafless, saprophytic nature of the species.

TYPE SPECIES: *Aphyllorchis pallida* Blume

Twenty-one leafless, little-known, uncommon saprophytes widespread in deep humus, low to upper elevation, swamps, savannas, along river banks and hill scrub to montane evergreen forests of Sri Lanka, India, southern China (Xizang, Yunnan to Guangdong), Hong Kong, Malaysia, Indonesia, northeastern Australia (Queensland) and New Guinea. These plants, often forming large colonies, have erect, slender, pale brown to purple, unbranched stems subtended by several, short sheaths borne at the nodes. The extremely tall, few to numerous-flowered inflorescence has well-spaced, delicate, pale cream to yellow-green flowers that are often purple-streaked or blotched. The shortly clawed, obscurely trilobed or entire lip has small, triangular side lobes and a relatively large, concave midlobe with a wavy margin. The flowers have a slender, curved, wingless, footless column.

APISTA

Blume

Bijdr. Fl. Ned. Ind.   **7**: 296 (1825).

ETYMOLOGY: Greek for uncertain. Alluding to a similarity to *Podochilus*, a genus of orchids.

TYPE SPECIES: *Apista tenuis* Blume

Now recognized as belonging to the genus *Podochilus*, *Apista* was previously considered to include one tiny, moss-like lithophyte found in low elevation, moss laden woodlands of Indonesia and Malaysia. This tiny plant has long, slender branching stems, each with small (moss-like), narrow leaves twisted at the base. The short, terminal, few-flowered inflorescence, borne at the stem's tip, has small, white flowers not opening fully. The white, narrowly clawed, trilobed lip has two purple basal spots, a narrowly curved appendage on each side near the base, and a bluntly triangular shape.

APLECTRA

An orthographic variant introduced in *First Cat. Gard. Transylv. Univ.*, 13 (1824). The correct spelling is *Aplectrum*.

APLECTRUM

Nuttall

Gen. N. Amer. Pl. (Nuttall)   **2**: 197 (1818).

Name published without a description. Today this name is most often referred to *Aplectrum* Torrey.

APLECTRUM

(Nuttall) Torrey

Comp. Fl. N. Middle States   322 (1826).

Not *Aplectrum* Blume (1831) Melastomataceæ.

Epidendroideæ ⚘ **Calypsoeæ**

ETYMOLOGY: Greek for without or negative and a spur. Referring to the absence or lack of a spur.

TYPE SPECIES: *Aplectrum hyemale*
(Mühlenberg ex Willdenow) Torrey
(*Cymbidium hyemale* Mühlenberg ex Willdenow)

One sympodial terrestrial is found in moist, cool, low to mid elevation, open deciduous (beech and sugar maple) woodlands of

eastern North America from eastern Canada (southern Quebec and Ontario) to northern Georgia (United States) and Minnesota to Oklahoma. This small, often colony-forming plant has erect, unbranched stems borne from a small corm. The solitary, broad, heavily pleated, gray-green leaf has white veins, is green-purple underneath, appears first in autumn, persists until spring, and usually is withered by flowering time. The erect, few-flowered inflorescence has green-purple to green flowers suffused yellow, magenta or purple-brown and do not open widely. The long, slender petals converge over the small, slender, pale green, compressed, wingless column forming a hood. The white, trilobed lip has ovate side lobes, and an expanded midlobe with a wavy, scalloped margin suffused magenta or purple.

NOTE: The plants were used by the early colonists for glue and medicine, and even the corms were used as a food starch.

APLOSTELIS

An orthographic variant introduced in *Revis. Gen. Pl.*, **2**: 647 (1898). The correct spelling is *Aplostellis*.

APLOSTELLIS

Thouars

Hist. Orchid.   Table 1, sub 2g, t. 24 (1822).

Name published without a description. Today this name is most often referred to *Nervilia*.

APLOSTELLIS

A. Richard

Mém. Soc. Hist. Nat. Paris   **4**: 36 (1828), and *Dict. Class. Hist. Nat.*   **1**: 509 (1827).

ETYMOLOGY: Greek for simple or single and to bring together or to bind. In reference to the simplicity of the small, leafless, solitary-flowered plant.

TYPE SPECIES: *Aplostellis ambigua* A. Richard nom. illeg.
Nervilia petraea (Afzelius ex Swartz) Summerhayes
(*Arethusa petraea* Afzelius ex Swartz)

Now recognized as belonging to the genus *Nervilia*, *Aplostellis* was previously considered to include six terrestrials found in low to mid elevation, hill forests, wooded savannas, and nutrient-poor sandy areas of central and eastern Africa, eastern Saudia Arabia to Yemen and Australia. The solitary, dark olive-green leaf, appearing soon after flowering, has silvery rays decorating the topside and is purple colored on the underside. The erect, solitary-flowered inflorescence has a brown-green to green flower, opening for just a few short hours, that has long, narrow, tapering segments. The

narrow, white, trilobed lip has various degrees of wavy margin and is marked or speckled red or purple.

APODA-PROPEPENTIA

Luer

Monogr. Syst. Bot. Missouri Bot. Gard. **95**: 255 (2004).

ETYMOLOGY: Greek for footless or spurless and Latin for creeping or undecided. Refers to the habit of the hanging or crawling rhizome.

TYPE SPECIES: *Apoda-prorepentia testaefolia* (Swartz) Luer
(*Epidendrum testaefolium* Swartz)

Not validly published, this name is referred to *Pleurothallis*. *Apoda-Prorepentia* was proposed to include seven epiphytes found from Cuba to Jamaica, Hispaniola, Guatemala to Ecuador, Venezuela and southern Brazil.

APOROPSIS

(Schlechter) M.A. Clements & D.L. Jones

Orchadian   **13**(11): 485 (2002).

ETYMOLOGY: Greek for to be uncertain or without and callus formation. Refers to the disc that is without any callus on the lip.

TYPE SPECIES: *Aporopsis macfarlanei*
(F. Mueller) M.A. Clements & D.L. Jones
(*Dendrobium macfarlanei* F. Mueller)
not *Dendrobium macfarlanei* Reichenbach f.

Now recognized as belonging to the genus *Dendrobium*, *Aporopsis* was proposed to include two epiphytes found in low elevation, gullies and along river banks of New Guinea and neighboring islands usually growing in large masses on *Casuarina* trees in full sunlight. These small, clump-forming plants have purple-brown or green, spindle-shaped, often hanging stems. The several, leathery leaves have unequally bilobed tips and are usually concave on the upper surface. The several, few-flowered inflorescences have white to pale yellow, fragrant flowers with narrow, recurved sepals and clawed, diamond-shaped petals with wavy margins. The trilobed lip has oblong, rounded side lobes, with numerous, purple streaks, that enfold the tiny column, and an oblong midlobe tapering to a sharp point with a large, green basal tooth.

Currently Accepted   Validly Published   Invalidly Published   Published Pre-1753   Superfluous Usage   Orthographic Variant   Fossil

O r c h i d   G e n e r a   • **30**

APOROSTYLIS

Rupp & Hatch

Proc. Linn. Soc. New South Wales, ser. 2
70: 60 (1946).

Orchidoideæ ⚘ Diurideæ • Caladeniinæ

ETYMOLOGY: Greek for to be in uncertainty, and style. Referring to the column structure that is intermediate between the orchid genera *Caladenia* and *Chiloglottis*.

TYPE SPECIES: *Aporostylis bifolia*
(Hooker f.) Rupp & Hatch
(*Caladenia bifolia* Hooker f.)

One uncommon, sympodial terrestrial is found in wet, humid, low to mid elevation, hill scrub to montane forests and grasslands of New Zealand and the surrounding islands of Stewart, Codfish, Antipodes, Campbell and Auckland. The whole, quite hairy, erect plant has short, unbranched stems, each with two basal, red-splotched, green leaves, and one leaf slightly larger than the other. The erect, one- to two-flowered inflorescence has small, dull white flowers with the concave dorsal sepal forming a hood over the small, footless column. The similar, narrow lateral sepals and petals are wide-spreading. The broad, entire lip has a scalloped, upcurved margin and two thickened, lobed, central ridges with yellow markings.

APORUM

Blume

Bijdr. Fl. Ned. Ind. **7**: 334, *t.* 39 (1825).

ETYMOLOGY: Greek for poor or hard to discover. Descriptive of the tiny flowers.

TYPE SPECIES: *None designated*

Now recognized as belonging to the genus *Dendrobium* as a section, *Aporum* was previously considered to include forty-five mostly small epiphytes or lithophytes widespread in southeastern Asia and Indonesia with the largest group concentrated in Myanmar and Borneo. These small, often hanging plants have short to moderately long, thin, leafy stems, each with flattened, usually sharp-pointed, fleshy leaves (closely spaced or overlapping) arranged in two ranks. The several, solitary-flowered inflorescences are borne from a cluster of chaffy bracts. The small to tiny, showy, pale yellow to white, transparent flowers, appearing in succession, are somewhat short-lived. The petals are smaller than the dorsal sepal which in turn is much smaller than the broad lateral sepals. The clawed, trilobed lip, attached to the short column, has a green, red or yellow blotch in the center.

APOSTASIA

Blume

Bijdr. Fl. Ned. Ind. **8**: 423, *t.* 5 (1825).

Apostasioideæ ⚘

ETYMOLOGY: Greek for separation or divorce. Probably referring to the three partitions in the ovary that separate this genus from other orchids.

TYPE SPECIES: *Apostasia odorata* Blume

Seven smooth, sympodial terrestrials are found in shady, moist, low to mid elevation, hill scrub and montane evergreen forests of southern China, India, Sri Lanka, Myanmar to Vietnam, Indonesia, New Guinea, northern Australia (Queensland), the Philippines and southern Japan. These evergreen plants have thin to slender stems densely covered with veined, grass-like, pleated, spirally arranged leaves. The terminal, erect, few-flowered inflorescence branches a little and has small, dull white or yellow, star-shaped flowers with almost equal, usually widespreading sepals and petals. The unusual flowers open widely, are sometimes irregularly ribbed, and lack a distinct lip, but sometimes the entire lip is the slightly larger segment. The flowers have a curved or erect column with two, fertile stamens.

NOTE: These species, along with the genus *Neuweidia*, are considered by some taxonomists not to really belong to the Orchid family because they have two, fertile stamens and a poorly developed column.

APPENDICULA

Blume

Bijdr. Fl. Ned. Ind. **7**: 297, *t.* 40 (1825).

Not *Appendicula* A.P. de Candolle (1828) Melastomataceæ.

Epidendroideæ ⚘ Podochileæ • Podochilinæ

ETYMOLOGY: Latin for little appendix or a small appendage. Referring to the calli found on the lip.

LECTOTYPE: *Appendicula alba* Blume

One hundred forty-two sympodial epiphytes, lithophytes or rare terrestrials are found in humid, low to upper elevation, scrub to montane forests from southeastern China (Guangdong to Hainan), northern India (Assam), Myanmar to Vietnam, to New Caledonia and the Philippines with the center of development on Sumatra (Indonesia). These small to large, almost fern-like plants have long, slender, often compressed, erect or hanging stems, sometimes branching, with closely spaced, oblong, veined leaves arranged in two rows, and often flattened in one direction. The short to long, numerous to few-flowered, axillary inflorescence has tiny, uninteresting flowers ranging from green-yellow, pale green, and white to pale pink. The broad based lateral sepals are joined to the column foot, forming a chin-like protuberance

with lip. The entire or obscurely trilobed lip has roundish or concave basal appendages that are sometimes lengthened into small keels, and the small midlobe often has a median keel. The flowers have a small, short column.

APPENDICULOPSIS

(Schlechter) Szlachetko

Fragm. Florist. Geobot. **3**(Suppl.): 119 (1995).

ETYMOLOGY: *Appendicula*, a genus of orchids and Greek for appearance. Referring to a similarity.

TYPE SPECIES: *Appendiculopsis stipulata*
(Griffith) Szlachetko
(*Appendicula stipulata* Griffith)

Now recognized as belonging to the genus *Agrostophyllum*, *Appendiculopsis* was proposed to include ten epiphytes found in low elevation, hill forests throughout Thailand, Malaysia, and Indonesia (Sumatra and Borneo). Several of the species have similar vegetative appearances but have quite distinct flowers. The plants have conspicuously crowded leaves, forming a right angle with the axils of the stem and are abruptly terminated at their base with a small leaf base. The slender plants have a terminal, few-flowered inflorescence with white or pale yellow-brown flowers. The small, trilobed lip has short, triangular side lobes connected by a low, fleshy partition and the tiny midlobe forms a right angle to the sac-like base. The flowers have a short column.

APULARIA

An orthographic variant introduced in *Dict. Univ. Hist. Nat.*, **1**: 584 (1841). The correct spelling is *Tipularia*.

APURATIA

An orthographic variant introduced in *Prakt. Stud. Orchid.*, 192 (1854). The correct spelling is *Apaturia*.

ARACAMUNIA

Carnevali & I. Ramírez

Ann. Missouri Bot. Gard. **76**(4): 962 (1989).

Orchidoideæ ⚘ Cranichideæ • Spiranthinæ

ETYMOLOGY: Named for Cerro Aracamuni (4,724 ft./ 1,440 m) a flat, table-top, sandstone mountain (located in the southern portion of the Venezuelan state of Amazonas) where the type species was discovered.

TYPE SPECIES: *Aracamunia liesneri*
Carnevali & I. Ramírez

One terrestrial is found on the mid elevation summit of Cerro Aracamuni in southern Venezuela (Amazonas). This unique orchid plant is scattered in swampy, boggy areas along with sundews, bladderworts and pitcher plants. This small plant has short stems, each with several, smooth leaves forming a loose rosette. The leaf axils have one to two, prominent, club-like processes covered by multicellular, short hairs. The erect, sparsely hairy, few-flowered inflorescence has small, narrowly tubular, white flowers. The narrowly clawed, oblong, entire lip has fine, papillose or ciliate-like hairs found at the tip. The flowers have a long, slender, slightly club-shaped, wingless, footless column.

ARACBNAHENIS

An orthographic variant introduced in *Hist. Orchid., t. 18* (1822). The correct spelling is *Arachnabenis*.

ARACCANTHE

An orthographic variant introduced in *Orchids India*, ed. 2, 99 (1999). The correct spelling is *Arachnanthe*.

ARACHNABENIS

Thouars
Hist. Orchid.   Table 1, sub 1e (1822).

Name published without a description. Today this name is most often referred to *Habenaria*.

ARACHNANTE

An orthographic variant introduced in *Bull. Fed. Soc. Hort. Belgique*, **4**: 139 (1864). The correct spelling is *Arachnanthe*.

ARACHNANTHE

Blume
Fl. Javæ   **1**: Praef. vi (1828), and
Rumphia   **4**: 55, t. 196 (1849).
ETYMOLOGY: Greek for spider and flower. From the cobweb-like markings on the type species.
TYPE SPECIES: *None designated*

Now recognized as belonging to the genera *Arachnis* and *Esmeralda*, *Arachnanthe* was previously considered to include twelve epiphytes found in moist, upper elevation, montane shady valleys of the Himalayas, Myanmar, southern China and Thailand. These scrambling plants have hanging stems, each with thick, leathery, narrow leaves. The often hanging or arching, few-flowered inflorescence has large, long-lived, fragrant, bright chestnut-brown flowers covered with broad, pale yellow stripes. The roundish, white to yellow, trilobed lip is streaked red, and has a fleshy, centrally keeled midlobe.

ARACHNARIA

Szlachetko
Richardiana   **3**(4): 153 (2003).
ETYMOLOGY: Greek for spider and strap. Referring to the spidery appearance of these flowers with their narrow petals, lip and spur.
TYPE SPECIES: *Arachnaria armatissima*
    (Reichenbach f.) Szlachetko
    (*Habenaria armatissima* Reichenbach f.)

Recognized as belonging to the genus *Habenaria*, *Arachnaria* was proposed to include fifteen terrestrials found from Mali to Sudan and Somalia to Namibia, Zaire and Mozambique growing singly or in small groups on termite mounds, wet woodlands, nutrient-poor grasslands or dense scrub. These erect plants have unbranched stems, each with a few heart-shaped, basal leaves. The few-flowered inflorescence has a bract encasing each delicate green, yellow or white flower. The flowers often emit a sweet nocturnal fragrance to attract moths. The erect dorsal sepal is hood-shaped, and has narrow to thread-like, bilobed petals. The trilobed lip has broad to narrow, thread-like side lobes, a spear-shaped midlobe, and a long, cylindrical spur with a swollen tip.

ARACHNIS

Blume
Bijdr. Fl. Ned. Ind.   **8**: 365, t. 26 (1825).
Epidendroideæ • Vandeæ • Aeridinæ
ETYMOLOGY: Greek for spider. From the fanciful resemblance of the flower with its usually striped sepals to that of a spider.
TYPE SPECIES: *Arachnis moschifera* Blume nom. illeg.
    This type name is now considered a synonym of
LECTOTYPE: *Arachnis flos-aeris*
    (Linnaeus) Reichenbach f.
    (*Epidendrum flos-aeris* Linnaeus)

Eleven often tall, vine-like epiphytes, lithophytes and sometimes terrestrials. These plants are some of the showiest and robust of the monopodial species and are found most often in wet areas with their clambering stems and roots extending up the neighboring trees. The species are found in low to mid elevation, hill to montane valleys and on cliff faces in southern China (Yunnan to Hainan), Taiwan, northern India (Assam), Myanmar to Vietnam, New Guinea, the Philippines and the Solomons with the largest development occurring in Indonesia and Malaysia. These climbing or scrambling plants have long, branched stems with oblong, rigid, strap-like leaves and rigid, often long, numerous to few-flowered inflorescences. The large, showy, long-lasting, fleshy, musky to sweetly fragrant

flowers are spidery in appearance with the lateral sepals and petals often bent downward. The flowers have a wide range of color, and are used extensively in the cut flower trade. The short, trilobed lip (base is sac-like or has a short spur), attached to the column base by a short stalk, has a raised ridge or callus. The flowers have a short, stout, wingless column.

ARACHNITES

F.W. Schmidt
Fl. Boëm. Cent. 1   **1**: 74, t. 99 (1793).
Name ICBN rejected vs. *Arachnitis* Philippi (1864) Burmanniaceæ.
ETYMOLOGY: Greek for spider. An allusion to the shape of the lip that resembles the body of a spider.
TYPE SPECIES: *None designated*

Although validly published this rejected name is now referred to *Ophrys*. *Arachnites* was considered to include twenty-one terrestrials ranging from Britain to Afghanistan and Morocco to Tunisia. These small plants have unbranched stems, each with a basal rosette of leaves. The few-flowered inflorescence has widely varying flowers with a trilobed lip.

ARACHNITIS

An orthographic variant introduced in *Kultuur Orchid.*, 120 (1856). The correct spelling is *Arachnis*.

ARACHNODENDRIS

Thouars
Hist. Orchid.   Table 3, sub 3q, t. 88 (1822).

Name published without a description, today this name is most often referred to *Aeranthes*.

ARACHNORCHIS

D.L. Jones & M.A. Clements
Orchadian   **13**(9): 392 (2001).
ETYMOLOGY: Greek for spider and orchid. Refers to a common vernacular name applied to these species.
TYPE SPECIES: *Arachnorchis patersonii*
    (R. Brown) D.L. Jones & M.A. Clements
    (*Caladenia patersonii* R. Brown)

Recognized as belonging to the genus *Caladenia*, *Arachnorchis* was proposed to include one hundred fifty terrestrials found in low elevation, sandy, open forests and woodlands of Australia. These erect, wiry, hairy plants have unbranched stems, each with a solitary, narrow leaf. The tall, few-flowered inflorescence has green-red, white to pale yellow

Currently Accepted   Validly Published   Invalidly Published   Published Pre-1753   Superfluous Usage   Orthographic Variant   Fossil

Orchid Genera • **32**

flowers with the narrow, extended petals and sepals thickened into club-like segments. The broad, recurved, entire lip has bands of dark colored, club-like calli crowded in the center and numerous, red-brown nerves. The flowers have a long, incurved, winged column with two usually yellow, gland-like, basal structures.

ARACO

Hernández

Rerum Med. Nov. Hisp. Thes. 38 cum icon (1651).

ETYMOLOGY: Latin for a kind of leguminous plant (pea family). Perhaps refers to the similarity of its long seed pod to those of beans.

TYPE SPECIES: *Araco aromatico* Hernández

Pre-1753, therefore not validly published in fulfillment of nomenclatural rules; this name is most often referred to *Vanilla*. *Araco* was previously considered to include one epiphyte found in low elevation, wet forests and woodlands from the southeastern United States (Florida), Cuba to Trinidad, the Guianas, Venezuela, central Mexico to Bolivia, Brazil and Paraguay. This aerial climbing plant has fleshy, oblong leaves borne at intervals along the stout stem. The few-flowered inflorescence has short-lived, pale green to yellow-green flowers. The tubular, narrowly clawed, entire lip, united to the long, slender column, is covered with short, yellow hairs and has a fringed, rolled backward margin. This name is now usually considered a synonym of *Vanilla planifolia* Jackson ex Andrews.

NOTE: The *Vanilla* genus is cultivated throughout the tropics as a primary source of the vanilla essence that is used today in a wide variety of products.

ARACUS

An orthographic variant cited in *Cat. Pl. Jamaica*, 221 (1696). The correct spelling is *Araco*.

ARATOCHILUS

Ridley

J. Straits Branch Roy. Asiat. Soc. 27: 67 (1894).

ETYMOLOGY: Latin for plowed or plow-shaped and lip. Probably an allusion to the two, ear-like structures located on the column.

TYPE SPECIES: *Aratochilus orchidous* (J. König) Ridley
(*Epidendrum orchideum* J. König)

Not validly published, this name is referred to *Trichoglottis*. *Aratochilus* was considered to include one epiphyte found in eastern India (Nicobar Island), Malaysia, Thailand and Laos. The above type name is now considered a synonym of *Trichoglottis orchidea* (J. König) Garay.

NOTE: Gunnar Seidenfaden in *The descriptiones Epidendrorum of J.G. König 1791*, page 22 concluded that Ridley must have accidentally misspelled the name *Ceratochilus*.

ARCHINEOTTIA

S.C. Chen

Acta Phytotax. Sin. 17(2): 12 (1979).

ETYMOLOGY: Greek for first or primitive and *Neottia*, a genus of orchids. A supposedly primitive segregate of *Neottia*.

TYPE SPECIES: *Archineottia gaudissartii*
(Handel-Mazzetti) S.C. Chen
(*Neottia gaudissartii* Handel-Mazzetti)

Now recognized as belonging to the genus *Neottia*, *Archineottia* was previously considered to include two primitive saprophytes, one found in cool, mid elevation, montane forest litter of northern China (Shanxi) and the other species in central Japan (Nagano). This slender plant has erect, unbranched, leafless, yellow stems subtended with several sheaths. The hairy, numerous to few-flowered inflorescence has small, hairy, purple-red to pale yellow flowers. The flowers do not open widely, have an incomplete or primitive column structure and a terminal stigma. The erect stamen has a free filament attached to the back of the column and no rostellum.

ARCHIVEA

Christenson & Jenny

Orchids (West Palm Beach) 65(5): 497 (1996).

Epidendroideæ ⚬ Cymbidieæ • Stanhopeinæ

ETYMOLOGY: Named for the archives of the Orchid Herbarium established in 1841 with the collection of William Hooker's herbaria that became the basis of the herbarium at the Royal Botanic Gardens, Kew in Britain. This herbarium continues to expand, and today now contains more than seven million specimens of plants and fungi.

TYPE SPECIES: *Archivea kewensis* Christenson & Jenny

One sympodial epiphyte found in Brazil which today is known only from a drawing located in the archives at the Royal Botanic Gardens, Kew (Britain). This plant has ovoid, strongly ribbed pseudobulbs, each with a solitary, ribbed leaf. The hanging, few-flowered inflorescence, borne from the base of the pseudobulb, has widespreading, white flowers with long, narrow sepals, and smaller, narrow petals, which all taper to sharp tips. The clawed, trilobed lip has narrow, tiny side lobes and a very long, incurved midlobe with a blunt point. The flowers have a short, straight column that is dilated toward the tip, the clinandrium terminal and at 90° to the column, the stigma ventral, surrounded by narrow wings.

ARELDIA

(Luer) Luer

Monogr. Syst. Bot. Missouri Bot. Gard. 95: 255 (2004).

ETYMOLOGY: An acronym of RLD, Robert Louis Dressler (1927-), an American systematic botanist, orchidologist and author of numerous books and articles on orchids. He first collected this species.

TYPE SPECIES: *Areldia dressleri* (Luer) Luer
(*Pleurothallis dressleri* Luer)

Recognized as belonging to the genus *Pleurothallis*, *Areldia* was proposed to include one epiphyte found in wet, mid elevation, montane rain forests of eastern Panama. This tiny, creeping plant has a flat, roundish, minute, pale green, leathery leaf veined dark green and speckled with minute, translucent pits or dark dots. The hair-like, one- to three-flowered inflorescence has large, yellow-brown flowers borne in succession. The flowers have small, yellow petals and the smooth, thinly textured sepals are mottled or striped with purple; the dorsal sepal is boat-shaped, and the ovate, lateral sepals are united for a short length. The broad to heart-shaped, red-brown, clawed, entire lip has a disc with a pair of fringed crests, an erect, finger-like appendage at the base and a rounded tips. The flowers have a short, concave column.

ARETHUSA

Linnaeus

Sp. Pl. (Linnaeus), ed. 1 2: 950 (1753), and *Gen. Pl.*, ed. 5 407 (1754).

Epidendroideæ ⚬ Arethuseæ • Arethusinæ

ETYMOLOGY: Greek Mythology. Named for the lovely, river nymph Arethusa, a companion of the goddess Artemis, who loved enjoying the beauty of nature. Noticing a river during the course of an adventure, she was beckoned by the promise of a bath, but soon realized she was not alone. The god of this river (Alpheus) fell in love with her and pursued her, but Arethusa wanted nothing to do with his advances. She called upon the goddess Artemis to help rescue her and was transformed into a spring on the island of Ortygia. Alpheus, not be denied, changed himself to flow underground. Probably refers to the wet habitat usually preferred by this genus.

LECTOTYPE: *Arethusa bulbosa* Linnaeus

One sympodial terrestrial is widely scattered in cool, low to mid elevation, sphagnum bogs, dense swamps and wet meadows of southeastern Canada (Ontario, Quebec to Newfoundland), and the northeastern United States (eastern Minnesota to Maine and northern Illinois to New Jersey with a small patch found in western North Carolina). This erect plant has slender, unbranched stems, each with a solitary, narrow, deciduous, grass-like leaf, borne from subterranean corm-like bulbs, The stem continues to elongate after the flower blooms. The large, solitary (rarely two), fragrant, showy, pink, lavender to rare white flower has the dorsal and lateral sepals forming a hood, and the petals curve above the lip. The obscurely trilobed lip has a yellow keel covered with numerous hairs or yellow crests which become fringed toward the tip. The flowers have a long, delicate, pink, curved, footless column that resembles the lip and has broad, flattened, lateral wings.

NOTE: The little corms were used by local natives and early settlers to treat toothaches.

ARETHUSA

J.F. Gronovius

Fl. Virgin.   **2**: 184 (1743).

Pre-1753, therefore not validly published in fulfillment of nomenclatural rules; this name is most often referred to *Arethusa* Linnaeus.

ARETHUSAE

An orthographic variant cited in *Nomencl. Bot. (Steudel)*, ed. 2, **1**: 558 (1840). The correct spelling is *Arethusa*.

ARETHUSANTHA

Finet

Bull. Soc. Bot. France   **44**(4): 179, *t. 5* (1897).

ETYMOLOGY: *Arethusa*, a genus of orchids and Greek for flower. In reference to the flowers' resemblance to those of *Arethusa*.

TYPE SPECIES: *Arethusantha bletioides* Finet

Now recognized as belonging to the genus *Cymbidium*, *Arethusantha* was previously considered to include one epiphyte found in mid elevation, montane forests from southern China (Yunnan) and northeastern India (Assam) to Laos. This plant has small pseudobulbs, each with several, narrow leaves. The arching, numerous-flowered inflorescence has fragrant, bell-shaped, pale yellow flowers with only the flowers at the tip of the long, floral spike opening. The trilobed lip has oblong, erect side lobes and the small, some-times red spotted midlobe is marked with two, orange lines. The flowers have a slender, hairy column. The above type name is currently unplaced with any species.

ARETUSA

An orthographic variant introduced in *Nov. Veg. Descr.*, **2**: 14 (1825). The correct spelling is *Arethusa*.

ARGYNOCHIS

An orthographic variant introduced in *J. Roy. Hort. Soc.*, **7**(1): 98 (1886). The correct spelling is *Argyrorchis*.

ARGYRORCHIS

Blume

Fl. Javæ Nov. Ser.   101 (1858), and
Coll. Orchid.   120, *tt. 31, 36* (1858).

ETYMOLOGY: Latin for silver and orchid. Referring to the silvery markings and rims of the leaves.

TYPE SPECIES: *Argyrorchis javanica* Blume
  This type name is now considered a synonym of
   Macodes petola (Blume) Lindley;
    basionym
     Neottia petola Blume

Now recognized as belonging to the genus *Macodes*, *Argyrorchis* was previously considered to include one terrestrial found in low to mid elevation, hill and montane forests of central Indonesia (Java). This plant has velvety, dark olive-green leaves in a spiraling, loose rosette with blotches of pale green and gold veins and has pink to purple-green undersides. The erect, hairy, numerous-flowered inflorescence has small, insignificant, pink to red-brown flowers covered with soft hairs on the outside segments. The white, twisted, shortly clawed, entire lip is sac-like at the base. The flowers have a small, twisted column.

ARHYNCHIUM

Lindley

Paxton's Fl. Gard.   **1**: 142 (1851).

ETYMOLOGY: Greek for without and snout. Referring to the rostellum which is not extended into a long neck.

TYPE SPECIES: *Arhynchium labrosum*
   Lindley & Paxton

Now recognized as belonging to the genus *Arachnis*, *Arhynchium* was previously considered to include one epiphyte distributed in warm, mid elevation, montane forests from northeastern India (Assam), Myanmar, Thailand and Vietnam to Taiwan. This plant has erect stems, subtended by leaf-like sheaths, each with several, oblong, distichous leaves that are broadly and unequally bilobed. The lengthy, few-flowered inflorescence has long-lasting, waxy, fragrant, green-yellow flowers suffused red-brown. The long, narrow sepals and petals are barred red-brown along the margins. The small, white or yellow, shortly clawed, obscurely trilobed lip has small side lobes, the long, narrow midlobe has three brown keels, and a small, horn-like spur. The flowers have a short, stout, wingless column.

ARIANTHERA

An orthographic variant introduced in *Dict. Univ. Hist. Nat.*, **9**: 169 (1847). The correct spelling is *Acianthera*.

ARIANTHUS

An orthographic variant introduced in *Bibliogr. Bot. Handbuch*, 287 (1841). The correct spelling is *Acianthera*.

ARICO

An orthographic variant introduced in *Hist. Orchid.*, 16 (1972). The correct spelling is *Araco*.

ARIDES

An orthographic variant introduced in *Bull. Fed. Soc. Hort. Belgique*, **16**: 15 (1875). The correct spelling is *Aerides*.

ARIETINIUM

An orthographic variant introduced in *Dict. Univ. Hist. Nat.*, **9**: 170 (1847). The correct spelling is *Arietinum*.

ARIETINUM

L.C. Beck

Bot. North. Middle States   352 (1833).

ETYMOLOGY: Latin for ram. Alluding to the resemblance of the flower shape to a ram's head.

TYPE SPECIES: *Arietinum americanum*
     (R. Brown) L.C. Beck
    (*Cypripedium arietinum* R. Brown)

Now recognized as belonging to the genus *Cypripedium*, *Arietinum* was previously considered to include one terrestrial found in cool, mid to upper elevation, montane forests, sphagnum bogs and limestone slopes of the northeastern United States (northern Wisconsin to Maine), Canada (central Manitoba to southern Quebec, Prince Edward Island and Nova Scotia) and south-western China (Yunnan). This small, frail plant has erect, slender stems, subtended by brown, tubular sheaths, and are leafy near the middle of the stem. The hairy, solitary-flowered inflorescence has a short-lived, fragrant, brown-green to purple-brown flower. The white, sac-like lip has a small, orifice covered in long hairs, strongly mottled and veined purple, and is elongate downward into a blunt cone-shape. The above type name is now considered a synonym of *Cypripedium arietinum* R. Brown.

| Currently Accepted | Validly Published | Invalidly Published | Published Pre-1753 | Superfluous Usage | Orthographic Variant | Fossil |

O R C H I D   G E N E R A   •   **34**

ARISANORCHIS

Hayata
Icon. Pl. Formosan. **4**: 109, *t. 57* (1914).
ETYMOLOGY: Named for Mount Arisan (7,326 ft./
2,232 m) located at the southern tip of Taiwan (an
island off the southeastern coast of China), where
the type species was collected. And Greek for
orchid.
TYPE SPECIES: *Arisanorchis takeoi* Hayata

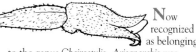

Now
recognized
as belonging
to the genus *Cheirostylis*, *Arisanorchis* was
previously considered to include two rather
insignificant terrestrials native in dense forests
from Japan to Taiwan. These small plants have
short, unbranched stems, each with several,
pale velvety green, basal leaves. The erect,
few-flowered inflorescence has green, slightly
hairy, small flowers. The sepals are joined for
half of their length forming a swollen tube,
and the oblong petals lie flat against the dorsal
sepal. The white, entire lip is recurved at the
tip. The flowers have a short, green column.
Both of the species are now considered
synonyms of *Cheirostylis takeoi* (Hayata) Schlechter.

ARISTOTELEA

Loureiro
Fl. Cochinch. **2**: 516, 522 (1790).
Not *Aristotelea* Sprengel (1825) Tiliaceæ.
ETYMOLOGY: Dedicated to Aristotle (384-322 BC),
Greek philosopher and scientist, born in northern
Greece (Macedonia). Aristotle and Plato (427-347
BC) were the most influential philosophers of
western tradition.
TYPE SPECIES: *Aristotelea spiralis* Loureiro
not *Ophrys spiralis* Linnaeus
This type name is now considered a synonym of
Spiranthes sinensis (Persoon) Ames;
basionym
Neottia sinensis Persoon

Now recognized as belonging
to the genus *Spiranthes*,
Aristotelea was previously
considered to include
one terrestrial found in low to
upper elevation, meadows,
pastures and piney woodlands from
eastern Russia (Amur, Kuril to Sakhalin), Iran
to Nepal, throughout China, Korea, Japan to
Indonesia, and Australia to the southwestern
Pacific Archipelago. This tall, erect plant
grows a basal rosette of leaves for the next
season alongside this year's flowering stems.
The tall, spiraling, numerous-flowered inflorescence has small, showy, bright magenta to
pink, slightly fragrant flowers. The white,
concave, entire lip has a wavy margin.

ARISTOTELIA

An orthographic variant introduced in *Fl.
Tellur.*, **2**: 86 (1836)[1837]. The correct spelling
is *Aristotelea*.

ARMODORUM

Breda
Gen. Sp. Orchid. Asclep., fasc. II   *t. 6* (1829).
Epidendroideæ ◊ Vandeæ • Aeridinæ
ETYMOLOGY: Greek for a crack in walls, nail or peg
and a gift. Alluding to its habit of growing in the
crevices of rocks.
TYPE SPECIES: *Armodorum distichum* Breda
This type name is now considered a synonym of
Armodorum sulingi (Blume) Schlechter;
basionym
Aerides sulingi Blume

Three uncommon, monopodial
epiphytes are found in low
elevation, forests and
scrub from Myanmar to Thailand
and Indonesia (Sumatra to Bali).
These rather vine-like plants
often grow to several feet in length. The rigid,
short or long, simple or branching, numerous
to few-flowered inflorescence has large,
fragrant, waxy, brown to green-yellow flowers
with long, narrow segments, and open all at
once. The small, brightly colored, trilobed lip
has small, erect side lobes, and the fleshy,
tongue-like midlobe has brown keels, usually
with two basal calli that almost obscure the
mouth of the short, thick spur. The flowers
have a short, slightly curved, wingless column.
NOTE: These plants are vegetatively similar to
Arachnis, but the trilobed lip has a dorsally flattened
midlobe.

ARNEDINA

An orthographic variant cited in *Deut. Bot.
Herb.-Buch*, 52 (1841). The correct spelling is
Arundina.

ARNOTTIA

A. Richard
Mém. Soc. Hist. Nat. Paris   **4**: 29, *t. 7* (1828), and
Monogr. Orchid. Bourbon   33, *t. 7* (1828).
Orchidoideæ ◊ Orchideæ • Orchidinæ
ETYMOLOGY: Dedicated to George Arnott Walker-
Arnott (1799-1868), a Scottish botanist, professor
of botany at Glasgow University and author of
numerous papers on mosses and the flora of India.
TYPE SPECIES: *Arnottia mauritiana* A. Richard

Four, rather common
sympodial terrestrials or
epiphytes are found
in low elevation,
hill rain forests of
Réunion, the Mascarene and
Mauritius Islands. These erect,
unbranched plants have a solitary leaf located
midway up the stem. The erect, hairy, few-
flowered inflorescence has rather large,
widespreading, white flowers, sometimes with
solid lilac lateral sepals. The strongly concave,
carmine rose, lilac or dark violet dorsal sepal
and small petals converge, forming a hood
over the tiny, erect column. The small, oblong,

entire lip is usually the same color as the
petals. These species are often included in
Cynorkis.

AROPHYLLUM

An orthographic variant introduced in *Gen.
Pl. (Endlicher)*, 193 (1837). The correct
spelling is *Arpophyllum*.

ARPHOPHYLLUM

An orthographic variant introduced in *Fl.
World Gard. Guide*, **6**: 88 (1863). The
correct spelling is *Arpophyllum*.

ARPOPHYLLUM

Lexarza
Nov. Veg. Descr.   **2**: 19 (1825).
Epidendroideæ ◊ Epidendreæ • Laeliinæ
ETYMOLOGY: Greek for sickle or scimitar and leaf.
Refers to the sickle-shaped leaves of the type species.
TYPE SPECIES: *Arpophyllum spicatum* Lexarza

Four spectacular, sympodial
epiphytes, lithophytes or
terrestrials, often called
hyacinth orchids, that
are found in low to upper
elevation, hill and
montane evergreen to
oak-pine forests of
Jamaica, Belize to Costa Rica, Colombia and
Venezuela with the most diversity occurring in
Mexico. These plants are highly variable in
their vegetative appearance and floral
dimensions, but can be readily identified by
their slender, compressed, stem-like pseudobulbs that are sometimes over a foot (30 cm)
tall, subtended by several, tubular sheaths, and
topped by a solitary, rigid, often channeled,
long-lasting, fleshy to leathery leaf. The small,
vividly hued, pink to purple, bell-shaped
flowers are borne on a tightly packed,
numerous-flowered, cylindrical inflorescence
that is subtended by a single, large bract. The
lateral sepals are united with the erect, slightly
curved, wingless column and have small,
oblong petals. The basally sac-like, entire lip,
usually smaller than the petals, has an entire,
irregularly notched or toothed margin.
NOTE: When Lexarza originally published the name
he misspelled it with just one 'L' - *Arpophylum*.

ARRHYCHIUM

An orthographic variant introduced in
Orchids India, ed. 2, 99 (1999). The correct
spelling is *Arhynchium*.

ARRHYNCHIUM

An orthographic variant introduced in *Ann.
Bot. Syst.*, **3**(3): 567 (1852). The correct
spelling is *Arhynchium*.

ARRHYNOCHIUM

An orthographic variant introduced in *Fl. Taiwan*, **5**: 882 (1978). The correct spelling is *Arhynchium*.

ARRYNCHIUM

An orthographic variant introduced in *Orchids Burma*, 262 (1895). The correct spelling is *Arhynchium*.

ARTHROCHILIUM

(Irmisch) Beck

Fl. Nieder-Osterreich **1**: 194, 212 (1890).

ETYMOLOGY: Greek for a joint and lip. Referring to the sharp distinction between the three parts of the lip that gives it the appearance of joints.

TYPE SPECIES: *Arthrochilium palustre* (Linnaeus) Beck (*Serapias helleborine* var. *palustris* Linnaeus)

Now recognized as belonging to the genus *Epipactis*, *Arthrochilium* was previously considered to include one terrestrial widely distributed in low to mid elevation, damp meadows, wet dunes and hollows from Britain to Poland, Spain to Romania, Turkey to Mongolia, Ukraine to Uzbekistan, Kazakhstan, Turkmenistan and central Russia (Krasnoyarsk). This erect plant has slender, unbranched stems, each with several, narrow leaves. The erect, few-flowered, hairy inflorescence has olive-green to red-brown flowers with slightly hairy sepals, and white to red petals. The white, trilobed lip has two orange stripes on each of the erect side lobes; the shortly clawed, broad midlobe has a wavy margin and toothed, yellow-edged basal swellings. The flowers have a short, curved column.

ARTHROCHILUM

An orthographic variant cited in *Handb. Orchid.-Namen*, 107, 329 (2005). The correct spelling is *Arthrochilium*.

ARTHROCHILUS

F. Mueller

Fragm. (Mueller) **1**(2): 42 (1858).

Orchidoideæ ⚘ Diurideæ • Thelymitrinæ

ETYMOLOGY: Greek for joint and lip. Alluding to the articulated, mobile lip.

TYPE SPECIES: *Arthrochilus irritabilis* F. Mueller

Ten highly interesting, sympodial terrestrials (one species a leafless saprophyte) distributed in low elevation, open coastal forests and savanna woodlands of eastern Australia (Queensland to Victoria), Tasmania and southern New Guinea. These colony-forming plants range from loose groups to densely congested mats. The erect, short, unbranched stem has a basal rosette or a solitary leaf, that is withered or absent at flowering time. The wiry, few to numerous-flowered inflorescence has dull green or red, insect-like flowers. The erect or slightly curved, narrow dorsal sepal is found behind the column and the narrow petals are thread-like. The mobile, entire lip, hinged to the underside of the column foot, has a large callus which dominates the lip's surface, and is ornamented with numerous, warts, cilia and shiny calli. The flowers have a curved, slender, footless column with two small, wing-like projections.

ARTHROCHYLIUM

An orthographic variant introduced in *Orchid.-Buch*, 83 (1892). The correct spelling is *Arthrochilium*.

ARTORIMA

Dressler & G.E. Pollard

Phytologia **21**(7): 439 (1971).

Epidendroideæ ⚘ Epidendreæ • Laeliinæ

ETYMOLOGY: Latin for narrow and cleft. Referring to the stigma located between the column wings, which has a T-shaped slit that is used to catch the feet of pollinator bees.

TYPE SPECIES: *Artorima erubescens* (Lindley) Dressler & G.E. Pollard (*Epidendrum erubescens* Lindley)

One sympodial epiphyte or rare lithophyte is found in cold, upper elevation, montane evergreen to oak-pine forests of southwestern Mexico (Guerrero and Oaxaca) that have nocturnal, cold to freezing temperatures. This plant has plump, short, purple or brown, widely-spaced, ovoid pseudo-bulbs, separated by thick rhizomes, each with a few distichous, narrow to oblong leaves. The numerous to few-flowered, purple inflorescence has showy, fragrant, pale pink to magenta, long-lasting flowers with darker colored veins. The trilobed lip, united to the slightly curved, footless column, has oblong side lobes, and a spoon-shaped midlobe with a splash of magenta at the bilobed tip. The unusual stigma has a T-shaped slit that catches the foot of the pollinating bee.

ARTHROSIA

(Luer) Luer

Monogr. Syst. Bot. Missouri Bot. Gard. **105**: 248, *f.* 5 (2006).

ETYMOLOGY: Greek for a joint. Refers to the distinct joint or attachment of the lip and column foot.

TYPE SPECIES: *Arthrosia auriculata* (Lindley) Luer (*Pleurothallis auriculata* Lindley)

Recognized as belonging to the genus *Acianthera*, *Arthrosia* was proposed to include eleven epiphytes found from southeastern Brazil (São Paulo, Rio de Janeiro, and Minas Gerais to Paraná) to northern Argentina (Misiones). These small, erect, tufted, often clump-forming plants have slender, compressed stems, subtended by a closely fitting, tubular sheath, each with a solitary, narrow, leathery leaf midway up the stem. The erect, few-flowered inflorescence has yellow to orange-tan flowers with an erect dorsal sepal and shallowly concave, lateral sepals that are united nearly to the tip. The small, translucent petals have irregular margins. The purple, trilobed lip has erect side lobes, and the midlobe has a rounded tip, slightly irregular margins and a disc with a pair of wedge-shaped calli. The flowers have a small, stout column.

ARUNDENIA

An orthographic variant introduced in *Icon. Pl. Ind. Orient. (Wight)*, **5**(1): 8 (1851). The correct spelling is *Arundina*.

ARUNDINA

Blume

Bijdr. Fl. Ned. Ind. **8**: 401, *t.* 73 (1825).

Epidendroideæ ⚘ Arethuseæ • Arethusinæ

ETYMOLOGY: Latin for a reed or cane. Referring to the reed-like appearance of the plants.

LECTOTYPE: *Arundina speciosa* Blume

This type name is now considered a synonym of *Arundina graminifolia* (D. Don) Hochreutiner; basionym *Bletia graminifolia* D. Don

One large, reed-like, sympodial terrestrial is widespread in the tropics extending from low to upper elevation, hill woodlands, scrub, montane forests, meadows and along river banks of northern India, southern China (Yunnan to Fujian), Myanmar to Vietnam, Malaysia and Indonesia to the adjacent Pacific Archipelago. These tall, erect, clump-forming, slender plants have rigid, unbranched stems, each with several, narrow, grass-like leaves. The erect, simple or branched, few-flowered inflorescence has highly variable,

Currently Accepted   Validly Published   Invalidly Published   Published Pre-1753   Superfluous Usage   Orthographic Variant   Fossil

Orchid Genera • **36**

large, short-lived, showy, purple-red to white flowers. The broad, trumpet-shaped, obscurely trilobed lip is usually a contrasting or darker color than the other floral segments, and envelopes the long, slender, footless column.

NOTE: This is a widely cultivated genus that has naturalized throughout much of the tropics. And in some areas these plants are considered weeds.

ARUNDINEA

An orthographic variant introduced in *Itin. Pl. Khasyah Mts.*, 316 (1848). The correct spelling is *Arundina*.

ASARCA

Poeppig ex **Lindley**

Quart. J. Sci. Lit. Arts, ser. 2   **1**(1): 52 (1827).

ETYMOLOGY: Greek for without or negative and flesh. Referring to the absence of fleshy glands in parts of the lip.

TYPE SPECIES: *Asarca speciosa* Lindley

Now recognized as belonging to the genera *Chloraea* or *Gavilea*, *Asarca* was originally considered to include one terrestrial found in rocky, low to mid elevation, hill to montane windswept grasslands of Chile, eastern Argentina and the Falkland Islands. This tall, erect, leafy plant has several, narrow leaves clasping the unbranched stem. The tall, wiry, few-flowered inflorescence has creamy-pink to yellow-orange flowers. The concave dorsal sepal and small petals converge, forming a hood over the small, yellow column. The lateral sepals are widespreading. The broad, trilobed lip, adorned with green warts, has broad, oblong, yellow side lobes and a long, narrow midlobe with a wavy margin. The above type name is now considered a synonym of *Chloraea chrysantha* Poeppig.

ASCIDIERIA

Seidenfaden

Nordic J. Bot.   **4**(1): 44 (1984).

ETYMOLOGY: Greek for bladder or a bag and *Eria*, a genus of orchids. Referring to the pitcher-like lip and its relationship to *Eria*.

TYPE SPECIES: *Ascidieria longifolia*
(Hooker f.) Seidenfaden
(*Eria longifolia* Hooker f.)

Now recognized as belonging to the genus *Eria*, *Ascidieria* was proposed to include one epiphyte found in low to upper elevation, hill to montane forests and woodlands throughout Thailand, Malaysia and Indonesia. This plant has long, slender stems, often swollen at the base, subtended by distichous leaf bases or by pale brown sheaths throughout, each with several, narrow leaves toward the tip. The one to two, erect or arching, unbranched inflores-

cences, borne just below the stem tip, are either covered with fine hairs or are smooth. The numerous-flowered inflorescence has tiny to minute, white flowers arranged in tight whorls, with each whorl containing up to ten blooms. The outer flora surfaces are densely covered in fine hairs. The boat-shaped, obscurely trilobed or trilobed lip is attached to the base of the short, club-shaped column foot. The flowers have a short column that is held at a right angle to the ovary.

ASCOCENTROPSIS

Senghas & Schildhauer

J. Orchideenfr.   **7**(4): 289 (2000).

Epidendroideæ 〰 Vandeæ • Aeridinæ

ETYMOLOGY: *Ascocentrum*, a genus of orchids, and Greek for appearance. Referring to a similarity with *Ascocentrum*.

TYPE SPECIES: *Ascocentropsis pusilla*
(Averyanov) Senghas & Schildhauer
(*Ascocentrum pusillum* Averyanov)

One uncommon, monopodial epiphyte is found in low elevation, hill forests of Thailand, Laos, Cambodia and Vietnam. This small, erect to climbing plant has short stems, each with several, strap-like, green or pale brown-green leaves. The several, slender, few-flowered inflorescences have small, thinly textured, pale purple to purple-red flowers with equal-sized sepals and petals. The trilobed lip has incurved side lobes closing the entrance to a long, thin-walled spur, and a small, fleshy, triangular midlobe. There are conspicuous lamellate calli found at the base of the midlobe protruding back into the spur. The flowers have a red to magenta, short, stout, wingless column.

ASCOCENTRUM

Schlechter

Repert. Spec. Nov. Regni Veg. Beih.   **1**: 975 (1913).

Epidendroideæ 〰 Vandeæ • Aeridinæ

ETYMOLOGY: Greek for a bag and spur. For the large, bag-like spur that hangs from the base of the lip.

LECTOTYPE: *Ascocentrum miniatum*
(Lindley) Schlechter
(*Saccolabium miniatum* Lindley)

Thirteen dwarf, compact growing, monopodial epiphytes are found in humid, low to upper elevation, hill scrub to montane evergreen forests from northern India (Assam), southern China (Yunnan), Bhutan, Myanmar to Vietnam, Indonesia (Java, Borneo and Sulawesi) and Taiwan to the Philippines. These plants have short, simple or forked stems, each with several, distichous, thick, channeled, strap-like leaves that are irregularly notched at the tips and arranged in two ranks. The short, stiffly erect,

numerous-flowered inflorescence has small, flat-faced, brightly hued, long-lived flowers. The yellow, orange, red, magenta to violet, showy flowers open simultaneously along the whole length of the inflorescence. The immobile, trilobed lip is attached to the base of a short, footless column. The midlobe is tongue-shaped, the small side lobes are united with the short, stout, wingless column, and the short spur has a small opening at the mouth.

ASCOCHILOPSIS

Carr

Gard. Bull. Straits Settlem.   **5**(1-2): 21 (1929).

Epidendroideæ 〰 Vandeæ • Aeridinæ

ETYMOLOGY: *Ascochilus*, a genus of orchids and Greek for appearance. Refers to its similarity to *Ascochilus*.

TYPE SPECIES: *Ascochilopsis myosurus* (Ridley) Carr
(*Saccolabium myosurus* Ridley)

Two uncommon, monopodial epiphytes are found in low elevation, evergreen hill, woodlands from Thailand and Malaysia to Indonesia. This small plant has short, erect stems, each with several, thick, fleshy, narrow leaves. The several, thickened, few-flowered inflorescences, borne from leaf nodes, are sparsely spotted with short, furry hair. The small, yellow to yellow-orange flowers open in succession with only one to four open at a time, but lasting only a single day, and all are borne at the tip or in hollows along the thick rachis. The immobile, white, trilobed lip has orange, basal spots, is joined to the base of the small, footless column, and has a fleshy, white, flattened, thick spur.

ASCOCHILUS

Blume

Fl. Javæ   **1**: Praef. vi (1828).

Name published without a description. Today this name is most often referred to *Geodorum*.

ASCOCHILUS

Ridley

J. Linn. Soc., Bot.   **32**: 374 (1896).

Not *Ascochilus* Blume (1828) Orchidaceæ. Although considered a homonym by ICBN code this name by Ridley is currently accepted.

Epidendroideæ 〰 Vandeæ • Aeridinæ

ETYMOLOGY: Greek for a bag or wine skin and lip. Refers to the cup-like spur into which the claw of the lip widens.

LECTOTYPE: *Ascochilus siamensis* Ridley

Six monopodial epiphytes are found in mid elevation, montane forests of Thailand, Malaysia, Indonesia and the Philippines. These small plants have short, leafy stems, each with either narrow and curved or long and pencil-like leaves. The short, numerous to few-flowered inflorescence has small, short-lived flowers appearing in succession or in successive clusters. The pale yellow to green flowers have the lateral sepals united with the column foot. The white, fleshy, trilobed lip has large, curved side lobes and the midlobe is either large or small sized with a narrow, thin, almost tube-like structure that extends the full length. The flowers have a short, club-shaped or slender, wingless column that is either footless or has an obscure foot.

NOTE: Vegetatively these species are similar to *Pteroceras* and were often included in either the genus *Sarcanthus* or *Sarcochilus*.

ASCOGLOSSUM

Schlechter

Repert. Spec. Nov. Regni Veg. Beih.
1(13): 974 (1913).

Epidendroideæ ⚬ Vandeæ • Aeridinæ

ETYMOLOGY: Greek for bag and tongue. Referring to the distinctly spurred lip.

TYPE SPECIES: *Ascoglossum calopterum*
(Reichenbach f.) Schlechter
(*Saccolabium calopterum* Reichenbach f.)

One monopodial epiphyte is native in low elevation, hill rain forests, scrub and mangroves of New Guinea, eastern Indonesia (Maluku) and the Philippines. This hard to find, medium to large-sized plant has slender, erect stems, borne near base of strap-like, fleshy to leathery leaves arranged in two rows and with unequally bilobed tips. The multibranched, numerous-flowered, pink inflorescence has small, lovely flowers lasting for a few weeks. The showy, swept-back, intensely magenta-purple to red flowers are among the most highly colored of any orchid. The orange suffused, trilobed lip has erect side lobes attached to the short, curved, wingless, footless column, a small, ovate, tongue-shaped midlobe, and a club-shaped spur.

ASCOLABIUM

S.S. Ying

Coloured Ill. Indig. Orchids Taiwan **1**(2): 53 (1977).

ETYMOLOGY: Greek for a bag and Latin for lip. In reference to the unusually shaped lip.

TYPE SPECIES: *Ascolabium pumilum*
(Hayata) S.S. Ying
(*Saccolabium pumilum* Hayata)

Now recognized as belonging to the genus *Ascocentrum*, *Ascolabium* was previously considered to include one epiphyte found in mid to upper elevation, montane evergreen forests of Taiwan.

This miniature plant has erect, short stems, subtended by leaf-like sheaths, each with needle-like, channeled, leathery, green to brown-green, distichous leaves. The short, slender, few-flowered inflorescence has pale pink-red to purple-red flowers with equally sized, oblong sepals and petals. The trilobed lip, attached to the column base, has small, erect, roundish, yellow, side lobes, an oblong, concave midlobe, and a small, cylindrical, green-brown spur. The flowers have a short column.

ASCOTAENIA

An orthographic variant introduced in *Repert. Spec. Nov. Regni Veg. Beih.*, **4**: 246 (1919). The correct spelling is *Ascotainia*.

ASCOTAINIA

Ridley

Mat. Fl. Malay. Penins. **1**: 115 (1907).

ETYMOLOGY: Greek for a bag or wine skin and band or ribbon. Refers to the spurred lip, thus differentiating it from the spurless orchid genus *Tainia*.

TYPE SPECIES: *None designated*

Now recognized as belonging to the genus *Tainia*, *Ascotainia* was previously considered to include fourteen rather attractive terrestrials found in low to upper elevation, hill scrub to montane forest slopes and along river banks. Their range extends from northeastern India (Sikkim to Assam), Myanmar to Vietnam, southern China (Yunnan to Hainan) and Indonesia. These blue-green plants have prominently ribbed pseudobulbs with numerous internodes and rather fragile, stalked foliage. The wand-like, few-flowered inflorescence has large, yellow flowers covered with several, brown stripes. The lateral sepals, united to the column foot forming a chin-like protuberance, are not hinged but spurred. The white, yellow-tinged, entire or obscurely trilobed lip, attached to the column foot, is often sprinkled with tiny, red dots. The flowers have a rather slender, somewhat curved, winged column.

ASPASIA

Lindley

Gen. Sp. Orchid. Pl.   139 (1833), and
J. Bot. (Hooker) **1**: 7 (1834).

Not *Aspasia* Salisbury (1866) Liliaceæ, and not
Aspasia E. Meyer ex Pfeiffer (1873) Labiatæ.

Epidendroideæ ⚬ Cymbidieæ • Oncidiinæ

ETYMOLOGY: Greek for glad or delightful or welcome kindly. An allusion to the beauty of the flowers.

Or perhaps, most likely, for the historical Athenian woman, Asparia, beloved by Pericles (495-429 BC), who as an Athenian politician and military leader built Athens into a strong and beautiful city.

TYPE SPECIES: *Aspasia epidendroides* Lindley

Seven sympodial epiphytes or lithophytes are dispersed in wet, low elevation, rain forests from Guatemala to Bolivia, Trinidad, the Guianas, Venezuela and Brazil. These plants have stalked, large, ovoid, glossy, pale green pseudobulbs, often ridged with age, subtended by leaf-bearing sheaths, each with one to two narrow, long, semi-leathery leaves. The erect or arching, solitary to few-flowered inflorescence has showy, long-lived, often rather large, fragrant flowers in combinations of green, purple and white. The green, narrow sepals are often spotted or blotched bronze or brown, the shorter, slightly broader petals are green, dull white or red, and the erect, concave dorsal sepal is united to the column base. The dull white, shortly clawed, entire or obscurely trilobed lip, attached to the lower portion of the erect, wingless, footless column, has purple blotches, and is constricted in the middle thus appearing trilobed.

ASPEGRENIA

Poeppig & Endlicher

Nov. Gen. Sp. Pl. (Poeppig & Endlicher)
2(1-2): 12, *t. 116* (1836).

ETYMOLOGY: Dedicated to Gustav Karsten Aspegren (1791-1828), a Swedish botanist, naturalist, and author of *Försök till en Blekingsk Flora*.

TYPE SPECIES: *Aspegrenia scirpoidea*
Poeppig & Endlicher

Now recognized as belonging to the genus *Octomeria*, *Aspegrenia* was previously considered to include one epiphyte found in Peru and southern Venezuela. This erect plant has unbranched stems, subtended by tubular sheaths, each with a solitary, extremely long, narrow, channeled leaf. The short, solitary-flowered inflorescence has a small, lemon-yellow flower not opening widely. The rosy, deeply trilobed lip has a rounded tip. The flowers have a short, slender column.

Currently Accepted   Validly Published   Invalidly Published   Published Pre-1753   Superfluous Usage   Orthographic Variant   Fossil

O r c h i d   G e n e r a • **38**

ASPEREGRENIA

An orthographic variant introduced in *Dict. Univ. Hist. Nat.*, **2**: 224 (1842). The correct spelling is *Aspegrenia*.

ASPIDOGYNE

Garay

Bradea **2**(28): 200 (1977).

Orchidoideæ 🍃 Cranichideæ • Goodyerinæ

ETYMOLOGY: Greek for shield and woman, female or womb. In reference to the large rostellum whose recurved sides resemble a shield.

TYPE SPECIES: *Aspidogyne foliosa*
(Poeppig & Endlicher) Garay
(*Pelexia foliosa* Poeppig & Endlicher)

Nineteen sympodial terrestrials are found in low to mid elevation, hill and montane forests, swampy to sandy river banks and woodland litter from Honduras to Ecuador, Brazil, Paraguay and northern Argentina (Misiones, Corrientes and Chaco). These erect plants have unbranched stems, each with well-spaced, spirally arranged, broad, green to coppery leaves that have tubular bases and prominently raised silver veins, and which gradually taper to a point. The usually hairy, numerous to few-flowered, red to green inflorescence has brick-red, brown-red or green flowers that are often white at the base and do not open fully. The external surface of the sepals are covered with scattered hairs. The white, trilobed lip has oblong, entire to curly side lobes, a broad, entire or bilobed midlobe whose tip strongly curves downward, and a long, swollen spur. The flowers have a short, footless column.

ASPLA

An orthographic variant cited in *Deut. Bot. Herb.-Buch*, 50 (1841). The correct spelling is *Aopla*.

ASTEROGLOSSUS

An orthographic variant cited in *Lex. Gen. Phan.*, 50 (1904). The correct spelling is *Astroglossus*.

ASTROGLOSSUS

Reichenbach *filius* **ex Bentham**

Gen. Pl. (Bentham & Hooker f.) **3**(2): 588 (1883).

Name published without a description. Today this name is most often referred to *Stellilabium*.

ATE

Lindley

Gen. Sp. Orchid. Pl. 326 (1835).

ETYMOLOGY: Greek Mythology. Ate is a goddess of infatuation, mischief, and guilt. Because of Ate's propensity for leading men to commit actions that they later would rue, Zeus, her father, exiled her from Olympus, and thereafter she wandered the Earth, causing misery and hardship, and seeking mischief and strife wherever she could. The meaning, if any, is obscure.

TYPE SPECIES: *Ate virens* Lindley

Now recognized as belonging to the genus *Habenaria*, *Ate* was previously considered to include two terrestrials found in wet, mid elevation, montane grasslands of southeastern India and Sri Lanka. These small, erect plants have unbranched stems, each with several, narrow, veined leaves. The long, few-flowered inflorescence has small, yellow-green flowers whose long, thread-like, bilobed petals exceed the length of the small, broad dorsal sepal. The long, pale yellow, trilobed lip has long, thread-like segments, and a hanging, cylindrical spur. This genus has a horn-like, recurved tooth that arises from the spur and curves down upon the lip. The flowers have a short column. The above type name is now considered a synonym of *Habenaria barbata* Wight ex Hooker f.

ATOPOGLOSSUM

Luer

Monogr. Syst. Bot. Missouri Bot. Gard. **95**: 255 (2004).

ETYMOLOGY: Greek for extraordinary, strange or disgusting and tongue or lip. Refers to the eccentric lip.

TYPE SPECIES: *Atopoglossum ekmanii*
(Schlechter) Luer
(*Pleurothallis ekmanii* Schlechter)

Recognized as belonging to the genus *Pleurothallis*, *Atopoglossum* was proposed to include three epiphytes, all are found in low elevation, hill scrub and forests of eastern Cuba. These erect, small, creeping plants have secondary stems, subtended by a loose tubular sheath, each with a solitary, narrow, thick, leathery leaf. The short, erect, solitary to few-flowered inflorescence, borne at the leaf axils, has small, thinly textured, purple flowers borne successively. The oblong, concave dorsal sepal, along with the lateral sepals, are joined for almost their whole length and have large, narrow petals. The ovate, green, trilobed lip has a minutely notched midlobe with an elevated basal callus, and short, thick, broadly rounded side lobes, and is attached to the column foot. The flowers have a slender, narrowly winged column.

ATRICHOGLOTTIS

Endlicher ex Wittstein

Etym.-Bot.-Handw.-Buch, ed. 1 86 (1852).

Name published without a description. Today this name is most often referred to as a section of *Trichoglottis*.

AULIZA

Salisbury

Trans. Hort. Soc. London **1**: 294 (1812).

ETYMOLOGY: Greek for lodge or to camp out. The meaning could possibly refer to its habitat.

TYPE SPECIES: *Auliza ciliaris* (Linnaeus) Salisbury
(*Epidendrum ciliaris* Linnaeus)

Now recognized as belonging to the genus *Epidendrum*, *Auliza* was previously considered to include fourteen epiphytes found from the southeastern United States (Florida), Mexico to Panama, and Puerto Rico to Trinidad, the Guianas, Venezuela, Colombia to Peru and northern Brazil. These plants are highly variable in their vegetative structure and have erect, slender or stout stems, each with several, leathery, usually glossy green leaves. The short, few-flowered inflorescence has large, fragrant, long-lived, green to yellow-green flowers. The white, trilobed lip has a bright yellow disc, and large, wide, wing-like side lobes, and the long, narrow midlobe is sharply pointed or tapers.

AULIZEUM

Lindley ex Wittstein

Etym.-Bot.-Handw.-Buch, ed. 1 86 (1852).

Name published without a description. Today this name is most often referred to *Epidendrum*.

AULOSEPALUM

Garay

Bot. Mus. Leafl. **28**(4): 298 (1980)[1982].

Orchidoideæ 🍃 Cranichideæ • Spiranthinæ

ETYMOLOGY: Greek for tube or flute and sepal. Refers to the sepaline tube formed by the sepals.

TYPE SPECIES: *Aulosepalum tenuiflorum*
(Greenman) Garay
(*Spiranthes tenuiflora* Greenman)

Six sympodial epiphytes are found in mid to upper elevation, mixed deciduous, seasonally dry forests and woodlands from central Mexico to Costa Rica. These erect plants have short, unbranched stems, each with a basal rosette of narrow leaves that are absent or withered at flowering time. The tall, thick, densely packed, numerous-flowered inflorescence has large, brown bracts, and the rather small, narrow to shortly tubular, green-white to white flowers do not open fully. The sepals and petals have a faint, green nerve and the lateral sepals are fused at the base (along with the lip), forming a conspicuous, chin-like nectary. The bright white, long-clawed, obscurely trilobed lip usually forms a long nectary with the column foot, and has a green midvein. The outer surface of the whole plant, including the flowers, is covered with short, soft hairs. The flowers have a long to short, small, short footed column fused to the dorsal sepal for half its length.

AULOSTYLIS

Schlechter

Repert. Spec. Nov. Regni Veg. Beih.
1(5): 392 (1912).

Etymology: Greek for tube or flute and style. Refers to the margins of the column that form a tube.

Type species: *Aulostylis papuana* Schlechter

Now recognized as belonging to the genus *Calanthe*, *Aulostylis* was previously considered to include one epiphyte found in misty, mid elevation, montane forests of New Guinea. This shade-loving, tiny plant has ovoid pseudobulbs, each with several large, pleated leaves that are usually absent during flowering. The erect or arching, few to numerous-flowered inflorescence has yellow-white flowers that have a wide, entire lip that is free from the straight, stout column. The upper part of the column forms a tube in which the stigma and rostellum are completely enclosed.

AURINOCIDIUM

Romowicz & Szlachetko

Polish Bot. J. **51**(1): 43 (2006)[2007].

Etymology: Latin for donkey and *Oncidium*, a genus of orchids. Refers to the form of the leaves, which resemble donkey ears.

Type species: *Aurinocidium pulvinatum*
(Lindley) Romowicz & Szlachetko
(*Oncidium pulvinatum* Lindley)

Recognized as belonging to the genus *Oncidium*, *Aurinocidium* was proposed to include seven epiphytes found in mid elevation, montane forests and grasslands from Brazil to northern Argentina and Paraguay. These plants have compressed, small, oblong pseudobulbs, each with a solitary, stiff, leathery, yellow-green leaf. The slender, erect or arching, loosely branched, numerous-flowered inflorescence has small, yellow to yellow-green flowers with a red-brown or red-orange basal tinge. The entire lip has a raised, cushion-shaped, basal protuberance usually covered with warts, soft hairs or small points (glands). The flowers have an erect, club-

shaped, footless column. The above type name is now considered a synonym of *Oncidium divaricatum* Lindley.

AUSTRALORCHIS

Brieger

Orchideen (Schlechter), ed. 3   **1**(11-12): 741 (1981).

Etymology: Latin for southern and Greek for orchid. Refers to being found on a southern continent.

Type species: *Australorchis monophylla*
(F. Mueller) Brieger
(*Dendrobium monophyllum* F. Mueller)

Now recognized as belonging to the genus *Dendrobium*, *Australorchis* was previously considered to include four epiphytes or lithophytes found in low elevation, subtropical rain forests of Australia (central Queensland to northern New South Wales) growing in masses on tree limbs and rocks usually in full sunlight. These small, creeping plants have numerous short, thick, erect pseudobulbs, becoming bleached and ribbed with age, each with a solitary, oblong to narrow, flat leaf. The long, slender, few-flowered inflorescence, borne from the tip of the pseudobulb, has small, often fragrant, bright yellow, white or orange, nodding flowers. The deep yellow, trilobed lip has small side lobes, and a broad, triangular midlobe with or without contrasting color or markings. The flowers have a short, broad, winged column.

AUXOPUR

An orthographic variant introduced in *Orchids India*, ed. 2, 261 (1999). The correct spelling is *Auxopus*.

AUXOPUS

Schlechter

Westafr. Kautschuk-Exped.   275 (1900), and
Bot. Jahrb. Syst.   **38**: 3 (1905).

Epidendroideæ ◊ Gastrodieæ

Etymology: Greek for to increase or strengthen and a foot. An allusion to the pedicel that greatly elongates after fertilization.

Type species: *Auxopus kamerunensis* Schlechter

Three diminutive terrestrials or saprophytes are found in shady, seasonally dry, low elevation, dense deciduous woodlands of Ivory Coast to Gabon, Zaire to Uganda, north-western Madagascar and the Mascarene Islands. These tall, leafless plants have weak, yellow-brown, unbranched stems subtended by small, sheathing scales. The compact headed, few-flowered, inflorescence has dull brown to green-brown, short-lived flowers not opening widely. The pedicels continue to elongate after

it flowers, so that the seed capsules are borne on long stalks. The lateral sepals are united along the ventral margins for most of their length forming a tube-like structure. The white, tongue-shaped, clawed, entire or obscurely lobed lip is united to the base of the long, erect, slender, winged, footless column and has a shallow notch at the tip of the lip and a basal disc with a pair of yellow calli.

AVICEPS

Lindley

Gen. Sp. Orchid. Pl.   345 (1838).

Etymology: Latin for little bird and head. The flower's shape, in a certain way, simulates a bird's head.

Type species: *Aviceps pumila* (Thunberg) Lindley
(*Satyrium pumilum* Thunberg)

Now recognized as belonging to the genus *Satyrium*, *Aviceps* was previously considered to include one terrestrial found in dry, low elevation, coastal woodlands of southwestern South Africa. This tiny, rosette-like plant sits but a little bit above the ground and usually just barely breaks the soil surface. The short, few-flowered inflorescence has rather large flowers that are dull green on the outside, dark maroon on the inside, and sometimes banded or mottled. The large, broad, concave dorsal sepal has red splashes sprinkled on the inside and is hood-like over the short, footless column. The flowers' fragrance ranges from faint to strongly putrid. The broad, cup-like, dark red, entire lip has a yellow splash toward the tip and a small spur. The flowers have a slender, slightly curved, footless column. The above type name is now considered a synonym of *Satyrium pumilum* Thunberg.

AZADEHDELIA

Braem

Schlechteriana   **1**(2): 34 (1988).

Etymology: Named in honor of Henry (Habib) Azadehdel (1955-), an Armenian-born British shopkeeper in Nothingham, Iranian diplomat, and amateur botanist who discovered and collected many new species.

Type species: *Azadehdelia brachyceras*
(Summerhayes) Braem
(*Aerangis brachyceras* Summerhayes)

Not validly published, this name is referred to *Cribbia*. *Azadehdelia* was considered to include one epiphyte found in Ethiopia, Kenya, Uganda, Tanzania, Zambia and Angola.

Currently Accepted   Validly Published   Invalidly Published   Published Pre-1753   Superfluous Usage   Orthographic Variant   Fossil

Orchid Genera • **40**

BACHIA

Schomburgk ex Lindley

Gen. Sp. Orchid. Pl. 410 (1840).

ETYMOLOGY: Dedicated to U.D.F. or U.J.T. Bach, a German from Jever, Oldenburg with a coffee plantation on the Demerara River near Georgetown, Guyana. He provided assistance to Moritz Richard Schomburgk (1811-1890) during his travels.

TYPE SPECIES: *None designated*

Name published without a description. Today this name is most often referred to *Cleistes*.

BACLARDIA

An orthographic variant introduced in *Fragm. Florist. Geobot.*, **3**(Suppl.): 92 (1995). The correct spelling is *Beclardia*.

BALBOPHYLLUM

An orthographic variant introduced in *Maori-Polynesian Comp. Dict.*, 340 (1891). The correct spelling is *Bulbophyllum*.

BANILLAS

Sloane

Cat. Pl. Jamaica 70 (1696).

Pre-1753, therefore not validly published in fulfillment of nomenclatural rules; this name is most often referred to *Vanilla*.

BAPTISTANIA

An orthographic variant introduced in *Index Gen. Phan.*, 404 (1888). The correct spelling is *Baptistonia*.

BAPTISTONIA

Barbosa Rodrigues

Gen. Sp. Orchid. **1**: 95, *t. 130* (1877).

ETYMOLOGY: Named in honor of Baptista (Baptisto) Caetano de Almeida Noguéira (1826-1882), a Brazilian poet, ethnologist, philologist and historian.

TYPE SPECIES: *Baptistonia echinata* Barbosa Rodrigues

Now recognized as belonging to the genus *Oncidium*, *Baptistonia* was previously considered to include one epiphyte found

in cool to hot, mid elevation, coastal montane forests of southeastern Brazil (Rio de Janeiro and São Paulo). This plant has compressed, oblong, tightly clustered pseudobulbs, partially subtended by several distichous, overlapping, leafless sheaths, each with two leathery leaves at the tip. The long, often branched, hanging, numerous-flowered inflorescence has pale yellow-green flowers with pink streaks. The dorsal sepal and small petals converge, forming a hood over the erect column. The trilobed lip has a maroon-purple to almost black midlobe and erect, solid yellow side lobes. The flowers have a long, shortly haired, conspicuously winged, footless column that is decurved at the tip. The above type name is now considered a synonym of *Oncidium brunleesianum* Reichenbach f.

BARBOSELLA

Schlechter

Repert. Spec. Nov. Regni Veg. **15**: 259 (1918).

Epidendroideæ ⚘ Epidendreæ • Pleurothallidinæ

ETYMOLOGY: In honor of João Barbosa Rodrigues (1842-1909), a Brazilian naturalist, explorer, publisher, botanical artist, director of Jardím Botânico in Rio de Janeiro, and author of *Genera et species Orchidearum novarum*. And Latin for diminutive.

LECTOTYPE: *Barbosella gardneri* (Lindley) Schlechter (*Pleurothallis gardneri* Lindley)

Eighteen sympodial epiphytes, lithophytes or terrestrials are distributed in wet, low to upper elevation, hill and montane forests from Cuba, Hispaniola, Jamaica, Guadeloupe, Martinique, southern Mexico to Bolivia, Venezuela, eastern Brazil and northern Argentina. These miniature, colony-forming plants have clustered, creeping, erect stems, subtended by overlapping, thin sheaths, each with a solitary, thick, leathery, narrow to elliptical leaf. The several, long, delicate, one- to two-flowered inflorescences, borne from the leaf base, have fleshy flowers varying from green, dark purple, and orange to pale yellow, with an erect, slender dorsal sepal. The lateral sepals are united nearly to their tips, forming a long, spreading structure and are drawn out almost to a point. The ovate to tongue-shaped, entire or obscurely trilobed lip, hinged to the column foot, is much smaller than the tiny petals and is concave at the base. The flowers have a short, erect to slightly curved, winged column.

BARBRODIA

An orthographic variant introduced in *Fragm. Florist. Geobot.*, **3**(Suppl.): 76 (1995). The correct spelling is *Barbrodria*.

BARBRODRIA

Luer

Selbyana **5**(3-4): 386 (1981).

ETYMOLOGY: Dedicated to João Barbosa Rodrigues (1842-1909), a Brazilian naturalist.

TYPE SPECIES: *Barbrodria miersii* (Lindley) Luer (*Pleurothallis miersii* Lindley)

Not validly published, this name is referred to *Barbosella*. *Barbrodria* was considered to include one epiphyte found in eastern Brazil (Espírito Santo to Santa Catarina).

BARKERA

An orthographic variant cited in *Lex. Gen. Phan.*, 60 (1904). The correct spelling is *Barkeria*.

BARKERIA

Knowles & Westcott

Fl. Cab. **2**: 7, *t. 49* (1838).

Epidendroideæ ⚘ Epidendreæ • Laeliinæ

ETYMOLOGY: Named in honor of George Barker (1776-1845), a British solicitor, horticulturist and orchid grower from Springfield, England who imported and then flowered the type species.

TYPE SPECIES: *Barkeria elegans* Knowles & Westcott
    This type name is now considered a synonym of
    Barkeria uniflora (Lexarza) Dressler & Halbinger;
        basionym
    Pachyphyllum uniflorum Lexarza

Fifteen sympodial epiphytes or sometimes lithophytes, are found in dry, low to mid elevation, oak-pine forests from central Mexico to Costa Rica. These plants have slender, spindle-shaped to cane-like pseudobulbs, subtended by leaf-sheaths, each with narrow to broadly ovate, distichous leaves that taper to a point. The pyramidal or cylindrical, few-flowered inflorescence has showy, pale to vivid pink, lilac, deep purple or even white flowers that have a bright yellow or white callus. The large, kite-like, entire lip has red lines radiating out from the short or long, widely-winged, footless column. The lip usually has a wavy margin and a blotch of bright color at the tip. The whole flower can be variously spotted with lilac or black.

BARLAA

An orthographic variant introduced in *Consp. Fl. France*, 257 (1927). The correct spelling is *Barlia*.

BARLAEA

Reichenbach *filius*

Linnaea **41**: 54 (1877)[1876].
Not *Barlaea* P.A. Saccardo (1889) Fungi-Pezizales.

ETYMOLOGY: A derivative of *Barlia*, a genus of orchids. Barla was a friend of Reichenbach.

TYPE SPECIES: *Barlaea calcarata*
        (Reichenbach f.) Reichenbach f.
        (*Stenoglottis calcarata* Reichenbach f.)

This type name is now considered a synonym of *Cynorkis squamosa* (Poiret) Lindley; basionym replaced with *Orchis squamosa* Poiret

Now recognized as belonging to the genus *Cynorkis*, *Barlaea* was previously considered to include one rather common terrestrial or epiphyte found in low to mid elevation, rain forests and among the tree mosses of Réunion and Mauritius islands. This erect plant has one to two, narrow, basal leaves and an erect, red-brown, few-flowered inflorescence. The small, white flowers, tinged with purple-rose, have widespreading lateral sepals. The concave dorsal sepal and small petals converge, forming a hood over the tiny column. The white, obscurely trilobed lip is speckled with variable purple dots and has a ruffled margin.

BARLIA

Parlatore

Fl. Ital. (Parlatore) **3**(2): 445 (1858)[1860], and *Nuov. Gen. Sp. Monocot.* 5 (1858).

Orchidoideæ ⚜ Orchideæ • Orchidinæ

ETYMOLOGY: Commemorating Joseph (Jérome) Hieronymus Jean Baptiste Barla (1817-1896), a French mycologist, director of the natural history museum in Nice, collector, author and illustrator of *Les champignons de la province de Nice ...*

TYPE SPECIES: *Barlia longibracteata*
        (Bivona-Bernardi) Parlatore
        (*Orchis longibracteata* Bivona-Bernardi)

This type name is now considered a synonym of *Barlia robertiana* (Loiseleur-Deslongchamps) Greuter; basionym replaced with *Orchis robertiana* Loiseleur-Deslongchamps

Two uncommon, sympodial terrestrials are found in low to mid elevation, grasslands, woodlands and pine scrub throughout the Mediterranean (Spain, Balearic Islands, Corsica, Sardinia, Sicily, Italy, Crete, Morocco to Libya, Greece and Turkey). One species is found only in the Canary Islands (Tenerife). These small, erect plants have unbranched, stout stems, each with several, ovate to narrow, basal leaves. The short, roundish, densely packed, numerous-flowered inflorescence has fragrant, pale olive-green flowers suffused brown or purple. The dorsal sepal and petals converge, forming a hood over the small column. The lateral sepals are widespreading. The pale rose, deeply trilobed lip is dotted or splashed with purple, has wide, wavy side lobes. The broad, bilobed midlobe has a wavy margin and a short, cone-shaped spur.

BARLINGTONIA

An orthographic variant introduced in *Bull. Fed. Soc. Hort. Belgique*, **5**: 139 (1864). The correct spelling is *Burlingtonia*.

BAROMBIA

Schlechter

Orchideen (Schlechter), ed. 1   600 (1914).

ETYMOLOGY: Named for the location, Barombi Station in southwestern Cameroon, where the type species was collected. There are many crater lakes of volcanic origin found in this region.

TYPE SPECIES: *Barombia gracillima*
        (Kraenzlin) Schlechter
        (*Angraecum gracillimum* Kraenzlin)

Now recognized as belonging to the genus *Aerangis*, *Barombia* was previously considered to include one epiphyte found in humid, low elevation, shady forests and woodlands of Cameroon and Gabon. This small plant has short, leafy stems, each with large, flat, leathery, dull green leaves that are arranged in a whorl. The hanging, wiry, few-flowered inflorescence has large, green-white flowers arranged in two rows. The flowers have similar, narrow sepals and petals with pale pink tips. The long, narrow, tapering, entire lip has a faintly rust-colored, thread-like, hanging spur that is almost ten inches (28 m) long. The flowers have a long, slender, club-shaped column.

BAROMBIELLA

Szlachetko

Ann. Bot. Fenn. **40**(1): 69 (2003).

ETYMOLOGY: *Barombia*, a genus of orchids and Greek for like. Referring to a similarity with the genus *Barombia*.

TYPE SPECIES: *Barombiella schliebenii*
        (Mansfeld) Szlachetko
        (*Leptocentrum schliebenii* Mansfeld)

Now recognized as belonging to the genus *Rangaeris*, *Barombiella* was proposed to include one epiphyte found in montane and river forests of Tanzania. This small plant has long, leafy stems, subtended by persistent leaf-like sheaths, each with several, distichous, leathery, unequally bilobed leaves. The few-flowered inflorescence has small, white flowers with narrow, spreading, inrolled segments. The obscurely trilobed lip has a long, tapering point and a long, thread-like, cylindrical, green-orange spur with a wide mouth. The flowers have a short, slender, footless column.

BARTERIA

An orthographic variant introduced in *Bull. Fed. Soc. Hort. Belgique*, **5**: 139 (1864). The correct spelling is *Barkeria*.

BARTHOLINA

R. Brown

Hortus Kew., ed. 2   **5**: 194 (1813).

Orchidoideæ ⚜ Orchideæ • Orchidinæ

ETYMOLOGY: Commemorating Thomas Bartholin (1616-1680), a Danish physician, naturalist, philologist, and professor of mathematics and anatomy at the University of Copenhagen. He was the first to describe the entire lymphatic system.

TYPE SPECIES: *Bartholina pectinata*
        (Thunberg) R. Brown nom. illeg.
        (*Orchis pectinata* Thunberg nom. illeg.)
    Bartholina burmanniana (Linnaeus) Ker-Gawler
        (*Orchis burmanniana* Linnaeus)

Two sympodial terrestrials are found in low elevation, pebbly, veld scrub from Namibia to the Cape Province of South Africa often forming dense colonies. These dwarf plants have erect, slender stems, each with a small, solitary, hairy, almost circular, basal leaf that lies flat on the ground. The erect, solitary-flowered inflorescence is densely covered with long, spreading hairs. The large, spidery, pale green and violet flowers have hairy to smooth, green sepals, and erect, smooth, white or green petals. The large, fan-shaped, cream-colored,

Currently Accepted   Validly Published   Invalidly Published   Published Pre-1753   Superfluous Usage   Orthographic Variant   Fossil

O r c h i d   G e n e r a • **42**

obscurely trilobed lip has numerous, hair-like, purple to white segments, and a short, tapering to cone-like spur. The flowers have a small, club-shaped, wingless column.

BARTHOLINIA

An orthographic variant introduced in *Dict. Class. Hist. Nat.*, **2**: 204 (1822). The correct spelling is *Bartholina*.

BASAALA-poulou

Rheede

Hort. Malab. **12**: 53-54, *t. 27* (1693).

ETYMOLOGY: A local Malayalam word for leafy grasses and epiphytes.

TYPE SPECIES: *Basaala-poulou-maravara* Rheede

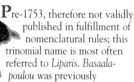

Pre-1753, therefore not validly published in fulfillment of nomenclatural rules; this trinomial name is most often referred to *Liparis*. *Basaala-poulou* was previously considered to include one epiphyte found in shady, low to mid elevation, hill to montane semi-evergreen forests of Malaysia, Thailand, Indonesia (Sumatra, Java, Borneo) and New Guinea. This plant has clustered pseudobulbs, each with several, thinly textured leaves. The long, red, dark purple to green, numerous-flowered inflorescence has small, green to maroon flowers with narrow sepals and petals. The dark purple to yellow, recurved, entire lip is V-channeled and widens considerably toward the tip. The flowers have a slender, arching column. This name is usually now considered a synonym of *Liparis rheedei* Lindley.

BASAALE

An orthographic variant introduced in *Dict. Class. Hist. Nat.*, **2**: 208 (1822). The correct spelling is *Basaala*.

BASIGYNE

J.J. Smith

Bull. Jard. Bot. Buitenzorg, sér. 2 **25**: 4 (1917).

ETYMOLOGY: Greek for base or pedestal and female or woman. Refers to the characteristic basal stigma.

TYPE SPECIES: *Basigyne muriculata* J.J. Smith

Now recognized as belonging to the genus *Dendrochilum*, *Basigyne* was previously considered to include one epiphyte or sometimes terrestrial found in eastern Indonesia (Sulawesi). This small plant has pear-shaped pseudobulbs, each with a solitary, flat, narrow, leathery leaf. The wiry, few-flowered inflorescence has red flowers; the petals and lip are hairy on both sides. There are minute, black calli on the base of the entire lip, which is attached to the short, footless, winged column at a right angle.

BASIPHYLLAEA

Schlechter

Repert. Spec. Nov. Regni Veg. **17**: 77 (1921).

Epidendroideæ ⚬ Epidendreæ • Bletiinæ

ETYMOLOGY: Greek for base or order and leaf. Refers to the basal position of the single leaf.

TYPE SPECIES: *Basiphyllaea sarcophylla*
(Reichenbach f.) Schlechter
(*Bletia sarcophylla* Reichenbach f.)

Seven uncommon, inconspicuous, sympodial terrestrials are found in low to mid elevation, grassy to rocky pine scrub or savannas from the southeastern United States (Florida), the Bahamas, Cuba to Hispaniola and Puerto Rico. These tiny, slender plants are exceedingly difficult to find, do not bloom annually, and may remain dormant for long periods. They have erect, smooth, sometimes branched stems, each with one to two, deciduous, dark green leaves. The leaves are sometimes absent during flowering. When in bloom the erect, entire or sometimes branched, wiry, few-flowered inflorescence has dull yellow-green flowers with narrow sepals and petals, which do not open widely. The white, trilobed lip has broad, roundish side lobes clasping the slender, slightly curved column, and the small midlobe has a notched tip.

BASKERVILLA

Lindley

Gen. Sp. Orchid. Pl. 505 (1840).

Orchidoideæ ⚬ Cranichideæ • Cranichidinæ

ETYMOLOGY: Dedicated to John Baskerville (1706-1775), a British engraver, type designer and printer from Birmingham who transformed English printing and type founding.
Or possibly honoring Thomas Baskerville (1812-1840), a British physician, botanist and author of *Affinities of Plants*.

TYPE SPECIES: *Baskervilla assurgens* Lindley

Seven sympodial terrestrials and epiphytes are distributed in mid to upper elevation, montane cloud forests or shady, disturbed forests from Nicaragua to Bolivia, the Guianas, Venezuela and south-eastern Brazil (Rio de Janeiro to São Paulo). These erect plants have a basal rosette consisting of velvety leaves or several, long, petiolate, dorsally ribbed leaves ascending up the unbranched stems. The erect, numerous-flowered inflorescence has small, green, brown-green to pink flowers. The clawed petals are united to the back of the erect, club-shaped, winged, footless column. The deeply concave or sac-like, entire lip has small calli forming a tubular entrance to the short spur.

BASKERVILLEA

An orthographic variant introduced in *J. Roy. Hort. Soc.*, **7**(1): 99 (1886). The correct spelling is *Baskervilla*.

BATEMANIA

An orthographic variant introduced in *Gen. Pl. (Endlicher)*, 197 (1837). The correct spelling is *Batemannia*.

BATEMANNIA

Lindley

Edwards's Bot. Reg. **20**: *t. 1714* (1834).

Epidendroideæ ⚬ Cymbidieæ • Zygopetalinæ

ETYMOLOGY: Commemorating James Bateman (1811-1897), a British orchidologist, botanist, horticulturist and author of *Orchidaceæ of Mexico and Guatemala* and *Monograph of Odontoglossums*.

TYPE SPECIES: *Batemannia colleyi* Lindley

Five sympodial epiphytes are found in wet, low to mid elevation, hill and montane forests from Colombia to Bolivia, Venezuela and Brazil. These plants have clustered, four-angled, one-noded pseudobulbs, subtended by several, short-lived sheaths, each with two pleated, semi-rigid, dull olive-green leaves. The curved to hanging, few to numerous-flowered inflorescence has showy, claret or green, fragrant flowers that are often suffused dark brown and tipped in green with a white or cream base. The dorsal sepal is hooded, the narrow lateral sepals are strongly curved sideways (inrolled), and the oblong petals are slightly larger than the dorsal sepal. The white, trilobed lip is suffused yellow and has a flattened ridge. The erect side lobes have jagged tips and the large, spreading midlobe curves downward. The flowers have a small, stout, club-shaped, wingless column.

BATHIEA

Schlechter

Beih. Bot. Centralbl. **33**(2): 440 (1915), and
Beih. Bot. Centralbl. **36**(2): 180 (1918).

ETYMOLOGY: Dedicated to Joseph Maria Henri Perrier de la Bâthie (1873-1958), a French mining prospector and natural history botanist. He studied and collected the flora and fauna of Madagascar and authored *Biogéographie des Plantes de Madagascar*.

TYPE SPECIES: *Bathiea perrieri* (Schlechter) Schlechter
(*Aeranthes perrieri* Schlechter)

Not validly published, this name is referred to *Neobathiea*. *Bathiea* was considered to include one epiphyte found in Madagascar.

BATHIORCHIS

Bosser & P.J. Cribb

Adansonia, sér. 3   **25**(2): 229 (2003).

Orchidoideæ ⁄ Cranichideæ • Goodyerinæ

ETYMOLOGY: In honor of Joseph Maria Henri Perrier de la Bâthie (1873-1958). And Greek for orchid.

TYPE SPECIES: *Bathiorchis rosea*
　　　(H. Perrier) Bosser & P.J. Cribb
　　　(*Gymnochilus roseum* H. Perrier)

One sympodial terrestrial is found in humid, mid elevation, montane rain forests at the northern tip of Madagascar (Perinet) in the Analamazoatra Special Reserve. This erect plant has unbranched stems on a creeping rhizome, with several leaves ascending up each stem. The numerous-flowered inflorescence has tiny, thinly textured flowers not opening widely with narrow, nerved sepals and petals. The broad, almost spoon-shaped, entire lip has notches at the tip with longitudinal lines and expansions. The flowers have an unusual S-shaped column that has thin, minute appendages and a spear-shaped cap. This plant is similar to *Platylepis* but here the column is totally different.

BAYNILLA

Humboldt

Vers. Neu-Spanien   **4**: 125 (1812).

ETYMOLOGY: A local spanish word for *Vanilla*, a genus of orchids, used to describe the local plants found in Mexico.

TYPE SPECIES: *None designated*

Not validly published, this name is now referred to *Vanilla*. *Baynilla* was considered to include four epiphytes found from central Mexico to Paraguay, Cuba to Trinidad, the Guianas and Venezuela. These are usually vine-like plants with viny stems that are essentially leafless; the leaves are reduced to scale-like bracts. The short, several-flowered inflorescence has large, fragrant flowers that fade after only a few hours. The entire to variously lobed lip is fused to the slender, slightly curved, stout column. These species are now considered as synonyms of *Vanilla planifolia* Jackson ex Andrews.

BEADLEA

Small

Fl. S.E. U.S.   319, 1329 (1903).

ETYMOLOGY: In memory of Chauncey Delos Beadle (1866-1950), a Canadian-born horticulturist and botanist employed as a curator at the Biltmore Herbarium in North Carolina, specialist on the flora of North America and author of *Biltmore Herbarium*.

TYPE SPECIES: *Beadlea storeri* (Chapman) Small
　　　(*Spiranthes storeri* Chapman)

This type name is now considered a synonym of *Cyclopogon cranichoides* (Grisebach) Schlechter; basionym replaced with *Pelexia cranichoides* Grisebach

Now recognized as belonging to the genus *Cyclopogon* while some authors refer them to *Spiranthes*. *Beadlea* was previously considered to include seven terrestrials found in low to mid elevation, forests and woodlands of the southeastern United States (central Florida), Cuba to Puerto Rico, Belize and Honduras, northern Venezuela and the Guianas usually in decaying humus. These inconspicuous, small plants have short, erect, unbranched stems, each with a basal rosette of coppery green leaves covered with white spots (only on a few species). The slightly twisted, few-flowered, purple inflorescence has small, green-brown, elongate flowers with the dorsal sepal and petals converge, forming a hood over the column. The tubular, white, shortly clawed, trilobed lip is suffused with pink and curves downward.

BECAISNEA

An orthographic variant cited in *Etym.-Bot.-Handw.-Buch*, ed. 1, 266 (1852). The correct spelling is *Decaisnea*.

BECLARDIA

A. Richard

Mém. Soc. Hist. Nat. Paris   **4**: 69 (1828), and *Monogr. Orchid. Bourbon*   78, t.11 (1828).

Epidendroideæ ⁄ Vandeæ • Aerangidinæ

ETYMOLOGY: In memory of Pierre Augustin Béclard (1785-1825), a French professor of anatomy and surgery at the Faculty of Medicine in Paris and an editor of *Nouveau journal de médecine*.

TYPE SPECIES: *Beclardia macrostachya*
　　　(Thouars) A. Richard
　　　(*Epidendrum macrostachyum* Thouars)

One monopodial epiphyte is found in humid, mid elevation, deciduous, rain forests of Madagascar, Réunion, and the Mascarene Islands. This small, fan-shaped plant has short stems, each with several, overlapping,

leathery leaves arranged in two rows. The few-flowered inflorescence, borne from the leaf nodes, has coarse-textured, pure white or red-white, long-lasting flowers. The trilobed or four-lobed lip is usually wider than it is long, and the side lobes are quite large. The deeply bilobed or notched midlobe has a wavy margin, is covered with several warts down the center, and has a bright yellow to green, basal splash. The short, swollen, wide mouthed, white spur has a blunt, green or yellow tip. The flowers have a slender column.

BEGONIA

Linnaeus

Sp. Pl. (Linnaeus), ed. 1   **2**: 1056 (1753).

ETYMOLOGY: In honor of Michel Bégon (1638-1710), a French-born governor, appointed by Louis XIV, for Santo Domingo (Hispaniola) and later French Canada and an amateur botanist. This name was first published by Charles Plumier (1646-1704) in *Nova Plantarum Americanarum Genera*, 1703.

TYPE SPECIES: *Not Orchidaceæ*

Linnaeus did not include this genus in Orchidaceæ. However there is one species (originally based on a leaf sample) from this genus recognized as belonging to *Nervilia*. This terrestrial species is found throughout Africa (Ghana to Zimbabwe), Madagascar, Réunion, Mauritius, Yemen and Oman. This erect plant has a large, solitary, kidney-shaped, heavily veined and pleated leaf, held well above the ground, which appears only after the solitary to few-flowered inflorescence has withered. The green flower has a pale green, obscurely trilobed lip with purple or dark green veins. The species (*Begonia monophylla* Pourret ex A.P. de Candolle, *Prod. (DC)*, **15**(1): 403 (1864)) was originally mistakenly included in the Begoniaceæ family. The name should now be correctly identified as a synonym of *Nervilia bicarinata* (Blume) Schlechter, *Bot. Jahrb. Syst.*, **45**: 405 (1911).

BEINERIA

An orthographic variant introduced in *Icon. Pl. Trop.*, ser. 2, 209 (1989). The correct spelling is *Bieneria*.

Currently Accepted　Validly Published　Invalidly Published　Published Pre-1753　Superfluous Usage　Orthographic Variant　Fossil

O r c h i d   G e n e r a • **44**

BELA-pola

Rheede

Hort. Malab. **11**: 69-70, *t. 35* (1692).

ETYMOLOGY: A local Malayalam word for white or water, and pola means sheath.

TYPE SPECIES: *Bela-pola-maravara* Rheede

Pre-1753, therefore not validly published in fulfillment of nomenclatural rules; this trinomial name is most often referred to *Geodorum*. Bela-pola was previously considered to include one terrestrial found in Malaysia, Thailand, Myanmar and Indonesia (Sumatra, Java to Borneo). This erect plant has roundish, subterranean pseudobulbs, each with oblong to narrow, pleated leaves. The erect, numerous-flowered inflorescence (arching at the tip) has a succession of waxy, fragrant pink or white flowers with a sickening, soapy fragrance. The white, erect, sac-like, entire lip is purple striped, and is constricted with two, round lobes that are veined or warty at the tips. This name is usually now considered a synonym of *Geodorum densiflorum* (Lamarck) Schlechter, *Repert. Spec. Nov. Regni Veg. Beih.*, **4**: 259 (1919).

BELOGLOTTIS

Schlechter

Beih. Bot. Centralbl. **37**(2): 364 (1920).

Orchidoideæ ⚘ Cranichideæ • Spiranthinæ

ETYMOLOGY: Greek for dart or arrow and tongue. Alluding to the lip shape of the flower that when flattened resembles an arrowhead.

LECTOTYPE: *Beloglottis costaricensis* (Reichenbach f.) Schlechter (*Spiranthes costaricensis* Reichenbach f.)

Seven inconspicuous, sympodial lithophytes, epiphytes or occasional terrestrials are found in low to mid elevation, hill to montane evergreen and semi deciduous forests and woodlands distributed from the southeastern United States (Florida), Hispaniola, southern Mexico to Bolivia, Trinidad, the Guianas, Venezuela, Brazil and northern Argentina (Salta). These small, erect plants have short, unbranched stems, each with a basal rosette of somewhat iridescent leaves that are usually present during flowering. The slender, few-flowered inflorescence has inconspicuous, small to tiny, tubular, fragrant, white, creamy to green flowers with bright green midveins. The exterior of the sepals is covered with fine hairs, and the joined sepals form a shallow, tubular-shaped cup with spreading tips. The clawed, white, trilobed lip has erect, basal appendages and rounded side lobes, and the finely notched midlobe has a rounded tip. The flowers have a short, massive, slightly club-shaped column.

BENTHAMIA

A. Richard

Mém. Soc. Hist. Nat. Paris **4**: 37, *t. 2* (1828), and
Monogr. Orchid. Bourbon 43, *t. 2* (1828).
Not Benthamia Lindley (1833) Cornaceæ, and not Benthamia Lindley (1830) Boraginaceæ.

Orchidoideæ ⚘ Orchideæ • Orchidinæ

ETYMOLOGY: Honoring George Bentham (1800-1884), a British systematic botanist, taxonomist, secretary and later president of the Royal Horticultural Society and co-author of *Genera Plantarum*.

LECTOTYPE: *Benthamia latifolia* A. Richard
This type name is now considered a synonym of *Benthamia chlorantha* (Sprengel) Garay & G.A. Romero; basionym (*Habenaria chlorantha* Sprengel)

Thirty-one sympodial terrestrials or epiphytes are found in cool, low to mid elevation, deeply shaded, hill to montane forests, grasslands and seasonal marshes of eastern Zimbabwe, Madagascar and the Mascarene Islands. These tall, thin, erect plants have unbranched stems that are leafy in the lower part. There are one to several of these narrow, ovate basal leaves. The erect, few to numerous-flowered inflorescence has small flowers in various pale shades of white, yellow or green with lighter venation. The sepals often converge, forming a hood over the short, erect column, and the narrow petals do not spread widely. The entire or more often trilobed lip has a short, testicle-shaped or cylindrical spur that is entire or bilobed at the tip.

BENZINGIA

Dodson

Icon. Pl. Trop., ser. 2 **5**: sub *t. 406* (1989), and
Validated: *Lindleyana* **10**(2): 74 (1995).

Epidendroideæ ⚘ Cymbidieæ • Zygopetalinæ

ETYMOLOGY: In honor of David Hill Benzing (1937-), an American professor of biology at Ohio's Oberlin College, author and botanist with interests in epiphytes, especially Bromeliaceæ and Orchidaceæ.

TYPE SPECIES: *Benzingia hirtzii* Dodson ex Dodson

Eight sympodial epiphytes are found in cool, low to mid elevation, hill and montane forests of western Ecuador. These small plants appear almost stemless, but are subtended by distichous, overlapping, leaf-bearing sheaths, each with the gray-green leaves arranged in fan-shaped ranks and basally overlapping. The upper surfaces of these leaves have a pebbly appearance. The wiry, erect to hanging, solitary-flowered inflorescence is usually borne from each leaf sheath. The yellow and white flower is spotted red-brown with widespreading segments. The scoop-shaped or sac-like, yellow, entire lip is

abundantly red spotted and hinged to the base of the column foot, and has a flat or slightly raised callus down the center, and an entire margin. The flowers have a slender, lightly arching or curved column that is winged below or lateral to the transverse stigma, and has a short, hairy foot.

BERTAUXIA

Szlachetko

Richardiana **4**(2): 56 (2004).

ETYMOLOGY: Named in honor of Pierre Bertaux (1955-), a French head horticulturist responsible for the orchid collection at Jardin du Luxembourg in Paris, and author of *Lycastes and Anguloa: Des Orchidées hors du commun*.

TYPE SPECIES: *Bertauxia vaupellii* (Reichenbach f. & Warming) Szlachetko (*Habenaria vaupellii* Reichenbach f. & Warming)

Recognized as belonging to the genus *Habenaria*, Bertauxia was proposed to include three terrestrials found in wet, low elevation, hill forests, savannas and prairies from Belize to Panama, Venezuela, the Guianas and Brazil to Paraguay. These tall, erect, robust plants have unbranched, slightly ribbed stems, each with several, narrow leaves decreasing in size up the stem. The erect, few-flowered inflorescence has small, inconspicuous flowers whose white or cream, bilobed or entire petals have narrow segments and broad, green sepals. The tiny, white or cream, trilobed lip has long, narrow side lobes, a spear-shaped midlobe, and a cylindrical, hanging spur. The above type name is now considered a synonym of *Habenaria johannensis* Barbosa Rodrigues.

BHUTANTHERA

Renz

Edinburgh J. Bot. **58**(1): 99 (2001).

Orchidoideæ ⚘ Orchideæ • Orchidinæ

ETYMOLOGY: Named for the Kingdom of Bhutan (this small landlocked country is located between northern India and Tibet), where most of the species are located. And Greek for flower.

TYPE SPECIES: *Bhutanthera albomarginata* (King & Pantling) Renz (*Habenaria albomarginata* King & Pantling)

Six small, sympodial terrestrials are found in cool, upper elevation, montane meadows and slopes of Bhutan and northern India (Sikkim) at Jongri on the south flank of Kinchinjung (14,000 m). These plants have stout stems, each with two, unequal, oblong leaves (narrow toward the base) that are strongly nerved. The erect, few-flowered inflorescence (large, leaf-like bracts on the lower spike and minute, triangular bracts on the upper) has rather large flowers with white or green sepals and red or white petals. The red, deeply trilobed lip has oblong, weakly sickle-shaped side lobes, an oblong midlobe, and a short, cone-like spur. The flowers have a small, stout column. Some of these species were formerly included in *Peristylus*.

BIAURELLA

Lindley ex **Wittstein**
Etym.-Bot.-Handw.-Buch, ed. 1   86 (1852).

Name published without a description. Today this name is most often referred to as a section of *Thelymitra*.

BICCHIA

Parlatore
Fl. Ital. (Parlatore)   3(2): 396 (1858)[1860].
ETYMOLOGY: Dedicated to Cesare Bicchi (1822-1906), an Italian physician, amateur botanist, director of Lucca Botanical Garden and collector of Italian flora.
TYPE SPECIES: *Bicchia albida* (Linnaeus) Parlatore
(*Satyrium albidum* Linnaeus)

Now recognized as belonging to the genus *Pseudorchis*, *Bicchia* was previously considered to include one terrestrial found in upper elevation, montane grasslands of Europe from Ireland to Poland, Germany to Spain and France to Romania. This small, erect plant has several, oblong to narrow leaves borne along the unbranched stem. The densely packed, numerous-flowered inflorescence has tiny, white, green or pale yellow flowers. The sepals and petals converge, forming a hood over the tiny column. The ovate lip is trilobed at the tip, has a tapered midlobe, and a minute, blunt cylindrical spur.

BICORNELLA

Lindley
Edwards's Bot. Reg.
20: sub 1701, section no. 26 (1834), and
Gen. Sp. Orchid. Pl.   334 (1835).
ETYMOLOGY: Latin for two and diminutive of horn. Referring to the small staminodial process located on the sides of the column.
TYPE SPECIES: *None designated*

Now recognized as belonging to the genus *Cynorkis*, *Bicornella* was previously considered to include nine terrestrials found in the montane regions of Madagascar, the Comoros and Mascarene Islands. These slender, erect plants have unbranched stems, each with several, narrow, grass-like leaves. The few-flowered inflorescence, subtended by long, narrow bracts, has small, purple or rosy-colored flowers sprinkled with darker colored spots.

The oblong, obscurely trilobed lip has a short roundish spur.

BIDOUPIA

Averyanov & Christenson ex **Senghas**
Orchideen (Schlechter), ed. 3   2758 (2002).
ETYMOLOGY: Named in honor of Bì Đúp - Nui Ba nature reserve in southern Vietnam where the type species was collected.
TYPE SPECIES: *Bidoupia bicamerata*
Averyanov & Christenson ex Senghas

Not validly published, this name is referred to *Schoenorchis*. *Bidoupia* was proposed to include one epiphyte found in low elevation, woodlands of southern Vietnam (Lam Dong). This species though similar to *Schoenorchis* differs on technical details.

BIDUPIA

An orthographic variant introduced in *Orchideen (Schlechter)*, ed. 3, 2758. (2002). The correct spelling is *Bidoupia*.

BIENERIA

Reichenbach *filius*
Bot. Zeitung (Berlin)   11: 3, t. 1 (1853).
ETYMOLOGY: Dedicated to Friedrich August Biener (1787-1861), a German physician from Dresden, and the first law dean at the Humboldt-Universität of Berlin, who shared his herbarium with Reichenbach.
TYPE SPECIES: *Bieneria boliviana* Reichenbach f.

Now recognized as belonging to the genus *Chloraea*, *Bieneria* was previously considered to include one terrestrial found in humid, upper elevation, rocky canyons of central Bolivia (Cochabamba) and northwestern Argentina (Tucumán). This erect plant has its leaves diminishing in size as they proceed up the stout, unbranched stem. The few-flowered inflorescence has yellow flowers with a slight green tinge. The broad, entire lip has a ruffled margin. The flowers have a slightly curved column with a yellow anther cap.

BIERMANNIA

King & Pantling
J. Asiat. Soc. Bengal, Pt. 2, Nat. Hist.
66(2): 591 (1897).
Epidendroideæ · Vandeæ · Aeridinæ
ETYMOLOGY: In honor of Johann Carl Adolph Biermann (1798-1879), a German-born British curator at the Royal Botanic Garden (Calcutta, Indian Botanic Garden), who was killed by a tiger on the garden's grounds.
TYPE SPECIES: *Biermannia quinquecallosa*
King & Pantling

Ten dwarf, monopodial epiphytes are found in low elevation, forest scrub of northeastern India (Assam), Thailand, Vietnam and Malaysia to Indonesia (Sumatra). These small, short-stemmed plants have fleshy, unequally bilobed, green-yellow leaves. The several, short, few-flowered inflorescences have small, fragrant (almond-scented), short-lived, white flowers appearing one at a time. The fleshy, movable, trilobed lip (attached at a right angle to a short but distinct column foot so that it is parallel with the shorter column) has brown or violet blotches, and a flat, brown-yellow callus. The base of the lip often has a cavity but never a distinct spur or sac. The flowers have a stout column that varies between the species, erect to curved, slender, sometimes wingless with an obscure to prominent foot.

BIFOLIUM

Dodoens
Stirp. Hist. Pempt.   242 (1583).

Pre-1753, therefore not validly published in fulfillment of nomenclatural rules; this name is most often referred to *Ophrys*.

BIFOLIUM

Petiver ex **Nieuwland**
Amer. Midl. Naturalist   3(4): 128 (1913).
Not *Bifolium* P.G. Gaertner et al. (1799) Liliaceæ.
ETYMOLOGY: Greek for two and a leaf. Referring to the slender stem with its two leaves.
TYPE SPECIES: *None designated*

Not validly published because of a prior use of the name, this homonym was replaced by *Listera*.

Currently Accepted   Validly Published   Invalidly Published   Published Pre-1753   Superfluous Usage   Orthographic Variant   Fossil

ORCHID GENERA • 46

BIFRENARIA

Lindley

Gen. Sp. Orchid. Pl.   152 (1832).

Epidendroideæ ◊ Cymbidieæ • Maxillariinæ

ETYMOLOGY: Latin for two or twice and rein or strap. An allusion to the two straps connecting the pollinia and the glands, a characteristic that distinguishes this genus from *Maxillaria*.

LECTOTYPE: *Bifrenaria atropurpurea*
(Loddiges) Lindley
(*Maxillaria atropurpurea* Loddiges)

Twenty-six sympodial epiphytes or lithophytes are found in low to mid elevation, rain forests of Colombia to Bolivia, the Guianas, Trinidad, Venezuela and northern Brazil. These plants, often forming huge masses, have angular, glossy, yellow to olive-green, ovoid to cone-like pseudobulbs, often with a black collar at the tip, and often ridged. Each pseudobulb has a solitary, broad, ribbed, leathery leaf with at least three, prominent veins on the underside. These somewhat compressed, hard pseudobulbs are well-spaced along thick, branching rhizomes. The short, few-flowered inflorescence has showy, large, waxy, yellow-green to wine-red, highly fragrant flowers, produced singly or a few at a time. The widespreading petals are smaller than the sepals. The clawed, trilobed or obscurely trilobed lip, joined to the tip of the prominent column foot, has erect side lobes, a square or roundish midlobe with a reflexed, wavy or a entire margin, a central, velvety callus, and a small spur. The flowers have an oblong, stout, slightly curved, wingless column.

BILABRELA

An orthographic variant cited in *Handb. Orchid.-Namen*, 117, 374 (2005). The correct spelling is *Bilabrella*.

BILABRELLA

Lindley

Edwards's Bot. Reg.
20: sub 1701, section no. 23 (1834).

ETYMOLOGY: Greek for two and upper lip. Descriptive of the petals, the lip is situated underneath giving the suggestion of an upper, additional lip.

TYPE SPECIES: *Bilabrella falcicornis* Lindley

Now recognized as belonging to the genus *Habenaria*, *Bilabrella* was previously considered to include three terrestrials found in seasonally wet, low elevation, marshy grasslands from western South Africa to Zimbabwe. These tall, slender, robust plants have a few narrow leaves with the smaller-sized leaves proceeding up the stem. The numerous to few-flowered inflorescence has narrow, smooth to hairy bracts. The small flowers have green sepals and white, deeply bilobed petals with an erect, upper lobe and an ovate, spreading lower lobe. The shortly clawed, deeply trilobed lip has narrow, equal length lobes or a slightly longer midlobe, and has a long slender, incurved spur. The flowers have a small column.

BINOTIA

Rolfe

Orchid Rev.   **13**(154): 296 (1905).

Epidendroideæ ◊ Cymbidieæ • Oncidiinæ

ETYMOLOGY: Commemorating Pedro Maria Binot (1855-1911), a Brazilian plant collector and nurseryman, for his many botanical discoveries. He was knighted by Leopold II of Belgium for his horticultural contributions to Belgium.

TYPE SPECIES: *Binotia brasiliensis* (Rolfe) Rolfe
(*Cochlioda brasiliensis* Rolfe)

One uncommon, sympodial epiphyte or occasionally lithophyte is found in low elevation, coastal forests of eastern Brazil (Minas Gerais, Rio de Janeiro and São Paulo). This small, tufted plant has ovoid, compressed pseudobulbs, partially subtended by short, leafless sheaths, each with two rather leathery, oblong leaves. The gracefully arching, often branched, few-flowered inflorescence has small, green-white to yellow-green, brown suffused flowers opening widely. The similar, narrow sepals and widespreading, slightly shorter petals are all sharply pointed. The long, arrow-shaped, white, trilobed lip is tipped with green. It is joined to the small, winged column, and has rose-colored, basal calli bearing a mass of short, yellow hairs or pimple-like projections.

BIPENNULA

An orthographic variant cited in *Nomencl. Bot. (Steudel)*, ed. 2, **1**: 128, 206 (1840). The correct spelling is *Bipinnula*.

BIPINNULA

Commerson ex Jussieu

Gen. Pl. (Jussieu)   65 (1789).

Orchidoideæ ◊ Cranichideæ • Chloraeinæ

ETYMOLOGY: Latin for two and the diminutive of a feather or wing. In reference to the elaborate wing-like sepals that are characteristic of this genus.

LECTOTYPE: *Bipinnula biplumata*
(Linnaeus f.) Reichenbach f.
(*Arethusa biplumata* Linnaeus f.)

Eleven bizarrely structured, sympodial terrestrials are found in cool, low to mid elevation, coastal and rocky grasslands of Chile, southern Brazil, Uruguay and Argentina (Buenos Aires). This genus has some of the more unusual and pleasing floral shapes of the orchid family. These erect plants have unbranched stems, each with several, narrow, bright green, basal leaves that are sometimes present during flowering. The stout, solitary to few-flowered inflorescence has small, green flowers with an erect dorsal sepal that is much broader than the unusual, long lateral sepals which have a curious fringing at the margin tips. The lobed or scalloped petals often converge with the triangular dorsal sepal, forming a hood over the long, curved column. The white, shortly clawed, entire lip has an entire or fringed, green margin with several, thick papillae.

BIPINULLA

Thouin ex Linnaeus *filius*
Suppl. Pl.   405 (1782).

Name published without a description. Today this name is most often referred to *Bipinnula*.

BIRCHEA

A. Richard

Ann. Sci. Nat., Bot., sér. 2   **15**: 66, t. 10 (1841).

ETYMOLOGY: Dedicated to de Burgh Birch (1799-1871), a British East India Company assistant surgeon hired by the Madras Presidency in 1824. He was stationed at Mount Ootacamund (7,263 ft./2,200 m) in western Tamil Nadu "Nilgiris" near the south-western tip of India and was an amateur naturalist.

TYPE SPECIES: *Birchea teretifolia* A. Richard

Now recognized as belonging to the genus *Luisia*, *Birchea* was previously considered to include one epiphyte found in southwestern India and Sri Lanka. This plant is quite variable in both size and shape of its flowers and vegetative segments. The plants have rigid, stout, noded stems, each with fleshy, pencil-like, blunt leaves. The green flowers are often decorated with fine, red dots along the margins. The thick, trilobed lip is black at the base, dark purple toward the tip, while the small, green side lobes are covered with fine, purple dots, and the broad midlobe has several, warty ridges. The above type name is now considered a synonym of *Luisia tenuifolia* Blume.

BISONEA

O'Neil

Amer. Orchid Soc. Bull. **64**(4): 372 (1995).

ETYMOLOGY: *Bison* is a North American, hoofed mammal with short horns and massive, shaggy, humped shoulders roaming the prairies of United States and Canada.

TYPE SPECIES: *Bisonea buffalophila* O'Neil

Not validly published in fulfillment of nomenclatural rules; published as an April fools joke.

One terrestrial reportedly found in the grasslands, plains and buffalo wallows of central and midwestern United States. This small, erect plant has unbranched stems, each with several, grass-like leaves. The erect, few-flowered inflorescence has large, showy, brilliantly blue flowers with similar segments and a highly repellent fragrance.

BITI-maram

Rheede

Hort. Malab. **12**: 5, *t. 2* (1693).

ETYMOLOGY: This Malayalam (a language from south India) word refers to a species of *Dalbergia latifola* (Veeti) and mararm means tree. This name refers to the host tree upon which this orchid grows.

TYPE SPECIES: *Biti-maram-maravara* Rheede

Pre-1753, therefore not validly published in fulfillment of nomenclatural rules; this trinomial name is most often referred to *Rhynchostylis*. *Biti-maram* was previously considered to include one epiphyte found in open, low elevation, hill forests of southern India, Sri Lanka, Myanmar, and Thailand. This is a highly ornamental, robust, semi-erect plant, often growing in large profusion, has curved, narrow, leathery, green-gray, channeled leaves. The several, hanging to drooping, numerous-flowered inflorescence has fragrant, pink to white flowers speckled purple. The lateral sepals are united to the column foot. The concave, wedge-shaped, entire lip has an entire or notched tip, is laterally compressed, and has a sac-like spur. The flowers have a short, stout, wingless column. This name is usually now considered a synonym of *Rhynchostylis retusa* (Linnaeus) Blume.

BLEPHARIDOGLOTTIS

An orthographic variant introduced in *Contr. Bot. Dept. Nebraska Univ.*, **3**(1): 54 (1902). The correct spelling is *Blephariglotis*.

BLEPHARIGLOTIS

Rafinesque

Fl. Tellur. **2**: 38 (1836)[1837].

ETYMOLOGY: Greek for eyelash and tongue. Referring to the fringed lip of the flower.

LECTOTYPE: *Blephariglotis albiflora* (Michaux) Rafinesque (*Orchis ciliaris* var. *alba* Michaux)

This type name is now considered a synonym of *Platanthera blephariglottis* (Willdenow) Lindley; basionym replaced with *Orchis blephariglottis* Willdenow

Now recognized as belonging to the genera *Platanthera*, *Pseudorchis* and *Habenaria*. *Blephariglotis* was previously considered to include seventeen terrestrials found in low to mid elevation, grasslands, bogs and woodland meadows from Canada (Ontario to Nova Scotia) and the United States (Maine to Wisconsin, eastern Texas to Georgia). These erect plants have stout, unbranched stems, each with several, narrow leaves, sheathing the stem below and then becoming bracts above. The erect, numerous-flowered inflorescence has showy, small, white, green-white to golden-yellow, fragrant flowers. The broad dorsal sepal and petals often converge, forming a hood over the short, erect column. The ovate, trilobed lip is heavily fringed, and has a tiny to long, club-shaped spur.

NOTE: Rafinesque originally spelled this genus with only one 't', but later authors changed the spelling to the currently accepted spelling with two t's.

BLEPHAROCHILUM

M.A. Clements & D.L. Jones

Orchadian **13**(11): 499 (2002).

ETYMOLOGY: Greek for eyelid and lip. Referring to hairy lip of the species.

TYPE SPECIES: *Blepharochilum macphersonii* (F.M. Bailey) M.A. Clements & D.L. Jones (*Bulbophyllum purpurascens* F.M. Bailey)

Recognized as belonging to the genus *Bulbophyllum*, *Blepharochilum* was proposed to include two epiphytes found in low elevation, coastal rain forests and inland river banks of northeastern Australia (Queensland). These small, densely matted plants have tiny, inconspicuous pseudobulbs, somewhat flattened on the top, each with several, erect, green to red, fleshy, channeled leaves. The long, erect, solitary to few-flowered inflorescence has tiny, deep red or dark purple flowers. The narrow dorsal sepal is held at a right angle to the inflorescences, and the slightly wider lateral sepals are parallel to the orange, strap-shaped, entire lip that is uppermost. The small petals are triangular in shape. The flowers have a tiny, footless column.

BLEPHAROGLOTTIS

An orthographic variant cited in *Lex. Gen. Phan.*, 70, 71 (1904). The correct spelling is *Blephariglotis*.

BLETIA

Ruiz & Pavón

Fl. Peruv. Prodr. 119, *t. 26* (1794).

Epidendroideæ ⚬ Epidendreæ • Bletiinæ

ETYMOLOGY: Honoring Luis Blet (*fl.* 1775s-1790s), a Spanish apothecary and botanist, who had a famous botanic garden in the port city of Algeciras located in southwestern Spain.

LECTOTYPE: *Bletia catenulata* Ruiz & Pavón

Thirty-four showy, sympodial terrestrials, lithophytes or semi-aquatics are found in low to upper elevation, mixed forests, prairies and grassy hillsides of the southeastern United States (Florida), Mexico to north-western Argentina and Bolivia. These plants have small corms or below-ground pseudobulbs (joined in long chains), each with several, thinly textured, deciduous, pleated, veined (on the underside) leaves that are sometimes up to 3 feet (1 m) long and may be present or absent at the time of flowering. The erect, numerous to few-flowered inflorescence has spectacular, large to small, pink to purple flowers, borne successively over a long period of time on a simple or branched inflorescence. In many instances the flowers do not open

Currently Accepted | Validly Published | Invalidly Published | Published Pre-1753 | Superfluous Usage | Orthographic Variant | Fossil

O r c h i d   G e n e r a   • **48**

fully. The entire or deeply trilobed lip, attached to the column base, has erect side lobes, and the broad midlobe curves downward or is erect, with a curled, notched or lobed margin. The lip has one to several, minutely toothed, yellow crests down the middle. The flowers have a white or green, long, slightly curved, footless column.

BLETIAE

An orthographic variant introduced in *Itin. Pl. Khasyah Mts.*, 146 (1848). The correct spelling is *Bletia*.

BLETIANA

Rafinesque
Amer. Monthly Mag. & Crit. Rev. **2**: 268 (1818).
ETYMOLOGY: A substitute name derived from *Bletia*, a genus of orchids.
TYPE SPECIES: *None designated*

A superfluous name proposed as a substitute for *Bletia*.

BLETILLA

Reichenbach *filius*
Fl. Serres Jard. Eur., ser. 1 **8**: 246 (1853).
Name ICBN conserved vs. *Jimensia* Rafinesque (1838) Orchidaceæ, and type name also conserved.

Epidendroideæ ⚘ Arethuseæ • Coelogyninæ

ETYMOLOGY: Diminutive of *Bletia*, a genus of orchids. Implying a resemblance to *Bletia*.
TYPE SPECIES: *Bletilla gebina* (Lindley) Reichenbach f. (*Bletia gebina* Lindley)
This type name is now considered a synonym of *Bletilla striata* (Thunberg) Reichenbach f.; basionym replaced with *Limodorum striatum* Thunberg

Five showy, sympodial terrestrials are restricted to cool, low to upper elevation, hill and montane meadows and forest glens in bright or full sunlight of China (Xizang to Guangxi and Anhui), Taiwan, Japan, Korea, Myanmar to Vietnam and Thailand. These plants have a swollen stem base which forms a distinct corm, subtended by overlapping sheaths, each with several, narrow, pleated, deciduous leaves that are sometimes variegated. The erect, zig-zagged, few-flowered inflorescence (rarely branched) arises from the center of expanding new growth. The large, narrow, bell-shaped flowers have a sweet fragrance and are delightfully colored rose-magenta, pink, yellow or white. The trilobed lip has a pink callus in the center; the erect side lobes enfold the slender, slightly curved, club-shaped column that has an obscure foot to footless, and the almost rectangular midlobe curves downward.

BLUMEORCHIS

Szlachetko
Ann. Bot. Fenn. **40**(1): 68 (2003).
ETYMOLOGY: Named in honor of Carl Ludwig von Blume (1796-1862), a German-born Dutch physician, botanist and author who studied and wrote about the flora of Indonesia. And Greek for orchid.
TYPE SPECIES: *Blumeorchis crochetii* (Guillaumin) Szlachetko (*Sarcanthus crochetii* Guillaumin)

Recognized as belonging to the genus *Cleisostoma*, *Blumeorchis* was proposed to include one epiphyte found in Thailand and Laos. This tiny, hanging plant has short stems with an often branched, few-flowered inflorescence that has white to green flowers turning yellow with age; the sepals and petals are suffused purple toward the tips. The white, purple to magenta tinged, trilobed lip, joined to the column foot, has erect, forward pointing, horn-shaped side lobes and has a small, scope- to arrowhead-shaped midlobe tapering into a blunt spur. There is a flap-like cover over the mouth of the spur. The flowers have a short, erect, wingless column.

BLUMIA

Meyen ex d'Orbigny
Dict. Univ. Hist. Nat. **9**: 170 (1847).
Not *Blumia* Nees ex Blume (1823) Magnoliaceæ, and not *Blumia* Sprengel (1826) Ternstroemiaceæ.

Name published without a description. Today this name is most often referred to *Podochilus*.

BOBOPHYLLUM

An orthographic variant introduced in *Itin. Pl. Khasyah Mts.*, 110 (1848). The correct spelling is *Bulbophyllum*.

BOGORIA

J.J. Smith
Orch. Java **1**: 566 (1905).

Epidendroideæ ⚘ Vandeæ • Aeridinæ

ETYMOLOGY: Named for the city of Bogor (founded in 1745 and formerly part of the Dutch East Indies), which is located on the Indonesian island of Java. Site of the Buitenzorg Botanical Gardens that was founded in 1817 by Casper Georg Carl Reinwardt, the first director.
TYPE SPECIES: *Bogoria raciborskii* J.J. Smith

Four small, monopodial epiphytes are found wet to fairy dry, low elevation, forest scrub from New Guinea to the Philippines. These plants have short stems, each with several, leathery leaves that have unequally bilobed tips. The long, slender, multibranched,

few-flowered inflorescence has only a few flowers open at a time. The minute, relatively short-lived, white or green-yellow flowers open widely and are produced in succession. The white, trilobed lip forms a pouch-like sac with the rim often marked with bright crimson, which is joined immovably to the long, broad, channel-like column foot, and has a small spur. The flowers have a short, straight, wingless column.

BOLBIDIUM

Brieger
Orchideen (Schlechter), ed. 3 **1**(11-12): 721 (1981).
ETYMOLOGY: Greek for a bulbous plant. Because of the conspicuous pseudobulb.
TYPE SPECIES: *Bolbidium pumilum* (Kuntze) Brieger (*Callista pumila* Kuntze)
This type name is now considered a synonym of *Dendrobium pachyphyllum* (Kuntze) Bakhuizen f.; basionym replaced with *Callista pachyphylla* Kuntze

Now recognized as belonging to the genus *Dendrobium* as a section. *Bolbidium* was previously considered to include eight epiphytes found in low to mid elevation, hill and montane forests from Myanmar to the Philippines. These small plants' short, club-shaped stems are thin basally with only the terminal internode swollen into a pseudobulb, each with two leaves at the tip. The solitary-flowered inflorescence has white or cream-colored flowers variously veined or suffused purple or pink. The short-lived, fragrant flowers open simultaneously when triggered by a sudden change in temperature. The white, entire lip has a wavy margin, is usually slightly notched at the tip and has a long, chin-like protuberance.

BOLBIDIUM

Lindley
Veg. Kingd. 181 (1846).

Name published without a description. Today this name is most often referred to *Cymbidium*.

BOLBODIUM

An orthographic variant introduced in *J. Proc. Linn. Soc.*, **3**: 19 (1859). The correct spelling is *Bolbidium*.

BOLBOPHYLLARIA

Reichenbach *filius*

Bot. Zeitung (Berlin) **10**: 934 (1852).

ETYMOLOGY: *Bulbophyllum*, a genus of orchids and Greek for resembling.

TYPE SPECIES: *Bolbophyllaria bracteolata*
(Lindley) Reichenbach f.
(*Bulbophyllum bracteolatum* Lindley)

Now recognized as belonging to the genus *Bulbophyllum*, *Bolbophyllaria* was previously considered to include eight epiphytes ranging from the southeastern United States (Florida) to the Guianas, Venezuela, Colombia and northern Brazil. These plants have sharp, four-edged pseudobulbs, each with paired, leathery, glossy leaves. The stiff, pale green, numerous-flowered inflorescence has intense maroon spotting, with small, green-brown sheaths at the nodes and a thick, swollen tip. The tiny, green-yellow to purple flowers are sprinkled with purple spots and have a foul fragrance.

BOLBOPHYLLOPSIS

Reichenbach *filius*

Bot. Zeitung (Berlin) **10**: 933 (1852).

ETYMOLOGY: *Bulbophyllum*, a genus of orchids and Greek for appearance or likeness.

TYPE SPECIES: *Bolbophyllopsis morphologorum*
Reichenbach f.

Now recognized as belonging to the genus *Bulbophyllum*, *Bolbophyllopsis* was previously considered to include two epiphytes found from the eastern Himalayas, Myanmar, Thailand to Vietnam and Taiwan. These plants have ovoid pseudobulbs, spaced along the rhizome, each with a solitary, thick, ovate leaf. The erect, drooping, numerous-flowered inflorescence has flowers that do not open widely, somewhat varying in color, but are usually a dirty yellow or yellow-green with purple lines and dots. The long dorsal sepal is concave; the lateral sepals have a broad base but narrow to a blunt tip and has small petals. The hinged, maroon to dark purple, mobile, entire lip tapers to a sharp point. The above type name is now considered a synonym of *Bulbophyllum umbellatum* var. *umbellatum* Lindley.

BOLBOPHYLLUM

An orthographic variant introduced in *Syst. Veg. (Sprengel)*, ed. 16, **3**: 681, 732 (1826). The correct spelling is *Bulbophyllum*.

BOLBORCHIS

Zollinger & Moritzi

Syst. Verz. (Moritzi et al.) 89 (1846).

ETYMOLOGY: Greek for bulb and orchid. From the conspicuous ovoid pseudobulbs.

TYPE SPECIES: *Bolborchis crociformis*
Zollinger & Moritzi

Now recognized as belonging to the genus *Nervilia*, *Bolborchis* was previously considered to include one terrestrial found in woodlands, evergreen forests and grasslands of Africa (Guinea to Zimbabwe), Saudi Arabia, northern India (Assam), Nepal, Thailand to the Philippines, Indonesia, Australia and the southwestern Pacific Archipelago. This erect, unbranched plant has a solitary, broadly heart-shaped, basal leaf appearing after flowering. The erect, solitary-flowered inflorescence has a narrow to widespreading, fragrant, brown-green flower with rather long, narrow sepals and petals. The white, entire lip is rolled over the small, club-shaped column, has short triangular side lobes, a roundish midlobe with fringed margins, and a yellow center often suffused pale lilac.

BOLBORKIS

An orthographic variant introduced in *Gen. Orchid.*, **4**: 517 (2005). The correct spelling is *Bolborchis*.

BOLLEA

Reichenbach *filius*

Bot. Zeitung (Berlin) **10**: 667 (1852).

ETYMOLOGY: Dedicated to Carl August Bolle (1821-1909), a German naturalist, dairy businessman, poet, a student of medicine and natural science, dendrologist, ornithologist and a patron of orchid horticulture.

TYPE SPECIES: *Bollea violacea* (Lindley) Reichenbach f.
(*Huntleya violacea* Lindley)

Now recognized as belonging to the genus *Pescatoria*, *Bollea* was previously considered to include twelve epiphytes found in western Brazil, Peru and Ecuador with the largest center of concentration found in Colombia. These tufted plants have short stems, each with several, distichous, narrow, overlapping leaves arranged in a fan shape. The curving downward to hanging, solitary-flowered inflorescence has showy, fragrant, thick, waxy-textured flowers that are vividly colored in soft, pastel combinations. The ovate sepals and petals are a similar shape. The pouched, entire lip is firmly attached to the tip of the column foot, and the short, broad, hooded column has lateral margins protruding over the semi-circular callus.

BOLUSIELLA

Schlechter

Beih. Bot. Centralbl. **36**(2): 105 (1918).

Epidendroideæ ⚭ Vandeæ • Aerangidinæ

ETYMOLOGY: Dedicated to Harry Bolus (1834-1911), a British-born South African stockbroker, banker, amateur botanist, and botanical illustrator. Author of *Orchids of South Africa*, *The Orchids of the Cape Peninsula*, and *Icones Orchidearum Austro-Africanorum Extratropicarum*. And Latin for diminutive.

LECTOTYPE: *Bolusiella maudae* (Bolus) Schlechter
(*Angraecum maudae* Bolus)

Six tufted, monopodial epiphytes or occasional lithophytes are found in low to mid elevation, woodlands and montane evergreen forests from the Ivory Coast to Equatorial Guinea, Malawi, Zambia, Tanzania and South Africa. These dwarf, fan-shaped plants have short, erect stems, each with several, overlapping, straight or curved leaves arranged in a fan shape. The minute to small, white flowers are on long, numerous-flowered inflorescences supported by a conspicuous, black bract. The flowers open first at the tip of the inflorescence spike and then bloom in a downward succession. The entire or obscurely trilobed lip has roundish side lobes, a long, recurved midlobe, and a short, green spur that curves forward below the lip. The flowers have a short, slightly curved, wingless, footless column.

BONATEA

Willdenow

Sp. Pl. (Willdenow), ed. 4 **4**: 5, 43 (1805).

Orchidoideæ ⚭ Orchideæ • Orchidinæ

ETYMOLOGY: Honoring Guiseppe Antonio Bonato (1753-1836), an Italian professor of botany at the University of Padova and author of *Osservazioni sopra i Funghi mangerecci estese*.

TYPE SPECIES: *Bonatea speciosa*
(Linnaeus f.) Willdenow
(*Orchis speciosa* Linnaeus f.)

Seventeen intriguing, sympodial terrestrials are found in dry, low to mid elevation, open woodlands, grasslands, scrub and coastal sand dunes from southwestern Saudi Arabia (Yemen), Ethiopia, Somalia southward to Zambia, Malawi, Mozambique and South Africa. These robust plants have erect, stout stems that are leafy throughout; sometimes the dark green leaves are withered by flowering time. The solitary to numerous-flowered inflorescence has large, showy, white, yellow or green flowers that have a strong but sweetly nocturnal fragrance. The dorsal sepal usually forms a hood with the lower petals lobes, which are bilobed with stigmatic arms. The long-clawed, trilobed lip, united in the basal part to the stigmatic arm and lateral sepals, has thread-like side lobes,

Currently Accepted   Validly Published   Invalidly Published   Published Pre-1753   Superfluous Usage   Orthographic Variant   Fossil

Orchid Genera • **50**

and a long to short, cylindrical spur with a tooth front of the mouth opening. The large column has distinctive stigmatic arms.

BONATOA

An orthographic variant cited in *Lex. Gen. Phan.*, 73 (1904). The correct spelling is *Bonatea*.

BONNIERA

Cordemoy

Rev. Gén. Bot. **11**: 416 (1899).

Epidendroideæ ⁓ **Vandeæ • Angraecinæ**

ETYMOLOGY: In appreciation of Eugene Marie Gaston Bonnier (1853-1922), a French botanist, editor of *Revue Générale de Botanique* and publisher of Cordemoy's notes on the orchids of Réunion.

TYPE SPECIES: *None designated*

Two uncommon, monopodial epiphytes are found only in low elevation, bushy rain forest vegetation of Réunion. These plants have longish, several noded, stout, woody stems, each with small, well-spaced, oblong, leathery, bilobed leaves that are arranged in alternating rows. The short, solitary-flowered inflorescence, borne from the leaf axils, has a pale yellow, pale brown to green-white flower with narrow, tapering sepals. The long petals have usually curved, thread-like segments. The broad, obscurely trilobed lip also has a long, thread-like midlobe. The flowers have a short, white column.

BONTIA

Not *Bontia* Linnaeus (1753) Myoporaceæ, and not *Bontia* Linnaeus (1759) Verbenaceæ.

An orthographic variant introduced in *Hort. Cliff.*, 430 (1738). The correct spelling is *Bontiana*.

BONTIANA

Petiver

Gaz. **1**: 70, *t. 44, f. 10* (1704).

ETYMOLOGY: In honor of Jacobus Bontius (1592-1631), a Dutch-born physician and naturalist who toured the Moluccas and Timor, but was stationed at Batavia where he worked in several positions. He was the first to describe the tea plant.

LECTOTYPE: *Bontiana luzonica* Petiver
designated by P.J. Cribb, *Taxon*, **48**: 47 (1999).

Pre-1753, therefore not validly published in fulfillment of nomenclatural rules; this name is most often referred to *Dendrobium. Bontiana* was previously considered to included one epiphyte found on the Philippines islands of Mindoro, Baguio, Rizal and Zambales in wet, open sandy areas. This small plant has swollen, branched stems with three to four internodes, that are thickened below into spindle-shaped pseudobulbs, each with several, fleshy leaves. The solitary-flowered inflorescence has pale green-yellow to white, sweetly fragrant flowers with brown or maroon markings. The short-clawed, obscurely trilobed lip has a dark purple blotch at the base and a tufted disc in the middle. Today this name is now a synonym of *Dendrobium carinatum* (Linnaeus) Willdenow.

BOOMHEADIA

An orthographic variant introduced in *Icon. Pl. Ind. Orient. (Wight)*, **5**(1): 19 (1851). The correct spelling is *Bromheadia*.

BORMIERA

An orthographic variant introduced in *Just's Bot. Jahresber.*, **27**(1): 463 (1901). The correct spelling is *Bonniera*.

BOTHRIOCHILUS

Lemaire

Jard. Fleur. **3**: sub 325 (1853), and
Ill. Hort. **3**(Misc.): 30 (1856).

ETYMOLOGY: From the Greek for shallow pit or small hole and lip. Refers to the sac-like base of the lip.

TYPE SPECIES: *Bothriochilus bellus* (Lemaire) Lemaire
(*Bifrenaria bella* Lemaire)

This type name is now considered a synonym of
Coelia bella (Lemaire) Reichenbach f;
basionym
Bifrenaria bella Lemaire

Recognized as belonging to the genus *Coelia, Bothriochilus* was previously considered to include four epiphytes, lithophytes or sometimes terrestrials found in low to mid elevation, hill and montane rain forests from central Mexico to Panama. These plants have clustered, olive-green, glossy, ovoid to pear-shaped pseudobulbs, each with several, narrow, softly textured, ribbed or pleated leaves clustered at the tip of the pseudobulb. The erect, numerous-flowered inflorescence, borne amid the sheaths, has large, showy, semi-transparent, broadly tubular to bell-shaped, ivory, sweetly fragrant flowers, not opening fully, that are variously marked rose or violet. The entire lip, deeply sac-like at the base, is trilobed near the tip, has small, roundish side lobes and has a triangular, golden-yellow to orange midlobe. The erect, long, slender, wingless column is minutely toothed at the tip along with the conspicuous spur, and the foot is as long as the column itself.

BOULETIA

(Schlechter) M.A. Clements & D.L. Jones

Orchadian **13**(11): 485 (2002).

ETYMOLOGY: Named in honor of Marcel Boulet (1945-), a New Caledonian retired head of Environment Services for the southern province of New Caledonia.

TYPE SPECIES: *Bouletia finetiana*
(Schlechter) M.A. Clements & D.L. Jones
(*Dendrobium finetianum* Schlechter)

Recognized as belonging to the genus *Dendrobium, Bouletia* was proposed to include one epiphyte that is found in high humidity, wet, low elevation, hill forests of New Caledonia with year-round rain fall. This small plant has long, slender, slightly zig-zagged stems, each with small leaves spaced along the upper half and arranged in two ranks. The short, few-flowered inflorescence, borne opposite the leaves on the upper stem, has small, fragrant, green-yellow flowers often sprinkled or suffused red-brown. The deep red-brown, hinged, trilobed lip has a bilobed midlobe with a white margin, and a small spur. The flowers have a white, recurved column.

BOURLINGTONIA

An orthographic variant introduced in *Gen. Pl. (Endlicher)*, 202 (1837). The correct spelling is *Broughtonia*.

BRAASIELLA

Braem, Lückel & Rüssmann

Orchidee (Hamburg) **35**(3): 115 (1984).

ETYMOLOGY: Named in honor of Lothar Alfred Braas (1942-1995), a German herbal specialist, author of numerous orchid articles and horticulturist from Siegen. And Latin for diminutive.

TYPE SPECIES: *Braasiella arizajuliana*
(Withner & Jiménez) Braem, Lückel & Rüssmann
(*Oncidium arizajulianum* Withner & Jiménez)

Now recognized as belonging to the genus *Tolumnia, Braasiella* was proposed to include one tiny, delicate epiphyte found in Hispaniola on tree branches overhanging rivers. The roots on the short, leafy stems emerge below each growth. The overlapping, distichous, bilaterally flattened leaves are channeled on their upper surface. The long, few-flowered inflorescence has showy, flat-faced flowers with yellow sepals and petals heavily barred red-brown. The broad, red-brown, trilobed lip has a white, transverse band, small side lobes and has an entire, arrow-shaped midlobe with a bright yellow callus. The whole shape and structure of the flower gives an impression of flight. The flowers have a small, erect, footless column with round or pointed, petal-like wings.

BRACHIONIDIUM

Lindley

Fol. Orchid. **8**: *Brachionidium*, 8 (1859).

Epidendroideæ ⚘ Epidendreæ • Pleurothallidinæ

ETYMOLOGY: Greek for diminutive of armlet or small arm. Alluding to the short arms on the column that do not bear stigmas.

LECTOTYPE: *Brachionidium parvifolium*
(Lindley) Lindley
(*Restrepia parvifolia* Lindley)

Sixty-five uncommon, sympodial epiphytes, lithophytes or terrestrials are found in misty, upper elevation, montane cloud forests from Guatemala to Bolivia, Venezuela, Guyana and southern Brazil, with a few species sprinkled from Cuba to Saint Vincent. These small to large, erect or creeping plants with a few often viny species, have short stems, subtended by overlapping, funnel-shaped, long pointed, scurfy to scaly sheaths, each with a solitary to several, smooth, leathery leaves. The solitary-flowered, hanging inflorescence has a spectacular, large, brightly to dull-colored flower open for only a short time. The thinly textured, delicate sepals and petals have long, thread-like tails, and the lateral sepals (synsepal) are united, concave and sometimes hood-like. The small, thick, entire or trilobed lip, wider than it is long, is hinged to the column foot, has an entire, fringed or a broad, flat basal callus. The flowers have a short, stout column.

BRACHISTEPIS

Thouars

Hist. Orchid. Table 3, sub 3p, t. 84 (1822).

Name published without a description. Today this name is most often referred to *Beclardia*.

BRACHTIA

Reichenbach *filius*

Linnaea **22**: 853 (1850).

Name ICBN conserved vs. *Brachtia* Trevisan de Saint-Leon (1848) Algae.

Epidendroideæ ⚘ Cymbidieæ • Oncidiinæ

ETYMOLOGY: In honor of Adalbert von Bracht (1804-1848), an Italian-born, Austro-Hungarian army officer, who collected plants in northeastern Italy and was killed during a revolution in Hungary that was later crushed.

TYPE SPECIES: *Brachtia glumacea* Reichenbach f.

Seven sympodial epiphytes or terrestrials are found in wet, upper elevation, montane cloud forests of the Andes from Venezuela and

Colombia to Ecuador. These plants have compressed, two-edged pseudobulbs, completely subtended by overlapping sheaths, each with one to two leaves. The inflorescences, borne in the axils of the sheaths of mature pseudobulbs, have large, flattened floral bracts that nearly hide the flowers. The small, fleshy, bright yellow or green flowers do not open fully, develop slowly, and last for a long period of time. The dorsal sepal is hood-shaped and is somewhat broader, than the concave petals. The wedge-shaped, fleshy, entire lip is swollen at its base forming a sac-like spur and has a two-ridge callus. The flowers have a short, stout, winged column.

BRACHYCLADIUM

(Luer) Luer

Monogr. Syst. Bot. Missouri Bot. Gard.
103: 307 (2005).

Not *Brachycladium* Corda (1838) Fungi, and not *Brachycladium* M.J. Berkeley (1848) Fossil.

ETYMOLOGY: Greek for short stems. Referring to the unusual secondary stems (ramicauls) that are shorter than the primary plant stems.

TYPE SPECIES: *Brachycladium nummularium*
(Reichenbach f.) Luer
(*Lepanthes nummularia* Reichenbach f.)

Not validly published because of a prior use of the name, this homonym was replaced by *Lepanthes*.

BRACHYCORIS

An orthographic variant introduced in *Gen. Pl., Suppl. 1 (Endlicher)*, 1366 (1840). The correct spelling is *Brachycorythis*.

BRACHYCORITHIS

An orthographic variant introduced in *Syn. Pl. (D. Dietrich)*, **5**: 14, 157 (1852). The correct spelling is *Brachycorythis*.

BRACHYCORYTHIS

Lindley

Gen. Sp. Orchid. Pl. 363 (1838).

Orchidoideæ ⚘ Orchideæ • Orchidinæ

ETYMOLOGY: Greek for short and helmet. Referring to the hood-shaped perianth which may vaguely resemble a helmet.

TYPE SPECIES: *Brachycorythis ovata* Lindley

Thirty-six uncommon, sympodial terrestrials or rare epiphytes and saprophytes are found in low to mid elevation, boggy swamps, grasslands and savannas to dry or wet, mixed deciduous and bamboo forests from Guinea to Zaire, Ethiopia to Mozambique, Madagascar, northern India

(Kashmir to Assam), southern China (Yunnan to Guangdong), Bangladesh to Vietnam and Taiwan. These erect plants have unbranched, slender stems, each with numerous to several, overlapping leaves or are rarely covered in scales. The often cylindrical, numerous to few-flowered inflorescence has leaf-like bracts often longer than the flowers. The mauve, white, yellow, pink or purple flowers are not large, but are presented in sufficient quantities to be showy, often with darker colored spots. The two-part lip has a basal hypochile with a small, sometimes bag-like or boat-shaped, to even an obscure spur, while the upper, flattened epichile is entire, bilobed or trilobed and usually projects forward. The flowers have an erect, usually short, stout column.

BRACHYONIDIUM

An orthographic variant introduced in *Bull. Soc. Roy. Bot. Belgique*, **43**: 344 (1906). The correct spelling is *Brachionidium*.

BRACHYPEZA

Garay

Bot. Mus. Leafl. **23**(4): 163 (1972).

Epidendroideæ ⚘ Vandeæ • Aeridinæ

ETYMOLOGY: Greek for short or bottom and foot. Referring to the small size of the characteristically short column foot.

TYPE SPECIES: *Brachypeza archytas* (Ridley) Garay
(*Saccolabium archytas* Ridley)

Seven monopodial epiphytes are found in low elevation, evergreen and limestone forests from Malaysia, Laos then south to Indonesia, New Guinea, northern Australia and the southwestern Pacific Archipelago. These small plants have short stems, each with several, fleshy, broad leaves suffused purple. The short, numerous-flowered, thickened inflorescence has close-set, short-lived flowers with only a few open at a time. The white or yellow, tiny flowers are blotched or mottled dark red. The hanging, highly mobile, trilobed lip has large, erect side lobes, and a small, recurved midlobe with almost its whole length consisting of a narrow spur. The flowers have a slender, forward bent, wingless column.

NOTE: These plants are vegetatively similar to *Phalaenopsis*, but the small flowers are similar to *Pteroceras*.

y Accepted | Validly Published | Invalidly Published | Published Pre-1753 | Superfluous Usage | Orthographic Variant | Fossil

Orchid Genera • 52

BRACHYSTELE

Schlechter

Beih. Bot. Centralbl. **37**(2): 370 (1920).

Orchidoideæ ⚬ Cranichideæ • Spiranthinæ

ETYMOLOGY: Greek for short and column, pillar or cylinder. An allusion to the very short rostellum.

LECTOTYPE: *Brachystele unilateralis*
(Poiret) Schlechter
(*Ophrys unilateralis* Poiret)
designated by Cabrera, *DAGI Publ. Técn.*, **1**(6): 16 (1942).

LECTOTYPE: *Brachystele guayanensis*
(Lindley) Schlechter
(*Goodyera guayanensis* Lindley)
designated superfluously by Burns-Balogh, *Amer. J. Bot.*, **69**(7): 1131 (1982).

Twenty inconspicuous, sympodial terrestrials are found in dry to marshy, low to mid elevation, pine-oak forest openings, scrub and grasslands from the southeastern Unites States (Florida), Mexico to Panama, the Guianas, Trinidad, Venezuela, Colombia to Chile and northern Argentina. These small, slender, inconspicuous plants have unbranched stems, each with a solitary leaf or a loose, basal rosette of leaves that are absent at flowering. The long, erect, delicate, congested (usually hairy throughout) inflorescence has small to minute, more or less tubular, green-white to yellow flowers not opening fully. Some species are fragrant and the strongly curved petals have papillate or ciliate margins. The white, clawed, trilobed lip has a broad base fused to the sides of the short, club-shaped, channeled column, with tufts of longer hairs near the base, and is recurved at the notched tip. These species were formerly included in *Spiranthes*.

BRACHYSTEPIS

An orthographic variant introduced in *Hist. Orchid.*, t. 83 (1822). The correct spelling is *Brachistepis*.

BRACISEPALUM

J.J. Smith

Bot. Jahrb. Syst. **65**: 464 (1933).

Epidendroideæ ⚬ Arethuseæ • Coelogyninæ

ETYMOLOGY: Latin for trousers and sepal. Refers to the lateral sepals that are united into a shortly bilobed extension that encloses the equally sac-like back of the lip; the latter is, so to speak 'clad in trousers.'

TYPE SPECIES: *Bracisepalum selebicum* J.J. Smith

Two uncommon, sympodial epiphytes are found in mid elevation, montane forests of eastern Indonesia (Sulawesi). Vegetatively these plants cannot usually be distinguished from those of *Dendrochilum*. These small plants have clustered, ovoid pseudobulbs, each with a solitary, thinly textured, fleshy leaf. The

long, hanging to arching, wiry, spirally arranged, numerous-flowered inflorescence has small, delicate, pale pink to red-yellow flowers opening simultaneously and have sickled-shaped petals. The deeply lobed lateral sepals, inserted at the base of the column, are joined to the basal portion of the broad, golden-yellow, entire lip that has two, sac-like extensions. The flowers have a slender, straight, winged column with a trilobed hood.

BRAEMIA

Jenny

Orchidee (Hamburg) **36**(1): 36 (1985).

ETYMOLOGY: In honor of Guido Jozef Braem (1944-), a Belgian-born German biologist, orchid taxonomist, art historian and author of several works on Cattleyas and Paphiopedilums.

TYPE SPECIES: *Braemia vittata* (Lindley) Jenny
(*Houlletia vittata* Lindley)

Now recognized as belonging to the genus *Polycycnis*, *Braemia* was proposed to include one epiphyte found in low elevation, forests and scrub from Brazil, the Guianas, Venezuela and Peru. This plant has pear-shaped to ovoid pseudobulbs, subtended by short-lived sheaths, each with a solitary, pleated, thinly textured, heavily veined leaf located at the tip. The stiffly, erect, numerous to few-flowered inflorescence has showy, yellow flowers intensely streaked with so much red-brown that it is impossible to see the base color. The narrowly clawed, trilobed lip has short, narrow, slightly concave side lobes, and the flat midlobe is obscurely trilobed, has a low, central keel, and an upcurved, horn-like callus. The flowers have a long, slender, arching, slightly club-shaped, winged column.

BRAENDLING

Aretius

Stocc Hornii et Nessi 234b (1561).

ETYMOLOGY: An old German word for something burnt. Refers to the color of the burned orchid - *Orchis ustulata*.

TYPE SPECIES: *None designated*

Pre-1753, therefore not validly published in fulfillment of nomenclatural rules; this name is most often referred to *Orchis*. *Braendling* was previously considered to include one terrestrial widespread from Britain to central Russia (West Siberia) and Germany to Greece. This stout plant has erect, unbranched stems, each with several, basal leaves. The erect, few to numerous-flowered inflorescence has the dark black-brown flowers with the dorsal sepal and petals converging to form a hood over the small column. The white, deeply trilobed lip has widespreading side lobes, a bilobed midlobe

and a slender spur. The above name is now considered a synonym of *Orchis ustulata* Linnaeus.

BRASAVOLA

An orthographic variant introduced in *Encycl. Pl.*, 762 (1829). The correct spelling is *Brassavola*.

BRASIA

An orthographic variant introduced in *Paxton's Mag. Bot.*, **4**: 235 (1838). The correct spelling is *Brassia*.

BRASILAELIA

Campacci

Colet. Orquídeas Brasil. **4**(Pré-anexo): 99 (2006).

ETYMOLOGY: Honoring Brazil and *Laelia*, a genus of orchids. Brazil is the largest country found in South America.

TYPE SPECIES: *Brasilaelia crispa* (Lindley) Campacci
(*Laelia crispa* Lindley)

Recognized as belonging to the genus *Hadrolaelia*, *Brasilaelia* was proposed to include one epiphyte or occasional lithophyte found in low to mid elevation, hill to montane forests of Brazil (Espírito Santo, Rio de Janeiro and Minas Gerais). This plant has long, compressed, club-shaped, grooved stems, each with a solitary, oblong leaf that has a notched tip. The few-flowered inflorescence, subtended by a compressed sheath, has showy, fragrant, white flowers suffused purple at the base. The narrow sepals and petals have wavy, crisp margins. The trilobed lip has large, broad, erect side lobes that surround the long, club-shaped column, has an oblong midlobe with deep purple-red radiating veins, a deep yellow basal callus and a crisped margin.

BRASILIDIUM

Campacci

Colet. Orquídeas Brasil. **3**: 78 (2006).

ETYMOLOGY: Honoring Brazil and *Oncidium*, a genus of orchids. Brazil is the largest country found in South America.

TYPE SPECIES: *Brasilidium crispum*
(Loddiges) Campacci
(*Oncidium crispum* Loddiges)

Recognized as belonging to the genus *Oncidium*, *Brasilidium* was proposed to include ten epiphytes found in Ecuador and southeastern Brazil. These plants have clustered, oblong, dark brown or purple-brown, compressed, ribbed pseudobulbs, each with several, oblong, leathery leaves. The erect or arching, multibranched, numerous-flowered inflorescence, borne from the pseudobulb base, has variable sized, chestnut-brown flowers that have wavy, yellow lined margins. The trilobed lip has ear-like side lobes, and the large, broadly clawed midlobe has a large, basal callus that is horn-like and multi-toothed. The flowers have a short, slightly curved, winged column.

BRASILIORCHIS

R. Singer, S. Koehler & Carnevali
Novon **17**(1): 94 (2007).
ETYMOLOGY: Named for the country of origin and Greek for orchid. Indicating that this is essentially a Brazilian orchid genus.
LECTOTYPE: *Brasiliorchis picta*
    (Hooker) R. Singer, S. Koehler & Carnevali
    (*Maxillaria picta* Hooker)

Recognized as belonging to the genus *Maxillaria*, *Brasiliorchis* was proposed to include thirteen epiphytes found in low elevation, Atlantic rain forests of southeastern Brazil (Rio Grande do Sul to Bahia) with three species found in north-eastern Argentina (Misiones) and Ecuador. These plants have small, pear-shaped, ridged to deeply grooved pseudobulbs, subtended by dry sheaths, each with two strap-like, folded leaves. The erect, solitary-flowered inflorescence, borne from the pseudobulb base, has a showy, bell-shaped, long-lasting, fragrant, cream to yellow-cream flower sprinkled with purple dots. The flowers have an almost straight column.

BRASILOCYCNIS

G. Gerlach & Whitten
J. Orchideenfr. **6**(3): 188 (1999).
ETYMOLOGY: Honoring the Federative Republic of Brazil (the largest country and site of the most important ecological rain forest in South America). And *Cycnis* (Greek for swan).
TYPE SPECIES: *Brasilocycnis breviloba*
    (Summerhayes) G. Gerlach & Whitten
    (*Polycycnis breviloba* Summerhayes)
This type name is now considered a synonym of *Lueckelia breviloba* (Summerhayes) Jenny; basionym
    Polycycnis breviloba Summerhayes

Now recognized as belonging to the genus *Lueckelia*, *Brasilocycnis* was proposed to include one epiphyte found in moist, low to mid elevation, forests of Brazil (Amazonas, Pará and Mato Grosso). This slender plant has oblong pseudobulbs, each with several, broad leaves. The erect to hanging, numerous-flowered inflorescence has small, yellow flowers covered with tiny, red spots and splashes. The

narrow, white, trilobed lip, sprinkled with several, red spots, has a narrow, obscurely trilobed, midlobe.

BRASSAEVOLA

An orthographic variant introduced in *Arch. Pharm.*, **15**: 266 (1865). The correct spelling is *Brassavola*.

BRASSAFOLA

An orthographic variant introduced in *Ann. Rep. Park Comm. Milwaukee*, 117 (1906). The correct spelling is *Brassavola*.

BRASSAVOLA

R. Brown
Hortus Kew., ed. 2   **5**: 216 (1813).
Name ICBN conserved vs. *Brassavola* Adanson (1763) Asteraceæ.

Epidendroideæ ⚬ Epidendreæ • Laeliinæ
ETYMOLOGY: Dedicated to Antonio Musa Brassavola (1500-1555), a Venetian nobleman, physician, botanist and a professor of logic, medicine and physics in Ferrara, Italy.
TYPE SPECIES: *Brassavola cucullata*
    (Linnaeus) R. Brown
    (*Epidendrum cucullatum* Linnaeus)

Twenty popular, showy sympodial epiphytes or lithophytes are found in low to mid elevation, coastal to montane forests, mangroves, rocky crevices and cliff faces from Mexico to Bolivia, Brazil and Jamaica. These plants, often forming large clumps, have slender or some-what thickened stems (dark green or purple), subtended by white, dry, tubular sheaths, each usually with one or rarely two, narrow, flattened, leathery to fleshy leaves at the tip. The arching to hanging, short, solitary to few-flowered inflorescence, borne at a leaf insertion or from the rhizome, has large, long-lasting, nocturnally fragrant, showy flowers that are sometimes white, creamy or green-yellow. The shape of the clawed, entire lip varies from wedge-shaped, long and slender, to short with no point and has margins that are either entire or fringed. The lip has a tubular claw enfolding a very short, club-shaped, usually winged, footless column that has a tooth at the tip and winged in the front.

NOTE: The popular species *digbyana* and *glauca* are now referred to the segregate genus *Rhyncholaelia*.

BRASSAVOLAEA

An orthographic variant introduced in *Gen. Pl.* (Sprengel), ed. 9, **2**: 676 (1831). The correct spelling is *Brassavola*.

BRASSAVOLEA

An orthographic variant introduced in *Syst. Veg.* (*Sprengel*), ed. 16, **3**: 682, 744 (1826). The correct spelling is *Brassavola*.

BRASSAVOLLA

An orthographic variant introduced in *Dict. Sci. Nat.*, **36**: 304 (1825). The correct spelling is *Brassavola*.

BRASSEVOLA

An orthographic variant introduced in *Rad. Jugoslav. Akad. Znan.*, **21**: 115 (1872). The correct spelling is *Brassavola*.

BRASSIA

R. Brown
Hortus Kew., ed. 2   **5**: 215 (1813).
Not *Brassia* A. Massalongo (1860) Lichen.

Epidendroideæ ⚬ Cymbidieæ • Oncidiinæ
ETYMOLOGY: Dedicated to William Brass (x-1783), a British botanist who was employed to collected plants in Guinea and South Africa, and also worked as an illustrator for Joseph Banks (1743-1820).
TYPE SPECIES: *Brassia maculata* R. Brown

Thirty-four sympodial epiphytes, occasional lithophytes or terrestrials are widespread in the American tropics from low to upper elevation, hill to montane forests, mangroves and scrub of the southeastern United States (Florida), Cuba to Trinidad, the Guianas, Venezuela, Mexico to Bolivia and Brazil. These plants are easily distinguished by their spider-like flowers that have long, yellow or green lateral sepals. The large, flat, oblong to ovoid pseudobulbs, subtended by overlapping sheaths, each with one to two, narrow leaves that are veined on the underside. The basal, simple, erect or hanging, numerous to few-flowered inflorescence is pale, yellow to lime green, long-lived flowers striped or barred with white, dark brown or maroon. A few of the species have extremely long sepals (five to six inches [12 cm]) and inward curved petals that taper to a sharp point. Almost all have a pervading fragrance that ranges from pleasant to putrid. The spreading, fiddle-shaped, entire or obscurely trilobed lip, shorter than the sepals or petals, has two or more ridges of heavily warted calli at the base. The flowers have a short, stout, wingless, footless column.

Currently Accepted   Validly Published   Invalidly Published   Published Pre-1753   Superfluous Usage   Orthographic Variant   Fossil

Orchid Genera · **54**

BRASSVOLA

An orthographic variant introduced in *Etim. Orquidofilos*, 15 (1998). The correct spelling is *Brassavola*.

BRASSOVALA

An orthographic variant introduced in *Hamburger Garten- Blumenzeitung*, **16**: 421 (1860). The correct spelling is *Brassavola*.

BRASSIOPSIS

Szlachetko & Górniak

Biodivers. Res. Conservation **1-2**: 11 (2006).

Not *Brassaiopsis* Decaisne & Planchon (1854) Araliaceæ, and not *Brassopsis* Shaw (2004) Orchidaceæ.

ETYMOLOGY: *Brassia*, a genus of orchids, and Greek for resemblance. Referring a similarity between *Brassia* and *Ada*.

TYPE SPECIES: *Brassiopsis keiliana*
(Reichenbach f. ex Lindley) Szlachetko & Górniak
(*Brassia keiliana* Reichenbach f. ex Lindley)

Recognized as belonging to the genera *Brassia* and *Ada*, *Brassiopsis* was proposed to include thirteen epiphytes found in mid elevation, montane cloud forests from Nicaragua to Peru and Venezuela. These plants have ovoid, compressed pseudobulbs, subtended by several, overlapping sheaths, each with leathery, narrow, erect to arching leaves. The erect, few-flowered inflorescence has orange-yellow to lime green, showy, waxy, faintly fragrant flowers with long, narrow sepals and petals that are variously barred red-brown. The obscurely trilobed lip is spear shaped, heavily keeled and has a recurved tip. The flowers have a short, small, footless column.

BRENESIA

Schlechter

Repert. Spec. Nov. Regni Veg. Beih. **19**: 200 (1923).

ETYMOLOGY: Honoring Alberto Manuel Brenes y Mora (1870-1948), a Costa Rican botanist, pharmacist and professor of pharmacy at the University of Santo Tomás in San José.

LECTOTYPE: *Brenesia costaricensis* Schlechter
This type name is now considered a synonym of
Acianthera johnsonii (Ames) Pridgeon & M.W. Chase;
basionym
Pleurothallis johnsonii Ames

Now recognized as belonging to the to the genus *Acianthera*, *Brenesia* was previously considered to include eleven epiphytes found in upper elevation, montane cloud forests from Costa Rica to Panama. These cluster-forming, rather stout, rigid, erect plants have several, solitary-flowered inflorescences with red to red-brown flowers that are spotted purple on their inner surfaces, do not open widely and have a foul fragrance. The long, narrow sepals have warts on all their surfaces and long, white hairs along the upper margins.

The flowers have small, triangular petals. The clawed, wedge to tongue-shaped, entire lip is concave. The flowers have a long, club-shaped, slightly curved column.

BREVILONGIUM

Christenson

Richardiana **6**(1) 47 (2006).

ETYMOLOGY: Latin for short and long. Refers to the two different types of inflorescences.

TYPE SPECIES: *Brevilongium globuliferum*
(Kunth) Christenson
(*Oncidium globuliferum* Kunth)

Recognized as belonging to the genus *Otoglossum*, *Brevilongium* was proposed to include eight epiphytes or terrestrials found in low to mid elevation, hill and montane forests from Costa Rica to Ecuador. These unusual tufted, large, stout plants have small, compressed pseudobulbs, subtended by leaf-like bracts when young, each with a solitary, oval to elliptical, leathery leaf. After a while the young plant bares a long, slender, usually sterile inflorescence that produces keikis at the nodes. These keikis mature and produce a fertile, twining, solitary-flowered inflorescence with a dull purple to bright yellow flower with similar, spreading sepals and petals. The broad, trilobed lip has small, erect to spreading side lobes and a large, spreading, bilobed midlobe with a wavy margin. The flowers have a short, stout column.

BRIEGERIA

Senghas

Orchidee (Hamburg) **31**(1): 29 (1980).

ETYMOLOGY: Dedicated to Fredrich Gustav Brieger (1900-1985), a German-born Brazilian geneticist, professor at the University of São Paulo, taxonomist and author of numerous articles on orchids.

TYPE SPECIES: *Briegeria teretifolia* (Swartz) Senghas
(*Epidendrum teretifolium* Swartz)

Now recognized as belonging to the genus *Jacquiniella*, *Briegeria* was previously considered to include five epiphytes found in low to mid elevation, hill and montane cloud forests from Mexico to Panama, Venezuela, Colombia to northern Brazil, the Guianas and Cuba to Puerto Rico. These small, tufted plants have cylindrical, succulent leaves spaced along the slender stems that are subtended by thin, dry, tubular sheaths. The solitary to numerous-flowered inflorescence has tiny, inconspicuous, olive-brown, red to yellow flowers with similar sepals and petals. The small, shortly clawed, entire lip, joined to the column base, has an entire or trilobed tip. The flowers have a short, small column.

BROCCEBEGENS

Rivinus

Icon. Pl. Fl. Hexspet. (Rivinus) t. 3 (1764).

ETYMOLOGY: Latin for a local mountain, Mount Brocken (3,746 ft./1,142 m), found in central eastern Germany (Hartz mountain range) and is not far from Leipzig, where the German physician and botanist Augustus Quirinus Rivinus (1652-1723) lived.

TYPE SPECIES: *None designated*

Name published without a description. Today this name is most often referred to *Dactylorhiza*.

BROMHAEDIA

An orthographic variant introduced in *Zastosowania*, **1**: 169, 170 (2000). The correct spelling is *Bromheadia*.

BROMHEADEA

An orthographic variant introduced in *Icon. Pl. Ind. Orient. (Wight)*, **3**: t. 1740 (1851). The correct spelling is *Bromheadia*.

BROMHEADIA

Lindley

Edwards's Bot. Reg.
27(Misc.): 89, section no. 184 (1841).

Epidendroideæ ⚭ Cymbidieæ • Bromheadiinæ

ETYMOLOGY: In honor of Edward Thomas (Ffrench) French Bromhead (1789-1855), an Irish baronet, lawyer from Lincolnshire, mathematician, high steward of Lincoln, founder of Cambridge Analytical Society and an amateur botanist.

TYPE SPECIES: *Bromheadia palustris* Lindley
This type name is now considered a synonym of
Bromheadia finlaysoniana (Lindley) Miquel;
basionym
Grammatophyllum finlaysonianum Lindley

Twenty-eight sympodial terrestrials or epiphytes are found in low to mid elevation, scrub and open forests from Sri Lanka, Malaysia, Indonesia and New Guinea to northern Australia. These erect plants' stems usually have two types of leaves; dorso-ventrally or laterally flattened, that are joined with the sheath and are almost parallel with the slender stem. The inflorescence has several, small to medium-sized, white or pale yellow flowers with red-purple and yellow markings and have narrow, spreading sepals and petals. The fragrant flowers open in the early morning, and last only for a few short hours. They bloom one to two at a time, in opposite rows and have regularly, alternating bracts. The boat-shaped, trilobed lip has erect side lobes, a recurved midlobe that is parallel with the long, slender, slightly curved, footless, winged column, and has a thickened, hairy disk.

BROOMHEADIA

An orthographic variant introduced in *Icon. Pl. Ind. Orient. (Wight)*, **5**(1): 18 (1851). The correct spelling is *Bromheadia*.

BROUGHTONIA

R. Brown

Hortus Kew., ed. 2   **5**: 217 (1813).

Epidendroideæ ◊ Epidendreæ • Laeliinæ

ETYMOLOGY: Dedicated to Arthur Broughton (1758-1796), a British physician and botanist who later settled in Jamaica and collected the West Indies flora, and author of *Enchiridion Botanicum* (1782).

TYPE SPECIES: *Broughtonia sanguinea*
(Swartz) R. Brown
(*Epidendrum sanguineum* Swartz)

Six sympodial epiphytes or lithophytes are confined in humid, low elevation, forest scrub of Jamaica, Cuba, the Bahamas and Puerto Rico. These plants have clustered, somewhat flattened, dull green to gray pseudobulbs, each with one to four, leathery or fleshy leaves at the tip. The long, simple to sometimes branching, few-flowered inflorescence has minute bracts and is borne from the tip of the pseudobulb that becomes grooved with age. This plant, when properly grown, is almost ever blooming. The brilliant candy striped, crimson, white, yellow to pale pink flowers have slightly incurved, oblong sepals and smaller petals. The broad to tubular, roundish, entire or obscurely trilobed lip has purple veins radiating out from the yellow or ivory colored base, and either a crisp or sightly notched margin. The flowers have a long, stout, footless column.

BROUGHTONIA

Wallich ex Lindley

Gen. Sp. Orchid. Pl.   35 (1830).

Name published without a description. Today this name is most often referred to *Otochilus*.

BROWMLEEA

An orthographic variant introduced in *Etim. Orquidofilos*, 29 (1998). The correct spelling is *Brownleea*.

BROWNLEA

An orthographic variant introduced in *Bot. Jahrb. Syst.*, **31**: 135 (1902). The correct spelling is *Brownleea*.

BROWNLEEA

Harvey ex Lindley

London J. Bot.   **1**: 16 (1842).

Orchidoideæ ◊ Orchideæ • Brownleeinæ

ETYMOLOGY: In honor of John Brownlee (1791-1871), a Scottish missionary and gardener who collected the type species while stationed at King William's Town in Caffraria, South Africa. He sent many plant specimens to William Henry Harvey (1811-1866).

LECTOTYPE: *Brownleea parviflora* Harvey ex Lindley

Seven or more sympodial terrestrials or occasional epiphytes are found in high rainfall, low to mid elevation, gravelly to sandy grasslands from Zaire, Cameroon, Kenya to eastern South Africa and Madagascar. These small plants have slender to stout, unbranched stems, each with one to two, ovate to narrow, deciduous leaves that become bract-like as they ascend up the stem. The head-like to long, densely clustered, numerous to few-flowered inflorescence has small, showy, white, pink or mauve flowers sprinkled with darker colored spots. The somewhat recurved, helmet-like dorsal sepal has a long, slender or short, club-like spur, is joined to the oblong, erect petals, and has spreading, ovate to narrow lateral sepals. The minute, entire to obscurely trilobed lip is fused to the stout, footless column base.

BRUGHTONIA

An orthographic variant introduced in *Dict. Sci. Nat.*, ed. 2, **13**: 56 (1819). The correct spelling is *Broughtonia*.

BRYOBIUM

Lindley

Intr. Nat. Syst. Bot., ed. 2   446 (1836), and *Edwards's Bot. Reg.*
24(Misc.): 79, section no. 145 (1838).

Epidendroideæ ◊ Podochileæ • Eriinæ

ETYMOLOGY: Greek for moss (to swell or teem with) and life. In reference to the plant's epiphytic habit growing among mosses.

TYPE SPECIES: *Bryobium pubescens* Lindley
This type name is now considered a synonym of
Bryobium retusum (Blume) Y.P. Ng & P.J. Cribb;
basionym
Dendrolirium retusum Blume

Seven sympodial epiphytes or lithophytes are widespread in low to mid elevation, hill forests from northern India (Assam) to Hong Kong and southward through Malaysia, Indonesia and northern Australia (Queensland). These tall plants have flattened, fleshy, few noded, ovoid to spindle-shaped pseudobulbs, each with several, upward curved, leathery leaves. The few-flowered inflorescence, covered in white, woolly hairs, has small, unpleasantly fragrant, pale green, white or pale yellow flowers which turn yellow as they age and are hairy on their backsides. The white, yellow or dull purple, entire or trilobed lip has small, roundish side lobes. The midlobe is as wide as it is long, has a wavy margin and short, fleshy calli. The flowers have a short, slightly curved, club-shaped column that has a slender base and then greatly expands toward the tip.

BRYOLOBIUM

An orthographic variant introduced in *Gen. Pl., Suppl. 1 (Endlicher)*, 1362 (1840). The correct spelling is *Bryobium*.

BUCCELLA

Luer

Monogr. Syst. Bot. Missouri Bot. Gard.
105: 7 (2006).

ETYMOLOGY: Latin for a cheek or inflated and like. Referring to the dilated lateral sepals.

TYPE SPECIES: *Buccella nidifica* (Reichenbach f.) Luer
(*Masdevallia nidifica* Reichenbach f.)

Recognized as belonging to the genus *Masdevallia*, *Buccella* was proposed to include nine epiphytes or lithophytes found in low to mid elevation, dense hill and montane forests from Nicaragua to Panama and Colombia to Ecuador. These small plants have short, erect stems, subtended by tubular bracts, each with a solitary, ovate, leathery leaf. The wiry, solitary-flowered inflorescence has a small, yellow-green to creamy-yellow flower often spotted and striped that are minutely hairy inside. The somewhat transparent, cup-shaped, lateral sepals taper into long, slender to thread-like tails and has small petals. The oblong, fiddle-shaped, entire is slightly curved. The flowers have an elongate, more or less club-shaped column.

BUCCULINA

Lindley

Companion Bot. Mag.   **2**(19): 209 (1837).
Not *Bucculina* V.S. Malyavkina (1949) Fossil.

ETYMOLOGY: Latin for little cheek. Alluding to the fleshy, broadly toothed, concave petals.

TYPE SPECIES: *Bucculina aspera* Lindley

Now recognized as belonging to the genus *Holothrix*, *Bucculina* was previously considered to include one terrestrial found in dry scrub of South Africa. This small, deciduous, erect plant

Currently Accepted   Validly Published   Invalidly Published   Published Pre-1753   Superfluous Usage   Orthographic Variant   Fossil

Orchid Genera • **56**

has slender, unbranched stems, each with two basal leaves that lie flat on the ground. The thick, water-storing upper leaf layer appears translucent. The hairy, few-flowered inflorescence has small, white-green flowers with fleshy, lobed petals. The pale mauve, entire lip, attached to the column base, has long, darker stripes and a short, broad, yellow-green, sharply inflexed spur. The flowers have a short, small column.

BUCHTIENIA

Schlechter

Repert. Spec. Nov. Regni Veg.   **27**: 33 (1929).

Orchidoideæ ⸙ Cranichideæ • Spiranthinæ

ETYMOLOGY: Commemorating Otto August Buchtien (1859-1946), a German botanist hired by the Bolivian government to organize the Museo Nacional in La Paz, he gathered the type species while collecting in Bolivia and Brazil. These specimens were later sold to different herbaria.

TYPE SPECIES: *Buchtienia boliviensis* Schlechter

Three uncommon, sympodial terrestrials are confined to very wet, low to mid elevation, hill and montane forests of Ecuador to Bolivia and a small area in southeastern Brazil (Mato Grosso). These large, erect plants have unbranched stems, each with several, thinly textured, oblong leaves forming a basal rosette that is present at flowering time. The very tall, numerous-flowered inflorescence (smooth or hairy above) is partly concealed by sheathing bracts, and has small, fleshy, rosy or green flowers with a concave, erect dorsal sepal. The long, narrow, widespreading lateral sepals taper to a point and has small, sickle-shaped petals. The small trilobed lip, shorter than the other segments, has erect, pointed to rounded side lobes enfolding the erect, short, slightly curved column and has a sharply pointed, decurved midlobe.

BUESELLA

An orthographic variant introduced in *Biodivers. Res. Conserv.*, **1-2**: 6. (2006). The correct spelling is *Buesiella*.

BUESIELLA

C. Schweinfurth

Bot. Mus. Leafl. **15**: 153. (1952).

ETYMOLOGY: Dedicated to Rudolf Adolf Christian Bües (1841-1948), a German-born Peruvian who ran a small natural history museum in Lima and extensively collected the orchids and bromeliads of Peru. And Latin for diminutive.

TYPE SPECIES: *Buesiella pusilla* C. Schweinfurth

Now recognized as belonging to the genus *Cyrtochilum*, *Buesiella* was previously considered to include five epiphytes found in upper elevation, montane

cloud forests of Peru and central Bolivia. These fragile, inconspicuous plants have ovate pseudobulbs, each with a long, narrow, solitary leaf. The few-flowered inflorescence has tiny, bell-shaped, fragrant, white flowers spotted magenta and with oblong sepals and ovate petals. The longitudinally, concave, white, trilobed lip has a thickened base, without side lobes, and the midlobe has a pair of erect, flat ridges that are parallel to the club-shaped, wingless, footless column.

BULBODICTIS

Rafinesque

Fl. Tellur.   **4**: 45 (1836)|1837].

ETYMOLOGY: Greek for bulb and net or lattice-like. Refers to the texture of the dry sheaths.

TYPE SPECIES: *None designated*

Name published without a description. Today this name is most often referred to *Epidendrum*.

BULBOPHILLUM

An orthographic variant introduced in *Orquideas Afic.*, 27 (1961). The correct spelling is *Bulbophyllum*.

BULBOPHYLLARIA

S. Moore

Fl. Mauritius   346 (1877).

ETYMOLOGY: Greek for bulb and rein or strap. Refers to the small inflorescence.

TYPE SPECIES: *Bulbophyllaria clavata*
(Thouars) S. Moore
(*Bulbophyllum clavatum* Thouars)

Not validly published, this name is most often referred to *Bulbophyllum*. *Bulbophyllaria* was considered to include one epiphyte found in the Mascarene and Réunion Islands.

BULBOPHYLLUM

Thouars

Hist. Orchid.   Table 3, sub 3u, *tt. 93-110* (1822).
Name ICBN conserved vs. *Phyllorkis* Thouars (1809), and type name also conserved.

Epidendroideæ ⸙ Dendrobiinæ • Currently unplaced

ETYMOLOGY: Greek for bulb and leaf. Referring to the single-noded pseudobulb with its solitary leaf.

LECTOTYPE: *Bulbophyllum nutans* Thouars

The largest genus of the entire orchid family with an estimated one thousand, eight hundred extraordinarily shaped, polymorphic, creeping epiphytes, lithophytes or rare terrestrials. They vary in size from minute, often forming large mats, to often massive, climbers. They have a wide range of habitats throughout the

tropical and subtropical regions of the globe. African species have small but occasionally quite striking plants and flowers. The American species have stiff, uninteresting plants with small, drab flowers. Asian species have multi-leaved plants usually with delightful flowers. But the greatest diversity is found in New Guinea. These plants have small to large, single-noded, stout pseudobulbs each with one to two leaves that develop along a creeping rhizome and have basal inflorescences. The enormously diverse flowers are often furnished with a strong fragrance, sometimes pleasant or sometimes fetid, but almost always suffocating in its intensity. Some flowers are so tiny they are only visible with the help of a magnifying lens. The dorsal sepal is free, the lateral sepals are often united and attached to the column foot, and the petals are usually smaller than sepals. The flowers possess an extraordinary articulated, often hairy, thin to rigid, entire or trilobed lip that is sensitive to even the slightest touch or breeze. Its function is to unbalance the visiting insect and tumble it against the short, erect column, thus the unsuspecting insect becomes attached to the pollinia and carries it to another flower. The dazzling, sensuous floral colors range through virtually every hue imaginable except blue. Many of the species were formerly included in the genus *Cirrhopetalum*.

BULBOPHYLUM

An orthographic variant introduced in *Wild Orchids Myanmar*, **2**: 106 (2003). The correct spelling is *Bulbophyllum*.

BULLEYA

An orthographic variant introduced in *Gen. Coelogyne*, 3 (2002). The correct spelling is *Bulleyia*.

BULLEYIA

Schlechter

Notes Roy. Bot. Gard. Edinburgh
5(24): 108, *t. 82* (1912).

Epidendroideæ ⸙ Arethuseæ • Coelogyninæ

ETYMOLOGY: Honoring Arthur Kilpin Bulley (1861-1942), a British cotton broker, naturalist and a seed company founder. He started Liverpool's Ness Botanic Garden and engaged George Forrest (1873-1932) to collect the flora and seeds of southern China.

TYPE SPECIES: *Bulleyia yunnanensis* Schlechter

One uncommon, sympodial epiphyte or lithophyte is found in low to upper elevation, mixed hill and montane forests of southern China (western Yunnan), north-eastern India (Assam), Bhutan and northern Bangladesh. This creeping plant has crowded, ovoid pseudobulbs, subtended by persistent, overlapping leaf-sheaths, each with two long, pleated, deciduous leaves. The whip-like, zig-zagged, hairy, few-flowered inflorescence has numerous, overlapping bracts on the upper portion; the small, white or yellow flowers have similar sepals (spreading lateral sepals are sometimes bent downward) and slightly narrower petals with their tips often converging. The forward coiled, tubular spur has a swollen nob at the base. The pale brown, entire lip is deeply constricted in the middle, has a notched or blunt tip, and has a small, thickened, curved spur. The flowers have a long, red-brown, slender, footless column.

BUNOCHILUS

D.L. Jones & M.A. Clements
Austral. Orchid Res. **4**: 66 (2002).
ETYMOLOGY: Greek for mound or knob and lip. Refers to the knob-like swelling at the base of the lip.
TYPE SPECIES: *Bunochilus longifolius*
   (R. Brown) D.L. Jones & M.A. Clements
   (*Pterostylis longifolia* R. Brown)

Recognized as belonging to the genus *Pterostylis*, *Bunochilus* was proposed to include seven terrestrials found in wet, open forest woodlands throughout Australia. These erect plants have slender, unbranched stems, each with a basal rosette of narrow, leaves that are usually withered during flowering. There are several, smaller leaves clasping the stem upward. The erect, few-flowered inflorescence has green flowers with each subtended by a leafy bract. The sepals and petals converge, forming a hood over the long, incurved column. The lateral sepals are directed downward and are joined for most of their length, but separate into two sharp points. The shortly clawed, oblong, obscurely trilobed lip has tiny side lobes and an upturned, bilobed, brown tipped midlobe.

BURLINGTONIA

Lindley
Edwards's Bot. Reg. **23**: t. 1927 (1837).
ETYMOLOGY: In honor of Blanche Georgiana Howard (1812-1840), the British Countess of Burlington and wife of William George Spencer Cavendish (1790-1858) the 6th Duke of Devonshire. He had engaged John Lindley to develop a garden at Chiswick.
TYPE SPECIES: *Burlingtonia candida* Lindley

Now recognized as belonging to the genus *Rodriguezia*, *Burlingtonia* was previously considered to include twenty-three epiphytes distributed in wet, low to upper elevation, hill and montane cloud forests from Trinidad, the Guianas, Venezuela and Panama to Peru with the greatest concentration found in Brazil. These small plants have short, strongly flattened, often widely-spaced pseudobulbs, each with one to two,

leathery leaves. The erect or hanging, branching, numerous to few-flowered inflorescence has showy, faintly fragrant, white, rosy pink, to yellow flowers. The broad, thinly textured, shallowly notched, bilobed lip has an inrolled margin, a yellow callus and has a short spur. The flowers have a footless, white column.

BURMIERA

An orthographic variant introduced in *Just's Bot. Jahresber.*, **27**(2): 463 (1901). The correct spelling is *Bonniera*.

BURNETTIA

Lindley
Gen. Sp. Orchid. Pl. 517 (1840).
Not *Burnettia* Grout (1903) Brachytheciaeæ.
Orchidoideæ ⚘ **Diurideæ** • **Thelymitrinæ**
ETYMOLOGY: In commemoration of Gilbert Thomas Burnett (1800-1835), a British professor of botany at King's College in London and author of *Outlines of Botany*.
TYPE SPECIES: *Burnettia cuneata* Lindley

One uncommon, dwarf saprophyte is found in wet, low elevation, boggy scrub of southeastern Australia and Tasmania. This small, erect plant is totally leafless but has thick, unbranched stems, each with overlapping, red-brown sheaths on the lower portion and several, distant ones upward. The solitary to few-flowered inflorescence has red-brown, white or pale blue flowers opening widely, with red markings on the exterior, while the interior is pure white, but it can occasionally be pink. The concave dorsal sepal forms a hood over the erect, slender, footless column. Considering the tiny size of the plant, the flowers are quite large. The broad, squared, entire lip curves upward, has two irregular lobed ridges or a few blunt calli and a wavy margin.

BURNSBALOGHIA

Szlachetko
Folia Geobot. Phytotax. **26**(4): 400 (1991).
ETYMOLOGY: Dedicated to Pamela Burns-Balogh (1949-), an American taxonomist and book publisher, for her study of *Spiranthinæ*.
TYPE SPECIES: *Burnsbaloghia diaphana*
   (Lindley) Szlachetko
   (*Spiranthes diaphana* Lindley)

Now recognized as belonging to the genus *Deiregyne*, *Burnsbaloghia* was proposed to include one terrestrial found in upper elevation, montane oak-pine forests of southern Mexico (Oaxaca).

This tall, erect plant has stout, unbranched stems, each with several leaves that are usually withered by flowering time. The erect, stiff, numerous to few-flowered inflorescence is completely covered with smooth bracts and white, brown-veined, smooth-textured floral sheaths. The relatively large, tubular, white flowers have the narrow sepals fused together at the base and the narrow petals are parallel to and glued together with the green veined dorsal sepal. The concave dorsal sepal and petals converge, forming a hood over the long, flattened column. The long-clawed, tongue-like, entire lip has a thick, V-shaped, hairy callus.

BYRSELLA

Luer
Monogr. Syst. Bot. Missouri Bot. Gard. **105**: 7 (2006).
ETYMOLOGY: Greek for leather and Latin for diminutive or looking like. Alluding to the texture of the leaves.
TYPE SPECIES: *Byrsella coccinea* (Lindley) Luer
   (*Masdevallia coriacea* Lindley)

Recognized as belonging to the genus *Masdevallia*, *Byrsella* was proposed to include forty-two epiphytes or lithophytes found in mid to upper elevation, montane cloud forests from Costa Rica to Colombia. These small, tufted plants have erect, short, stout stems, subtended basally by a few tubular sheaths, each with a thick, keeled, leathery leaf. The short, solitary-flowered inflorescence has a pale green, yellow to white flower spotted and/or striped dull purple to brown-red. The fleshy, united sepals form a tube or cup shape, are often warty on the inside and taper into long or short tails. The small, flexible, oblong petals are hard and tough in texture but without a prominent appendage. The thick, oblong, entire lip has a blunt or roundish tip and often has a warty texture. The flowers have an elongate, more or less club-shaped column.

BYURLINGTONIA

An orthographic variant cited in *Vasc. Pl. Fam. Gen.*, 75 (1992). The correct spelling is *Burlingtonia*.

Currently Accepted   Validly Published   Invalidly Published   Published Pre-1753   Superfluous Usage   Orthographic Variant   Fossil

Orchid Genera • **58**

CABAESTUM

An orthographic variant introduced in *Wonders Veg.*, 219 (1872). The correct spelling is *Catasetum*.

CACTUS

Linnaeus
Syst. Nat., ed. 10   **2**: 1054 (1759).
ETYMOLOGY: Latin for a prickly plant with edible stalks or for anything thorny. Refers to the thick, fleshy stems that function as leaves.
TYPE SPECIES: *Not Orchidaceæ*

Linnaeus did not include this genus in Orchidaceæ. However he described a plant as **repens, teres, striatus, muticus** which he refers to Sloane's *Voy. Jamaica* (*Sloane*), 224, *ff. 3-4* (1707) as reference. This specimen has a herbarium sheet (**7**: 86) found at the Natural History Museum in London (Britain) that is clearly *Vanilla claviculata*. Linnaeus also refers to Plumier's *Pl. Amer.*, 176, *f. 2* (1755), but this most likely is a species of *Rhipsalis* (Cactusaceæ). Linnaeus later repeats the same diagnosis in *Species Plantarum*, ed. 2, 668 (1762), but here he drops the reference to Sloane and instead sites **Cactus parasiticus inermis** and gives the credits to Browne (sheet #238). In the Linnaean Herbarium there is a specimen sheet labeled from Browne, that is titled **Cactus parasicus** by Linnaeus himself, but there is no flower or fruit with this specimen. It must be surmised that this specimen is either *Dendrophylax funalis* (Swartz) Bentham ex Rolfe or some other leafless species belonging to the genus *Campylocentrum*.

CADADENIA

An orthographic variant introduced in *Ill. Hort.*, **33**: 131 (1886). The correct spelling is *Caladenia*.

CADETIA

Gaudichaud-Beaupré
Freycinet's *Voy. Uranie, Bot.*   422, *t. 33* (1826)[1829].
Epidendroideæ ⚘ Dendrobiinæ • Currently unplaced
ETYMOLOGY: In memory of Louis Claude Cadet de Gassicourt (1769-1821), a French lawyer, chemist, pharmacist, apothecary and author of a dictionary on chemical terms, he also devised many chemical formulas.
TYPE SPECIES: *Cadetia umbellata* Gaudichaud-Beaupré

Sixty sympodial epiphytes or lithophytes are found mostly in low elevation, rain forests and mangroves of New Guinea with a few species found in northern Australia, New Caledonia, the Solomons and the Philippines. These dwarf, tufted plants grow in small clumps and have clustered, often cylindrical stems with one node. The solitary, flat, stiff leaf is usually bilobed. The numerous, solitary (rarely two) flowered inflorescences emerge one at a time in succession over a period of months and are borne from a cluster of papery bracts at the tip of the stem. These small, white or pale pink flowers are sometimes marked with purple on the lip. The lateral sepals are united at the base along with the column foot, forming a small spur. The broad, white, yellow, orange or purple, entire or trilobed lip is ornamented with hairs usually on the outside portion. The flowers have a short, slightly curved, footless column that is also hairy underneath.

CAELIA

An orthographic variant introduced in *Hort. Brit.* (*Sweet*), ed. 3, 637 (1839). The correct spelling is *Coelia*.

CAELOGLOSSUM

An orthographic variant cited in *Nomencl. Bot.* (*Steudel*), ed. 2, **1**: 247, 394 (1840). The correct spelling is *Coeloglossum*.

CAELOGYNE

An orthographic variant introduced in *Coll. Bot.* (*Lindley*), sub 33 (1821). The correct spelling is *Coelogyne*.

CAEMIDIA

An orthographic variant introduced in *Syn. Pl.* (*D. Dietrich*), **5**: 19 (1852). The correct spelling is *Cnemidia*.

CAESTICHIS

Thouars
Hist. Orchid.   Table 3, sub 3r, *t. 90* (1822).

Name published without a description. Today this name is most often referred to *Liparis*.

CAHYA

An orthographic variant introduced in *J. Proc. Roy. Soc. New South Wales*, **15**: 229 (1882). The correct spelling is *Caleya*.

CALADENIA

R. Brown
Prodr. Fl. Nov. Holland.   323 (1810).
Orchidoideæ ⚘ Diurideæ • Caladeniinæ
ETYMOLOGY: Greek for beautiful and gland. Refers to the glandular disk of the lip.
LECTOTYPE: *Caladenia flava* R. Brown designated by Pfitzer, *Nat. Pflanzenfam.*, **2**(6): 104 (1889), not *Caladenia catenata* (Smith) Druce (N. Hallè 1977), not *Caladenia carnea* R. Brown (M.A. Clements 1989)

Two hundred fifty sympodial terrestrials are found in low to mid elevation, open forests, grasslands and tall scrub of eastern Indonesia (Bali to Maluku), New Guinea, New Caledonia, New Zealand, Tasmania with most of the species found in eastern to southwestern coastal areas of Australia. These small, hairy plants have erect, unbranched stems, subtended by a multilayered, persistent fibrous tunic, each with a solitary, narrow or oblong, basal leaf. They often form vast colonies arising from the production of daughter-tubers. The often wiry, solitary to few-flowered inflorescence has a fairly simple, delicate, fragrant, long-tailed flower with a fan-shaped arrangement of petals and lateral sepals. The incurved dorsal sepal forms a hood over the column and the floral segments are either long, tail-like or short. The small, usually trilobed lip, attached by a short, mobile claw to the anterior column base, is adorned with a callus of warts, small projections (papillae) or hairs. The flowers have a slender, incurved or erect column.

CALADENIASTRUM

Szlachetko

Ann. Bot. Fenn. **40**(2): 144 (2003).

ETYMOLOGY: *Caladenia*, a genus of orchids and Latin for thick. Refers to the thick column.

TYPE SPECIES: *Caladeniastrum flavum*
(R. Brown) Szlachetko
(*Caladenia flava* R. Brown)

Recognized as belonging to the genus *Caladenia*, *Caladeniastrum* was proposed to include six terrestrials found in low elevation, coastal scrub to granite outcrops of south-western Australia. These hairy plants have underground woolly and knotty stems, each with a rather large, basal leaf and a leaf-like sheath midway up the stem. The flexible, few-flowered inflorescence has large, yellow flowers with the dorsal sepal and petals having distinct scarlet lines or blotches along the center. The broad, deeply trilobed lip has a concave claw, the long midlobe is bordered with a few rows of club-shaped calli. The flowers have a thick, incurved column that is two-winged.

CALAENA

An orthographic variant introduced in *Linnaea*, **2**: 528 (1827). The correct spelling is *Caleana*.

CALANDENIA

An orthographic variant cited in *Orchid. Lex.*, ed. 1, 38 (1969). The correct spelling is *Caladenia*.

CALANTE

An orthographic variant introduced in *Sempervirens*, **28**(2): 16 (1889). The correct spelling is *Calanthe*.

CALANTHA

An orthographic variant introduced in *Beih. Bot. Centralbl.*, **8**(4-5): 312 (1899). The correct spelling is *Calanthe*.

CALANTHE

R. Brown

Bot. Reg. **7**: sub 578 (1821), and
Bot. Reg. **9**: t. 720 (1823).

Name ICBN conserved vs. *Alismorkis* Thouars (1809) Orchidaceæ.

Epidendroideæ ⚹ Collabiinæ • Currently unplaced

ETYMOLOGY: Greek for beautiful and flower. An allusion to the beautiful flowers of most of the species.

LECTOTYPE: *Calanthe veratrifolia* nom. illeg.
(Willdenow) R. Brown ex Ker Gawler
(*Limodorum veratrifolium* Willdenow)
This type name is now considered a synonym of *Calanthe triplicata* (Willemet) Ames; basionym replaced with *Orchis triplicata* Willemet

A popular genus of upward of one hundred eighty-seven primarily sympodial terrestrials or rare epiphytes with a huge area of dispersal, are found in low to upper elevation, hill scrub and montane evergreen forests, along river banks and grasslands throughout southern Africa and Madagascar to northern India (Kashmir to Assam), China (Xizang to Hainan, Gansu to Zhejiang), Japan, Myanmar to Vietnam, Indonesia, and eastern Australia to New Zealand with one species in tropical America, but most species are found from Thailand to the Philippines. These plants have a short, fast-growing season. Some of the species have large, silvery pseudobulbs that lose their leaves in the dry season, flowering only when bare of leaves, and the inflorescence emerges from the base of a leafless pseudobulb. A few other species have minute to stout pseudobulbs, each with broad, evergreen leaves and a densely packed inflorescence. These plants have rather sizeable, usually distinctly pleated, dark green leaves. The erect or arching, densely packed to loosely arranged, numerous to few-flowered inflorescence, and can often be several feet in length. The short-lived flowers occur in almost every imaginable color combination, and have usually spreading, similar sepals and petals. The entire, bilobed, trilobed or four-lobed lip, united at the base to the entire length of the column, has a midlobe that is often deeply bilobed, adorned with a callus of warts and usually has a slender, decurved spur. The flowers have a long or short, club-shaped, footless column that is united along its underside to the lip.

CALANTHEA

Not *Calanthea* (A.P. de Candolle) Miers (1865) Capparaceæ.

An orthographic variant introduced in *Itin. Pl. Khasyah Mts.*, 174 (1848). The correct spelling is *Calanthe*.

CALANTHIDIUM

Pfitzer

Nat. Pflanzenfam. **2**(6): 151, 153 (1889).

ETYMOLOGY: *Calanthe*, a genus of orchids and Greek for diminutive.

TYPE SPECIES: *Calanthidium labrosum*
(Reichenbach f.) Pfitzer
(*Calanthe labrosa* Reichenbach f.)

Now recognized as belonging to the genus *Calanthe*, *Calanthidium* was previously considered to include one terrestrial found from southern China (Yunnan) to Myanmar and Thailand. This plant has rather small, ovoid or cone-shaped pseudobulbs, subtended by large, leafy sheaths, each with several leaves. The erect, few-flowered inflorescence is covered in soft hairs, as is the outside surface of the flowers. The white to pale yellow flowers have a faint purple or pale pink tint, and turns orange-red as it ages. The pale purple, trilobed lip has the side lobes embracing the short, thick, footless column, the midlobe has a wavy margin, is covered with purple-red spots, and a long, slightly hairy, pale yellow spur.

CALANTHIDUM

An orthographic variant introduced in *Vasc. Pl. Fam. Gen.*, 76 (1992). The correct spelling is *Calanthidium*.

CALANYHE

An orthographic variant cited in *World Checkl. Seed Pl. (Govaerts)*, **1**(2): 5 (1995). The correct spelling is *Calanthe*.

CALAPOGON

An orthographic variant introduced in *Dict. Class. Hist. Nat.*, **9**: 426 (1826). The correct spelling is *Calopogon*.

CALASETUM

An orthographic variant introduced in *Beitr. Morph. Biol. Orchid.*, 22 (1863). The correct spelling is *Catasetum*.

CALATHE

An orthographic variant cited in *Orchid. Lex.*, ed. 1, 38 (1969). The correct spelling is *Calanthe*.

Currently Accepted   Validly Published   Invalidly Published   Published Pre-1753   Superfluous Usage   Orthographic Variant   Fossil

Orchid Genera • 60

CALAUTHE

An orthographic variant cited in *Nomencl. Bot. (Steudel)*, ed. 2, **1**: 75 (1840). The correct spelling is *Calanthe*.

CALCARAMPHIS

Thouars
Hist. Orchid.   Table 1, sub 1b, *t. 4* (1822).

Name published without a description. Today this name is most often referred to *Cynorkis*.

CALCEANGIS

Thouars
Hist. Orchid.   *t. 78* (1822).

Name published without a description. Today this name is most often referred to *Angraecum*.

CALCEARIA

Blume
Bijdr. Fl. Ned. Ind.   **8**: 417, *t. 33* (1825).
ETYMOLOGY: Latin for shoe or slipper. Referring to the large, conspicuous lip shaped like a shoe.
TYPE SPECIES: *Calcearia picta* Blume

Now recognized as belonging to the genus *Corybas*, *Calcearia* was previously considered to include two tiny terrestrials found in Indonesia (Sumatra, Java and Borneo) and Malaysia often forming dense colonies. These plants have short stems, each with a solitary, heart-shaped, dark green leaf veined white or pink. The solitary-flowered inflorescence has a large, maroon flower that is marked with white in the throat of the entire lip and has translucent, white and purple sepals and petals. The above type name is now considered a synonym of *Corybas pictus* (Blume) Reichenbach f.

CALCEOLANGIS

Thouars
Hist. Orchid.   Table 2, sub 3o (1822).

Name published without a description. Today this name is most often referred to *Angraecum*.

CALCEOLAR

An orthographic variant cited in *Lex. Gen. Phan.*, 89 (1904). The correct spelling is *Calceolaria*.

CALCEOLARIA

Heister
Syst. Pl. Gen.   5 (1748).
Not *Calceolaria* Loefling (1758) Violaceæ, and not *Calceolaria* Linnaeus (1770) Scrophulariaceæ which was conserved.
ETYMOLOGY: Latin for shoe. Referring to the large, conspicuous lip that is shaped like a shoe.
TYPE SPECIES: *None designated*

Not validly published because of the prior use of a conserved name, this homonym was replaced by *Cypripedium*.

CALCEOLUS

Gesner
Hort. German. (Gesner)   245b (1561).

Pre-1753, therefore not validly published in fulfillment of nomenclatural rules; this name is most often referred to *Cypripedium*.

CALCEOLUS

P. Miller
Gard. Dict. Abr., ed. 4   (1754).
ETYMOLOGY: Latin for carrying a small shoe. From the shape of the large, conspicuous lip.
TYPE SPECIES: *None designated*

Now recognized as belonging to the genus *Cypripedium*, *Calceolus* was previously considered to include two terrestrials ranging from Britain, Scandinavia to eastern Russia (Amur, Primorye, Kamchatka), Denmark southeast to Greece. These erect plants have short, unbranched stems, each with several, broad, ovoid leaves. The erect, usually solitary-flowered inflorescence has a small, dainty, fragrant flower with a bright yellow, slipper-shaped lip. And has long, narrow, slightly twisted, green, dark brown to brown-green dorsal sepal and petals.

CALEANA

R. Brown
Prodr. Fl. Nov. Holland.   329 (1810).
Orchidoideæ ◊ Diurideæ • Thelymitrinæ
ETYMOLOGY: Commemorating George Caley (1770-1829), a British botanist, and superintendent at the West Indies Botanic Gardens in St.Vincent. While in employ of Joseph Banks (1743-1820), he was sent to New South Wales, Australia to collect the local flora.
LECTOTYPE: *Caleana major* R. Brown

Seven rather dull, sympodial terrestrials are found in low elevation, coastal scrub and rocky, timbered slopes of southeastern and southwestern Australia, Tasmania and northern New

Zealand. These slender, small plants are of interest primarily to botanists. These plants grow in colonies (reproduction is solely from seed) and have erect, short, unbranched stems, each with a solitary, narrow, hairy, basal leaf that is more or less dull red. The solitary to few-flowered inflorescence has upside down, red-brown, bizarre shaped flowers with dark purple markings. The long-clawed, entire lip is folded and curved to resemble the body of an insect. The lip is then hinged to the tip of the long, slender, incurved column and upon contact with a pollinator the lamina folds (forming a bowl-like structure) into the broad column wings.

CALEYA

An orthographic variant introduced in *Hortus Kew.*, ed. 2, **5**: 204 (1813). The correct spelling is *Caleana*.

CALEYANA

An orthographic variant cited in *Lex. Gen. Phan.*, 89 (1904). The correct spelling is *Caleana*.

CALIPOGON

An orthographic variant introduced in *Atlantic J.*, **1**(4): 148 (1832). The correct spelling is *Calopogon*.

CALISTA

An orthographic variant introduced in *Schriften Ges. Beförd. Gesammten Naturwiss. Marburg*, **2**: 125 (1831). The correct spelling is *Callista*.

CALLANTHE

An orthographic variant cited in *Lex. Gen. Phan.*, 89 (1904). The correct spelling is *Calanthe*.

CALLIPHYLLON

Bubani
Fl. Pyren. (Bubani)   **4**: 56 (1901).
ETYMOLOGY: Greek for beautiful and leaf. Descriptive of its attractive leaf or pretty petals.
TYPE SPECIES: *None designated*

Now recognized as belonging to the genus *Epipactis*, *Calliphyllon* was previously considered to include two unusually large terrestrials found from Norway to Turkey and northern Africa (Morocco to Libya). These erect plants have several, green leaves clasping the unbranched stem upward. The numerous to few-flowered inflorescence has green, green-yellow or brown flowers heavily suffused and veined with purple. One species is now considered a synonym of *Epipactis helleborine* (Linnaeus) Crantz and the other a synonym of *Epipactis palustris* (Linnaeus) Crantz.

CALLIPHYLLUM

An orthographic variant introduced in *Orchideen (Schlechter)*, ed. 3, **5**(6): 290 (1973). The correct spelling is *Calliphyllon*.

CALLISIA

Not *Callisia* Loefling (1758) Commelinaceæ, nor *Callisia* Linnaeus (1760) Asteraceæ.

An orthographic variant introduced in *Orchids India*, ed. 2, 198 (1999). The correct spelling is *Callista*.

CALLISTA

Loureiro

Fl. Cochinch. **2**: 516, 519 (1790).

Name ICBN rejected vs. *Dendrobium* Swartz (1799), and not *Callista* D. Don (1834) Ericaceæ.

ETYMOLOGY: Greek for very beautiful. Referring to the outstanding beauty of the flowers.

TYPE SPECIES: *Callista amabilis* Loureiro

Although validly published this rejected name is now referred to *Dendrobium*. *Callista* was considered to include ten epiphytes often forming, large clumps with a relatively small distribution in Myanmar and the surrounding countries. The erect, club-shaped pseudobulbs vary from short to thick and are elongate with several internodes, each with several, persistent, leathery leaves grouped at the end of the stem. The long, drooping to hanging, numerous-flowered inflorescence has large, fragrant flowers with thinly textured sepals and the smaller petals often have notched margins. The entire lip lacks side lobes and is densely hairy on the inner surface. The above type name is now considered a synonym of *Dendrobium amabile* (Loureiro) O'Brien.

CALLITHRONUM

Ehrhart

Beitr. Naturk. (Ehrhart) **4**: 149 (1789).

ETYMOLOGY: Greek for beauty and seat. Referring to its beautiful lip that might be likened to an ornate armchair.

TYPE SPECIES: *None designated*

Now recognized as belonging to the genus *Cephalanthera*, *Callithronum* was previously considered to include one terrestrial found in mid elevation, woodland scrub from Britain to central Russia (West Siberia) and western Iran, Norway to Spain through Romania, and northern Africa (Morocco to Tunisia). This erect plant has unbranched stems, each with several, narrow leaves at the base and several, scale-like leaves on the hairy stem. The few-flowered inflorescence has pale to deep lilac-red flowers not opening widely that are also hairy on the outer surfaces. The sharply pointed, trilobed lip is paler than the other segments.

CALLOGRAPHIS

An orthographic variant introduced in *Dict. Class. Hist. Nat.*, **3**: 61 (1823). The correct spelling is *Calographis*.

CALLOSTILIS

An orthographic variant introduced in *Tab. Pl. Jav. Orchid.*, t. 74 (1825). The correct spelling is *Callostylis*.

CALLOSTYLIS

Blume

Bijdr. Fl. Ned. Ind. **7**: 340, t. 74 (1825).

ETYMOLOGY: Greek for beautiful and column or style. The column is a conspicuous part of the flower.

TYPE SPECIES: *Callostylis rigida* Blume

Recognized as belonging to the genus *Eria*, *Callostylis* was previously considered to include three epiphytes or rare terrestrials found in low to upper elevation, hill to montane moss laden forests and swamps of northern India, Myanmar to Vietnam and Malaysia to Indonesia (Borneo). These plants have well-spaced, short, erect pseudobulbs, each with two to three, curving, rather tough, leathery, deep green leaves. The short, erect or spreading, numerous to few-flowered inflorescence are borne sometimes from the upper nodes but rarely from the basal nodes. The cream, white, green-yellow, yellow, brown to orange colored flowers are suffused pale yellow on the outside. The segments are sometimes appear white or brown because of the covering of short, dense hairs. The mobile, heart-shaped, entire or trilobed lip is clawed at the base and is attached to the short column foot. The flowers have a long, strongly curved column. The above type name is now considered a synonym of *Eria discolor* Lindley.

CALLOTA

An orthographic variant introduced in *Bull. Herb. Boissier*, ser. 1, **6**(11): 858 (1898). The correct spelling is *Calota*.

CALOCHILOS

An orthographic variant introduced in *Syst. Veg. (Sprengel)*, ed. 16, **3**: 678, 713 (1826). The correct spelling is *Calochilus*.

CALOCHILUS

R. Brown

Prodr. Fl. Nov. Holland. 320 (1810).

Orchidoideæ ⬥ Diurideæ ● Thelymitrinæ

ETYMOLOGY: Greek for beautiful and lip. From the lip that is usually densely bearded with long hairs which have a metallic sheen.

LECTOTYPE: *Calochilus paludosus* R. Brown

Twenty-three sympodial terrestrials are found in cool, low elevation, sparse hill forests, grasslands, bogs and coastal scrub of Australia, Tasmania, northern New Zealand, New Caledonia and southern New Guinea with all species reproducing solely from seed. These plants have short, erect, unbranched stems with thin, bud-scales at each node, each with a solitary, deciduous, basal leaf that has rolled up margins. The slender, numerous to few-flowered inflorescence has showy, fragrant, green, purple or red-brown flowers opening widely in hot weather. The dorsal sepal is hood-shaped over the short, winged, footless column. The small petals often have hooked tips. The large, obscurely lobed lip has its margin entire or with numerous, coarse, colorful hairs giving the flower an appearance of having a bristly beard. The flower emits a fragrance that sexually attracts certain species of wasps.

CALODISA

Endlicher ex Wittstein

Etym.-Bot.-Handw.-Buch, ed. 1 143 (1852).

Name published without a description. Today this name is most often referred to as a section of *Disa*.

CALOGLOSSUM

Schlechter

Repert. Spec. Nov. Regni Veg. **15**: 212 (1918).

ETYMOLOGY: Greek for beautiful or fine and tongue. Refers to the complex, beautiful, tongue-like lip.

TYPE SPECIES: *None designated*

Now recognized as belonging to the genus *Cymbidiella*, *Caloglossum* was previously considered to include four terrestrials or epiphytes found in Madagascar. These tall (only when in flower), large

Currently Accepted   Validly Published   Invalidly Published   Published Pre-1753   Superfluous Usage   Orthographic Variant   Fossil

Orchid Genera • **62**

plants have several, thinly textured leaves with pale-colored veins. The numerous-flowered inflorescence has small, green-yellow to green flowers. The broad, red-brown to yellow, trilobed lip is often spotted and lined or edged with red and has a red-brown edged, wavy margin.

CALOGRAPHIS

Thouars
Hist. Orchid.   Table 2, sub 3n, *tt. 43-44* (1822).

Name published without a description. Today this name is most often referred to *Eulopidium*.

CALOGYNE

Jussieu
Dict. Sci. Nat.   **36**: 304 (1825).
Not *Calogyne* R. Brown (1810) Goodeniaceæ.

Name published without a description. Today it is not known which genus is referred to by this name.

CALONEMA

Lindley ex **Wittstein**
Etym.-Bot.-Handw.-Buch, ed. 1   144 (1852).

Name published without a description. Today this name is most often referred to as a section of *Caladenia*.

CALONEMA

(Lindley) D.L. Jones & M.A. Clements
Orchadian   **13**(9): 400 (2001).
Not *Calonema* Morgan (1893) Trichianceæ.
ETYMOLOGY: Greek for beautiful and threads. Refers to the thread-like segments of some of the species.
TYPE SPECIES: *Calonema filiferum*
(Lindley) D.L. Jones & M.A. Clements
(*Caladenia filifera* Lindley)

Not validly published because of a prior use of the name, this homonym was replaced by *Calonemorchis*.

CALONEMA

(Lindley) Szlachetko
Polish Bot. J.   **46**(1): 15 (2001).
Not *Calonema* Morgan (1893) Trichianceæ.
ETYMOLOGY: Greek for beautiful and threads. Refers to the thread-like segments of some of the species.
TYPE SPECIES: *Calonema filifera* (Lindley) Szlachetko
(*Caladenia filifera* Lindley)

Not validly published because of a prior use of the name, this homonym was replaced by *Calonemorchis*.

CALONEMORCHIS

Szlachetko
Polish Bot. J.   **46**(2): 137 (2001).
ETYMOLOGY: *Calonema*, a genus of orchids and Greek for orchid. Referring to the thread-like segments of some of the species.
TYPE SPECIES: *Calonemorchis filifera*
(Lindley) Szlachetko
(*Caladenia filifera* Lindley)

Recognized as belonging to the genus *Caladenia*, *Calonemorchis* was proposed to include seventy-four terrestrials found in low elevation, woodlands, grasslands or scrub of Australia and New Zealand. These small, erect, hairy plants have short, unbranched stems, each with a solitary, long, narrow basal leaf. The usually solitary to rarely few-flowered inflorescence has tiny, spidery, yellow-green to blue flower streaked red. The sepals are usually smaller than the long, narrow petals. The minute but broad, mobile, shortly clawed, entire lip has dark red veins and has a fringed or notched margin. The rather long, thick, shiny calli are crowded along the center that are either arranged in two or more rows or are irregularly scattered. The flowers have an erect or incurved, winged column.

CALOPOGON

R. Brown
Hortus Kew., ed. 2   **5**: 204 (1813).
Name ICBN conserved.

Epidendroideæ ◊ Arethuseæ • Arethusinæ
ETYMOLOGY: Greek for beautiful and beard. Alluding to the brightly hued, fringed crest or protuberances on the lip.
LECTOTYPE: *Calopogon pulchellus*
(Salisbury) R. Brown nom. illeg.
(*Limodorum pulchellum* Salisbury nom. illeg.)
designated by M.L. Green, *Prop. Brit. Bot.*, 100 (1929).

This type name is now considered a synonym of
LECTOTYPE: *Calopogon tuberosus*
(Linnaeus) Britton, Sterns & Poggenburg)
(*Limodorum tuberosum* Linnaeus)
designated by Mackenzie, *Rhodora*, **27**: 194 (1925).

Five sympodial terrestrials are found in low to mid elevation, bogs, wet scrub and savannas of the eastern United States (Maine to Florida and Minnesota to Louisiana) and southeastern Canada (Ontario and Quebec) with often intensely acidic soils, but one species ranges from Newfoundland (Canada) to western Cuba and the northern Bahamas. These small, erect plants have smooth, unbranched stems, borne from small corms, each with a solitary to several, deciduous, tall, grass-like, prominently veined leaves. The tall, solitary to few-flowered, green to purple inflorescence bears proportionately large, bright magenta, pink or rare white flowers with varying degrees of

fragrance. The erect, uppermost, hinged, obscurely trilobed lip has small, fleshy side lobes, and the spoon-shaped or shallowly notched midlobe is furnished with beard-like, yellow hairs and papillae. The flowers have a green to white, flattened, slender, winged, footless column.

CALOPOGONEM

An orthographic variant introduced in *Gen. Pl.*, *Suppl. 1* (Endlicher), 1367 (1840). The correct spelling is *Calopogon*.

CALORCHIS

Barbosa Rodrigues
Gen. Sp. Orchid.   **1**: 195, *t. 458* (1877).
ETYMOLOGY: Greek for beautiful and orchid. Refers to the flower's beauty, and its resemblance to a species of *Orchis*.
TYPE SPECIES: *Calorchis phaenoleuca*
Barbosa Rodrigues

Now recognized as belonging to the genus *Ponthieva*, *Calorchis* was previously considered to include one terrestrial found in eastern Brazil (Minas Gerais). This small, erect plant has short, unbranched stems, each with a few elliptical, basal leaves that have sharp, tapering tips. The tall, few-flowered inflorescence bears small, white flowers that are all facing in one direction on the rachis. The dorsal sepal is oblong and the ovate lateral sepals are asymmetrical with the upper margin greatly expanded into an ear-like shape. The clawed petals are fused to the club-shaped, wingless column at the base. The clawed, sac-like, trilobed lip has a tongue-like midlobe and is attached to the middle of the column.

CALOSTYLIS

An orthographic variant introduced in *J. Roy. Hort. Soc.*, **7**: 101 (1886). The correct spelling is *Callostylis*.

CALOTA

Harvey ex **Lindley**
Gen. Sp. Orchid. Pl.   365 (1838).
ETYMOLOGY: Greek for beautiful. Refers to the beauty of the flowers.
TYPE SPECIES: *None designated*

Name published without a description. Today this name is most often referred to *Ceratandra*.

CALUERA

Dodson & Determann

Amer. Orchid Soc. Bull. **52**(4): 375 (1983).

Epidendroideæ ‰ **Cymbidieæ** • **Oncidiinæ**

ETYMOLOGY: Named in honor of Carlyle August Luer (1922-), an American orchid taxonomist, physician and author of numerous works on *Pleurothallidinæ*.

TYPE SPECIES: *Caluera surinamensis*
Dodson & Determann

Two dwarf, psygmoid epiphytes are located in low elevation, rain forests of northern Brazil (Pará), Colombia to Ecuador (Napo), Venezuela and the Guianas. These tiny, fan-shaped plants have short stems, each with several, distichous, oblong leaves that are united to somewhat swollen sheaths. The wiry inflorescence, borne from the leaf axils, has an umbel of usually four, small, white flowers. The oblong petals are covered with pink spots or blotches and the slender sepal are widespreading. The ovate, white, entire lip has a large, bright yellow, cushion-like callus in the center. The flowers have a strongly hooked, long column with a T-shaped anther.

CALYMANTHERA

An orthographic variant introduced in *Repert. Spec. Nov. Regni Veg.*, **1**(1): xlii (1914). The correct spelling is *Calymmanthera*.

CALYMMANTHERA

Schlechter

Repert. Spec. Nov. Regni Veg. Beih.
1(12): 955 (1913).

Epidendroideæ ‰ **Vandeæ** • **Aeridinæ**

ETYMOLOGY: Greek for a covering and anther. Refers to the hooded, covered condition of the anther.

LECTOTYPE: *Calymmanthera tenuis* Schlechter

Five uncommon, monopodial epiphytes are found in mid to upper elevation, moss laden tree branches of New Guinea and adjacent islands. These small, inconspicuous plants, often forming dense, spreading colonies, have short to elongate, erect to hanging stems (frequently branching near the base), each with a few long, narrow, distichous, thick leaves. The branching, numerous to few-flowered inflorescence has tiny, short-lived, translucent white to yellow (changing color as they age) flowers not opening widely that have narrow, pointed sepals and petals. The small, mobile, pure white, trilobed lip is very thick and fleshy, has erect side lobes and a tongue-shaped midlobe with a deep V-shaped disc. The flowers have an erect, short, wingless column.

CALYPSO

Salisbury

Parad. Lond. **2**: t. 89 (1807).

Name ICBN conserved vs. *Calypso* Thouars (1804) Hippocrateaceæ.

Epidendroideæ ‰ **Calypsoeæ**

ETYMOLOGY: Greek Mythology. Named for Calypso, a sea-nymph, daughter of Atlas and Queen of Ogygia, in Homer's *Odyssey*. She lived on the island of Ogygia and there entertained Ulysses after the sack of Troy. Although she offered to make him immortal if he would remain, Ulysses spurned the offer and continued his journey. Her name means hiding or concealment.

TYPE SPECIES: *Calypso borealis* (Swartz) Salisbury nom. illeg. (*Cymbidium boreale* Swartz)

This type name is now considered a synonym of *Calypso bulbosa* (Linnaeus) Oakes (*Cypripedium bulbosum* Linnaeus)

One sympodial terrestrial which forms dense colonies and ranges throughout the northern temperate zones in damp, low to upper elevation, hill and montane pine forests, leaf mold, coarse sand and sphagnum moss from Sweden to Lithuania, western Russia (Amur to Khabarovsk) to Japan, Mongolia, northern China (Nei Mongol to Jilin), Canada (Yukon Territory to Newfoundland and Nova Scotia), the United States (Alaska, Washington to New Mexico, Arizona and northern Minnesota to Maine). This small, dainty plant has a tiny, corm-like pseudobulb, subtended by thin sheaths at the base, each with a solitary, oblong leaf that has a wavy margin. The leaves produced in autumn are withered by spring. The erect, solitary-flowered inflorescence has a slightly nodding, vanilla fragrant, small to large, showy flower found in various color shades from bright rose to magenta with long, narrow segments. The slipper-like or fiddle-shaped, entire lip has short, soft hairs on the front margins of the mouth with a broad, widespread front section, and two flat lying, long spurs at the tip. The flowers have a broad, hooded, white or pink column.

CALYPSODIUM

Link

Handbuch (Link) **1**: 252 (1829).

ETYMOLOGY: Diminutive of *Calypso*, a genus of orchids.

TYPE SPECIES: *Calypsodium boreale* (Swartz) Link (*Cymbidium boreale* Swartz)

Now recognized as belonging to the genus *Calypso*, *Calypsodium* was previously considered to include one terrestrial ranging across the northern temperate areas of Europe, Russia to Korea, Canada and the United States. This small, erect plant has

slender, unbranched stems, each with a solitary, basal leaf. The erect, solitary-flowered inflorescence has a wonderfully fragrant, rose to magenta flower with white tufts of hairs, and an irregularly blotched, short, lobed lip. The above type name is now considered a synonym of *Calypso bulbosa* (Linnaeus) Oakes.

CALYPTROCHILUM

Kraenzlin

Bot. Jahrb. Syst. **22**: 30 (1895).

Epidendroideæ ‰ **Vandeæ** • **Angraecinæ**

ETYMOLOGY: Greek for covering or veil and lip. In reference to the translucent veil-like, broad fall of the lip.

TYPE SPECIES: *Calyptrochilum preussii* Kraenzlin

This type name is now considered a synonym of *Calyptrochilum emarginatum* (Afzelius ex Swartz) Schlechter; basionym *Limodorum emarginatum* Afzelius ex Swartz

Two monopodial epiphytes or occasional lithophytes are found in low to mid elevation, woodlands and river forests of western Ethiopia to Gambia, Ghana south to Zimbabwe and Madagascar. These clump-forming plants have woody, long, hanging or spreading stems, each with several, distichous, oblong, unequally bilobed leaves twisted at the base to lie in one plane. The short, often zig-zagging, numerous to few-flowered inflorescence has fleshy, white, creamy or pale green, nocturnally fragrant flowers that turn orange as they age and the sepals are slightly shorter than petals. The spreading, green, yellow or orange, trilobed lip has roundish side lobes, the oblong midlobe has a notched tip. The blunt, yellow base or entirely green spur has a wide mouth, is constricted in the middle, the tip is often at strongly bent to the base of the spur and has a swollen tip. The flowers have a short, stout, fleshy column with a small foot.

CALYPTROCHILUS

An orthographic variant introduced in *Nat. Pflanzenfam., Nachtr.*, **1**: 113 (1897). The correct spelling is *Calyptrochilum*.

CALYPTRORCHIS

(Pabst) Brieger

Orchideen (Schlechter), ed. 3 **7**(25-28): 428 (1975).

ETYMOLOGY: Greek for covering, large loose hood or monk's hood and orchid.

TYPE SPECIES: *None designated*

Name published without a description. Today this name is most often referred to *Specklinia*.

| Currently Accepted | Validly Published | Invalidly Published | Published Pre-1753 | Superfluous Usage | Orthographic Variant | Fossil |

O r c h i d G e n e r a • **64**

CAMAEORCHIS

C. Bauhin
Prodr. (Bauhin), ed. 1   29 (1620).

Pre-1753, therefore not validly published in fulfillment of nomenclatural rules; this name is most often referred to *Chamorchis.*

CAMARIDIUM

Lindley
Bot. Reg.   **10**: *t. 844* (1824).
ETYMOLOGY: Greek for arched or vault. Descriptive of the shape of the half-rounded column.
TYPE SPECIES: *Camaridium ochroleucum* Lindley

Now recognized as belonging to the genus *Maxillaria, Camaridium* was previously considered to include seventy-eight epiphytes found in low to mid elevation, tropical forests from Costa Rica to Bolivia, northern Brazil, Trinidad to Venezuela and the Guianas. These clump-forming plants have numerous, tightly packed, compressed pseudobulbs producing several, solitary-flowered inflorescences that are borne from the pseudobulb base. The usually large, fragrant, variously colored, showy, short-lived flowers have a yellow, trilobed lip. The above type name is now considered a synonym of *Maxillaria lutescens* Scheidweiler.

CAMAROTIS

Lindley
Gen. Sp. Orchid. Pl.   219 (1833).
ETYMOLOGY: Greek for an arch or vaulted. Refers to the shape of the chambered structured lip.
TYPE SPECIES: *Camarotis purpurea* Lindley
This type name is now considered a synonym of *Micropera rostrata* (Roxburgh) N.P. Balakrishnan; basionym *Aerides rostrata* Roxburgh

Now recognized as belonging to the genus *Micropera, Camarotis* was previously considered to include fourteen epiphytes ranging from northeastern India (Arunachal Pradesh), Bangladesh, Myanmar, Malaysia, Indonesia and New Guinea to the Philippines. These climbing plants have long, erect stems, each with well-spaced, narrow, leathery leaves. The erect or drooping, numerous to few-flowered inflorescence has waxy, long-lasting, fragrant, dark crimson to pearl-white flowers suffused pale pink to purple. The sac-like, immobile, trilobed lip has short, broad side lobes; and the tiny midlobe is flat, lying to the front margins of the side lobes. The cone-like, hollow spur appears in the front of the lip. The rostellum is twisted, thus yielding an asymmetrical flower.

CAMELOSTALIX

Pfitzer
Pflanzenr. (Engler)   **IV.50**(II.B.7): 159 (1907).
ETYMOLOGY: Greek for camel and club or stake. Referring to the club-shaped column, which has two humps in side view.
TYPE SPECIES: *Camelostalix reichenbachii* Pfitzer

Now recognized as belonging to the genus *Pholidota, Camelostalix* was previously considered to include one epiphyte found in mid elevation, heavily shaded forests of Indonesia (Java and Sumatra). This plant has closely grouped, oblong pseudobulbs, each with two narrow leaves. Arising from the side of the pseudobulb is a hanging, zig-zagging, numerous-flowered inflorescence that has small, pale brown or green flowers arranged in two rows. The obscurely trilobed lip is sac-like at the base. The flowers have a short, straight column. The above type name is now considered a synonym of *Pholidota camelostalix* Reichenbach f.

CAMERIDIUM

An orthographic variant introduced in *Linnaea,* **22**: 857 (1849). The correct spelling is *Camaridium.*

CAMEROTIS

An orthographic variant introduced in *Hort. Universel,* ser. 2, **1**: 58 (1846). The correct spelling is *Camarotis.*

CAMILLEUGENIA

Frappier ex Cordemoy
Fl. Reunion   234 (1895).
ETYMOLOGY: Honoring two French brothers for furthering our knowledge about the flora of Réunion: Camille de Cordemoy (1840-1909), and Eugène Jacob de Cordemoy (1835-1911), who was the author of *Flore de l'Ile de Reunion.*
TYPE SPECIES: *Camilleugenia coccinelloides* Frappier ex Cordemoy

Now recognized as belonging to the genus *Cynorkis, Camilleugenia* was previously considered to include one terrestrial found in Madagascar and Réunion. This tall, slender unbranched plant has one to two, small, grass-like leaves usually lying against the ground. The erect, wiry, few-flowered inflorescence has tiny, white or violet flowers with colored veins. The flowers, each subtended by narrow bracts, have similar petals and sepals, and a tiny, five-lobed lip.

CAMPANEMIA

An orthographic variant cited in *Lex. Gen. Phan.,* 95, 474 (1904). The correct spelling is *Capanemia.*

CAMPANULORCHIS

Brieger
Orchideen (Schlechter), ed. 3   **1**(11-12): 750 (1981).
ETYMOLOGY: Latin for little bell-shaped and Greek for orchid. Referring to the fanciful resemblance of the little flower to a bell.
TYPE SPECIES: *Campanulorchis globifera* (Rolfe) Brieger (*Eria globifera* Rolfe)

Now recognized as belonging to the genus *Eria, Campanulorchis* was previously considered to include three epiphytes or lithophytes found growing in low to mid elevation, hill scrub and montane evergreen forests, mosses, peaty swamps or among limestone rocks of Myanmar, Thailand and Vietnam. These tiny plants have ovoid pseudobulbs, spaced along the rhizome, each with one to two, leathery leaves. The short, solitary-flowered inflorescence, subtended by brown sheaths, has a small, cream to pink flower densely covered with soft hairs on the outside of the floral segments. The entire or trilobed lip has small, erect side lobes and a tongue-shaped midlobe that has a thickened margin and tapers to a blunt point. The flowers have a small, slightly curved, club-shaped column.

CAMPYLOCENTRON

An orthographic variant introduced in *Gen. Pl. (Bentham & Hooker f.),* **3**(2): 585 (1883). The correct spelling is *Campylocentrum.*

CAMPYLOCENTRUM

Bentham
J. Linn. Soc., Bot.   **18**(110): 337 (1881).
Epidendroideæ Vandeæ • Angraecinæ
ETYMOLOGY: Greek for crooked or bent and a spur or point. Refers to the shape of the long, slender, sharply curved spur.
TYPE SPECIES: *Todaroa micrantha* A. Richard & Galeotti not *Campylocentrum micranthum* (Lindley) Rolfe This type name is now considered a synonym of *Campylocentrum schiedei* (Reichenbach f.) Bentham ex Hemsley; basionym *Angraecum schiedei* Reichenbach f.

Seventy-three monopodial epiphytes or lithophytes are found in humid, low to mid elevation, woodlands and forests from the southeastern United States (central Florida), Cuba to Trinidad, the

Guianas and Mexico southward to Argentina. These rambling plants, often growing in large masses, have leafy stems or are leafless on short stems with massive clusters of roots. The leaves if present are oblong to narrow, leathery, distichous and have unequally bilobed tips. The root tips are usually suffused orange-brown or tan. The short, numerous to few-flowered inflorescence, borne from the stem's internode, has extremely small, usually white or yellow flowers. The small flowers are arranged in two ranks along the rachis. The flat or concave, entire or trilobed lip (similar in shape to the sepals and petals) has a long, often recurved, club-shaped, short to quite long spur. The flowers have a short, wingless, footless column.

CAMPYLOCNETRUM

An orthographic variant cited in *Dict. Gen. Names Seed Pl.*, 299 (1995). The correct spelling is *Campylocentrum*.

CAMPYSTES

Salisbury

Monthly Rev., ser. 2 **75**: 81 (1814).

ETYMOLOGY: Greek for crooked or bent and column. Refers to the shape of the column.

TYPE SPECIES: *None designated*

A superfluous name proposed as a substitute for *Cephalanthera*.

CANACORCHIS

Guillaumin

Bull. Mus. Natl. Hist. Nat., sér. 2 **35**(6): 653 (1964).

ETYMOLOGY: Latin for groove and Greek for orchid. Refers to the grooves found on the pseudobulbs.

TYPE SPECIES: *Canacorchis lophoglottis* Guillaumin

Now recognized as belonging to the genus *Bulbophyllum*, *Canacorchis* was previously considered to include one epiphyte found in upper elevation, montane scrub of New Caledonia. This small plant has ovoid, grooved on the sides pseudobulbs, each with a solitary, leathery leaf. The several, long, whip-like, solitary-flowered, red inflorescence, borne from the pseudobulb base, has a tiny, dark red-brown flower with equally long, narrow sepals and has very tiny petals. The elongate, slender, entire lip is heavily bearded or fringed in dark pink-red. The flowers have a small, stout, wingless column with a slender tooth at the tip.

CANNAEORCHIS

M.A. Clements & D.L. Jones

Lasianthera **1**(3): 132 (1998).

ETYMOLOGY: Greek for reed or cane and orchid. Referring to the cane-like appearance of the plants.

TYPE SPECIES: *Cannaeorchis fractiflexa* (Finet) M.A. Clements & D.L. Jones (*Dendrobium fractiflexum* Finet)

Now recognized as belonging to the genus *Dendrobium*, *Cannaeorchis* was proposed to include eleven terrestrials or sometimes epiphytes found exclusively in mid elevation, rocky margins of stunted rain forests of New Caledonia. These large plants have cane-like, simple or branched stems, each with the narrow leaves arranged in two ranks along its length. The older stems are subtended by persistent leaf sheaths. The thin to wiry, erect or hanging, solitary, in pairs or few-flowered inflorescence is borne off nodes opposite the leaves. The long-lived, white or creamy, green to brown flower opens widely and is often suffused pink. The narrow, entire or obscurely trilobed lip has three to rare five, basal calli, and has a prominent chin-like projection. The flowers have a straight, wingless column with a shallowly incurved foot that is slightly longer than the column.

CAPANEMIA

Barbosa Rodrigues

Gen. Sp. Orchid. **1**: 137, *t. 354* (1877).

Epidendroideæ ⚘ Cymbidieæ • Oncidiinæ

ETYMOLOGY: Honoring Guilherme Schüch, Barão de Capanema (1824-1908), a Brazilian naturalist, engineer and physicist. He constructed the first telegraph lines and meteorological stations in Brazil.

LECTOTYPE: *Capanemia micromera* Barbosa Rodrigues

Fourteen miniature, sympodial epiphytes are found in low to mid elevation, coastal montane forests and along river banks of eastern Brazil, Paraguay and northeastern Argentina. These clump-forming, plants have small, narrow, ovoid pseudobulbs, subtended by several, papery to thinly textured sheaths, each with a solitary, small, flat to curved, needle-like, channeled, slightly leathery leaf that is either green to red-green. The several, numerous to few-flowered inflorescences have tiny to minute, white or green, translucent, lightly fragrant flowers. The spreading lateral sepals are sometimes slightly united. The clawed, entire lip, borne from the base of the column, has a bright yellow or orange, basal callus. The flowers have an erect, minute, footless column.

CARAIA

An orthographic variant introduced in *Orchid Fl. Kamrup Distr. Assam*, 148 (2001). The correct spelling is *Ceraia*.

CARALLORHIZA

An orthographic variant introduced in *J. Educ. Upper Canada*, **13**(8): 119 (1860). The correct spelling is *Corallorhiza*.

CARDAMOMUM

Sloane

Cat. Pl. Jamaica 61, 220 (1696), and *Voy. Jamaica* **1**: 166, *t. 103, f. 3* (1707).

ETYMOLOGY: Greek for heart or Latin for a spice or a type of water plantin. Cardamom was known and used in Ancient Greece as a cooking spice and in traditional medicine.

Or possibly referring to a similarity of the orchid plant to that of the ginger (Zingiberaceæ) family which was used for its aromatic flavor.

TYPE SPECIES: *Cardamomum minus pseudo-asphodeli follis* Sloane

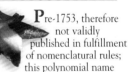

Pre-1753, therefore not validly published in fulfillment of nomenclatural rules; this polynomial name is most often referred to *Stenorrhynchos*. *Cardamomum* was previously considered to include one terrestrial widespread from Mexico to Peru, Cuba to Puerto Rico and Venezuela. This damp loving plant has erect, unbranched stems, each with several, dark green, basal leaves. The erect, sometimes nodding, numerous-flowered inflorescence is often bright red and quite hairy. The tubular, bright red flowers have the dorsal sepal and petals fused together for most of their length. The lateral sepals are united, forming a chin-like projection with the base of the lip. The narrow, white to pale pink, entire lip has a slightly, recurved tip and thickened, hairy sides. This name is usually now considered a synonym of *Stenorrhynchos speciosum* (Jacquin) Richard.

CARDIOCHILOS

P.J. Cribb

Kew Bull. **32**(1): 183 (1977).

Epidendroideæ ⚘ Vandeæ • Aerangidinæ

ETYMOLOGY: Greek for a heart and lip. In reference to the fleshy, heart shape of the lip.

TYPE SPECIES: *Cardiochilos williamsonii* P.J. Cribb

One small, monopodial epiphyte is found only in mid elevation, montane forests of northern Malawi (Nyika

Currently Accepted   Validly Published   Invalidly Published   Published Pre-1753   Superfluous Usage   Orthographic Variant   Fossil

Orchid Genera • **66**

Plateau) and southern Tanzania. This small plant has short, erect stems, each with several, distichous, pleated, narrow, unequal bilobed leaves arranged in two rows. The long, one- to two-flowered inflorescence, borne from the axils of the lower leaves, is covered with short hairs, and has pale green to yellow-orange flowers with similar sepals and petals. The white, heart-shaped, obscurely trilobed lip is inflated in the midsection with a sharp tip, and the distinct horizontal, elongate spur is swollen in the middle and has a wide mouth. The flowers have a short, erect, wingless, footless column.

CARDIOPHYLLUM

Ehrhart
Beitr. Naturk. (Ehrhart) **4**: 148 (1789).
ETYMOLOGY: Greek for heart and leaf.
TYPE SPECIES: *None designated*

Name published without a description. Today this name is most often referred to *Listera*.

CARENIDIUM

Baptista
Colet. Orquídeas Brasil. **3**: 90 (2006).
ETYMOLOGY: Greek for head, peak or crest and two. Refers to the shape of the high keels that are widely varied from very simple to quite complex.
TYPE SPECIES: *Carenidium concolor*
(Hooker) D.H. Baptista
(*Oncidium concolor* Hooker)

Recognized as belonging to the genus *Oncidium*, *Carenidium* was proposed to include ten epiphytes found in cool, mid elevation, coastal forests from south-eastern Brazil (Bahia, Rio de Janeiro and Minas Gerais) to northern Argentina. These plants have clustered, ovate to oblong, compressed, strongly ribbed pseudobulbs, each with several, bright green, oblong to narrow, leathery leaves. The loosely, hanging, few-flowered inflorescence, borne from the pseudobulb base, has bright yellow-green to red-brown flowers with the lateral sepals joined for about half their length. The bright yellow, long-clawed, obscurely four-lobed lip has a basal callus with a minute peg or nob on each side of the ridge. These flowers have a small, erect column with roundish wings.

CARPANGIS

Thouars
Hist. Orchid. Table 2, sub 3o, *t.* 76 (1822).

Name published without a description. Today this name is most often referred to *Angraecum*.

CARPAROMORCHIS

M.A. Clements & D.L. Jones
Orchadian **13**(11): 499 (2002).
ETYMOLOGY: Greek for fruit, aroma and orchid. Refers to the fruity smell when the plant is in bloom.
TYPE SPECIES: *Carparomorchis macrantha*
(Lindley) M.A. Clements & D.L. Jones
(*Bulbophyllum macranthum* Lindley)

Recognized as belonging to the genus *Bulbophyllum*, *Carparomorchis* was proposed to include two epiphytes or occasional lithophytes found in low to mid elevation, coastal to montane forests and swamps from northern India (Assam), Myanmar to Vietnam, Indonesia to the Philippines, New Guinea and northeastern Australia. The stout, creeping rhizomes of these plants often form dense masses, and have short, angular, usually wrinkled pseudobulbs, each with a solitary, rather thick, channeled leaf. The several, but solitary-flowered inflorescences have a sweetly fragrant (though somewhat pungent), pale yellow to white, densely spotted crimson to dark red-brown flower. The thick, arched, tongue-shaped, mobile, entire lip is channeled below. The flowers have a straight, wingless column with a strongly incurved or inflexed foot.

CARRIA

V.P. Castro & K.G. Lacerda
Orchids (West Palm Beach) **74**(9): 694 (2005).
Not *Carria* G. Gardner (1846) Theaceæ.
ETYMOLOGY: Named in honor of George Francis Carr (1935-), an American retired US Foreign Service, airlines and insurance representative who has greatly expanded the knowledge of *Cycnoches*.
TYPE SPECIES: *Carria colorata*
(Königer & J.G. Weinmann) V.P. Castro & K.G. Lacerda
(*Oncidium coloratum* Königer & J.G. Weinmann)

Not validly published because of a prior use of the name, this homonym was replaced by *Carriella*.

CARRIELLA

V.P. Castro & K.G. Lacerda
Icon. Orchid. Brasil., ser. 2 *t.* 123 (2006), and COAB **63**: 67 (2006).
Epidendroideæ ⑯ Cymbidieæ • Oncidiinæ
ETYMOLOGY: *Carria*, a genus of orchids and Latin for diminutive.
TYPE SPECIES: *Carriella colorata*
(Königer & J.G. Weinmann) V.P. Castro & K.G. Lacerda
(*Oncidium coloratum* Königer & J.G. Weinmann)

One sympodial epiphyte is found in humid, mid elevation, montane rain forests of Brazil (Espírito Santo and Bahia). This small plant has laterally compressed to ovate pseudobulbs, partially subtended by thin, dry bracts, each with a solitary, narrow, thick, leathery leaf. The wiry, solitary to three-flowered inflorescence, borne from the base of the pseudobulb, has a small, green-yellow flower with widespreading petals that have brightly colored, orange-red tips. The clawed, lateral sepals can be solid yellow-green or blotched orange-red at the base. The trilobed lip has narrow, erect, incurved side lobes that are colored orange-red and the small, yellow midlobe is arrowhead-shaped with a blunt tip. The flowers have a short, hairy, slightly wingless column.

CARTERETIA

A. Richard
d'Urville's Voy. Astrolabe **2**: 10, *t.* 4 (1834).
ETYMOLOGY: In memory of Philip Carteret (1733-1796), a British rear admiral who voyaged around the world and was the first European explorer to visit New Ireland (a small island northeast of New Guinea), where the type species was collected.
TYPE SPECIES: *Carteretia paniculata* A. Richard
This type name is now considered a synonym of
Cleisostoma quinquefidum (Lindley) Garay;
basionym
Saccolabium quinquefidum Lindley

Now recognized as belonging to the genus *Cleisostoma*, *Carteretia* was previously considered to include one epiphyte found in New Guinea. This robust, clump-forming plant has stout stems at the base, each with strap-shaped, distichous, leathery leaves. The older, yellow-brown stems have a large, gray leaf scar around each node. The multibranched, numerous-flowered inflorescence has small, olive-green flowers with pale brown-maroon stripes. The white, trilobed lip has a thick, tongue-shaped midlobe with a hairy, basal callus that almost closes the entrance to the stout, swollen spur. The flowers have a small, broad column.

CARTERIA

Small
Torreya **10**: 187 (1910).
Not *Carteria* Diesing (1866) Algae.
ETYMOLOGY: Dedicated to Joel Jackson Carter (1843-1912), an American from Pleasant Grove, Pennsylvania who collected the type species and other flora of eastern United States.
TYPE SPECIES: *Carteria corallicola* Small

Not validly published because of a prior use of the name, this homonym was replaced by *Basiphyllaea*.

CARUNASTYLIS

An orthographic variant introduced in *Orchideen (Schlechter)*, ed. 1, 88 (1914). The correct spelling is *Corunastylis*.

CARYANTHES

An orthographic variant introduced in *Hort. Universel*, **5**: 57 (1844). The correct spelling is *Coryanthes*.

CASTASETUM

An orthographic variant introduced in *Neue Allg. Garten- Blumenzeitung*, **1**: 325 (1845-46). The correct spelling is *Catasetum*.

CASTROA

Guiard

Richardiana   **6**(3): 162 (2006).

Epidendroideæ 🌿 Cymbidieæ • Oncidiinæ

ETYMOLOGY: Honoring Vitorino Paiva Castro y Neto (1946-), a Brazilian chemical engineer, orchid taxonomist and author of *Botanique Orchidees Bresil Amerique*.

TYPE SPECIES: *Castroa calimaniana* Guiard

One sympodial epiphyte is found in mid elevation, montane forests of Brazil (Espírito Santo). This dwarf plant has compressed, ovoid pseudo-bulbs, subtended by bracts, each with a solitary, leathery leaf. The erect, wiry, few-flowered inflorescence has bright yellow flowers with similar sepals and petals banded red-brown. The lateral sepals are united for a short distance. The yellow, trilobed lip has small, triangular side lobes and a broad yellow midlobe with a center notch and raised, basal appendages. The flowers have a short, erect, winged, footless column.

CATACHAETUM

Hoffmannsegg

Verz. Orchid.   22 (1842).

ETYMOLOGY: Greek for below or downward and Latin for bristle or mane. Referring to the antenna-like appendages on the column of the male flower.

TYPE SPECIES: *None designated*

Now recognized as belonging to the genus *Catasetum*, *Catachaetum* was previously considered to include seven epiphytes ranging from Trinidad and the Guianas to northern Brazil. These large plants have spindle-shaped or ovoid pseudobulbs, subtended by several, leaf-sheaths, each with oblong, deciduous, pleated leaves borne at the tip. The erect or arching to hanging, few-flowered inflorescence has unisexual (male or female), green or yellow-green flowers spotted purple; these unisexual blooms can be borne on the same plant. The female flowers have a helmet-shaped, rigid lip

and the male flowers emit a strong fragrance to attract male bee pollinators.

NOTE: Today, there is no copy of Hoffmannsegg's publication available; this name is based on a secondary report that was published in *Linnaea*, **16**(Litt.): 231 (1842).

CATASETO

An orthographic variant introduced in *Syn. Pl. (Kunth)*, **1**: 331 (1822). The correct spelling is *Catasetum*.

CATASETUM

Richard ex Kunth

Syn. Pl. (Kunth)   **1**: 330 (1822).

Epidendroideæ 🌿 Cymbidieæ • Catasetinæ

ETYMOLOGY: Greek for downward or below and Latin for bristle. For the two appendages or antenna-like processes of the column that turn downward in the male flowers of most species.

TYPE SPECIES: *Catasetum macrocarpum* Richard ex Kunth

One hundred fifty-seven large, sympodial epiphytes and sometimes as terrestrials or lithophytes are found in low to mid elevation, hill and montane deciduous to evergreen forests and scrub from Mexico to Bolivia, Trinidad, the Guianas, Venezuela, Argentina and Paraguay with the largest center of development in Brazil. This genus includes some quite unusual orchids with their unisexual, rarely bisexual flowers. These unusual morphological features make this an extremely difficult genus to classify. Sex of the flowers is determined by light intensity and growing conditions. The female flowers, borne on separate inflorescences, are mostly green, and do not vary much between the various species. Full, bright sunlight triggers female flowers, and shade produces male flowers. The flowers vary in shape and color, and admit a strong, musky fragrance to attract specific species of male bees, which are attracted to the odor. The bees proceed to scratch at the source releasing the viscidium that is thrown by a tension-bound stipe onto the back of the bee. The viscidium is then deposited on the stigmatic surface of a female flower. The male flowers have an erect, thickened, slightly curved column that is with or without a pair of antennae at the base. The females flowers have a shorter, thicker column that is without antennae, but is bent forward at the tip. The plants have fleshy, ovoid, cone-like or spindle-shaped pseudobulbs, subtended by leaf sheaths when young, each with several, large, pleated, deciduous leaves.

CATHEA

Salisbury

Trans. Hort. Soc. London   **1**: 300 (1812).

ETYMOLOGY: Latin for a barbed spear. An allusion to the densely bearded lip.

TYPE SPECIES: *Cathea pulchella* (Salisbury) Salisbury
(*Limodorum pulchellum* Salisbury)

This type name is now considered a synonym of *Calopogon tuberosus* (Linnaeus) Britton; basionym replaced with *Limodorum tuberosum* Linnaeus

Now recognized as belonging to the genus *Calopogon*, *Cathea* was previously considered to include one terrestrial found from southeastern Canada to the southern United States (Florida). This tiny, erect plant has several, narrow, basal leaves. The erect, few-flowered, green-purple inflorescence has deep pink to white flowers opening almost simultaneously. The obscurely trilobed lip has a disk of pale purple bristles with yellow tipped hairs.

CATLEYA

An orthographic variant introduced in *Bull. Sci. Nat. Geol.*, **26**: 58 (1831). The correct spelling is *Cattleya*.

CATLEYE

An orthographic variant introduced in *Fl. Serres Jard. Angleterre*, *t. 3742* (1839). The correct spelling is *Cattleya*.

CATTLEAY

An orthographic variant introduced in *Repert. Spec. Nov. Regni Veg. Beih.*, **9**: 154 (1921). The correct spelling is *Cattleya*.

CATTLEIA

An orthographic variant cited in *Nomencl. Bot. (Steudel)*, ed. 2, **1**: 311, 559 (1841). The correct spelling is *Cattleya*.

CATTLEJA

An orthographic variant introduced in *Physiol. Gew.*, **2**: 357 (1838). The correct spelling is *Cattleya*.

| Currently Accepted | Validly Published | Invalidly Published | Published Pre-1753 | Superfluous Usage | Orthographic Variant | Fossil |

O r c h i d   G e n e r a • **68**

CATTLEY

An orthographic variant introduced in *Hamburger Garten- Blumenzeitung*, **30**: 184 (1881). The correct spelling is *Cattleya*.

CATTLEYA

Lindley
Coll. Bot. (Lindley)   tt. 33, 37 (1821).
Epidendroideæ ⚘ Epidendreæ • Laeliinæ
ETYMOLOGY: Dedicated to William Cattley (1788-1835), a British merchant, horticulturist, collector of rare tropical plants and one of the earliest British growers to build a collection of tropical orchids.

The type species first arrived in England in 1817 as packing material around ferns collected by William Swainson during a plant gathering trip in eastern Brazil. This species, only preserved as a horticultural curiosity at first, was brought to flower in Cattley's (Barnet) greenhouse in November 1818.

TYPE SPECIES: *Cattleya labiata* Lindley

Fifty-four sympodial epiphytes or lithophytes, with innumerable varieties and forms, that serve as the basis for thousands of hybrids, both natural and manmade. It is without a doubt one of the most popular and widely grown genera of the whole orchid family. Its members are often synonymous with the very word "orchid." The genus is widespread in the American tropics with two major centers of development: the Andes of northern and western South America with the largest group found along the Atlantic coastal regions of eastern Brazil. They are found in dry to wet, low to mid elevation, woodlands and montane forests. These plants have thickened, club-shaped pseudobulbous stems, often subtended by thin, dry sheaths, becoming furrowed with age, each with one or three, leathery or fleshy leaves. The solitary to few-flowered inflorescence has small to large, showy flowers. These spectacular, often highly fragrant flowers have a wide variety of rich colors and lovely pastels, the available color combinations of yellow, white and purple are nearly unlimited but unfortunately there are no blues, blacks or true reds. The entire or weakly trilobed, usually tubular lip is free or rarely joined to the column base and is usually deep notched. The flowers have a club-shaped, two-winged, footless column.

CATTLEYAOPSIS

An orthographic variant introduced in *Sempervirens*, **20**(39): 466 (1891). The correct spelling is *Cattleyopsis*.

CATTLEYELLA

van den Berg & **M.W. Chase**
Bol. CAOB   **52**: 100 (2003).
Epidendroideæ ⚘ Epidendreæ • Laeliinæ
ETYMOLOGY: *Cattleya*, a genus of orchids and Latin for diminutive. Refers to a resemblance to *Cattleya*.
TYPE SPECIES: *Cattleyella araguaiensis*
(Pabst) Van den Berg & M.W. Chase
(*Cattleya araguaiensis* Pabst)

One sympodial epiphyte is found in humid, low elevation, dense forests of east central Brazil (Tocantins). This plant has small, slim, spindly pseudobulbs, each with a solitary, oblong, leathery leaf. The solitary to two-flowered inflorescence has a long-lasting flower with similar narrow to elliptical, yellow-green sepals and petals heavily spotted red-brown. The funnel-shaped, entire to obscurely trilobed lip has white, oblong side lobes that envelope the long, club-shaped, footless column; and a red-brown midlobe that has a scalloped margin and a basal splash of magenta.

CATTLEYOPSIS

Lemaire
Jard. Fleur.   **4**(Misc.): 59 (1854).
ETYMOLOGY: *Cattleya*, a genus of orchids and Greek for resembling or likeness.
TYPE SPECIES: *Cattleyopsis delicatula* Lemaire
This type name is now considered a synonym of
Broughtonia lindenii (Lindley) Dressler;
basionym
Laelia lindenii Lindley

Now recognized as belonging to the genus *Broughtonia*, *Cattleyopsis* was previously considered to include three epiphytes found growing in humid, low elevation, hill forests of the Bahamas and Cuba usually in full sunlight. These dwarf to medium-sized plants have small, clustered, ovoid to egg-shaped pseudobulbs, each with one to two, fleshy-rigid leaves that have minutely notched margins. The long, erect, few-flowered inflorescence has small, showy, pastel colored flowers lasting in perfection for several weeks. The broad, entire lip, tubular at the base, is widespreading in the front with pairs of papillae on the central veins. The flowers have a slender, club-shaped, footless column.

CATTLEZA

An orthographic variant introduced in *Florist Hort. J.*, **3**: 153 (1854). The correct spelling is *Cattleya*.

CATTLLEYA

An orthographic variant introduced in *Xenia Orchid.*, **2**: 173 (1873). The correct spelling is *Cattleya*.

CATTLYLA

An orthographic variant introduced in *Tijdschr. Natuurl. Gesch. Physiol.*, **6**: 78 (1839). The correct spelling is *Cattleya*.

CAUCAEA

Schlechter
Repert. Spec. Nov. Regni Veg. Beih.   **7**: 189 (1920).
Epidendroideæ ⚘ Cymbidieæ • Oncidiinæ
ETYMOLOGY: Named for the Department (state) of Cauca (an area located in southwestern region of the Republic of Colombia along the Pacific Ocean) where the type species was collected.
TYPE SPECIES: *Caucaea obscura*
(F. Lehmann & Kraenzlin) Schlechter
(*Rodriguezia obscura* F. Lehmann & Kraenzlin)
This type name is now considered a synonym of
Caucaea radiata (Lindley) Mansfeld;
basionym replaced with
Abola radiata Lindley

Twenty sympodial epiphytes are found in upper elevation, montane forests of Venezuela and Colombia to Peru. These plants have compressed pseudobulbs, subtended by over-lapping leaf sheaths, each with one to two leathery leaves. One species has tiny flowers and all the other species have large-sized flowers. The fleshy, dull purple flowers suffused maroon, have pale green tips and minute warts on the outer surfaces. The sepals and petals are slightly longer than the white, entire lip that is sprinkled with purple spots and has a yellow callus. The lateral sepals are united for almost their whole length. The flowers have a very short column with fleshy, wing-like lobes.

CAULANGIS

Thouars
Hist. Orchid.   Table 2, sub 3o, t. 75 (1822).

Name published without a description. Today this name is most often referred to *Mystacidium*.

CAULARTHRON

Rafinesque

Fl. Tellur. **2**: 40 (1836)[1837].

Epidendroideæ ⚘ Epidendreæ • Laeliinæ

ETYMOLOGY: Greek for stem or stalk and a joint. Descriptive of the persistent leaf bases that give the elongate pseudobulbs the appearance of being jointed.

LECTOTYPE: *Caularthron bicornutum*
(Hooker) Rafinesque
(*Epidendrum bicornutum* Hooker)

Four sympodial epiphytes or lithophytes are found in seasonally dry, low to mid elevation, tropical hill forests, cliff faces and along river banks from southern Mexico to Ecuador, Venezuela, Trinidad, the Guianas and Brazil, usually growing in full sunlight. They are commonly called the Virgin Orchid. In the wild these plants have spindle-shaped pseudobulbs, subtended by persistent, white, leaf-bases, each with several, oblong, fleshy to leathery leaves. There is one species that has its older, hollow pseudobulbs inhabited by ants. The erect, numerous to few-flowered inflorescence has showy, waxy, fragrant, long-lasting, white or pink-white flowers opening widely that change color as they age or are pollinated. The trilobed lip has small, erect, rounded side lobes, and the narrow midlobe has a yellow callus often sprinkled with purple spots and specks and hollow, horn-like processes. The flowers have a short, flat to arched, winged, footless column.

CELCEOLUS

An orthographic variant introduced in *Orchids India*, ed. 2, 35 (1999). The correct spelling is *Calceolus*.

CELOGYNE

An orthographic variant introduced in *Revue Hort. (Paris)*, **36**: 335 (1866). The correct spelling is *Coelogyne*.

CENTRANTHERA

Scheidweiler

Allg. Gartenzeitung **10**(37): 293 (1842).

Not *Centranthera* R. Brown (1810) Scrophulariaceæ.

ETYMOLOGY: Greek for a spur or point and anther. Referring to the pointed anthers.

TYPE SPECIES: *Centranthera punctata* Scheidweiler
This type name is now considered a synonym of
Pleurothallis centranthera Lindley

Not validly published because of a prior use of the name, this homonym was replaced by *Pleurothallis*.

CENTROCHILUS

Schauer

Nov. Actorum Acad. Caes. Leop.-Carol. Nat. Cur., ser. 3 **19**(Suppl. 1): 435, *t. 13C* (1843), or *Observ. Bot.* **16**(Suppl. 2): 435, *t. 13C* (1843).

ETYMOLOGY: Greek for a spur and lip. Descriptive of the slender, club-like spur on the lip.

TYPE SPECIES: *Centrochilus gracilis* Schauer
This type name is now considered a synonym of
Habenaria linguella Lindley

Now recognized as belonging to the genus *Habenaria*, *Centrochilus* was previously considered to include one terrestrial found in low to upper elevation, montane forests and grasslands of southern China (Guangxi, Guangdong, Guizhou, Hainan, Yunnan to Hong Kong) and northern Vietnam. This tall, slender plant has unbranched stems, each with numerous, soft leaves and a few-flowered inflorescence. The green flowers have small, orange suffused petals that converge with the erect, dorsal sepal, forming a hood over the small column. The white, trilobed lip has small side lobes, a long, notched midlobe, and a long, yellow to green spur.

CENTROGENIUM

Schlechter

Beih. Bot. Centralbl. **37**(2): 451 (1920), and *Repert. Spec. Nov. Regni Veg. Beih.* **6**: 54 (1919).

ETYMOLOGY: Greek for a spur and chin or beard. Refers to the shape of the spur that is formed by the lateral sepals and the column foot.

LECTOTYPE: *Centrogenium calcaratum*
(Swartz) Schlechter
(*Neottia calcarata* Swartz)

Now recognized as belonging to the genus *Eltroplectris*, *Centrogenium* was previously considered to include fifteen terrestrials found in low elevation, hill scrub and along river banks from the south-eastern United States (Florida) to Brazil. These tall, erect plants have unbranched stems, each with several, thinly textured, deep blue-green, basal leaves. These brown spotted leaves are usually withered by flowering time. The erect, hairy, purple, few-flowered inflorescence has attractive, fragrant, green, purple, white or pale brown flowers with long, narrow segments. These segments are united at the bases with the column foot forming a blunt spur. The narrow, fringed, entire lip is notched above the middle and recurved. The flowers have a short, stout column.

CENTROGLOSSA

Barbosa Rodrigues

Gen. Sp. Orchid. **2**: 234 (1882).

Epidendroideæ ⚘ Cymbidieæ • Oncidiinæ

ETYMOLOGY: Greek for a spur and tongue. An allusion to the elongate lip which opens in front of the column.

LECTOTYPE: *Centroglossa tripollinica*
(Barbosa Rodrigues) Barbosa Rodrigues
(*Ornithocephalus tripollinica* Barbosa Rodrigues)

Five unusual, tufted, sympodial epiphytes are found in low to mid elevation, rain forests of southeastern Brazil (Minas Gerais to Santa Catarina). These tiny plants have ovoid, slightly compressed pseudobulbs, each with a solitary, narrow, slightly folded, leathery, leaf. The several, short, erect, few-flowered inflorescence, borne from a mature pseudo-bulb, has small, showy, green, yellow, purple or white flowers with similar sepals and petals. The tiny, trilobed lip has erect side lobes, and an unusual, deeply cup-shaped midlobe with a central callus, radiating green veins and has a tiny spur. The flowers have a short, erect column.

CENTROPETALUM

Lindley

Sert. Orchid. *t. 21* (1838).

ETYMOLOGY: Latin for center and petal. Referring to the shape of the hooded clinandrium that is characteristic of this genus.

TYPE SPECIES: *Centropetalum distichum* Lindley
This type name is now considered a synonym of
Fernandezia subbiflora Ruiz & Pavón

Now recognized as belonging to the genus *Fernandezia*, *Centropetalum* was previously considered to include seven epiphytes found in wet, upper elevation, montane cloud forests in the Andes of Colombia, Venezuela, Ecuador and Peru; also found in Costa Rica. These dwarf, distichous, fleshy-leafed plants have small, needle-like leaves and proportionately large, red or scarlet flowers with a funnel-shaped, broadly winged column structure. The several, short, solitary-flowered inflorescences have flowers produced in rapid succession. The brightly colored flowers have the entire lip at its base clasping a callus.

Currently Accepted   Validly Published   Invalidly Published   Published Pre-1753   Superfluous Usage   Orthographic Variant   Fossil

Orchid Genera • 70

CENTROSIA

A. Richard

Mém. Soc. Hist. Nat. Paris **4**: 39, t. 7 (1828).

ETYMOLOGY: Greek for a spur. Referring to the conspicuously spurred lip.

TYPE SPECIES: *Centrosia aubertii* A. Richard

This type name is now considered a synonym of
Calanthe sylvatica (Thouars) Lindley;
basionym
Centrosis sylvatica Thouars

Now recognized as belonging to the genus *Calanthe*, *Centrosia* was previously considered to include one terrestrial found in low to upper elevation, evergreen rain forests from Africa (Sierra Leone to Cameroon, Gabon to Angola, Uganda to South Africa), Madagascar, the Mascarene Islands, southeastern China, Japan and India to Indonesia. This plant has small, cone-shaped, noded pseudobulbs, subtended by leafy bases, each with several, narrow, pleated, ribbed, softly hairy leaves. The erect, hairy, numerous to few-flowered inflorescence has large, deep to pale violet, widespreading flowers. The trilobed lip has oblong side lobes, the midlobe has a wavy margin with a notched tip and has a slender, incurved spur.

CENTROSIS

Thouars

Hist. Orchid. Table 1, sub 2l, tt. 35-36 (1822).

ETYMOLOGY: Greek for a spur or any sharp point. Refers to the conspicuously spurred lip.

TYPE SPECIES: *Centrosis sylvatica* Thouars

Now recognized as belonging to the genus *Calanthe*, *Centrosis* Thouars was previously considered to include five terrestrials found in low to mid elevation, hill scrub and montane rain forests of Madagascar, as well as the Comoros, Mascarenes and Seychelles Islands. These plants have elliptical to cone-shaped pseudobulbs, each with several, oblong leaves. The terminal, numerous to few-flowered inflorescence, often as long as the leaves, has large, widespreading, deep violet flowers that are hairy on the outside segments. The yellow to mauve, trilobed lip, joined to the column base, has oblong, sickle-shaped side lobes. The shortly clawed, fan or wedged-shaped midlobe has a notched tip, a wavy margin and a slender, incurved spur.

CENTROSIS

Swartz

Adnot. Bot. 52 (1829).

Not *Centrosis* Thouars (1822) Orchidaceæ.

ETYMOLOGY: Greek for a spur. Referring to the lip that is conspicuously spurred.

TYPE SPECIES: *Centrosis abortiva* (Linnaeus) Swartz

This type name is now considered a synonym of
Limodorum abortivum (Linnaeus) Swartz;
basionym
Orchis abortiva Linnaeus

Not validly published because of a prior use of the name, this homonym was replaced by *Limodorum*.

CENTROSTIGMA

Schlechter

Bot. Jahrb. Syst. **53**: 522 (1915).

Orchidoideæ ⚘ Orchideæ • Orchidinæ

ETYMOLOGY: Latin for a center and stigma. Refers to the stigmatic concavity that has a central position on the flower.

LECTOTYPE: *Centrostigma occultans*
(Welwitsch ex Reichenbach f.) Schlechter
(*Habenaria occultans* Welwitsch ex Reichenbach f.)
designated by Summerhayes, *Kew Bull.*, **11**: 219 (1951).

LECTOTYPE: *Centrostigma schlechteri*
(Kraenzlin) Schlechter
(*Habenaria schlechteri* Kraenzlin)
designated by Phillips, *Gen. S. African Fl. Pl.* ed. 2, 232 (1951).

Three sympodial terrestrials are found in mid elevation, grasslands and marshes from Tanzania to north-eastern South Africa. These robust, erect plants have unbranched, leafy stems that are both striking and unusual looking as whole plant turns black once the flowers die off. The few-flowered inflorescence usually has rather showy, white, creamy-yellow or even green flowers. The trilobed lip has erect or combed, tooth-like side lobes that form a hood over the erect, curved column and has a cylindrical, exceedingly long spur. The flowers have a complex column structure with adjacent anther chambers. The parallel, branched, stigmatic processes are bilobed, the lower lobes are receptive, and the upper lobes are sterile and project upward in front of the anther.

CEOLOGLOSSUM

An orthographic variant introduced in *Orchids India*, ed. 2, 143 (1999). The correct spelling is *Coeloglossum*.

CEOLOGYNE

An orthographic variant introduced in *Planze*, **2**: 245 (1897). The correct spelling is *Coelogyne*.

CEPHALANCEROPSIS

An orthographic variant introduced in *Native Orchids Taiwan*, ed. 3, 133 (1985). The correct spelling is *Cephalantheropsis*.

CEPHALANGRAECUM

Schlechter

Beih. Bot. Centralbl. **36**(2): 135 (1918).

ETYMOLOGY: Greek for head and *Angraecum*, a genus of orchids, thus differentiating the genus by its short, congested, head-like inflorescence.

TYPE SPECIES: *None designated*

Now recognized as belonging to the genus *Ancistrorhynchus*, *Cephalangraecum* was previously considered to include nine hanging epiphytes found in shady, low to mid elevation, evergreen forests from Ghana, Ivory Coast, Togo and Nigeria to Uganda. These plants have short stems, subtended by persistent leaf-bases, each with several, overlapping, stiff, leathery, unequally bilobed leaves. The numerous-flowered inflorescence, borne from the lower leaf axils, has tiny, mostly white flowers with similar sepals and petals. The entire or trilobed lip, often marked with a blotch of green, has a straight, S-shaped or an abruptly bent (like a knee) spur, that sometimes has a swollen tip and/or mouth. The flowers have a short column.

CEPHALANTHERA

Richard

De Orchid. Eur. 21, 29, 38 (1817), and *Mém. Mus. Hist. Nat.* **4**: 51 (1818).

Epidendroideæ ⚘ Neottieæ

ETYMOLOGY: Greek for head and anther or stamen. Referring to the head-shaped anther.

LECTOTYPE: *Cephalanthera damasonium*
(Miller) Druce
(*Serapias damasonium* Miller)

Twenty sympodial terrestrials or saprophytes are widespread in Old World northern temperate zones in moist to dry, low to upper elevation, woodlands, sand dunes, open piney woods and meadows, extending from Sweden to throughout Europe, Russia, Turkey to Kyrgyzstan, northwestern Africa (Morocco to Tunisia), Cyprus to Iran and Pakistan, northern India (Kashmir to Assam) Nepal, Myanmar with one species in western Canada (British Colombia) and the western United States (Washington to northern California). These erect plants (heavily dependent on the mycorrhiza fungus) have a slender to stout, unbranched stem, subtended by basal sheaths, each with several, narrow to oblong leaves, alternating up the stem. The showy flowers are produced at the top of long, numerous to few-flowered inflorescences. The often complex, mostly white, rosy or green flowers not opening widely, are subtended by green bracts. The dorsal sepal and petals converge, forming a hood over the slender, erect, footless column and have widespreading lateral sepals. The heart-shaped, bilobed lip is divided into two portions by a median constriction and has a reduced, short spur or is spurless. The hypochile is sac-like below the long, slightly curved to erect, footless column. The recurved epichile has fleshy, bright yellow ridges and a wavy margin.

CEPHALANTHEROPSIS

Guillaumin

Bull. Mus. Natl. Hist. Nat., sér. 2
32(2): 188 (1960).

Epidendroideæ ⁄ Collabiinæ • Currently unplaced

ETYMOLOGY: *Cephalanthera*, a genus of orchids and Greek for appearance or looking like.

TYPE SPECIES: *Cephalantheropsis lateriscapa*
Guillaumin

This type name is now considered a synonym of *Cephalantheropsis longipes* (Hooker f.) Ormerod; basionym *Calanthe longipes* Hooker f.

Five sympodial terrestrials or epiphytes are scattered in low to upper elevation, hill and montane evergreen forests from northeastern India (Sikkim to Assam), southern China (Tibet to Fujian), Myanmar to Vietnam, Malaysia, Taiwan, southern Japan (Ryukyu Islands) and extending to the Philippines. These plants have bamboo-like, leafy stems, each with several, pleated, thinly textured leaves. The shortly hairy, few-flowered inflorescence (often two or more) has small, showy white, yellow, to cream-colored flowers facing in all directions. The sepals are hairy on the outside with both the sepals and petals being slightly reflexed. The long lip is trilobed in the middle and has erect side lobes surrounding the short column. The shortly clawed, bilobed midlobe has yellow ridges down the center, a notched tip, and a strong wavy margin. The flowers have a fleshy, hairy, footless column.

CEPOBACULUM

M.A. Clements & **D.L. Jones**
Orchadian   **13**(11): 486 (2002).

ETYMOLOGY: Greek for onion or head and stick. Referring to the local, common name for the type species - onion orchid.

TYPE SPECIES: *Cepobaculum canaliculatum* (R. Brown) M.A. Clements & D.L. Jones (*Dendrobium canaliculatum* R. Brown)

Recognized as belonging to the genus *Dendrobium*, *Cepobaculum* was proposed to include eight epiphytes or occasional lithophytes found in low elevation, *Melaleuca* scrub and open forests of northeastern Australia and New Guinea. These small plants have ovoid or spindle-shaped pseudobulbs, each with several, almost cylindrical leaves that have a deep groove on their upper surfaces. The erect, numerous to few-flowered inflorescence has flowers varying in color. The predominantly pale yellow-green, fragrant flowers have narrow, somewhat twisted sepals and petals. The white, trilobed lip has purple markings, erect, rounded side lobes, and an oval midlobe with several raised keels. The flowers have a short column with the column foot joined to the lip and lateral sepals.

CEPRIPIDIUM

An orthographic variant introduced in *Icon. Pl. Ind. Orient. (Wight)*, **5**(1): 22 (1852). The correct spelling is *Cypripedium*.

CERAEA

An orthographic variant cited in *Lex. Gen. Phan.*, 110 (1904). The correct spelling is *Ceraia*.

CERAIA

Loureiro
Fl. Cochinch.   **2**: 518 (1790).
Name ICBN rejected vs. *Dendrobium* Swartz (1799)
Orchidaceæ.

ETYMOLOGY: Greek for horn. Referring to the cornucopia-like shaped spur.

TYPE SPECIES: *Ceraia simplicissima* Loureiro

Although validly published this rejected name is now referred to *Dendrobium. Ceraia* was considered to include one epiphyte or lithophyte found in India, Sri Lanka, Myanmar to Vietnam, Taiwan, Indonesia, New Guinea and the Philippines. This plant has erect, thin stems or deeply ridged to wrinkled, three or four-noded pseudobulbs, each with rather rigid, leathery leaves that are eventually deciduous.

The erect, few-flowered inflorescence has strongly fragrant, small flowers which last for just a few short hours. The trilobed lip is attached to the base of the column foot, forming a short, chin-like spur; has small side lobes, and a broad midlobe. The above type name is often now included as a synonym of *Dendrobium crumenatum* Swartz.

CERAJA

An orthographic variant introduced in *Nouv. Dict. Hist. Nat.*, **7**: 179 (1803). The correct spelling is *Ceraia*.

CERASTOTYLIS

An orthographic variant introduced in *Bot. Centralbl.*, **101**(22): 588 (1906). The correct spelling is *Ceratostylis*.

CERATANDRA

Ecklon ex **F.A. Bauer**
Ill. Orch. Pl. (Bauer & Lindley)   t. 16 (1837).

Orchidoideæ ⁄ Orchideæ • Disinæ

ETYMOLOGY: Greek for horn and a man or stamen. Referring to the horn-like appendages on the anther.

TYPE SPECIES: *Ceratandra chloroleuca* Ecklon ex F.A. Bauer

This type name is now considered a synonym of
LECTOTYPE: *Ceratandra atrata* (Linnaeus) T. Durand & Schinz (*Ophrys atrata* Linnaeus)

Six uncommon, sympodial terrestrials are found in seasonally wet, low elevation, western coastal marshes and hills in the Cape area of South Africa. These erect plants have slender to stout, unbranched stems sometimes in bundle of four. The mostly dissimilar leaves consist of several, narrow leaves spaced along the stem and a basal rosette of rather narrow, pointed leaves borne from the thick roots. The tall, terminal, numerous to few-flowered inflorescence has yellow-green, striking yellow-orange, white or even dull pink flowers suffused red or orange, with a most unpleasant, soap-like fragrance. The broad, semi-circular or anchor-shaped, entire lip is uppermost and often filled with a small callus. The flowers have a small, short column.

NOTE: These species are stimulated by fire to bloom and this usually produces a sudden mass of flowering plants.

Currently Accepted   Validly Published   Invalidly Published   Published Pre-1753   Superfluous Usage   Orthographic Variant   Fossil

Orchid Genera • **72**

CERATANDROPSIS

Rolfe

Fl. Cap. (Harvey) **5**(3): 266 (1913).

ETYMOLOGY: *Ceratandra*, a genus of orchids and Greek for appearance. Refers to a similarity with *Ceratandra*.

LECTOTYPE: *Ceratandropsis grandiflora*
(Lindley) Rolfe
(*Ceratandra grandiflora* Lindley)

Now recognized as belonging to the genus *Ceratandra*, *Ceratandropsis* was previously considered to include one terrestrial found in South Africa. This tall, erect plant has unbranched stems, each with several, narrow leaves. The densely packed, numerous-flowered inflorescence has bright yellow to white flowers with the dorsal sepal and petals joined together. The small flower is without a lip appendage.

CERATHANDRA

An orthographic variant introduced in *Beitr. Morph. Biol. Orchid.*, 39 (1863). The correct spelling is *Ceratandra*.

CERATIUM

Blume

Bijdr. Fl. Ned. Ind. **7**: 341, *t.* 46 (1825).
Not *Ceratium* Schrank (1793) Algae, and not *Ceratium* Albertini & Schweinitz (1805) Fungi.

ETYMOLOGY: Greek for little horn or pod. Descriptive of the long capsule that is divided by a membranous partition.

TYPE SPECIES: *Ceratium compressum* Blume

Not validly published because of a prior use of the name, this homonym was replaced by *Eria*.

CERATOBIUM

M.A. Clements & D.L. Jones

Orchadian **13**(11): 486 (2002).

ETYMOLOGY: Greek for horn and life. Referring to the resemblance of the petals and sepals to the long, twisted horns of an antelope.

TYPE SPECIES: *Ceratobium antennatum*
(Lindley) M.A. Clements & D.L. Jones
(*Dendrobium antennatum* Lindley)

Recognized as belonging to the genus *Dendrobium*, *Ceratobium* was proposed to include twelve epiphytes found in humid, low to mid elevations, semi-exposed scrub and often occurring in association with ant infested plants in both New Guinea and northeastern Australia. These plants have short, compact, yellow-green pseudobulbs that are roughly angled with a slender tip, each with several, succulent, narrow, variably sized leaves. The erect or arching, few-flowered inflorescence, borne from pointed nodes, has showy, fragrant, long-lived flowers with white sepals and long, upright, green, purple or green-yellow petals that are slightly or spirally twisted. The white, trilobed lip has purple veins, erect side lobes and has an ovate, pointed midlobe with a ridged callus.

CERATOCENTRON

Senghas

Orchidee (Hamburg) **40**(3): 89 (1989).

Epidendroideæ Vandeæ • Aeridinæ

ETYMOLOGY: Greek for a horn and spur. Refers to the large spur and the horn-like projection on the lip.

TYPE SPECIES: *Ceratocentron fesselii* Senghas

One monopodial epiphyte is found in mid elevation, montane forests of the northern Philippines (Luzon). This tiny plant has short stems, each with several, leathery, dark green leaves. The several, short, erect, solitary to two-flowered inflorescences have miniature, widespreading, orange to bright crimson flowers that almost hide the tiny plant when in bloom. The minute, white or two-tone pink, fleshy, obscurely trilobed lip has fine, wine-red dots sprinkled down the center, and the large, bilaterally compressed, long spur (forward and upward pointing) has a solid, fleshy horn just below the lip. The flowers have a very short, fleshy, wingless, footless column.

CERATOCHILUS

Blume

Bijdr. Fl. Ned. Ind. **8**: 358, *t.* 25 (1825).
Not *Ceratochilus* Lindley ex Loddiges (1829) Orchidaceæ.

Epidendroideæ Vandeæ • Aeridinæ

ETYMOLOGY: Greek for a horn and lip. Refers to the two, horn-like calluses at the mouth of the lip.

TYPE SPECIES: *Ceratochilus biglandulosus* Blume

One monopodial epiphyte is found in upper elevation, montane cloud forests of Indonesia (Java, Sumatra and Borneo) among the mosses. This dwarf plant has tiny, red tinged, green leaves spaced along the stem. The short, solitary-flowered inflorescence has a proportionately large, flat-faced, translucent, pristine white flower that lasts for just one week, but turns a bright red as it ages. The tiny, trilobed or obscurely trilobed lip is cup-shaped over the bright green, short, slightly curved backward column, that has a black anther cap. It has two horn-like projections on either side of the mouth to the green, short or long, cylindrical to bilaterally flattened spur. The flowers have a small, stout column.

CERATOCHILUS

Lindley ex **Loddiges**

Bot. Cab. **15**: *t.* 1414 (1829).
Not *Ceratochilus* Blume (1825) Orchidaceæ.

ETYMOLOGY: Greek for horn and lip. Referring to the two, horn-like calluses located at the mouth of the lip.

TYPE SPECIES: *Ceratochilus grandiflorus* Loddiges

Not validly published because of a prior use of the name, this homonym was replaced by *Stanhopea*.

CERATOPETALORCHIS

Szlachetko, Górniak & Tukallo

Richardiana **3**(4): 158 (2003).

ETYMOLOGY: Greek for horn, petals and orchid. Referring to the appearance of these flowers with their narrow upright petals.

TYPE SPECIES: *Ceratopetalorchis cornuta*
(Lindley) Szlachetko, Górniak & Tukallo
(*Habenaria cornuta* Lindley)

Recognized as belonging to the genus *Habenaria*, *Ceratopetalorchis* was proposed to include twelve terrestrials found in mid elevation, forest scrub, savannas, marshes or grasslands from Guinea to Ethiopia, Sudan to South Africa and Madagascar growing singly or in small groups. These small to medium-sized plants have erect, unbranched stems, each with several leaves ascending upward. The few-flowered inflorescence has a bract encasing, each delicate, green, yellow or white flower. The concave dorsal sepal is hood shaped, and the long, narrow to thread-like petals are held upright above the dorsal sepal and curve strongly inward. The trilobed lip has narrow side lobes with notched margins, a narrow spear-shaped midlobe, and a long, cylindrical spur with a swollen tip.

CERATOPSIS

Lindley

Gen. Sp. Orchid. Pl. 383 (1840).

ETYMOLOGY: Greek for a horn and resembling. From the conspicuous, horn-like spur of the lip.

TYPE SPECIES: *Ceratopsis rosea* (D. Don) Lindley
(*Limodorum roseum* D. Don)

Now recognized as belonging to the genus *Epipogium*, *Ceratopsis* was previously considered to include one saprophyte found in low to mid elevation, evergreen forests and thickets from Ghana to Kenya and Uganda, India to southern China, Japan, Taiwan to the Philippines and Fiji to northern Australia. A remarkable and unusual plant with development of the inflorescence, the opening of the flowers, to final seed dispersal taking place within just five total days. This leafless plant has hollow, erect stems that are brown at their base graduating to nearly white at the top with several, leaf-like sheaths. The numerous-flowered inflorescence has wide-spreading, white flowers often suffused or speckled with pink or magenta. The trilobed lip has broad, triangular side lobes; a heart-shaped midlobe, often flecked or suffused red; a notched margin; and a rather broad, often bent spur. The flowers have a tiny column.

CERATOSTYLIS

Blume

Bijdr. Fl. Ned. Ind.   **7**: 304, t. 56 (1825).

Epidendroideæ ❧ Podochileæ • Eriinæ

ETYMOLOGY: Greek for a horn and style or pillar. Refers to the usually fleshy column that appear to have a horn-like appearance.

LECTOTYPE: *Ceratostylis subulata* Blume
designated by Butzin, *Taxon*, **32**: 630 (1983).

LECTOTYPE: *Ceratostylis graminea* Blume
designated by P.J. Cribb, *Gen. Orch.*, **4**: 546 (2005).

One hundred forty-five sympodial epiphytes are found in low to upper elevation, hill scrub and montane forests from southern China (Xizang to Hainan), northern India (Sikkim), Nepal, Myanmar to Vietnam, Indonesia to the Philippines and New Caledonia with the largest concentration found in New Guinea. These simple or branched, erect or hanging, closely tufted or creeping, slender to thick plants have short, rarely leafless stems, each with thin leaves or long stems with large, pencil-shaped, leathery or fleshy leaves. The several, short, solitary-flowered inflorescences have a tiny, white, yellow, red or bright orange flower often occurring in clusters. These clusters, opening all at once, are produced in great abundance just below the base of the leaves. The yellow to white, tiny, entire or trilobed lip, joined to the column foot by a long claw, has a curved, thickened blade. The flowers have a short, wingless column.

CERATOSTYLUS

An orthographic variant introduced in *Tab. Pl. Jav. Orchid.*, t. 5 (1825). The correct spelling is *Ceratostylis*.

CERATOSYLIS

An orthographic variant introduced in *Acta Bot. Fenn.*, **173**: 37 (2002). The correct spelling is *Ceratostylis*.

CEREO

Sloane

Cat. Pl. Jamaica   198 (1696), and
Voy. Jamaica   **2**: 160, t. 224, ff. 3-4 (1725).

ETYMOLOGY: Latin for waxen. Referring to the texture of the flowers.

TYPE SPECIES: *Cereo affinis scandens* Sloane

Pre-1753, therefore not validly published in fulfillment of nomenclatural rules; this trinomial name is most often referred to *Vanilla*. *Cereo* was previously considered to include one epiphyte wide-spread from Puerto Rico, Hispaniola, Cuba and the Cayman Islands to Jamaica in low elevation woodlands. This multibranched, climbing or aerial plant has succulent stems, each with several, small, fleshy, rigid leaves borne at the nodes which later with age fall off. The few-flowered inflorescence has fragrant, large, short-lived, yellow-green flowers with a white, funnel-shaped, trilobed lip that has two red, basal blotches. The flowers have a long, footless column. This name is now usually considered a synonym of *Vanilla claviculata* (Swartz) Swartz.

NOTE: The plant has long, pod-like seed pods that when dried and cured, have a delicate fragrance from which a flavoring extract is made.

CEROCHILUS

Lindley

Gard. Chron., ser. 1   **1854**: 87 (1854).

ETYMOLOGY: Greek for a horn and lip. Refers to the two, horn-like glands at the sides of the lip.

TYPE SPECIES: *Cerochilus rubens* Lindley
This type name is now considered a synonym of
Hetaeria affinis (Griffith) Seidenfaden & Ormerod;
basionym
Goodyera affinis Griffith

Now recognized as belonging to the genus *Hetaeria*, *Cerochilus* was previously considered to include one terrestrial found in upper elevation, montane forests and along river banks from northeastern India, Bhutan, northern Myanmar, southern China (Yunnan) and Thailand to Vietnam. This erect plant has leafy stems, each with broad, veined, fleshy leaves that are distinctly stalked. The erect, numerous-flowered inflorescence has large bracts and small, green flowers not opening widely that are tipped pink. The sepals are similar and the hammer-shaped, clawed petals are pinched on one side. The flowers are densely covered with soft hairs and the uppermost, entire lip has a sac-like base. The flowers have a short column.

CERRHOPETALUM

An orthographic variant introduced in *Icon. Pl. Ind. Orient. (Wight)*, **3**: t. 1658 (1851). The correct spelling is *Cirrhopetalum*.

CERTOCHILUS

An orthographic variant introduced in *Ceiba*, **5**(4): 182 (1956). The correct spelling is *Ceratochilus*.

CERUTANDRA

An orthographic variant introduced in *J. Soc. Hort. Seine-et-Oise.*, **1896**: 45 (1896). The correct spelling is *Ceratandra*.

CESPIPHYLIS

An orthographic variant introduced in *Hist. Orchid.*, t. 103 (1822). The correct spelling is *Coespiphylis*.

CESTICHES

An orthographic variant introduced in *Orchideen (Schlechter)*, ed. 1, 161 (1915). The correct spelling is *Cestichis*.

CESTICHIS

Thouars

Hist. Orchid.   t. 90 (1822).

Name published without a description. Today this name is most often referred to *Stichorkis*.

CESTICHIS

Thouars ex Pfitzer

Entwurf Anordn. Orch.   56, 101 (1887).

ETYMOLOGY: Greek for a serrated instrument. Refers to the margins of the toothed lip.

LECTOTYPE: *Cestichis caespitosa* (Lamarck) Ames
(*Epidendrum caespitosum* Lamarck)

Now recognized as belonging to the genus *Stichorkis*, *Cestichis* was previously considered to include thirty-six epiphytes or lithophytes found from Malaysia and Indonesia to the Philippines. These erect plants have compressed pseudobulbs, each with a solitary, long, narrow leaf. The erect, numerous to few-flowered inflorescence has tiny, two-ranked bracts, and equally tiny, red-brown to green flowers. The trilobed or entire lip has a narrow

Currently Accepted   Validly Published   Invalidly Published   Published Pre-1753   Superfluous Usage   Orthographic Variant   Fossil

Orchid Genera • 74

base from which the down turned blade, grooved down the midline, broadly widens.

CESTICHUS

An orthographic variant introduced in *Orchid. Philipp.*, 137 (2001). The correct spelling is *Cestichis*.

CHAEMAEREPES

An orthographic variant cited in *Dict. Fl. Pl.*, ed. 8, 233 (1973). The correct spelling is *Chamaerepes*.

CHAENANTHE

Lindley

Edwards's Bot. Reg.
24(Misc.): 38, section no. 60 (1838).

ETYMOLOGY: Greek for gape (open mouth) and flower. Refers to the fanciful resemblance of the flower, when viewed from its side, to a panting dog with its tongue hanging out.

TYPE SPECIES: *Chaenanthe barkeri* Lindley

Now recognized as belonging to the genus *Diadenium*, *Chaenanthe* was previously considered to include one epiphyte found in wet, low to mid elevation, hill and montane forests of northern Brazil (Pernambuco and Pará) and eastern Ecuador. This plant has flattened, ovate pseudobulbs, each with a solitary, oblong leaf. The often hanging, few-flowered inflorescence has pink flowers whose united lateral sepals lengthen into a bag-shape that hangs down in front of the ovary. The entire lip, joined along the column for nearly its whole length, has a long, sepaline spur.

CHAERADOPLECTRON

An orthographic variant introduced in *Gen. Pl., Suppl. 3 (Endlicher)*, **3**: 62 (1843). The correct spelling is *Choeradoplectron*.

CHAERODOPLECTRON

An orthographic variant cited in *Lex. Gen. Phan.*, 113 (1904). The correct spelling is *Choeradoplectron*.

CHAEROPLECTRON

An orthographic variant introduced in *Orchid.-Buch*, 517 (1892). The correct spelling is *Choeradoplectron*.

CHAETOCEPHALA

Barbosa Rodrigues

Gen. Sp. Orchid. **2**: 37, t. 802 (1881).

ETYMOLOGY: Greek for hair, bristle or mane and head. Refers to the hair covering the tip of the anthers in the type species.

LECTOTYPE: *Chaetocephala punctata*
Barbosa Rodrigues

Now recognized as belonging to the genus *Myoxanthus*, *Chaetocephala* was previously considered to include two epiphytes found in dry, mid elevation, woodland scrub of Serra do Mar of southeastern Brazil (Minas Gerais to Paraná). These large, wiry plants have secondary stems, sometimes swollen at the base, each with several, narrow leaves. The several, solitary-flowered inflorescences have a green or yellow-nerved flower variously dotted purple, with similar sepals and the long, tail-like petals have knob-like tips. The dark orange, trilobed lip is suffused purple at the base, and the anther cap has tufted hairs.

CHAMACORCHIS

An orthographic variant introduced in *Naturgesch. Pflanzenr.*, 85 (1890). The correct spelling is *Chamorchis*.

CHAMAEANGIS

Schlechter

Validated: *Beih. Bot. Centralbl.* **36**(2): 107 (1918), *Bot. Jahrb. Syst.* **53**: 597 (1915), and *Beih. Bot. Centralbl.* **33**(2): 426 (1915).

Epidendroideæ ※ Vandeæ • Aerangidinæ

ETYMOLOGY: Greek for low growth or on the ground and vessel. Referring to the swollen, vessel-like spur of these small flowers.

LECTOTYPE: *Chamaeangis gracilis*
(Thouars) Schlechter
(*Angraecum gracile* Thouars)

Ten small, monopodial epiphytes are found in low to upper elevation, hill to montane rain forests and river scrub from Ivory Coast to Uganda, São Tomé, Angola to Tanzania, Madagascar and the Mascarene Islands. These plants have short, hanging to erect, leafy stems (becoming woody with age), each with several, distichous, narrow, usually fleshy, unequally bilobed leaves. The several, long, hanging, numerous to few-flowered inflorescence has whorls of minute, intricate flowers borne at the nodes. The fragrant, green, yellow, orange or creamy-colored flowers do not open widely. The broad, entire lip has a blunt or rounded tip, and have an exceedingly long, decurved spur with a swollen tip. The flowers have a short, stout,

fleshy, footless column that is either winged or wingless.

CHAMAEANTHUS

Schlechter

Orch. Java **1**: 552 (1905).
Not *Chamaeanthus* Ule (1908) Commelinaceæ.

Epidendroideæ ※ Vandeæ • Aeridinæ

ETYMOLOGY: Greek for dwarfness or low growth and flower. Refers to the tiny, insignificant flower and its low growth habit.

TYPE SPECIES: *Chamaeanthus brachystachys*
Schlechter

Two small, monopodial epiphytes are found in low elevation, hill forests from Malaysia to New Caledonia and the Philippines. These dwarf, inconspicuous plants form dense mats, and have short stems, each with only a few leaves. One species has somewhat fleshy leaves. The short, numerous-flowered inflorescence, borne from stem nodes, has tiny, short-lived, green-yellow flowers that open only slightly and with only a few open at any one time. The trilobed lip, attached to the end of the column foot, has erect, thin side lobes, and a fleshy, triangular midlobe with a somewhat thread-like margin. The flowers have a short, erect to slightly bow-shaped, wingless column.

CHAMAEGASTRODIA

Makino & Maekawa

Bot. Mag. (Tokyo) **49**(585): 596 (1935).

Orchidoideæ ※ Cranichideæ • Goodyerinæ

ETYMOLOGY: Greek for lowly or on the ground and *Gastrodia*, a genus of orchids. Referring to a similarity to a small *Gastrodia* species.

TYPE SPECIES: *Chamaegastrodia shikokiana*
(Makino) Makino & Maekawa
(*Gastrodia shikokiana* Makino)

Five small, odd, leafless saprophytes are found in mid to upper elevation, hill scrub and montane evergreen forests of Korea, Japan, southern China (Xizang, Yunnan and Sichuan), northeastern India (Assam), Nepal and Thailand to Vietnam. These erect plants have leafless, unbranched, yellow, yellow-brown, pale brown-red or suffused purple-red stems, each with numerous, sheath-like, red, clasping scales spaced upward. The few-flowered, hairy to smooth inflorescence (with clasping sheaths) has a unique, yellow or pale brown-red flower with the petals and sepals united into a tubular shape. The mobile, trilobed lip has a sac-like hypochile, and the mesochile along with the epichile is T-shaped. The flowers have a short, stout, footless column. The outer surface of the flowers has a rough or warty appearance. Some of the species were formerly included in *Evrardianthe*.

ROSEWARNE LEARNING CENTRE

CHAMAEGASTRODIUM

An orthographic variant introduced in *Orchideen (Schlechter)*, ed. 3, **6**(17-20): 307 (1976). The correct spelling is *Chamaegastrodia*.

CHAMAELEORCHIS

Senghas & Lückel

Orchideen (Schlechter), ed. 3 **I/C**(33-36): 2305 (1997).

ETYMOLOGY: Latin for chameleon and orchid. Refers to the unclear position of the type species (*Miltonia warscewiczii*) that did not fit into any genus.

TYPE SPECIES: *Chamaeleorchis warscewiczii* (Reichenbach f.) Senghas & Lückel (*Miltonia warscewiczii* Reichenbach f.)

Now recognized as belonging to the genus *Oncidium*, *Chamaeleorchis* was proposed to include one epiphyte found in mid elevation, montane forests from Panama to Peru. This plant has clustered, compressed pseudobulbs, each with a solitary, leathery leaf. The few to numerous-flowered inflorescence has fragrant, wide-spreading, waxy, white flowers opening all at once and tipped brown-red or yellow. The rosy-purple to red-brown, oblong, entire lip has a wide, white margin, is deeply bilobed at the tip, and has a disc with two small, yellow teeth. The flowers have a short, stout column. The above type name is now considered a synonym of *Oncidium fuscatum* Reichenbach f.

CHAMAELOPHYTON

An orthographic variant cited in *Handb. Orchid.-Namen*, 186 (2005). The correct spelling is *Chamelophyton*.

CHAMAEORCHIS

C. Bauhin

Pinax 84 (1623).

Pre-1753, therefore not validly published in fulfillment of nomenclatural rules; this name is most often referred to *Chamorchis*.

CHAMAEORCHIS

Hudson

Fl. Angl. (Hudson), ed. 2 **2**: 390 (1778).
ETYMOLOGY: Greek for lowly or small and orchid.
TYPE SPECIES: *None designated*

Name published without a description. Today this name is most often referred to *Chamorchis*.

CHAMAEREPENS

An orthographic variant cited in *Handb. Orchid.-Namen*, 186 (2005). The correct spelling is *Chamaerepes*.

CHAMAEREPES

Sprengel

Syst. Veg. (Sprengel), ed. 16. **3**: 676, 702 (1826).
ETYMOLOGY: Greek for lowly or prostrate and Latin for to creep. Referring to the growth habit of the plant as it hugs the ground in an almost creeping habit.

TYPE SPECIES: *Chamaerepes alpina* (Linnaeus) Sprengel (*Ophrys alpina* Linnaeus)

Now recognized as belonging to the genus *Chamorchis*, *Chamaerepes* was previously considered to include one terrestrial found in upper elevation, montane rocky scrub, nutrient-poor meadows from Sweden to northwestern Russia and France, Germany to Romania. This small, erect plant has unbranched, stout stems, each with several, narrow, grass-like leaves. The numerous-flowered inflorescence has tiny, green flowers suffused brown-purple with the sepals and petals converge, forming a hood over the small column. The tiny, yellow-green, entire lip is tongue-shaped. The above type name is now considered a synonym of *Chamorchis alpina* (Linnaeus) Richard.

CHAMAESTYRAX

Fuchs ex Gesner

Opera Bot. **2**: 21 (1770).
ETYMOLOGY: Greek for lowly and resin or fragrance. Refers to the small, dark colored, fragrant flowers.
TYPE SPECIES: *None designated*

Name published without a description. Today this name is most often referred to *Nigritella*.

CHAMELOPHYTON

Garay

Orquideologia **9**(2): 115 (1974).
Epidendroideæ ⚘ Epidendreæ • Pleurothallidinæ
ETYMOLOGY: Greek for lowly or creeping and plant. In reference to the growth habit of the genus.

TYPE SPECIES: *Chamelophyton kegelii* (Reichenbach f.) Garay (*Restrepia kegelii* Reichenbach f.)

One sympodial epiphyte is found in shady, mid to upper elevation, montane forests of northeastern Venezuela and the Guianas. This tiny, creeping plant, often forming dense mats, has a thick, leathery, roundish leaf that is dark green, warty on top and purple underneath. The solitary-flowered inflorescence has a pale brown flower with maroon overlays and barely opens. The fleshy, pale brown, trilobed lip, hinged at the base of the column foot, is suffused or spotted maroon, has upward curved side lobes, a forward pointing, rounded midlobe with a broadly rounded tip and has a pair of calli near the middle. The flowers have a small, yellow, slightly club-shaped, narrowly winged column and anther cap.

CHAMORCHIS

Richard

De Orchid. Eur. 20, 27, 35 (1817), and *Mém. Mus. Hist. Nat.* **4**: 49 (1818).
Orchidoideæ ⚘ Orchideæ • Orchidinæ
ETYMOLOGY: Greek for lowly or dwarf and orchid. Referring to the small size of the plant.

TYPE SPECIES: *Chamorchis alpina* (Linnaeus) Richard (*Ophrys alpina* Linnaeus)

One sympodial terrestrial is confined to upper elevation, montane rocky meadows and grasslands, that have only a slight covering of snow in winter. They range from the European Alps, across Sweden, northern Norway, northern Finland, and a small area of the Carpathian Mountains (Poland, Slovakia, Ukraine and eastern Romania). This tiny, erect plant, often forming large colonies, has unbranched, erect stems, each with several, grass-like, basal leaves. The short, numerous to few-flowered inflorescence has small, yellow-green flowers suffused brown. The sepals and small petals converge, forming a hood over the minute, wingless, footless column. The tongue-shaped, obscurely trilobed or entire lip has two basal swellings.

CHANGNIENIA

S.S. Chien

Contr. Biol. Lab. Sci. Soc. China, Bot. Ser. **10**: 89 (1935).
Epidendroideæ ⚘ Calypsoeæ
ETYMOLOGY: Dedicated to Chang-nien Chen (1900-x), a Chinese botanical collector from the Research Institute of Biology in Nanjing, who collected the type species.

TYPE SPECIES: *Changnienia amoena* S.S. Chien

One sympodial terrestrial is found in humid, low to mid elevation, open evergreen forests and valley slopes of southeastern China (Anhui, Hubei, Hunan, Jiangsu, Jiangxi, Shaanxi, Sichuan, Zhejiang and Xizang). This small, charming plant has ovoid to corm-shaped pseudobulbs (found below ground), each with a solitary, broadly oval leaf that is purple on the underside. The short, slender, solitary-flowered inflorescence, borne from the tip of the

Currently Accepted | Validly Published | Invalidly Published | Published Pre-1753 | Superfluous Usage | Orthographic Variant | Fossil

Orchid Genera • **76**

pseudobulb, has a large, white, pink to pale purple flower with similar sepals and spreading petals. The broad, white, trilobed lip has erect side lobes surrounding the small, incurved, winged column. The spreading, purple spotted midlobe has a wavy margin, and a large, stiffly swollen, tapering, curved, horn-like spur.

NOTE: The little pseudobulbs are used by the local people as a medical treatment for sores and snakebites.

CHARADOPLECTRON

An orthographic variant cited in *Handb. Orchid.-Namen*, 186 (2005). The correct spelling is *Choeradoplectron*.

CHASEELLA

Summerhayes

Kirkia   **1**: 88 (1961).

Epidendroideæ ⚘ Dendrobiinæ • Currently unplaced

ETYMOLOGY: Honoring Norman Centlivres Chase (1888-1970), a British-born plant collector who contributed much to our knowledge of Zimbabwe and Zambian orchids. And Latin for diminutive.

TYPE SPECIES: *Chaseella pseudohydra* Summerhayes

One tiny, sympodial epiphyte is found in upper elevation, evergreen forests of Zimbabwe (Honde and Haroni Valleys), Kenya and eastern Zambia. This minuscule plant is extremely difficult to locate among the tree branches. Each of its tiny, roundish, gray-green pseudobulbs, borne well-spaced along the rhizome, have a radiating topknot or rosette of tiny, stiff, needle-like leaves. The solitary-flowered inflorescence has a minute, dark red to pale yellow flower with a cup-shaped dorsal sepal, broad lateral sepals that taper to sharp points, and small, roundish petals. The red-brown to orange, tongue-shaped, mobile, obscurely trilobed or entire lip is somewhat recurved and has a short claw. The flowers have an erect, white, slightly curved, stout column with long, broad wings.

CHAUBARDIA

Reichenbach *filius*

Bot. Zeitung (Berlin)   **10**: 671 (1852).

Epidendroideæ ⚘ Cymbidieæ • Zygopetalinæ

ETYMOLOGY: Dedicated to Louis Anthanase (Anastase) Chaubard (1785-1854), a French lawyer, botanist, nurseryman and co-author of *Nouvelle flore du Peloponnèse et des Cyclade*.

TYPE SPECIES: *Chaubardia surinamensis* Reichenbach f.

Five sympodial epiphytes are found in wet, low elevation, tropical forests of Trinidad, the Guianas, Brazil and Ecuador to Bolivia. These plants have small, fan-like clusters of thin, distichous leaves or may have only one leaf on a small, often inconspicuous, concealed pseudobulb that is subtended by lateral or sheathing leaves. The several, short, erect to arching, solitary-flowered inflorescences, borne from the leaf axils, have a small, flat, pale green to white flower while some species have glossy sepals streaked chestnut brown. The narrow, spreading sepals and petals have margins that are sometimes strongly curved. Edges of the shortly clawed, fleshy, obscurely trilobed lip are violet-blue to pink with a prominent raised, toothed callus. The flowers have a long, slightly curved, broadly winged column.

CHAUBARDIELLA

Garay

Orquideologia   **4**: 146 (1969).

Epidendroideæ ⚘ Cymbidieæ • Zygopetalinæ

ETYMOLOGY: *Chaubardia*, a genus of orchids and Latin for diminutive. Referring to the similarity of the flowers to those of *Chaubardia*.

TYPE SPECIES: *Chaubardiella tigrina*
(Garay & Dunsterville) Garay
(*Chaubardia tigrina* Garay & Dunsterville)

Eight sympodial epiphytes are found in low to mid elevation, tropical forests from Costa Rica to Peru. These small, fan-shaped plants have short, leafy stems with distichous, thin, narrowly oblong leaves. The short, slender inflorescence, borne from the axils of leaf sheaths, often lays on the ground or is hanging. The solitary-flowered inflorescence has a showy, cream to yellow flower heavily marbled with irregular maroon bars and bands giving the flower an appearance of being brown colored. The strongly concave, shortly clawed, shallowly cup-shaped, entire lip has a callus in the middle with a slender, elongate tooth on each side. The flowers have a short, stout, fleshy, hairy, broadly, triangular winged column.

CHAULIODON

Summerhayes

Bot. Mus. Leafl.   **11**: 163 (1943).

Epidendroideæ ⚘ Vandeæ • Aerangidinæ

ETYMOLOGY: Greek for with outstanding or projecting teeth. An allusion to the enormous tooth on the lip.

TYPE SPECIES: *Chauliodon buntingii* Summerhayes
This type name is now considered a synonym of
Chauliodon deflexicalcaratum (De Wildeman) L. Jonsson;
basionym
Angraecum deflexicalcaratum De Wildeman

One monopodial epiphyte is found in low to mid elevation, hill scrub and rain forests from Liberia to southern Nigeria, Gabon and Zaire. This short-stemmed, dwarf plant is completely leafless but has a mass of clambering, tangled roots. The several, hanging, few-flowered inflorescences have tiny, brown-rose or white flowers whose segments curve abruptly backward in the middle. The most distinctive feature is the balloon-like, entire lip with the lamina reduced to a tooth-like point. The tall, erect callus is found in front of the spur mouth, and the cylindrical spur is abruptly bent downward at a sharp angle. The flowers have a long, wingless, footless column.

CHAULIODUM

An orthographic variant introduced in *Bot. Mus. Leafl.*, **11**: 163 (1943). The correct spelling is *Chauliodon*.

CHEILOGLOTIS

An orthographic variant introduced in *Not. Pl. Asiat.*, **3**: 271 (1851). The correct spelling is *Chiloglottis*.

CHEIRADEMIA

An orthographic variant introduced in *Etim. Orquidofilos*, 33 (1998). The correct spelling is *Cheiradenia*.

CHEIRADENIA

Lindley

Fol. Orchid.   **4**: *Cheiradenia*, 1 (1853).

Epidendroideæ ⚘ Cymbidieæ • Zygopetalinæ

ETYMOLOGY: Greek for hand and gland. From the elevated callus terminating in a finger-like protuberance on the lip.

TYPE SPECIES: *Cheiradenia cuspidata* Lindley

One uncommon, nondescript, epiphyte or occasionally lithophyte is found in low elevation, rain forests from the Guianas, Venezuela and northern Brazil. This small plant has slender, thinly textured leaves arranged in a fan or tuft-shape. The wand-like, few-flowered, green-brown inflorescence has white flowers backed by a rosette of bracts. The petals are often suffused with dark purple marks. The deeply, cup-shaped, obscurely trilobed lip has a forward projecting callus of two elongate teeth, and the side lobes tend to curve inward over the top of the callus. The flowers have a short, broad, slightly curved column.

CHEIRADOPLECTUM

An orthographic variant cited in *Etym.-Bot.-Handw.-Buch*, ed. 1, 187 (1852). The correct spelling is *Choeradoplectron*.

CHEIROPTEROCEPHALUS

Barbosa Rodrigues

Gen. Sp. Orchid. **1**: 28, *t. 396* (1877).

ETYMOLOGY: Greek for a hand, wing and head. Descriptive of the bizarre flower that resembles a bat's head.

TYPE SPECIES: *Cheiropterocephalus sertuliferus* Barbosa Rodrigues

This type name is now considered a synonym of *Malaxis excavata* (Lindley) Kuntze; basionym *Microstylis excavata* Lindley

Now recognized as belonging to the genus *Malaxis*, *Cheiropterocephalus* was previously considered to include one terrestrial found in cool, mid to upper elevation, montane forests from Mexico to southeastern Brazil and northern Argentina. This inconspicuous, small plant has short stems to cone-like pseudobulbs, subtended by a few leafless sheathing bracts, each with two long, clasping leaves that taper to a point. The short, head-like, numerous-flowered inflorescence has tiny, green flowers with a broad, triangular to oblong, heart-shaped, green, entire lip. The flowers have a small, yellow column.

CHEIRORCHIS

Carrière

Gard. Bull. Straits Settlem. **7**: 40 (1932).

ETYMOLOGY: Greek for a hand and orchid. Refers to the distinct, hand-like growth habit.

LECTOTYPE: *Cheirorchis breviscapa* Carrière

Now recognized as belonging to the genus *Cordiglottis*, *Cheirorchis* was previously considered to include five epiphytes found in wet, low elevation, woodland and scrub of Thailand and Malaysia. These small, hanging plants have short stems, each with several, flattened, slightly curved, dull yellow-green leaves that have overlapping basal sheaths. The short, few to numerous-flowered inflorescence, borne from lower leaf axils, has tiny, short-lived, translucent, creamy flowers suffused pale rosy-mauve. The mobile, tiny, clawed, obscurely trilobed lip has insignificant, short side lobes, and a densely powdery, ovate midlobe. The flowers have a short column with long wings.

CHEIROSTYLIS

Blume

Bijdr. Fl. Ned. Ind. **8**: 413, *t. 16* (1825).

Orchidoideæ ⚘ Cranichideæ • Goodyerinæ

ETYMOLOGY: Greek for a hand and pillar or style. Refers to the lobed tip of the column (clinandrium) that bears a striking resemblance to a hand.

TYPE SPECIES: *Cheirostylis montana* Blume

Forty-seven insignificant, sympodial epiphytes or terrestrials are found in low to upper elevation, dense forests and scrub from Ethiopia, Nigeria to Uganda, Madagascar, the Comoros Islands, southern China, northeastern India (Assam), Indonesia to the Philippines and New Guinea to Australia. These small, erect creeping plants have short to long, slender stems, each with green to purple-green, softly textured leaves that are sometimes withered by flowering and/or lightly veined. The hairy or smooth, long or short, few-flowered inflorescence has small, pale olive-green to white flowers. The tube-like, slender, smooth or hairy (on the outer surfaces) sepals are joined for nearly their entire length, enclosing the base to all of the lip. The pristine white, trilobed lip has a sac-like hypochile with several, papillose glands, a short, narrowly clawed mesochile, and the entire epichile is deeply bilobed near the tip. The flowers have a short, footless column.

CHEIROSTYLUS

An orthographic variant introduced in *Nat. Syst. Bot.*, ed. 2, 341 (1836). The correct spelling is *Cheirostylis*.

CHELANTHERA

An orthographic variant introduced in *J. Hort. Prat. Belgique*, ser. 2, 168 (1858). The correct spelling is *Chelonanthera*.

CHELOGYNE

An orthographic variant introduced in *Enum. Phan. Born.*, 204 (1942). The correct spelling is *Coelogyne*.

CHELONANTHERA

Blume

Bijdr. Fl. Ned. Ind. **8**: 382, *t. 51* (1825).

ETYMOLOGY: Greek for turtle and anther. Alluding to the two-valved anther and its fancied resemblance to a turtle.

LECTOTYPE: *Chelonanthera gibbosa* Blume

This type name is now considered a synonym of *Pholidota gibbosa* (Blume) Lindley ex de Vriese; basionym *Chelonanthera gibbosa* Blume

Now recognized as belonging to the genera *Pholidota* and *Coelogyne*, *Chelonanthera* was previously considered to include eight epiphytes distributed from Malaysia to Indonesia and the Solomons to the southwestern Pacific Archipelago. These plants have well-spaced, cylindrical pseudobulbs, each with one to two, fleshy leaves. The slender, few to numerous-flowered inflorescence, borne at the tip of new pseudobulbs, is conspicuously zig-zagged in two alternating ranks. The small, creamy, faintly pink, yellow-green to pale brown flowers have concave sepals and similar or narrower petals. The trilobed or obscurely trilobed lip has small side lobes and a broad, deeply cleft midlobe. The flowers have a short, winged, footless column.

CHELONENTHERA

An orthographic variant introduced in *Orchid Fl. Kamrup Distr. Assam*, 185 (2001). The correct spelling is *Chelonanthera*.

CHELONISTELE

Pfitzer

Pflanzenr. (Engler) **IV.50**(II.B.7): 136 (1907).

Epidendroideæ ⚘ Arethuseæ • Coelogyninæ

ETYMOLOGY: Greek for tortoise shell and column. Refers to the winged column hood, which resembles the dorsal portion of a turtle shell.

TYPE SPECIES: *Chelonistele sulphurea* (Blume) Pfitzer (*Chelonanthera sulphurea* Blume)

Twelve epiphytes or lithophytes are found in low to upper elevation, hill to montane forests and scrub from Malaysia, Indonesia (Sumatra, Java and Borneo) and the southern Philippines with most of the species found in Borneo. These plants have clustered, ovoid or cone-shaped, pencil-like to flattened pseudobulbs, all turned to one side of the rhizome, each with two usually tough, deciduous, pleated, narrow leaves. The erect to spreading or curved, numerous to few-flowered inflorescence is subtended by floral bracts and borne from the

Currently Accepted   Validly Published   Invalidly Published   Published Pre-1753   Superfluous Usage   Orthographic Variant   Fossil

O r c h i d   G e n e r a   • **78**

tips of new pseudobulbs. The fragrant, creamy to white flowers range from thin to rather fleshy-textured. They open widely or barely open, and has a few open or all will open at the same time. The white, sometimes obscurely trilobed or bilobed lip, downward hanging, has a dark colored callus at the narrow, sac-like or concave base. The flowers have a wedge-shaped, winged, footless column.

CHELROSTYLIS

An orthographic variant cited in *Icon. Bot. Index*, 255 (1855). The correct spelling is *Cheirostylis*.

CHELYORCHIS

Dressler & N.H. Williams
Orchids Venezuela, ed. 2   **3**: 1130 (2000).

Epidendroideæ ⚘ Cymbidieæ • Oncidiinæ

ETYMOLOGY: Greek for turtle or tortoise, and orchid. In reference to the flattened, bumpy, spotted pseudobulbs that look like a cluster of small, lumpy turtle-shells.

TYPE SPECIES: *Chelyorchis ampliata*
(Lindley) Dressler & N.H. Williams
(*Oncidium ampliatum* Lindley)

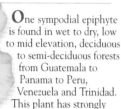

One sympodial epiphyte is found in wet to dry, low to mid elevation, deciduous to semi-deciduous forests from Guatemala to Panama to Peru, Venezuela and Trinidad. This plant has strongly compressed, ridged, bright green pseudobulbs sprinkled with purple spots, each with two, elliptical, leathery leaves. The multibranched, erect or arching, flat-topped, numerous-flowered inflorescence has bright yellow flowers with clawed, ear-like petals. The slightly smaller sepals are densely covered with chestnut spots or blotches. The bright yellow, clawed, deeply trilobed lip is almost white on the backside, has tiny, erect side lobes, has a broad, bilobed midlobe that is kidney-shaped to oblong, and has a wavy margin. The flowers have a short, erect, winged column.

CHENOPLESIUM

An orthographic variant introduced in *Syn. Pl. (D. Dietrich)*, **5**: 173 (1852). The correct spelling is *Genoplesium*.

CHICHILTIC

Hernández
Rerum Med. Nov. Hisp. Thes.   **1**: 368 (1651).

ETYMOLOGY: A local Nahuatl (Aztec) word for red, mountain or volcano, and flower.

TYPE SPECIES: *Chichiltic tepetlauhxochitl* Hernández

Pre-1753, therefore not validly published in fulfillment of nomenclatural rules; this name is most often referred to *Laelia*. *Chichiltic* was previously considered to include one epiphyte found over a wide area of the central Mexico plateau and surrounding highlands on oak trees in open, dry, deciduous, stunted forests. This small plant has pear-shaped pseudobulbs, each with two oblong, leathery leaves. The solitary or rarely two-flowered inflorescence has a large, showy flower ranging from dark to pale lavender with lavender dots sprinkled on the white lip. This name is usually now considered as a synonym of *Laelia speciosa* (Kunth) Schlechter.

CHICHULTIC

An orthographic variant cited in *Herb. Amboin. (Rumphius)*, **6**: 106 (1750). The correct spelling is *Chichiltic*.

CHILOCHISTA

An orthographic variant introduced in *Icon. Pl. Ind. Orient. (Wight)*, **3**: t. *1741* (1851). The correct spelling is *Chiloschista*.

CHILOGLOTTIS

R. Brown
Prodr. Fl. Nov. Holland.   322 (1810).

Orchidoideæ ⚘ Diurideæ • Thelymitrinæ

ETYMOLOGY: Greek for lip and gullet, tongue or mouth. From the resemblance of the lip and callus to a human throat.

TYPE SPECIES: *Chiloglottis diphylla* R. Brown

This type name is now considered a synonym of
Chiloglottis reflexa (Labillardière) Druce;
basionym
Epipactis reflexa Labillardière

Twenty-seven small, sympodial terrestrials are found in moist, low to mid elevation, forest litter of eastern Australia, Tasmania, New Zealand, Chatham, Stewart and Campbell Islands. These tiny, erect plants have short, unbranched stems, each with two roundish, basal leaves held opposite each other against the ground. They reproduce solely by seed and often form large, free-flowering colonies. The short, solitary-flowered inflorescence (elongates after

pollination) has a dull green to red-brown flower marked with purple or brown. The broad dorsal sepal is incurved over the prominent, slightly curved column, and the lateral sepals are united at the base. The shortly clawed, large, entire lip has tremulous or limited movement, a group or line of various shaped and sized calli that resemble the appearance and with the fragrance of a female wasp.

CHILOPOGON

Schlechter
Repert. Spec. Nov. Regni Veg. Beih. **1**(5): 325, 332 (1912).

Epidendroideæ ⚘ Podochileæ • Podochilinæ

ETYMOLOGY: Greek for lip and beard. In reference to the bearded claw of the lip.

TYPE SPECIES: *None designated*

Three uncommon, sympodial epiphytes or lithophytes are found in typically wet, low to mid elevation, hill scrub and montane rain forests of New Guinea and the Solomon Islands. These tufted plants, forming small colonies, have creeping, erect to often hanging stems, subtended by small, overlapping, dark green leaves. The solitary-flowered inflorescence is subtended by several, large sheaths that have sharp-pointed bristled, white margins. The small, white or yellow flower, darkens as it ages and has only one flower open at a time. The concave lateral sepals extend into sharp-pointed, hollow horns, and has tiny, roundish petals. The widespread, white, wedge-shaped, entire lip has a basal disc separated from the short spur by long, white, tangled hairs. The flowers have an erect, short, footless column.

CHILOSCHISTA

Lindley
Edwards's Bot. Reg.   **18**: sub 1522 (1832).

Epidendroideæ ⚘ Vandeæ • Aeridinæ

ETYMOLOGY: Greek for lip and cleft or to cut. Alluding to the cleft (cut almost to the middle) of the lip.

TYPE SPECIES: *Chiloschista usneoides* (D. Don) Lindley
(*Epidendrum usneoides* D. Don)

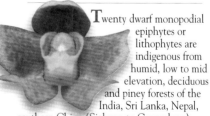

Twenty dwarf monopodial epiphytes or lithophytes are indigenous from humid, low to mid elevation, deciduous and piney forests of the India, Sri Lanka, Nepal, southern China (Sichuan to Guangdong), Taiwan, Myanmar to Thailand, Indonesia, New Guinea to northern Australia and the southwestern Pacific Archipelago. These short-stemmed (often without a distinct stem), leafless plants or rarely with only several, small leaves, have an entangled mass of roots that grasps the host. The hairy or smooth, branched or unbranched, numerous to few-flowered inflorescence has small, showy, white to golden yellow, lightly fragrant flowers. The flowers often have crimson spots ranging from several specks to large blotches and the backside of these flowers are often quite hairy. The clawed, trilobed lip forms a small pouch and has large, erect side lobes. The very short and small or slightly longer, widespreading midlobe has congested keels or callus. The flowers have a very short, erect, wingless column.

CHILOTERUS

D.L. Jones & M.A. Clements
Orchadian **14**(8: Sci. Suppl.): xiii (2004).
ETYMOLOGY: Greek for nose and bag. Refers to the pouch-structure at the base of the united sepals which encloses the column foot and lip base.
TYPE SPECIES: *Chiloterus cucullatum*
(Reichenbach f.) D.L. Jones & M.A. Clements
(*Prasophyllum cucullatum* Reichenbach f.)

Recognized as belonging to the genus *Prasophyllum*, *Chiloterus* was proposed to include two terrestrials found in low elevation, swamp and boggy margins of southwestern Australia. These small, erect plants have slender, unbranched stems, each with a narrow, grass-like leaf that is fused to the stem for much of its length. The erect, numerous-flowered inflorescence breaks through the leaf. The sweetly fragrant, white flowers have bright purple markings. The lateral, incurved sepals are united to their tips forming a hood above and in front of the lip. The entire lip, attached to a long claw, is erect for much of its length and has a wavy, scalloped and finely notched margin. The flowers have column appendages of variable length with a backward bent tip.

CHILYATHUM

T. Post & Kuntze
Lex. Gen. Phan. 119 (1904).
ETYMOLOGY: Greek for lip and flower.
TYPE SPECIES: *None designated*

Name published without a description. Today this name is most often referred to as a section of *Oncidium*.

CHIOGLOTTIS

An orthographic variant introduced in *Syn. Pl.* (D. Dietrich), **5**: 177 (1852). The correct spelling is *Chiloglottis*.

CHIRADENIA

An orthographic variant cited in *Lex. Gen. Phan.*, 117, 120 (1904). The correct spelling is *Cheiradenia*.

CHIRONIELLA

Braem
Richardiana **6**(2): 108 (2006).
Epidendroideæ Cymbidieæ • Oncidiinæ
ETYMOLOGY: Honoring Guy Robert Chiron (1944-), a French naturalist and author of *Pahiopedilum* and *Cattleya, Laelia et Genres Allies*. And Latin for diminutive.
TYPE SPECIES: *Chironiella crispa* (Lindley) Braem
(*Laelia crispa* Lindley)

One sympodial epiphyte or occasional lithophyte is found in low to mid elevation, hill and montane forests of Brazil (Espírito Santo, Rio de Janeiro and Minas Gerais). This often massively clumped plant has compressed, club-shaped, long, grooved stems, each with a solitary, oblong leaf that has a notched tip. The few-flowered inflorescence, subtended by a compressed sheath, has showy, fragrant, long-lasting, white flowers suffused purple toward the base. The narrow sepals and petals have wavy, crisp margins. The trilobed lip has large, broad, erect side lobes that surround the long, club-shaped column and has an oblong midlobe with deep purple-red radiating veins, a deep yellow basal callus and a crisped margin.

CHIROSTYLIS

An orthographic variant cited in *Lex. Gen. Phan.*, 118, 120 (1904). The correct spelling is *Cheirostylis*.

CHIRRHAEA

An orthographic variant introduced in *Gartenbeobachter*, **4**: 113 (1840). The correct spelling is *Cirrhaea*.

CHISIS

An orthographic variant introduced in *Neue Allg. Garten- Blumenzeitung*, **1**: 319 (1845-46). The correct spelling is *Chysis*.

CHITONANTHERA

Schlechter
Nachtr. Fl. Schutzgeb. Südsee 193 (1905).
ETYMOLOGY: Greek for tunic, covering or cloak and anther. Refers to the projection of the clinandrium that surrounds the anther like a tunic.
TYPE SPECIES: *None designated*

Now recognized as belonging to the genus *Octarrhena*, *Chitonanthera* was previously considered to include

twenty-four epiphytes found in misty, upper elevation, forest canopies of New Guinea. These uncommon, dwarf plants have erect, spreading or branched stems, each with small, flattened or pencil-shaped, jointed or unjointed leaves. The tufts of erect inflorescences are borne between the leaf nodes. The solitary to few-flowered inflorescence has tiny, often dull red, minutely hairy flowers with similar sepals, tiny, rounded petals and a tongue-shaped, entire lip. The flowers have a small, footless column.

CHITONOCHILUS

Schlechter
Nachtr. Fl. Schutzgeb. Südsee 134 (1905).
ETYMOLOGY: Greek for tunic, covering or cloak and lip. Refers to the lip that surrounds the column like a tunic.
TYPE SPECIES: *Chitonochilus papuanum* Schlechter

Now recognized as belonging to the genus *Agrostophyllum*, *Chitonochilus* was previously considered to include one epiphyte found in misty, upper elevation, montane forests of New Guinea in the Torricelli and Kani ranges. This large, robust, uninteresting plant has thin stems, each with several, narrow, small leaves. The several, few-flowered inflorescences have heads of small, white flowers with broad sepals. The petals spread outward from an erect, slender, footless column and the concave, entire lip's tip is held erect. The above type name is now considered a synonym of *Agrostophyllum neoguinense* Kittredge.

CHLOIDIA

Lindley
Gen. Sp. Orchid. Pl. 484 (1840).
ETYMOLOGY: Greek for grass-like. Referring to the habit of a branching grass-like leaves rather than that of an orchid plant.
LECTOTYPE: *Chloidia polystachya*
(Swartz) Reichenbach f.
(*Serapias polystachya* Swartz)

Now recognized as belonging to the genera *Corymborkis* and *Tropidia*, *Chloidia* was previously considered to include five terrestrials found in the Bahamas, Cuba to Puerto Rico and central Mexico to Ecuador. These erect, leafy plants have their inflorescence almost concealed in tube-shaped, leaf-bearing sheaths. The tiny, inconspicuous, translucent or pale yellow flowers have a yellow, entire lip without calli or any other appendages. The flowers have a long, slender, pale green column. The above type name is now considered a synonym of *Tropidia polystachya* (Swartz) Ames.

Currently Accepted | Validly Published | Invalidly Published | Published Pre-1753 | Superfluous Usage | Orthographic Variant | Fossil

O r c h i d   G e n e r a • **80**

CHLORAEA

Lindley

Quart. J. Sci. Lit. Arts, ser. 2   **1**(1): 47 (1827).

Orchidoideæ ⚬ Cranichideæ • Chloraeinæ

ETYMOLOGY: Greek for pale and green. Referring to the floral color of several of the species.

TYPE SPECIES: *Chloraea gavilu* Lindley nom. illeg.
(*Cymbidium luteum* Willldenow)

This type name is now considered a synonym of

LECTOTYPE: *Chloraea virescens* (Willdenow) Lindley
(*Cymbidium virescens* Willdenow)

A complex genus of fifty-one sympodial terrestrials are found in cool, mid to upper elevation, rocky to grassy slopes, thorny thickets and along river banks from southern Brazil, Uruguay, Argentina, the Falkland Islands, Peru and Bolivia with the most species found in Chile. These robust plants have erect, unbranched stems, each with a basal rosette or has flat, narrow to ovate, shiny leaves scattered along the stem. The erect, slender to robust, few to numerous-flowered inflorescence has large, brightly colored to boldly patterned, white, green, yellow, orange or red flowers. The lateral sepals (with or without wart-like outgrowths) have short to long, swollen tips. The short, broad petals (entire or with tooth margins) are joined to the dorsal sepal. The entire or trilobed (usually hairy and often a different color) lip has a long to short claw, without or with a callus of crests, and has entire or usually pinnately cleft, toothed or wavy margins. The flowers have a long, slightly curved column.

CHLOREA

An orthographic variant introduced in *Ann. Sci. Nat. (Paris)*, ser. 2, **4**: 314 (1835). The correct spelling is *Chloraea*.

CHLOROSA

Blume

Bijdr. Fl. Ned. Ind.   **8**: 420, t. 31 (1825).

ETYMOLOGY: Greek for green. Referring to the color of the flower.

TYPE SPECIES: *None designated*

Now recognized as belonging to the genus *Cryptostylis*, *Chlorosa* was previously considered to include two nondescript terrestrials found on Mount Kinabalu in Malaysia (Sabah) and also Indonesia (Java). These erect plants have several, softly textured, broad leaves with a more or less distinct network of dark colored veins that are often spotted purple. The erect, few-flowered inflorescence has small, waxy, yellow-green flowers suffused dull red with very narrow segments.

CHOERADOPLECTRON

Schauer

Nov. Actorum Acad. Caes. Leop.-Carol. Nat. Cur., ser. 3   **19**(Suppl. 1): 436 (1843), or
Observ. Bot.   **16**(Suppl. 2): 436 (1843).

ETYMOLOGY: Greek for neck or gland and spur. Refers to the long spur that is apically somewhat swollen and resembles a gland.

TYPE SPECIES: *Choeradoplectron spiranthes* Schauer

This type name is now considered a synonym of
Peristylus lacertifer (Lindley) J.J. Smith;
basionym
Coeloglossum lacertiferum Lindley

Now recognized as belonging to the genus *Peristylus*, *Choeradoplectron* was previously considered to include one terrestrial found in Myanmar, Thailand, Malaysia and Indonesia. This plant has erect, unbranched stems, each with a few leaves close to the base and has several, bract-like leaves spaced up the stem. The long, few-flowered inflorescence has small, pale green flowers not opening widely. The dorsal sepal and petals converge over the short column, and the long lateral sepals point upward. The broad, trilobed lip has narrow, curved side lobes, the midlobe is shorter with a roundish tip, and the short, forward bent spur has a blunt point.

CHOERODOPLECTRON

An orthographic variant cited in *Hist. Nat. Veg. (Spach)*, **12**: 181 (1846). The correct spelling is *Choeradoplectron*.

CHONDORRHYNCHA

An orthographic variant introduced in *Repert. Spec. Nov. Regni Veg. Beih.*, **19**: 301 (1923). The correct spelling is *Chondrorhyncha*.

CHONDRADENIA

Maximowicz ex Makino

Bot. Mag. (Tokyo)   **11**: 413 (1897).

Not validly published, this name is most often referred to *Chondradenia* Maximowicz ex Maekawa.

CHONDRADENIA

Maximowicz ex Maekawa

Wild Orchids Japan Colour   456 (1971).

ETYMOLOGY: Greek for cartilage and gland. Refers to the cartilage-like material found in front of the spur entrance.

TYPE SPECIES: *Chondradenia fauriei*
(Finet) Sawada ex Maekawa
(*Orchis fauriei* Finet)

Now recognized as belonging to the genus *Orchis*, *Chondradenia* was previously considered to include two terrestrials found in mid to upper elevation, montane grasslands of southern Japan (Honshu), northern Myanmar and southwestern China (Yunnan). These small, uncommon plants have short stems, each with one or two, broad, ovate leaves midway up the stem. The erect or nodding, few-flowered inflorescence has leafy, floral bracts often longer than the small flowers. The white or pink flowers have somewhat spreading to narrow sepals and oblong petals with minute teeth on the upper margins. The wedged-shaped, trilobed lip is notched at the tip with a small, central tooth, and has a small, swollen spur. The flowers have a short column.

CHONDRORHYNCA

An orthographic variant introduced in *Rev. Hort. Belge Étrangère*, **30**: 71 (1904). The correct spelling is *Chondrorhyncha*.

CHONDRORHYNCHA

Lindley

Orchid. Linden.   12 (1846).

Epidendroideæ ⚬ Cymbidieæ • Zygopetalinæ

ETYMOLOGY: Greek for cartilage or grain of wheat and snout, horn or beak. Refers to the snout-like column.

TYPE SPECIES: *Chondrorhyncha rosea* Lindley

Thirty fascinating sympodial epiphytes are widespread in wet, low to upper elevation, hill to montane forests from Cuba, southern Mexico to Brazil with the largest concentration occurring in the Colombian Andes. These plants have short stems, each with oblong, pleated, nerved leaves. All are joined to the leaf-sheaths and are arranged in a fan shape. The solitary-flowered inflorescence, borne from the leaf axils, has a showy flower. The yellow or pale green flower has the sepals attached to the thick, club-shaped column base. The white, broad, funnel-shaped, entire lip is spotted rosy red, fades to a pale green at the base, and has a basal, toothed callus. The petals and lip can have either a plain or extremely frilly margin, and forms a somewhat tubular structure. The lip has a notch on either side of its base producing a false spur along with the lateral sepals that are swept backward.

CHONDRORRHYNCHA

An orthographic variant introduced in *Refug. Bot.*, **2**: sub 107 (1882). The correct spelling is *Chondrorhyncha*.

CHONDRORYNCHA

An orthographic variant introduced in *Ill. Hort.*, **28**: 80 (1881). The correct spelling is *Chondrorhyncha*.

CHONDROSCAPHE

(Dressler) Senghas & G. Gerlach
Orchideen (Schlechter), ed. 3 **1/B**(27): 1655 (1993).

Epidendroideæ ʷ Cymbidieæ • Zygopetalinæ

ETYMOLOGY: Greek for cartilage and tub, basin, bowl or boat. In reference to the lip that has a hard and tough, but flexible structure.

TYPE SPECIES: *Chondroscaphe flaveola*
(Linden & Reichenbach f.) Senghas & G. Gerlach
(*Zygopetalon flaveolum* Linden & Reichenbach f.)
This type name is now considered a synonym of
Chondroscaphe fimbriata
(Linden & Reichenbach f.) Dressler;
basionym replaced with
Stenia fimbriata Linden & Reichenbach f.

Twelve showy, psygmoid epiphytes are found in upper elevation, montane forests from Venezuela and Colombia to Peru. These fan-shaped plants have short stems, each with overlapping, thinly textured, strap-shaped, narrow leaves. The often hanging, solitary-flowered inflorescence has a large, showy, pale yellow, highly fragrant flower. The petals have finely fringed margins, and sepals have entire margins. The broad, pale yellow, roundish, entire or obscurely trilobed lip has a few chestnut blotches, an entire margin that is irregularly long to short, highly fringed, and a trilobed basal callus. The flowers have a stout to slender, slightly curved, wingless column.

CHRISTENSENIA

Not *Christensenia* Maxon (1905) Marattiaceæ.

An orthographic variant introduced in *Fragm. Florist. Geobot.*, **3**(Suppl.): 88 (1995). The correct spelling is *Christensonia*.

CHRISTENSONELLA

Szlachetko, Mytnik, Górniak & Śmiszek
Polish Bot. J. **51**(1): 57 (2006)[2007].

Epidendroideæ ʷ Cymbidieæ • Maxillariinæ

ETYMOLOGY: Dedicated to Eric Alston Christenson (1956-). And Latin for diminutive.

TYPE SPECIES: *Christensonella nardoides*
(Kraenzlin) Szlachetko, Mytnik, Górniak & Śmiszek nom. illeg.
(*Maxillaria nardoides* Kraenzlin)
Christensonella subulata
(Lindley) Szlachetko, Mytnik, Górniak & Śmiszek
(*Maxillaria subulata* Lindley)

Twenty sympodial epiphytes or lithophytes are found in moist to seasonally dry, low elevation, hill forests from southern Mexico to Bolivia, the Guianas, and Brazil to northern Argentina (Misiones). These small, clump-forming, hanging to erect plants have ovoid to pear-shaped, wrinkled to ridged, channeled pseudobulbs, subtended by overlapping, distichous, papery sheaths, each with a few long, narrow leaves. The leaves are erect to twisted, flat or folded lengthwise, leathery to fleshy or rarely thin. The short, solitary-flowered inflorescence has a small, brown or red-brown flower with widespreading segments. The entire or obscurely trilobed lip is strongly recurved to middle of the disc, has a rounded to blunt tip and an entire to notched margin. The midlobe (in most species) has a shiny purple to dark red spot covered by a hair-like mass to papillae. The flowers have a slender, slightly curved column.

CHRISTENSONIA

Haager
Orchid Digest **57**(1): 40 (1993).

Epidendroideæ ʷ Vandeæ • Sarcanthinæ

ETYMOLOGY: Named in honor of Eric Alston Christenson (1956-), an American research taxonomist specializing in orchids of southeast Asia, a prolific taxonomical and horticultural author.

TYPE SPECIES: *Christensonia vietnamica* Haager

One elegant monopodial epiphyte is found low elevation, semi-deciduous to deciduous, coastal scrub and savanna woodlands of southern Vietnam. This dwarf plant has stout stems, each with numerous, well-spaced, tough, leathery, strap-shaped leaves. The several, short, few-flowered inflorescences, borne from the leaf axils, have green-yellow flowers. The large, flat, immobile, trilobed lip has oblong, green side lobes, a broad, white midlobe with a wavy or fringed margin and a long, yellow-green spur. The flowers have a short, stout, wingless column with a short foot that is continuous with the lip.

CHROMATOTRICCUM

M.A. Clements & D.L. Jones
Orchadian **13**(11): 493 (2002).

ETYMOLOGY: Greek for color and a small bird. An allusion to the colorful flowers that are pollinated by small birds.

TYPE SPECIES: *Chromatotriccum lawesii*
(F. Mueller) M.A. Clements & D.L. Jones
(*Dendrobium lawesii* F. Mueller)

Recognized as belonging to the genus *Dendrobium*, *Chromatotriccum* was proposed to include eighty-seven epiphytes found in low to upper elevation, hill scrub and montane cloud forests from Thailand, Indonesia and New Guinea to the Solomon Islands (Bougainville to Guadalcanal). These showy plants are noted for their brightly colored flowers and certain color variants are found in only to certain small individual areas. These plants have long, slender, leafy, usually hanging stems, each with narrow, ovate, distichous, often suffused purple leaves arranged in two ranks along the length of the stem. The small, hanging inflorescences have long-lasting flowers, borne on leafless stems, with a wide range of color from pink, red, purple, orange to yellow the most common. The oblong, fringed, entire lip folds inwards on the lower margins and appears boat-shaped. The flowers have a small, short column.

CHRONDRORHYNCHA

An orthographic variant introduced in *Selbyana*, **7**(2-4): 357 (1984). The correct spelling is *Chondrorhyncha*.

CHRONIOCHILUS

J.J. Smith
Bull. Jard. Bot. Buitenzorg, sér. 2 **26**: 81 (1918).

Epidendroideæ ʷ Vandeæ • Aeridinæ

ETYMOLOGY: Greek for persistent or long-continued and lip. Descriptive of the unusually long-lasting flowers of the type species.

TYPE SPECIES: *Chroniochilus tjidadapensis* J.J. Smith
This type name is now considered a synonym of
Chroniochilus minimus (Blume) J.J. Smith;
basionym
Dendrocolla minima Blume

Four monopodial epiphytes are found in low to mid elevation, tropical forests of Thailand, Malaysia, Indonesia and Fiji. These small, inconspicuous plants have short, stout stems, each with several, small, flat, fleshy, unequally bilobed leaves. The short, zig-zagged, few-flowered inflorescence has small, very fragrant, short-lived, pale

Currently Accepted   Validly Published   Invalidly Published   Published Pre-1753   Superfluous Usage   Orthographic Variant   Fossil

Orchid Genera • 82

yellow to yellow-green flowers covered with brown blotches, are hairy on their outer segments, and open widely. The mobile, broadly clawed, trilobed lip has large, ear-like, minutely hairy side lobes, and a cone-shaped, oblong midlobe. The flowers have a long, curved, stout column.

CHRYPTOSTYLIS

An orthographic variant introduced in *Orchids Thailand*, **1**: 53 (1959). The correct spelling is *Cryptostylis*.

CHRYSOBAPHUS

Wallich
Tent. Fl. Napal.   37, t. 27 (1826).
ETYMOLOGY: Greek for gold and a dye. Descriptive of the bright goldish color of the leaf veins.
TYPE SPECIES: *Chrysobaphus roxburghii* Wallich

Now recognized as belonging to the genus *Anoectochilus*, *Chrysobaphus* was previously considered to include one terrestrial found in damp, low to mid elevation, evergreen forests and along river banks from southern China (Xizang to Zhejiang), Bangladesh, northern India (Kashmir to Assam), Laos, Thailand and Vietnam. This erect plant has unbranched stems, each with several, dark velvety-green, dark purple to black leaves in a basal rosette. The leaves have distinct golden yellow midveins, and are often suffused red toward the margins. The tall, hairy, few-flowered, pale red inflorescence has small, green to pale pink flowers. The white, Y-shaped, trilobed lip has a spurred, hypochile tapering to a minute structure, the mesochile is irregularly toothed or fringed, and the epichile is bilobed. The above type name is now considered a synonym of *Anoectochilus setaceus* Blume.

CHRYSOBOPHUS

An orthographic variant introduced in *Hort. Praticien*, **6**: 5 (1862). The correct spelling is *Chrysobaphus*.

CHRYSOCYCHNIS

An orthographic variant cited in *Man. Dict. Fl. Pl.*, ed. 4, 144 (1919). The correct spelling is *Chrysocycnis*.

CHRYSOCYCNIS

Linden & Reichenbach *filius*
Bonplandia   **2**(23): 280 (1854).
Epidendroideæ 🌱 Cymbidieæ • Maxillariinæ
ETYMOLOGY: Greek for golden and swan. Refers to the fanciful resemblance of the flowers to a swan because of the bent, exposed column.
TYPE SPECIES: *Chrysocycnis schlimii*
Linden & Reichenbach f.

Four uncommon, sympodial epiphytes are found in mid to upper elevation, montane forests from Costa Rica to Ecuador and Venezuela. These strange, climbing plants have a unique growing habit that is either vining or dimorphic. The erect plants have comparatively large, leathery leaves borne along simple or branched stems. Pseudobulbs are borne at the base of the plant or along the stem. The solitary-flowered inflorescence, borne from the base of the pseudobulb or along the stem, has a flat-faced, orange-brown flower spotted and barred chestnut. The small, hairy, brown to yellow, trilobed lip has oblong, spreading side lobes, a larger midlobe with a swollen mound of calli. The flowers have a strongly curved, hairy, footless column.

CHRYSOGLOSELLA

An orthographic variant introduced in *Orchideen (Schlechter)*, ed. 3, **14**: 849 (1984). The correct spelling is *Chrysoglossella*.

CHRYSOGLOSSELLA

Hatusima
Sci. Rep. Yokosuka City Mus.   **13**: 29 (1967).
ETYMOLOGY: Greek for golden, tongue and Latin for diminutive. Referring to the small golden lip.
TYPE SPECIES: *Chrysoglossella japonica* Hatusima

Now recognized as belonging to the genus *Hancockia*, *Chrysoglossella* was previously considered to include one terrestrial found in damp, mid elevation, forest slopes and valleys of southwestern China (Yunnan), northern Vietnam and Japan (Ryukyu Islands). This small, creeping plant has erect, unbranched stems. The solitary leaf, sprinkled with minute, wart-like spots, has a wavy to scalloped margin with many, parallel fine veins. The solitary-flowered inflorescence, borne from a specialized, leafless shoot, has a small, thinly textured, pink flower. The broad, golden, trilobed lip, attached to the column at the base, has an entire to slightly wavy margin, and has a long, slender, tubular spur with a double-crested keel inside on the mid-vein. The flowers have a slender, footless column. The above type name is now considered a synonym of *Hancockia uniflora* Rolfe.

CHRYSOGLOSSUM

Blume
Bijdr. Fl. Ned. Ind.   **7**: 337, t. 7 (1825).
Epidendroideæ 🌱 Collabiinæ • Currently unplaced
ETYMOLOGY: Greek for golden and tongue. Alluding to the color of the lip in the type species.
LECTOTYPE: *Chrysoglossum ornatum* Blume

Four sympodial terrestrials or rare epiphytes are found in shady, humid, low to mid elevation, hill and montane forests and slopes from northern India (Sikkim), Nepal, Sri Lanka, southern China (Yunnan), Taiwan, Thailand to Vietnam, Malaysia, Indonesia, the Philippines and New Guinea to the southwestern Pacific Archipelago. These plants have large, upright, green pseudobulbs, each with a solitary, somewhat large, pleated, thinly textured leaf. The erect, red-brown, numerous-flowered inflorescence has pale green flowers heavily spotted red. The lateral sepals united with the column foot, form a short, small, chin-like projection or spur that has a narrow entrance. The mobile, pure white, trilobed lip, narrowly attached to the column foot, has erect side lobes, and a concave midlobe with three, deeply lobed keels which are sometimes sprinkled with red spots. The flowers have a slender, erect, winged column that is curved forward.

CHUSUA

Nevski
Komarov's *Fl. URSS*   **4**: 509, 574 (1935).
ETYMOLOGY: The local native (Nawari) name for this orchid in Nepal – choo-swa.
TYPE SPECIES: *Chusua secunda* Nevski nom. illeg.
(*Orchis pauciflora* Fischer ex Lindley, not Tenore)
This type name is now considered a synonym of *Ponerorchis chusua* (D. Don) Soó; basionym replaced with *Orchis chusua* D. Don

Now recognized as belonging to the genus *Ponerorchis*, *Chusua* was previously considered to include twenty terrestrials found in mid to upper elevation, forest scrub and montane meadows of eastern Russia (Amur to Primorye), northern China (Gansu, Hebei, Henan to Sichuan), Korea, Japan, northern India and Bhutan. These erect plants have unbranched stems, subtended by two tubular, basal sheaths, each with several, narrow leaves. The densely packed, numerous to few-flowered inflorescence has violet-purple, pink, violet-red or rare yellow flowers spotted or blotched with a darker shade. The concave dorsal sepal and erect, veined petals converge, forming a hood over the short, erect column. The trilobed lip has a broad, oblong or squarish midlobe sprinkled with purple splashes; side lobes strongly curved sideways and a small spur. The flowers have a short, erect column.

CHYSIS

Lindley

Edwards's Bot. Reg. **23**: *t. 1937* (1837).

Epidendroideæ ⚘ **Arethuseæ** • **Bletiinæ**

ETYMOLOGY: Greek for melting or flushing. Alluding to the self-fertilizing ability of the flowers that causes the pollinia to appear to be fused together by the time the flower fully opens.

TYPE SPECIES: *Chysis aurea* Lindley

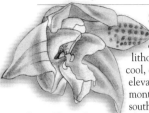

Seven variable, sympodial epiphytes or lithophytes are found cool, damp, low to mid elevation, hill and montane forests from southern Mexico to Peru. These plants have clustered, usually hanging, fleshy, spindle-shaped pseudobulbs, subtended by dry, thinly textured sheaths, each with several, pleated, deciduous leaves heavily veined on the underside. The short, few-flowered inflorescence, borne from newly developed growth, has large, showy, waxy flowers that are long-lived, highly fragrant, lemon-yellow, pink, creamy to purple and are suffused brown. The white to yellow, deeply trilobed lip has erect, oblong side lobes, and the notched midlobe is marked maroon or brown, with a crisp, wavy margin. The flowers have a short, incurved, broadly winged column with a prominent foot.

CHYTROGLOSSA

Reichenbach *filius*

Hamburger Garten-Blumenzeitung **19**: 546 (1863).

Epidendroideæ ⚘ **Cymbidieæ** • **Oncidiinæ**

ETYMOLOGY: Greek for pot, well or deep hole and tongue. Referring to the joining at the stigmatic, concave surface with the base of the pot-shaped lip.

LECTOTYPE: *Chytroglossa aurata* Reichenbach f.

Three uncommon, dwarf, sympodial epiphytes are native in low elevation, coastal cloud forests of southeastern Brazil (Rio de Janeiro and São Paulo). These plants have short stems, each with several, narrow, leathery leaves arranged in a fan shape. The few-flowered inflorescence has attractive, small, golden yellow to pale yellow flowers with long, narrow segments. The trilobed lip has white, triangular side lobes each with a large, purple spot, and the tongue-shaped midlobe is sprinkled with several, dark red spots. The flowers have an erect, slender column with a hooded tip.

CICLOPOGON

An orthographic variant introduced in *Enum. Pl. Hort. Bot. Fluminensi*, 19 (1893). The correct spelling is *Cyclopogon*.

CIMBIDIUM

An orthographic variant introduced in *Expos. Fam. Nat.*, **1**: 164 (1805). The correct spelling is *Cymbidium*.

CINOSORCHIS

An orthographic variant introduced in *Hort. Eystet.*, *t. 132* (1613). The correct spelling is *Cynosorchis*.

CIONISACCUS

Breda

Gen. Sp. Orchid. Asclep., fasc. II   *t. 8* (1829).

ETYMOLOGY: Greek for column or pillar and sac. Refers to the lip that is bag-like at the base of the column.

TYPE SPECIES: *Cionisaccus lanceolatus* Breda
This type name is now considered a synonym of
Goodyera procera (Ker Gawler) Hooker;
basionym
Neottia procera Ker Gawler

Now recognized as belonging to the genus *Goodyera*, *Cionisaccus* was previously considered to include one small terrestrial widespread in China (Anhui to Xizang), India, Sri Lanka, Taiwan, Japan, Malaysia, Indonesia to the Philippines and Thailand to Cambodia. This variable plant, often overlooked because of its small size, has erect, unbranched stems that are leafy at their base. The numerous-flowered inflorescence has small, white flowers and the entire lip has a pair of antennae at the tip.

CIONOSACCUS

An orthographic variant introduced in *Orchideen (Schlechter)*, ed. 1, 114 (1914). The correct spelling is *Cionisaccus*.

CIORISACCUS

An orthographic variant introduced in *J. Gener. Litter.*, **1828**(11): 323 (1828). The correct spelling is *Cionisaccus*.

CIPRIPEDIUM

An orthographic variant introduced in *Deutsch. Mag. Garten- Blumenk.*, **1849**: 245 (1849). The correct spelling is *Cypripedium*.

CIRIPEDIUM

An orthographic variant introduced in *Fl. Pedem.*, **1**: 18 (1829). The correct spelling is *Cypripedium*.

CIRRAEA

An orthographic variant cited in *Lex. Gen. Phan.*, 126 (1904). The correct spelling is *Cirrhaea*.

CIRRHAAE

An orthographic variant introduced in *Hort. Reg.*, **3**(31): 41 (1834). The correct spelling is *Cirrhaea*.

CIRRHAEA

Lindley

Edwards's Bot. Reg. **18**: *t. 1538* (1832).

Epidendroideæ ⚘ **Cymbidieæ** • **Stanhopeinæ**

ETYMOLOGY: Latin for tendril or curl of hair. Descriptive of the rostellum that is prolonged like a tendril.

TYPE SPECIES: *Cirrhaea loddigesii* (Loddiges) Lindley
(*Cymbidium dependens* Loddiges)

Nine exquisite, sympodial epiphytes or lithophytes are found in cool, mid elevation, montane forests of central and southern Brazil (Espírito Santo to São Paulo). These strangely shaped plants have strongly ribbed, egg-shaped, densely grouped pseudobulbs, each with a solitary, deeply veined, pleated leaf. The hanging, numerous-flowered inflorescence, borne from the pseudobulb base, has lightly fragrant, waxy, long-lasting, oddly shaped flowers whose shape varies differently even on the same rachis and do not open fully. They vary in color from green-yellow, yellow to dark brown-red. The narrow, spreading or forward pointing sepals and petals are often sprinkled or heavily covered with red-brown spots and bars. The long-clawed, trilobed lip, attached to the short column foot, has backward bent side lobes, and the narrowly triangular to broad, shell-shaped midlobe has a callus with a raised, fleshy bump. The flowers have a white, slender, incurved, club-shaped column.

CIRRHAEAM

Lindley

Bot. Reg. **11**: sub 930 (1825).

Name published without a description. Today this name is most often referred to *Cirrhaea*.

| Currently Accepted | Validly Published | Invalidly Published | Published Pre-1753 | Superfluous Usage | Orthographic Variant | Fossil |

O r c h i d   G e n e r a   • **84**

CIRRHEA

An orthographic variant introduced in *J. Hort. Prat. Belgique*, 139 (1847). The correct spelling is *Cirrhaea*.

CIRRHOEA

An orthographic variant introduced in *Hort. Reg.*, **5**(64): 391 (1836). The correct spelling is *Cirrhaea*.

CIRRHOPATALUM

An orthographic variant introduced in *Gartenflora*, **15**: 251 (1866). The correct spelling is *Cirrhopetalum*.

CIRRHOPETALAE

An orthographic variant introduced in *Itin. Pl. Khasyah Mts.*, 123 (1848). The correct spelling is *Cirrhopetalum*.

CIRRHOPETALO

An orthographic variant introduced in *Itin. Pl. Khasyah Mts.*, 166 (1848). The correct spelling is *Cirrhopetalum*.

CIRRHOPETALUM

Lindley
Gen. Sp. Orchid. Pl.   45, 58 (1830), and
Bot. Reg.   **10**: sub 832 (1824) nom illeg.
Name ICBN conserved vs. *Ephippium* Blume (1825), and vs. *Zygoglossum* Reinwardt (1825) Orchidaceæ.

ETYMOLOGY: Greek for tendril or curl and petal. Refers to the long, strap-shaped, lateral sepals, that are the most salient feature of the genus and thus providing the allusion of locks or curls on a persons head.

TYPE SPECIES: *Cirrhopetalum thouarsii* Lindley nom. illeg.
Cirrhopetalum umbellatum
(J.G. Forster) Frappier ex Cordemoy nom. illeg.
(*Epidendrum umbellatum* J.G. Forster
This type name is now considered a synonym of
Bulbophyllum longiflorum Thouars

Now recognized as belonging to the genus *Bulbophyllum*, *Cirrhopetalum* was previously considered to include one hundred forty-eight epiphytes found in low to mid elevation, hill and montane forests and woodlands from India, Sri Lanka, China (Xizang to Fujian, Gansu to Anhui), Myanmar, Vietnam, southern Japan (Ryukyu Islands), Taiwan and the southern Pacific Archipelago. These intriguing plants vary in size from minute to large, have clustered, oblong pseudobulbs, each with a solitary, leathery leaf. The inflorescence has several flowers produced in a semi-circle tier. These unusual flowers have extremely long, tapering, united lateral sepals notched at

the tip, short stumpy petals and usually with either a foul or pleasant fragrance. Long, dark colored hairs are often found on the dorsal sepal and petals. Each flower has a short, stout column attached to a highly mobile, strongly curved, entire lip that flutters in the slightest of breezes. The small, often glossy or wet-looking, projecting lip attracts flies on the lookout for raw meat.

NOTE: These species are often included in *Bulbophyllum* today and the taxonomists are still unsure of their placement.

CIRROPETALUM

An orthographic variant introduced in *Rep. Bot. Gard. Calcutta*, 9 (1843). The correct spelling is *Cirrhopetalum*.

CIRTOPODIUM

An orthographic variant cited in *Hist. Nat. Veg. (Spach)*, **12**: 178 (1846). The correct spelling is *Cyrtopodium*.

CIRTOSIA

An orthographic variant introduced in *Identif. Guide Vietnamese Orchids*, 77 (1994). The correct spelling is *Cyrtosia*.

CISCHWEINFIA

Dressler & **N.H. Williams**
Amer. Orchid Soc. Bull.   **39**(11): 991 (1970).
Epidendroideæ ≠ Cymbidieæ • Oncidiinæ

ETYMOLOGY: Named in honor of Charles Samuel Schweinfurth (1890-1970), an American botanist, taxonomist, curator of the Oakes Ames Herbarium and author of *Orchids of Peru*.

TYPE SPECIES: *Cischweinfia pusilla*
(C. Schweinfurth) Dressler & N.H. Williams
(*Aspasia pusilla* C. Schweinfurth)

Eleven sympodial epiphytes are found in wet, low to mid elevation, hill scrub and montane forests from Costa Rica to Bolivia. These miniature plants have small, clustered, flattened, sharply two-edged pseudobulbs, partially subtended by distichous, leaf-bearing sheaths, each with a solitary, slender to strap-shaped, slightly leathery leaf. The several, short, few-flowered inflorescences, borne from the base of the pseudobulb, have small, colorful, green to green-yellow flowers mottled cream to purple with similarly shaped sepals and petals. The funnel-shaped, entire lip is broadly wedge-shaped, tapers to a pointed tip, covered with pink spots, and is hairy within. The lip is basally united to both sides of the short, erect, hooded, footless column, forming a short, nectary-like spur.

CISTELA

An orthographic variant introduced in *Fl. Javæ*, **1**: Praef. vi (1828). The correct spelling is *Cistella*.

CISTELLA

Blume
Bijdr. Fl. Ned. Ind.   **7**: 293, *t*. 55 (1825).
Name ICBN rejected vs. *Cistella* Quélet (1886) Fungi.

ETYMOLOGY: Latin for small box or small chest. From the form or shape of the anther that bears the pollinia as if in a small container.

TYPE SPECIES: *Cistella cernua* (Willdenow) Blume
(*Malaxis cernua* Willdenow)
This type name is now considered a synonym of
Geodorum densiflorum (Lamarck) Schlechter;
basionym replaced with
Limodorum densiflorum Lamarck

Although validly published this rejected name is now referred to *Geodorum*. *Cistella* was considered to include one terrestrial found from the Philippines, Myanmar, Indonesia, Malaysia and Thailand to southern China (Sichuan to Hainan).

CISTILLA

An orthographic variant introduced in *Hort. Donat.*, 142 (1858). The correct spelling is *Cistella*.

CITHERIS

An orthographic variant introduced in *Fl. Brit. Ind.*, **5**: 818 (1890). The correct spelling is *Cytheris*.

CITRABENIS

Thouars
Hist. Orchid.   Table 1, sub 1e (1822).

Name published without a description. Today this name is most often referred to *Habenaria*.

CITRAHENIS

An orthographic variant introduced in *Hist. Orchid.*, *t*. 16 (1822). The correct spelling is *Citrabenis*.

CITRANGIS

Thouars
Hist. Orchid.   Table 2, sub 3o, *t*. 61 (1822).

Name published without a description. Today this name is most often referred to *Angraecum*.

CITRINABENIS

Thouars

Hist. Orchid. t. 16 (1822).

Name published without a description. Today this name is most often referred to *Habenaria*.

CLADERIA

Hooker *filius*

Fl. Brit. Ind. **5**: 810 (1890).
Name ICBN conserved vs. *Claderia* Rafinesque (1838) Rutaceæ.

Epidendroideæ ⚘ **Collabiinæ** • **Currently unplaced**

ETYMOLOGY: Greek for a branch and *Eria*, a genus of orchids. From the stretched growth and the similarity to *Eria*.

TYPE SPECIES: *Claderia viridiflora* Hooker f.

Two sympodial semi-terrestrials or rare epiphytes are found in humid, low elevation, forests with nutrient-poor soil from Malaysia, Thailand, Indonesia (Borneo, Sumatra and Sulawesi) to New Guinea. These climbing plants have short stems, each with several, pleated, mottled leaves. The long, creeping rhizomes have leafy shoots. The simple or branched, stout inflorescence slowly lengthens and bears a succession of several, green-yellow flowers with deep green veins but have only one to two open at a time. The dorsal sepal is erect or curved over the slender, wingless, footless column and widespreading lateral sepals. The pale green, sac-like, trilobed lip has striking, darker green veins, and large side lobes with the wider midlobe being much longer that has a hairy, club-shaped basal ridge.

CLADOBIUM

Lindley

Intr. Nat. Syst. Bot., ed. 2   446 (1836).

ETYMOLOGY: Greek for a branch or shoot and life. In reference to the plant's epiphytic growth habit.

TYPE SPECIES: *Cladobium violaceum* Lindley
This type name is now considered a synonym of
Scaphyglottis graminifolia
(Ruiz & Pavón) Poeppig & Endlicher;
basionym
Fernandezia graminifolia Ruiz & Pavón

Now recognized as belonging to the genus *Scaphyglottis*, *Cladobium* Lindley was previously considered to include one epiphyte found in wet, low to mid elevation, hill and montane forests of the Guianas, Venezuela, Colombia to Bolivia and northern Brazil. This plant is quite variable in size, and the few-flowered inflorescence produces flowers in

succession with only one to two open at a time. The rose purple to violet flower has a small tooth on each side of its straight, wingless, footless column and has a thick, rigid, clawed, entire lip.

CLADOBIUM

Schlechter

Beih. Bot. Centralbl. **37**(2): 431 (1920).
Not *Cladobium* Lindley (1836) Orchidaceæ.

ETYMOLOGY: Greek for branch and life. In reference to the plants epiphytic growth habit.

LECTOTYPE: *Cladobium ceracifolium*
(Barbosa Rodrigues) Schlechter
(*Spiranthes ceracifolia* Barbosa Rodrigues)

Not validly published because of a prior use of the name, this homonym was replaced by *Lankesterella*.

CLADORHIZA

Rafinesque

Amer. Monthly Mag. & Crit. Rev.   **1**: 429 (1817).

ETYMOLOGY: Greek for twig or branch and a root. Refers to the fleshy, multibranched roots.

TYPE SPECIES: *Cladorhiza maculata* Rafinesque

Now recognized as belonging to the genus *Corallorhiza*, *Cladorhiza* was previously considered to include two saprophytes commonly found in shady, mid to upper elevation, scrub from Canada (British Colombia to Labrador), the northern United States (Oregon to Virginia) and central Mexico to Guatemala. These erect, colony-forming plants have a leafless, unbranched stem arising from decaying humus that varies from deep purple to a clear yellow. The basic color of the flower matches the stem's color. The size of the plant and flowers varies throughout its range. The white, trilobed lip has small side lobes, the midlobe has a wavy margin and is usually spotted purple. The flowers have a small, curved column.

CLAVOPHYLIS

Thouars

Hist. Orchid.   Table 3, sub 3u, t. 99 (1822).

Name published without a description. Today this name is most often referred to *Bulbophyllum*.

CLEDOBIUM

An orthographic variant introduced in *Reis. Br.-Guiana*, **3**: 909 (1848). The correct spelling is *Cladobium*.

CLEIDOSTOMA

Blume

Fl. Javæ   **1**: Praef. vi (1828).
ETYMOLOGY: Greek for to small key and mouth.
TYPE SPECIES: *None designated*

Name published without a description. Today this name is most often referred to *Phalaenopsis*.

CLEIOSOSTOMA

An orthographic variant cited in *Hist. Nat. Veg. (Spach)*, **12**: 179 (1846). The correct spelling is *Cleisostoma*.

CLEIOSTOMA

Not *Cleiostoma* Rafinesque (1838) Convolvulaceæ.

An orthographic variant cited in *Deut. Bot. Herb.-Buch*, 54 (1841). The correct spelling is *Cleisostoma*.

CLEISEOSTOMA

An orthographic variant introduced in *Cat. Pl. Hort. Bot. Bogor.*, 44 (1844). The correct spelling is *Cleisostoma*.

CLEISOCENTRON

Brühl

Guide Orchids Sikkim   136 (1926).

Epidendroideæ ⚘ **Vandeæ** • **Aeridinæ**

ETYMOLOGY: Greek for lock, key or bar to shut and a sharp point or spur. Descriptive of the spur that is almost completely closed by a thickening of its wall.

TYPE SPECIES: *Cleisocentron trichromum*
(Reichenbach f.) Brühl
(*Saccolabium trichromum* Reichenbach f.)
This type name is now considered a synonym of
Cleisocentron pallens
(Cathcart ex Lindley) N. Pearce & P.J. Cribb;
basionym replaced with
Saccolabium pallens Cathcart ex Lindley

Three dwarf, monopodial epiphytes are found in mid to upper elevation, montane forests and river scrub from India (Kashmir to Assam), Myanmar and Vietnam to Indonesia (northern Borneo). These plants have long, hanging stems, each with a laxly, two-rank arrangement of leathery, pencil-like or strap-like leaves. The short, numerous to few-flowered inflorescence has waxy, fleshy, long-lived, fragrant, often spectacular flowers found in shades of yellow, pink-white, red-brown or pastel blue and are covered with purple spots or blotches. The immobile, trilobed lip has erect sides lobes and a broadly triangular midlobe. The curved, cylindrical

Currently Accepted   Validly Published   Invalidly Published   Published Pre-1753   Superfluous Usage   Orthographic Variant   Fossil

spur contains either an upward pointing, central protuberance on the back wall or a decurved, shelf-like back wall with a flap-like callus. The flowers have an erect, wingless column with a prominent foot.

CLEISOMERIA

Lindley ex G. Don

Loudon's *Encycl. Pl.*, new ed., Suppl.
2: 1447, 1472 (1855).

Epidendroideæ ⚬ Vandeæ • Aeridinæ

ETYMOLOGY: Greek for closed or to lock and a portion or a part. Refers to the lip enclosing the column.

TYPE SPECIES: *Cleisomeria lanatum* Lindley ex G. Don

Two monopodial epiphytes are found in low elevation, semi-deciduous, deciduous and savanna scrub from Myanmar, Thailand, Laos, Cambodia, Vietnam and Malaysia to eastern Indonesia (Borneo). These plants have stout, erect stems, each with numerous internodes, closely spaced leaves overlapping at the base, that curve outward and downward. The hanging to erect, slender, often branching, shortly hairy, numerous-flowered inflorescence has large floral bracts. The green to dark red-brown flowers have an erect, hooded dorsal sepal, widespreading lateral sepals, and small, roundish petals with hairy margins edged in pale green and red-brown veins. The trilobed lip has thin, pale green side lobes, the cup-shaped midlobe has two, narrow lobes at the tip, and the tiny spur has its entrance nearly closed or blocked by fleshy cushions. The flowers have a stout, footless column.

CLEISOSTOMA

Blume

Bijdr. Fl. Ned. Ind. **8**: 362, t. 27 (1825).

Not *Cleistostoma* Bridel (1826) Calymperaceæ, and not *Cleistostoma* Rafinesque (1836) Convolvulaceæ.

Epidendroideæ ⚬ Vandeæ • Aeridinæ

ETYMOLOGY: Greek for closed or locked and mouth. Referring to the prominent calli that can appear to block the opening into the lip pouch.

LECTOTYPE: *Cleisostoma sagittatum* Blume

Eighty-seven monopodial epiphytes or occasionally lithophytes are found in low elevation, woodlands, scrub and mangroves from southern China (Hainan, Yunnan to Guizhou), India, Sri Lanka, Myanmar to Vietnam, Taiwan, Indonesia, the Philippines, New Guinea and the adjacent southwestern Pacific Archipelago with the center of development in Thailand. These small to medium-sized plants have short or long, erect or arching stems, each with several, flat or pencil-like, fleshy leaves. The short or long, erect or

hanging, simple or branched, numerous-flowered inflorescence has small, fleshy, red-brown, orange to purple flowers (subtended by small bracts) with the margins and mid-ribs varying from brown-black to green. The short, white to yellow, cone-shaped, trilobed lip has a pair of curious outgrowths resembling horns located at the tip. The flowers have a short, stout, wingless column.

CLEISOSTOMOPSIS

Seidenfaden

Opera Bot. **114**: 370, 372 (1992).

Epidendroideæ ⚬ Vandeæ • Aeridinæ

ETYMOLOGY: *Cleisostoma*, a genus of orchids and Greek for resembling or likeness.

TYPE SPECIES: *Cleisostomopsis eberhardtii*
(Finet) Seidenfaden
(*Saccolabium eberhardtii* Finet)

One monopodial epiphyte is found in low elevation, hill forests of Vietnam and southeastern China (Guangxi). This small, hanging plant has several, narrow, pencil-like leaves spaced along the long, slender stem. The short, numerous-flowered inflorescence has tiny, magenta flowers with similar, widespreading sepals and petals. The short, cup-like, trilobed lip has Y-shaped appendages on the back wall of the long, swollen spur. The flowers have a short, wingless column with an obscure foot.

CLEISOSTOMPSIS

An orthographic variant introduced in *Fragm. Florist. Geobot.*, **3**(Suppl.): 88 (1995). The correct spelling is *Cleisostomopsis*.

CLEISOSTONIA

An orthographic variant introduced in *Rad. Jugoslav. Akad. Znan.*, **21**: 37 (1872). The correct spelling is *Cleisostoma*.

CLEISOSTOSTOMA

An orthographic variant cited in *Handb. Orchid.-Namen*, 651 (2005). The correct spelling is *Cleisostoma*.

CLEISOTOMA

An orthographic variant introduced in *Nat. Pflanzen-Syst.*, 197 (1829). The correct spelling is *Cleisostoma*.

CLEISTES

Richard

Mém. Mus. Hist. Nat. **4**: 31 (1818).

Name published without a description. Today this name is most often referred to *Cleistes* Lindley.

CLEISTES

Richard ex Lindley

Gen. Sp. Orchid. Pl. 409 (1840).

Vanilloideæ ⚬ Pogoniieæ

ETYMOLOGY: Greek for closed. Alluding to the narrow, funnel-shaped whorl of the petals and lip whose parts do not spread, giving the flowers a closed appearance even when the plant is in full bloom.

TYPE SPECIES: *Cleistes lutea* Lindley nom. illeg.
Cleistes grandiflorum (Aublet) Schlechter
(*Limodorum grandiflorum* Aublet)

Sixty-three showy, sympodial terrestrials are found in low to upper elevation, savannas, grasslands and marshes from the eastern United States (New Jersey to northern Florida) and from Costa Rica to Bolivia, Venezuela, the Guianas and then southward with the vast majority found in Brazil. These slender plants have erect, unbranched, hollow stems, each with a solitary leaf midway up the stem or several, clasping leaf-like floral bracts and one to two leaves on the flowering stems. The solitary to few-flowered inflorescence often has large, showy flowers invariably brightly colored with white, pink, yellow and green but brown is often predominate. The petals and lip usually form a tube shape. In some species the flowers open widely and in others they barely open. The rather tubular, obscurely trilobed at the tip or entire lip has a central, longitudinal callus. The flowers have a slender, footless column. These species were often included in *Pogonia*.

CLEISTHES

An orthographic variant introduced in *J. Hort. Prat. Belgique*, ser. 2, 203 (1858). The correct spelling is *Cleistes*.

CLEISTOCENTRON

An orthographic variant cited in *CRC World Dict. Pl.*, **1**: 554 (1999). The correct spelling is *Cleisocentron*.

CLEISTOGAMA

An orthographic variant introduced in *Bot. Centralbl.*, **70**(19-20): 217 (1897). The correct spelling is *Cleisostoma*.

CLEISTOMA

An orthographic variant introduced in *Not. Pl. Asiat.*, **3**: 357 (1851). The correct spelling is *Cleisostoma*.

CLEISTOSTOMA

An orthographic variant introduced in *Repert. Spec. Nov. Regni Veg. Beih.*, **4**: 291 (1919). The correct spelling is *Cleisostoma*.

CLEMATEPISTEPHIUM

N. Hallé

Fl. Nouvelle Caledonie & Depend.   **8**: 403 (1977).

Vanilloideæ 🍃 **Vanillineæ**

ETYMOLOGY: Greek for twig or tendril and *Epistephium*, a genus of orchids. Referring to the vining growth habit and the *Epistephium*-like leaves.

TYPE SPECIES: *Clematepistephium smilacifolium*
(Reichenbach f.) N. Hallé
(*Epistephium smilacifolium* Reichenbach f.)

One sympodial terrestrial is found in dark, low to mid elevation, rain forests of New Caledonia. This unusual, climbing plant has long, almost woody stems which twines without the aid of aerial roots. The large, prominent, net-veined leaves, one at each node, have a leathery texture. The dark red flowers, each subtended by a small bract, develop into a cluster at the end of the vine, protruding well beyond the supporting plant. The trilobed lip has upright side lobes, and the midlobe has a distinct notch and row of bristles. The flowers have a slender, slightly incurved, footless column. The plant only flowers in full sunlight and then only after having attained considerable height.

CLINHYMENIA

A. Richard & Galeotti

Compt. Rend. Hebd. Séances Acad. Sci. **18**: 512 (1844).

ETYMOLOGY: Greek for a bed, slope or recline and membrane. Referring to the shape of the elongated lip.

TYPE SPECIES: *Clinhymenia pallidiflora*
A. Richard & Galeotti

Now recognized as belonging to the genus *Cryptarrhena*, *Clinhymenia* was previously considered to include one epiphyte found from Mexico to Panama, Jamaica, Trinidad and Colombia to Peru. This small plant has narrow leaves borne in a fan shape and a numerous to few-flowered inflorescence with small, yellow-green flowers. The long-clawed, unusual four-lobed lip has long, narrow side lobes that taper to fine points, and has a short, blunt midlobe

with a bilobed tip. The above type name is considered a synonym of *Cryptarrhena lunata* R. Brown.

CLISOSTOMA

An orthographic variant cited in *Lex. Gen. Phan.*, 130 (1904). The correct spelling is *Cleisostoma*.

CLISTES

An orthographic variant cited in *Lex. Gen. Phan.*, 129, 130 (1904). The correct spelling is *Cleistes*.

CLOIDIA

An orthographic variant introduced in *Ceiba*, **5**(4): 48 (1956). The correct spelling is *Chloidia*.

CLOVESIA

An orthographic variant cited in *Etym.-Bot.-Handw.-Buch*, ed. 1, 208 (1852). The correct spelling is *Clowesia*.

CLOWESIA

Lindley

Edwards's Bot. Reg.   **29**: t. 39 (1843), and Misc. 25, section no. 39 (1843).

Epidendroideæ 🍃 **Cymbidieæ** • **Catasetinæ**

ETYMOLOGY: Dedicated to John H. Clowes (1777-1846), a British church administrator and minister from Broughton Hall in Manchester, who was the first to flower the type species. He gave his vast orchid collection to Kew upon his death.

TYPE SPECIES: *Clowesia rosea* Lindley

Seven sympodial epiphytes are found in low to mid elevation, hill and montane oak-pine forests from south-western Mexico to Ecuador, Venezuela, the Guianas and northern Brazil. These plants have ovoid, several noded, grooved when old pseudobulbs, each with several, thinly textured, pleated, heavily veined, deciduous leaves. The hanging, numerous-flowered inflorescence has complex, but fairly showy, pale green or pink flowers that can be rather sickly and/or sweetly fragrant, and the petals have finely notched margins. Unlike their close relative *Catasetum*, these flowers are bisexual with both the anther and stigma functional. The interesting, spurred or bag-like, trilobed lip has a rolled margin, the oblong, front lobe is often heavily to thinly fringed at the tip or entire and has a callus with irregular toothed margins. The short to fairly long, erect, usually wingless column has

an explosive trigger mechanism that attaches its pollinia onto visiting pollinators.

CLYNHYMENIA

An orthographic variant introduced in *Ann. Sci. Nat., Bot.*, ed. 3, **3**: 24 (1845). The correct spelling is *Clinhymenia*.

CNEMIDIA

Lindley

Edwards's Bot. Reg.   **19**: sub 1618 (1833).

ETYMOLOGY: Greek for spoke of a wheel or legging. Referring to the basally united perianth parts that resemble the spokes of a wheel at the hub.

TYPE SPECIES: *Cnemidia angulosa* Lindley

Now recognized as belonging to the genus *Tropidia*, *Cnemidia* was previously considered to include four terrestrials found in low to mid elevation, primary and disturbed forests from India to the southwestern Pacific Archipelago. These medium to rather large-sized plants have erect, leafy stems. The simple or few-branched, numerous-flowered inflorescence has small, white or pale yellow flowers not opening widely. The entire lip, much larger than the other floral segments, is basally sac-like or pouched, and often with a short spur. The flowers have a short to obscure, fleshy column.

COAGULUM

C. Bauhin

Pinax   86 (1623).

Pre-1753, therefore not validly published in fulfillment of nomenclatural rules. The name was used by Pliny (ancient Greek writer) and others and is most often referred to *Orchis*.

COATZONTE

Hernández

Rerum Med. Nov. Hisp. Thes.   **1**: 266 (1651), and *Opera (Hernández)*   **1**: 241 (1790).

ETYMOLOGY: A Nahuatl word (a language spoken by the peoples that inhabited the central valley of Mexico, whose speakers included the Aztecs) for a serpent or snake (viper's head), plant and flower.

TYPE SPECIES: *Coatzonte coxochitl, Lyncis flore. feu Lyncea* Hernández

Pre-1753, therefore not validly published in fulfillment of nomenclatural rules; this polynomial name is most often referred to *Stanhopea. Coatzonte coxochitl* was previously considered to include

Currently Accepted   Validly Published   Invalidly Published   Published Pre-1753   Superfluous Usage   Orthographic Variant   Fossil

O r c h i d   G e n e r a • **88**

one epiphyte, terrestrial or lithophyte found in mid to upper elevation, montane forests and rocky slopes of central Mexico (Morelos, Mexico, Michoacán and Guerrero). This plant has ovoid pseudobulbs, subtended by thin, dry sheaths, each with a solitary, rigid, pleated leaf. The hanging, stout, few-flowered inflorescence, borne from the base of the pseudobulb, has large, fragrant, waxy, pale yellow or yellow-orange flowers heavily spotted red-brown. The huge, ivory colored, trilobed lip is stained, blotched and speckled purple. The flowers have a long, club-shaped column that is stippled red-brown. This name is usually now considered as a synonym of *Stanhopea hernandezii* (Kunth) Schlechter.

COATZONTECOMAXOCHITL

An orthographic variant introduced in *Gen. Hist. Things New Spain*, **11**: 211 (1590). The correct spelling is *Coatzonte*.

COCCINEORCHIS

Schlechter

Beih. Bot. Centralbl. **37**(2): 434 (1920).

Orchidoideæ ῼ Cranichideæ • Spiranthinæ

ETYMOLOGY: Greek for scarlet or crimson and orchid. Referring to the flower color of the type species that in ancient times was obtained from the Coccoidea family of insects.

TYPE SPECIES: *Coccineorchis corymbosa*
(Kraenzlin) Schlechter
(*Spiranthes corymbosa* Kraenzlin)

This type name is now considered a synonym of *Coccineorchis cernua* (Lindley) Garay; basionym replaced with *Stenorrhynchos cernuum* Lindley

Four sympodial terrestrials or epiphytes are found in low to upper elevation, hill to montane cloud forests and woodlands from Nicaragua to Bolivia. These erect, leafy plants have unbranched stems, each with a basal rosette of broadly ovate, deep green, nerved leaves. The short, erect, hairy, numerous-flowered inflorescence with several, scape-like bracts, has large, showy, tubular flowers that are bright yellow to brick-red. The dorsal sepal and petals converge, forming a hood over the straight, slender, slightly club-shaped column. The yellow, hairy, clawed, obscurely trilobed lip has a scarlet to white tip and is basally attached to the lateral sepals forming a short, tunnel-like access to the nectary.

COCHLEANTHES

Rafinesque

Fl. Tellur. **4**: 45 (1836)[1838].

Epidendroideæ ῼ Cymbidieæ • Zygopetalinæ

ETYMOLOGY: Greek for snail or spiral shell and flower. Indicating the appearance of the flowers, referring to the shell-like form of the lip.

TYPE SPECIES: *Cochleanthes fragrans*
Rafinesque nom. illeg.
Cochleanthes flabelliformis
(Swartz) R.E. Schultes & Garay
(*Epidendrum flabelliforme* Swartz)

Fourteen sympodial epiphytes are widely distributed in low to mid elevation, hill scrub and montane forests from Nicaragua, Costa Rica to Bolivia and Brazil. These plants have short stems, each with numerous, distichous, bright green, thinly textured leaves borne in a fan-like arrangement. The short, solitary-flowered inflorescence, borne from the leaf axils, has a showy, long-lasting, fragrant flower that is relatively large-sized, and varies in color from white, pink, purple to pale yellow. The dorsal sepal is erect to hooded, and the lateral sepals are often bend inward with inrolled margins. The white, blue to purple veined, shortly clawed, entire or obscurely trilobed lip has the sides embracing the short, erect, often club-like column.

COCHLIA

Blume

Bijdr. Fl. Ned. Ind. **7**: 320, *t.* 59 (1825).

ETYMOLOGY: Greek for snail-shell or anything spirally twisted. Descriptive of the lip that resembles a snail with two feelers.

TYPE SPECIES: *Cochlia violacea* Blume

Now recognized as belonging to the genus *Bulbophyllum*, *Cochlia* was previously considered to include one epiphyte or lithophyte found along sandstone ridges, in low to mid elevation, hill and montane forests of Indonesia and Malaysia. This plant has tiny, elongate pseudobulbs, each with a solitary, convex leaf. The few-flowered inflorescence has a dense, globular head of dark violet flowers that are almost black in color. The white, entire lip has black side lobes sticking out laterally, like horns and is reflexed at the tip. The above type name is now considered a synonym of *Bulbophyllum cochlia* Garay, Hamer & Siegerist.

COCHLIODA

Lindley

Fol. Orchid. **4**: *Cochlioda*, 1 (1853).

Epidendroideæ ῼ Cymbidieæ • Oncidiinæ

ETYMOLOGY: Greek for spiral or snail-shell. An allusion to the appearance of the linear calli on the lip.

TYPE SPECIES: *Cochlioda densiflora* Lindley

Seven sympodial epiphytes or lithophytes are found in mid to upper elevation, montane cloud forests of the Andes from Colombia to Bolivia. These densely clustered plants have short, compressed or flattened, oblong to ovate pseudobulbs, subtended by several, distichous, leaf-like sheaths, each with one or two, narrow to oblong leaves. The one or two, erect, hanging or arching, numerous to few-flowered inflorescence, borne from the axils of the upper sheaths, has large or small bracts. Has spectacular, typically large, rich, brilliant red, scarlet, orange, purple to bright pink flowers. They differ from *Odontoglossum* by their distinctly trilobed lip that is fused to the long, slender to stout, curved, footless column. The erect, long-clawed, trilobed lip has oblong or rounded side lobes, and an entire or prominently bilobed midlobe.

NOTE: Some of these species are used extensively in intergeneric hybridizing because of their rich color.

COCKTOWNIA

An orthographic variant introduced in *Ann. Bot. Fenn.*, **40**: 144 (2003). The correct spelling is *Cooktownia*.

COCLEORCHIS

Szlachetko

Fragm. Florist. Geobot. **39**(2): 557 (1994).

ETYMOLOGY: Named after Coclé, a province located in central Panama facing the Pacific Ocean, where the type species was collected.

TYPE SPECIES: *Cocleorchis sarcoglottidis* Szlachetko

Now recognized as belonging to the genus *Cyclopogon*, *Cocleorchis* was proposed to include two terrestrials found in a small, restricted forested area on the Pacific side of central Panama. These delicate plants have erect, unbranched stems, each with a basal rosette of several, ovate leaves. The twisted, almost erect, few-flowered inflorescence has usually small, thinly textured, tubular, green flowers with long, narrow, nerved sepals and petals fused together at the base. The shortly clawed, trilobed lip has a thinly textured, obscurely fiddle-shaped hypochile, the mesochile has a fleshy, thickened margin, and the kidney-shaped epichile has a minutely notched margin. The above type name is now considered a synonym of *Cyclopogon dressleri* Szlachetko.

CODONORCHIS

Lindley

Gen. Sp. Orchid. Pl. 410 (1840).

Orchidoideæ ⸬ **Codonorchideæ**

ETYMOLOGY: Greek for a small bell or cowbell and orchid. Alluding to the bell shape formed by the petals and lip.

LECTOTYPE: *Codonorchis lessonii* (d'Urville) Lindley
(*Epipactis lessonii* d'Urville)

Two uncommon, sympodial terrestrials are found in chilly, low to upper elevation, windswept pampas, shady rain forests and coastal woodlands with the most southern distribution in southern Chile, south-eastern Brazil (a very tiny area of Rio Grande do Sul) to western Argentina, even extending into the inhospitable terrain of the Straits of Magellan and the Falkland Islands. These erect plants, often forming local colonies, have unbranched stems, each with a whorl of several, ovate leaves midway up the stem. The wiry, erect, solitary-flowered inflorescence has a large, showy, white or pink flower sprinkled with tiny, red spots. The small petals converge over the lip. The shortly clawed, entire or trilobed lip, attached to the thin, curved column base, has erect side lobes, the midlobe is covered with numerous, small appendages and has an entire or wavy margin. The flowers have a long, slender column.

CODONOSIPHON

Schlechter

Repert. Spec. Nov. Regni Veg. Beih.
1(9): 682 (1912), and **1**(12): 893 (1913).

ETYMOLOGY: Greek for bell and tube. Referring to the sepals that are partly united into a bell-shaped tube.

TYPE SPECIES: *None designated*

Now recognized as belonging to the genus *Bulbophyllum*, *Codonosiphon* was previously considered to include three epiphytes found in misty, upper montane, montane forests of New Guinea and Indonesia (Sulawesi). These plants have small, clustered, egg-shaped pseudo-bulbs, subtended by thin, dry sheaths, each with a solitary, deciduous, narrow, leathery, heavily grooved leaf. The wiry, solitary-flowered inflorescence, borne from the base of the pseudobulb, has a tiny, dark red to black-red flower. The sepals are united forming a bell-shaped tube and the inside surface of the floral segments are hairy. The immobile, entire lip is firmly attached to the slender, almost footless column that has a yellow tip.

COELANDRIA

Fitzgerald

Austral. Orch. **1**(7): t. 2 (1882).

ETYMOLOGY: Greek for hollow and anther. The pollen masses are united into a thin, hollow scale.

TYPE SPECIES: *Coelandria smillieae*
(F. Mueller) Fitzgerald
(*Dendrobium smillieae* F. Mueller)

Now recognized as belonging to the genus *Dendrobium*, *Coelandria* was previously considered to include eight robust epiphytes or occasionally lithophytes found in mid elevation, open rain forests of northeastern Australia and New Guinea. These robust plants form large clumps of non-branching stems, subtended by thin, dry sheaths, each with several, thinly textured to leathery, seasonally deciduous, twisted or curved leaves. The tightly packed inflorescence, borne toward the tip of the leafless stem, is bottle-brush like. The rigid, shiny, thick, waxy and fleshy flowers' segments have bases of pink graduating to white, cream or pale green at the tips with the lip often a contrasting color. The small dorsal sepal is oblong, the lateral sepals are ovate to spatula-shaped, and the small petals are similar to the dorsal sepal. The thick, uppermost, entire lip embraces the short column.

COELIA

Lindley

Gen. Sp. Orchid. Pl. 36 (1830).

Epidendroideæ ⸬ **Arethuseæ** • **Bletiinæ**

ETYMOLOGY: Greek for hollow. Based on a drawing by Bauer that suggested a hollow body; the drawing was in error.

TYPE SPECIES: *Coelia baueriana* Lindley nom. illeg.

Coelia triptera (Smith) G. Don ex Steudel
(*Epidendrum tripterum* Smith)

Five attractive, sympodial epiphytes, lithophytes or terrestrials are found in low to upper elevation, hill scrub to montane rain and oak-pine forests of south eastern Mexico to Panama, Cuba and Jamaica. These plants often form huge colonies, have clustered, oval to roundish, one-noded pseudo-bulbs, subtended by papery sheaths, each with several, narrow, grass-like, thinly textured leaves. The few-flowered inflorescence, subtended by several, distichous, overlapping sheaths, are borne from the base of the pseudobulb. The small, fleshy, white, cream or buff flowers have a strong, sweet fragrance. The small, arrowhead-shaped, entire lip is distinctly channeled with an inrolled margin and minute papillate. The flowers have a short, stout, broadly winged column.

COELIOPSIS

Reichenbach *filius*

Gard. Chron., ser. 1 **1872**: 9 (1872).

Epidendroideæ ⸬ **Cymbidieæ** • **Coelioposidinæ**

ETYMOLOGY: *Coelia*, a genus of orchids and Greek for appearance or likeness. Referring to a similarity.

TYPE SPECIES: *Coeliopsis hyacinthosma*
Reichenbach f.

One attractive, sympodial epiphyte is found in wet, low elevation, hill forests from Costa Rica to Colombia and Ecuador. This small plant has roundish, often wrinkled pseudobulbs, subtended by papery, basal sheaths, each topped by several, pleated leaves that are prominently veined on the underside. The short, few-flowered inflorescence grows downward or sideways. The small, creamy-white to brown, fragrant flowers do not open widely. They are packed in a head-like structure and are rigidly fleshy and waxy. The petals are much smaller than the sepals, and the lateral sepals are united, forming a sac-like or chin-like, basal projection. The trilobed lip has erect side lobes with a spreading, fringed margin. The rectangular or ovate midlobe has a bright orange blotch near the base, is strongly bent downward, and has a fringed margin. The flowers have a short, slightly club-shaped, winged column.

COELOBOGYNE

Not *Coelobogyne* J. Smith (1839) Euphorbiaceæ.

An orthographic variant introduced in *Wochenschr. Vereines Beford. Gartenbaues Konigl. Preuss. Staaten*, **11**(47): 375 (1868). The correct spelling is *Coelogyne*.

COELOGINE

An orthographic variant introduced in *Tijdschr. Ned. Indië*, **17**(2): 123 (1855). The correct spelling is *Coelogyne*.

COELOGLOSSUM

Hartman

Handb. Skand. Fl., ed. 1 323, 329 (1820).

Name ICBN rejected vs. *Dactylorhiza* Nevski (1937) Orchidaceæ.

ETYMOLOGY: Greek for hollow and tongue. From the form of the lip.

LECTOTYPE: *Coeloglossum viride* (Linnaeus) Hartman
(*Satyrium viride* Linnaeus)

Although validly published this rejected name is now referred to *Dactylorhiza*, *Coeloglossum* was previously considered to include one quite common terrestrial found in low to upper elevation, grasslands and montane

Currently Accepted | Validly Published | Invalidly Published | Published Pre-1753 | Superfluous Usage | Orthographic Variant | Fossil

forests across Canada, the United States (Alaska, Washington to Virginia), Scandinavia to Italy, Britain to eastern Russia (Amur to Kamchatka), Turkey to Mongolia, Korea, Japan and Taiwan. This tiny, inconspicuous but extremely variable plant has smooth, unbranched stems, subtended by tubular, basal sheaths and has simple, green, tubular flowers. This plant is hard to locate in their habitats, as they easily blend in with the native grasses. The erect, lax to rather densely packed, few to numerous-flowered inflorescence has tiny, green-yellow flowers. The sepals and petals converge, forming a well-rounded hood over the short, stout column. The yellow, wedge-shaped, entire or obscurely trilobed lip is three toothed at the tip, suffused red-brown along the margin, and has a short, sac-like spur.

NOTE: Current DNA analysis shows that *Coeloglossum* is clearly nested within *Dactylorhiza*.

COELOGLOSSUM

Lindley

Edwards's Bot. Reg.   **20**: sub 1701, no. 27 (1834).
Not *Coeloglossum* Hartman (1820) Orchidaceæ.

ETYMOLOGY: Greek for hollow or cavity and tongue. Refers to the lip of these species.

TYPE SPECIES: *None designated*

Not validly published because of a prior use of the name, this homonym was replaced by *Peristylus*.

COELOGNE

An orthographic variant introduced in *Enum. Phan. Born.*, 204 (1942). The correct spelling is *Coelogyne*.

COELOGROSSUM

An orthographic variant introduced in *Ill. Fl. Japan*, 701 (1949). The correct spelling is *Coeloglossum*.

COELOGYME

An orthographic variant introduced in *Orchid. Nepal*, 75 (1978). The correct spelling is *Coelogyne*.

COELOGYNA

An orthographic variant introduced in *Itin. Pl. Khasyah Mts.*, 159 (1848). The correct spelling is *Coelogyne*.

COELOGYNE

Lindley

Coll. Bot. (Lindley)   sub t. 33 (1821), and
Coll. Bot. (Lindley)   t. 37 (1825).

Epidendroideæ ⚬ **Arethuseæ** • **Coelogyninæ**

ETYMOLOGY: Greek for hollow and woman, female or pistil. Suggestive of the deeply excavated stigma.

LECTOTYPE: *Coelogyne cristata* Lindley

One hundred eighty-two sympodial epiphytes, lithophytes or rare terrestrials are found in low to upper elevation, coastal to montane forests, swampy scrub and rocky cliffs with a vast range extending from Sri Lanka through southern China (Xizang to Yunnan, Guangxi to Jiangxi, Hainan and Hong Kong), India (Kashmir to Assam), Nepal, Myanmar to Vietnam, Indonesia, the Philippines and to the southwestern Pacific Archipelago. The greatest diversity is found in Borneo and Sumatra. These plants have large, ovoid, cone-shaped or cylindrical pseudobulbs, crowded or remotely spaced on the rhizome, each with a pair of elliptical to narrow, evergreen leaves, borne from the tip of the pseudobulb. The small to fairly large, showy flowers are produced singly, in pairs, or more commonly on long, multifloral inflorescences. The inflorescence is developed in one of four ways: **a**) produced on a separate shoot that does not develop to produce a pseudobulb and leaves; **b**) produced on a mature shoot with full-grown leaves; **c**) produced before the pseudobulbs and leaves on the same shoot; and **d**) produced at the same time as the pseudo-bulbs and leaves. The typically fragrant, pristine white, green, yellow-green to coppery brown flowers are rather short-lived, and come in a variety of shapes and sizes. The petals range from narrow to thread-like in shape and the sepals are small to rather large. Some species the flowers open in succession and in other species they open simultaneously. Many species have intricate dark brown or bright yellow mottling or blotches on the complexly keeled, callused, and usually trilobed lip. The flowers have a rather long, footless column.

NOTE: These species are often taxonomically difficult to identify especially when dried.

COELOSTYLIS

Not *Coelostylis* Torrey & A. Gray ex Endlicher & Fenzl (1939) Loganiaceæ, nor *Coelostylis* (A. Jussieu) Kuntze (1891) Malpighiaceæ.

An orthographic variant cited in *Lex. Gen. Phan.*, 134, 135 (1904). The correct spelling is *Coilostylis*.

COEMACTRA

An orthographic variant introduced in *Beih. Bot. Centralbl.*, **8**(4-5): 312 (1899). The correct spelling is *Cremastra*.

COENADENIUM

(Summerhayes) Szlachetko

Ann. Bot. Fenn.   **40**(1): 70 (2003).

ETYMOLOGY: Greek for hollow or cavity and with a gland. Referring to the large, swollen spur.

TYPE SPECIES: *Coenadenium brevilobum*
            (Summerhayes) Szlachetko
        (*Angraecopsis breviloba* Summerhayes)

Recognized as belonging to the genus *Angraecopsis*, *Coenadenium* was proposed to include three epiphytes found in Tanzania and Kenya. These dwarf plants have tiny, unbranched stems, often appearing leafless, that have small, dull green leaves with the roots often being more prominent than the leaves. The long, numerous-flowered inflorescence has funnel-like, distichous, black bracts and has pale green or yellow-green flowers with narrow segments. The obscurely trilobed lip has small, ear-like side lobes and a long, swollen, club-shaped spur. The flowers have a slender, curved, wingless column.

COESPIPHYLIS

Thouars

Hist. Orchid.   Table 3, sub 3u (1822).

Name published without a description. Today this name is most often referred to *Bulbophyllum*.

COESTICHIS

Thouars

Hist. Orchid.   Table 3, sub 3r (1822).

Name published without a description. Today this name is most often referred to *Liparis*.

COGNIAUXIOCHARIS

(Schlechter) Hoehne

Arq. Bot. Estado São Paulo, n.s.   **1**(6): 132 (1944).

ETYMOLOGY: Dedicated to Alfred (Celestin) Cogniaux (1841-1916), a Belgian botanist who worked extensively on the orchids of Brazil, the West Indies, and the Americas and was co-author of *Orchidees Dictionnaire Iconographique*. And Latin for to honor or dedicate.

TYPE SPECIES: *Cogniauxiocharis glazioviana*
            (Cogniaux) Hoehne
        (*Pelexia glazioviana* Cogniaux)

Now recognized as belonging to the genus *Pteroglossa*, *Cogniauxiocharis* was previously considered to include two terrestrials found in south-eastern Brazil (Espírito Santo and Minas Gerais). These erect, small, leafy plants have unbranched stems, each with several, broad leaves lightly veined on the underside. The erect, hairy, red, few-flowered inflorescence has small, green to pink flowers not opening widely, whose outer surfaces are covered with fine hairs. The clawed, obscurely trilobed lip has small specs found scatted on the tip and has a short, blunt spur. The flowers have a more or less erect, slender, wingless, footless column.

COHNIA

Reichenbach *filius*

Bot. Zeitung (Berlin) **10**: 928 (1852).

Not *Cohnia* Kunth (1850) Liliaceæ.

ETYMOLOGY: In honor of Ferdinand Julius Cohn (1828-1898), a German founder of bacteriology. He is noted for his studies of algae, bacteria and other microorganisms. He devised a systematic classification of bacteria into genera and species.

TYPE SPECIES: *Cohnia quekettioides* Reichenbach f.

Not validly published because of a prior use of the name, this homonym was replaced by *Cohniella*.

COHNIELLA

Pfitzer

Nat. Pflanzenfam. **2**(6): 193, 194 (1889).

Not *Cohniella* Schroeder (1897) Scenedesmaceæ.

Epidendroideæ ⚘ Cymbideæ • Oncidiinæ

ETYMOLOGY: *Cohnia*, a genus of orchids and Latin for diminutive.

TYPE SPECIES: *Cohniella quekettioides*
(Reichenbach f.) Pfitzer
(*Cohnia quekettioides* Reichenbach f.)

Once consisting of eleven sympodial epiphytes found in low elevation, evergreen forests from Guatemala to Nicaragua, but now reduced to just one species. These plants, often called rat-tailed *Oncidiums*, have inconspicuous pseudobulbs, subtended by distichous, leaf-like sheaths, each with a solitary, long, thick, cylindrical leaf. The long, simple or branched, numerous-flowered inflorescence has wide-spreading, bright yellow flowers covered with red-brown spots. The yellow lateral sepals are deeply concave. The trilobed lip has a central, red-brown claw, small, erect side lobes are often spotted red-brown and has a wide-spreading, bilobed midlobe. The flowers have a short, stout, footless, incurved column.

NOTE: Most of these species were formerly included in *Oncidium*, but recent DNA studies now place these species in *Trichocentrum*.

COILLON

Guéroult

Hist. Pl. 388 (1558).

Pre-1753, therefore not validly published in fulfillment of nomenclatural rules; this name is most often referred to *Satyrium*.

COILOCHILUS

Schlechter

Bot. Jahrb. Syst. **39**: 36 (1906).

Orchidoideæ ⚘ Diurideæ • Cryptostylidinæ

ETYMOLOGY: Greek for hollow and lip. In reference to the concave lip.

TYPE SPECIES: *Coilochilus neocaledonicum*
Schlechter

One sympodial terrestrial is found in humid, low to mid elevation, forest scrub and gullies of eastern New Caledonia. This small, erect plant has slender, unbranched stems, each with a basal rosette of one narrow leaf per shoot. The tall, wiry, numerous-flowered inflorescence has tiny, dull green-yellow flowers that are self-pollinating and will change color as they age. The tiny, cup-shaped, entire lip is somewhat similar to the size, shape and coloration of the sepals and petals. The flowers have an obscure column with a short, massive foot.

COILOSTYLIS

Rafinesque

Fl. Tellur. **4**: 37 (1836)[1837].

ETYMOLOGY: Greek for hollow and style. Alluding to the cavity in which the stigma and anthers are carried.

LECTOTYPE: *Coilostylis emarginata* Rafinesque
This type name is now considered a synonym of
Epidendrum ciliare Linnaeus

Now recognized as belonging to the genus *Epidendrum, Coilostylis* was previously considered to include two epiphytes or sometimes lithophytes found in wet, low to mid elevation, hill scrub and montane forests from Puerto Rico to Trinidad, the Guianas, Venezuela, Mexico to Peru and Brazil. These plants have spindle-shaped to cylindrical stems, subtended by overlapping, papery sheaths, each with several, leathery, glossy leaves. The few-flowered inflorescence, borne on a newly maturing pseudobulb, has fragrant, pale green to green-yellow flowers. The white, trilobed lip has deeply fringed side lobes and a long, slender, upcurved midlobe. The flowers have a long, slender, club-shaped column.

COLAX

Lindley ex Sprengel

Syst. Veg. (Sprengel), ed. 16 **3**: 680, 727 (1826).

ETYMOLOGY: Greek for parasite. Referring to the species epiphytic habit.

TYPE SPECIES: *None designated*

Now recognized as belonging to the genus *Bifrenaria, Colax* Sprengel was previously considered to include six epiphytes or lithophytes found in low elevation, hill forests and rocky crevices from Trinidad, the Guianas, Venezuela, Colombia to Peru and Brazil usually in full sunlight. These plants have narrow or stem-like, clustered pseudobulbs, each with several, pleated, thinly textured leaves. The erect to arching, few-flowered inflorescence has showy, fragrant, white, yellow-green or pale green flowers with spreading sepals and smaller petals. The white to yellow-orange, clawed, obscurely trilobed lip has erect side lobes and the midlobe has a lobed callus.

COLAX

Lindley

Edwards's Bot. Reg.
29(Misc): 50, section no. 65 (1843).

Not *Colax* Lindley ex Sprengel (1826) Orchidaceæ.

ETYMOLOGY: Greek for parasite. Referring to the plants' epiphytic habitat.

TYPE SPECIES: *None designated*

Not validly published because of a prior use of the name, this homonym was replaced by *Pabstia*.

COLLABIOPSIS

S.S. Ying

Coloured Ill. Indig. Orchids Taiwan **1**(2): 112 (1977).

ETYMOLOGY: *Collabium*, a genus of orchids, and Greek for resembling.

TYPE SPECIES: *Collabiopsis formosana*
(Hayata) S.S. Ying
(*Collabium formosanum* Hayata)

Now recognized as belonging to the genus *Collabium, Collabiopsis* was previously considered to include six terrestrials found in moist, low to mid elevation, evergreen forests of northern Taiwan, China (Yunnan to Guangdong) and Myanmar to Vietnam. These erect, unbranched plants, often forming dense mats, have a solitary, basal leaf with wavy margins, dark green blotches and numerous veins. The erect, few-flowered inflorescence has a red base and is pale green toward the tip. The showy, yellow-green flowers suffused purple-red, have narrow segments. The lip is

Currently Accepted Validly Published Invalidly Published Published Pre-1753 Superfluous Usage Orthographic Variant Fossil

held at right angles to the other floral segments. The trilobed lip has incurved side lobes, the shallowly notched midlobe has two keels marked or lined purple-red, and has a small, tubular spur.

COLLABIUM

Blume

Bijdr. Fl. Ned. Ind. **8**: 357 (1825).

Epidendroideæ ⚘ Collabiinæ • Currently unplaced

ETYMOLOGY: Latin for neck and lip. Refers to the lateral sepals that are inserted on the spur of the lip and embrace the column like a collar.

TYPE SPECIES: *Collabium nebulosum* Blume

Fourteen, uncommon sympodial terrestrials or rare epiphytes are found in low to mid elevation, hill scrub and montane rocky slopes and valleys from southern China (Xizang, Yunnan to Hubei), Taiwan, northern India (Assam), Myanmar to Vietnam and Indonesia to the southwestern Pacific Archipelago. These plants have narrow, cylindrical pseudobulbs with one noded and tubular sheaths, each with a broad, papery, blotched leaf that is yellow or dark green on the topside and blue-green on the underside. The few-flowered inflorescence has rather showy, green-yellow flowers stained purple-red. The narrow lateral sepals are joined with the column foot forming a long chin-like, spur projection or is spurless. The white, immobile, clawed, trilobed lip has erect side lobes, the broad midlobe is suffused red or yellow near the keels and has a notched margin. The flowers are arranged on the floral rachis half twisted and slightly asymmetric. The flowers have a long, somewhat club-shaped, slightly forward curved column.

COLLAEA

Not *Collaea* A.P. de Candolle (1825) Fabaceæ, and not *Collaea* Sprengel (1826) Asteraceæ.

An orthographic variant introduced in *Gen. Pl. (Endlicher)*, 213 (1837). The correct spelling is *Collea*.

COLLARE-STUARTENSE

Senghas & Bockermühl

J. Orchideenfr. **4**(2): 73 (1997).

ETYMOLOGY: Latinized form of *Stuart collar*. Refers to the column wings and the fused collar of the column resembling an old-fashioned starched, lace collar that was fashionable during Stuart period (1603-1688).

TYPE SPECIES: *Collare-stuartense multistellare* (Reichenbach f.) Senghas & Bockermühl (*Odontoglossum multistellare* Reichenbach f.)

Now recognized as belonging to the genera *Odontoglossum* and *Miltonioides*. *Collare-stuartense* was proposed to include six epiphytes found in upper elevation, montane cloud forests of Ecuador to Bolivia. These plants have ovate, flattened pseudobulbs, subtended at the base by distichous, leaf-bearing sheaths, each with several leathery leaves. The multi-flowered inflorescence has large, green-yellow flowers with pale brown stripes or blotches. The white, trilobed lip has roundish side lobe with various notches on the margins. The narrow, smooth midlobe tapers to a sharp point and has a few brown blotches.

COLLEA

Lindley

Bot. Reg. **9**: sub 760 (1823).

Name ICBN rejected vs. *Pelexia* Poiteau ex Lindley (1826) Orchidaceæ.

ETYMOLOGY: Either named in honor of Thomas Colley (1801-1862), an English orchid collector who worked for James Bateman (1811-1897) in the Guianas.

Or possibly named for Luigi Aloysius Colla (1766-1848), an Italian botanist and horticulturist from Turin and author of *Hortus Ripulensis, Herbarium Pedemontanum*.

TYPE SPECIES: *None designated*

Although validly published this rejected name is now referred to the genera *Pelexia* and *Eltroplectris*. *Collea* was considered to include two terrestrials found from Cuba to Puerto Rico, southern Mexico to Colombia and Venezuela. These erect plants have unbranched stems, each with a basal rosette of leaves. They are a shiny on the upper face and the dull backside is deeply nerved. The erect, hairy, few-flowered inflorescence has flowers with the dorsal sepal and petals forming a hood over the short, footless column. The erect, entire lip is attached to the base of the column.

COLLOSTYLIS

An orthographic variant introduced in *Dict. Class. Sci. Nat.*, **4**: 168 (1838). The correct spelling is *Callostylis*.

COLOGYNE

An orthographic variant introduced in *Itin. Pl. Khasyah Mts.*, 163 (1848). The correct spelling is *Coelogyne*.

COLOMBIANA

Ospina

Orquideologia **8**(3): 230 (1973).

ETYMOLOGY: Named in honor of the Republic of Colombia (located on the northwestern area of South America), where the type species was collected.

TYPE SPECIES: *Colombiana garayana* Ospina

Now recognized as belonging to the genus *Pleurothallis*, *Colombiana* was previously considered to include two terrestrials found in upper elevation, montane forests of northwestern Colombia (Antioquia). These small plants have slender, erect stems, each with long, narrow leaves. The several, few-flowered inflorescences have small, red flowers, borne toward the spikes' tip, opening in succession.

COMERSOPHYLIS

An orthographic variant introduced in *Hist. Orchid.*, *t.* 97 (1822). The correct spelling is *Commersophylis*.

COMMERSIS

Thouars

Hist. Orchid. Table 3, sub 3v (1822).

Name published without a description. Today this name is most often referred to *Bulbophyllum*.

COMMERSOPHYLIS

Thouars

Hist. Orchid. Table 3, sub 3u (1822).

Name published without a description. Today this name is most often referred to *Bulbophyllum*.

COMMERSORCHIS

Thouars

Hist. Orchid. Table 3, sub 3v (1822).

ETYMOLOGY: Commemorating Philibert Commerçon (1737-1773), a French doctor and naturalist. He joined Louis Antoine de Bougainville on his circum-navigational voyage (1766-1769). On the return voyage, he remained at the islands of Madagascar and Mauritius where he died.

TYPE SPECIES: *None designated*

Name published without a description. Today this name is most often referred to *Bulbophyllum*.

COMPARETIA

An orthographic variant introduced in *Prakt. Stud. Orchid.*, 44, 221 (1854). The correct spelling is *Comparettia*.

COMPARETTIA

Poeppig & Endlicher

Nov. Gen. Sp. Pl. (Poeppig & Endlicher)
1(7-10): 42, *t. 73* (1836).

Epidendroideæ ◊ Cymbidieæ • Oncidiinæ

ETYMOLOGY: Dedicated to Andrea Comparetti (1745-1801), an Italian botanist, explorer, plant physiologist, professor of botany at the University of Padua and author of *Osservazioni sulle propriete della China del Brasile.*

LECTOTYPE: *Comparettia falcata*
Poeppig & Endlicher
indirectly designated by Reichenbach f., *Ann. Bot. Syst.*,
6: 688 (1863), and
designated by Britton & Wilson, *Sci, Surv. Porto Rico,*
5(2): 211 (1924).

Seven sympodial epiphytes are found in low to upper elevation, hill to montane forests from Cuba to Puerto Rico, Mexico to Panama with the greatest development occurring in the Andes of Venezuela, Colombia to Bolivia and Brazil. These showy, small plants have tiny, densely clustered, flattened pseudobulbs, each with a solitary, fleshy, proportionately large leaf. The long, wiry, arching, simple to branched, numerous to few-flowered inflorescence has nodding, brightly colored flowers with small sepals and petals. The lateral sepals are extended into a spur-like sheath into which the spur of the lip is inserted. The uniquely structured, spreading, shortly clawed, trilobed lip has two tail-like spurs at the base, that in turn are enclosed by the long, lateral sepals, thus appearing as if three spurs are present. The flowers have an erect, wide, wingless, footless column.

COMPERIA

K. Koch

Linnaea **22**: 287 (1849).

Orchidoideæ ◊ Orchideæ • Orchidinæ

ETYMOLOGY: Derived from the name of the type species, *Orchis comperiana* (named by vonSteven in *Nouv. Mém. Soc. Imp. Naturalistes Moscou*, **1**: 259 1829) - honoring a Mr. D. Compère (x-1847), a French-born Crimean (Krym) landowner and amateur botanist who collected the flora of western Crimea, and never got to publish his work *Flora Laspiana.*

LECTOTYPE: *Comperia comperiana*
(Steven) Ascherson & Graebner
(*Orchis comperiana* Steven)

One sympodial terrestrial is found in seasonally dry, low to mid elevation, deciduous, open piney woodlands and always on limestone soil from Ukraine (Crimea), Turkey to western Iran, Syria and Lebanon. This small, erect plant has stout, unbranched stems, each with several, basal leaves often arranged upward. The short, somewhat densely packed, few to numerous-flowered inflorescence has large, showy, green or maroon flowers suffused brown-purple or rose. The sepals and petals converge, forming a hood, and the petals have a few marginal teeth. The trilobed lip has its ends drawn out into four long, thread-like extensions and has a swollen, incurved spur. The flowers have a short, footless column.

COMPYLOCENTRUM

An orthographic variant cited in *Pl. Alkaloids*, 155 (1996). The correct spelling is *Campylocentrum.*

CONCHIDIUM

Griffith

Not. Pl. Asiat. **3**: 321, *t. 310* (1851).

Epidendroideæ ◊ Podochileæ • Eriinæ

ETYMOLOGY: Greek for mussel, hollow or seashell. Refers to the bulbs that are shaped like a closed shell.

TYPE SPECIES: *Conchidium pusillum* Griffith

Ten sympodial epiphytes or lithophytes are found in low to upper elevation, dense hill and montane forests, mosses and lichens from northern India (Kashmir to Assam), Myanmar to Vietnam, southern China (Xizang to Fujian) and Hong Kong. These minute plants have long, creeping rhizomes and the tiny, roundish pseudobulbs are usually in pairs; each with one to two, thinly textured leaves that have a long bristle at the tip. The erect, wiry, few-flowered inflorescence has small, white flowers not opening widely. The triangular lateral sepals are united with the column foot forming a chin-like protuberance. The slightly recurved, narrow, entire or trilobed lip, attached to the column foot, has finely serrated margins and tapers to a sharp point. The flowers have a small column with a curving foot. These species were formerly included in *Eria.*

CONCHOCHILUS

Hasskarl

Tijdschr. Natuurl. Gesch. Physiol. **9**: 146 (1842).

ETYMOLOGY: Greek for mussel or seashell and lip. Descriptive of the white spotted lip that resembles a mussel shell.

TYPE SPECIES: *Conchochilus oppositiflorus* Hasskarl
This type name is now considered a synonym of
Appendicula cristata Blume

Now recognized as belonging to the genus *Appendicula*, *Conchochilus* was previously considered to include one epiphyte found in eastern Indonesia (Sumatra to Borneo). This low-growing plant has flattened, often branching stems subtended by narrow, deep green leaves. The long, often branching, numerous-flowered inflorescence gradually lengthens over time. The tiny, green-yellow flowers have brown nerves and are violet suffused. The yellow or white, trilobed lip is suffused crimson or pink and has a few intricate calli. The flowers have a small, deep crimson column.

CONCHOCHYLUS

An orthographic variant introduced in *Cat. Pl. Hort. Bot. Bogor.*, 300 (1844). The correct spelling is *Conchochilus.*

CONCHOGLOSSUM

Breda

Gen. Sp. Orchid. Asclep., fasc. IIII, n.s.   (1830).

ETYMOLOGY: Latin for shell and tongue. Refers to the shape of the lip.

TYPE SPECIES: *None designated*

Now recognized as belonging to the genera *Cyrtosia* and *Galeola*, *Conchoglossum* was previously considered to include two terrestrials found from northeastern India (Assam), Taiwan, Myanmar to Vietnam, Indonesia (Borneo to Java) and the Philippines. These erect plants have red, unbranched stems, each with several, dark green, checkered patterned leaves that have slightly wavy margins. The few-flowered inflorescence has pale yellow to creamy flowers with the dorsal sepal and petals converge, forming a hood over the small, short column. The entire lip has a sac-like base or small spur.

Currently Accepted   Validly Published   Invalidly Published   Published Pre-1753   Superfluous Usage   Orthographic Variant   Fossil

O r c h i d   G e n e r a   • **94**

CONCOCIDIUM

Romowicz & Szlachetko

Polish Bot. J. **51**(1): 44 (2006)[2007].

ETYMOLOGY: Latin for one color and *Oncidium*, a genus of orchids. Refers to the sectional name of *Concoloria* used by Kraenzlin.

TYPE SPECIES: *Concocidium concolor*
(Hooker) Romowicz & Szlachetko
(*Oncidium concolor* Hooker)

Recognized as belonging to the genus *Oncidium*, *Concocidium* was proposed to include eight epiphytes found in mid elevation, montane forests from Bolivia, Brazil to northeastern Argentina and Mexico (Chiapas) to Costa Rica. These plants have clustered, ovate to oblong, wrinkled pseudobulbs, each with several, leathery leaves borne at the tip. The slender, hanging, few to numerous-flowered inflorescence has small to large, bright canary-yellow, brown-green, purple-brown to bright orange flowers. The erect dorsal sepal is concave, the lateral sepals are united almost to the middle, the oblong petals have rounded tips and have slightly wavy margins. The short to long-clawed, entire lip has a basal callus with a number of parallel keels or lobed crest and a notched tip. The flowers have an erect, short, footless column.

CONDYLAGO

Luer

Orquideologia **15**(2-3): 118 (1982).

ETYMOLOGY: Latin for knuckle or joint. An allusion to the articulation of the lip to the column foot.

TYPE SPECIES: *Condylago rodrigoi* Luer

Now recognized as belonging to the genus *Stelis*, *Condylago* was proposed to include one epiphyte found in mid to upper elevation, montane forests of northwestern Colombia (Antioquia) and southern Panama. This small plant has erect, unbranched stems, subtended by tubular sheaths, each with a solitary, thinly textured, leathery leaf. The several, erect, slender, zig-zagged, few-flowered inflorescences bloom successively and will continue to bloom for years. The small, green to red-brown flowers are covered with purple spots, and the inner surface of the sepals is densely covered with fine, white hairs. The dark purple, entire lip has an unusual mechanism (slender, flexible strap or hinge) capable of forcibly lifting a pollinator upward against the green-white, winged column that has a prominent-bent foot.

CONIPHYLIS

Thouars

Hist. Orchid. Table 3, sub 3u, *t. 100* (1822).

Name published without a description. Today this name is most often referred to *Bulbophyllum*.

CONOPSEA

Wittstein

Etym.-Bot.-Handw.-Buch, ed. 1 222 (1852).

Name published without a description. Today this name is most often referred to *Gymnadenia*.

CONOPSIDIUM

Wallroth

Linnaea **14**: 147 (1840), and
Beitr. Bot. (Wallroth) 101 (1842).

ETYMOLOGY: Greek for gnat or mosquito and vault or chamber. Alluding to the shape of the small petals.

TYPE SPECIES: *Conopsidium stenantherum*
Wallroth nom. illeg.
Platanthera bifolia (Linnaeus) Richard
(*Orchis bifolia* Linnaeus)

Now recognized as belonging to the genus *Platanthera*, *Conopsidium* was previously considered to include two terrestrials found in low to mid elevation, open meadows and woodlands with nutrient-poor soil from Scandinavia, Britain to western Russia (Belarus to Ukraine) and northern Africa (Tunisia to Algeria). These erect plants have slender, unbranched stems, each with several basal leaves. The few-flowered inflorescence has sweetly fragrant, white or pale green flowers with widespreading lateral sepals. The hooded, heart-shaped dorsal sepal and the tiny, incurved petals converge over the short column. The long, tongue-shaped, entire lip has a long, cylindrical, green spur that is usually upward curved.

CONOSTALIX

(Kraenzlin) Brieger

Orchideen (Schlechter), ed. 3 **1**(11-12): 659 (1981).

ETYMOLOGY: Greek for a cone and staff or stake. Referring to the straight, cone-shaped spur.

TYPE SPECIES: *Conostalix calcaratum* (Lindley) Brieger
(*Dendrobium calcaratum* Lindley nom. illeg.)
not *Dendrobium calcaratum* A. Richard and
not *Dendrobium conostalix* Reichenbach f.

Now recognized as belonging to the genus *Dendrobium*, *Conostalix* was previously considered to include nine terrestrials and epiphytes distributed in low elevation, swamps, sandy soils and shallow river banks from Myanmar to Australia with most

species found in eastern Indonesia (Borneo). These slender, inconspicuous plants have wiry, reed-like stems, each with several, narrow, stiff, grass-like leaves. The leaf-like sheaths have irregular, twisted, short, brown or black hairs. The small, dull green to creamy flowers appear singly or in pairs from every node, are veined red-brown and are laid against the stem. The broad, almost white, trilobed lip is the most visible part of the flower and has small, tooth-like side lobes and a notched, rounded midlobe. The base of the lip, joined to the sides of the column foot, forms a closed spur. The above type name is now considered a synonym of *Dendrobium lobbii* Teijsmann & Binnendijk.

CONSTANTIA

Barbosa Rodrigues

Gen. Sp. Orchid. **1**: 78, *t. 245* (1877).

Epidendroideæ ◊ Epidendreæ • Laeliinæ

ETYMOLOGY: Dedicated to Constança Eufrosina da Borba Pacca (1844-1920), the third wife of the Brazilian botanist João Barbosa Rodrigues (1842-1909). Together they had 13 children, six boys and seven girls.

TYPE SPECIES: *Constantia rupestris* Barbosa Rodrigues

Six delightful, sympodial epiphytes are found in low to mid elevation, scrub of southern Brazil (Minas Gerais, Santa Catarina and Rio de Janeiro) where they grow mainly on *Vellozia* bushes usually in full sunlight. These dwarf plants have tiny, green or brown pseudobulbs, tightly arranged in masses, each with a pair of oblong, leathery or fleshy leaves that lay flat and have white ridges. The erect, solitary or rare two-flowered inflorescence has a tiny, pale green, pink, dark red-brown or creamy white flower with narrow to ovate, fleshy sepals and petals. The spear-shaped, trilobed lip tapers to a sharp point and has a bright yellow, prominent, ridged callus located at the base. The flowers have a short, white, pink or dark red column.

CONVALLARIA

Plumier

Pl. Amer. 171, *t. 176, f. 3* (1758).

Not *Convallaria* Linnaeus (1753) Liliaceæ.

ETYMOLOGY: Latin for kettle-shaped or valley. Refers to the shape of the small flowers.

TYPE SPECIES: *Convallaria caule articulato, unifolio, bifloro* Plumier

Not validly published because of a prior use of the name, this homonym was replaced by *Octomeria*. This name is now considered as a synonym of *Octomeria graminifolia* (Linnaeus) R. Brown.

COOKTOWNIA

D.L. Jones

Austrobaileya **5**(1): 74 (1997).

Orchidoideæ ⚘ Orchideæ • Orchidinæ

ETYMOLOGY: Named for the nearest population center in eastern Australia to where the type species was collected, Cooktown. This town name honors Captain James Cook (1728-1779), a British explorer and navigator, who sailed around the world twice.

TYPE SPECIES: *Cooktownia robertsii* D.L. Jones

One strange, sympodial terrestrial is found in low elevation, woodlands of northeastern Australia (Queensland). This small plant has short, erect stems, each with two roundish basal leaves. The wiry, few-flowered inflorescence has green flowers with darker colored veins. The sepals and petals are narrow but the petals have green-white margins. The spurless, entire lip has an incurved margin. The flowers have a small, dark green column.

COPPENSIA

Dumortier

Nouv. Mém. Acad. Roy. Sci. Bruxelles **9**(3): 10 (1835).

ETYMOLOGY: Probably named to honor Bernard Benoit Coppens (1756-1801), a Belgian physician.

TYPE SPECIES: *Coppensia bifolia* (Sims) Dumortier (*Oncidium bifolium* Sims)

Now recognized as belonging to the genus *Oncidium*, *Coppensia* was previously considered to include one epiphyte found in cool, mid to upper elevation, montane forests and along river banks of southern Brazil and Uruguay. This small plant has clustered, ovoid to oblong pseudobulbs, become deeply grooved with age, each with one to two, narrow, somewhat leathery leaves. The erect, simple to few-branched, numerous-flowered inflorescence has showy, yellow flowers. The sepals, petals and callus are densely covered with red-brown spots. The somewhat kidney-shaped, trilobed lip has small side lobes, and the much larger, vivid yellow midlobe is deeply notched. The flowers have a short column.

CORALLIOCYPHOS

An orthographic variant introduced in *Orchideen (Schlechter)*, ed. 1, 116 (1914). The correct spelling is *Coralliokyphos*.

CORALLIOKYPHOS

Fleischmann & Rechinger

Denkschr. Kaiserl. Akad. Wiss., Wien. Math.-Naturwiss Kl. **85**: 252, t. 3, f. 1 (1910).

ETYMOLOGY: Greek for coral and hump or hunchback. Alluding to the coral-like humps at the base of the lip.

TYPE SPECIES: *Coralliokyphos candidissimum* Fleischmann & Rechinger

This type name is now considered a synonym of *Moerenhoutia heteromorpha* (Reichenbach f.) Bentham & Hooker f.; basionym *Platylepis heteromorpha* Reichenbach f.

Now recognized as belonging to the genus *Moerenhoutia*, *Coralliokyphos* was previously considered to include one terrestrial found in low elevation, hill forests of western Indonesia (Maluku) and Samoa. This erect plant has several, thinly textured leaves. The numerous-flowered inflorescence bears, white flowers with a prominent, three-ridged callus.

CORALLIORHIZA

An orthographic variant introduced in *Fl. Brandenburg*, **1**: 697 (1864). The correct spelling is *Corallorhiza*.

CORALLIORRHIZA

An orthographic variant introduced in *Bull. Soc. Roy. Bot. Belgique.*, **3**: 226, 227 (1864). The correct spelling is *Corallorhiza*.

CORALLORCHIZA

An orthographic variant cited in *Nomencl. Bot. (Steudel)*, ed. 2, **1**: 128 (1840). The correct spelling is *Corallorhiza*.

CORALLORHIZA

Haller

Enum. Meth. Stirp. Helv. **1**: 278 (1742).

Pre-1753, therefore not validly published in fulfillment of nomenclatural rules. This name is most often referred to *Corallorhiza* Gagnebin.

CORALLORHIZA

Gagnebin

Acta Helv. Phys.-Math. **2**: 61 (1755).

Orthographic name ICBN conserved vs. *Corallorhiza* Châtelain (1760) Orchidaceæ.

Epidendroideæ ⚘ Calypsoeæ

ETYMOLOGY: Greek for coral and root. Describing the often brittle, coral-like appearance or texture of the branched, underground rhizomes.

TYPE SPECIES: *Corallorhiza trifida* (Linnaeus) Châtelain (*Ophrys corallorrhiza* Linnaeus)

Eleven uncommon, inconspicuous saprophytes are found in low to upper elevation, rich, decaying humus native across Canada, the United States (Alaska and Washington to Florida) and central Mexico to Guatemala, but also extending into Europe (Scandinavia, Britain to Kazakhstan), subarctic Russia (Amur to Magadan, Kamchatka to the Kuril Islands), Mongolia to Nepal, China (Xinjiang to Hebei) and Korea. They are often found in clusters of large colonies growing in dark or shady, damp woods or rocky slopes in rich, decaying humus and rotten leaves. These odd, slender, leafless plants have an underground tangle of rhizomes that are invaded by strands of mycorrhiza. There are various genera of fungi known to be associated with *Corallorhiza*. The erect, unbranched stem has the flowers located at the top of a succulent, yellow-green, brown or purple numerous-flowered inflorescence. These inconspicuous to showy, small flowers vary in color depending upon the degree of light to which they are subjected during the growing season and are suffused with varying degrees of purple. They are usually self-pollinating, and the widespreading flowers do not open fully. The broad, entire or trilobed lip often has two, small side lobes that are narrowed at the claw; the wide midlobe has a wavy margin and is either plain or variously spotted magenta or red. The flowers have a small, slightly curved, wingless, footless column that is often spotted.

CORALLORIZA

An orthographic variant introduced in *Nomencl. Fl. Danic.*, 19 (1827). The correct spelling is *Corallorhiza*.

CORALLORRHIZA

An orthographic variant introduced in *Acta Helv. Phys-Math.*, **2**: 57 (1755). The correct spelling is *Corallorhiza*.

| Currently Accepted | Validly Published | Invalidly Published | Published Pre-1753 | Superfluous Usage | Orthographic Variant | Fossil |

O r c h i d   G e n e r a   • **96**

CORALORHIZA

An orthographic variant introduced in *Amer. Monthly Mag. & Crit. Rev.*, **2**: 119 (1817). The correct spelling is *Corallorhiza*.

CORCURBORCHIS

Thouars

Hist. Orchid. Table 1, sub 2m (1822).

Name published without a description. Today this name is most often referred to *Corymborkis*.

CORDANTHERA

L.O. Williams

Lilloa **6**: 244 (1941).

ETYMOLOGY: Latin for the heart and Greek for flower. In reference to the heart-shaped anthers.

TYPE SPECIES: *Cordanthera andina* L.O. Williams

Now recognized as belonging to the genus *Stellilabium*, *Cordanthera* was previously considered to include one epiphyte found in mid to upper elevation, dense montane forests of Venezuela, Colombia and Ecuador. This small, short-lived plant has short stems that are usually sheathed by yellow-green, distichous leaves. The erect, few-flowered inflorescence has pale green-brown flowers veined dull red. The bases of the narrow petals are suffused maroon and have darker blotches of the same color. The chestnut-brown, trilobed lip has small, horn-like side lobes and a large, scoop-shaped midlobe. The flowers have a short, stumpy, hairy column with a long, hook-like beak, and a bright red cap.

CORDIGLOTTIS

J.J. Smith

Bull. Jard. Bot. Buitenzorg, sér. 3 **5**: 95 (1922).

Epidendroideæ ◊ Vandeæ • Aeridinæ

ETYMOLOGY: Latin for heart and tongue. Descriptive of the heart-shaped lip of the species.

TYPE SPECIES: *Cordiglottis westenenkii* J.J. Smith

Seven monopodial epiphytes are distributed in low elevation, hill forests of southern Thailand, Malaysia and Indonesia (Sumatra and Borneo). These small plants have short, hanging, purple stems, each with several, thick, narrow or compressed, slightly curved leaves arranged in two rows. They are subtended completely by overlapping, leaf bearing sheaths. The short or long, numerous to few-flowered inflorescence has small, creamy white to dark red flowers suffused mauve, lasting only one day, and open

one at a time in succession. The mobile, slightly sac-like, often S-curved in profile, trilobed lip has erect side lobes with a usually powdery callus between them, and the fleshy midlobe is hairy or powdery. The flowers have a short, slightly curved column.

CORDULA

Rafinesque

Fl. Tellur. **4**: 46 (1836)[1837].

Name ICBN rejected vs. *Paphiopedilum* Pfitzer (1886) Orchidaceæ.

ETYMOLOGY: Named for a nymph, but none exists in classical literature with this name.

TYPE SPECIES: *Cordula insignis* (Wallich ex Lindley) Rafinesque (*Cypripedium insigne* Wallich ex Lindley)

Although validly published this rejected name is now referred to *Paphiopedilum*. *Cordula* was considered to include fifty-three epiphytes distributed from India, southern China, and Myanmar to Vietnam, Indonesia and the Philippines. These often showy plants have short stems, each with fans of several or numerous, leathery leaves, frequently mottled with light or dark markings. The often hairy, few-flowered inflorescence has large flowers heavily marked with veins. The large dorsal sepal has brown spots, the petals are lined with tufts of stiff hairs, warts and bumps and the united lateral sepals form a single bract-like segment. The sac or pouch-like lip has incurved side lobes.

CORDYLA

Blume

Bijdr. Fl. Ned. Ind. **8**: 416 (1825).

Not *Cordyla* Loureiro (1790) Fabaceæ.

ETYMOLOGY: Greek for club. Refers to the club-shaped column.

TYPE SPECIES: *None designated*

Not validly published because of a prior use of the name, this homonym was replaced by *Nervilia*.

CORDYLESTILIS

An orthographic variant introduced in *J. Bot. (Hooker)*, **4**(26): 74 (1842). The correct spelling is *Cordylestylis*.

CORDYLESTYLIS

Falconer

J. Bot. (Hooker) **4**(26): 75 (1842).

ETYMOLOGY: Greek for club and style. Refers to the shape of the column.

TYPE SPECIES: *Cordylestylis foliosa* Falconer
This type name is now considered a synonym of *Goodyera procera* (Ker Gawler) Hooker; basionym *Neottia procera* Ker Gawler

Now recognized as belonging to the genus *Goodyera*, *Cordylestylis* was previously considered to include one small terrestrial widespread in Japan, southern China, Hong Kong, the Philippines and India, Indonesia and Malaysia to Thailand. This variable plant has erect stems that are leafy in the basal third with narrow, petiolate leaves. The numerous-flowered inflorescence has small, white flowers. The dorsal sepal and petals converge, forming a hood over the short column. The roundish, entire lip has a pair of white appendages at the base.

CORDYLESTYLLIS

An orthographic variant cited in *Handb. Orchid.-Namen*, 212 (2005). The correct spelling is *Cordylestylis*.

CORDYLOSTYLIS

An orthographic variant cited in *Hist. Nat. Veg. (Spach)*, **12**: 181 (1846). The correct spelling is *Cordylestylis*.

CORI-coazonte coxochitl

An orthographic variant introduced in *Hort. Donat.*, 138 (1858). The correct spelling is *Cozticcoatzonte*.

CORILOSTYLIS

An orthographic variant introduced in *Orchideen (Schlechter)*, ed. 1, 190 (1914). The correct spelling is *Coilostylis*.

CORISANTHES

Not *Corisanthes* Martius (1824) Violaceæ.

An orthographic variant introduced in *Encycl. (Lamarck), Suppl.*, **2**: 365 (1811). The correct spelling is *Criosanthes*.

CORTICOATZOATE

An orthographic variant introduced in *Fl. Serres Jard. Angleterre, t. 3742* (1839). The correct spelling is *Cozticcoatzonte*.

An orthographic variant introduced in *Nov. Veg. Descr.*, **2**: 22 (1825). The correct spelling is *Cozticcoatzonte*.

CORUNASTYLIS

Fitzgerald

Austral. Orch. **2**(3): *t. 1* (1888).

ETYMOLOGY: Greek for club and style. Refers to the column that is thickened or somewhat club shaped at the tip.

TYPE SPECIES: *Corunastylis apostasioides* Fitzgerald
This type name is now considered a synonym of *Genoplesium apostasioides* (Fitzgerald) D.L. Jones & M.A. Clements; basionym *Corunastylis apostasioides* Fitzgerald

Now recognized as belonging to the genus *Genoplesium*, *Corunastylis* was previously considered to include forty-eight terrestrials found in low elevation, hill scrub of Australia, New Zealand and New Caledonia. These small, slender, erect, unbranched plants have tubers that are replaced annually and a sheathing bract subtending the inflorescence. The numerous to few-flowered inflorescence has green-yellow flowers. The deeply concave dorsal sepal is marked with crimson, and the margins have short hairs. The short petals have prominent markings. The oblong, shortly clawed, entire lip is densely fringed with long, fine hairs. Some species have an odor of fermenting fruit or other offensive odors. Many of these species were formerly included in *Prasophyllum*.

CORYANTHES

Hooker

Bot. Mag. **58**: *t. 3102* (1831).

Epidendroideæ · Cymbidieæ · Stanhopeinæ

ETYMOLOGY: Greek for helmet and flower. Referring to the helmet-like epichile of the lip.

TYPE SPECIES: *Coryanthes maculata* Hooker

Thirty-eight sympodial epiphytes are found in humid, low to mid elevation, woodland to montane rain forests and of Honduras, Guatemala to Bolivia and Brazil. These large plants have short to long, clustered, ovoid to pear-shaped pseudobulbs, each with two large, pleated, fleshy to leathery leaves. The hanging, few-flowered inflorescence has short-lived, waxy flowers. Flower color varies widely even within a certain species making identification quite difficult. The flowers are extraordinary for the complexity of their unusual pollination mechanism and typically have a strong, penetrating and musty fragrance. The unusual bucket-shaped, long-clawed lip has a cup-shaped hypochile from which emerges the slender, tube-like mesochile that expands into the large, bucket-shaped epichile. The trilobed epichile has a claw-like midlobe that almost touches the stout, arched, winged column. The flowers have a footless column with liquid-producing glands dripping a sugary substance into the bucket.

CORYANTHUS

An orthographic variant introduced in *Paxton's Mag. Bot.*, **2**: 131 (1836). The correct spelling is *Coryanthes*.

CORYBAS

Salisbury

Parad. Lond. **2**: *t. 83* (1807).

Orchidoideæ · Diurideæ · Acianthinæ

ETYMOLOGY: Greek Mythology. A drunken man or a priest who danced (after becoming suitably sozzled), in honor of the goddess Rhea Cybele (an ancient Asian goddess of nature and fertility).

Referring perhaps to the shape of these warrior's helmets or the nodding head of a drunk.

TYPE SPECIES: *Corybas aconitiflorus* Salisbury

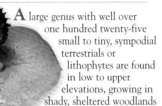

A large genus with well over one hundred twenty-five small to tiny, sympodial terrestrials or lithophytes are found in low to upper elevations, growing in shady, sheltered woodlands and moss laden rocky crevices. These exquisite little plants are exacting in their habitat requirements and have a wide range extending from India (Kashmir to Assam), Thailand, Malaysia, Indonesia, New Guinea, Australia, the Philippines, New Zealand and the southern Pacific Archipelago. Along with the plants' diminutive stature, they exhibit a most unusual beauty even when not in bloom. These erect plants have short, unbranched stems, each with a solitary, dark green, heart-shaped leaf often purple-red on the underside. The comparatively large, stalkless, solitary flower ranges from purple to pink and white. The large dorsal sepal is helmet-shaped, and the lateral sepals and petals are often thread-like. The large, recurved, entire lip, attached at its base to the column base, has incurved or flat, entire, scalloped or toothed margins with two short, basal spurs or appendages. The flowers have a tiny, slender to squat column that is straight or incurved.

CORYCIUM

Swartz

Kongl. Vetensk. Acad. Nya Handl., ser. 2 **21**: 220, *t. 3g* (1800).

Orchidoideæ · Orchideæ · Disinæ

ETYMOLOGY: Greek for helmet or leather bag and Latin for quality, or nature of. Refers to the helmet-shaped hood.

LECTOTYPE: *Corycium orobanchoides* (Linnaeus f.) Swartz (*Satyrium orobanchoides* Linnaeus f.)

Fifteen sympodial terrestrials are found in low to mid elevation, grasslands and scrub of South Africa and Lesotho with disjunctive populations in Malawi and Tanzania. These colony forming, erect plants have tall, slender to robust, unbranched stems, each with transparent leaf sheaths below the clustered (in the lower portion), narrow leaves. The erect, densely packed, numerous-flowered inflorescence (narrow bracts as long or longer than the flowers) has small, intricate flowers in various combinations of green, white, yellow, mauve and purple. The dorsal sepal along with the strongly concave or sac-like petals are united, forming a hood over the erect, shield-like, entire lip that has various appendages. The flowers have a short, stout column.

CORYDANDRA

Reichenbach

Deut. Bot. Herb.-Buch 53 (1841).

ETYMOLOGY: Greek for helmet and flower. Referring to the helmet-shaped head or cap over the anther.

TYPE SPECIES: *None designated*

A superfluous name proposed as a substitute for *Galeandra*.

CORYMBIS

Thouars

Hist. Orchid. Table 1, sub 2m, *tt. 37-38* (1822).

ETYMOLOGY: Greek for cluster or comb. Referring to the flat-topped or convex inflorescence.

TYPE SPECIES: *None designated*

A superfluous name proposed as a substitute for *Corymborkis*.

An orthographic variant introduced in *Hist. Orchid.*, Table 4, sub 2, *t. 37* (1822). The correct spelling is *Corymborkis*.

Currently Accepted   Validly Published   Invalidly Published   Published Pre-1753   Superfluous Usage   Orthographic Variant   Fossil

Orchid Genera · 98

CORYMBORKIS

Thouars
Nouv. Bull. Sci. Soc. Philom. Paris
1(19): 318 (1809).

Epidendroideæ ❧ Tropidieæ

ETYMOLOGY: Greek for a cluster or corymb and orchid. Referring to the cluster or corymb-like inflorescence of some of the species.

TYPE SPECIES: *Corymborkis corymbis* Thouars

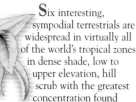

Six interesting, sympodial terrestrials are widespread in virtually all of the world's tropical zones in dense shade, low to upper elevation, hill scrub with the greatest concentration found from southern China, Japan to Indonesia, northeastern Australia and the southwestern Pacific Archipelago. There are two species are found throughout the West Indies, Central and South America, Africa, Madagascar and the Mascarene Islands. These evergreen plants have tough, woody, simple to sometimes branched, slender, reed-like stems (rather long, often with several arising from one rhizome). The large, papery, pleated leaves alternate on the upper half of the stem and often appear spiraling. These primitive plants simulate a ginger plant. The several, often branched inflorescences, borne from the leaf axils, have short-lived, slender, often pleasantly fragrant, sometimes showy, green, white or yellow flowers that are distichous and do not open widely. The narrow sepals are equal in length, the slender, slightly shorter petals embrace the column, which are united or fused at the base usually forming a basal claw. The hairy, erect, broadly ovate, entire lip has a long, folded claw (equal in length to sepals and petals) that embraces the slender, club-shaped, footless column, has two longitudinal keels also clasping the column.

CORYNANTHES

An orthographic variant introduced in *Bot. Zeitung (Berlin)*, **6**: 65 (1848). The correct spelling is *Coryanthes*.

CORYNOSTYLIS

Not *Corynostylis* Martius (1824) Violaceæ.

An orthographic variant cited in *Lex. Gen. Phan.*, 36 (1904). The correct spelling is *Corunastylis*.

CORYNOSTYLUS

An orthographic variant cited in *Lex. Gen. Phan.*, 143, 144 (1904). The correct spelling is *Corunastylis*.

CORYPHAEA

Lindley ex Wittstein
Etym.-Bot.-Handw.-Buch, ed. 1   231 (1852).

Name published without a description. Today this name is most often referred to as a section of *Disa*.

CORYSANTHES

R. Brown
Prodr. Fl. Nov. Holland.   328 (1810).

ETYMOLOGY: Greek for helmet and flower. Descriptive of the helmet-like lip of the flower.

LECTOTYPE: *Corysanthes fimbriata* R. Brown

Now recognized as belonging to the genus *Corybas*, *Corysanthes* was previously considered to include sixty-two terrestrials found in decaying humus, low to upper elevation, forests, scrub and moss laden cliffs from southern China (Guangxi to Yunnan), Thailand to Vietnam, Indonesia, the Philippines and New Zealand with the largest concentration found in Australia. These tiny, short-stemmed plants have a solitary, round to heart-shaped, frosty green to dark velvety green leaf that hugs the ground. The showy, solitary, small, often red-purple flower is dominated by a broad lip and usually sits on the leaf surface. The large, entire lip has a lacerated or heavily fringed margin and is sometimes two spurred. The dorsal sepal forms a large, cup-shaped hood over the whole flower. The flowers have a short, fleshy, winged column.

CORYSANTHIS

An orthographic variant introduced in *Gen. Pl., Suppl. 1 (Endlicher)*, 1367 (1840). The correct spelling is *Corysanthes*.

CORYTANTHES

An orthographic variant introduced in *Fl. Serres Jard. Eur.*, **1**: 211 (1845). The correct spelling is *Coryanthes*.

CORYTHANTES

An orthographic variant introduced in *Rev. Hort. (Paris)*, **37**: 18 (1866). The correct spelling is *Coryanthes*.

CORYTHANTHES

An orthographic variant introduced in *Fl. Serres Jard. Eur.*, **1**: 207 (1845). The correct spelling is *Coryanthes*.

CORYZANTHES

An orthographic variant introduced in *Dict. Class. Hist. Nat.*, **4**: 516, 530 (1823). The correct spelling is *Corysanthes*.

COSMOSANDALOS

Gesner ex Haller
Enum. Meth. Stirp. Helv.   **1**: 276 (1742).

Pre-1753, therefore not validly published in fulfillment of nomenclatural rules. This name is most often referred to *Cypripedium*.

COSTARICAEA

Schlechter
Repert. Spec. Nov. Regni Veg. Beih.   **19**: 30 (1923).

ETYMOLOGY: Honoring the Republic of Costa Rica (located in Central America between Panama and Nicaragua) where the type species was collected.

TYPE SPECIES: *Costaricaea amparoana* Schlechter

Now recognized as belonging to the genus *Scaphyglottis*, *Costaricaea* was previously considered to include one epiphyte found in Nicaragua, Costa Rica and Panama. This small plant has clustered, slender, ridged pseudobulbs produced apically from the tips of older pseudobulbs and appear tufted or shrubby. The small, green, suffused red flowers are borne on short-stalked terminal clusters. The white, entire lip, united to the base of the short column, has a center splash of bright yellow, and a tongue-like tip.

COTTONIA

Wight
Icon. Pl. Ind. Orient. (Wight) **5**(1): 21, t. 1755 (1851).

Epidendroideæ ❧ Vandeæ • Aeridinæ

ETYMOLOGY: Honoring Frederic Conyers Cotton (1807-1901), a British army lieutenant colonel of the Madras engineers, who collected and cultivated the orchids from around the Malabar (southwestern coastal) region in India.

TYPE SPECIES: *Cottonia macrostachys* Wight
This type name is now considered a synonym of *Cottonia peduncularis* (Lindley) Reichenbach f.; basionym *Vanda peduncularis* Lindley

One monopodial epiphyte is found in low to mid elevation, hill to montane forests from Sri Lanka and southwestern India. This unusual, robust climbing plant has narrow, sickle-shaped, channeled, bilobed leaves that are spaced along a long stem. The long, wiry, branched, few-flowered inflorescence, borne at the internodes, has small, unusually shaped, dirty orange flowers with similar, widespreading, red-veined sepals and petals. The broad, fleshy, trilobed lip has small, yellow side lobes covered with short hairs, and the midlobe has dark purple streaks which perfectly mimics an insect. The flower is probably pollinated by pseudocopulation. The flowers have a slender, short column with two wing-like projections.

COTYLOLABIUM

Garay

Bot. Mus. Leafl.   **28**(4): 307 (1980)[1982].

Orchidoideæ ⚘ Cranichideæ • Spiranthinæ

ETYMOLOGY: Greek for cavity or anything hollow and lip. Referring to the concave shape of the lip base.

TYPE SPECIES: *Cotylolabium lutzii* (Pabst) Garay (*Stenorrhynchos lutzii* Pabst)

One sympodial terrestrial is found in low elevation, grasslands in a small area of southeastern Brazil (Minas Gerais). This erect plant has unbranched stems, each with a few well-spaced, relatively small and somewhat bract-like leaves. The spirally twisted, few-flowered inflorescence (almost completely subtended by leafy bracts) has showy, large, yellow flowers that do not open widely, but in slow succession, with all facing to one side of the rachis. The large, erect, entire or obscurely trilobed lip is cup-shaped at its slightly notched tip and concave at the base. The flowers have a club-shaped column that is footless or has an obscure foot.

COUILLON

Mattioli

Comment. M.P.A. Matthiole   491, 492 (1572).

Pre-1753, therefore not validly published in fulfillment of nomenclatural rules; this name is most often referred to *Ophrys* and *Dactylorhiza*.

COZTICCOATZONTE

Hernández

Opera (Hernández)   1: 240 (1790).

ETYMOLOGY: A Nahuatl (Aztec) word for yellow, snake or serpent and plant.

TYPE SPECIES: *Cozticcoatzontecoxochitl, se planta fores ferente luteos, colubri capiti persimiles* Hernández

Pre-1753, therefore not validly published in fulfillment of nomenclatural rules; this polynomial name is most often referred to *Prosthechea*. *Cozticcoatzonte* was previously considered to include one epiphyte found in central Mexico.

This erect or hanging plant has egg or pear-shaped pseudobulbs, each with several, gray-green leaves that are covered in a fine powdery "film." The hanging, solitary-flowered inflorescence has a fragrant, bright citron-yellow to orange flower not opening fully with similar sepals and petals. The large, trilobed lip (usually a deeper yellow) has side lobes clasping the small column, the midlobe is frilled along its white margin, has a golden splash in the center and a basal callus. This name is usually now considered as a synonym of *Prosthechea citrina* (Lexarza) W.E. Higgins.

NOTE: The flowers were used by local natives to treat stomach disorders.

COZTICOATZONTECOXOCHITL

An orthographic variant introduced in *Dicc. Nombres Vulg. Pl.*, 66 (1871). The correct spelling is *Cozticcoatzonte*.

COZTICZACATZACUXOCHITL

An orthographic variant introduced in *Nov. Veg. Descr.*, **2**: 13 (1825). The correct spelling is *Cozticcoatzonte*.

CPPRIPEDIUM

An orthographic variant introduced in *Orchid. Gen. Sp.*, **6**: 40 (1901). The correct spelling is *Cypripedium*.

CRANACHIS

An orthographic variant introduced in *Nouv. Dict. Hist. Nat.*, **6**: 477 (1803). The correct spelling is *Cranichis*.

CRANGONORCHIS

D.L. Jones & M.A. Clements

Austral. Orchid Res.   **4**: 67 (2002).

ETYMOLOGY: Greek for shrimp and orchid. Refers to the common name of the flower 'prawn greenhood.'

TYPE SPECIES: *Crangonorchis pedoglossa* (Fitzgerald) D.L. Jones & M.A. Clements (*Pterostylis pedoglossa* Fitzgerald)

Recognized as belonging to the genus *Pterostylis*, *Crangonorchis* was proposed to include two terrestrials found in low elevation, coastal scrub of eastern Australia and Tasmania. These erect, fragile, dainty plants, sometimes forming large colonies, have slender, unbranched stems, each with several leaves arranged in a loose rosette. The solitary-flowered inflorescence has a usually green flower suffused red-brown toward the tips. The dorsal sepals and petals taper to long, thread-like points and converge, forming a

hood over the straight column. The long-clawed, heart-shaped, entire lip has a rather thick, shallowly notched tip.

CRANICHES

An orthographic variant introduced in *Beih. Bot. Centralbl.*, **36**(2): 430 (1918). The correct spelling is *Cranichis*.

CRANICHIA

An orthographic variant introduced in *Orchid.-Buch*, 165 (1892). The correct spelling is *Cranichis*.

CRANICHIS

Swartz

Prodr. (Swartz)   8: 120 (1788).

Orchidoideæ ⚘ Cranichideæ • Cranichidinæ

ETYMOLOGY: Greek for helmet. An allusion to the uppermost, almost helmet-shaped lip that is borne over the column.

LECTOTYPE: *Cranichis muscosa* Swartz

Fifty-four small, sympodial terrestrials or lithophytes are found in low to upper elevation, hill and montane rain forests, sphagnum woodlands and scrub from the southeastern United States (Florida) and Guatemala to Bolivia, Venezuela, Brazil and north-western Argentina. These plants have short, erect, unbranched stems, each with a basal rosette of one to several leaves or with the leaves spaced upward along the stem. The long, erect, numerous to few-flowered inflorescence has tiny, white, pink or green, exquisite, thinly textured flowers that are complex in shape. The small to tiny petals often have numerous, fine hairs along the margin. The more or less concave, uppermost, entire or lobed lip is somewhat sac-shaped or hood-like, and often conspicuously marked or heavily veined. The white lip often has a minutely ciliate margin and a blunt tip. The flowers have a short, fleshy, footless column.

CRANICHYS

An orthographic variant introduced in *Dict. Class. Hist. Nat.*, **11**: 515 (1827). The correct spelling is *Cranichis*.

CRANIECHIS

An orthographic variant introduced in *Cat. Descr. Orquid., Estac. Exp. Agron. Santiago, Cuba*, **60**: 45 (1938). The correct spelling is *Cranichis*.

Currently Accepted   Validly Published   Invalidly Published   Published Pre-1753   Superfluous Usage   Orthographic Variant   Fossil

Orchid Genera · 100

CRASSANGIS

Thouars

Hist. Orchid. Table 2, sub 3o, tt. 70-71 (1822).

Name published without a description. Today this name is most often referred to *Angraecum*.

CREMASTRA

Lindley

Gen. Sp. Orchid. Pl. 172 (1833).

Epidendroideæ ⚬ Calypsoeæ

ETYMOLOGY: Greek for flower stalk. Descriptive of the long, hanging, conspicuous ovary of the flower.

TYPE SPECIES: *Cremastra wallichiana* Lindley nom. illeg.
Cremastra appendiculata (D. Don) Makino
(*Cymbidium appendiculatum* D. Don)

Four unusual sympodial terrestrials are widespread in humid, low to upper elevation, hill scrub to montane broad leaf forests of eastern Russia (Sakhalin and Kuril Islands), northern India (Assam), Nepal, Bhutan, southern Korea, Japan, Taiwan, China (Yunnan to Henan) and Thailand to Vietnam. These small, and inconspicuous plants (often forming large clumps) have clustered, ovoid to corm-shaped pseudobulbs closely connected or well-spaced and are subtended by tubular sheaths. The one or two, pleated leaves are borne from tip of the pseudobulb. The erect, densely packed, few to numerous-flowered inflorescence has narrow, tubular, strongly fragrant, drooping flowers ranging from pink, purple to buff-colored and do not open widely. The slender, white, shortly clawed, trilobed lip has either the lower part or the upper part trilobed and is slightly sac-like at the base. The flowers have a long, slender, wingless, footless column.

CREORCHIS

An orthographic variant introduced in *Beih. Bot. Centralbl.*, **8**(4-5): 312 (1899). The correct spelling is *Georchis*.

CREPIDIUM

Blume

Bijdr. Fl. Ned. Ind. **8**: 387, *t. 63* (1825).
Not *Crepidium* Tausch (1828) Asteraceæ.

ETYMOLOGY: Greek for shaped like a sandal or slipper. Perhaps in reference to the sac-like base of the lip.

LECTOTYPE: *Crepidium rheedii* Blume
This type name is now considered a synonym of
Malaxis acutangula (Hooker f.) Kuntze;
basionym
Microstylis acutangula Hooker f.

Now recognized as belonging to the genera *Dienia* and *Malaxis*, *Crepidium* was previously considered to include two hundred terrestrials or rare epiphytes found

mostly in low to upper elevation, montane forests litter of southern China (Yunnan to Fujian, Hainan), northern India (Sikkim), Vietnam, Thailand, Malaysia, Indonesia, the Philippines and Australia. These softly textured plants have spindle-shaped to cylindrical pseudobulbs, each with several, channeled, broad, pleated, thin to fleshy leaves often suffused purple or brown that have wavy margins. The erect, numerous to few-flowered inflorescence has small to tiny, green, brown, yellow, pink or purple flowers that turn yellow as they age. The erect, delicate, thinly textured, entire to lobed lip has small side lobes with various teeth, and the triangular midlobe is distinctly notched at the tip and usually concave at the base. The flowers have a short, slightly curved, footless column.

CRIBBIA

Senghas

Orchidee (Hamburg) **36**(1): 19 (1985).

Epidendroideæ ⚬ Vandeæ • Aerangidinæ

ETYMOLOGY: Named in honor of Phillip James Cribb (1946-), a British botanist, Deputy Keeper and Curator of the Orchid Herbarium, Royal Botanic Gardens, Kew, and author of numerous books and articles on/about orchids.

TYPE SPECIES: *Cribbia brachyceras*
(Summerhayes) Senghas
(*Aerangis brachyceras* Summerhayes)

Four small, monopodial epiphytes or lithophytes restricted in humid, low to mid elevation, hill forests of Kenya, Tanzania, Zambia and São Tomé. These plants have short, upright or arching stems, subtended by overlapping leaf-sheaths. The thinly textured, distichous, narrow to oblong, unequally bilobed leaves are twisted at the base to lie in one plane. The several, numerous to few-flowered inflorescences, borne from the base of the plant, have small, well-spaced, fragrant, almost translucent, pale green, pale yellow-brown or pure white flowers. The entire lip has no callus but has a decurved to straight, cylindrical spur tapering from the funnel-shaped mouth. The flowers have a short, wingless, footless column.

CRINONIA

Blume

Bijdr. Fl. Ned. Ind. **7**: 338, *t. 41* (1825).

ETYMOLOGY: Greek for bed of lilies. Descriptive of the flowers that bear a superficial resemblance to a lily.

TYPE SPECIES: *None designated*

Now recognized as belonging to the genus *Pholidota*, *Crinonia* was previously considered to include five epiphytes common in shady, upper elevation, montane forests from Thailand, Malaysia and Indonesia (Java and Borneo) to the

Philippines. These plants have small oblong or oval pseudobulbs, each with one to two, narrow leaves. The hanging, few-flowered inflorescence has small, salmon to pink flowers presented in a zig-zagged pattern. The small, S-shaped, yellow, entire lip is sac-like at the base.

CRIOGENES

Salisbury

Monthly Rev., ser. 2 **75**: 81 (1814).

ETYMOLOGY: Greek for ram's head and to generate. Referring to the "charging ram" look of the flowers.

TYPE SPECIES: *None designated*

A superfluous name proposed as a substitute for *Cypripedium*.

CRIOSANTHES

Rafinesque

J. Phys. Chim. Hist. Nat. Arts **89**: 102 (1819), and *Amer. Monthly Mag. & Crit. Rev.* **2**: 268 (1818).

ETYMOLOGY: Greek for ram and flower. Referring to the unusual shape of the lip in relation to the other parts of the flower.

TYPE SPECIES: *Criosanthes borealis* Rafinesque

Now recognized as belonging to the genus *Cypripedium*, *Criosanthes* was previously considered to include two terrestrials found in dry, low to mid elevation, oak-pine woodlands from Canada (Yukon Territory to Newfoundland), the United States (Alaska, Washington to Oregon, Minnesota eastward to Maine and northern Georgia westward to northern Louisiana) and southwestern China (Yunnan). These small plants have a basal rosette of pale blue-green, basal leaves spiraled around the stem. The erect, solitary to four-flowered inflorescence has green, purple to rare white flowers with a broadly ovate to helmet-shaped dorsal sepal. The narrow lateral sepals and petals are slightly twisted and incurved around the lip. The unusual basin-shaped, green to purple lip is densely hairy, has purple to magenta veins and an incurved margin. The above type name is now considered a synonym of *Cypripedium arietinum* R. Brown.

CRIPRIPEDILUM

An orthographic variant introduced in *Man. Vasc. Pl. Yangtze Valley*, 532 (1958). The correct spelling is *Cypripedium*.

CRIPTANGIS

Thouars

Hist. Orchid. Table 3, sub 3o, *t. 50* (1822).

Name published without a description. Today this name is most often referred to *Mystacidium*.

CRIPTOPHYLIS

Thouars

Hist. Orchid.   Table 3, sub 1u (1822).

Name published without a description. Today this name is most often referred to *Bulbophyllum*.

CROCODEILANTHE

Reichenbach *filius* & **Warszewicz**

Xenia Orchid.   **1**: 10, t. 6 (1854), and
Bonplandia   **2**(9): 113 (1854).

ETYMOLOGY: Greek for crocodile and flower. Alluding to a fanciful resemblance of the flower to the head of a crocodile.

TYPE SPECIES: *Crocodeilanthe xiphizusa*
        Reichenbach f. & Warszewicz

Now recognized as belonging to the genus *Stelis*, *Crocodeilanthe* was previously considered to include four epiphytes found in cool, upper elevation, montane forests of northern Peru and Ecuador. These large, stout, tufted, clump-forming plants have erect, stout stems, subtended by loose, tubular sheaths, each with a solitary, elliptical, leathery leaf. The several, erect, solitary-flowered inflorescences, opening simultaneously, have small, yellow flowers often suffused brown, and sprinkled with several, purple spots. The flowers have large, floral bracts that are inflated. The fleshy, oblong, entire lip has a broadly rounded tip and a pair of low, crescent-shaped calli slightly above the middle. The flowers have a small, stout column.

CROCODILANTHE

An orthographic variant introduced in *Fol. Orchid., Pleurothallis*, 1 (1859). The correct spelling is *Crocodeilanthe*.

CROCODYLANTHE

An orthographic variant introduced in *Orchid.-Buch*, 165 (1892). The correct spelling is *Crocodeilanthe*.

CROSSANGIS

Schlechter

Beih. Bot. Centralbl.   **36**(2): 141 (1918).

ETYMOLOGY: Greek for little fringe and vessel or cup. Descriptive of the side lobes of the lip.

TYPE SPECIES: *Crossangis polydactyla*
        (Kraenzlin) Schlechter
        (*Listrostachys polydactyla* Kraenzlin)

Now recognized as belonging to the genus *Rhipidoglossum*, *Crossangis* was previously considered to include one epiphyte found in the upper elevation, montane forests of south-western Cameroon. This plant has short stems, each with the several, fleshy leaves bunched at the tip. The few-flowered inflorescence has small, green-white flowers. The trilobed lip has a small midlobe that is almost tooth-like and the side lobes curve around the small column.

CROSSOGLOSSA

Dressler & **Dodson**

Native Ecuadorian Orchids   **1**: 148 (1993), and
Validated: *Lindleyana*   **10**(2): 2 (1995).

Epidendroideæ ⚘ Malaxideæ

ETYMOLOGY: Greek for fringe and tongue or lip. Descriptive of the serrated lip margin of some of the species.

TYPE SPECIES: *Crossoglossa blephariglottis*
        (Schlechter) Dressler & Dodson
        (*Microstylis blephariglottis* Schlechter)

Twenty-one epiphytes or terrestrials are found primarily in wet, low to upper elevation, hill scrub and montane forest litter from Costa Rica to Bolivia usually at the base of trees. These plants have short or creeping, hanging or arching, leafy stems, subtended by the bases of distichous, evenly spaced, thinly textured leaves. The leaves are arranged in a basal fan or scattered along the length of the stem and have wavy or crisped margins. The numerous-flowered inflorescence has small, mostly green to green-yellow flowers with transparent, forward curved, usually narrow petals that have a prominent midvein. The five-nerved, heart-shaped, entire, bilobed or obscurely trilobed lip has a somewhat rolled back, flat or concave, entire or notched margin. The collar-like, thick callus clasps the short, erect, club-shaped, footless column, and then extends as a short flap onto the blade of the lip.

CRYBE

Lindley

Intr. Nat. Syst. Bot., ed. 2   446 (1836), and
Edwards's Bot. Reg.   **22**: t. 1872 (1836).

ETYMOLOGY: Greek for to hide. In reference to the column that is hidden, as the flower never fully opens.

TYPE SPECIES: *Crybe rosea* Lindley

Now recognized as belonging to the genus *Bletia*, *Crybe* was previously considered to include one terrestrial found in dry, mid to upper elevation, oak-pine forests, meadows, cliff faces and along river banks from southern Mexico to Nicaragua. This seldom seen, plant has an inflorescence arising on a stem separate from the few pleated leaves. The erect, sometimes branching, few-flowered inflorescence has showy, nodding, almost tubular, dark purple, purple-red to white flowers not opening fully that are often arranged on one side of the spike. The trilobed lip, usually a brighter color, has a white base, and a ruffled margin. The above type name is now considered a synonym of *Bletia purpurata* A. Richard & Galeotti.

CRYPTANGIS

An orthographic variant introduced in *Dict. Class. Hist. Nat.*, **5**: 151 (1824). The correct spelling is *Criptangis*.

CRYPTANTHEMIS

Rupp

Proc. Linn. Soc. New South Wales, ser. 2
57: 58, tt. 1-9 (1931).

ETYMOLOGY: Greek for hidden and stamen. Refers to the section of the column that covers the anther.

TYPE SPECIES: *Cryptanthemis slateri* Rupp

Now recognized as belonging to the genus *Rhizanthella*, *Cryptanthemis* was previously considered to include one uncommon, subterranean saprophyte found in southeastern and western Australia; only grows in harmony with the broom honey myrtle (*Melaleuca*) scrub. This plant has numerous, tiny flowers produced in a whorl, and their size changes as they proceed inward. The flowers are colored waxy-white but slowly darken to a dull purple-brown when exposed to light and have a hood-like arrangement of the sepals and petals. The thick, fleshy, entire lip is covered with fine hairs and has a unique hinge.

CRYPTANTHEMUM

An orthographic variant introduced in *Proc. Linn. Soc. New South Wales*, ser. 2, **57**: 58 (1932). The correct spelling is *Cryptanthemis*.

| Currently Accepted | Validly Published | Invalidly Published | Published Pre-1753 | Superfluous Usage | Orthographic Variant | Fossil |

Orchid Genera • **102**

CRYPTARRHENA

R. Brown

Bot. Reg. **2**: *t. 153* (1816).

Epidendroideæ ⚘ Cymbidieæ • Zygopetalinæ

ETYMOLOGY: Greek for hidden and male or stamen. Refers to the "cowled part of the column that covers the anther."

TYPE SPECIES: *Cryptarrhena lunata* R. Brown

Four uncommon, epiphytes are found in humid, low to mid elevation, woodland and montane rain forests from southern Mexico to Peru, Jamaica, Trinidad, the Guianas, Venezuela and Brazil. These small plants have short, leafy stems or small, bilaterally compressed pseudobulbs, each with several, distichous, overlapping, leathery leaves. The arching to hanging, numerous-flowered inflorescence has tiny, fleshy, but attractive, widespreading, green flowers. The anchor-shaped, yellow, four-lobed to five-lobed lip has a prominent, long claw. The narrow or triangular ovate lobes has two short basal lobes and has two longer, narrow recurved lobes. The flowers have an erect, short, wingless, footless column with a distinct basal tooth.

CRYPTARRHENIA

An orthographic variant introduced in *Cat. Pl. Trinidad*, 85 (1870). The correct spelling is *Cryptarrhena*.

CRYPTERPIS

Thouars

Hist. Orchid.   Table 1, sub 2i, *t. 28, t. 30* (1822).

Name published without a description. Today this name is most often referred to *Platylepis*.

CRYPTOCENTRUM

Bentham

J. Linn. Soc., Bot.   **18**: 325 (1881).

Epidendroideæ ⚘ Cymbidieæ • Maxillariinæ

ETYMOLOGY: Greek for hidden and a spur or sharp point. Referring to the spur which is formed by the sepals and is hidden in a leaf-like bract.

TYPE SPECIES: *Cryptocentrum jamesonii* Bentham
    This type name is now considered a synonym of
    Cryptocentrum lehmannii (Reichenbach f.) Garay;
    basionym
    Aeranthes lehmannii Reichenbach f.

Nineteen sympodial epiphytes are found in wet, low to upper elevation, hill and montane forests from Costa Rica to Peru. These small plants have erect, rarely branched stems or rare solitary leafed pseudobulbs, each with

spirally arranged, extremely narrow, leathery to fleshy, flat leaves. The several, wiry, solitary-flowered inflorescences, borne from the base of the stem or sheath axils, have a small, dull-green, green-tan, sometimes purple or totally red-purple, usually star-shaped flower with long, narrow sepals and tiny petals. The small, tongue-like, entire or obscurely trilobed lip is united with the base of the column foot. The prominent, long spur is enclosed in the floral bract. The flowers have a short, wingless, footless column.

CRYPTOCHILOS

An orthographic variant introduced in *Gen. Pl. (Sprengel)*, **2**: 676 (1831). The correct spelling is *Cryptochilus*.

CRYPTOCHILUS

Wallich

Tent. Fl. Napal.   **2**: 36, *t. 26* (1824).

Epidendroideæ ⚘ Podochileæ • Eriinæ

ETYMOLOGY: Greek for hidden and lip. Referring to the lip that is obscured from view by the urn-shaped sepals and petals.

TYPE SPECIES: *Cryptochilus sanguineus* Wallich

Four sympodial epiphytes or lithophytes are found in low to upper elevation, hill and montane forests from northeastern India (Sikkim), Bhutan, Nepal to southern China (Xizang and Yunnan), Thailand, Laos and Vietnam. These plants have clustered, ovoid to egg-shaped pseudobulbs, sometimes entirely subtended by sheaths, each with two to three, drooping, leathery or fleshy, usually small leaves. The several, tall, numerous-flowered inflorescences have tiny flowers arranged in two rows, either with all facing the same side or in totally opposite directions. The floral bracts exceed the flowers in size. The urn- or bell-shaped, yellow or brilliant scarlet flowers have finely hairy outside surfaces. The sepals, united in the basal two-thirds, form an unusual tubular shape, and the small petals are hidden inside. The oblong, entire or trilobed lip, united to the free tip of the column foot, has erect sides, and the midlobe is slightly recurved. The flowers have a short, slightly curved column with a very long foot.

CRYPTOGLOTTIS

Blume

Bijdr. Fl. Ned. Ind.   **7**: 296, *t. 42* (1825).

ETYMOLOGY: Greek for hidden or to hide and tongue. Descriptive of the lip.

TYPE SPECIES: *Cryptoglottis serpillifolia* Blume

Now recognized as belonging to the genus *Podochilus*, *Cryptoglottis* was previously considered to

include one epiphyte found in Myanmar, Indonesia, Malaysia and the Philippines. This creeping, tiny, branching plant has thread-like stems, each with several, small, leathery leaves tapering to a sharp point. The short, zig-zagging, few-flowered inflorescence has tiny, pale green or bright white flowers not opening fully that are often suffused pink or magenta. The oblong sepals and petals are similar and are united forming a tubular shape for most of their length. The tiny, entire lip has a bright purple patch or is purple suffused, has two slender appendages near the base, and has a large, spur-like protuberance. The flowers have a long, erect column. The above type name is now considered a synonym of *Podochilus serpyllifolius* (Blume) Lindley.

CRYPTOPHORANTHUS

Barbosa Rodrigues

Gen. Sp. Orchid.   **2**: 79, *t. 476* (1881).

ETYMOLOGY: Greek for hidden, bearing or to bear and flower. An allusion to the sepals that are united at the base and tip thus hiding the petals, lip and other parts.

LECTOTYPE: *Cryptophoranthus fenestratus*
    (Barbosa Rodrigues) Barbosa Rodrigues
    (*Pleurothallis fenestrata* Barbosa Rodrigues)
    designated by Butzin, *Taxon*, **32**: 631 (1983), and
    Acuña, *Cat. Descr. Orquideas Cuba.*, **60**: 115 (1939).
    This type name is now considered a synonym of
    Acianthera fenestrata
    (Barbosa Rodrigues) Pridgeon & M.W. Chase;
    basionym
    Pleurothallis fenestrata Barbosa Rodrigues

Now recognized as belonging to the genus *Acianthera*, *Cryptophoranthus* was previously considered to include twenty epiphytes ranging from western to southern Brazil. These small plants have well developed stems. The several inflorescences, borne from the leaf axils, have either a solitary flower or a cluster of brightly to dull-colored flowers often sprinkled with red-brown spots and covered with short hairs on the outer surfaces. The large sepals are joined together at their tips, and are opened by a long, media slit. The tiny petals, a hinged, entire lip, and long column are borne within this structure.

CRYPTOPHYLIS

Thouars

Hist. Orchid.   *tt. 93-94* (1822).

Name published without a description. Today this name is most often referred to *Bulbophyllum*.

CRYPTOPUS

Lindley

Bot. Reg. **10**: sub 817 (1824).

Epidendroideæ ◊ Vandeæ • Angraecinæ

ETYMOLOGY: Greek for hidden and foot. Referring to Lindley's belief that the filaments and glands of the pollinia are hidden in a pouch.

TYPE SPECIES: *Cryptopus elatus* (Thouars) Lindley
(*Angraecum elatum* Thouars)

Four unusual, monopodial epiphytes are found in mid elevation, montane forests of Madagascar, the Mascarene Islands, Réunion and Mauritius. These twig plants have long, slender, simple or branched leafy stems, each with tough, leathery leaves arranged in two ranks along the length of the stem. The erect to spreading, simple to multibranched, numerous to few-flowered inflorescence emerges through the leaf sheaths opposite the distichous leaves. The showy, white to green-yellow flowers have distinct, deeply lobed petals that resemble the lip somewhat and short, narrow sepals. The trilobed or four-lobed lip has a small, red, orange or yellow blush in the center, it has strongly recurved side lobes, the midlobe is narrowly clawed and has a small, short spur. The flowers have a green, short, slightly bent, footless column.

CRYPTOPYLOS

Garay

Bot. Mus. Leafl. **23**(4): 176 (1972).

Epidendroideæ ◊ Vandeæ • Aeridinæ

ETYMOLOGY: Greek for hidden and gate or door. In reference to the small aperture of the lip cavity that is concealed within the fleshy tip.

TYPE SPECIES: *Cryptopylos clausus* (J.J. Smith) Garay
(*Sarcochilus clausus* J.J. Smith)

One monopodial epiphyte is found in low elevation, evergreen hill forests of Thailand, Cambodia, Laos, Vietnam and Indonesia (Sumatra). This plant has short stems, each with several, oblong, pale green leaves. Vegetatively the plant resembles a *Phalaenopsis* in habit, although the stem is a bit longer. The hanging, few-flowered inflorescence has small, well-spaced, yellow-brown flowers with all opening simultaneously. Hidden inside the complex, mobile lip is a small opening to the particularly closed spur cavity with a horizontal plate that rises from the back wall of the lip that is united to the long column foot. The inside of the white, obscurely trilobed lip is pale yellow with a violet ring found at the mouth of spur opening. The flowers have a long, slender, club-shaped, wingless column.

CRYPTORCHIS

Makino

Bot. Mag. (Tokyo) **1**: 118 (1887).

ETYMOLOGY: Greek for hidden and orchid. Refers to the small size of the plant.

TYPE SPECIES: *Cryptorchis aphylla* Makino
This type name is now considered a synonym of
Taeniophyllum glandulosum Blume

Not validly published, this name is referred to *Taeniophyllum*. *Cryptorchis* was previously considered to include one epiphyte widespread from northeastern India to southern China (Yunnan to Hainan), Taiwan, Korea, Japan, Malaysia, Indonesia, New Guinea and Australia.

CRYPTOSACCUS

An orthographic variant cited in *Biol. Cent.-Amer., Bot.*, **3**: 289 (1884). The correct spelling is *Cryptosanus*.

CRYPTOSANUS

Scheidweiler

Allg. Gartenzeitung **11**(13): 101 (1843).

ETYMOLOGY: Greek for hidden and style. Refers to the column that is enclosed in a small chamber formed by the lower part of the lip.

TYPE SPECIES: *Cryptosanus scriptus* Scheidweiler

Now recognized as belonging to the genus *Leochilus*, *Cryptosanus* was previously considered to include one epiphyte found in shady, wet, low to mid elevation, tropical forests of Cuba and from Mexico to Ecuador. This small plant has compressed pseudobulbs, each with several, pale green leaves. The arching, sometimes branched, few-flowered inflorescence has small, green-yellow, fragrant flowers with purple or red-brown markings or spots. The entire or trilobed lip has a deep, cup-like, hairy callus at the base and has a shallowly notched or bilobed tip. The flowers have a short, stout, footless column with a slender projection on each side in the middle.

CRYPTOSTYLIS

R. Brown

Prodr. Fl. Nov. Holland. 317 (1810).

Orchidoideæ ◊ Diurideæ • Cryptostylidinæ

ETYMOLOGY: Greek for hidden and pillar or column. Refers to the short column that is enclosed in a small chamber formed by the lower part of the lip.

LECTOTYPE: *Cryptostylis longifolia* R. Brown nom. illeg.
Cryptostylis subulata (Labillardière) Reichenbach f.
(*Malaxis subulata* Labillardière)
designated by Averyanov,
Vasc. Pl. Syn. Vietnamese Fl. Orch., **1**: 165 (1990).

LECTOTYPE: *Cryptostylis erecta* R. Brown
designated by N. Hallé, *Fl. Nouvelle Caledonie & Depend.*,
8: 481 (1977).

Twenty-five stemless, sympodial terrestrials and a few saprophytes are found in moist to seasonally dry, low to upper elevation, woodlands and evergreen montane forests from northern India (Assam), Sri Lanka, Thailand to Vietnam, Taiwan, western Indonesia (Java and Sumatra), the southern Philippines (Mindanao), Australia, Tasmania, New Zealand and Vanuatu to Samoa. These robust, clump-forming, erect plants have slender, unbranched stems, each with a solitary leaf or are leafless. The leaves are variegated and/or spotted, with even a few species having darker veins on pale backgrounds. The wiry to stout, few-flowered inflorescence has spidery, green and purple flowers sometimes tinted red with only one to three open at a time. The often inconspicuous, inrolled, narrow sepals and petals have a narrow appearance. The large, colorful, entire lip is uppermost, covered with short glandular bristles, and the margins are variously curved. The flowers have a short, footless column.

NOTE: These flowers mimic a female insect and emit a fragrance to attract and lure male wasps for pollination.

CRYPTOSTYLUS

An orthographic variant introduced in *Remarques Fl. Polynésie*, 33 (1890). The correct spelling is *Cryptostylis*.

CTENORCHIS

K. Schumann

Just's Bot. Jahresber. **27**(1): 467 (1901).

ETYMOLOGY: Greek for a comb and orchid. From the arrangement of the leaves that resemble the teeth of a comb.

TYPE SPECIES: *Ctenorchis pectinata*
(Thouars) K. Schumann
(*Angraecum pectinatum* Thouars)

Now recognized as belonging to the genus *Angraecum*, *Ctenorchis* was previously considered to include one epiphyte found in the Mascarene

Islands. This small, often clump-forming plant has several, rigid stems, each with short, stiff, narrow, needle-like, dark green, leathery leaves. The short-lived, solitary-flowered inflorescence, borne from the leaf axils, has a small to minute, white flower with similar narrow sepals and petals. The slightly broader, entire lip has a small, almost straight, stiff spur.

CUCULINA

Rafinesque
Fl. Tellur. **4**: 49 (1836)[1837].
ETYMOLOGY: Latin for a hood or cap. Referring to the cap-shaped lip.
TYPE SPECIES: *None designated*

A superfluous name proposed as a substitute for *Catasetum*.

CUCULLA

Blume ex d'Orbigny
Dict. Univ. Hist. Nat. **9**: 170 (1847).

Name published without a description. Today this name is most often referred to as a section of *Aerides*.

CUCULLANGIS

Thouars
Hist. Orchid. Table 3, sub 3u, t. 48 (1822).

Name published without a description. Today this name is most often referred to *Angraecum*.

CUCUMERIA

Luer
Monogr. Syst. Bot. Missouri Bot. Gard. **95**: 257 (2004).
ETYMOLOGY: Latin for with cucumber-shaped bulbs. Referring to the cucumber-like texture on the outer surface of the flower.
TYPE SPECIES: *Cucumeria cucumeris* (Luer) Luer
(*Pleurothallis cucumeris* Luer)

Recognized as belonging to the genus *Pleurothallis*, *Cucumeria* was proposed to include one epiphyte found in mid elevation, montane forests of Panama. This erect plant has long, erect stems, subtended by tubular sheaths, each with a solitary, leathery leaf. The short, few-flowered inflorescence, borne from the base of the leaf, has tiny, pale green-yellow flowers whose outer surface looks like the skin of a cucumber (Cucurbitaceæ family). This surface is covered with numerous, warty extrusions. The lateral sepals are united for a short length, the lateral sepals form a synsepal. The tiny petals, and the entire lip is encased within the tube shape. The flowers have a small, club-shaped column.

CUITLANZINA

An orthographic variant introduced in *Orchid. Scelet.*, 15 (1826). The correct spelling is *Cuitlauzina*.

CUITLAUZINA

Lexarza
Nov. Veg. Descr. **2**: 32 (1825).
Epidendroideæ ⁙ **Cymbidieæ** • **Oncidiinæ**
ETYMOLOGY: Named in honor of Cuitlahuatzín (x-1520), an Aztec nobleman, former governor of Iztapalapa who installed public gardens in western Mexico and was Emperor for just eighty days before dying of smallpox brought by the Spanish.
TYPE SPECIES: *Cuitlauzina pendula* Lexarza

Six graceful, sympodial epiphytes are found in mid to upper elevation, montane oak-pine forests from southwestern Mexico (Sinaloa, Jalisco and Michoacán) to Panama. These densely clustered plants have large, flattened, glossy pseudobulbs, subtended by several, overlapping sheaths (which become wrinkled with age), each with two leathery leaves. The long, hanging to arching, numerous to few-flowered inflorescence has long-lived, showy, waxy, lemon fragrant, flat-faced, pure white to pale pink flowers. The white to rosy-pink, notched, kidney-shaped, bilobed lip has a narrow, yellow claw, also sprinkled with red spots, and has a prominent, fleshy callus. The flowers have a short, erect, winged column.

CUITLAUZINIA

An orthographic variant cited in *Deut. Bot. Herb.-Buch*, 54 (1841). The correct spelling is *Cuitlauzina*.

CUITZAULINA

An orthographic variant introduced in *Fragm. Florist. Geobot.*, **3**(Suppl.): 103 (1995). The correct spelling is *Cuitlauzina*.

CULICES

An orthographic variant introduced in *Inst. Rei Herb.*, **1**: 433 (1700). The correct spelling is *Cullices*.

CULLICES

L'Obel
Icon. Stirp. 179, f. 1 (1591).

Pre-1753, therefore not validly published in fulfillment of nomenclatural rules. This name is most often referred to *Orchis*.

CULTRIDENDRIS

Thouars
Hist. Orchid. Table 3, sub 3q, t. 87 (1822).

Name published without a description. Today this name is most often referred to *Polystachya*.

CURVANGIS

Thouars
Hist. Orchid. Table 3, sub 3o, t. 56 (1822).

Name published without a description. Today this name is most often referred to *Jumellea*.

CURVOPHYLIS

Thouars
Hist. Orchid. Table 3, sub 3u, t. 95 (1822).

Name published without a description. Today this name is most often referred to *Bulbophyllum*.

CUTSIS

Burns-Balogh, E.W. Greenwood & R. González
Phytologia **51**(5): 297 (1982).
ETYMOLOGY: A local native indigenous name used for this orchid from western central Mexico.
TYPE SPECIES: *Cutsis cinnabarina* (Lexarza) C. Nelson
(*Neottia cinnabarina* Lexarza)

Now recognized as belonging to the genus *Dichromanthus*, *Cutsis* was proposed to include one terrestrial found in low to upper elevation, dry scrub to tropical deciduous forests, lava fields and grasslands ranging from the southeastern United States (Texas) to western Guatemala. This showy, erect plant has unbranched stems that are commonly leafy during flowering, each with several, narrow, dark green, basal leaves becoming bracts up the stem. The tall, densely packed, cylindrical, numerous-flowered inflorescence has large, vermilion red, tubular flowers that are red on the outside, pale yellow-red to white on the inner surfaces. The segments have flaring, pointed tips and are spirally arranged on the rachis but become disarrayed during flowering. The narrow, yellow, entire lip is slightly concave in the middle and has a vermilion tip. The flowers have a long, slender, club-shaped column.

CYAENORCHIS

An orthographic variant introduced in *Nat. Pflanzenfam.*, **2**(6): 220 (1889). The correct spelling is *Cyaneaorchis*.

CYANACORCHIS

An orthographic variant introduced in *Bull. Soc. Roy. Bot. Belgique*, **43**: 348 (1906). The correct spelling is *Cyanaeorchis*.

CYANAEORCHIS

Barbosa Rodrigues

Gen. Sp. Orchid. **1**: 112, *t. 408* (1877).

Epidendroideæ ✧ **Cymbidieæ** • **Eulophiinæ**

ETYMOLOGY: Greek Mythology. Named for Cyané, a Sicilian water-nymph who resisted Hades when he kidnapped a friend, Kore, and tried taking him to the underworld. Referring to the species preference for a wet habitat. Greek for orchid.

TYPE SPECIES: *Cyanaeorchis arundinae*
(Reichenbach f.) Barbosa Rodrigues
(*Eulophia arundinae* Reichenbach f.)

Two uncommon, sympodial terrestrials are found in moist, low elevation, meadows and marshes of southeastern Brazil, Paraguay and north-eastern Argentina (Chaco, Buenos Aires and Entrerios). These small, tufted plants are typically found fully exposed to bright sunlight. The erect plants have several, narrow, pencil-like leaves arranged up the thin stem. The long, slender, few-flowered inflorescence has a loose arrangement of small, white flowers opening successively with the small petals converging over the small, curved, wingless, footless column. The ovate sepals are widespreading. The shortly clawed, trilobed lip has a bright yellow midlobe ornamented with yellow calli.

CYANAEROCHIS

An orthographic variant cited in *Pl. Alkaloids*, 158 (1996). The correct spelling is *Cyanaeorchis*.

CYANICULA

Hopper & **A.P. Brown**

Lindleyana **15**(2): 120 (2000).

Orchidoideæ ✧ **Diurideæ** • **Caladeniinæ**

ETYMOLOGY: Greek for blue and small. Referring to the color of these small, blue flowers.

TYPE SPECIES: *Cyanicula gemmata*
(Lindley) Hopper & A.P. Brown
(*Caladenia gemmata* Lindley)

Ten sympodial terrestrials are found in low elevation, forests, swamps, scrub and rocky crevices of southwestern Australia with two species found in eastern coastal regions. These erect, clump-forming plants have short,

unbranched, hairy stems, subtended by a multilayered fibrous tunic, each with a solitary, long, narrow, basal leaf. The erect, hairy, solitary to few-flowered inflorescence has brightly colored blue, rare yellow or white flowers that are heat sensitive, usually blooming only after a fire. The small, ovate, entire lip, attached by a short claw to the anterior column base, is heavily adorned with dark colored calli and has its margin, spreading or erect, entire or weakly, to strongly toothed. The flowers have a slender, incurved, footless column. These species were formerly included in *Caladenia*.

CYANORCHIS

An orthographic variant introduced in *Hist. Orchid.*, Table 1, sub 1d, *tt. 33-34* (1822). The correct spelling is *Cyanorkis*.

CYANORKIS

Thouars

Nouv. Bull. Sci. Soc. Philom. Paris **1**(19): 317 (1809).

ETYMOLOGY: Greek for blue and orchid. The flowers are colored a delicate blue-violet.

TYPE SPECIES: *Epidendrum tetragonum* Thouars

Now recognized as belonging to the genus *Phaius*, *Cyanorkis* was previously considered to include one terrestrial found from the Mascarenes to the Seychelles. This small plant has several, broad, thinly textured, pleated leaves borne midway up the stem. The erect, few-flowered inflorescence is borne from large, leaf bracts. The small, yellow-brown flowers do not open widely, have a tubular, cup-shaped lip adorned with yellow calli and a small, ovate spur. The lip remains on the fruit long after the petals have fallen away.

CYATHOGLOTTIS

Poeppig & **Endlicher**

Nov. Gen. Sp. Pl. (Poeppig & Endlicher) **1**(7-10): 55, *t. 94* (1836).

ETYMOLOGY: Greek for little cup or ladle and tongue. Refers to the shape of the lip.

TYPE SPECIES: *None designated*

Now recognized as belonging to the genus *Sobralia*, *Cyathoglottis* was previously considered to include three terrestrials or epiphytes found in Venezuela, Ecuador and Peru. These reedy plants have the stem's strongly nerved leaves falling off as they grow, leaving only a few at the top and has dull gray-green sheaths spotted red-brown. The solitary-

flowered inflorescence (produced in succession) has a short-lived, white to pale green flower with creamy sepals and petals. The tubular, white, entire or obscurely trilobed lip, united to the column base, is streaked and suffused orange-yellow, has numerous, basal calli and a wavy margin. The flowers have a short, winged, footless column.

CYATOGLOTTIS

An orthographic variant introduced in *Bull. Fed. Soc. Hort. Belgique*, 225 (1887). The correct spelling is *Cyathoglottis*.

CYBEBUS

Garay

Bot. Mus. Leafl. **26**(1): 15 (1978).

Orchidoideæ ✧ **Cranichideæ** • **Spiranthinæ**

ETYMOLOGY: Greek for stooping with head bent. In reference to the bent shape of the flowers. Or possibly Greek Mythology. Cybele was a goddess of the Earth Mother, who embodied the fertile earth, a goddess of caverns and mountains, nature, wild animals (especially lions and bees).

TYPE SPECIES: *Cybebus grandis* Garay

One sympodial terrestrial is found in extremely wet, mid to upper elevation, marshy scrub from southwestern Colombia (Nariño) to northern Ecuador (Carchi). This erect plant has short, unbranched stems, each with a few elliptical leaves, forming a basal rosette. The erect, few-flowered inflorescence (smooth below and hairy above) has large, white (sometimes suffused pink), showy, fragrant flowers. The long, narrow sepals form a distinct, bent tube with the lateral sepals spreading beyond the tube and are recurved at their tips. The clawed, strongly recurved, entire lip has the blade forming a tunnel-like access to the nectary. The erect, strongly curved, slender column, partially joined with the dorsal sepal and petals, has its base extended into a prominent column foot that is almost as long as the column itself.

CYBELE

Falconer ex **Lindley**

Veg. Kingd., ed. 2 183 (1847).

Not *Cybele* Salisbury ex J. Knight (1809) Proteaceæ.

ETYMOLOGY: Greek Mythology. Cyebele was also known as Magna Mater and the Mother of the Gods. She was the goddess of nature and fertility, and she presided over mountains and fortresses.

TYPE SPECIES: *None designated*

Name published without a description. Today this name is most often referred to *Herminium*.

| Currently Accepted | Validly Published | Invalidly Published | Published Pre-1753 | Superfluous Usage | Orthographic Variant | Fossil |

Orchid Genera • **106**

CYBELION

Sprengel

Syst. Veg. (Sprengel), ed. 16   **3**: 679, 721 (1826).

ETYMOLOGY: Greek for head. Descriptive of the flowers that barely open thus giving the appearance of little, rounded heads.

TYPE SPECIES: *None designated*

Now recognized as belonging to the genus *Ionopsis*, *Cybelion* was previously considered to include six epiphytes found in low elevation, hill scrub and forests from the southeastern United States (Florida), Cuba to Trinidad, the Guianas, Venezuela and Mexico to Paraguay. These plants are with or without, small pseudobulbs that are leafless or each with a solitary, rigid, leathery leaf. The numerous to few-flowered, often branching inflorescence has showy, small to medium-sized, sweetly fragrant flowers and have a range of color from yellow-white to pale pink. The united lateral sepals form a short pouch below the clawed, entire or bilobed lip that is much larger than the other segments.

CYBELIUM

An orthographic variant cited in *Nomencl. Bot. (Steudel)*, ed. 2, **1**: 558, 814 (1840). The correct spelling is *Cybelion*.

CYBIDIUM

An orthographic variant introduced in *Mag. Nat. Hist. & J. Zool.*, **1**: 280 (1829). The correct spelling is *Cymbidium*.

CYCHNOCHES

An orthographic variant introduced in *Fl. Cab.*, **1**: 71 (1837). The correct spelling is *Cycnoches*.

CYCLOPOGON

C. Presl

Reliq. Haenk.   **1**(2): 93, t. 13, f. 1 (1827).

Orchidoideæ ⚬ Cranichideæ • Spiranthinæ

ETYMOLOGY: Greek for circle, round or ring and beard. Probably in reference to the disposition of a circle of beards around the opening of the basal sepaline tube.

TYPE SPECIES: *Cyclopogon ovalifolius* C. Presl

Eighty-two sympodial terrestrials, lithophytes or epiphytes are distributed in damp to dry, low to upper elevation, oak-pine forests, scrubby meadows, along shady river banks, mangroves or tree filled depressions in lava flows throughout the Bahamas, Cuba to Trinidad, the southeastern United States (Florida), southern Mexico to Bolivia and Argentina with the largest concentration found in Brazil. One species has naturalized in Hong Kong, Indonesia (Java), Samoa and Sri Lanka. These erect plants have short, delicate, unbranched stems, each with a basal rosette of green leaves suffused purple, and are withered by or just after flowering. The slender, smooth to hairy, numerous to few-flowered inflorescence has small, tubular, pale green, creamy, green-brown to olive-brown flowers sometimes suffused with red-brown marks or streaks. The translucent petals have a conspicuous mid-vein. The white, fiddle to spear-shaped, clawed, trilobed or obscurely trilobed lip has a fleshy lobe in the form of a hook on each side at the base. The flowers have a slender, small to long, curved, slightly hairy column.

CYCLOPTERA

Endlicher

Enchir. Bot. (Endlicher)   113 (1841).

Not *Cycloptera* (R. Brown) Spach (1841) Proteaceæ.

ETYMOLOGY: Greek for circle and wing.

TYPE SPECIES: *None designated*

Name published without a description. Today this name is most often referred to *Spiranthes*.

CYCLOSIA

Klotzsch

Allg. Gartenzeitung   **6**(39): 305 (1838).

ETYMOLOGY: Latin for circle and tiny. Referring to the numerous, tiny blotches.

TYPE SPECIES: *Cyclosia maculata* Klotzsch

Now recognized as belonging to the genus *Mormodes*, *Cyclosia* was previously considered to include one epiphyte found in restricted to the low to mid elevation, along the northern slopes of the Sierra Norte in Mexico (Oaxaca). This plant has clustered, spindle-shaped pseudobulbs, subtended by dull white leaf sheaths, each with several, narrow, deciduous leaves. The one-sided, numerous-flowered inflorescence has showy, deep yellow flowers facing upward that are sparsely to densely spotted, brown-maroon, and have a strong, most unpleasant fragrance. The trilobed lip has a large, tapering midlobe, and even the side lobes taper to a point. The flowers have a thick, erect, footless column that is twisted to one side in male flowers.

CYCNAUKEN

An orthographic variant introduced in *Fl. Serres Jard. Eur.*, **1**: 207, 210 (1845). The correct spelling is *Cycnoches*.

CYCNOCHES

Lindley

Gen. Sp. Orchid. Pl.   154 (1832).

Epidendroideæ ⚬ Cymbidieæ • Catasetinæ

ETYMOLOGY: Greek for a swan and neck or throat. Referring to the slender, gracefully arched column of the male flowers.

TYPE SPECIES: *Cycnoches loddigesii* Lindley

These fabulous, swan orchids are some of the most prized of the American orchids. There are about thirty-three species, plus several variants of these large, sympodial epiphytes or terrestrials found ranging in seasonally dry to wet, low to mid elevation, hill scrub and montane forests of southern Mexico to Bolivia, the Guianas, Venezuela and northern Brazil. These plants have long, spindle-shaped, several noded pseudobulbs, each with thin, heavily veined, deciduous, pleated leaves. The erect, arching or hanging, numerous to few-flowered inflorescence has small to large-sized, showy flowers that are unisexual, fragrant, and sometimes waxy. The flower sex is determined by light intensity, the male (thinly textured and with a long, thin column) and female (fleshy and with a short, stout column) flowers can be morphologically similar or distinctly different. The thin to fleshy, often distinctly clawed, entire or lobed lip is narrow to orbicular, and crested to fringed. The flowers have a short, slender to stout, arched, wingless column.

CYCNOCHIS

An orthographic variant introduced in *Pansey*, 45 (1835). The correct spelling is *Cycnoches*.

CYDONIORCHIS

Senghas

J. Orchideenfr.   **1**(1): 11 (1994).

ETYMOLOGY: Greek for quince and orchid. In reference to the fragrance given off by the flowers.

TYPE SPECIES: *Cydoniorchis tetragona*
  (Lindley) Senghas
  (*Lycaste tetragona* Lindley)

Now recognized as belonging to the genus *Bifrenaria*, *Cydoniorchis* was proposed to include two epiphytes or lithophytes found in wet, low to mid elevation, coastal montane forests of eastern Brazil. These plants have markedly four-angled, ovoid pseudobulbs, each with a few narrow, pleated, fleshy leaves. The short, few-flowered inflorescence has large, waxy, unpleasantly fragrant, long-lasting flowers with the sepals and petals streaked and suffused red-brown or maroon. The green, trilobed lip is suffused red-brown or violet toward the base.

CYENOCHES

An orthographic variant introduced in *Land Bolivar*, **2**: 196 (1878). The correct spelling is *Cycnoches*.

CYHESIA

An orthographic variant introduced in *Icon. Pl. Ind. Orient. (Wight)*, **3**: *t. 1751-52* (1851). The correct spelling is *Cytheris*.

CYLINDRILOBUS

An orthographic variant introduced in *Feddes Repert.*, **94**(7-8): 444 (1983). The correct spelling is *Cylindrolobus*.

CYLINDROCHILUS

Thwaites

Enum. Pl. Zeyl. (Thwaites) 307 (1861).
ETYMOLOGY: Greek for long and round and lip. An allusion to the lip that is curled upward like a cylinder.
TYPE SPECIES: *Cylindrochilus pulchellus* Thwaites

Now recognized as belonging to the genus *Thrixspermum*, *Cylindrochilus* was previously considered to include one epiphyte found in Sri Lanka. This small, non-pseudobulbous plant has short stems, each with several, strap-shaped leaves spaced along the stem. The long, slender, few-flowered inflorescence has spiny floral bracts. The short-lived, white flowers have a broad, trilobed lip with a few scurfy hairs on the lower margin. The above type name is now considered a synonym of *Thrixspermum pulchellum* (Thwaites) Schlechter.

CYLINDROLOBUS

Blume

Fl. Javæ **1**: Praef vi (1828).

Name published without a description. Today this name is most often referred to *Clylindrolobus* Brieger.

CYLINDROLOBUS

(Blume) Brieger

Orchideen (Schlechter), ed. 3 **1**(11-12): 664 (1981).
ETYMOLOGY: Greek for cylinder and a lobe or pod. Referring to the shape of the lip.
TYPE SPECIES: *Cylindrolobus compressus*
(Blume) Brieger
(*Ceratium compressum* Blume)

Not validly published, this name is referred to as a section of *Eria*. *Cylindrolobus* was previously considered to include thirty-four epiphytes found in India, Sri Lanka, Thailand, Indonesia and New Guinea.

CYMBIDIELLA

Rolfe

Orchid Rev. **26**(303): 58 (1918).
Epidendroideæ ✿ Cymbidieæ • Eulophiinæ
ETYMOLOGY: *Cymbidium*, a genus of orchids and Latin for diminutive.
LECTOTYPE: *Cymbidiella flabellata* (Thouars) Rolfe
(*Cymbidium flabellatum* Thouars)
Lectotype designated here

Three remarkable epiphytes or terrestrials are found in humid, low to mid elevation, areas of Madagascar. Each species is invariably found growing among very specific species of plants: *C. flabellata* – grows terrestrially, usually under certain shrubs, peaty bogs and rocky ground; *C. falcigera* – grows only on the trunks of one specific species of palm, *Raphia*; and *C. pardalina* – grows on a specific species of staghorn fern, *Platycerium*. These large, striking plants have elongate, clustered pseudobulbs, each with the distichous, pleated leaves arranged in a fan shape that more or less cover the pseudobulb. The erect, numerous-flowered inflorescence has showy, pale green to green-yellow flowers. The dorsal sepal and petals converge, forming a hood over the small column. The lateral sepals and petals are shortly united to the column foot; the petals are heavily marked or spotted black or purple-black. The large, trilobed or four-lobed lip has erect side lobes encircling the short column and has a prominent basal callus. The large, pale green to red, bilobed or entire midlobe has a wavy margin.

CYMBIDIUM

Swartz

Nova Acta Regiæ Soc. Sci. Upsal., ser. 2 **6**: 70 (1799).
Epidendroideæ ✿ Cymbidieæ • Cymbidiinæ
ETYMOLOGY: Greek for boat shaped or skiff and cup. An allusion to the boat-shaped lip.
LECTOTYPE: *Cymbidium aloifolium* (Linnaeus) Swartz
(*Epidendrum aloifolium* Linnaeus)

One of the better known and widely popular flowers of the orchid family.

There are sixty-seven of these sympodial terrestrials, lithophytes, epiphytes or rare saprophytes are found in low to upper elevation, hill and montane evergreen, semi-deciduous, deciduous forests and savanna scrub ranging from India, Sri Lanka, Myanmar to Vietnam, Korea, Japan, Indonesia, the Philippines, New Guinea and Australia. Most species are found in north central China (Shaanxi to Henan) but also ranging southward from Xizang, Yunnan to Hainan. These warm to cool growing, often tall growing plants have short, slightly elongate to indistinct, strongly compressed to ovoid pseudobulbs, often subtended completely with leafy sheaths (rarely absent and replaced by a slender stem), each with several, long, strap-like, obscurely bilobed leaves. The erect or arching, solitary to numerous-flowered inflorescence has showy, small to large, waxy, often fragrant flowers. The floral shape is diverse as is the coloration. These plants can stay in bloom for periods of up to three months or more. The trilobed lip is free or fused to the column base, the side lobes are erect around the long, often forward bent, winged column, and the midlobe is recurved.

NOTE: This genus is used extensively for the cut flower industry. There are many artificial hybrids numbering well into the thousands.

CYMBIDRUM

An orthographic variant cited in *Nomencl. Bot. (Steudel)*, ed. 2, **1**: 30 (1840). The correct spelling is *Cymbidium*.

CYMBIDUM

An orthographic variant introduced in *Icon. Pl. Ind. Orient. (Wight)*, **5**(1): 21 (1852). The correct spelling is *Cymbidium*.

Currently Accepted | Validly Published | Invalidly Published | Published Pre-1753 | Superfluous Usage | Orthographic Variant | Fossil

O r c h i d G e n e r a • **108**

CYMBIGLOSSUM

Halbinger

Orquidea (Mexico City), n.s.   **9**(1): 1-2 (1983).

ETYMOLOGY: Greek for a boat-shaped or cup and tongue. In reference to the flower shape.

TYPE SPECIES: *None designated*

Not validly published, this name is referred to *Rhynchostele*, *Cymbiglossum* was previously considered to include fourteen epiphytes found from Mexico to Panama and Venezuela.

CYMBOGLOSSUM

(J.J. Smith) Brieger

Orchideen (Schlechter), ed. 3   **1**(11-12): 649 (1981).

ETYMOLOGY: Greek for a boat and tongue. In reference to the flower shape.

TYPE SPECIES: *None designated*

Not validly published, this name is referred to *Eria*. *Cymboglossum* was proposed to include three epiphytes found from northern India to Indonesia (Sumatra, Sulawesi and Borneo).

CYMBYDIUM

An orthographic variant introduced in *Hist. County Berkshire, Mass.*, 54 (1829). The correct spelling is *Cymbidium*.

CYNAENORCHIS

An orthographic variant introduced in *Orchid Conservation*, 88 (2003). The correct spelling is *Cyanaeorchis*.

CYNOCHES

An orthographic variant introduced in *Orchidaceæ (Ames)*, 25 (1844). The correct spelling is *Cycnoches*.

CYNORCHIS

Persoon

Syn. Pl. (Persoon)   503 (1807).

Name published without a description. Today this name is most often referred to *Cynorkis*.

CYNORCHIS

An orthographic variant introduced in *Hist. Orchid.*, Table 4, sub 1, *t. 13* (1822). The correct spelling is *Cynorkis*.

CYNORCHYS

An orthographic variant introduced in *Beih. Bot. Centralbl.*, **33**(2): 398 (1915). The correct spelling is *Cynorkis*.

CYNORKIS

Thouars

Nouv. Bull. Sci. Soc. Philom. Paris **1**(19): 317 (1809).

Orchidoideæ ※ **Orchideæ** ● **Orchidinæ**

ETYMOLOGY: Greek for dog and orchid. From the small tubers that have a fanciful resemblance to canine testicles.

LECTOTYPE: *Cynorkis fastigata* Thouars

There are about one hundred sixty of these large, mainly sympodial terrestrials or occasional epiphytes are usually found in wet, low to upper elevation, marshes, swamps, bogs, damp grasslands, rocky crevices and along river banks throughout Madagascar, the Mascarene Islands. A few species are found in tropical Africa with even one species found in the south-western Pacific Archipelago. These erect plants have unbranched, often hairy stems, each with a solitary leaf or several, large leaves borne in a ground-hugging rosette that have distinctively colored veins. The long, slender, solitary to numerous-flowered inflorescence has small, showy, mauve, orange, red to lilac, occasionally white or yellow flowers. In some species the flowers turn yellow, then orange as they age. The dorsal sepal often converges with the petals forming a hood over the short, broad column and has widespreading lateral sepals. The entire, trilobed or even five-lobed lip is often much larger than the other segments and has a long to short, slender spur at the base.

CYNOSORCHEOS

An orthographic variant introduced in *Cruyde Boeck*, 382 (1644). The correct spelling is *Cynosorchis*.

CYNOSORCHIM

Pliny

Hist. Nat.   **XXVII**: 65 (AD 56).

Pre-1753, therefore not validly published in fulfillment of nomenclatural rules; this name is most often referred to *Orchis*.

CYNOSORCHIN

An orthographic variant introduced in *Herb. (Brunfels)*, 107 (1532). The correct spelling is *Cynosorchis*.

CYNOSORCHIOS

An orthographic variant introduced in *Fl. Coron. Herb. Hist.*, 201 (1578). The correct spelling is *Cynosorchis*.

CYNOSORCHIS

Brunfels

Herb. (Brunfels)   107 (1532).

Pre-1753, therefore not validly published in fulfillment of nomenclatural rules; this name is most often referred to *Orchis*.

CYNOSORCHIS

Thouars

Hist. Orchid.   Table 1, sub 1d, *tt. 14-15* (1822).

Name published without a description. Today this name is most often referred to *Cynorkis*.

CYNOSORCHOS

An orthographic variant introduced in *Herb. Gen. Hist. Pl.*, 207 (1633). The correct spelling is *Cynosorchis*.

CYONISACCUS

An orthographic variant introduced in *Ann. Hort. Bot.*, **5**: 160 (1862). The correct spelling is *Cionisaccus*.

CYONOCHES

An orthographic variant introduced in *Various Contr. Orchids*, 220, 224 (1889). The correct spelling is *Cycnoches*.

CYORKIS

An orthographic variant cited in *World Checkl. Seed Pl. (Govaerts)*, **1**(2): 6 (1995). The correct spelling is *Cynorkis*.

CYOTOPERA

An orthographic variant introduced in *Cat. Pl. Trinidad*, 82 (1870). The correct spelling is *Cyrtopera*.

CYPERERCHIS

An orthographic variant introduced in *Orchid. Nepal*, 89 (1978). The correct spelling is *Cyperorchis*.

CYPEROCHIS

An orthographic variant cited in *Vasc. Pl. Fam. Gen.*, 125 (1992). The correct spelling is *Cyperorchis*.

CYPERORCHIS

Blume

Rumphia **4**: 47 (1849), and
Mus. Bot. **1**: 48 (1849).

ETYMOLOGY: Greek for a sedge or rush and orchid. Descriptive of the long, sedge-like leaves.

TYPE SPECIES: *Cyperorchis elegans* (Lindley) Blume (*Cymbidium elegans* Lindley)

This type name is now considered a synonym of *Cyperorchis longifolium* (D. Don) Schlechter; basionym replaced with *Cymbidium longifolium* D. Don

Now recognized as belonging to the genus *Cymbidium*, *Cyperorchis* was previously considered to include six epiphytes, lithophytes or sometimes terrestrials found in damp, mid to upper elevation, forests and cliff faces of northeastern India (Sikkim to Assam), and Myanmar to southern China (Sichuan, Xizang and Yunnan). These plants have bilaterally flattened, ovoid pseudobulbs, each with several, narrow, distichous leaves minutely bilobed at the tip. The slender, hanging, numerous-flowered inflorescence has bell-shaped, showy, faintly fragrant, pale yellow, white to green flowers with only those at the tip of the long inflorescence opening. The yellow to white, trilobed lip has erect side lobes, and the small, slightly curved, often bilobed midlobe is spotted bright red or red-purple. The flowers have a long, slender, hairy column.

CYPHOCHILUS

Schlechter

Repert. Spec. Nov. Regni Veg. Beih. **1**(5): 325, 358 (1912).

Epidendroideæ ◊ Podochileæ • Podochilinæ

ETYMOLOGY: Greek for bent, curved or hump and lip. Refers to the bent position of the lip.

TYPE SPECIES: *None designated*

Seven sympodial terrestrials are found in low to mid elevation, hill and montane rain forests of New Guinea and New Caledonia in windy, exposed and shrubby areas. These tufted plants have several stiff, often wire-like, branched stems, each with small, narrow, distichous leaves. The few-flowered inflorescence has yellow-green, green, pale yellow to white flowers with narrow, erect petals. The lateral sepals, united to the column foot, form an obtuse, chin-like protuberance. The large, broad, narrowly clawed, white, shallowly bilobed lip has appendages with a tubercle toward the front; these are separated by a broad furrow covered by fine hairs. The flowers have a small column.

CYPHOLOLORON

An orthographic variant cited in *Handb. Orchid.-Namen*, 234 (2005). The correct spelling is *Cypholoron*.

CYPHOLORON

Dodson & Dressler

Phytologia **24**(4): 285 (1972).

Epidendroideæ ◊ Cymbidieæ • Oncidiinæ

ETYMOLOGY: Greek for bent, curved or tumor and strap or thong. In reference to the bent shape of the pollinarium.

TYPE SPECIES: *Cypholoron frigida* Dodson & Dressler

Two sympodial epiphytes are found in wet, upper elevation, montane cloud forests of Venezuela and Ecuador (Loja). These minute plants have tiny, ovoid pseudobulbs, subtended by overlapping sheaths, each with a solitary, slender, red-green leaf. The several, erect, wiry inflorescences, opening in succession, are borne from the axils of the leaf sheath. The unusual, comparatively large, white flower has narrow segments covered with broad pink stripes. The heart-shaped, entire lip has a long claw, and is shallowly notched at the tip. The flowers have a long, slender, footless column that is somewhat arched and has a tri-pronged, slender tip.

CYPREPEDIUM

An orthographic variant introduced in *Fl.-Gard.*, 109 (1858). The correct spelling is *Cypripedium*.

CYPREPIDIUM

An orthographic variant introduced in *Cat. Pl. Trinidad*, 85 (1870). The correct spelling is *Cypripedium*.

CYPRIDEDIUM

An orthographic variant introduced in *Rev. Hort. Belge Étrangère*, **30**: 196 (1904). The correct spelling is *Cypripedium*.

CYPRIDIPEDIUM

An orthographic variant introduced in *Ill. Hort.*, **2**: sub 64 (1855). The correct spelling is *Cypripedium*.

CYPRIDOPEDILUM

An orthographic variant introduced in *Fl. Nordostdeut. Flachl.*, 204 (1898). The correct spelling is *Cypripedium*.

CYPRIDOPEDIUM

An orthographic variant introduced in *Contr. Bot. Dept. Nebraska Univ.*, **3**(1): 54 (1902). The correct spelling is *Cypripedium*.

CYPRIEDIUM

An orthographic variant introduced in *Voy. Louisiane*, **3**: 353 (1807). The correct spelling is *Cypripedium*.

CYPRIPEDILEN

An orthographic variant introduced in *Bot. Jahrb. Syst.*, **19**: 38 (1895). The correct spelling is *Cypripedium*.

CYPRIPEDILON

An orthographic variant introduced in *Bull. Soc. Bot. France*, **14**: 278 (1867). The correct spelling is *Cypripedium*.

CYPRIPEDILUM

An orthographic variant introduced in *Fl. Brandenburg*, **1**: 700 (1864). The correct spelling is *Cypripedium*.

CYPRIPEDIUM

Linnaeus

Sp. Pl. (*Linnaeus*), ed. 1 **2**: 951 (1753).

Cypripedioideæ ◊

ETYMOLOGY: Greek Mythology. Named for *Aphrodite* (Venus) a goddess who was born on the sacred island of Cyprus (located in the eastern Mediterranean Sea). And Greek for slipper or sandal.

There is a neat tale about the slipper. Venus and her lover, Adonis, were out hunting when overtaken by a tremendous storm and took shelter. They used this enforced time to their full advantage, leading Venus to mislay her slipper. After the storm had passed, the slipper was found by a mortal, but before he could pick it up the slipper was transformed into a flower whose central petal was shaped like a slipper.

LECTOTYPE: *Cypripedium calceolus* Linnaeus

These true lady slippers number about fifty species that are widespread in dry to wet, mid to upper elevation, bogs, marshes and scrub. These uncommon sympodial terrestrials are found from Norway to eastern Russia (Amur to Primorye),

Currently Accepted   Validly Published   Invalidly Published   Published Pre-1753   Superfluous Usage   Orthographic Variant   Fossil

Orchid Genera • 110

Britain to Turkey, and Ukraine to Japan, Korea, Canada and the United States with a few species extending into Mexico and Guatemala, northern Pakistan, Bhutan, Nepal to Myanmar but the largest concentration is found throughout China. These erect, showy plants have short to long, often hairy, unbranched stems, each with one to several, deciduous, often pleated leaves. These are often prominently veined, smooth textured or covered with soft hairs. The slender, solitary to few-flowered inflorescence has yellow-green, white, deep maroon-purple to pink flowers. The erect dorsal sepal has an entire or wavy margin, the lateral sepals are united forming the synsepalum (that is held behind the lip), and the spreading, narrow petals are more or less twisted. The stalkless, slipper or sac-shaped lip, colored differently from the other segments, has an inrolled margin and is somewhat grooved along the veins.

NOTE: This genus name was originally used by early authors to include all species of orchids that had a slipper-shaped lip; these included species now considered distinct that are included in *Paphiopedilum*, *Phragmipedilum* and *Selenipedilum*.

CYPRIPEDIVM

An orthographic variant introduced in *Fl. Jap. (Thunberg)*, 30 (1784). The correct spelling is *Cypripedium*.

CYPRIPODIUM

An orthographic variant introduced in *Jahrb. Lit.*, **5**(8): 136 (1821). The correct spelling is *Cypripedium*.

CYPRISEDIUM

An orthographic variant introduced in *Tijdschr. Ned. Indië*, **17**(2): 123 (1855). The correct spelling is *Cypripedium*.

CYRIPEDIUM

An orthographic variant introduced in *Hist. Settlem. Indian*, 99 (1852). The correct spelling is *Cypripedium*.

CYRRHOPETALUM

An orthographic variant introduced in *Prakt. Stud. Orchid.*, 33 (1854). The correct spelling is *Cirrhopetalum*.

CYRRIPEDIUM

An orthographic variant introduced in *Syst. Nat. (Linnaeus)*, ed. 12, **12**: 595 (1767). The correct spelling is *Cypripedium*.

CYRSTOSTYLIS

An orthographic variant cited in *Syn. Bot., Suppl.*, 9 (1870). The correct spelling is *Cyrtostylis*.

CYRTHOCHILUM

An orthographic variant cited in *Handb. Orchid.-Namen*, 242, 520 (2005). The correct spelling is *Cyrtochilum*.

CYRTHOPODIUM

An orthographic variant introduced in *Hort. Spaarn-Berg.*, 28 (1839). The correct spelling is *Cyrtopodium*.

CYRTIDIORCHIS

Rauschert

Taxon   **31**(3): 560 (1982).

Epidendroideæ ⚘ Cymbidieæ • Maxillariinæ

ETYMOLOGY: *Cyrtidium*, a genus of orchids and Greek for orchid.

LECTOTYPE: *Cyrtidiorchis rhomboglossa*
(F. Lehmann & Kraenzlin) Rauschert
(*Chrysocycnis rhomboglossa* F. Lehmann & Kraenzlin)

Four sympodial epiphytes are found in mid to upper elevation, montane forests from Colombia (Antioquia and Santander) to central Peru (Junín) and north-western Venezuela. These dimorphic plants have globose or ovoid, wrinkled pseudobulbs, each with one or two flat, leathery leaves. One growth consists of sterile, tufted, ovoid pseudobulbs subtended by leaf-like bracts. And the second growth has erect, branched, well-spaced, leafy flowering pseudobulbs. The several, short, solitary to few-flowered inflorescences, borne from the leaf axils, have a small, fleshy, yellow-brown or orange flower borne singly but in succession. The widespreading to strongly recurved petals are often finely veined in maroon with bronze edging. The small, hairy, trilobed or shallowly trilobed lip is has a concave midlobe sprinkled with violet-black hairs. The prominently arched, winged but footless, pale brown column widens toward the tip.

CYRTIDIUM

Schlechter

Repert. Spec. Nov. Regni Veg. Beih.   **27**: 178 (1924). Not *Cyrtidium* Vainio (1921) Fungi.

ETYMOLOGY: Composed from *Cyrtoglottis*, for the resemblance of its lip, and *Camaridium*, for the habit of the plant.

LECTOTYPE: *Cyrtidium rhomboglossum*
(F. Lehmann & Kraenzlin) Schlechter
(*Chrysocycnis rhomboglossa* F. Lehmann & Kraenzlin)

Not validly published because of a prior use of the name, this homonym was replaced by *Cyrtidiorchis*.

CYRTOCHILA

An orthographic variant introduced in *Xenia Orchid.*, **1**: 42 (1858). The correct spelling is *Cyrtochilum*.

CYRTOCHILES

An orthographic variant introduced in *Deutsch. Mag. Garten- Blumenk.*, **1849**: 245 (1849). The correct spelling is *Cryptostylis*.

CYRTOCHILOIDES

N.H. Williams & M.W. Chase

Lindleyana   **16**(4): 284 (2001).

Epidendroideæ ⚘ Cymbidieæ • Oncidiinæ

ETYMOLOGY: *Cyrtochilum*, a genus of orchids, and Greek for resembling.

TYPE SPECIES: *Cyrtochiloides ochmatochila*
(Reichenbach f.) N.H. Williams & M.W. Chase
(*Oncidium ochmatochilum* Reichenbach f.)

Three large robust, sympodial epiphytes or sometimes terrestrials are distributed in low to mid elevation, hill scrub to montane forests and coffee plantations from southern Mexico (Chiapas) to Peru. These plants have small, pear-shaped to ovoid pseudobulbs, subtended by large, overlapping leaf sheaths, each with numerous, distichous, overlapping, dull-colored leaves (usually two) with prominent veins. The often inconspicuous pseudobulbs are hidden by the leaf bases. The several, upright, numerous-flowered inflorescence is multi-branched. The small, fragrant, brown and white flowers (until they fade to yellow) have a dorsal sepal with a prominent keel. The narrowly trilobed lip has obscurely triangular side lobes, a widespreading, often large midlobe with a callus of several keels, ridges or projections. The flowers have a small, red, winged column.

CYRTOCHILOS

An orthographic variant introduced in *Syst. Veg. (Sprengel)*, ed. 16, **3**: 680, 729 (1826). The correct spelling is *Cyrtochilum*.

CYRTOCHILUM

Kunth
Nov. Gen. Sp.   **1**: 349, *t. 84* (1816).
Epidendroideæ 🌿 Cymbidieæ • Oncidiinæ
ETYMOLOGY: Greek for curved or arched and lip. Descriptive of the lip shape of the type species.
LECTOTYPE: *Cyrtochilum undulatum* Kunth

About one hundred nineteen large, sympodial epiphytes or terrestrials are found in cool, mid to upper elevation, montane forests from Costa Rica to Bolivia, Venezuela, Puerto Rico and Jamaica. These, often large, evergreen plants have clustered to remote, ovoid, cone to pear-shaped, sometimes compressed pseudobulbs, each with several, very long leaves borne at the tip of the pseudobulb. The simple to branched inflorescence is erect, curved to arching, and sometimes long, scrambling to vining through the surrounding vegetation. The inflorescence also has numerous clusters of small to large, often spectacularly showy, yellow, brown or purple flowers that vary widely in size. The broad spreading sepals have wavy margins, and the petals are usually slightly smaller than the sepals. The arrow-shaped, entire or obscurely trilobed lip is much smaller than those of *Oncidium*, and has a ridged, basal callus. The flowers have a short, erect, winged column.

CYRTOCHILUS

An orthographic variant introduced in *Bot. Reg.*, **10**: sub 832 (1824). The correct spelling is *Cyrtochilum*.

CYRTOCHYLUM

An orthographic variant introduced in *Isis (Oken)*, **7**(8): 884 (1825). The correct spelling is *Cyrtochilum*.

CYRTOGLOTTIS

Schlechter
Repert. Spec. Nov. Regni Veg. Beih.   **7**: 181 (1920).
ETYMOLOGY: Greek for curved or arched and tongue. In reference to the curved and ample fleshy lip.
TYPE SPECIES: *Cyrtoglottis gracilipes* Schlechter

Now recognized as belonging to the genus *Mormolyca*, *Cyrtoglottis* was previously considered to include one epiphyte found in upper elevation, montane forests of Colombia and Venezuela. This creeping plant has somewhat compressed, clustered pseudobulbs, each with a solitary, narrow leaf. The several, slender, solitary-flowered inflorescences have a brown-yellow to red flower with tiny petals and long, ovate sepals that taper to sharp points. The tiny, trilobed lip has erect, small side lobes and a large, roundish midlobe. The flowers have a strongly curved, wingless, footless column.

CYRTOPEDIUM

An orthographic variant introduced in *Not. Pl. Asiat.*, 271 (1851). The correct spelling is *Cyrtopodium*.

CYRTOPERA

Lindley
Gen. Sp. Orchid. Pl.   189 (1833), and
Numer. List.   246, no. 7362-64 (1831).
ETYMOLOGY: Greek for curved or arched and a pouch. Referring to the pouch-like shaped spur of the lip.
LECTOTYPE: *Cyrtopera woodfordii* (Sims) Lindley
(*Cyrtopodium woodfordii* Sims)
This type name is now considered a synonym of *Eulophia alta* (Linnaeus) Fawcett & Rendle; basionym replaced with *Limodorum altum* Linnaeus

Now recognized as belonging to the genus *Eulophia*, *Cyrtopera* was previously considered to include forty-six terrestrials widespread throughout Asia and Africa with one species found in North and South America where in some instances they are considered weeds. These tall erect plants have unbranched stems, each with several, narrow, dark green leaves. The erect, few to numerous-flowered inflorescence arises from a subterranean, corm-like stem. The showy, green flowers have a brown-green to red, entire or trilobed lip with a sac-like appendage.

CYRTOPERAX

An orthographic variant introduced in *Beih. Bot. Centralbl.*, **36**(2): 482 (1918). The correct spelling is *Cyrtopera*.

CYRTOPHIA

An orthographic variant introduced in *Orchids India*, ed. 2, 246 (1999). The correct spelling is *Cyrtopera*.

CYRTOPODIUM

R. Brown
Hortus Kew., ed. 2   **5**: 216 (1813).
Epidendroideæ 🌿 Cymbidieæ • Catasetinæ
ETYMOLOGY: Greek for bent, curved or convex and a small foot. Refers to the upcurved, bent column-foot.
TYPE SPECIES: *Cyrtopodium andersonii*
(Lambert ex Andrews) R. Brown
(*Cymbidium andersonii* Lambert ex Andrews)

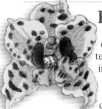

Forty-four quite large to medium-sized, sympodial epiphytes, lithophytes, or terrestrials are indigenous in virtually all parts of the American tropics in low to upper elevation, coastal to montane forests, scrub, mangroves and cypress swamps. They are found from the southeastern United States (Florida), Cuba to Trinidad, the Guianas, Venezuela, Mexico southward to Bolivia, Argentina and Paraguay with the largest concentration found in southeastern Brazil. These plants have large, spindle-shaped to cane-like pseudobulbs, subtended by clasping leaf sheaths, each with several, long (3 feet/ 91 cm), erect to arching, thinly textured, pleated, dark green, deciduous leaves. The erect, usually branching, numerous to few-flowered inflorescence, borne from the pseudobulb base, has highly colored (usually yellow), long-lasting, waxy, fragrant flowers with blotches or markings of darker colors. The floral bracts are as large, and just as colorful as the flowers themselves. The trilobed lip has rounded side lobes that are incurved over the short, stout, slightly curved, narrowly winged or wingless column, and the slightly smaller midlobe has a warty, entire or wavy margin.

NOTE: The dried and ground pseudobulbs were often used by the local natives as a source of glue.

CYRTOPOPERA

An orthographic variant introduced in *Repert. Spec. Nov. Regni Veg. Beih.*, **7**: 257 (1920). The correct spelling is *Cyrtopera*.

Currently Accepted   Validly Published   Invalidly Published   Published Pre-1753   Superfluous Usage   Orthographic Variant   Fossil

O r c h i d   G e n e r a   • **112**

An orthographic variant introduced in *Rev. Hort. Belge Étrangère*, **28**: 203 (1902). The correct spelling is *Cyrtopera*.

CYRTORCHIS

Schlechter

Orchideen (Schlechter), ed. 1   595 (1914).

Epidendroideæ ⚘ Vandeæ • Aerangidinæ

ETYMOLOGY: Greek for curved or arched and orchid. Descriptive of the arching, recurved floral segments.

LECTOTYPE: *Cyrtorchis arcuata* (Lindley) Schlechter (*Angraecum arcuatum* Lindley)

Fifteen monopodial epiphytes or rare lithophytes are found in low to upper elevation, open woodlands, montane and river forests from Guinea to Congo, Angola to southern Ethiopia then south to Zambia, Zimbabwe and South Africa usually growing in bright sunlight. These plants have erect or hanging stems, subtended by leaf-sheaths, each with distichous, leathery or fleshy, flat or pleated, unequally bilobed leaves and arranged in two ranks. The erect stems are leafless along the lower portions and hang due to age. The several, short, numerous to few-flowered inflorescences have small to large, usually pure white, ivory to green flowers (change to pale orange or yellow with age) that are star or bell-shaped and have a strong nocturnal, sweetly fragrance. The flowers have large, pale bracts that turn black or dark brown as the flower opens. The entire or obscurely trilobed lip has a long, tapering, curved, green or pink spur. The flowers have a short, fleshy, slender, downward bent column with an inconspicuous foot.

CYRTOSIA

Blume

Bijdr. Fl. Ned. Ind.   **8**: 396, *t. 6* (1825).

Vanilloideæ ⚘ Vanillineæ

ETYMOLOGY: Greek for curved or swollen. Referring to the bow-shaped pollen mass on the column.

LECTOTYPE: *Cyrtosia javanica* Blume

Five leafless saprophytes are found in low to upper elevation, montane and bamboo forests ranging from northeastern India (Assam), Sri Lanka, Malaysia, China (Guangxi, Guizhou and Zhejiang), Japan, Taiwan, Indonesia, Thailand, Laos, Vietnam and New Guinea to the Philippines. These plants have large, underground rhizomes and erect, yellow-brown or red-brown, simple or branched stems often with several emerging from one rhizome. The slowly elongating, numerous-flowered inflores-

cence has several, scale-like bracts, and produces flowers opening in succession. The small, dirty white, pale green, pale brown or yellow flowers open only slightly and are hairy on their outside segments. The entire or obscurely trilobed lip has a shortly hairy, red margin that are raised on either side of the white, slightly curved, footless column base and becomes yellow toward the tip.

CYRTOSTYLIS

R. Brown

Prodr. Fl. Nov. Holland.   322 (1810).

Orchidoideæ ⚘ Diurideæ • Acianthinæ

ETYMOLOGY: Greek for curved or arched and column or style. Refers to the fluted, curved enlargement of the column.

TYPE SPECIES: *Cyrtostylis reniformis* R. Brown

Three sympodial terrestrials are found in moist, humus-rich, low elevation, hill forests, grasslands and coastal woodlands of southern Australia, Tasmania and New Zealand. These erect plants, often growing in crowded colonies, have short, unbranched stems, each with a solitary, kidney-shaped or oblong, prominently veined basal leaf. The solitary to few-flowered inflorescence has translucent, red-brown, green to yellow-orange flowers that glisten when exposed to bright sunlight. The flowers have narrow lateral sepals and petals with the longer, erect dorsal sepal concave over the slender, arched, footless column. The broadly oblong, flat, entire lip dominates the flower, is weakly toothed but not lobed, and is slightly angled to allow droplets of nectar to run downward. The flowers have a short column.

CYSTOCHILUM

Barbosa Rodrigues

Gen. Sp. Orchid.   1: 197, *t. 468* (1877).

ETYMOLOGY: Greek for bladder or pouch and lip. Refers to the bladder shape of the lip.

TYPE SPECIES: *Cystochilum candidum* Barbosa Rodrigues

Now recognized as belonging to the genus *Cranichis*, *Cystochilum* was previously considered to include one terrestrial found in shady, mid elevation, woodlands and forests of southeastern Brazil (Paraná) and northern Argentina (Salta and Misiones). This small plant has erect, unbranched stems, each with a basal rosette of leaves that have ruffled margins. The tall, numerous-flowered inflorescence has tiny, pink flowers whose minute petals curve forward or downward over the large, ovate dorsal sepal. The more or less concave, oblong, entire lip, often sprinkled with a few brown specs or spots, is uppermost.

An orthographic variant cited in *Lex. Gen. Phan.*, 146 (1904). The correct spelling is *Cystochilum*.

An orthographic variant introduced in *Jorn. Sci. Math. Phys. Nat.*, **4**(14): 184 (1873). The correct spelling is *Cyrtopera*.

CYSTOPUS

Blume

Fl. Javæ Nov. Ser.   **1**: 69 (1858), and *Coll. Orchid.*   **1**: 82, *tt. 21 & 23G* (1858).

Not *Cystopus* Léveillé (1847) Fungi.

ETYMOLOGY: Greek for a bladder and a foot. Referring to the inflated base of the lip.

TYPE SPECIES: *None designated*

Not validly published, this name is referred to *Pristiglottis* and *Odontochilus*. *Cystopus* was considered to include sixteen terrestrials widespread from Malaysia, Indonesia, New Caledonia and New Guinea to the south-western Pacific Archipelago.

CYSTORCHIS

Blume

Fl. Javæ Nov. Ser.   **1**: 73, *t. 24* (1858), and *Coll. Orchid.*   **1**: 87, *tt. 34, 36* (1858).

Orchidoideæ ⚘ Cranichideæ • Goodyerinæ

ETYMOLOGY: Greek for a bladder and orchid. In reference to the sac formed by the basal part of the lip and the lateral sepals.

LECTOTYPE: *Cystorchis variegata* Blume

Twenty-one small, complex, sympodial terrestrials or saprophytes are found in cool, misty, low to mid elevation, hill scrub and montane rain forests of Thailand, Malaysia, Indonesia, New Guinea, Vanuatu and the Philippines. These small, leafy plants are grown more for their attractive, occasionally variegated leaves. The leafs' upper surface may be dark brown, purple-green, dark green or yellow-green but with or without pale olive-green or white areas between the nerves. These plants have stems with several leaves or the saprophyte species have just a few brown scales. The slender, numerous-flowered inflorescence covered with short hairs has insignificant, white to pale brown, fragrant flowers not opening widely. The dorsal sepal and petals converge, forming a hood over the short, footless column. The lateral sepals partially or entirely enclose the base of the narrow, white to yellow, immobile, entire lip which ends in the front as a raised plate, and has a short, slightly decurved, bladder-like spur with two or three lobes. The flowers have a small, footless column.

CYTHERA

An orthographic variant introduced in *Fl. Alaska Yukon*, **3**: 494 (1943). The correct spelling is *Cytherea*.

CYTHEREA

Salisbury

Parad. Lond. **2**(1): errata (1807), and
Trans. Hort. Soc. London **1**: 301 (1812).

ETYMOLOGY: Greek Mythology. A surname of *Venus*, the Roman goddess of love, beauty, and reproduction. She is identified with the Greek goddess *Aphrodite* who was borne by Dione to Zeus. She had a magic girdle that made all men fall in love with her.

TYPE SPECIES: *Cytherea borealis* (Swartz) Salisbury (*Cymbidium boreale* Swartz)

A superfluous name proposed as a substitute for *Calypso*.

CYTHERIA

An orthographic variant introduced in *Hort. Thenensis*, 185 (1895). The correct spelling is *Cytheris*.

CYTHERIS

Lindley

Gen. Sp. Orchid. Pl. 128, 129 (1831), and
Numer. List. 131, no. 3750 (1830).

ETYMOLOGY: Greek Mythology. A name used as a surname of Venus for beauty.

TYPE SPECIES: *Cytheris cordifolia* Lindley

Now recognized as belonging to the genus *Nephelaphyllum*, *Cytheris* was previously considered to include one terrestrial found in shady, low to mid elevation, mixed forests from Bangladesh to northeastern India (Assam). This creeping, often branching plant has long, almost stem-like pseudobulbs with one-internode, each with a solitary, heart-shaped, often mottled, dark purple leaf. The few-flowered inflorescence, borne from a specialized shoot, has small, green-brown flowers with long, often recurved or spreading, narrow segments. The pale yellow, wedge-shaped, trilobed lip has narrow side lobes; the midlobe has three, thick nerves ending in flattened spines and has a short, knob-like spur. The flowers have a short, slightly winged column.

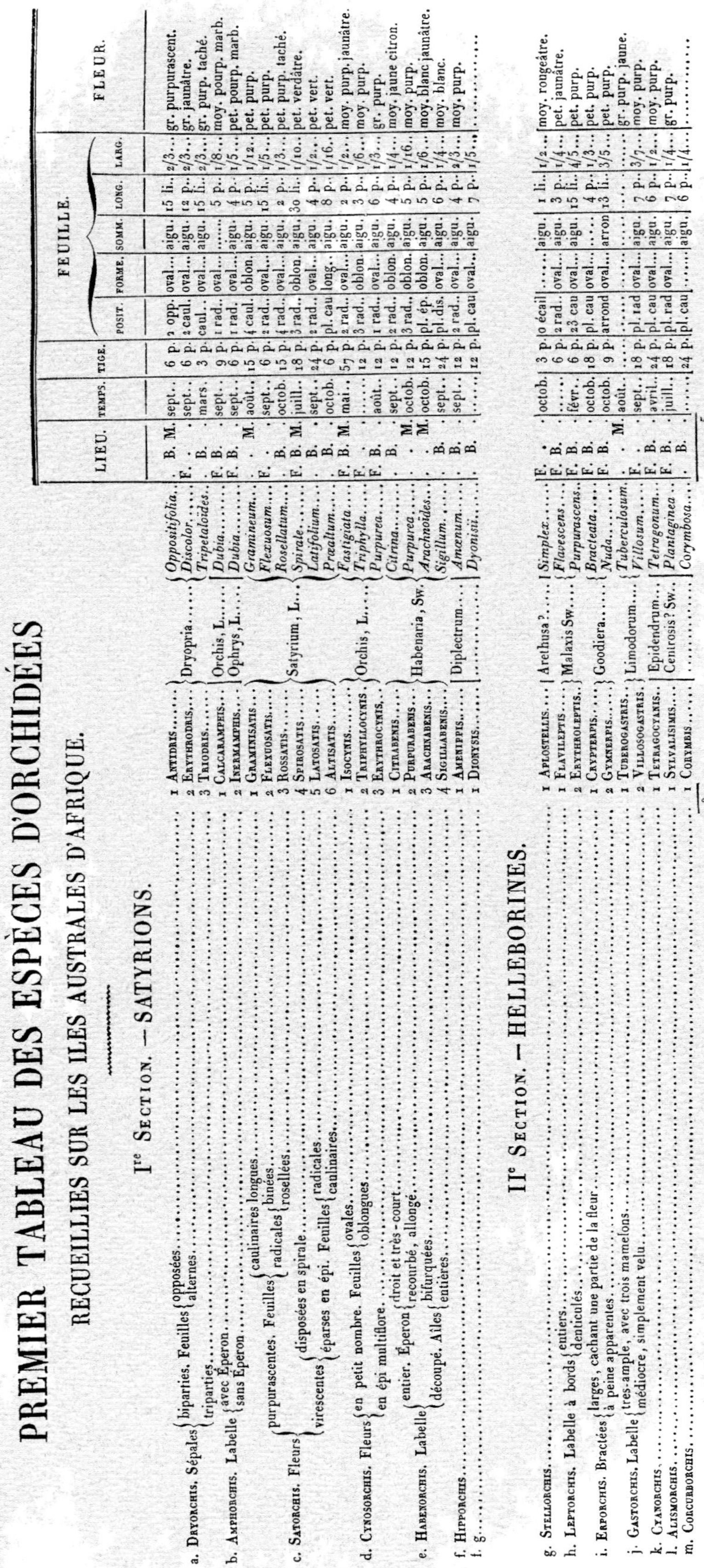

Thouars
Histoire Particulière des Plantes Orchidees
table one (1822).

PREMIER TABLEAU DES ESPÈCES D'ORCHIDÉES
RECUEILLIES SUR LES ILES AUSTRALES D'AFRIQUE.

[Rotated botanical table — "Ire SECTION. — SATYRIONS." and "IIe SECTION. — HELLEBORINES." listing genera and species with columns for LIEU, TEMPS, TIGE, FEUILLE (POSIT., FORME, SOMM., LONG., LARG.), and FLEUR.]

Currently Accepted | Validly Published | Invalidly Published | Published Pre-1753 | Superfluous Usage | Orthographic Variant | Fossil

Orchid Genera · **114**

DACTYLORCHIS

(Klinge) P. Vermeulen
Stud. Dactylorch. 64 (1947).
ETYMOLOGY: Greek for finger and orchid. Refers to the regular branching, long or short digitate tubers.
TYPE SPECIES: *Dactylorchis incarnata*
(Linnaeus) P. Vermeulen
(*Orchis incarnata* Linnaeus)

A superfluous name proposed as a substitute for *Dactylorhiza*.

DACTYLORHIZA

Necker ex Nevski
Trudy Bot. Inst. Akad. Nauk S.S.S.R., ser. 1
Fl. Sist. Vyssh. Rast. **4**: 332 (1937).
Name ICBN conserved vs. *Coeloglossum* Hartman (1820)
Orchidaceæ.

Orchidoideæ ❧ Orchideæ • Orchidinæ
ETYMOLOGY: Greek for a finger and root. Refers to the finger-like lobes of the tubers of the more primitive species, which contrast with the rounded tubers of *Orchis* proper.
LECTOTYPE: *Dactylorhiza umbrosa*
(Karelin & Kirilov) Nevski
(*Orchis umbrosa* Karelin & Kirilov)

Some forty-two temperate sympodial terrestrials are found in wet to dry, low to upper elevation, grasslands, bogs and nutrient-poor soils often forming large colonies and usually growing in full sunlight. They are widespread from Iceland, Norway to Greece, Bulgaria to Turkey and Morocco to Libya, Ukraine to eastern Russia (Yakutiya to Kamchatka and Primorye), Mongolia, northern to southwestern China (Heilongjiang to Xizang), Japan, the Aleutian Islands (United States) and Canada (Yukon Territory to Prince Edward Island). These small, leafy plants have unbranched, slender to stout stems, each with a basal rosette of leaves that are unspotted or variously spotted purple and sometimes suffused red-purple on the upper surface. The erect, numerous-flowered inflorescence has leafy floral bracts often exceeding the length of the purple, lilac, red, yellow or rare white flowers. The flowers are often heavily spotted in darker colors, and the dorsal sepal and petals converge, forming a loose hood over the small, erect column. The entire and concave, or flat and trilobed lip, often with a darker pattern of lines, loops or dots, has three basal calli, and a cylindrical, cone-shaped or extremely short spur.

NOTE: Natural hybridization is quite common between the different species of this genus, and because of this constant hybridization, classification of this genus can often be confusing.

DACTYLORHYNCHOS

An orthographic variant introduced in *Orchideen (Schlechter)*, ed. 3, **13**: 765 (1983). The correct spelling is *Dactylorhynchus*.

DACTYLORHYNCHUS

Schlechter
Repert. Spec. Nov. Regni Veg. Beih.
1(9): 682 (1912), and
Repert. Spec. Nov. Regni Veg. Beih.
1(12): 890 (1913).
ETYMOLOGY: Greek for a finger and snout or horn. An allusion to the finger like column.
TYPE SPECIES: *Dactylorhynchus flavescens* Schlechter

Now recognized as belonging to the genus *Bulbophyllum*, *Dactylorhynchus* was previously considered to include one epiphyte found in upper elevation, montane forests of western Indonesia and New Guinea. This uncommon, dwarf, tufted plant has tiny, somewhat flattened pseudobulbs held at right angles to the rhizomes, each with a solitary leaf (the leaf and inflorescence are enclosed in sheaths). The one- to two-flowered inflorescence has minute, pale green to yellow flowers opening only moderately. The yellow, slightly curved, fiddle-shaped, shortly clawed, entire lip is rather thick textured. The flowers have a short, wingless column. The above type name is now considered a synonym of *Bulbophyllum latipes* J.J. Smith.

DACTYLORRHIZA

An orthographic variant introduced in *Elem. Bot. (Necker)*, **3**: 402 (1790). The correct spelling is *Dactylorhiza*.

DACTYLOSTALIX

Reichenbach *filius*
Bot. Zeitung (Berlin) **36**: 74 (1878).
Epidendroideæ ❧ Calypsoeæ
ETYMOLOGY: Greek for a finger and stake. An allusion to the several elongate finger-like crests on the lip.
TYPE SPECIES: *Dactylostalix ringens* Reichenbach f.

One sympodial terrestrial is found in cold, mid elevation, montane forests of Japan and southeastern Russia (Sakhalin and Kuril Islands). This small, erect plant has short, slender stems, each with a solitary, broad, heart-shaped basal leaf. The tall, solitary-flowered inflorescence has two tubular sheaths and a delicate, slightly nodding flower, which is rather large for the size of the plant. The pale olive-green to green-yellow flower is purple spotted on the basal sections. The fairly large, white, trilobed lip has broad, ovate side lobes sprinkled with purple spots or blotches, and the spotted midlobe has a recurved, wavy margin. The flowers have a long, slender, flat, footless column.

DACTYLOSTYLES

An orthographic variant introduced in *Dict. Univ. Hist. Nat.*, **9**: 171 (1847). The correct spelling is *Dactylostylis*.

DACTYLOSTYLIS

Scheidweiler
Allg. Gartenzeitung **7**(51): 405 (1839).
ETYMOLOGY: Greek for a finger and column. From the prominent staminodes found on the column.
TYPE SPECIES: *Dactylostylis fimbriata* Scheidweiler

Now recognized as belonging to the genus *Zygostates*, *Dactylostylis* was previously considered to include one epiphyte found in misty, mid elevation, moss laden montane forests of Paraguay, Argentina and southeastern Brazil. This small, fan-shaped plant has short stems, subtended by persistent sheaths, each with narrow to oblong leaves that are joined at the base. The arching, numerous to few-flowered inflorescence has minute, white or yellow flowers stained green. The narrow sepals and large, roundish petals have deeply and irregularly serrated margins. The green-yellow, cup-shaped, entire lip has two thick calli, and has an entire or serrated margin. The flowers have a downward curved, wingless column. The above type name is now considered a synonym of *Zygostates lunata* Lindley.

DAIOTYLA

Dressler

Lankesteriana **5**(2): 92 (2005).

Epidendroideæ ⚘ **Cymbidieæ** • **Zygopetalinæ**

ETYMOLOGY: Greek for to divide and knot or callus. Refers to the basal callus.

TYPE SPECIES: *Daiotyla albicans* (Rolfe) Dressler (*Chondrorhyncha albicans* Rolfe)

Three sympodial epiphytes or terrestrials are found in shady, humid, low to mid elevation, hill scrub and montane forests from Costa Rica to Panama and Colombia. These plants have their leaves overlapping forming a fan shape. The several, solitary-flowered inflorescences, borne from the axils of the leaf sheaths, have a pale yellow to white flower. The narrow sepals are in sharp contrast to the broad petals. The white, broadly tubular, entire lip has a splash of yellow at the base, has a wavy, slightly notched to entire margin and a long, slender, green-yellow spur. The species differ mainly with their thick, two-part basal callus that reaches to the middle of the lip. The flowers have a long, curved, club-shaped column.

DAMASONIUM

Dodoens

Fl. Coron. Herb. Hist. 77 (1578).

Not *Damasonium* P. Miller (1754) Alismaceæ, not *Damasonium* Adanson (1763) Alismaceæ, and not *Damasonium* Schreber (1789) Hydrocharitaceæ.

ETYMOLOGY: Latin and Greek name for a water-plantain (*Alisma*).

TYPE SPECIES: *None designated*

There are many species of *Cephalanthera*, *Epipactis* and even *Cypripedium* which were published under this name, but today this name is now considered a genus of aquatic plants found in North America, Europe and Australia. The pre-1753 botanists considered these orchid plants as belonging to this group because of their preference for wet or damp growing habitats.

DANHATCHIA

Garay & Christenson

Orchadian **11**(10): 469, *f.* 471 (1995).

Orchidoideæ ⚘ **Cranichideæ** • **Goodyerinæ**

ETYMOLOGY: In honor of Edwin Daniel Hatch (1919-), a New Zealand accountant, amateur naturalist, orchidologist from Auckland and co-author of the *Field Guide to the New Zealand Orchids*.

TYPE SPECIES: *Danhatchia australis* (Hatch) Garay & Christenson (*Yoania australis* Hatch)

One elusive, dull-colored saprophyte is found only in low elevation, forests of northern New Zealand. This totally leafless plant has erect, finely haired, unbranched stems lacking chlorophyll and has several, white inflated sheaths with pink veins. The erect, few-flowered inflorescence has white to pink-brown, tubular flowers which do not open widely. They are suffused purple toward their base and have white tips. The sac-like, entire lip, joined to the sides of the small, slightly curved, club-shaped column, has several, stiff hairs or bristles. The plant appears to self-pollinate and is parasitic on a puffball fungus, which in turn grows in mycorrhizal association with the rootlets of *taraire* trees and/or *nikau* palms.

DARWINIELLA

Braas & Lückel

Orchidee (Hamburg) **33**(5): 168 (1982).

Not *Darwiniella* Spegazzini (1888) Fungi.

ETYMOLOGY: Named in honor of Charles Robert Darwin (1809-1882), a British naturalist who revolutionized biology with his theory of evolution through the process of natural selection from a few common ancestors and author of *The Origin of the Species*. And Latin for diminutive.

TYPE SPECIES: *Darwiniella bergoldii* (Garay & Dunsterville) Braas & Lückel (*Trichoceros bergoldii* Garay & Dunsterville)

Not validly published because of a prior use of the name, this homonym was replaced by *Darwiniera*.

DARWINIERA

Braas & Lückel

Orchidee (Hamburg) **33**(6): 212 (1982).

ETYMOLOGY: A derivative of *Darwiniella*, a genus of orchids.

TYPE SPECIES: *Darwiniera bergoldii* (Garay & Dunsterville) Brass & Lückel (*Trichoceros bergoldii* Garay & Dunsterville)

Now recognized as belonging to the genus *Stellilabium*, *Darwiniera* was previously considered to include one epiphyte found in

the upper elevation, montane forests of Venezuela. This small plant has pseudobulbs, stacked upward, each with several, ovate, finely grooved or channeled leaves. The short, erect, few-flowered inflorescence, borne from the axils of the upper leaves, has pale green-yellow flowers with equally pale pink nerves. The trilobed lip has erect or spreading side lobes and an ovate midlobe. The flowers have a deep raspberry-red, cup-shaped, short but stout column with numerous, long hairs adorning the tip.

DASYGLOSSUM

Königer & Schildhauer

Arcula **1**: 5 (1994).

ETYMOLOGY: Greek for thick with hair, shaggy or rough and tongue. Refers to the hairy lip callus that lies close to the underside of the column.

TYPE SPECIES: *Dasyglossum myanthum* (Lindley) Königer & Schildhauer (*Odontoglossum myanthum* Lindley) This type name is now considered a synonym of *Cyrtochilum myanthum* (Lindley) Kraenzlin; basionym *Odontoglossum myanthum* Lindley

Now recognized as belonging to the genera *Odontoglossum*, *Oncidium* and *Cyrtochilum*. *Dasyglossum* was proposed to include twenty-two epiphytes found in mid to upper elevation, montane cloud forests from southern Mexico to Ecuador and Peru. These robust plants have ovate, flattened pseudobulbs, subtended by overlapping, distichous sheaths, each with a solitary, narrow leaf. The erect, often branching, numerous-flowered inflorescence has small, brown-yellow flowers. The lower half of the trilobed lip is parallel to the long, slender column and adjacent to a simple callus. The inflorescence also has the unusual ability to produce keikis.

DAVEJONESIA

M.A. Clements

Orchadian **13**(11): 487 (2002).

ETYMOLOGY: Honoring David Lloyd Jones (1944-), an Australian horticulturist and botanical illustrator, who has described, named, renamed and illustrated numerous orchids.

TYPE SPECIES: *Davejonesia lichenastra* (F. Mueller) M.A. Clements (*Dendrobium lichenastrum* F. Mueller)

Recognized as belonging to the genus *Dendrobium*, *Davejonesia* was proposed to include three epiphytes or occasional lithophytes found in wet, low elevation, rain forests of northeastern Australia (Queensland). These small plants have creeping rhizomes forming dense mats

Currently Accepted   Validly Published   Invalidly Published   Published Pre-1753   Superfluous Usage   Orthographic Variant   Fossil

O r c h i d   G e n e r a   • **116**

over tree branches. Each short stem has a solitary, fleshy leaf with the leaves either close-set or well-spaced. The short, solitary-flowered inflorescence, borne from the leaf base, has a tiny, yellow, creamy, green to pink flower with or without purple tinges. The brightly colored lip is entire or has tiny lobes. All the species are now considered synonyms of *Dendrobium lichenastrum* (F. Mueller) Kraenzlin.

DECAISNEA

Brongniart

Duperrey's Voy. Monde, Phan.
1(6): 192, *t.* 39 (1829).

Name ICBN rejected vs. *Decaisnea* Hooker f. & Thomson (1855) Lardizabalaceæ.

ETYMOLOGY: Dedicated to Joseph Decaisne (1807-1882), a Belgian-born horticulturist and botanical illustrator, author of numerous works and a professor and a director of botany at Jardin des Plantes in Paris.

TYPE SPECIES: *Decaisnea densiflora* Brongniart

Although validly published this rejected name is now referred to *Prescottia*. *Decaisnea* was considered to include one terrestrial found from southeastern Brazil to Uruguay. This erect plant has stout, unbranched stems, each with several leaves in a basal rosette. The tall, densely packed, numerous-flowered inflorescence has minute flowers with the lateral sepals and small petals united at the base forming a chin-like protuberance. The ovate dorsal sepal has curled margins. The deeply concave, entire lip is borne uppermost.

DECAISNIA

An orthographic variant introduced in *Bot. Reg.*, **19**: sub 1618 (1833). The correct spelling is *Decaisnea*.

DECANISNEA

Lindley

Numer. List.   247, no. 7388 (1832).

ETYMOLOGY: The meaning here is not clear, but it could be a typo for Decaisnea.

TYPE SPECIES: *Decanisnea angulosa* Lindley

Not validly published, this name is referred to *Tropidia*. *Decanisnea* was considered to include one terrestrial found in northern India (Assam), Bhutan, Myanmar to Vietnam, Malaysia and Indonesia to the Philippines.

DECEPTOR

Seidenfaden

Opera Bot.   **114**: 361, 363 (1992).

Epidendroideæ 🌿 **Vandeæ** • **Aeridinæ**

ETYMOLOGY: Greek for to deceive or cheating. An allusion to the size of the tiny flowers in relationship to the large size of the plant.

TYPE SPECIES: *Deceptor bidoupensis*
(Tixier & Guillaumin) Seidenfaden
(*Saccolabium bidoupense* Tixier & Guillaumin)

One monopodial epiphyte is found in upper elevation, montane forests of southern Vietnam. This stout plant has thick, leathery, overlapping, deciduous, leaves arranged in two rows. The multibranched, hanging, numerous-flowered inflorescence has tiny, green-yellow flowers with purple dots and blotches at the base. There small, sac-like, obscurely lobed lip has an unusual ring of hairs at the entrance to the small, swollen spur sac. The flowers have a white, short, erect, wingless, footless column with two purple blotches.

DECKERIA

Klotzsch ex Czerwiakowski

Cat. Pl. (*Warszewicz*)   62 (1864).

Not *Deckeria* H. Karsten (1857) Arecaceæ.

ETYMOLOGY: Named for Rudolph Decker (*fl.* 1850s), a German royal printer and book binder from Berlin, who financed the collection travels of Gustav Karl Wilhelm Hermann Karsten (1817-1908), a German botanist and geologist.

TYPE SPECIES: *Deckeria speciosa*

Name published without a description, by both Czerwiakowski (1864) and Sander (*Sander's Orchid Guide*, ed. 4, 163 (1927)). Today this name is most often referred to *Schomburgkia*.

DECRYPTA

An orthographic variant introduced in *Pansey*, 45 (1835). The correct spelling is *Dicrypta*.

DEDICIEA

An orthographic variant introduced in *Beih. Bot. Centralbl.*, **8**(4-5): 311 (1899). The correct spelling is *Didicea*.

DEGRANVILLEA

Determann

Amer. Orchid Soc. Bull.   **54**(2): 174 (1985).

Orchidoideæ 🌿 **Cranichideæ** • **Spiranthinæ**

ETYMOLOGY: Honoring Jean Jacques de Granville (1943-), a French-born scientist, botanist, authority on the flora conservation of French Guiana, and author of numerous conservation studies.

TYPE SPECIES: *Degranvillea dermaptera* Determann

One sympodial saprophyte or terrestrial is found in seasonally dry, low elevation, hill forests and scrub of central French Guiana (Saül-Inini). This small, leafless plant lacks chlorophyll and depends on mycorrhizal fungus. The erect, fragile, hairy, white, few-flowered inflorescence is quite weak and has just several, leaf-like bracts. The small, tubular, sparsely hairy, translucent, off-white flowers all open simultaneously and are suffused pale purple toward the segments tips. The lateral sepals are united forming a narrow, sepaline spur and the narrow, brown petals fade to pale purple at the tips. The shortly clawed, pale purple, trilobed lip is tubular (united with the dorsal sepal) on the lower two-thirds, has a recurved, wavy margin and radiating, basal veins. The flowers have a slender column.

DEIREGYNE

Schlechter

Beih. Bot. Centralbl.   **37**(2): 426 (1920).

Orchidoideæ 🌿 **Cranichideæ** • **Spiranthinæ**

ETYMOLOGY: Greek for neck or throat and pistil, woman or female. In reference to the position of the sepals, that sits perpendicularly on top of the ovary as a neck-like extension.

LECTOTYPE: *Deiregyne hemichrea* (Lindley) Schlechter
(*Spiranthes hemichrea* Lindley)
designated by Burns-Balogh, *Amer. J. Bot.*,
69(7): 1131 (1982).
now considered a synonym of *Aulosepalum hemichrea*

LECTOTYPE: *Deiregyne chloreaeformis* [*chloreiformis*]
(A. Richard & Galeotti) Schlechter
designated by Garay, *Bot. Mus. Leafl.*, **28**: 313 (1980).
now considered a synonym of *Deiregyne diaphana*
The choice of *Deiregyne chloreaeformis* is in conflict with the protologue, see Szlachetko, *Fragm. Florist. Geobot.*, **40**: 794 (11 Dec 1995).

Nineteen sympodial terrestrials or lithophytes are found in mid to upper elevation, grassy slopes, meadows and oak-pine forests from the southwestern United States (Texas), Mexico, and Nicaragua to Panama. These erect plants have unbranched, usually stout stems, each with several, narrow, basal leaves generally absent or are withering during flowering. The tall, hairy, densely packed, numerous-flowered inflorescence, usually subtended by tubular white bracts that have yellow-brown to red-brown veins. The small, pure white, yellow to pink flowers are usually spirally arranged and the dorsal sepal and petals converge over the flattened column forming a hood. The strongly curved lateral sepals are united in the basal third or below. The papery-thin, fragrant, semi-transparent, tubular flowers have a white, short to long-clawed, trilobed lip with green or yellow running down the center midvein, and has a slightly wavy margin. The flowers have a long, slightly curved or straight, slender column.

DEIREGYNOPSIS

Rauschert
Taxon **31**(3): 560 (1982).
ETYMOLOGY: *Deiregyne*, a genus of orchids and Greek appearance or likeness.
TYPE SPECIES: *Deiregynopsis tenuiflorum*
    (Greenman) Rauschert
    (*Spiranthes tenuiflora* Greenman)

Not validly published, this name is referred to *Aulosepalum*. *Deiregynopsis* was previously considered to include one terrestrial found from Mexico to Nicaragua.

DEMORCHIS

D.L. Jones & M.A. Clements
Orchadian **14**(8: Sci. Suppl.): xiii (2004).
ETYMOLOGY: Greek for plump, fat or bulky and *Orchis*, a genus of orchids. Descriptive of the small, inflated flowers.
TYPE SPECIES: *Demorchis queenslandica*
    (Dockrill) D.L. Jones & M.A. Clements
    (*Gastrodia queenslandica* Dockrill)

Recognized as belonging to the genus *Gastrodia*, *Demorchis* was proposed to include two saprophytes found in low elevation, moist, sheltered forests of northeastern Australia and New Guinea with deep, thick, humus litter. These small, erect, inconspicuous plants have slender, unbranched and leafless stems. The numerous to few-flowered inflorescence has dull-colored flowers with a rough, exterior surface. The short, tubular floral segments are united into a five-lobed bell shape with the thick, fleshy sepals fused along their margins. The overlapping, smaller petals have free tips. The long, narrow, entire lip is on a movable, wide claw. The flowers have a long column with a distinct foot.

DENDOBIUM

An orthographic variant introduced in *Wochenschr. Vereines Beford. Gartenbaues Konigl. Preuss. Staaten*, **1**(46): 366 (1858). The correct spelling is *Dendrobium*.

DENDOBRIUM

An orthographic variant introduced in *Aphor. Bot.*, 188 (1823). The correct spelling is *Dendrobium*.

DENDROBATES

M.A. Clements & D.L. Jones
Orchadian **13**(11): 487 (2002).
Not *Dendrobates* Cope (1865) Dendrobatidæ-Anura.
ETYMOLOGY: Greek for tree and walker. Referring to the plants' growth habit.
TYPE SPECIES: *Dendrobates virotii*
    (Guillaumin) M.A. Clements & D.L. Jones
    (*Dendrobium virotii* Guillaumin)

Not validly published, this name is referred to *Dendrobium*. *Dendrobates* was proposed to include one epiphyte found in New Caledonia.

DENDROBEUM

An orthographic variant introduced in *Not. Pl. Asiat.*, **3**: 255 (1851). The correct spelling is *Dendrobium*.

DENDROBINM

An orthographic variant introduced in *Index Seminum Hort. Petrop.*, Suppl.: 14 (1864). The correct spelling is *Dendrobium*.

DENDROBIUM

Swartz
Nova Acta Regiæ Soc. Sci. Upsal., ser. 2 **6**: 82 (1799).
Name ICBN conserved vs. *Callista* Loureiro (1790), and vs. *Ceraia* Loureiro (1790) Orchidaceæ.

Epidendroideæ ⚘ Dendrobiinæ • Currently unplaced
ETYMOLOGY: Greek for a tree and life. Referring to the epiphytic habit of the genus, meaning 'living on a tree.'
TYPE SPECIES: *Dendrobium moniliforme*
    (Linnaeus) Swartz
    (*Epidendrum moniliforme* Linnaeus)

One of the larger genera within the orchid family, exceeding one thousand, one hundred eighty-four species of mainly sympodial epiphytes but occasionally lithophytes or terrestrials. This genus has a wide, gigantic range including India, Sri Lanka, Korea, Japan, southeast Asia, Indonesia to Australia, and New Zealand to the southwestern Pacific Archipelago with the greatest diversity found in New Guinea.

They can be found growing from steamy hot coastal areas to the foothills of snow-swept mountains. These plants have cane-like stems that are either **a)** rhizomatous, **b)** erect with numerous nodes, **c)** erect with one to several nodes, or **d)** lacks a rhizome but has new stems with numerous nodes arising from the base of the old stems. These tough stems are swollen at the base or along their whole length. They are often pseudobulbous, subtended by sheathing leaf bases and bladeless sheaths which have either deciduous or evergreen, papery to leathery leaves. The erect, horizontal or hanging, terminal or lateral, solitary to numerous-flowered inflorescences have showy, short to long-lived flowers. These flowers can be extremely diverse in dimension, color, shape and texture and are usually fragrant. The genus has one species, *D. cuthbertsonii* where the flowers often last for eight to ten months. The entire or trilobed lip has its base joined to the long column foot, often forming a more or less prominent, closed spur with the lateral sepals, and has a disc with a few keels. The flowers have a mostly short, stout column with a massive to pronounced column foot.

NOTE: The sheer number of species and morphology has led to the erection of numerous sections to a generic level, to help make this genus more workable, but even this has been the subject of much varied criticism.

DENDROBRIUM

An orthographic variant introduced in *Dict. Class. Hist. Nat.*, **2**: 519 (1822). The correct spelling is *Dendrobium*.

DENDROBUM

An orthographic variant introduced in *Handb. Singapore*, 119 (1892). The correct spelling is *Dendrobium*.

DENDROCALLA

An orthographic variant introduced in *Fl. Taiwan*, **5**: 1113 (1978). The correct spelling is *Dendrocolla*.

DENDROCHILUM

Blume
Bijdr. Fl. Ned. Ind. **8**: 398, t. 52 (1825).
Epidendroideæ ⚘ Arethuseæ • Coelogyninæ
ETYMOLOGY: Greek for tree and either lip or green food. Alluding to either the prominent lip or to the epiphytic habit.
LECTOTYPE: *Dendrochilum aurantiacum* Blume

There are over two hundred sixty-four of these sympodial epiphytes, lithophytes or occasional

Currently Accepted   Validly Published   Invalidly Published   Published Pre-1753   Superfluous Usage   Orthographic Variant   Fossil

Orchid Genera • **118**

terrestrials found in low to upper elevation, hill and montane, rain forests from Myanmar to New Guinea with the center of diversity in the Philippines and Indonesia (Sumatra and Borneo). The plants often form large clumps on moss-covered trees where there is very little temperature variation. A common name for these plants is chain orchid. These miniature, evergreen plants have dense to loosely tufted, narrow, spindle-shaped or ovoid, clustered to sparsely spaced pseudobulbs, each with a solitary, thinly textured to rigid leaf borne at the tip. These plants often look more like a grass than an orchid. The several, wiry, at first erect then becoming hanging, numerous-flowered inflorescences have showy, extremely fragrant, star-like, thinly textured, long-lasting, small flowers that are carefully arranged on crowded chains in two distinct rows. The cream, yellow, green to red flowers have a lip often colored in darker hues. The trilobed or obscurely trilobed lip usually has small to tiny side lobes, and the large midlobe has a disk with two to three, small keels. The flowers have a short column that is with or without a foot.

DENDROCHILUS

An orthographic variant introduced in *Fl. Javæ*, **1**: Praef. vi (1828). The correct spelling is *Dendrochilum*.

DENDROCHIS

An orthographic variant introduced in *Beih. Bot. Centralbl.*, **34**(2): 323 (1917). The correct spelling is *Dendrorkis*.

DENDROCHYLUM

An orthographic variant introduced in *Enum. Pl. Mus. Paris*, ed. 2, 72 (1850). The correct spelling is *Dendrochilum*.

DENDROCOLLA

Blume
Bijdr. Fl. Ned. Ind.　　**7**: 286, *t.* 67 (1825).
ETYMOLOGY: Greek for tree and glue. Referring to its epiphytic growth.
LECTOTYPE: *Dendrocolla hystrix* Blume

Now recognized as a section belonging the genus *Thrixspermum*, *Dendrocolla* was previously considered to include forty-two epiphytes found in low elevation, swamps, scrub and grasslands ranging from Sri Lanka, India, Thailand to Vietnam and Indonesia to the southwestern Pacific Archipelago. These hanging plants have flattened stems with short internodes, each with several, closely spaced leaves or long, climbing stems with several, well-spaced leaves. The long or short, whip-like, few-flowered inflorescence has small, pale yellow to white flowers crowning the tip with similar, long or short sepals and petals. The immovable, trilobed lip attached to the column foot, has a scalloped margin, and the long or short midlobe is usually fleshy. The flowers have a short to long, thick column.

DENDROCORYNE

(Lindley) Brieger
Orchideen (Schlechter), ed. 3　　**1**(11-12): 724 (1981).
ETYMOLOGY: Greek for a tree and club. Referring to the club-shaped pseudobulbs.
TYPE SPECIES: *Dendrocoryne speciosum*
　　　　　　(Smith) Brieger
　　　　　　(*Dendrobium speciosum* Smith)

Not validly published, this name is referred to *Dendrobium*. *Dendrocoryne* was previously considered to include one lithophyte found in northeastern Australia and New Guinea.

DENDROLIRION

An orthographic variant introduced in *J. Linn. Soc., Bot.*, **18**(110): 303 (1881). The correct spelling is *Dendrolirium*.

DENDROLIRIUM

Blume
Bijdr. Fl. Ned. Ind.　　**7**: 343, *t.* 69 (1825).
ETYMOLOGY: Greek for a tree and lily. Referring to the epiphytic habit.
LECTOTYPE: *Dendrolirium ornatum* Blume
　　This type name is now considered a synonym of
　　　　　Eria ornata (Blume) Lindley;
　　　　　　basionym
　　　　　Dendrolirium ornatum Blume

Now recognized as belonging to the genus *Eria*, *Dendrolirium* was previously considered to include twenty-two epiphytes found in hot, low to mid elevation, hill and montane forests of Thailand, Malaysia, Indonesia and the Philippines. These robust plants have short, flattened, thick, spindle-shaped to ovoid, laterally compressed pseudobulbs, subtended by basal sheaths, each with several, fleshy, narrow to oblong, yellow-green leaves. The long, erect to hanging, cottony to densely hairy, few-flowered inflorescence, covered with red-brown hairs, has green-yellow flowers not opening widely. The smaller petals often have a red median streak. The forward pointing, red, trilobed lip is slightly lobed with ridges, grooved down the middle has darker colored and crisped edges.

DENDROLOBIUM

An orthographic variant cited in *Dict. Gen. Names Seed Pl.*, 303 (1995). The correct spelling is *Dendrolirium*.

DENDROPHYLAX

Reichenbach *filius*
Ann. Bot. Syst.　　**6**: 903 (1864).
Epidendroideæ · Vandeæ · Angraecinæ
ETYMOLOGY: Greek for tree and guardian. Probably an allusion to the roots that tightly clasp the branches of the trees.
TYPE SPECIES: *Dendrophylax hymenanthus*
　　　　　(Grisebach) Reichenbach f.
　　　　　(*Aeranthes hymenantha* Grisebach)
　　This type name is now considered a synonym of
　　　　Dendrophylax varius (J.F. Gmelin) Urban;
　　　　　basionym replaced with
　　　　　Orchis varia J.F. Gmelin

Nine monopodial epiphytes are native in humid to dry, low elevation, swampy forests from the Bahamas, the southeastern United States (Florida), Cuba to Puerto Rico, southeastern Mexico to El Salvador with most species found in Hispaniola. No leaves appear on the adult, twig-like plants that have short, woody stems with densely clustered, silvery-gray roots (tips are always green) tightly clasping the tree. The simple or branching, long, solitary to few-flowered inflorescence has striking, small to large, white to green flowers opening in succession with a few species being nocturnally fragrant. The narrow, spreading sepals and petals are similar. The large to small, entire, bilobed or trilobed lip has short side lobes, is deeply notched at the tip, and continuous with the broad, short, footless column. The slender, long to tiny spur has a broad mouth.

DENDROPHYLLAX

An orthographic variant introduced in *Fragm. Florist. Geobot.*, **3**(Suppl.): 93 (1995). The correct spelling is *Dendrophylax*.

DENDRORCHIS

An orthographic variant introduced in *Hist. Orchid.*, Table 3, sub 3q, *t.* 85 (1822). The correct spelling is *Dendrorkis*.

DENDRORKIS

Thouars
Nouv. Bull. Sci. Soc. Philom. Paris
1(19): 318 (1809).
Name ICBN rejected vs. *Polystachya* Hooker (1824) Orchidaceæ.
ETYMOLOGY: Greek for a tree and orchid. In reference to the epiphytic habit.
TYPE SPECIES: *None designated*

Although validly published this rejected name is now referred to *Polystachya*. *Dendrorkis* was considered to include ten epiphytes found in both the Old and New Worlds. These variable plants have rhizomes with erect stems that are usually pseudobulbous at the base, have one to several nodes, each with one to several leaves. The erect inflorescence, densely covered with fine hairs, has tiny flowers that do not open widely. The lateral sepals form a chin-like projection with the column foot. The trilobed lip, with or without a hairy callus, is often recurved.

DENGRANVILLEA

An orthographic variant introduced in *Fragm. Florist. Geobot.*, **3**(Suppl.): 43 (1995). The correct spelling is *Degranvillea*.

DENSLOVIA

Rydberg

Brittonia   **1**: 85 (1931).

ETYMOLOGY: Honoring Herbert McKenzie Denslow (1852-1944), an American Episcopalian minister who was an original member and later served as president of the Torrey Botanical Club of New York.

TYPE SPECIES: *Denslovia clavellata* (Michaux) Rydberg (*Orchis clavellata* Michaux)

Now recognized as belonging to the genus *Platanthera*, *Denslovia* was previously considered to include one terrestrial commonly found in swampy forests or along shady river beds of southeastern Canada (Ontario to Newfoundland) and the eastern United States (Maine to eastern Texas). This erect plant has one to two, narrow leaves just below the middle of the slender, unbranched stem. The erect, wispy, few-flowered inflorescence has white-green to yellow-green flowers, slightly rotated on the rachis, that have small, roundish sepals and petals. The obscurely trilobed lip has a small, club-shaped spur varying in both width and length. The flowers have a short, broad column.

DENSOPHYLIS

Thouars

Hist. Orchid.   Table 3, sub 3u, *t. 108* (1822).

Name published without a description. Today this name is most often referred to *Bulbophyllum*.

DENTARIA

Clusius

Rar. Stirp. Hisp. Obs. Hist.   450 (1576).

Not *Dentaria* Linnaeus (1753) Brassicaceæ.

Pre-1753, therefore not validly published in fulfillment of nomenclatural rules; this name is most often referred to *Corallorhiza*.

DEPPEA

Not *Deppea* Chamisso & D.F.L. Schlechtendal (1830) Rubiaceæ.

An orthographic variant cited in *Lex. Gen. Phan.*, 31, 168 (1904). The correct spelling is *Deppia*.

DEPPIA

Rafinesque

Fl. Tellur.   **2**: 51 (1836)[1837].

Not *Deppea* Chamisso & D.F.L. Schlechtendal (1830) Rubiaceæ.

ETYMOLOGY: Dedicated to Ferdinand Deppe (1794-1861), a Prussian botanist, landscape painter, and an early explorer and collector of the flora and fauna of southwestern United States and Mexico.

TYPE SPECIES: *Deppia mexicana* Rafinesque nom. illeg.
      Lycaste deppei (Loddiges ex Lindley) Lindley
      (*Maxillaria deppei* Loddiges ex Lindley)

Now recognized as belonging to the genus *Lycaste*, *Deppia* was previously considered to include one epiphyte found in wet, mid elevation, montane forests from southern Mexico (Chiapas and Tamaulipas) to Nicaragua (Jinotega). This plant has ovoid, compressed pseudobulbs, subtended by dried sheaths, each with two pleated leaves. The solitary-flowered inflorescence has a showy flower with the pale green sepals heavily suffused and flecked with red, and green-white, red speckled petals that converge, forming a hood over the long, curved column. The orange-yellow, trilobed lip has prominently nerved side lobes forming a tube around the column, and the midlobe has bright brown-red spots and a small toothed margin.

DEROEMERA

Reichenbach *filius*

De Pollin. Orchid.   29 (1852).

ETYMOLOGY: Dedicated to Rudolph Benno von Römer (1803-1870), a German amateur botanist from Leipzig, a friend of Reichenbach. He donated his botanical library to the University of Leipzig.

TYPE SPECIES: *Deroemera squamata* (Hochstetter ex A. Richard) Reichenbach f. (*Peristylus squamatus* Hochstetter ex A. Richard)

Now recognized as belonging to the genus *Holothrix*, *Deroemera* was previously considered to include three terrestrials found from Ethiopia to Uganda and Tanzania. These small, erect plants have unbranched stems, each with a solitary, basal, round leaf that withers during flowering. The tall, hairy, densely packed, numerous-flowered inflorescence has small, white, tubular flowers

sparsely covered with long hairs. The lip has numerous, unequal lobes, and the club-shaped spur is strongly recurved.

DEROEMERIA

An orthographic variant introduced in *J. Bot.*, **33**: 277 (1895). The correct spelling is *Deroemera*.

DEROMERIA

An orthographic variant introduced in *Nat. Pflanzenfam.*, **2**(6): 93 (1888). The correct spelling is *Deroemera*.

DESCAISNEA

An orthographic variant introduced in *Hort. Donat.*, 158 (1858). The correct spelling is *Decaisnea*.

DESMOTRICHIUM

An orthographic variant introduced in *Hort. Universel*, **1**(3): 82 (1847). The correct spelling is *Desmotrichum*.

DESMOTRICHUM

Blume

Bijdr. Fl. Ned. Ind.   **7**: 329, *t. 35* (1825).

Name ICBN rejected vs. *Desmotrichium* Kützing (1845) Algae, and not *Desmotrichum* J.H. Léveillé (1843) Fungi.

ETYMOLOGY: Greek for connection or a bond and hair. Refers to the connection between the anther and the column.

LECTOTYPE: *Desmotrichum angulatum* Blume

Not validly published because of a prior use of the name, this homonym was replaced by *Flickingeria*. At the same time, a similar observation was made by Hunt and Summerhayes and they proposed the name *Ephemerantha*. But, because Hawkes's name was published (6 Jan 1961) earlier than the name proposed (2 Jun 1961) by Hunt & Summerhayes, the name *Flickingeria* has priority.

DESPERIS

An orthographic variant introduced in *Jorn. Sci. Math. Phys. Nat.*, **4**(14): 184 (1873). The correct spelling is *Disperis*.

DETERMANIA

An orthographic variant introduced in *Zastosowania*, **1**: 169 (2000). The correct spelling is *Determannia*.

Currently Accepted   Validly Published   Invalidly Published   Published Pre-1753   Superfluous Usage   Orthographic Variant   Fossil

Orchid Genera · **120**

DETERMANNIA

Szlachetko

Fragm. Florist. Geobot. **3**(Suppl.): 101, 105 (1995).

ETYMOLOGY: Named for Ronald Oskar Determann (1957-), an American superintendent of the Fuqua Conservatory at the Atlanta Botanical Garden in Atlanta, Georgia.

TYPE SPECIES: *None designated*

Name published without a description. Today this name is most often referred to *Scelochilopsis*. This genus name was attributed to Dodson and Chase in error.

DEVOGELIA

A. Schuiteman

Blumea **49**(2-3): 362, f. 1 (2004).

Epidendroideæ ⬦ Currently unplaced

ETYMOLOGY: In honor of Eduard Ferdinand de Vogel (1942-), a Dutchman from the National Herbarium at Leiden who has expanded our knowledge of the Indonesian region orchids, author of several orchid monographs and collector of the type species.

TYPE SPECIES: *Devogelia intonsa* A. Schuiteman

One sympodial terrestrial is found in low elevation, limestone hill forests of eastern Indonesia (Obi Islands - Maluku) and western New Guinea. This locally common plant has short, black-green pseudobulbs, each with a solitary, narrow, pleated, rather stiff leaf. The tall, erect, few-flowered inflorescence, borne from the axils of the uppermost leaf, has small, green-yellow flowers. The shortly clawed, immobile, yellow or white, deeply trilobed lip has yellow stripes in the center and along the midlobe that is basally, densely covered with hairs. The flowers have an slender, slightly curved column.

NOTE: This plant, *Devogelia*, vegetatively resembles *Plocoglottis* or *Tainia*, but because of its various characteristics this species could belong to *Cymbidieæ*.

DIACRIUM

(Lindley) Bentham

J. Linn. Soc., Bot. **18**(110): 312 (1881).

ETYMOLOGY: Greek for two or double and point. Refers to the horn-shaped protuberances that project up from the upper surface of the lip.

TYPE SPECIES: *Diacrium bicornutum* (Hooker) Bentham
(*Epidendrum bicornutum* Hooker)

Now recognized as belonging to the genus *Caularthron*, *Diacrium* was previously considered to include four epiphytes found in low elevation, coastal forests or along river banks from Mexico to Colombia, Venezuela, the Guianas, Trinidad and Brazil. These plants have elongate, hollow pseudobulbs of several nodes, subtended by pale gray sheaths, each

with several, thick, oblong leaves. The few to numerous-flowered inflorescence has showy, thick, pure white flowers that sometimes self-pollinate before opening. The trilobed lip, sprinkled with crimson spots, has two large, fleshy calli.

DIADENIA

An orthographic variant introduced in *Bot. Mitt. Tropen*, **2**: 15 (1888). The correct spelling is *Diadenium*.

DIADENIOPSIS

Szlachetko

Polish Bot. J. **51**(1): 39 (2006)[2007].

ETYMOLOGY: *Diadenium*, a genus of orchids and Greek for appearance. Alluding to a similarity to *Diadenium*.

TYPE SPECIES: *Diadeniopsis bennettii*
(Garay) Szlachetko
(*Diadenium bennettii* Garay)

Recognized as belonging to the genus *Systeloglossum*, *Diadeniopsis* was proposed to include one epiphyte found in mid elevation, rain forests of central Peru (Junín). This small, tufted plant has oblong, slightly compressed pseudobulbs, subtended by several, overlapping, leaf-bearing sheaths, each with a solitary, leathery leaf borne at the tip. The erect, few-flowered inflorescence has small, dull green-brown flowers suffused purple with an erect dorsal sepal and petals. The lateral sepals are united forming a synsepal. The long-clawed, entire lip has a concave, deeply notched tip. The flowers have a slender, slightly curved column.

DIADENIUM

Poeppig & Endlicher

Nov. Gen. Sp. Pl. (Poeppig & Endlicher)
1(7-10): 41, t. 71 (1836).

Epidendroideæ ⬦ Cymbidieæ • Oncidiinæ

ETYMOLOGY: Greek for through or separate and gland. Refers to the two, waxy pollen masses.

TYPE SPECIES: *Diadenium micranthum*
Poeppig & Endlicher

Two uncommon, small epiphytes are indigenous in low elevation, tropical hill forests of Venezuela, northwestern Brazil and Ecuador to Peru. These plants have small, ovoid to spindle-shaped, bright green pseudobulbs, subtended by distichous sheaths with the upper ones becoming almost leaf-like, each with a solitary, oblong leaf. The tall, numerous-flowered inflorescences, borne from mature pseudo-bulbs, have small, pink, white or green-white flowers. The united lateral sepals form a

recurved spur at their base, and the petals run down the column foot. The long-clawed, white, entire lip has a narrow, obtuse midlobe that is united to the underside of the column foot and extends to the tip of the sepaline spur. The flowers have a long, club-shaped column.

DIALISSA

Lindley

Ann. Mag. Nat. Hist. **15**(96): 107 (1845).

ETYMOLOGY: Latin for both or separate and stuck together. Descriptive of the joined sepals forming an urn-shaped flower that is the principal character of this genus.

TYPE SPECIES: *Dialissa pulchella* Lindley

Now recognized as belonging to the genus *Stelis*, *Dialissa* was previously considered to include three terrestrials found in upper elevation, montane forests of Colombia, Ecuador and Peru. These large plants have slender stems, each with narrow leaves. The erect, numerous-flowered inflorescence has small to medium-sized, yellow, white to green flowers arranged in a zig-zagged pattern up the stem. The connection of the sepals form a sepaline tube. The above type name is now considered a synonym of *Stelis dialissa* Reichenbach f.

DIANEA

An orthographic variant introduced in *Orchid.-Buch*, 214 (1892). The correct spelling is *Dienia*.

DIANIA

An orthographic variant introduced in *Nat. Pflanzenfam.*, **2**(6): 130 (1888). The correct spelling is *Dienia*.

DIAPHANANTHE

Schlechter

Orchideen (Schlechter), ed. 1 593 (1914).

Epidendroideæ ⬦ Vandeæ • Aerangidinæ

ETYMOLOGY: Greek for transparent and flower. Refers to the membranaceous (thin) texture of various parts of the flower.

LECTOTYPE: *Diaphananthe pellucida*
(Lindley) Schlechter
(*Angraecum pellucidum* Lindley)

Some twenty-four monopodial epiphytes are found in wet, low to mid elevation, evergreen forests of Africa (Ethiopia, Ivory Coast to Zimbabwe) and São Tomé. These plants have long or short stems, subtended by sheathing leaf-bases and are leafy throughout. The curved, unequally bilobed, distichous, leathery to fleshy leaves are often twisted at the base to lie in one plane. The several, long, arching or hanging, densely packed, numerous-flowered inflorescence has small, translucent or colorless, delightfully fragrant, rarely showy, pale green, pale yellow, salmon-pink or white flowers produced in vast quantities. The broad, white, usually entire or obscurely trilobed lip has a notched, wavy margin and has a distinct, tooth-like callus in the mouth of the long to short, slender spur. The flowers have a fairly short, wingless, footless column.

DIAPHANATHE

An orthographic variant cited in *Dict. Fl. Pl.*, ed. 8, 964 (1973). The correct spelling is *Diaphananthe*.

DIAPHANTHE

An orthographic variant introduced in *Fl. Trop. E. Africa*, **3**: 169 (1989). The correct spelling is *Diaphananthe*.

DIARIUM

An orthographic variant introduced in *Hamburger Garten- Blumenzeitung*, **40**: 154 (1884). The correct spelling is *Diacrium*.

DICERATOSTELE

Summerhayes

Bull. Misc. Inform. Kew **1938**(1): 151 (1938).

Epidendroideæ ⚘ Triphoreæ

ETYMOLOGY: Greek for double, horn and column. Referring to the two characteristic appendages at the tip of the column.

TYPE SPECIES: *Diceratostele gabonensis* Summerhayes

One obscure and puzzling, sympodial terrestrial is found low elevation, woodlands, swamp and along river banks of the Ivory Coast, Liberia, Nigeria, Cameroon, Congo and Gabon. This erect, rigid, nearly woody, reed-like plant has long, pleated, narrow, spirally arranged leaves that get smaller in size as they ascend up the stem. The few-flowered (erect sympodium of racemes) inflorescence has translucent, tiny, white, narrow flowers with sparsely hairy sepals. The long, entire lip, united to the column base, is constricted in the middle, has two, basal crests; tapers to either a point or has a blunt tip and a wavy margin. There are two flattened, horn-like appendages located at the top of the long, slender, footless column that is winged on the upper half with the erect anther borne on a small stalk at the top of the column.
NOTE: The plant is vegetatively similar to the genus *Corymborkis*.

DICEROSTYLIS

Blume

Fl. Javæ Nov. Ser. 98 (1858).

ETYMOLOGY: Greek for two, horn and style. Refers to the column that has two horn-like processes.

TYPE SPECIES: *Dicerostylis lanceolata* Blume

Now recognized as belonging to the genus *Hylophila*, *Dicerostylis* was previously considered to include three terrestrials found in damp, low elevation, hill forests of Taiwan, Malaysia and Indonesia to the Philippines. These erect plants, grown mostly for their foliage, have a hairy, red-brown, numerous-flowered inflorescence. The minute, tightly packed, pale green, pink to orange flowers are suffused red-brown, and have a hairy, sac-like, veined, entire lip. The white tipped dorsal sepal and petals converge, forming a hood that encloses the whole flower. The flowers have a forward curved, footless column.

DICHAEA

Lindley

Gen. Sp. Orchid. Pl. 208 (1833), and
J. Bot. (Hooker) **1**: 5 (1834).

Epidendroideæ ⚘ Cymbidieæ • Zygopetalinæ

ETYMOLOGY: Greek for twofold or for leaves arranged in two ranks. In reference to the two-ranked foliage that is typical of this genus.

LECTOTYPE: *Dichaea echinocarpa* (Swartz) Lindley nom. illeg.
(*Epidendrum echinocarpon* Swartz nom. illeg. superfl.)

Nomenclaturally Correct Name:
Dichaea pendula (Aublet) Cogniaux
(*Limodorum pendulum* Aublet)
designated by Britton & P. Wilson,
Sci. Surv. Porto Rico, **5**: 214 (1924).

Over one hundred ten pseudomonopodial epiphytes or lithophytes are found in wet, mid elevation, montane forests from Cuba, Mexico to Peru and northern Brazil. These plants have cane-like, hanging or erect, thickened stems, branching at the base, each with strap-shaped, close-set, evergreen or semi-distichous, somewhat leathery leaves that are arranged in two ranks. The smooth or stiff leaves are covered with course hairs and/or have notched margins. They are grown as much for their foliage as for the unique, often brightly hued, solitary, star-shaped flower borne from the axils of the leaf. For all of their small floral size, they often give off an amazingly powerful fragrance. The short, solitary-flowered inflorescence has spreading to incurved sepals and petals. Some species are self-pollinating. The spade-shaped, concave, clawed, trilobed or rare entire lip is rigidly united to the short column foot. The flowers have a short, erect column.

DICHAEASTRUM

Cogniaux ex **Brieger**

Orchideen (Schlechter), ed. 3 **1/B**(30): 1854 (1995).

ETYMOLOGY: *Dichaea*, a genus of orchids and Latin for swollen.

TYPE SPECIES: *None designated*

Name published without a description. Today this name is most often referred to as a section of *Dichaea*.

DICHAEOPSIS

Pfitzer

Entwurf Anordn. Orch. 107 (1887), and
Nat. Pflanzenfam. **2**(6): 206-207 (1889).

ETYMOLOGY: *Dichaea*, a genus of orchids and Greek for appearance or likeness.

LECTOTYPE: *Dichaeopsis graminoides* (Swartz) Schlechter
(*Epidendrum graminoides* Swartz)

Now recognized as belonging to the genus *Dichaea*, *Dichaeopsis* was previously considered to include seven epiphytes found from Mexico to Bolivia and Cuba to Puerto Rico. These small, sprawling plants have erect to often hanging stems and rather irregularly arranged leaves that are often of variable sizes and shape. The solitary-flowered inflorescence has a thinly textured, pale cream flower sprinkled with a few purple spots at the base, borne on a long, thread-like stalk. The broad, fiddle-shaped, trilobed lip is fused to the column foot.

DICHEA

An orthographic variant introduced in *Cat. Pl. Trinidad*, 85 (1870). The correct spelling is *Dichaea*.

DICHOPUS

Blume

Mus. Bot. **2**(11): 176 (1856).

ETYMOLOGY: Greek for double or divided and foot. Refers to the fleshy cuneiform appendage located at the base of the column.

TYPE SPECIES: *Dichopus insignis* Blume

Now recognized as belonging to the genus *Dendrobium*, *Dichopus* was previously considered to include one epiphyte found in low elevation, coastal forests from Indonesia to the Solomon Islands. This plant forms large, straggly clumps of long stick-like, brittle, leafy stems, each with ovate, often purple suffused leaves that are large on the basal portion and much smaller toward the tip. The short inflorescence has a pair of

Currently Accepted   Validly Published   Invalidly Published   Published Pre-1753   Superfluous Usage   Orthographic Variant   Fossil

Orchid Genera • 122

short-lived, fragrant, bright yellow flowers opening widely that are heavily blotched and/or barred red-brown. The white to pale yellow, trilobed lip has small, narrow, erect side lobes, and the recurved midlobe is often sprinkled with brown splashes and has a wavy margin. The above type name is now considered a synonym of *Dendrobium insigne* (Blume) Reichenbach f. ex Miquel.

DICHRAEA

An orthographic variant introduced in *Refug. Bot.*, **2**: sub 84 (1869). The correct spelling is *Dichaea*.

DICHROMANTHUS

Garay
Bot. Mus. Leafl.   **28**(4): 313 (1980)[1982].

Orchidoideæ ◊ Cranichideæ • Spiranthinæ

ETYMOLOGY: Greek for two, color and flower. Refers to the beautiful flowers being predominantly of two colors.

TYPE SPECIES: *Dichromanthus cinnabarinus*
(Lexarza) Garay
(*Neottia cinnabarina* Lexarza)

One sympodial terrestrial is found in low to upper elevation, hill and montane slopes and open scrub of the southwestern United States (Texas) and Mexico to Honduras. This strikingly showy, erect, unbranched plant is commonly leafy during flowering, each with narrow, dark green leaves forming a basal rosette becoming bracts as they proceed up the stem. The tall, cylindrical, densely packed, numerous-flowered inflorescence has large, tubular to urn-shaped flowers that are vermilion-red on the outside and white to pale yellow-red on the inner surfaces. The narrow sepals united only at the base have flared tips. The narrow, yellow, clawed, entire lip, slightly concave in the middle, forms a narrow, tunnel-like entrance to the nectary and has a vermilion-colored tip. The flowers have a long, slender, hairy, club-shaped column.

DICKASONIA

L.O. Williams
Bot. Mus. Leafl.   **9**: 37 (1941).

Epidendroideæ ◊ Arethuseæ • Coelogyninæ

ETYMOLOGY: Honoring Frederick Garrett Dickason (1904-1990), an American Baptist missionary, professor of botany, English and Bible studies in both Burma and India. He also wrote numerous articles on and about the ministry.

TYPE SPECIES: *Dickasonia vernicosa* L.O. Williams

One uncommon, sympodial epiphyte is found in deeply shaded, mid to upper elevation, montane forests of Bhutan,

northeastern India and northern Myanmar. This small plant has clustered, shiny, ovoid pseudobulbs, subtended by overlapping, leaf-like sheaths, each with a solitary, prominently nerved leaf. The short, hanging to arching, few-flowered inflorescence has small (all facing one direction), semi-transparent, white, nerved, tiny flowers. The flowers are shallowly cup-shaped or sac-like at the base and each is subtended by a large bract. The oblong, immobile, entire lip, attached to the short, slender column, has a sac-like base, a wavy margin and a small spur.

DICRANOTAENIA

Finet
Bull. Soc. Bot. France   **54**(9): 47 (1907).

ETYMOLOGY: Greek for two-branched, helmet and band or ribbon. The meaning here is unclear.

TYPE SPECIES: *Dicranotaenia dahomeensis* Finet
This type name is now considered a synonym of
Microcoelia konduensis (De Wildeman) Summerhayes;
basionym
Angraecum konduense De Wildeman

Now recognized as belonging to the genus *Microcoelia*, *Dicranotaenia* was previously considered to include one epiphyte found in low to mid elevation, rain forests and woodlands of Ivory Coast, Ghana, Benin, Nigeria, Uganda, Zaire, and Cameroon. This plant has several, short, stout stems with scale-like, nerved leaves and numerous, twisted roots. The several, descending, few-flowered inflorescences, opening simultaneously, have tiny, white flowers suffused orange-brown. The large, white, entire to obscurely trilobed lip is suffused green around the mouth of the distinctly incurved, small spur.

DICROPHILA

An orthographic variant cited in *Gen. Siphon.*, 96 (1900). The correct spelling is *Dicrophyla*.

DICROPHYLA

Rafinesque
Fl. Tellur.   **4**: 39 (1836)[1837].

ETYMOLOGY: Greek for two color and leaf. An allusion to the distinct foliage that is colored purple and gold.

TYPE SPECIES: *Dicrophyla elegans* Rafinesque nom. illeg.
Ludisia discolor (Ker-Gawler) A. Richard
(*Goodyera discolor* Ker-Gawler)

Now recognized as belonging to the genus *Ludisia*, *Dicrophyla* was previously considered to include one terrestrial found in Myanmar, Thailand, southeastern China, Hong Kong and Vietnam. This small, erect plant has stems with purple leaves veined and cross veined red or gold. The hairy, few-flowered inflorescence has small, white flowers. The dorsal sepal and petals converge, forming a concave hood over

the long, slender column that is twisted in the opposite direction of the long-clawed, shallowly bilobed lip.

DICROPHYLLA

An orthographic variant introduced in *Orchideen (Schlechter)*, ed. 3, **5**(6): 305 (1974). The correct spelling is *Dicrophyla*.

DICRYPTA

Lindley
Gen. Sp. Orchid. Pl.   44, 152 (1830).

ETYMOLOGY: Greek for double and hidden or to hide. Alluding to the manner in that the anther is set into a cavity of the clinandrium.

TYPE SPECIES: *Dicrypta baueri* Lindley
This type name is now considered a synonym of
Heterotaxis crassifolia Lindley

Now recognized as belonging to the genus *Heterotaxis*, *Dicrypta* was previously considered to include ten epiphytes found from the southeastern United States (Florida), Cuba to Hispaniola, and Mexico to Brazil. These often large, clump-forming plants have compressed pseudobulbs mostly subtended in dark green, leathery, narrow, overlapping leaf-sheaths. The short, solitary-flowered inflorescence, borne from the leaf axils, has a short-lived, thick, pale yellow-green to yellow flower with the outer surfaces suffused maroon. The obscurely trilobed lip has side lobes that appear as mere bulges. The flowers have a long, arching, wingless column.

DICTYOPHYLLARIA

Garay
Bot. Mus. Leafl.   **30**(4): 231 (1986).

Vanilloideæ ◊ Vanilleæ

ETYMOLOGY: Greek for mesh or net and small leaf. Referring to the net-like pattern or conspicuous network of veins on the reduced leaves.

TYPE SPECIES: *Dictyophyllaria dietschiana*
(Edwall) Garay
(*Vanilla dietschiana* Edwall)

One sympodial terrestrial is found in upper elevation, Serra do Mar forest of eastern Brazil (São Paulo). This tall, slender plant has erect, branched stems, each with small, triangular, rigid leaves that have prominent differentiated, net-veined bracts. The solitary-flowered inflorescence, borne from upper leaf bracts, has small, bright green to olive-green flowers with thinly textured, similar sepals and petals. The broad, creamy, entire lip is rolled into a tubular shape which has a flared tip, a wavy margin and is free from the long, slightly arched, unadorned column.

DIDACTULUS

An orthographic variant introduced in *Monogr. Syst. Bot. Missouri Bot. Gard.*, **95**: 257 (2004). The correct spelling is *Didactylus*.

DIDACTYLE

Lindley

Fol. Orchid. **1**: *Didactyle*, 1 (1852).

ETYMOLOGY: Greek for twice or two and a finger. Refers to the two extra, tendril-like appendages that are borne on the column.

TYPE SPECIES: *None designated*

Now recognized as belonging to the genus *Bulbophyllum*, *Didactyle* was previously considered to include nineteen epiphytes or lithophytes found in Venezuela, the Guianas to southeastern Brazil, and Colombia to Peru usually growing in full sunlight. These plants have small, egg-shaped pseudobulbs usually with four well-defined edges, each with a solitary, oblong, leathery to fleshy leaf. The erect, slender, few-flowered inflorescence has small, pale yellow-brown to creamy-colored flowers opening in slow succession. The narrow sepals and petals have dark chestnut markings on the inner face. The tiny, trilobed lip has purple hairs along the margin. The flowers have a long, club-shaped column.

DIDACTYLUS

(Luer) Luer

Monogr. Syst. Bot. Missouri Bot. Gard. **26**: 257 (2004), and

Validated: *Monogr. Syst. Bot. Missouri Bot. Gard.* **27**: 310 (2005).

ETYMOLOGY: Greek for twice and column. Referring to the two pronged rostellum.

TYPE SPECIES: *Didactylus butcheri* (L.O. Williams) Luer (*Pleurothallis butcheri* L.O. Williams)

Recognized as belonging to the genus *Acianthera*, *Didactylus* was proposed to include four epiphytes found from Honduras, Costa Rica and Panama to Ecuador in low elevation, moss laden forests. These hanging plants have slender, purple stems, each with a solitary, long, narrow leaf. The long, wiry, few-flowered inflorescence has small, yellow-green flowers covered with purple spots. There are long hairs covering the sepals; the lateral sepals are joined and the tiny, oblong petals are translucent. The thick, obscurely trilobed lip, hinged to the column foot, has erect, tiny side lobes and has a long, narrow midlobe with a minutely, serrated margin.

DIDICIEA

King & Prain ex King & Pantling

J. Asiat. Soc. Bengal, Pt. 2, Nat. Hist. **65**(2): 118 (1896).

ETYMOLOGY: Dedicated to David Douglas Cunningham (1843-1914), a British physician and army assistant surgeon, who collected the type species while serving in Bengal, India. The initial consonants of his names was used for the epithet.

TYPE SPECIES: *Didiciea cunninghamii* King & Prain ex King & Pantling

Recognized as belonging to the genus *Tipularia*, *Didiciea* was previously considered to include two terrestrials found in mid to upper elevation, montane pine forests from northern India (Sikkim and Garhwal) and also in central Taiwan and southern Japan. These small, erect plants have corm-like pseudobulbs (closely arranged in a row), each with a solitary, nearly triangular leaf that is brown-purple on the underside. The slender, tall, few-flowered inflorescence has small, translucent white to yellow-green flowers not opening widely. The oblong, concave, entire lip is obscurely trilobed at the tip and has a minute, cone-shaped spur. The flowers have a short, stout, wingless column.

DIDIMOPLEXIELLA

An orthographic variant introduced in *Arch. Jard. Bot. Rio de Janeiro*, **13**: 33 (1954). The correct spelling is *Didymoplexiella*.

DIDOTHION

Rafinesque

Fl. Tellur. **4**: 39 (1836)[1837].

ETYMOLOGY: Greek for twice or double and a small abscess. Referring to the two basal hard and thick calli on the lip.

TYPE SPECIES: *Didothion clavatum* (Lindley) Rafinesque (*Epidendrum clavatum* Lindley nom. illeg.) not J. König

Epidendrum purpurascens Focke

Now recognized as belonging to the genus *Epidendrum*, *Didothion* was previously considered to include one epiphyte found in Costa Rica, Colombia, Venezuela, the Guianas and northern Brazil. This plant has dark brown-olive, compressed pseudobulbs (not sharp edged), subtended by ragged sheaths, each with a solitary, stiff leaf borne at the tip. The long, few-flowered inflorescence, borne from new growth, is entirely concealed at the base with several, large bracts, and has long-lasting, fragrant, pale yellow-green flowers. The sepals and petals have recurved margins. The white, trilobed lip has two small, basal calli; the side lobes are finely notched and a spade-shaped midlobe.

DIDYMOPLEIS

An orthographic variant introduced in *Mat. Fl. Malay. Penins.*, **1**: 12 (1907). The correct spelling is *Didymoplexis*.

DIDYMOPLEXIELLA

Garay

Arch. Jard. Bot. Rio de Janeiro **13**: 33 (1954).

Epidendroideæ ⚘ Gastrodieæ

ETYMOLOGY: *Didymoplexis*, a genus of orchids and Latin for diminutive.

TYPE SPECIES: *Didymoplexiella ornata* (Ridley) Garay (*Leucolena ornata* Ridley)

Six leafless saprophytes are found in humid, low to mid elevation, evergreen hill to montane forests and scrub of southern China (Hainan), Taiwan, southern Japan, Thailand, Vietnam and Indonesia (Sumatra to Borneo). These small, slender, erect plants have simple, unbranched stems, each with scale-like sheaths. The numerous to few-flowered inflorescence, sometimes thickened on its upper part, has closely arranged flowers and tiny, tubular bracts. The small, brown-green or white flowers are streaked pale pink at their base, and open in succession. The lateral sepals are united for more than half their length. The white, entire or obscurely trilobed lip has large side lobes, a smaller, oblong, upcurved midlobe with a pink or purple center, and a small, bilobed, basal callus. The flowers have a small, broad, winged, footless column. These species differ from *Didymoplexis* by their long, tooth-like projections located at the tip of the column and on either side of the anther.

DIDYMOPLEXIOPSIS

Seidenfaden

Contr. Orchid Fl. Thailand **13**: 13 (1997).

Epidendroideæ ⚘ Gastrodieæ • Currently unplaced

ETYMOLOGY: *Didymoplexis*, a genus of orchids and Greek for appearance.

TYPE SPECIES: *Didymoplexiopsis khiriwongensis* Seidenfaden

One saprophyte is found in low elevation, tropical forests of southwestern Thailand, Laos and Vietnam. This leafless, erect plant has thin, unbranched stems, each with a few minute, triangular floral bracts. The erect, few-flowered inflorescence has fragile flowers opening successively, one at a time. The pure white, short-lived flower has a bilobed or entire lip attached to the column foot for a portion of its length. The column foot has rows of tiny, red dots. The triangular, entire lip's surface has calli with red blotches at the base and tip.

Currently Accepted   Validly Published   Invalidly Published   Published Pre-1753   Superfluous Usage   Orthographic Variant   Fossil

Orchid Genera • **124**

DIDYMOPLEXIS

Griffith

Calcutta J. Nat. Hist. **4**: 383, t. 17 (1844).

Epidendroideæ ⚘ Gastrodieæ

ETYMOLOGY: Greek for in pairs or divided into two lobes and Latin for interwoven. Refers to the two, small column wings that form an abbreviated, bilobed floral tube.

TYPE SPECIES: *Didymoplexis pallens* Griffith

Seventeen saprophytes are found in low to mid elevation, hill to montane rain and bamboo forest litter from Afghanistan, northern India (Sikkim), Bangladesh, Thailand, southern Japan (Ryukyu Islands), Taiwan, Malaysia, New Guinea, northeastern Australia and the Philippines to the southwestern Pacific Archipelago and tropical Africa (Ghana to northeastern South Africa) and eastern Madagascar. These small to tiny, slender, leafless plants have pale brown to pink, unbranched, erect stems without chlorophyll, and several, scale-like sheaths. These plants are not easily detected in the leaf litter where they grow. The solitary to numerous-flowered inflorescence has delicate, white or creamy, small flowers usually suffused pink-brown and are open for only a few short hours. The lateral sepals are untied to the middle forming a shallow cup or tubular-shape. The dorsal sepal and petals are united to the middle, then converge, forming a hood over the long, winged column. The broadly clawed, entire or obscurely lobed lip has yellow warts sprinkled down the middle, is joined to the column foot, and has a blunt front margin.

DIDYMOSTIGMA

Brieger

Orchideen (Schlechter), ed. 3 **6**(21-24): 328 (1976).
Not *Didymostigma* W.T. Wang (1984) Gesneriaceæ.

ETYMOLOGY: Greek for double and stigma. Refers to the illusion having of two columns.

TYPE SPECIES: *Didymostigma obliqua* Brieger
This type name is now considered a synonym of
Cyclopogon obliquus (J.J. Smith) Szlachetko;
basionym
Spiranthes obliqua J.J.Smith

Not validly published, this name is referred to *Cyclopogon*. *Didymostigma* was previously considered to include one terrestrial that is widespread from El Salvador to Costa Rica, Guadeloupe, Cuba, northern Argentina, Brazil, Sri Lanka, Indonesia (Java) and Hong Kong.

DIENA

An orthographic variant cited in *Consp. Regn. Veg.*, 69 (1828). The correct spelling is *Dienia*.

DIENIA

Lindley

Bot. Reg. **10**: sub 825 (1824).

Epidendroideæ ⚘ Malaxideæ • Currently unplaced

ETYMOLOGY: Greek for two years old. Referring to the belief that the plant only flowers every two years.

TYPE SPECIES: *Dienia congesta* Lindley
This type name is now considered a synonym of
Dienia ophrydis (J. König) Seidenfaden;
basionym
Epidendrum ophrydis J. König

Eleven sympodial terrestrials or rare epiphytes are found in hot to cool, low elevation, tropical rain, mixed to piney forests and along river banks from Taiwan, southern China (Yunnan to Fujian), northern India, Myanmar to Vietnam, Indonesia, the Philippines and northern Australia to the southwestern Pacific Archipelago. These erect, often creeping plants have tall, tapered pseudobulbs, subtended by thin, dry sheaths, each with a solitary to several, softly textured, oblong to rounded, pleated, often purple leaves. The stout, erect, densely packed, numerous-flowered inflorescence has small to tiny, short to long-lived, yellow-green, brown, green, pink or purple flowers that have a combination of various colors. The squarish, trilobed lip has broad, blunt side lobes and a narrow, oblong midlobe that is either entire or notched. The flowers have a small, club-shaped, footless column.

DIGLYPHIS

An orthographic variant introduced in *Fl. Javæ*, **1**: Praef. vi (1828); and *Fl. Javæ Nov. Ser.*, 138 (1858). The correct spelling is *Diglyphosa*.

DIGLYPHOSA

Blume

Bijdr. Fl. Ned. Ind. **7**: 336, t. 60 (1825).

Epidendroideæ ⚘ Collabiinæ • Currently unplaced

ETYMOLOGY: Greek for two or twice and to cleave or carve. Descriptive of the front margin of the anther that is drawn out into two, triangular lobes separated by an incision.

TYPE SPECIES: *Diglyphosa latifolia* Blume

Three sympodial terrestrials are found in dark, mid elevation, montane forests from northeastern India (Sikkim), Nepal, southern China (Yunnan), Vietnam, Malaysia, Indonesia and New Guinea to the Philippines. These creeping plants have slender, purple-brown pseudobulbs, each with a solitary, green, papery leaf that has wavy margins and are usually blotched dark green. The erect, sometimes branched, purple, numerous-flowered inflorescence, borne from undeveloped pseudobulbs, has several, dark purple, tubular bracts. The tiny, orange-yellow to pink flowers do not open widely but all open simultaneously, have purple markings and have a disgusting fragrance. The mobile, entire, obscurely trilobed or trilobed lip is slightly contracted near the middle and divided into a reflexed epichile with a sharp tip, and a small, thick hypochile with concave central section. The flowers have a long, slender, curved, wingless, footless column.

DIGLYPHYS

Spach

Hist. Nat. Veg. (Spach) **12**: 176 (1846).

ETYMOLOGY: Greek for two or double and notch.

TYPE SPECIES: *None designated*

Name published without a description. Today this name is most often referred to *Diglyphosa*.

DIGMOPHROTIS

An orthographic variant introduced in *Fl. Bras. (Martius)*, **3**(4): 18 (1893). The correct spelling is *Digomphotis*.

DIGNANTHE

An orthographic variant introduced in *Ann. Hort.*, **5**: 232 (1850). The correct spelling is *Dignathe*.

DIGNATHE

Lindley

J. Hort. Soc. London **4**: 268 (1849).

Epidendroideæ ⚘ Oncidiinæ

ETYMOLOGY: Greek for twice and jaw or cheek. Refers to the two, fleshy plates on the lip, thus giving the appearance of a gaping jaw.

TYPE SPECIES: *Dignathe pygmaea* Lindley

One sympodial epiphyte is found in low to mid elevation, dry oak-pine forests of central Mexico (Hidalgo). This minute plant has ovoid, laterally compressed pseudobulbs, subtended by papery sheaths, each with a solitary leaf. The plant often produces long strings of pseudobulbs that intermingle in the humus and live moss, forming dense colonies. The solitary-flowered inflorescence has a translucent, white to pale green flower covered with yellow spots and blotches. The broad, fleshy, obscurely trilobed lip, attached to the column base, has a bright yellow, fleshy callus. The flowers have a white, short, footless column.

DIGOMPHOTIS

Rafinesque

Fl. Tellur. **2**: 37 (1836)[1837].

ETYMOLOGY: Greek for twice, nail and ear. Refers to the club-like or ear-like appendages on the column.

TYPE SPECIES: *Digomphotis undulata* Rafinesque

This type name is now considered a synonym of *Peristylus goodyeroides* (D. Don) Lindley; basionym *Habenaria goodyeroides* D. Don

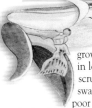

Now recognized as belonging to the genus *Peristylus*. *Digomphotis* was previously considered to include two terrestrials found in low to upper elevation, hill scrub to montane forests and grassy slopes. The designated type species is distributed from northern India, China (Yunnan to Jiangxi), Myanmar to Vietnam, Indonesia, the Philippines and New Guinea. This erect plant, usually leafless at the base, has several, dark green leaves in a whorl, midway up the unbranched stem. The numerous-flowered inflorescence has small, widespreading flowers with the green sepals often turning red with age. The wider, thicker-textured, triangular petals are a dull gray-olive green. The dull gray-green, trilobed lip has a small, sac-like, roundish spur. The second species (*Digomphotis cordata* (Willdenow) Rafinesque) is found in the Azores, Madeira, the Canary and Cape Verde Islands, and the western Mediterranean region. And is now considered a synonym of *Gennaria diphylla* (Link) Parlatore.

DIKYLIKOSTIGMA

Kraenzlin

Notizbl. Bot. Gart. Berlin-Dahlem **7**: 321 (1919).

ETYMOLOGY: Greek for twice, saucer-shaped and stigma. For the two separate, bent outward, stigmatic surfaces that are usually discolored.

TYPE SPECIES: *Dikylikostigma preussii* Kraenzlin

This type name is now considered a synonym of *Discyphus scopulariae* (Reichenbach f.) Schlechter; basionym *Spiranthes scopulariae* Reichenbach f.

Now recognized as belonging to the genus *Discyphus*, *Dikylikostigma* was previously considered to include one terrestrial found in low elevation, grasslands and scrub of Trinidad, Brazil, Panama and Venezuela. This slender, erect plant has unbranched stems, each with a solitary or several, ovate, basal leaves. The erect, numerous to few-flowered inflorescence has small, tubular, white flowers suffused pale green, covered with short hairs and has a tiny, trilobed lip.

DILOCHIA

Lindley

Gen. Sp. Orchid. Pl. 38 (1830), and *Numer. List* 53, no. 1952 (1832).

Epidendroideæ ◊ Arctheuseæ • Coelogyninæ

ETYMOLOGY: Greek for double or two, rank (double company) and rows. In reference to the arrangement of the leaves along the stem.

TYPE SPECIES: *Dilochia wallichii* Lindley

Eight sympodial terrestrials, rare lithophytes or low growing epiphytes are found in low to upper elevation, hill scrub, montane forests and swamps usually with nutrient-poor soil ranging from Myanmar, Thailand, Malaysia to Indonesia and New Guinea to the Philippines. These large plants have cane-like to broad, leafy stems, each with stiff, distichous, leathery leaves. The simple or multibranched, numerous-flowered inflorescence has small but attractive, short-lived flowers that are produced one by one and do not open fully. The dull yellow-green or white flowers, subtended by creamy-white, concave bracts are suffused pink on the outside surfaces. The dorsal sepal is hood-like over the small to long, slender, slightly curved, wingless to narrowly winged, footless column. The bright red to yellow, trilobed lip, suffused brown-orange, has erect side lobes and the often bilobed midlobe has a disk with five, dark red keels from base to the tip.

DILOCHIOPSIS

(Hooker *filius*) **Brieger**

Orchideen (Schlechter), ed. 3 **1**(11-12): 662 (1981).

ETYMOLOGY: *Dilochia*, an orchid genus and Greek for appearance or likeness.

TYPE SPECIES: *Dilochiopsis scortechinii* (Hooker f.) Brieger (*Eria scortechinii* Hooker f.)

Now recognized as belonging to the genus *Eria*, *Dilochiopsis* was previously considered to include one epiphyte or terrestrial found in mid elevation, montane forests of Malaysia. This slender, erect plant has thin stems, each with a solitary, narrow, strongly nerved, leathery leaf borne at each node. The multibranched, numerous-flowered inflorescence has small, hairy, nerved, white flowers suffused pink or blue whose outer surfaces are covered with fine, rusty-colored hairs. The short, trilobed lip has large, oblong, erect side lobes, and the broad, notched midlobe has a central keel of fine, spreading, lilac hairs. The flowers have a short, winged column.

NOTE: When Brieger originally published this genus he misspelled the name as *Dilochopsis*.

DILOCHUS

An orthographic variant introduced in *Fl. Ind. Batav.*, or alternate title *Fl. Ned. Ind.*, **3**: 669 (1859). The correct spelling is *Dilochia*.

DILOMILIS

Rafinesque

Fl. Tellur. **4**: 43 (1836)[1837].

Epidendroideæ ◊ Epidendreæ • Pleurothallidinæ

ETYMOLOGY: Greek for twice or two and fringe or border. Refers to the two, parallel crests on the lip.

TYPE SPECIES: *Dilomilis serrata* Rafinesque nom. illeg. *Dilomilis montana* (Swartz) Summerhayes (*Epidendrum montanum* Swartz)

Five sympodial terrestrials, epiphytes or lithophytes are found mostly in humid, low elevation, rain forests and highlands of western Cuba, Hispaniola, Jamaica and Puerto Rico. These erect plants have simple to multibranched, cane-like stems, each with narrow, elliptical or very slender, hairy, leathery leaves. The slightly nodding, simple to branching, few-flowered inflorescence has iridescent white to yellow flowers open simultaneously. The lower flowers are much larger than those at the tip. The white, triangular, trilobed lip is purple spotted and has a yellow midline. The flowers have a small, slender, purple and yellow, narrowly winged column.

DIMERANDRA

Schlechter

Repert. Spec. Nov. Regni Veg. Beih. **17**: 43 (1922).

Epidendroideæ ◊ Epidendreæ • Laeliinæ

ETYMOLOGY: Greek for twice, part and stamens. An allusion to the two large, lobes located on both sides of the column.

LECTOTYPE: *Dimerandra rimbachii* (Schlechter) Schlechter (*Epidendrum rimbachii* Schlechter)

This type name is now considered a synonym of *Dimerandra emarginata* (G. Meyer) Hoehne; basionym replaced with *Oncidium emarginatum* G. Meyer

Six quite delightful, sympodial epiphytes are found in seasonally dry, low elevation, dense swampy forests of Jamaica, Mexico to Peru, the Guianas, Trinidad, Venezuela and northern Brazil (Amazonas to Amapá). These erect plants have clustered, fleshy, cane-like stems, subtended by thin, overlapping leaf sheaths, each with flat, oblong to tongue-shaped, unequally bilobed leaves arranged in two ranks. The clustered, short inflorescences,

Currently Accepted | Validly Published | Invalidly Published | Published Pre-1753 | Superfluous Usage | Orthographic Variant | Fossil

O r c h i d G e n e r a • **126**

produced in succession, have showy, flat-faced flowers produced in pairs or singly that are often self-pollinating. The rosy to magenta flowers have spreading to cup-shaped lateral sepals and elliptical petals. The obscurely heart-shaped, shortly clawed, entire lip has a white and yellow, basal spot, and is basally united to the dark pink, short, footless column.

DIMORPHORCHIS

Rolfe

Orchid Rev. **27**(321-322): 149 (1919).

Epidendroideæ *Vandeæ* • Aeridinæ

ETYMOLOGY: Greek for having two forms and orchid. Referring to a remarkable habit of producing flowers of two separate kinds on the same inflorescence.

TYPE SPECIES: *Dimorphorchis lowii* (Lindley) Rolfe (*Vanda lowii* Lindley)

Two extraordinary, monopodial epiphytes are found in humid, low elevation, hill forests of eastern Indonesia (Borneo) usually in bright sunlight. These large, hanging plants have long, branching, arched to erect stems, each with distichous, strap-shaped, leathery leaves arranged in two ranks. The extremely long, hanging, numerous-flowered inflorescences have large, fleshy flowers well-spaced along the length of the rachis, and fragrant for the first few days. The basal flowers are structurally different from the rest of flowers on the inflorescence. These upper flowers do not open fully and are heavily covered with maroon or red-purple blotches. The lower, bright yellow flowers are lightly covered with small, maroon or purple blotches, spots or bars. They open fully, and their outer surfaces are quite hairy. The sac-like, trilobed lip has triangular side lobes with incurved margins. The fleshy, compressed midlobe is at an obtuse angle to the base part of the lip and extends into an upturned, long tapering tip. There is a yellow, finger-like appendage from the central basal disk. The flowers have a short, erect, wingless column.

DINEMA

Lindley

Orchid. Scelet. 16 (1826), and
Gen. Sp. Orchid. Pl. 111 (1831).
Not *Dinema* Perty (1852) Euglenophyceæ-Peranemataceæ.

Epidendroideæ *Epidendreæ* • Laeliinæ

ETYMOLOGY: Greek for twice and thread or filament. From the two, fine processes located on the column.

TYPE SPECIES: *Dinema polybulbon* (Swartz) Lindley (*Epidendrum polybulbon* Swartz)

One small, sympodial epiphyte or rare lithophyte is found in moist, humid, low to mid elevation, open pine-oak and mixed forests of Cuba, Jamaica, Mexico, Belize and Honduras to Nicaragua. This dwarf, creeping plant has pale yellow-green ovoid pseudobulbs, widely spaced along the chain-like rhizome, each with two narrow, dark green leaves. The short, solitary-flowered inflorescence has a fairly large, sweetly fragrant, green-yellow flower suffused or streaked brown-red, with similar, narrow sepals and petals. The broad, shortly clawed, yellow-white, entire lip, attached to the short, fleshy, winged, footless column, has a fine toothed or wavy margin.

DINKLAGEELLA

Mansfeld

Repert. Spec. Nov. Regni Veg. **36**: 63 (1934).

Epidendroideæ *Vandeæ* • Aerangidinæ

ETYMOLOGY: Honoring Max Julius Dinklage (1864-1935), a German diplomat, merchant, store clerk in Liberia and the Cameroons, who collected the flora of western Africa (Liberia). And Latin for diminutive.

TYPE SPECIES: *Dinklageella liberica* Mansfeld

Four uncommon, monopodial epiphytes are found in low elevation, woodlands of Liberia, Guinea to Gabon, Cameroon, Zaire, São Tomé and the Gulf of Guinea Islands. These low, creeping, hanging plants have long, slender stems, each with small, widely spaced leaves arranged in two rows and has numerous, sprawling roots. The long, few-flowered inflorescences have small, flat-faced, white or cream flowers that open widely and are sometimes suffused yellow or orange. The trilobed lip has large, roundish side lobes, and an oblong midlobe. The wide mouth, long, S-shaped spur is swollen at the tip. The flowers have a short, robust, wingless, footless column.

DIODONOPSIS

Pridgeon & M.W. Chase

Lindleyana **16**(4): 252 (2001).

Epidendroideæ *Epidendreæ* • Pleurothallidinæ

ETYMOLOGY: *Diodon*, generic name for porcupine-fish and Greek for appearance. Refers to the overall appearance of the flower that is covered with numerous, small, soft protuberances.

TYPE SPECIES: *Diodonopsis pygmaea* (Kraenzlin) Pridgeon & M.W. Chase (*Masdevallia pygmaea* Kraenzlin)

Five sympodial epiphytes are found in low to upper elevation, hill to montane cloud forests from Costa Rica to Bolivia among tree mosses. These small, erect, tufted plants have short stems, subtended by several sheaths, each with a solitary, leathery, narrow leaf. The erect, solitary to few-flowered inflorescence is borne from a twig-like, leafy base. The large, fleshy, white to yellow-brown flowers has a fleshy, ovate dorsal sepal that is free with a long or short, tail-like extension with a knob-like tip and the tiny petals have notched margins. The ovate, lateral sepals have long to short, tail-like extensions also with knob tips and are united along their sides forming a chin-like protuberance surrounding the column foot. The border or edge of the variable, entire lip is hinged at the base. The flowers have a small, slightly curved, wingless column marked wine-red.

DIONYSIS

Thouars

Hist. Orchid. Table 1, sub 1fg (1822).

ETYMOLOGY: Greek Mythology. Dionysus was the god of wine, the son of Zeus and Semele, and he granted Midas the power to turn whatever he touched into gold.

TYPE SPECIES: *None designated*

Name published without a description, and placement for this name is currently unknown. But was though to be a section of *Satyrium*.

DIOSTOMAEA

An orthographic variant introduced in *Reis. Br.-Guiana*, **3**: 915 (1848). The correct spelling is *Distomaea*.

DIOTHILOPHIS

An orthographic variant cited in *Dict. Fl. Pl.*, ed. 8, 369 (1973). The correct spelling is *Diothilophis*.

DIOTHONAEA

An orthographic variant introduced in *Ann. Bot. Syst.*, **3**(3): 567 (1852). The correct spelling is *Diothonea*.

DIOTHONEA

Lindley

J. Bot. (Hooker)   **1**: 12 (1834).

ETYMOLOGY: Greek for two-fold and fine linen or sails. Alluding to the two membranes stretched from the column to the lip, like jibs from the foremast to the bowsprit of a ship.

TYPE SPECIES: *Diothonea lloensis* Lindley

Now recognized as belonging to the genus *Epidendrum*, *Diothonea* was previously considered to include five epiphytes or terrestrials found in wet, mid to upper elevation, montane forests of western Venezuela, Colombia, Ecuador and Peru to central Bolivia. These plants have cylindrical, cane-like stems that are leafy for much of their length and branch toward the tip. The several, long to short, numerous to few-flowered inflorescence has small to large, pale pink-red, brown or green-yellow, fragrant flowers. The large, green to brown-green, entire or trilobed lip is completely or obliquely united to the sides of the short, stout, footless column that has a four-lobed tip.

DIPERA

Sprengel

Syst. Veg. (Sprengel), ed. 16   **3**: 676, 696 (1826).

ETYMOLOGY: Latin for two or double and pouch or sac. Refers to the appendages found on the column.

TYPE SPECIES: *None designated*

A superfluous name proposed as a substitute for *Disperis*.

DIPERIS

An orthographic variant introduced in *Icon. Pl. Ind. Orient. (Wight)*, **3**: *t. 1719* (1851). The correct spelling is *Disperis*.

DIPHRYLLUM

Rafinesque

Med. Repos., ser. 2   **5**: 357 (1808).

Name ICBN rejected vs. *Listera* R. Brown (1813) Orchidaceæ.

ETYMOLOGY: Greek for twice and leaf. Alluding to the two, sub-opposite leaves borne on the stem.

TYPE SPECIES: *Diphryllum bifolium* Rafinesque

This type name is now considered a synonym of *Neottia bifolia* Rafinesque

Although validly published this rejected name is now referred to *Neottia*. *Diphryllum* was considered to include nine terrestrials found from southeastern Canada (Ontario to Nova Scotia) and the eastern United States (New York to Florida and eastern Texas to Georgia). These small, erect, inconspicuous plants have two, heart-shaped leaves midway up the unbranched stem. The few-flowered inflorescence has tiny, dull-colored flowers with a disproportionately large lip varying from entire to deeply bilobed.

DIPHYES

Blume

Bijdr. Fl. Ned. Ind.   **7**: 310, *t. 66* (1825).

Not *Diphyes* Cookson (1965) Fossil.

ETYMOLOGY: Greek for of double and shape or nature. Refers to the two kinds of growth habit; one with distichous leaves and without pseudobulbs; and the other has pseudobulbs with each having a solitary leaf at the tip.

TYPE SPECIES: *None designated*

Now recognized as belonging to the genus *Bulbophyllum*, *Diphyes* was previously considered to include twenty-two epiphytes found in humid, low to mid elevation, hill to montane forests, grasslands and mangroves from Thailand, Malaysia and Indonesia to New Guinea. These small plants have tiny, close-set to clustered, narrowly ovoid pseudobulbs, scattered along a creeping rhizome, each with a solitary, flat, thick leaf. The erect to arching, short to long, solitary to few-flowered inflorescence has brown-yellow bracts in rows, that often completely conceal the tiny, fragrant, red, yellow, pale green or white flowers that have a small, tongue-shaped, entire lip. The lateral sepals are united at the base forming a chin-like protuberance and has tiny petals.

DIPHYLAX

Hooker *filius*

Hooker's Icon. Pl.   **19**: *t. 1865* (1889).

Orchidoideæ ⚘ Orchideæ • Orchidinæ

ETYMOLOGY: Greek for double and guardian or protector. Refers to the two, guard-like staminodes found on either side of the anther.

TYPE SPECIES: *Diphylax urceolata*
(C.B. Clarke) Hooker f.
(*Habenaria urceolata* C.B. Clarke)

Three uncommon sympodial terrestrials are found in upper elevation, montane forests of Pakistan, Nepal, Bhutan, India, Afghanistan and southwestern China (Yunnan and Guizhou). These small, erect plants have several leaves. If there is only one leaf then it is located midway on the long, unbranched stem; if there are two or more leaves these are usually basal. The slender, numerous to few-flowered inflorescence has small, white and pink or purple, and sometimes suffused green flowers. The narrow sepals and petals are nearly equal in length and converge, forming a hood over the short column. The sometimes hairy, entire or distally trilobed lip is usually decurved, narrow or tongue-shaped, nearly as long as sepals, with a slightly concave base. It has an inward-rolled margin and forms a tube above the middle. The short, swollen spur has a contracted neck. These species are often considered as a section of *Habenaria*.

DIPHYLLUM

An orthographic variant introduced in *Herb. Raf.*, 73 (1833). The correct spelling is *Diphryllum*.

DIPLACORCHIS

Schlechter

Beih. Bot. Centralbl.   **38**(2): 127 (1921).

ETYMOLOGY: Greek for double-folded and orchid. Referring to two, parallel keels located on the lip.

TYPE SPECIES: *Diplacorchis tenuior*
(Reichenbach f.) Schlechter
(*Brachycorythis tenuior* Reichenbach f.)

Now recognized as belonging to the genus *Brachycorythis*, *Diplacorchis* was previously considered to include one terrestrial found in mid elevation, open savannas and grasslands from Madagascar to South Africa. This rather common plant has erect, unbranched stems, each with overlapping, narrow leaves. The packed, semi-cylindrical inflorescence has purple, rose or white-pink flowers. The bend downward, entire to trilobed lip has a fleshy, concave

Currently Accepted   Validly Published   Invalidly Published   Published Pre-1753   Superfluous Usage   Orthographic Variant   Fossil

Orchid Genera • 128

midlobe, and either a short, wide, bilobed spur or a sac-like protuberance. The flowers have a long, slender column.

DIPLANDRORCHIS

S.C. Chen

Acta Phytotax. Sin. **17**(1): 2 (1979).

ETYMOLOGY: Greek for double, man or stamen and orchid. Referring to the one disk-like, flat-topped stigma and the two anthers.

TYPE SPECIES: *Diplandrorchis sinica* S.C. Chen

Now recognized as belonging to the genus *Neottia*, *Diplandrorchis* was previously considered to include one saprophyte found in low elevation, grassy slopes of northeastern China (Liaoning) in *Tilia* forests. This erect, slender plant has unbranched, leafless stems, subtended by several sheaths. The few-flowered inflorescence has thinly textured, green-white to pale green flowers with a hairy, outer surface on the oblong sepals. The entire lip is identical in its shape to the petals. The flat-topped stigma has a disk-like appendage at the tip of the erect column. There is no rostellum, and there are two anthers found on the upper portion of the column.

DIPLANTHERA

Rafinesque

Herb. Raf. 73 (1833).

Not *Diplanthera* Schrank (1821) Acanthaceæ, not *Diplanthera* Banks & Solander ex R. Brown (1810) Bignoniaceæ, not *Diplanthera* Thouars (1806) Cymodoceaceæ, and not *Diplanthera* J.G. Gleditsch (1764) Acanthaceæ.

ETYMOLOGY: Greek for double and a split anther.

TYPE SPECIES: *None designated*

Name published without a description. Today this name is most often referred to *Platanthera*.

DIPLECTHRUM

Persoon

Syn. Pl. (Persoon) **2**: 508 (1807).

ETYMOLOGY: Greek for double and spur. Referring to the double spurs typically found in these species.

TYPE SPECIES: *None designated*

Not validly published, this name is referred to *Satyrium*. *Diplecthrum* was considered to include twelve terrestrials found in various parts of South Africa and one species is found in Madagascar, Réunion and the Comoros Islands.

DIPLECTRADEN

Rafinesque

Fl. Tellur. **2**: 90 (1836)[1837].

ETYMOLOGY: Greek for twice, spur and gland. Describing the spurred lip and the two knobs or knots located on the anther.

TYPE SPECIES: *Diplectraden leptoceras*
(Hooker) Rafinesque
(*Habenaria leptoceras* Hooker)

Now recognized as belonging to the genus *Habenaria*, *Diplectraden* was previously considered to include one terrestrial found in mid elevation, montane grasslands and woodlands of eastern Brazil (São Paulo). This tall plant has thick stems, surrounded by several, narrow, pale green leaves that diminish in size as they proceed up the stem. The erect, densely packed, numerous-flowered inflorescence has tiny, pale green-yellow flowers. The dorsal sepal is fused with the petals forming a hood over the small column. The long, obscurely trilobed lip has minuscule side lobes, a sword-shaped midlobe, and a long, white, cylindrical spur.

DIPLECTRUM

Salisbury

Trans. Hort. Soc. London **1**: 287 (1812).

ETYMOLOGY: Greek for double and spur. Referring to the double spurs typically found in these species.

LECTOTYPE: *Diplectrum cucullifolium*
(Linnaeus) Salisbury
(*Orchis bicornis* Linnaeus)

A superfluous name proposed as a substitute for *Satyrium*.

DIPLOCAULOBIUM

(Reichenbach *filius*) Kraenzlin

Pflanzenr. (Engler) **21**(IV.50.II.B): 331 (1910).

Epidendroideæ ⚬ Dendrobiinæ • Currently unplaced

ETYMOLOGY: Greek for double, stem and life. Refers to the pseudobulbs that grow in two dissimilar shapes.

TYPE SPECIES: *Diplocaulobium nitidissimum*
(Reichenbach f.) Kraenzlin
(*Dendrobium nitidissimum* Reichenbach f.)

Ninety-one sympodial epiphytes or sometimes lithophytes are found in low elevation, swamps and mangroves ranging from Malaysia and Indonesia through Fiji with the center of development in New Guinea. These clump-forming plants have long, tapering to rather flattened, clustered or widespread, one-noded pseudobulbs each with a solitary, narrow leaf. The several, erect inflorescences, have one to two flowers and are borne from the leaf axis.

The dull to showy, white, yellow or red flowers last less than a day, are small to often large, and spider-like. The sepals and petals are usually slender to thread-like with some species having a narrow shape, but all are united to the column foot forming a distinct chin-like protuberance. They are borne singly, but their gregarious flowering is triggered by a sudden change in temperature that can cause the plant to be literally covered in masses of flowers in just a few short days. The entire to obscurely trilobed lip has small side lobes. The midlobe has a rather long callus of longitudinal keels and a wavy margin. The flowers have a short, fleshy, slightly curved column.

DIPLOCENTRON

An orthographic variant introduced in *Edwards's Bot. Reg.*, **24**: sub 68 (1838). The correct spelling is *Diplocentrum*.

DIPLOCENTRUM

Lindley

Edwards's Bot. Reg. **18**: sub 1522 (1832).

Epidendroideæ ⚬ Vandeæ • Aeridinæ

ETYMOLOGY: Greek for double and spur. Referring to the two spurs found on the lip.

TYPE SPECIES: *Diplocentrum recurvum* Lindley

Two monopodial epiphytes are found in mid elevation, montane forests and scrub of southern India (Karnataka, Kerala and Tamil Nadu) and Sri Lanka. These stunted-looking plants have woody stems subtended by the bases of old fallen leaves. The long, thinly textured, deep yellow-green, semi-terete leaves have unequally bilobed tips. The rather long, multibranching, densely packed, numerous-flowered inflorescences have small, pale green, deep pink or white flowers with dark pink streaks in the center. The crimson, magenta or white, tongue-like, entire lip has blotches of pink. The prominent callus is slightly recurved and has two short, twin spurs. The flowers have a short, stout, wingless, footless column.

DIPLOCHILOS

An orthographic variant introduced in *Edwards's Bot. Reg.*, **18**: sub 1499 (1832). The correct spelling is *Diplochilus*.

DIPLOCHILUS

Lindley

Edwards's Bot. Reg. **18**: sub 1499 (1832).

ETYMOLOGY: Greek for double and lip. Referring to the similarity of the lip to the petals that gives the flower the appearance of being duplicated.

TYPE SPECIES: *None designated*

Now recognized as belonging to the genus *Diplomeris*, *Diplochilos* was previously considered to include two terrestrials found from northern India to northern Vietnam and southern China. These tiny plants have large leaves and an erect, hairy, few-flowered inflorescence. The pale pink to white flowers have an unusually long, curved spur.

DIPLOCONCHIUM

Schauer

Nov. Actorum Acad. Caes. Leop.-Carol. German. Nat. Cur., ser. 3 **19**(Suppl. 1): 428, *t. 12, f. A* (1843), or *Observ. Bot.* **16**(Suppl. 2): 428, *t. 12* (1843).

ETYMOLOGY: Greek for double and mussel or sea shell. Refers to the concave lip shape of the hypochile and the epichile.

TYPE SPECIES: *Diploconchium inocephalum* Schauer

Now recognized as belonging to the genus *Agrostophyllum*, *Diploconchium* was previously considered to include one epiphyte found in low to mid elevation, hill and montane forests ranging from southern Taiwan to the Philippines. This large plant has clustered, flattened stems, each with several, narrow, two-ranked leaves joined to the overlapping sheathing bases. The clustered, terminal, head-like, numerous-flowered inflorescences have small, white flowers, turning yellow as they age, and lasting for a few short days. The entire lip is concave at the base, contracted in the middle and then sac-like toward the tip. The flowers have a small, footless column.

DIPLODIUM

Swartz

Ges. Naturf. Freunde Berlin Mag. Neuesten Entdeck. Gesammten Naturk. **4**: 84, *t. 3* (1810).

Name ICBN rejected vs. *Pterostylis* R. Brown (1810) Orchidaceæ.

ETYMOLOGY: Greek for double. Alluding to the form of the two lateral sepals being united to about the middle forming a segment twice as wide as the other segments.

TYPE SPECIES: *Diplodium alatum* (Labillardière) Swartz
(*Disperis alata* Labillardière)

Although validly published this rejected name is now referred to *Pterostylis*. *Diplodium* was considered to include one terrestrial found in wet forests to sandy scrub of New Zealand, Tasmania and southeastern Australia, often forming dense colonies. This slender-stemmed, unbranched plant has its few bract-like leaves withered by flowering time. The solitary-flowered inflorescence has a pale flower with longitudinal stripes. The hood-like dorsal sepal curves forward with a rather blunt tip. The united lateral sepals are erect and have two, hair-like tips that are separated by a wide space. These two, long tips are forward and curved at the tip. The long, tapered, entire lip narrows to a blunt tip.

DIPLOGASTRA

Welwitsch ex Reichenbach *filius*

Flora **48**(12): 183 (1865).

ETYMOLOGY: Greek for double and belly or pouch. Referring to the basally doubled sac-like lip.

TYPE SPECIES: *Diplogastra angolensis*
Welwitsch ex Reichenbach f.
This type name is now considered a synonym of *Platylepis glandulosa* (Lindley) Reichenbach f.; basionym
Notiophrys glandulosa Lindley

Now recognized as belonging to the genus *Platylepis*, *Diplogastra* was previously considered to include one terrestrial found in shady, low elevation, swampy forests or along river banks from the Ivory Coast to Uganda and Gabon to Zimbabwe. This is a small, creeping plant at its base that becomes erect and leafy on the pencil-thick, soft stems. The erect, densely packed, hairy, numerous-flowered inflorescence has several sterile sheaths. The small, green-white or pink-brown flower's outer surface is conspicuously glandular-hairy, and the tiny petals form a hood along with the dorsal sepal.

DIPLOLABELLUM

Maekawa

J. Jap. Bot. **11**(5): 305, *t. 8* (1935).

ETYMOLOGY: Greek for doubling and a little lip. Refers to the pleated or folded lip.

TYPE SPECIES: *Diplolabellum coreanum*
(Finet) Maekawa
(*Oreorchis coreana* Finet)
This type name is now considered a synonym of *Oreorchis patens* subsp. *coreana* (Finet) Y.N. Lee; basionym
Oreorchis coreana Finet

Now recognized as belonging to the genus *Oreorchis*, *Diplolabellum* was previously considered to include one saprophyte found in cool, mid elevation, montane forests of Korea and Japan. This plant has small, corm-like pseudobulbs, each with a few grass-like leaves. The erect, few-flowered inflorescence has small, olive-green flowers not opening fully. Both the petals and lip's midlobe can be sprinkled with magenta spots. The white, trilobed lip has erect, flag-like side lobes and a broad midlobe with a wavy margin with two ridges. The flowers have a yellow, erect column.

DIPLOMERIS

D. Don

Prodr. Fl. Nepal. 26 (1825).

Orchidoideæ · Orchideæ · Orchidinæ

ETYMOLOGY: Greek for double and a portion or a part. Referring to the two, appendix-like projections on the column.

TYPE SPECIES: *Diplomeris pulchella* D. Don

Five charming, uncommon, sympodial terrestrials are found in low to upper elevation, grasslands and steep montane rocky slopes of northeastern India (Assam), Nepal, central China (Xizang, Yunnan, Guizhou and Sichuan), Myanmar to Vietnam. These dwarf plants are more or less prostrate and have short stems, each with one to two large, roundish or sword-shaped, hairy or smooth leaves. The arching to spreading, one- to two-flowered inflorescence has a showy, comparatively large, roundish, white flower; the large petals are much broader than the sepals. The large, fan-shaped, entire or minutely trilobed lip, joined to the base of the short column by a long, yellow claw, and has a slender hanging, green, curved spur.

DIPLOPRORA

Hooker *filius*

Fl. Brit. Ind. **6**(1): 26 (1890).

Epidendroideæ · Vandeæ · Aeridinæ

ETYMOLOGY: Greek for double and prow or front. Descriptive of the spreading, bilobed tip of the lip.

TYPE SPECIES: *Diploprora championii*
(Lindley) Hooker f.
(*Cottonia championii* Lindley)

Two monopodial epiphytes are native in low to mid elevation, montane valleys and forests to India (Kerala), Sri Lanka, southern China (Fujian to Yunnan), Taiwan, Hong Kong and Thailand to Vietnam. These small plants have long, slender, slightly compressed, often hanging stems, each with several, narrow, thinly textured, distichous leaves spaced along the stem. The short, few-flowered inflorescence has small, yellow or white, fragrant flowers opening in succession with similar sepals and petals. The broad, immobile, white and yellow spotted, entire lip has its margins united to both sides of the short, stout, wingless, footless column and is divided into two shallow, small, fork-like segments or tails at the tip.

Currently Accepted   Validly Published   Invalidly Published   Published Pre-1753   Superfluous Usage   Orthographic Variant   Fossil

DIPLORRHIZA

Ehrhart

Beitr. Naturk. (Ehrhart) **4**: 147 (1789).

ETYMOLOGY: Greek for double and root.

TYPE SPECIES: *Satyrium viride* Linnaeus

Not validly published, this name is most often referred to as a synonym of *Habenaria*.

DIPODIUM

R. Brown

Prodr. Fl. Nov. Holland. 330 (1810).

Epidendroideæ ⁞⁄ Cymbidieæ • Eulophiinæ

ETYMOLOGY: Greek for double and a little foot. Alluding to the two stipes of the pollinia that are fixed to the rostellum.

TYPE SPECIES: *Dipodium punctatum* (Smith) R. Brown
(*Dendrobium punctatum* Smith)

This type name is now considered a synonym of *Dipodium squamatum* (G. Forster) R. Brown; basionym replaced with *Ophrys squamata* G. Forster

A remarkable genus consisting of twenty-four sympodial or monopodial saprophytes, leafy terrestrials, and climbing epiphytes are found in open, low to mid elevation, swampy woodlands and nutrient-poor soil from Cambodia to Vietnam, Malaysia, Indonesia, New Guinea, Australia and the Philippines to the south-western Pacific Archipelago. These sprawling plants may start as a terrestrial and then creep along the forest floor until finding a nearby tree or vertical rock to climb. Once the basal portion of the stem dies, it will continue growing as an epiphyte or lithophyte. The plants have short or elongate, slender stems with or without leaves that overlap at the base or are spaced along the stem in two ranks. The erect, red to brown-red, solitary to few-flowered inflorescence, arising from the leaf axils, has waxy or heavily textured, creamy white, pink, deep red, yellow to yellow-green flowers usually spotted and/or blotched red. The trilobed or obscurely trilobed lip has narrow side lobes, and an often densely hairy midlobe. The flowers have a short, stout, footless column.

DIPTERANTHUS

Barbosa Rodrigues

Gen. Sp. Orchid. **2**: 232, t. 196 (1882).

ETYMOLOGY: Greek for two, a wing and flower. An allusion to the two appendages of the column and the consequent resemblance of the flower to a gnat or a small fly.

TYPE SPECIES: *Dipteranthus pseudobulbiferus*
(Barbosa Rodrigues) Barbosa Rodrigues
(*Ornithocephalus pseudobulbiferus* Barbosa Rodrigues)

Now recognized as belonging to the genus *Zygostates*, *Dipteranthus* was previously considered to include two dwarf epiphytes found in southern Brazil, Peru and Ecuador. These unusual small plants have tiny, tightly clustered, ovoid pseudobulbs, each with a solitary, flattened, thick, leathery, bright green leaf. The short, often hanging, few-flowered inflorescence, borne from the base of the pseudobulb in the axils of the upper leaf sheath, bears clusters of minute, translucent, white, yellow or green-yellow flowers. The dorsal sepal and petals converge, forming a hood over the bright yellow, footless, wingless column. The larger lateral sepals have a blotch of green at the base, and strongly curve inward toward the concave, trilobed lip. The above type name is now considered a synonym of *Zygostates pellucida* Reichenbach f.

DIPTEROSTELE

Schlechter

Repert. Spec. Nov. Regni Veg. Beih. **8**: 106 (1921).

ETYMOLOGY: Greek for two-winged and column or stamen. Descriptive of the two, wing-like processes on the sides of the small stigma.

TYPE SPECIES: *Dipterostele microglossa* Schlechter

Now recognized as belonging to the genus *Stellilabium*, *Dipterostele* was previously considered to include thirteen epiphytes found in mid to upper elevation, montane forests from southern Mexico to Costa Rica, Ecuador and Bolivia. These small, slender, delicate plants have erect stems, each with narrow, distichous leaves. The erect, branched, few-flowered inflorescences bear small, yellow-brown flowers. The red, trilobed lip has a hairy base and the callus has a broad cushion. The flowers have a short column the tip of which has a long, up-turned hook.

DIREMA

An orthographic variant introduced in *Nat. Syst. Pl.*, 300 (1832). The correct spelling is *Dimema*.

DISA

P.J. Bergius

Descr. Pl. Cap. 348 (1767).

Orchidoideæ ⁞⁄ Orchideæ • Disinæ

ETYMOLOGY: Swedish Mythology. According to some sources the name is derived from a mythical queen of Sweden, Queen Disa, whom legend says appeared before the King of Swea wrapped only in a fishing net when commanded to appear neither naked nor clothed.

Or possibly for the Goddesses or Disas who were worshiped in the Uppsala regions of eastern Sweden during early pagan times of the middle ages.

TYPE SPECIES: *Disa uniflora* P.J. Bergius

Approximately one hundred sixty-nine sympodial terrestrials or rare epiphytes are found in wet, low to upper elevation, nutrient-poor marsh, rocky crevices, grasslands or along river banks from Ethiopia to South Africa, Madagascar and Réunion with one species found in Yemen. These showy, erect plants have unbranched, leafy stems, each with narrow, overlapping to lax, soft to somewhat rigid, green leaves. The leaves are occasionally barred red, and the undersides are suffused purple or are entirely deep red. The numerous to few-flowered inflorescence has long or short bracts, and small to large, hooded flowers. Structure of the richly colored, showy flower is most unusual because the dominating structure is not the lip but the often spurred, frequently ornately formed, dorsal sepal usually forming a hood over the small, short, broad column. The club-shaped spur is sac-like or elongate, cylindrical or thread-like, and curves downward, upward or is horizontal. The simple, oblong petals are tucked inside the dorsal sepal or protrude from it, and sometimes are twisted to obscure the helmet entrance. The usually small, narrow, entire lip has an entire or rarely fringed margin.

DISCYPHUS

Schlechter

Repert. Spec. Nov. Regni Veg. **15**: 417 (1919).

Orchidoideæ ⁞⁄ Cranichideæ • Spiranthinæ

ETYMOLOGY: Greek for double and cup or jug. Refers to the two separate and distinct, cup-like stigmas.

TYPE SPECIES: *Discyphus scopulariae*
(Reichenbach f.) Schlechter
(*Spiranthes scopulariae* Reichenbach f.)

One sympodial terrestrial is found in low elevation, scrub of Panama, Venezuela, Trinidad and northeastern Brazil (Piauí, Bahia, Rio Grande do Norte and Paraíba). This small plant has short, unbranched stems, each with a solitary, heart-shaped leaf lying flat on the ground. The erect, hairy (brown), few-flowered inflorescence has widely spaced bracts, and the small, tubular, hairy, dull green-white flowers are suffused pale green and have a concave dorsal sepal. The long-clawed, trilobed lip has a wide hypochile with two large lobes at the base that have roundish ends, and the obscurely trilobed epichile has fleshy, soft protuberances. The whole plant is covered with stiff, short hairs. The flowers have a slender, club-shaped, footless column.

DISELLA

Lindley ex Wittstein
Etym.-Bot.-Handw.-Buch, ed. 1   294 (1852).
Not *Disella* E.L. Greene (1906) Malvaceæ.

Name published without a description. Today this name is most often referred to as a section of *Disa*.

DISERIS

An orthographic variant introduced in *Icon. Pl. Ind. Orient. (Wight)*, **5**(1): 15 (1851). The correct spelling is *Disperis*.

DISIA

An orthographic variant cited in *World Checkl. Seed Pl. (Govaerts)*, **1**(2): 1 (1995). The correct spelling is *Disa*.

DISKAYPHOGYNE

An orthographic variant cited in *Orchideen (Schlechter): Liter. Reg. Band I/A, B, and C*, 165 (2003). The correct spelling is *Diskyphogyne*.

DISKYPHOGYNE

Szlachetko & R. González
Fragm. Florist. Geobot.   **41**(1): 494 (1996).
ETYMOLOGY: Greek for twice, cup and female. In reference to the cup-like lateral lobes of the stigma.
TYPE SPECIES: *Diskyphogyne scabrilingua*
(Szlachetko) Szlachetko & R.González
(*Brachystele scabrilingua* Szlachetko)

Now recognized as belonging to the genus *Brachystele*, *Diskyphogyne* was previously considered to include three terrestrials found in Brazil, Paraguay and Uruguay. These erect, tall plants have slender, unbranched stems, each with distinct, narrow leaves in a basal rosette that are usually present during flowering. The minute, tubular, dull-colored flowers are arranged in densely packed, spirally arranged, multi-flowered inflorescences that can resemble small bottle-brushes. The usually shortly clawed, entire lip has a broad base that

sometimes has tiny, basal thickenings or horn-like appendages. The flowers have a short, erect column with the column foot that is relatively massive.

DISPARIS

An orthographic variant introduced in *Atti Soc. Ital. Sci. Nat.*, **16**: 335 (1873). The correct spelling is *Disperis*.

DISPERANTHOCEROS

Mytnik & Szlachetko
Richardiana   **7**(2): 65 (2007).
ETYMOLOGY: Greek for twice, flower and horn. Refers to the shape of the flowers.
TYPE SPECIES: *Disperanthoceros anthoceros*
(la Croix & P.J. Cribb) Mytnik & Szlachetko
(*Polystachya anthoceros* la Croix & P.J. Cribb)

Recognized as belonging to the genus *Polystachya*, *Disperanthoceros* was proposed to include one epiphyte or terrestrial found in humid, low to mid elevation, forests and woodlands of northern Nigeria (Plateau Mambilla). These plants have small, clustered, pear-shaped pseudobulbs each with two long, narrow, grass-like leaves. The few-flowered inflorescence has a foul smelling, pale brown to white flowers with similar sepals and petals suffused purple. The large, clawed, trilobed lip has small, erect side lobes and an ovate midlobe. The flowers have a short column.

DISPERIS

Swartz
Kongl. Vetensk. Akad. Nya Handl., ser. 2
21: 218, t. 3f (1800).
Orchidoideæ ⁝ Orchideæ • Brownleeinæ
ETYMOLOGY: Greek for twice and wallet or bag. Alluding to the pouches formed by the lateral sepals.
TYPE SPECIES: *Disperis secunda*
(Thunberg) Swartz nom. illeg.
(*Arethusa secunda* Thunberg) nom. illeg.
This type name is now considered a synonym of
LECTOTYPE: *Disperis circumflexa*
(Linnaeus) T. Durand & Schinz
(*Ophrys circumflexa* Linnaeus)
designated by both
E.P. Phillips, *Gen. S. Afr. Fl. Pl.*, ed 2, 237 (1951), and
H.P. Linder & Kurzweil, *Orchid S. Afr.*, 299 (1999).

Upward of seventy-six sympodial terrestrials are found in low to mid elevation, rain and cloud forests and dense moss laden forests, grasslands and woodlands from Togo, Ethiopia to South Africa with a few species found in Madagascar, the Mascarene Islands and southern India (Karnataka, Kerala and Tamil Nadu), Sri Lanka, southern Japan, Taiwan, Thailand and New Guinea to the Philippines. These colony forming, slender

plants have a smooth or hairy, unbranched stems, each with several, softly textured, basal leaves or are borne along the stem. The smooth or rarely hairy, small leaves are sometimes purple underneath. The few-flowered inflorescence has exceedingly complex flowers varying in size from tiny to rather large, and found in a wide range of shades from white, pink, magenta, yellow to green. The dorsal sepal is united to the sickle-shaped petals, but rarely extends into a prominent spur; the erect petals converge, forming a hood with the dorsal sepal behind the short, erect, mostly stout column. The lateral sepals each have a sac-like spur in the middle or near the inner margin (spur lacking in a few species). The highly modified, variable lip, usually hidden within the hood, has horn-like side lobes, always has an entire or bilobed appendage and is united by a claw to the face of the column.

DISPERSIS

An orthographic variant cited in *Man. Dict. Fl. Pl.*, ed. 4, 223 (1919). The correct spelling is *Disperis*.

DISPIRES

An orthographic variant introduced in *Icon. Pl. Ind. Orient. (Wight)*, **2**: t. 930 (1851). The correct spelling is *Disperis*.

DISSORHYNCHIUM

Schauer
Nov. Actorum Acad. Caes. Leop.-Carol. German. Nat. Cur., ser. 3   **19**(Suppl. 1): 434, t. 13A (1843), or
Observ. Bot.   **16**(Suppl. 2): 434, t. 13A (1843).
ETYMOLOGY: Greek for double and snout or horn. Refers to the deeply clefted rostellum that along with its two points project forward.
TYPE SPECIES: *Dissorhynchium muricatum* Schauer

Now recognized as belonging to the genus *Habenaria*, *Dissorhynchium* was previously considered to include one terrestrial found in low elevation, swampy forests or slopes from southeastern China (Guangdong to Hainan), Indonesia (Borneo) and the Philippines. This is a creeping plant at the base that becomes erect, leafy on the stem's lower section and bract-like above. The erect, stout, ridged inflorescence has several, sterile sheaths. The white, green-white or pink-brown flower's outer surface is conspicuously glandular-hairy. The small, narrow petals converge, forming a hood with the erect, concave dorsal sepal. The trilobed lip has long, narrow side lobes and midlobe that are thread-like. The long, club-shaped spur has a swollen tip. The above type name is now considered a synonym of *Habenaria hystrix* Ames.

| Currently Accepted | Validly Published | Invalidly Published | Published Pre-1753 | Superfluous Usage | Orthographic Variant | Fossil |

DISSORRHYNCHIUM

An orthographic variant cited in *Lex. Gen. Phan.*, 181 (1904). The correct spelling is *Dissorhynchium*.

DISSORYNCHIUM

An orthographic variant cited in *Lex. Gen. Phan.*, 181 (1904). The correct spelling is *Dissorhynchium*.

DISTICHIS

Thouars

Hist. Orchid.   Table 3, sub 3r, *tt.* 89-90 (1822).

Name published without a description. Today this name is most often referred to *Stichorkis*.

DISTICHOLIPARIS

Margońska & Szlachetko

Orchidee (Hamburg)   **55**(2): 175 (2004).

ETYMOLOGY: Greek for in two rows or ranks and *Liparis*, an orchid genus. Referring to the type of leaf arrangement typically found in this genus.

TYPE SPECIES: *Districholiparis disticha*
(Thouars) Margońska & Szlachetko
(*Malaxis disticha* Thouars)

A superfluous name proposed as a substitute for *Stichorkis*.

DISTICHORCHIS

M.A. Clements & D.L. Jones

Orchadian   **13**(11): 487 (2002).

ETYMOLOGY: Greek for in two rows and orchid. Refers to the two rank arrangement of the leaves.

TYPE SPECIES: *Distichorchis cerina*
(Schlechter) M.A. Clements & D.L. Jones
(*Dendrobium cerinum* Schlechter, nom. illeg.)

Recognized as belonging to the genus *Dendrobium*, *Distichorchis* was proposed to include forty-three epiphytes or lithophytes found in low elevation, rain forests of New Guinea and throughout the southwestern Pacific Archipelago with year-round rainfall. This plant has long, cylindrical stems (pseudobulbous or non-pseudobulbous) that become hanging with age, each with small, oblong leaves arranged in two ranks along the stem. The solitary-flowered inflorescence, borne from the leaf axils, has a small, waxy, greenwhite or white flower, changing to dark yellow or orange as it ages. The sepals and petals are strongly recurved. The large, trilobed lip has roundish, erect side lobes, and the broad, scope-shaped, bilobed midlobe has a wavy margin, and fleshy, brown keels. The flowers

have a short, concave column. The above type name is now considered a synonym of *Dendrobium austrocaledonicum* Schlechter.

DISTOMAE

An orthographic variant introduced in *Repert. Spec. Nov. Regni Veg. Beih.*, **4**: 140 (1919). The correct spelling is *Distomaea*.

DISTOMAEA

Spenner

Fl. Friburg.   **1**: 245 (1825).

ETYMOLOGY: Greek for twice and cut or cut off. In reference to the slit found in the middle of the lip.

TYPE SPECIES: *None designated*

Now recognized as belonging to the genus *Listera*, *Distomaea* was previously considered to include three small terrestrials widely distributed in the northern hemisphere from Denmark to Ukraine, Russia to northern China, Korea, Japan, Canada to Greenland, Iceland and the United States (Washington to northern New Mexico, Maine to West Virginia). They are most difficult to find in the wet sphagnum bogs because of their small size. These erect plants have a slightly hairy, unbranched stem with a pair of oblong leaves located midway up the stem. The fewflowered inflorescence has tiny, nearly invisible, green-brown flowers with a wedgeshaped, bilobed lip that is divided in two for up to half of its length. The flowers have a short, thick column.

NOTE: One can only see the details and appreciate the real beauty of these flowers by using a strong magnifying glass.

DISTOMAIA

An orthographic variant introduced in *Handb. Bot. (Spenner)*, **3**: 186 (1836). The correct spelling is *Distomaea*.

DISTYLODON

Summerhayes

Kew Bull.   **20**: 197 (1966).

Epidendroideæ ◊ Vandeæ • Aerangidinæ

ETYMOLOGY: Greek for two, column or style and tooth. Descriptive of the column that has two teeth.

TYPE SPECIES: *Distylodon comptum* Summerhayes

One monopodial epiphyte is found in mid elevation, hill forests of southwestern Uganda. This dwarf plant has short, flattened stems, each with the few distichous, narrow, unequal bilobed leaves twisted at the base; thus

appearing to lie in one plane. The slender, solitary-flowered inflorescence has an insignificant, small, pale green flower not opening widely that has long, narrow sepals and petals. The obscurely trilobed lip has erect side lobes. The narrow midlobe is much longer and the straight, cylindrical spur has a narrow mouth. The flowers have a short, erect, footless column.

DITEILIS

Rafinesque

Herb. Raf.   73 (1833).

ETYMOLOGY: Greek for double and flocks or down. Descriptive of the two warts on the lip.

TYPE SPECIES: *Diteilis nepalensis* Rafinesque nom. illeg.
Liparis nervousa subsp. *nervousa*
(*Cymbidium bituberculatum* Hooker)

Now recognized as belonging to the genus *Liparis*, *Diteilis* was previously considered to include one terrestrial or lithophyte found from Korea, southern Japan (Ryukyu Islands), northern India (Kashmir to Assam) to the southwestern Pacific Archipelago, tropical Africa (Ghana to Zimbabwe), Cuba to Trinidad, southeastern United States (Florida), Mexico to Panama and Brazil. This plant has stems forming long pseudobulbs, each with one to two, thinly textured, narrow leaves. The erect, densely packed, numerous-flowered inflorescences have small, green or yellowgreen flowers often with a dark purple, entire lip. The flowers have a long, arched column.

DITHRIX

(Hooker *filius*) Schlechter

Notizbl. Bot. Gart. Berlin-Dahlem   **9**: 583 (1926).

ETYMOLOGY: Greek for two and hair. Referring to the deeply lobed lip.

TYPE SPECIES: *Habenaria decipiens* Hooker f. nom. illeg.
not *Habenaria decipiens* Wight (1851)
This type name is now considered a synonym of
Diphylax griffithii (Hooker f.) Kraenzlin
(*Habenaria griffithii* Hooker f.)

Now recognized as belonging to the genus *Diphylax*, *Dithrix* was previously considered to include one terrestrial found in mid elevation, montane forests of southwestern India. This tall plant has slender, erect, unbranched stems, each with narrow or oblong leaves on the lower stem or with the upper leaves utilized as sheathing bracts. The short, few-flowered inflorescence has large, fragrant, fleshy flowers. The white, ovate lateral sepals and narrow, sharply pointed petals are obscurely nerved. The deeply trilobed lip has wedge-shaped side lobes with thread-like tips; a narrow midlobe and has a long, green, cylindrical spur.

DITHYRIDANTHUS

Garay

Bot. Mus. Leafl. **28**(4): 315 (1980)[1982].

ETYMOLOGY: Greek for with two doors or entrances and flower. Describing the two lateral openings formed by the dorsal and lateral sepals at the base of the flower.

TYPE SPECIES: *Dithyridanthus densiflorus*
(C. Schweinfurth) Garay
(*Spiranthes densiflora* C. Schweinfurth)

Now recognized as belonging to the genus *Schiedeella*, *Dithyridanthus* was previously considered to include one terrestrial found in mid elevation, oak-pine forests of Mexico. This erect plant has stout, unbranched stems, each with a basal cluster of dark green leaves often withered at flowering time. The numerous to few-flowered inflorescence has brown, attractively veined floral bracts partially covering each, usually dull-colored flower. The flowers have narrow sepals and petals united at the base forming a tubular shape and each has a strongly recurved tip. The narrowly clawed, red-thickened, entire lip has an erect or bent epichile, a widely varied hypochile and has two prominent basal appendages or are without. The flowers have a long, slender column.

DITUILIS

An orthographic variant introduced in *Fl. Tellur.*, **4**: 49 (1836)[1837]. The correct spelling is *Diteilis*.

DITULIMA

Rafinesque

Fl. Tellur. **4**: 41 (1836)[1837].

ETYMOLOGY: Greek for two and knob or swelling. Refers to the two, wart-like structures located on the stigma.

TYPE SPECIES: *Ditulima anceps* (Swartz) Rafinesque
(*Dendrobium anceps* Swartz)

Now recognized as belonging to the genus *Dendrobium*, *Ditulima* was previously considered to include one epiphyte found in low to mid elevation, tropical and subtropical valley forests and scrub of northeastern India, Nepal, Bhutan, Bangladesh, Andaman Islands, Nicobar Islands and Thailand to Vietnam. This large plant has somewhat flattened stems, each with several, fleshy, overlapping, ovate to narrow leaves. The short, solitary-flowered inflorescences borne prolifically along the center line, near the tip; have a small, green-yellow flower. The pale yellow, wedge-shaped, obscurely trilobed lip, sprinkled with tiny, red spots, has a wavy margin with a shallow notch. The flowers have a short column.

DITULINA

An orthographic variant introduced in *Orchideen (Schlechter)*, ed. 1, 249 (1914). The correct spelling is *Ditulima*.

DIURIS

Smith

Trans. Linn. Soc. London, Bot. **4**: 222 (1798).

Orchidoideæ ⁖ Diurideæ • Diuridinæ

ETYMOLOGY: Greek for two and a tail. An allusion to the two lateral sepals in the form of tails that project below the lip.

LECTOTYPE: *Diuris aurea* Smith

Fifty-eight colony forming, sympodial terrestrials are found in low elevation, grasslands, slopes, scrub and coastal dunes of Australia (Queensland to Victoria and Western Australia) and Tasmania with one species endemic to Timor. These erect plants have short, unbranched stems, subtended by thin, leaf-like sheaths at each node, each with one to several, grass-like, distichous or spirally arranged leaves. The erect, wiry, solitary to few-flowered inflorescence has attractive, pea-like flowers that are colored predominantly yellow. The short dorsal sepal forms a hood over the column. The lip is patterned with darker red, brown or purple markings and blotches, and is attached by its base to the anterior column base. The strongly trilobed lip, at the base, has side lobes flanking the erect, short, winged column, and the midlobe is keeled or folded longitudinally with a spreading margin.

DOCKRILLA

An orthographic variant introduced in *Fl. Vit. Nova*, **5**: 410 (1991). The correct spelling is *Dockrillia*.

DOCKRILLIA

Brieger

Orchideen (Schlechter), ed. 3 **1**(11-12): 745 (1981).

ETYMOLOGY: Named in honor of Alick William Dockrill (1915-), an Australian orchidologist, herbarium keeper and author of *Australian Indigenous Orchids*.

TYPE SPECIES: *Dockrillia linguiforme* (Swartz) Brieger
(*Dendrobium linguiforme* Swartz)

Now recognized as belonging to the genus *Dendrobium*, *Dockrillia* was previously considered to include twenty-one epiphytes or lithophytes found in low to mid

elevation, rain forests from Australia and New Guinea to the southwestern Pacific Archipelago. These rambling to creeping plants, often forming large colonies, have numerous, thick, tough, dark green to red, conspicuously ribbed, fleshy leaves, spaced along a thin, wiry, short stem. Most have hanging to erect, short to long, numerous to few-flowered inflorescences with small, white or green-yellow flowers that have slender, sometimes curled sepals and petals. The flowers change color as they age. The uppermost trilobed lip has several, faintly purple markings, and a ruffled, recurved midlobe. The flowers have a short, stout column.

DODSONIA

Ackerman

Selbyana **5**(2): 118 (1979).

ETYMOLOGY: Honoring Calaway Homer Dodson (1928-), an American botanist, author of numerous orchid articles, books, and a former director of the Marie Selby Botanical Gardens in Sarasota, Florida.

TYPE SPECIES: *Dodsonia saccata* (Garay) Ackerman
(*Stenia saccata* Garay)

Now recognized as belonging to the genus *Stenia*, *Dodsonia* was previously considered to include two terrestrials or epiphytes found in wet, mid elevation, montane forests from Costa Rica to Peru. These small plants have several, fan-like growths of lightly veined leaves, and the short, lower leaves are almost bract-like. The solitary-flowered inflorescence has a white to pale green-yellow flower with its petals attached to nearly the full length of the column foot. The deeply sac-like, trilobed lip (sprinkled with red spots) has side lobes longer than the short, triangular midlobe that has its front margin adorned with two sickle-shaped, minutely papillose callosities. The flowers have an erect, stout column.

DOLABRIFOLIA

(Pfitzer) Szlachetko & Romowicz

Richardiana **7**(2): 54 (2007).

ETYMOLOGY: Latin for axe or pick-shaped and leaf. Refers to the shape of the leaves.

TYPE SPECIES: *Dolabrifolia disticha*
(Lindley) Szlachetko & Romowicz
(*Angraecum disticha* Lindley)

Recognized as belonging to the genus *Angraecum*, *Dolabrifolia* was proposed to include five epiphytes or terrestrials distributed in humid, low to mid elevation, forests from the Ivory Coast to Cameroon, and Zaire to Angola and Uganda. These plants have curved to sprawling, leafy stems each with distichous, overlapping, flattened, fleshy leaves. The short, solitary-flowered inflorescence has a

Currently Accepted Validly Published Invalidly Published Published Pre-1753 Superfluous Usage Orthographic Variant Fossil

small, long-lived, fragrant, white flower with oblong sepals and slightly shorter petals. The obscurely trilobed lip has rounded side lobes, a triangular midlobe and a small spur. The flowers have a very short column.

DOLICHANGIS

Thouars
Hist. Orchid. Table 2, sub 3o, *tt.* 66-67 (1822).

Name published without a description. Today this name is most often referred to *Angraecum*.

DOLICHOCENTRUM

(Schlechter) Brieger
Orchideen (Schlechter), ed. 3 **1**(11-12): 659 (1981).
ETYMOLOGY: Latin for long and spur. Descriptive of the long spur on the sepals.
TYPE SPECIES: *Dolichocentrum furcatum*
(Reinwardt ex Lindley) Brieger
(*Dendrobium furcatum* Reinwardt ex Lindley)

Now recognized as belonging to the genus *Dendrobium* as a section, *Dolichocentrum* was previously considered to include two epiphytes found in mid elevation, montane rain forests of eastern Indonesia (northeastern Sulawesi) with year-round rainfall. Thes plants have occasionally branching, thin stems, each with narrow, almost grass-like leaves arranged in two ranks for most of their length. The short, few-flowered inflorescence, borne laterally or near the tip of the stem, has large, white to pale pink flowers. The clawed, trilobed lip has inrolled margins and a long spur formed by the fused bases of the lateral sepals.

DOMINGOA

Schlechter
Symb. Antill. **7**: 496 (1913).

Epidendroideæ ◊ Epidendreæ ● Laeliinæ

ETYMOLOGY: For Santo Domingo, a former Spanish colony established on the West Indies island of Hispaniola, now known as the Dominican Republic.
LECTOTYPE: *Domingoa haematochila*
(Reichenbach f.) Carabia
(*Epidendrum haematochilum* Reichenbach f.)

Two small, uncommon but attractive epiphytes or lithophytes are found in low to mid elevation, hill and montane forests of Cuba, Puerto Rico and Hispaniola. These plants have clustered, elongate pseudobulbs, subtended by papery sheaths, each with a solitary, narrow, flattened, stiff, papery leaf. The erect, long, solitary to few-flowered inflorescence produces blooms borne successively on the same stem for two to three years. The disproportionately large, faintly fragrant, pale green-yellow to brown

flowers are almost translucent and have purple lines. The long narrow sepals have sharply pointed tips. The dark purple-brown, entire lip is shallowly to deeply notched at the tip and has two large calli on the disc. The flowers have a long, slightly curved column.

DONACOPSIS

Gagnepain
Bull. Mus. Natl. Hist. Nat., sér. 2 **4**(5): 593 (1932).
ETYMOLOGY: Greek for reed and resemblance. Referring to the plants' reed-like habit.
TYPE SPECIES: *Donacopsis laotica* Gagnepain

Now recognized as belonging to the genus *Eulophia*, *Donacopsis* was previously considered to include one terrestrial originally collected on one occasion on low elevation, deciduous forests or savannas of Laos. But now also found in Thailand, Cambodia and Vietnam. This erect plant has several, narrow, grass-like leaves and a wiry, few-flowered inflorescence subtended by several, leaf-like bracts. The pink-brown flower has long, narrow, brown-green sepals and large, ear-like, pink-brown petals. The white to pale pink, obscurely trilobed lip has small, oblong side lobes, and the broad, magenta striped midlobe has a notched, wavy margin, and a small spur. The above type name is now considered a synonym of *Eulophia pauciflora* Guillaumin.

DONDODIA

Luer
Monogr. Syst. Bot. Missouri Bot. Gard. **105**: 85, *f.* 42 (2006).
ETYMOLOGY: Named for Donald Dungan Dod (1912-), an American-born Dominican Episcopalian clergyman and plant collector. The Donald Dod National Park (Sierra del Bahoruco), ecological reserve along the Haiti border was named for him.
TYPE SPECIES: *Dondodia erosa* (Garay) Luer
(*Cryptophoranthus erosa* Garay)

Recognized as belonging to the genus *Pleurothallis*, *Dondodia* was proposed to include one epiphyte found in Hispaniola. This small, tufted plant has stout, erect stems, subtended by thin, tubular sheaths, each with a thick, leathery leaf that is minutely notched as if gnawed. The erect, solitary-flowered inflorescence has a large, purple flower that does not open widely. The deeply concave lateral sepals form a synsepal and the ovate dorsal sepal is also concave. The tiny, smooth-textured petals are held within the flower as well as the thick, broadly ovate, entire lip that has a rounded tip; there is a pair of low, warty calli near the middle. The lip is hinged by a narrow, slender claw to the tip of the column. The flowers have a small, slightly arched, winged column.

DORITES

An orthographic variant introduced in *Orchids Nepal Himalaya*, 500 (1984). The correct spelling is *Doritis*.

DORITIS

Lindley
Gen. Sp. Orchid. Pl. 178 (1833).
ETYMOLOGY: Greek for a spear. Referring to the triangular or arrowhead shaped lip.

Greek Mythology. Or perhaps for *Doritis*, one of the many names used for the Greek goddess *Aphrodite*.
TYPE SPECIES: *Doritis pulcherrima* Lindley

Now recognized as belonging to the genus *Phalaenopsis*, *Doritis* was previously considered to include two lithophytes found in low elevation, evergreen forests, savannas and along river banks ranging from southern China (Hainan), northeastern India, Myanmar, Thailand, Laos, Vietnam to Indonesia (Sumatra). These extremely variable, small to medium-sized plants have short, leafy stems, each with flat, distichous, leathery leaves arranged in two rows. The erect, often three-foot (1 m) long, numerous-flowered inflorescence produces showy flowers opening in succession over a long period, in varying shades of pale rosy-purple and the lateral sepals are united at the base to the column foot forming a spur-like projection. The clawed, trilobed lip is abruptly bent in the middle, has narrow, erect side lobes on either side of the claw, and the oblong midlobe has a short, sharp point with the basal disc having a callus between the narrow lobes on the claw. The flowers have a long, flattened, more or less winged column.

DORSINIA

An orthographic variant introduced in *Viti*, 443 (1862). The correct spelling is *Dossinia*.

DORYCHEILE

Reichenbach
Deut. Bot. Herb.-Buch 56 (1841).
ETYMOLOGY: Greek for a spear or shaft and lip. Refers to the spear shape of the lip.
LECTOTYPE: *Dorycheile rubra* (Linnaeus) Fuss
(*Serapias rubra* Linnaeus)

Now recognized as belonging to the genus *Cephalanthera*, *Dorycheile* was previously considered to include one terrestrial found in scrub and shady woodlands of Europe (rare in Britain), northern Africa (Morocco to

Tunisia), Greece, Turkey and Georgia to Iran. This erect plant has slender to stout, unbranched stems, each with several, basal sheaths and narrow leaves. The mostly white, rosy or green flowers open widely and are subtended by green bracts. The dorsal sepal and petals converge, forming a hood over the long column, and has widespreading lateral sepals. The long, yellow, heart-shaped, trilobed lip, divided into two portions, has brown, longitudinal stripes and has either a reduced spur or is spurless.

DORYCHILUS

An orthographic variant cited in *Lex. Gen. Phan.*, 185 (1904). The correct spelling is *Dorycheile*.

DORYPHORA

Reichenbach

Deut. Bot. Herb.-Buch 56 (1841).

Not *Doryphora* Endlicher (1938) Monimiaceæ.

ETYMOLOGY: Greek for a spear or shaft.

TYPE SPECIES: *None designated*

Name published without a description. Today this name is most often referred to as a section of *Cephalanthera*.

DOSSINIA

C. Morren

Ann. Soc. Roy. Agric. Gand **4**: 171 (1848).

Orchidoideæ ⚘ Cranichideæ • Goodyerinæ

ETYMOLOGY: Honoring Pierre-Étienne Dossin (1777-1852), a Belgian botanist and pharmacist from Liége, who published a small catalogue of plants in 1804.

TYPE SPECIES: *Dossinia marmorata* C. Morren

One sympodial terrestrial or occasional lithophyte is found in low elevation, limestone hill forests of southern Malaysia (Sarawak) region of northern Borneo. This small plant is grown mostly for its showy rosette of foliage. The leaves' upper surface is dark velvety green, lined with pale ochre, green-yellow or pink, and the pale yellow underside is suffused rose. The erect, numerous-flowered inflorescence has rather small, pale brown flowers tipped in white or pink-white, and whose outside surface is covered in fine hairs. The trilobed lip has a bilobed, sac-like hypochile, a short tapered mesochile, and a bilobed, somewhat squarish epichile. The flowers have a small, erect, stout, slightly twisted, weakly curved column. This species vegetatively resembles those of *Macodes*.

DOSSYNIA

An orthographic variant introduced in *Prakt. Stud. Orchid.*, 33 (1854). The correct spelling is *Dossinia*.

DOTHILIS

Rafinesque

Fl. Tellur. **2**: 60 (1836)[1837].

ETYMOLOGY: Greek for a small abscess or boil and crowd or throng. Alluding to the lip that is covered with small, soft protuberances.

TYPE SPECIES: *Dothilis grandiflora* (Hooker) Rafinesque (*Neottia grandiflora* Hooker)

Now recognized as belonging to the genus *Sarcoglottis*, *Dothilis* was previously considered to include one terrestrial found in low to mid elevation, seasonally dry, hill and montane forests of Venezuela, Brazil and Ecuador. This large, erect plant has unbranched stems, each with a few narrow leaves in a basal rosette that are present at flowering. The basally clasping leaves gradually taper to tubular, floral bracts. The erect, numerous to few-flowered inflorescence has small flowers with green sepals, and white to yellow-green petals. The long, narrow lateral sepals are united for almost their whole length. The white to yellow-green, entire lip is covered with darker green veins and lays flat against the curved tips of the lateral sepals.

DOTHILOPHIS

Rafinesque

Fl. Tellur. **4**: 39 (1836)[1837].

ETYMOLOGY: Greek for a small abscess or boil and crest. An allusion to the warty crests on the lip.

TYPE SPECIES: *Dothilophis purpurea* Rafinesque nom. illeg. *Barkeria skinneri* (Bateman ex Lindley) Paxton (*Epidendrum skinneri* Bateman ex Lindley)

Now recognized as belonging to the genus *Barkeria*, *Dothilophis* was previously considered to include one slender epiphyte or lithophyte found in low to mid elevation, hill and montane oak-pine forests ranging from southern Mexico (Chiapas) to northwestern Guatemala. This plant has clustered, spindle-shaped pseudobulbs, each with several, distichous, elliptical to narrow, pale green leaves. The numerous to few-flowered inflorescence has long-lived, pale to vivid pink, lilac, deep purple or even white flowers. The white to pink, tongue-shaped, entire lip, united to the column for a short distance, has three, long, raised, bright yellow keels. The flowers have a tiny, slightly club-shaped column.

DOTTULIS

An orthographic variant introduced in *Beih. Bot. Centralbl.*, **37**(2): 416 (1920). The correct spelling is *Dothilis*.

DOXOSMA

Rafinesque

Fl. Tellur. **4**: 9 (1836)[1837].

ETYMOLOGY: Greek for glory or honor and fragrance. An allusion to the strong fragrance of the type species.

TYPE SPECIES: *Doxosma gracilis* (Lindley) Rafinesque (*Epidendrum gracile* Lindley)

Now recognized as belonging to the genus *Encyclia*, *Doxosma* was previously considered to include one epiphyte or terrestrial found in low elevation, hill forests and woodlands of the Bahamas to the Turks and Caicos Islands. This plant, often forming large clumps, has ovoid, dull brown pseudobulbs, each with narrow, leathery leaves borne at the tip. The erect, numerous-flowered inflorescence has fragrant, green-yellow flowers suffused with brown and widespreading, similar sepals and petals. The white to yellow, trilobed lip has purple veins radiating from the base, large, erect, green side lobes, and the broad midlobe has a notched, wavy margin. The flowers have a long, club-shaped column.

DRACOMONTICOLA

H.P. Linder & Kurzweil

Willdenowia **25**(1): 229 (1995).

ETYMOLOGY: Greek for dragon, mountain and dweller. Referring to the Drakensberg area in South Africa where the type species grows.

TYPE SPECIES: *Dracomonticola virginea* (Bolus) H.P. Linder & Kurzweil (*Platanthera virginea* Bolus)

Now recognized as belonging to the genus *Neobolusia*, *Dracomonticola* was proposed to include one terrestrial found in upper elevation, grassy to south-facing rocky ledges and crevices of western South Africa and Lesotho. This erect plant has a solitary, basal leaf and a small, single leaf that clasps the slender, unbranched stem. The head-like, few-flowered, slightly drooping inflorescence has white flowers consisting of concave petals that are one-third the length of the sepals and fold over the short column. The fiddle-shaped, pale pink, obscurely trilobed lip has a flat, triangular epichile with minute side lobes, and a shallow, concave hypochile with a basal callus. The above type name is now considered a synonym of *Neobolusia virginea* (Bolus) Schlechter.

| Currently Accepted | Validly Published | Invalidly Published | Published Pre-1753 | Superfluous Usage | Orthographic Variant | Fossil |

Orchid Genera • **136**

DRACONANTHES

(Luer) Luer

Monogr. Syst. Bot. Missouri Bot. Gard.
61(1): 2 (1996).

Epidendroideæ ⚘ Epidendreæ • Pleurothallidinæ

ETYMOLOGY: Greek for dragon-like and flower. For the flowers' similarity to the mythological monster.

TYPE SPECIES: *Draconanthes aberrans*
(Schlechter) Luer
(*Lepanthes aberrans* Schlechter)

Two sympodial epiphytes, lithophytes or terrestrials are found in upper elevation, montane cloud forests of Venezuela and Colombia to Bolivia. These small plants have erect stems, each with a solitary, leathery, green leaf that is purple on the underside. The initially erect, few-flowered inflorescence later curves downward as the flowers appear in succession. The small flowers are covered with short, brisk hairs on the outer surfaces. The dull green, rigid dorsal sepal has a purple center; the dull purple lateral sepals have green veins and are united for a short length at the base. The rigid, quite narrow to oblong, unlobed petals are yellow-orange. The orange, trilobed lip, united to base of the column, has a red stripe, the thick side lobes surround the long, wingless, footless column and the short midlobe has a curved, roundish tip. The strange side lobes hang downward and are strongly notched.

DRACONTIA

(Schlechter) Luer

Monogr. Syst. Bot. Missouri Bot. Gard.
95: 257 (2004).

ETYMOLOGY: Latin for dragon-like. Referring to the fierce looking shape of the flowers.

TYPE SPECIES: *Dracontia tuerckheimii*
(Schlechter) Luer
(*Pleurothallis tuerckheimii* Schlechter)
This type name is now considered a synonym of
Stelis megachlamys (Schlechter) Pupulin;
basionym replaced with
Pleurothallis megachlamys Schlechter

Recognized as belonging to the genus *Stelis*, *Dracontia* was proposed to include seventeen epiphytes found in mid to upper elevation, mixed oak-pine to cloud forests from central Mexico to Panama and Cuba to Jamaica. These small, erect plants have secondary stems, each with strap-like leaves that are bright green on the upper surface and blue-green below. The several, suberect, few-flowered inflorescences have drooping, purple and white or creamy flowers opening simultaneously. The lateral sepals are united almost to their tips, and the tiny, hood-shaped, yellow petals have a few red stripes. The narrow, recurved, entire lip has two calli at the base. The flowers have a short, footless column.

DRACULA

Luer

Selbyana **2**(2-3): 190 (1978).

Epidendroideæ ⚘ Epidendreæ • Pleurothallidinæ

ETYMOLOGY: Latin for dragon. Refers to the bizarre sinister and fancied shape of the flowers. Romanian Mythology. A reference to a fictional vampire, Vlad Tepes, known as the Count Dracula (1431-1476), a prince of Wallachia. He is known for his gruesome and bloody atrocities committed during his many regnal periods.

TYPE SPECIES: *Dracula chimaera*
(Reichenbach f.) Luer
(*Masdevallia chimaera* Reichenbach f.)

One hundred eleven tufted, sympodial commonly epiphytes or terrestrials are found mostly in shady, low to upper elevation, woodlands and montane cloud forests of southeastern Mexico (Chiapas) to northern Peru with the center of diversity found in Ecuador. These plants each with long, textured leaves that rib and taper solitary to few-bizarre, flat to large lateral or more of their on the inner in a dense mass Colombia and have short stems, somewhat thinly have a prominent mid-toward the base. The flowered inflorescence has bell-shaped flowers. The sepals are joined for a third length, are are shortly hairy surface. Each sepal is covered of hairs, warts or nodules and has long tails. The small to minute, warty petals flank the small, short column. The small, two part lip, hinged to the base of the column foot, has a fleshy, oblong, clawed hypochile, and a roundish, shell-shaped, sac-like or flat epichile adorned with radiating grooves or is veined. The flower provides an allusion of a small face appearing outward toward the viewer.

DRAKAEA

Lindley

Sketch Veg. Swan R. Appendix: 55 (1840).

Orchidoideæ ⚘ Diurideæ • Thelymitrinæ

ETYMOLOGY: Honoring Sarah "Ducky" Anne Drake (1803-1857), a British botanical illustrator who worked exclusively for John Lindley. Her beautiful and highly prized illustrations appeared in *Edwards's Botanical Register, Curtis' Botanical Magazine* and *Sertum Orchidaceum*.

TYPE SPECIES: *Drakaea elastica* Lindley

Nine sympodial terrestrials are confined in low elevation, scrub of southwestern Australia. The flowers have a highly complex structure in order to attract the males of certain wasp species. These erect plants have unbranched stems, each with a solitary, thick, spongy, ground-hugging, heart-shaped leaf that appears in late autumn and winter. The plants

often sparsely colonize disturbed tracts and embankments. The wiry, solitary-flowered inflorescence bears a green-yellow and purple flower with a distinct fetid fragrance. The mobile, entire lip, hinged to the tip of the column foot by a short, narrow claw has prominent, black, glistening, wart-like glands and short, branched hairs. The flowers have a slender, winged column that is abruptly incurved and folded in the middle to resemble the body of a wasp.

DRAKEA

An orthographic variant introduced in *Enchir. Bot. (Endlicher)*, 114 (1841). The correct spelling is *Drakaea*.

DRAKONORCHIS

**(Hopper & A.P. Brown)
D.L. Jones & M.A. Clements**

Orchadian **13**(9): 403 (2001).

ETYMOLOGY: Greek for a dragon and orchid. Referring to the common name of the flower which can resemble a dragon.

TYPE SPECIES: *Drakonorchis barbarossa*
(Reichenbach f.) D.L. Jones & M.A. Clements
(*Caladenia barbarossa* Reichenbach f.)

Recognized as belonging to the genus *Caladenia*, *Drakonorchis* was proposed to include four terrestrials found in low elevation, sandy, coastal forests of western Australia. These erect, usually hairy plants have unbranched stems, each with a solitary, narrow leaf close to the ground. The wiry, solitary-flowered inflorescence has a pale green to green-yellow flower with red markings or stripes. The narrow dorsal sepal is incurved over the strongly curved column and has spreading or bent downward petals. The bizarre, tightly hinged, hairy, trilobed lip, remarkably insect-like in form, has two, erect side lobes with fleshy, horn-like appendages, and the midlobe or lamina is incurved.

DRESSLERELLA

Luer

Selbyana **3**(1-2): 1 (1976).

Epidendroideæ ⚘ Epidendreæ • Pleurothallidinæ

ETYMOLOGY: Honoring Robert Louis Dressler (1927-). And Latin for diminutive.

TYPE SPECIES: *Dresslerella pertusa* (Dressler) Luer
(*Pleurothallis pertusa* Dressler)

Nine sympodial epiphytes are found in Guatemala and Nicaragua to Peru in moist, low to upper elevation, hill and montane cloud forests. These miniature, erect to hanging plants have clustered stems, each with thick, heavily veined, leathery leaves that often have varying degrees of hairiness and sometimes even lie along the ground in a rosette. The several, solitary-flowered inflorescences, borne from the leaf axils, have fleshy, translucent, red, dark purple to green-yellow, tubular flowers (also quite hairy) with bright red veins and spots. The hairy dorsal sepal is free or united in the basal part to the often inflated lateral sepals that are converged almost to their tips. The arrowhead or fiddle-shaped, trilobed lip has a minute callus. The flowers have a slender, winged column.

DRESSLERIA

Dodson

Selbyana **1**(2): 131 (1975).

Epidendroideæ ⚘ Cymbidieæ • Catasetinæ

ETYMOLOGY: Named in honor of Robert Louis Dressler (1927-), an American systematic botanist, taxonomist, orchidologist and author of several books and articles on orchids.

TYPE SPECIES: *Dressleria dilecta*
(Reichenbach f.) Dodson
(*Catasetum dilectum* Reichenbach f.)

Ten sympodial epiphytes or lithophytes are found in low to mid elevation, hill and montane forests from Nicaragua, Costa Rica and Panama to Peru commonly perch on dead tree limbs. These plants have spindle-shaped, fleshy, clustered pseudobulbs with numerous nodes, subtended by distichous, leaf-bearing sheaths, each with thickly textured, heavily veined leaves. The numerous to few-flowered inflorescence, borne from the base of the pseudobulb, has lustrous cream or green, waxy extremely fragrant flowers that are variable in shape and bisexual (pollinarium and stigma are always functional). The fleshy, clawed, trilobed lip is united to the base and sides of the short to stout, or long to slender column. The sensitive anther strikingly releases the pollinia when the anther cap is lifted. The stigma will not accept fertilization until the pollen has been removed. After the pollen has been removed, the column straightens and raises back to expose the stigma now ready for pollination.

DRESSLERIELLA

Brieger

Orchideen (Schlechter), ed. 3 **9**(33-36): 555 (1977).

ETYMOLOGY: Honoring Robert Louis Dressler (1927-). And Latin for diminutive.

TYPE SPECIES: *None designated*

Not validly published, this name is referred to *Jacquiniella*. *Dressleriella* was previously considered to include six epiphytes found from Mexico to Peru, Brazil, Cuba to Trinidad, the Guianas and Venezuela.

DRIMODA

An orthographic variant introduced in *Prakt. Stud. Orchid.*, 45 (1854). The correct spelling is *Drymoda*.

DRYADELLA

Luer

Selbyana **2**(2-3): 207 (1978).

Epidendroideæ ⚘ Epidendreæ • Pleurothallidinæ

ETYMOLOGY: Greek Mythology. Named for various divinity dryads or nymphs that are found in the trees and forests. And Latin for diminutive.

TYPE SPECIES: *Dryadella elata* (Luer) Luer
(*Masdevallia elata* Luer)

Forty-two dwarf, sympodial epiphytes found in low to upper elevation, hill to montane cloud forests and scrub ranging from southern Mexico to Bolivia, Venezuela, southeastern Brazil (Bahia to Rio Grande do Sul) and Paraguay. These clump-forming plants have short, erect stems, subtended by tubular sheaths, each with a solitary, small, densely tufted, narrow, dark green, thick leaf. The short, solitary-flowered inflorescence has a small to minute flower varying from ochre to golden yellow, often densely spotted maroon or bright purple, and many of the species have a foul fragrance. The united lateral sepals are slightly hood-shaped, tailed at the tips, and have a transverse callus across their base. The small, short, broad to narrow petals are multi-angled. The flower is always buried deeply within the foliage. They have a transverse callus across the bases of the lateral sepals. The small, oblong to obtuse, entire lip has a slender claw, and a shovel-shaped lamina. The flowers have a slender, winged column.

DRYADORCHIS

Schlechter

Repert. Spec. Nov. Regni Veg. Beih. **1**(13): 976 (1913).

Epidendroideæ ⚘ Vandeæ • Aeridinæ

ETYMOLOGY: Greek for woodland nymph and orchid. An allusion to its habitat in upper, misty forests.

LECTOTYPE: *Dryadorchis barbellata* Schlechter

Four extremely isolated, monopodial epiphytes are found in upper elevation, montane cloud forests of New Guinea (four species are found in Papua and one species is only found in western New Guinea). These small plants have short, unbranched stems, each with dull green leaves arranged in a fan shape (often purple on the undersides). The plants

have a rather insignificant appearance and resemble *Sarcochilus* in vegetative habit. The few-flowered, purple inflorescence has faintly fragrant, short-lived, pale yellow to white flowers heavily banded or spotted red-brown to violet-pink on the inside, and are white on the outside surfaces. The short column foot is attached to the mobile, trilobed lip with a short claw. The lip has small, erect, spotted or banded side lobes, and the white, sac-like midlobe has an orange-yellow, basal callus. The flowers have a long, stout, slightly incurved column.

DRYMOANTHUS

Nicholls

Vict. Naturalist **59**: 173 (1942).

Epidendroideæ ⚘ Vandeæ • Aeridinæ

ETYMOLOGY: Greek for forest and flower. In reference to the plants usual habitat of forested lands.

TYPE SPECIES: *Drymoanthus minutus* Nicholls

Four uncommon, diminutive, monopodial epiphytes are found in mid elevation, forests and scrub of northeastern Australia, New Caledonia and New Zealand. These small plants have short stems, each with a few flattened, oblong, curved or twisted leaves arranged in one plane and has numerous, widespreading, gray roots. The short, few-flowered inflorescence has tiny, dull green to green-white, fragrant flowers opening in succession. The immobile, white, green to yellow, cup-shaped, entire lip has no prominent calli, and has a smooth margin. The flowers have a short, erect, slightly curved, wingless column with two, almost horizontal teeth in front.

DRYMODA

Lindley

Sert. Orchid. t. 8c (1838).

Epidendroideæ ⚘ Dendrobiinæ • Currently unplaced

ETYMOLOGY: Greek for forest or thicket. In reference to their epiphytic habit.

TYPE SPECIES: *Drymoda picta* Lindley

Three remarkable, sympodial epiphytes are found in low elevation, premontane forests of Myanmar, Thailand and Laos. These small plants have closely spaced, disk-like, wrinkled, purple pseudobulbs, each with one to two, ovate, short-lived leaves at the tip that wither and are absent during flowering. The long, thin, solitary-flowered inflorescence has a yellow or yellow-green flower heavily streaked with maroon and is quite large for the size of the tiny plant. The minute, thread-like petals are spotted or blotched with rosy-purple. The large

Currently Accepted   Validly Published   Invalidly Published   Published Pre-1753   Superfluous Usage   Orthographic Variant   Fossil

Orchid Genera • 138

lateral sepals are either widespreading or strongly curved inward and are joined to the tip of the column foot. The small, dark rosy-purple, highly mobile, entire lip is attached at the very long column foot. The flowers have a short, winged column.

DRYOPAEIA

An orthographic variant introduced in *Orchid. Scelet.*, 12 (1826). The correct spelling is *Dryopria*.

DRYOPEIA

An orthographic variant introduced in *Hist. Orchid.*, *tt. 1-3* (1822). The correct spelling is *Dryopria*.

DRYOPEJA

An orthographic variant cited in *Lex. Gen. Phan.*, 187 (1904). The correct spelling is *Dryopeia*.

DRYOPERA

An orthographic variant cited in *Handb. Orchid.-Namen*, 288 (2005). The correct spelling is *Dryopria*.

DRYOPOEIA

An orthographic variant introduced in *Nat. Syst. Pl.*, 301 (1832). The correct spelling is *Dryopeia*.

DRYOPRIA

Thouars
Hist. Orchid.　　Table 1, sub 1a, *t. 1* (1822).
ETYMOLOGY: Greek for a woodland nymph (Dryas). The origin and meaning is unknown.
TYPE SPECIES: *None designated*

Not validly published, this name is referred to *Disperis*. *Dryopria* was considered to include three terrestrials found in Madagascar, the Comoros, Réunion and Mascarene Islands.

DRYORCHIS

An orthographic variant introduced in *Hist. Orchid.*, Table 1, sub 1a, *t. 1* (1822). The correct spelling is *Dryorkis*.

DRYORKIS

Thouars
Nouv. Bull. Sci. Soc. Philom. Paris **1**(19): 316 (1809).
ETYMOLOGY: Greek Mythology. *Dryas* was the son of King Lycurgus of Thrace. He was killed when his father went insane and mistook him for a patch of ivy, a plant holy to the god Dionysus, and Greek for orchid. The meaning as used here is unclear, unless referring to the forest habitat.
LECTOTYPE: *Dryorkis tripetaloides* Thouars

Now most often recognized as belonging to the genus *Disperis*, *Dryorkis* was previously considered to include three terrestrials found in Madagascar, the Comoros Islands, Réunion, and the Mascarene Islands. These erect plants have just a few leaves above the center of the stem. The few-flowered inflorescence has flowers that are netted with dark veins.

DUBOISIA

H. Karsten
Allg. Gartenzeitung **15**(50): 394 (1847).
Not *Duboisia* R. Brown (1810) Solanaceæ.
ETYMOLOGY: Dedicated to Emil Heinrich du Bois-Reymond (1818-1896), a French-born German physiologist whose studies of muscle reflexes demonstrated that electrical changes accompany muscle action, which contributed to early findings of electrophysiology.
TYPE SPECIES: *Duboisia reymondii* H. Karsten

Not validly published because of a prior use of the name, this homonym was replaced by *Dubois-Reymondia*.

DUBOIS-RAYMONDIA

An orthographic variant cited in *Cat. Pl. (Warszewicz)*, 58 (1864). The correct spelling is *Dubois-Reymondia*.

DUBOIS-REYMONDIA

H. Karsten
Bot. Zeitung (Berlin) **6**: 397 (1848).
ETYMOLOGY: *Duboisia*, a genus of orchids, with du Bois's second name (Reymond) added.
TYPE SPECIES: *Dubois-Reymondia palpigera* (H. Karsten) H. Karsten (*Duboisia reymondii* H. Karsten)
This type name is now considered a synonym of *Myoxanthus reymondii* (H. Karsten) Luer; basionym replaced with *Duboisia reymondii* H. Karsten

Now most often recognized as belonging to the genus *Myoxanthus*, *Dubois-Reymondia* was previously considered to include seven epiphytes found in mid to upper elevation, montane rain forests of Venezuela and Colombia to Ecuador. These wiry, thin, rigid plants have

long stems, each with pale green leaves borne in papery sheaths that have short, bristly hairs. The one- to three-flowered inflorescence has yellow-brown, insect-like flowers that are also covered on their outer surfaces with short hairs. The lateral sepals are toad-like, the petals are shaped like insect antennae, and the short-clawed, entire lip is tongue-like with a rounded tip. The flowers have a slightly curved column. These species were originally included in *Pleurothallis*.

DUCKEELLA

Porto & Brade
Anais Reunião Sul-Amer. Bot. **3**(1): 32 (1938)[1940].
Vanilloideæ ⚘ Pogoniieæ
ETYMOLOGY: In honor of Walter Adolpho Ducke (1876-1959), a Brazilian botanist, entomologist and Amazonian naturalist, who wrote about and collected the flora and fauna of Brazil especially in the Amazonian region. And Latin for diminutive.
TYPE SPECIES: *Duckeella adolphii* Porto & Brade

Three sympodial terrestrials are found in seasonally wet, low to mid elevation, Amazon River basin and nutrient-poor savannas from northwestern Brazil to south-eastern Venezuela (Bolivar and Amazonas) and Colombia (Vichada). The plants will even grow on floating river vegetation. These rather tall, erect plants have numerous, long, narrow, leathery leaves borne at the base of the flowering stem. The terminal, branched or simple, few-flowered inflorescence has showy, orange to bright yellow flowers, each subtended by small, leafy bracts. The ovate petals are usually broader than the sepals. The yellow, trilobed (at base) lip has a flattened tip, and is generally indistinct from the petals except for several, slightly raised, longitudinal crests. The flowers have a slender, footless column.

DUNGSIA

Chiron & V.P. Castro
Richardiana **2**(1) 11 (2002).
ETYMOLOGY: Honoring Gunther Friedrich (Fritz) Dungs (1915-1977), a German-born Brazilian orchid collector, botanist and co-author of *Orchidaceae Brasilienses*.
TYPE SPECIES: *Dungsia harpophylla* (Reichenbach f.) Chiron & V.P. Castro (*Laelia harpophylla* Reichenbach f.)

Recognized as belonging to the genus *Hoffmannseggella*, *Dungsia* was proposed to include three epiphytes found in shady, low elevation, scrub and forests only in south-eastern Brazil (Minas Gerais and Espírito Santo). These robust plants have clustered, slender stems, each with a solitary, broad, terete, leathery, dark green leaf often suffused maroon. The short, few-flowered inflorescence, subtended at the base by a short sheath, has large, bright orange-red flowers with narrow, sepals and petals. The long, deeply trilobed lip has side lobes that are erect over the arched, small column often forming a long tube-like structure, and the strongly curled, small midlobe is cream-colored with orange veins.

NOTE: Some authors consider the species of *Dungsia* as being a part of *Sophronitis*.

DUNSTERVILLEA

Garay

Venez. Orchid. Ill. **5**: 70 (1972).

Epidendroideæ ⚘ Cymbidieæ • Oncidiinæ

ETYMOLOGY: Honoring Galfrid Charles Kenneth Dunsterville (1905-1988), a British-born Venezuelan petroleum engineer, botanist and author, who along with his wife Ellinor "Nora" Freeman (1904-2004) collected, described and illustrated the orchids and flora of Venezuela.

TYPE SPECIES: *Dunstervillea mirabilis* Garay

One psygmoid epiphyte is found in wet, low to mid elevation, hill to montane forests of eastern Venezuela (Bolivar) to Ecuador (Pastaza) on slender tree limbs. This minute plant has its succulent-like leaves arranged more or less in one plane. The short, erect, solitary-flowered inflorescence, borne from the leaf sheaths, has a minute, starry-shaped, white or yellow-green flower that is almost larger than the rest of the plant. The short sepals and petals are similar to each other. The base of the white, entire or cup-shaped lip is rigidly attached to the short, erect column, and the triangular, internally hairy spur is produced between the column foot and the lip.

DURABACULUM

M.A. Clements & D.L. Jones

Orchadian **13**(11): 487 (2002).

ETYMOLOGY: Latin for hard staff. Referring to the long lasting, stiff stems with their two rank arrangement of leaves.

TYPE SPECIES: *Durabaculum undulatum*
(R. Brown) M.A. Clements & D.L. Jones
(*Dendrobium undulatum* R. Brown)

Recognized as belonging to the genus *Dendrobium*, *Durabaculum* was proposed to include fifty-four epiphytes found in humid, low elevation, coastal sand dunes, mangroves and cliff faces from Indonesia, northeastern Australia, New Guinea and the southwestern Pacific Archipelago. These plants have numerous to a few, cylindrical stems that are leafy in the upper two thirds, each with several, distichous, ovate to elliptical, leathery leaves. The two or more, numerous-flowered inflorescences, borne from the apical nodes, have wide opening, long-lasting, fragrant, pale yellow, white or green flowers suffused brown, that often become darker with age. The long sepals and petals are strongly twisted. The trilobed lip has three or more calli along the midlobe and a wavy margin. The above type name is now considered a synonym of *Dendrobium discolor* Lindley.

DYAKIA

Christenson

Orchid Digest **50**(2): 63 (1986).

Epidendroideæ ⚘ Vandeæ • Aeridinæ

ETYMOLOGY: Named in honor of the Dyak aborigines of Borneo (an island in the Indonesian Archipelago in the western Pacific Ocean).

TYPE SPECIES: *Dyakia hendersoniana*
(Reichenbach f.) Christenson
(*Saccolabium hendersonianum* Reichenbach f.)

One miniature, monopodial epiphyte is found in low elevation, seasonally swampy forests and along river banks of eastern Indonesia (Borneo). This plant has short to long, leafy stems, each with several, pale green, broad, flat, distichous, obtusely bilobed leaves. The erect, densely packed, cylindrical, numerous-flowered inflorescence is taller than the plant and has showy, bright to vivid rose pink, sweetly fragrant, fleshy flowers with a dark purple spot found at the base of each lateral sepal. The tiny, sac-like, white, obscurely trilobed lip has minute side lobes, a prominent callus on the back wall, and has a compressed hanging, club-like spur. The flowers have a short, erect, wingless column with a stout foot. This species is still sometimes included in *Ascocentrum*.

DYONISIS

An orthographic variant introduced in *Hist. Orchid., t.* 23 (1822). The correct spelling is *Dionysis*.

DYSSORHYNCHIUM

An orthographic variant cited in *Hist. Nat. Veg. (Spach)*, **12**: 180 (1846). The correct spelling is *Dissorhynchium*.

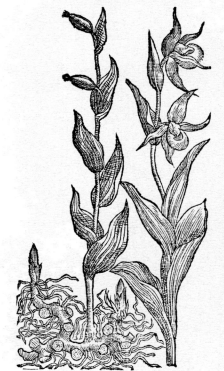

272   Pſeudodamaſonium.

STIRP. PANNON. HIST.   273

in longum & obliquum ſumma tellure ſeſe ſpargẽs, multiſque fibris donata, atque ſuperiorum annorum caulis veſtigia impreſſa habens, vt in pſeudocorallio fere conſpicimus, extremitatibus ſemper in nouum germen extuberantibus: amariuſcula eſt ſi deguſtetur.

Inuenitur nonnullis ſiluoſis locis Leyteberg ſupra Bruterſtorf: reperi et apud Cloſterneuburg prato quodam ſub fruticibus coryli, & in ſiluis Entzeſtorf vicinis: ſed omnium abundãtiſſimè in Pannonica quadã ſilua, magno miliari ab arce munitiſſima Nemethwywar Ill. Dn. Balthaſaris de Batthyan. Jn Hercinia item ſilua, plurimiſque aliis Germaniæ locis copioſe naſci ab amicis intellexi.   Floret Maio.

Sunt qui dicant flore albò inueniri, quod ſanè nondum mihi videre contigit, quemadmodum nec id quod in œnipontinis montibus obſeruauit doctiſſimus & diligentiſſimus noſter Matthias de Lobel, vtriculo purpureo.

Similis ſanè cum Pannonico coloris florem ferre mihi retulerunt quod in Hercinia ſilua naſcitur, & ab incolis Marien ſchuch *appellari. Nec etiam colore differebat, quem è poſtremis Pannoniæ limitibus Daciæ vicinis collectũ ante paucos annos mihi oſtendebat Jll. Dn. de Batthyan, cùm ex ea peregrinatione rediſſet. Vngaris Ezerethgyw fiu, id eſt millebona herba dicitur.*

C. V. Geſnerus in epiſtolis frequentem in Heluetiis inueniri ait, illi verò luteum etiam florem tribuit, & ad Aliſmatis ſpecies refert. Coſmoſandalos Pauſaniæ fortè fuerit, inquit, nam & ſandalij formam refert flos, & punctis ceu literis quibuſdam notatur, etſi Pauſanias Hyacinthum eſſe coniicit, ſed huic cum ſandalio nihil. Quidam vir doctus Lonchitin primam eſſe putat. Vnſer frawen ſchuch *appellant, hoc eſt calceolos Virginis, à forma floris.*   S   Ioſias

Carolus Clusius
Rariorum aliquot Stirpium, per Pannoniam   page 272-273 (1583).

Currently Accepted   Validly Published   Invalidly Published   Published Pre-1753   Superfluous Usage   Orthographic Variant   Fossil

EARINA

Lindley

Edwards's Bot. Reg. **20**: sub 1699 (1834).

Epidendroideæ ⁄ Agrostophyllinæ • Currently unplaced

ETYMOLOGY: Greek for springtime. Referring to the flowering season of the type species.

TYPE SPECIES: *Earina mucronata* Lindley nom. illeg.
Earina autumnalis (G. Forster) Hooker f.
(*Epidendrum autumnale* G. Forster)

Six attractive, sympodial epiphytes (some terrestrials) or lithophytes are found in low to mid elevation, hill forests to coastal cliffs from Samoa to New Zealand and New Caledonia to the Tonga Archipelago. These tufted, erect to hanging plants have thick, unbranched, leafy stems, each with narrow, sharply pointed leaves arranged in alternating rows. The leaves are attached by long, overlapping sheaths that completely enclose the stem. The hanging, numerous-flowered inflorescence has small, heavily to light but rather unpleasant fragrance, usually white to pale yellow flowers in small clusters, which do not open widely. The white to yellow-orange, entire to trilobed lip has an entire or wavy margin and a bright orange-yellow, basal callus. The flowers have an erect, curved column.

EBURNANGIS

Thouars

Hist. Orchid. Table 2, sub 3o, *t.* 65 (1822).

Name published without a description. Today this name is most often referred to *Angraecum*.

EBUROPHYTON

A. Heller

Muhlenbergia **1**(4): 48 (1904).

ETYMOLOGY: Latin for ivory and Greek for plant. From the whitish color of this saprophyte.

TYPE SPECIES: *Eburophyton austiniae*
(A. Gray) A. Heller
(*Chloraea austiniae* A. Gray)

Now recognized as belonging to the genus *Cephalanthera*, *Eburophyton* was previously considered to include one saprophyte found in mid to upper elevation, montane pine forests of the western United States (Washington to California) in deep shade. This erect, leafless plant has unbranched, completely colorless stems subtended at the base with white sheaths that become bracts as they proceed upward. The few-flowered inflorescence has colorless flowers except for a bright yellow spot on the midlobe of the trilobed lip. Even the seed capsule is white. The plant itself has a cool, clammy feel and looks like the white Indian pipe (*Monotropa*) plant.

ECHINELLA

Pridgeon & M.W. Chase

Lindleyana **16**(4): 253 (2001).

Not *Echinella* Acharius (1810) Desmidiaeæ; and not *Echinella* Massee (1895) Fungi.

ETYMOLOGY: Latin for hedgehog and diminutive. Referring to the appearance of the flowers.

TYPE SPECIES: *Echinella aspasicensis*
(Reichenbach f.) Pridgeon & M.W. Chase
(*Pleurothallis aspasicensis* Reichenbach f.)

Not validly published because of a prior use of the name, this homonym was replaced by *Echinosepala*.

ECHINOGLOSSUM

An orthographic variant cited in *Deut. Bot. Herb.-Buch*, 54 (1841). The correct spelling is *Echioglossum*.

ECHINORHYNCHA

Dressler

Lankesteriana **5**(2): 94 (2005).

Epidendroideæ ⁄ Cymbidieæ • Zygopetalinæ

ETYMOLOGY: Greek for sea urchin or hedgehog and beak. Refers to the appendages under the column.

TYPE SPECIES: *Echinorhyncha litensis*
(Dodson) Dressler
(*Chondrorhyncha litensis* Dodson)

Four sympodial epiphytes are found in low to mid elevation, hill to montane forests from Colombia to northern Ecuador (Esmeraldas). These small plants have short stems, subtended by overlapping, distichous, leafy sheaths, each with long, narrow leaves. The wiry, solitary-flowered inflorescence has a yellow-white flower with the erect dorsal sepal curved backward and widespreading lateral sepals. The entire lip, bilobed at the tip, has a raised, toothed, basal callus and has a finely notched margin. The flowers have a small, winged column with two or more, bristly, sea urchin-like appendages on its underside.

ECHINOSEPALA

Pridgeon & M.W. Chase

Lindleyana **17**(2): 100 (2002).

Epidendroideæ ⁄ Epidendreæ • Pleurothallidinæ

ETYMOLOGY: Latin for hedgehog and sepal. Refers to the densely hairy appearance of the sepals in most of the species.

TYPE SPECIES: *Echinosepala aspasicensis*
(Reichenbach f.) Pridgeon & M.W. Chase
(*Pleurothallis aspasicensis* Reichenbach f.)

Eight sympodial epiphytes, rare lithophytes or terrestrials are distributed in moist, low to mid elevation, hill and montane cloud forests to rocky crevices from Jamaica, Belize to Colombia, the Guianas, Venezuela, Bolivia and northern Brazil. These small plants have creeping rhizomes and numerous, stout stems, subtended by loose sheaths, each with a solitary, elliptical to ovate, leathery leaf. The short, solitary-flowered inflorescence is borne from either the rhizome, basal nodes of the stem or the stem tip. The small, fleshy flower has external hairy sepals with maroon nerves on a yellow base; the lateral sepals are united, and the fleshy, yellow petals have maroon nerves. The maroon, trilobed lip has erect, oblong or hooked side lobes; the midlobe has two lateral hooks in the middle and a broad, elevated, horseshoe-shaped, red, thickenings at the base with lateral keels. The flowers have a slender, white, hairy column stippled red.

ECHIOGLOSSA

An orthographic variant introduced in *Cat. Pl. Hort. Bot. Bogor.*, 45 (1844). The correct spelling is *Echioglossum*.

ECHIOGLOSSUM

Blume

Bijdr. Fl. Ned. Ind. **8**: 364, *t.* 28 (1825).

ETYMOLOGY: Greek for viper and tongue. From the blade of the lip that has a tongue-like shape which resembles a snake's tongue.

TYPE SPECIES: *Echioglossum javanicum* Blume

Now recognized as belonging to the genus *Cleisostoma*, *Echioglossum* was previously considered to include twelve epiphytes widespread in low to mid elevation, evergreen forests from northern India (Sikkim to Assam), southern China (Yunnan, Guangxi and Hainan), Myanmar to Vietnam, Thailand and Indonesia (Sumatra to Java). These erect to hanging plants have robust, cylindrical, short or long, stout stems, each with pencil-like or flat leaves arranged on the upper half. The thick leaves are either unlobed or blunt with unequally bilobed tips. The short, simple to branched, numerous-flowered inflorescence has showy, yellow-green, yellow to purple-brown flowers sprinkled with several to numerous, purple spots. The large, pale purple to yellow, trilobed lip is almost saddle-shaped; the erect side lobes have sharp tips, the midlobe has two thin, deeply lobed tails at the tip, and a small spur. The flowers have a short, thick, wingless, footless column.

ECKARDIA

An orthographic variant introduced in *Gen. Pl., Suppl. 2 (Endlicher)*, **2**: 17 (1842). The correct spelling is *Eckartia*.

ECKARDUA

An orthographic variant introduced in *Sander's Orch. Guide*, ed. 4, 194 (1927). The correct spelling is *Eckartia*.

ECKARTIA

Reichenbach

Deut. Bot. Herb.-Buch 53 (1841).

ETYMOLOGY: The meaning for this is unknown.

TYPE SPECIES: *None designated*

A superfluous name proposed as a substitute for *Peristeria*.

ECUADORIA

Dodson & Dressler

Orquideologia **19**(2): 133 (1994).

ETYMOLOGY: In honor of Ecuador (a republic located in northwestern coastal region of South America), where the type species was collected.

TYPE SPECIES: *Ecuadoria intagana* Dodson & Dressler

Now recognized as belonging to the genus *Microthelys*, *Ecuadoria* was proposed to include one terrestrial found in wet, mid elevation, montane cloud forests of northern Ecuador (Imbabura). This small, erect, plant has unbranched, short stems terminating with a few-flowered inflorescence. The rachis is subtended by sheaths and has large, floral bracts which are longer than the flowers. The small, green flowers have a brown, entire lip with a pair of orange blotches on the underside. The narrow dorsal sepal is united with the base of the lateral sepals forming a short tube. The flowers have a pencil-like column that is flattened on the underside and slightly swollen toward the tip. The above type name is now considered a synonym of *Microthelys intagana* (Dodson & Dressler) Szlachetko.

EFFUSIELLA

Luer

Monogr. Syst. Bot. Missouri Bot. Gard. **112**: 106 (2007).

ETYMOLOGY: Latin for dispersed or disorderly and diminutive. Refers to loosely arranged inflorescence.

TYPE SPECIES: *Effusiella amparoana* (Schlechter) Luer (*Pleurothallis amparoana* Schlechter)

Recognized as belonging to the genus *Pleurothallis*, *Effusiella* was proposed to include forty epiphytes or occasional lithophytes found in low to mid elevation, hill to montane forests and woodlands from southern Mexico (Chiapas) to Bolivia and Venezuela. These dwarf plants have thin ramicauls, subtended by tubular sheaths, each with a solitary, oblong, leathery, dark green leaf. The several, solitary to few-flowered inflorescence, borne from a spathe at the leaf base, has small, translucent, usually (slightly to densely) hairy, pale yellow, red, yellow-green to deep black flowers opening widely. The deeply concave lateral sepals are united, an erect dorsal sepal and has tiny, narrow petals with tapered tails. The tiny, entire lip is usually tongue-shaped. The flowers have a tiny, stout column.

EGGELINGIA

Summerhayes

Bot. Mus. Leafl. **14**: 235 (1951).

Epidendroideæ ⚘ Vandeæ • Aerangidinæ

ETYMOLOGY: Honoring William Julius Eggeling (1909-1992), a Scottish botanist, conservationist, a conservator of forests in Uganda who collected and furthered our understanding of the orchids from the eastern Africa region.

TYPE SPECIES: *Eggelingia ligulifolia* Summerhayes

Three monopodial epiphytes are found in mid elevation, evergreen forests and lava flows in the main rift valley of central Africa from Uganda to Ghana. This inconspicuous, easily overlooked, tiny plant has long, slender, often hanging stems, each with stiff, narrow or tongue-shaped, leathery or fleshy, strap-like, distichous leaves. The leaves have persistent leaf sheaths bearing a hair-like, membranous scale at the tip opposite the leaf. The short, few-flowered inflorescence, borne from the leaf axils, has small, pristine white or yellow-white flowers. The sac-like to concave, ovate, entire lip has a short, almost thread-like, straight spur and a dark green splash. The flowers have a short, erect, fleshy, wingless, footless column.

EICOSIA

An orthographic variant introduced in *Fl. Javæ*, **1**: Praef. vii (1828). The correct spelling is *Eucosia*.

ELANGIS

Thouars

Hist. Orchid. Table 3, sub 3o, *tt.* 79-80 (1822).

Name published without a description. Today this name is most often referred to *Cryptopus*.

ELA-pola

Rheede

Hort. Malab. **11**: 71, *t.* 36 (1692).

ETYMOLOGY: A local Malayalam name for leaf. And pola means sheath.

TYPE SPECIES: *Ela-pola* Rheede

Pre-1753, therefore not validly published in fulfillment of nomenclatural rules; this binomial name is most often referred to *Eulophia*. *Ela-pola* was previously considered to include one terrestrial widespread in low elevation, swamps, grasslands and roadcuts from India, Sri Lanka, the Himalayas, southern China, Thailand, Malaysia, New Guinea to Fiji and Tonga. This

Currently Accepted   Validly Published   Invalidly Published   Published Pre-1753   Superfluous Usage   Orthographic Variant   Fossil

Orchid Genera • **142**

plant has almost round pseudobulbs, borne below the ground, each with several, stalked leaves. The erect, few-flowered inflorescence has olive-green flowers. The sepals have dark green or maroon nerves, and the creamy or white petals have pink nerves. The pale pink-mauve, trilobed lip has raised nerves on the disc. This name is usually now considered as a synonym of *Eulophia spectabilis* (Dennstedt) Suresh.

ELASMATIUM

Dulac
Fl. Hautes-Pyrénées   121 (1867).

ETYMOLOGY: Greek for metal plate or flat end. Alluding to the pattern on the leaves that gives the appearance of a metallic sheen.

TYPE SPECIES: *Elasmatium repens* (Linnaeus) Dulac
(*Satyrium repens* Linnaeus)

Now recognized as belonging to the genus *Goodyera, Elasmatium* was previously considered to include one terrestrial widespread in dry to damp, mid elevation, pine-oak forests, grassland and tundra from Alaska to the eastern United States, Scandinavia, Poland to Romania, across Russia (West Siberia to Primorye), eastern Turkey to northern India, northeastern China, and Korea to Japan. This erect plant generally has unbranched stems, each with reptile-like mottling on the basal rosette leaves. The erect, narrow, densely packed, numerous-flowered inflorescence has fragrant, insignificant, white to creamy, hairy flowers arranged in a tight spiral on the rachis. The dorsal sepal and petals converge, forming a hood over the small, short column. The small, trilobed lip is quite hairy.

ELASMATUM

An orthographic variant introduced in *Hort. Thenensis*, 186 (1895). The correct spelling is *Elasmatium*.

ELASMIUM

Blume ex Ridley
J. Linn. Soc., Bot.   **22**(145): 296 (1887).

ETYMOLOGY: Latin for illusion or deceit. Refers to the unusual small size of the thread-like petals.

TYPE SPECIES: *Elasmium parviflorum* Blume ex Ridley
This type name is now considered a synonym of
Liparis parviflora (Blume) Lindley;
basionym
Malaxis parviflora Blume

Not validly published, this name is referred to *Liparis. Elasmium* was considered to include one epiphyte found from Thailand, Malaysia, Indonesia, New Guinea and the Philippines.

ELEANTHES

An orthographic variant introduced in *Gen. Pl. (Endlicher)*, 190 (1837). The correct spelling is *Elleanthus*.

ELEANTHUS

An orthographic variant cited in *Etym.-Bot.-Handw.-Buch*, ed. 1, 316 (1852). The correct spelling is *Elleanthus*.

ELEORCHIS

Maekawa
J. Jap. Bot.   **11**(5): 297 (1935).

Epidendroideæ ⚘ Arethuseæ • Arethusinæ

ETYMOLOGY: Greek for marsh and orchid. Refers to the plant's preferred swampy or wet habitat.

TYPE SPECIES: *Eleorchis japonica* (A. Gray) Maekawa
(*Arethusa japonica* A. Gray)

One uncommon, sympodial terrestrial is found in cold, mid elevation, montane bogs and marshes of Japan (Hokkaido and northern Honshu) and far eastern Russia (Kuril Islands). This small, slender, erect plant has tiny, ovoid to cone-like pseudobulbs, each with a solitary, narrow, deciduous, grass-like leaf. The erect, solitary or rarely two-flowered, green inflorescence, borne from the leaf axils, has a showy, thinly textured, rosy-red flower with long, narrow segments and which does not open widely. The long, entire or obscurely lobed lip has a bright white crest or is noncrested and is shallowly notched along the margin. The flowers have a small, footless column that is ridged on each side.

ELEUTHEROGLOSSUM

M.A. Clements & D.L. Jones
Orchadian   **13**(11): 489 (2002).

ETYMOLOGY: Greek for free or separate and tongue. Refers to the lip which is not connected.

Or Greek Mythology: *Eleuther*, a son of Apollo and Aethusa (daughter of Poseidon), won a Pythian victory at the games for his loud and sweet voice.

TYPE SPECIES: *Eleutheroglossum closterium*
(Schlechter) M.A. Clements & D.L. Jones
(*Dendrobium eleutheroglossum* Schlechter)

Recognized as belonging to the genus *Dendrobium. Eleutheroglossum* was proposed to include five epiphytes or lithophytes found in low to mid elevation, open forests or skimpy rain forests of New Caledonia and northeastern Australia. These small plants have club-shaped pseudobulbs, subtended by a distinct sheath, each with several, leathery leaves grouped near the tip of the stem. The erect, few-flowered

inflorescence, borne near the tip of the stem, has small, yellow flowers with maroon or purple markings, and the flowers turn orange as they age. The prominent, lateral sepals are typically arranged at a 45° angle. The short, trilobed lip has erect, rounded side lobes, and the somewhat kidney-shaped midlobe has a clefted tip. The flowers have a stout, yellow column.

ELLEANTHUS

C. Presl
Reliq. Haenk.   **1**: 97 (1827).

Epidendroideæ ⚘ Sobralieæ

ETYMOLOGY: Greek for to be shut in and flower. A reference to the bracts that enclose the flowers.

Or possibly Greek Mythology. Helle and Phrixus were the children of Athamas, king of Orkhomenos and his nymph-wife, Nephele (Cloud). Athamas later rejected Nephele for a woman who plotted to have Helle and Phrixus offered as a sacrifice. Nephele and the god, Hermes, devised the escape of Helle and Phrixus on a magical ram with golden fleece.

LECTOTYPE: *Elleanthus lancifolius* C. Presl

A complex genus of one hundred six sympodial, mostly terrestrials or with a few epiphytes found in low to upper elevation, hill to montane cloud forests from Cuba to Trinidad, southern Mexico to Panama, with the greatest concentration in the South American Andes and Brazil. These erect plants have cane or reed-like, simple or branched, leafy stems that are subtended by sheaths toward the tip. The narrow to ovate, distichous, pleated leaves, arranged in two ranks along the stem, are coated with a fine dust and sometimes sparsely hairy. The long, densely packed, numerous-flowered inflorescences has small, brightly colored flowers arranged in tight, ball-like heads or in two ranks along a zig-zagged rachis. In all cases the flowers are almost obscured by large, overlapping, and sometimes hairy bracts that in some species are as colorful as the flowers. The entire or obscurely trilobed lip encloses the erect, winged, footless column and has an entire, toothed or a finely fringed margin.

ELLEBORINE

Clusius
Rar. Pl. Hist.   **3**: 272, 273 (1601).

Pre-1753, therefore not validly published in fulfillment of nomenclatural rules; this name is most often referred to *Cephalanthera* and *Cypripedium*.

ELONGATIA

(Luer) Luer

Monogr. Syst. Bot. Missouri Bot. Gard.
95: 257 (2004).

ETYMOLOGY: Latin for lengthen or extend. Referring to the long inflorescences.

TYPE SPECIES: *Elongatia restrepioides* (Lindley) Luer
(*Pleurothallis restrepioides* Lindley)

Recognized as belonging to the genus *Stelis*, *Elongatia* was proposed to include ten epiphytes or rarely lithophytes found in wet, low to upper elevation, hill and montane forests of the Amazon River basin of northern Brazil, Venezuela and Colombia to Peru. These small plants have slender, cylindrical stems, subtended by several, tubular sheaths, each with one to two, leathery leaves. The long, few-flowered inflorescence has large, hanging, fragrant, showy, yellow-green flowers with the sepals and petals (notched margins) that are a red to mauve on the outer surface. The clawed, golden yellow to red, entire or obscurely trilobed lip has a red to mauve center with an orange-pink callus, and a wavy margin. The flowers have an erect column with a short, thick, pedestal-like foot.

ELOYELLA

P. Ortíz

Orquideologia **13**(3): 234 (1979).

Epidendroideæ ⚘ Cymbidieæ • Oncidiinæ

ETYMOLOGY: Named in honor of Eloy Valenzuela (1756-1834), a Spanish-born Colombian priest and botanist. He accompanied Antonio Góngora and Jose Mutis to Nueva Granada in 1783, and in 1810 Valenzuela headed the provisional government of Colombia. And Latin for diminutive.

TYPE SPECIES: *Eloyella antioquiensis* (P. Ortíz) P. Ortíz
(*Phymatidium antioquiensis* P. Ortíz)

Six psygmoid epiphytes are found in wet, low elevation, hill forests of Panama, Colombia, Ecuador and Peru. These dwarf plants have an arrangement of fan-shaped, bi-laterally flattened, distichous, thick, leathery leaves. The erect, stout, few-flowered inflorescence has tiny, green and white to yellow-green flowers, opening in succession, with widespreading similar sepals and petals. The dark yellow-green, entire lip has prominent, thick calli and a toothed margin. The flowers have a slender, erect, slightly curved, footless column.

ELTROPLECTRIS

Rafinesque

Fl. Tellur. **2**: 51 (1836)[1837].

Orchidoideæ ⚘ Cranichideæ • Spiranthinæ

ETYMOLOGY: Greek (corruption) for free and spur. Referring to the prominent spur that is formed by the joined bases of the lateral sepals and lip.

TYPE SPECIES: *Eltroplectris acuminata*
Rafinesque nom. illeg.

This type name is now considered a synonym of

LECTOTYPE: *Eltroplectris calcarata*
(Swartz) Garay & H.R. Sweet
(*Neottia calcarata* Swartz)

Thirteen sympodial terrestrials are found in shady, low to mid elevation, forest margins from the southeastern United States (Florida), the Bahamas, Cuba to Trinidad, Mexico to Bolivia, Brazil and Paraguay to Argentina. These erect plants have unbranched stems, each with several, (one to two) attractive, satiny, deciduous, blue-green to dark green leaves in a basal rosette or cluster that are sometimes absent at flowering. The erect, stout, smooth, maroon to pink, hairy, loosely arranged, numerous to few-flowered inflorescence is subtended by several, loose bracts. The showy, fragrant, green-white to pale brown flowers have long, narrow, lateral sepals that are joined for variable lengths. The thinly textured, delicately fringed, entire lip, notched in the middle, is joined at the base of the lateral sepals forming a spur that is cylindrical to club-like and is incurved or recurved near its tip. The flowers have a white, long, slender, club-shaped column that is flat or channeled, and smoothly textured to shortly hairy.

ELYTHRANTHE

Not *Elythranthe* Reichenbach (1841) Loranthaceæ.

An orthographic variant introduced in *Dict. Univ. Hist. Nat.*, **9**: 172 (1847). The correct spelling is *Elythranthera*.

ELYTHRANTHERA

(Endlicher) A.S. George

W. Austral. Naturalist **9**: 6 (1963).

Orchidoideæ ⚘ Diurideæ • Caladeniinæ

ETYMOLOGY: Greek for cover or sheath and Latin for anther. Referring to the column wings that extend over the column.

TYPE SPECIES: *Elythranthera brunonis*
(Endlicher) A.S. George
(*Glossodia brunonis* Endlicher)

Two sympodial terrestrials are found in low elevation, coastal scrub, open forests and sandy *Banksia* scrub of southwestern Australia. These small, erect plants have short, hairy, unbranched stems, subtended by a multi-layered, fibrous sheath, each with a solitary, hairy, narrow, deciduous leaf, often purple on the underside. This withers during the long, hot summer and reappears in the cool of autumn. The equally hairy, slender, one- to four-flowered inflorescence has small flowers in a wide range of pink to purple colors. These remarkable flowers have a glossy luster on the inside and a dull, drab, blotched appearance on the outside of the floral segments. The small, entire lip has one to two, basal calli on a flattened claw. The flowers have an erect, footless column that is prominent and widely winged.

ELYTRANTHERA

An orthographic variant cited in *Etym.-Bot.-Handw.-Buch*, ed. 1, 319 (1852). The correct spelling is *Elythranthera*.

EMBREEA

Dodson

Phytologia **46**(6): 389 (1980).

Epidendroideæ ⚘ Cymbidieæ • Stanhopeinæ

ETYMOLOGY: Honoring Alvin Embree (1926-2001), an American business executive, owner of a travel bus company, orchidologist and orchid judge.

TYPE SPECIES: *Embreea rodigasiana*
(Claes ex Cogniaux) Dodson
(*Stanhopea rodigasiana* Claes ex Cogniaux)

Two sympodial epiphytes with an unusual trans-Andean distribution in very wet, low to mid elevation, hill to montane cloud forests from western Colombia (Antioquia) and southeastern Ecuador. These plants have densely clustered, sharply four-angled pseudobulbs, subtended by overlapping, dry sheaths, each with a solitary, pleated, gray-green leaf. The several, hanging, solitary-flowered inflorescences have a spectacular, large, pale pink to white flower densely spotted brown on the topside. The fleshy, distinctly shaped flower is short-lived and has a concave dorsal sepal with ovate lateral sepals and recurved, narrow petals. The broad sepals are heavily spotted red-brown on the inside surfaces and lightly spotted on the outside. The waxy, gray or blue-white, trilobed lip is spotted bright red or chestnut brown. The wings of the mesochile are T-shaped and incurved, each with a distinctive, fang-shaped horn. The flowers have a club-shaped, narrowly winged column.

Currently Accepted   Validly Published   Invalidly Published   Published Pre-1753   Superfluous Usage   Orthographic Variant   Fossil

O r c h i d   G e n e r a • **144**

EMPUSA

Lindley

Bot. Reg. **10**: sub 825 (1824).

Not *Empusa* Cohn (1855) Fungi.

ETYMOLOGY: Greek for a hobgoblin with a vampire's appetite. Alluding to the fantastic form of the flowers.

TYPE SPECIES: *Empusa paradoxa* Lindley

Now recognized as belonging to the genus *Liparis*, *Empusa* was previously considered to include one terrestrial widespread from northern India, Bhutan, Nepal, southern China, Taiwan and Thailand to Malaysia. This small plant has sheathed, narrowly ovoid pseudobulbs, each with several, large, narrow, strongly veined leaves. The long, few-flowered inflorescence has fragrant, pale brown, white to green-yellow flowers. The dark purple or green, squarish, entire lip is recurved in the middle, with a finely toothed, upper margin, and has a shallow notched tip. The flowers have a slightly forward curved column.

EMPUSARIA

Reichenbach

Consp. Regn. Veg. 69 (1828).

ETYMOLOGY: Derivative of *Empusa*, a genus of orchids. Suggesting a relationship.

TYPE SPECIES: *None designated*

A superfluous name proposed as a substitute for these species now referred to *Liparis*.

EMPUSELLA

(Luer) Luer

Monogr. Syst. Bot. Missouri Bot. Gard. **95**: 258 (2004).

ETYMOLOGY: Greek for a hobgoblin with a vampire's appetite and Latin for diminutive. Referring to the flower's fancied appearance.

TYPE SPECIES: *Empusella endotrachys*
(Reichenbach f.) Luer
(*Pleurothallis endotrachys* Reichenbach f.)

Recognized as belonging to the genus *Specklinia*, *Empusella* was proposed to include one epiphyte found in mid to upper elevation, montane cloud forests from southern Mexico to Colombia and Venezuela. This small, clump-forming plant has stout, clustered stems, each with a narrow, fleshy leaf that has minutely toothed tips. The several, erect, few-flowered inflorescences have small, orange-red to bright red flowers which open in succession. The large lateral sepals, united in the basal half, form a shallow, chin-like projection. The tiny petals are rounded and the inner surface of both the petals and sepals have a rough or wrinkled appearance. The

fleshy, curved, entire lip has a callused margin. The flowers have a minute column.

ENCHEIRIDION

Summerhayes

Bot. Mus. Leafl. **11**: 161 (1943).

ETYMOLOGY: Greek for dagger or knife handle. Referring to the long, dagger-like rostellum.

TYPE SPECIES: *Encheiridion macrorrhynchium*
(Schlechter) Summerhayes
(*Angraecum macrorrhynchium* Schlechter)

Now recognized as belonging to the genus *Microcoelia*, *Encheiridion* was previously considered to include three epiphytes found in low to mid elevation, rain forests and dense woodlands of western Africa from Liberia to Central African Republic, Equatorial Guinea to Zaire, Uganda and Zambia. These leafless plants have a short, erect stems, each with several, scale-like leaves. The several, short, erect to hanging, numerous-flowered inflorescences have lovely, small, frosty-white or yellow flowers suffused pink-tan. The small, white, trilobed lip has tiny side lobes; the large, broad, deeply notched midlobe has a yellow-green, basal splash and a wavy margin. The long, strongly recurved, orange-pink spur becomes swollen at the tip with age and has a plate-like thickening protecting the spur mouth.

ENCHEIRIDIUM

An orthographic variant cited in *Handb. Orchid.-Namen*, 468 (2005). The correct spelling is *Encheiridion*.

ENCYCLIA

Hooker

Bot. Mag. **55**: *t. 2831* (1828).

Epidendroideæ ⦙ Epidendreæ • Laeliinæ

ETYMOLOGY: Greek for to encircle. Descriptive of the side lobes of the lip that enclose the column instead of being fused to it.

TYPE SPECIES: *Encyclia viridiflora* Hooker

One hundred fifty-four, highly variable, clump-forming, evergreen, sympodial epiphytes or terrestrials are found in seasonally dry to wet, low to upper elevation, hill to montane oak-pine and rain forests of the Bahamas, the United States (southern Florida), Cuba to Trinidad, Belize to Bolivia, Brazil, Paraguay and northern Argentina with the greatest concentration found in Mexico. This genus can be distinguished from most species of *Epidendrum* by the presence of stems forming more or less pear-shaped to ovoid pseudobulbs,

partially subtended below by several, thin, dry sheaths, each with two or three, fleshy, strap-like leaves borne toward the tips. The slender, often multibranched, numerous to few-flowered inflorescence, borne from the stem tip, has showy, wonderfully fragrant flowers found in a wide range of colors and shades of yellow, brown, green or rare pink. The flowers have similar sepals and petals. The widely varied, entire or trilobed lip encircles the stout or slender, footless column, but is never fully attached.

NOTE: These species are related to *Cattleya*; however, *Encyclia* flowers are smaller than those of the usually larger *Cattleya* species.

ENCYCLIA

Poeppig & Endlicher

Nov. Gen. Sp. Pl. (Poeppig & Endlicher) **2**: 10 (1838).

Not validly published, this name is most often referred to *Polystachya*.

ENCYCLIUM

Lindley ex Stein

Orchid.-Buch 224 (1892).

Not validly published, this name is most often referred to *Epidendrum*.

ENCYLIA

An orthographic variant introduced in *Bonplandia*, **4**(14): 213 (1856). The correct spelling is *Encyclia*.

ENDEISA

Rafinesque

Fl. Tellur. **2**: 52 (1836)[1837].

ETYMOLOGY: Greek Mythology. Dedicated to *Endeis*, wife of Acacus, King of Aegina and mother of Telamon and Peleus. Peleus was the father of Achilles, who was the hero in Homer's *Iliad*.

TYPE SPECIES: *Endeisa flava* Rafinesque nom. illeg.
Dendrobium densiflorum Lindley

Now recognized as belonging to the genus *Dendrobium*, *Endeisa* was previously considered to include one epiphyte or lithophyte found in low elevation, evergreen hill forests from northeastern India (Sikkim), Nepal, Bhutan, Myanmar, northern Thailand and southern China (Xizang to Guangdong). This spectacular, showy, tufted, erect plant has clustered, almost four-angled stems, each with several, narrow, leathery leaves near the tip. The arching to hanging, densely packed, numerous-flowered inflorescence, borne near the tip of stem, has showy, short-lived, thinly textured, delicately fragrant, yellow flowers.

The broad, roundish, shortly clawed, entire lip has a rich, dark yellow or orange center and a heavily fringed margin. The flowers have a short, orange-yellow column.

ENDISA

An orthographic variant cited in *Lex. Gen. Phan.*, 197 (1904). The correct spelling is *Endeisa*.

ENDRESIELLA

Schlechter
Repert. Spec. Nov. Regni Veg. **17**: 13 (1921).
ETYMOLOGY: Dedicated to A.R. Endrés (x-1875), a European who collected (mostly likely for George Skinner and later for H.G. Reichenbach) flora and fauna in Costa Rica, Panama and later was murdered in Riohacha, Colombia. And Latin for diminutive.
TYPE SPECIES: *Endresiella zahlbruckneriana*
Schlechter

Now recognized as belonging to the genus *Trevoria, Endresiella* was previously considered to include one epiphyte found in wet, mid to upper elevation, montane cloud forests from Nicaragua to Panama and Colombia to Bolivia. This plant has cone-like pseudobulbs, each with a solitary, green leaf. The short, hanging, few-flowered inflorescence has creamy white flowers with narrow petals and broad, concave sepals. The pale tan to white, trilobed lip, united with the long column foot, has an incurved (hood-shaped), unlobed, fleshy hypochile. The concave mesochile has an orange-yellow disk, and a rigid, triangular-shaped epichile. The flowers have a short, fleshy column.

ENOTHREA

Rafinesque
Fl. Tellur. **4**: 43 (1836)[1837].
ETYMOLOGY: Apparently dedicated to a nymph but none can be found in the classical literature.
Greek Mythology. In Hesiod's (*fl.* 800 B.C.) poem *Theogony* (a codified genealogy of the many myths of the Greek gods) there is mentioned some three thousand different sea-nymphs.
TYPE SPECIES: *Enothrea graminifolia*
(Linnaeus) Rafinesque
(*Epidendrum graminifolium* Linnaeus)
Octomeria graminifolia (Linnaeus) R. Brown

Now recognized as belonging to the genus *Octomeria, Enothrea* was previously considered to include one epiphyte found from Belize to Ecuador, Venezuela and Trinidad. This small, creeping plant has short, secondary stems, each with a solitary

leaf. The solitary-flowered inflorescence, borne from below the leaf base, has a green-white flower with a fleshy, trilobed lip. The flowers have a slender, short footed column.

ENPUSA

An orthographic variant introduced in *Rad. Jugoslav. Akad. Znan.*, **21**: 126 (1872). The correct spelling is *Empusa*.

ENSIFERA

Blume ex d'Orbigny
Dict. Univ. Hist. Nat. **9**: 169 (1847).

Name published without a description. Today this name is most often referred to *Oberonia*.

ENTATICUS

Gray
Nat. Arr. Brit. Pl. **2**: 198, 205 (1821).
ETYMOLOGY: Greek for stimulating and plant. Refers to an old-time medical virtue that may have been once associated with this plant.
TYPE SPECIES: *None designated*

Not validly published, this name is referred to *Coeloglossum viride* and *Pseudorchis albida*. *Entaticus* was generally considered to include two terrestrials found across Europe (Britain to Turkey).

ENTOMOPHOBIA

deVogel
Blumea **30**(1): 199 (1984).
Epidendroideæ ⚬ Arethuseæ • Coelogyninæ
ETYMOLOGY: Greek for insects and fear or panic. In reference to the flower entrance being obstructed or closed, thus preventing pollination.
TYPE SPECIES: *Entomophobia kinabaluensis*
(Ames) deVogel
(*Pholidota kinabaluensis* Ames)

One sympodial epiphyte or lithophyte is found in low to upper elevation, hill to montane forests of eastern Indonesia (Sulawesi) and southern Malaysia (Sabah). This plant has small, clustered pseudobulbs, all facing to one side of the rhizome, subtended by thin, dry sheaths, each with two narrow, stiff, thinly leathery leaves. The erect, few-flowered inflorescence (continues to elongate after flowering) has white to creamy flowers encased in persistent floral bracts. They are probably self-pollinating, almost entirely closed and all opening simultaneously. The green, obscurely trilobed lip has a deeply sac-like base, is separated from the front by a transverse, slightly bent, fleshy callus and has a wavy margin. The flowers have an arching, conspicuously winged, footless column.

EOORCHIS

J. Mehl
Ber. Arb. Heimische Orch. **1**: 9 (1984).
ETYMOLOGY: Greek for true and orchid. Refers to the species being a true, fossil orchid.
TYPE SPECIES: *Eoorchis miocaenica* J. Mehl

One fossil orchid is from the Upper Miocene epoch (twenty-five million years ago) and was found in freshwater limestone beds. The specimen was discovered at Öhningen-Wangen, which is located near Lake Constance on the border between Germany, Austria and Switzerland.

EPARMATOSTIGMA

Garay
Bot. Mus. Leafl. **23**(4): 178 (1972).
Epidendroideæ ⚬ Vandeæ • Aeridinæ
ETYMOLOGY: Greek for swelling and stigma. In reference to the shape of the stigma that protrudes from the column like an inflated bubble.
TYPE SPECIES: *Eparmatostigma dives*
(Reichenbach f.) Garay
(*Saccolabium dives* Reichenbach f.)

One monopodial epiphyte, which is found in low elevation, montane evergreen forests of central Vietnam (Song Be). This small, short-stemmed plant has long, narrow, channeled, leathery, unequally bilobed leaves arranged in two rows. The several, numerous-flowered inflorescences have small, white-yellow flowers opening widely and then lasting for only a short duration. The inflated, bubble-like, vertical stigma is unique to this genus. The short, stout, wingless, footless column is not attached to the large, sac-like, white, trilobed lip for most of the length.

EPEPACTIS

An orthographic variant introduced in *Icon. Pl. Ind. Orient. (Wight)*, **3**: t. 1723 (1851). The correct spelling is *Epipactis*.

EPHEMERANTHA

P.F. Hunt & Summerhayes
Taxon **10**(4): 102 (1961).
ETYMOLOGY: Greek for a very short duration or temporary and flower. Refers to the ephemeral flowers that typically last for one, short day.
TYPE SPECIES: *Ephemerantha angulata*
(Blume) P.F. Hunt & Summerhayes
(*Desmotrichum angulatum* Blume)

Because of a previous publication, by a few days, these species are now included in *Flickingeria*.

Currently Accepted   Validly Published   Invalidly Published   Published Pre-1753   Superfluous Usage   Orthographic Variant   Fossil

O r c h i d   G e n e r a   • 146

EPHIPPIANTHUS

Reichenbach *filius*

Flora **51**(3): 33 (1868), and
Reis. Amur-Land., Bot. 180, *t.* 5 (1868).

Epidendroideæ 🌿 Calypsoeæ

ETYMOLOGY: Greek for saddle and flower. From the saddle-like shape of the lip.

TYPE SPECIES: *Ephippianthus schmidtii* Reichenbach f.
This type name is now considered a synonym of *Ephippianthus sachalinensis* Reichenbach f.

Two inconspicuous, but delicate, sympodial terrestrials are found in mid elevation, moss laden montane forests and piney woodlands of Japan and eastern Russia (Kuril Islands to Khabarovsk). This dwarf, slender plant has erect, unbranched stems, each with a solitary, round to heart-shaped, silver spotted, basal leaf. The slender, few-flowered inflorescence has dainty, small, white to yellow-green flowers with several nerves on the sepals and petals. The shortly clawed, entire lip has hairy, red blotches down the middle and a fleshy, red callus on each side near the base. The flowers have a slender, curved column.

EPHIPPIUM

Blume

Bijdr. Fl. Ned. Ind. **7**: 308, *t.* 65 (1825).

Name ICBN rejected vs. *Cirrhopetalum* Lindley (1830) Orchidaceæ; and not *Ephippium* Vekshina (1959) Fossil.

ETYMOLOGY: Greek for saddle. An allusion to the saddle-shaped lip.

LECTOTYPE: *Ephippium ciliatum* Blume

Although validly published this rejected name is now referred to a section of the genus *Bulbophyllum*. *Ephippium* was considered to include nine epiphytes found from Malaysia, Laos, Thailand, Vietnam, Indonesia (Java and Borneo), the Philippines and New Guinea to northern Australia. These creeping plants have small, narrow, cone-shaped, widely separated pseudobulbs, each with a solitary, leathery leaf. The long, solitary-flowered inflorescence has a flower with long, tail-like or short, roundish sepals. The erect dorsal sepal is finely fringed toward the base with the lateral sepals united or not joined for most of their length. They have narrow petals that are quite small. The tiny, tongue-shaped, entire lip is prolonged into a narrow tail.

EPIBATOR

(Luer) Luer

Monogr. Syst. Bot. Missouri Bot. Gard. **95**: 201 (2004).

ETYMOLOGY: Greek for a climber. Referring to the plant's vine-like growth habit.

TYPE SPECIES: *Epibator hirtzii* (Luer) Luer
(*Zootrophion hirtzii* Luer)

Recognized as belonging to the genus *Zootrophion*, *Epibator* was proposed to include three epiphytes found in upper elevation, montane cloud forests of Ecuador. These small, tufted plants, often clump-forming, have an unusual vine-like habit and have small, leathery leaves. The several, solitary-flowered inflorescences, borne below the leaf node, have a yellow flower characterized by the union of the sepals at their tips only, thus creating a window on either side of the tubular flower. The trilobed lip, hinged to the column foot, has marginal side lobes near the middle, the tiny petals and even the small column are all hidden inside the flower.

EPIBLASTUS

Schlechter

Nachtr. Fl. Schutzgeb. Südsee 136 (1905).

Epidendroideæ 🌿 Podochileæ • Eriinæ

ETYMOLOGY: Greek for above or upon and bud, shoot or sprout. Refers to the growth habit of the shoots, which are branched and grow superimposed so that one is above the other.

LECTOTYPE: *Epiblastus ornithidioides* Schlechter

Twenty-two uncommon, sympodial terrestrials or epiphytes are found in low to upper elevation, hill and montane moss laden forests from Indonesia (Sulawesi) and New Guinea to the Philippines. These rather large, scrambling, colony forming plants have superposed stems, each with new growth arising from near the tip of the previous older stem. The stem has its base subtended by overlapping sheaths, each with a solitary, narrow leaf at the tip. Each of the several, erect or hanging, solitary to few-flowered inflorescences, subtended by a leafy base, has a tiny, waxy, usually red-orange to scarlet-red flower which does not open fully. The lateral sepals are united at the base forming a chin-like protuberance. The tongue-shaped, obscurely trilobed lip has a raised, basal disk and is deeply sac-like. The flowers have a small, slightly curved, wingless column.

EPIBLEMA

R. Brown

Prodr Fl. Nov. Holland. 315 (1810).

Orchidoideæ 🌿 Diurideæ • Diuridinæ

ETYMOLOGY: Greek for upon or over and coverlet or garment. Suggestive of the column wings that might be likened to a bedcover or comforter.

TYPE SPECIES: *Epiblema grandiflorum* R. Brown

One interesting, uncommon, sympodial terrestrial is found in low elevation, coastal swamps and damp peaty scrub of south-western Australia. This colony-forming plant has short, unbranched stems, each with a solitary, slender, narrow leaf. The wiry, solitary to few-flowered inflorescence has roundish, lilac-blue to deep mauve flowers heavily blotched and marked along the veins. The segments are of equal size and shape, but the petals are more heavily blotched. The tongue-shaped, shortly clawed, entire lip has a basal callus, which is entire or bilobed with a tuft of projecting, thread-like appendages. The flowers have a short, footless column.

EPICLADIUM

(Lindley) Small

Fl. Miami 56 (1913).

ETYMOLOGY: Greek for upon or on and a small branching twig. Referring to its epiphytic habitat.

TYPE SPECIES: *Epicladium boothianum* (Lindley) Small
(*Epidendrum boothianum* Lindley)

Now recognized as belonging to the genus *Prosthechea*, *Epicladium* was previously considered to include one epiphyte found in the south-eastern United States (southern Florida), Mexico to Belize, the Bahamas and Cuba to Hispaniola. This plant has laterally compressed pseudobulbs, each with several, slick, shiny, yellow-green leaves that are slightly twisted. The few-flowered inflorescence has yellow-green flowers with irregular, brown-purple blotches. The yellow-green, obscurely trilobed lip has a basal disc with the callus edged in purple. It has strongly curved side lobes and the white midlobe has a wavy margin. This species was formerly included in *Encyclia*.

EPICRANTES

An orthographic variant introduced in *Bull. Mus. Natl. Hist. Nat.*, ser. 2, **28**: 486 (1957). The correct spelling is *Epicranthes*.

EPICRANTHES

Blume

Bijdr. Fl. Ned. Ind. **7**: 306, *t.* 9 (1825).

ETYMOLOGY: Greek for sail yard, yard-arm or headdress and flower. Refers to the column that has seven hanging, sail-like processes or projections.

TYPE SPECIES: *Epicranthes javanica* Blume

Now recognized as belonging to the genus *Bulbophyllum*, *Epicranthes* was previously considered to include twenty-eight epiphytes found in damp, low to mid elevation, evergreen forests from Indonesia to the Philippines. These plants have small, oblong pseudobulbs, each with a solitary, thick leaf. The solitary to few-flowered inflorescence, borne from the base of the pseudobulb, has a thick-textured, yellow flower opening widely, that is sprinkled with several, violet spots. The minute, tape-like petals have a number of extremely mobile, white ornaments with dark spots. The fleshy, tongue-shaped lip has a hairy (numerous, small, foam-like, sticky protuberances) cushion near the base, and a dark violet tip. The mobile, extremely fleshy, entire lip often appears sac-like and has a deep central groove. The flowers have a short, stout column. The above type name is now considered a synonym of *Bulbophyllum epicranthes* Hooker f.

EPICRIANTHES

An orthographic variant introduced in *Fl. Javæ*, **1**: Praef. vii (1828). The correct spelling is *Epicranthes*.

EPIDANTHUS

L.O. Williams

Bot. Mus. Leafl. **8**: 148 (1940).

ETYMOLOGY: In reference to its resemblance to *Epidendrum*, a genus of orchids and Greek for flower.

TYPE SPECIES: *Epidanthus paranthicus* (Reichenbach f.) L.O. Williams (*Epidendrum paranthicum* Reichenbach f.)

Now recognized as belonging to the genus *Epidendrum*, *Epidanthus* was previously considered to include three epiphytes found along the margins of wet, mid elevation, cloud forests from Mexico (Chiapas) to Ecuador. These dwarf plants form dense masses of slender, multi-branched stems, each with several, needle-like leaves. The few-flowered, zig-zagging inflorescence is borne from the tip. The tiny, fleshy, green, creamy to bright yellow flowers have large subtending bracts. The variable trilobed or entire lip has upturned side lobes that nearly surrounds the column for its entire

length, and the midlobe gradually tapers to a point. The flowers have two, waxy masses of pollinia attached to an oblong disk.

EPIDENDENDRUM

An orthographic variant introduced in *Orquideas Afic.*, 120 (1961). The correct spelling is *Epidendrum*.

EPIDENDRE

Descourtilz

Delessert's Bibliogr.
Unpublished, located at Institut de France (1820).

ETYMOLOGY: Greek for upon. Refers to the plant's preferred growing habits.

TYPE SPECIES: *None designated*

Not validly published, this name is most often referred to a variety of different orchid genera including *Cattleya, Sophronitis, Miltonia, Leptotes, Maxillaria, Ionopsis, Huntleya* and *Bifrenaria*.

There are numerous orchid species in this collection of floral and fauna drawings by Michael Étienne Descourtilz (1775-1836) which were owned and collected by Jules Paul Benjamin Delessert (1773-1847) a French industrialist, banker, philanthropist and amateur botanist.

EPIDENDRIUM

An orthographic variant introduced in *Malay. Penins.*, 523 (1834). The correct spelling is *Epidendrum*.

EPIDENDRON

Hermann

Parad. Batav. 187, *t.* 187 (1698).

Pre-1753, therefore not validly published in fulfillment of nomenclatural rules; this name is most often referred to *Epidendrum*.

EPIDENDROPSIS

Garay & Dunsterville

Venez. Orchid. Ill. **6**: 39 (1976).

ETYMOLOGY: *Epidendrum*, a genus of orchids and Greek for appearance.

TYPE SPECIES: *Epidendropsis violascens* (Ridley) Garay & Dunsterville (*Epidendrum violascens* Ridley)

Now recognized as belonging to the genus *Epidendrum*, *Epidendropsis* was previously considered to include three lithophytes found in wet, low to upper elevation, hill to montane forests

and woodlands from Puerto Rico, Hispaniola to Trinidad, the Guianas, Venezuela, Costa Rica to Peru and northern Brazil. These small plants have cane-like, branched, leafy stems. The lightly branched, thread-like, few-flowered inflorescence has pale green-yellow flowers often suffused maroon with similar shaped sepals and narrow petals. The entire lip, united to the small, wingless, footless column to its tip, is covered by minute, fleshy papillae.

EPIDENDRSM

An orthographic variant introduced in *Repert. Spec. Nov. Regni Veg. Beih.*, **7**: 69 (1919). The correct spelling is *Epidendrum*.

EPIDENDRUM

Linnaeus

Sp. Pl. (Linnaeus), ed. 1 **2**: 952 (1753).

Name ICBN rejected vs. *Epidendrum* Linnaeus (1763) Orchidaceæ.

ETYMOLOGY: Greek for upon and orchid. From the epiphytic habit of the species.

LECTOTYPE: *Epidendrum nodosum* Linnaeus

Although validly published this rejected name is now referred to *Brassavola*. *Epidendrum* Linnaeus was considered to include a rather large and widely varied group of epiphytic orchids.

EPIDENDRUM

Linnaeus

Sp. Pl. (Linnaeus), ed. 2 **2**: 1347 (1763).

Name ICBN conserved vs. *Epidendrum* Linnaeus (1753) Orchidaceæ, and type name also conserved.

Epidendroideæ · Epidendreæ · Laeliinæ

ETYMOLOGY: Greek for upon and a tree. Refers to the growth habit of most species of the genus that grow upon other plants. Originally considered to be parasitic, but it was later shown that they are not.

LECTOTYPE: *Epidendrum nocturnum* Jacquin not *Epidendrum nodosum* (Linnaeus) Britton & Wilson

A large genus in excess of one thousand, one hundred twenty-five sympodial epiphytes, but also including terrestrials and uncommon lithophytes are found in wet to dry, low to mid elevation with a wide range of habitats. These species are exclusively American, ranging from the eastern United States (North Carolina to Florida), the Bahamas, Cuba to Trinidad, Mexico to Peru, the Galapagos Islands, Argentina and Paraguay with centers of development in Mexico, the Andes and Brazil usually growing in full sunlight. These slender, erect, hanging to creeping plants have thin, cane-like to reed-stemmed, thickened, simple to branching stems with narrow, fleshy to leathery leaves. With few exceptions the

Currently Accepted   Validly Published   Invalidly Published   Published Pre-1753   Superfluous Usage   Orthographic Variant   Fossil

Orchid Genera · 148

numerous to few-flowered inflorescence is terminal, simple or profusely branched, and bears from one to numerous flowers which vary from excessively small to quite large, opening successively or simultaneously. The smooth or thickened (hardened), entire or trilobed lip is united to the straight or slightly arched, footless column.

NOTE: At one time most of the species of *Encyclia* and *Prosthechea* were included in *Epidendrum*. The name *Epidendrum* was used by early botanists and writers to place and describe many of the newly discovered epiphyte type plants.

EPIDENDUM

An orthographic variant introduced in *Handb. Indian Fl.*, **3**: 361 (1869). The correct spelling is *Epidendrum*.

EPIDORCHIS

An orthographic variant introduced in *Hist. Orchid.*, Table 1, sub 2i, *t. 81* (1822). The correct spelling is *Epidorkis*.

EPIDORKIS

Thouars
Nouv. Bull. Sci. Soc. Philom. Paris
1(19): 318 (1809).
ETYMOLOGY: Greek for upon or on top and orchid. Referring to the epiphytic habit.
TYPE SPECIES: *None designated*

Not validly published, this name is referred to the genera *Jumellea, Angraecum, Microcoelia, Solenangis, Oeonia* and *Mystacidium. Epidorkis* was considered to include forty-three epiphytes found from Tanzania to South Africa, Madagascar and the Mascarene Islands.

EPIGENEIUM

Gagnepain
Bull. Mus. Natl. Hist. Nat., sér. 2   **4**: 594 (1932).
Epidendroideæ ⚘ Dendrobiinæ • Currently unplaced
ETYMOLOGY: Greek for upon and chin or bread. Refers to the position of the petals and lateral sepals on the column foot.
TYPE SPECIES: *Epigeneium fargesii* (Finet) Gagnepain
(*Dendrobium fargesii* Finet)

Thirty-eight somewhat uncommon sympodial epiphytes or lithophytes are found in low to upper elevation, montane rain or moss laden forests ranging from northeastern India (Sikkim to Assam), China (Anhui to Yunnan), Taiwan, Myanmar to Vietnam, Indonesia (Java, Sumatra and Borneo) and New Guinea to the Philippines. These plants, often forming large clumps, usually have a creeping habit with clustered or scattered, ovoid to cone-shaped pseudobulbs consisting of one internode, each

with one to three, oblong to ovate, leathery, bilobed leaves. The erect to slightly curved, solitary to few-flowered inflorescence borne at the tip of the pseudobulb that is subtended by a papery, large or small bract. The often showy, waxy, fragrant, small to large, pale green to white, long-lasting flowers can be variously spotted and striped in red, purple or maroon shades. The dorsal sepal encloses the short, slightly curved column, and the lateral sepals form a chin-like protuberance along with the long column foot. The oblong, trilobed or entire lip has rounded side lobes, and the midlobe has calli or ridges at the base.

EPIGOGIUM

An orthographic variant introduced in *Arch. Bot. (Leipzig)*, 40 (1796). The correct spelling is *Epipogium*.

EPILLASTUS

An orthographic variant introduced in *Bot. Centralbl.*, **108**(48): 588 (1908). The correct spelling is *Epiblastus*.

EPILYNA

Schlechter
Beih. Bot. Centralbl.   **36**(2): 374 (1918).
Epidendroideæ ⚘ Sobralieæ
ETYMOLOGY: Greek for upon and Latin for *lynx*, a genus of wild, sometimes spotted cats. Refers to the various spotted flowers.
TYPE SPECIES: *Epilyna jimenezii* Schlechter

Three sympodial epiphytes are found in extremely wet, low to upper elevation, hill scrub to montane cloud forests from Costa Rica to Ecuador. These small, erect plants have slender, cane-like stems, each with several, narrow, distichous, almost toothpick-like, papery leaves that have prominent veins and are not attached to the floral sheaths. The stem and floral bracts are sprinkled with numerous red-brown specs. The terminal, compact, few-flowered inflorescence has distinctly arranged, tiny, white to brown-cream flowers with soft, black, scale-like hairs on the outer surface. The entire to obscurely trilobed lip, sac-like at the base, has a pair of kidney-shaped, fleshy calli and a notched margin. The flowers have a short, footless column.

NOTE: *Epilyna* is similar to *Elleanthus* but is clearly distinct on a number of characters.

EPIPACTES

An orthographic variant introduced in *Arch. Pharm.*, 46: 372 (1846). The correct spelling is *Epipactis*.

EPIPACTIDES

Irmisch
Linnaea   **19**: 118 (1847).

Name published without a description. Today this name is most often referred to *Epipactis*.

EPIPACTIS

Besler
Hort. Eystet.   *t. 130, 196* (1613).

Pre-1753, therefore not validly published in fulfillment of nomenclatural rules; this name is most often referred to *Cephalanthera*.

EPIPACTIS

Séguier
Pl. Veron.   **3**: 253 (1754).
Name ICBN rejected vs. *Epipactis* Zinn (1757) Orchidaceæ.
ETYMOLOGY: Greek for rupture-wort. An ancient name employed by Theophrastus (371-287 BC), a Greek botanist, for a plant used to curdle milk.
TYPE SPECIES: *Satyrium repens* Linnaeus

Although validly published this rejected name is now referred to *Goodyera*.

EPIPACTIS

Zinn
Cat. Pl. Hort. Gott.   85 (1757).
Name ICBN conserved vs. *Epipactis* Séguier (1754) Orchidaceæ, and type name also conserved.
Epidendroideæ ⚘ Neottieæ
ETYMOLOGY: Greek for rupture-wort. An ancient name employed by Theophrastus (371-287 BC), a Greek philosopher/botanist (sometimes called the father of Botany), for a plant used to curdle (turn, sour, ferment) milk in the manuscript *Enquirey into Plants*.
TYPE SPECIES: *Epipactis helleborine* (Linnaeus) Crantz
(*Serapias helleborine* Linnaeus)

Sixty-four large, sympodial terrestrials or occasionally saprophytes are found in low to upper elevation, wetlands, dunes, marshy scrub and along river banks in the northern temperate zones from Norway to Spain, Britain to across Russia (to Buryata), Afghanistan, throughout China, northern India (Kashmir to Assam) to Myanmar with a few species found in eastern Canada (Ontario), the United States to Mexico and Ethiopia to Malawi. In some areas these species are so common they are considered weeds. This is a difficult genus taxonomically and not generally attractive. These plants have erect stems with spirally arranged leaves that proceed up the stem with leaf-like floral bracts often exceeding the size of the flowers. The numerous to few-flowered inflorescence usually has dull yellow, green-yellow, red or brown flowers heavily suffused and veined purple, usually turned to one side on the rachis, that are either widespreading or loosely converging. The bilobed lip is divided into a basal part (hypochile) with or without side lobes, that is often deeply concave or sac-like, and a flat, triangular part (epichile) that is not lobed but often has a pair of calli. The flowers have a short, footless column that curves over the lip.

EPIPACTUM

An orthographic variant introduced in *Schriften Ges. Beförd. Gesammten Naturwiss. Marburg*, **2**: 125 (1831). The correct spelling is *Epipactis*.

EPIPACTYS

An orthographic variant introduced in *Fl. Frisica*, 123 (1840). The correct spelling is *Epipactis*.

EPIPAETIS

An orthographic variant introduced in *Fl. Javæ, t. 64* (1858). The correct spelling is *Epipactis*.

EPIPHANES

Blume

Bijdr. Fl. Ned. Ind.   **8**: 421, *t. 4* (1825).
ETYMOLOGY: Greek for clearly evident or in full view. From the prominently stalked flowers arranged in a spike.
TYPE SPECIES: *Epiphanes javanica* Blume
This type name is now considered a synonym of
Gastrodia javanica (Blume) Lindley;
basionym
Epiphanes javanica Blume

Now recognized as belonging to the genus *Gastrodia*, *Epiphanes* was previously considered to include one saprophyte found in moist, low elevation, dense hill forests and woodlands from southern Taiwan, southern Japan (Ryukyu Islands), Indonesia, Malaysia and the Philippines. This erect, leafless, pale brown plant has unbranched stems subtended by several, scale-like sheaths on the lower section. The few to numerous-flowered inflorescence has dark yellow flowers. The sepals and petals are joined, and the united lateral sepals form a small, swollen structure. The yellow, slightly diamond-shaped, entire lip is joined to the end of the distinct column foot, and has a longitudinal, green line on the lower surface.

EPIPHANES

Reichenbach *filius* ex **Pfitzer**

Nat. Pflanzenfam.   **2**(6): 219 (1889).
ETYMOLOGY: Greek for upon and bearing or carrying. Referring to its habitat.
TYPE SPECIES: *None designated*

Not validly published, this name is referred to *Pogoniopsis*.

EPIPHORA

Lindley

Compan. Bot. Mag.   **2**(19): 201 (1837).
Not *Epiphora* Nylander (1876) Fungi.
ETYMOLOGY: Greek for upon and to carry. Refers to the epiphytic habit of growing on other plants.
TYPE SPECIES: *Epiphora pubescens* Lindley

Now recognized as belonging to the genus *Polystachya*, *Epiphora* was previously considered to include three epiphytes or lithophytes found in mid elevation, exposed sandstone outcrops and woodlands from Guinea to Cameroon and Zambia, Zimbabwe to South Africa. These plants have clustered, cone-shaped pseudobulbs, each with several, narrow, unequally bilobed leaves. The erect, flattened, fuzzy, few-flowered inflorescence has inverted, fragrant, bright yellow to orange flowers with the interior surface of the sepals and the small lip streaked with red. The trilobed lip has small, erect side lobes, and a spear-shaped midlobe covered with white hairs. The flowers have a short column.

EPIPOGION

An orthographic variant introduced in *Fam. Pl.*, **2**: 554 (1763). The correct spelling is *Epipogium*.

EPIPOGIUM

Ehrhart

Beitr. Naturk. (Ehrhart)   **4**: 149 (1789).

Name published without a description. Today this name is most often referred to *Epipogium* Borkhausen.

EPIPOGIUM

J.F. Gmelin ex **Borkhausen**

Tent. Disp. Pl. German.   139 (1792).
Epidendroideæ ⚹ **Nervilieæ**
ETYMOLOGY: Greek for upon or upward and beard. Referring to the turned-up lip, that has a fanciful resemblance to a beard.
TYPE SPECIES: *Epipogium aphyllum* Swartz
(*Satyrium epipogium* Linnaeus)

Four, cool-growing saprophytes are found in low to upper elevation, hill to montane dense to open forests, mossy slopes and woodlands with a wide range from Norway to Greece, Britain to Ukraine, Ghana to Uganda, Angola to South Africa, Madagascar, Réunion, Mauritius, and across Russia (West Siberia to Primorye), India, Sri Lanka, Malaysia, Indonesia to Japan, Korea, Mongolia, China (Heilongjiang to Yunnan), Taiwan, New Guinea, northeastern Australia and the Philippines to Fiji. These leafless, scaly, thick-stemmed, erect plants produce relatively large, numerous, complex flowers that are erratic in appearance from year to year. The nodding, usually white to pale green flowers do not open widely, and are sometimes suffused pink. The narrow sepals and slightly wider petals are similar. The whole plant has a short life cycle, needing only a few days for the development of the scape, flowering, and release of the seeds. The broad, entire or trilobed lip is basally produced into a distinct short, small spur. The flowers have a short, club-shaped column with an obscure foot.

EPIPOGON

An orthographic variant introduced in *Handb. Bot. (Breslau)*, **3**(1): 361 (1884). The correct spelling is *Epipogium*.

EPIPOGUM

J.G. Gmelin

Fl. Sibir. (J.G. Gmelin)   **1**: 11, *t. 2, f. 2* (1747).

Pre-1753, therefore not validly published in fulfillment of nomenclatural rules; this name is most often referred to *Epipogium* Borkhausen.

EPIPOPON

An orthographic variant introduced in *Repert. Spec. Nov. Regni Veg. Beih.*, **4**: 152 (1919). The correct spelling is *Epipogium*.

| Currently Accepted | Validly Published | Invalidly Published | Published Pre-1753 | Superfluous Usage | Orthographic Variant | Fossil |

Orchid Genera · 150

EPISTEFIUM

An orthographic variant introduced in *Orquideas Colomb.*, 31 (1958). The correct spelling is *Epistephium*.

EPISTEPHIUM

Kunth

Syn. Pl. (Kunth)   **1**: 340 (1822).

Vanilloideæ ⚘ Vanillineæ

ETYMOLOGY: Greek for garlanded or crowned with. Referring to the persistent, crown-like or urn-shaped ring at the tip of the ovary.

TYPE SPECIES: *Epistephium elatum* Kunth

A group of twenty-three sympodial terrestrials that are restricted in hot to cold, low to mid elevation, hill to montane rain forests, open savannas, grasslands and boggy meadows from the Guianas, Venezuela, Colombia to Peru and Brazil with one species occurring in Trinidad and Belize. These erect, mostly large, cane-like plants have long, robust, simple or branched stems that may grow horizontally near the base of the plants, giving the appearance of a rhizome, before turning to grow vertically. The variable size and shape, striking leathery foliage has prominent, red venation. The terminal, several-flowered inflorescence bears large, showy, brightly colored, pale pink, dark purple to rare green flowers opening successively, but are short-lived. The entire or obscurely trilobed lip has a simple to extremely wavy margin, is rolled, forming a tube around the slender, footless column, and has numerous hairs, bristles, scales or thickened grooves forming a crest to the center of the lip.

EPISTYCHIUM

An orthographic variant introduced in *Hamburger Garten- Blumenzeitung*, **9**: 80 (1853). The correct spelling is *Epistephium*.

EPITHACIA

An orthographic variant introduced in *Icon. Pl. Rar. (Link)*, **2**: 89 (1844). The correct spelling is *Epithecia*.

EPITHECIA

Knowles & Westcott

Fl. Cab.   **2**: 167, t. 87 (1838).

ETYMOLOGY: Greek for appendage. Descriptive of the clinandrium that is "roundish, entire and has a short but sharp point at the base, with a roundish fleshy appendage immediately below ..."

TYPE SPECIES: *Epithecia glauca*
(Knowles & Westcott) Knowles & Westcott
(*Prosthechea glauca* Knowles & Westcott)

A superfluous name proposed as a substitute for *Prosthechea*.

EPITHECIUM

An orthographic variant introduced in *Gen. Pl. (Bentham & Hooker f.)*, **3**: 529, 1239 (1883). The correct spelling is *Epithecia*.

EQUITIRIS

Thouars

Hist. Orchid.   Table 3, sub 3t, t. 92 (1822).

Name published without a description. Today this name is most often referred to *Oberonia*.

ERANA

An orthographic variant introduced in *Deutsch. Mag. Garten- Blumenk.*, 365 (1853). The correct spelling is *Eria*.

ERASANTHE

P.J. Cribb, Hermans & D.L. Roberts

Adansonia, ser. 3   **29**(1): 28 (2007).

ETYMOLOGY: The name is derived from an anagram of *Aeranthes*, a genus of orchids.

TYPE SPECIES: *Erasanthe henrici*
(Schlechter) P.J. Cribb, Hermans & D.L. Roberts
(*Aeranthes henrici* Schlechter)

Recognized as belonging to the genus *Aeranthes*, *Erasanthe* was proposed to include one epiphyte found in humid, low elevation, evergreen forests and open woodlands of Madagascar. This plant has a short stem, each with several, overlapping, pale green, oblong to narrow, leathery leaves that have wavy margins. The several, stout, hanging, solitary-flowered inflorescences have a white to pale green flower blooming simultaneously that has long, narrow, tapering segments. The shortly clawed, dark green, obscurely trilobed lip has large, oblong side lobes, a long, narrow midlobe with all the margins notched and a long, slender spur. The flowers have a small, short column.

ERECTOROSTELLATA

Brieger

Orchideen (Schlechter), ed. 3   **7**(25-28): 416 (1975).

ETYMOLOGY: Greek for erect and beak-shaped. Refers to the rostellum.

TYPE SPECIES: *None designated*

Name published without a description. Today this name is most often referred to *Pleurothallis*.

ERECTOROSTRATA

Brieger

Orchideen (Schlechter), ed. 3   **7**(25-28): 428 (1975).

ETYMOLOGY: Greek for erect and beaked.

TYPE SPECIES: *None designated*

Name published without a description. Today this name is most often referred to *Pleurothallis*.

EREMORCHIS

D.L. Jones & M.A. Clements

Austral. Orchid Res.   **4**: 72 (2002).

ETYMOLOGY: Greek for solitary or lonely and orchid. Refers to the plants' geographical and morphological isolation.

TYPE SPECIES: *Eremorchis allantoidea*
(R.S. Rogers) D.L. Jones & M.A. Clements
(*Pterostylis allantoidea* R.S. Rogers)

Recognized as belonging to the genus *Pterostylis*, *Eremorchis* was proposed to include one terrestrial found in low elevation, coastal woodlands of western Australia. This tiny, erect plant has slender, unbranched stems, each with a basal rosette that has numerous, overlapping, pale green leaves with wavy margins. The plant has a ovate, leafy bract near the rosette, which has a hairy margin and tapers to a long, fine tip. The solitary-flowered inflorescence has a green flower with a decurved hood that has dark purple stripes and markings. The dark colored lateral sepals extend to thread-like tips that greatly exceed the length of the dorsal sepal. The mobile, sausage-like, red-brown, entire lip is channeled above, and slightly recurved. The flowers have an erect column.

ERI

An orthographic variant introduced in *Mat. Fl. Malay. Penins.*, **1**: 109 (1907). The correct spelling is *Eria*.

ERIA

Lindley

Bot. Reg. **11**: *t.* 904 (1825).
Name ICBN conserved.

Epidendroideæ ✹ **Podochileæ** • **Eriinæ**

ETYMOLOGY: Greek for woolly. Referring to the hairy flowers and inflorescences of some species.

LECTOTYPE: *Eria stellata* Lindley

This type name is now considered a synonym of
Eria javanica (Swartz) Blume;
basionym
Dendrobium javanicum Swartz

A large genus with four hundred four sympodial epiphytes, lithophytes or rare terrestrials are found in low to upper elevation, hill to montane evergreen forests, scrub, peaty swamps and mangroves. The species range from southern China (Yunnan to Hainan), India, and Sri Lanka to Samoa and Fiji with the greatest development occurring in Indonesia and New Guinea. This is a diverse genus ranging from small, tufted, creeping plants to large, robust plants. These problematic and under described plants have pseudobulbous or cane-like stems that are either short or long, each with two to numerous leaves, but rarely one leaf. The several, long or short, solitary to numerous-flowered inflorescence sometimes has large, conspicuously colored bracts. The small to tiny, often not showy, pale brown, creamy, yellow-green, green to rosy, sometimes fragrant flowers have a rather distinctive shape but are short-lived. Some species have flowers densely covered in soft hairs, some just the inflorescence, and still other species have the entire plant covered in soft hairs. The entire or usually trilobed lip is attached but not stalked on the prominent column foot, and this foot forms a long to short, spur-like, pouch or even a roundish protuberance. The flowers have a short, broad to stout column.

ERIAE

An orthographic variant introduced in *Not. Pl. Asiat.*, **3**: 304 (1851). The correct spelling is *Eria*.

ERIAXIS

Reichenbach *filius*

Linnaea **41**: 63 (1877).

Vanilloideæ ✹ **Vanillineæ**

ETYMOLOGY: Greek for woolly and Latin for axis. Descriptive of the hairy inflorescence, ovary and sepals in the type species.

TYPE SPECIES: *Eriaxis rigida* Reichenbach f.

One terrestrial is found in low elevation, hill forests and open scrub of New Caledonia. This large, stiff plant has hollow, occasionally branching, leafy stems. A solitary, thick, leathery leaf, midway up the stem, is characterized by numerous, free vein endings. This leaf appears at each node. The terminal, sometimes branched, few-flowered inflorescence has showy, short-lived, white to pale pink flowers. The number of flowers often depends upon the amount of sunlight received. The dark purple to bright magenta, trilobed lip has yellow margins, and the erect side lobes form an unfused floral tube around the curved, slender, footless column.

ERICKSONELLA

(Reichenbach *filius*) Hopper & A.P. Brown

Austral. Syst. Bot. **17**(2): 208 (2004).

Orchidoideæ ✹ **Diurideæ** • **Caladeniinæ**

ETYMOLOGY: Named in honor of Frederica (Rica) Lucy Erickson née Sandilands (1908-), an Australian school teacher, naturalist, illustrator and author of *Orchids of the West*. And Latin for diminutive.

TYPE SPECIES: *Ericksonella saccharata*
(Reichenbach f.) Hopper & A.P. Brown
(*Caladenia saccharata* Reichenbach f.)

One sympodial terrestrial is found in low elevation, woodlands of south-western Australia. This slender plant, often forming large colonies, has erect, unbranched stems, each with a solitary, long, narrow, hairy, pale yellow-green leaf. The solitary-flowered inflorescence has a fragrant, bright white flower whose upper surface is violet colored and has glandular tipped hairs on the outer surface. The erect dorsal sepal is slightly incurved, and the lateral sepals are widespreading. The shortly clawed, trilobed lip has prominent, violet side lobes, and a large, rounded, yellow or white midlobe with two rows of yellow, club-shaped calli. The flowers have a red-purple, incurved column.

ERIOCHILOS

An orthographic variant introduced in *Syst. Veg. (Sprengel)*, ed. 16, **3**: 678, 714 (1826). The correct spelling is *Eriochilus*.

ERIOCHILUM

An orthographic variant introduced in *Schriften Ges. Beförd. Gesammten Naturwiss. Marburg*, **2**: 125 (1831). The correct spelling is *Eriochilus*.

ERIOCHILUS

R. Brown

Prodr. Fl. Nov. Holland. 323 (1810).

Orchidoideæ ✹ **Diurideæ** • **Caladeniinæ**

ETYMOLOGY: Greek for woolly and a lip. Referring to the glandular hair-like outgrowth on the lip that appears woolly.

TYPE SPECIES: *Eriochilus autumnalis* R. Brown nom. illeg.
Eriochilus cucullatus (Labillardière) Reichenbach f.)
(*Epipactis cucullata* Labillardière)

Twelve sympodial terrestrials are found in low elevation, coastal woodlands and sphagnum bogs of southwestern and eastern Australia and Tasmania. These erect, slender plants have hairy, unbranched stems, each with a solitary, ovate leaf (appearing mid-stem) or sometimes reduced to a small bract. The leaf often does not appear until long after flowering, usually during the autumn rains. The thin, wiry, solitary to few-flowered inflorescence has pale to bright pink, mauve or even white flowers with the small petals narrower than the lateral sepals. The small dorsal sepal forms a hood over the short, erect, winged column. The densely hairy, obscurely trilobed lip comes in various shades, and the broad, thick midlobe is adorned with clusters of bristle-like growths.

ERIOCHYLUS

An orthographic variant introduced in *Nat. Syst. Pl.*, 302 (1832). The correct spelling is *Eriochilus*.

Currently Accepted | Validly Published | Invalidly Published | Published Pre-1753 | Superfluous Usage | Orthographic Variant | Fossil

Orchid Genera • **152**

ERIODES

Rolfe

Orchid Rev. **23**(275): 326 (1915).

Epidendroideæ 🌿 Collabiinæ • Currently unplaced

ETYMOLOGY: Greek for woolly. The name is base on *Erioidea*, which was applied to a specimen collected by William Griffith (1810-1845). An allusion to the resemblance of the type species to the orchid genus *Eria*.

TYPE SPECIES: *Eriodes barbata* (Lindley) Rolfe (*Tainia barbata* Lindley)

One sympodial epiphyte or lithophyte is found in cool, mid elevation, montane forests from northern India (Assam), Bhutan, Myanmar to Vietnam and Thailand to southern China (Yunnan). This plant has large, clustered, egg-shaped to roundish, rigid pseudobulbs, each with two short-stalked, prominently veined leaves. The few-flowered inflorescence (upper portion branched) has faintly fragrant, yellow flowers striped brown-purple. The strongly veined flowers have a concave dorsal sepal, broad, strongly reflexed lateral sepals and narrow petals. The soft, downy-covered inflorescence has an irregular line of flat, brown hairs on one side of the pedicel. The narrow, mobile, brown, entire lip is recurved. The flowers have a short, thick, strongly-angled column.

ERIOIDEA

Griffith

Itin. Pl. Khasyah Mts. 83 (1848), and
Icon. Pl. Asiat. **3**: t. 301 (1848).

Name published without a description. Today this name is most often referred to *Dendrobium*.

ERIOPEXIS

(Schlechter) Brieger

Orchideen (Schlechter), ed. 3 **1**(11-12): 656 (1981).

ETYMOLOGY: *Eria*, a genus of orchids and Greek for tight or fastening. Referring to the hairy lip.

TYPE SPECIES: *Eriopexis schlechteri* Brieger

Now recognized as belonging to the genus *Dendrobium*, *Eriopexis* was previously considered to include six epiphytes found in upper elevation, montane cloud forests of New Guinea. These erect or hanging plants have broad, swollen stems, subtended by prominently flattened, leaf-like sheaths, each with its several leaves arranged in two ranks. The inflorescence has large, fleshy, often white flowers, borne in lateral pairs from the leaf axils, that last for only a day and do not open widely. The small, five-lobed lip has a blunt tip and is covered with small warts. The flowers

have a long column foot that forms a sac-like chin. The above type name is now considered a synonym of *Dendrobium eriopexis* Schlechter.

ERIOPSIS

Lindley

Edwards's Bot. Reg. **33**: sub 9, t. 18 (1847).

Epidendroideæ 🌿 Cymbidieæ • Eriopsidinæ

ETYMOLOGY: *Eria*, a genus of orchids and Greek for appearance. Suggesting that the plants (particularly the flowers) are like those of *Eria*.

TYPE SPECIES: *Eriopsis biloba* Lindley

Five sympodial epiphytes, lithophytes and sometime terrestrials are found in wet, low to mid elevation, hill to montane forests ranging from Costa Rica to Bolivia, Venezuela and Brazil on rocky or clay slopes. These plants have clustered, stoutly ovoid to pear-shaped, dark green to almost black pseudobulbs, subtended by overlapping sheaths, each with several, heavily veined, leathery or papery leaves. The graceful, erect to arching, numerous-flowered inflorescence, borne from the base of a newly matured pseudobulb. The fragrant, showy, waxy, creamy, yellow-orange to purple flowers have similar sepals and slightly smaller petals, which open simultaneously and are uniquely multi-colored. The white, trilobed lip has large, broad, erect to incurved, orange side lobes, and a smaller, white to creamy, kidney-shaped, entire to bilobed midlobe with dark maroon blotches or spots. The disc has toothed or entire crests or a pair of flattened, horn-like calli. The flowers have a long, arching column.

ERIOXANTHA

Rafinesque

Gard. Mag. & Reg. Rural Domest. Improv. **8**: 247 (1832).

ETYMOLOGY: *Eria*, a genus of orchids and Greek for flower. Referring to a similarity to *Eria*.

TYPE SPECIES: *None designated*

A superfluous name proposed as a substitute for *Eria*.

ERIURA

Lindley ex Stein

Orchid.-Buch 248 (1892).

Name published without a description. Today this name is most often referred to as a section of *Eria*.

ERPORCHIS

An orthographic variant introduced in *Hist. Orchid.*, Table 1, sub 2i, t. 28 (1822). The correct spelling is *Erporkis*.

ERPORKIS

Thouars

Nouv. Bull. Sci. Soc. Philom. Paris **1**(19): 317 (1809).

Name ICBN rejected vs. *Platylepis* A. Richard (1828) Orchidaceæ.

ETYMOLOGY: Greek for to creep or crawl and orchid. Refers to the creeping rhizome.

LECTOTYPE: *Goodyera occulta* Thouars

Although validly published this rejected name is now referred to the genera *Platylepis* and *Cheirostylis*. *Erporkis* was considered to include two terrestrials widespread in shady, low to mid elevation, rain forests from Ghana to Zaire, Ethiopia to Tanzania, Angola to Mozambique, Madagascar, Réunion, Seychelles to Vanuatu and New Caledonia. These erect plants generally have unbranched, thick stems, each with several, shiny, ovate leaves. The thick, hairy, few to numerous-flowered inflorescence has tiny flowers that do not open fully. The species are now considered as synonyms of *Platylepis occulta* (Thouars) Reichenbach f. and *Cheirostylis nuda* (Thouars) Ormerod.

ERVARDIANTHE

An orthographic variant cited in *Dict. Gen. Names Seed Pl.*, 258 (1995). The correct spelling is *Evrardianthe*.

ERYA

An orthographic variant introduced in *Tijdschr. Natuurl. Gesch. Physiol.*, **6**: 78 (1839). The correct spelling is *Eria*.

ERYCINA

Lindley

Fol. Orchid. **2**: Erycina 1 (1853).

Epidendroideæ 🌿 Cymbidieæ • Oncidiinæ

ETYMOLOGY: Greek Mythology. *Erycina*, the Aphrodite of Mount Eryx in Sicily, was equated with the Greek goddess Aphrodite and assumed many of her aspects. She is associated with the queen bee of the heather. The name is used in reference to the beauty of the flower.

TYPE SPECIES: *Erycina echinata* (Kunth) Lindley (*Oncidium echinatum* Kunth)

Seven sympodial epiphytes are native in seasonally dry, low to upper elevation, coastal, deciduous or thorn forests from western Mexico to Panama, Colombia to Ecuador and Trinidad. These small plants have clustered, ovate pseudobulbs, sheathed at the base; each with several, narrow, distichous, bright green, thinly textured leaves. The arching to hanging, entire to branched, few-flowered inflorescence, borne near the base of the pseudobulb, has showy, cup-shaped, mainly yellow flowers with green or brown sepals and tiny petals. The golden or bright yellow, trilobed lip is longer than the other segments and has fan-shaped, somewhat incurved side lobes and a kidney-shaped midlobe. The flowers have a very short, curved, wingless column with a red anther cap.

ERYCINE

An orthographic variant cited in *Syn. Bot.*, 104 (1870). The correct spelling is *Erycina*.

ERYTHORCHIS

An orthographic variant introduced in *Veg. Kingd.*, ed. 1, 183 (1853). The correct spelling is *Erythrorchis*.

ERYTHROCYNIS

Thouars

Hist. Orchid.   Table 1, sub 1d (1822).

Name published without a description. Today this name is most often referred to *Cynorkis*.

ERYTHRODEN

An orthographic variant introduced in *Coll. Orchid.*, 96 (1858). The correct spelling is *Erythrodes*.

ERYTHRODES

Blume

Bijdr. Fl. Ned. Ind.   **8**: 410, *t. 72* (1825).

Orchidoideæ ⚘ Cranichideæ • Goodyerinæ

ETYMOLOGY: Greek for red and likeness. Refers to the red-brown color of the inflorescences and flowers.

TYPE SPECIES: *Erythrodes latifolia* Blume

Some twenty-seven taxonomically complex, sympodial terrestrials or rare epiphytes are widespread in shady, low to mid elevation, primary forest litter and along river banks that are usually found from southern (Yunnan to Guangdong), northeastern India (Assam), Bhutan, Sri Lanka, Taiwan, Myanmar to Vietnam, Thailand, Indonesia, the Philippines and the southwestern Pacific Archipelago. These usually creeping, erect plants have unbranched stems, each with loose, leafy rosettes or several, scattered, green to red, frequently patterned or variegated leaves arising from a mainly red rhizome. The erect, hairy inflorescence is green basally then becoming red toward the tip. The small, drab-colored, white, pale green or red-brown flowers are often of great complexity and can be extremely difficult

to interpret and describe. The slender, often white, entire or obscurely trilobed lip lacks glands or warts, is attached to the short, slender, footless column at the base, and has an inflated bladder-like, tubular spur. The neotropical species are usually segregated to the genus *Microchilus*.

ERYTHRODRIS

Thouars

Hist. Orchid.   Table 1, sub 1a (1822).

Name published without a description. Today this name is most often referred to *Disperis*.

ERYTHRODRYS

An orthographic variant introduced in *Hist. Orchid.*, *t. 2* (1822). The correct spelling is *Erythrodris*.

ERYTHROLEPTIS

Thouars

Hist. Orchid.   Table 1, sub 2h (1822).

Name published without a description. Today this name is most often referred to *Liparis*.

ERYTHRORCHIS

Blume

Rumphia   **1**(10-12): 200, *t. 70* (1837).

Vanilloideæ ⚘ Vanillineæ

ETYMOLOGY: Greek for red and orchid. Referring to the reddish stem of many of the species.

TYPE SPECIES: *Erythrorchis altissima* (Blume) Blume
      (*Cyrtosia altissima* Blume)

Three large saprophytes are found in partly shaded, low elevation, swampy evergreen and bamboo forests from China (Hainan), Taiwan, southern Japan, northeastern India, Myanmar to Vietnam, Malaysia, Indonesia and eastern Australia (Queensland to New South Wales). These plants have thin, dark brown to red-brown, branching stems, often forming extensive, tangled masses and are spectacular climbers with their leaves reduced to mere scales (one at each node). The simple or branched, smooth, numerous-flowered inflorescence has small, green-yellow, pale yellow-brown or brown flowers opening in succession with only one or two open at a time as the rachis lengthens. The wedge-shaped, white, essentially entire or weakly trilobed lip has its lateral margin rolled upward, forming a floral tube around the slightly curved, footless column; has a wavy or fringed margin and a hairy, fleshy callus.

ESMERALDA

Reichenbach *filius*

Xenia Orchid.   **2**: 38 (1862).

Epidendroideæ ⚘ Vandeæ • Aeridinæ

ETYMOLOGY: Greek for emerald green. Referring to the jewel-like beauty of the flower or possibly in reference to the deep green of the leaves.

TYPE SPECIES: *Esmeralda cathcartii*
      (Lindley) Reichenbach f.
      (*Vanda cathcartii* Lindley)

Two exquisite, monopodial epiphytes, lithophytes or terrestrials are found in moist, mid elevation, forest valleys of north-eastern India, Nepal, southern China (Hainan) and Myanmar to Thailand. These sometimes climbing plants have stout, pencil-like stems, each with several, distichous, deep green, oblong, leathery leaves arranged in two rows. These leaves are twisted at the base to face one direction and have unequally bilobed tips. The erect, stout, few-flowered inflorescence, longer than the leaves, has showy, large, slightly to strongly fragrant, long-lived, waxy, thick, pale yellow flowers heavily barred with darker colors; the ovate sepals and petals are usually similar. The flowers are off-white on the undersides. The mobile, cup-shaped, trilobed lip has small, erect side lobes, and the clawed, kidney-shaped midlobe has raised calli and an upturned, irregularly notched margin. The flowers have a short, stout, wingless, yellow column.

ESTELIS

An orthographic variant introduced in *Cat. Descr. Orquid.*, *Estac. Exp. Agron. Santiago, Cuba*, **60**: 61 (1938). The correct spelling is *Stelis*.

ESTOCHYLOS

An orthographic variant introduced in *Prakt. Stud. Orchid.*, 43, 248 (1854). The correct spelling is *Sestochilos*.

ETAERIA

Blume

Bijdr. Fl. Ned. Ind.   **8**: 409, *t. 14* (1825).

Orthography ICBN rejected vs. *Hetaeria* Blume (1825)
      Orchidaceæ.

ETYMOLOGY: Greek for companionship. Referring to the intimate association of this genus with others in the tribe *Neottieæ*.

TYPE SPECIES: *None designated*

Although validly published this rejected name is now referred to *Hetaeria*. *Etaeria* was considered to include three terrestrials widely distributed from Indonesia, New Guinea and

Currently Accepted   Validly Published   Invalidly Published   Published Pre-1753   Superfluous Usage   Orthographic Variant   Fossil

O r c h i d   G e n e r a   • **154**

Australia to the Philippines. These creeping plants have short stems, each with several, well-spaced leaves that clasp upward along the slender stem and are often withered by flowering time. The erect, slender, hairy, numerous-flowered inflorescence has tiny flowers with the dorsal sepal and petals forming a hood. The concave, entire lip has a tip with an incurved margin.

EUANTHE

Schlechter
Orchideen (Schlechter), ed. 1   567 (1914).
Epidendroideæ ⚬ **Vandeæ** • **Aeridinæ**
ETYMOLOGY: Greek for blooming or well-flowered. Referring to the beauty of these spectacular flowers.
TYPE SPECIES: *Euanthe sanderiana*
(Reichenbach f.) Schlechter
(*Vanda sanderiana* Reichenbach f.)

One monopodial epiphyte is found in low elevation, coastal scrub of the southern Philippines (Mindanao). This massive plant has elongate stems, subtended by overlapping sheathing bases, each with several, distichous, recurved, leathery leaves that are centrally grooved. The erect, few-flowered inflorescence has large, showy, three-toned flowers. The dorsal sepal and petals are similar in color, but the tawny-yellow lateral sepals have red-brown net-venation. The small, streaked, veined or stained, trilobed lip has a concave base with roundish, erect side lobes, and a fleshy, shortly clawed, oblong midlobe that has three central ridges and a recurved, red-brown tip. The flowers have a short, stout, wingless column.
NOTE: This genus differs from *Vanda*, although often included in *Vanda*, because of technical details.

EUCALADENIA

Endlicher ex Wittstein
Etym.-Bot.-Handw.-Buch, ed. 1   340 (1852).

Name published without a description. Today this name is most often referred to as a section of *Caladenia*.

EUCERATANDRA

Lindley ex Wittstein
Etym.-Bot.-Handw.-Buch, ed. 1   341 (1852).

Name published without a description. Today this name is most often referred to as a section of *Ceratandra*.

EUCHILE

(Dressler & G.E. Pollard) Withner
Cattleyas & Relatives   5: 137 (1998).
ETYMOLOGY: Greek for beautiful or true and lip. Refers to the broad trilobed lip of the type species.
TYPE SPECIES: *Euchile mariae* (Ames) Withner
(*Epidendrum mariae* Ames)

Recognized as belonging to the genus *Prosthechea*, *Euchile* was proposed to include two epiphytes found in seasonally dry, mid to upper elevation, montane oak-pine forests of central and southern Mexico. These small, plants have hanging, clustered, cone-shaped to ovoid, often flattened, gray-green pseudobulbs, each with two leathery leaves that have a unique gray, waxy coating. The hanging, solitary to few-flowered, nodding inflorescence has yellow to green, sweetly fragrant flowers which do not open fully. The broad, white, softly ruffled, trilobed lip has green veining at the base. The side lobes have crisp edges, and the broad, fiddle-shaped midlobe has a notched tip. The flowers have a pale green to white, short, wingless, footless column that has a central tooth projecting beyond the anther cap.

EUCNEMIA

An orthographic variant cited in *Deut. Bot. Herb.-Buch*, 53 (1841). The correct spelling is *Eucnemis*.

EUCNEMIS

Lindley
Gen. Sp. Orchid. Pl.   161 (1833).
ETYMOLOGY: Greek for good or well and knee or joint. Referring to the lateral sepals that are joined to the column with a short foot.
TYPE SPECIES: *Eucnemis brevilabris* Lindley
This type name is now considered a synonym of
Govenia liliacea (Lexarza) Lindley;
basionym
Maxillaria liliacea Lexarza

Now recognized as belonging to the genus *Govenia*, *Eucnemis* was previously considered to include one terrestrial found in mid elevation, montane forests from Mexico to Argentina. This plant has corm-like pseudobulbs, each with two rather large, deciduous, leathery leaves (normally leafless during the dry season). The erect, numerous-flowered inflorescence has white or creamy flowers. The finely banded, pale rose dorsal sepal and petals converge, forming a hood over the erect column. The erect, entire lip is suffused pink-brown below and spotted red-brown toward the tip.

EUCODIA

An orthographic variant introduced in *Dict. Bot. Prat.*, 490 (1882). The correct spelling is *Eucosia*.

EUCOSIA

Blume
Bijdr. Fl. Ned. Ind.   8: 415, t. 18 (1825).
ETYMOLOGY: Greek for good or fine and ornament. Referring to the beauty of the flowers.
TYPE SPECIES: *Eucosia carnea* Blume
This type name is now considered a synonym of
Goodyera viridiflora (Blume) Blume;
basionym
Neottia viridiflora Blume

Now recognized as belonging to the genus *Goodyera*, *Eucosia* was previously considered to include three dwarf terrestrials found in shady, low to upper elevation, hill to montane forests and along river banks of Japan (Ryukyu Islands), Taiwan, eastern China (Jiangxi to Hainan, Yunnan), northern India, Nepal, Thailand, Vietnam, Indonesia, New Guinea, the Philippines and northeastern Australia (Queensland) to the southwestern Pacific Archipelago. These small plants are grown mostly for their magnificent, variegated, velvety, dark brown-green foliage that is covered with rosy-red to silvery veins. The erect, few to numerous-flowered inflorescence has small, white to pale green-white flowers often suffused pink and which do not open widely. The dorsal sepal and petals converge, forming a hood over the short, footless column. The long entire lip has a curved tip with one to two notches.

EUCYCLIA

An orthographic variant introduced in *Orchid.-Buch*, 248 (1892). The correct spelling is *Encyclia*.

EUCYMBIDIUM

Lindley ex Wittstein
Etym.-Bot.-Handw.-Buch, ed. 1   344 (1852).

Name published without a description. Today this name is most often referred to as a section of *Cymbidium*.

EUDISA

Endlicher ex Wittstein
Etym.-Bot.-Handw.-Buch, ed. 1   345 (1852).

Name published without a description. Today this name is most often referred to as a section of *Disa*.

EUDISANTHEMA

Necker ex **T. Post** & **Kuntze**

Lex. Gen. Phan. Prosp. 215 (1903).

ETYMOLOGY: Greek for good, strong or beautiful, Latin for rich or grand and Greek for anther. Refers to the unusual shape of the flowers.

TYPE SPECIES: *Eudisanthema cucullata*
(Linnaeus) R. Brown
(*Epidendrum cucullatum* Linnaeus)

Not validly published, this name is referred to *Brassavola*. *Eudisanthema* was considered to include one epiphyte distributed from Mexico to Colombia, Hispaniola to Trinidad, the Guianas and Venezuela.

EUEPIDENDRUM

Lindley ex **Wittstein**

Etym.-Bot.-Handw.-Buch, ed. 1 345 (1852).

Name published without a description. Today this name is most often referred to as a section of *Epidendrum*.

EUGLOSSODIA

Endlicher ex **Wittstein**

Etym.-Bot.-Handw.-Buch, ed. 1 346 (1852).

Name published without a description. Today this name is most often referred to as a section of *Glossodia*.

EULOPHIA

R. Brown ex **Lindley**

Bot. Reg. **7**: sub 578 [573], as *Eulophus* (1821), and
Bot. Reg. **8**: t. 686 (1822).

Name and orthography ICBN conserved vs. *Graphorkis* Thouars (1809); vs. *Lissochilus* R. Brown (1821); and not *Eulophia* C.A. Agardh (1822) Hookeraceæ.

Epidendroideæ ⚘ Cymbidieæ • Eulophiinæ

ETYMOLOGY: Greek for well or good and a plume or crest. Alluding to to the crest on the lip.

TYPE SPECIES: *Eulophia guineensis* Lindley

More then two hundred eleven sympodial terrestrials or rare lithophytes that are widespread in all the tropical and subtropical regions of the globe and are found in low to mid elevation, hill to montane valleys, slopes and meadows. The greatest development occurs in the grasslands of Africa (Ethiopia to South Africa, Gambia to Uganda and Cameroon to Botswana). Most of the plants have angular pseudobulbs, each usually with two or more, pleated, leathery or fleshy, narrow to widespread, deciduous, pleated, green leaves. Some species have brown or buff-colored leaves that are reduced to being scale-like. The simple to rarely branching, numerous to few-flowered inflorescence bears often small to large flowers opening successively over a rather long period of time. Several of the African species are quite showy and among the most robust with their inflorescences attaining heights often in excess of fifteen feet (4.5 m). The entire or trilobed lip has erect side lobes, a spreading midlobe with a basal disc bearing erect calli, papillae or hairs, and is sac-like sometimes having a slender, tubular spur at the base. The flowers have a long to short, stout, winged or wingless column that is with or without a foot. The lateral sepals are sometimes fused to the column foot. There are also has a few saprophytic species found in this genus that may have poorly developed leaves.

EULOPHIDIUM

Pfitzer

Entwurf Anordn. Orch. 87, 106 (1887), and
Nat. Pflanzenfam. **2**(6): 186, 188 (1889).

ETYMOLOGY: *Eulophia*, a genus of orchids and Greek for to resemble.

TYPE SPECIES: *Eulophidium maculatum*
(Lindley) Pfitzer
(*Angraecum maculatum* Lindley)

Now recognized as belonging to the genera *Oeceoclades* and *Eulophia*, *Eulophidium* was previously considered to include ten terrestrials or uncommon epiphytes found in low to mid elevation, hill forests, woodlands and rocky slopes from Tanzania to South Africa and Angola to Madagascar and the Comoros Islands with one species found from the southeastern United States (southern Florida) to Brazil. These plants have elongate to ovoid, green-brown pseudobulbs, each with one to several, leathery leaves at the tip. These plants are often grown for their handsome, often variegated leaves. The simple or branched, few-flowered inflorescence has thinly textured, brown to green flowers which do not open widely. The pale yellow, trilobed or four-lobed lip has a dull red blotch in the center, and has a short to long, slender spur. The flowers have a short column.

EULOPHIDUM

An orthographic variant cited in *Dict. Gen. Names Seed Pl.*, 256 (1995). The correct spelling is *Eulophidium*.

EULOPHIELLA

Rolfe

Lindenia **7**: 77 (1891).

Epidendroideæ ⚘ Cymbidieæ • Eulophiinæ

ETYMOLOGY: *Eulophia*, a genus of orchids and Latin for diminutive.

TYPE SPECIES: *Eulophiella elisabethæ* Linden & Rolfe

Five robust, highly specialized, sympodial epiphytes or rare terrestrials are found in wet, low to mid elevation, rain forests of Madagascar and then only growing on certain species of *Vonitra* (Palm family) or *Pandanus* (Screw Pine). These large plants have widely spaced, compressed, spindle-shaped pseudobulbs, borne on a stout creeping rhizome, each with several, long, thinly textured, pleated, grass-like leaves. The arching, sometimes branched, few-flowered inflorescence has large, ornate, fragrant, waxy, pink-white flowers suffused rose pink on the outside. The flowers open over a long period of time. The trilobed lip, attached to the column's prominent foot, has oblong side lobes; a circular midlobe with a large, yellow, basal blotch, a raised horse-shoe-shaped callus and a notched tip. The flowers have a small, fleshy, slightly curved column.

EULOPHIODIUM

An orthographic variant cited in *Handb. Orchid.-Namen*, 501 (2005). The correct spelling is *Eulophidium*.

EULOPHIOPSIS

Pfitzer

Entwurf Anordn. Orch. 105 (1887), and
Nat. Pflanzenfam. **2**(6): 182, 183 (1889).

ETYMOLOGY: *Eulophia*, a genus of orchids and Greek for appearance. Refers to a likeness to *Eulophia*.

TYPE SPECIES: *Eulophiopsis scripta* (Thouars) Pfitzer
(*Limodorum scriptum* Thouars)

This type name is now considered a synonym of *Graphorkis concolor* var. *alphabetica* F.N. Rasmussen

Now recognized as belonging to the genus *Graphorkis*, *Eulophiopsis* was previously considered to include five epiphytes found in low elevation, hill forests from Ivory Coast to Uganda and Zimbabwe to Madagascar and the Mascarene Islands to the Seychelles. These plants have bright yellow, cone-like pseudobulbs that become strongly furrowed with age, each with several leaves borne at the tip. The erect, branching, numerous-flowered inflorescence

| Currently Accepted | Validly Published | Invalidly Published | Published Pre-1753 | Superfluous Usage | Orthographic Variant | Fossil |

Orchid Genera • **156**

has small but attractive, yellow flowers with purple-brown or maroon markings and/or blotches. The white to pale yellow, trilobed lip has small, erect, oblong side lobes, the midlobe has raised, basal keels and a forward curving spur. The flowers have a slender, arched column has a hairy mound at the base.

EULOPHUS

R. Brown

Bot. Reg. **7**: sub 578 [573] (1821).

Orthography ICBN rejected vs. *Eulophia* R. Brown (1821) Orchidaceæ; and not *Eulophus* Nuttall ex A.P. Candolle (1829) Apiaceæ.

ETYMOLOGY: Greek for well and crest or nape of neck or ridge.

TYPE SPECIES: *Eulophus virens* (Roxburgh) R. Brown (*Limodorum virens* Roxburgh)

This type name is now considered a synonym of *Eulophia epidendraea* (J. König ex Retzius) C.E.C. Fischer; basionym replaced with *Serapias epidendraea* J. König ex Retzius

Not validly published, this name is referred to *Eulophia*. *Eulophus* was considered to include two terrestrials or epiphytes found in southwestern India (Maharashtra, Kerala and Tamil Nadu), Sri Lanka and Bangladesh.

EULOPIA

An orthographic variant introduced in *Hort. & J. Rural Art Rural Taste*, **3**: 55 (1857). The correct spelling is *Eulophia*.

EUNANNOS

Porto & Brade

Arq. Inst. Biol. Veg. **2**(2): 210, 212 (1935).

ETYMOLOGY: Greek for good, properly or true and small or dwarf. Refers to the small size of the plant to the size of the beautiful flower.

TYPE SPECIES: *Eunannos grandiflora* (Lindley) Porto & Brade (*Sophronitis grandiflora* Lindley)

This type name is now considered a synonym of *Sophronitis coccinea* (Lindley) Reichenbach f.; basionym *Sophronitis grandiflora* Lindley

Not validly published, this name is referred to *Sophronitis*. *Eunannos* was considered to include one epiphyte or lithophyte found in southeastern Brazil and northern Argentina (Misiones).

EUORCHIS

An orthographic variant introduced in *Field Guide Orchids*, 258 (1991). The correct spelling is *Eoorchis*.

EUOTHONAEA

Reichenbach *filius*

Bot. Zeitung (Berlin) **10**: 722 (1852).

ETYMOLOGY: Greek for beautiful or good and sail or membrane. Referring to the outer segments of the flower that resemble sails.

TYPE SPECIES: *None designated*

Now recognized as belonging to the genus *Scaphyglottis*, *Euothonaea* was previously considered to include two epiphytes or lithophytes found in low to mid elevation, hill forests to woodlands of Mexico to Panama, Colombia to Peru, the Guianas and Brazil. These small plants have clustered pseudobulbous stems, each with numerous nodes and thinly textured, grass-like leaves. The short, solitary-flowered inflorescence has a small, red-salmon flower subtended by a tightly compressed white bract. The lateral sepals and the entire lip are united to the column foot forming a chin-like protuberance.

EUPHLEBIUM

(Kraenzlin) Brieger

Orchideen (Schlechter), ed. 3 **1**(11-12): 722 (1981).

ETYMOLOGY: Greek for genuine or good and vein. Referring to the beautiful, radiating veins of the lip.

TYPE SPECIES: *Euphlebium spurium* (Blume) Brieger (*Dendrocolla spuria* Blume)

Now recognized as belonging to the genus *Dendrobium*, *Euphlebium* was previously considered to include six epiphytes or lithophytes found in low to mid elevation, hill and montane rain forests and swamps of Malaysia, Indonesia, the Philippines and New Guinea. These miniature plants have club-shaped, angled stems (often becoming hanging with age) with numerous internodes, each with two to three, narrow, dark green leaves located at the tip. The solitary-flowered inflorescences, borne near the stems' tips, emerge at the nodes of bare stems with the flower lasting only one day. The tiny, white to creamy flower opens fairly widely and the shortly clawed, concave, entire lip widens to a broad, roundish, creamy to pink-colored blade with radiating purple-brown veins. The flowers have a long, slender column.

EUPHROBOSCES

An orthographic variant introduced in *Icon. Pl. Ind. Orient. (Wight)*, **5**(1): 17 (1852). The correct spelling is *Euproboscis*.

EUPHROBOSCIS

An orthographic variant cited in *Icon. Pl. Ind. Orient. (Wight)*, **3**: t. 1732 (1851). The correct spelling is *Euproboscis*.

EUPROBISCIS

An orthographic variant introduced in *Orchideen (Schlechter)*, ed. 3, **6**(21-24): 363 (1976). The correct spelling is *Euproboscis*.

EUPROBOSCIS

Griffith

Calcutta J. Nat. Hist. **5**: 371, t. 37 (1845).

ETYMOLOGY: Greek for good and proboscis or nose. Descriptive of the anthers that are parallel with the column and prolonged into a long beak.

TYPE SPECIES: *Euproboscis pygmaea* Griffith

Now recognized as belonging to the genus *Thelasis*, *Euproboscis* was previously considered to include one epiphyte or lithophyte widely distributed in mid elevation, montane forests, cliff faces, valleys, river banks and rocky crevices from southern China (Yunnan to Hainan), northern India (Sikkim to Assam), Myanmar to Vietnam, Taiwan, Thailand, Malaysia and the Philippines to New Guinea. This miniature plant forms dense clusters from which each compressed pseudobulb bears two unequal, glossy leaves with prominent mid-veins. The numerous-flowered inflorescence has slightly purple bracts and tiny, uniformly pale green to yellow-green flowers that do not open widely. The obscurely trilobed lip has erect, roundish side lobes and an oblong midlobe with a blunt tip. The flowers have a short, footless column.

EUROPEDIUM

An orthographic variant introduced in *J. Hort. Cottage Gard.*, ser. 2, **4**: 275 (1863). The correct spelling is *Uropedium*.

EURYBLEMA

Dressler

Lankesteriana **5**(2): 94 (2005).

Epidendroideæ ◊ Cymbidieæ • Zygopetalinæ

ETYMOLOGY: Greek for broad and blanket or cover. Refers to the shape of the basal callus.

TYPE SPECIES: *Euryblema anatona* (Dressler) Dressler (*Cochleanthes anatona* Dressler)

Two sympodial epiphytes are found in mid elevation, montane forests from Panama to Colombia. These small plants have short stems, subtended by overlapping, distichous, purple spotted, leafy sheaths. The solitary-flowered inflorescence, borne from the axils of the leaf sheaths, has a large, showy, white to cream-colored, fragrant flower. The oblong dorsal sepal has a backward arching tip. The yellow to white, entire lip is deeply concave, densely covered with purple-brown spots, a broad, toothed callus, and a wavy margin. The flowers have a straight, slender column.

EURYCAULIS

M.A. Clements & D.L. Jones
Orchadian **13**(11): 490 (2002).
ETYMOLOGY: Greek for broad and stem. Referring to the wide, flattened pseudobulbs.
TYPE SPECIES: *Eurycaulis lamellatus*
(Blume) M.A. Clements & D.L. Jones
(*Onychium lamellatum* Blume)

Recognized as belonging to the genus *Dendrobium, Eurycaulis* was proposed to include five epiphytes in low to mid elevation, rain forests ranging from Myanmar, Thailand, Indonesia and New Guinea to the southwestern Pacific Archipelago. These plants have long, spindle-shaped, laterally flattened stems that are initially erect, then hanging with age. The thinly textured leaves are arranged in two ranks along most of the stem while older stems are leafless. The numerous to few-flowered inflorescence has white, creamy to yellow flowers, which are not long-lasting and turn darker as they age. The spoon-shaped, trilobed lip has a few rounded, fleshy keels, without distinct side lobes, has a bilobed midlobe and a chin-like protuberance. The above type name is now considered a synonym of *Dendrobium lamellatum* (Blume) Lindley.

EURYCENTRUM

Schlechter
Nachtr. Fl. Schutzgeb. Südsee 89 (1905).
Orchidoideæ ⚘ Cranichideæ • Goodyerinæ
ETYMOLOGY: Greek for broad or large and a spur. Referring to the conspicuously broad spur of the lip.
LECTOTYPE: *Eurycentrum obscurum*
(Blume) Schlechter
(*Cystorchis obscura* Blume)

Seven uncommon, sympodial terrestrials are found in shady, low to mid elevation, hill to montane forests of New Guinea and the Solomon Islands usually in deep humus soil. These erect to ascending plants have elongate stems, each with variegated or mottled, ovate, dark green-brown leaves that have purple undersides. The short to long, slightly hairy, few-flowered inflorescence has small, intricate, thinly textured, off-white to pale red-brown flowers with a bright red, deeply concave dorsal sepal. All the flowers face in one direction on the spike. The

tiny, entire or bilobed lip has a large, cone-like spur with a single, fleshy appendage on each side. The flowers have a short, wingless, footless column.

EURYCHONE

Schlechter
Beih. Bot. Centralbl. **36**(2): 134 (1918).
Epidendroideæ ⚘ Vandeæ • Aerangidinæ
ETYMOLOGY: Greek for broad and funnel. In reference to the funnel-shaped entrance to the spur.
TYPE SPECIES: *None designated*

Two uncommon, dwarf monopodial epiphytes are found in dark to shady, high humidity, low to mid elevation, hill to montane rain forests and scrub from the Ivory Coast to Angola and Zaire. Vegetatively, these small plants resemble *Phalaenopsis*. These plants have short stems, each several, broad, thick, leathery, dull olive-green leaves (set close together) that have wavy margins and unequally bilobed tips. The hanging, short, few-flowered inflorescence has relatively showy, translucent, large, sweetly fragrant, white to pink flowers usually hidden under the leaves. The broad, funnel to tubular-shaped, obscurely trilobed lip, which narrows into a long, club-shaped spur, has dark green or pink markings. The flowers have a short, stout, footless column.

EURYSTYLES

Wawra
Oesterr. Bot. Z. **13**: 223 (1863).
Not *Eurystylus* Bouché (1845) Cannaceæ.
Orchidoideæ ⚘ Cranichideæ • Spiranthinæ
ETYMOLOGY: Greek for broad or large and pillar or column. Refers to the short, broad column of the type species. This was in error, as the plant used to described the species by Wawra was deformed.
TYPE SPECIES: *Eurystyles cotyledon* Wawra

Eighteen diminutive sympodial epiphytes are restricted to damp, warm to cool, low to upper elevation, hill to montane cloud, evergreen and semi-deciduous forests from Cuba to Trinidad, Guatemala to Peru, Venezuela, the Guianas and northern Argentina (Misiones) with the largest concentration found in eastern Brazil. These small plants have a basal rosette of tiny, thinly textured leaves from which arises an erect to hanging, delicate, almost wiry, densely hairy inflorescence usually with a few sheaths similar to the leaves. The spirally arranged (clustered heads), numerous-flowered inflorescence has minute to small, tubular, mostly

white, dull pink to pale brown flowers with a green base; the thin, semi-transparent segments have a dark green midvein and often thickened tips. The sepals have concave bases and are covered on the outside by cilia or sharply pointed bristles. The distinctly clawed, entire lip is fused to the base of the lateral sepals. The flowers have a variable, long, slender column that occur in several different forms even within a single population.
NOTE: This genus, which had just one species when described by Wawra in 1863, was then found in the Brazilian state of Bahia. It was originally placed in the Zingiberaceæ (Gingers and wild Bananas) family by Wawra, but in 1904 Engler & Schumann (*Pflanzenr.*, **4**(46): 437) placed it correctly in the Orchidaceæ family.

EURYSTYLIS

An orthographic variant introduced in *Altas Orchid Poll.*, 80 (1995). The correct spelling is *Eurystyles*.

EUTHONAEA

An orthographic variant introduced in *Bot. Zeitung (Berlin)*, **10**: 772 (1852). The correct spelling is *Euothonaea*.

EVELEYNA

An orthographic variant cited in *Nomencl. Bot. (Steudel)*, ed. 2, **1**: 620 (1840). The correct spelling is *Evelyna*.

EVELINA

An orthographic variant introduced in *Enum. Pl. Mus. Paris*, ed. 2, 73 (1850). The correct spelling is *Evelyna*.

EVELYNA

Poeppig & Endlicher
Nov. Gen. Sp. Pl. (Poeppig & Endlicher)
1(7-10): 32, t. 56 (1836).
Not *Evelyna* Rafinesque (1838) Lauraceæ.
ETYMOLOGY: Commemorating John Evelyn (1620-1706), a British scholar, who to escape the English civil war, embarked on a period of travel in Italy and France. He was at the center of the intellectual, social, political, and ecclesiastical world of his day.
LECTOTYPE: *Evelyna capitata* Poeppig & Endlicher designated by Dressler, *Gen. Orch.*, **4**: 598 (2005), and Pfeiffer, *Nomencl. Bot. (Pfeiffer)*, **1**(2): 1321 (1874).

Now recognized as belonging to the genus *Elleanthus, Evelyna* was previously considered to include forty-six terrestrials and epiphytes found from Cuba to Trinidad, the Guianas, Venezuela and southern Mexico to

Currently Accepted | Validly Published | Invalidly Published | Published Pre-1753 | Superfluous Usage | Orthographic Variant | Fossil

Orchid Genera • **158**

Peru. These erect plants have reed-like, simple or branched stems, each with several, thinly textured, papery leaves toward their tips. The tightly compact, numerous-flowered inflorescence has colorful flowers, appearing successively, and are all concealed by extremely tight, brightly colored bracts usually exceeding the flower. These brightly colored, thinly textured flowers have a sac-like, entire lip. The flowers have an erect, footless column.

EVOTA

Rolfe
Fl. Cap. (Harvey) **5**(3): 268 (1913).
ETYMOLOGY: Greek for well or good and ear. Refers to the expanded arms of the rostellum.
LECTOTYPE: *Evota harveyana* (Lindley) Rolfe
(*Ceratandra harveyana* Lindley)

Now recognized as belonging to the genus *Ceratandra*, *Evota* was proposed to include three terrestrials found in low to mid elevation, coastal sandy soil and marshes of the Cape region in southwestern South Africa. These slender, showy plants have numerous, narrow leaves scattered along the erect, unbranched stem. The few-flowered inflorescence has white, yellow or green, fragrant flowers smelling of soap. The deeply bilobed lip is divided into two horns (rostellum), bent backward. The lip and gynostemium are fused together forming a large structure on a short stalk. These plants flower mainly after a fire sweeps through the local grasslands.

EVOTELLA

Kurzweil & H.P. Linder
Pl. Syst. Evol. **75**(3-4): 215 (1991).
Orchidoideæ 🌿 Orchideæ • Disinæ
ETYMOLOGY: *Evota*, a genus of orchids and Latin for diminutive.
TYPE SPECIES: *Evotella rubiginosa*
(Sonder ex Bolus) Kurzweil & H.P. Linder
(*Pterygodium rubiginosum* Sonder ex Bolus)

One sympodial terrestrial is found in mid elevation, grasslands and open scrub of the southwestern corner of the southern Cape area of South Africa. This robust, slender plant has erect, unbranched stems subtended by colorless leaf sheaths below the several, semi-pencil-like, fleshy leaves. The densely packed, numerous-flowered inflorescence is filled with cup-shaped flowers that have maroon, red to pink petals often lightly to heavily suffused maroon. The strikingly white, broadly triangular, hairy, entire lip has a hanging claw. The flowers have an erect column. The plant will usually only bloom after the disturbance of a fire.

EVRARDIA

Gagnepain
Bull. Mus. Natl. Hist. Nat., sér. 2 **4**(5): 596 (1932).
Not *Evrardia* Adanson (1763) Anacardiaceæ.
ETYMOLOGY: Dedicated to François Evrard (1885-1957), a French botanist and plant collector who donated his collection of plants from Indochina to the Paris Museum.
TYPE SPECIES: *Evrardia poilanei* Gagnepain

Not validly published because of a prior use of the name, this homonym was replaced by *Chamaegastrodia*.

EVRARDIANA

Averyanov
Russk. Bot. Zhurn. **73**(3): 432 (1988).
Not *Evrardia* Gagnepain (1932) Orchidaceæ.
ETYMOLOGY: *Evrardia*, a genus of orchids, and Greek for from.
TYPE SPECIES: *Evrardiana poilanei*
(Gagnepain) Averyanov
(*Evrardia poilanei* Gagnepain)

A superfluous name proposed as a substitute for *Evrardianthe*.

EVRARDIANTHA

An orthographic variant cited in *Orchideen* (Schlechter): *Liter. Reg. Band I/A, B, and C*, 166 (2003). The correct spelling is *Evrardianthe*.

EVRARDIANTHE

Rauschert
Feddes Repert. **94**(7-8): 433 (1983).
ETYMOLOGY: *Evrardia*, a genus of orchids and Latin for flower.
TYPE SPECIES: *Evrardianthe poilanei*
(Gagnepain) Rauschert
(*Evrardia poilanei* Gagnepain)

Now recognized as belonging to the genus *Odontochilus*, *Evrardianthe* was proposed to include one uncommon, saprophyte found in mid to upper elevation, montane evergreen forests from Japan, southwestern China (Xizang to Yunnan), Vietnam and northern Thailand. This dwarf, erect plant has branched, purple-red, stout stems that are mostly a series of overlapping, sheath-like bracts or scales that lack chlorophyll. The several, numerous-flowered, hairy inflorescences have dull purple-red, fragrant flowers. The dorsal sepal and petals converge, forming a hood over the column. The flared, deep yellow, bilobed lip is somewhat Y-shaped. The slightly dilated hypochile is concave or sac-like with two rounded calli at base. The mesochile has a short-claw, and the dilated, bilobed epichile has two horn-like, broad spreading, V-shaped

lobes at the tip. The flowers have a short, thick, footless column with two large, tooth-like projections below the stigma.

EXALARIA

Garay & G.A. Romero
Harvard Pap. Bot. **4**(2): 479 (1999).
Orchidoideæ 🌿 Cranichideæ • Cranichidinæ
ETYMOLOGY: Latin for without or lacking, and wing. Refers to the column structure that is without a winged portion which usually contains the anther.
TYPE SPECIES: *Exalaria parviflora*
(C. Presl) Garay & G.A. Romero
(*Ophrys parviflora* C. Presl)

One insignificant, sympodial terrestrial is widespread in low to upper elevation, hill to montane forests, woodlands, scrub, rocky to sandy cliff faces and roadsides of the northern Andes from Venezuela to Peru. This colony-forming, tufted plant has unbranched, erect stems, each with a basal rosette of leaves. The erect, densely packed, few-flowered inflorescence has tiny, white flowers with a single (usually green) nerve on each segment, and the flower's outside surface is covered with soft hairs. The small, obscurely trilobed lip is slightly sac-like at its base. The flowers have a short, stout, erect, wingless, footless column.

EXERIA

Rafinesque
Fl. Tellur. **4**: 49 (1836)[1837].
ETYMOLOGY: Greek for from and *Eria*, a genus of orchids. A new name derived from *Eria*.
TYPE SPECIES: *None designated*

A superfluous name proposed as a substitute for *Eria*.

EXOCHANTHUS

M.A. Clements & D.L. Jones
Orchadian **13**(11): 496 (2002).
ETYMOLOGY: Greek for projecting and flower. Refers to the upward position of the lip.
TYPE SPECIES: *Exochanthus pleianthus*
(Schlechter) M.A. Clements & D.L. Jones
(*Dendrobium pleianthum* Schlechter)

Recognized as belonging to the genus *Dendrobium*, *Exochanthus* was proposed to include three epiphytes or terrestrials growing in low elevation, peat or on land slips of New Guinea and the Solomon Islands. These large plants have erect to suberect, slender to flattened stems, each with narrow, slightly drooping, leathery leaves spaced along the stem's length that are twisted to all face in one direction. The several, short, few-flowered inflorescences has tiny, white to pale yellow flowers, not always opening widely, with a wide dorsal sepal and slightly narrower, lateral sepals. The wedge-shaped trilobed lip has small, erect side lobes with a warty, orange-yellow callus at the base of the midlobe which is edged in dark maroon.

EXOPHYA

Rafinesque

Fl. Tellur. **2**: 63 (1836)[1837].

ETYMOLOGY: Latin for outer and growth. Alluding to the drawing by Rafinesque that appears to show a lateral inflorescence. Of some note, there are no records that any of Rafinesque's illustrations exist today.

TYPE SPECIES: *Exophya fuscata* Rafinesque nom. illeg.
Epidendrum patens Swartz

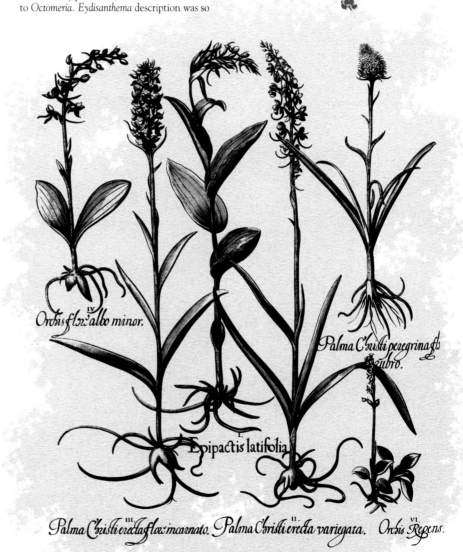

Now recognized as belonging to the genus *Epidendrum*, *Exophya* was previously considered to include one epiphyte or occasional lithophyte found in low to mid elevation, hill to montane forests and swamps from Puerto Rico to Trinidad and the Guianas. The whole plant changes color from red to maroon when exposed to bright sunlight, and when shaded, will fade to green. This plant has small, pear-shaped pseudobulbs, each with two narrow, grass-like leaves. The few-flowered inflorescence has long-lasting, rigid, small, yellow-green to red-brown flowers often suffused purple. The trilobed lip has large, oblong side lobes and a short, bilobed midlobe. The flowers have a long, slender column with a broad tip.

EXPANGIS

Thouars

Hist. Orchid. Table 2, sub 3o, *t. 57* (1822).

Name published without a description. Today this name is most often referred to *Angraecum*.

EXPEDICULA

Luer

Monogr. Syst. Bot. Missouri Bot. Gard. **103**: 308 (2005).

ETYMOLOGY: Latin for improper or immoral. Refers to the small, roundish flowers.

TYPE SPECIES: *Expedicula apoda*
(Garay & Dunsterville) Luer
(*Pleurothallis apoda* Garay & Dunsterville)

Recognized as belonging to the genus *Pleurothallis*, *Expedicula* was proposed to include two epiphytes or occasional lithophytes found in upper elevation, montane forests of Venezuela, Colombia and Ecuador to Bolivia. These dwarf,

creeping plants have erect stems, each with a solitary, dark purple-green, fleshy, rough surfaced leaf. The few-flowered inflorescence has small, translucent, brown-red to bright maroon-pink flowers opening widely and singly in succession. The deeply concave lateral sepals are united for half their length and the narrower petals have tapered tails. The tiny, yellow, entire lip is usually cup-shaped with the side lobes standing upright along side the short, footless, wingless column. The midlobe is found buried in the cup of the lateral sepals.

EYDISANTHEMA

Necker

Elem. Bot. (Necker) **3**: 133 (1790).

ETYMOLOGY: Greek for not like and flower. Refers perhaps to not being like *Disa*, a genus of orchids.

TYPE SPECIES: *None designated*

Not validly published, this name is referred to *Octomeria*. *Eydisanthema* description was so vague that when Rafinesque (*Fl. Tellur.*, **4**: 36 (1836)[1837]) reviewed the description, he could only conclude that the name might belong with *Octomeria*. But Theophile Durand (*Index Genera Phranerogamorum*, 587 (1888)) thought that the name might belong with *Epidendrum*.

EYDISENTHEMA

An orthographic variant introduced in *Hort. Donat.*, 172 (1858). The correct spelling is *Eydisanthema*.

EYDYSANTHEMA

An orthographic variant introduced in *Dict. Hist. Nat.*, **6**: 384 (1824). The correct spelling is *Eydisanthema*.

Orchis flor. albo minor.

Palma Christi peregrina fl. rubro.

Epipactis latifolia

Palma Christi erecta flor. incarnato. *Palma Christi erecta variegata.* *Orchis Regens.*

Besler *Hortus Eystettensis* plate 196 (1613).

Currently Accepted   Validly Published   Invalidly Published   Published Pre-1753   Superfluous Usage   Orthographic Variant   Fossil

Orchid Genera · **160**

FAJUS

An orthographic variant introduced in *Séance Publique Soc. Argic.*, 194 (1852). The correct spelling is *Phaius*.

FARICARIA

An orthographic variant introduced in *J. Roy. Hort. Soc.*, **7**(1): 112 (1886). The correct spelling is *Forficaria*.

FELIPOGON

An orthographic variant introduced in *Sin. Fl. Cuzco*, 199 (1941). The correct spelling is *Telipogon*.

FENSOA

An orthographic variant introduced in *Orchid Fl. Kamrup Distr. Assam*, 128 (2001). The correct spelling is *Jensoa*.

FERDINANDEZIA

An orthographic variant introduced in *Ill. Hort.*, **29**: 51 (1882). The correct spelling is *Fernandezia*.

FERNANDESIA

An orthographic variant introduced in *Syn. Pl. (Persoon)*, **2**: 517 (1807). The correct spelling is *Fernandezia*.

FERNANDEZIA

Ruiz & Pavón
Fl. Peruv. Prodr.   123, *t.* 27 (1794).

Epidendroideæ ⚬ **Cymbidieæ** • **Oncidiinæ**

ETYMOLOGY: Dedicated to Gregorio García Fernández (*fl.* late 1700s), a Spanish physician, botanist and vice president of the real academia medica Matritense (Madrid) and institue of botany.

LECTOTYPE: *Fernandezia subbiflora* Ruiz & Pavón

Nine tiny, monopodial epiphytes are found in wet, cold, windy, upper elevation, montane cloud forests of Costa Rica and Venezuela to Peru. These plants have erect, hanging to horizontal, fleshy stems, each with tiny, needle-like, dark green leaves that have only the growing tips curved upward. The stems are concealed by distichous, overlapping, leaf-bearing sheaths. The several, short, solitary-flowered inflorescences have a small, showy flower ranging from brilliant pink to bright vermilion red with the petals usually larger than the sepals. The broad, large, usually entire lip is often fan-shaped. The flowers have a broadly winged, sac-like column with notched margins, which clasp the lip callus. Many of these species were formerly included in *Nasonia*.

FERNANDEZIA

Lindley
Gen. Sp. Orchid. Pl.   207 (1833), and
Edwards's Bot. Reg.   **21**: *t.* 1806 (1835).

Not validly published, this name is most often referred to *Lockhartia*.

FERRUMINARIA

Garay, Hamer & Siegerist
Nordic J. Bot.   **14**(6): 635 (1994).

ETYMOLOGY: Latin for cement or bind and join. In reference to the lip that is continuous with the column foot.

TYPE SPECIES: *Ferruminaria brastagiensis* (Carr) Garay, Hamer & Siegerist (*Bulbophyllum brastagiense* Carr)

Now recognized as belonging to the genus *Bulbophyllum*, *Ferruminaria* was proposed to include three epiphytes found in low elevation, hill forests of Malaysia, Indonesia and New Guinea. These small plants have numerous, clustered, grooved pseudobulbs, each with a solitary, fleshy leaf. The several, clustered, solitary-flowered inflorescences have small, widespreading, green, orange to yellow flowers opening in succession. The flowers have a free column foot and lack a hinged lip. The flowers have a small, trilobed lip with tiny, erect, white side lobes and an oblong, dark red midlobe. The sepals have red markings and hairy margins; the small, pale green petals are covered with black dots. The flowers have a small column. The above type name is now considered a synonym of *Bulbophyllum crepidiferum* J.J. Smith.

FIELDIA

Gaudichaud-Beaupré
Freycinet's Voy. Uranie, Bot.   424, *t.* 36 (1826)[1829].
Not *Fieldia* A. Cunningham (1825) Gesneriaceæ.

ETYMOLOGY: Dedicated to Barron Field (1786-1846), a British-born Australian judge in the high court located at Port Jackson, New South Wales, where he assisted botanical collectors with their work in the Spice Islands (Maluku are located in the eastern Indonesian Archipelago).

TYPE SPECIES: *Fieldia lissochiloides* Gaudichaud-Beaupré

Not validly published because of a prior use of the name, this homonym was replaced by *Vandopsis*.

FILANGIS

Thouars
Hist. Orchid.   Table 2, sub 3o, *t.* 52 (1822).

Name published without a description. Today this name is most often referred to *Angraecum*.

FIMBRIELLA

Farwell ex **Butzin**
Willdenowia   **11**(2): 323 (1981).

ETYMOLOGY: Latin for fringed or shreds and diminutive. Refers to both the small size of the plant and the fringed lip.

TYPE SPECIES: *Fimbriella lacera* (Michaux) Butzin (*Orchis lacera* Michaux)

Now recognized as belonging to the genus *Platanthera*, *Fimbriella* was previously considered to include one terrestrial found in cold, low to mid elevation, sphagnum bogs of eastern Canada (Ontario, New Brunswick and Nova Scotia) and the eastern United States (Minnesota to Maine and Arkansas to South Carolina). This tall, erect plant has several, narrow, dark green leaves clasping the erect, unbranched stem. The numerous-flowered inflorescence has large flowers in various shades of purple, pale yellow, green to pure white. The deeply trilobed lip curves upward, has a shallow to deeply, heavily fringed margin, and has a long, slender spur. The flowers have a small column.

FIMBRORCHIS

Szlachetko

Orchidee (Hamburg) **55**(4): 489 (2004).

ETYMOLOGY: Latin for thread-like or shaped and Greek for orchid. Refers to the narrow fringe or slender processes on the lip's extravagant side lobes.

TYPE SPECIES: *Fimbrorchis trichosantha*
(Wallich ex Lindley) Szlachetko
(*Habenaria trichosantha* Wallich ex Lindley)

Recognized as belonging to the genus *Habenaria*, *Fimbrorchis* was proposed to include ten terrestrials found in low to mid elevation, hill to montane forests and grasslands from eastern Russia (Amur to Primorye), Korea to Japan, eastern China (Anhui to Guangdong), Bhutan, Myanmar to Vietnam, Indonesia (Borneo, Sulawesi and Maluku), Thailand and Malaysia. These erect plants have long or short, unbranched stems, each with narrow, grass-like leaves. The numerous to few-flowered inflorescence has green to yellow-green flowers. The spoon or hood-shaped dorsal sepal and narrow petals converge, forming a hood over the short column. The pure white, trilobed lip has side lobes with numerous, long, slender, multibranched segments, a narrow or slightly trilobed midlobe, and has a long, narrow, green, slightly swollen spur.

FINETIA

Schlechter

Beih. Bot. Centralbl. **36**(2): 140 (1918).

Not *Finetia* Gagnepain (1917) Combretaceæ.

ETYMOLOGY: Dedicated to Achille Eugène Finet (1863-1913), a French botanist, laboratory assistant, editor of *Notulae systematicae*, and a superb illustrator who specialized in the orchids of southeast Asia.

TYPE SPECIES: *Finetia falcata* (Thunberg) Schlechter
(*Orchis falcata* Thunberg)

Not validly published because of a prior use of the name, this homonym was replaced by *Neofinetia*.

FINGARDIA

Szlachetko

Fragm. Florist. Geobot. **3**(Suppl.): 134 (1995).

ETYMOLOGY: In honor of Finn Nygaard Rasmussen (1948-), a Danish botanist and professor of theoretical taxonomy and evolution in Orchidaceæ at the Botanical Institute in Copenhagen.

TYPE SPECIES: *Fingardia nephroglossa*
(Schlechter) Szlachetko
(*Microstylis nephroglossa* Schlechter)

Now recognized as belonging to the genus *Malaxis*, *Fingardia* was proposed to include ten terrestrials found in leaf litter or swampy soils of low elevation, hill forests from Malaysia, Indonesia, the Philippines and New Guinea to Australia. These plants have spindle-shaped pseudobulbs, each with brown-purple leaves that have pale green bands. The tiny flowers are highly complex in structure and are borne on compact, densely packed inflorescences. The dull green-yellow flowers have conspicuously nerved sepals and petals. The broad, trilobed lip is often suffused purple-brown, has a prominent finger-like, basal callus and a shallowly notched midlobe.

FISSIA

(Luer) Luer

Monogr. Syst. Bot. Missouri Bot. Gard. **105**: 9 (2006).

ETYMOLOGY: Latin for split or to divide. Referring to its separation from *Masdevallia*.

TYPE SPECIES: *Fissia picturata* (Reichenbach f.) Luer
(*Masdevallia picturata* Reichenbach f.)

Recognized as belonging to the genus *Masdevallia*, *Fissia* was proposed to include three epiphytes or lithophytes found in wet, mid to upper elevation, montane cloud forests from Costa Rica to Bolivia, and the Guianas. These small plants have short, erect stems, subtended by thinly textured, tubular sheaths, each with a solitary, narrow to ovate, leathery leaf. The erect, solitary-flowered inflorescence has a widely varied in color and pattern flower with the large sepals tapering into long, slender tails. The small, erect petals have a rounded appendage above the base, sharply, toothed tips and are found alongside the slender, more or less club-shaped column. The oblong, entire lip has marginal folds dividing it into epichile and hypochile sections.

FISSIPES

Small

Fl. S.E. U.S. 311, 1329 (1903).

ETYMOLOGY: Latin for divide or to split and foot. Referring to the cleft lip.

TYPE SPECIES: *Fissipes acaulis* (Aiton) Small
(*Cypripedium acaule* Aiton)

Now recognized as belonging to the genus *Cypripedium*, *Fissipes* was previously considered to include one terrestrial found in low to mid elevation, boggy swamps of Canada (Northwest Territories to Nova Scotia and Labrador) and the eastern United States (Minnesota to Maine and South Carolina). This erect, unbranched plant has a pair of soft, bright green leaves that are almost sticky from dense hairs. The solitary-flowered inflorescence, borne on a slightly hairy rachis, has a flower found in various shades from yellow-green to green-brown. The twisted, lateral sepals and petals are suffused purple. The narrow, slightly cup-shaped, dorsal sepal forms a hood over the column. The large, sac-like lip varies from pink to pure white with darker colored veins. The pouched shaped lip has a longitudinal cleft down the center and has a deeply inrolled margin.

FITZGERALDIA

F. Mueller

S. Sci. Rec. **2**: 56 (1882).

Not *Fitzgeraldia* F. Mueller (1867) Annonaceæ.

ETYMOLOGY: In honor of Robert Desmond (David) FitzGerald (1830-1892), an Irish-born Australian deputy surveyor general in New South Wales, an ornithologist, botanical illustrator and author of *Australian Orchids*.

TYPE SPECIES: *Fitzgeraldia ellipticus* F. Mueller

Not validly published because of a prior use of the name, this homonym was replaced by *Pyrorchis*.

FITZGERALDIELLA

Schlechter

Notizbl. Bot. Gart. Berlin-Dahlem **9**(88): 590 (1926).

ETYMOLOGY: Commemorating Robert Desmond FitzGerald (1830-1892). And Latin for diminutive.

TYPE SPECIES: *None designated*

Name published without a description. Today this name is most often referred to *Sarcochilus*.

Currently Accepted   Validly Published   Invalidly Published   Published Pre-1753   Superfluous Usage   Orthographic Variant   Fossil

Orchid Genera • **162**

FLABELLOGRAPHIS

Thouars
Hist. Orchid. Table 2, sub 3n, *t. 39* (1822).

Name published without a description. Today this name is most often referred to *Cymbidiella*.

FLABELLORCHIS

An orthographic variant introduced in *Hist. Orchid.*, *t. 40* (1822). The correct spelling is *Flabellographis*.

FLAGELLARIA

Noroña
Verh. Batav. Genootsch. Kunsten, ed. 1 **5**: 16 (1790).
Not *Flagellaria* Linnaeus (1753) Flagellariaceæ, and not *Flagellaria* Stackhouse (1809) Phaeophyceæ-Gracilariaceæ.
ETYMOLOGY: Greek for whip-like. Refers to the long, thin, supple shoots.
TYPE SPECIES: *Flagellaria araneiflora*
(Linnaeus) Noroña
(*Epidendrum flos-aeris* Linnaeus)
This type name is now considered a synonym of
Arachnis flos-aeris (Linnaeus) Reichenbach f.
basionym
Epidendrum flos-aeris Linnaeus

Not validly published because of a prior use of the name, this homonym was replaced by *Arachnis*.

FLAVILEPTIS

Thouars
Hist. Orchid. Table 1, sub 2h, *t. 25* (1822).

Name published without a description. Today this name is most often referred to *Liparis*.

FLEXUOSATIS

Thouars
Hist. Orchid. Table 1, sub 1c, *t. 7, t. 12f* (1822).

Name published without a description. Today this name is most often referred to *Schizodium*.

FLICKINGERIA

A.D. Hawkes
Orchid Weekly **2**(46): 451 (1961).
Epidendroideæ 〰 Dendrobiinæ • Currently unplaced
ETYMOLOGY: Named for Edward A. Flickinger (fl. 1950-1970s), a British-born American publisher of garden journals, and editor of both the *Orchid Weekly* (1958-66) and the *Orchid Journal* (1955-59).
TYPE SPECIES: *Flickingeria angulata*
(Blume) A.D. Hawkes
(*Desmotrichum angulatum* Blume)

Seventy sympodial epiphytes or rare terrestrials are found in low to mid elevation, open hill to montane forests and along river banks from southern China (Yunnan to Hainan), India (Andaman and Nicobar islands), Myanmar to Vietnam, Indonesia, the Philippines, New Guinea and Australia to the southwestern Pacific Archipelago. These plants have tufted, branched, erect or hanging stems with one internode dilated into one to several thickened, club-like to spindle-shaped pseudobulbs, each with a solitary, terminal leaf. The inflorescence is borne from the tip of the pseudobulb or a little below the tip, but this seems to even change with the age of the plant. The number and length of the nodes on stems below the first pseudobulb seems to increase with the plant's age. The usually solitary-flowered inflorescence has a small, fragrant, white, green or bright yellow flower lasting for only a day and even then is often closed by mid-day. The flowers have their lateral sepals fused to the column's long, distinct foot producing a chin-like projection. The trilobed or rarely entire lip has two to three keels, erect side lobes and the midlobe varies widely in shape and decoration. The flowers have a short, fleshy column.

FLOS

Rumphius
Herb. Amboin. (*Rumphius*) **6**: 115, *t. 52, f. 2* (1750).
ETYMOLOGY: Latin for flower.
TYPE SPECIES: *None designated*

Pre-1753, therefore not validly published in fulfillment of nomenclatural rules. There were three orchids published using the same first name of *Flos* and all are terrestrials. *Flos triplicatus, Helleborus amboinicus* is one widespread herb from Africa to India, Sri Lanka, southern China, Japan, Indonesia and Australia to Fiji. This highly variable plant has ovoid pseudobulbs, each with several, deep green or silvery, ribbed leaves that are hairy on the underside. The numerous-flowered inflorescence has showy, white flowers with pale green tips on the sepals. The trilobed lip has a deeply divided midlobe, a bright yellow or red callus, and a slender, curved spur. This name is now usually considered a synonym of *Calanthe triplicata* (Willemet) Ames.

Another published name, also a terrestrial, *Flos susannae* (**8**: 286, *t. 99, f. 2*), is a widespread herb found from southern China, northern India, Myanmar to Vietnam, Malaysia and Japan. This robust plant has thick, leafy stems, subtended by several, bladeless sheaths at the base, each with several, oblong leaves. The few-flowered inflorescence has large, white, nocturnally fragrant flowers with an extravagantly fringed, trilobed lip and a long cylindrical spur. The flower has an erect column. This name is now usually considered a synonym of *Pecteilis susannae* (Linnaeus) Rafinesque.

The third name, also a terrestrial, is called a *smaller kind* (**8**: 288). This plant is found scattered from Laos, Thailand and Indonesia to northern Australia. A widely variable plant that has erect, unbranched stems, each with several, narrow, grass-like leaves scattered along the stem. The few-flowered inflorescence has tiny, white, yellow or purple flowers. The dorsal sepal and petals converge, forming a hood over the stout column. The trilobed lip has narrow side lobes and midlobe and has a long, narrow spur. This name is now usually considered a synonym of *Habenaria rumphii* (Brongniart) Lindley.

FOLIUM

Rumphius
Herb. Amboin. (*Rumphius*) **6**: 93, *t. 41, f. 3* (1750).
ETYMOLOGY: Latin for leaf.
TYPE SPECIES: *Folium petolatum* Rumphius

Pre-1753, therefore not validly published in fulfillment of nomenclatural rules. There are two different terrestrials found in Indonesia (Java and Sumatra), India and Sri Lanka among the fallen leaves of tropical wet, mid elevation, evergreen forests growing in small groups. The first herb is grown mostly for its green-black leaves that have an intricate network of silvery white veins. The erect, few-flowered inflorescence has tiny, green flowers with red tips and has an unusually fringed, large, white, bilobed lip. This name is now usually considered a synonym of *Anoectochilus setaceus* Blume.

The other erect herb also has dark green leaves, but with longitudinal, golden-yellow veins, that resembles a local textile pattern - Patola. It has small, red-brown flowers with a white, trilobed lip. This name is now usually considered a synonym of *Macodes javanica* (Blume) Hooker f.

FORBESINA

Ridley

J. Bot. **63**(Suppl.): 120 (1925).

ETYMOLOGY: Honoring Henry Ogg Forbes (1851-1932), a Scottish scientist, orchid collector and explorer of South America and the Malaysian Archipelago. He was later a director of the Canterbury Museum in New Zealand.

TYPE SPECIES: *Forbesina eriiformis* Ridley
This type name is now considered a synonym of *Eria appendiculata* (Blume) Lindley; basionym *Dendrolirium appendiculatum* Blume

Now recognized as belonging to the genus *Eria*, *Forbesina* was previously considered to include one epiphyte found in wet, low to mid elevation, hill to montane forests from Indonesia (Sumatra) to northern Australia. This plant often grows into large, dense mats with all of the segments being hairy. The plant has finger-like, clustered pseudobulbs, subtended by sheaths when young, each with two or three, thick leaves. The few-flowered, hairy inflorescence has tiny, pale purple to yellow-brown flowers opening occasionally, not opening fully or even sometimes not at all. The trilobed lip has purple side lobes, and a curved, white midlobe with an erect, mauve disk.

FORFICARIA

Lindley

Gen. Sp. Orchid. Pl. 362 (1838).

ETYMOLOGY: Latin for a pair of scissors. Descriptive of the flower when in bud.

TYPE SPECIES: *Forficaria graminifolia* Lindley

Now recognized as belonging to the genus *Disa*, *Forficaria* was previously considered to include one terrestrial found in low elevation, well-drained, pebbly ground of the extreme southern Cape region of South Africa. This erect plant has unbranched stems, each with several, narrow, grass-like leaves. The slender, few-flowered inflorescence has yellow, green-yellow or bright blue-purple flowers. The bright blue-purple or white, entire lip is edged in dark blue or purple and often extravagantly fringed. The above type name is now considered a synonym of *Disa forficaria* Bolus.

FORNICARIA

Blume ex d'Orbigny

Dict. Univ. Hist. Nat. **9**: 170 (1847).
Not *Fornicaria* Rafinesque (1838) Asteraceæ.

Name published without a description. Today this name is most often referred to as a section of *Aerides*.

FORSYTHMAJORA

An orthographic variant introduced in *Fl. Madagasc.*, 90 (1936). The correct spelling is *Forsthmajoria*.

FORSYTHMAJORIA

Kraenzlin ex Schlechter

Orchideen (Schlechter), ed. 1   73 (1914).

ETYMOLOGY: In honor of Charles Immanuel Forsythmajor (1843-1923), a Swiss botanist, zoologist and vertebrate paleontologist who travelled widely and collected the flora of Madagascar and Italy.

TYPE SPECIES: *Forsythmajoria pulchra* Kraenzlin ex Schlechter (*Bicornella pulchra* Schlechter)
This type name is now considered a synonym of *Cynorkis lilacina* var. *pulchra* (Kraenzlin ex Schlechter) H. Perrier;

Not validly published, this name is referred to *Cynorkis*. *Forsythmajoria* was considered to include one terrestrial widespread in Madagascar and the Comoros Islands.

FRACTIUNGUIS

Schlechter

Anexos Mem. Inst. Butantan, Secç. Bot. **1**(4): 55 (1922).

ETYMOLOGY: Latin for week or feeble and a nail. Descriptive of the long, bent claw of the lip.

LECTOTYPE: *Fractiunguis reflexa* (Reichenbach f.) Schlechter (*Hexisea reflexa* Reichenbach f.)

Now recognized as belonging to the genus *Scaphyglottis*, *Fractiunguis* was previously considered to include three epiphytes found in wet, low to mid elevation, hill forests and woodlands from Trinidad, the Guianas, Venezuela, Costa Rica to Bolivia and Brazil. These unremarkable plants have slender, usually hanging, branched stems, each with two long, pencil-like, deeply grooved leaves. The short, few-flowered inflorescence, borne from the leaf axils, usually has only one, short-lived, green-brown flower open at a time. The tiny, inconspicuous, pale green flowers have a few purple markings but are of no great beauty. The flowers have a short, footless column.

FRAGRANGIS

Thouars

Hist. Orchid.   Table 2, sub 3o, t. 54 (1822).

Name published without a description. Today this name is most often referred to *Jumellea*.

FREGEA

Reichenbach *filius*

Bot. Zeitung (Berlin)   **10**: 712 (1852).

ETYMOLOGY: In honor of Christian Gottlieb Frege (1778-1855), a German entrepreneur, merchant, banker and counselor from Leipzig, who was a friend of Reichenbach.

TYPE SPECIES: *Fregea amabilis* Reichenbach f.

Now recognized as belonging to the genus *Sobralia*, *Fregea* was previously considered to include two terrestrials or epiphytes that are found in cool, mid to upper elevation, montane forests and pastures of Costa Rica and Panama. These plants have cane-like stems, each with thinly textured, heavily veined, leathery, dark green leaves united to the tubular leaf-sheaths. The short, solitary to few-flowered inflorescence has a small but showy, thinly textured, short-lived, intensely bright or deep red-purple color flower. The tubular, trilobed lip, attached to the column base, lacks either a prominent calli or disk. The flowers have a short column with a trilobed tip.

FRONDARIA

Luer

Monogr. Syst. Bot. Missouri Bot. Gard. **15**: 29 (1986).

Epidendroideæ ⚬ Epidendreæ • Pleurothallidinæ

ETYMOLOGY: Latin for a crown of leaves or foliage. Refers to the leaf-like sheaths that adorn the stem.

TYPE SPECIES: *Frondaria caulescens* (Lindley) Luer (*Pleurothallis caulescens* Lindley)

One sympodial epiphyte that is restricted to upper elevation, montane forests of the Andes from Colombia to central Bolivia. This tiny plant has slender, erect stems, subtended by small, narrow, leaf-like sheaths occurring upward along the stem, each with several, leathery leaves. The several, erect, numerous to few-flowered inflorescence has minute, nodding to hanging, transparent pale yellow or green-yellow flowers with long, narrow sepals, and much smaller, roundish petals. All the flowers open simultaneously. The minuscule, ovate lip is trilobed below the middle, the rounded side lobes curve upward and the ovate to oblong midlobe is rounded and shallowly notched. The flowers have a short, slightly curved, wingless column.

Currently Accepted   Validly Published   Invalidly Published   Published Pre-1753   Superfluous Usage   Orthographic Variant   Fossil

Orchid Genera • **164**

FROSCULA

Rafinesque

Fl. Tellur. **4**: 44 (1836)[1837].

ETYMOLOGY: Said to be dedicated to a nymph but none of this name is known in classical literature.

Greek Mythology. Hesiod's (fl. 800 BC) poem *Theogony* (a codified genealogy of the many myths of the Greek gods) mentions there are some three thousand different sea-nymphs.

TYPE SPECIES: *Froscula hispida* Rafinesque nom. illeg.
Dendrobium longicornu Lindley

Now recognized as belonging to the genus *Dendrobium*, *Froscula* was previously considered to include one epiphyte found in cool to humid, mid to upper elevation, mixed, piney and moss-laden forests of the northwestern India (Assam), Bhutan and Myanmar to southern China (Guangxi). This small, slender plant has leafy stems. The young, apple green stems have short, black hairs with the older, ridged stems becoming darker and often leafless. The several, one- to two-flowered inflorescences are borne from a tip of the older internodes. The small, generally drooping, long-lasting, white flowers, often not opening fully, have a blotch of orange-yellow on the trilobed lip. The side lobes have pale apricot, colored veins, the midlobe is beautifully fringed, and a small spur.

FRUTICICOLA

M.A. Clements & D.L. Jones

Orchadian **13**(11): 499 (2002).

ETYMOLOGY: Latin for a dweller in bushy areas. Refers to the preferred growth of hanging from the tree limbs.

TYPE SPECIES: *Fruticicola albopunctata*
(Schlechter) M.A. Clements & D.L. Jones
(*Bulbophyllum fruticicola* Schlechter)

Recognized as belonging to the genus *Bulbophyllum*, *Fruticicola* was proposed to include two epiphytes found in wet, low to mid elevation, rain forests and woodlands of New Guinea and northeastern Australia (Queensland) hanging from trees. These small, creeping plants have tiny, slightly roundish pseudobulbs, each with a solitary, narrow, channeled leaf. The short, several (in bundles), solitary-flowered inflorescences have a minute, white or pink flower with several, dark red stripes. The slightly concave, erect dorsal sepal has three nerves, and the minute, erect petals are hairy along their margin. The mobile, pink, entire lip is recurved above the middle and has a hairy margin. The flowers have a short, stout column. The above type name is now considered a synonym of *Bulbophyllum fruticicola* Schlechter.

FU

Kaempfer

Am. Exot. 864, t. 865 (1712).

ETYMOLOGY: A local, Japanese name for wind.

TYPE SPECIES: *Fu ran* Kaempfer

Pre-1753, therefore not validly published in fulfillment of nomenclatural rules; this binomial name is most often referred to *Dendrobium*. *Fu* was previously considered to include one epiphyte found in low to mid elevation, hill and montane forests of south-eastern China (Guangxi) and northern Taiwan. This erect plant has somewhat flattened and sparsely branched stems often swollen into club-shaped, noded pseudobulbs, each with several, oblong, leathery leaves. The few-flowered inflorescence, borne toward the apical portion of the leafless stems, has fragrant, white flowers heavily suffused pink to purple toward the tips. The shortly clawed, entire lip clasps the short column below middle This name is now usually considered a synonym of *Dendrobium linawianum* Reichenbach f.

FUERTESIELLA

Schlechter

Symb. Antill. **7**: 492 (1913).

Orchidoideæ ⊩ Cranichideæ • Cranichidinæ

ETYMOLOGY: In honor of Pére Miguel Domingo Fuertes de Lorén (1871-1926), a Spanish-born Cuban priest who collected and studied the flora of Cuba and Hispaniola. And Latin for diminutive.

TYPE SPECIES: *Fuertesiella pterichoides* Schlechter

One uncommon sympodial terrestrial is found in mid elevation, pine and montane moss laden forests of eastern Cuba and a small area in the central Dominican Republic. This small, erect plant has simple, unbranched stems, each with one or two, heart-shaped to oval, basal leaves usually withered by flowering time. The erect, then nodding, slender, congested, hairy, few-flowered inflorescence has tubular bracts. The proportionately large, brown flowers are subtended by tapering sheaths. The nerved, narrow sepals are sparsely, long haired on the outer surfaces, and the short, narrow petals are joined to the dorsal sepal. The white, heart-shaped, entire or obscurely trilobed lip has a flattened margin and a V-shaped, yellow and brown spotted callus. The flowers have a short, inconspicuous column.

FUNCKIELLA

An orthographic variant introduced in *Bot. Mus. Leafl.*, **28**(4): 320 (1980)[1982]. The correct spelling is *Funkiella*.

FUNKIELLA

Schlechter

Beih. Bot. Centralbl. **37**(2): 430 (1920).

Orchidoideæ ⊩ Cranichideæ • Spiranthinæ

ETYMOLOGY: Dedicated to Nicolas Funck (1816-1896), a Luxemburg naturalist, director of the Zoological Gardens in Brussels and Cologne, and an explorer and orchid collector in Central and South America. And Latin for diminutive.

TYPE SPECIES: *Funkiella hyemalis*
(A. Richard & Galeotti) Schlechter
(*Spiranthes hyemalis* A. Richard & Galeotti)

Four sympodial terrestrials or occasional epiphytes are found in mid to upper elevation, montane meadows, humus soil, leaf litter, rocky scrub and oak-pine forests from the south-western United States (southern Texas) and Mexico to Costa Rica. These slender, erect to bow-shaped plants, leafless during flowering, have unbranched, delicate to stout stems, each with a basal rosette of pale green leaves. The erect, few-flowered inflorescence, smooth throughout or densely hairy above, has large, tubular, bright yellow to white flowers with an erect, concave dorsal sepal. The erect, short to obscurely clawed, boat-shaped, rarely entire lip forms a narrow, tunnel-like access to the nectary, has a red, thick callus in the center or has no thickenings, and has veins on the margin and outer surface. The flowers have a straight, short to obscure, footless column.

FUSIDENDRIS

Thouars

Hist. Orchid. Table 3, sub 3q, t. 86 (1822).

Name published without a description. Today this name is most often referred to *Polystachya*.

GABERTIA

Gaudichaud-Beaupré

Freycinet's Voy. Uranie, Bot. 425 (1826)[1829].

ETYMOLOGY: Dedicated to a Mr. Gabert (*fl.* in early 1800s), a French-born secretary to the expedition on which Gaudichaud sailed and worked.

TYPE SPECIES: *Gabertia scripta*
(Linnaeus) Gaudichaud-Beaupré
(*Epidendrum scriptum* Linnaeus)

Now recognized as belonging to the genus *Grammatophyllum*, *Gabertia* was previously considered to include one epiphyte always found in low elevation, coastal trees, lagoons and coconut plantations of Indonesia, New Guinea, and the Philippines to the Solomon Islands. This plant has long, clustered pseudobulbs that become slightly furrowed with age, each with several, leathery, waxy, yellow-green leaves. The erect or arching, numerous-flowered inflorescence has flowers opening over an extended period of time. The heavily textured, waxy flowers are variable in color but are generally yellow-green with dark brown blotches on the inner surface and more green on the outside surface.

GALEANDRA

Lindley

Ill. Orch. Pl. (Bauer & Lindley) t. 8 (1832).

Epidendroideæ ⚘ Cymbidieæ • Catasetinæ

ETYMOLOGY: Latin for helmet and Greek for anther or male. Refers to the helmet-like anther cap.

TYPE SPECIES: *Galeandra baueri* Lindley

Thirty-four, sympodial epiphytes, uncommon terrestrials or lithophytes are widespread in low to mid elevation, open to piney forests from the United States (southern Florida), Mexico to Bolivia, Brazil and northern Argentina with the greatest diversity found in the Amazon River basin region. These robust plants have erect, spindle-shaped pseudobulbs, subtended by the purple-spotted leaf-sheaths, each with several, thick, pleated, deciduous leaves. Some species have a few or no leaves at flowering. The erect, arching or hanging,

terminal, simple or branched, numerous to few-flowered inflorescence has large, showy, yellow-brown, green to green-brown, fragrant, long-lived flowers, often appearing as if suspended in mid air. The tubular, white or purple-veined, entire or obscurely lobed lip has a dark rosy tip, and a prominent, tapering, sometimes cone-like to funnel-shaped spur. The flowers have a stout, shallow-winged or wingless column.

GALEARIS

Rafinesque

Herb. Raf. 71 (1833).

Orchidoideæ ⚘ Orchideæ • Orchidinæ

ETYMOLOGY: Latin for helmet. Alluding to the appearance of the petals and sepals that form a hood over the column.

LECTOTYPE: *Galearis spectabilis*
(Linnaeus) Rafinesque
(*Orchis spectabilis* Linnaeus)

One sympodial terrestrial is found in thick, low to mid elevation, decaying woodland forests of eastern Canada (southern Ontario) and the eastern United States (Wisconsin to Maine and Missouri to North Carolina). These erect plants have stout, unbranched stems, each with a pair of basal leaves and leaf-like floral bracts that surpass the flower in length. The erect, few-flowered inflorescence has relatively large, showy flowers. The purple to white sepals and petals converge, forming a hood over the small, stout column. The long, narrow or ovate, white or pale pink, hanging, entire or obscurely trilobed lip has a wavy margin and a small, stout spur. The flowers have a small, short, stout column.

GALEOGLOSSUM

A. Richard & Galeotti

Ann. Sci. Nat., Bot., sér. 3 **3**: 31 (1845).

ETYMOLOGY: Latin for helmet and Greek for tongue. Descriptive of the helmet-shaped lip.

TYPE SPECIES: *Galeoglossum prescottioides*
A. Richard & Galeotti
This type name is now considered a synonym of *Prescottia tubulosa* (Lindley) L.O. Williams;
basionym
Cranichis tubulosa Lindley

Now recognized as belonging to the genus *Prescottia*, *Galeoglossum* was previously considered to include one terrestrial found in mid to upper elevation, deep, damp loam and leaf mold of oak-pine forests from Mexico and Guatemala. This erect plant develops several, ovate, basal rosette leaves, but is leafless during flowering. The long, few to numerous-flowered inflorescence has small, thinly textured, pale green-white to gray-white flowers. The pale yellow, helmet-like, entire or obscurely trilobed lip is uppermost and forms a tubular shape over the flower.

GALEOLA

Loureiro

Fl. Cochinch. **2**: 516, 520 (1790).

Vanilloideæ ⚘ Vanillineæ

ETYMOLOGY: Latin for a hollow vessel shaped like a helmet. In reference to the shape of the anther with its pair of projecting appendages.

TYPE SPECIES: *Galeola nudifolia* Loureiro

Seven extraordinary, mainly leafless, apparently pseudomonopodial saprophytes are scattered in wet, shady, low to mid elevation, decaying timber, rocky ground and along river banks throughout Madagascar, the Comoros Islands, southern China (Xizang to Hainan), India (Kashmir to Assam), Nepal, Taiwan, Thailand to Vietnam, Indonesia, New Guinea, New Caledonia and the Philippines. Although widespread, they are quite uncommon, seldom seen and impossible to cultivate. Some of these vining species have tiny, red leaves; some species are erect plants without aerial roots,

Currently Accepted   Validly Published   Invalidly Published   Published Pre-1753   Superfluous Usage   Orthographic Variant   Fossil

O r c h i d   G e n e r a   •   **166**

while still other species are virtually leafless. The long, flexible, stout, yellow-brown or red-brown stems can attain lengths in excess of 60 feet (18 m). The immense inflorescences covered in rusty-brown hairs, produce literally thousands of yellow or green-yellow flowers suffused brown, and most are only 1/2 inch (1 cm) across. The concave, entire lip is streaked brown or red and has a callus with patches of fuzz. The flowers have a strongly curved, club-shaped, wingless column.

GALEORCHIS

Rydberg

Man. Fl. N. States (Britton)   292 (1901).

ETYMOLOGY: Latin for helmet and Greek for orchid. An allusion to the sepals that unite to form a hood over the column.

TYPE SPECIES: *None designated*

A superfluous name proposed as a substitute for *Galearis* and *Platanthera*.

GALEOTIA

An orthographic variant introduced in *Bot. Mag.*, **92**: sub 5567 (1866). The correct spelling is *Galeottia*.

GALEOTIELLA

An orthographic variant introduced in *Polish Bot. Stud.*, **20**: 34 (2005). The correct spelling is *Galeottiella*.

GALEOTTIA

A. Richard & Galeotti

Ann. Sci. Nat., Bot., sér. 3   **3**: 25 (1845).

Although currently accepted this name does not have priority according to ICBN code; not *Galeottia* Ruprecht ex H.G. Galeotti (1842) Poaceæ, and not *Galeottia* Nees (1847) Acanthaceæ.

Epidendroideæ ⫸ Cymbidieæ • Zygopetalinæ

ETYMOLOGY: Honoring Henri Guillaume Galeotti (1814-1858), a French-born Belgian botanist who collected the flora, fauna and fossils of Central America (especially Mexico). Also an illustrator and author of *Enumeratio Graminearum et Cyperacearum*.

TYPE SPECIES: *Galeottia grandiflora*
A. Richard & Galeotti

Twelve epiphytes or terrestrials are distributed in moist, low to mid elevation, open forests from southern Mexico to Bolivia, Venezuela and Brazil. These plants have clustered, ovoid, pale green pseudo-bulbs, changing color as they age, each with two large, pleated leaves. The few-flowered inflorescence has fleshy, long-lasting, showy, waxy, fragrant, pale green flowers that are broadly striped dark green to pale brown on the outer surfaces. The white, red streaked, trilobed lip has a erect side lobes; the ovate midlobe has a fan-shaped callus with a thread-like margin and is strongly recurved at the tip. The flowers have a slender to short, stout, slightly curved column with maroon stripes.

GALEOTTIELLA

Schlechter

Beih. Bot. Centralbl.   **37**(2): 360 (1920).

Orchidoideæ ⫸ Cranichideæ • Galeottiellinæ

ETYMOLOGY: Honoring Henri Guillaume Galeotti (1814-1858). And Latin for diminutive.

LECTOTYPE: *Galeottiella sarcoglossa*
(A. Richard & Galeotti) Schlechter
(*Spiranthes sarcoglossa* A. Richard & Galeotti)

Three sympodial terrestrials or epiphytes are distributed in mid to upper elevation, montane forests, rocky grasslands, open slopes or on oak tree branches from central Mexico to Guatemala. These short, erect plants have stout, unbranched stems, each with small, narrow leaves, rigidly ascending with several, sunken veins on the upper surface, sunken on the underside, and minute, translucent margins. The slender, few-flowered inflorescence has small, oblong, pale green bracts. The tiny to small, inconspicuous, tubular, pale green-white flowers turn brown-red as they age. The narrow, strongly curved petals have papillate margins. The tiny, concave, short or long-clawed, trilobed lip has roundish, erect side lobes and a thickened callus on the midlobe. The flowers have a short, slightly curved column.

GALERA

Blume

Bijdr. Fl. Ned. Ind.   **8**: 415, *t. 3* (1825).

Not *Galera* (E.M. Fries) Kummer (1871) Fungi.

ETYMOLOGY: Latin for hood or cap. Referring to the dorsal sepal and petals that cover the column.

TYPE SPECIES: *Galera nutans* Blume
This type name is now considered a synonym of
Epipogium roseum (D. Don) Lindley;
basionym
Limodorum roseum D. Don

Now recognized as belonging to the genus *Epipogium, Galera* was previously considered to include five saprophytic species found in moist, shady, low to mid elevation, deciduous, evergreen forests and woodlands of Africa (Ghana to Uganda), India, Nepal, Pakistan, Japan, Taiwan, Thailand to Vietnam, Indonesia and northern Australia to the southwestern Pacific Archipelago. These erect plants have thick, hollow, fleshy, leafless, scaly stems. The hollow stem is brown basally then becomes nearly white towards the tip. The numerous to few-flowered inflorescence has large, white or pale green flowers suffused pink. The entire lip has two rows of minute warts down the center.

GALLEOTIA

An orthographic variant introduced in *Prakt. Stud. Orchid.*, 32 (1854). The correct spelling is *Galeottia*.

GAMARIA

Rafinesque

Fl. Tellur.   **4**: 49 (1836)[1837].

ETYMOLOGY: The origin and meaning of this word is unknown.

TYPE SPECIES: *Gamaria cornuta* (Linnaeus) Rafinesque
(*Orchis cornuta* Linnaeus)

Now recognized as belonging to the genus *Disa, Gamaria* was previously considered to include one terrestrial found in the Cape grasslands of South Africa and Zimbabwe. This erect, leafy plant has unbranched stems, each with a few-flowered inflorescence that has purple to silvery green flowers. The concave dorsal sepal (white inside and purple outside) forms a hood over the small, stout, curved, broadly winged column, and the small, strongly curved petals usually lie within the hood. The large, oblong, white lateral sepals have a short, blunt, purple tip. The small, oval, entire lip is bright yellow with a large, brown splash.

GAMOPLEXIS

Falconer

Proc. Linn. Soc. London   **1**: 320 (1847), and
Trans. Linn. Soc. London   **20**: 293, *t. 13* (1847).

ETYMOLOGY: Greek for to marry or bind together and weaving. Referring to the cohesion of the perianth segments.

TYPE SPECIES: *Gamoplexis orobanchoides* Falconer

Now recognized as belonging to the genus *Gastrodia, Gamoplexis* was previously considered to include one saprophyte found in upper elevation, montane forests and grasslands from Pakistan, northern India (Kashmir) to Nepal. This stout, leafless plant has unbranched stem. The erect, numerous-flowered inflorescence has tubular, pale red-brown flowers not opening widely and are often yellow fringed. The above type name is now considered a synonym of *Gastrodia falconeri* D.L. Jones & M.A. Clements.

GAMOSEPALUM

Schlechter

Beih. Bot. Centralbl.   **37**(2): 429 (1920).

Not *Gamosepalum* Haussknecht (1897) Brassicaceæ.

ETYMOLOGY: Greek for marriage and Latin for sepal. Alluding to the union of the sepals with the petals and lip into a tube.

TYPE SPECIES: *Gamosepalum tenuiflorum*
(Greenman) Schlechter
(*Spiranthes tenuiflora* Greenman)

Not validly published because of a prior use of the name, this homonym was replaced by *Aulosepalum*.

GANGORA

An orthographic variant introduced in *Ill. Hort.*, **30**: 182 (1883). The correct spelling is *Gongora*.

GARAYA

Szlachetko

Polish Bot. Stud., Guideb. Ser.   **5**: 4 (1993).

ETYMOLOGY: Honoring Leslie Andres Garay (1924-).

TYPE SPECIES: *Garaya atroviridis*
(Barbosa Rodrigues) Szlachetko
(*Cyclopogon atroviridis* Barbosa Rodrigues)

Now recognized as belonging to the genus *Mesadenella*, *Garaya* was previously considered to include one terrestrial found in low elevation, coastal evergreen forests of southeastern Brazil (São Paulo to Santa Catarina). This erect plant has unbranched stems, each with several, ovate, veined, basal leaves. The wiry, erect, few-flowered inflorescence is more or less spirally twisted and has small, well-spaced sheaths. The tubular, green flowers have dissimilar sepals that are hairy on the outer surfaces. The shortly clawed, entire lip is decurved near the tip. The flowers have a long, club-shaped column with a tiny or reduced column foot.

GARAYANTHUS

Szlachetko

Fragm. Florist. Geobot.   **3**(Suppl.): 136 (1995).

ETYMOLOGY: Honoring Leslie Andres Garay (1924-). And Greek for flower.

TYPE SPECIES: *Garayanthus duplicilobus*
(J.J. Smith) Szlachetko
(*Sarcanthus duplicilobus* J.J. Smith)

Now recognized as belonging to the genus *Cleisostoma*, *Garayanthus* was proposed to include six epiphytes found in low to mid elevation, hill to montane forests from eastern

China (Jiangxi to Hainan), Taiwan, Thailand, Laos, Vietnam and Indonesia to the Philippines. These small, erect plants have stout stems, each with well-spaced, narrow, bilobed, fleshy to leathery leaves. The short to long, red-brown, multibranched, few-flowered inflorescence has small, fleshy, deep red-brown flowers with a green median line and margins. The strongly bent, trilobed lip has small, erect side lobes, the fleshy midlobe has red bars, a yellow callus and a straight, tubular spur. The flower's most distinctive feature is a massive, saddle-like, sticky part of the viscidium. The flowers have a thick, short to slender, wingless column.

GARAYELLA

Brieger

Orchideen (Schlechter), ed. 3   **7**(25-28): 425 (1975), and
Validated: *Trab. 26 Congr. Nac. Bot., Rio de Janeiro*
26: 42 (1977).

ETYMOLOGY: In honor of Leslie Andres Garay (1924-), a Hungarian-born American botanist, orchidologist, curator of the Oaks Ames Orchid Herbarium at Harvard University, and co-author of *Venezuelan Orchids Illustrated*. And Latin for diminutive.

TYPE SPECIES: *Garayella hexandra*
(Garay & Dunsterville) Brieger
(*Pleurothallis hexandra* Garay & Dunsterville)

This type name is now considered a synonym of *Chamelophyton kegelii* (Reichenbach f.) Garay; basionym replaced with *Restrepia kegelii* Reichenbach f.

Now recognized as belonging to the genus *Chamelophyton*, *Garayella* was previously considered to include one terrestrial or epiphyte found in mid to upper elevation, montane forests of northeastern Venezuela and the Guianas. This miniature plant forms dense mats and has narrow leaves that are dark green on the topside and purple on the underside. The several, solitary-flowered inflorescences have a pale brown flower not opening fully, with overlays of maroon. The pale brown, hinged, trilobed lip is suffused or spotted maroon. The flowers have a short, yellow column and anther cap.

GASTORCHIS

An orthographic variant introduced in *Hist. Orchid.*, Table 1, sub 2j, t. 31 (1822). The correct spelling is *Gastorkis*.

GASTORKIS

Thouars

Nouv. Bull. Sci. Soc. Philom. Paris
1(19): 317 (1809).

ETYMOLOGY: Greek for belly and orchid. In reference to the belly-shaped lip.

TYPE SPECIES: *None designated*

Now recognized as belonging to the genus *Phaius*, *Gastorkis* was previously considered to include six epiphytes or terrestrials found in Madagascar and the Mascarene Islands. Certain species grow exclusively on a single species of trees. These plants have tightly clustered pseudobulbs, each with broad, heavily textured leaves. The erect, few-flowered inflorescence has large, white to red flowers suffused pale rose and they open successively over a long period of time. The large, trilobed lip is quite variable in color.

GASTRIDIUM

Blume

Fl. Javæ   **1**: Praef. vii (1828), and
Bijdr. Fl. Ned. Ind.   **7**: 333 (1825).

Not *Gastridium* Palisot de Beauvois (1812) Poaceæ, and not *Gastridium* Lyngbye (1819) Champiaceæ.

Not validly published because of a prior use of the name, this homonym was replaced by *Dendrobium*.

GASTROCHILUS

D. Don

Prodr. Fl. Nepal.   32 (1825).

Name ICBN rejected vs. *Saccolabium* Blume (1825); and not *Gastrochilus* Wallich (1829) Zingiberaceæ.

ETYMOLOGY: Greek for pot-belly or belly and a lip. In reference to the belly-like, swollen sac of the lip.

TYPE SPECIES: *Gastrochilus calceolaris*
(Buchanan-Hamilton ex Smith) D. Don
(*Aerides calceolare* Buchanan-Hamilton ex Smith)

Although validly published this rejected name is now referred to *Saccolabium*. *Gastrochilus* was considered to include fifty-five epiphytes found in cool to humid, low to mid elevation, dense evergreen hill to montane forests from southern India (Karnataka, Kerala, Tamil Nadu and Orissa), Sri Lanka to Indonesia and the Philippines. These plants have short to long, branched or unbranched stems, each with several, leathery, distichous, unequally bilobed leaves. The short, few-flowered inflorescence has small to rather large, long-lived, waxy, slightly fragrant, hairy, flowers variously spotted, barred or heavily blotched. The small, sac-like, immobile, entire or trilobed lip has its sides firmly joined to the base of the column. The flowers have a short, stout, wingless, footless column.

Currently Accepted   Validly Published   Invalidly Published   Published Pre-1753   Superfluous Usage   Orthographic Variant   Fossil

Orchid Genera · **168**

GASTRODIA

R. Brown
Prodr. Fl. Nov. Holland. 330 (1810).

Epidendroideæ Gastrodieæ

ETYMOLOGY: Greek for pot-bellied or stomach-like and likeness. In reference to the urn-shaped sepals that are inflated at the base in front giving the flower a stomach-like appearance.

TYPE SPECIES: *Gastrodia sesamoides* R. Brown

Forty-one uncommon saprophytes are found in low to upper elevation, hill and montane forests' decaying litter ranging from Africa (Cameroon) to eastern Russia (Kamchatka to Kuril), Japan to the Philippines, Indonesia, Australia and New Zealand with the largest concentration found throughout China. These erect plants have long to short, scaly, yellow-brown stems. The plants usually appear at the start of the wet season. The several, dull purple-brown, few to solitary-flowered inflorescences have white, dull brown, pale brown, brown-yellow to dark green-brown flowers. The sepals and petals are united into an unusual, warty or roughened, five-lobed tube with a swollen, sac-like basal portion. The small, yellow or white, broadly clawed, entire or trilobed lip, united to the end of the column foot, has two to three keels. Sometimes it has glandular basal calli and a blunt or wavy margin. The flowers have a long, slender, winged column.

GASTRODIUM

An orthographic variant introduced in *Anal. Fam. Pl.*, 56 (1829). The correct spelling is *Gastrodia*.

GASTROGLOTTIS

Blume
Bijdr. Fl. Ned. Ind. **8**: 397 (1825).

ETYMOLOGY: Greek for belly and tongue. Descriptive of the basal pouch or swelling of the lip.

TYPE SPECIES: *Gastroglottis montana* Blume
This type name is now considered a synonym of
Dienia ophrydis (J. König) Seidenfaden;
basionym
Epidendrum ophrydis J. König

Now recognized as belonging to the genus *Dienia*, *Gastroglottis* was originally considered to include one epiphyte found in moist, low to mid elevation, hill to montane rain and piney forests from India, southeastern China (Hainan), Myanmar to Vietnam, Malaysia, Indonesia and New Guinea to northeastern Australia (Queensland). This attractive plant has erect, unbranched stems, subtended by leaf-like sheaths, each with numerous, basal leaves that have wavy margins. The erect to arching, numerous to few-flowered inflorescence has small to tiny, yellow-green, brown or purple flowers with even combinations of the three colors. The long, narrow petals droop downward almost covering the tiny flower. The flowers have an ovate, more or less flat, tiny, trilobed lip.

GASTROPODIUM

Lindley
Ann. Mag. Nat. Hist., ser. 1 **15**: 107 (1845).

ETYMOLOGY: Greek for belly and little foot or shoe. Descriptive of the slipper-shape lip.

TYPE SPECIES: *Gastropodium violaceum* Lindley

Now recognized as belonging to the genus *Epidendrum*, *Gastropodium* was previously considered to include one epiphyte or terrestrial found in wet, mid elevation, montane cloud forests from Panama, Colombia to Peru and Brazil. This branching, reed-like plant has its new stems subtended by thin, dry sheaths, and are produced from nodes of older stiff, distichous leaves. The short, head-like, densely packed, few-flowered inflorescence has small, showy, thinly textured, bright purple to pink flowers which do not open fully. The tongue-shaped, concave, entire lip is fused to the column and has a yellow, basal callus. The flowers have a small, violet-black column. The above type name is now considered a synonym of *Epidendrum gastropodium* Reichenbach f.

GASTRORCHIS

Schlechter
Repert. Spec. Nov. Regni Veg. Beih. **33**: 166 (1924).

Epidendroideæ Collabiinæ • Currently unplaced

ETYMOLOGY: Greek for belly and orchid. From the basally inflated or sac-like lip.

TYPE SPECIES: *Gastrorchis tuberculosa*
(Thouars) Schlechter
(*Limodorum tuberculosum* Thouars)

Nine sympodial terrestrials or rare epiphytes are found in warm to cool, low to mid elevation, semi-deciduous forests with most species found in eastern Madagascar and one in the Mascarene Islands. These extremely rare plants are closely related to *Phaius*, and some species are found exclusively on a single species of trees. The small, round to spindle-shaped pseudobulbs, each with several, long, narrow to broad, pleated to grass-like leaves. The tall, erect, few-flowered inflorescence has long-lasting, heavily textured, small flowers with pure white sepals and petal, and open successively over an extended period. The broad, obscurely trilobed lip has erect, yellow side lobes covered with red spots, and the small, white midlobe has a lilac or violet spotted margin, with a yellow disc and callus. The flowers have a long, white, curved column that is footless or with a small foot.

GASTROSIPHON

M.A. Clements & D.L. Jones
Orchadian **13**(10): 447 (2002).

ETYMOLOGY: Greek for belly and tube-like. In reference to the shape of the swollen lip tube.

TYPE SPECIES: *Gastrosiphon schlechteri*
(Schlechter) M.A. Clements & D.L. Jones
(*Corybas gastrosiphon* Schlechter)

Recognized as belonging to the genus *Corybas*, *Gastrosiphon* was proposed to include twenty-nine terrestrials found humid, wet, low to mid elevation, woodlands from Malaysia to New Guinea and northeastern Australia. These dwarf plants have short, unbranched stems, each with a solitary, ovate or kidney-shaped, prominently veined, basal leaf. The short, solitary-flowered inflorescence is sometimes found within the leaf. The flower has an erect, concave, hood-shaped dorsal sepal, and tiny lateral sepals and petals. The prominently swollen, erect, entire lip is broadly tubular with its margins shortly incurved and tooth-like, and it has a short, closed spur. The flowers have a short, erect, footless column.

GATASETUM

An orthographic variant introduced in *Bull. Sci. Nat. Geol.*, **10**: 269 (1827). The correct spelling is *Catasetum*.

GAVILA

An orthographic variant introduced in *Linnaea*, **2**: 528 (1827). The correct spelling is *Gavilea*.

GAVILEA

Poeppig
Fragm. Syn. Pl. 18 (1833).

Orchidoideæ Cranichideæ • Chloraeinæ

ETYMOLOGY: From the vernacular (local Indian) name used for the plant in Chile, gavilú.

LECTOTYPE: *Gavilea leucantha* Poeppig

Fourteen sympodial terrestrials are distributed in cold, mid to upper elevation, meadows, rocky fields and cliffs in temperate and extreme cold of southern Argentina, Juan Fernández and Falklands Islands with the greatest concentration found in southern Chile. These erect, unbranched plants (survives in extremes of heat, cold and dryness) have several, flat, narrow leaves arranged in a basal rosette or scattered along the stem. The erect, slender to stout, numerous to few-flowered inflorescences have white, green or yellow flowers. The entire or trilobed lip has erect side lobes usually with two, basal structures that resemble glands. It has wart-like outgrowths, and appendages of various sorts along the veins. The margin tips are entire or lobed clefts and have a toothed or warty margin. The flowers have a short, stout, winged column that is sometimes enclosed by a neck at the base.

GAVILLEA

An orthographic variant cited in *Nomencl. Bot. (Steudel)*, ed. 2, **1**: 666 (1840). The correct spelling is *Gavilea*.

GEERINCKIA

Mytnik & Szlachetko
Richardiana   **7**(2): 62 (2007).
ETYMOLOGY: Named for Daniel Geerinck (1945-), a Belgian professor of systematic botany and phytosociology at the Université Libre de Bruxelles.
TYPE SPECIES: *Geerinckia couloniana*
   (Geerinck & Arbonnier) Mytnik & Szlachetko
   (*Polystachya couloniana* Geerinck & Arbonnier)

Recognized as belonging to the genus *Polystachya*, *Geerinckia* was proposed to include one epiphyte or terrestrial found in low to mid elevation, grasslands from Burundi to Congo. These plants have small, ovoid pseudobulbs each with narrow, bright green leaves. The erect, solitary-flowered inflorescence has a pale rosy flower with similar sepals and petals and a large, entire lip. The flowers have a short column.

GEESINKORCHIS

deVogel
Blumea   **30**(1): 199 (1984).
Epidendroideæ ◊ Arethuseæ • Coelogyninæ
ETYMOLOGY: In honor of Robert Geesink (1945-1992), a Dutch botanist from the Rijksherbarium (Netherlands) in Leiden, who collected the type species and authored *Scala millettiearum*. And Greek for orchid.
TYPE SPECIES: *Geesinkorchis alaticallosa* deVogel

Two sympodial epiphytes or terrestrials are found in moist, low to mid elevation, hill and montane forests from western Malaysia to Indonesia (Sumatra to northern Borneo). These plants have flattened pseudobulbs, grouped close together and turned to one side on the rhizome, each with two narrow, stiff, leathery leaves. The erect, numerous-flowered inflorescence has flowers opening in succession but with only one or two open at a time; the rachis continues to lengthen during flowering. The yellow-brown to pale green-white flowers have a deeply concave dorsal sepal; slightly hairy lateral sepals, and narrow petals that curve or are rolled backward. The broad, white, trilobed lip curves downward, has a splash of red-orange, and tiny, roundish side lobes. The flowers have a deeply concave, footless column.

GEISSANTHERA

Schlechter
Nachtr. Fl. Schutzgeb. Südsee   231 (1905).
ETYMOLOGY: Greek for cornice or tile and flower. Refers to the bristle-like secondary bracts opposite each leaf that look like adorned ledges.
TYPE SPECIES: *Geissanthera papuana* Schlechter

Now recognized as belonging to the genus *Microtatorchis*, *Geissanthera* was previously considered to include three epiphytes found in misty, upper elevation, montane forests of New Guinea. These mostly leafless, dwarf plants have chlorophyll in their roots. The numerous-flowered inflorescence has small, extremely complex, dull-colored flowers. The sepals and petals of which are fused into a tube shape.

GENEOSPLESIUM

An orthographic variant cited in *Syn. Bot., Suppl.*, 9 (1874). The correct spelling is *Genoplesium*.

GENNARIA

Parlatore
Fl. Ital. (Parlatore)   **3**: 404 (1860).
Orchidoideæ ◊ Orchideæ • Orchidinæ
ETYMOLOGY: In honor of Patrizio Gennari (1820-1897), an Italian botanist, founder of the Botanical Garden of Cagliari, Sardinia and author of *La Storia naturale in Sardegna nell'ultimo ventennio*.
Or possibly for Benedetto Gennari's (1550-1610), the elder and (1633-1715), the younger, Italian religious painters. Some of their paintings hang in the Vatican (Rome) and Kensington Palace (London).
LECTOTYPE: *Gennaria diphylla* (Link) Parlatore
   (*Satyrium diphyllum* Link)

One unusual, sympodial terrestrial is found in low elevation, coastal piney and evergreen forests of the western Mediterranean (Sardinia, Corsica, Spain, Portugal and Bulgaria), Morocco to Tunisia and the Canary Islands. This tiny, erect plant has one to two, sheathing scale, basal leaves and two heart-shaped leaves clasping the unbranched stem. The plant produces long-stalked leaves from time to time over several years before flowering. The erect to slightly curved, numerous-flowered inflorescence has small, yellow-green flowers not opening widely and usually with all facing one direction. The forward pointing sepals have cowl-shaped points and the petals curve backward. The tongue-shaped, trilobed lip has downward-turned tips and a short, pouch-shaped, grooved spur. The flowers have a short column.

GENOPLASIUM

An orthographic variant introduced in *Dict. Sci. Nat.*, **36**: 304 (1825). The correct spelling is *Genoplesium*.

GENOPLESIUM

R. Brown
Prodr. Fl. Nov. Holland.   319 (1810).
Orchidoideæ ◊ Diurideæ • Prasophyllinæ
ETYMOLOGY: Greek for race or kind and near. Alluding to a close affinity with *Prasophyllum*, a genus of orchids.
TYPE SPECIES: *Genoplesium baueri* R. Brown

Forty-five sympodial terrestrials and saprophytes are found in low to mid elevation, grassy forests, bogs and coastal woodlands of New Caledonia, southern Australia, Tasmania and New Zealand. These often brittle, succulent, slender, erect plants have unbranched stems, subtended by leaf-like sheaths, each with several, leaves or scale-like leaves. The leaves of sterile plants are hollow, but in fertile plants the leaf and flowering stem are fused and develop as a single unit. The plants reproduce solely from seed. The erect, solitary to few-flowered inflorescence has small, dull-colored, green and red flowers with a fruity fragrance. The flowers have a short, broad dorsal sepal; widespreading lateral sepals and short, notched petals that are dissimilar in size, shape and coloration of the sepals. The thick, narrow, entire lip, attached to the column foot by a short claw, quivers in the slightest breeze, and has an incurved margin. The flowers have a long to short, slender, winged column.

Currently Accepted | Validly Published | Invalidly Published | Published Pre-1753 | Superfluous Usage | Orthographic Variant | Fossil

Orchid Genera • **170**

GENYORCHIS

Schlechter

Westafr. Kautschuk-Exped. 280 (1900), and
Bot. Jahrb. Syst. **38**: 11 (1905)[1907].

Name ICBN conserved vs. *Taurostalix* Schlechter (1852)
Orchidaceæ, and type name conserved.

Epidendroideæ ⚬ Dendrobiinæ • Currently unplaced

ETYMOLOGY: Greek for jaw or a mouth with teeth
and orchid. Alluding to the resemblance of the
flower to an open jaw.

TYPE SPECIES: *Genyorchis pumila* (Swartz) Schlechter
(*Dendrobium pumilum* Swartz)

Ten uncommon, small, creeping epiphytes or lithophytes are found in low to mid elevation, rain forests and mangroves from the Ivory Coast to Uganda, and Equatorial Guinea to Zaire. These small plants have well-spaced, ovoid or cylindrical, four-angled pseudobulbs, each with one to two, narrow, fleshy or leathery leaves. The few-flowered inflorescence has tiny, pale cream or green flowers not opening widely and often suffused purple. The small, purple to white petals have a yellow patch at the base. The small, fleshy, bright purple to yellow, obscurely trilobed lip has a recurved tip covered with papillae. The flowers have a short, winged column with a long foot.

GEOBINA

Rafinesque

Fl. Tellur. **4**: 49 (1836)[1837].

ETYMOLOGY: Greek for earth and to have illicit
intercourse. In reference to its terrestrial habit.

TYPE SPECIES: *None designated*

A superfluous name proposed as a substitute for *Eria*.

GEOBLASTA

Barbosa Rodrigues

Vellosia, ed. 2 **1**: 132 (1891).

Orchidoideæ ⚬ Cranichideæ • Chloraeinæ

ETYMOLOGY: Greek for earth and sprout or bud. An
allusion to the enclosed, bud-like blooms that emerge
from the ground.

TYPE SPECIES: *Geoblasta teixeirana* Barbosa Rodrigues
This type name is now considered a synonym of
Geoblasta penicillata
(Reichenbach f.) Hoehne ex M.N. Corrêa;
basionym
Chloraea penicillata Reichenbach f.

Two sympodial terrestrials are found in dry, cool, low elevation, hill forest grasslands and rocky crevices of southeastern Brazil, southern Uruguay and northeastern Argentina (Buenos Aires). These erect plants, which survive in extreme heat and dryness, have unbranched, erect stems, each with a basal cluster of leaves. The solitary-flowered inflorescence has a large, showy, bright green to yellow-green and white flower. The narrow, heavily veined sepals and petals are crossed veined in red-green. The large, entire lip, covered with dark red or maroon blotches, has a basal callus of elevated, cushion-like, white hairs. The flowers have an erect, incurved, wingless column.

GEOCALPA

(Kraenzlin) Brieger

Orchideen (Schlechter), ed. 3 **7**(25-28): 440 (1975).

ETYMOLOGY: Greek for earth and cup or jug. Refers to
the tiny size of the plant and the curled flowers.

TYPE SPECIES: *None designated*

Not validly published, this name is referred to *Acianthera*, *Geocalpa* was considered to include two tiny epiphytes found in southeastern Brazil (Minas Gerais).

GEODORA

An orthographic variant introduced in *Nouv. Dict. Hist. Nat.*, ed. 2, **13**: 17 (1817). The correct spelling is *Geodorum*.

GEODORUM

Jackson

H.C. Andrews' Bot. Repos. **10**: t. 626 (1811).

Epidendroideæ ⚬ Cymbidieæ • Eulophiinæ

ETYMOLOGY: Greek for ground or the earth and gift.
In reference to their terrestrial habitat.

TYPE SPECIES: *Geodorum citrinum* Jackson

Thirteen, sympodial terrestrials are found in low to mid elevation, hill and montane forests, along river banks, slopes and savannas from southern China (Sichuan to Hainan, Yunnan), India, Bangladesh, Myanmar to Vietnam, Indonesia, the Philippines, New Guinea and northern Australia to the southwestern Pacific Archipelago. These plants have fleshy, corm-like or roundish, clustered pseudobulbs, arising at or just below the soil surface, each with several, deciduous, pleated leaves on long to short stems. The hanging, densely packed, numerous-flowered inflorescence (arranged in heads), is borne on a separate stem. It is held upright for the most part but curves over into a hook shape at the top when flowering, and later straightening for the dispersal of seeds. The bell- to tubular-shaped, delicately colored, waxy, usually delightfully fragrant flowers are not long lasting and do not open widely. The entire or obscurely trilobed lip has a short sac-like base. The flowers have a short column with a distinct foot.

GEODYERA

An orthographic variant introduced in *Rad. Jugoslav. Akad. Znan.*, **21**: 23 (1872). The correct spelling is *Goodyera*.

GEORCHIS

Lindley

Edwards's Bot. Reg. **19**: sub 1618 (1833), and
Numer. List. 247, no. 7379 (1831).

ETYMOLOGY: Greek for earth and orchid. Referring
to its terrestrial habitat.

TYPE SPECIES: *Georchis biflora* Lindley

Now recognized as belonging to the genus *Goodyera*, *Georchis* was previously considered to include ten terrestrials found in damp, low to upper elevation, hill and montane valley slopes of northern India (Sikkim), Nepal, southern China (Shanxi to Xizang), Korea, Japan, Taiwan and Indonesia to New Guinea. These erect plants have unbranched stems, each with several, dark green, silvery-white veined leaves in a basal rosette that are sometimes suffused purple-red. The erect, tall, somewhat spiraled, hairy, numerous-flowered inflorescence has tubular, white, pink to pale green flowers. The narrow, white, entire lip has yellow margins and is sac-like at the base with gland-like hairs inside and slightly recurved at the tip. The flowers have a short, deeply divided column.

GERARDOA

(Luer) Luer

Monogr. Syst. Bot. Missouri Bot. Gard.
105: 86, f. 43 (2006).

ETYMOLOGY: Named for Gerardo Herrera y Chacón
(1948-), a Costa Rican landscape architect, field
botanist and plant collector.

TYPE SPECIES: *Gerardoa montezumae* (Luer) Luer
(*Pleurothallis montezumae* Luer)

Recognized as belonging to the genus *Pleurothallis*, *Gerardoa* was proposed to include one epiphyte found in low elevation, hill forests of central Costa Rica. This small plant has erect, slender stems, subtended by brown, tubular sheaths, each with a solitary, erect, large, leathery leaf. The two-flowered inflorescence has orange-brown flowers borne successively. The dorsal sepal is concave below the middle. The concave lateral sepals are united to the middle, forming a synsepal and a small, chin-like, basal protuberance. The small petals are minutely pointed. The oblong, warty, entire lip has a disk shallowly channeled between converging calli. The flowers have a long, slender, wingless column.

GERLACHIA

Szlachetko

Richardiana   **7**(2): 48 (2007).

ETYMOLOGY: In honor of Günter Gerlach (1953-), a German curator at Botanic Garden Münich of Nymphenburg and botanist who specializes in Stanhopeinæ.

TYPE SPECIES: *Gerlachia tricornis* (Lindley) Szlachetko (*Stanhopea tricornis* Lindley)

Recognized as belonging to the genus *Stanhopea*, *Gerlachia* was proposed to include one epiphyte found in shady, wet, low to mid elevation, hill to montane forests along the western slopes of the Andes from Colombia to Peru. These plants have ovate, dark green, ribbed pseudobulbs, subtended by overlapping, thin, papery bracts, each with a solitary, pleated leaf. The hanging, few-flowered inflorescence, borne from a mature pseudobulb, has showy, fragrant, creamy-white flowers with the smaller, yellow petals tipped or suffused orange or pink and tightly curve around the long, slender, broadly winged column. The complex, fleshy, trilobed lip has a thick, concave hypochile dotted purple, and the indistinct mesochile has two orange, sickle-shaped horns curving over the oblong epichile that has a slightly trilobed tip.

GERSINIA

Néraud ex Gaudichaud-Beaupré

Freycinet's *Voy. Uranie, Bot.*   25, 27 (1826)[1829].

Not validly published, this name is most often referred to *Bulbophyllum*.

GHIESBRECHTIA

An orthographic variant introduced in *Dict. Univ. Hist. Nat.*, **9**: 171 (1847). The correct spelling is *Ghiesbreghtia*.

GHIESBREGHTIA

A. Richard & Galeotti

Ann. Sci. Nat., Bot., sér. 3   **3**: 28 (1845).

Not *Ghiesbreghtia* A. Gray (1873) Scrophulariaceæ.

ETYMOLOGY: Commemorating Auguste Boniface Ghiesbreght (1810-1893), a Belgian geologist, botanical explorer in Mexico, patron of botany and a collaborator with Jean Linden (1817-1898).

TYPE SPECIES: *Ghiesbreghtia calanthoides*
A. Richard & Galeotti

Now recognized as belonging to the genus *Calanthe*, *Ghiesbreghtia* was previously considered to include two terrestrials found in wet, cool to warm, mid to upper elevation, dense montane forests from Mexico to Colombia and Cuba to Jamaica. These erect plants have pale green corms, subtended by sheathing leaf bases and two large, broad, prominently veined leaves. The terminal, pink to brown, numerous-flowered inflorescence has spirally arranged, densely hairy, white or pink flowers marked red-brown. The widespreading lateral sepals curve backward at the pointed tips and much smaller petals. The fleshy, hairy, obscurely trilobed lip, attached to the column, thus forming a short tube, has a bright yellow basal splash and a short spur. Both species are now considered synonyms of *Calanthe calanthoides* (A. Richard & Galeotti) Hamer & Garay.

GHIESEBREGHTIA

An orthographic variant introduced in *Fol. Orchid.*, **1**: *Ghiesebreghtia*, 3 (1854). The correct spelling is *Ghiesbreghtia*.

GHISBREGHTIA

An orthographic variant introduced in *Symb. Antill.*, **6**: 569 (1910). The correct spelling is *Ghiesbreghtia*.

GIESBREGHTIA

An orthographic variant introduced in *Orchid.-Buch*, 257 (1892). The correct spelling is *Ghiesbreghtia*.

GIGLIOGLIA

An orthographic variant cited in *Lex. Gen. Phan.*, 248 (1904). The correct spelling is *Gigliola*.

GIGLIOLA

An orthographic variant introduced in *Fl. Bras. (Martius)*, **3**(4): 600 (1893). The correct spelling is *Gigliolia*.

GIGLIOLIA

Barbosa Rodrigues

Gen. Sp. Orchid.   **1**: 25, *t.* 393 (1877).

Not *Gigliolia* Beccari (1877) Arecaceæ.

ETYMOLOGY: In honor of Enrico Hillyer Giglioli (1845-1909), a British-born Italian naturalist, zoologist, ethnologist and a professor of comparative anatomy and zoology at the Institute de Studi Superiori in Florence.

LECTOTYPE: *Gigliolia geraensis* Barbosa Rodrigues

Now recognized as belonging to the genus *Octomeria*, *Gigliolia* was previously considered to include two epiphytes found in southeastern Brazil. These small, creeping, whip-like plants have erect stems, subtended by several sheaths, each with a solitary, narrow, leathery leaf located at the tip. The short, few-flowered inflorescence, borne from the leaf axils, has tiny, creamy to pale green flowers that emerge from a basal rosette of small bracts. The trilobed lip has ovate, erect side lobes and the midlobe has a recurved tip. The flowers have a small, slender, slightly curved column.

GIODORUM

An orthographic variant introduced in *Icon. Pl. Ind. Orient. (Wight)*, **3**(1): 10 (1850). The correct spelling is *Geodorum*.

GIROSTACHIS

An orthographic variant introduced in *Fl. Tellur.*, **2**: 87 (1836)[1837]. The correct spelling is *Gyrostachys*.

GIROSTACHYS

An orthographic variant cited in *Index Raf.*, 102 (1949). The correct spelling is *Gyrostachys*.

GIULIANETTIA

Rolfe

Hooker's Icon. Pl.   **27**: *t.* 2616 (1899).

ETYMOLOGY: In honor of Amedeo Giulianetti (x-1901), an Italian who explored and collected natural history objects in New Guinea, a government agent of the interior for the Mekeo district, and author of *Nella Nuova Guinea britannica*.

TYPE SPECIES: *Giulianettia tenuis* Rolfe

Now recognized as belonging to the genus *Glomera*, *Giulianettia* was previously considered to include fourteen epiphytes or terrestrials found in New Guinea. These small, slender, multibranched stemmed plants have narrow, tubular leaves. The short, solitary-flowered inflorescence has an insignificant, dark pink or green, fragrant, widespreading flower with narrow sepals and petals. The broadly heart-shaped, entire lip has a pale brown or black tip and a conspicuous, club-shaped spur. The flowers have a short, stout column.

GLADIANGIS

Thouars

Hist. Orchid.   Table 2, sub 3o, *t.* 53 (1822).

Name published without a description. Today this name is most often referred to *Angraecum*.

Currently Accepted   Validly Published   Invalidly Published   Published Pre-1753   Superfluous Usage   Orthographic Variant   Fossil

O r c h i d   G e n e r a   • 172

GLOMERA

Blume

Bijdr. Fl. Ned. Ind. **8**: 372, *t.* 68 (1825).

Epidendroideæ ⚘ Arethuseæ • Coelogyninæ

ETYMOLOGY: Latin for to wind into a ball or clustered. Refers to the ball-like cluster of flowers on the inflorescence.

TYPE SPECIES: *Glomera erythrosma* Blume

One hundred twenty-seven sympodial epiphytes or terrestrials are found in low to upper elevation, hill to montane evergreen rain forests from Malaysia, Laos to Indonesia and the Philippines to the southwestern Pacific Archipelago with New Guinea being the center of distribution. These small stature, erect to hanging, often branching plants have fairly long, hard, leafy stems, each with distichous, narrow leaves arranged in two rows toward the tip. The flattened, sometimes pencil-like leaves are papery to fleshy, smooth or sometimes hairy, often warty and the margins are often fringed or ciliate. The head-like, each with several, individual flowers, inflorescences are subtended by leaf bases. The small, predominantly white, green, orange, brown-pink or yellow flowers do open widely and have little resemblance to an orchid. The entire or obscurely trilobed lip, united to the column, often has a red tinge or spot at the tip and a minute spur. The flowers have a white, small, somewhat curved column that is footless or with a small foot and has a black or brown anther cap.

GLOMEZIA

An orthographic variant introduced in *Gart.-Zeitung (Berlin)*, **2**: 156 (1883). The correct spelling is *Gomesa*.

GLOSSADENIA

Welwitsch ex Ascherson & Graebner

Syn. Mitteleur. Fl. **3**: 655 (1907).

ETYMOLOGY: Greek for tongue-like and gland-like or swelling. Referring to the enlarged lip.

TYPE SPECIES: *Glossadenia broteroi*
Welwitsch ex Ascherson & Graebner
This type name is now considered a synonym of
Ophrys bombyliflora Link

Not validly published, this name is referred to *Ophrys*. *Glossadenia* was considered to include one terrestrial found in open woodlands and meadows of the Mediterranean region (Spain, Balearic Islands, southern France, Corsica, Sardinia, Italy to Turkey, and Morocco to Libya) and the Canary Islands.

GLOSSAPIS

An orthographic variant introduced in *Dansk Bot. Ark.*, **31**(3): 41 (1977). The correct spelling is *Glossaspis*.

GLOSSASPIS

Sprengel

Syst. Veg. (Sprengel), ed. 16 **3**: 675, 694 (1826).

ETYMOLOGY: Greek for a tongue and shield or boss. From the mid-lobe of the tongue-shaped lip.

TYPE SPECIES: *Glossaspis tentaculata*
(Lindley) Sprengel
(*Glossula tentaculata* Lindley)

Now recognized as belonging to the genus *Peristylus*, *Glossaspis* was previously considered to include two terrestrials found in damp, low elevation, on hilly slopes and grasslands from southern China (Yunnan to southern Fujian), Hong Kong, Cambodia and Thailand to Vietnam. These miniature, slender plants have several, small, narrow to oblong, clustered leaves. The tall, erect, few-flowered inflorescence has tiny, green or yellow-green flowers not opening widely. The trilobed lip has long, almost thread-like, yellow-green side lobes that spread at right angles to the narrowly oblong midlobe and a long, slightly bilobed, hanging spur. The flowers have a small, thick column.

GLOSSOCHILOPSIS

Szlachetko

Fragm. Florist. Geobot. **3**(Suppl.): 122 (1995).

ETYMOLOGY: Greek for tongue and appearance. Refers to the large tongue-shaped rostellum.

TYPE SPECIES: *Glossochilopsis chamaeorchis*
(Schlechter) Szlachetko
(*Microstylis chamaeorchis* Schlechter)

Now recognized as belonging to the genus *Malaxis*, *Glossochilopsis* was previously considered to include three terrestrials found in mid elevation, open montane mixed and pine forests from southern China (Hainan), Taiwan, northern India (Sikkim), Bhutan, Nepal, Andaman Islands, Myanmar to Vietnam, Taiwan, Indonesia, the Philippines, New Caledonia and New Guinea to northern Australia (Queensland). These erect plants have narrow, tapering pseudobulbs to fleshy cylindrical stems, each with several, deciduous leaves and has several, sheath-like leaves clasping the lower stem. The tall, numerous-flowered inflorescence has small, long-lasting, green, white or red-purple flowers with narrow segments. The cup-like, entire lip has a few short, thick ridges. The flowers have a small, erect to slightly curved, stout, footless column.

GLOSSODIA

R. Brown

Prodr. Fl. Nov. Holland. 325 (1810).

Orchidoideæ ⚘ Diurideæ • Caladeniinæ

ETYMOLOGY: Greek for tongue-shaped and likeness. Refers to the tongue-like appendage at the base of the column.

LECTOTYPE: *Glossodia major* R. Brown

Two showy, sympodial terrestrials are found in low elevation, coastal scrub, dunes and eucalyptus forests of eastern and southern Australia and Tasmania. These erect plants, often forming large colonies, have short, unbranched stems, subtended by a multilayered fibrous tunic, each with a solitary, hairy, narrow, basal leaf. The slender, wiry, hairy, one- to two-flowered inflorescence has spectacular blue to purple or rare white, sweetly fragrant flowers with a glossy surface on the inside and hairy on the outer surfaces. The small, heart-shaped, waxy-textured, entire lip is bright white at the base and has two, basal calli on a flattened, curved claw. The flowers have an erect, incurved column.

GLOSSOIDA

An orthographic variant cited in *Dict. Gen. Names Seed Pl.*, 59 (1995). The correct spelling is *Glossodia*.

GLOSSOPSIS

An orthographic variant cited in *Lex. Gen. Phan.*, 251 (1904). The correct spelling is *Glossaspis*.

GLOSSORHYNCHA

Ridley

J. Linn. Soc., Bot. **28**(195): 341, *t.* 44 (1891).

ETYMOLOGY: Greek for tongue and snout or horn. Referring to the large, tongue-shaped rostellum.

TYPE SPECIES: *Glossorhyncha amboinensis* Ridley

Now recognized as belonging to the genus *Glomera*, *Glossorhyncha* was previously considered to include eighty epiphytes, lithophytes or rare terrestrials found in misty, low to upper elevation, hill and montane forests for the most part to New Guinea, but a few species are also found in the Solomons, Vanuatu, New Caledonia and Fiji. These green, sometimes suffused orange, strongly branched, tiny plants form dense, spreading masses in tree mosses. The erect or hanging stems are usually slender, multibranched and each with several, narrow leaves at the tip. The slender, solitary-flowered inflorescence has a distinctive structure where each flower has two opposing bracts. The sweetly fragrant, delicate white flower, large for the size of the plant, has similar, narrow sepals and petals with yellow tips and an obscurely trilobed lip. The flowers have a short, slender column.

GLOSSORRHYNCHA

An orthographic variant introduced in *Nat. Pflanzenfam., Nachtr.*, **1**: 105 (1897). The correct spelling is *Glossorhyncha*.

GLOSSORYNCHA

An orthographic variant cited in *Lex. Gen. Phan.*, 251 (1904). The correct spelling is *Glossorhyncha*.

GLOSSULA

Lindley
Bot. Reg. **10**: t. 862 (1824).
Name ICBN rejected vs. *Peristylus* Blume (1825) Orchidaceæ; and not *Glossula* (Rafinesque) Reichenbach (1837) Aristolochiaceæ.
ETYMOLOGY: Diminutive of Greek for tongue. Refers to the lip's unusual midlobe.
TYPE SPECIES: *Glossula tentaculata* Lindley

Although validly published this rejected name is referred to *Peristylus*. *Glossula* was considered to include four terrestrials found from northern India (Assam), southern China (Yunnan to Fujian), Thailand, Cambodia and Vietnam. These small, erect plants have smooth, slender stems, each with clustered, narrow to oblong leaves. The tall, cylindrical inflorescence has tiny flowers with a concave dorsal sepal and widespreading lateral sepals. The small petals converge but are not fused to the dorsal sepal. The unusual, deeply trilobed lip has very long, thread-like side lobes, a small, narrow midlobe and a hanging spur.

GLYCORCHIS

D.L. Jones & M.A. Clements
Orchadian **13**(9): 404 (2001).
ETYMOLOGY: Greek for sweet and orchid. The local Aussie common name is applied to this species.
TYPE SPECIES: *None designated*

Not validly published, this name is referred to *Ericksonella*. *Glycorchis* was considered to include one terrestrial found in southwestern Australia.

GNEMIDIA

An orthographic variant introduced in *Orchideen (Schlechter)*, ed. 1, 127 (1915). The correct spelling is *Cnemidia*.

GOADBYELLA

R.S. Rogers
Trans. & Proc. Roy. Soc. South Australia **51**: 294 (1927).
ETYMOLOGY: Named in honor of Bede Theodoric Goadby (1863-1944), an Indian-born Australian lieutenant colonel, army engineer, orchid enthusiast and amateur botanist. And Latin for diminutive.
TYPE SPECIES: *Goadbyella gracilis* R.S. Rogers

Now recognized as belonging to the genus *Microtis*, *Goadbyella* was previously considered to include one terrestrial found in wet, low elevation habitats of western Australia. This inconspicuous, slender, robust plant has unbranched stems each with several, narrow, tapering leaves. The erect, numerous-flowered inflorescence has tiny, crisp white to dull green flowers with a prominent, concave dorsal sepal. The long, white, bilobed lip has large and broad, or long and narrow lobes with a crisp or wavy, fringed or scalloped margin. The unusual callus has an oblong or an irregular, hard thickening along the center and sometimes has a pair of calli. The above type name is now considered a synonym of *Microtis alba* R. Brown.

GODOYERA

An orthographic variant introduced in *Nouv. Dict. Hist. Nat.*, ed. 2, **30**: 242 (1819). The correct spelling is *Goodyera*.

GODYERA

An orthographic variant introduced in *Nomencl. Fl. Danic.*, 181 (1827). The correct spelling is *Goodyera*.

GOLDSCHMIDTIA

Dammer
Orchis (Ledien & Witt) **4**(1): 86 (1910).
ETYMOLOGY: Honoring Hans Goldschmidt (1861-1923), a German chemist who discovered the thermite reaction used in the welding of steel and an orchid enthusiast from Essen.
TYPE SPECIES: *Goldschmidtia gracilis* Dammer
This type name is now considered a synonym of *Dendrobium hercoglossum* Reichenbach f.

Not validly published, this name is referred to *Dendrobium*. *Goldschmidtia* was considered to include one epiphyte found from Thailand to Vietnam, Hong Kong, China (Anhui to Yunnan), Malaysia, and Indonesia (Sumatra) to the Philippines.

GOLERA

An orthographic variant introduced in *Fl. Taiwan*, **5**: 980 (1978). The correct spelling is *Galera*.

GOMERA

An orthographic variant introduced in *Bonplandia*, **4**(20): 322 (1856). The correct spelling is *Gomesa*.

GOMESA

R. Brown
Bot. Mag. **42**: t. 1748 (1815).
Epidendroideæ • Cymbidieæ • Oncidiinæ
ETYMOLOGY: Honoring Bernardino Antônio Gomes (1769-1823), a Portuguese-born botanist, doctor who went to Brazil as a naval physician, and author of *Plantas medicinais do Brasil*.
TYPE SPECIES: *Gomesa recurva* R. Brown

Seventeen small, sympodial epiphytes or lithophytes are found in moist, humid, mid elevation, montane forests of southern and central Brazil, Paraguay, Uruguay and northeastern Argentina. These plants have tightly clustered to well-spaced, translucent green, oval, cone-shaped to strongly compressed pseudobulbs, partially subtended by pale green, leafless sheaths, each with two oblong, leathery to thinly textured leaves. Some species have large spaces between the pseudobulbs spaced along the short rhizome. The arching, densely packed, numerous-flowered inflorescence has small to tiny, insignificant, faintly fragrant, long-lived, white, yellow or green flowers. The entire or trilobed lip, attached to the column base, has erect side lobes, and a spreading or curved midlobe with two basal calli. The flowers have an erect, slender, footless column.

Currently Accepted   Validly Published   Invalidly Published   Published Pre-1753   Superfluous Usage   Orthographic Variant   Fossil

Orchid Genera • **174**

GOMESIA

Not *Gomesia* La Llave (1832) Compositæ.

An orthographic variant introduced in *Nouv. Dict. Hist. Nat.*, ed. 2, **13**: 284 (1817). The correct spelling is *Gomesa*.

GOMEZA

An orthographic variant introduced in *Bot. Cab.*, **9**: t. 806 (1824). The correct spelling is *Gomesa*.

GOMEZIA

Hoffmannsegg

Verz. Orchid. 50 (1842), and
Bot. Zeitung (Berlin) **1**: 832 (1843).

Not *Gomezia* Bentham & Hooker f. (1873) Compositæ, not *Gomezia* Mutis (1821) Rubiaceæ, and not *Gomezia* Bartling (1830) Orchidaceæ.

ETYMOLOGY: Honoring Bernardino Antônio Gomes (1769-1823).

TYPE SPECIES: *Gomezia densiflora* Hoffmannsegg

This type name is now considered a synonym of
Gomesa recurva R. Brown

Not validly published because of a prior use of the name, this homonym was replaced by *Gomesia*.

GOMEZIA

An orthographic variant introduced in *Ord. Nat. Pl.*, 58 (1830). The correct spelling is *Gomesa*.

GOMPHICHES

An orthographic variant introduced in *Repert. Spec. Nov. Regni Veg. Beih.*, **6**: 15 (1919). The correct spelling is *Gomphichis*.

GOMPHICHIS

Lindley

Gen. Sp. Orchid. Pl. 446 (1840).

Orchidoideæ ⚘ Cranichideæ • Cranichidinæ

ETYMOLOGY: Greek for nail, peg or pin. Refers to the hairs on the flower, which are quite stiff, upstanding like nails that are partly driven into a surface.

TYPE SPECIES: *Gomphichis goodyeroides* Lindley

Twenty-five, sympodial terrestrials or occasional epiphytes are found in wet, cool, mid to upper elevation, montane grasslands from Costa Rica to Bolivia, Venezuela, Guyana and western Brazil. These large, erect plants have simple, stout, leafy stems, each with several, narrow, fleshy leaves grouped together near the base. The terminal, downy covered, numerous-flowered inflorescence has several, leafy bracts and the tiny, pale yellow to creamy flowers have hairy margins. The slender sepals have densely woolly, rigid or soft, slender hairs and the petals have ciliate to slender processes. The hairy, concave, entire or trilobed lip is uppermost and has a thickened basal disk. The flowers have a club-shaped, footless column that is bent at a right angle.

GOMPHOSTYLIS

Wallich ex Lindley

Gen. Sp. Orchid. Pl. 43 (1830).

Not *Gomphostylis* Rafinesque (1837) Melanthiaceæ.

ETYMOLOGY: Greek for nail and style. Referring to the size and shape of the column.

TYPE SPECIES: *Gomphostylis candida*
Wallich ex Lindley
(*Coelogyne maculata* Lindley)
This type name is now considered a synonym of
Pleione maculata (Lindley) Lindley;
basionym
Coelogyne maculata Lindley

Not validly published, this name is referred to *Pleione*. *Gomphostylis* was considered to include one epiphyte or lithophyte found in northern India, southern China, Myanmar and Thailand.

GONATOSTYLIS

Schlechter

Bot. Jahrb. Syst. **39**: 56 (1906).

Orchidoideæ ⚘ Cranichideæ • Goodyerinæ

ETYMOLOGY: Greek for jointed, angle and pillar or style. Descriptive of the bent column.

TYPE SPECIES: *Gonatostylis vieillardii*
(Reichenbach f.) Schlechter
(*Rhamphidia vieillardii* Reichenbach f.)

Two uncommon, sympodial terrestrials are found in humid, low to mid elevation, hill and montane forests, scrub and savanna of New Caledonia. These medium-sized, erect plants have short, unbranched stems, subtended entirely by leaf sheaths, each with several, spear-shaped, variegated, green or dark purple-red leaves that have pale colored margins. The tall, slender, numerous-flowered inflorescence has tiny flowers opening progressively, but not widely. The concave lateral sepals are slightly larger than the dorsal sepal, and the oblong petals are thinly textured. The fiddle-shaped, entire lip has two fleshy ridges within the concave area, and incurved margins. The flowers have a slender, strongly curved (at the tip), footless column.

GONGONA

An orthographic variant introduced in *Orchideen (Schlechter)*, ed. 1, 114 (1914). The correct spelling is *Gongora*.

GONGORA

Ruiz & Pavón

Fl. Peruv. Prodr. 117, t. 25 (1794).

Epidendroideæ ⚘ Cymbidieæ • Stanhopeinæ

ETYMOLOGY: In dedication to Antonio Caballero y Góngora (1723-1796), Bishop of Córdoba, Spain, the Viceroy of New Granada (Colombia and Ecuador), Governor of Peru, and a patron of the Spanish botanist, naturalist and physician Jose Celestino Bruno Mutis (1732-1808).

TYPE SPECIES: *Gongora quinquenervis* Ruiz & Pavón

About fifty-eight sympodial epiphytes are found in wet, low to mid elevation, hill and montane forests of southern Mexico (Chiapas) to Panama, Trinidad, the Guianas, Venezuela, Ecuador and Peru to northern Brazil with the center of distribution in Colombia. These plants have strongly ribbed, ovoid to elongated pseudobulbs, each with two thinly textured, heavily veined leaves. The long, hanging, numerous to few-flowered inflorescences (often three feet or more in length and borne from the base of the pseudo-bulb) have intricate, short-lived, waxy, highly colored flowers, and most species are strongly fragrant. With a fascinating lip shape, often defying a verbal description, the trilobed lip, continuous with the column foot, has erect side lobes, and the midlobe is compressed or sac-like. The flowers have a slender, slightly arched column that is more or less winged on the margins.

GONGORAS

Hoffmannsegg

Verz. Orchid. 53 (1843), and
Bot. Zeitung (Berlin) **1**: 833 (1843).

ETYMOLOGY: In dedication to Antonio Caballero y Góngora.

TYPE SPECIES: *Gongoras irrorata* Hoffmannsegg
This type name is now considered a synonym of
Gongora bufonia Lindley

Not validly published, this name is referred to *Gongora*. *Gongoras* was considered to include one epiphyte found in Brazil (São Paulo, Rio de Janeiro, Santa Catarina, Paraná and Pernambuco).

GONIOBULBON

D.F. Blaxell

Orchid. German-Neu-Guinea 42 (1982).

Not validly published, this name was incorrectly referred to as a genus, in the English translation of *Orchidaceen von Deutsch-Neu-Guinea* by R.S. Rogers, but today is considered a section of *Diplocaulobium*.

GONIOCHILUS

M.W. Chase

Contr. Univ. Michigan Herb. **16**: 124 (1987).

Epidendroideæ ╲ Cymbidieæ • Oncidiinæ

ETYMOLOGY: Latinized Greek for jointed and lip. In reference to the lip that is bent downward like a knee.

TYPE SPECIES: *Goniochilus leochilinus* (Reichenbach f.) M.W. Chase (*Rodriguezia leochilina* Reichenbach f.)

One sympodial epiphyte is found in low to mid elevation, hill to montane cloud forests, coffee and citrus groves from Nicaragua and Costa Rica to Peru. This small, red-purple plant has clusters of tiny, flattened pseudobulbs, subtended by distichous, overlapping sheaths, each with a solitary leaf that has its two sides, folded together lengthwise. The several, hanging, few-flowered inflorescences have bell-shaped, green-yellow flowers covered with red-brown or brown spots. The white, trilobed lip, sprinkled with a few rosy red blotches, has small side lobes. The downward hanging midlobe has a wavy margin that is notched in the middle, and has a basal, plate-like callus with a raised hump. The flowers have a small, club-shaped, winged column.

GONOGONA

An orthographic variant introduced in *Nat. Syst. Bot.*, ed. 2, 341 (1836). The correct spelling is *Gonogora*.

GONOGORA

Link

Enum. Hort. Berol. Alt. **2**: 369 (1822).

ETYMOLOGY: The origin and meaning of this name is unknown.

TYPE SPECIES: *None designated*

Now recognized as belonging to the genera *Ludisia* and *Goodyera*, *Gonogora* was previously considered to include two terrestrials found from Myanmar to Vietnam, southern China (Yunnan to Hainan) and Malaysia. One species is highly variable, often grown for its showy, purple-red leaves that have red or golden-yellow veins. The few-flowered inflorescence has small, white flowers with a strangely twisted, long-clawed, entire to bilobed lip. The flowers have a small column with a bright yellow anther. One species is now considered a synonym of *Ludisia discolor* (Ker Gawler).

A. Richard, and the other species is a synonym of *Goodyera repens* (Linnaeus) R. Brown.

GOODIERA

An orthographic variant introduced in *Hist. Orchid.*, Table 1, sub 2i, *tt.* 28-29 (1822). The correct spelling is *Goodyera*.

GOODIREA

An orthographic variant introduced in *Comp. Fl. Ital. (Arcangeli)*, ed. 2, 159, 162 (1894). The correct spelling is *Goodyera*.

GOODIYERA

An orthographic variant introduced in *Bot. Centralbl.*, **53**(51): 475 (1899). The correct spelling is *Goodyera*.

GOODYEARA

An orthographic variant introduced in *Trans. Wisconsin Acad. Sci.*, **3**: 56 (1876). The correct spelling is *Goodyera*.

GOODYERA

R. Brown

Hortus Kew., ed. 2 **5**: 197 (1813).

Orchidoideæ ╲ Cranichideæ • Goodyerinæ

ETYMOLOGY: In honor of John Goodyer (1592-1664), a British botanist and Greek scholar who maintained an herbal garden in Petersfield, where in 1655 he translated *The Greek Herbal of Dioscorides: Illustrated by a Byzantine …*

LECTOTYPE: *Goodyera repens* (Linnaeus) R. Brown (*Satyrium repens* Linnaeus)

Ninety-six evergreen, sympodial terrestrials, rare epiphytes or lithophytes are widespread in almost all parts of the globe, except Africa, in shady, low to upper elevation, montane forests, grasslands and roadsides. The largest group is found from northern India (Sikkim) to Vietnam, Indonesia (Sumatra), Mongolia, China (Jilin to Xizang), Korea and Japan (Hokkaido to Honshu). But are also found in Canada to Mexico, Europe, Russia and Madagascar. These erect, small plants have short to long, white to red-brown, unbranched stems, each with commonly crowded, spirally arranged, basal or clustered, slightly fleshy leaves that have showy, reptile-like, leaf mottlings of silvery veins and markings. These attractive, checkered or veined leaves are retained for several growing seasons. The erect, hairy, narrow, densely packed, numerous to few-flowered inflorescence has tight, spirally arranged flowers with

smooth to hairy outer surfaces. The insignificant, often rather small, white, green, yellow or pale brown flowers do not open widely. The dorsal sepal and petals (sometimes joined near their tips) converge, forming a hood over the slender, erect, short or prominent, footless column. The hollow, narrowly sac-like or deeply concave, hairy, obscurely trilobed or entire lip is attached for much of its length to the lower column margins. The roundish to oblong spur, if present, has several appendages.

NOTE: These species are most often grown for their attractive leaves, rather than for their drab flowers.

GOODYERIA

An orthographic variant introduced in *Neue Jahr. Phil. Paedag.*, 644 (1877). The correct spelling is *Goodyera*.

GOODYRA

An orthographic variant introduced in *Bot. Zeitung (Leipzig)*, **33**: 352 (1874) The correct spelling is *Goodyera*.

GOOYERA

An orthographic variant introduced in *Enum. Pl. Jap.*, **2**: 519 (1879). The correct spelling is *Goodyera*.

GORDYERA

An orthographic variant introduced in *Beih. Bot. Centralbl.*, **33**(2): 410 (1915). The correct spelling is *Goodyera*.

GORENIA

An orthographic variant cited in *Pl. Vasc. Gen. (Meisner)*, **2**: 283 (1842). The correct spelling is *Govenia*.

GORGOGLOSSUM

F. Lehmann

Gard. Chron., ser. 3 **21**: 346 (1897).

ETYMOLOGY: Greek for the terrible or fierce and for tongue. Alluding to the excessively thread-like margins of the lip and petals.

Or perhaps, Greek Mythology. Referring to the fancied resemblance of the snake-covered heads of the *Gorgons*. The Gorgons were three hideous sisters (Medusa, Stheno and Euryale) who lived in the far west and were the offspring of sea-gods. They had live snakes instead of hair.

TYPE SPECIES: *Gorgoglossum reichenbachiana* F. Lehmann

Not validly published, this name is referred to *Sievekingia*. *Gorgoglossum* was considered to include one epiphyte found from southwestern Colombia to northern Bolivia.

Currently Accepted | Validly Published | Invalidly Published | Published Pre-1753 | Superfluous Usage | Orthographic Variant | Fossil

GOVENIA

Lindley

Bot. Cab. **18**: *t. 1709* (1831), and
Gen. Sp. Orchid. Pl. 153 (1832).

Epidendroideæ ⚘ Calypsoeæ

ETYMOLOGY: Commemorating James Robert Gowen (x-1862), a British gardener to the 3rd Earl of Carnarvon, horticulturist, secretary and a treasurer of the Royal Horticultural Society. He collected the flora of eastern India.

TYPE SPECIES: *Govenia superba* (Lexarza) Lindley
(*Maxillaria superba* Lexarza)

Nineteen, sympodial terrestrials are distributed in moist, humid to cool, mid elevation, montane and pine-oak forests from Mexico to Bolivia, Brazil, Argentina and Paraguay with one species found in the Bahamas, Cuba to Puerto Rico and the south-eastern United States (Florida). These plants have short stems reduced to corm-like or egg-shaped pseudobulbs, subtended by leaf-sheaths, each with one to three, thinly textured, strongly veined, pleated leaves. The erect, numerous to few-flowered inflorescence has pale yellow to white flowers varying tremendously in color even within a single species and only open partially. The concave, large dorsal sepal and strongly curved, erect petals (finely banded pale rose inside) converge, forming a hood over the incurved, fleshy, winged column that is with or without a foot. The strongly erect, shortly clawed, entire lip has a downward curved tip.

NOTE: This is a taxonomically difficult genus to identify because the various differences usually disappear in the dried herbarium material.

GOVINDOOIA

Wight

Icon. Pl. Ind. Orient. (Wight) **6**: 34, *t. 2090* (1853).

ETYMOLOGY: Dedicated to Mr. Govindoo, a local Indian native artist who produced the illustrations used for the last three volumes of Robert Wight's (1796-1872) *Icones* series on the flora of India.

TYPE SPECIES: *Govindooia nervosa* Wight

This type name is now considered a synonym of
Tropidia angulosa (Lindley) Blume;
basionym
Cnemidia angulosa Lindley

Now recognized as belonging to the genus *Tropidia*, *Govindooia* was previously considered to include one terrestrial distributed in low to mid elevation, humid, shady, evergreen forests of southern China (Yunnan to Guangxi), Taiwan, northern India (Sikkim), Myanmar to Vietnam, Thailand, Malaysia and Indonesia. This simple to sometimes branching plant has rather thin, woody stems, subtended by loose sheaths, each with several, unequal leaves near the stem's tip. The erect, few-flowered inflorescence has small, white or pale yellow flowers not opening widely, and the oblong, entire lip has a small spur.

GOVINDOVIA

An orthographic variant introduced in *Ann. Bot. Syst.*, **6**: 158 (1861). The correct spelling is *Govindooia*.

GOWENIA

An orthographic variant cited in *Lex. Gen. Phan.*, 213, 255 (1904). The correct spelling is *Govenia*.

GRAASTIDIUM

An orthographic variant introduced in *Orchids India*, ed. 2, 210 (1999). The correct spelling is *Grastidium*.

GRACIELANTHUS

R. González & Szlachetko

Fragm. Florist. Geobot. **40**(2): 760 (1995).

ETYMOLOGY: Honoring Graciela Calderón y Rzedowski (1931-), a Polish-born Mexican botanist and taxonomist who has written numerous articles furthering our knowledge of Mexican botany. And Latin for flower.

TYPE SPECIES: *Gracielanthus pyramidalis*
(Lindley) R. González & Szlachetko
(*Spiranthes pyramidalis* Lindley)

Now recognized as belonging to the genus *Kionophyton*, *Gracielanthus* was proposed to include two terrestrials, occasionally epiphytes or lithophytes found in leaf mold among lava rocks or deep humus in mid elevation, oak-pine forests from Mexico to Nicaragua. These erect plants have unbranched stems with overlapping sheaths and rosulate leaves. The leaves are partly withered by flowering time. The tall, spirally arranged, densely packed, numerous-flowered, thick inflorescence has small, mostly pale brown to green-brown, tubular flowers with white veins. The spear-shaped, long to shortly clawed, ovate, entire lip has two small, thick projections located near the base. The flowers have a short, curved, densely hairy column.

GRACILANGIS

Thouars

Hist. Orchid. Table 2, sub 3o, *t. 77* (1822).

Name published without a description. Today this name is most often referred to *Chamaeangis*.

GRACILOPHYLIS

Thouars

Hist. Orchid. Table 3, sub 3u, *t. 101* (1822).

Name published without a description. Today this name is most often referred to *Bulbophyllum*.

GRAFIA

A.D. Hawkes

Phytologia **13**(5): 305 (1966).
Not *Grafia* Reichenbach (1837) Apiaceæ.

ETYMOLOGY: Dedicated to Alfred Bryd Graf (1901-2001), an American horticulturist, botanical photographer, magazine editor and the author of books on tropical flora including *Exotica*.

TYPE SPECIES: *Grafia parishii*
(Reichenbach f.) A.D. Hawkes
(*Phalaenopsis parishii* Reichenbach f.)

Not validly published because of a prior use of the name, this homonym was replaced by *Phalaenopsis*.

GRAMATOPHYLLUM

An orthographic variant introduced in *Neue Allg. Garten- Blumenzeitung*, **1**: 321 (1845-46). The correct spelling is *Grammatophyllum*.

GRAMINISATIS

Thouars

Hist. Orchid. Table 1, sub 1c, *t. 6, t. 12a* (1822).

Name published without a description. Today this name is most often referred to *Cynorkis*.

GRAMMANGIS

Reichenbach *filius*

Hamburger Garten- Blumenzeitung **16**: 520 (1860).

Epidendroideæ ⚘ Cymbideæ ⚘ Eulophiinæ

ETYMOLOGY: Greek for a thread or line and vessel. Significance is obscure, unless referring to the conspicuous red-purple lines on the lip.

TYPE SPECIES: *Grammangis ellisii*
(Lindley) Reichenbach f.
(*Grammatophyllum ellisii* Lindley)

Two sympodial, epiphytes are found in shady, low to mid elevation, coastal rain forests of eastern Madagascar. These large, robust plants have densely packed, numerous-flowered inflorescences, borne from the base of a tall, spindle-shaped pseudobulb. Each bulb has several, oblong, leathery, glossy, dark green leaves. These long-lived, waxy, strikingly colored brown flowers with a heavy pervading fragrance, have glossy, widespreading, brown lateral sepals spotted yellow. The smaller, creamy-colored petals are pink-yellow above, and the arching dorsal sepal has a wavy margin with the tip bent backward. The white, trilobed lip, joined at the tip of the column foot, has strongly curved side lobes, and the long, narrow midlobe is pale pink-orange above with a white callus. The flowers have a small, fleshy, winged column with a short, thick foot.

GRAMMATOPHYLLUM

Blume
Bijdr. Fl. Ned. Ind. **8**: 377, t. 20 (1825).

Epidendroideæ ◊ Cymbidieæ • Cymbidiinæ

ETYMOLOGY: Greek for letters or line and leaf. Refers to the dark and conspicuous markings of the sepals and petals.

TYPE SPECIES: *Grammatophyllum speciosum*
(Linnaeus) Blume
(*Epidendrum scriptum* Linnaeus)

Eleven sympodial epiphytes found in humid, low to mid elevation, coastal rain and evergreen forests, and along river banks from Myanmar, Malaysia, Indonesia, New Guinea, the Solomon Islands and Fiji to the Philippines. These often prodigious orchids include one species conceded to be the largest of the pseudobulbous orchids. These bulbs can reach lengths in excess of twenty-five feet (7.5 m) but average nine to ten feet (2.7 to 3 m) in length. Some species have cane-like stems each with several, alternating leaves giving an impression of a palm. Other species have thick, compact pseudobulbs, subtended by several sheaths, each with oblong, pleated leaves at the tip. All of these clump-forming species are spectacular with their huge, arching, numerous-flowered inflorescences that have showy, long-lasting, large, multi-colored, waxy flowers. The color and intensity of the flower varies, with the lowest flowers on the rachis sterile and often misshapen. The small, usually hairy, trilobed lip has oblong, bluntly pointed, erect side lobes, and the broad, ovate midlobe has three small, basal calli. The flowers have a short, club-shaped, footless column.

GRAMMATOPHYLUM

An orthographic variant introduced in *Rumphia*, **4**: 50 (1849). The correct spelling is *Grammatophyllum*.

GRAMMINGIS

An orthographic variant introduced in *Hamburger Garten- Blumenzeitung*, **18**: 84 (1862). The correct spelling is *Grammangis*.

GRANDIPHYLLUM

Docha Neto
Colet. Orquídeas Brasil. **3**: 75 (2006).

ETYMOLOGY: Latin for big or showy and leaf. Refers to the leaves of the plant that are proportionally large when compared with the other parts.

TYPE SPECIES: *Grandiphyllum divaricatum*
(Lindley) Docha Neto
(*Oncidium divaricatum* Lindley)

Recognized as belonging to the genus *Oncidium*, *Grandiphyllum* was proposed to include ten epiphytes found in mid elevation, montane forests of eastern Peru and southeastern Brazil to northern Argentina. These small plants have tightly clustered, roundish, strongly compressed, yellow-green pseudobulbs, each with a solitary, narrow to oblong, leathery leaf that is strongly keeled on the backside. The long, multi-branched, dull purple, numerous-flowered inflorescence has small, fragrant flowers with shortly clawed sepals and petals. These are colored chestnut-brown with a golden yellow blotch near the tips. The trilobed lip has large, roundish side lobes spotted red-brown and the oblong, yellow midlobe has a cushion-like callus.

GRANICHIS

An orthographic variant introduced in *Lilloa*, **3**: 476 (1938). The correct spelling is *Cranichis*.

GRAPHORCHIS

An orthographic variant introduced in *Hist. Orchid.*, Table 4, sub 3, t. 39 (1822). The correct spelling is *Graphorkis*.

GRAPHORKIS

Thouars
Nouv. Bull. Sci. Soc. Philom. Paris **1**(19): 318 (1809).
Name ICBN conserved, and type name also conserved.

Epidendroideæ ◊ Cymbidieæ • Cymbidiinæ

ETYMOLOGY: Greek for painted, marked with letters or to write and for orchid. Refers to the variegated markings or patterns on the flower.

TYPE SPECIES: *Graphorkis concolor* (Thouars) Kuntze
(*Limodorum concolor* Thouars)

Four sympodial epiphytes are found in humid, low elevation, hill forests of Madagascar and the Mascarene Islands with one species found in tropical Africa from

southern Ethiopia to Ghana and south to Zambia. These small plants have clustered, ovoid to cylindrical pseudobulbs, subtended by dry sheaths, each with several leaves. The leaves, borne at the tip, appear only after the flowers have faded. The plants are vegetatively similar to *Ansellia* but this genus has spurred flowers. The branched, numerous to few-flowered inflorescence has small, dull yellow-green flowers with or without brown or purple markings on the front side of the sepals and petals. The backside is usually a solid, pale green-yellow. The bright yellow, trilobed lip has small, erect side lobes; a broad, pale yellow midlobe with several calli and has a bent, sharply forward spur that is nearly as long as the lip. The flowers have an erect or bent, wingless column with a hairy mound on each side at the base.

GRASTIDIAM

An orthographic variant introduced in *Orchids India*, ed. 2, 204 (1999). The correct spelling is *Grastidium*.

GRASTIDIUM

Blume
Bijdr. Fl. Ned. Ind. **7**: 333, 433 (1825).

ETYMOLOGY: Greek for grass or green fodder. Alluding to the green of the entire plant.

LECTOTYPE: *Grastidium salaccense* Blume

Now recognized as belonging to the genus *Dendrobium*, as a section *Grastidium* was previously considered to include one hundred fifty-seven epiphytes, lithophytes or terrestrials found in low to mid elevation, hill and montane forests from India to the southwestern Pacific Archipelago with the largest concentration found in New Guinea sometimes growing in full sunlight. These erect or arching plants have long, slender, wiry stems, with one to several internodes, or they sometimes form small pseudobulbs. The thin, well-spaced, grass-like, green to dull yellow leaves have sheathing bases. The several, solitary-flowered inflorescences have a small, pale green, bright yellow or pale yellow flowers borne in pairs from leaf nodes and lasting for only a day. The showy, white to yellow, trilobed lip has brown markings and a prominent chin-like protuberance which is attached or fused at the base of the column foot. Plant colonies will often synchronize their blooming times together.

GRASTRIDIUM

An orthographic variant cited in *Lex. Gen. Phan.*, 256 (1904). The correct spelling is *Grastidium*.

Currently Accepted   Validly Published   Invalidly Published   Published Pre-1753   Superfluous Usage   Orthographic Variant   Fossil

Orchid Genera • **178**

GREENWOODIA

Burns-Balogh

Orquidea (Mexico City), n.s.　　**10**(1): 1 (1986).

ETYMOLOGY: In honor of Edward Warren Greenwood (1918-2002), a Canadian engineering chemist and amateur botanist who worked on the taxonomy of western Mexican orchids from the Oaxaca region.

TYPE SPECIES: *Greenwoodia sawyeri*
(Standley & L.O. Williams) Burns-Balogh
(*Spiranthes sawyeri* Standley & L.O. Williams)

Now recognized as belonging to the genus *Kionophyton*, *Greenwoodia* was previously considered to include one terrestrial found in sunny, mid elevation, open forests of northeastern Mexico. This erect plant has slender, unbranched stems, each with clasping basal leaves that wither soon after flowering commences. The numerous-flowered inflorescence has slightly overlapping bracts. The small green-yellow, tubular flowers are covered with several, pale tan spots, each subtended by a bract. The narrow dorsal sepal, lateral sepals and petals each have three nerves. The white, entire lip forms a tube-like entrance, has yellow margins, and red-brown lines on the callus. The flowers have a short, narrow white column.

GROBIA

An orthographic variant introduced in *Hamburger Garten- Blumenzeitung*, **27**: 218 (1871). The correct spelling is *Grobya*.

GROBYA

Lindley

Edwards's Bot. Reg.　　**20**: t. 1740 (1835).

Epidendroideæ ⚘ Cymbidieæ • Catasetinæ

ETYMOLOGY: Honoring George Harry Grey (1802-1835), a British Lord of Groby at Dunham Massey Hall (located near Altrincham in Cheshire), an early orchid grower and patron of horticulture. He was a direct descendant of Lady Jane Grey (1537-1554), the nine day Queen of England.

TYPE SPECIES: *Grobya amherstiae* Lindley

Four unusual, attractive, sympodial epiphytes are found in humid, low elevation, rain forests of southeastern Brazil; one species is found in Ecuador. These small plants have densely tufted, ovoid, fleshy pseudobulbs, subtended by persistent, white, leafy bases, each with long, narrow, slightly grooved, pleated to grass-like leaves at the tip. The arching to hanging, numerous to few-flowered inflorescence has large, showy, fragrant, yellow, pale green to orange flowers suffused green and/or purple and are usually marked or spotted with yellow-brown tones. The usually large dorsal sepal along with the erect, broad petals form a hood over the erect, broad, slender or short, wingless column. The shortly united, narrow lateral sepals are spreading or reflexed, inrolled, twisted and claw-like. The small, trilobed lip has curved to erect side lobes. The flat, spreading midlobe has rounded ends, and the toothed disk has numerous, wart-like tubercles.

GROMMATOPHYLLUM

An orthographic variant introduced in *Not. Pl. Asiat.*, **3**: 344 (1851). The correct spelling is *Grammatophyllum*.

GROSOURDIA

An orthographic variant introduced in *J. Linn. Soc., Bot.*, **18**(110): 332 (1881). The correct spelling is *Grosourdya*.

GROSOURDYA

Reichenbach *filius*

Bot. Zeitung (Berlin)　　**22**: 297 (1864).

Epidendroideæ ⚘ Vandeæ • Aeridinæ

ETYMOLOGY: Honoring René (Renato) de Grosourdy (fl. 1836-1864), a German who specialized in the medical plants of South America and author of *El médico botánico criollo* and *Chimie Médicale*.

TYPE SPECIES: *Grosourdya elegans* Reichenbach f.

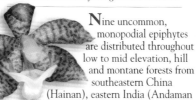

Nine uncommon, monopodial epiphytes are distributed throughout low to mid elevation, hill and montane forests from southeastern China (Hainan), eastern India (Andaman Islands), Myanmar to Vietnam, Thailand and Malaysia to the Philippines, with most found in Indonesia. These small plants have short stems, each with a few to several, flat, fleshy, distichous, sharply bilobed leaves that are arranged in two ranks. The several, slender, rough to prickly, few-flowered inflorescences have tiny, short-lived, usually pale or deep yellow flowers covered with red spots, and they open in succession over a long period of time. The yellow or white, trilobed lip has erect side lobes. It is hinged to the long, slender, slightly curved column that is bent forward at an obtuse angle and has a rounded, slightly elongated or swollen spur with a constricted mouth. These species were formerly included in *Pteroceras* or *Sarcochilus*.

GROSOWIDYA

An orthographic variant introduced in *Index Kew.*, **1**(2): 1067 (1893). The correct spelling is *Grosourdya*.

GROSSOURDYA

An orthographic variant introduced in *Bot. Zeitung (Berlin)*, **22**: 1, 6 (1864). The correct spelling is *Grosourdya*.

GUANCHESIA

An orthographic variant introduced in *Int. J. Plant Sci.*, **163**(6): 1055 (2002). The correct spelling is *Guanchezia*.

GUANCHEZIA

Romero & Carnevali

Orchids Venezuela, ed. 2　　**3**: 1135 (2000).

Epidendroideæ ⚘ Cymbidieæ • Maxillariinæ

ETYMOLOGY: Dedicated to Francisco J. Guánchez y Meza (1953-), a Venezuelan-born ethnobotanist from Cornell University (New York) and Dominican Republic's Punta Cana who has contributed greatly to our knowledge of the plants.

TYPE SPECIES: *Guanchezia maguirei*
(Schweinfurth) Romero & Carnevali
(*Bifrenaria maguirei* Schweinfurth)

One sympodial terrestrial or uncommon epiphyte, found in boggy, mid elevation, cerro summits of Aracamuni, Autana and Duida from southern Venezuelan (Amazonas). This plant has oblong pseudobulbs, each with a large, solitary, strongly ribbed leaf that is often a shiny purple. The erect, one- to two-flowered inflorescence has rather variable, dull yellow flowers suffused red, and the sepals margins are often rolled inwards with age. The broad, flat, white, obscurely trilobed lip has dark purple nerves radiating out from the base and a thin, white margin. The flowers have a short, stout, pale green column.

GUARIANTHE

Dressler & W.E. Higgins

Lankesteriana　　**7**(1): 37 (2003).

Epidendroideæ ⚘ Epidendreæ • Laeliinæ

ETYMOLOGY: From the Nahuatl (Aztec language) for tree and Greek for flower. Refers to the local name applied to this flower that grows on a tree.

TYPE SPECIES: *Guarianthe skinneri*
(Bateman) Dressler & W.E. Higgins
(*Cattleya skinneri* Bateman)

Four sympodial epiphytes are found in seasonally moist, low to mid elevation, hill to montane forests or cliff banks from southwestern Mexico, Belize to Panama, Trinidad, northern Colombia and northern Venezuela. These plants have slightly compressed, thickened, often densely clustered, club-shaped stems, each with two to four, oblong, leathery leaves borne at the tip. The short but usually erect, numerous to few-flowered inflorescence, borne from mature stems, has showy, rosy to bright purple flowers that are slightly to strongly fragrant, and has narrow, widespreading sepals and slightly wider petals. The white or creamy-colored throat of the entire or obscurely trilobed lip forms a funnel around the small, slender to club-shaped column.

GUDRUNIA

Braem

Schlechteriana   4(1-2): 24 (1993).

ETYMOLOGY: In honor of Gudrun Braem (1951-) née Schluckebier from Mengeringhausen, the German-born wife of Guido Braem (1944-), a Belgian art historian, orchidologist and author of numerous books on *Cattleya* and *Paphiopedilum*.

TYPE SPECIES: *Gudrunia tuerckheimii*
(Cogniaux) Braem
(*Oncidium tuerckheimii* Cogniaux)

Now recognized as belonging to the genus *Tolumnia*, *Gudrunia* was proposed to include one epiphyte found in cool, mid elevation, montane forests and scrub of Hispaniola and Cuba. This small, hanging plant has an attractive, fan-like shape with the triangular, long leaves overlapping at the bases. The long, wiry, few-flowered inflorescence has large, showy, long-lasting, bright yellow flowers covered with bold brown-purple blotches. The large, trilobed lip has small side lobes and a four-lobed midlobe with a red striped callus. The flowers have a small, stout, winged column.

GUEBINA

Brongniart

Enum. Pl. Mus. Paris, ed. 2   77 (1850).

Name published without a description. Today this name is most often referred to *Vanilla*.

GUILIANETTIA

An orthographic variant introduced in *Orchid. Icon. Index*, **4**: 269 (1934). The correct spelling is *Giulianettia*.

GULARIA

Garay

Bot. Mus. Leafl.   **28**(4): 321 (1980)[1982].

ETYMOLOGY: Greek for gullet or throat. In reference to the appearance of the tubular flowers.

TYPE SPECIES: *Gularia trilineata* (Lindley) Garay
(*Spiranthes trilineata* Lindley)

Now recognized as belonging to the genera *Deiregyne* and *Schiedeella*, *Gularia* was previously considered to include two terrestrials found in mid elevation, oak-pine forests from Mexico to Costa Rica usually in full sunlight. These small to tiny, inconspicuous plants are leafless during flowering. The delicate, few-flowered, white to pale brown inflorescence has small, white, tubular flowers suffused pink and green nerved. The dorsal sepal is united to the back of the column; the lateral sepals run down the column-foot forming a cylindrical nectary, and the petals converge with the dorsal sepal. The long-clawed, obscurely trilobed lip has basal appendages, and a rather fleshy, recurved, tip that is conspicuously constricted and has small, soft protuberances.

GUNIA

An orthographic variant introduced in *Prakt. Stud. Orchid.*, 32 (1854). The correct spelling is *Gunnia*.

GUNNARELLA

Senghas

Orchidee (Hamburg)   **39**(2): 71 (1988).

Epidendroideæ ⚘ **Vandeæ** • **Aeridinæ**

ETYMOLOGY: Dedicated to Gunnar Seidenfaden (1908-2001). And Latin for diminutive.

TYPE SPECIES: *Gunnarella carinata*
(J.J. Smith) Senghas
(*Chamaeanthus carinatuis* J.J. Smith)

Nine monopodial epiphytes are found in low elevation, rain forests, mangrove swamps, coastal woodlands and savannas from New Guinea, the Solomons and New Caledonia to Vanuatu. These tiny plants, often overlooked because of their size, have short to long, leafy stems in a fan-shaped arrangement, each with leathery, flattened, bilobed leaves that turn red when exposed to bright sunlight. The long, zig-zagged, hanging, numerous-flowered inflorescence has small, translucent white to creamy-white, sweetly fragrant, short-lived, delicate flowers opening sporadically or simultaneously but not widely. The sepals are free or shortly united with the petals at the base. The mobile,

fleshy, obscurely trilobed lip is yellow. The flowers have a long column.

GUNNARORCHIS

Brieger

Orchideen (Schlechter), ed. 3   **1**(11-12): 650 (1981).

ETYMOLOGY: In honor of Gunnar Seidenfaden (1908-2001), a Danish diplomat, explorer, naturalist, expert on tropical Asiatic orchids, author of numerous articles on Thai orchids and co-author of *The Orchids of Peninsular Malaysia and Singapore*. And Greek for orchid.

TYPE SPECIES: *Gunnarorchis perpusilla*
(C.S.P. Parish & Reichenbach f.) Brieger
(*Eria perpusilla* C.S.P. Parish & Reichenbach f.)

Now recognized as belonging to the genus *Eria*, *Gunnarorchis* was previously considered to include one epiphyte found in Myanmar, Thailand, Laos and Vietnam. This small plant has tiny, roundish, flattened, ribbed pseudobulbs, subtended by gray-green sheaths, but are usually leafless or sometimes with two fleshy, deciduous, thinly textured leaves. The long, stout, few to numerous-flowered inflorescence has white flowers that do not open widely and usually appear only after the leaves have withered. The oblong, obscurely trilobed lip has a recurved tip. The flowers have a short, stout column.

GUNNARRELLA

An orthographic variant introduced in *Fragm. Florist. Geobot.*, **3**(Suppl.): 89 (1995). The correct spelling is *Gunnarella*.

GUNNIA

Lindley

Edwards's Bot. Reg.   **20**: sub 1699 (1834).

Not *Gunnia* F. Mueller (1858) Aizoaceæ.

ETYMOLOGY: In honor of Ronald Campbell Gunn (1808-1881), a South African-born Australian army officer, Tasmania police magistrate and amateur botanist who provided numerous plant specimens to both John Lindley and William J. Hooker.

TYPE SPECIES: *Gunnia australis* Lindley

Now recognized as belonging to the genus *Sarcochilus*, *Gunnia* was previously considered to include three epiphytes found in dry, low elevation, woodlands of eastern Australia (New South Wales, Victoria and Tasmania). These plants have short stems, subtended by overlapping sheaths, each with several, slightly twisted, narrow, leathery leaves. The hanging, few-flowered inflorescence has small, fragrant flowers varying from brown to pale yellow-green. The white, trilobed lip has oblong,

Currently Accepted   Validly Published   Invalidly Published   Published Pre-1753   Superfluous Usage   Orthographic Variant   Fossil

O r c h i d   G e n e r a   •   **180**

upward curved, yellow side lobes almost as long as the shorter petals, that are covered with purple blotches and streaks. The lip has a small, white, sac-like midlobe, and a cone-shaped spur. The flowers have a slender, short to long, curved column.

GUNUIA

An orthographic variant introduced in *Syn. Pl.* (D. Dietrich), **5**: 113 (1852). The correct spelling is *Gunnia*.

GUSSONEA

A. Richard

Mém. Soc. Hist. Nat. Paris **4**: 67, *t. 11* (Sept. 1828), and *Dict. Class. Hist. Nat.* **12**: 509 (1827).

Not *Gussonea* Tornabene (1848) Lichens, not *Gussonea* J. Presl & G. Presl (Jul/Dec 1828) Cyperaceæ, and not *Gussonea* Parlatore (1838) Favaceæ.

ETYMOLOGY: Dedicated to Giovanni Gussone (1787-1866), a Neapolitan botanist, director of Bocca di Falco Botanical Garden at Palermo and author of *Enumeratio Plantum Vascularium ...*

TYPE SPECIES: *Gussonea aphylla* (Thouars) A. Richard (*Angraecum aphyllum* Thouars)

Not validly published, this name is referred to *Solenangis*. *Gussonea* was considered to include twenty-eight epiphytes found in low elevation, scrub of Kenya to Mozambique and Zimbabwe, and Madagascar to the Mascarene Islands.

GUSSONIA

Not *Gussonia* Sprengel (1820) Euphorbiaceæ.

An orthographic variant introduced in *Gen. Pl.* (Sprengel), **2**: 664 (1831). The correct spelling is *Gussonea*.

GYALADENIA

Schlechter

Beih. Bot. Centralbl. **38**(2): 124 (1921).

ETYMOLOGY: Greek for hollow and gland. Referring to the concave, hood-shaped lobes of the rostellum.

TYPE SPECIES: *Gyaladenia mac-owaniana* (Reichenbach f.) Schlechter (*Brachycorythis mac-owaniana* Reichenbach f.)

Now recognized as belonging to the genus *Brachycorythis*, *Gyaladenia* was previously considered to include ten terrestrials found in mid elevation, grasslands of South Africa, Burundi, Rwanda, Zambia, Malawi and Madagascar. These erect plants, usually flowering only after a fire, have slender, unbranched stems, each with the numerous, narrow leaves decreasing in size up the stem and then grading into bracts. The numerous-flowered inflorescence has flowers with brown to green sepals and pale green

petals and lip. The trilobed lip has triangular-shaped side lobes and the broad, kidney-shaped midlobe has a shallow notch.

GYALANTHOS

Szlachetko & Margońska

Polish Bot. J. **46**(2): 116 (2001)[2002].

ETYMOLOGY: Greek for hollow and flower. Refers to the flower form.

TYPE SPECIES: *Gyalanthos mirabilis* (Schlechter) Szlachetko & Margońska (*Pleurothallis mirabilis* Schlechter)

Recognized as belonging to the genus *Pabstiella*, *Gyalanthos* was proposed to include two epiphytes found in cool, moist, mid elevation, montane coastal forests of eastern Brazil. These small plants have long, wiry stems, each with a solitary leaf located midway up the stem. The long, few-flowered inflorescence, borne in the leaf axils, has small, white, long-chinned flowers often suffused pink. The long-clawed, arrowhead-shaped, hinged, entire lip, united to the column foot, is strongly bent at a right angle in the middle and has a long, swollen spur. The flowers have a swollen column foot that is quite long.

GYAS

Salisbury

Trans. Hort. Soc. London **1**: 299 (1812).

ETYMOLOGY: Greek for a giant with a hundred arms or for the curved piece of wood. The origin and its meaning are unknown.

TYPE SPECIES: *None designated*

Now recognized as belonging to the genus *Bletia*, *Gyas* was previously considered to include three terrestrials found from low to upper elevation, grasslands to woodlands with well drained soil throughout Cuba, Jamaica, the southeastern United States (Florida), the Guianas, Venezuela and Mexico to Bolivia. These plants have short stems, each with two fairly large leaves. The few-flowered inflorescence has deep purple flowers that are white toward the base, and the broad petals have wavy margins. The purple, trilobed lip has erect side lobes; the midlobe is white toward the base with a yellow callus in the center, and a wavy margin. The flowers have a long, curved column.

GYMADENIA

An orthographic variant introduced in *Beih. Bot. Centralbl.*, **33**(2): 406 (1915). The correct spelling is *Gymnadenia*.

GYMNADENIA

R. Brown

Hortus Kew., ed. 2 **5**: 191 (1813).

Orchidoideæ ⚬ Orchideæ • Orchidinæ

ETYMOLOGY: Greek for naked and gland. Referring to the sticky disk of the pollinia that is free on each side of the rostellum and not in the pouch-like expansion of the stigma.

TYPE SPECIES: *Gymnadenia conopsea* (Linnaeus) R. Brown (*Orchis conopsea* Linnaeus)

Twenty-four sympodial terrestrials are found growing in low to upper elevation, montane meadows, marshes, fens and chalk or limestone banks. They are widespread from Scandinavia to eastern Russia (Kamchatka to Kuril Islands), Denmark to Uzbekistan, and extending into China (Xizang to Jilin), Japan, northern India (Kashmir to Assam) and Bhutan. These erect, dwarf plants have slender, unbranched stems, each with two or three, scale-like leaves at the base along with three or four, fleshy leaves. The erect, few to numerous-flowered inflorescence (in a tapering, cylindrical spike) has small, showy, fragrant flowers varying in color from pink, purple-red, yellow-green or white. Some species have the dorsal sepal and petals converging to form a hood over the short, erect column, and the down curved lateral sepals are widespreading. In other species all the segments are widespreading. The broad, entire, trilobed or shortly trilobed lip has a short or long, often thread-like spur that curves downward, and is with or without a swollen tip.

GYMNADENIOPSIS

Rydberg

Man. Fl. N. States (Britton) 293 (1901).

ETYMOLOGY: *Gymnadenia*, a genus of orchids and Greek for appearance. Alluding to a similarity to *Gymnadenia*.

LECTOTYPE: *Gymnadeniopsis nivea* (Nuttall) Rydberg (*Orchis nivea* Nuttall)

Now recognized as belonging to the genus *Platanthera*, *Gymnadeniopsis* was previously considered to include three terrestrials found in cool, low to mid elevation, open bogs and sunny, wet meadows of eastern Canada (Ontario to Newfoundland) and the United States (New Jersey to eastern Texas). These tall, slender plants have blue-green, fluted stems, each with several, long leaves below and narrow, pointed bracts above. The densely packed, numerous to few-flowered, cylindrical inflorescence has small, green, pure white or orange-yellow flowers. The uppermost, entire lip is bent backward at the center, and the stiff horizontal spur is often longer than the ovary. The flowers have a tiny, bright yellow column.

GYMNERPIS

Thouars
Hist. Orchid.   Table 1, sub 2i, *tt. 29-30* (1822).

Name published without a description. Today this name is most often referred to *Goodyera*.

GYMNOCHILUS

Blume
Coll. Orchid.   107, *t. 32* (1859), and
Fl. Javæ Nov. Ser.   **1**: 90, *t. 32* (1858).
Not *Gymnochilus* Clements (1896) Fungi.
ETYMOLOGY: Greek for naked and lip. In reference to the lip that is naked or unadorned.
TYPE SPECIES: *None designated*

Now recognized as belonging to the genus *Cheirostylis*, *Gymnochilus* was previously considered to include three terrestrials inhabiting humid, evergreen forests from Tanzania to South Africa, and Madagascar to the Mascarene Islands. These uncommon, erect plants have unbranched stems, each with several, three veined, oval to narrow leaves. The erect, few-flowered inflorescence has tiny, pink flowers with long, narrow veined petals. The small, obscurely trilobed lip tapers to a point, and is united to the golden-yellow, slender, slightly curved, footless column.

GYMNODENIA

An orthographic variant introduced in *Schriften Ges. Beförd. Gesammten Nauturwiss. Marburg*, **2**: 126 (1831). The correct spelling is *Gymnadenia*.

GYMNOSTYLIS

Wallich ex Pfitzer
Pflanzenr. (Engler)   **IV.50**(II.B.7): 127 (1907).
Not *Gymnostylis* Rafinesque (1818) Asteraceæ.
ETYMOLOGY: Greek for naked and column or pillar. Referring to the size and shape of the column.
TYPE SPECIES: *Gymnostylis candida* (Lindley) Pfitzer
        (*Coelogyne maculata* Lindley)

A superfluous name proposed as a substitute for *Gomphostylis*.

GYNIZDON

An orthographic variant cited in *Handb. Orchid.-Namen*, 367 (2005). The correct spelling is *Gynizodon*.

GYNIZODON

Rafinesque
Fl. Tellur.   **4**: 40 (1836)[1837].
ETYMOLOGY: Greek for stigma in orchids and tooth. Descriptive of the two toothed stigmatic area.
TYPE SPECIES: *Gynizodon russelliana*
        (Lindley) Rafinesque
        (*Oncidium russellianum* Lindley)

Now recognized as belonging to the genus *Miltonia*, *Gynizodon* was previously considered to include one epiphyte found in cool, mid elevation, montane forests of eastern Brazil (Rio de Janeiro, São Paulo, Paraná, Santa Catharina and Rio Grande do Sol). This plant has oblong, laterally compressed, closely set pseudobulbs, subtended by leaf-bearing sheaths, each with two narrow leaves. The erect or arching, few-flowered inflorescence has mottled, purple scapes and brown bracts. The large, red-brown flowers, not opening widely, are tipped pale yellow. The broad, pale purple, shortly clawed, entire lip has white or pale yellow blotches. The flowers have a short, footless column.

GYNOGLOTTIS

J.J. Smith
Recueil Trav. Bot. Neerl.   **1**: 49, *t. 2* (1904).
Epidendroideæ ⚜ Arethuseæ • Coelogyninæ
ETYMOLOGY: Greek for woman or female and lip or tongue. In reference to the lips' claw that is joined to the column forming a basally inflated, constricted tube suggestive of a mammalian female organ.
TYPE SPECIES: *Gynoglottis cymbidioides*
        (Reichenbach f.) J.J. Smith
        (*Coelogyne cymbidioides* Reichenbach f.)

One uncommon, sympodial epiphyte is found in wet, mid elevation, montane moss laden forests of Indonesia (west central Sumatra) and New Guinea. This plant has large, shiny, close-set, cone-shaped, one-noded pseudobulbs, subtended by large, leafy sheaths, each with two narrow, thinly textured, leathery leaves that last through several growing seasons. The erect, numerous-flowered inflorescence, borne from a young pseudobulb, has pure white, rather small, fragrant flowers with boat-shaped, strongly keeled lateral sepals. The golden-yellow, tubular, trilobed lip, united to the slender, slightly curved, footless column for

much of its length, has a white margin, and is unequally swollen or inflated on one side.

GYROROSTACHYS

An orthographic variant introduced in *Amer. Midl. Naturalist*, **6**(9): 206 (1920). The correct spelling is *Gyrostachys*.

GYROSTACHIS

Persoon
Syn. Pl. (Persoon), ed. 2   511 (1807).
ETYMOLOGY: Greek for rounded and spike. Refers to the twisted shape of the inflorescence.
TYPE SPECIES: *None designated*

Name published without a description. Today this name is most often referred to *Gyrostachys*.

GYROSTACHYS

Dumortier
Fl. Belg. (Dumortier)   134 (1827).

Not validly published, this name is most often referred to *Spiranthes*.

GYROSTACHYS

Persoon ex Blume
Coll. Orchid.   127 (1859).
ETYMOLOGY: Greek for rounded or a ring and spike. From the twisted shape of the inflorescence.
LECTOTYPE: *Gyrostachys spiralis* (Linnaeus) Kuntze
        (*Ophrys spiralis* Linnaeus)

Not validly published, this name is referred to *Spiranthes*. *Gyrostachys* was previously considered to include one hundred twenty terrestrials ranging from Mexico to Panama, and the southern United States (Florida), with one species found from central Russia (West Siberia) to Vietnam and Australia.

GYROSTAICHY

An orthographic variant introduced in *Amer. Naturalist*, **31**: 796 (1897). The correct spelling is *Gyrostachys*.

Currently Accepted   Validly Published   Invalidly Published   Published Pre-1753   Superfluous Usage   Orthographic Variant   Fossil

Orchid Genera · **182**

HABENAREA

An orthographic variant introduced in *Icon. Pl. Ind. Orient. (Wight)*, **2**: *t. 922* (1851). The correct spelling is *Habenaria*.

HABENARIA

Willdenow

Sp. Pl. (Willdenow), ed. 4   **4**(1): 5, 44 (1805).

Orchidoideæ ✿ Orchideæ • Orchidinæ

ETYMOLOGY: Latin for rein or strap. Refers to some species in which the spur is long and shaped like a strap or the division of the petals and lip are long and strap-like.

LECTOTYPE: *Habenaria macroceratitis* Willdenow
(*Orchis habenaria* Linnaeus)
designated by Kraenzlin, *Bot. Jahrb. Syst.*, **16**: 58 (1892).

LECTOTYPE: *Habenaria monorrhiza*
(Swartz) Reichenbach f.
(*Orchis monorrhiza* Swartz)
not validly designated by Lindley, *Bot. Reg.*,
18: sub 1499 (1832).

This type name is now considered a synonym of
Habenaria quinqueseta var. *macroceratitis*
(Willdenow) Luer;
basionym replaced with
Habenaria macroceratitis Willdenow

This large genus has an estimated eight hundred forty-eight sympodial terrestrials or rare epiphytes found in low to upper elevation, grasslands, meadows to open forests with many species found in deep shade. They have a cosmopolitan distribution but are particularly abundant in Brazil and Africa (Ethiopia to South Africa, Cameroon to Zambia and Madagascar), with a few species found in Asia (Afghanistan to Korea) and from Cuba, central Mexico to northern Argentina. These erect plants have unbranched stems, each with several to a few thinly textured leaves spaced along the stem, clustered at the base or in the middle or one to two, basal leaves lying flat or pressed to the ground. The sometimes showy to very plain flowers are mostly green and white, rare with a yellow, pink or red lip. The dorsal sepal often converges, forming a hood with the petals that are either entire, bilobed or divided into two shallow segments. The terminal, numerous to few-flowered inflorescence has insignificant to showy flowers varying tremendously in appearance and structure. Most species have the lip making up the most distinctive, prominent portion of the flower. The entire or trilobed lip has the side lobes sometimes further divided. The long or short, slender or sac-like spur often inflated at the tip, is either bent or straight. The flowers have a small, unique column that often has pointed staminodes rising above the anther or protruding above the entrance of the spur.

HABENELLA

Small

Fl. S.E. U.S.   316, 1329 (1903).

ETYMOLOGY: Diminutive of *Habenaria*, a genus of orchids, and Latin for diminutive. Indicating a relationship to *Habenaria*.

TYPE SPECIES: *Habenella garberi* (Porter) Small
(*Habenaria garberi* Porter)

Now recognized as belonging to the genus *Habenaria*, *Habenella* was previously considered to include two terrestrials found in dry, low to mid elevation, woodland scrub from the United States (southern Florida), Cuba, Puerto Rico, Hispaniola and southern Mexico to Panama. These robust, erect, unbranched plants have glossy, deep green leaves proceeding up the stem. The few-flowered inflorescence has yellow-green flowers. The deeply concave dorsal sepal and petals converge, forming a hood over the column, the lateral sepals are widespreading, and the yellow petals are obscurely trilobed at the tip. The narrow, yellow, entire lip has a pair of small projections at the base and a slender, pale green spur. The above type name is now considered a synonym of *Habenaria floribunda* Lindley.

HABENORCHIS

An orthographic variant introduced in *Hist. Orchid.*, Table 1, sub 1e (1822). The correct spelling is *Habenorkis*.

HABENORKIS

Thouars

Nouv. Bull. Sci. Soc. Philom. Paris
1(19): 317 (1809).

ETYMOLOGY: *Habenaria*, a genus of orchids, and Greek for orchid.

TYPE SPECIES: *None designated*

A superfluous name proposed as a substitute for *Habenaria*.

HABENURIA

An orthographic variant introduced in *Bull. Soc. Roy. Bot. Belgique*, **43**: 273 (1906). The correct spelling is *Habenaria*.

HABERARIA

An orthographic variant introduced in *Bot. Mag. (Tokyo)*, **1**: 120 (1887). The correct spelling is *Habenaria*.

HABERIARIA

An orthographic variant introduced in *Icon. Pl. Ind. Orient. (Wight)*, **3**: *t. 1700* (1851). The correct spelling is *Habenaria*.

HADROLAELIA

(Schlechter) Chiron & V.P. Castro

Richardiana   **2**(1): 11 (2002).

Epidendroideæ ✿ Epidendreæ • Laeliinæ

ETYMOLOGY: Greek for water serpent and *Laelia*, a genus of orchids. Referring to its wet habitat and alluding to its relationship to *Laelia*.

TYPE SPECIES: *Hadrolaelia pumila*
(Hooker) Chiron & V.P. Castro
(*Cattleya pumila* Hooker)

Nineteen sympodial epiphytes or lithophytes that are sometimes included in *Sophronitis* and are found in low elevation, moist, savannas, prairies and forest slopes of southeastern Brazil (Espírito Santo, Rio de Janeiro and Minas Gerais). These robust plants have club-shaped, compressed, grooved stems, each with a solitary, oblong, leathery, pale green leaf that is notched at the tip. The erect, few-flowered inflorescence, subtended by compressed sheaths, has showy, white, rosy-purple to lavender flowers with narrow sepals, and petals suffused purple toward the base. The white to deep magenta, deeply trilobed or obscurely trilobed lip has deep rosy-purple veins with a deep yellow base, distinctive keels or crests and a wavy margin. The lateral side lobes enfold upward and envelope the long, club-shaped column.

HAEMARIA

Lindley

Orchid. Scelet. 9 (1826), and
Edwards's Bot. Reg. **19**: sub 1618 (1833).

ETYMOLOGY: Greek for blood-red. Descriptive of the sheathing bracts that are bright red beneath.

TYPE SPECIES: *Haemaria discolor* (Ker Gawler) Lindley (*Goodyera discolor* Ker Gawler)

A superfluous name proposed as a substitute for *Ludisia*.

HAEMATORCHIS

Blume

Rumphia **4**: t. 200B (1848)[1849].

ETYMOLOGY: Greek for blood-red and orchid. From the color of the inflorescence.

TYPE SPECIES: *Haematorchis altissima* (Blume) Blume (*Cyrtosia altissima* Blume)

Now recognized as belonging to the genus *Erythrorchis*, *Haematorchis* was previously considered to include one saprophyte found climbing on trees and bamboo thickets in low elevation, grassy forests from northeastern India, southeastern China (Hainan), Taiwan, Myanmar to Vietnam, Malaysia and the Philippines. The long, leafless, red-brown or green-brown stems are twining, zig-zagged, and can have several branches. The simple or branched, numerous-flowered inflorescence has small, yellow or brown flowers often faintly spotted, that do not open widely. The wedge-shaped, suffused tan, obscurely trilobed lip has a wavy or fringed margin and a hairy callus.

HAGSATERA

R. González

Orquidea (Mexico City), n.s. **3**(11): 343 (1974).

Epidendroideæ • Epidendreæ • Laeliinæ

ETYMOLOGY: Honoring Eric Hágsater (1945-), a Mexican, member of the Mexican Pharmaceutical Association, orchidologist, editor of *Orquídea* and co-author of *Icones Orchidacearum*.

TYPE SPECIES: *Hagsatera brachycolumna* (L.O. Williams) R. González (*Epidendrum brachycolumna* L.O. Williams)

Two sympodial epiphytes are found in dry, mid elevation, oak-pine forests of western Mexico (Guerrero and Oaxaca) and Guatemala. These plants' growth habit is quite distinctive, mature growths consist of a slender, erect stem terminating in a pseudobulbous swelling at whose base new stems arise forming a tall, wand-like growth, which tends to lack aerial roots and has a dark red-purple color. The plants may be as much as a foot high (30 cm),

nodding in the wind with no more support than the roots of the old pseudobulbs. The terminal, few-flowered inflorescence has clustered, hanging, facing downward flowers. These have a faint to harsh fragrance, are colored olive to lime-green, sometimes suffused purple; have stiff, spreading sepals, and the concave petals have a sharp point. The pale yellow-green, trilobed lip is strongly to intensely streaked, edged in bright red-brown or dark purple, has minute side lobes, and the midlobe has a slightly inrolled margin. The flowers have a short, footless column.

HAHENORCHIS

An orthographic variant introduced in *Hist. Orchid.*, t. 16 (1922). The correct spelling is *Habenorchis*.

HAKONEASTA

An orthographic variant introduced in *Phylogeny Classif. Orchid Fam.*, 271 (1993). The correct spelling is *Hakoneaste*.

HAKONEASTE

Maekawa

Bot. Mag. (Tokyo) **49**: 598 (1935).

ETYMOLOGY: Named in honor of Hakone (a Japanese mountain resort located southeast of Mount Fuji in the Kanagawa prefecture). And Greek for inhabitant.

TYPE SPECIES: *Hakoneaste sawadana* Maekawa
This type name is now considered a synonym of *Ephippianthus sawadanus* (Maekawa) Ohwi; basionym
Hakoneaste sawadana Maekawa

Now recognized as belonging to the genus *Ephippianthus*, *Hakoneaste* was previously considered to include one terrestrial found in the extinct volcano Mount Hakone region of Japan (south central Honshu). This small, delicate plant has erect, unbranched stems, each with a solitary, oblong leaf. The slender, few-flowered inflorescence has several, scale-like bracts on the lower portion. The tiny, yellow-green flowers have nerved sepals and petals with pale brown-purple tips. The entire lip has a notched, ragged margin and a pale brown blotch or streak down the center. The flowers have a slender, curved column.

HALENARIA

An orthographic variant introduced in *Beih. Bot. Centralbl.*, **33**(2): 404 (1915). The correct spelling is *Habenaria*.

HALLACKIA

Harvey

Thes. Cap. **2**(1): 2, t. 102 (1863).

ETYMOLOGY: Dedicated to Russell Hallack (1824-1903), a South African businessman, amateur botanist and plant collector from Port Elizabeth.

TYPE SPECIES: *Hallackia fimbriata* Harvey

Now recognized as belonging to the genus *Huttonaea*, *Hallackia* was previously considered to include two terrestrials found in cool, forests of South Africa. These slender, erect plants have unbranched stems, each with two, distant leaves. The erect, few-flowered inflorescence has small to tiny, white flowers whose outer segment margins are shortly fringed as is the broad, fan-shaped, entire lip.

HALLEORCHIS

Szlachetko & Olszewski

Fl. Cameroun **34**: 246, t. 85 (1998).

Orchidoideæ • Cranichideæ • Goodyerinæ

ETYMOLOGY: Dedicated to Nicolas Hallé (1927-), a French botanist who studied the flora of eastern Africa and the southwest Pacific Islands. He is the author of *Flore de la Nouvelle-Calédonie et Dépendences*. And Greek for orchid.

TYPE SPECIES: *Halleorchis aspidogynoides* Szlachetko & Olszewski

One sympodial terrestrial is found only in the humid, low elevation, woodlands from Cameroon to Gabon. This plant has erect, stout stems, each with the arranged spirally leaves on lower portion. The erect, tall, hairy, densely packed, numerous-flowered inflorescence has minute, delicate, rosy flowers not opening widely that are covered with soft hairs on the outside segments. The hood-shaped dorsal sepal and the shell-shaped lateral sepals enclose the base of the lip. The entire or deeply cleft lip, constricted near the middle, has a shell-shaped or concave basal portion, a flat frontal portion, and its margin is attached to the lower third of the short, footless column.

HAMARIA

Not *Hamaria* Fourreau (1868) Leguminosæ, and not *Hamaria* Kunze ex Baillon (1892) Polygonaceæ.

An orthographic variant introduced in *Dict. Class. Hist. Nat.*, **11**: 515 (1827). The correct spelling is *Haemaria*.

Currently Accepted   Validly Published   Invalidly Published   Published Pre-1753   Superfluous Usage   Orthographic Variant   Fossil

O r c h i d   G e n e r a   • **184**

HAMMARBYA

Kuntze

Revis. Gen. Pl. **2**: 665 (1891).

Epidendroideæ Malaxideæ

ETYMOLOGY: Named for Hammarby, a summer estate located 9 miles (15 km) southeast of Uppsala in western central Sweden, which was acquired in 1758 by Carl von Linné (1707-1778).

TYPE SPECIES: *Hammarbya paludosa* (Linnaeus) Kuntze
(*Ophrys paludosa* Linnaeus)

One sympodial terrestrial is found in low to mid elevation, boggy and wet dunes of the cool, northern temperate zones from Sweden to eastern Russia, Britain to Romania, Japan, the United States (Alaska and Minnesota) and western Canada. This small, erect plant has a swollen, unbranched stem base that is pseudobulbous (this usually sits atop last year's bulb), each with several, small, oval, fleshy leaves. The plant sometimes has tiny plantlets or bulbils sprouting from the tips of the leaves. The erect, numerous to few-flowered inflorescence has tiny, flat-shaped, green to yellow-green flowers. The unusual bowl-shaped, entire or obscurely trilobed lip is uppermost and has dark green veins. The flowers have a short, erect, footless column.

HAMULARIA

Averyanov & Averyanova

Komarovia **4**: 18 (2005), and
J. Orchideenfr. **13**(1): 72 (2006).

ETYMOLOGY: Greek for stalk. Refers to the pollinia stalk that is characteristic of the species.

TYPE SPECIES: *Hamularia puluongensis*
Averyanov & Averyanova

Now recognized as belonging to the genus *Bulbophyllum*, *Hamularia* was previously considered to include four epiphytes found in mid elevation, evergreen forests of northern Vietnam, Indonesia, the Philippines, Brunei and New Guinea. These creeping plants have egg-shaped pseudobulbs, each with a solitary, thinly textured leaf. The solitary-flowered inflorescence, borne from the pseudobulb base, has a dull yellow flower covered with numerous red spots and does not open fully. The long-clawed, thinly hinged, red-purple, entire lip has several, raised ridges. The flowers have a short column with a large, massive, fleshy, triangular stipe that covers the tip and frontal portion of the column. These species are closely related to *Sunipia*.

HANCOCKIA

Rolfe

J. Linn. Soc., Bot. **36**(249): 20 (1903).

Epidendroideæ Collabiinæ • Currently unplaced

ETYMOLOGY: Dedicated to William Hancock (1847-1914), an Irish amateur botanist, who worked for the Chinese Maritime Customs and collected flora in China for the Royal Botanic Gardens at Kew, Maximowicz in St. Petersburg and Hance in Hong Kong.

TYPE SPECIES: *Hancockia uniflora* Rolfe

One sympodial terrestrial is found in moist, mid elevation, montane valleys and slopes of south-western China (Yunnan), northern Vietnam and southern Japan (Ryukyu Islands). This small, creeping plant has erect, unbranched stems subtended by persistent tubular sheaths. The few leaves, sprinkled with minute, wart-like spots, have a wavy to scalloped margin and numerous, fine, parallel veins. The solitary-flowered inflorescence, borne from a specialized leafless shoot, has a small, pink flower with large, papery floral bracts, narrow sepals and petals; does not open widely. The broad, trilobed lip, attached to the column base, has an entire, slightly wavy margin, and a long, slender, tubular spur with a double crested keel inside on the mid-vein. The flowers have a slender, club-shaped column.

HAPALOCHILUS

(Schlechter) Senghas

Orchidee (Hamburg) **29**(6): 248 (1978).

ETYMOLOGY: Greek for delicate, soft or tender and a lip. In reference to the long, soft textured lip that dominates the flower.

TYPE SPECIES: *Hapalochilus nitidus*
(Schlechter) Senghas
(*Bulbophyllum nitidum* Schlechter)

Now recognized as belonging to the genus *Bulbophyllum*, *Hapalochilus* was previously considered to include fifty epiphytes found in low to mid elevation, dense hill and montane rain forests of Indonesia (Java and Borneo) to New Guinea. These small, clump-forming plants have flattened, purple stained pseudobulbs, each with a solitary, leathery leaf. The erect, solitary-flowered inflorescence has a brightly colored flower with translucent, yellow, cream, red-brown or white, long, narrow sepals that have dark purple veins and sprinkled with blotches or spots. The petals are quite tiny. The equally long, narrow, yellow to red tipped, roundish, entire lip is also sprinkled with blotches and tapers to a long or blunt point.

HAPALORCHIS

Schlechter

Repert. Spec. Nov. Regni Veg. Beih.
6: 30, 52 (1919), and
Beih. Bot. Centralbl. **37**(2): 361 (1920).

Orchidoideæ Cranichideæ • Spiranthinæ

ETYMOLOGY: Greek for delicate or soft and orchid. Referring to the delicate texture of the plant and flowers.

TYPE SPECIES: *Hapalorchis cheirostyloides* Schlechter

LECTOTYPE: *Hapalorchis candidus*
Schlechter (Kraenzlin)
(*Sauroglossum candidium* Kraenzlin)

These type names are now considered synonyms of *Hapalorchis lineatus* (Lindley) Schlechter; basionym replaced with *Spiranthes lineata* Lindley

Eight sympodial terrestrials, epiphytes or lithophytes are found in shady, wet, low to upper elevation, montane tropical evergreen and subtropical forests from Cuba to Puerto Rico, the Guianas, Venezuela and Guatemala south to northern Argentina. These erect, delicate plants have unbranched stems, each with a solitary or several, heart-shaped leaves in a basal rosette. The tall, slender, few-flowered inflorescence, partially subtended by sheaths, has small, white or pale yellow-green, loosely tubular flowers opening one at time; all facing in the same direction on the rachis and are often suffused pink. The white, trilobed lip has incurved side lobes, the broad midlobe has an inrolled margin with bright green mid-nerves. The flowers have a long, erect, club-shaped column.

HAPLOCHILUS

Endlicher

Enchir. Bot. (Endlicher) 113 (1841), and
Gen. Pl., Suppl. (Endlicher) **2**: 20 (1842).

ETYMOLOGY: Greek for single or simple and lip. Referring to the long lip that dominates the flower.

TYPE SPECIES: *None designated*

Now recognized as belonging to the genus *Zeuxine*, *Haplochilus* was previously considered to include eight terrestrials found from India to the Philippines. These tall plants have unbranched, erect, shortly hairy stems, each with several, ovate leaves located near the base. The few-flowered inflorescence has hairy, white flowers. The thinly textured, three-nerved, sac-like, bilobed lip has an inrolled margin that is united to the base of the short column. They are closely related to *Hetaeria*, but these flowers have their lip located lower than most.

HAPLOSTELIS

An orthographic variant cited in *Deut. Bot. Herb.-Buch*, 56 (1841). The correct spelling is *Aplostellis*.

HAPLOSTELLIS

An orthographic variant introduced in *Gen. Pl. (Endlicher)*, 219 (1837). The correct spelling is *Aplostellis*.

HARAELLA

Kudô

J. Soc. Trop. Agric. **2**: 26 (1930).
Not *Haraella* K. Hara & Hino (1955) Fungi.

Epidendroideæ ⚘ Vandeæ • Aeridinæ

ETYMOLOGY: Honoring Hiroshi (Yoshie) Hara (1911-1986), a Japanese collector for the Taihoku Imperial University of Formosa (Taiwan) who collected the type species. And Latin for diminutive.

LECTOTYPE: *Haraella retrocalla* (Hayata) Kudô
(*Saccolabium retrocallum* Hayata)

One monopodial epiphyte is found in low to mid elevation, hill and montane forests on the island of Taiwan. This tiny plant has short stems, each with loose fans of tough, strap-shaped, distichous leaves sheathing the stem at the base. The solitary to few-flowered inflorescence, borne from the leaf axils, has small, showy, waxy, yellow to yellow-green, heavily fragrant flowers. The distinctive, translucent, off white, insect-like, shallowly trilobed lip is blotched with maroon and contracted in the middle forming two equal-sized sections. The notched midlobe is minutely fringed. The flowers have a short, wingless, footless column.

HARPOPHYLLUM

An orthographic variant introduced in *Orch. Exot.*, 785 (1894). The correct spelling is *Arpophyllum*.

HARRIESILLA

An orthographic variant introduced in *Beih. Bot. Centralbl.*, **36**(2): 87 (1918). The correct spelling is *Harrisella*.

HARRISELLA

Fawcett & Rendle

J. Bot. **47**(559): 265 (1909).

Epidendroideæ ⚘ Vandeæ • Angraecinæ

ETYMOLOGY: Dedicated to William H. Harris (1860-1920), an Irish superintendent of the Public Gardens and Plantations of Jamaica, prolific collector of local flora and author of *History of the Introduction of the Economic Plants of Jamaica*. And Latin for diminutive.

TYPE SPECIES: *Harrisella porrecta*
(Reichenbach f.) Fawcett & Rendle
(*Aeranthus porrectus* Reichenbach f.)
This type name is now considered a synonym of
Dendrophylax porrectus
(Reichenbach f.) Carlsward & Whitten;
basionym replaced with
Aeranthes porrecta Reichenbach f.

Now recognized as belonging to the genera *Campylocentrum* and *Dendrophylax*. *Harrisella* was previously considered to include three easily overlooked epiphytes that are usually found in low elevation, old citrus groves, hardwood hammocks and junipers in the southeastern United States (Florida), southern Mexico and throughout the Caribbean region. These short-stemmed, scale-like to leafless plants have clusters of small, silvery-green chlorophyllous roots. The hair-like, often branching, few-flowered inflorescences have tiny to minute, pale yellow to green-yellow flowers, opening in succession, with a nocturnal fragrance. The deeply concave, pale yellow, entire lip is uppermost and has a long to short, often swollen spur. The flowers have a pale green, short, thick, footless column. After flowering the ripened fruits, often larger than the flowers, hang in little clusters and turn brown when mature, spilling forth fuzzy seeds reminiscent of milkweed.

HARRISIELLA

An orthographic variant introduced in *Orchideen (Schlechter)*, ed. 1, 590 (1914). The correct spelling is *Harrisella*.

HARTWEGIA

Lindley

Edwards's Bot. Reg. **23**: sub 1970 (1837).
Not *Hartwegia* Nees von Esenbeck (1831) Liliaceæ.

ETYMOLOGY: Dedicated to Karl Theodore Hartweg (1812-1871), a German plant collector who explored Mexico, California and the South American Andes for the Horticultural Society of London. He was later a director for the gardens of the Gran Duchy of Schwetzingen in Baden, Germany.

TYPE SPECIES: *Hartwegia purpurea* Lindley

Not validly published because of a prior use of the name, this homonym was replaced by *Nageliella*.

HEBENARIA

An orthographic variant introduced in *Fortsetz. Allg. Teutsch. Gart.-Mag.*, **7**(4): 162 (1823). The correct spelling is *Habenaria*.

HECABE

Rafinesque

Fl. Tellur. **4**: 44 (1836)[1837].

ETYMOLOGY: Greek Mythology. Dedicated to Hecabe, the wife of King Priam of Troy. She was the mother of Paris, who because of his abduction of Helen from the Greek kingdom of Lakedaimon, brought about the ten-year war that led to the total destruction of Troy by the united Greek kingdoms. After the sack of Troy (1184 BC), Hecabe was given as a prize to Ulysses, she cast herself off his ship while he sailed home through the Hellespont.

TYPE SPECIES: *Hecabe lutea* Rafinesque nom. illeg.
Phaius flavus (Blume) Lindley
(*Limodorum flavum* Blume)

Now recognized as belonging to the genus *Phaius*, *Hecabe* was previously considered to include one terrestrial found in humid, shady, low to mid elevation, evergreen forests from Japan, northern India (Sikkim to Assam), Sri Lanka, southern China (Yunnan to Hainan), Taiwan, Vietnam, Indonesia and New Guinea to the Philippines. This plant has large, cone-like to ovoid pseudobulbs, completely subtended by leafy sheaths, each with several, dark green leaves spotted yellow or white. The long, erect, few-flowered inflorescence has showy, long-lived, fragrant, pale yellow to yellow-green flowers. The hairy, trilobed lip has red-brown, lacerated margins and a long, white to pale yellow spur. The flowers have a slender column.

HEDERORCHIS

An orthographic variant introduced in *Hist. Orchid.*, Table 3, sec. 3s, t. 91 (1822). The correct spelling is *Hederorkis*.

HEDERORKIS

Thouars

Nouv. Bull. Sci. Soc. Philom. Paris **1**(19): 319 (1809).

Epidendroideæ ⚘ Vandeæ • Polystachyinæ

ETYMOLOGY: Latin for vine or ivy and Greek for orchid. Refers to the climbing habit of the plant.

TYPE SPECIES: *Hederorkis scandens* Thouars
(*Neottia scandens* Thouars)

Two saprophytes are found found in low elevation, woodlands on the islands of Mauritius and the Seychelles. These

Currently Accepted   Validly Published   Invalidly Published   Published Pre-1753   Superfluous Usage   Orthographic Variant   Fossil

Orchid Genera • **186**

robust, climbing plants have fleshy, often squarish stems with several small nodes that have the leaves reduced to tiny, sheathing scales or have oblong, leathery leaves in pairs along the stem. The several, curving, few-flowered inflorescences have fairly complex, dingy brown, purple-brown, cream or purple flowers with narrow sepals and petals. The bag-like or curved, oblong, entire lip has a deep cleft at the tip. The flowers have a slender, slightly curved, narrowly winged column.

HELCIA

Lindley
Edwards's Bot. Reg.
31(Misc.): 17, section no. 27 (1845).

Epidendroideæ ✹ Cymbidieæ • Oncidiinæ

ETYMOLOGY: Latin for horse-collar or yoke. From the hollow, hairy pit at the base of the lip which, when seen from the front, looks like the starched, high collars such as the ladies wore during the reign of Queen Elizabeth I (1533-1603).

TYPE SPECIES: *Helcia sanguinolenta* Lindley

Four sympodial epiphytes are found in low to upper elevation, hill to montane forests of Colombia, Ecuador and Peru. These plants have thick, tightly packed, oblong pseudobulbs, partially subtended by overlapping, dry sheaths, each with a solitary, thick, narrow, leathery leaf. The solitary-flowered inflorescence has a large, showy, fragrant, long-lasting, yellow flower heavily spotted or barred chocolate brown. The oblong, bright white to yellow, entire or obscurely trilobed lip has broken, crimson veins, an wavy margin, a hairy basal disc and a notched or bilobed tip. The flowers have a slender, erect, club-shaped, footless column.

HELICIA

Not *Helicia* Persoon (1805) Loranthaceæ, and not *Helicia* Loureiro (1790) Proteaceæ.

An orthographic variant introduced in *Syn. Pl. (D. Dietrich)*, **5**: 6, 75 (1852). The correct spelling is *Helcia*.

HELICTONIA

Ehrhart
Beitr. Naturk. (Ehrhart) **4**: 148 (1789).
Not *Heliconia* Linnaeus (1771) Musaceæ.

ETYMOLOGY: Greek for twisted or rolled. Refers to the floral spike.

TYPE SPECIES: *Ophrys spiralis* Linnaeus

Not validly published, this name is most often referred to as a synonym of *Spiranthes*.

HELLEBORINE

Plumier
Nov. Pl. Amer. (1703, 1758 and 1759).
ETYMOLOGY: Greek for a ranunculaceous plant (buttercup family). From a superficial resemblance to some species of *Helleborus*.
TYPE SPECIES: *None designated*

Pre-1753, therefore not validly published in fulfillment of nomenclatural rules; this name is today considered as a synonym of many different genera including *Bletia, Brassavola, Brassia, Cyrtopodium, Dendrophylax, Eulophia, Isochilus, Maxillaria, Octomeria, Oncidium, Pleurothallis, Prosthechea, Psychilis, Sacoila, Spiranthes* and *Tetramica*.

HELLEBORINE

Martyn ex Kuntze
Revis. Gen. Pl. **2**: 665 (1891).
Not *Helleborine* P. Miller (1754) Orchidaceæ, and not *Helleborine* Moench (1794) Orchidaceæ.
ETYMOLOGY: Greek for a ranunculaceous plant (buttercup family). From a superficial resemblance to some species of *Helleborus*.
TYPE SPECIES: *None designated*

Because of a prior use of the name, this homonym was replaced by *Calopogon*.

HELLERIELLA

A.D. Hawkes
Phytologia **14**(1): 4 (1966).
Epidendroideæ ✹ Epidendreæ • Ponerinæ
ETYMOLOGY: Honoring Alfonse Henry Heller (1894-1973). And Latin for diminutive.
TYPE SPECIES: *Helleriella nicaraguensis* A.D. Hawkes

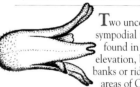

Two uncommon sympodial epiphytes or lithophytes are found in mid to upper elevation, montane cloud forests from southern Mexico to Panama. These large, erect to hanging plants have irregular, branched, compressed stems (woody and bamboo-like), leafy only on the upper main stem and branches, each with several, distichous leaves. The short, few-flowered, subsessile inflorescence has stiff, long-lasting, green, yellow-white to white flowers conspicuously nerved with either purple or green. The large sepals are broader than the small petals. The white to green, shortly clawed, mobile, obscurely trilobed lip has bright yellow calli, and the side lobes have splashes of bright red with upper, finely notched to entire margins. The flowers have a short, white, wingless column with a short foot.

HELLERORCHIS

A.D. Hawkes
Orchid J. **3**(6): 275 (1959).
ETYMOLOGY: Dedicated to Alfonse Henry Heller (1894-1973), a German-born, American mining engineer who lived in Nicaragua and collected and studied the local flora. And Greek for orchid.

TYPE SPECIES: *Hellerorchis gomezoides*
(Barbosa Rodrigues) A.D. Hawkes
(*Theodorea gomezoides* Barbosa Rodrigues)

A superfluous name proposed as a substitute for *Rodrigueziella*.

HELLICTONIA

An orthographic variant cited in *Orchideen* (Schlechter): *Liter. Reg. Band I/A, B, and C*, 215 (2003). The correct spelling is *Helictonia*.

HELONEMA

Not *Helonema* Suessenguth (1943) Cyperaceæ.

An orthographic variant introduced in *Phylogeny Classif. Orchid Fam.*, 120, 268 (1993). The correct spelling is *Helonoma*.

HELONOMA

Garay
Bot. Mus. Leafl. **28**(4): 327 (1980)[1982].
Orchidoideæ ✹ Cranichideæ • Spiranthinæ
ETYMOLOGY: Greek for living in a marsh or bog. Descriptive of the plants' habitat.

TYPE SPECIES: *Helonoma americana*
(C. Schweinfurth & Garay) Garay
(*Manniella americana* C. Schweinfurth & Garay)

Two uncommon, sympodial terrestrials are found in low to upper elevation, boggy river banks or ridges in small areas of Guyana, southern Venezuela (Amazonas and Bolivar) Ecuador and northern Brazil. These unusually slender, fleshy plants have erect, unbranched stems, each with the small, yellow-blotched leaves forming a basal rosette. The tall, few-flowered, green to red inflorescence with widely spaced, tubular (below) or narrow (above) bracts. The small, green at their base, and white toward the tip, flowers (held to one side) have their fused sepals forming a tube of variable length to which the long claw of the obscurely trilobed lip is attached. The flowers have a short to somewhat long, club-shaped column.

HELORCHIS

Schlechter

Repert. Spec. Nov. Regni Veg. Beih. **33**: 35 (1924).

ETYMOLOGY: Greek for marsh or low ground and orchid. From its bog-growing habitat.

TYPE SPECIES: *Helorchis filiformis*
(Kraenzlin) Schlechter
(*Peristylus filiformis* Kraenzlin)

This type name is now considered a synonym of *Cynorkis papillosa* (Ridley) Summerhayes; basionym replaced with *Habenaria papillosa* Ridley

Now recognized as belonging to the genus *Cynorkis*. *Helorchis* was previously considered to include one terrestrial found in peat bogs and damp scrub of Madagascar. This very tall, slender, unbranched plant has few leaves and can be leafless during flowering. The erect, numerous-flowered inflorescence has tiny, white flowers with long lateral sepals; the concave dorsal sepal and petals converge over the column. The obscurely trilobed lip has a broad splash of violet or magenta toward the upturned tip, is strongly nerved and has a small spur.

HELOTHRIX

Not *Helothrix* Nees (1841) Cyperaceæ.

An orthographic variant introduced in *Syn. Pl. (D. Dietrich)*, **5**: 14, 132 (1852). The correct spelling is *Holothrix*.

HEMIBABENARIA

An orthographic variant introduced in *Orchideen (Schlechter)*, ed. 1, 64 (1914). The correct spelling is *Hemihabenaria*.

HEMIHABENARIA

Finet

Rev. Gén. Bot. **13**: 532 (1902).

ETYMOLOGY: Greek for half and *Habenaria*, a genus of orchids. Alluding to a close relationship with *Habenaria*.

TYPE SPECIES: *None designated*

Now recognized as belonging to the genus *Pecteilis*, *Hemihabenaria* was previously considered to include four terrestrials found in mid to upper elevation, montane grasslands and valley slopes from the northern India (Sikkim), Nepal, Myanmar to Vietnam, southern China (Yunnan to Gansu, Hainan to Jiangxi), Korea, Japan, far eastern Russia (Primorye) and Indonesia. These plants have stout, erect stems leafy throughout or with a basal rosette. The solitary to few-flowered inflorescence bears large, usually white, yellow or pale green flowers. The small

petals and the dorsal sepal converge, forming a hood over the erect column. These showy, nocturnally fragrant flowers have a trilobed lip with the side lobes extravagantly fringed or minutely toothed. The long, narrow midlobe is entire, and the long spur is slightly curved.

HEMINILIA

An orthographic variant introduced in *Index Gen. Phan.*, 403 (1888). The correct spelling is *Hemipilia*.

HEMIPERIS

Frappier ex **Cordemoy**

Fl. Reunion 235 (1895).

ETYMOLOGY: Greek for half and scrotum. Descriptive of the two, filament-like caudicles that are immersed on the under surface in the epidermis of the rostellum.

TYPE SPECIES: *None designated*

Now recognized as belonging to the genus *Cynorkis*, *Hemiperis* was previously considered to include twenty terrestrials or uncommon epiphytes found in leaf litter of montane moss laden forests. The species are fairly common in Madagascar, but are also found on other islands within the western Indian Ocean area. These erect, thinly leaved plants have a few-flowered inflorescence with brightly colored flowers. The dorsal sepal and petals converge, forming a hood over the small column.

HEMIPILIA

Lindley

Gen. Sp. Orchid. Pl. 296 (1835).

Orchidoideæ ⦿ Orchideæ • Orchidinæ

ETYMOLOGY: Greek for semi, somewhat, and felt, hat or cap. Referring to the irregular, felty covering of hairs on the lip.

TYPE SPECIES: *Hemipilia cordifolia* Lindley

Eighteen attractive, robust sympodial terrestrials are found in mid to upper elevation, montane forests and moss laden slopes of northern India (Kashmir to Assam), Nepal, Taiwan and Myanmar to Vietnam with the most species found in southern China (Xizang to Shaanxi). These small plants have erect, unbranched stems, each with a solitary, fleshy, oval to heart-shaped, green basal leaf mottled or flecked dark purple on the upper surface. The numerous to few-flowered inflorescence has showy, somewhat trumpet-shaped, purple to pink flowers. The dorsal sepal and small petals sometimes joins or converge, forming a hood over the small, erect, hood-like column. The broad spreading, entire or trilobed lip has a wavy or fringed margin. There are two calli

at the base near the mouth of the straight or occasionally incurved, rather long to short spur which often has fine, small protuberances inside. The flowers have a distinct, small column.

HEMIPILIOPSIS

Y. Luo & S.C. Chen

Orchid Rev. **111**(1249): 48 (2003), and
Validated: *Novon* **13**(4): 450 (2003).

Orchidoideæ ⦿ Orchideæ • Orchidinæ

ETYMOLOGY: *Hemipilia*, a genus of orchids, and Greek for appearance or likeness. Refers to a similarity to *Hemipilia*.

TYPE SPECIES: *Hemipiliopsis purpureopunctata*
(K.Y. Lang) Y. Luo & S.C. Chen
(*Habenaria purpureopunctata* K.Y. Lang)

One sympodial terrestrial is found in upper elevation, montane evergreen to oak-pine forests, grassy slopes and along sandy river banks of southeastern China (Xizang) and north-eastern India (Assam). This small, erect plant has unbranched stems, each with a basal rosette of leaves covered with purple spots. The wiry, hairy, purple spotted, numerous to few-flowered inflorescence has pale purple, veined flowers with widespreading lateral sepals. The oblong, concave dorsal sepal and straight petals converge, forming a hood over the small column. The fan-shaped or broad, trilobed lip has a club-shaped projection located above the center notch and a small, roundish spur.

HEMISCLERIA

Lindley

Fol. Orchid. **4**: *Hemiscleria*, 1 (1853).

ETYMOLOGY: Greek for half and hard or dry. Refers to the harsh texture of the vegetative segments.

TYPE SPECIES: *Hemiscleria nutans* Lindley

Now recognized as belonging to the genus *Epidendrum*, *Hemiscleria* was previously considered to include one epiphyte found in upper elevation, montane cloud forests of Ecuador and Peru. This plant has erect or hanging, short, stiff stems, each with several narrow leaves. The small, bright red to yellow, multi-flowered, club-like inflorescence has a swollen, strongly curved stalk. The bright orange, rigid flowers have their lateral sepals attached to the short, thick, winged column and also surround the base of the lip that is longer than the other segments. The trilobed lip has erect side lobes and a blunt tipped midlobe. The above type name is now considered a synonym of *Epidendrum hemiscleria* Reichenbach f.

Currently Accepted   Validly Published   Invalidly Published   Published Pre-1753   Superfluous Usage   Orthographic Variant   Fossil

O r c h i d   G e n e r a • **188**

HEMPILIA

An orthographic variant introduced in *Repert. Spec. Nov. Regni Veg. Beih.*, **4**: 87 (1919). The correct spelling is *Hemipilia*.

HENICOSTEMA

Blume

Fl. Javæ **1**: Praef. vii (1828).

ETYMOLOGY: Greek for union and to bridge or a relationship.

TYPE SPECIES: *None designated*

Name published without a description. Today this name is most often referred to *Bulbophyllum*.

HENOSIS

Hooker *filius*

Fl. Brit. Ind. **5**: 771, and **6**: 189 (1890).

ETYMOLOGY: Greek for union. Alluding to the attachment of the sepals to the column foot.

TYPE SPECIES: *Henosis longipes*
      (Reichenbach f.) Hooker f.
      (*Bulbophyllum longipes* Reichenbach f.)

Now recognized as belonging to the genus *Monomeria*, *Henosis* was previously considered to include one epiphyte found in mid elevation, montane forests and scrub of Myanmar, Thailand and Malaysia. This small plant has smooth, ovoid to pear-shaped pseudobulbs, each with a solitary, leathery, strap-shaped leaf. The long, wiry, few-flowered inflorescence has transparent, small, yellow flowers with the minute, thinly textured petals united to the column foot. The long, narrow lateral sepals and the hinged, narrowly ovate, entire lip (covered in soft hairs) are attached to the column foot. The flowers have a large, broadly winged column.

HERANTHES

An orthographic variant introduced in *Mém. Acad. Sci. Toulouse*, **7**: 310 (1875). The correct spelling is *Aeranthes*.

HERBA-supplex

Rumphius

Herb. Amboin. (Rumphius)   **6**: *t. 50, f. 2* (1750).

ETYMOLOGY: Latin for plant.

TYPE SPECIES: *Herba supplex prima* Rumphius

Pre-1753, therefore not validly published in fulfillment of nomenclatural rules. There were six different epiphytic species published by Rumphius that used the same first name of *Herba* that are orchids.

Herba supplex major prima (111, *t. 50, f. 2*) is found in the hot, humid rain forests of Myanmar, Thailand, Cambodia, Vietnam, Malaysia, and Indonesia. This plant has long stems densely subtended by flattened, overlapping leaves. The few-flowered inflorescence has tiny, bright yellow flowers. This name is usually referred to as a synonym of *Dendrobium concinnum* Miquel.

Herba supplex major quinta (111-112, *t. 51, f. 2*) is found in eastern Indonesia (Maluku) and surrounding islands. This plant has flattened, leafy stems that are overlapping, alternating in two rows, and falling off with age. The small fragile, white flowers have an entire lip. This name is usually referred to as a synonym of *Dendrobium calceolum* Roxburgh.

Herba supplex minor (110, *t. 50, f. 2*) found from Malaysia to New Guinea. This plant has small, overlapping, variable leaves with a tiny, dark purple flower borne at the leaf nodes. This name is usually referred to as a synonym of *Dendrobium atropurpureum* (Blume) Miquel.

There are three additional descriptions: *Herba supplex major secunda* (111) is a creeping epiphyte or lithophyte with thin, stiff stems and long, narrow leaves; *Herba supplex major tertia* (111) an epiphyte with thick stems and flat leaves; and *Herba supplex major quarta* (111) an epiphyte with long stems and small flowers draped at the top (that could possibly be *Dendrobium confusum* J.J. Smith). These names could be referred to *Dendrobium* but the vague descriptions are without illustrations to allow for accurate identifications.

HERMAPHRODITICA

L'Obel

Icon. Stirp.   178, *f. 2* (1591).

Pre-1753, therefore not validly published in fulfillment of nomenclatural rules; this name is most often referred to *Helleborine*.

HERMININM

An orthographic variant introduced in *Orchid. Nepal*, 26 (1978). The correct spelling is *Herminium*.

HERMINIORCHIS

Foerster

Fl. Excurs. Aachen   348 (1878).

ETYMOLOGY: Greek for bedpost and orchid. The meaning as applied here is unclear.

TYPE SPECIES: *Herminiorchis monorchis*
      (Linnaeus) Foerster
      (*Ophrys monorchis* Linnaeus)

Not validly published, this name is referred to *Herminium*, *Herminiorchis* was previously considered to include one terrestrial found from Scandinavia to eastern Russia (Primorye), Germany to Ukraine, China (Heilongjiang to Xizang, Yunnan), Korea, Japan and northern India (Kashmir) to Nepal.

HERMINIUM

Linnaeus

Opera Var.   251 (1758), and
Fl. Lapp. (Linnaeus)   247 (1737).

Orchidoideæ ⚘ Orchideæ • Orchidinæ

ETYMOLOGY: Greek for bedpost. Probably descriptive of the two knob-like staminodia that stand on either side of the anther or to the tubers, both of which resemble a carved bedpost.

Or Greek Mythology. Named for *Hermes*, the god of commerce, invention, travel and thievery, who also served as a messenger and herald for other gods. He is often identified with Roman god *Mercury*.

TYPE SPECIES: *Herminium monorchis*
      (Linnaeus) R. Brown
      (*Orchis monorchis* Linnaeus)

Twenty-eight, small, insignificant terrestrials are scattered in low to upper elevation, hill and montane forests, woodlands and grasslands from Sweden to western Russia, Denmark to Bulgaria, Turkey to throughout China, Mongolia, northern India (Assam), Myanmar to Vietnam Malaysia, Indonesia (Java and Timor) and the Philippines. These tall, erect plants have unbranched stems, subtended by wide tubular, basal sheaths, each with several, oblong leaves, closely spaced on the lower half of the stem or a solitary leaf with two or three, scale-like leaves at the base. The long, slender, numerous to few-flowered inflorescence has small to tiny, often spidery, pale green or yellow, fragrant flowers with a darker shade on the outer surface. The dorsal sepal and the small petals converge, forming a hood over the short column. The spreading or hanging, short-clawed, entire, bilobed, trilobed or rare five-lobed lip is flat, obscurely bag-like or concave. The lip has narrowly triangular side lobes, and an oblong, blunt midlobe that is continuous with the short, thick column base.

HERMINUM

An orthographic variant introduced in *Dict. Sci. Nat.*, **36**: 304 (1825). The correct spelling is *Herminium*.

HERORCHIS

Lindley
Bot. Reg.   **20**: sub 1701 (1834).

Name published without a description. Today this name is most often referred to as a section of *Orchis*.

HERPETHOPHYTON

An orthographic variant introduced in *Orchideen (Schlechter)*, ed. 3, **1**(11-12): 660 (1981). The correct spelling is *Herpethophytum*.

HERPETHOPHYTUM

(Schlechter) Brieger
Orchideen (Schlechter), ed. 3   **1**(11-12): 660 (1981).

Name published without a description. Today this name is most often referred to as a section of *Dendrobium*.

HERPETOPHYTUM

Rauschert
Feddes Repert.   **94**(7-8): 454 (1983).
ETYMOLOGY: Greek for crawling or reptile and a plant. Refers to their creeping and growing habit.
TYPE SPECIES: *Herpetophytum schlechteri*
(Schlechter) Brieger
(*Dendrobium herpetophytum* Schlechter)

Now recognized as belonging to the genus *Dendrobium*, *Herpetophytum* was previously considered to include fifteen epiphytes restricted to mid to upper elevation, montane cloud forests of New Guinea. These small plants, often growing in dense moss, have branched, wiry, hanging stems with the small leaves (with a sheathing base) spaced along their length. The short, flattened, one- to two-flowered inflorescence has tiny, white to yellow flowers, which last for only a day. The lateral sepals are flushed to their tips, forming a spur that surrounds the stout, wingless, footless column that has a large, blunt tooth. The entire lip has radiating red veins. The above type name is now considered a synonym of *Dendrobium herpetophytum* Schlechter.

HERPISMA

An orthographic variant cited in *Dict. Gen. Names Seed Pl.*, 59 (1995). The correct spelling is *Herpysma*.

HERPORCHIS

An orthographic variant cited in *Lex. Gen. Phan.*, 178, 276 (1904). The correct spelling is *Herorchis*.

HERPYSMA

Lindley
Edwards's Bot. Reg.   **19**: sub 1618 (1833), and *Numer. List*   247, no. 7389 (1831).
Orchidoideæ ⚘ Cranichideæ • Goodyerinæ
ETYMOLOGY: Greek for to creep or creeping. Referring to the creeping growth habit of this genus.
TYPE SPECIES: *Herpysma longicaulis* Lindley

One sympodial terrestrial is found in low to mid elevation, hill and montane forests margins from southern China (Yunnan), northern India (Sikkim), Nepal, Myanmar to Vietnam, Indonesia (Sumatra) and Thailand. This ground-hugging plant has long stems, each with several, ovate leaves that taper at either end. The slender, densely packed, hairy inflorescence has somewhat large, showy, white flowers suffused orange-red to pink. The dorsal sepal and petals converge, forming a hood, and the white lateral sepals are tipped with orange or scarlet. The short, trilobed lip has two triangular keels on the blade between the two side lobes that are joined on both sides to the base of the short, footless, slightly decurved column. The long, slender spur is notched at the tip.

HERSCHELIA

Lindley
Gen. Sp. Orchid. Pl.   362 (1838).
Not *Herschelia* Bowdick (1825) Solanaceæ.
ETYMOLOGY: Honoring John Frederick William Herschel (1792-1871), a British astronomer, founder of the Royal Astronomical Society, chemist and philosopher.
TYPE SPECIES: *Herschelia coelestis* Lindley

Not validly published because of a prior use of the name, this homonym was replaced by *Herschelianthe*, but today these species are now included in *Disa*.

HERSCHELIANTHE

Rauschert
Feddes Repert.   **94**(7-8): 434 (1983).
ETYMOLOGY: *Herschelia*, a genus of orchids, and Greek for flower. For its similarity to *Herschelia*.
TYPE SPECIES: *Herschelianthe graminifolia*
(Ker Gawler ex Sprengel) Rauschert
(*Disa graminifolia* Ker Gawler ex Sprengel)

Now recognized as belonging to the genus *Disa*, *Herschelianthe* was previously considered to include sixteen terrestrials found in low to mid elevation, scrub and grasslands native mostly to the Cape area of South Africa but also from Ethiopia to Zimbabwe. These erect, slender, reed-like plants have almost grass-like leaves borne along the erect, unbranched stem. The erect, few-flowered inflorescence has attractive, fragrant flowers in various shades of mauve to even a true blue. The erect, hood-shaped dorsal sepal is spurred and the small, spoon-shaped petals are clawed and often lie inside the hood. The large, narrow, pale colored, entire lip has a deeper shade of blue on its ornately fringed margins.

HERSCHELIODISA

(Linder) Szlachetko & Rutkowski
Acta Bot. Fenn.   **169**: 81 (2000).

Name published without a description. Today this name is most often referred to *Disa*.

HETAERIA

Blume
Bijdr. Fl. Ned. Ind.   **8**: 409, *t. 14* (1825).
Name ICBN conserved vs. *Etaeria* Blume (1825) Orchidaceæ, type name also conserved; and not *Hetaeria* Endlicher (1836) Philydraceæ.
Orchidoideæ ⚘ Cranichideæ • Goodyerinæ
ETYMOLOGY: Greek for companionship or brotherhood. Referring to the many similarities of this genus with the species of *Goodyera*.
LECTOTYPE: *Hetaeria oblongifolia* Blume

Thirty-two sympodial terrestrials or lithophytes are found in low to upper elevation, evergreen montane forests ranging from western Africa (Cameroon to Zaire), the Comoros Islands, southern China (Yunnan to Hainan), Taiwan, northern India (Sikkim), Malaysia, Indonesia and New Guinea to Fiji. Several of these small, creeping species have showy, colorful leaves and a tallish, numerous-flowered inflorescence that is extremely hairy and has small, dull yellow to pale green flowers. The small dorsal sepal and slightly narrower petals converge or with a small gap, forming a hood over the short, footless column that along with the lateral sepals, enclose the

| Currently Accepted | Validly Published | Invalidly Published | Published Pre-1753 | Superfluous Usage | Orthographic Variant | Fossil |

O r c h i d   G e n e r a   •   **190**

lip base. Only a few flowers are open at any one time. The entire lip is deeply pouched at the base, has thin to fleshy appendages near the base and has a rarely short or broad spur.

HETERANTHOCIDIUM

Szlachetko, Mytnik & Romowicz
Polish Bot. J.   **51**(1): 54 (2006)[2007].

ETYMOLOGY: Greek for varying or differently flowered and *Oncidium*, a genus of orchids. Refers to the structure of the flowers, which are double shaped.

TYPE SPECIES: *Heteranthocidium heteranthum*
(Poeppig & Endlicher) Szlachetko, Mytnik & Romowicz
(*Oncidium heteranthum* Poeppig & Endlicher)

Recognized as belonging to the genus *Oncidium*, *Heteranthocidium* was proposed to include fifteen epiphytes found in mid elevation, montane forests from Costa Rica to Bolivia, Venezuela and the Guianas. These small plants have clustered, slightly grooved, ovoid, compressed, pale green pseudobulbs with two sharp edges, subtended by short, leaf-bearing sheaths, each with several, narrow leaves. The slender, erect, arching to drooping, numerous-flowered inflorescence has small, long-lasting, pale yellow-green flowers with maroon blotches or bars. These flowers are borne on a mature pseudobulb, which have both lipless, sterile and normal flowers. The fertile flowers appear toward the tip with the lower, sterile flowers not fully developed and usually a pale yellow. The entire or obscurely trilobed lip has small side lobes with recurved margins, the shortly clawed, kidney-shaped midlobe is deeply bilobed and the basal, brown callus is toothed and crested. The flowers have a small, stout column.

HEXEROTAXIS

Lindley
Bot. Reg.   **12**: t. 1028 (1826).

Epidendroideæ ⚘ Cymbidieæ • Maxillariinæ

ETYMOLOGY: Greek for other or differing and order. An allusion to the genus having an affinity with *Arethusa*, but it may be a connecting link between *Arethuseæ* and *Epidendreæ*.

TYPE SPECIES: *Heterotaxis crassifolia* Lindley

Fourteen sympodial epiphytes or lithophytes are found in wet, low to mid elevation, hill to montane forests and scrub from the southeastern United States (southern Florida), Cuba to Jamaica, and Mexico to Peru, the Guianas, Venezuela and southeastern Brazil. These plants have oblong, clustered, strongly compressed, shinny pseudobulbs, subtended by leaf-bearing sheaths, each with a solitary, narrow leaf borne at the base. The erect, short, solitary-flowered inflorescence has a bell-shaped, pale yellow, orange

to orange-red flower. The flower, borne at the leaf axils, does not open widely and has purple markings. The yellow to dark purple, obscurely trilobed lip has a pale purple center streak and a hairy callus in basal half, with its margins entire or toothed. The flowers have a slender, arched column.

HETEROZEUXINE

T. Hashimoto
Ann. Tsukuba Bot. Gard.   **5**: 21 (1986).

ETYMOLOGY: Greek for other or different and *Zeuxine*, a genus of orchids. Refers to a similarity to *Zeuxine*.

TYPE SPECIES: *Heterozeuxine odorata*
(Fukuyama) T. Hashimoto
(*Zeuxine odorata* Fukuyama)

Now recognized as belonging to the genus *Zeuxine*, *Heterozeuxine* was previously considered to include seven terrestrials found from southern Japan to Malaysia. These tall plants have several, small leaves well-spaced on the unbranched stem's lower half. The long, few-flowered inflorescence has well-spaced flowers whose ovary is slightly hairy; the sepals are smooth textured. The shortly clawed, entire lip is widely sac-like at the base with a callus on either side and has an incurved, cone-shaped tooth on each margin. The broad, white midlobe has two broad lobes. The flowers have a short, incurved column with large, basal wings.

HEXADENIA

An orthographic variant introduced in *Syn. Pl. (D. Dietrich)*, **5**: 4 (1852). The correct spelling is *Hexadesmia*.

HEXADESMIA

Brongniart
Ann. Sci. Nat., Bot., ser. 2   **17**: 44 (1842).

ETYMOLOGY: Greek for six and a bond or bundle. An allusion to the pollinia that are connected by six filaments.

TYPE SPECIES: *Hexadesmia fasciculata* Brongniart
This type name is now considered a synonym of *Scaphyglottis lindeniana*
(A. Richard & Galeotti) L.O. Williams;
basionym
Hexadesmia lindeniana A. Richard & Galeotti

Now recognized as belonging to the genus *Scaphyglottis*, *Hexadesmia* was previously considered to include fifteen epiphytes found in low elevation, woodlands from central Mexico to Peru, the Guianas and Venezuela. These small plants have tufted, slender,

spindle-shaped, sometimes stalked pseudobulbs, each with two bright green, leathery leaves. The solitary to numerous-flowered inflorescence has small, showy, semi-transparent, pale white flowers with pink nerves and spreading segments. The white, oblong lip (trilobed at base) has a bilobed tip and a wavy margin. The flowers have a yellow-green, erect or incurved, club-shaped column.

HEXADSEMIA

An orthographic variant introduced in *Hort. Donat.*, 176 (1858). The correct spelling is *Hexadesmia*.

HEXALECTRIS

Rafinesque
Neogenyton   4 (1825).

Epidendroideæ ⚘ Epidendreæ • Bletiinæ

ETYMOLOGY: Greek for six and cock. In reference to the wavy crests on the lip that bear some resemblance to a cock's comb.

TYPE SPECIES: *Hexalectris aphylla* (Nuttall) Rafinesque
(*Bletia aphylla* Nuttall)
This type name is now considered a synonym of *Hexalectris spicata* (Walter) Barnhart;
basionym replaced with *Arethusa spicata* Walter

Seven unusual saprophytes are found in dry, low to mid elevation, open scrub and pine-oak forests from the southern and southwestern United States (Texas to Arizona) and Mexico to Guatemala. These solitary to sometimes colony forming, leafless plants have purple, pink to yellow-brown, erect, unbranched stems and lack chlorophyll. They live in association with a specific mycorrhizal fungus. The several, few-flowered inflorescences have nodding, yellow, magenta, tan, purple or maroon flowers with purple-brown stripes. The shallow, red-violet, trilobed lip has a wavy margin and several, bright purple basal crests. The flowers have a white, strongly curved, winged column. The number and size of plants found will vary from year to year depending on rainfall.

HEXALETRIS

An orthographic variant introduced in *Herb. Raf.*, 74 (1833). The correct spelling is *Hexalectris*.

HEXAMERIA

R. Brown
Pl. Jav. Rar. (Bennett) 26, t. 7 (1838).
Not *Hexameria* Torrey & Gray (1839) Cucurbitaceæ.
ETYMOLOGY: Greek for six and part. Referring to the six similar sepals, petals and lip segments.
TYPE SPECIES: *Hexameria disticha* R. Brown
This type name is now considered a synonym of *Podochilus serpyllifolius* (Blume) Lindley; basionym *Cryptoglottis serpyllifolia* Blume

 **N**ow recognized as belonging to the genus *Podochilus*, *Hexameria* was previously considered to include one epiphyte found in Indonesia (Borneo). This tiny, moss-like plant has long, branching stems that are both creeping and free hanging with small leaves. The few-flowered inflorescence has tiny, white flowers not fully opening. The pink tipped sepals and petals are united forming a tubular shape for most of their length. The narrow, entire lip has two slender appendages near the base and has a large, spur-like protuberance.

HEXESIA

An orthographic variant introduced in *J. Roy. Hort. Soc.*, **7**(1): 115 (1886). The correct spelling is *Hexisea*.

HEXISEA

Lindley
J. Bot. (Hooker) **1**: 7 (1834).
Name ICBN rejected vs. *Scaphyglottis* Poeppig & Endlicher (1836) Orchidaceæ.
ETYMOLOGY: Greek for six and equal or similar. Refers to the equal size and a similarity in shape of the perianth segments.
TYPE SPECIES: *Hexisea bidentata* Lindley

Although validly published this rejected name is now referred to *Scaphyglottis*. *Hexisea* was considered to include five epiphytes or lithophytes are found in misty, warm to cool, low to mid elevation, hill forests ranging from Cuba to Hispaniola, Mexico to Peru, Venezuela, the Guianas and northern Brazil.

HEXISIA

An orthographic variant introduced in *Gen. Pl. (Bentham & Hooker f.)*, **3**: 469, 524 (1883). The correct spelling is *Hexisea*.

HEXOPEA

An orthographic variant cited in *Nomencl. Bot. (Steudel)*, ed. 2, **1**: 757 (1840). The correct spelling is *Hexopia*.

HEXOPIA

Bateman ex Lindley
Edwards's Bot. Reg.
26(Misc.): 46, section no. 90 (1840).
ETYMOLOGY: Greek for six and appearance. Referring to the six pollinia.
TYPE SPECIES: *Hexopia crurigera* Bateman ex Lindley

Now recognized as belonging to the genus *Scaphyglottis*, *Hexopia* was previously considered to include one epiphyte found in wet, low to mid elevation, hill and montane rain forests from Mexico to Ecuador. This plant has dense clumps of white to gray roots, spindle-shaped to stalked pseudobulbs, each with a narrow, bilobed leaf. The slightly zig-zagged, blue-green, few-flowered inflorescence has pink to white flowers with narrow segments. The lateral sepals are united with the column foot forming a prominent chin-like projection. The oblong to wedge-shaped, entire lip has a bilobed tip. The flowers have a short, club-like column.

HIMANTHOGLOSSUM

An orthographic variant introduced in *Syn. Fl. Germ. Helv.*, ed. 1, 689 (1837). The correct spelling is *Himantoglossum*.

HIMANTHOGLOSUM

An orthographic variant introduced in *Thes. Lit. Bot.*, 435 (1872). The correct spelling is *Himantoglossum*.

HIMANTOGLOSSUM

Sprengel
Syst. Veg. (Sprengel), ed. 16 **3**: 675, 694 (1826).
Name ICBN conserved, and type name also conserved.
Orchidoideæ • Orchideæ • Orchidinæ
ETYMOLOGY: Greek for strap or thong and tongue. For the long, strap-like projection of the lip.
TYPE SPECIES: *Himantoglossum hircinum*
(Linnaeus) Sprengel
(*Satyrium hircinum* Linnaeus)

Seven sympodial terrestrials, known as lizard orchids, are found mainly in mid elevation, grasslands, scrub, open woodlands and sand dunes from Britain to Greece, Morocco to Tunisia, Turkey, the Caucasus Mountains, Israel, Jordan and Iran usually growing in full sunlight. These large, robust plants are vaguely reptilian in their markings and have a strong, foul fragrance. These plants have erect, leafy, unbranched stems, each with the lower leaves

withered and brown when the flowers begin to appear. This occurs because the leaves are produced during the previous growing season and then endure through the rigors of winter. The erect, numerous-flowered inflorescence has green, purple to brown-white flowers with the sepals and narrow, tiny petals forming a blunt hood over the small, stout column. The trilobed lip has short side lobes and a curiously elongate, slightly twisted, ribbon-like midlobe, with an entire to wavy margin that has short to long bilobed, entire to wavy tips, and has a small, cone-shaped spur.

HINTONELLA

Ames
Bot. Mus. Leafl. **6**(9): 186 (1938).
Epidendroideæ • Cymbidieæ • Oncidiinæ
ETYMOLOGY: Dedicated to George Boole Hinton (1882-1943), a British-born American metallurgist and botanist who collected orchids and other flora in central Mexico. Latin for diminutive.
TYPE SPECIES: *Hintonella mexicana* Ames

One uncommon, sympodial epiphyte is found in humid, mid elevation, steep hillsides, canyon cliffs, and oak-pine to dense deciduous forests of central Mexico (Jalisco, Guerrero, Morelos, Michoacán and Oaxaca). This tiny plant has minute, oblong to roundish pseudobulbs, subtended by leaf-bearing sheaths, each with a solitary, fleshy, channeled leaf. The short, few-flowered inflorescence has tiny, long-lasting, green-yellow to white, slightly fragrant flowers. The hairy, glandular, obscurely trilobed lip has red-brown spots, a recurved, fleshy, basal callus, and a transverse keel on the upper portion. The flowers have a short, straight column.

HIPPEOGLOSSUM

An orthographic variant introduced in *Repert. Spec. Nov. Regni Veg.*, **32**: 315 (1933). The correct spelling is *Hippoglossum*.

HIPPEOPHYLLUM

Schlechter
Nachtr. Fl. Schutzgeb. Südsee 107 (1905).
Epidendroideæ • Malaxideæ
ETYMOLOGY: Greek for horseman or rider and leaf. Referring to the shape of the compressed leaves.
TYPE SPECIES: *Hippeophyllum micranthum* Schlechter

Thirteen sympodial epiphytes are found in low to mid elevation, cliff faces and along river banks from southern China (Gansu), Taiwan, Malaysia, Indonesia and New

Currently Accepted | Validly Published | Invalidly Published | Published Pre-1753 | Superfluous Usage | Orthographic Variant | Fossil

Orchid Genera • 192

Guinea to the Solomon Islands. These tiny, scrambling plants have long, creeping, rigid rhizomes with short stems, subtended in a leafy base, each with the distichous, flattened, leathery leaves arranged in two rows. The densely packed, numerous-flowered, sometimes hairy inflorescence, borne from the center of the leaf bases, has upwards of 200, extremely small, pale green to white flowers. The slightly reflexed sepals are widespreading, and the narrow petals curl forward. The yellow, usually trilobed lip is uppermost, has erect side lobes, a downward curved midlobe with notched margins, and has a concave base sometimes with two calli. The flowers have a short, erect, slender, wingless, footless column.

HIPPOGLOSSUM

Breda

Gen. Sp. Orchid. Asclep., fasc. III   *t. 14* (1827).

Not *Hippoglossum* Hill (1756) Liliaceæ, and not *Hippoglossum* Hartman (1832) Boraginaceæ.

ETYMOLOGY: Greek for horse and tongue. Descriptive of the dominate, saddle-shaped lip.

Or possibly Greek Mythology. Hippo was a beautiful sea nymph and daughter of Oceanus and Tethys, from Hesiod's Theogony poem describing the birth of the Greek gods and goddesses.

TYPE SPECIES: *Hippoglossum umbellatum* Breda

This type name is now considered a synonym of *Bulbophyllum umbellatum* Lindley

Not validly published because of a prior use of the name, this homonym was replaced by *Bulbophyllum*.

HIPPOPODIUM

Harvey ex Lindley

Gen. Sp. Orchid. Pl.   364 (1838).

ETYMOLOGY: Greek for horse and foot.

TYPE SPECIES: *None designated*

Name published without a description. Today this name is most often referred to *Ceratandra*.

HIPPORCHIS

An orthographic variant introduced in *Hist. Orchid.*, Table 1, sub 1f, *t. 21* (1822). The correct spelling is *Hipporkis*.

HIPPORKIS

Thouars

Nouv. Bull. Sci. Soc. Philom. Paris 1(19): 317 (1809).

ETYMOLOGY: Greek for horse and orchid. Descriptive of the two spurs on the dorsal sepal that give the appearance of a horse's head with attached reins.

TYPE SPECIES: *None designated*

A superfluous name proposed as a substitute for *Satyrium*.

HIRTZIA

Dodson

Icon. Pl. Trop., ser. 1   **10**: *t. 924* (1984).

Epidendroideæ 🍃 Cymbidieæ • Zygopetalinæ

ETYMOLOGY: Honoring Alexander Charles Hirtz (1951-), an Ecuadorian-born American geologist and orchidologist who helps run the Tropica 2000 Foundation for the preservation of the Andes and built a museum to house his Valdivian artifacts.

TYPE SPECIES: *Hirtzia benzingii* Dodson

Two sympodial, twig epiphytes are found in wet, mid to upper elevation, montane forests of Ecuador and Colombia (Antioquia). These small plants have short stems, each with several, stiff, flattened, overlapping leaves arranged in a fan shape and are covered in short, white hairs. The few-flowered inflorescence has triangular, floral bracts. The nodding, bright yellow to green-yellow flowers are barred dark red. The dorsal sepal is concave over the large, red column and has narrow petals and lateral sepals. The white, entire lip, obscurely lobed on each side toward the tip, is concave in front of the yellow callus and sprinkled with red spots. The flowers have a slender, strongly curved, red column.

HISPANIELLA

Braem

Orchidee (Hamburg)   **31**(4): 144 (1980).

ETYMOLOGY: Name of an island in the West Indies - Hispaniola (located in the Caribbean Sea and occupied by both the Republic of Haiti and the Dominican Republic). And Latin for diminutive.

TYPE SPECIES: *Hispaniella henekenii* (Schomburgk ex Lindley) Braem (*Oncidium henekenii* Schomburgk ex Lindley)

Now recognized as belonging to the genus *Tolumnia*, *Hispaniella* was previously considered to include one epiphyte found on the island of Hispaniola. This miniature, distinctive, twig-like plant grows on certain spiny shrubs and cacti. The short, leafy stems have fleshy, compressed, strongly curved, distichous leaves with irregular, minutely notched margins. The long, zig-zagged, few-flowered inflorescence has bee-like, off yellow to creamy flowers suffused purple. There is rarely more than one flower open at any given time but will continue blooming successively over several months and actually increases in length after each old flower has dropped, and then produces another. The hairy, dark maroon, obscurely trilobed or entire lip has a distinct yellow margin with numerous, hairy protuberances on each side in front. The flowers have a short column with tiny, narrow wings.

HOEHNEELLA

Ruschi

Orquid. Nov. Estad. Espirito Santo   3 (1945).

ETYMOLOGY: In honor of Frederico Carlos Hoehne (1882-1959), a German-born Brazilian professor at Instituto Botânico de São Paulo, in the department of botany and agronomy, a director of the Botanic Garden of Rio de Janeiro and author of *Flora Brasilica*. And Latin for diminutive.

TYPE SPECIES: *Hoehneella gehrtiana* (Hoehne) Ruschi (*Warcewiczella gehrtiana* Hoehne)

Now recognized as belonging to the genus *Chaubardia*, *Hoehneella* was previously considered to include three uncommon, epiphytes found in humid, low to mid elevation, shady bush and woodlands of southeastern Brazil (São Paulo, Rio de Janeiro and Espírito Santo). These attractive plants have small, compressed pseudobulbs becoming grooved with age, subtended by leaf-like sheaths, each with a solitary, narrow, oblong, deciduous, leathery leaf. The erect, solitary-flowered inflorescence, borne from the base of the leaf-like sheaths, has a green-yellow flower with petals that are white at their tips and pale green toward the base. The white, broad, oblong, entire lip, often suffused green, has a wavy margin. The flowers have a straight, wingless column with a short foot.

HOFFMANNSEGGELLA

H.G. Jones

Acta Bot. Acad. Sci. Hung.   **14**: 69 (1968).

Epidendroideæ 🍃 Epidendreæ • Laeliinæ

ETYMOLOGY: In honor of Johann Centurius von Hoffmannsegg (1766-1849), a German count, botanist, entomologist, ornithologist and naturalist who worked on identifying the plants and animals of South America. He is the author of *Flore Portugaise*. And Latin for diminutive.

TYPE SPECIES: *Hoffmannseggella cinnabarina* (Bateman ex Lindley) H.G. Jones (*Laelia cinnabarina* Bateman ex Lindley)

Twenty-five sympodial epiphytes or rare lithophytes are found in low to mid elevation, hill and montane forests of eastern Brazil (Rio de Janeiro, Minas Gerais and São Paulo). These plants have cylindrical stems swollen at the base, subtended by white sheaths, each with one or rarely two, narrow, erect to spreading leaves suffused purple. The short to long, few-flowered inflorescence has long-lasting, bright yellow, orange-red to purple flowers. The long, distinctly trilobed lip has narrow, ovate midlobe with a crisped margin that is strongly reflexed at the tips. The triangular side lobes enfold over the short, stout, winged column forming a tube.

HOFFMEISTERELLA

An orthographic variant introduced in *J. Roy. Hort. Soc.*, **7**(1): 115 (1886). The correct spelling is *Hofmeisterella*.

HOFMEISTERA

Reichenbach *filius*

De Pollin. Orchid. 30 (1852).

Not *Hofmeisteria* Walpers (1846) Asteraceæ.

ETYMOLOGY: Dedicated to Wilhelm Friedrich Benedict Hofmeister (1824-1877), a German botanist, microscopist, and a professor at the Universities of Heidelberg and Tübingen.

TYPE SPECIES: *Hofmeistera eumicroscopica* Reichenbach f.

Not validly published because of a prior use of the name, this homonym was replaced by *Hofmeisterella*.

HOFMEISTERELLA

Reichenbach *filius*

Ann. Bot. Syst. **3**(3): 563 (1852).

Epidendroideæ ◊ Cymbidieæ • Oncidiinæ

ETYMOLOGY: *Hofmeistera*, a genus of orchids and Latin for diminutive.

TYPE SPECIES: *Hofmeisterella eumicroscopica* (Reichenbach f.) Reichenbach f. (*Hofmeistera eumicroscopica* Reichenbach f.)

One uncommon, somewhat psygmoid epiphyte is found in cool, mid to upper elevation, montane cloud forests of Venezuela and Colombia to Bolivia. This small, stemless plant has narrow, pencil-like, distichous, fleshy leaves in a fan-shaped arrangement. The several, erect to curved, flattened, few-flowered inflorescence is borne from the axils of the leaves. The small, citron-yellow flowers have narrow sepals and petals, and the trilobed lip has small, erect side lobes. The midlobe has a bright red to maroon spot on the sharply tapering tip and a smooth disc with a few obscure keels. The flowers have a slender, footless column that has broad, rounded wings at the very broad base. The recurved rostellum is fang- or hook-like.

HOLCOGLOSSUM

Schlechter

Repert. Spec. Nov. Regni Veg. Beih. **4**: 285 (1919).

Epidendroideæ ◊ Vandeæ • Aeridinæ

ETYMOLOGY: Greek for strap and tongue. From the strap-like spur on the lip.

TYPE SPECIES: *Holcoglossum quasipinifolium* (Hayata) Schlechter (*Saccolabium quasipinifolium* Hayata)

Ten monopodial epiphytes are found in mid to upper elevation, montane forests of northeastern India (Assam), southern China (Yunnan to Hainan), Myanmar to Vietnam, Thailand and Taiwan. These plants have rather short to long stems, each with needle-shaped leaves taking on a red appearance when exposed to full sunlight. The simple or branched, numerous to few-flowered inflorescence has small to large, thinly textured, showy, fragrant flowers ranging from white, pink-purple to yellow and have similar, slightly twisted segments with wavy margins. The dark rose to purple, trilobed lip has small, yellow, erect side lobes sprinkled red-brown and a large, white or magenta midlobe with appendages at the base. The sharply curved, elongate spur is sometimes absent. The flowers have a short, stout, wingless column.

NOTE: There is one self-fertilized species found in southern China (Yunnan) where *Holcoglossum amesianum* has developed an adaptation to the dry and insect-scarce habitat. The pollen-bearing anther uncovers itself and then rotates into position for insertion into the stigma cavity. This unusual fertilization is accomplished without the help of sticky fluids or other self-pollinating methods. This sexual relationship is so exclusive that each individual flower does not transfer pollen to the other flowers on the same plant.

HOLMESIA

P.J. Cribb

Kew Bull. **32**(1): 175 (1977).

Not *Holmesia* J.G. Agardh (1890) Rhodophyceæ-Delesseriaceæ.

ETYMOLOGY: Named in honor of W.D. Holmes (1925-), a British-born conservator of forests in NW Zambia who collected the flora of Zambia and Malawi for the Salisbury's herbarium in Rhodesia and for the Oxford and Kew herbariums in England and author of *Bark-hive Bee-keeping in Zambia*.

TYPE SPECIES: *Holmesia parva* P.J. Cribb

Not validly published because of a prior use of the name, this homonym was replaced by *Angraecopsis*.

HOLOCOGLOSSUM

An orthographic variant introduced in *J. Geobot.*, **16**(1): 7 (1968). The correct spelling is *Holcoglossum*.

HOLOGYNE

Pfitzer

Pflanzenr. (Engler) **IV.50**(II.B.7): 131 (1907).

ETYMOLOGY: Greek for whole or complete and woman or female. The description is clear but the application to this genus is obscure.

TYPE SPECIES: *Hologyne miniata* (Blume) Pfitzer (*Chelonanthera miniata* Blume)

Now recognized as belonging to the genus *Coelogyne*, *Hologyne* was previously considered to include two epiphytes found in warm to cool, mid elevation, montane forests of Indonesia and New Guinea. These plants have tall, thin, cylindrical pseudobulbs, each with two thinly textured leaves. The short, zig-zagging, few-flowered inflorescence has orange-red to yellow-green flowers with narrow petals and similar sepals. The short portion of the spoon-shaped, entire lip has five sides with two, deep red keels and a notched or fringed margin. Both species are now considered as synonyms of *Coelogyne miniata* (Blume) Lindley.

HOLOPOGON

Komarov & Nevski

Komarov's Fl. URSS **4**: 471, 571 (1935).

ETYMOLOGY: Greek for entire and beard. From the hairy surface of the leaves, scapes and sepals.

TYPE SPECIES: *Holopogon ussuriensis* Komarov & Nevski

Now recognized as belonging to the genus *Neottia*, *Holopogon* was previously considered to include six saprophytes found in mid to upper elevation, mixed forests and scrub of southeastern Russia (southern Primorye), China (Sichuan, Shaanxi and Henan), Japan and northern India (Kashmir to Assam). These uncommon, small, hairy, erect plants have essentially leafless, chlorophyllous, unbranched stems. The short, few-flowered inflorescence has small, white flowers with narrow, nerved sepals that are slightly hairy on the backside and the smooth petals have a blunt or rounded tip. The drooping, slightly concave, entire lip has a bilobed tip. The flowers have a short column.

HOLOTHRIX

Richard

De Orchid. Eur. 33 (1817), and *Mém. Mus. Hist. Nat.* **4**: 55 (1818).

Name published without a description, today this name is most often referred to *Holothrix* Lindley.

Currently Accepted   Validly Published   Invalidly Published   Published Pre-1753   Superfluous Usage   Orthographic Variant   Fossil

O r c h i d   G e n e r a   • **194**

HOLOTHRIX

Richard ex Lindley

Gen. Sp. Orchid. Pl. 257, 283 (1835).

Name ICBN conserved vs. *Monotris* Lindley (1834), vs. *Scopularia* Lindley (1834), vs. *Saccidium* Lindley (1835), and vs. *Tryphia* Lindley (1835) Orchidaceæ.

Orchidoideæ ⚘ Orchideæ • Orchidinæ

ETYMOLOGY: Latin for whole or complete and hair. Refers to the densely hairy leaves of the type species.

TYPE SPECIES: *Holothrix parvifolia* Lindley nom. illeg.

This type name is now considered a synonym of *Holothrix hispidula* (Linnaeus f.) T. Durand & Schinz
basionym
(*Orchis hispidula* Linnaeus f.)

A genus of some forty-four sympodial terrestrials are found in dry, low to upper elevation, arid and rocky scrub of Nigeria to Kenya, Malawi, Zimbabwe, South Africa and southwestern Saudia Arabia. These unusual, little, erect, deciduous plants have unbranched stems, each with two typically hairy, ovate or roundish, basal leaves that hug the ground and sometimes are withered before flowering begins. The upper, water-storing, thick leaf appears translucent and is sometimes withered by flowering time. The slender, few-flowered inflorescence, with or without sheaths, has tiny flowers varying from white, cream, yellow, green to pink-cream. The long petals are entire or lobed with three or more, finger-like lobes and rather fleshy. The usually lobed, toothed or rare entire lip has many species with hair-like lobes and has a small, curved spur. The flowers have a small to tiny, erect, wingless column.

HOLOTRIX

An orthographic variant introduced in *Dict. Class. Hist. Nat.*, 12: 308 (1827). The correct spelling is *Holothrix*.

HOMALOPETALUM

Rolfe

Hooker's Icon. Pl. 25: t. 2461 (1896).

Epidendroideæ ⚘ Epidendreæ • Laeliinæ

ETYMOLOGY: Greek for even, uniform and petal. Refers to the similarity of the sepals and petals.

TYPE SPECIES: *Homalopetalum jamaicense* Rolfe

This type name is now considered a synonym of *Homalopetalum vomeriforme* (Swartz) Fawcett & Rendle;
basionym
Epidendrum vomeriforme Swartz

Four exceptionally interesting, sympodial epiphytes or lithophytes are found in moist, mid to upper elevation, montane moss laden to cloud forests from Cuba, Hispaniola, and Jamaica, then from Mexico to Panama, Colombia, Ecuador, Peru and a few small areas of Venezuela and southeastern Brazil. These creeping, erect or hanging, densely clustered, dwarf to minute plants have tiny, ovoid pseudobulbs, subtended at the base by short, flat lying sheaths, each with a small, solitary, gray-green, fleshy leaf suffused dark purple. The slender, solitary-flowered inflorescence has an inconspicuous and small to large and showy, star-shaped, translucent, green-yellow, yellow to pale green flower variously suffused and/or dotted maroon or purple. The flower supported by a slender scape, allows the flower to flex with the wind. The petals, similar to the sepals, converge along their upper margins. The large, clawed or not, entire lip has a pair of keel-like calli at the base. The flowers have a small, slightly curved column that is winged along its whole length or is wingless.

HOMOCOLLETICON

(Summerhayes) Szlachetko & Olszewski

Fl. Cameroun 36: 727 (2001).

ETYMOLOGY: Greek for equal, similar or likeness and collection or group. Referring to the likeness among the flowers' sepals, petals and lip.

TYPE SPECIES: *Homocolleticon monteiroae* (Reichenbach f.) Szlachetko & Olszewski (*Cyrtorchis monteiroae* Reichenbach f.)

Now recognized as belonging to the genus *Cyrtorchis*, *Homocolleticon* was proposed to include seven epiphytes found in humid, low elevation, woodlands and evergreen forests of Sierra Leone to Uganda, then south to Angola. These small plants have long, hanging stems with oblong, tapering, strap-like, overlapping, dark green leaves that have visible cross veins. The stems are subtended by the brittle remains of old leaf sheaths. The short, numerous to few-flowered inflorescence has widely-spaced, fragrant, white or creamy flowers arranged in two ranks. The flowers turn pale orange with age and have similar shaped sepals and petals. The broad, entire or obscurely trilobed lip has a long, green-orange tinged, tapering, slightly incurved spur. The flowers have a slender, downward bent column.

HONGORA

An orthographic variant introduced in *Bot. Centralbl.*, 80(13): 505 (1899). The correct spelling is *Gongora*.

HORDEANTHOS

Szlachetko

Richardiana 7(2): 88 (2007).

ETYMOLOGY: Latin for *Hordeum*, a genus of grass, and Greek for flower. Refers to large, tight bundle of flowers that looks like a grass seed head.

TYPE SPECIES: *Hordeanthos lemniscatum* (C.S.P. Parish ex Hooker f.) Szlachetko (*Bulbophyllum lemniscatum* C.S.P. Parish ex Hooker f.)

Recognized as belonging to the genus *Bulbophyllum*, *Hordeanthos* was proposed to include three epiphytes found in low elevation, hill forests of Myanmar and Thailand. These plants have clustered, small, heavily wrinkled, roundish, pseudobulbs each with three, small leaves borne from the base of the pseudobulb. These leaves are usually withered by flowering time. The slender, numerous-flowered inflorescences have tiny to minute, deep purple to red-purple flowers with each hairy sepal having a very long appendage variously banded white and red. Has tiny, narrow, white petals covered with red or purple streaks. The tiny, entire lip is recurved and dark blue-purple.

HORICHIA

Jenny

Orchidee (Hamburg) 32(3): 107 (1981).

Epidendroideæ ⚘ Cymbidieæ • Stanhopeinæ

ETYMOLOGY: In honor of Clarence Klaus Horich (1921-1994), a German-born Costa Rican coffee plantation owner who collected and discovered many new flora species of Central America.

TYPE SPECIES: *Horichia dressleri* Jenny

One sympodial epiphyte is found in humid, mid elevation, montane forests of Costa Rica and Panama. This small plant has clustered, ovoid, smooth pseudobulbs, each with a solitary, pleated leaf when young. The erect, few-flowered inflorescence has deep red-brown flowers with a pale suffusion of color toward the edges. The small dorsal sepal recurves sharply. The petals and lateral sepals are similar in shape and size. The bright golden-yellow, deeply trilobed lip has long, narrow, curled side lobes, and a narrow, downward hanging midlobe that tapers to a sharp point. The flowers have a straight, footless, wingless column.

HORMIDIUM

Lindley ex Heynhold

Nom. Bot. Hort. **2**: 880 (1841).

Not *Hormidium* Kützing (1843) Chlorophyceæ-Prasiolaceæ.

ETYMOLOGY: Greek for necklace. Referring to the rhizomatose habit of the pseudobulbs being distantly placed along the rhizome.

TYPE SPECIES: *Hormidium uniflorum*
(Lindley) Heynhold
(*Epidendrum uniflorum* Lindley)
This type name is now considered a synonym of
Prosthechea pygmaea (Hooker) W.E. Higgins;
basionym replaced with
Epidendrum pygmaeum Hooker

Now recognized as belonging to the genus *Prosthechea*, *Hormidium* was previously considered to include eight epiphytes found in wet, low to mid elevation, hill and montane forests and woodlands from the southeastern United States (southern Florida), southern Mexico to Brazil, Cuba to Trinidad, the Guianas and Venezuela. These dwarf plants form dense colonies of spindle-shaped pseudobulbs, each with several, narrow, leathery leaves, borne at the tip of the pseudo-bulb. The short, few-flowered inflorescence has inconspicuous, small, yellow-green flowers that appear nestled between pairs of dwarf leaves. The white, trilobed lip has prominent, upcurved side lobes, and the short pointed midlobe has a bright purple tip. The flowers have a long column.

HORVATIA

Garay

Stud. Phytologica 40 (1977).

Epidendroideæ ⚘ Cymbidieæ • Maxillariinæ

ETYMOLOGY: In honor of Adolf Olivér Horvát (1907-1997), a Hungarian high school teacher of botany and chemistry, professor of botany at the University of Pécs, and a priest of the Cistercian Order.

TYPE SPECIES: *Horvatia andicola* Garay

One robust, sympodial epiphyte is found in cool, wet, upper elevation, montane valley forests of central Ecuador (Cañar). This hanging plant has a long, creeping, leafless rhizome between which are found small, well-spaced, ovoid pseudobulbs, subtended by thin, dry, red sheaths, each with a long, solitary, narrow, leathery leaf. The solitary-flowered inflorescence, borne most unusually from the rhizome and between pseudobulbs, has a small, star-shaped, white flower with long, narrow, widespreading segments. The small, mobile, shortly clawed, obscurely lobed lip is attached to the short column foot. The flowers have a small, short, roundish, wingless column.

NOTE: The tiny plant is somewhat similar to *Bulbophyllum*, but much more so to *Teuscheria*.

HOULETIA

An orthographic variant cited in *Cat. Pl.* (*Warszewicz*), 66 (1864). The correct spelling is *Houlletia*.

HOULETTIA

An orthographic variant introduced in *Gart.-Zeitung*, **1**: 387 (1882). The correct spelling is *Houlletia*.

HOULLETIA

Brongniart

Ann. Sci. Nat., Bot., ser. 2 **15**: 37 (1841), and *Hort. Universel* **3**: 132 (1841).

Epidendroideæ ⚘ Cymbidieæ • Stanhopeinæ

ETYMOLOGY: In commemoration of a Mr. R. de J.B. Houllet (c. 1815-1890), a French horticulturist who collected (together with Jean Baptiste Antoine Guillemin {1796-1842}) the type species and was head gardener at the Jardin des Plantes in Paris.

TYPE SPECIES: *Houlletia stapeliiflora* Brongniart
This type name is now considered a synonym of
Houlletia brocklehurstiana Lindley

Nine sympodial terrestrials or rare epiphytes are found in wet, cool to humid, mid elevation, montane forests from Guatemala to Bolivia and Brazil. These large, stout plants have clustered, ovoid, ridged pseudobulbs, often subtended by gray sheaths, each with large, pleated, heavily veined leaves. The arching to hanging, solitary to few-flowered inflorescence, borne from the base of the pseudobulb, has large, showy, fragrant, dark maroon, yellow, to orange, widespreading flowers heavily spotted red-brown or mostly unspotted. The white to yellow, deeply trilobed lip, continuous with the column base, is lined and spotted below with pink-red. The side lobes are erect and the midlobe has two narrow, arched horns. The flowers have a pale brown, slender, wingless, erect column with a yellow-green tip with a bright red foot.

HUEBNERIA

Schlechter

Beih. Bot. Centralbl. **42**(2): 96 (1925).

Not *Huebneria* Reichenbach (1841) Clusieæ.

ETYMOLOGY: Dedicated to Georg Hübner (1862-1935), a German explorer who through his photo imagery of Manaus documented the Amazonian flora and peoples with his iconography. These visual memories stored at the Botanic Museum in Berlin were destroyed in 1945 by the bombing of the city.

TYPE SPECIES: *Huebneria yauaperyensis*
(Barbosa Rodrigues) Schlechter
(*Orleanesia yauaperyensis* Barbosa Rodrigues)

Not validly published because of a prior use of the name, this homonym was replaced by *Orleanesia*.

HUMBOLDTIA

Ruiz & Pavón

Fl. Peruv. Prodr. 121, t. 27 (1794).

Name ICBN rejected vs. *Humboldtia* Vahl (1794) Fabaceæ; and not *Humboldtia* F. Thiergart & U. Frantz (1963) Fossil.

ETYMOLOGY: Dedicated to Friedrich Wilhem Heinrich Alexander von Humboldt (1769-1859), a Prussian baron, scientific explorer, student of natural history and author of numerous scientific works.

LECTOTYPE: *Humboldtia purpurea* Ruiz & Pavón
This type name is now considered a synonym of
Stelis purpurea (Ruiz & Pavón) Willdenow;
basionym
Humboldtia purpurea Ruiz & Pavón

Although validly published this rejected name is now referred to the genera *Stelis* and *Pleurothallis*. *Humboldtia* was considered to include three hundred epiphytes distributed in low to especially upper elevation, hill and montane forests and woodlands from the southeastern United States (southern Florida), Cuba to Trinidad, and southern Mexico to Brazil and Bolivia. These highly variable, small to relatively large plants have erect, stout to thin stems, each with a solitary, leathery leaf. The often several, short to long, erect to arching, solitary to numerous-flowered inflorescences have small to tiny, nodding flowers in a wide range of colors and shapes. The petals are usually smaller than the sepals. The usually small to tiny, entire or obscurely trilobed lip is united to the column foot and has a central disc with keels or calli. The flowers have a small to tiny column with or without a foot.

NOTE: Ruiz & Pavón originally published the genus spelled (*Humboltia*), without the 'D', but they corrected the spelling in *Syst. Veg. Fl. Peruv. Chil.*, 233 (1798).

Currently Accepted   Validly Published   Invalidly Published   Published Pre-1753   Superfluous Usage   Orthographic Variant   Fossil

O r c h i d   G e n e r a • **196**

HUNTLEYA

Bateman ex **Lindley**

Edwards's Bot. Reg. **23**: sub 1991 (1837).

Epidendroideæ ◊ Cymbidieæ • Zygopetalinæ

ETYMOLOGY: In honor of the John Thomas Huntley (1792-x), a British clergyman (rector of Binbrooke Linc), gardener, and an orchid-fancier from Kimbolton Hunts (Huntingdonshire).

TYPE SPECIES: *Huntleya meleagris* Lindley

Thirteen magnificent, sympodial epiphytes are found in extremely wet, low to mid elevation, hill and montane forests ranging from Costa Rica to Venezuela, Brazil and Trinidad. These fan-like plants lack pseudobulbs but have short stems, each with narrow, lightly veined, semi-leathery to thinly textured leaves, that overlap at the base and are arranged in a fan shape. The solitary-flowered inflorescence has an often large, flat-faced, showy, lustrous flower with widely spreading segments. They are delightfully colored, fragrant, waxy-textured as if they had just been freshly lacquered, and the flower lasts for more than a month. The lateral sepals are joined at the base and inserted on the column foot. The flat, short-clawed, obscurely trilobed lip is furnished with almost hair-like, fine fringe or shallowly cut, at the tip of each, small side lobe. The flowers have a short, stout column.

HUTTONAEA

Harvey

Thes. Cap. **2**(1): 1, *t. 101* (1863).

Orchidoideæ ◊ Orchideæ • Huttonaeinæ

ETYMOLOGY: Dedicated to Caroline R. Hutton née Atherstone (1826-1908) a South African, who along with her husband, Henry Hutton (1825-1896), collected the type species and other flora of southern Africa.

TYPE SPECIES: *Huttonaea pulchra* Harvey

Five uncommon, sympodial terrestrials are found in mid to upper elevation, montane forests, grasslands and woodlands with high summer-rainfalls of the eastern Cape area in South Africa. These small, erect plants have short to tall, slender, unbranched stems, each with several, broad, ovate, softly textured leaves. When young the plants have a solitary, somewhat heart-shaped leaf and sometimes a small leaf will be found mid stem. The erect, simple to branched, solitary to few-flowered inflorescence has large, bizarre, usually white to pale green flowers with purple markings. The ornate, conspicuously, deeply and heavily fringed petals are sac-like, and even the ovate, shortly clawed, entire lip is also deeply fringed. The flowers have a yellow, short, footless column.

HUTTONIA

An orthographic variant introduced in *J. Linn. Soc., Bot.*, **19**: 339 (1882). The correct spelling is *Huttonaea*.

HYACINTHORCHIS

Blume

Mus. Bot. **1**(3): 48, *t. 16* (1849).

ETYMOLOGY: *Hyacinthus*, a genus of lilies and Greek for orchid. Referring to the inflorescence which looks like that of *Hyacinthus*.
Or Greek Mythology. The son of Clio and Pierus, King of Macedonia, Hyakinthos was accidentally killed by Apollo who made a flower from his tears, the hyacinth, of his friend's spilled blood.

TYPE SPECIES: *Hyacinthorchis variabilis* Blume
This type name is now considered a synonym of *Cremastra appendiculata* var. *variabilis* (Blume) I.D. Lund;
basionym
Hyacinthorchis variabilis Blume

Now recognized as belonging to the genus *Cremastra*, *Hyacinthorchis* was previously considered to include one terrestrial found in low to upper elevation, hill and montane forests of northern India (Sikkim), China (Anhui to Yunnan, Xizang), Taiwan, Vietnam, Thailand and Japan. This plant has ovoid pseudobulbs, each with a solitary, narrow leaf. The erect, few-flowered inflorescence has tubular, pink to creamy flowers not opening widely that have long, narrow sepals and petals. The trilobed lip has a small projection on the midlobe and is slightly sac-like at the base. The flowers have a long, slender, wingless, footless column.

HYALOSEMA

Rolfe

Orchid Rev. **27**(319-320): 130 (1919).

ETYMOLOGY: Greek for glassy or crystalline and mark or standard. Alluding to the translucent markings located on the dorsal sepal.

TYPE SPECIES: *Hyalosema grandiflorum* (Blume) Rolfe
(*Bulbophyllum grandiflorum* Blume)

Now recognized as belonging to the genus as a section of *Bulbophyllum*, *Hyalosema* was previously considered to include fifteen epiphytes found in low elevation, rain forests from Malaysia, Indonesia, the Philippines and New Guinea to the Solomons. These plants have widely spaced, bright green but tough, small pseudobulbs, subtended by dry sheaths, each with a solitary, oblong, leathery leaf. The erect to arching, solitary-flowered inflorescence, borne from the rhizome, has exceedingly large, green, brown-green or pink flowers with the large dorsal sepal forming a hood over the column. They are certainly among the most distorted or ugly and foul smelling of all the orchids.

HYBOCHILUS

Schlechter

Repert. Spec. Nov. Regni Veg. **16**: 429 (1920).

ETYMOLOGY: Greek for hump-backed and lip. Referring to the hump-like swelling in the middle part of the lip.

TYPE SPECIES: *Hybochilus inconspicuus* (Kraenzlin) Schlechter
(*Rodriguezia inconspicua* Kraenzlin)

Now recognized as belonging to the genus *Trichocentrum*, *Hybochilus* was previously considered to include one uncommon, dwarf epiphyte found in mid elevation, montane cloud forests from Costa Rica to Panama. This short-lived, twig plant has clustered, ovoid to oblong pseudobulbs, each with one to two, leathery, unequally bilobed leaves. The short, highly branched, numerous-flowered inflorescence, subtended by leafy-sheaths, has minute, weakly colored, white flowers sprinkled with several, pale brown-purple spots and has rosy-purple margins. The long, white, trilobed lip, attached to the column, has a few red spots, a green-yellow basal splash and a slightly rough surface. The flowers have a short, stout, footless column with a beak-like anther. The above type name is now considered a synonym of *Trichocentrum candidum* Lindley.

HYDRANTHUS

Kuhl & **Hasskarl** ex **Reichenbach** *filius*

Xenia Orchid. **2**: 20 (1862).

ETYMOLOGY: Greek for moist, wet or water and flower. Referring to the plants' favorite habitat.

TYPE SPECIES: *Hydranthus scandens* (Blume) Kuhl & Hasskarl ex Reichenbach f.
(*Leopardanthus scandens* Blume)

Now recognized as belonging to the genus *Dipodium*, *Hydranthus* was previously considered to include one epiphyte found in low elevation, woodlands from Thailand, Malaysia, Indonesia, northern Australia (Queensland) to Vanuatu and the Solomons. This erect, tufted or climbing plant has slender stems, each with rather long, curved leaves. The erect, few-flowered inflorescence has pale yellow flowers with crimson blotches on their backsides, that faintly show through to the front. The narrow, somewhat folded, trilobed lip is purple striped and has several, wooly hairs on the front section. The flowers have a short, thick column.

HYDRORCHIS

D.L. Jones & M.A. Clements

Orchadian   **13**(10): 462 (2002).

ETYMOLOGY: Latin for water and orchid. Alluding to this species' preferred habitat.

TYPE SPECIES: *Hydrorchis orbicularis*
  (R.S. Rogers) D.L. Jones & M.A. Clements
  (*Microtis orbicularis* R.S. Rogers)

Recognized as belonging to the genus *Microtis*, *Hydrorchis* was proposed to include one terrestrial found in low elevation, swampy scrub of southern Australia (Victoria to Western Australia) and Tasmania growing with great abundance in watery swamps. This erect, slender, unbranched plant has a solitary leaf found just below the inflorescence at an angulation of the stem. The few-flowered inflorescence breaks through the leaf after elongation and has small, red to pale brown flowers. The dorsal sepal is hood-like, and the tiny, widespreading petals are slightly recurved. The plain, entire lip is oval-shaped and has an upcurved margin. The flowers have a minute column.

HYGROCHILUS

Pfitzer

Nat. Pflanzenfam. Nachtr.   **1**(II-IV): 112 (1897).

Epidendroideæ ⚘ Vandeæ • Aeridinæ

ETYMOLOGY: Greek for moist or damp and lip. In reference to the nectar-producing channel at the base of the lip.

TYPE SPECIES: *Hygrochilus parishii*
  (Veitch & Reichenbach f.) Pfitzer
  (*Vanda parishii* Veitch & Reichenbach f.)

Two monopodial epiphytes or terrestrials are found in low to mid elevation, forests and slopes from northern India (Assam), southern China (Yunnan), Myanmar to Vietnam and Thailand. These stout but short or slightly elongated stemmed plants have several, thick, flat, leathery leaves arranged in two rows. The erect, numerous to few-flowered inflorescence has large, showy, heavily textured, long-lived, green-yellow, fragrant flowers covered with red-brown blotches. The small, pale yellow to bright magenta, mobile, bipartite or obscurely trilobed lip is attached to the column foot. The hypochile has a narrow, nectar-filled channel with a fleshy, raised basal callus between the small side lobes. The ovate or broadly clawed epichile has a central, raised ridge. The flowers have a long, forward bent, wingless, footless column. This species was formerly included in *Vandopsis*.

HYLAEORCHIS

Carnevali & G.A. Romero

Orchids Venezuela, ed. 2   **3**: 1136 (2000).

Epidendroideæ ⚘ Cymbidieæ • Maxillariinæ

ETYMOLOGY: Greek for belonging to forest or woodland and orchid. A term used in biogeographical and ecological literature referring to the lowland Amazonian forests.

TYPE SPECIES: *Hylaeorchis petiolaris*
  (Schlechter) Carnevali & Romero
  (*Maxillaria petiolaris* Schlechter)

One sympodial epiphyte or occasional lithophyte is found in hot, humid, low elevation, heavily flooded forests of the Guianas, south-eastern Venezuela and northern Brazil. This plant has compressed pseudobulbs, subtended in persistent sheaths, each with a solitary, leathery leaf. The short, solitary-flowered inflorescence, borne from the base of the pseudobulb, has a dull peachy-yellow flower suffused pale maroon with the inner surface often spotted maroon. The tongue-shaped trilobed lip has short, erect side lobes, the midlobe has a shiny, dark claret basal splash and almost white margins. The flowers have a short, erect, stout column.

HYLOBIUM

An orthographic variant introduced in *Gart.-Zeitung*, **1**: 205 (1882). The correct spelling is *Xylobium*.

HYLOGLOSSUM

An orthographic variant introduced in *J. Gener. Litter.*, **1828**(11): 323 (1828). The correct spelling is *Styloglossum*.

HYLOPHILA

Lindley

Edwards's Bot. Reg.   **19**: sub 1618 (1833), and
Numer. List   247, no. 7396 (1831).
Not *Hylophila* Quélet (1886) Fungi.

Orchidoideæ ⚘ Cranichideæ • Goodyerinæ

ETYMOLOGY: Greek for forest or a wood and lover or loving. Alluding to both its terrestrial and favorite forest habitat.

TYPE SPECIES: *Hylophila mollis* Lindley

Ten large, sympodial terrestrials, occasional lithophytes or rare epiphytes are found in damp, low to mid elevation, evergreen hill moss or humus from Taiwan, Thailand, Indonesia and New Guinea to the Philippines. These creeping, jewel orchids are grown more for their colored foliage than their minute, taxonomically difficult flowers. The erect stem has several, pale to dark green, narrow to ovate leaves and a hairy, numerous-flowered, red-brown inflorescence. The tightly bunched, small to tiny, translucent, pale green, pink to orange flowers do not open widely, but have white tips and colored midveins. The large dorsal sepal and petals converge, forming a hood that encloses the whole flower and the small to obscure, footless column. The deeply sac-shaped, bilobed lip is quite hairy.

HYLOPHYLA

An orthographic variant cited in *Handb. Orchid.-Namen*, 389 (2005). The correct spelling is *Hylophila*.

HYMANTHOGLOSSUM

An orthographic variant introduced in *Orchid. Sicul.*, 67 (1842). The correct spelling is *Himantoglossum*.

HYMENERIA

D.L. Jones & M.A. Clements

Orchadian   **13**(11): 501 (2002).

ETYMOLOGY: Greek for membrane or thin and *Eria*, a genus of orchids. Referring to the somewhat shapeless stem that has thinly textured leaves.

TYPE SPECIES: *Hymeneria obesa*
  (Lindley) D.L. Jones & M.A. Clements
  (*Eria obesa* Lindley)

Recognized as belonging to the genus *Eria*, *Hymeneria* was proposed to include three epiphytes found in low elevation, hill forests of northern India (Assam), Nepal, Myanmar, Thailand, Indonesia, New Guinea, northern Australia (Queensland), Solomon Islands and Samoa. These plants have stout, cylindrical or somewhat compressed, silvery-green pseudo-bulbs, subtended by persistent leaf sheaths, each with several, narrow leaves. The several, few-flowered inflorescences, borne from the upper nodes of the pseudobulb, have large, pale white bracts and usually only flower after shedding their leaves. The small, white flowers fade to green toward the base. The obscurely trilobed lip has a blunt tip, is without distinct side lobes, and has three keels on the midlobe.

Currently Accepted   Validly Published   Invalidly Published   Published Pre-1753   Superfluous Usage   Orthographic Variant   Fossil

Orchid Genera • **198**

HYMENOCHILUS

D.L. Jones & M.A. Clements

Austral. Orchid Res.   **4**: 72 (2002).

ETYMOLOGY: Greek for membrane and tongue. Refers to the thin texture of the lip.

TYPE SPECIES: *Hymenochilus muticus*
(R. Brown) D.L. Jones & M.A. Clements
(*Pterostylis mutica* R. Brown)

Recognized as belonging to the genus *Pterostylis*, *Hymenochilus* was proposed to include nine terrestrials found in dry, low elevation, open grasslands and sandy, hillside pastures of southern Australia, Tasmania and New Zealand. These robust, slender plants have a smooth, unbranched stem with a basal rosette crowded with narrow leaves that are often withered by flowering time. The erect, few-flowered inflorescence has occasionally spirally arranged, green flowers. The dorsal sepal and petals converge, forming a hood over the incurved column. The broadly clawed, green to white, entire lip has a wavy margin, a raised callus and a dark green protuberance.

HYMENORCHIS

Schlechter

Repert. Spec. Nov. Regni Veg. Beih.
1(13): 994 (1913).

Epidendroideæ ※ Vandeæ • Aeridinæ

ETYMOLOGY: Greek for a membrane and orchid. Descriptive of the delicate texture of the flowers.

TYPE SPECIES: *Hymenorchis javanica*
(Teysmann & Binnendijk) Schlechter
(*Oeceoclades javanica* Teysmann & Binnendijk)

Ten monopodial epiphytes are found in misty, mid elevation, montane forests from Indonesia (Java), New Guinea and New Caledonia to the Philippines. The fleshy to leathery, slightly hairy leaves of these small plants have minutely notched margins and will slit the leaf sheaths when emerging. The hairy, few-flowered inflorescence has small, bell-shaped, translucent, white or pale green flowers with only a few open at any one time. The flowers, covered with white hairs, do not open widely and are fairly large in proportion to the small size of the plant. The diamond-shaped sepals and petals have a prominent central ridge and have serrated and notched margins. The tiny, usually contrasting dark green, scoop-shaped, entire lip, attached to the column, has a white tip, a serrated margin and a large, swollen, pale green spur. The flowers have a short, footless column.

HYPODAEMATIUM

An orthographic variant introduced in *Orchideen (Schlechter)*, ed. 3, 217 (2003). The correct spelling is *Hypodematium*.

HYPODEMA

Reichenbach

Deut. Bot. Herb.-Buch   56 (1841).

ETYMOLOGY: Latin for rounded.

TYPE SPECIES: *None designated*

Name published without a description. Today this name is most often referred to *Cypripedium*.

HYPODEMATIUM

A. Richard

Tent. Fl. Abyss.   **2**: 286, t. 83 (1850).

Not *Hypodematium* G. Kunze (1833) Dryopteridaceæ, and not *Hypodematium* A. Richard (1848) Rubiaceæ.

ETYMOLOGY: Greek for sandal. Descriptive of the shape of the lip.

TYPE SPECIES: *Hypodematium abyssinicum*
A. Richard
This type name is now considered a synonym of *Eulophia streptopetala* Lindley

Not validly published because of a prior use of the name, this homonym was replaced by *Eulophia*.

HYSTERIA

Reinwardt

Syll. Pl. Nov.   **2**: 5 (1825).

ETYMOLOGY: Greek for latter or behind and womb or uterus. The application of this name as a description is unclear.

TYPE SPECIES: *Hysteria veratrifolia* Reinwardt

Now recognized as belonging to the genus *Corymborkis*, *Hysteria* was previously considered to include one terrestrial found in low to mid elevation, hill and montane forests of south-eastern China (Yunnan), southern Japan, Taiwan, India (Assam, Nicobar and Andaman Islands), Bangladesh, Thailand, Vietnam, Indonesia to northeastern Australia, the Philippines and the south-western Pacific Archipelago. This erect, inconspicuous, often clump-forming plant has slender, woody and rather long stems, each with several, minutely notched, papery leaves subtended by clasping sheaths at the base. The few to numerous-flowered, simple to sometimes branched, erect, spreading or hanging inflorescence has uniformly white or pale green, fragrant, variable-sized flowers with long, narrow sepals and petals. The long-clawed, entire lip clasps the erect, slender column.

HYTERIA

An orthographic variant introduced in *Bibliogr. Bot. Handbuch*, 286 (1841). The correct spelling is *Hysteria*.

Jarava
Historia de las Yervas y Plantas
pages 314 & 405 (1557).

IANTHA

Hooker

Exot. Fl. **2**(12): *t. 113* (1824).

Not *Ianthe* Salisbury (1866) Hypoidaceæ.

ETYMOLOGY: Greek for violet and flower. Suggesting a similarity of the flowers to some species of violets.

Or Greek Mythology. *Iantha* was a beautiful sea nymph and daughter of Oceanus and Tethys, from Hesiod's *Theogony* poem which describes the birth of the various Greek gods and goddesses.

TYPE SPECIES: *Iantha pallidiflora* Hooker

This type name is now considered a synonym of
Ionopsis utricularioides (Swartz) Lindley;
basionym
Epidendrum utricularioides Swartz

Now recognized as belonging to the genus *Ionopsis*, *Iantha* was previously considered to include one epiphyte found from the south-eastern United States (Florida) and Mexico to Brazil. This plant is highly variable in both its vegetation and floral dimensions. The small plant has compact pseudobulbs, each with one to two, leathery leaves. The long, branching, numerous to few-flowered inflorescence has pastel to bright pink flowers with purple veins. The shortly clawed, large, flat, heart-shaped, entire lip has a bilobed tip with an entire or wavy margin. The flowers have a small, stout, wingless, footless column.

IBIDIUM

Salisbury

Trans. Hort. Soc. London **1**: 291 (1812).

ETYMOLOGY: Greek for diminutive of *ibis*, a species of birds. Alluding to a resemblance of the flowers to the neck and head of the ibis.

LECTOTYPE: *Ibidium spirale* (Linnaeus) Salisbury
(*Ophrys spiralis* Linnaeus)

Now recognized as belonging to the genus *Spiranthes*, *Ibidium* was previously considered to include thirty terrestrials found mainly in low to mid elevation, grassy fields and meadows of mainly the eastern United States (Michigan to eastern Texas and New Hampshire to Florida), Canada (Yukon Territory to Labrador), Mexico to Panama, the Bahamas and Cuba to Trinidad. These erect plants have stout to slender, unbranched stems with the leaves varying from narrow to broadly ovate. In some species the leaves are not present at the time of flowering. The erect, numerous to few-flowered inflorescence has small to tiny, white to purple-brown flowers. The dorsal sepal and petals converge, forming a hood over the tiny column. The shortly clawed, entire or rare lobed lip is usually flanked by a pair of minute protuberances.

NOTE: In this group of orchids the typical spiranthoid floral twist is so irregular it cannot be distinguished in some species, while other species are tight enough to present the flowers in three or more distinct vertical ranks.

ICHTHYOSTOMUM

D.L. Jones, M.A. Clements & Molloy

Orchadian **13**(11): 499 (2002).

ETYMOLOGY: Greek for fish and mouth. Referring to the capsule that opens like a fishes mouth.

TYPE SPECIES: *Ichthyostomum pygmaeum*
(Smith) M.A. Clements & D.L. Jones
(*Dendrobium pygmaeum* Smith)

Recognized as belonging to the genus *Bulbophyllum*, *Ichthyostomum* was proposed to include one epiphyte found in low to mid elevation, growing as mossy mats on trees, also sometimes on rocks as a lithophyte in New Zealand and Lord Howe Island. This tiny plant has minute, almost matchhead-sized, squat, yellow-green pseudobulbs, each with a tiny, solitary, ovate leaf. The short, solitary-flowered inflorescence has a minute, thinly textured, creamy-green flower that opens briefly but will remain attached to its capsule even when the flower withers. This unusual capsule has two upper valves that remain together, so that when the fruit opens it gives it an appearance of a bivalve. These tiny flowers self-pollinate. The flowers have a short, winged column.

IDA

A. Ryan & Oakeley

Orchid Digest **67**(1): 9 (2003).

Epidendroideæ • Cymbidieæ • Maxillariinæ

ETYMOLOGY: Cretan Mythology: *Ida* was a hunter from a band of beautiful, unadorned virgin warriors whose red, dusty cheeks were suffused with sweat, and they were led by Queen Latonia (a nymph of the woods and stars). Latonia along with her sister Adrasteia and the virgin warrior Dactyls nurtured the infant Zeus without the knowledge of his father (Kronos). They put him in a golden cradle hung upon the trees and executed war dances around the cradle, and beat bronze shields with swords, so that Kronos could not hear the baby crying nor find him either on the earth, or in the sky, or in the sea. Zeus later transferred these ladies into the heavens and designated them as a constellation that he named the Bears.

TYPE SPECIES: *Ida locusta*
(Reichenbach f.) A. Ryan & Oakeley
(*Lycaste locusta* Reichenbach f.)

Thirty-five sympodial epiphytes, lithophytes or terrestrials are found in wet, cool to warm, low to upper elevation, hill to montane forests, grasslands, coastal swamps and river banks of Jamaica, Cuba, Hispaniola, Colombia to Bolivia, Venezuela and Brazil. These plants have large, spindle-shaped to ovoid pseudo-bulbs, subtended by brown bracts borne from the tip, each with several, large, broad leaves. The erect, wiry, solitary-flowered inflorescence, borne from the pseudobulb base, has a large, nodding, green, white, orange to yellow, nocturnally fragrant flower with similar sepals. The broad to narrow petals are either widespreading or converge, forming a hood over the long, slender, curved column. The prominent trilobed lip has a narrow hypochile, side lobes that rise vertically but do not form a side wall to the hypochile, and the midlobe often has a fringed margin or entire margin.

IEBINE

Rafinesque

Fl. Tellur. **4**: 39 (1836)[1837].

ETYMOLOGY: The name is apparently derived from the Japanese vernacular name for *Calanthe*.

TYPE SPECIES: *Iebine nervosa* (Thunberg) Rafinesque
(*Ophrys nervosa* Thunberg)

Now recognized as belonging to the genus *Liparis*, *Iebine* was previously considered to include one terrestrial or lithophyte widespread in wet, low to mid elevation, open forests, woodlands and road-sides from Cuba to Trinidad, the Guianas, Venezuela, southern Mexico to Peru, Brazil

| Currently Accepted | Validly Published | Invalidly Published | Published Pre-1753 | Superfluous Usage | Orthographic Variant | Fossil |

O r c h i d   G e n e r a   • 200

and Paraguay, Africa and India to New Guinea. This plant has pale green pseudobulbs usually subtended by dried up, old leaves. The softly textured, wrinkled leaves are shiny, pale green on top and velvety, pale green on the underside. The erect, few-flowered inflorescence has pale green flowers suffused pink to maroon. The thick, broad, green, entire lip has a dark pink-maroon blotch toward the tip. The flowers have a long, slender, erect column.

IMERINAEA

Schlechter

Repert. Spec. Nov. Regni Veg. Beih. **33**: 151 (1925).

Epidendroideæ · Vandeæ • Polystachyinæ

ETYMOLOGY: A location in central Madagascar (East Imerina) where the type species was collected. Merina was a kingdom in Madagascar made up of Malayo-Indonesian descendent peoples, which was wracked by intermittent civil war, and by 1863 the kingdom included all of Madagascar except for the south and a western portion of the island. This monarchy was later abolished in 1897.

TYPE SPECIES: *Imerinaea madagascarica* Schlechter

One uncommon, sympodial terrestrial or sometimes lithophyte that is found in humid, mid elevation, montane forests and woodlands of Madagascar (Antananarivo, Antsiranana, Fianarantsoa and Toamasina) and the Comoros Islands. This plant has small, ovoid pseudobulbs, subtended by leaf-sheaths, each with a solitary, oblong leaf. The very tall, slender, few-flowered inflorescence, both the leaf and spike, are borne from the tip of the pseudobulb. The tiny, yellow-white flowers, not opening fully, are covered with fine hairs on both sides, as is the short, broad, entire lip which is uppermost and has a notched, front margin. The flowers have a long, slender column with minute papillose at the base.

IMERINORCHIS

Szlachetko

Orchidee (Hamburg) **56**(1): 68 (2005).

ETYMOLOGY: Latin for landscape and Greek for orchid. Refers to the area where found.

TYPE SPECIES: *Imerinorchis galeata*
(Reichenbach f.) Szlachetko
(*Cynosorchis galeata* Reichenbach f.)

Recognized as belonging to the genus *Cynorkis, Imerinorchis* was proposed to include thirteen terrestrials found in humid, low to mid elevation, marshes and prairies of Madagascar, Comoros and the Mascarene Islands. These erect, slender plants have a delicate, unbranched stem with a basal rosette. The numerous to few-flowered inflorescence has rather small, purple-white to pale pink flowers with large, widespreading lateral sepals. The short to long, narrow petals are united with the lip base and converge with the dorsal

---

sepal forming a hood over the broad, horizontal column. The long, narrow, entire, obscurely trilobed to four-lobed lip has a cylindrical or thread-like spur.

INCAEA

Luer

Monogr. Syst. Bot. Missouri Bot. Gard. **105**: 87, *f.* 44 (2006).

ETYMOLOGY: South American Indian people living in the central Andes. When the Spanish conquest began in the early 1530s, the Inca empire covered most of modern Ecuador and Peru, much of Bolivia, and parts of Argentina and Chile. The word inca in the Quechua language means literally lord or royal person.

TYPE SPECIES: *Incaea yupanki*
(Luer & R. Vásquez) Luer
(*Pleurothallis yupanki* Luer & R. Vásquez)

Recognized as belonging to the genus *Phloeophila, Incaea* was proposed to include one lithophyte found in mid elevation, montane forests of central Bolivia (Santa Cruz). This minute, creeping plant has tiny, overlapping, elliptical, thick, leathery leaves suffused dark purple and are appressed to moss laden stones. The solitary-flowered inflorescence has a large, purple flower. The concave, fleshy, dorsal sepal and lateral sepals are united forming a roundish tube. The concave lateral sepals are united toward the middle then are bifid with sharp points and small, oblong, smooth petals. The smooth, obscurely trilobed lip has short, erect side lobes, a wide, tongue-shaped midlobe with a rounded tip and is hinged by a narrow strap to the column foot. The flowers have a long, slender column.

INDIA

A.N. Rao

J. Econ. Taxon. Bot. **22**(3): 701 (1998)[1999].

Epidendroideæ · Vandeæ • Aeridinæ

ETYMOLOGY: Honoring the country where the species was collected. The Republic of India is located in the subcontinent of southeast Asia and separated from Asia by the Himalayan mountains.

TYPE SPECIES: *India arunachalensis* A.N. Rao

One monopodial epiphyte is found in cool, upper elevation, montane evergreen forests of the far northeastern corner of India (Arunachal Pradesh). This small plant has slender stems, each with several, alternating, strap-shaped leaves. The hanging, few-flowered inflorescence has small, cup-shaped, pale green flowers that do not fully open. The similar, small dorsal sepal and petals converge, forming a hood over the short, hammer-shaped column. The trilobed lip has a long spur (internally hairy), small erect, triangular side lobes, and a dark purple, backwall callus. This

---

genus is known from a single collection and is similar to *Uncifera*.

INERMAMPHIS

Thouars

Hist. Orchid. Table 1, sub 1b, *t.* 5 (1822).

Name published without a description. Today this name is most often referred to *Amottia*.

INOBULBON

(Schlechter) Schlechter & Kraenzlin

Pflanzenr. (Engler) **IV 50**(Heft 45): 316 (1910).

ETYMOLOGY: Greek for fiber or strength and a bulb. Refers to the fibrous or scale-like leaves surrounding the pseudobulbs that shred into masses of fibers.

TYPE SPECIES: *Inobulbon muricatum* (Finet) Kraenzlin
(*Dendrobium muricatum* Finet)

Now recognized as belonging to the genus *Dendrobium, Inobulbon* was previously considered to include three epiphytes with two species found in New Caledonia in low elevation, hill forests with either shade or full sunlight. One species is widespread from Africa (Uganda to South Africa), Madagascar to the Seychelles and Indonesia, the Philippines, and northern Australia to the southwestern Pacific Archipelago. These plants have large, ovoid pseudobulbs, subtended by numerous, stiff, upright fibers, each with several, reasonably large, leathery leaves. These fibers create distinctive rings of erect bristles and are formed from the remains of the old leaf bases at each node. The long, branched, few-flowered inflorescence has yellow-green flowers, which close at night and open in the morning, are sprinkled with red blotches. The stiff, white, deeply trilobed lip has erect side lobes, and the long, narrow midlobe has a wavy edge sprinkled in red. The flowers have a stout, wingless column.

INOBULBUM

An orthographic variant cited in *Man. Dict. Fl. Pl.*, ed. 4, 342 (1919). The correct spelling is *Inobulbon*.

INOPSIS

An orthographic variant cited in *Nomencl. Bot. (Steudel)*, ed. 1, **1**: 432 (1821). The correct spelling is *Ionopsis*.

INTI

M.A. Blanco

Lankesteriana **7**(3): 524 (2007).

ETYMOLOGY: Inca Mythology. Named for the sun god, *Inti*, of the Inca religion. The long, narrow leaves that radiate out from a congested shoot are reminiscent of the rays of a rising sun.

TYPE SPECIES: *Inti chartacifolia*
(Ames & C. Schweinfurth) M.A. Blanco
(*Maxillaria chartacifolia* Ames & C. Schweinfurth)

Recognized as belonging to the genus *Maxillaria*, *Inti* was proposed to include two epiphytes found in low elevation, scrub from Costa Rica to Peru. These large plants have inconspicuous, small pseudobulbs, subtended by densely overlapping, distichous sheaths, each with narrow, mid-nerved, papery leaves arranged in a fan shape. The solitary-flowered inflorescence has a fetid smelling, yellow flower with widespreading, oblong sepals and smaller petals. The red-brown, obscurely trilobed lip has short, erect side lobes, a tongue-shaped midlobe with a rounded, yellow tip. The flowers have a stout, slightly curved column.

IONE

Lindley

Fol. Orchid. **2**: *Ione*, 1 (1853).

ETYMOLOGY: Greek Mythology. Dedicated to the sea nymph, *Ione*, one of some fifty nymphs listed by Apollodorus (2nd century BC) in *The Library*. These sisters dwelt with their father Nereus at the bottom of the sea, had the power to change into any form they chose, and were often depicted as youthful, beautiful maidens - sometimes clothed, sometimes naked and often shown holding fish in their hands.

TYPE SPECIES: *None designated*

Now recognized as belonging to the genus *Sunipia*, *Ione* was previously considered to include twenty-two epiphytes found in upper elevation, montane forests of northern India (Kashmir to Assam), Nepal, southern China (Yunnan), Myanmar to Vietnam, Thailand and Taiwan. These plants have well-spaced, ovoid pseudobulbs, each with a solitary, leathery leaf. The erect, few-flowered inflorescence has subtending sheaths, and the flowers have short, tiny petals with inrolled edges and entire to notched margins. The white to pale yellow dorsal sepal is heavily striped dark red-purple. The simple, entire lip is deep yellow to dark red-purple.

IONOPSIS

Kunth

Nov. Gen. Sp. **1**: 348, *t.* 83 (1815).

Epidendroideæ ✿ Cymbidieæ • Oncidiinæ

ETYMOLOGY: Greek for violet and appearance or likeness. Refers to a fancied resemblance of the form and color of these flowers to violets.

TYPE SPECIES: *Ionopsis pulchella* Kunth
This type name is now considered a synonym of
Ionopsis utricularioides (Swartz) Lindley;
basionym
Epidendrum utricularioides Swartz

Six sympodial epiphytes are found over a widespread area in low to mid elevation, hardwood forests from the southeastern United States (Florida), Cuba to Trinidad, the Guianas, Venezuela, Mexico to the Bolivia, Paraguay and the Galapagos Islands. These plants have tiny, inconspicuous, flattened pseudobulbs, usually hidden in the base of the leaf sheaths, each with several, narrow, coarse, leathery leaves. Some species have a thickened stem with the narrow leaves arranged in two parallel rows. The simple to delicately branched, arching to hanging, numerous to few-flowered inflorescence, borne from the pseudobulb base, has small, showy, fragile-looking flowers with the lateral sepals united at the base forming a short sac below the lip. The shortly clawed, large, flat to slightly concave, entire or bilobed lip is joined to the stout, short, footless, wingless or obscurely winged column base. The flowers vary tremendously in size and degree of coloration from dark purple to pure white even within the same colony.

IONORCHIS

An orthographic variant cited in *CRC World Dict. Pl.*, **2**: 1307 (1999). The correct spelling is *Jonorchis*.

IPSE

An orthographic variant introduced in *Orchid.-Buch*, 282 (1892). The correct spelling is *Ipsea*.

IPSEA

Lindley

Gen. Sp. Orchid. Pl. 124 (1831).

Epidendroideæ ✿ Collabiinæ • Currently unplaced

ETYMOLOGY: Latin for self. Lindley considered this genus rather isolated from other orchids.
Or possibly Greek for woodworm or bindweed. Alluding to the corky network formed by the large fibrous roots.

TYPE SPECIES: *Ipsea speciosa* Lindley

Three sympodial terrestrials are found in mid elevation, montane grasslands of southern India, Sri Lanka and Thailand. These plants have subterranean pseudobulbs with one to a few internodes, and the narrow, solitary, or rarely two, leaf is withered by flowering time. The erect, few-flowered, hairy inflorescence has delightful, rather long-lived, fragrant, waxy flowers that are a bright golden-yellow, and the oblong dorsal sepal is hood-like. The yellow, trilobed lip has bright orange spots on the large, erect side lobes; the recurved midlobe is spade-shaped, and has a scalloped ridge callus. The flowers have a slender, curved, club-shaped, winged column.

IPSIA

An orthographic variant introduced in *Icon. Plé. Ind. Orient. (Wight)*, **3**: *t.* 1663 (1851). The correct spelling is *Ipsea*.

IRENEA

Szlachetko, Mytnik, Górniak & Romowicz

Biodivers. Res. Conservation **1-2**: 5 (2006).

ETYMOLOGY: Dedicated to Irene Elisabeth Bock née Steiner (1939-), a German orchid collector, retired teacher and currently editor of the *Die Orchidee*.

TYPE SPECIES: *Irenea myantha*
(Lindley) Szlachetko, Mytnik, Górniak & Romowicz
(*Odontoglossum myanthum* Lindley)

Recognized as belonging to the genus *Cyrtochilum*, *Irenea* was proposed to include eleven epiphytes or terrestrials found in mid to upper elevation, montane cloud forests along steep slopes from Colombia to Peru. These robust plants have ovoid to narrowly pear-shaped, laterally compressed to flattened pseudobulbs, subtended by overlapping, distichous sheaths, each with a solitary, narrow leaf. The erect, often branching, numerous-flowered inflorescence has small, brown-yellow, bright yellow or vermillion flowers. The lower half of the trilobed lip is parallel to the long or short, slender column and adjacent to a simple callus.

| Currently Accepted | Validly Published | Invalidly Published | Published Pre-1753 | Superfluous Usage | Orthographic Variant | Fossil |

Orchid Genera • **202**

IRIDIORCHIS

An orthographic variant introduced in *Fl. Brit. Ind.*, **6**: 12 (1890). The correct spelling is *Iridorchis*.

IRIDORCHIS

Blume

Fl. Javæ Nov. Ser. **1**: 75 (1858), and *Coll. Orchid.* 90 (1859).

Not *Iridorchis* Thouars (1822) Orchidaceæ.

ETYMOLOGY: Greek for iridescent or multicolored and orchid. Refers to various colored flowers.

TYPE SPECIES: *Iridorchis gigantea* Blume nom. illeg.

This type name is now considered a synonym of *Cymbidium iridioides* D. Don; basionym *Cymbidium giganteum* Wallich ex Lindley, nom. illeg.

Not validly published because of a prior use of the name, this homonym was replaced by *Cymbidium*.

IRIDORCHIS

An orthographic variant introduced in *Hist. Orchid.*, Table 3, sub 3t, *t*. 92 (1822). The correct spelling is *Iridorkis*.

IRIDORKIS

Thouars

Nouv. Bull. Sci. Soc. Philom. Paris **1**(19): 319 (1809).

Name ICBN rejected vs. *Oberonia* Lindley (1830) Orchidaceæ.

ETYMOLOGY: Greek for rainbow and orchid. Refers to the various colors of the little flowers.

TYPE SPECIES: *Epidendrum distichum* Lamarck

Although validly published this rejected name is referred to *Oberonia. Iridorkis* was considered to include one epiphyte found in densely shaded rain forests from Ghana to Kenya, Uganda, Madagascar and the Comoros Islands. These plants have numerous, overlapping, iris-like leaves arranged in two rows, giving the plant a flat, compressed appearance. The long, densely packed, numerous-flowered inflorescence has miniscule flowers that need magnification for their delicate shapes to be clearly seen.

IRIORCHIS

An orthographic variant introduced in *Orchid Fl. Kamrup Distr. Assam*, 125 (2001). The correct spelling is *Iridorchis*.

ISABELIA

Barbosa Rodrigues

Gen. Sp. Orchid. **1**: 75 (1877).

Not *Isabelia* Lentin & G.L. Williams (1976) Fossil.

Epidendroideæ 🌱 **Epidendreæ** • **Laeliinæ**

ETYMOLOGY: In honor of Isabel Cristina Leopoldina Augusta Alcântara (1846-1921) Countess d'Eu, a Brazilian princess, patron of floriculture and science, and who in 1888, while her father, Emperor Pedro II was in Europe, signed a law abolishing slavery in Brazil.

TYPE SPECIES: *Isabelia virginalis* Barbosa Rodrigues

Three sympodial epiphytes are found in damp, warm to cool, low to mid elevation, coastal to montane forests of southeastern Brazil (Bahia to Rio Grande do Sul), Paraguay and northeastern Argentina (Misiones). These dwarf, creeping plants form dense mats of clustered or well-spaced pseudobulbs that are clad in fibrous netting, each with a solitary, slender, needle-like leaf. The short, solitary to few-flowered inflorescence has a small, waxy, snow-white to off-white, long-lived flower suffused with rose-violet or pale purple. The lateral sepals are joined at the base forming a small sac with the lip. The roundish, creamy-white, entire lip is sac-like at the base and is appressed to the red or dark magenta, fleshy, wingless, recurved column.

ISABELLA

An orthographic variant introduced in *Nat. Pflanzenfam.*, **2**(6): 220 (1889). The correct spelling is *Isabelia*.

ISANTHEUM

Burbidge

Cool Orchids 149 (1874).

ETYMOLOGY: Greek for equal and anther.

TYPE SPECIES: *Isantheum laeve* Lindley

Name published without a description. Today this name is most often referred to *Odontoglossum*.

ISCHNOCENTRUM

Schlechter

Repert. Spec. Nov. Regni Veg. Beih. **1**(4): 318 (1912).

ETYMOLOGY: Greek for thin, weak or withered and a spur. Refers to the long, thread-like spur.

TYPE SPECIES: *Ischnocentrum myrtillus* Schlechter

Now recognized as belonging to the genus *Glomera*, *Ischnocentrum* was previously considered to include two epiphytes restricted to misty, upper

elevation, montane forests of New Guinea. These small, sometimes red to brown plants grow in vast colonies often completely covering the branches of the host trees. The plants have hard, erect stems subtended by leaf bases. The delicate, dark salmon-brown, showy flowers have a flat, entire lip that is bent downward at a sharp angle. These flowers have a short, obscure or footless column which is united to the lip margins forming a sac-like spur.

ISCHNOGYNE

Schlechter

Repert. Spec. Nov. Regni Veg. **12**: 106 (1913).

Epidendroideæ 🌱 **Arethuseæ** • **Coelogyninæ**

ETYMOLOGY: Greek for weak, thin or slender and women or female. Refers to the really long, slender column.

TYPE SPECIES: *Ischnogyne mandarinorum* (Kraenzlin) Schlechter (*Coelogyne mandarinorum* Kraenzlin)

One uncommon creeping, sympodial epiphyte or lithophyte is found in low to mid elevation, sparse hill and montane forests of central China (Shaanxi, Guizhou, Sichuan, Gansu and Hubei). This small, creeping, inconspicuous plant has erect or bent, densely wrinkled stems or pseudobulbs, each with a solitary, oblong to narrow, thinly leathery leaf that has a stalk-like base. The erect, solitary-flowered inflorescence has a rather large, white, uniquely structured flower with the lateral sepals forming a sac-like base. The white, narrow, trilobed lip has two, purple-red spots at the base, small, roundish side lobes; has a squarish, notched midlobe with a V-shaped tip, a wavy margin and a bright yellow, basal splash. The short spur is partly enclosed by the two lateral sepals at the base. The flowers have a long, slender, footless column.

ISIAS

De Notaris

Mem. Reale Accad. Sci. Torino, ser. 2 **6**: 413 (1844).

Not *Isia* D.L. Hawksworth & C. Manoharachary (1978) Fungi.

ETYMOLOGY: Egyptian Mythology. *Isis* is a goddess of fertility, wisdom, magic, and life. She was an important source of the pharaoh's powers, and her cult was popular throughout ancient Egypt. *Isis* was the sister-wife of *Osiris* the Egyptian god of the underworld.

TYPE SPECIES: *Isias triloba* De Notaris

Now recognized as belonging to the genus *Serapias*, *Isias* was previously considered to include one terrestrial found in olive groves, pinewoods and damp meadows along the French Mediterranean and Italian coastal regions and on the islands of Elba, Corsica and Sardinia. This short, erect plant has unbranched stems, each with one to two, basal leaves. The erect, few-flowered inflorescence has dull gray-violet flowers with the dorsal sepal forming a hood over the small column. The above type name is now considered a synonym of *Serapias neglecta* De Notaris.

ISOCHELIUS

An orthographic variant introduced in *Cat. Descr. Orquid., Estac. Exp. Agron. Santiago, Cuba,* **60**: 53 (1938). The correct spelling is *Isochilus.*

ISOCHILOS

An orthographic variant introduced in *Gen. Pl.* (Sprengel), **2**: 671 (1830). The correct spelling is *Isochilus.*

ISOCHILUS

R. Brown
Hortus Kew., ed. 2   **5**: 209 (1813).

Epidendroideæ 🌿 **Epidendreæ** • **Ponerinæ**

ETYMOLOGY: Greek for equal and lip. Most likely, calling attention to the fact that the lip is usually equal to the sepals and petals in size.

LECTOTYPE: *Isochilus linearis* (Jacquin) R. Brown
(*Epidendrum lineare* Jacquin)
indirectly designated by Reichenbach f., *Bonplandia,*
2: 22 (1854), and
designated by Pfeiffer, *Nomencl. Bot.* (Pfeiffer),
1(2): 1767 (1872).

Twelve unusual, sympodial terrestrials, epiphytes or rare lithophytes all variable to an extreme, are found in moist, low to upper elevation, hill and montane cloud, oak-pine and evergreen forests, woodlands, swamp and mangroves ranging from Cuba to Trinidad, southern Mexico to Peru, Venezuela, the Guianas, Brazil and northern Argentina. These graceful, small, tufted or creeping plants often form gigantic colonies cloaking almost every possible available spot. They are grown as much for their strange, grass-like vegetation as for their sometimes flowers that range from orange, pink, lilac to magenta. The erect, slender stem has narrow to oblong, leathery to semi-leathery, distichous, dark green leaves. On mature plants the top leaves sometimes change color; these purple tones only appear before flowering begins. The several, terminal, dense-ly clustered, few to numerous-flowered inflorescences have usually brightly colored, tiny to small, tubular flowers blooming almost any time during the year. The lateral sepals are free or united to the middle with the dorsal sepal and petals free. Many of the species are self pollinating, rarely open and the flowers are usually borne or arranged on one side of the rachis. The tiny, shortly clawed, mostly erect, entire or obscurely trilobed lip is S-shaped at

the base, parallels the column and is joined at the base to the column. The flowers have an erect to arched, wingless column that is either footless or with an obscure foot.

ISOCYNIS

Thouars
Hist. Orchid.   Table 1, sub 1d, *t. 13* (1822).

Name published without a description. Today this name is most often referred to *Cynorkis.*

ISOTRIA

Rafinesque
Med. Repos., hexade 2   **5**: 357 (1808), and
J. Bot. (Desvaux)   **1**: 220 (1808).

Vanilloideæ 🌿 **Pogoniieæ**

ETYMOLOGY: Greek for equal or likeness and in threes. Referring to the arrangement of the sepals that are of similar size, shape and color.

TYPE SPECIES: *Isotria verticillata*
(Mühlenberg ex Willldenow) Rafinesque
(*Arethusa verticillata* Mühlenberg ex Willldenow)

Two uncommon, sympodial terrestrials are distributed in strongly acidic soils of shady, mid elevation, moist scrub with a mixture of pine or entirely deciduous forests of eastern Canada (Ontario) and the eastern United States (Michigan to Georgia). This genus has strong mycorrhizal fungi associations and dormancy requirements. These erect, colony-forming plants have smooth, hollow, unbranched, maroon to pale green stems, each topped with a unique whorl of several (usually five to six), oblong leaves. The short, usually solitary to two-flowered inflorescence has striking, large, pale red-purple and yellow-green to green flowers with the tiny petals arching over the white, slender, footless column. The white to yellow-green, trilobed lip has triangular, inrolled, red-purple side lobes, and the white midlobe has a wavy surface with a fleshy, yellow midridge. These species were once included in *Pogonia.*

ITACULUMIA

Hoehne
Bol. Mus. Nac. Rio de Janeiro   **12**(3/4): 79 (1936).

ETYMOLOGY: Named for the type collection locality of the genus, Serra do Itaculumi, a mountain range located in the southeastern Brazilian state of Minas Gerais.

TYPE SPECIES: *Itaculumia ulaei* Hoehne

Now recognized as belonging to the genus *Habenaria, Itaculumia* was previously considered to include three terrestrials found primarily in south-eastern Brazil (Minas Gerais). These erect, wiry

plants have unbranched stems, subtended by long, narrow bracts, each with several, narrow, grass-like leaves. The few-flowered inflorescence has minute, green flowers with veined, similar sepals and petals that open widely. The trilobed lip has long, narrow, pointed side lobes, and a small, roundish midlobe. The flowers have a small column. The above type name is now considered a synonym of *Habenaria itaculumia* Garay.

IXYOPHORA

Dressler
Lankesteriana   **5**(2): 95 (2005).

Epidendroideæ 🌿 **Cymbidieæ** • **Zygopetalinæ**

ETYMOLOGY: Greek for waist and bearer or carrier. Refers to the narrow waist of the stipe.

TYPE SPECIES: *Ixyophora viridisepala*
(Senghas) Dressler
(*Chondrorhyncha viridisepala* Senghas)

Three sympodial epiphytes are found in wet, warm to cool, low to mid elevation, hill to montane forests and woodlands from Colombia to Peru. These slightly fan-shaped plants have erect stems, each with a solitary, broad, leathery leaf. The arching, solitary-flowered inflorescence, borne from the leaf axils, has a yellow, green-yellow to white flower with long, narrow, strongly curved sepals and broad petals. The scoop-shaped, white to dull green, entire lip has a notched margin and surrounds the broad column.

IZOCHILUS

An orthographic variant introduced in *Schriften Ges. Beförd. Gesammten Naturwiss. Marburg,* **2**: 125 (1831). The correct spelling is *Isochilus.*

IZTACTEPETZACUXOCHITL

An orthographic variant introduced in *Nov. Veg. Descr.,* **2**: 13 (1825). The correct spelling is *Yztactepetzacuxochitl.*

Currently Accepted   Validly Published   Invalidly Published   Published Pre-1753   Superfluous Usage   Orthographic Variant   Fossil

Orchid Genera • 204

JACQUINIELLA

Schlechter

Repert. Spec. Nov. Regni Veg. Beih. **7**: 123 (1920).

Epidendroideæ ⚘ **Epidendreæ** • **Laeliinæ**

ETYMOLOGY: Commemorating Nikolaus Joseph von Jacquin (1727-1817), an Austrian-born Dutch professor of botany and chemistry at Chemnitz and Vienna, who collected and wrote about the flora of the West Indies region. And Latin for diminutive.

LECTOTYPE: *Jacquiniella globosa*
(Jacquin) Schlechter
(*Epidendrum globosum* Jacquin)

Six rather nondescript, mainly tufted, sympodial epiphytes or lithophytes are found in low to upper elevation, hill and montane forests from Mexico to Peru, Brazil, Cuba to Trinidad, the Guianas, and Venezuela in woodlands and scrub with cool, dry winters. These erect, sprawling plants have small, slender, cane-like stems, entirely subtended in leaf-sheaths, each with distichous, fleshy, flattened, pencil-like or channeled, green or bronze leaves. The several, solitary to few-flowered inflorescences have a minute, cup-shaped, delicate, yellow or green flower not opening fully that is borne singly or in a cluster at the tip of the stem. The sepals and petals are all similarly shaped. The yellow-green to pale green, thick, entire to trilobed lip has a concave center. The flowers have a short, stout, erect to slightly curved, footless column.

JAENIOPHYLLUM

An orthographic variant introduced in *Prakt. Stud. Orchid.*, 45, 255 (1854). The correct spelling is *Taeniophyllum*.

JAINIA

An orthographic variant introduced in *Bot. Centralbl.*, **107**(20): 527 (1908). The correct spelling is *Tainia*.

JAMAICELLA

An orthographic variant introduced in *Phylogeny Classif. Orchid Fam.*, 273 (1993). The correct spelling is *Jamaiciella*.

JAMAICIELLA

Braem

Orchidee (Hamburg) **31**(3): 120 (1980).

ETYMOLOGY: In honor of the Caribbean island of Jamaica (located just south of Cuba) where the type species was collected. And Latin for diminutive.

TYPE SPECIES: *Jamaiciella triquetra* (Swartz) Braem
(*Epidendrum triquetrum* Swartz)

This type name is now considered a synonym of
Tolumnia triquetra (Swartz) Nir;
basionym
Epidendrum triquetrum Swartz

Now recognized as belonging to the genus *Tolumnia*, *Jamaiciella* was previously considered to include one epiphyte found in low elevation scrub on the island of Jamaica. This miniature, fan-shaped plant has short, leafy, rampant stems, each with several, distichous, flattened, tongue-shaped leaves. The slender, simple to branched, numerous to few-flowered inflorescence has showy, long-lasting, slightly waxy, pink to pale purple flowers mottled with white. The pillow-like, trilobed lip has small side lobes, and the entire midlobe has a crisp margin and no callus. The flowers have a short, stout, prominently winged column.

JANSENIA

Barbosa Rodrigues

Vellosia, ed. 2 **1**: 124, *t*. 857 (1891).

ETYMOLOGY: Honoring José Jansen Ferreira, Junior (*fl.* 1880s), a Brazilian governor (1884-85) of the Amazonas province, who also gave assistance to the Museu Botânico do Amazonas.

TYPE SPECIES: *Jansenia cultrifolia* Barbosa Rodrigues

Now recognized as belonging to the genus *Plectrophora*, *Jansenia* was previously considered to include one epiphyte found in low elevation, humid forests from the Guianas, Venezuela and northern Brazil. This plant has tiny, pale green, compressed pseudobulbs, subtended by leaf-like sheaths, each with a solitary, narrow leaf. The several, solitary-flowered inflorescences have a yellow, citrus-fragrant flower that is fairly rigid. The bell-shaped, white to yellow, obscurely trilobed lip forms an elongated, hollow, thick, green spur

at the base that is sprinkled with numerous, dark yellow splashes and a wavy margin. The flowers have a stout, wingless, footless column.

JANTHA

An orthographic variant cited in *Nomencl. Bot. (Steudel)*, ed. 2, **1**: 458, 797 (1840). The correct spelling is *Iantha*.

JEBINE

An orthographic variant introduced in *Dict. Sci. Nat.*, **24**: 218 (1822). The correct spelling is *Iebine*.

JEJEWOODIA

Szlachetko

Fragm. Florist. Geobot. **3**(Suppl.): 135 (1995).

Epidendroideæ ⚘ **Vandeæ** • **Aeridinæ**

ETYMOLOGY: Dedicated to Jeffrey James Wood (1952-), a British orchidologist who has worked and collected in Borneo, author of *The Plants of Mount Kinabalu*, *Dendrochilum of Borneo* and co-author of *The Orchids of Peninsular Malaysia and Singapore*.

TYPE SPECIES: *Jejewoodia jiewhoei*
(J.J. Wood & Shim) Szlachetko
(*Ceratochilus jiewhoei* J.J. Wood & Shim)

One monopodial epiphyte is found in low elevation, oak-laurel hill forests of southern Malaysia (Sabah) on the island of Borneo. This dwarf plant has unbranched stems, subtended by sheathing bases, each with several, stiff, flattened leaves, spaced along the stem. The solitary-flowered inflorescence, borne along the upper portion of the stem, has a pristine white, translucent flower with roundish petals and sepals that taper to a point. Sometimes there is a small, yellow spot or splash in the center of the trilobed lip. The flowers have a short, stout, wingless, footless column.

JEJOSEPHIA

A.N. Rao & Mani

J. Econ. Taxon. Bot. **7**(1): 217 (1985).

Epidendroideæ ⚘ Dendrobiinæ • Currently unplaced

ETYMOLOGY: In honor of J.E. Joseph (1928-2000), an Indian botanist and author of *Orchids of Nilgiris*.

TYPE SPECIES: *Jejosephia pusilla*
(J. Joseph & H. Deka) A.N. Rao & Mani
(*Trias pusilla* J. Joseph & H. Deka)

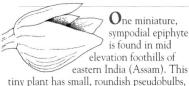

One miniature, sympodial epiphyte is found in mid elevation foothills of eastern India (Assam). This tiny plant has small, roundish pseudobulbs, each with a solitary, leathery leaf. The short, solitary-flowered inflorescence has a brown-green flower that does not open fully. The small, trilobed lip has side lobes longer than the spear-shaped midlobe that is further trilobed and has three lamellae on the disc. The flowers have a short, stout column.

JENMANIA

Rolfe

Bull. Misc. Inform. Kew **1898**: 198 (1898).

Not *Jenmania* Wächter (1897) Lichenes.

ETYMOLOGY: Dedicated to George Samuel Jenman (1845-1902), an English horticulturist and botanist who worked in Jamaica and served as a superintendent of Guyana's Botanic Gardens in Georgetown.

TYPE SPECIES: *Jenmania elata* Rolfe

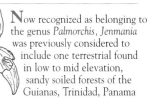

Now recognized as belonging to the genus *Palmorchis*, *Jenmania* was previously considered to include one terrestrial found in low to mid elevation, sandy soiled forests of the Guianas, Trinidad, Panama and northern Brazil. This tall, clump-forming plant has several, broad, veined, pleated leaves. The tightly packed, few-flowered inflorescence has large bracts and small, white to yellow flowers. The yellow and white, trilobed lip has several, red streaks and a wavy margin. The flowers have a long, slender column. The above type name is now considered a synonym of *Palmorchis pubescentis* Barbosa Rodrigues.

JENMANNIA

An orthographic variant cited in *Handb. Orchid.-Namen*, 393, 540 (2005). The correct spelling is *Jenmania*.

JENNYELLA

Lückel & Fessel

Caesiana **13**: 3 (1999).

ETYMOLOGY: Dedicated to Rudolf Jenny (1953-), a Swiss water chemist, orchidologist and author who writes numerous articles on the orchid subtribe Stanhopeinæ. And Latin for diminutive.

TYPE SPECIES: *Jennyella sanderi* (Rolfe) Lückel & Fessel
(*Houlletia sanderi* Rolfe)

Now recognized as belonging to the genus *Houlletia*, *Jennyella* was proposed to include four epiphytes or terrestrials found in wet, mid elevation, montane forests of Colombia, Ecuador, Peru and Bolivia. These plants are similar to *Houlletia*, but the side lobes of the large, broad trilobed lip have a narrow base with a lower, toothed margin. The pear-shaped, grooved pseudobulbs, subtended by thin, dry sheaths, each with a solitary, narrow leaf. The erect, few-flowered inflorescence has translucent, pale yellow to white, strongly fragrant flowers with indistinct markings. The hypochile portion of the trilobed lip has two, broadly spathe-shaped side lobes with a blunt tooth in front, The fleshy, oblong mesochile is abruptly terminated, and the terminated epichile has small notches at the tip. The flowers have a long, slender column with a short foot.

JENSOA

Rafinesque

Fl. Tellur. **4**: 38 (1836)[1837].

ETYMOLOGY: Dedicated to an unknown Japanese botanist whose work was consulted by Carl Peter Thunberg (1743-1828) for his *Flora Japonica*.

TYPE SPECIES: *Jensoa ensata* Rafinesque nom. illeg.
Cymbidium ensifolium (Linnaeus) Swartz
(*Epidendrum ensifolium* Linnaeus)

Now recognized as belonging to the genus *Cymbidium*, *Jensoa* was previously considered to include one terrestrial or lithophyte found in low to mid elevation, hill to montane evergreen forests and limestone moss laden rocks ranging from Sri Lanka, India, southern China, Japan, Thailand, Malaysia and Indonesia to New Guinea. This robust plant has small, often subterranean pseudobulbs, each with a few to several, grass-like, tufted leaves often having minutely toothed tips. The erect, few-flowered inflorescence has fragrant, pale yellow, pale brown to green flowers, and the sepals have a few red lines. The pale yellow or green, trilobed lip has red-streaked, roundish, erect side lobes that clasp the long, slightly bent forward, wingless, footless column and a red to red-brown blotched or spotted midlobe with a wavy margin.

JIMENSIA

Rafinesque

Fl. Tellur. **4**: 38 (1836)[1837].

Name ICBN rejected vs. *Bletilla* Reichenbach f. (1853) Orchidaceæ.

ETYMOLOGY: Dedicated to an unknown Japanese botanist whose work was consulted by Carl Peter Thunberg (1743-1828) for his *Flora Japonica*.

TYPE SPECIES: *Jimensia nervosa* Rafinesque nom. illeg.
Bletilla striata (Thunberg) Reichenbach f.
(*Limodorum striatum* Thunberg)

Although validly published this rejected name is now referred to *Bletilla*. *Jimensia* was considered to include ten terrestrials found only in cool, montane forests and grasslands of China, Japan and Taiwan. These plants have small, compressed, roundish, sticky, corm-like pseudobulbs, each with a few oblong to narrow leaves. The erect, few-flowered inflorescence (rarely branched) typically has rosy-purple or pink flowers not opening widely. The white, purple-red tinged, trilobed lip has long, oblong side lobes and raised, deep purple keels on the almost rectangular-shaped midlobe.

JONATHANIA

Yam ex Nyman

Arditti's Fundamentals Orchid Biol. **1**: 97 (1992).

Name published without a description, this fictitious name was used as an example to show the reader the correct way to create a new genus name.

JONE

An orthographic variant introduced in *Stat. Account Bengal*, **20**: 189 (1877). The correct spelling is *Ione*.

JONESIOPSIS

Szlachetko

Polish Bot. J. **46**(1): 14 (2001).

ETYMOLOGY: Named to honor David Lloyd Jones (1944-), an Australian orchidologist and author of numerous books and articles on orchids. And Latin for diminutive.

TYPE SPECIES: *Jonesiopsis multiclavia*
(Reichenbach f.) Szlachetko
(*Caladenia multiclavia* Reichenbach f.)

Now recognized as belonging to the genus *Caladenia*, *Jonesiopsis* was proposed to include forty-nine wiry terrestrials found in sandy or gravelly soil of southwestern Australia. These wispy, erect, hairy plants have unbranched stems, each with a few narrow leaves. The one- to two-flowered inflorescence has red-pink to green flowers. The narrow, spidery sepals and petals are often striped with red and yellow and the segments

Currently Accepted   Validly Published   Invalidly Published   Published Pre-1753   Superfluous Usage   Orthographic Variant   Fossil

Orchid Genera • **206**

have upcurved tips. The tightly curved, diamond-shaped, trilobed lip has a massive patch of black calli with prominent red and yellow stripes at the base.

JONESYELLA

An orthographic variant introduced in *Polish Bot. J.*, **46**(1): 14 (2001). The correct spelling is *Jonesiopsis*.

JONOPSIS

An orthographic variant introduced in *Nov. Gen. Sp. (Kunth)*, **1**: 335, *t. 83* (1815). The correct spelling is *Ionopsis*.

JONORCHIS

Beck

Fl. Nieder-Osterreich   **1**: 195, 215 (1890).

ETYMOLOGY: Greek for violet-blue and orchid. Refers to the color of the flowers.

TYPE SPECIES: *Jonorchis abortiva* (Linnaeus) Beck
(*Orchis abortiva* Linnaeus)

Now recognized as belonging to the genus *Limodorum*, *Jonorchis* was previously considered to include one saprophyte found in shady, mid elevation, scrub and grassy areas from Austria to France, Spain to Iran and Morocco to Tunisia. This erect, robust, leafless plant has numerous scales on its unbranched stem. The erect, numerous to few-flowered inflorescence has pale pink, white to violet flowers. The concave dorsal sepal forms a hood over the erect, slender column. The triangular, yellow and violet, trilobed lip has a wavy margin, and a long, slender, green spur. The above type name is now considered a synonym of *Limodorum abortivum* (Linnaeus) Swartz.

JOSEPHA

Not *Josepha* Vellozo (1825) Nyctaginaceæ.

An orthographic variant introduced in *Gen. Pl. (Bentham & Hooker f.)*, **3**: 468, 516 (1883). The correct spelling is *Josephia*.

JOSEPHIA

Wight

Icon. Pl. Ind. Orient. (Wight)
5(1): 19, *tt. 1742-1743* (1851).

Not *Josephia* R. Brown ex Knight (1809) Proteaceæ, and not *Josephia* Steudel (1840) Nyctaginaceæ.

ETYMOLOGY: Dedicated to Joseph Dalton Hooker (1817-1911), a British botanist, explorer, a director of the Royal Botanic Gardens, Kew and co-author of *Genera Plantarum* and *The Floral of British India*.

TYPE SPECIES: *Josephia lanceolata* Wight

Not validly published because of a prior use of the name, this homonym was replaced by *Sirhookera*.

JOSTIA

Luer

Monogr. Syst. Bot. Missouri Bot. Gard.
79: 2 (2000).

ETYMOLOGY: Named in honor of Lou Jost (1957-), an Ecuadorian orchid biologist from Baños, ornithological guide and nature artist who noted the moveable lip of this species.

TYPE SPECIES: *Jostia teaguei* (Luer) Luer
(*Masdevallia teaguei* Luer)

Recognized as belonging to the genus *Masdevallia*, *Jostia* was proposed to include one epiphyte found in mid elevation, montane cloud forests from Colombia to southern Ecuador. This small plant has slender, erect stems, subtended by tubular sheaths, each with a solitary, dark green leaf. The congested, successively flowered inflorescence has red-brown to red-purple flowers fading to yellow-orange at the base. The united sepals form a gaping, funnel-shaped tube with the tips extended into short, slender tails, and it has tiny petals. The small to tiny, tongue-shaped, entire lip is sensitive to disturbances, causing the lip to flip upward, just beneath the straight to slightly curved, wingless column, and a few minutes later the lip returns to its normal position.

JOUYELLA

Szlachetko & Margońska

Polish Bot. J.   **46**(2): 124 (2002).

ETYMOLOGY: Named in honor of Alain Daniel Jouy (1933-) a French editor of *l'Orchidophilie* for the Société Française d'Orchidophilie, an orchid photographer and author of articles on orchids. And Latin for diminutive.

TYPE SPECIES: *Jouyella fimbriata*
(Poeppig) Szlachetko & Margońska
(*Chloraea fimbriata* Poeppig)
This type name is now considered a synonym of
Bipinnula fimbriata (Poeppig) I.M. Johnston
Basionym
(*Chloraea fimbriata* Poeppig)

Recognized as belonging to the genus *Bipinnula*, *Jouyella* was proposed to include four terrestrials found in cool, mid elevation, exposed, rocky montane regions of central Chile. These small plants have stout, erect, unbranched stems, subtended by tubular sheaths, each with a basal rosette of several, rather fleshy, oblong leaves. The congested, successively flowered, branched inflorescence has green to white flowers. The green dorsal sepal and white petals converge, forming a hood over the white, thinly textured, lip. The clawed, entire lip is striped in green, and usually has long to short, club-shaped protuberances along the margin. The green lateral sepals are heavily fringed and also have

numerous, club-shaped protuberances. The flowers have a short, slightly curved column.

JSOCHILUS

An orthographic variant introduced in *Repert. Spec. Nov. Regni Veg.*, **10**: 360 (1912). The correct spelling is *Isochilus*.

JULOTIS

An orthographic variant introduced in *Fl. Bras. (Martius)*, **3**(4): 18 (1893). The correct spelling is *Tulotis*.

JUMELLEA

Schlechter

Orchideen (Schlechter), ed. 1   609 (1914).

Epidendroideæ ⚬ Vandeæ • Angraecinæ

ETYMOLOGY: Dedicated to Henri Lucien Jumelle (1866-1935), a French plant physiologist, professor of botany (Marseille) who collected and studied the flora of Madagascar. And Latin for diminutive.

LECTOTYPE: *Jumellea recurva* (Thouars) Schlechter
(*Angraecum recurvum* Thouars)
This type name is now considered a synonym of
Jumellea recta (Thouars) Schlechter
basionym
Angraecum recurvum Thouars

Fifty-eight, mainly tufted, monopodial epiphytes or lithophytes are found in hot to cool, low to mid elevation, open tropical and moss laden forests with the vast majority found in Madagascar, the Comoros and the Mascarene Islands. A few species are also found from Kenya to South Africa. These plants are most noted for the uniformity of the petals and lip within the genus. Since the species have similar flowers, the vegetative portions are quite important for correct identification. These plants have short to long, rarely branched stems with distichous, strap-shaped, bilobed leaves spaced along the stem or arranged in a fan shape. There are also a few climbing species with clasping roots found along the stem's length. The narrow, pristine white to green-white, nocturnally fragrant to spicy flowers, pollinated by night-flying moths, are borne singly but in vast quantities. The narrow, obscurely trilobed lip does not surround the short, tiny, winged or wingless column as it does in *Angraecum*. The nectar-filled, hollow spur varies widely from short to quite long, slender to thread-like.

NOTE: During the Victorian era the dried foliage of these species was used for a delicately flavored tea called "Faham Tea".

KAEFERSTEINIA

An orthographic variant introduced in *Wochenschr. Vereines Beford. Gartenbaues Konigl. Preuss. Staaten*, **6**(17): 136 (1863). The correct spelling is *Kefersteinia*.

KALIMPONGIA

Pradhan

Orchid Digest   **41**(5): 172 (1977).

ETYMOLOGY: Named for the town in the Dārjiling district of northeastern (Sikkim) India that is well known for its wide variety of orchid species.

TYPE SPECIES: *Kalimpongia narajitii* Pradhan

Now recognized as belonging to the genus *Dickasonia*, *Kalimpongia* was previously considered to include one epiphyte found in upper elevation, montane forests of northeastern India (Bihar, Assam and Manipur) and Myanmar. This plant has small, clustered, smooth pseudobulbs, each with one to two, leathery leaves. The hanging to arching, few-flowered inflorescence is fairly large to small, translucent, white flowers with a musky fragrance. The flowers have a short, rounded spur and an extremely short column. The above type name is now considered a synonym of *Dickasonia vernicosa* L.O. Williams.

KALOPTERNIX

Garay & Dunsterville

Venez. Orchid. Ill.   **6**: 40 (1976).

ETYMOLOGY: Greek for shortened stem of plant. Refers to the reduced upright stems in relationship to other species of *Epidendrum*.

TYPE SPECIES: *Kalopternix deltoglossus*
        (Garay & Dunsterville) Garay & Dunsterville
        (*Epidendrum deltoglossum* Garay & Dunsterville)

Now recognized as belonging to the genus *Epidendrum*, *Kalopternix* was proposed to include three epiphytes found in mid to upper elevation, montane forests with constant moisture of Venezuela, Ecuador and Peru. These tiny, hanging plants have branching rhizomes from which the fleshy leaves and minute pseudo-

bulbs arise. The pseudobulbs are subtended by distichous, overlapping, narrow, ballooning sheaths. The short, few-flowered inflorescence has a succession of pale green-brown to purple flowers with maroon veining, and the margins have a sprinkling of small hairs. The pale brown, trilobed lip, tapering to a long or short, sharp tip, has a darker green-brown, wavy margin with the underside having a few pale maroon nerves showing.

KANSJIRAM-maravara

Rheede

Hort. Malab.   **12**: 17-18, *t*. 8 (1693).

ETYMOLOGY: A local Malayalam (this Dravidian language is from southeastern India and is closely related to the Tamil language) word for *Strychnos nuxvomica*, a tree species upon which this orchid was found growing.

TYPE SPECIES: *Kansjiram-maravara* Rheede

Pre-1753, therefore not validly published in fulfillment of nomenclatural rules; this binomial name is most often referred to *Cymbidium*. *Kansjiram-maravara* was previously considered to include one epiphyte found in low to mid elevation, hill and montane forests, woodlands, along river banks and cliff faces of India (Sikkim), southern China (Guizhou to Guangdong), Sri Lanka, Myanmar to Vietnam, Malaysia, Thailand and Indonesia (Java). This plant, forming huge, hanging colonies, has egg-shaped to ovoid pseudobulbs, each with strap-shaped, curved, leathery leaves. The hanging, numerous-flowered inflorescence has lightly fragrant, yellow flowers with broad, brown-maroon median stripes. The trilobed lip has veined, erect side lobes and the ovate, recurved midlobe has a yellow, ridged callus. The flowers have a long column. This name is usually now considered a synonym of *Cymbidium aloifolium* (Linnaeus) Swartz.

KANSYRAM

An orthographic variant introduced in *Nouv. Dict. Hist. Nat.*, ed. 2, **17**: 45 (1817). The correct spelling is *Kansjiram*.

KARORCHIS

An orthographic variant introduced in *Orchadian*, **13**(11): 499 (2002). The correct spelling is *Kaurorchis*.

KATHARINEA

An orthographic variant introduced in *Phylogeny Classif. Orchid Fam.*, 276 (1993). The correct spelling is *Katherinea*.

KATHERINEA

A.D. Hawkes

Lloydia   **19**: 94 (1956).

ETYMOLOGY: In honor of Katherine H. Chatham, the mother of American orchidologist Alex Drum Hawkes (1927-1977). He was the author of *Encyclopaedia of Cultivated Orchids*.

TYPE SPECIES: *Katherinea ampla*
        (Lindley) A.D. Hawkes
        (*Dendrobium amplum* Lindley)

Now recognized as belonging to the genus *Epigeneium*, *Katherinea* was previously considered to include thirty epiphytes or scrambling terrestrials found in mid to upper elevation, montane moss laden forests from north-eastern India (Assam), Bhutan, Nepal, southern China (Xizang to Guangxi), Myanmar to Vietnam, Malaysia, the Philippines, Indonesia and New Guinea. These plants have angled, grooved pseudo-bulbs, subtended by thinly textured sheaths, each with two to three, thick, dark green leaves suffused maroon. The solitary to few-flowered inflorescence has white, yellow-green or crimson, sweetly fragrant flowers often suffused purple on the outside surfaces. The prominently trilobed lip has a short, chin-like protuberance, erect side lobes and a diamond-shaped midlobe with a recurved tip. The flowers have a long, stout column.

KATHOU

An orthographic variant introduced in *Schlüessel Hortus Malab.*, 39 (1818). The correct spelling is *Katou*.

Currently Accepted   Validly Published   Invalidly Published   Published Pre-1753   Superfluous Usage   Orthographic Variant   Fossil

Orchid Genera · **208**

KATONG-ging

Kaempfer

Am. Exot. 868 (1712).

ETYMOLOGY: A local Malayalam name for wild, as found in nature.

TYPE SPECIES: *Katong-ging* Kaempfer

Pre-1753, therefore not validly published in fulfillment of nomenclatural rules; this binomial name is most often referred to *Arachnis*. *Katong-ging* was previously considered to include one terrestrial found in low elevation, mangroves and along river banks of Thailand, Malaysia, Indonesia and the Philippines. This large, climbing or scrambling plant has pencil-like stems, each with tongue-shaped to narrow, bilobed leaves. The simple or branching, few-flowered inflorescence has showy, fragrant, dark green or yellow flowers variously barred with maroon. The trilobed lip has recurved side lobes, an ovate midlobe and a small spur. This name is usually now considered a synonym of *Arachnis flos-aeris* (Linnaeus) Reichenbach f.

KATOU-kaida

Rheede

Hort. Malab. 12: 51-52, t. 26 (1693).

Not *Katou-tsjeroe* Adanson (1763) Anacardianceæ.

ETYMOLOGY: A local Malayalam name for wild, as found in nature. Kaida generally refers to the leaves of *Pandanus*, thus indicating a resemblance of Katou's leaves with those of *Pandanus*.

TYPE SPECIES: *Katou-kaida-maravara* Rheede

Pre-1753, therefore not validly published in fulfillment of nomenclatural rules; this trinomial name is most often referred to *Eulophia*. *Katou-kaida* was previously considered to include one terrestrial or rare epiphyte found in Sri Lanka, India and Myanmar. This plant has roundish to ovoid pseudobulbs, either buried or partially exposed, each with several, long, narrow leaves. The slender, few-flowered inflorescence has waxy, fragrant, white to green flowers. The trilobed lip has violet, basal keels and a slightly curved, cylindrical spur. This name is usually now considered a synonym of *Eulophia epidendraea* (J. König ex Retzius) C.E.C. Fischer.

Rheede also published a second name *Katou-theka-maravara* (12: 49, t. 25) that is only illustrated by rather immature bulbs. This terrestrial plant is found in low elevation, hill scrub from southern China, Taiwan and northern India to the Philippines. The plant has ovoid pseudobulbs, each with several, narrow, deciduous leaves. The erect, slender, few-flowered inflorescence has green flowers with spreading sepals and petals suffused brown-purple. The small, white, trilobed lip has erect side lobes enfolding the short column; the midlobe has a basal disc with thread-like papillae and a small, club-like spur. This name is usually now considered a synonym of *Eulophia graminea* Lindley.

KATOU-ponnam

Rheede

Hort. Malab. 12: 55, t. 28 (1693).

ETYMOLOGY: A local Malayalam word for wild, as for something found in nature. Ponnam means gold.

TYPE SPECIES: *Katou-ponnam-maravara* Rheede

Pre-1753, therefore not validly published in fulfillment of nomenclatural rules; this trinomial name is most often referred to *Liparis*. *Katou-ponnam* was previously considered to include one epiphyte found in low to mid elevation, open swampy areas and among the grasses of northern India, Nepal, Myanmar, Thailand, Laos, Vietnam, southern China (Hainan), Taiwan, Japan and Guam. This plant has short, swollen stems, each bearing several, broad leaves. The erect, stout, numerous-flowered inflorescence has pale yellow-green, fragrant flowers with a purple, entire lip. This name is usually now considered a synonym of *Liparis odorata* (Willdenow) Lindley.

KATTOU

An orthographic variant introduced in *Sp. Pl.* (*Willdenow*), ed. 4, **4**(1): 91 (1805). The correct spelling is *Katou*.

KAURORCHIS

D.L. Jones & M.A. Clements

Orchadian **14**(8 Sci. Suppl.): xv (2004).

ETYMOLOGY: Greek for brittle and orchid. Refers to the texture of these tiny plants.

TYPE SPECIES: *Kaurorchis evasa*
(T.E. Hunt & Rupp) D.L. Jones & M.A. Clements
(*Bulbophyllum evasum* T.E. Hunt & Rupp)

Recognized as belonging to the genus *Bulbophyllum*, *Kaurorchis* was proposed to include one epiphyte or lithophyte found in cool, low elevation, misty, hill forests of northeastern Australia among the moss laden rocks or on tree branches. This extremely brittle, tiny plant has small pseudobulbs fused to the rhizome, and are subtended by sheathing bracts, each with flat, oval or almost circular, rather thick leaves arranged in strings along the thin stem. The wiry, maroon, few to numerous-flowered inflorescence has tiny, inconspicuous, bell-shaped, maroon to pink flowers, borne in a tight, ball-like head at the tip of the spike, They do not open widely and have dark red stripes that at a casual glance makes the whole flower appear red. The narrow, thick, heart-shaped, entire lip is deeply channeled and densely covered with small glands.

KEFERSTEINIA

Reichenbach *filius*

Bot. Zeitung (Berlin) 10: 633 (1852).

Epidendroideæ \ Cymbidieæ • Zygopetalinæ

ETYMOLOGY: In honor of Christian Keferstein (1784-1866), a German geologist, paleontologist, mineralogist and orchid grower from Kröllwitz, who gathered an amazing group of orchids.

LECTOTYPE: *Kefersteinia graminea*
(Lindley) Reichenbach f.
(*Zygopetalon gramineum* Lindley)

Sixty-one sympodial epiphytes or rare terrestrials are found in wet, humid, mid to upper elevation, montane forests of southern Mexico to Panama and Colombia to Bolivia. These small, compact plants have short stems, each with narrow, erect to arching, thinly textured leaves arranged in a fan-like presentation. The several, hanging, solitary-flowered inflorescences, borne from the axils of the leaf sheaths, have small, thinly textured, creamy-white, yellow-white to pale green flowers covered with red to violet specks on the petals. The shortly clawed, roundish, concave, obscurely trilobed or entire lip is often heavily spotted, has a wavy, notched or fringed margin and the tip is either straight or curves downward. The basal callus is either low and long or short and high, supported by a distinct stipe. The flowers have an erect, stout column with a distinct, vertical keel in front.

KEFERSTEINIANA

An orthographic variant introduced in *Prakt. Stud. Orchid.*, 256 (1854). The correct spelling is *Kefersteinia*.

KEFFERSTEINIA

An orthographic variant cited in *Cat. Pl.* (*Warszewicz*), 64 (1864). The correct spelling is *Kefersteinia*.

KEIFERSTEINIA

An orthographic variant introduced in *J. Roy. Hort. Soc.*, **7**(1): 80 (1886). The correct spelling is *Kefersteinia*.

KEGELIA

Reichenbach *filius*

Bot. Zeitung (Berlin) **10**: 670 (1852).

Not *Kegelia* Schultz-Bipontinus (1848) Asteraceæ.

ETYMOLOGY: Commemorating Hermann Aribert Heinrich Kegel (1819-1856), a German who collected flora in Dutch Guiana (Surinam) and was a head gardener for the Botanical Gardens in Halle, Germany.

TYPE SPECIES: *Kegelia houtteana* Reichenbach f.

Not validly published because of a prior use of the name, this homonym was replaced by *Kegeliella*.

KEGELIELLA

Mansfeld

Repert. Spec. Nov. Regni Veg. Beih. **36**: 60 (1934).

Epidendroideæ ⁜ Cymbidieæ • Stanhopeinæ

ETYMOLOGY: *Kegelia*, a genus of orchids and Latin for diminutive.

TYPE SPECIES: *Kegeliella houtteana*
(Reichenbach f.) L.O. Williams
(*Kegelia houtteana* Reichenbach f.)

Three uncommon, dwarf, sympodial epiphytes comprise this genus, and are found in only a few scattered localities in low to mid elevation, hill and montane forests from southern Mexico, Costa Rica to Panama, Venezuela, Colombia, Trinidad and Surinam. These strange plants simulate a small *Gongora*, and the ovoid, somewhat compressed pseudobulbs, subtended by leaf-like bracts, each with two or three, conspicuously nerved leaves borne at the tip. The several, few-flowered inflorescences have small, white to dull brown flowers that have hairy segments covered with red-brown bars throughout. The thinly textured, bright green to yellow, trilobed lip, sometimes heavily spotted red, has large, spreading side lobes, and a small, triangular midlobe with an erect, yellow-green callus. The flowers have a long, more or less curved, green column with two broad wings.

KERANTHUS

Loureiro ex Endlicher

Gen. Pl. (Endlicher) 193 (1836).

ETYMOLOGY: Latin for heart and flower.

TYPE SPECIES: *None designated*

Name published without a description. Today this name is most often referred to *Dendrobium*.

KERGELIELLA

An orthographic variant introduced in *Orchids Venezuela*, ed. 2, 1136 (2000). The correct spelling is *Kegeliella*.

KERIGOMNIA

P. Royen

Contr. Herb. Austral. **12**: 1 (1976).

ETYMOLOGY: Named for Kerigomna Camp which is found on the eastern slope of Mount Wilhelm (4,200 ft./1,280 m) along the northern coast of Papua New Guinea in Chimbu (Simbu) Province where the type species was collected.

TYPE SPECIES: *Kerigomnia bilabrata* P. Royen

Now recognized as belonging to the genus *Octarrhena*, *Kerigomnia* was previously considered to include one epiphyte found in upper elevation, montane forests of New Guinea. This small bushy plant has branched or simple stems with numerous, warty, laterally compressed leaves. The solitary to few-flowered inflorescence has brown-orange flowers with small petals and large sepals which are joined at the base. The immobile, thick, purple, entire lip has a narrow ridge of hairs. The flowers have a short column with a bilobed appendage. The above type name is now considered a synonym of *Octarrhena bilabrata* (P. Royen) W. Kittredge.

KINETOCHILUS

(Schlechter) Brieger

Orchideen (Schlechter), ed. 3 **1**(11-12): 686 (1981).

ETYMOLOGY: Latin for movable and lip. Referring to the movable lip that is fastened to the column foot by a flexible link.

TYPE SPECIES: *Kinetochilus pectinatus* (Finet) Brieger
(*Dendrobium pectinatum* Finet)

Now recognized as belonging to the genus *Dendrobium*, *Kinetochilus* was previously considered to include three epiphytes or lithophytes found in mid elevation, montane rain forests of New Caledonia, Christmas and Cocos islands. These plants have long, slender to thick stems, each with their small, leathery leaves arranged like teeth on a comb. The several, short, more or less upright, few-flowered inflorescence has small, pale to bright yellow-green flowers spotted pink or maroon and not opening fully. The strongly upward curved, entire lip is quite movable. The flowers have a short, curved column. The above type name is now considered a synonym of *Dendrobium pectinatum* Finet.

KINGIDIUM

P.F. Hunt

Kew Bull. **24**: 97 (1970).

ETYMOLOGY: A substitute name derived from *Kingiella*, a genus of orchids.

TYPE SPECIES: *Kingidium taeniale* (Lindley) P.F. Hunt
(*Aerides taenialis* Lindley)

This type name is now considered a synonym of *Phalaenopsis taenialis* (Lindley) Christenson & Pradhan; basionym *Aerides taenialis* Lindley

Now recognized as belonging to the genus *Phalaenopsis*, *Kingidium* was previously considered to include five epiphytes found in mid to upper elevation, montane forests of southern China (Xizang to Yunnan), northern India (Kashmir to Assam), Nepal and Myanmar. These clump-forming plants are vegetatively similar to *Phalaenopsis*. The plants have short stems, each with several thinly textured, large or small, broad or narrow, deciduous leaves. The numerous to few-flowered inflorescence has showy, small, white to pink flowers. Sometimes the purple spotted lateral sepals are united to the short column foot. The shortly clawed, trilobed lip has erect, curved side lobes and a large, forward spreading midlobe that is slightly sac-like at the base. The flowers have a slender, erect, narrowly winged column.

KINGELLA

Not *Kingella* Tieghem (1895) Loranthaceæ.

An orthographic variant introduced in *Malayan Nat. J.*, **36**(1): 21 (1982). The correct spelling is *Kingiella*.

KINGIELLA

Rolfe

Orchid Rev. **25**(297): 196 (1917).

Not *Kingella* van Tieghem (1895) Loranthaceæ.

ETYMOLOGY: Named in honor of George King (1840-1909), a Scottish explorer and botanist who, along with Robert Pantling (1856-1910), wrote *Orchids of the Sikkim-Himalayas*. And Latin for diminutive.

LECTOTYPE: *Kingiella taenialis* (Lindley) Rolfe
(*Aerides taenialis* Lindley)

Not validly published because of a prior use of the name, this homonym was replaced by *Kingidium*.

Currently Accepted   Validly Published   Invalidly Published   Published Pre-1753   Superfluous Usage   Orthographic Variant   Fossil

Orchid Genera • 210

KIONOPHYTON

Garay

Bot. Mus. Leafl. **28**(4): 329 (1980)[1982].

Orchidoideæ ⚘ Cranichideæ • Spiranthinæ

ETYMOLOGY: Greek for pillar or column and plant. Refers to the pillar-like base of the stem that is found below the spreading basal rosette.

TYPE SPECIES: *Kionophyton seminuda*
(Schlechter) Garay
(*Spiranthes seminuda* Schlechter)

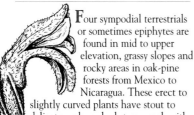

Four sympodial terrestrials or sometimes epiphytes are found in mid to upper elevation, grassy slopes and rocky areas in oak-pine forests from Mexico to Nicaragua. These erect to slightly curved plants have stout to delicate, unbranched stems, each with several leaves forming a basal rosette that is withered before the flowers appear. The hairy above, numerous to few-flowered inflorescence has several, thin, pale brown bracts covering the dull white, yellow or green, tubular flowers. The lateral sepals form a prominent nectary. The shortly clawed, ovate to elliptical, entire lip is attached to the sides of the slender, delicate, club-shaped column forming a tunnel-like access to the nectary. These species are sometimes included in *Stenorrhynchos*.

KITIGORCHIS

Maekawa

Wild Orchids Japan Colour 469 (1971).

ETYMOLOGY: Japanese for north and Greek for orchid. Referring to the locality of the type species.

TYPE SPECIES: *Kitigorchis itoana* Maekawa

Now recognized as belonging to the genus *Oreorchis*, *Kitigorchis* was previously considered to include five terrestrials found in mid to upper elevation, montane meadows from northern Japan (Honshu) and southern China (Xizang to Sichuan) and northern India (Assam) to Myanmar. These small plants have ovate pseudobulbs, each with a solitary, rigid, narrow leaf (borne at the tip of the pseudobulb) that has prominent nerves. The erect, numerous to few-flowered inflorescence has small, olive-green to yellow flowers with most opening simultaneously. The yellow to white, trilobed lip, sprinkled purple-red, has a wavy margin, and poorly developed calli.

KLEBERIELLA

V.P. Castro & Catharino

Richardiana **6**(3): 158 (2006).

Epidendroideæ ⚘ Cymbidieæ • Oncidiinæ

ETYMOLOGY: Honoring Kleber Garcia de Lacerda, Jr. (1950-), a Brazilian tropical diseases physician, naturalist, botanical illustrator and author of *Brazilian Orchids*. And Latin for diminutive.

TYPE SPECIES: *Kleberiella uniflora*
(Booth ex Lindley) V.P. Castro & Catharino
(*Oncidium uniflorum* Booth ex Lindley)

Six sympodial epiphytes or occasional lithophytes are found in cool, mid elevation, montane forests, dry savannas and along river banks from southeastern Brazil, Paraguay, Uruguay to northeastern Argentina.
This dwarf plant has clustered, strongly compressed, grooved, ovate pseudobulbs, subtended by thin, dry, leafless sheaths, each with a solitary, bright green, narrow leaf. The erect, few-flowered inflorescence has widespreading flowers with similar, narrow, yellow-green sepals and petals. The trilobed lip has small, wing-like side lobes and the broadly oblong, bilobed midlobe has small, orange, butterfly-like ridges. The flowers have an erect winged column.

KOCHIOPHYTON

Schlechter ex Cogniaux

Fl. Bras. (Martius) **3**(6): 574 (1906).

ETYMOLOGY: Dedicated to Theodor Koch-Grünberg (1872-1924), a German anthropologist, ethnologist, linguistic interpreter, and explorer of northwestern Brazil and Colombia. And Greek for plant.

TYPE SPECIES: *Kochiophyton negrense*
Schlechter ex Cogniaux
This type name is now considered a synonym of *Aganisia cyanea* (Lindley) Reichenbach f.;
basionym
Acacallis cyanea Lindley

Now recognized as belonging to the genus *Aganisia*, *Kochiophyton* was previously considered to include two epiphytes found in Colombia, Venezuela and Brazil. These dwarf plants have ovoid pseudobulbs, subtended by papery bracts, each with a solitary, dark green, bilobed leaf. The erect or arching, slender, few-flowered inflorescence has showy, fragrant flowers with mauve outside and lavender-blue inside. The kidney-shaped, concave, trilobed lip is golden-bronze to red-purple with a yellow-orange callus. The flowers have an erect, slender column.

KOELLEINSTEINIA

An orthographic variant introduced in *Bull. Soc. Roy. Bot. Belgique*, **43**: 346 (1906). The correct spelling is *Koellensteinia*.

KOELLENSTEINIA

Reichenbach *filius*

Bonplandia **2**(2): 17 (1854).

Epidendroideæ ⚘ Cymbidieæ • Zygopetalinæ

ETYMOLOGY: Dedicated to Captain Frédéric baron of Kellner von Koellenstein (*fl.* 1850s), an Austrian military officer and a friend of Reichenbach.

TYPE SPECIES: *Koellensteinia kellneriana*
Reichenbach f.

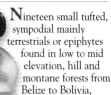

Nineteen small tufted, sympodial mainly terrestrials or epiphytes found in low to mid elevation, hill and montane forests from Belize to Bolivia, Venezuela, the Guianas and Brazil. These attractive, showy plants have short, leafy stems, often thickening with age into conspicuous pseudobulbs. These have one to three, narrow, pleated, lightly veined leaves. The erect, slender, numerous to few-flowered inflorescence has small, fragrant, yellow or white flowers. These are barred magenta, rose or violet and suffused pink on the outside. The trilobed lip has spreading or erect, small side lobes, a larger, broad midlobe that is entire or somewhat bilobed and has a bilobed, erect callus. The flowers have a very short, wingless or winged column with a conspicuous foot.

KOLLI-tsierou

Rheede

Hort. Malab. **12**: 13, *t.* 6 (1693).

ETYMOLOGY: A local Malayalam name for a short and sparsely branched variety of Mango tree.

TYPE SPECIES: *Kolli-tsierou-mau-maravara* Rheede

Pre-1753, therefore not validly published in fulfillment of nomenclatural rules; this polynomial name is most often referred to *Cleisostoma*. *Kolli-tsierou* was previously considered to include one epiphyte found in southern India (Karnataka, Kerala and Tamil Nadu), Sri Lanka and Thailand. This hanging, often branched plant has short stems, each with flat, narrow, leathery leaves. The few-flowered inflorescence, borne from the leaf axils, has tiny flowers with brown-red, recurved sepals and petals. The trilobed lip has small, white, erect side lobes and a broad, concave, bright magenta midlobe with a raised protuberance at the base. The flowers have a short column. This name is usually now considered a synonym of *Cleisostoma tenuifolium* (Linnaeus) Garay.

KOLONG

An orthographic variant introduced in *Sp. Pl.* (*Linnaeus*), ed. 1, **2**: 952 (1753). The correct spelling is *Katong*.

KONANTZIA

An orthographic variant introduced in *Phytologia*, **46**(6): 387 (1980). The correct spelling is *Konanzia*.

KONANZIA

Dodson & N.H. Williams

Native Ecuadorian Orchids **2**: 374 (1996).

ETYMOLOGY: In honor of Max Nicolás Konanz (1926-), an Ecuadorian industrialist, importer and businessman from Guayaquil, an art collector, and orchidologist who collected the type species.

TYPE SPECIES: *Konanzia minutiflora*
Dodson & N.H. Williams

Now recognized as belonging to the genus *Ionopsis*, *Konanzia* was previously considered to include one terrestrial or epiphyte found in wet, low to mid elevation, coastal to montane cloud forests of Ecuador (Chimborazo and Cotopaxi). This tiny plant has slightly flattened, sharp edged pseudobulbs, subtended by overlapping, leaf sheaths, each with a pair of thick, fleshy, small leaves. The erect, multi-branched, densely packed, few-flowered inflorescence has tiny, white to pale green, bell-shaped flowers not opening widely. The concave, hood-like dorsal sepal and narrow, pink tipped petals form a tube around the short, slightly curved column. The bases of the lateral sepals are united with the long column foot forming a chin-like protuberance. The white, tongue-shaped, clawed, entire lip has a recurved tip and is sprinkled with purple spots.

KORNASIA

Szlachetko

Fragm. Florist. Geobot. **3**(Suppl.): 120 (1995).

ETYMOLOGY: In honor of Jan Kazimierz Kornaś (1923-1994), a Polish botanist and author of *Vascular Plants of Pogorze Ciezkowickie*.

TYPE SPECIES: *Kornasia maclaudii* (Finet) Szlachetko
(*Microstylis maclaudii* Finet)

Now recognized as belonging to the genus *Malaxis*, *Kornasia* was proposed to include three terrestrials found in the mid elevation, rain forests of Sierra Leone, Guinea, Ghana, Liberia and Nigeria. These inconspicuous, small plants have spindle-shaped pseudobulbs, subtended by sheathing bases, each with several, ovate or narrow, basal leaves. The elongate to head-like inflorescence has minute, green to deep rose, fragrant flowers that have small hairs along the margins of the sepals and petals. The fan-shaped, entire lip has calli with needle-like projections located at the base and a fringed margin. The flowers have a short, footless column.

KOTONG

An orthographic variant introduced in *Sp. Pl.* (*Linnaeus*), ed. 1, **2**: 1348 (1763). The correct spelling is *Katong*.

KRAENZLINELLA

Kuntze

Lex. Gen. Phan. 310 (1903).

Epidendroideæ ⚘ Epidendreæ • Pleurothallidinæ

ETYMOLOGY: Dedicated to Friedrich (Fritz) Wilhelm Ludwig Kränzlin (1847-1934), a German taxonomist, professor of botany at Grauen Kloster monastery in Berlin and author of several monographs on orchids. And Latin for diminutive.

TYPE SPECIES: *Kraenzlinella tunguraguae*
(F. Lehmann & Kraenzlin) Kuntze ex Engler & Prantl
(*Otopetalum tunguraguae* F. Lehmann & Kraenzlin)
This type name is now considered a synonym of
Kraenzlinella otopetalum (Schlechter) Luer;
basionym replaced with
Pleurothallis otopetalum Schlechter

Five small, sympodial epiphytes, lithophytes or terrestrials are found in low to upper elevation, hill and montane rain forests of Mexico, El Salvador, Costa Rica to Colombia, Venezuela and Surinam. These erect plants have erect, slender, unbranched stems, subtended by a few overlapping sheaths, each with a solitary, elliptical, ovate to pencil-like, leathery leaf. The erect, few-flowered inflorescence has bright red to green-yellow flowers graduating to white on the triangular to ovate sepals, and the tiny petals are bright red to yellow. The green, fleshy, tiny, oblong to ovate, entire or trilobed lip is hinged to the column foot and curved toward the base. The flowers have a long, slender, winged column.

KRAENZLINIELLA

An orthographic variant introduced in *Phylogeny Classif. Orchid Fam.*, 275 (1993). The correct spelling is *Kraenzlinella*.

KRAENZLINORCHIS

Szlachetko

Orchidee (*Hamburg*) **55**(1): 57 (2004).

ETYMOLOGY: Dedicated to Friedrich Kraenzlin (1847-1934), a German taxonomist and professor who wrote a revision and monograph of the genus *Habenaria*. And Greek for orchid.

TYPE SPECIES: *Kraenzlinorchis mandersii*
(Collett & Hemsley) Szlachetko
(*Habenaria mandersii* Collett & Hemsley)

Recognized as belonging to the genus *Habenaria*, *Kraenzlinorchis* was proposed to include four terrestrials found in montane forests and grasslands from northern India to the Philippines. These tall, erect plants have unbranched stems subtended by several, narrow leaves decreasing upward in size. The numerous-flowered inflorescence has small, white flowers with an erect dorsal sepal, spreading lateral sepals and entire petals. The oblong, entire or obscurely trilobed lip has a long, cylindrical, slightly sac-like spur. The flowers have a short column.

KREODANTHUS

Garay

Bradea **2**(28): 198 (1977).

Orchidoideæ ⚘ Cranichideæ • Goodyerinæ

ETYMOLOGY: Greek for fleshy and flower. In reference to the substance and texture of the flowers.

TYPE SPECIES: *Kreodanthus simplex*
(C. Schweinfurth) Garay
(*Erythrodes simplex* C. Schweinfurth)

Six trailing, sympodial terrestrials are found in shady, mid to upper elevation, montane forests and woodlands from Cuba and southern Mexico to Peru. These tall, slender plants have unbranched stems, each with several leaves. These leaves clasp the stem at various intervals upward and have curled margins. The short to long, hairy, green to orange, few-flowered inflorescence has small, fleshy, green to orange flowers. The dorsal sepal and petals converge, forming a hood over the small to long, strongly curved, footless column, and the lateral sepals hang downward. The fleshy, yellow-green, concave to tongue-shaped, entire lip has a conspicuous, long, incurved, sac-like spur.

KRYPTOSTOMA

(Summerhayes) Geerinck

Bull. Jard. Bot. Belg. **52**(1-2): 149 (1982).

ETYMOLOGY: Greek for hidden or secret and mouth. Referring to the spur entrance that is hidden by the floral segments.

TYPE SPECIES: *Kryptostoma tentaculigerum*
(Reichenbach f.) Geerinck
(*Habenaria tentaculigera* Reichenbach f.)

Now recognized as belonging to the genus *Habenaria*, *Kryptostoma* was previously considered to include thirteen terrestrials found growing in mid elevation, marshes of tropical eastern Africa (Kenya to Zimbabwe). These small plants have slender, erect stems that are leafy throughout; with the lower mostly reduced to sheaths and the uppermost to leafy bracts. The tall, numerous to few-flowered inflorescence has showy, fragrant, pale green and white flowers with usually bilobed petals. The trilobed lip, narrow at the base, is divided into numerous segments. The widespreading side

| Currently Accepted | Validly Published | Invalidly Published | Published Pre-1753 | Superfluous Usage | Orthographic Variant | Fossil |

O r c h i d   G e n e r a • **212**

lobes usually have numerous segments on the outer edges, and the long or short cylindrical spur is swollen at the tip.

KUHLHASSELLTIA

An orthographic variant introduced in *Fragm. Florist. Geobot.*, **3**(Suppl.): 40 (1995). The correct spelling is *Kuhlhasseltia*.

KUHLHASSELTIA

J.J. Smith

Icon. Bogor.   **4**: 1, t. 301 (1910).

Orchidoideæ • Cranichideæ • Goodyerinæ

ETYMOLOGY: In honor of two Dutchmen, Heinrich Kuhl (1796-1821) and Johan Coenraad vanHasselt (1797-1823), who pioneered the study of orchids in Java (Indonesia).

LECTOTYPE: *Kuhlhasseltia javanica* J.J. Smith

Twelve rather small, sympodial terrestrials are distributed in dark, humid low to mid elevation, hill and montane forest slopes from Korea, southern Japan, Taiwan, the Philippines, southeastern Malaysia (Sabah and Sarawak) and Indonesia to New Guinea. These erect plants have creeping rhizomes and slender, unbranched stems, each with several, leaf-like bracts midway on the stem. The several, small, dark red-black leaves often have purple undersides and notched, wavy margins. The erect, hairy, few-flowered inflorescence has small, off-white to pale green flowers subtended by notched, pale brown bracts. The dorsal sepal forms a hood over the massive, footless column that is basally attached to the lip margin. The trilobed lip has narrow, long to short side lobes, a long, entire to bilobed midlobe that abruptly spreads at the tip or is shallowly blunt and has a shallow spur.

KUSIBABELLA

Szlachetko

Richardiana   **4**(2): 58 (2004).

ETYMOLOGY: In honor of Tadeusz Wladyslaw Kusibab (1957-), a Polish nurseryman and photographer from Kraków, who specializes in ericaceous plants, *Catasetinæ, Dracula* and *Stanhopeinæ*. And Latin for diminutive.

TYPE SPECIES: *Kusibabella gourlieana*
       (Gillies ex Lindley) Szlachetko
       (*Habenaria gourlieana* Gillies ex Lindley)

Recognized as belonging to the genus *Habenaria*, *Kusibabella* was proposed to include eight terrestrials found in low to mid elevation, grasslands and scrub from southern Mexico to northern Argentina. These tall, erect plants have unbranched stems, each with several, narrow leaves. The numerous-flowered inflorescence has green flowers with bilobed petals whose narrow, upper lobe converges with the concave, erect dorsal sepal, forming a hood over the small, erect column. The trilobed lip has long, narrow side lobes, a small to long, narrow midlobe, and a long, cylindrical spur.

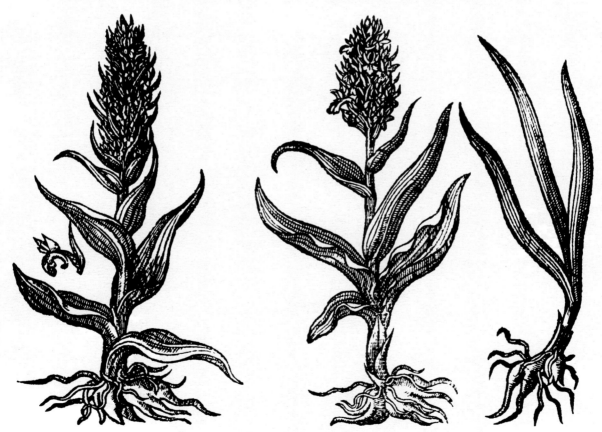

190   ICONES STIRPIVM.

Scrapias paluſtris latifolia L. 95. T. 224.   Scrapias paluſtris altera leptophylla. L. 96. T. 224.

L'Obel   *Icones Stirpium*   page 190 (1591).

LACAENA

Lindley

Edwards's Bot. Reg.
29(Misc.): 68, section no. 101 (1843), and
Edwards's Bot. Reg.   **30**: *t.* 50 (1844).

Epidendroideæ ⚘ **Cymbidieæ** • **Stanhopeinæ**

ETYMOLOGY: From the Greek *Lakaina*, meaning a woman of Laconia (a city in southern Greece) and an alternative name for Helen of Troy because of her abduction from her husband (King of Sparta) by Paris, a prince of Troy (modern day Ilium in north-western Turkey). This ancient city was totally destroyed by the united Greek kingdoms about 1250 BC as told in Homer's tales of the *Iliad* and *Odyssey*.

Or may possibly be derived from Greek for *lakis*, a cleft. An allusion to the divisions of the lip.

TYPE SPECIES: *Lacaena bicolor* Lindley

Two uncommon, sympodial epiphytes are found in mid elevation, montane oak-pine forests, palms and steep embankments from Mexico to Colombia. These large-growing plants have pseudobulbous stems, each with several, heavily pleated leaves. The hanging, numerous-flowered inflorescence has showy, cup-shaped, yellow, white or pink, waxy, fragrant flowers stained or streaked violet. The lateral sepals form a chin-like protuberance with the column foot, and the smaller petals are similar to the dorsal sepal. The obscurely to distinctly clawed, deeply trilobed lip has erect side lobes, and the heart-shaped to slender midlobe has two, prominent, hairy, brown-violet calli and is densely spotted. The flowers have a more or less long, slightly curved, club-shaped column. These plants are similar in habit to *Acineta* or *Lueddemannia*.

LACEAENA

An orthographic variant introduced in *Prakt. Stud. Orchid.*, 58 (1854). The correct spelling is *Lacaena*.

LACROIXIA

Szlachetko

Ann. Bot. Fenn.   **40**(1): 69 (2003).

ETYMOLOGY: In honor of Isobyla Florence la Croix (1933-), a British botanist who worked and lived for several years in various African countries, co-author of *Orchids of Malawi* and *African Orchids in the Wild* and editor of the *Orchid Review*.

TYPE SPECIES: *Lacroixia minor*
          (Summerhayes) Szlachetko
          (*Dinklageella minor* Summerhayes)

Recognized as belonging to the genus *Dinklageella*, *Lacroixia* was proposed to include one epiphyte found in low elevation, coastal woodlands of Ghana and Liberia. This low, creeping, hanging plant has short stems, each with narrow leaves arranged in two rows and has numerous sprawling roots. The short, few-flowered inflorescence has white flowers with narrow sepals and oblong petals. The trilobed (only in the upper third) lip has narrow lobes and a short, sac-like, small mouthed spur that has a swollen tip. The flowers have a short, erect, footless column.

LAELIA

Lindley

Gen. Sp. Orchid. Pl.   96, 115 (1831).

Name ICBN conserved, and type name also conserved; vs.
     Laelia Adanson (1763) Brassicaceæ, and not
     Laelia Persoon (1806) Brassicaceæ.

Epidendroideæ ⚘ **Epidendreæ** • **Laeliinæ**

ETYMOLOGY: Roman Mythology. Dedicated to *Laelia*, one of the six Vestal Virgins who attended the sacred fire in the temple of Vesta (a goddess of the hearth, identified with the Greek goddess Hestia) and held written wills for citizens in ancient Rome.

Or possibly the name borne by females of the ancient Roman family of *Laelius*.

LECTOTYPE: *Laelia grandiflora* (Lexarza) Lindley
          (*Bletia grandiflora* Lexarza)

This type name is now considered a synonym of
     Laelia speciosa (Kunth) Schlechter;
     basionym replaced with
     Bletia speciosa Kunth

Twenty-five sympodial epiphytes, lithophytes or terrestrials are found in moist to dry, mid to upper elevation, oak-pine to deciduous forests from northern Mexico to Costa Rica, Cuba and Jamaica

often growing in full sunlight. They are sometimes subject to cold winters or can be found in hot, tropical forests to even on canyon cliffs. After a recent revision, the genus now contains only a few species, but there are literally thousands of hybrids of these showy flowers. These semi-dwarf plants have ovoid, cone-shaped, roundish or cylindrical pseudo-bulbs, subtended by papery bracts at the base, each with a solitary, fleshy or leathery leaf. There are even a few species that have two to three leaves. The inflorescences vary with several species attaining heights in excess of six feet (1.8 m), while others bear solitary, brightly colored flowers usually with each species having a distinct fragrance. The flowers are usually vivid in shades of white, yellow, pink or purple with several hues in between. They can resemble *Cattleya* but have narrower sepals and a far less showy lip. The flower size can range up to four inches (10 cm) across. The outside margin of the trilobed lip matches the color of the sepals and petals but has contrasting stripes in the throat; the side lobes enfold and surround the usually long, semi-club-shaped, footless column or are separate from the lip.

LAELIOPSIS

Lindley & Paxton

Paxton's Fl. Gard.   **3**: 155, *t.* 105 (1853).

ETYMOLOGY: *Laelia*, a genus of orchids and Greek for appearance.

TYPE SPECIES: *Laeliopsis domingensis*
          (Lindley) Lindley & Paxton
          (*Cattleya domingensis* Lindley)

Now recognized as belonging to the genus *Broughtonia*, *Laeliopsis* was previously considered to include one epiphyte found in low to mid elevation, woodlands and montane forests on the Caribbean islands of Mona and Hispaniola under hot, dry desert-like conditions. These plants have clustered, somewhat compressed, ovoid to spindle-shaped pseudobulbs, each with two or three, stiff, narrow, pointed leaves that have rough or notched margins. The numerous to few-flowered inflorescence has short-lived, showy, faintly fragrant, rose to lilac, purple veined flowers not opening widely. The flowers are clustered at the tip and open in succession over a long period. The obscurely trilobed lip has side lobes forming a tube, and the midlobe

Currently Accepted   Validly Published   Invalidly Published   Published Pre-1753   Superfluous Usage   Orthographic Variant   Fossil

O r c h i d   G e n e r a   • **214**

has a purple-banded disc. The flowers have a slender, pink, club-shaped column.

LAMIUM

Not *Lamium* Linnaeus (1754) Lamiaceæ.

An orthographic variant introduced in *J. Roy. Hort. Soc.*, **7**(1): 116 (1886). The correct spelling is *Lanium*.

LAN

Chao Shih-keng

Chin Chang Lan Pu   (1233).

ETYMOLOGY: An early Chinese name referring to a fragrant grass which later authors attribute to an orchid, *Cymbidium*. Lan in early ancient writings seems to refer to common fragrant plants rather than exclusively to orchids. The earliest orchid reference of lan is mentioned in Chinese literature (*Shih Ching* and *Li Chi*) written about 900-600 BC.

TYPE SPECIES: *None designated*

An early book (*Treatise on Orchids of Chin Chang*) describes some twenty-two kinds of orchid plants. Another book, *Lan Pu* (Treatise on Orchids) by Wang Kuei-hsueh (1247) from Fujian province, describes some thirty-seven different orchid species. Orchid plants (in the Far East) have been held in high esteem and cultivated for some 800 years before the birth of Christ.

There are many other early published works on Chinese orchids:
Lan Yi (Changes of Orchid) by Lu Ting-Wong (1250); *Lan Shih* (A History of Orchids) by Tan Hsi-tzu (1368); *Lan Hui Ching* (Orchid Mirror) by Tu Yung-ning (1811); *Lan Hui Tung Hsin Lu* (Reports of both Lan and Hui) by Hsu Chi-lou (1865); and *Lan Yen Shu Lue* (A Brief Description of Orchids) by Yuen Shih-chun (1876).

NOTE: The influence of Confucius' (551-479 BC) teachings helped in assigning the name of lan to the various species of *Cymbidium*. The Chinese were the first to cultivate and describe orchids, and they were almost certainly the first to describe orchids for medicinal use.

LANCEANA

An orthographic variant cited in *Cat. Pl.* (*Warszewicz*), 66 (1864). The correct spelling is *Lacaena*.

LANIUM

Lindley ex Bentham

Hooker's Icon. Pl.   **14**: 24, t. 1334 (1881).

ETYMOLOGY: Latin for wool. In reference to the woolly hairs on the inflorescence, sepals, and seed capsules.

LECTOTYPE: *Lanium avicula* (Lindley) Bentham
(*Epidendrum avicula* Lindley)

Now recognized as belonging to the genus *Epidendrum*, *Lanium* was previously considered to include nine epiphytes or lithophytes found in wet, mid elevation, montane forests of western Brazil (Paraná, Mato Grosso and Mato Grosso do Sul), the Guianas and Ecuador to Bolivia. These dwarf, uncommon, clustered, creeping plants have thickened, cane-like stems, subtended by short-lived sheaths, each with distichous, fleshy to leathery, flat, stiff, short, red-green leaves whose upper surface is slightly wrinkled. The erect, numerous to few-flowered, thinly textured, maroon inflorescence has small, fragrant, yellow-brown, pale green-red or yellow-green flowers sprinkled with fine red spots and has small, woolly hairs on the backside of the sepals. The concave, pointed, entire lip has a pair of basal calli and is united to the short, stout, footless column at the tip, forming a short tube.

LANKESTERELLA

Ames

Sched. Orchid.   **4**: 3 (1923).

Orchidoideæ • Cranichideæ • Spiranthinæ

ETYMOLOGY: In honor of Charles Herbert Lankester (1879-1969), a British-born explorer, plant collector, horticulturist, and coffee grower in Costa Rica who created the Lankester Botanic Gardens in Paraíso, now part of the University of Costa Rica. And Latin for diminutive.

TYPE SPECIES: *Lankesterella costaricensis* Ames
This type name is now considered a synonym of
Lankesterella orthantha (Kraenzlin) Garay;
basionym
Spiranthes orthantha Kraenzlin

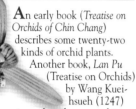

Eleven sympodial epiphytes are found in shady, wet, low to upper elevation, forests, scrub and on moss-laden tree branches from eastern Cuba, Hispaniola, Costa Rica to Peru, Venezuela, eastern Brazil (Minas Gerais to Rio Grande do Sul), northern Argentina and Uruguay. These dwarf plants have short, erect, unbranched stems, each with minute often clustered basal rosettes of delicate, shiny, evergreen leaves that have hairy margins. The erect to arched, delicate, few-flowered inflorescence, densely covered with long, soft hairs, has small, inconspicuous, tubular flowers held to one side, in various shades of emerald-green and white. They are proportionately large for the size of the plant. The sepals and petals

converge, have faint green stripes, a margin tooth from the midpoint to the tip, and the lateral sepals along with the long column foot form a distinct chin-like protuberance. The entire to shallowly trilobed lip is sac-like to concave at the base with thickenings along the margin. The flowers have a short, erect, channeled column that is hairy on the underside and has a short to prominent, massive foot.

LAPORUM

An orthographic variant introduced in *Enum. Phan. Born.*, 164 (1942). The correct spelling is *Aporum*.

LARICORCHIS

Szlachetko

Richardiana   **7**(1): 27 (2007).

ETYMOLOGY: Latin for pine and Greek for orchid. Refers to the shape of the pine-needle like leaves.

TYPE SPECIES: *Laricorchis aggregata*
(Kunth) Szlachetko
(*Dendrobium aggregatum* Kunth)

Recognized as belonging to the genus *Maxillaria*, *Laricorchis* was proposed to include one epiphyte found in upper elevation, montane cloud forests from northwestern Venezuela and Colombia to Peru. The small plant has long pseudobulbs, subtended by gray or brown, tubular sheaths, each with tightly overlapping, small, flat, folded leaves borne toward the tip. The short, pale pink to magenta, numerous-flowered inflorescence, borne from the leaf axils, has small, creamy pink to yellow flowers not opening fully. The dorsal sepal and petals converge, forming a hood over the long, slender column. The white to pale yellow, entire lip is tongue-shaped and has a thickened mid disc.

LARNANDRA

Rafinesque

Neogenyton   4 (1825).

ETYMOLOGY: Greek for box or cell and anther. In reference to the anthers that have a lid like structure.

TYPE SPECIES: *Larnandra magnolia*
(Mühlenberg) Rafinesque
(*Epidendrum magnoliae* Mühlenberg)

Now recognized as belonging to the genus *Epidendrum*, *Larnandra* was previously considered to include two epiphytes or lithophytes found in low to mid elevation, oak-pine forests of the southeastern United States (eastern Carolinas to southern Louisiana) and northeastern Mexico. These plants have simple, reed-like stems, each with several, narrow leaves. The erect, terminal, few-flowered inflorescence has green, coppery-brown to yellow-green, oily fragrant flowers opening simultaneously. The heart-shaped, trilobed lip has roundish side lobes, and the ovate-triangular midlobe has a shallow notch and a central keel. The above type name is now considered a synonym of *Epidendrum magnoliae* Mühlenberg.

LARNAUDRA

An orthographic variant introduced in *Orchideen (Schlechter)*, ed. 1, 190 (1914). The correct spelling is *Larnandra*.

LATHRISIA

Swartz
Adnot. Bot. 48 (1829).
ETYMOLOGY: Greek for hidden, secret or concealed. The meaning as applied here is unknown.
TYPE SPECIES: *Lathrisia pectinata*
(Thunberg) Swartz nom. illeg.
(*Orchis pectinata* Thunberg)
Bartholina burmanniana (Linnaeus) Ker Gawler
(*Orchis burmanniana* Linnaeus)

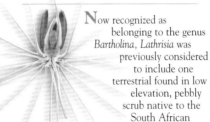

Now recognized as belonging to the genus *Bartholina, Lathrisia* was previously considered to include one terrestrial found in low elevation, pebbly scrub native to the South African Cape area. This slender, erect plant has unbranched stems, each with a solitary, basal leaf that is almost circular in shape. The wiry, solitary-flowered inflorescence is densely covered with long hairs. The pale green and violet flower has narrow sepals and petals converging, forming a hood over the column. The unusual fan-shaped, obscurely trilobed lip has several, radiating, hair-like segments.

LATISATIS

An orthographic variant introduced in *Hist. Orchid.*, t. 10, t. 12c (1822). The correct spelling is *Latosatis*.

LATOSATIS

Thouars
Hist. Orchid. Table 1, sub 1c (1822).

Name published without a description. Today this name is most often referred to *Habenaria*.

LATOUREA

An orthographic variant introduced in *Gen. Pl. (Bentham & Hooker f.)*, **3**: 466, 501 (1883). The correct spelling is *Latouria*.

LATOURIA

Blume
Rumphia **4**: 41, *t. 195 & 199* (1849).
Not *Latouria* (Endlicher) Lindley (1847) Goodeniaceæ.
ETYMOLOGY: Dedicated to a Mr. Latour (*fl.* 1830s) who drew specimens, prepared lithographic plates, applied hand coloring to the finished prints and was a personal friend of Carl Blume (1796-1862).
TYPE SPECIES: *Latouria spectabilis* Blume

Not validly published because of a prior use of the name, this homonym was replaced by *Dendrobium*.

LATOURORCHIS

Brieger
Orchideen (Schlechter), ed. 3 **1**(11-12): 727 (1981).
ETYMOLOGY: *Latouria*, a genus of orchids and Greek for orchid.
TYPE SPECIES: *Latourorchis spectabilis* (Blume) Brieger
(*Latouria spectabilis* Blume)

A superfluous name proposed as a substitute for *Latouria*.

LEAOA

Schlechter & Porto
Arch. Jard. Bot. Rio de Janeiro **3**: 292 (1922).
ETYMOLOGY: Complimenting Antonio E. Pacheco (de Area) Leão (1872-1931), a Brazilian botanist, anthropologist and director of the Botanical Garden in Rio de Janeiro.
TYPE SPECIES: *Leaoa monophylla*
(Barbosa Rodrigues) Schlechter & Porto
(*Hexadesmia monophylla* Barbosa Rodrigues)
This type name is now considered a synonym of *Scaphyglottis livida* (Lindley) Schlechter;
basionym replaced with
Isochilus lividus Lindley

Now recognized as belonging to the genus *Scaphyglottis, Leaoa* was previously considered to include one epiphyte found in low to mid elevation, hill forests and coffee trees growing occasionally in northern Brazil, Venezuela, Mexico to Honduras and Colombia to Bolivia. This plant has minute, densely branched, narrow, spindle-shaped pseudobulbous stems, each with one to two, long, narrow leaves that have bilobed tips. The erect or hanging, one- to two-flowered inflorescence has pale green to green-yellow flowers overlaid with brown, and the floral base is suffused pink. The flowers are held close to the tip of the pseudobulb. The abruptly terminated, shallowly notched, obscurely trilobed lip is pale green. The flowers have a small, short-footed column.

LECANORCHIS

Blume
Mus. Bot. **2**(12): 188 (1856).
Vanilloideæ Vanillineæ
ETYMOLOGY: Greek for basin or pot and orchid. Refers to the urn or cup-shaped sack at the base of the lip.
LECTOTYPE: *Lecanorchis javanica* Blume

Fourteen odd, robust saprophytes are found in dark, humid, low to mid elevation, mixed to evergreen forests ranging from northern India (Sikkim), Taiwan, Malaysia, Indonesia and New Guinea to the Philippines with Japan (Honshu) having the largest concentration. These leafless, erect plants have simple or branched, brittle, black stems (lasting long after flowering). The erect, numerous to few-flowered inflorescence has inconspicuous, varying-colored, pale green-yellow or pale brown flowers with similar, thinly textured sepals and petals and has a small, toothed cup or collar-like structure found just below the sepals. The white to pale lavender, hairy, entire or trilobed lip is attached along its margins to the base of the slender, footless column forming a short tube, and the tip of the lip forms a shallow spoon-shape.

LECTANDRA

J.J. Smith
Bull. Dépt. Agric. Indes Néerl. **13**: 55 (1907), and *Repert. Spec. Nov. Regni Veg.* **5**: 299 (1908).
ETYMOLOGY: Greek for gathered or chosen and male or stamen. Alluding to the concentration of the flowers on the short inflorescence located below the leaves.
TYPE SPECIES: *Lectandra parviflora* J.J. Smith
This type name is now considered a synonym of *Poaephyllum pauciflorum* (Hooker f.) Ridley;
basionym
Agrostophyllum pauciflorum Hooker f.

Now recognized as belonging to the genus *Poaephyllum, Lectandra* was previously considered to include four epiphytes found in misty, low elevation, evergreen forests of New Guinea, Thailand, Indonesia and the Philippines. These plants have erect, stiff stems, each with compressed, rather large leaves arranged in two rows. The short, few-flowered inflorescence continues to develop as the newer buds open. The small to tiny, white flowers have petals with slightly notched tips and the lateral sepals have pointed tips. The obscurely trilobed lip has erect, inrolled side lobes with a basal, hairy

Currently Accepted   Validly Published   Invalidly Published   Published Pre-1753   Superfluous Usage   Orthographic Variant   Fossil

Orchid Genera • **216**

callus, and the spear-shaped midlobe has minute, red spots.

LEDGERIA

F. Mueller
Fragm. (Mueller) **1**(10): 238 (1859).

ETYMOLOGY: Dedicated to Charles Ledger (1818-1905), a British-born Australian naturalist, adventurer and importer of *Cinchona* seeds to Java that provided the world's supply of quinine for many years.

TYPE SPECIES: *Ledgeria aphylla* F. Mueller
This type name is now considered a synonym of
Erythrorchis cassythoides
(A. Cunningham ex Lindley) Garay;
basionym
Dendrobium cassythoides A. Cunningham ex Lindley

Now recognized as belonging to the genera *Erythrorchis* and *Pseudovanilla*, *Ledgeria* was previously considered to include two large saprophytes found in the tropics and subtropics from New Guinea to the Solomons and northeastern Australia. These spectacular, leafless vining plants often attain heights in excess of ten feet (3 m) and have literally hundreds of honey fragrant flowers with many of them opening at one time. The short-lived, pale yellow to orange flowers are quite conspicuous with their bright crimson-red lip. The broad, trilobed lip curves around the column. It has short and erect or obsolete side lobes, and the midlobe has a wavy, yellow margin with two long, raised, basal calli. The flowers have a long, slender, curved column.

LEIMODORON

Clusius
Rar. Pl. Hist. 270 (1601).

Pre-1753, therefore not validly published in fulfillment of nomenclatural rules; this name is most often referred to *Limodorum*.

LEIOANTHUM

M.A. Clements & D.L. Jones
Orchadian **13**(11): 490 (2002).

ETYMOLOGY: Greek for smooth and flower. Refers to the waxy appearance of the flowers.

TYPE SPECIES: *Leioanthum bifalce*
(Lindley) M.A. Clements & D.L. Jones
(*Dendrobium bifalce* Lindley)

Recognized as belonging to the genus *Dendrobium*, *Leioanthum* was proposed to include one epiphyte or lithophyte found in hot, low elevation, steamy rain forests or baking on rocks from New Guinea, northern Australia, to the Solomons. This large plant has spindle-shaped pseudobulbs, each with several, clustered, oval, yellow-green, leathery leaves. The erect, few-flowered inflorescence has waxy, green to yellow flowers speckled and dotted red-brown. The narrow petals are smaller than the other segments. The trilobed lip has erect, almost pointed, brown side lobes, and the bilobed, brown to yellow midlobe with a cleft in the center, has a green, entire margin and a raised white keel. The flowers have a stout, short, wingless column.

LEIOCHILUS

Not *Leiochilus* Hooker f. (1873) Rubiaceæ.

An orthographic variant introduced in *Fl. Serres Jard.*, **23**: 249 (1880). The correct spelling is *Leochilus*.

LEJOCHILUS

An orthographic variant cited in *Lex. Gen. Phan.*, 321 (1904). The correct spelling is *Leochilus*.

LELIA

An orthographic variant introduced in *Dict. Univ. Hist. Nat. Atlas*, 15, *t.* 19 (1849). The correct spelling is *Laelia*.

LEMBOGLOSSUM

Halbinger
Orquidea (Mexico City), n.s. **9**(2): 348 (1984).

ETYMOLOGY: Greek for boat or fishing boat and tongue. Referring to the boat-shaped lip.

TYPE SPECIES: *Lemboglossum rossii*
(Lindley) Halbinger
(*Odontoglossum rossii* Lindley)

Now recognized as belonging to the genus *Rhynchostele*, *Lemboglossum* was previously considered to include fourteen epiphytes, lithophytes or rare terrestrials found in humid, mid to upper montane, mixed to deciduous forests from southern Mexico to Panama and Colombia. These plants have rounded, ovoid or elongate pseudobulbs, subtended by papery sheaths, each with two thinly textured, narrow leaves. The simple or few-branched, erect to hanging, numerous to few-flowered inflorescence is borne from the basal sheaths. The showy, short-lived, yellow-green, white or pink, thinly textured flowers are heavily barred or spotted brown or red-brown. The shortly clawed, trilobed lip, fused to the column, is white or pale pink, has small, erect side lobes, a large, heart-shaped midlobe with a yellow to white, basal callus and has a wavy margin. The flowers have a long, broad or slender column.

LEMNISCOA

Hooker *filius*
Bot. Mag. **98**: sub 5961 (1872).

ETYMOLOGY: Greek for a colored ribbon. Refers to the long, ribbon-like sepals.

TYPE SPECIES: *Lemniscoa parishii*
C.S.P. Parish ex Hooker *filius*

Not validly published, this name is referred to *Bulbophyllum*. *Lemniscoa* was considered to include one epiphyte found in Myanmar and Thailand. The above type name is now considered a synonym of *Bulbophyllum lemniscatum* C.S.P. Parish ex Hooker f.

LEMURANTHE

Schlechter
Repert. Spec. Nov. Regni Veg. Beih. **33**: 84 (1924).

ETYMOLOGY: *Lemuria*, a paleogeographic landmass and Greek for flower. Refers to the landmass that includes Madagascar and India that persisted into the late Cretaceous period. And Latin for flower.

Or possibly named for the unique endemic, arboreal primates Lemurs.

TYPE SPECIES: *Lemuranthe gymnochiloides*
(Schlechter) Schlechter
(*Habenaria gymnochiloides* Schlechter)

Now recognized as belonging to the genus *Cynorkis*, *Lemuranthe* was previously considered to include one terrestrial found in mid elevation, montane rocky forests of Madagascar and the Comoros Islands. This tall, erect plant has unbranched stems, each with several leaves and a short, few-flowered inflorescence. The tiny, purple flowers have an entire lip. The flowers have a small column that bears a rostellum with tiny arms.

LEMURELLA

Schlechter
Repert. Spec. Nov. Regni Veg Beih. **33**: 366, 367 (1925).

Epidendroideæ • Vandeæ • Angraecinæ

ETYMOLOGY: *Lemuria*, a paleographic land mass and Latin for diminutive.

TYPE SPECIES: *Lemurella ambongensis*
(Schlechter) Schlechter
(*Angraecum ambongense* Schlechter)
This type name is now considered a synonym of
Lemurella culicifera (Reichenbach f.) H. Perrier;
basionym replaced with
Angraecum culiciferum Reichenbach f.

Four small, monopodial epiphytes are found in low to mid elevation, moss laden forests and sandy scrub of western Madagascar and the Comoros Islands. These dwarf plants have short, thin, compressed, curved or hanging stems, subtended by persistent leaf bases, each with several, oblong to ovate, leathery, unequally bilobed leaves. The short, erect, few-flowered inflorescence has tiny, nearly transparent, inverted, yellow to green flowers. The trilobed lip has erect, rounded side lobes, a basal callus, a long, blunt midlobe with a downward pointing tip, and a long, cylindrical spur that curves upward. The flowers have a short, slightly bent, footless column.

LEMURORCHIS

Kraenzlin

Bot. Jahrb. Syst. **17**: 58 (1893).

Epidendroideæ ⚘ Vandeæ • Angraecinæ

ETYMOLOGY: *Lemuria*, a paleographic land mass and Greek for orchid.

TYPE SPECIES: *Lemurorchis madagascariensis*
Kraenzlin

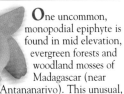

One uncommon, monopodial epiphyte is found in mid elevation, evergreen forests and woodland mosses of Madagascar (near Antananarivo). This unusual, tall plant has long to short stems, each with narrow, leathery, bilobed leaves that are folded in the lower portion but strap-shaped above. The hanging, numerous-flowered inflorescence, borne from the leaf axils, has large bracts completely covering the buds that are released when the small to tiny, white, yellow to orange flowers open widely. The distinctly trilobed lip, attached to the base of the erect, slender column, has large, rounded side lobes. The circular midlobe has a small callus in front of the spur mouth and a bilobed tip. The cylindrical, blunt spur is bent upward like a knee.

LEOCHILUM

An orthographic variant introduced in *Cat. Descr. Orquid., Estac. Exp. Agron. Santiago, Cuba*, **60**: 188 (1938). The correct spelling is *Leochilus*.

LEOCHILUS

Knowles & Westcott

Fl. Cab. **2**: 143 (1838).

Epidendroideæ ⚘ Cymbidieæ • Oncidiinæ

ETYMOLOGY: Greek for smooth and lip. Referring to the smooth surface of the lip.

TYPE SPECIES: *Leochilus oncidioides*
Knowles & Westcott

Eleven sympodial epiphytes or lithophytes are found in low to mid elevation, evergreen forests from the United States (southern Florida), Cuba to Trinidad, central Mexico to Ecuador, Brazil and Venezuela. These dwarf, tufted plants have pseudobulbous

stems, subtended by compressed leaf-sheaths, each with one to two, narrow, leathery, unequally bilobed leaves. The arching to hanging, one to two, zig-zagging, purple, numerous to few-flowered inflorescence has small (mostly inconspicuous), fragrant, gray-green to yellow-green flowers often suffused brown or purple. The sepals are similar to the slightly smaller, wider petals. The entire or obscurely trilobed lip, joined to the base of the column, is often longer than the petals with a cup-shaped, short hairy callus. The flowers have a short, footless column.

LEOPARDANTHUS

Blume

Rumphia **4**: 47 (1849), and
Mus. Bot. **1**(3): 47, *t. 15* (1849).

ETYMOLOGY: Greek for a spotted leopard and flower. Referring to the conspicuously spotted perianth segments.

TYPE SPECIES: *Leopardanthus scandens* Blume

Now recognized as belonging to the genus *Dipodium*, *Leopardanthus* was previously considered to include one epiphyte found in low elevation, woodlands from Thailand, Malaysia, Indonesia, northern Australia (Queensland) to Vanuatu and the Solomons. This erect plant has a few-flowered inflorescence with pale yellow flowers covered in dark crimson blotches on their backsides. These blotches show faintly through to the front. The narrow, somewhat folded, trilobed or obscurely trilobed lip is purple striped and has woolly hairs on the front section.

LEPANTES

An orthographic variant introduced in *J. Bot. (Schrader)*, **2**(2): 249 (1800). The correct spelling is *Lepanthes*.

LEPANTHANTHE

(Schlechter) Szlachetko

Richardiana **7**(2): 82 (2007).

ETYMOLOGY: Greek for small, scale or bark and flower. Refers to the size of the tiny flowers.

TYPE SPECIES: *Lepanthanthe lepanthiflorum*
(Schlechter) Szlachetko
(*Bulbophyllum lepanthiflorum* Schlechter)

Recognized as belonging to the genus *Bulbophyllum*, *Lepanthanthe* was proposed to include four epiphytes found in humid, low elevation, forests on moss laden branches of New Guinea along river banks. This small, hanging plant has tiny, green pseudobulbs, subtended by a triangular, gray to brown

sheath, each with a solitary, heart-shaped to ovate leaf that has a strongly decurved margin. The plant forms hanging, rope-like strands that sway in the breeze. The short, densely packed, numerous-flowered inflorescence has small, translucent white to pale yellow flowers with only a few opening at a time. The similar, widespread sepals have a central yellow nerve and tiny, erect petals. The flowers have a small, red-brown, hairy column.

LEPANTHES

Swartz

Nova Acta Regiæ Soc. Sci. Upsal. **6**: 85 (1799), and
Kongl. Vetensk. Acad. Nya Handl. **21**: 249 (1800).

Epidendroideæ ⚘ Epidendreæ • Pleurothallidinæ

ETYMOLOGY: Greek for scale, small or bark and flower. Referring to the minute, scale-like flowers of many of the species.

LECTOTYPE: *Lepanthes concinna* Swartz nom. illeg.

This type name is now considered a synonym of *Lepanthes ovalis* (Swartz) Fawcett & Rendle (*Epidendrum ovale* Swartz)

Over nine hundred of these tufted, sympodial epiphytes or lithophytes principally are found in low to upper elevation, hill to montane forests, woodlands and scrub from Cuba to Trinidad, southern Mexico to Bolivia, Venezuela, the Guianas and northern Brazil (Pará and Amapá). These dwarf to minute, cluster forming plants have slender to tufted stems, subtended by a series of tubular, ribbed, more or less overlapping, leaf sheaths. The leathery leaves sometimes have a velvety texture and often have colorful, attractive markings. The several, solitary or few-flowered inflorescences, often borne flat against the leaf surface, have a tiny to small, brightly colored flower, opening widely so as to appear almost flat. The flowers are short-lived, lasting for only two days. The minute, broad, variously shaped petals are almost always more brightly colored than the larger, widespreading sepals. The entire, bilobed or trilobed lip is highly specialized and varies tremendously in its design and size. The small side lobes surround the slender, wingless, footless column and the minute midlobe is variously shaped and often hairy.

Currently Accepted   Validly Published   Invalidly Published   Published Pre-1753   Superfluous Usage   Orthographic Variant   Fossil

LEPANTHOPSIS

(Cogniaux) Ames

Bot. Mus. Leafl. **1**(9): 3 (1933).

Epidendroideæ ⚘ Epidendreæ • Pleurothallidinæ

ETYMOLOGY: *Lepanthes*, a genus of orchids and Greek for like. Refers to the similarity of this genus to *Lepanthes*.

LECTOTYPE: *Lepanthopsis floripecten*
(Reichenbach f.) Ames
(*Pleurothallis floripecten* Reichenbach f.)

Thirty-eight sympodial epiphytes to lithophytes are found in low to upper elevation, hill and montane cloud forests and woodlands from the southeastern United States (southern Florida), Cuba to Puerto Rico and Honduras to Peru, the Guianas, Venezuela and northern and southeastern Brazil (Roraima and Santa Catarina). These miniscule, tufted plants have erect, delicate stems, subtended by tubular, ribbed sheaths, each with a solitary, leathery leaf. The total plant is usually only a meager three inches (7 cm) in height. The one to several, congested, numerous-flowered inflorescences, borne within the uppermost sheath, have minute, star-like, translucent flowers arranged in two rows (back to back) down the spike presenting an extremely formal appearance. All open simultaneously. The large, dominant sepals are often highly colored and the tiny, roundish, entire or rare trilobed lip surrounds the broad, short, wingless, footless column.

LEPANTHOS

An orthographic variant introduced in *Ann. Soc. Bot. Lyon*, **7**: 56 (1880). The correct spelling is *Lepanthes*.

LEPARIS

An orthographic variant introduced in *Icon. Pl. Ind. Orient.* (Wight), **3**(2): 9 (1844). The correct spelling is *Liparis*.

LEPENTHES

An orthographic variant introduced in *Contr. Fl. Guadeloupe*, 118 (1892). The correct spelling is *Lepanthes*.

LEPERVANCHEA

An orthographic variant introduced in *Beih. Bot. Centralbl.*, **33**(2): 438 (1915). The correct spelling is *Lepervenchea*.

LEPERVENCHEA

Cordemoy

Rev. Gén. Bot. **11**: 415, *f. 18* (1899).

ETYMOLOGY: Dedicated to Pierre de Lepervenche-Meziéres (fl. 1840s), a native French créole railroad employee who collected the flora of Reunion.

TYPE SPECIES: *Lepervenchea tenuifolia*
(Frappier ex Cordemoy) Cordemoy
(*Angraecum tenuifolium* Frappier ex Cordemoy)

Now recognized as belonging to the genus *Angraecum*, *Lepervenchea* was proposed to include one epiphyte found in mid elevation, rain forests on the tiny island of Réunion near Cilaos. This small plant has hanging, flattened stems, subtended by leafy bases, each with several, long, narrow leaves. The short, few-flowered, somewhat flattened inflorescence, borne from the leaf axils, has small, star-shaped, yellow-green flowers with similar, narrow sepals and petals. The narrow, concave, entire lip has a small, straight, cylindrical spur.

LEPHOTHES

An orthographic variant introduced in *Arch. Pharm.*, **15**: 266 (1865). The correct spelling is *Leptotes*.

LEPIANTHES

Not *Lepianthes* Rafinesque (1838) Piperaceæ.

An orthographic variant cited in *Lex. Gen. Phan.*, 323 (1904). The correct spelling is *Lepanthes*.

LEPIDOGYNA

An orthographic variant cited in *Lex. Gen. Phan.*, 324 (1904). The correct spelling is *Lepidogyne*.

LEPIDOGYNE

Blume

Coll. Orchid. **1**: 93, *t. 25* (1858)[1859], and *Fl. Javæ Nov. Ser.* 78, *t. 25* (1858).

Not *Lepidogyna* R.M. Schuster (1980) Lepidolaenaceæ.

Orchidoideæ ⚘ Cranichideæ • Goodyerinæ

ETYMOLOGY: Greek for scale and woman. Refers to the awl-shaped, scale-like rostellum of the column.

TYPE SPECIES: *Lepidogyne longifolia* (Blume) Blume
(*Neottia longifolia* Blume)

One sympodial terrestrial is found in deep shade, peaty soils, in low to mid elevation, hill and montane forests often among scrubby undergrowth from Malaysia, Indonesia (Java and Sumatra) and New Guinea to the Philippines. This robust plant has stout, short stems with numerous, long, fleshy, sword-shaped leaves grouped at the base. It has a most unusual appearance for an orchid, often attaining heights in excess of three feet (91 cm). The tall, thick, densely packed, hairy inflorescence has narrow, subtending bracts that are longer than the flowers. The remarkably showy, but small, fragile flowers, not opening widely, are in shades of red-brown and covered with short, soft hairs. The dorsal sepal and petals converge, forming a hood over the small, slightly curved, footless column and the lateral sepals are often fringed. The sac-like, trilobed lip has cone-like calli on the hypochile. The hypochile has erect side lobes; the epichile is strap-shaped, and some species even have long spurs.

LEPORELLA

A.S. George

Nuytsia **1**(2): 183 (1971).

Orchidoideæ ⚘ Diurideæ • Thelymitrinæ

ETYMOLOGY: Latin for hare and diminutive. A common name derived from its erect petals that resemble the ears of a hare.

TYPE SPECIES: *Leporella fimbriata*
(Lindley) A.S. George
(*Leptoceras fimbriata* Lindley)

One uncommon, sympodial terrestrial is found in low elevation, sandy plains and coastal scrub of southern Australia (southern Victoria and southwestern Western Australia). This stout, erect plant has unbranched stems, each with a solitary, leathery, distinctively red-veined leaf. The few-flowered inflorescence has strongly marked flowers with brown-red lines on a creamy background and is tipped in dark brown. The broad, concave dorsal sepal is incurved over the column, has erect, club-shaped petals, and has narrow, club-shaped, lateral sepals. The broad, obscurely trilobed lip is blotched and covered with red-brown hairs and has a fringed margin. The flowers have a short, curved column.

NOTE: A most unusual species in that it is pollinated only by winged bull ants.

LEPRRVANCHEA

An orthographic variant introduced in *Beih. Bot. Centralbl.*, **36**(2): 157 (1918). The correct spelling is *Lepervenchea*.

LEPTANTHES

An orthographic variant introduced in *Edinburgh Philos. J.*, **8**: 21 (1823). The correct spelling is *Lepanthes*.

LEPTANTHUS

Not *Leptanthus* Michaux (1803) Pontederiaceæ.

An orthographic variant cited in *Nomencl. Bot.* (Steudel), ed. 2, **1**: 558 (1840). The correct spelling is *Lepanthes*.

LEPTOCENTRUM

Schlechter

Orchideen (Schlechter), ed. 1   600 (1914).

ETYMOLOGY: Greek for delicate, thin or slender and a spur. Descriptive of the delicate, thread-like spur.

TYPE SPECIES: *Leptocentrum caudatum*
(Lindley) Schlechter
(*Angraecum caudatum* Lindley)

Now recognized as belonging to the genus *Plectrelminthus*, *Leptocentrum* was previously considered to include four epiphytes found in hot, low elevation, forests and scrub from Ghana to Zimbabwe and the Comoros Islands usually in full sunlight. These plants have short, leafy stems, each with numerous, pale yellow-green, distichous, close-set leaves. The hanging, few-flowered inflorescence, borne from the lower leaf axils, has fragrant, white and pale green flowers with an extremely long, cylindrical, coiled, green-yellow spur. The white, veined, trilobed lip has a broad, fan-shaped, sharply pointed midlobe. The flowers have a short, stout column.

LEPTOCERAS

(R. Brown) Lindley

Sketch Veg. Swan R.   **Append.**: 53 (1840), and
Gen. Sp. Orchid. Pl.   415 (1840).

Not *Leptoceras* Fitzgerald (1889) Orchidaceæ.

ETYMOLOGY: Greek for slender or thin and horn. Referring to the two, long, club shaped, apically swollen horn-like petals.

LECTOTYPE: *Leptoceras menziesii* (R. Brown) Lindley
(*Caladenia menziesii* R. Brown)

Now recognized as belonging to the genera *Caladenia*, *Leporella* and *Lyperanthus*, *Leptoceras* was previously considered to include six terrestrials found in low elevation, coastal forests and woodlands of eastern Australia (Queensland to Tasmania). These tiny plants often form large colonies but will flower only after a fire. The short, erect, unbranched stems each have a solitary, blue-green leaf, minutely sized during the dry season with prominent red veins. The erect, hairy, one- to three-flowered inflorescence has yellow to white flowers with dark red markings. The long tips of the erect, ear-like, dark red petals are quite glandular, and the concave dorsal sepal is hood-like over the slender, slightly curved, winged column. The obscurely trilobed lip has an erect, entire or slightly irregular margin.

LEPTOCERAS

Fitzgerald

Austral. Orch.   **2**(4): t. 4 (1888).

Name published without a description. Today this name is most often referred to *Leporella*.

LEPTOCEROS

An orthographic variant introduced in *Phylogeny Classif. Orchid Fam.*, 269 (1993). The correct spelling is *Leptoceras*.

LEPTORCHIS

An orthographic variant introduced in *Hist. Orchid.*, Table 1, sub 2h, t. 25 (1822). The correct spelling is *Leptorkis*.

LEPTORKIS

Thouars

Nouv. Bull. Sci. Soc. Philom. Paris
1(19): 317 (1809).

Name ICBN rejected vs. *Liparis* Richard (1817) Orchidaceæ.

ETYMOLOGY: Greek for slender or delicateness and orchid. Referred to a slender habit, when originally described by Thouars.

TYPE SPECIES: *None designated*

Although validly published this rejected name is now referred to *Liparis*. *Leptorkis* was considered to include one hundred forty-three terrestrials found worldwide, with the greatest concentration occurring in the Asian tropics (India to Indonesia, the Philippines and the southwestern Pacific Archipelago). These plants are highly variable in their vegetative characteristics, but most have pseudobulbs that are topped with relatively softly textured, fleshy, green leaves. The erect, few-flowered inflorescence has small flowers with wide-spreading sepals and narrow petals. The lip varies from trilobed to shallowly notched and is usually recurved. The flowers have a slender, curved column.

LEPTODES

An orthographic variant introduced in *Dict. Univ. Hist. Nat.*, **7**: 310 (1846). The correct spelling is *Leptotes*.

LEPTOTES

Lindley

Edwards's Bot. Reg.   **19**: t. 1625 (1833).

Epidendroideæ ⚬ Epidendreæ • Laeliinæ

ETYMOLOGY: Greek for tenderness, gracefulness or delicateness. Refers to the leaves of these species.

TYPE SPECIES: *Leptotes bicolor* Lindley

Six attractive, sympodial epiphytes or sometimes lithophytes are found in humid, low elevation, coastal forests and woodlands of southeastern Brazil (Bahia to Rio Grande do Sul), Paraguay and north-eastern Argentina. These dwarf plants forming tight clumps, have tiny, stick-like pseudobulbs, each with a solitary, almost pencil-like, channeled leaf. The solitary to few-flowered inflorescence, borne from the pseudobulb tip, has large, delicate, fragrant, delightful flowers often colored from sparkling white, yellow to pale lilac. The white to pink, narrow, trilobed lip, attached to the short column at the base, has white or green, erect or spreading side lobes, and a dark pink, white or yellow, narrow midlobe tipped in white. The flowers have a fleshy, erect, footless column that is green or purple.

NOTE: When dried and ripened the seed capsules of this genus contain a vanillin flavoring.

LEPTOTHERIUM

An orthographic variant introduced in *Syn. Pl.* (Persoon), **1**: 398 (1839). The correct spelling is *Leptothrium*.

LEPTOTHRIUM

Kunth

Nov. Gen. Sp.   **1**: 340 (1815).

Not *Leptothrium* Kunth (1829) Poaceæ.

ETYMOLOGY: Latin for slim or thin. Describing the small, thinly textured flowers.

TYPE SPECIES: *Leptothrium lineare* Kunth

Not validly published, this name is referred to *Isochilus*. *Leptothrium* was considered to include one epiphyte, lithophyte or terrestrial found from southern Mexico to Bolivia, Cuba to Trinidad, the Guianas, Venezuela, Brazil, Paraguay and Argentina.

Currently Accepted   Validly Published   Invalidly Published   Published Pre-1753   Superfluous Usage   Orthographic Variant   Fossil

Orchid Genera • 220

LEQUEETIA

Bubani

Fl. Pyren. (Bubani)   **4**: 57 (1901).

ETYMOLOGY: In memory of Nicolas Lequeet (*fl.* 1500s), who furnished many plants to Charles de l'Écluse (Carolus Clusius) d'Arras (1526-1609), a French aristocrat, lawyer, professor of botany at the University of Leiden and author of *Rariorum plantarum historia.*

TYPE SPECIES: *Lequeetia violacea* Bubani

This type name is now considered a synonym of *Limodorum abortivum* (Linnaeus) Swartz; basionym *Orchis abortiva* Linnaeus

Now recognized as belonging to the genus *Limodorum*, *Lequeetia* was previously considered to include two uncommon but rather attractive saprophytes found in low to mid elevation, open scrub and nutrient-poor grasslands from Austria to Spain, France to Turkey, Morocco to Tunisia, Iran, Syria, Lebanon and Israel. These erect plants have stout, unbranched, leafless stems which can easily attain heights of two feet (60 cm) and exhibit almost no chlorophyll. The erect, few-flowered inflorescence has mostly violet purple to pale purple flowers that open widely. The tongue-shaped, trilobed lip has a wavy margin and a long, tapering spur.

LEROCHILUS

An orthographic variant introduced in *Hamburger Garten- Blumenzeitung*, **40**: 154 (1884). The correct spelling is *Leochilus.*

LESLIEA

Seidenfaden

Opera Bot.   **95**: 190 (1988).

Epidendroideæ   Vandeæ • Aeridinæ

ETYMOLOGY: In honor of Leslie Andres Garay (1924-), a Hungarian-born American botanist, orchidologist, a former curator of the Oakes Ames Orchid Herbarium at Harvard University and co-author of *Venezuelan Orchids Illustrated.*

TYPE SPECIES: *Lesliea mirabilis* Seidenfaden

One uncommon, monopodial epiphyte is found in mid elevation, montane forests of Thailand. This minute plant has short stems, each with several, broad leaves arranged in two rows. The thin, often hanging, few-flowered, dark purple inflorescence has tiny, brown-green to yellow flowers opening in succession that have similar, widespreading sepals and petals. The white, distinctly lobed, cup-shaped lip, hinged by a small strap, has pale purple markings at the base and a short, broad spur with a wide mouth. The flowers have a short, erect column with an obscure foot.

LESQUETIA

An orthographic variant cited in *Index Raf.*, 102 (1949). The correct spelling is *Lequeetia.*

LESSOCHILUS

An orthographic variant introduced in *Paxton's Mag. Bot.*, **4**: 94 (1838). The correct spelling is *Lissochilus.*

LEUCANORCHIS

An orthographic variant introduced in *J. Roy. Hort. Soc.*, **7**(1): 116 (1886). The correct spelling is *Lecanorchis.*

LEUCHORCHIS

An orthographic variant introduced in *Orchid Gen. Thailand*, **6**: 177 (1986). The correct spelling is *Leucorchis.*

LEUCOCHLAENA

An orthographic variant cited in *Lex. Gen. Phan.*, 328 (1904). The correct spelling is *Leucolena.*

LEUCOCHYLE

An orthographic variant introduced in *Index Seminum Hort. Bot. Berol.*, Appendix 1 (1854). The correct spelling is *Leucohyle.*

LEUCOGLOSSUM

Burbidge

Cool Orchids   150 (1874).

ETYMOLOGY: Greek for white and tongue.

TYPE SPECIES: *Leucoglossum bictonense* (Bateman) Lindley (*Cyrtochilum bictoniense* Bateman)

Name published without a description. Today this name is most often referred to *Odontoglossum.*

LEUCOHILE

An orthographic variant introduced in *Cat. Descr. Orquid., Estac. Exp. Agron. Santiago, Cuba*, **60**: 178 (1938). The correct spelling is *Leucohyle.*

LEUCOHYLE

Klotzsch

Index Seminum Hort. Bot. Berol. 1854 **(App.):** 1 (1854).

ETYMOLOGY: Greek for white and a wood or forest. Refers to the white, woolly hairs found on the inflorescence.

TYPE SPECIES: *Leucohyle warscewiczii* Klotzsch

This type name is now considered a synonym of *Trichopilia subulata* (Swartz) Reichenbach f.; basionym *Epidendrum subulatum* Swartz

Now recognized as belonging to the genus *Trichopilia*, *Leucohyle* was previously considered to include three epiphytes found in low elevation, hill forests from Panama to Peru, the Guianas, Venezuela, Trinidad and northern Brazil (Amazonas to Amapá). These plants have short, erect, slightly swollen stems, each with a solitary, narrow leaf. The few-flowered inflorescence, borne from the terminal axils of the sheaths that cover the stems, has showy, almost translucent, white, slightly fragrant flowers. The broad, concave, entire or obscurely trilobed lip is erect around the base of the small, erect column and is spotted crimson to mauve.

LEUCOLAENA

Not *Leucolaena* (de Candolle) Bentham (1837) Apiaceæ.

An orthographic variant introduced in *J. Linn. Soc., Bot.*, **28**: *t. 43* (1891). The correct spelling is *Leucolena.*

LEUCOLENA

Ridley

J. Linn. Soc., Bot.   **28**(195): 340 (1891).

Not *Leucolaena* Bentham (1837) Apiaceæ.

ETYMOLOGY: Greek for white and cloak, blanket or covering. Refers to the fused sepals and petals.

TYPE SPECIES: *Leucolena ornata* Ridley

Not validly published because of a prior use of the name, this homonym was replaced by *Didymoplexiella.*

LEUCORCHIS

Blume

Mus. Bot. **1**(2): 31 (1849).

Not *Leucorchis* E. Meyer (1839) Orchidaceæ.

ETYMOLOGY: Greek for white and orchid. Referring to the plant's lack of green coloration.

TYPE SPECIES: *Leucorchis sylvatica* Blume

Now recognized as belonging to the genus *Didymoplexis*, *Leucorchis* Blume was previously considered to include eight saprophytes inhabiting a region from Afghanistan to the southwestern Pacific Archipelago. These erect plants have leafless, unbranched stems, each with several, triangular bracts. The small, pale olive-green to pink flower has its dorsal sepal united to the petals for half of their length. The lateral sepals are similarly attached for a short distance to the petals. The yellow-white, broad, entire lip, attached to the column foot, has raised sides with a row of yellow warts down the center. The above type name is now considered a synonym of *Didymoplexis pallens* Griffith.

LEUCORCHIS

E. Meyer

Preuss. Pflanzengatt. 50 (1839).

ETYMOLOGY: Greek for white and orchid. Descriptive of the numerous, tiny, white flowers.

TYPE SPECIES: *Leucorchis albida* (Linnaeus) E. Meyer
(*Satyrium albidum* Linnaeus)

Not validly published, this name is most often referred to *Pseudorchis*.

LEUCOSTACHYS

Hoffmannsegg

Verz. Orchid. 26 (1842).

ETYMOLOGY: Greek for white and ear of grain or a spike. Referring to the congested, cylindrical inflorescence of the small flowers.

TYPE SPECIES: *Leucostachys procera*
(Ker Gawler) Hoffmannsegg
(*Neottia procera* Ker Gawler)
This type name is now considered a synonym of
Goodyera procera (Ker Gawler) Hooker;
basionym
Neottia procera Ker Gawler

Now recognized as belonging to the genus *Goodyera*, *Leucostachys* was previously considered to include one terrestrial widespread in low to mid elevation, forests and woodlands from southern China (Anhui to Xizang), India, Thailand, Indonesia, Malaysia, Hong Kong and the Philippines. This exceedingly variable plant has erect, unbranched stems that are leafy at the base. The numerous-

flowered inflorescence has small, insignificant, uniformly white flowers. The concave dorsal sepal and petals converge, forming a hood over the short, fleshy column. The roundish to sac-like, entire lip has bristly hairs within, a pair of white tubercles at the base, and a recurved tip.

NOTE: There is no copy of Hoffmannsegg's publication available today. This name is based on a secondary report published in *Linnaea*, **16**(Litt.): 234 (1842).

LICASTE

An orthographic variant introduced in *Sin. Fl. Cuzco*, 197 (1941). The correct spelling is *Lycaste*.

LICHENORA

Wight

Icon. Pl. Ind. Orient. (*Wight*) **5**(1): t. 1738 (1851).

ETYMOLOGY: Greek for lichen. Refers to this species' flat, tiny pseudobulbs which adhere to tree branches upon which they grow and appear like lichens.

TYPE SPECIES: *Lichenora jerdoniana* Wight

Now recognized as belonging to the genus *Porpax*, *Lichenora* was previously considered to include one epiphyte found in mid elevation, evergreen forests of southwestern India and Andaman Islands. This tiny plant has numerous, flattened, disc-shaped pseudobulbs often covering tree branches; each has two, ovate leaves covered with blotched markings. The short, hairy, one- to two-flowered inflorescence has tiny, tubular, red-purple to brown, hairy flowers. The boat-shaped sepals are united forming a long tube (small petals are found inside) with a triangular-shaped mouth. The obscurely trilobed lip has a tongue-like projection with a ragged or notched margin.

LICHINORA

An orthographic variant introduced in *Icon. Pl. Ind. Orient.* (*Wight*), **5**(1): 18 (1851). The correct spelling is *Lichenora*.

LICHONORA

An orthographic variant introduced in *Prakt. Stud. Orchid.*, 260 (1854). The correct spelling is *Lichenora*.

LICHTERVELDEA

An orthographic variant introduced in *Hort. Donat.*, 191 (1858). The correct spelling is *Lichterveldia*.

LICHTERVELDIA

Lemaire

Ill. Hort. **2**: sub 59 (1855).

ETYMOLOGY: In honor of Louis de Lichtervelde (*fl.* 1850s), a Belgian count, political advisor, and chief cabinet minister to King Leopold I whose son Louis Hermann Marie Ghislain (1889-1959) was the bibliographer for King Leopold II of Belgium.

TYPE SPECIES: *Lichterveldia lindleyi* Lemaire

Now recognized as belonging to the genus *Cuitlauzina*, *Lichterveldia* was previously considered to include one epiphyte or sometimes terrestrial found in mid elevation, oak-pine forests of Mexico (Michoacán, Sinaloa and Jalisco). This plant has roundish, compressed, glossy pseudobulbs becoming wrinkled with age, subtended by several, overlapping sheaths, each with two dull or glossy, pale green, leathery leaves. The hanging, numerous to few-flowered inflorescence has waxy, long-lived, flat-faced, fragrant flowers that are typically white or pink, and sometimes dotted with dark pink. The bright mauve or pink, kidney-shaped, entire lip has a long, yellow claw, and is shallowly notched at the tip. The flowers have a short, erect, winged column. The above type name is now considered a synonym of *Cuitlauzina pendula* Lexarza.

LIDMODORUM

An orthographic variant cited in *Syn. Bot., Suppl.*, 9 (1870). The correct spelling is *Limodorum*.

LIGEOPHILA

Garay

Bradea **2**(28): 194 (1977).

Orchidoideæ • Cranichideæ • Goodyerinæ

ETYMOLOGY: Greek for shadowy or twilight and loving. In reference to the preferred deep, shady habitat of the plants.

TYPE SPECIES: *Ligeophila stigmatoptera*
(Reichenbach f.) Garay
(*Physurus stigmatopterus* Reichenbach f.)

Nine sympodial terrestrials or epiphytes are found in wet, low elevation, shady forests, swamp and river banks from southern Mexico to Peru, Venezuela, northern Argentina (Misiones) and western and north-eastern Brazil (Rondônia, Amazonas, Amapá and Pará). These stout, creeping plants have terminally erect stems, each with a loosely arranged rosette of oblong, thinly textured leaves. The long, numerous to few-flowered, smooth to hairy, pink-brown inflorescence has

Currently Accepted   Validly Published   Invalidly Published   Published Pre-1753   Superfluous Usage   Orthographic Variant   Fossil

Orchid Genera • 222

small, yellow to dark green flowers that have narrow sepals and petals with dark red tips. The uppermost, complex, white, trilobed or bilobed lip has broad side lobes with inrolled margins; and the narrow, small to tiny, bilobed midlobe then widens out with two horn-like protuberances, and has a small spur. The flowers have a short, incurved column.

LIMADORUM

An orthographic variant introduced in *Amer. Gard. Cal.*, 72, 461 (1806). The correct spelling is *Limodorum*.

LIMATODES

An orthographic variant introduced in *Gen. Sp. Orchid. Pl.*, 252 (1833). The correct spelling is *Limatodis*.

LIMATODIS

Blume

Bijdr. Fl. Ned. Ind.   **8**: 375, t. 62 (1825).

ETYMOLOGY: Greek for meadow or wet place. Refers to the plant's preferred growing habitat.

TYPE SPECIES: *Limatodis pauciflora* Blume

Now recognized as belonging to the genus *Phaius*, *Limatodis* was previously considered to include eight terrestrials found in low to mid elevation, dense forests and along river banks of Malaysia and Indonesia (Java and Sumatra). These large plants have spectacular, often four-foot (1.2 m) tall, close-set stems, each with foot long (30 cm), pleated leaves. The several, few-flowered inflorescences, borne from the stem below the leaves, have large, pale yellow flowers opening in succession, with violet spots. The orange-yellow, entire lip also has red spots arranged in lines and has a long, slender, pink spur that narrows evenly to the tip. Both species are now included as synonyms of *Phaius pauciflorus* (Blume) Blume.

LIMIDORNM

An orthographic variant introduced in *Mus. Bot.*, **2**(12): 178 (1852). The correct spelling is *Limodorum*.

LIMMODORUM

An orthographic variant introduced in *Dict. Sci. Nat.*, **36**: 305 (1825). The correct spelling is *Limodorum*.

LIMNAS

Ehrhart

Beitr. Naturk. (Ehrhart)   **4**: 146 (1789).

Not *Limnas* Trinius (1820) Poaceæ.

ETYMOLOGY: Greek for marsh or standing water. Refers to its bog-like habitat.

Or Greek Mythology. *Limniads* were protective nymphs ("nymph" is a Greek word meaning young woman, and was considered an important part of Greek religion) of lakes, marshes and swamps.

TYPE SPECIES: *Limnas paludosa* (Linnaeus) Ehrhart
(*Ophrys paludosa* Linnaeus)

Now recognized as belonging to the genus *Hammarbya*, *Limnas* was previously considered to include one terrestrial found in cold, low to mid elevation, sphagnum bogs of northern Europe, across northern Russia to Japan, northwestern United States (Alaska) and across Canada. This minute plant has a slender, erect, unbranched stem (sometimes a group will tightly cluster) with small, fleshy leaves that envelope the base of the small, roundish pseudobulb. Small, bulb-like bulbils develop on the front margins of the leaves, fall off and develop into new plants. The tall, twisted, numerous-flowered inflorescence has tiny, yellow-green flowers. The small, entire lip is uppermost, and has dark green veins. The flower has a minute, erect column.

LIMNODORUM

An orthographic variant introduced in *Rep. State Board Geol. Michigan*, 282 (1907). The correct spelling is *Limodorum*.

LIMNORCHIS

Rydberg

Mem. New York Bot. Gard.   **1**: 104 (1900).

ETYMOLOGY: Greek for pool or standing water and orchid. From the bog habitat of some of the species.

LECTOTYPE: *Limnorchis hyperborea* (Linnaeus) Rydberg
(*Orchis hyperborea* Linnaeus)

Now recognized as belonging to the genus *Platanthera*, *Limnorchis* was previously considered to include thirty terrestrials found in low elevation, boreal bogs or wet scrub from Greenland to Iceland, Canada, Alaska (US), far eastern Russia (Yakutiya to Kamchatka), Korea and northern Japan. These stout, erect plants have unbranched stems, each with several, narrow leaves that clasp the stem below, then become bracts upward. The tall, densely packed, few-flowered inflorescence has small, white, yellow, green to blue-green flowers. The dorsal sepal and petals converge, forming a hood over the short column. The narrow, entire lip tapers to a point and has a cylindrical or slightly club-like, hanging spur.

LIMODERUM

An orthographic variant introduced in *Fl. Brit. Ind.*, **6**: 37 (1890). The correct spelling is *Limodorum*.

LIMODONUM

An orthographic variant introduced in *Orchids India*, ed. 2, 388 (1999). The correct spelling is *Limodorum*.

LIMODORON

Dodoens

Stirp. Hist. Pempt.   552 (1616).

Pre-1753, therefore not validly published in fulfillment of nomenclatural rules; this name is most often referred to *Limodorum* Boehmer.

LIMODORON

An orthographic variant introduced in *Fl. Belg. Foed.*, 170 (1781). The correct spelling is *Limodorum*.

LIMODORUM

Linnaeus

Sp. Pl. (Linnaeus), ed. 1   **2**: 950 (1753).

Name ICBN rejected vs. *Limodorum* Boehmer (1760) Orchidaceæ.

ETYMOLOGY: Greek for meadow and gift. Referring to the plant's common habitat.

LECTOTYPE: *Limodorum tuberosum* Linnaeus

Although validly published this rejected name is now referred to *Calopogon*.

LIMODORUM

Boehmer

Ludwig's Def. Gen. Pl., ed. 3   358 (1760).

Name ICBN conserved vs. *Limodorum* Linnaeus (1753) Orchidaceæ.

Epidendroideæ ⁂ Neottieæ

ETYMOLOGY: Greek for meadow and gift. Possibly referring to the fact that the plants sometimes occur in meadows.

The name is more than likely a literary error made by the herbalist Rembert Dodoens (1517-1585), who applied the name of *haemodoron* to this plant that was used by Theophrastus (373-287 BC) to denote a red-flowered parasitic plant of unknown identity.

Or Greek Mythology. *Leimoniads* were nymphs (spirits) of the meadow and flowers.

TYPE SPECIES: *Limodorum abortivum*
(Linnaeus) Swartz
(*Orchis abortiva* Linnaeus)

Three uncommon saprophytes are found in low to upper elevation, hill and montane oak-pine, oak-beech forests, open woodlands and nutrient-poor scrub from Austria to Spain, France to Turkey, western Africa (Morocco to Tunisia), Iran, Syria, Lebanon and Israel. These erect plants have stout, leafless, unbranched stems that easily attain heights of two feet (60 cm), each with several, leaf-like sheaths and scarcely has any chlorophyll. The few-flowered inflorescence has showy, mostly violet-purple to rare white flowers that do open widely. The erect dorsal sepal is concave; the widespreading lateral sepals are flat and the narrow petals are usually erect. The entire or obscurely lobed (at the tip) lip has a wavy, up-turned margin and a downward pointing, slender spur. The flowers have a forward curved, slender, erect column.

LIMONDORUM

An orthographic variant introduced in *Rad. Jugoslav. Akad. Znan.*, **21**: 23 (1872). The correct spelling is *Limodorum*.

LIMONIAS

Ehrhart

Beitr. Naturk. (Ehrhart)   **4**: 147 (1789).

ETYMOLOGY: Latin for a citrus-like fragrance.

TYPE SPECIES: *None designated*

Name published without a description. Today this name is most often referred to *Epipactis*.

LINDBLOMIA

Fries

Bot. Not.   **1843**(9): 134 (1843).

ETYMOLOGY: Dedicated to Alexis Edvard Lindblom (1807-1853), a Swedish traveler, founder and editor of the journal *Botaniska Notiser*.

TYPE SPECIES: *None designated*

Not validly published, these species are now referred to *Dactylorhiza* and *Platanthera*.

LINDHEIMINA

D. McDonald

Sweet-Scented Fl.   69, 88 (1895).

ETYMOLOGY: Named for Ferdinand Jacob Lindheimer (1801-1879), a Germany-born American naturalist, newspaper editor and publisher of *Neu Braunfelser Zeitung*. He collected plants in Texas for Ash Gray and George Engelmann.

TYPE SPECIES: *Lindheimina texana* D. McDonald

Name published without a description. This name was published as belonging to Orchidaceæ which it is not, but the name should be referred to *Lindheimera* (Asteraceæ).

LINDLEYALIS

Luer

Monogr. Syst. Bot. Missouri Bot. Gard. **95**: 258 (2004).

ETYMOLOGY: Honoring John Lindley (1799-1865), a British botanist, professor of botany, and the foremost orchidologist of his time who was the first to work out a classification system for orchids. A prolific botanical writer and founder-editor of the newspaper *The Gardeners' Chronicle*.

TYPE SPECIES: *Lindleyalis hemirhoda* (Lindley) Luer (*Pleurothallis hemirhoda* Lindley)

This type name is now considered a synonym of *Pleurothallis nuda* (Klotzsch) Reichenbach f.; basionym replaced with *Restrepia nuda* (Klotzsch)

Recognized as belonging to the genus *Pleurothallis*, *Lindleyalis* was proposed to include six epiphytes found in upper elevation, montane forests of the Andes from Venezuela to Bolivia. These small, tufted plants have erect, green or dark purple stems, each with a solitary, narrow to oblong, minutely bilobed leaf. The short, solitary to few-flowered inflorescence, borne at the leaf axils, has a nodding, green, bright to dull yellow or red flower; the united lateral sepals form a synsepal, and it has a large, forward curved dorsal sepal, and long, quite narrow petals. The red-striped, tongue-shaped, entire lip has an incurved margin covered with short hairs. The flowers have a tiny, yellow column.

LINDLEYELLA

Schlechter

Orchideen (Schlechter), ed. 1   414 (1914).
Not *Lindleyella* Rydberg (1908) Rosaceæ.

ETYMOLOGY: Dedicated to John Lindley (1799-1865), a British botanist, horticulturist, professor of botany at University College, London and a prolific botanical writer. And Latin for diminutive.

TYPE SPECIES: *Lindleyella aurantiaca* (Lindley) Schlechter (*Bifrenaria aurantiaca* Lindley)

Not validly published because of a prior use of the name, this homonym was replaced by *Rudolfiella*.

LINDORUM

An orthographic variant introduced in *Orchids India*, ed. 2, 190 (1999). The correct spelling is *Limodorum*.

LINDSAYELLA

Ames & C. Schweinfurth

Bot. Mus. Leafl.   **5**(2): 33 (1937).

ETYMOLOGY: Dedicated to Walter Rae Lindsay (1906-1997), an American-born director of the Panama Canal Zone Experimental Gardens who collected the type species. And Latin for diminutive.

TYPE SPECIES: *Lindsayella amabilis* Ames & C. Schweinfurth not *Fregea amabilis* Reichenbach f.

Now recognized as belonging to the genus *Sobralia*, *Lindsayella* was previously considered to include one epiphyte or terrestrial found in low elevation, hill forests of Panama. This slender plant has erect, woody stems, subtended by leaf sheaths, each with narrow, pleated, distichous leaves on the upper portion. On the lower portion of the stem the leaves are much smaller. The solitary, rarely two-flowered inflorescence, borne from the stem's tip, has a delicate, rosy-pink, magenta or deep red, short-lived flower. A triggering mechanism, most likely a temperature change, will cause all the flowers in a certain area to open simultaneously; the next day there will be none. The large, entire lip surrounds the column and has a bilobed tip with an irregular scalloped margin and a bright orange callus. The above type name is now considered a synonym of *Sobralia callosa* L.O. Williams.

LINGUELLA

D.L. Jones & M.A. Clements

Austral. Orchid Res.   **4**: 74 (2002).

ETYMOLOGY: Latin for tongue shaped and diminutive. Referring to the tiny, dark green appendages found on the anterior side of the dorsal sepal.

TYPE SPECIES: *Linguella nana* (R. Brown) D.L. Jones & M.A. Clements (*Pterostylis nana* R. Brown)

Recognized as belonging to the genus *Pterostylis*, *Linguella* was proposed to include five terrestrials found in low elevation, heavy clay to sandy soil of well shaded woodlands of southwestern Australia and New Zealand. These small, erect plants have slender, sometimes branched stems, each with a small, basal rosette. The solitary to rarely two-flowered inflorescence has a translucent, white to pale green flower with white or dark green, longitudinal stripes. The dorsal sepal and petals converge, forming a hood over the erect column. The narrowly clawed, green, bilobed lip has a wide space between the bilobes that terminates in narrow or thread-like tips which are held high above the hood.

Currently Accepted   Validly Published   Invalidly Published   Published Pre-1753   Superfluous Usage   Orthographic Variant   Fossil

Orchid Genera • 224

An orthographic variant introduced in *Hort. Brit. (Loudon)*, 370 (1830). The correct spelling is *Limodorum*.

LIPARIS

Richard

De Orchid. Eur.   21, 30, 38, *f. 10* (1817).

Name ICBN conserved vs. *Leptorkis* Thouars (1809) Orchidaceæ.

Epidendroideæ ⚘ Malaxideæ

ETYMOLOGY: Greek for oily, greasy or shining. Refers to the smooth, shining surface of the leaves typical of many of these species.

LECTOTYPE: *Liparis loeselii* (Linnaeus) Richard
(*Ophrys loeselii* Linnaeus)

Approximately four hundred sympodial terrestrials, epiphytes or lithophytes are found in low to upper elevation, hill to montane rain and open forests, marshes, fens and rocky crevices. This large, cosmopolitan genus is found all across Europe, Russia, Asia and both North and South America, but the largest concentration is found in New Guinea usually growing in shady, moist to sunny areas with high humidity. These plants are closely related to *Malaxis*, have ovoid, cylindrical to cone-shaped, slightly compressed pseudobulbs, subtended by leaf sheaths, with one to several, leathery leaves at the top. The leaves can be thinly textured, persist after they wither, or become leathery and fall off as they age. The often fleshy, numerous to few-flowered inflorescence has tiny, small to medium-sized, highly unusual flowers often colored a drab green, yellow-green, purple or even dull orange to often translucent. The oblong to narrow sepals have rolled margins and the narrow to thread-like petals are tubular or strongly rolled. The oblong to fan-shaped, entire or trilobed lip is the largest segment in most instances, has a notched to a wavy margin and a shallowly notched, abruptly blunt or suddenly terminated tip. The flowers have a small, slender to stout, club-shaped, incurved, weak to strongly winged column.

NOTE: The flowers usually have a strong, putrid fragrance that is used to attract its pollinators.

An orthographic variant cited in *Syn. Bot., Suppl.*, 9 (1870). The correct spelling is *Lyperanthus*.

An orthographic variant introduced in *Jorn. Sci. Math. Phys. Nat.*, **4**(14): 184 (1873). The correct spelling is *Lissochilus*.

An orthographic variant introduced in *Prakt. Stud. Orchid.*, 45 (1854). The correct spelling is *Lissochilus*.

LISOWSKIA

Szlachetko

Fragm. Florist. Geobot.   **3**(Suppl.): 121 (1995).

ETYMOLOGY: Dedicated to Stanislaw Lisowski (1924-2004), a Polish botanist, bryologist and professor at the Adam Michiewicz University in Poznan, Poland and author of *Les Asteraceæ dans la flore d'Afrique Centrale* and *Flora of central Africa*.

TYPE SPECIES: *Lisowskia katangensis*
(Summerhayes) Szlachetko
(*Malaxis katangensis* Summerhayes)

Now recognized as belonging to the genus *Malaxis*, *Lisowskia* was proposed to include five terrestrials, found in damp, shady, mid elevation, rain forests from Ivory Coast to Zambia and Madagascar. These inconspicuous, tiny plants, often forming large colonies, have short, erect, unbranched secondary stems, each with several thinly textured, ovate leaves located at mid-stem. The long, erect, few-flowered inflorescence has tiny, flat, translucent, pale green or pale yellow-green flowers, turning orange with age and has narrow segments with roundish tips. The orange-green, ovate, entire lip gives the flower the appearance of a little face peeking over a wall. The flowers have a short, stout, footless column.

An orthographic variant cited in *Pl. Alkaloids*, 160 (1996). The correct spelling is *Lissochilus*.

An orthographic variant introduced in *Syst. Veg. (Sprengel)*, ed. 16, **3**: 679, 720 (1826). The correct spelling is *Lissochilus*.

LISSOCHILUS

R. Brown ex Lindley

Bot. Reg.   **7**: *t. 573*, sub 578 (1821), and
Coll. Bot. (Lindley)   *t. 31* (1822).

Name ICBN rejected vs. *Eulophia* R. Brown (1821) Orchidaceæ.

ETYMOLOGY: Greek for smooth and lip. In reference to the uncrested lip found in many of these species.

TYPE SPECIES: *Lissochilus speciosus* R. Brown ex Lindley

Although validly published this rejected name is now referred to *Eulophia*. *Lissochilus* was considered to include thirty-nine terrestrials found in Madagascar, the Comoros and Mascarenes Islands, Ethiopia to South Africa, Saudia Arabia and Yemen. These widely varied plants have angular pseudobulbs, each with two or more, leathery, widespreading leaves which most often appear after flowering. The numerous to few-flowered inflorescence has showy, long-lasting, fragrant flowers. The trilobed lip has erect side lobes united to the base of the short column, and an oblong midlobe with a blunt or roundish tip.

An orthographic variant introduced in *Fortsetz. Allg. Teutsch. Gart.-Mag.*, **8**(5): 215 (1824). The correct spelling is *Lissochilus*.

An orthographic variant introduced in *Syll. Pl. Nov.*, **1**: 125 (1824). The correct spelling is *Lissochilus*.

LISTERA

R. Brown

Hortus Kew., ed. 2   **5**: 201 (1813).

Name ICBN conserved, type name also conserved; vs. *Listera* Adanson (1763) Fabaceæ, and vs. *Diphryllum* Rafinesque (1808).

ETYMOLOGY: In honor of Martin Lister (1638-1711), a British physician and naturalist with interests in zoology, entomology, paleontology, geology and botany. He wrote numerous medical publications and a major classification *Tractatus de Araneis* on spiders.

LECTOTYPE: *Listera ovata* (Linnaeus) R. Brown
(*Ophrys ovata* Linnaeus)

Now recognized as belonging to the genus *Neottia*, *Listera* was previously considered to include twenty terrestrials widespread in damp, seasonally flooded, low to mid elevation, deciduous woodlands and scrub in northern temperate zones of Iceland, Greenland, Canada (Yukon Territory to Nova Scotia and Newfoundland), the United States (Alaska, Washington to northern New Mexico, and Maine to West Virginia), Sweden to Turkey, and northern India to China, central Russia (West Siberia), Japan and Taiwan. These insignificant, dwarf plants have short, erect, slender to stout stems, each with two or rarely three, green leaves usually suffused with red. The outer surface of the stem and flowers is sometimes sticky to the touch. The erect, terminal inflorescence may have a hundred or more of these small to minute, green-yellow, dark-green, blue-green, maroon or pink-tan flowers appearing over a long blooming season. They have a somewhat unpleasant fragrance. The similar, incurved sepals and petals form a lax hood over the short, thick, erect or slightly arching, footless column. The long, bilobed or rare entire lip has a basal nectary located in a groove down the middle, is bound at the sides by ridges, and is shallowly notched or trilobed.

LISTERIA

Not *Listeria* Necker ex Rafinesque (1820) Rubiaceæ.

An orthographic variant introduced in *Anleit. Kenntn. Gew.*, ed. 2, **2**(1): 293 (1817). The correct spelling is *Listera*.

LISTROSTACHIS

An orthographic variant introduced in *Fl. Reunion*, 216 (1895). The correct spelling is *Listrostachys*.

LISTROSTACHYS

Reichenbach *filius*

Bot. Zeitung (Berlin) **10**: 930 (1852).

Epidendroideæ ⚘ Vandeæ • Angraecinæ

ETYMOLOGY: Greek for spade or shovel and a spike or ear of wheat. Alluding to the compact inflorescences and distichous flowers.

TYPE SPECIES: *Listrostachys jenischiana* Reichenbach f.

This type name is now considered a synonym of *Listrostachys pertusa* (Lindley) Reichenbach f.; basionym *Angraecum pertusum* Lindley

Two monopodial epiphytes are found in humid, mid elevation, evergreen forests from Sierra Leone to Cameroon, Gabon, Zaire, São Tomé and the Mauritius Islands. These small plants have short stems, each with narrowly oblong or narrow, dark green, equal or slightly unequal, bilobed leaves. The long, erect or spreading, numerous-flowered, stout inflorescence has small to tiny, two ranked, mostly white flowers with similar sepals and petals. The sharply tapering, entire lip has a stout, red spur minutely decorated with small, red spots or warts, suffused with red toward the base and club-like at the tip. The mouth of the spur is some distance from the base of the lip and the short, stout, wingless column.

NOTE: Many of the original *Listrostachys* species, that were erroneously included under this name, have now been transferred to various other genera.

LISTROTACHYS

An orthographic variant cited in *Lex. Gen. Phan.*, 334 (1904). The correct spelling is *Listrostachys*.

LOBELIA

Linnaeus

Sp. Pl. (Linnaeus), ed. 1   **2**: 929 (1753).

Not *Lobelia* P. Miller (1754) Goodeniaceæ.

ETYMOLOGY: Named in honor of Matthias de L'Obel (1538-1616), a Flemish-born British curator and botanist at the Botanical Gardens of Oxford, physician to King James I (1566-1625) and author of *Plantarum seu stirpium historia*.

TYPE SPECIES: *Not Orchidaceæ*

Linnaeus did not include this genus in Orchidaceæ; however, in 1858 there was one species, *Lobelia futatsbagusa*, placed in the genus by Siebold. Blume (*Flora Javæ*, 115 (1858)) credited the name in the synonym list of *Listera cordata*. This small *Lobelia* is a terrestrial found throughout the northern hemisphere in damp, montane moss laden forests and thickets. This slender plant has two heart-shaped leaves clasping the stem midway up. The numerous to few-flowered inflorescence has small to tiny flowers with similar sepals and petals. The narrow, entire lip has a cleft for about half of its length, and a basal disk with a pair of spreading horns. The flowers have a short, thick column. The species was mistakenly included in the Campanulaceæ (Bell flower) family by Philipp Franz von Siebold, but the name should now be correctly identified as a synonym of *Listera cordata* (Linnaeus) R. Brown.

LOBOGYNA

An orthographic variant cited in *Lex. Gen. Phan.*, 335 (1904). The correct spelling is *Lobogyne*.

LOBOGYNE

Schlechter

Mém. Herb. Boissier, ser. 2   **21**: 65 (1900).

ETYMOLOGY: Greek for lobe and woman or pistil. The column is toothed and horned beneath the stigma.

TYPE SPECIES: *Lobogyne bracteosa* (Reichenbach f.) Schlechter (*Appendicula bracteosa* Reichenbach f.)

Now recognized as belonging to the genus *Appendicula*, *Lobogyne* was previously considered to include two epiphytes found in low elevation, rain forests of New Guinea and the southwestern Pacific Archipelago. These plants have erect or hanging, congested stems subtended by the tubular bases of the dark green, unequally bilobed leaves. The hanging or sometimes laxly branched, multi-flowered inflorescence has small, pale yellow-green to green-white flowers. The yellow, fleshy, oblong to fiddle-shaped, entire or obscurely trilobed lip has a red base. The flowers have a short, footless column.

LOBUS

Clusius

Exot. (Clusius)   72 (1605).

ETYMOLOGY: Latin for small pod or lobes. Refers to the shape of the fruit.

TYPE SPECIES: *Lobus oblongus aromatica* Clusius

Pre-1753, therefore not validly published in fulfillment of nomenclatural rules; this trinomial name is most often referred to *Vanilla*. *Lobus* was previously considered to include one epiphyte found in low elevation, wet woodlands from the southeastern United States (southern Florida) to the Caribbean, central Mexico to Panama and Colombia to Brazil. This aerial or climbing plant has pencil-like, fleshy, branching stems with oblong leaves spaced along the stem. The numerous-flowered inflorescence has fragrant, short-lived, pale yellow-green flowers opening in succession. The triangular lip has yellow hairs and veins in the midline. The flowers have a long, slender, downy covered column. This name is usually now considered a synonym of *Vanilla plantifolia* Jackson ex Andrews.

NOTE: This species is often cultivated throughout the tropics as a source of culinary vanilla essence.

LOCHILUS

An orthographic variant introduced in *Syn. Pl. (D. Dietrich)*, **5**: 11 (1852). The correct spelling is *Leochilus*.

LOCKARTIA

An orthographic variant introduced in *Struct. Orchid.*, t. 13, f. 5 (1883). The correct spelling is *Lockhartia*.

LOCKHARDTIA

An orthographic variant introduced in *Hort. Donat.*, 172 (1858). The correct spelling is *Lockhartia*.

LOCKHARTEA

An orthographic variant introduced in *Hamburger Garten- Blumenzeitung*, **16**: 179 (1860). The correct spelling is *Lockhartia*.

Currently Accepted   Validly Published   Invalidly Published   Published Pre-1753   Superfluous Usage   Orthographic Variant   Fossil

Orchid Genera • 226

LOCKHARTIA

Hooker

Bot. Mag. **54**: t. 2715 (1827).

Epidendroideæ ⚘ **Cymbidieæ** • **Oncidiinæ**

ETYMOLOGY: Commemorating David Lockhart (x-1846), a British-born botanist who was the first superintendent of the Royal Botanic Gardens in Trinidad and who collected the type species.

TYPE SPECIES: *Lockhartia elegans* Hooker

This type name is now considered a synonym of *Lockhartia imbricata* (Lamarck) Hoehne; basionym *Epidendrum imbricatum* Lamarck

Twenty-seven tufted, evergreen, psygmoid epiphytes are found in wet, low elevation, rain forests extending from southern Mexico to Peru, Brazil and Trinidad. These plants have erect to hanging, remarkably flattened stems, each with numerous, closely overlapping, sometimes tooth-like leaves forming two ranks along the entire length of the stem. The several, short, numerous to few-flowered inflorescences are borne in small groups between the leaf axils near the stem tip. The flowers superficially resemble those of *Oncidium*. The small, mostly yellow (with red markings) or white flowers are borne singly or in airy panicles that may continue to produce for a long time. The entire or trilobed lip has narrow, incurved or recurved side lobes, and the oblong midlobe has a two to four-lobed margin. The flowers have a short, stout, footless column.

LODDIGESIA

Luer

Monogr. Syst. Bot. Missouri Bot. Gard. **105**: 251 (2006).

Not *Loddigesia* Sims (1806) Fabaceæ.

ETYMOLOGY: Named for Conrad Loddiges (1739-1789), a German-born British nurseryman (Hackney) specializing in orchids and author of *Catalogue of Plants,* in the collection of Conrad Loddiges & Sons, nurserymen, at Hackney, near London.

TYPE SPECIES: *Loddigesia quadrifida* (Lexarza) Luer (*Dendrobium quadrifidum* Lexarza)

Not validly published because of a prior use of the name, this homonym was replaced by *Pleurothallis.*

LOEFGRENIANTHUS

Hoehne

Bol. Inst. Brasil. Sci. **2**: 352 (1927), and *Arq. Bot. Estado São Paulo* **1**(4): 592 (1927).

Epidendroideæ ⚘ **Epidendreæ** • **Laeliinæ**

ETYMOLOGY: Honoring Johan Alberto Constantin Löfgren (1854-1918), a Swedish-born Brazilian botanist, a director of the Botanical Garden of Rio de Janeiro, and collector of the type species. And Latin for flower.

TYPE SPECIES: *Loefgrenianthus blanche-amesii* (Löefgren) Hoehne (*Leptotes blanche-amesii* Löefgren)

One uncommon, sympodial epiphyte is found in cool, low to mid elevation, hill to montane forests of eastern Brazil (Minas Gerais to Paraná) on moss laden trees (*Podocarpus* and *Araucaria*). This small plant has a zig-zagging, hanging, flexible and curved stem usually with a solitary, narrow to ovate, flat leaf. The short, solitary to few-flowered inflorescence has an attractive, large, white flower. The dorsal sepal and lateral sepals are narrow and the smaller, oblong petals are usually slightly narrower in width. The orange or yellow, minutely cup-shaped, entire lip has an incurved, notched margin with magenta fringe. It has an oblong disc forming a spur-shaped nectary at the base, and a thickened, notched callus in the center. The flowers have a white, long, wingless column with a bright magenta cap that is irregularly toothed.

LOELIA

An orthographic variant introduced in *Ann. Sci. Nat., Bot.,* sér. 3, **3**: 23 (1845). The correct spelling is *Laelia.*

LOMAX

Luer

Monogr. Syst. Bot. Missouri Bot. Gard. **105**: 88, f. 45 (2006).

ETYMOLOGY: Latin for without meaning. Referring to the unknown relationship to other species.

TYPE SPECIES: *Lomax punctulata* (Reichenbach f.) Luer (*Physosiphon punctulatus* Reichenbach f.) not *Pleurothallis punctulata* Rolfe

Recognized as belonging to the genus *Stelis, Lomax* was proposed to include one epiphyte found in mid to upper elevation, montane oak forests of southern Mexico (Chiapas), Guatemala, southward to Venezuela and Ecuador. This small plant has short, stout stems, subtended by thin, tubular sheaths, each with a solitary, erect, thick, oblong, leathery leaf. The long, wiry, few-flowered inflorescence has tiny, fleshy, yellow

flowers suffused or spotted purple below the middle that bloom simultaneously and successively. The concave dorsal sepal is united to the oblong, shallowly concave, lateral sepals for a short length forming a short, cylindrical tube and has small, purple petals that are minutely warty. The oblong, purple, obscurely trilobed lip has a thick, warty tip and is hinged to the end of the column foot. The flowers have a slender, slightly curved column.

LOMEZA

An orthographic variant introduced in *Bot. Centralbl.*, **80**(13): 504 (1899). The correct spelling is *Gomesa.*

LONCHITIS

Bubani

Fl. Pyren. (Bubani) **4**: 50 (1901).

Not *Lonchitis* Linnaeus (1753) Pteridophyta.

ETYMOLOGY: Greek for lance and closely connected. An ancient name used by the Greek physician Dioscorides (AD 40-c. 90) for a species of fern. And a name applied to a plant used by Pliny (AD 23-79) for a tongue-shaped grass - *Satyrion.*

TYPE SPECIES: *Lonchitis cordigera* (Linnaeus) Bubani (*Serapias cordigera* Linnaeus)

Not validly published because of a prior use of the name, this homonym was replaced by *Serapias.*

LONCHOPHYLLUM

Ehrhart

Beitr. Naturk. (Ehrhart) **4**: 148 (1789).

ETYMOLOGY: Greek for lance and leaf. Refers to the spear-like leaves.

TYPE SPECIES: *Serapias lonchophyllum* Linnaeus

Not validly published, this name is most often referred to as a synonym of *Cephalanthera.*

LONGIPHYLIS

Thouars

Hist. Orchid. Table 3, sub 3u, t. 98 (1822).

Name published without a description. Today this name is most often referred to *Bulbophyllum.*

LONGORA

An orthographic variant introduced in *Bot. Centralbl.*, **80**(13): 506 (1899). The correct spelling is *Gongora.*

LOPHIARELLA

Szlachetko, Mytnik & Romowicz

Polish Bot. J. **51**(1): 53 (2006)[2007].

ETYMOLOGY: *Lophiaris*, a genus of orchids and Latin for diminutive. Alluding to a similarity to *Lophiaris*.

TYPE SPECIES: *Lophiarella microchilum*
(Lindley) Szlachetko, Mytnik & Romowicz
(*Oncidium microchilum* Lindley)

Recognized as belonging to the genus *Trichocentrum*, *Lophiarella* was proposed to include two terrestrials or lithophytes found in mid elevation, montane rain forests from Mexico to Guatemala and Brazil to northeastern Argentina and Paraguay. These small plants have ovoid to rounded, compressed pseudobulbs, subtended by overlapping, stiff, triangular, leafless sheaths, each with a solitary, leathery, thick leaf. The multibranched, few-flowered inflorescence has small, long-lasting, brown, yellow or red-brown flowers heavily blotched red-brown. The entire or obscurely trilobed lip has small, white side lobes and a small, red speckled midlobe with a large, central callus. The flowers have an erect, slender, slightly curved, footless column.

LOPHIARIS

Rafinesque

Fl. Tellur. **4**: 40 (1836)[1837].

ETYMOLOGY: Greek for crest or mane. Descriptive of the fleshy crest found on the lip.

TYPE SPECIES: *Lophiaris fragrans* Rafinesque nom. illeg.
Trichocentrum lanceanum
(Lindley) M.W. Chase & N.H. Williams
(*Oncidium lanceanum* Lindley)

Now recognized as belonging to the genus *Trichocentrum*, *Lophiaris* was previously considered to include nineteen epiphytes found in low elevation, tropical and subtropical forests of the Guianas, Trinidad, Venezuela, Colombia to Peru and northern Brazil. These plants' pseudobulbs are either lacking or, if present, they are minute and strongly compressed, each with a solitary, leathery leaf spotted purple. The long, numerous-flowered inflorescences have showy, waxy, fragrant, long-lasting, yellow flowers heavily spotted or blotched brown-purple. The rose to violet purple, trilobed lip has small, purple side lobes; the oblong, white midlobe is broadly clawed and has a rich dark violet callus. The flowers have a short, stout, winged column that is green-yellow below and dark purple above.

LOPHOGLOTIS

Rafinesque

Fl. Tellur. **4**: 49 (1836)[1837].

ETYMOLOGY: Greek for crest and lip. From the conspicuous crest at the base of the lip.

TYPE SPECIES: *None designated*

A superfluous name proposed as a substitute for *Sophronitis*.

LOPHOGLOTTIS

An orthographic variant introduced in *Fl. Bras. (Martius)*, **3**(5): 313 (1893). The correct spelling is *Lophoglotis*.

LORLEANESIA

An orthographic variant introduced in *Bot. Centralbl.*, **76**(49): 345 (1898). The correct spelling is *Orleanesia*.

LOROGLOSSUM

Richard

De Orchid. Eur. 19, 25, 32 (1817).

ETYMOLOGY: Greek for a thong or strap and tongue. Descriptive of the long, twisted lip.

TYPE SPECIES: *Loroglossum hircinum*
(Linnaeus) Richard
(*Satyrium hircinum* Linnaeus)

Now recognized as belonging to the genus *Himantoglossum*, *Loroglossum* was previously considered to include two terrestrials found in low to mid elevation, scrub and grasslands from Britain to Romania, Spain to Turkey, northern Africa (Morocco to Tunisia) and Iraq. These tall, stout plants have unbranched stems, each with several dark green leaves that have wavy margins. The numerous-flowered inflorescence has long, purple-green flowers. These foul smelling flowers have an elongate, trilobed lip with the ribbon-like midlobe sharply bilobed at the tip. The oblong sepals and petals converge, forming a tight hood over the small column.

LOTHANIA

An orthographic variant introduced in *Gard. Chron.*, ser. 3, **75**: 173 (1924). The correct spelling is *Lothiania*.

LOTHIANIA

Kraenzlin

Gard. Chron., ser. 3 **75**: 173 (1924).

ETYMOLOGY: In honor of Schomberg Henry Kerr (1833-1900), a British Marquis de Lothian of Newbattle Abbey who provided the means for Florence Helen Woolword's (1855-1936) beautiful *Monograph of Masdevallia* to be printed.

TYPE SPECIES: *Lothiania mordax*
(Reichenbach f.) Kraenzlin
(*Masdevallia mordax* Reichenbach f.)
This type name is now considered a synonym of *Porroglossum mordax* (Reichenbach f.) H.R. Sweet; basionym
Masdevallia mordax Reichenbach f.

Now recognized as belonging to the genera *Poroglossum* and *Masdevallia*, *Lothiania* was previously considered to include two epiphytes found in upper elevation, montane forests of western Colombia and Venezuela. These plants have slender, erect, dark brown stems, each with narrow, leathery leaves. The few-flowered inflorescence has pale green to yellow flowers suffused purple, and the sepals usually end in long, thick tails that are densely spotted red-brown and have ragged margins. The large flowers bloom in succession. The pale green, tiny, rounded, entire lip has a deep purple disc. The flowers have a short, winged column.

LOTHONIANIA

An orthographic variant introduced in *Gard. Chron.*, ser. 3, **75**: 173 (1924). The correct spelling is *Lothiania*.

LOUISIA

An orthographic variant introduced in *Xenia Orchid.*, **1**: 204 (1856). The correct spelling is *Luisia*.

LOWIORCHIS

Szlachetko

Orchidee (Hamburg) **55**(3): 314 (2004).

ETYMOLOGY: In honor of Hugh Low (1824-1905), a British administrator in the Malay Peninsula who spent 30 years as a civil servant on the small island of Labuan. As a botanical collector he discovered many spectacular new orchids and other plants that were sent to Kew. And Greek for orchid.

TYPE SPECIES: *Lowiorchis lowiana*
(Reichenbach f.) Szlachetko
(*Cynosorchis lowiana* Reichenbach f.)

Recognized as belonging to the genus *Cynorkis*, *Lowiorchis* was proposed to include five terrestrials, epiphytes or lithophytes found in mid elevation, grasslands of eastern Madagascar. These small plants have short, erect, unbranched stems, subtended by brown, tubular sheaths, each with a solitary, narrow

Currently Accepted   Validly Published   Invalidly Published   Published Pre-1753   Superfluous Usage   Orthographic Variant   Fossil

Orchid Genera · **228**

leaf. The slender, few-flowered inflorescence has large, rose suffused flowers. The sepals, petals and spur are often green, but there are widespread differences in both the colors and patterns found on these flowers. The long, broad, trilobed lip has oblong side lobes equal to the midlobe, and the clawed, bilobed midlobe is deeply notched and has a slender spur. The flowers have a short column.

LOXOMA

Garay
Bot. Mus. Leafl. **23**(4): 183 (1972).
Not *Loxoma* R. Brown ex A. Cunningham (1837) Loxsomaceæ, and not orthographic variant *Loxsoma*.
ETYMOLOGY: Greek for slanting and having the nature of. Referring to the reclining nature of the column.
TYPE SPECIES: *Loxoma maculatum* (Dalzell) Garay
(*Micropera maculata* Dalzell)

Not validly published because of a prior use of the name, this homonym was replaced by *Loxomorchis*.

LOXOMORCHIS

Rauschert
Taxon **31**(3): 561 (1982).
ETYMOLOGY: *Loxoma*, a genus of orchids and Greek for orchid.
TYPE SPECIES: *Loxomorchis maculata*
(Dalzell) Rauschert
(*Micropera maculata* Dalzell)

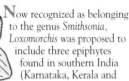

Now recognized as belonging to the genus *Smithsonia*, *Loxomorchis* was proposed to include three epiphytes found in southern India (Karnataka, Kerala and Tamil Nadu). These miniature plants have short stems with numerous roots. The inflorescence is not densely crowded but has fleshy, small, long-lasting and even slightly fragrant, creamy or dingy white flowers. The unusual lip looks like an English sidesaddle with two horns. The small, entire lip has an opening to the sac-like base between the two horns and is concealed by a downward hanging scale in the manner of saddle-flaps. The flowers have a short, stout, wingless, footless column.

LUDDEMANIA

An orthographic variant introduced in *Pescatorea*, **1**: t. 22 (1860). The correct spelling is *Lueddemannia*.

LUDDEMANNIA

An orthographic variant introduced in *J. Hort. Prat. Belgique*, **5**: 71 (1861). The correct spelling is *Lueddemannia*.

LUDISIA

A. Richard
Dict. Class. Hist. Nat **7**: 437 (1825).
Orchidoideæ · Cranichideæ · Goodyerinæ
ETYMOLOGY: The origin of the name is unknown but could possibly be named after the subject of an Ancient Greek elegy written by her widower.
LECTOTYPE: *Ludisia discolor* (Ker Gawler) A. Richard
(*Goodyera discolor* Ker Gawler)

One variable sympodial terrestrial or occasional lithophyte is found in humid, low to mid elevation, shady evergreen forests and along river banks from southern China (Yunnan to Hainan), Myanmar to Vietnam, Thailand and north central Indonesia (Anambas and Natuna islands) to the Philippines. This quite variable, creeping plant is most often grown for its beautifully iridescent, velvety, dark maroon foliage that has contrasting, metallic red or golden yellow veins. The erect or hanging plant has pink, red, green to brown with pale flecks, fleshy, twisted stems either lying on the ground or held upright, branching and rooting at nodes. The striking, dark green, almost black leaves are scattered along the creeping stem or in a loose rosette on upright stems and have brightly colored veins. The erect, hairy, numerous-flowered inflorescence has small, sparkling white, fragrant flowers. The dorsal sepal and petals converge, forming a hood over the glossy yellow column. The long, slender, footless column is twisted in the opposite direction of the lip. The flowers have a strangely twisted, yellow, entire to bilobed lip, united at the base of the column with a sac-like base and an oblong, cleft tip. This species has often been included in *Haemaria*.

LUECKELIA

Jenny
Austral. Orchid Rev. **64**(4): 15 (1999).
Epidendroideæ · Cymbidieæ · Stanhopeinæ
ETYMOLOGY: Named to honor Emil Lückel (1927-), a German print shop owner from Frankfurt and a former editor of the German orchid journal *Die Orchidee*.
TYPE SPECIES: *Lueckelia breviloba*
(Summerhayes ex E.W. Cooper) Jenny
(*Polycycnis breviloba* Summerhayes ex E.W. Cooper)

One slender, sympodial epiphyte is found in wet, humid, low to mid elevation, dense forests of Brazil (Amazonas, Pará, and Mato Grosso). This plant has oblong to ovoid pseudobulbs, each with several, broad, heavily veined, pleated leaves. The erect, numerous-flowered inflorescence has small, fragrant, yellow flowers with its narrow segments covered with small, red spots or bars. The long, narrow, white lip is

also sprinkled with several, red spots. The trilobed lip is smooth on the inside and quite hairy on the outside, and the unlobed hypochile is united to the base of the distinctly curved, slender, footless column. The broad, triangular epichile, connected under the hypochile, has downward curved margins and is usually covered by sparse, stiff, dark hairs.

LUEDDEMANIA

An orthographic variant introduced in *Repert. Spec. Nov. Regni Veg. Beih.*, **9**: 157 (1921). The correct spelling is *Lueddemannia*.

LUEDDEMANNIA

Linden & Reichenbach *filius*
Bonplandia **2**(23): 281 (1854).
Epidendroideæ · Cymbidieæ · Stanhopeinæ
ETYMOLOGY: Dedicated to a Mr. E.G. or G.A. Lüddemann (1821-1884), a German-born horticulturist, head gardner for J.P. Pescatore in Paris and a friend of both Linden and Reichenbach.
TYPE SPECIES: *Lueddemannia pescatorei*
(Lindley) Linden & Reichenbach f.
(*Cycnoches pescatorei* Lindley)

Two sympodial epiphytes are found in wet, low to mid elevation, hill and montane rain forests from Venezuela to Peru. These large, robust plants have clustered, ovoid, lightly ribbed, slightly compressed, one-noded pseudobulbs, each with long, narrow, pleated leaves heavily veined on the underside. The long, hanging, basal, densely packed, red-green, numerous-flowered inflorescence has sweetly fragrant, fleshy flowers. The red-brown sepals have red veins. The petals and lip are orange to bright yellow. The shortly clawed, waxy, red speckled, trilobed lip has erect, rounded side lobes. The triangular midlobe has a recurved, tapering tip and a basal callus with a flattened, hairy tooth. The flowers have a slender, slightly incurved, winged column.

LUEDEMANNIA

An orthographic variant introduced in *Gen. Pl. (Bentham & Hooker f.)*, **3**: 552 (1883). The correct spelling is *Lueddemannia*.

LUERANTHOS

Szlachetko & Margońska

Polish Bot. J. **46**(2): 117 (2001).

ETYMOLOGY: Honoring Carlyle August Luer (1922-). And Greek for flower.

TYPE SPECIES: *Lueranthos vestigipetalus*
(Luer) Szlachetko & Margońska
(*Pleurothallis vestigipetala* Luer)

Recognized as belonging to the genus *Andinia*, *Lueranthos* was proposed to include one epiphyte found in cool, upper elevation, montane forests of Venezuela, Colombia, Ecuador and Peru. This small, creeping plant has erect, stout stems, subtended by tubular sheaths, each with a solitary, erect, narrow, leathery leaf. The zig-zagged, few-flowered inflorescence has one, pale brown flower after another, opening in succession. The smooth, narrow, long, tapering sepals have hairy margins and the minute petals have short hairs. The long, narrow, thinly textured, hairy, translucent yellow, entire lip has inrolled side margins surrounding the long, slender, tubular, footless column that has a non-hooded tip and two small horns toward the base.

LUERELLA

Braas

Orchidee (Hamburg) **30**(3): 108 (1979).

ETYMOLOGY: Named to honor Carlyle August Luer (1922-), an American physician, orchidologist, author of numerous articles on Pleurothallidinæ and *The Orchids of North America and Canada*. And Latin for diminutive.

TYPE SPECIES: *Luerella pelecaniceps* (Luer) Braas
(*Masdevallia pelecaniceps* Luer)

Now recognized as belonging to the genus *Phloeophila*, *Luerella* was previously considered to include one epiphyte found in upper elevation, montane cloud forests of Panama. This small, tufted, clump-forming plant has erect stems, each with a solitary, leathery leaf. The several, erect, solitary-flowered inflorescences have a large, rigid, box-like, red flower that has a yellow, concave dorsal sepal; the lateral sepals (united for most of their length; synsepal) are covered with purple spots; the tiny petals are hidden inside. The tiny, entire lip has orange calli with purple spots. The flowers have a curved, yellow column.

LUISA

An orthographic variant introduced in *Gen. Pl. (Endlicher)*, 199 (1837). The correct spelling is *Luisia*.

LUISEA

An orthographic variant introduced in *Bot. Centralbl.*, **53**(51): 471 (1899). The correct spelling is *Luisia*.

LUISIA

Gaudichaud-Beaupré

Freycinet's Voy. Uranie, Bot. 426, t. 37 (1826)[1829].

Epidendroideæ · Vandeæ · Aeridinæ

ETYMOLOGY: Luis Váez de Torres (c. 1565-1640), a Spanish navigator, botanist, and illustrator who sailed the South Pacific and discovered the straits, named in his honor in 1606, thus proving that New Guinea was an island and not a part of the Australian subcontinent.

Or possibly dedicated to Luis de Torres (fl. 1490s), a Genoese linguist and botanist, who had to be baptized so that he could sail with Christopher Columbus. Never returning to Spain, he later settled in Cuba and there received a yearly salary as a representative for the Spanish government.

TYPE SPECIES: *Luisia teretifolia* Gaudichaud-Beaupré
This type name is now considered a synonym of
Luisia tristis (G. Forster) Hooker f.;
basionym
Epidendrum triste Hooker f.

Thirty-nine monopodial epiphytes are found in low to mid elevation, hill and montane forests distributed over a huge region from northern Korea, Japan, southern China (Yunnan to Hainan), northern India (Sikkim), Myanmar to Vietnam, Taiwan, Malaysia, Indonesia, the Philippines, northern Australia, New Guinea to New Caledonia and Fiji. These plants simulate the terete-leaved *Papilionanthe*, while the flowers often superficially resemble those of *Ophrys*. These erect or climbing plants have rigid, stout, noded stems often branching above the base forming a tufted habit, while other species form a single, long stem, each with several, fleshy leaves. The numerous-flowered inflorescence has small to medium-sized, fleshy, faintly foul smelling, waxy, long-lived flowers that continue to grow in size even after opening, often remarkably so. The yellow-green, stained and streaked sepals have various shades of red or maroon and small to large, usually green petals. The white, yellow or green, immobile, entire or lobed lip is a deep purple at the base and often streaked with paler colored veins. The kidney-shaped epichile has a broadly rounded tip and a four-angled hypochile portion. The flowers have a very short, fleshy, footless column.

LUISIOPSIS

C.S. Kumar & P.C.S. Kumar

Rheedea **15**(1): 46 (2005).

ETYMOLOGY: *Luisia*, a genus of orchids, and Greek for resemblance or likeness. Refers to a similarity to *Luisia*.

TYPE SPECIES: *Luisiopsis inconspicua*
(Hooker f.) C.S. Kumar & P.C.S. Kumar
(*Saccolabium inconspicuum* Hooker f.)

Recognized as belonging to the genus *Gastrochilus*, *Luisiopsis* was proposed to include one epiphyte found from northwestern India to Bangladesh. This plant has long, slender, sometimes branching stems, each with a few distichous, narrow, channeled leaves. The short, few-flowered inflorescence has tufts of small, yellow-green to green-white flowers with an erect, concave dorsal sepal, similar oblong, keeled lateral sepals and tiny, erect petals. The trilobed lip, united to the column base, has a purple spotted, sac-like hypochile and a heart-shaped, shortly clawed midlobe with a slightly bilobed tip. The flowers have an erect, stout column.

LUSIA

An orthographic variant introduced in *Orchid. Nilgiris*, 78 (1982). The correct spelling is *Luisia*.

LUZAMA

Luer

Monogr. Syst. Bot. Missouri Bot. Gard. **105**: 10 (2006).

ETYMOLOGY: The name is an anagram of Amaluza, a small town found in the upper Andes of southern Ecuador (Azuay Province) where the type species was collected.

TYPE SPECIES: *Luzama amaluzae* (Luer & Malo) Luer
(*Masdevallia amaluzae* Luer & Malo)

Recognized as belonging to the genus *Masdevallia*, *Luzama* was proposed to include thirty epiphytes found in mid to upper elevation, montane forests from Costa Rica to Bolivia with the largest group found in Ecuador. These small, tufted plants have short stems, subtended by thin, tubular sheaths, each with a solitary, elliptical, leathery leaf. The several, short, wiry, solitary-flowered inflorescence has a slender, yellow flower heavily striped red-brown, and blooms successively. The large sepals have thickened veins, minute, soft, pimple-like protuberances at the ovary, are united into an oblong, cup-shape and taper into slender tails. The small, oblong to narrow, entire lip is hinged to the column foot. The flowers have a small, slightly curved, more or less club-shaped column.

Currently Accepted | Validly Published | Invalidly Published | Published Pre-1753 | Superfluous Usage | Orthographic Variant | Fossil

LYCAST

An orthographic variant introduced in *Bot. Reg.*, **29**(Misc): 12 (1843). The correct spelling is *Lycaste*.

LYCASTE

Lindley
Edwards's Bot. Reg.
29(Misc.): 14, section no 64 (1843).

Epidendroideæ ⚘ Cymbidieæ • Maxillariinæ

ETYMOLOGY: A fanciful name, and according to Lindley (1843), *Lycaste* was a beautiful woman. This Greek name could have come from the anagram of the Greek for beautiful, *caliste*.

But according to **C. Lemaire** (1848), *Lycaste* was the wife of a man named Butes in ancient Greece famed for her beauty and nicknamed Venus. **Lempriére** (1808) states that *Lycaste* was a famous courtesan of Drepanum called Venus on account of her great beauty. She had a son called Eryx who was an excellent boxer but died when Heracles beat him in a match. **J. Hallett** (1993) claims that King Priam had no daughter by the name of *Lycaste*, but in a poem *Dionysiaca* by the Roman poet Nannos he states that the charming *Lycaste* was Nannos's daughter by a concubine and that she married Polydamas the son of Panthous and Phrontis. Also further study of **Julio-Claudian's** (AD 14-68) Roman mythology has a virgin hunter (*Lycaste*) from Crete who was led by *Latonia*, queen of the woods and stars.

LECTOTYPE: *Lycaste macrophylla*
(Poeppig & Endlicher) Lindley
(*Maxillaria macrophylla* Poeppig & Endlicher)
designated by A. Bullock, *Kew Bull.*, **13**: 254 (1958), and
Acuña, *Cat. Descr. Orquídeas Cuba.*, **60**: 165 (1939).

Fifty taxonomically perplexing, sympodial epiphytes, lithophytes or terrestrials are found in low to upper elevation, hill to montane forests and woodlands from Cuba, Haiti, Jamaica and central Mexico south to western Bolivia, Venezuela and the Guianas. These plants have clustered, thick to stout, ovoid pseudobulbs, each with a few large, pleated, deciduous leaves. The foliage is shed during winter or at the onset of new growth (only in the yellow-flowered *Lycastes*), often becoming spotted and yellow with age. The several, solitary-flowered inflorescences are borne from the base of the pseudobulb on leafless scapes. The unusually large, waxy, triangular, long-lasting, showy flowers are enchantingly fragrant or smell like old soap. The petals, often a different color from the widespreading sepals, arch over the trilobed lip. The midlobe of some species is fringed and in other species the lip is entire and finger-like. The side lobes usually enfold the long, slightly curved, winged or wingless column.

NOTE: Today these species are heavily utilized in hybridization with fascinating results.

LYCOCHILUS

An orthographic variant introduced in *Deutsch. Mag. Garten- Blumenk.*, **1849**: 245 (1849). The correct spelling is *Lissochilus*.

LYCOMORIUM

An orthographic variant introduced in *Orchid. Icon. Index*, **5**: 334 (1934). The correct spelling is *Lycomormium*.

LYCOMORMIUM

Reichenbach *filius*
Bot. Zeitung (Berlin)   **10**: 833 (1852).

Epidendroideæ ⚘ Cymbidieæ • Coelioposidinæ

ETYMOLOGY: Greek for wolf and hobgoblin. Refers to the large flower with its grotesque, fleshy lip.

TYPE SPECIES: *Lycomormium squalidum*
(Poeppig & Endlicher) Reichenbach f.
(*Anguloa squalida* Poeppig & Endlicher)

Six uncommon, sympodial epiphytes or terrestrials are restricted to very wet, low to mid elevation, hill and montane forests of Panama and Colombia to Peru. These robust plants have large, tightly clustered, ovoid to pear-shaped, slightly ribbed pseudobulbs, subtended by leaf-like sheaths, each with several, large, pleated, prominent veined leaves. The hanging, few-flowered inflorescence has showy flowers not opening widely. The fleshy, pale green-cream, pink to white flowers are externally and internally spotted red-brown. The somewhat concave sepals are united at the base forming a cup-shape. The entire lip, attached to the long, curved column foot, has two parts (rigid, erect epichile and a lobed, recurved hypochile that is trilobed at the tip). The flowers have a small, stout, wingless column.

LYEASTE

An orthographic variant introduced in *Refug. Bot.*, **2**(1): t. 131 (1872). The correct spelling is *Lycaste*.

LYPARIS

An orthographic variant introduced in *Séance Publique Soc. Argic.*, 194 (1852). The correct spelling is *Liparis*.

LYPERANTHUS

R. Brown
Prodr. Fl. Nov. Holland.   325 (1810).

Orchidoideæ ⚘ Diurideæ • Thelymitrinæ

ETYMOLOGY: Greek for mournful or sad and flower. Referring to the appearance or dull color of these orchids.

LECTOTYPE: *Lyperanthus suaveolens* R. Brown

Three sympodial terrestrials are found in damp, low elevation, hill scrub and sandy, open forests of extreme southwestern and southern coastal areas of Australia, Tasmania and New Zealand with a strong seasonal climate. These tall, erect plants, forming sparse colonies, have unbranched stems, each with one or two stiff, waxy, leathery leaves and large floral bracts. The tough, wiry to stout, few-flowered inflorescence has dull yellow-green to white, fragrant, short-lived flowers often marked with deep crimson spots and splashes. The long, narrow dorsal sepal forms a hood over the erect, incurved, slightly winged column. The curved, entire or trilobed lip has its nearest margins closely embracing the column; the distant margins are notched or fringed and have rows of overlapping calli. These long-lived flowers are often strongly fragrant in warm weather.

LYRAEA

Lindley
Gen. Sp. Orchid. Pl.   46 (1830).

ETYMOLOGY: Greek for lyre or fiddle shaped. In reference to the shape of the lip.

TYPE SPECIES: *Lyraea prismatica* (Thouars) Lindley
(*Bulbophyllum prismaticum* Thouars)

Now recognized as belonging to the genus *Bulbophyllum*, *Lyraea* was previously considered to include one epiphyte found in moss laden, mid elevation, montane rain forests of Réunion. This uncommon plant has oblong, sharply four-angled, yellow-green pseudobulbs, each with two small leaves. The several, erect, straggly, few-flowered inflorescences are held well above the leaves and have small, yellow flowers. The yellow, occasionally red-tinged, bilobed lip has its widely spaced tips curving sharply outward.

LYROGLOSSA

Schlechter

Beih. Bot. Centralbl. **37**(2): 448 (1920).

Orchidoideæ ⚘ Cranichideæ • Spiranthinæ

ETYMOLOGY: Greek for lyre and tongue. An allusion to the lyre (stringed musical instrument) shaped lip.

LECTOTYPE: *Lyroglossa grisebachii*
(Cogniaux) Schlechter
(*Spiranthes grisebachii* Cogniaux)
designated by Angely, *Fl. Analit. São Paulo*, **6**: 1277 (1973); cited by Szlachetko, *Fragm. Fl. Geobot.*, **39**: 122 (1994).

LECTOTYPE: *Lyroglossa bradei* Schlechter ex Mansfeld designated by Burns-Balogh, *Amer. J. Bot.*, **69**(7): 1132 (1982).

Two sympodial terrestrials are found in low to mid elevation, hill scrub, forests, woodlands and marshy grasslands of southern Mexico, Belize, Nicaragua, Trinidad, eastern Venezuela, the Guianas, Bolivia, southeastern Brazil (Minas Gerais to Paraná) and Paraguay. These plants have erect, unbranched stems, subtended by tubular sheaths, each with the small, cup-like leaves absent when in flower. The delicate, spiraled, hairy, few-flowered inflorescence has pale green, fleshy, nodding to erect, tubular flowers covered in soft hairs. The white, fiddle-shaped, shortly clawed, trilobed lip has two oblong, green calli or a basal margin. Has a diamond-shaped hypochile, a roundish, shallowly notched epichile and a minutely toothed to scalloped margin or is somewhat covered with small, soft protuberances. The flowers have a short, erect, small, rather massive column with an obscure foot.

LYSIAS

Salisbury

Trans. Hort. Soc. London **1**: 288 (1812).

ETYMOLOGY: Named for Lysias (459-380 BC), an Athenian orator and litigator from Syracuse (Sicily), whose most famous written speech was in the defense of a man charged with the destruction of a sacred olive tree.

TYPE SPECIES: *Lysias bifolia* (Linnaeus) Salisbury
(*Orchis bifolia* Linnaeus)

Now recognized as belonging to the genus *Platanthera*, *Lysias* was previously considered to include four terrestrials found in damp, rich humus of low to mid elevation, hill scrub and montane dense forests from eastern Canada (southern Ontario, New Brunswick, Nova Scotia, Prince Edward Island and Newfoundland), the northeastern United States (Maine to Pennsylvania) and down through the Appalachian Mountains (West Virginia to North Carolina) and Europe to eastern Russia (Kamchatka).

These erect, small plants have unbranched stems, each with two large, heart-shaped, basal leaves. The erect, numerous-flowered, scaly inflorescence has small, showy, white or pale green flowers. The lateral sepals widely curve backward behind the small, narrow petals. The slender spur is longer than the narrow, long, tapering, entire lip. The flowers have a tiny to large, stout column.

LYSIELLA

Rydberg

Mem. New York Bot. Gard. **1**: 104 (1900).

ETYMOLOGY: *Lysias*, a genus of orchids and Latin for diminutive. Thus alluding to a relationship to *Lysias*.

TYPE SPECIES: *Lysiella obtusata*
(Banks ex Pursh) Rydberg
(*Orchis obtusata* Banks ex Pursh)

Now recognized as belonging to the genus *Platanthera*, *Lysiella* was previously considered to include three terrestrials found in cold, low to mid elevation, woodland bogs and evergreen forests from northern Sweden to Finland, central and eastern Russia (Kamchatka), Alaska (US), Canada, the northeastern United States (Maine to New York, northern Michigan), and the central Rocky Mountains of the western United States (Oregon to Colorado). These erect, small plants have a solitary (rarely two), narrow leaf clasping the base of the unbranched stem. The few-flowered inflorescence has pale green-white to yellow flowers with widespreading lateral sepals. The narrow, tapering, entire lip has a grooved tip with a minute, downward hanging appendage. The flowers have a tapering spur and a tiny column.

LYSIMNIA

Rafinesque

Fl. Tellur. **4**: 43 (1836)[1837].

ETYMOLOGY: Supposedly named for a nymph, but none bearing this name can be found in classical literature. Nymphs were usually minor female deities or gods with each presiding over bodies of water, woods or other natural features. They were considered an important part of Greek religion.

TYPE SPECIES: *Lysimnia bicolor* Rafinesque nom. illeg.
Brassavola subulifolia Lindley

Now recognized as belonging to the genus *Brassavola*, *Lysimnia* was previously considered to include one epiphyte found in mid elevation, montane forests of Jamaica. This tall plant has robust, cylindrical pseudobulbs, each with a solitary, shiny, dark green, thickly fleshy, narrow, channeled leaf that tapers to a point. The erect to slightly arching, few-flowered

---

inflorescence has showy, creamy, white to pale green-white flowers that are nocturnally fragrant. The large, white, clawed, heart-shaped, entire lip has a long, tubular base and a recurved tip. The flowers have a short, erect, pale green column.

LYSSOCHILUS

An orthographic variant introduced in *Dict. Sci. Nat.*, **36**: 305 (1825). The correct spelling is *Lissochilus*.

SPEC. NAT. SYNARMOPHYTORUM. 133

PHADROSANTHUS. • *Faux-Epiderdre.* •

1474. CHAR. DIAGN. *Productum*, tubulatum, cujus pars inferior, diverfa; crinulato-cordata, quadrato-cordata, & reniformis.
CHAR. PEC. *Spadix*, fimplex.
Perigynanda propria, 4. 5-fepala.
Sepala: patula, repanda, undulata, obovata, inæqualia, ovato-oblonga, lanceolata.
Productum, tubulatum, cujus inferior pars crinulato-cordata, quadrato-cordata, reniformis.
Antheræ, 2, piftillo infertæ.
Stylus, brevis.
Stigma, infundibuliforme.
Germen, contortum, ypomenum.
Capfula, oblonga, 1-locularis, 3-valvis, polyfperma.
Proles in hac fpecie, fcapofæ.
Folia fimplicia. Quæd. Epidendr. Lin.
Obf. Fructificantes prolium diverfarum partes phadrofanthi etiam variæ: nam dantur quædam proles fepala exhibentes.repanda; aliæ: fepalis undulatis, obovatis, ovato-oblongis, tandem proles aliæ, fepala lanceolata profærentes. Inferior pars tubulati producti, quæ improprie nectarium, dicitur, crinulato-cordata, quadrato-cordata & reniformis.

EYDISANTHEMA. • *Eydifanthème.* •

1475. CHAR. DIAGN. *Productum*, breviter tubulatum. Hujus inferior pars, perampla, acuminato-cordata, bafin tubi amplectens.
Antheræ, 8, in cucullâ 4-loculari.
CHAR. PEC. *Spadice*, fimplex.
Perigynanda propria, 5-fepala; fingula, fepala, linearia, longa, patula, æqualia, quorum, 2, interiora, cæteris anguftiora.
Productum, breviter tubulatum, cujus inferior pars, ampla, acuminato cordata, erecta, bafin tubi columnaris amplectens.

I 3

Necker *Elementa Botanica*
3: page 133 (1790).

Currently Accepted   Validly Published   Invalidly Published   Published Pre-1753   Superfluous Usage   Orthographic Variant   Fossil

O r c h i d   G e n e r a • **232**

MACARANTHES

An orthographic variant introduced in *Bull. Sci. Nat. Geol.*, **22**: 282 (1830). The correct spelling is *Mycaranthes*.

MACCRAITHEA

M.A. Clements & D.L. Jones
Orchadian   **13**(11): 496 (2002).
ETYMOLOGY: Honoring Gerald McCraith (1940-), an Australian orchidologist, co-founder of the Australian Orchid Foundation, a creator of many *Odontoglossum* hybrids and a philanthropist.
TYPE SPECIES: *Maccraithea cuthbertsonii*
(F. Mueller) M.A. Clements & D.L. Jones
(*Dendrobium cuthbertsonii* F. Mueller)

Recognized as belonging to the genus *Dendrobium*, *Maccraithea* was proposed to include twelve epiphytes or terrestrials found in low to upper elevation, hill and montane grasslands, moss laden rock ledges, and cliff faces from New Guinea and Vanuatu to Fiji. These small, clump-forming plants have short, thick, roundish to spindle-shaped pseudobulbs, each with rough textured, dark green leaves. The leaves have prominent black warts on the upper surface and tinged purple below. The several, short, usually solitary-flowered inflorescences have a large, brightly colored (pink, white, bright red, magenta, yellow or orange) flowers that are extremely long lasting. The hood-shaped, blunt, obscurely entire to trilobed lip has upturned sides. The flowers have a short column.

MACDONALDIA

Gunn ex **Lindley**
Sketch Veg. Swan R.   **Appendix**: 50, *t. 9* (1840).
ETYMOLOGY: In honor of Charlotte Smith née Macdonald (1809-1838), an Australian who examined the orchids of Tasmania with great care and sent specimens to the South African-born Australian army officer and botanist Ronald Campbell Gunn (1808-1881).
LECTOTYPE: *Macdonaldia smithiana* Gunn ex Lindley

Now recognized as belonging to the genus *Thelymitra*, *Macdonaldia* was previously considered to include seven terrestrials principally found in low elevation, swamps and marshes of Australia, but a few species are found in Indonesia, New Guinea, the Philippines, New Zealand and Fiji. The flowers fully open only when exposed to bright sunlight. The wiry, zig-zagged, red, few-flowered inflorescence has small, pale yellow flowers. The smaller, entire lip is similar to the sepals and petals. The flowers have a slightly curved or erect, footless column. The above type name is now considered a synonym of *Thelymitra flexuosa* Endlicher.

MACODES

(Blume) Lindley
Gen. Sp. Orchid. Pl.   496 (1840).
Orchidoideæ ⚘ Cranichideæ • Goodyerinæ
ETYMOLOGY: Greek for long and denoting likeness. Alluding to the elongate midlobe of the lip.
TYPE SPECIES: *Macodes petola* (Blume) Lindley
(*Neottia petola* Blume)

Nine uncommon, sympodial terrestrials or occasional epiphytes are found in moist, low to mid elevation, rain forests, leaf litter and humus with low light and high humidity from Japan, Malaysia, eastern Vietnam, Indonesia, and New Guinea to the Solomon Islands. These jewel, evergreen orchids are grown mainly for their showy, attractively patterned, dark green to brown-green leaves. The plants have erect stems, each with the leaves sometimes suffused red, with varying degrees of silver to gold netting and are red-purple on the underside. The hairy, few-flowered inflorescence has small, asymmetric, dull-colored, white, brown to pink flowers, and the sepals' outer surfaces are hairy. The rusty-brown to white, trilobed lip (uppermost) has small side lobes; the midlobe has a narrow claw, twisted to one side. The flowers have a short, twisted, footless column.

MACRADENIA

R. Brown
Bot. Reg.   **8**: *t. 612* (1822).
Epidendroideæ ⚘ Cymbidieæ • Oncidiinæ
ETYMOLOGY: Greek for long or gland. Refers to the long stipe connecting the pollinia to the viscidium.
TYPE SPECIES: *Macradenia lutescens* R. Brown

Eleven inconspicuous sympodial epiphytes are found in low elevation, hill forests and woodlands from the southeastern United States (Florida), Mexico to Peru, the Bahamas, Cuba to Trinidad, the Guianas to Venezuela, Brazil and Paraguay. These small plants have clustered, cylindrical pseudobulbs, each with a solitary, fleshy or leathery, oblong leaf, borne from the pseudobulb tip. The hanging, few to numerous-flowered inflorescence has showy, small, dark maroon, pale orange, red to dull yellow flowers with yellow to white margins. The more or less spreading, narrow to oblong sepals and petals taper to a sharp point. The deeply trilobed lip has erect side lobes embracing the club-shaped, wingless, footless column and usually has a short, narrow midlobe with a shallow, basal callus, but several species have the midlobe distinctively curved to the side.

MACROCENTRON

An orthographic variant introduced in *Abh. Königl. Ges. Wiss. Göttingen*, **24**: 340 (1879). The correct spelling is *Macrocentrum*.

MACROCENTRUM

Philippi
Anales Univ. Chile   **36**: 200 (1870), and
Sert. Mendoc. Alt.   43 (1871).
Not *Macrocentrum* Hooker f. (1867) Melastomataceæ.
ETYMOLOGY: Greek for large and a spur. Referring to the rostellum, stigma and other processes that are attached to the column.
TYPE SPECIES: *Macrocentrum mendocinum* Philippi
This type name is now considered a synonym of
Habenaria gourlieana Gillies ex Lindley

Not validly published because of a prior use of the name, this homonym was replaced by *Habenaria*.

MACROCHILON

An orthographic variant introduced in *Orchid.-Buch*, 320 (1892). The correct spelling is *Macrochilus*.

MACROCHILUM

An orthographic variant introduced in *Orchid.-Buch*, 320 (1892). The correct spelling is *Macrochilus*.

MACROCHILUS

Knowles & Westcott

Fl. Cab.   **1**: 95, *t. 45* (1837).

Not *Macrochilus* C. Presl (1836) Campanulaceæ.

ETYMOLOGY: Greek for large or long and lip. An allusion to the unusually large, conspicuous lip.

TYPE SPECIES: *Macrochilus fryanus*
Knowles & Westcott

This type name is now considered a synonym of
Miltonia spectabilis Lindley

Not validly published because of a prior use of the name, this homonym was replaced by *Miltonia*.

MACROCHYLUS

An orthographic variant introduced in *Prakt. Stud. Orchid.*, 263 (1854). The correct spelling is *Macrochilus*.

MACROCLINIUM

Barbosa Rodrigues

Gen. Sp. Orchid.   **2**: 236, *t. 605* (1882).

Epidendroideæ ⚬ Cymbidieæ • Oncidiinæ

ETYMOLOGY: Greek for large or long and a little bed. Descriptive of the prominent clinandrium of some species.

TYPE SPECIES: *Macroclinium roseum*
Barbosa Rodrigues

Thirty-eight sympodial epiphytes are found in moist to humid, hot to cool, low to mid elevation, hill to montane forests from southern Mexico to Peru and Brazil. These fan-shaped, twig-like plants have tiny, compressed pseudobulbs or are submonopodial without any pseudobulbs, each usually have several, laterally flattened, rigid, fleshy, distichous leaves that are somewhat purple spotted. Sometimes the bases of the leaves are thickened forming a small pseudobulb. The often branched, thin to thread-like, erect or hanging, numerous to few-flowered inflorescence has small to miniature, short-lived, slightly fragrant, almost translucent pale green or white flowers suffused pale pink or rose-red.

The erect dorsal sepal is slightly concave and the long, narrow lateral sepals and petals have a drooping habit. The long-clawed, trilobed lip has narrow side lobes, and the narrowly ovate, concave, toothed, white midlobe has a violet spot at the midpoint. The flowers have a long, straight, slender, club-shaped column.

MACROCLINIUM

Barbosa Rodrigues ex Pfitzer

Nat. Pflanzenfam.   **2**(6): 220 (1889).

Name published without a description. Today this name is most often referred to *Macroclinium* Barbosa Rodrigues.

MACRODAENIA

An orthographic variant introduced in *Rad. Jugoslav. Akad. Znan.*, **21**: 95 (1872). The correct spelling is *Macradenia*.

MACROLEPIS

A. Richard

d'Urville's *Voy. Astrolabe*   **2**: 25, *t. 19* (1833).

ETYMOLOGY: Greek for large or long and scale. Referring to the numerous large floral bracts.

TYPE SPECIES: *Macrolepis longiscapa* A. Richard

Now recognized as belonging to the genus *Bulbophyllum*, *Macrolepis* was previously considered to include one epiphyte found in low elevation, rain forests of New Guinea, Fiji, Vanuatu and the Solomons. This erect, creeping plant has a few-flowered inflorescence borne from the base of the pseudobulb. The lemon-green flowers, opening one at a time, have an unpleasant fragrance and purple lines or blotches at their base. The tapering, maroon, trilobed lip has short, erect side lobes, a long, tongue-shaped midlobe that is yellow at the tip and base. The flowers have a small, yellow-white column.

MACROLINIUM

An orthographic variant cited in *Lex. Gen. Phan.*, 345 (1904). The correct spelling is *Macroclinium*.

MACROPLECTRUM

Pfitzer

Nat. Pflanzenfam.   **2**(6): 208, 214 (1889).

ETYMOLOGY: Greek for large or long and a spur. Descriptive of the long spur at the base of the lip.

TYPE SPECIES: *Macroplectrum sesquipedale*
(Thouars) Pfitzer
(*Angraecum sesquipedale* Thouars)

Now recognized as belonging to the genus *Angraecum*, *Macroplectrum* was previously considered to include twenty epiphytes found in humid, low to upper elevation, hill and montane forests with most species found in Madagascar, Comoros, Seychelles and the Mascarenes islands. These extraordinary plants have long or short stems, each with several, short, thick, narrow, leathery, bilobed leaves. The numerous to solitary-flowered inflorescence has small to quite large, pale white-green, green or yellow-green, long-lasting flowers with usually wide-spreading sepals and petals. The shell- or boat-shaped, entire lip is usually quite concave with a prominent spur of various lengths. The base of the lip is clasped around the small, stout, footless column.

MACROPODANTHUS

L.O. Williams

Bot. Mus. Leafl.   **6**(5): 103 (1938).

Epidendroideæ ⚬ Vandeæ • Aeridinæ

ETYMOLOGY: Greek for large or long, a foot and flower. Referring to the long column foot.

TYPE SPECIES: *Macropodanthus philippinensis*
L.O. Williams

Six uncommon, monopodial epiphytes are found in low to mid elevation, hill and montane forests from eastern India (Andaman and Nicobar Islands), Thailand, Malaysia and Indonesia (Sumatra, Java and Borneo) to the Philippines. Vegetatively similar to *Pteroceras*, but these differ only in their flower structure. These miniature to small plants have short stems, each with thick, fleshy, oblong to narrow, unevenly bilobed leaves arranged in two rows. The clustered, numerous-flowered inflorescences have small, sweetly fragrant, white, pale yellow to green flowers opening simultaneously. The inner surfaces of the petals and sepals have a white tinge and are covered with small, crimson spots or blotches. The mobile, trilobed lip, hinged at a right angle to the long column foot, has raised or narrow side lobes, a small, triangular midlobe that has different ornaments on the blade at the entrance to the large, cylindrical spur. The flowers have an erect, stout column.

Currently Accepted   Validly Published   Invalidly Published   Published Pre-1753   Superfluous Usage   Orthographic Variant   Fossil

O r c h i d   G e n e r a   • 234

MACROSTEPIS

Thouars

Hist. Orchid. Table 3, sub 3p, *t. 83* (1822).

Name published without a description. Today this name is most often referred to *Beclardia*.

MACROSTOMIUM

Blume

Bijdr. Fl. Ned. Ind. **7**: 335, *t. 37* (1825).

ETYMOLOGY: Greek for large or long and mouth. Alluding to the appearance of the flower that when opened has a yawning mouth.

TYPE SPECIES: *Macrostomium aloefolium* Blume
This type name is now considered a synonym of *Dendrobium aloefolium* (Blume) Reichenbach f.; basionym *Macrostomium aloefolium* Blume

Now recognized as belonging to the genus *Dendrobium*, *Macrostomium* was previously considered to include one epiphyte found in low elevation, hill scrub and forests of Myanmar to Vietnam, Malaysia, Thailand, Indonesia, the Philippines and New Guinea. This compact, tangled plant has clumped stems, each with short, bract-like leaves that overlap in two rows, subtending the long, red stem and are often purple. The plant is erect when young and later becomes hanging with age. The solitary-flowered inflorescence, borne from a cluster of bracts on the leafless portion of the stem, has a minute, white to creamy flower. The sepals and petals are bent backward, with or without purple-red stripes. The trilobed lip has small, oblong side lobes and a notched, flared, bilobed midlobe. The flowers have a small column.

MACROSTOMUM

An orthographic variant introduced in *Gen. Pl. (Bentham & Hooker f.)*, **3**: 499 (1883). The correct spelling is *Macrostomium*.

MACROSTYLIS

Breda

Gen. Sp. Orchid. Asclep., fasc. I *t. 2* (1828).
Not *Macrostylis* Bartling & H.L. Wendland (1824) Rutaceæ.

ETYMOLOGY: Greek for long and column or style. Refers to the unusual long length of the column.

TYPE SPECIES: *Macrostylis disticha* Breda
This type name is now considered a synonym of *Corymborkis veratrifolia* (Reinwardt) Blume; basionym *Hysteria veratrifolia* Reinwardt

Not validly published because of a prior use of the name, this homonym was replaced by *Corymborkis*.

MACROTIS

Breda

Gen. Sp. Orchid. Asclep., fasc. IIII, n.s. . (1830).
Not *Macrotis* Rafinesque (1834) Ranunculaceæ.

ETYMOLOGY: Greek for large or long and ears. Refers to the lobes.

TYPE SPECIES: *Macrotis anceps* Breda
This type name is now considered a synonym of *Ceratostylis anceps* Blume

Now recognized as belonging to the genus *Ceratostylis*, *Macrotis* was previously considered to include one epiphyte found in mid elevation, shady forests of Indonesia (Java). This plant has clustered, slender pseudobulbs, each with a solitary, small, slender, pencil-like leaf. The short, solitary-flowered inflorescence, borne from sheaths at the base of the leaf, has a small, pale orange flower. The small, entire lip is narrow at the base, usually curved and almost beak-like. The flowers have a short column.

MACRURA

(Kraenzlin) Szlachetko & Sawicka

Orchidee (Hamburg) **54**(3): 331 (2003).

ETYMOLOGY: Latin for large. Referring to the large showy flowers of the type species.

TYPE SPECIES: *Macrura perbella*
(Reichenbach f.) Szlachetko & Sawicka
(*Habenaria perbella* Reichenbach f.)

Recognized as belonging to the genus *Habenaria*, *Macrura* was previously considered to include seven terrestrials found from Sudan to Angola, Zambia and Cameroon. These erect plants have long or short, unbranched stems, each with several, narrow leaves that proceed up the stem, gradually changing into large, leafy bracts. The few to numerous-flowered inflorescence has large, showy, green to white flowers. The erect dorsal sepal is spoon or hood-shaped and the lateral sepals are bent backward. The bilobed petals are both unequal in size and form. The trilobed lip has various sized side lobes, a narrow midlobe and a long spur. The flowers have a short, massive column.

MADISONIA

(Luer) Luer

Monogr. Syst. Bot. Missouri Bot. Gard. **95**: 258 (2004).

ETYMOLOGY: Honoring Michael T. Madison (1948-), an American botanist, editor of *Aroideana*, now a retired carpenter, who collected the type species while collecting flora in Ecuador and Peru.

TYPE SPECIES: *Madisonia kerrii* (Braga) Luer
(*Pleurothallis kerrii* Braga)

Recognized as belonging to the genus *Pleurothallis*, *Madisonia* was proposed to include one epiphyte found in upper elevation, montane forests of northeastern Peru and western Brazil in the Amazon river basin. This small to tiny, erect plant has erect stems, subtended with ribbed sheaths, each with a solitary, elliptical, thick, leathery leaf that often lies prone. The long, few-flowered inflorescence has dark purple flowers blooming successively. The lateral sepals are united for most of their length and have narrow, veined petals. The tiny, trilobed lip has two rounded, erect side lobes, a long, tongue-shaped midlobe with a thick, warty callus and a minute, green-purple spur. The flowers have a tiny, creamy, curved column that is purple-tinged along the edges.

MAELENIA

Dumortier

Not. Maelenia 17 (1834), and
Mém. Acad. Roy. Sci. Belgique **9**: 13, *t. 10* (1834).

ETYMOLOGY: Dedicated to Philippe Marie Guillaume Vandermaelen (1795-1869), a Belgian cartographer, nursery owner and author of *Dictionaire Géographique du Luxembourg* who, along with his brother, Jean-François (1797-1872), was the first to flower this species that won a prize at the Floral Society of Brussels Horticultural Exposition.

TYPE SPECIES: *Maelenia paradoxa* Dumortier

Now recognized as belonging to the genus *Cattleya*, *Maelenia* was previously considered to include one epiphyte found in low elevation, coastal forests and woodlands of south-eastern Brazil (Rio de Janeiro to Santa Catarina). This plant has tall, compressed pseudobulbs becoming furrowed with age, subtended by several, membraneous sheaths, each with two narrow, rigid, leathery leaves. The erect, few-flowered inflorescence has waxy, heavily fragrant, long-lived and variable colored flowers. The typically yellow-green or olive-green flowers are often suffused purple-brown and has similar shaped sepals and petals. The white, somewhat tubular, trilobed lip is rosy suffused, and inside the yellow throat has radiating red veins. The above type name is now considered a synonym of *Cattleya forbesii* Lindley.

MAEROSTYLIS

An orthographic variant cited in *Etym.-Bot.-Handw.-Buch*, ed. 1, 549 (1852). The correct spelling is Macrostylis.

MALACHADENIA

Lindley

Edwards's Bot. Reg.
25(Misc.): 67, section no. 110 (1839).

ETYMOLOGY: Greek for weak or soft and gland. In reference to the soft character of the glands associated with the pollen masses.

TYPE SPECIES: *Malachadenia clavata* Lindley

Now recognized as belonging to the genus *Bulbophyllum*, *Malachadenia* was previously considered to include one epiphyte found along the low elevation, coastal forests of Brazil (São Paulo and Rio de Janeiro). This small plant has ovate pseudobulbs spaced along the rhizome, each with a solitary, leathery leaf. The erect, few-flowered inflorescence, borne from the pseudobulb base, has dull green flowers sprinkled brown-red and has minute, green petals. The mobile, fleshy, dark brown, entire lip tapers to a point. The above type name is now considered a synonym of *Bulbophyllum malachadenia* Cogniaux.

MALACHENIA

An orthographic variant introduced in *Edwards's Bot. Reg.*, **25**(Misc.): 67, section no. 110 (1839). The correct spelling is *Malachadenia*.

MALANIS

An orthographic variant introduced in *Exot. Fl.*, **3**(27): sub 179 (1825). The correct spelling is *Malaxis*.

MALAXIS

Solander ex Swartz

Prodr. (Swartz) **8**: 119 (1788), and
Kongl. Vetensk. Acad. Nya Handl. **21**: 233 (1800).

Epidendroideæ ⚘ Malaxideæ

ETYMOLOGY: Greek for softening or tender. Referring to the soft, tender texture of the leaves.

LECTOTYPE: *Malaxis spicata* Swartz
designated by Britton & Brown, *Ill. Fl. N.U.S.*, ed 2, **1**: 570 (1913).

LECTOTYPE: *Malaxis rheedii* Swartz
not validly designated by Ascherson, *Fl. Prov. Brandenb.*, **1**: 699 (1864).

A taxonomically complex genus with over four hundred usually sympodial terrestrials or rare epiphytes that are found in low to upper elevation, mixed and moss laden hill forests to montane evergreen forests from cold temperate climates to the hot tropics. These often creeping plants are cosmopolitan in their distribution (North America to South America, Europe and Africa) with the largest group found from China, Korea, Japan, Taiwan, Pakistan to Vietnam, Indonesia, the Philippines, northern Australia and the southwestern Pacific Archipelago, but are absent from New Zealand. All the species have pseudobulbous stems and some species are grown just for their colorful, thinly textured, shiny, deep purple, pleated, deciduous leaves and stems. The erect, compact, numerous to few-flowered inflorescence (can be cylindrical or flat-topped) has typically tiny, dull-colored, green, orange, yellow, brown, pink or dark purple flowers. The large, entire or trilobed lip is bilobed or split at the tip and may have an entire or toothed margin. The larger sepals are reflexed and the thread-like petals often curl behind the lip, giving the pollinator free access to the short column. Leaf color is an unreliable character, as many species exist in two distinct color forms, often both yellow-green and purple. These species differ from *Liparis* with their spurless lip not attached to the short to long, or short, stout, footless column.

MALLEOLA

J.J. Smith & Schlechter ex Schlechter

Repert. Spec. Nov. Regni Veg. Beih.
1(13): 979 (1913).

Epidendroideæ ⚘ Vandeæ • Aeridinæ

ETYMOLOGY: Latin for little hammer. Referring to the hammer-shaped, prominent spur on the lip.

LECTOTYPE: *Malleola sphingoides* J.J. Smith

Twenty-nine monopodial epiphytes or lithophytes are widespread in shady, low to mid elevation, seasonally rainy to evergreen montane forests from India to New Guinea and the Philippines. These tiny, often climbing plants have long to short, flattened stems subtended by leaf sheaths. The often red tinged leaves are arranged in two rows. The few-flowered inflorescence, borne from the leaf axils, has small, insignificant, thinly textured, usually drooping, white, orange to pale yellow-green, long-lived, fragrant flowers suffused purple, red or mauve; usually facing in all directions on the inflorescence. The trilobed lip, fused to the short, stout, footless column, has low, rounded side lobes, a small, fleshy, narrow midlobe that is strongly recurved, and a cone-like or sac-shaped spur.

MANIELLA

An orthographic variant introduced in *Westafr. Kautschuk-Exped.*, 276 (1900). The correct spelling is *Manniella*.

MANILLE

An orthographic variant introduced in *Bull. Fed. Soc. Hort. Belgique*, **5**: 139 (1864). The correct spelling is *Vanilla*.

MANNIELLA

Reichenbach *filius*

Otia Bot. Hamburg., fasc. 2   109 (1881).

Orchidoideæ ⚘ Cranichideæ • Manniellinæ

ETYMOLOGY: In honor of Gustav Mann (1836-1916), a German-born British forest engineer, botanist and explorer of Cameroon and the Gulf of Guinea; and later served as forestry administrator in northeastern India (Assam). And Latin for diminutive.

TYPE SPECIES: *Manniella gustavi* Reichenbach f.

Two uncommon, sympodial terrestrials are found in shady, mid elevation, evergreen forests, grasslands and swamps from Sierra Leone to Tanzania. These tall, slender plants have short, unbranched stems, each with an attractive rosette of deep green, white mottled, broad leaves with long petiolates. The erect, slender, numerous-flowered inflorescence has small, white, brown or pink, smooth or hairy flowers not opening widely. The helmet-shaped dorsal sepal and petals converge, forming a hood over the small column. The lateral sepals are united to one another. The long, obscurely bilobed lip, united below the lateral sepals, has numerous, basal papillae, and an upturned margin with a pointed tip. The flowers have a small, bent, footless column with two tooth-like wings.

MANTHA

An orthographic variant introduced in *Orchideen (Schlechter)*, ed. 3, **6**(21-24): 337 (1975). The correct spelling is *Ulantha*.

MAPINGUARI

Carnevali & R.B. Singer

Lankesteriana   **7**(3): 525 (2007).

ETYMOLOGY: Named for a mythical creature living in the Amazon region of northern Brazil. This was a ground-dwelling, sloth-like creature with red fur and a series of unnatural characteristics like long claws, caiman-like skin, backward feet and a second mouth on its belly.

TYPE SPECIES: *Mapinguari longipetiolata*
(Ames & C. Schweinfurth) Carnevali & R.B. Singer
(*Maxillaria longipetiolata* Ames & C. Schweinfurth)

Recognized as belonging to the genus *Maxillaria*, *Mapinguari* was proposed to include four epiphytes found in low elevation, scrub from southeastern Brazil (São Paulo and Rio de Janeiro) and Costa Rica

| Currently Accepted | Validly Published | Invalidly Published | Published Pre-1753 | Superfluous Usage | Orthographic Variant | Fossil |

Orchid Genera • 236

and Panama. These plants have long, ovoid pseudobulbs, each with a solitary, narrow, channeled, slightly leathery leaf. The short, solitary-flowered inflorescence has a brown, maroon or creamy pink flower with wide-spreading, narrow to oblong sepals and slightly smaller, erect petals. The trilobed lip has small, erect side lobes and a tongue-like midlobe with a thickened, basal callus. The flowers have a small column with a flattened front.

MARDEVALLIA

An orthographic variant introduced in *Bot. Jahrb. Syst.*, **26**: 452 (1899). The correct spelling is *Masdevallia*.

MARGELLIANTHA

P.J. Cribb
Kew Bull. **34**(2): 329 (1979).
Epidendroideæ ⚬ Vandeæ • Aerangidinæ
ETYMOLOGY: Greek for pearl and flower. For the resemblance of the little flower to a glistening pearl.
TYPE SPECIES: *Margelliantha leedalii* P.J. Cribb

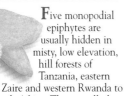

Five monopodial epiphytes are usually hidden in misty, low elevation, hill forests of Tanzania, eastern Zaire and western Rwanda to South Africa. These small plants have short, erect to hanging stems, each with distichous, leathery, unequally bilobed leaves. The several, hanging, few-flowered inflorescences have bell-shaped, delicate, glistening white, yellow-green or pale yellow flowers. They are most unusual because of their inrolled or incurved segments so that the flower remains partly closed. The fan-shaped, entire lip is notched at the tip, and the short, club-like spur is slightly incurved. The flowers have an erect, wingless, footless column with a bright green anther cap.

MARIARISQUETA

Guinea
Ensayo Geobot. Guin. Continent. Espan.
268, *f.* 46 (1946), and
Anales Jard. Bot. Madrid **6**(2): 469 (1946).
ETYMOLOGY: Named in honor of María Guinea née Arisqueta (fl. 1940s), wife of the Spanish botanist Emilio Guinea y López (1907-1985).
TYPE SPECIES: *Mariarisqueta divina* Guinea

Now recognized as belonging to the genus *Cheirostylis*, *Mariarisqueta* was previously considered to include one terrestrial found on damp, moss laden rocks in Sierra Leone, Ghana and Equatorial Guinea (Rio Muni). This small, creeping, erect plant has several, broad, ovate leaves spaced along the lower portion of the stem. The erect, hairy, few-flowered

inflorescence has small, white flowers with thinly textured, united sepals and petals. The long-clawed, bilobed lip is distinctly notched or toothed and has buff-colored spots on the basal claw. The flowers have a short column.

MARMODES

An orthographic variant cited in *Hist. Nat. Veg. (Spach)*, **12**: 177 (1846). The correct spelling is *Mormodes*.

MARSUPIARIA

Hoehne
Arq. Bot. Estado São Paulo, n.s. **2**(4): 69 (1947).
ETYMOLOGY: Greek for little bag or pouch. In reference to the bag-shaped sheaths at the base of the leaves, a distinct character of this genus.
TYPE SPECIES: *Marsupiaria iridifolia*
(Bateman ex Reichenbach f.) Hoehne
(*Dicrypta iridifolia* Bateman ex Reichenbach f.)
This type name is now considered a synonym of *Heterotaxis valenzuelana* (A. Richard) Ojeda & Carnevali; basionym replaced with *Pleurothallis valenzuelana* A. Richard

Now recognized as belonging to the genus *Heterotaxis*, *Marsupiaria* was previously considered to include six epiphytes or lithophytes found in wet, low to mid elevation, hill to montane forests from Cuba, Nicaragua to Ecuador, Venezuela and Brazil usually in full sunlight. These erect, short-stemmed plants have long, flat, leathery, blue-green, overlapping leaves arranged in a fan shape. The several, solitary-flowered inflorescences appear at the cleft of the leaves. The tiny, green-yellow to pale cream, spicy fragrant flowers do not open widely. The tongue-shaped, obscurely trilobed lip has a dark yellow, raised central keel with purple or maroon markings.

MASDAVALLIA

An orthographic variant introduced in *Timehri*, **5**: 171 (1886). The correct spelling is *Masdevallia*.

MASDESVALLIA

An orthographic variant introduced in *J. Soc. Centr. Hort. France*, ser. 3, **5**: 585 (1883). The correct spelling is *Masdevallia*.

MASDEVALIA

An orthographic variant introduced in *Fl. Peruv. Prodr.*, 122 (1794). The correct spelling is *Masdevallia*.

MASDEVALLIA

Ruiz & Pavón
Fl. Peruv. Prodr. 122, *t.* 27 (1794).
Epidendroideæ ⚬ Epidendreæ • Pleurothallidinæ
ETYMOLOGY: In honor of José Masdeval (x-1801), a Spanish physician in the court of King Charles III (1759-88) of Spain. He was an amateur botanist and he pioneered the hygienic methods used to treat fevers then rampant in the principality of Cataluña.
TYPE SPECIES: *Masdevallia uniflora* Ruiz & Pavón

There are over five hundred of these unusual epiphytes or less commonly found lithophytes or even terrestrials are found in cool, moist, low to usually upper elevation, hill and montane forests. Their range extends from Mexico and Belize to Bolivia, the Guianas, Venezuela and eastern Brazil with the greatest diversity found in Colombia. These plants have short, erect stems, subtended by thin, dry, over-lapping sheaths, each with a solitary, small to large, fleshy to leathery, oblong to narrow leaf. The several, solitary-flowered inflorescences have flowers varying in size from tiny to gigantic (1 ft/30 cm) tall. These showy, distinctive, triangular or tubular flowers are extraordinary for their amazing range of shapes, as well as the variety and beauty of the colors. The sepals, more or less unite at the base, forming a sepaline tube, and narrow toward the tips forming short to long-tails. They usually have small, narrow petals. The small to minute, straight or recurved, entire or trilobed lip is either stalked or shortly clawed. The flowers have a short, erect or curved, sometimes winged column that has a tiny segment tucked away in the sepaline tube.

MASDEVALLIANTHA

(Luer) Szlachetko & Margońska
Polish Bot. J. **46**(2): 117 (2001).
ETYMOLOGY: *Masdevallia*, a genus of orchids and Greek for flower. Referring to the similarity of the flowers to *Masdevallia*.
TYPE SPECIES: *Masdevalliantha masdevalliopsis*
(Luer) Szlachetko & Margońska
(*Pleurothallis masdevalliopsis* Luer)

Recognized as belonging to the genus *Pleurothallis*, *Masdevalliantha* was proposed to include two epiphytes found in cool, moist, mid to upper elevation, montane forests of Ecuador and Peru. These small, tufted plants have short, stout stems, subtended by tubular sheaths, each with a solitary, narrow, thick, leathery leaf. The several, solitary-flowered inflorescences have a pale green-white flower with tiny, roundish, translucent yellow petals. The concave dorsal sepal tapers into a long, slender tail; the ovate lateral sepals are united for a short length forming a cup shape and then also taper to a slender tail. The clawed, trilobed lip has tiny, roundish side lobes; a broad, recurved midlobe covered with tiny calli or warts; and a ragged margin. The flowers have a short, stout column.

MASDEWALIA

An orthographic variant introduced in *Dict. Sci. Nat.*, **36**: 304 (1825). The correct spelling is *Masdevallia*.

MASTIGION

Garay, Hamer & Siegerist
Nordic J. Bot. **14**(6): 635 (1994).

ETYMOLOGY: Greek for a diminutive of mastix, a small whip. In reference to the appearance of the of their long, whip-like tails.

TYPE SPECIES: *Mastigion appendiculatum*
(Rolfe) Garay, Hamer & Siegerist
(*Bulbophyllum appendiculatum* Rolfe)

Now recognized as belonging to the genus *Bulbophyllum*, *Mastigion* was proposed to include five epiphytes found in mid elevation, montane forests from northeastern India, Laos to Vietnam, Indonesia (Sumatra, Borneo) and the Philippines. These small plants have distinct pseudobulbs, each with a solitary, leathery leaf. The few-flowered inflorescence has a whorl or circlet of green and purple flowers with an unpleasant fragrance. The dorsal sepal has prominent, cilia-like appendages. The long, twisted lateral sepals are united along the outer margins, forming whip-like tails. The tiny petals have thick, fleshy hairs along their margins that are thread-like at the base, making them easily movable even in the slightest of breezes. The simple or entire lip is attached to the tip of the column foot, has erect margins and a three keeled disk. The flowers have a stout column.

MATURNA

Rafinesque
Fl. Tellur. **2**: 99 (1836)[1837].

ETYMOLOGY: Roman Mythology. Mātūta the goddess of dawn was more properly known as the goddess of childbirth and her festival, the Matralia, was attended only by married women.

TYPE SPECIES: *Maturna suaveolens*
(Lindley) Rafinesque nom. illeg.
(*Rodriguezia suaveolens* Lindley)
Gomesa foliosa (Hooker) Klotzsch ex Reichenbach f.
(*Pleurothallis foliosa* Hooker)

Now recognized as belonging to the genus *Gomesa*, *Maturna* was previously considered to include one epiphyte found in mid elevation, montane forests

of southeastern Brazil. This small plant has short, compressed pseudobulbs, each with several leaves. The hanging or bow-shaped, densely packed, numerous-flowered inflorescence has fragrant, showy, yellow flowers with similar sepals and petals. The entire lip is attached to the erect, footless column base.

MAXILARIA

An orthographic variant introduced in *Geogr. Estado Antioquia*, 81 (1885). The correct spelling is *Maxillaria*.

MAXILLARIA

Ruiz & Pavón
Fl. Peruv. Prodr. 116, t. 25 (1794).

Epidendroideæ ⬩ Cymbidieæ • Maxillariinæ

ETYMOLOGY: Latin for jawbone. An allusion to the yawning flowers and the fancied resemblance of the column foot and lip to the jaw of an ass (donkey).

LECTOTYPE: *Maxillaria ramosa* Ruiz & Pavón
designated by Garay & H.R. Sweet, *J. Arnold. Arbor.*, **53**: 524 (1972).
both of the following lectotypes are in conflict with protologue
LECTOTYPE: *Maxillaria longipetala* Ruiz & Pavón
designated by Acuña, *Cat. Descr. Orquideas Cuba.*, **60**: 171 (1939).
LECTOTYPE: *Maxillaria platypetala* Ruiz & Pavón
designated by Brieger & Hunt, *Taxon*, **18**: 602 (1969).

An estimated five hundred fifty-two sympodial or sometimes monopodial epiphytes, lithophytes or terrestrials have a wide range in low to upper elevation, hill and montane forests and scrub from the southeastern United States (southern Florida), Cuba to Trinidad, the Guianas and Mexico south to Argentina with the greatest development found in the Andes and Brazil. Varying greatly in structure, some species have clustered pseudobulbs; some have long stems between the pseudobulbs. Some species grow three or four feet (1 m) high, and are with or without pseudobulbs, other species are found in various combinations. Produced in vast numbers, each inflorescence has a solitary, small to large, sometimes showy flower with color varying widely from pure white to black-brown, with a range of fragrances from sweet to offensive. The lateral sepals are joined at the column foot, forming a chin-like protuberance and the petals are usually smaller. The concave, trilobed or entire lip is attached to the column foot, usually has a disk with a powdery or waxy callus. The flowers have an erect or curved, stout column that is semi-pencil-like, rarely winged, and usually with a conspicuous foot.

MAXILLARIELLA

M.A. Blanco & Carnevali
Lankesteriana **7**(3): 527 (2007).

ETYMOLOGY: *Maxillaria*, a genus of orchids and Latin for diminutive. Refers to a similarity to *Maxillaria*.

TYPE SPECIES: *Maxillariella diuturna*
(Ames & C. Schweinfurth) M.A. Blanco & Carnevali
(*Maxillaria diuturna* Ames & C. Schweinfurth)

Recognized as belonging to the genus *Maxillaria*, *Maxillariella* was proposed to include forty six epiphytes or occasional terrestrials found in low to upper elevation, hill and montane forests of southern Mexico (Chiapas) to northern Peru, Jamaica, Venezuela and southeastern Brazil. These plants have thin, wiry, laterally compressed, cane-like stems, completely subtended by overlapping, distichous sheaths, each with narrow, well-spaced, oblong leaves. The several, solitary-flowered inflorescence, borne from the leaf axils, has a small, yellow, red-yellow or yellow-green flower with widespreading, nerved sepals and smaller, oblong petals. The entire to obscurely trilobed lip has inrolled margins and a minutely papillose callus. The flowers have a stout, concave column.

MEASDENUS

An orthographic variant introduced in *Bot. Porto Rico*, 186 (1924). The correct spelling is *Mesadenus*.

MECAXÓCHITL

Petiver
Gaz. 72 (1704), and
Sahagún
Gen. Hist. Things New Spain **11**: 192 (1590).

Pre-1753, therefore not validly published in fulfillment of nomenclatural rules; this name is most often referred to *Tlilxochitl*.

MECOPODUM

D.L. Jones & M.A. Clements
Orchadian **14**(8: Sci. Suppl.): xiv (2004).

ETYMOLOGY: Greek for length and foot. Refers to the long column foot, elongated column wings and elongated rostellum.

TYPE SPECIES: *Mecopodum parvifolium*
(Lindley) D.L. Jones & M.A. Clements
(*Prasophyllum parvifolium* Lindley)

Recognized as belonging to the genus *Prasophyllum*, *Mecopodum* was proposed to include two terrestrials found in low elevation, along coastal margins of southwestern Australia. These small, erect plants have a slender, wiry, unbranched stem with a narrow, grass-like leaf fused for much of its length to the stem. The numerous to few-flowered

Currently Accepted   Validly Published   Invalidly Published   Published Pre-1753   Superfluous Usage   Orthographic Variant   Fossil

O r c h i d   G e n e r a   • **238**

inflorescence, breaking through the leaf, has white flowers with red-purple markings. The lateral sepals are united at the base with the short column forming a small pouch. The entire lip is attached to a short claw and is erect for much of its length. The flowers have a short, winged column that has a long, curved column foot with the lip attached to its tip.

MECOSA

Blume

Bijdr. Fl. Ned. Ind.   **8**: 403, *t. 1* (1825).

ETYMOLOGY: Greek for length. Descriptive of the long, linear lip.

TYPE SPECIES: *None designated*

Now recognized as belonging to the genus *Platanthera*, *Mecosa* was previously considered to include two terrestrials distributed in warm to cold, mid to upper elevation, moss laden montane ridges from Japan, Taiwan, Hong Kong, Thailand, Vietnam, Indonesia (Java and Sumatra) to New Guinea. These small plants have long, unbranched stems, each with several, well-spaced, dark veined, ovate leaves. The erect, few to numerous-flowered inflorescence has pale green flowers. The lateral sepals curve backward; the narrow, overlapped petals and dorsal sepal converge, forming a hood over the short, stout column. The triangular, entire lip has a long spur. The species are now considered as synonyms of *Platanthera angustata* (Blume) Lindley and *Platanthera blumei* Lindley.

MEDIOCALCAR

J.J. Smith

Bull. Inst. Bot. Buitenzorg, sér. 2   **7**: 3 (1900).

Epidendroideæ ⚘ **Podochileæ** • **Eriinæ**

ETYMOLOGY: Latin for middle and spur. From the hollowed out, sac-like shape of the lip, which folds at the base to form a sac-like structure.

TYPE SPECIES: *Mediocalcar bicolor* J.J. Smith
    This type name is now considered a synonym of
        Mediocalcar paradoxum subsp. *robustum*
            (Schlechter) Schuiteman;
            basionym
        Mediocalcar robustum Schlechter

Twenty-four sympodial epiphytes are found primarily to cool, low to upper elevation, hill and montane cloud forests of Indonesia (Sulawesi), New Guinea and the southwestern Pacific Archipelago. These small, creeping and scrambling plants, often forming dense clumps, have cone-shaped, one noded, pseudobulbous stems, subtended when young by sheaths, each with several, fleshy leaves. They are a rather aberrant genus with glossy, strange balloon-shaped, puffed flowers in brilliant combinations of red, yellow, green or white with bright contrasting colored tips. The

several, short, one- to two-flowered inflorescences have flowers lasting for a considerable time and are borne from the tip of old or developing pseudobulbs. The flowers range from bright red, pink to orange with usually yellow tips. The dorsal sepal is united with the lateral sepals for more than half their length. The base of the column foot forms a chin-like projection and the narrow, inconspicuous petals are hidden within the sepal structure. The shortly clawed, entire or obscurely trilobed lip has the hypochile separated from the sac-like epichile by a fleshy callus. The flowers have a short, fleshy, winged column.

MEDIOCALCAS

An orthographic variant cited in *Man. Dict. Fl. Pl.*, ed. 4, 415 (1914). The correct spelling is *Mediocalcar*.

MEDUSORCHIS

Szlachetko

Orchidee (Hamburg)   **55**(4): 487 (2004).

ETYMOLOGY: Greek Mythology. One of the three Gorgon sisters, who was once a beautiful maiden whose hair was her chief glory, but she dared to vie in beauty with Athena, who then deprived her of her charms, changed her beautiful ringlets into hissing serpents, and whose eyes would turn a beholder to stone if looked into. And Greek for orchid.

TYPE SPECIES: *Medusorchis ternatea*
            (Reichenbach f.) Szlachetko
            (*Habenaria ternatea* Reichenbach f.)

Recognized as belonging to the genus *Habenaria*, *Medusorchis* was proposed to include five terrestrials found in low to mid elevation, hill and montane forests from Japan to the Philippines, New Guinea, Laos, Thailand and eastern India (Andaman Islands). These erect plants have long or short, unbranched stems, each with narrow leaves that proceed up the stem, gradually changing into large, leafy bracts. The few to numerous-flowered inflorescence has green flowers. The spoon or hood-shaped dorsal sepal and the lateral sepals converge, forming a hood over the short column. The deeply lobed petals have thin, fringed segments. The trilobed lip has side lobes with numerous, long, slender segments, a narrow midlobe, with a long, narrow spur slightly swollen at the tip.

MEGACLINIUM

Lindley

Bot. Reg.   **10**: sub 832 (1824).

Name published without a description. Today this name is most often referred to *Megaclinium* Lindley.

MEGACLINIUM

Lindley

Bot. Reg.   **12**: *t.* 989 (1826).

ETYMOLOGY: Greek for wide or large and a little bed. Descriptive of the wide, flat spiraled inflorescence in which the flowers are embedded.

TYPE SPECIES: *Megaclinium falcatum* Lindley

Now recognized as belonging to the genus *Bulbophyllum*, *Megaclinium* was previously considered to include sixty-six epiphytes occasional lithophytes found in low to mid elevation, evergreen forests of Africa from Ghana to Rwanda. These plants have broad to ovoid pseudobulbs, each with two leathery leaves. The erect, smooth, stout, purple to green colored inflorescence often exceeds the length of the leaves. The tiny, quite variable, yellow-brown flowers, borne along both surfaces of the swollen or flattened rachis, are sprinkled red-brown on the outer surfaces and have a foul fragrance. The fleshy, oblong dorsal sepal has sharp edges, the lateral sepals are curved sideways, and the tiny petals are yellow tipped. The thinly textured, recurved, entire lip is purple-brown.

MEGALORCHIS

H. Perrier

Bull. Soc. Bot. France   **83**: 579 (1937).

Orchidoideæ ⚘ **Orchideæ** • **Orchidinæ**

ETYMOLOGY: Greek for big and orchid. Alluding to the large, beautiful flower.

TYPE SPECIES: *Megalorchis regalis*
            (Schlechter) H. Perrier
            (*Habenaria regalis* Schlechter)

One uncommon, sympodial terrestrial is found in mid elevation, montane moss laden forests of northern Madagascar. This erect plant has stout, leafy stems, each with numerous, spirally arranged, tongue-shaped leaves that become smaller upward. The tall, few-flowered inflorescence has large, strikingly pristine white flowers conspicuously veined. The spreading lateral sepals form with the base of the lip a large, chin-like projection, and the petals are united with the dorsal sepal, forming a hood over the short, broad column. The large, trilobed lip has erect side lobes; the clawed, tongue-shaped midlobe is strongly recurved in the middle, with a long, hanging spur.

MEGALOTIS

An orthographic variant introduced in *Phylogeny Classif. Orchid Fam.*, 207, 277 (1993). The correct spelling is *Megalotus*.

MEGALOTUS

Garay

Bot. Mus. Leafl. **23**(4): 184 (1972).

Epidendroideæ ⁄ Vandeæ • Aeridinæ

ETYMOLOGY: Greek for large or big and ear. Referring to the ear-like appendages on the column.

TYPE SPECIES: *Megalotus bifidus* (Lindley) Garay
(*Saccolabium bifidum* Lindley)

One monopodial epiphyte is widespread in low to mid elevation, forests and scrub of the Philippines. This small, often hanging plant has several, fleshy, oblong, unequally bilobed leaves suffused purple. The arching to hanging, numerous-flowered inflorescence has tiny, white, cream, pale yellow-green or purple flowers often marked or suffused dull purple. The white, trilobed lip has a purple spot at the base and small to tiny side lobes. The long, recurved midlobe has a sharply pointed, two prong tip, and a short spur constricted at the mouth with an inflated tip. The flowers have a short, winged, footless column.

MEGASTYLES

An orthographic variant cited in *Man. Dict. Fl. Pl.*, ed. 4, 416 (1919). The correct spelling is *Megastylis*.

MEGASTYLIS

(Schlechter) Schlechter

Bot. Jahrb. Syst. **45**: 379, 384 (1911).

Orchidoideæ ⁄ Cranichideæ • Chloraeinæ

ETYMOLOGY: Greek for large or big and pillar or column. Refers to the large, prominent column of the species.

LECTOTYPE: *Megastylis gigas*
(Reichenbach f.) Schlechter
(*Caladenia gigas* Reichenbach f.)

Six sympodial terrestrials or semi-lithophytes are found in wet, low to mid elevation, scrub and savannas for the most part endemic to New Caledonia. These orchids are of no particular beauty; some species grow in full sunlight and others in dense, shady rain forests. These robust, erect, clump-forming plants have short, unbranched stems (bud-scales at each node), each with several leaves per shoot. The leaf margins are entire or have minute, black teeth. The several, erect to arching, few-flowered inflorescences have green, white or bright yellow flowers. The concave dorsal sepal forms a hood over the slender, curved, footless, wingless column. The entire lip, attached by a short claw to the column base, has irregular rows of calli.

MEGEMA

Luer

Monogr. Syst. Bot. Missouri Bot. Gard. **105**: 11 (2006).

ETYMOLOGY: Greek for gigantic or large and a garment. Refers to the sheaths and bract.

TYPE SPECIES: *Megema cucullata* (Lindley) Luer
(*Masdevallia cucullata* Lindley)

Recognized as belonging to the genus *Masdevallia*, *Megema* was proposed to include seven epiphytes found in mid to upper elevation, montane forests from Colombia to eastern Ecuador. These large plants have stout stems, subtended by loose, overlapping sheaths, each with a solitary, leathery leaf. The solitary-flowered inflorescence has a large, dark maroon, rosy pink to yellow flower engulfed by a large, hood-shaped, floral bract. The sepals are slightly united into a rigid tube or cup shape and each tapers into long tails. The small, thick petals are more or less warty or are twisted. The entire lip has an epichile and hypochile sections. The flowers have an elongate, more or less club-shaped column.

MEIRACYLLIUM

Reichenbach *filius*

Xenia Orchid. **1**: 12, *t.* 6 (1854).

Epidendroideæ ⁄ Epidendreæ • Laeliinæ

ETYMOLOGY: Greek for stripling or little fellow. Undoubtedly in reference to its low, creeping habit.

TYPE SPECIES: *Meiracyllium trinasutum* Reichenbach f.

Two creeping, sympodial epiphytes or sometimes lithophytes are found in humid, seasonally dry, low to mid elevation, oak-pine forests, woodlands, savannas and coastal scrub of western Mexico (Sinaloa to Oaxaca), El Salvador and Guatemala. These charming, dwarf plants have short, creeping stems with the rhizomes subtended in persistent scales. Each growth has a small, solitary, broad to roundish, fleshy to leathery leaf. The short, few-flowered inflorescence, borne from the leaf axils, has delicate but large, showy, red-purple flowers. The erect, shorter petals are slightly wider than the widespreading sepals. The entire lip, fused to the inconspicuous column foot, is strongly concave or sac-like at the base and its upturned margin is lobed at the base. The flowers have a short, slender, wingless column.

MEIRACYLLUM

An orthographic variant introduced in *J. Roy. Hort. Soc.*, **3**(1): 120 (1886). The correct spelling is *Meiracyllium*.

MEJODA

An orthographic variant introduced in *Syn. Pl. (D. Dietrich)*, **5**: 168 (1852). The correct spelling is *Myoda*.

MELACHDENIA

An orthographic variant introduced in *Syn. Pl. (D. Dietrich)*, **5**: 14 (1852). The correct spelling is *Malachadenia*.

MELAENIA

An orthographic variant introduced in *Gen. Pl. (Endlicher)*, 194 (1837). The correct spelling is *Maelenia*.

MELAXIS

An orthographic variant cited in *Nomencl. Bot. (Steudel)*, ed. 2, **2**: 118 (1841). The correct spelling is *Malaxis*.

MELICLIS

Rafinesque

Fl. Tellur. **2**: 99 (1836)[1837].

ETYMOLOGY: Greek for honey and key or bolt. From the sac-like lip which collects liquid.

TYPE SPECIES: *Meliclis speciosa* (Hooker) Rafinesque
(*Gongora speciosa* Hooker)

Now recognized as belonging to the genus *Coryanthes*, *Meliclis* was previously considered to include one epiphyte found in low elevation, hill forests from Guatemala to Peru, Trinidad, the Guianas, Venezuela and Brazil. This large plant has squat, narrow, dark green, glossy pseudobulbs that become furrowed and ridged with age, each subtended by papery, gray bracts. Each pseudobulb has a solitary, narrow leaf prominently veined on the underside. The hanging, few-flowered inflorescence has large, grotesque, waxy, pale yellow flowers with an orange-red, bucket-shaped pouch often suffused red or tawny yellow. The flowers have a musky fragrance and last for only a few days. The hanging, clawed lip has three sections: the basal, concave hypochile is helmet-shaped and emerges from a slender, tube-like mesochile, that expands into the bucket-shaped, trilobed epichile with its claw-like midlobe almost touching the long, winged column. The above type name is now considered a synonym of *Coryanthes speciosa* Hooker.

Currently Accepted Validly Published Invalidly Published Published Pre-1753 Superfluous Usage Orthographic Variant Fossil

MELIORCHIS

S.R. Ramírez, Gravendeel, R.B. Singer,
C.R. Marshall & N.E. Pierce
Nature **448**: 1042 (2007).

ETYMOLOGY: The name of the Meliponine bees and
Greek for orchid. Refers to the type of extinct bees
that pollinated the sample.

TYPE SPECIES: *Meliorchis caribea*
S.R. Ramírez, Gravendeel, R.B. Singer,
C.R. Marshall & N.E. Pierce

One fossil based on the remains found
entombed in fossil amber. The unique
pollinium, entombed within the amber,
allowed the researchers to make a taxonomic
analysis. The fossil clearly falls within the
orchid family, sub-families, Orchidoideæ, and
subtribe Goodyerinæ. This sample was found
in a mine east of Stantiago, Cordillera
Septendtrional, Dominican Republic.

MELITTIAS

L'Obel
Icon. Stirp. 180, *f. 2* (1591).

Pre-1753, therefore not validly published in
fulfillment of nomenclatural rules; this name is
most often referred to *Orchis*.

MENADENA

Rafinesque
Fl. Tellur. **2**: 98 (1836)[1837].

ETYMOLOGY: Greek for crescent moon and gland.
Descriptive of the crescent shape of the glands.

TYPE SPECIES: *Menadena parkeri* (Hooker) Rafinesque
(*Maxillaria parkeri* Hooker)

Now recognized as belonging
to the genus *Maxillaria*,
Menadena was previously
considered to include
one epiphyte found in low to
upper elevation, hill and montane
forests of Venezuela, the Guianas,
Peru and northern Brazil. This
plant has clustered, ovoid, dark green,
generally roundish, somewhat compressed
pseudobulbs, subtended by large, gray sheaths,
each with a solitary, narrow leaf. The short,
solitary-flowered inflorescence has a thickly
textured, yellow to orange flower. The erect,
narrow, white petals have pale maroon
veining. The pale orange-yellow, trilobed lip
has a hairy, basal callus, erect side lobes and
an oblong, fleshy, white midlobe with a wavy
margin. The flowers have an erect, stout,
wingless column.

MENADENIA

An orthographic variant introduced in *Bull.
Soc. Roy. Bot. Belgique*, **43**: 340 (1906). The
correct spelling is *Menadena*.

MENADENII

An orthographic variant introduced in *Bull.
Soc. Roy. Bot. Belgique*, **43**: 342 (1906). The
correct spelling is *Menadena*.

MENADENIUM

Rafinesque
Fl. Tellur. **4**: 45 (1836)[1837].

Name published without a description.
Today this name is most often referred to
Menadenium Cogniaux.

MENADENIUM

Rafinesque ex Cogniaux
Fl. Bras. (Martius) **3**(5): 581 (1902).

ETYMOLOGY: Greek for crescent moon and bearing or
gland. An allusion to the crescent-shaped callus at
the base of the lip.

TYPE SPECIES: *None designated*

Now recognized as belonging to the
genus *Zygosepalum*, *Menadenium* was
previously considered to include four
epiphytes found in wet, low to mid
elevation, hill and montane forests
of the Guianas, Venezuela and
northern Brazil. These climbing plants
have ovoid to oblong pseudobulbs,
subtended by overlapping, distichous sheaths,
each with a solitary, oblong to narrow, dark
green leaf. The erect, usually solitary to few-
flowered inflorescence has a large, heavily
textured, showy, long-lived, fragrant flower
that is somewhat variable in its color range.
The large, shortly clawed, obscurely trilobed
lip is reflexed or hanging, and has a violet
basal calli. The flowers have a long, curved,
broadly winged column.

MENDONCELLA

A.D. Hawkes
Orquídea (Rio de Janeiro) **25**: 7 (1964).

ETYMOLOGY: Honoring Luyz de Mendonça e Silva
(1903-1974), a Brazilian physician, founder and
editor of the Brazilian orchid journal *Orquídea*. And
Latin for diminutive.

TYPE SPECIES: *Mendoncella grandiflora*
(A. Richard & Galeotti) A.D. Hawkes
(*Galeottia grandiflora* A. Richard & Galeotti)

A superfluous name proposed as a substitute
for *Galeottia*.

MENDONSELLA

An orthographic variant introduced in
Encycl. Cult. Orchids, 297 (1987). The correct
spelling is *Mendoncella*.

MENEPHORA

Rafinesque
Fl. Tellur. **4**: 46 (1836)[1837].

ETYMOLOGY: Greek for the crescent moon and
bearing. From its half-moon shaped sterile stamens.

TYPE SPECIES: *Menephora bicolor* Rafinesque
This type name is now considered a synonym of
Paphiopedilum purpuratum (Lindley) Stein;
basionym
Cypripedium purpuratum Lindley

Now recognized as belonging
to the genus *Paphiopedilum*,
Menephora was
previously considered
to include one
terrestrial or lithophyte found in
shady, low to mid elevation, steep
limestone cliffs of southeastern coastal China
(Hainan), Hong Kong and Vietnam. This
erect plant has short, unbranched stems, each
with basal leaves mottled dark and pale green.
The erect, purple, solitary-flowered inflorescence (with short, white hairs) has a flower
whose broad, white, dorsal sepal is streaked
with bold, brown-purple and the synsepal is
dark brown with the sides curved toward the
base. The long, purple-green petals are
sprinkled with small, black dots at the base
and wavy margins. The brown-purple, sac-like
lip has darker veins.

MENEZESIELLA

Chiron & V.P. Castro
Richardiana **6**(2): 103 (2006).

Epidendroideæ Cymbidieæ • Oncidiinæ

ETYMOLOGY: Honoring Lou Christian Menezes
(1943-), a Brazilian forestry engineer, ecologist and
botanist for the Instituto Brasileiro do Meio
Ambiente e dos Recursos Naturais Renovaveis
(Ibama). And Latin for diminutive.

TYPE SPECIES: *Menezesiella raniferum*
(Lindley) V.P. Castro & Chiron
(*Oncidium raniferum* Lindley)

Three sympodial epiphytes or
occasional lithophytes are found
in cool, moist, upper elevation,
montane forests of southeastern
Brazil (Rio de Janeiro and São
Paulo). These plants have oblong
to ovoid, clustered, flattened,
ribbed pseudobulbs, subtended by
several bracts, each with two narrow, thinly
leathery leaves. The erect, simple to branched,
numerous-flowered inflorescence has pale to
bright yellow, small to minute flowers with
similar, widespreading, bent backward sepals
and petals that are covered with red-brown
spots. The yellow, trilobed lip has small,
oblong to narrow, erect side lobes and a broad,
long, slightly bilobed midlobe with a large,
raised, pale brown to orange-brown, basal
callus. The flowers have a small, erect, short
column with ear-like appendages.

MENOPHORA

An orthographic variant cited in *Lex. Gen. Phan.*, 360 (1904). The correct spelling is *Menephora*.

MENOTRIS

An orthographic variant cited in *Syn. Bot.*, 106 (1870). The correct spelling is *Monotris*.

MESADENALLA

An orthographic variant introduced in *Acta Bot. Fenn.*, **169**: 259 (2000). The correct spelling is *Mesadenella*.

MESADENELLA

Pabst & Garay

Arch. Jard. Bot. Rio de Janeiro　**12**: 207 (1953).

Orchidoideæ ⚬ Cranichideæ • Spiranthinæ

ETYMOLOGY: *Mesadenus*, a genus of orchids and Latin for diminutive. Refers to the resemblance of the polliniae to those of *Mesadenus*.

LECTOTYPE: *Mesadenella esmeraldae*
　　(Linden ex Reichenbach f.) Pabst & Garay
　　(*Spiranthes esmeraldae* Linden ex Reichenbach f.)
This type name is now considered a synonym of *Mesadenella cuspidata* (Lindley) Garay; basionym replaced with
　　Spiranthes cuspidata Lindley

Seven sympodial terrestrials or lithophytes are usually found in leaf mold or humus in both tropical and subtropical, low elevation, hill forests and scrub from Guatemala to Costa Rica, Venezuela, the Guianas, Colombia to Bolivia and Brazil to northern Argentina (Misiones). These stout, variable plants have erect, unbranched stems, each with a flat, basal rosette of ovate leaves sometimes sprinkled with white spots on the upper surface. The slender, tall, numerous to few-flowered inflorescence have spirally twisted, inconspicuous to small, tubular, white or green flowers not opening fully and are often suffused brown to salmon-pink. The distinctly clawed, strongly arched, entire or obscurely trilobed lip has an abrupt (horn-like) protuberance, recurved at the tip, and a pair of fleshy calli at the base. The flowers have a long, club-shaped column.

MESADENUS

Schlechter

Beih. Bot. Centralbl.　**37**(2): 367 (1920).

Orchidoideæ ⚬ Cranichideæ • Spiranthinæ

ETYMOLOGY: Greek for in the middle and gland. An allusion to the conspicuous gland between the two pollinia.

LECTOTYPE: *Mesadenus galeottianus*
　　(A. Richard) Schlechter
　　(*Spiranthes galeottiana* A. Richard)
This type name is now considered a synonym of *Mesadenus polyanthus* (Reichenbach f.) Schlechter; basionym replaced with
　　Spiranthes polyantha Reichenbach f.

Six sympodial terrestrials are found in seasonally dry, low to upper elevation, scrub, woodlands, rocky fields and montane oak-pine forests from the southeastern United States (Florida), the Bahamas, Cuba to Puerto Rico, Costa Rica to Panama and Brazil. These erect plants have short, unbranched stems, each with a basal rosette of narrow, often iridescent leaves. The leaves are usually absent or withered by flowering time. The delicate, erect, numerous to few-flowered inflorescence, partially subtended by several, red to green, tubular bracts, has its blooms presented to one side on the rachis. The small to tiny, green-brown, tubular flowers have widespreading, narrow sepals and petals that are barely differentiated. The long-clawed, narrow, entire lip, channeled or grooved in the middle, has its sides clinging to the sides of the small, slender, slightly curved, club-shaped column.

MESICERA

Rafinesque

Neogenyton　4 (1825).

ETYMOLOGY: Greek for middle and horn. An allusion to the horn-like, stigmatic processes protruding from the flower.

TYPE SPECIES: *None designated*

Now recognized as belonging to the genus *Habenaria*, *Mesicera* was previously considered to include three terrestrials widespread in low to mid elevation, open slopes, grasslands, deciduous or oak-pine forests from the southeastern United States (Florida), the Bahamas, Cuba to Jamaica, Mexico to Colombia and Venezuela. These erect plants have numerous, soft, mid-nerved, ovate leaves spaced up the unbranched, stout stem. The few-flowered inflorescence has fleshy, green-white flowers with a green, concave dorsal sepal; oblong, green lateral sepals, and two-part, thread-like, white petals. The trilobed lip has long, thread-like side lobes, a long, narrow midlobe, and a long, white to green spur.

MESOCERAS

An orthographic variant cited in *Lex. Gen. Phan.*, 361 (1904). The correct spelling is *Mesicera*.

MESOCLASTES

Lindley

Gen. Sp. Orchid. Pl.　44 (1830).

ETYMOLOGY: Greek for in the middle and to break off. Alluding to the lip that is sharply interrupted in the middle.

TYPE SPECIES: *None designated*

Now recognized as belonging to the genera *Luisia* or *Papilionanthe*, *Mesoclastes* was previously considered to include two epiphytes found in low to upper elevation, open forests and valleys from southern China (Yunnan), Thailand and Vietnam to Malaysia. These plants have curved rather slender, several noded stems, each with several, fleshy leaves. The short, few-flowered inflorescence has all of the small, yellow to yellow-green flowers open simultaneously but not widely. The dorsal sepal and petals lie in almost one plane, while the lateral sepals are hidden under the lip, embracing the lip margin. The trilobed lip has a blunt, shallowly notched tip.

MESODACTYLIS

Wallich

Pl. Asiat. Rar.　**1**(4): 74, *t.* 84 (1830).

ETYMOLOGY: Latin for middle finger or large fingered.

TYPE SPECIES: *Mesodactylis deflexa* Wallich

Name published without a description. Today this name is most often referred to *Apostasia*.

MESODACTYLUS

An orthographic variant introduced in *Gen. Pl. (Endlicher)*, 221 (1837). The correct spelling is *Mesodactylis*.

Currently Accepted　　Validly Published　　Invalidly Published　　Published Pre-1753　　Superfluous Usage　　Orthographic Variant　　Fossil

O r c h i d　G e n e r a　• **242**

MESOGLOSSUM

Halbinger

Orquidea (Mexico City), n.s.　　**8**(2): 194 (1982).

Epidendroideæ ⚬ Cymbidieæ • Oncidiinæ

ETYMOLOGY: Greek for in the middle and tongue. Alluding to the position of this genus within the *Oncidium-Odontoglossum* alliance.

TYPE SPECIES: *Mesoglossum londesboroughianum* (Reichenbach f.) Halbinger (*Odontoglossum londesboroughianum* Reichenbach f.)

One sympodial lithophyte or terrestrial found in mid elevation, scrub and rocky crevices of southwestern Mexico (Guerrero) usually growing in full sunlight on east-facing slopes. This plant has wrinkled, ovoid to egg-shaped, olive-green pseudobulbs, subtended by dry sheaths, each with two deciduous, thinly textured leaves. The erect, long, slender, simple or occasionally branched, numerous-flowered inflorescence has showy, long-lasting, bright golden yellow flowers heavily marked or barred with red-brown bands. The bright yellow, trilobed lip, attached to the column base, has tiny side lobes, and a large, narrowly clawed midlobe that is widespreading and deeply notched. The flowers have a small, slender, curved, wingless column with a short foot.

MESOPTERA

Rafinesque

Herb. Raf.　　73 (1833).

Name ICBN rejected vs. *Mesoptera* Hooker f. (1873) Rubiaceæ

ETYMOLOGY: Greek for in the middle and wing. An allusion to the lateral wings on the column.

TYPE SPECIES: *None designated*

Although validly published this rejected name is referred to *Liparis*. *Mesoptera* was considered to include two terrestrials found in the eastern United States, Canada and central Europe to eastern Russia. These short, delicate plants have small pseudobulbs and the erect, few-flowered inflorescence has flowers with narrow to thread-like sepals and petals. The oblong, sickle-shaped, entire lip has a wavy, notched margin.

MESOSCLASTES

An orthographic variant introduced in *Syn. Pl. (D. Dietrich)*, **5**: 3 (1852). The correct spelling is *Mesoclastes*.

MESOSPENIDIUM

An orthographic variant introduced in *Prakt. Stud. Orchid.*, 268 (1854). The correct spelling is *Mesospinidium*.

MESOSPINIDIUM

Reichenbach *filius*

Bot. Zeitung (Berlin)　　**10**: 929 (1852).

Epidendroideæ ⚬ Cymbidieæ • Oncidiinæ

ETYMOLOGY: Greek for middle and diminutive of a small, chaf finch (found in Europe). Descriptive of the anther that resembles a bird's head when viewed from the side.

TYPE SPECIES: *Mesospinidium warscewiczii* Reichenbach f.

Seven sympodial epiphytes are found in shady, low to mid elevation, hill scrub and montane cloud forests from Guatemala to Ecuador and Peru. These plants have gray-green, laterally compressed, ovoid pseudobulbs, subtended by two or more leaf-bearing sheaths, each with two pale green leaves. The often, branched, numerous-flowered inflorescence, borne from a mature pseudobulb, has stiff flowers with widespreading segments. The rather fleshy, small, green or yellow flowers are covered with red or brown spots or blotches; the lateral sepals are united to the middle and the small petals are directed outward. The white or cream, wedge-shaped, entire lip is covered with orange blotches, has a wavy margin and a pair of fleshy (hairy between) keels at the base. The flowers have a small, stout column.

METACHILON

An orthographic variant cited in *Nomencl. Bot. (Steudel)*, ed. 2, **2**: 136 (1841). The correct spelling is *Metachilum*.

METACHILUM

Lindley

Gen. Sp. Orchid. Pl.　　74 (1830).

ETYMOLOGY: Greek for near or between and lip. An allusion to the union of the lip with the column foot.

TYPE SPECIES: *Metachilum cyathiferum* Lindley

Now recognized as belonging to the genus *Appendicula*, *Metachilum* was previously considered to include one terrestrial found in humid, low to upper elevation, moss laden forests of Indonesia, Malaysia, Thailand and the Philippines. This tall plant has laterally compressed, winged stems, subtended completely by overlapping sheaths, each with wide, bilobed leaves that have a bristle-like structure between the lobes. The short, zig-zagged inflorescence, borne from the upper leaf nodes, has minute bracts. The minute, few-flowered inflorescence has insignificant, yellow-green flowers. The white, entire lip, joined to the column foot, has a blunt tip. The above type name is now considered a synonym of *Appendicula anceps* Blume.

METACHILUS

An orthographic variant cited in *Lex. Gen. Phan.*, 362 (1904). The correct spelling is *Metachilum*.

METOPETALUM

An orthographic variant introduced in *Ann. Hort. Bot.*, **5**: 187 (1862). The correct spelling is *Mitopetalum*.

METOSTIGMA

An orthographic variant introduced in *Orchid.-Buch*, 517 (1892). The correct spelling is *Mitostigma*.

MEXICOA

Garay

Bradea　　**1**(40): 423 (1974).

Epidendroideæ ⚬ Cymbidieæ • Oncidiinæ

ETYMOLOGY: In honor of the Estados Unidos Mexicanos, a republic (located in the southwestern North American continent, between the Gulf of Mexico and the Pacific Ocean), where the type species was collected.

TYPE SPECIES: *Mexicoa ghiesbreghtiana* (A. Richard & Galeotti) Garay (*Oncidium ghiesbreghtianum* A. Richard & Galeotti)

One attractive, sympodial epiphyte is restricted in dry, upper elevation, montane oak-pine forests of western Mexico (Oaxaca, Michoacán and Guerrero). This clump-forming plant has ovoid to cone-shaped, compressed, grooved pseudobulbs, each with one to two, narrow, thinly leathery leaves that turn red when exposed to bright light. The short, few-flowered inflorescence has showy flowers with the maroon sepals and petals suffused white or yellow and are rosy veined. The bright yellow, trilobed lip dominates the flower with its spreading side lobes that are roundish in the front, a fan-shaped midlobe that is bilobed at the tip and a yellow-orange callus. The flowers have a small, strongly curved, wingless column.

MEXIPEDIUM

V.A. Albert & M.W. Chase

Lindleyana   **7**(3): 173 (1992).

Cypripedioideæ 🌿

ETYMOLOGY: Honoring the country of Mexico and Greek for sandal. Referring to the slipper-shaped lip.

TYPE SPECIES: *Mexipedium xerophyticum*
(Soto Arenas, Salazar & Hágsater) Albert & Chase
(*Phragmipedium xerophyticum* Soto Arenas, Salazar & Hágsater)

One small, quite attractive sympodial terrestrial or lithophyte is found in mid elevation, coastal scrub of south-western Mexico (Oaxaca) in dry, open scrub dominated by succulents and cacti or usually on exposed steep cliffs. This minute, inconspicuous, colony-forming plant has an erect, leafy stem with the base subtended by two to three, sterile bracts and has silvery-green leaves. The erect, hairy, sometimes branched, red, one- to two-flowered inflorescence has small, white, thinly textured flowers, borne successively. The flowers are densely covered with pale brown hairs on the outer sepal surfaces, and the dorsal sepal forms a hood over the lip. The tip of the dorsal sepal and short column are pink colored. The deeply pouched, inflated and slipper-shaped lip has obscure, incurved side lobes.

MEYRACYLLIUM

An orthographic variant introduced in *Ill. Hort.*, **29**: 68 (1882). The correct spelling is *Meiracyllium*.

MIANGIS

Thouars

Hist. Orchid.   Table 2, sub 3o (1822).

Name published without a description. Today this name is most often referred to *Angraecopsis*.

MIANTHUS

An orthographic variant introduced in *Séance Publique Soc. Argic.*, 195 (1852). The correct spelling is *Myanthus*.

MICARANTHUS

An orthographic variant introduced in *Dict. Class. Sci. Nat.*, **7**: 539 (1841). The correct spelling is *Mycaranthes*.

MICROCAELIA

An orthographic variant introduced in *Nat. Syst. Bot.*, ed. 2, 340 (1836). The correct spelling is *Microcoelia*.

MICROCATTLEYA

Chiron & V.P. Castro

Richardiana   **2**(1) 27 (2002).

ETYMOLOGY: Greek for small and *Cattleya*, a genus of orchids. Alluding to a relationship to *Cattleya*.

TYPE SPECIES: *Microcattleya cattleyioides*
(A. Richard) Chiron & V.P. Castro
(*Laelia cattleyioides* A. Richard)

Recognized as belonging to the genus *Sophronitis*, *Microcattleya* was proposed to include one epiphyte found from Bolivia and Brazil to northern Argentina (Misiones and Salta). This small, robust plant has oblong, compressed pseudo-bulbs, each with two fleshy, deeply channeled leaves. The short, one- to few-flowered inflorescence has white, fragrant flowers with narrow sepals and petals of equal width. The white, deeply trilobed lip has erect side lobes, a roundish midlobe with deep rosy-purple veins, and a wavy margin. The above type name is now considered a hybrid of *Microlaelia lundii* (Reichenbach f.) Chiron & V.P. Castro x *Cattleya loddigesii* Lindley.

MICROCHILUS

C. Presl

Reliq. Haenk.   **1**(2): 94 (1827).

Orchidoideæ 🌿 Cranichideæ • Goodyerinæ

ETYMOLOGY: Greek for small or short and lip. Refers to the small lip size of the blade.

LECTOTYPE: *Microchilus minor* C. Presl

Some eighty sympodial terrestrials, occasional lithophytes or rare epiphytes are found in low to mid elevation, evergreen forests from southern Mexico to Panama, Cuba to Trinidad, the Guianas, Venezuela, Colombia to northern Chile, Brazil, Paraguay, northern Argentina, and the Galapagos Islands. These erect to creeping plants have unbranched, stout to slender stems. The few to several, green to brown, variegated silver, plain or green leaves are usually spaced up the stem but sometimes bunched together at the base. The hairy, tightly spiraled, numerous-flowered inflorescence has small, brown-green flowers with a white, long, entire or bilobed lip. The cylindrical, thickened, often bilobed spur is filled with a clear, sweet-tasting liquid. The

flowers have a slender, short, slightly curved, wingless, footless column.

MICROCOELIA

Lindley

Gen. Sp. Orchid. Pl.   60 (1830).

Not *Microcoelia* J.G. Agardh (1876) Kallymeniceæ.

Epidendroideæ 🌿 Vandeæ • Aerangidinæ

ETYMOLOGY: Greek for small and hollow. Refers to the small lip that has a swollen area on one side.

TYPE SPECIES: *Microcoelia exilis* Lindley

Twenty-nine remarkable, monopodial epiphytes or uncommon lithophytes are found seasonally dry, low to upper elevation, coastal to montane forests and mixed deciduous woodlands throughout Ghana, Nigeria to Cameroon and east to Uganda and then south to Zimbabwe, Mozambique and Madagascar. These leafless, short-stemmed plants are attractive even when not in bloom. The branching, often flattened roots are silvery when dry, green when moist, and many species have gnarly roots covered with small bumps. The several, long or often short inflo-rescences arise from a woody stem and have small to tiny, brown bracts. The small to minute, bell-shaped, translucent white to creamy flowers, often produced in profusion are suffused pale pink or brown. The almost entire or obscurely trilobed lip has a thread-like or roundish, short to long spur with a green tinge. The flowers have a fleshy, stout, short to minute, wingless, footless column.

MICRODELIA

An orthographic variant cited in *Pl. Alkaloids*, 156 (1996). The correct spelling is *Microcoelia*.

MICROEPIDENDRUM

Brieger ex W.E. Higgins

Acta Bot. Mex.   **60**(1): 22 (2002).

Epidendroideæ 🌿 Epidendreæ • Laeliinæ

ETYMOLOGY: Greek for small and *Epidendrum*, a genus of orchids. Refers to the small plants similar to those of the allied *Epidendrum*.

TYPE SPECIES: *Microepidendrum subulatifolium*
(A. Richard & Galeotti) Brieger ex W.E. Higgins
(*Epidendrum subulatifolium* A. Richard & Galeotti)

One sympodial epiphyte or lithophyte is found in dry, mid elevation, oak-pine forests of western Mexico (Jalisco, Michoacán, Guerrero and Oaxaca). This small,

Currently Accepted   Validly Published   Invalidly Published   Published Pre-1753   Superfluous Usage   Orthographic Variant   Fossil

O r c h i d   G e n e r a   • **244**

inconspicuous, reed-like plant has slender stems with all new growth being red including the root tips, each with several, narrow, distichous, dark green or green leaves suffused purple-brown. The sometimes branched, numerous to few-flowered inflorescence has small, fragrant, yellow-brown to yellow-green flowers with red veins, which do not open widely. The broadly clawed, bright white, strongly recurved, entire lip has a yellow, basal callus, is deeply notched at the tip, and has a wavy or an irregularly toothed margin. The flowers have a small, stout, slightly curved column with a burgundy colored anther.

MICROHOLMESIA

P.J. Cribb

Mabberley's Pl.-Book   371 (1987).

ETYMOLOGY: Greek for small and *Holmesia*, a genus of orchids. Alluding to a relationship to *Holmesia*.

TYPE SPECIES: *Microholmesia parva*
(P.J. Cribb) P.J. Cribb
(*Holmesia parva* P.J. Cribb)

Now recognized as belonging to the genus *Angraecopsis*, *Microholmesia* was previously considered to include one epiphyte found in mid elevation, mixed evergreen and river forests of Cameroon, Tanzania, Zimbabwe, Malawi and Mozambique; also Madagascar and the Mascarene Islands. This miniature, short-stemmed plant appears almost leafless, with its gray-green roots often more conspicuous than the distichous, narrow or scythe-shaped, unequally lobed leaves. The long, hanging, numerous to few-flowered inflorescence has small to tiny, drab colored green flowers spirally arranged and not opening fully. The tiny, trilobed lip has a curved spur with a club-like, bilobed tip. The flowers have an erect, short, wingless, footless column.

MICROLAELIA

(Schlechter) Chiron & V.P. Castro

Richardiana   2(1) 11 (2002).

ETYMOLOGY: Greek for small and *Laelia*, a genus of orchids. Alluding to a relationship to *Laelia*.

TYPE SPECIES: *Microlaelia lundii*
(Reichenbach f. & Warming) Chiron & V.P. Castro
(*Bletia lundii* Reichenbach f. & Warming)
This type name is now considered a synonym of *Sophronitis lundii*
(Reichenbach f. & Warming) Van den Berg & M.W. Chase;
basionym
Bletia lundii Reichenbach f. & Warming

Recognized as belonging to the *Sophronitis*, *Microlaelia* was proposed to include one epiphyte or lithophyte found in dry, mid elevation, prairies and thickets from Bolivia to eastern Brazil (Minas Gerais) and northern Argentina (Misiones to Salta). This

small, robust plant has short, oblong to narrow, slightly compressed pseudobulbs, each with two small, fleshy, semi-cylindrical, deeply channeled leaves. The short, one- to few-flowered inflorescence has white flowers with narrow sepals and petals of equal width. The white, deeply trilobed lip has erect side lobes, a roundish midlobe with deep rosy-purple, radiating veins, a deep yellow base, and a wavy margin. The flowers have a short, broad column.

MICROPERA

Lindley

Edwards's Bot. Reg.   18: sub 1522 (1832).
Not *Micropera* Léveillé (1846) Fungi.

Epidendroideæ ⚘ Vandeæ • Aeridinæ

ETYMOLOGY: Greek for small and sac or pouch. Alluding to the small, sac-like spur on the lip.

TYPE SPECIES: *Micropera pallida* (Roxburgh) Lindley
(*Aerides pallida* Roxburgh)

Eighteen monopodial terrestrials or epiphytes are found in low elevation, often on dead trees usually growing in bright sunlight of northern India (Assam), Bhutan, Myanmar to Vietnam, Malaysia, Indonesia, New Guinea, northern Australia and the Solomons to the Philippines. These climbing, long-stemmed plants have numerous, narrow, fleshy leaves arranged in two rows. The simple or branching, numerous-flowered inflorescences have small, cream, rosy pink or yellow flowers with the lip uppermost. The strongly sac-like, trilobed lip has a glossy sheen and along with the short, twisted column makes the flowers appear nonsymmetric. The trilobed lip has a front wall consisting of two parallel calli. Inside the spur is a longitudinal dividing wall that has various ornaments at the entrance. The flowers have a variable, footless column with a long, beak-like rostellum.

MICROPERA

Dalzell

Hooker's J. Bot. Kew Gard. Misc.   3: 282 (1851).

ETYMOLOGY: Greek for small and sac. Alluding to the size of the small lip.

TYPE SPECIES: *Micropera maculata* Dalzell

Not validly published, this name is referred to *Smithsonia*. *Micropera* Dalzell was considered to include one epiphyte found in western India (Kerala, Karnataka and Tamil Nadu).

MICROPERAS

An orthographic variant introduced in *Syn. Pl.* (D. Dietrich), 5: 12 (1852). The correct spelling is *Micropera*.

MICROPHYTANTHE

(Schlechter) Brieger

Orchideen (Schlechter), ed. 3   1(11-12): 742 (1981).

ETYMOLOGY: Greek for tiny, plant and flower. Refers to the relatively large-sized flowers for such a small plant.

TYPE SPECIES: *Microphytanthe bulbophylloides*
(Schlechter) Brieger
(*Dendrobium bulbophylloides* Schlechter)

Now recognized as belonging to the genus *Dendrobium*, *Microphytanthe* was previously considered to include three epiphytes found in mid to upper elevation, montane forests of New Guinea. These tiny, usually creeping plants form dense mats on tree branches with their unusually swollen, cigar-shaped, brown, red-brown or green pseudobulbs bent like an 'L', each with a solitary, thick, fleshy leaf. The stout, short, solitary-flowered inflorescence, borne from the tip of the pseudobulb, has a yellow, orange or maroon, long-lasting flower. The large, widespreading lateral sepals form a cup-shape around the short, stout, wingless column. The shiny, dark colored lip is either entire or obscurely trilobed. The column has a long, incurved foot which forms a large, funnel-shaped protuberance.

MICROPORA

Not *Micropora* Hooker f. (1886) Lauraceæ.

An orthographic variant cited in *Lex. Gen. Phan.*, 366 (1904). The correct spelling is *Micropera*.

MICROSACCUS

Blume

Bijdr. Fl. Ned. Ind.   8: 367 (1825).

Epidendroideæ ⚘ Vandeæ • Aeridinæ

ETYMOLOGY: Greek for tiny and sac. Refers to the the small, sack-like spur.

TYPE SPECIES: *Microsaccus javensis* Blume

Thirteen monopodial epiphytes are found in low elevation, open forests of Thailand to Vietnam, Malaysia, Indonesia (Sumatra, Java and Borneo) and the Philippines. These miniature, tufted plants have long, often curved, thin, branching, laterally flattened, close-set stems, subtended by compressed, distichous, overlapping, mottled, fleshy leaves arranged in two rows. The short inflorescence, borne from the leaf axils, has a pair of small to tiny, white, somewhat fleshy flowers not opening widely; the lateral sepals are joined at the base of the relatively large, transversely flattened, rather large, stout spur.

The fleshy, entire lip is without appendages. The flowers have a short, stout column.

MICROSSACCUS

An orthographic variant introduced in *Dict. Bot. Prat.*, 490 (1882). The correct spelling is *Microsaccus*.

MICROSTIS

An orthographic variant introduced in *Prakt. Stud. Orchid.*, 47 (1854). The correct spelling is *Microtis*.

MICROSTYLIDIS

An orthographic variant introduced in *J. Linn. Soc., Bot.*, **24**: 197 (1888). The correct spelling is *Microstylis*.

MICROSTYLIS

(Nuttall) Eaton

Man. Bot., ed. 3   115, 347, 353 (1822).

Name ICBN conserved vs. *Achroanthes* Rafinesque (1819) Orchidaceæ.

ETYMOLOGY: Greek for small and column. Referring to the short, slender column of the type species.

TYPE SPECIES: *Microstylis ophioglossoides* (Mühlenberg ex Willdenow) Nuttall ex Eaton nom. illeg. (*Malaxis ophioglossoides* Mühlenberg ex Willdenow)

This type name is now considered a synonym of *Microstylis unifolia* (Michaux) Britton, Sterns & Poggenburg (*Malaxis unifolia* Michaux)

Now recognized as belonging to the genus *Malaxis*, *Microstylis* was previously considered to include over four hundred terrestrials found in dry, deeply shady, low to upper elevation, piney woodlands ranging from North America, Europe and Russia to southeastern Asia. These plants have ovate, keeled pseudobulbs produced in an upward series, each with one or more, soft green, thinly textured leaves. The short, few to numerous-flowered inflorescence has small to tiny, insignificant, green flowers with reflexed sepals and long, slender petals that are curled backward. The variable, trilobed or entire lip is flat to concave, but usually thickened with two rounded, ear-shaped lobes.

MICROSTYLLIS

An orthographic variant introduced in *Hort. Franc.*, ser. 2, **6**: 92 (1864). The correct spelling is *Microstylis*.

MICROTATORCHIS

Schlechter

Nachtr. Fl. Schutzgeb. Südsee   224 (1905).

Epidendroideæ ⚬ Vandeæ • Aeridinæ

ETYMOLOGY: Greek for smallest and orchid. Alluding to the minute habit of the plant.

LECTOTYPE: *Microtatorchis perpusilla* Schlechter

Fifty monopodial epiphytes or uncommon terrestrials are found in misty, upper elevation, montane forests of Taiwan, New Caledonia, the Philippines and the southwestern Pacific Archipelago with a center of distribution in New Guinea. These minute, predominantly leafless plants have chlorophyll-containing roots. The erect, small to tiny stems may have minute, narrow leaves with a long spine or none at all. The short, solitary to numerous-flowered inflorescence has small, dull yellow, yellow-orange, red-brown or green flowers not opening widely; with the sepals and short petals fused into a short tube. The entire or trilobed lip is firmly attached to the base of the short, footless column.

MICROTERANGIS

(Schlechter) Senghas

Orchidee (Hamburg)   **36**(1): 22 (1985).

Epidendroideæ ⚬ Vandeæ • Aerangidinæ

ETYMOLOGY: Greek for small or tiny and *Aerangis*, a genus of orchids. Refers to the spur of the tiny flower.

TYPE SPECIES: *Microterangis hariotiana* (Kraenzlin) Senghas (*Mystacidium hariotianum* Kraenzlin)

Seven monopodial epiphytes are found in low to mid elevation, hill and montane forests from Madagascar to the Comoros Islands. These small, short-stemmed, densely leafy plants are similar to *Chamaeangis* but differ in their column structure, pollinia, and short spurs. The fleshy to thinly leathery, oblong or ovate, bright green leaves are unequally and obtusely bilobed at the tips. The several, short to long, densely packed, numerous-flowered inflorescences, longer than the leaves, have small to tiny, dull yellow, yellow-orange or red-brown flowers with widespreading, triangular to elliptical sepals and petals. The notched, wedge-shaped or entire lip has a swollen, sac-shaped spur. The flowers have a short, straight, wingless, footless column.

MICROTHALLUS

Cohn

Pflanze   **2**: 244, 275 (1897).

ETYMOLOGY: Greek for small and minute.

TYPE SPECIES: *Microthallus ornatus* Cohn

Not validly published, this name is most often referred to as a synonym of *Pleurothallis*.

MICROTHECA

Schlechter

Repert. Spec. Nov. Regni Veg. Beih.   **33**: 76 (1924).

Not *Microtheca* Ehrenberg (1838) Algae.

ETYMOLOGY: Greek for small and chest or box. An allusion to the very small anther cavities.

TYPE SPECIES: *Microtheca madagascarica* Schlechter

Not validly published because of a prior use of the name, this homonym was replaced by *Cynorkis*.

MICROTHELYS

Garay

Bot. Mus. Leafl.   **28**(4): 336 (1980)[1982].

Orchidoideæ ⚬ Cranichideæ • Spiranthinæ

ETYMOLOGY: Greek for small or tiny and female. Describing the minute nature of the rostellum.

TYPE SPECIES: *Microthelys minutiflora* (A. Richard & Galeotti) Garay (*Spiranthes minutiflora* A. Richard & Galeotti)

Six slender, sympodial terrestrials, lithophytes or epiphytes are found in mid to upper elevation, montane oak-pine and fir forests from southern Mexico to Costa Rica, with one species found in northern Ecuador (Imbabura). These erect plants have short, unbranched stems, each with a loose, basal rosette. The narrow, gray-green leaves are usually withered by flowering time. The tall, somewhat twisted, smooth to sparsely hairy, few-flowered inflorescence has ascending to nodding, minute to small, tubular, fragrant, white to pale green flowers. The shortly clawed, entire or trilobed lip has a tunnel-like access to the nectary and has a bright red callus extending almost the whole length of the lip. The flowers have a straight, club-shaped column.

Currently Accepted   Validly Published   Invalidly Published   Published Pre-1753   Superfluous Usage   Orthographic Variant   Fossil

Orchid Genera • **246**

MICROTIDIUM

D.L. Jones & M.A. Clements
Orchadian **13**(10): 463 (2002).

ETYMOLOGY: *Microtis*, a genus of orchids and Latin for diminutive. Referring to a similarity.

TYPE SPECIES: *Microtidium atratum*
(Lindley) D.L. Jones & M.A. Clements
(*Microtis atrata* Lindley)

Recognized as belonging to the genus *Microtis*, *Microtidium* was proposed to include one terrestrial found in moist, low elevation, scrub and marshes of western Australia, often growing nearly submerged. This whole plant including the flowers is yellow-green. The tubular leaf, sheath wraps, around the floral rachis and its length often exceeds the small plant in height. The numerous-flowered inflorescence has minute flowers with a hood-like dorsal sepal. The spreading petals are shorter than the similar lateral sepals. The oblong, entire lip has a blunt tip and practically its entire margin is trimmed with small to minute glands.

MICROTIS

R. Brown
Prodr. Fl. Nov. Holland. 320 (1810).

Orchidoideæ ৸ Diurideæ • Prasophyllinæ

ETYMOLOGY: Greek for small and an ear. In reference to the small wings of the column that are projected forward.

LECTOTYPE: *Microtis rara* R. Brown

Eighteen attractive, sympodial terrestrials are found in moist, low to mid elevation, open forests, montane grassy slopes, meadows and marshy bogs from eastern China (Anhui to Guangxi), southern Japan, Taiwan, Malaysia, Indonesia, New Caledonia and New Zealand to the Philippines with the greatest concentration found in Australia and Tasmania. These small to tiny plants have erect, unbranched stems, each a solitary, long, narrow leaf. The wiry, loose to densely spiralled, numerous-flowered inflorescence emerges through a thin point on the upper part of the leaf. The small, inconspicuous, sweetly fragrant, green or pale green-white flowers have the dorsal sepal hood-like over the short column, and the petals are smaller than the widespreading lateral sepals. The lip is markedly dissimilar in size, shape and color. The flowers have a short or minute column with small, ear-like wings.

NOTE: These species are most unusual because they are pollinated by ants. Their pollen is resistant to the antifungal secretions of ants that usually kills most types of pollen.

MILTONIA

Lindley
Edwards's Bot. Reg. **23**: sub 1976 (1837).
Name ICBN conserved.

Epidendroideæ ৸ Cymbidieæ • Oncidiinæ

ETYMOLOGY: Dedicated to Charles William Wentworth (1786-1857) the 4th Earl of Fitzwilliam, Viscount Milton of Wentworth House in Yorkshire, a British patron of horticulture and orchids.

TYPE SPECIES: *Miltonia spectabilis* Lindley

Ten sympodial epiphytes, plus numerous natural and manmade hybrids, are found in warm, moist, low to mid elevation, hill forests and scrub of eastern Brazil (Pernambuco to Rio Grande do Sul) to north-eastern Argentina. These evergreen plants have narrow, oblong pseudobulbs often produced on a creeping rhizome, subtended by leaf-like bracts turning papery, each with two narrow, pointed, dark green leaves. The large, showy, flat-faced flowers have beautiful markings at the lip base that are striking and intricate. The short, erect or arching, solitary to numerous-flowered inflorescences, borne from the base of the pseudobulb, have star-shaped, waxy, sometimes slightly fragrant flowers. The petals often recurved along the lower half. The flower colors range from yellow to green and are marked with brown, purple or red. The broadly spreading, fiddle-shaped, entire lip is shortly to broadly clawed and attached to the base of the short, footless column at a right angle.

MILTONIOIDES

Brieger & Lückel
Orchidee (Hamburg) **34**(4): 130 (1983).

Epidendroideæ ৸ Cymbidieæ • Oncidiinæ

ETYMOLOGY: *Miltonia*, a genus of orchids and Greek for resembling. Indicating a similarity to *Miltonia*.

TYPE SPECIES: *Miltonioides karwinskii*
(Lindley) Brieger & Lückel
(*Cyrtochilum karwinskii* Lindley)

Five sympodial epiphytes or lithophytes are found in mid elevation, hill forests of Mexico, Costa Rica and Colombia to Peru. These plants have compressed, ovoid pseudobulbs, subtended at the base by leaf-bearing sheaths, each with one to two, leathery leaves. The few-flowered inflorescence has showy, flat, yellow-green, fragrant, waxy flowers with similar sepals and petals heavily barred brown-red. The fiddle-shaped, usually bicolored, entire lip has recurved margins with a broad, white tip and has several, yellow veins radiating from the base. The flowers have an erect, club-shaped, winged or wingless column.

MILTONIOPSIS

Godefroy-Lebeuf
Orchidophile (Argenteuil) **9**: 63 (1889).

Epidendroideæ ৸ Cymbidieæ • Oncidiinæ

ETYMOLOGY: *Miltonia*, a genus of orchids and Greek for appearance or likeness.

TYPE SPECIES: *Miltoniopsis vexillaria*
(Reichenbach f.) Godefroy-Lebeuf
(*Odontoglossum vexillarium* Reichenbach f.)

Five sympodial epiphytes are found in wet, low to upper elevation, hill to montane cloud forest margins and scrub from Guatemala to Panama, Colombia to Peru, and Venezuela. These showy flowers are often called the Pansy orchid. This genus differs from *Miltonia* by its clustered, compressed, ovoid to oblong pseudobulbs, subtended by distichous, overlapping, leaf-like bracts, each with a solitary, bilaterally flattened, fragile, thinly textured, blue-green to pale gray-green leaf. The slender, arching, solitary to few-flowered inflorescence, borne from the base of the pseudobulb, has large, decorative, flat-faced, delicately fragrant, white, pink or pale purple-red flowers with spreading sepals and petals. The broad, flattened, entire lip has a central keel and is united by a raised ridge with the short, footless, wingless column.

MINICOLUMNA

Brieger
Orchideen (Schlechter), ed. 3 **8**(29-32): 495 (1976).

ETYMOLOGY: Greek for small and column. Referring to the small size of the column.

TYPE SPECIES: *None designated*

Not validly published, this name is referred to *Epidendrum*. *Minicolumna* was considered to include two epiphytes found in Trinidad, the Guianas, northern Brazil, Venezuela and Colombia to Bolivia. Both species are now considered synonyms of *Epidendrum compressum* Grisebach.

MINUPHYLIS

Thouars
Hist. Orchid. Table 3, sub 3u, *t. 110* (1822).

Name published without a description. Today this name is most often referred to *Bulbophyllum*.

MIOXANTHUS

An orthographic variant introduced in *Nat. Pflanzenfam.*, **2**(6): 139 (1888). The correct spelling is *Myoxanthus*.

MIRACYLLIUM

An orthographic variant cited in *Lex. Gen. Phan.*, 357, 368 (1904). The correct spelling is *Meiracyllium*.

MIRANDOPSIS

Szlachetko & Margońska

Polish Bot. J. **46**(2): 117 (2001).

ETYMOLOGY: Latin for strange or causing wonder and likeness or appearance. An allusion to the unusual character of the species.

TYPE SPECIES: *Mirandopsis miranda*
(Luer) Szlachetko & Margońska
(*Pleurothallis miranda* Luer)

Recognized as belonging to the genus *Pleurothallis*, *Mirandopsis* was proposed to include one epiphyte found in cool, moist, mid elevation, montane forests of Ecuador. This plant has a well-developed, twig-like stem, subtended by leaf-like sheaths, each with a solitary, ovate leaf. The several, solitary-flowered inflorescences emerge from a conspicuous, spatula-shaped ring on the leaf stem. The flower has joined sepals; the tiny, pointed petals are hood-shaped. The squarish, hinged, entire lip strongly recurves under itself and has a pair of calli in the center. The flowers have a short, stout, footless column.

MIRANDORCHIS

Szlachetko & Kras-Lapinska

Orchidee (Hamburg) **54**(1): 84 (2003).

ETYMOLOGY: Latin for strange or causing wonder and Greek for orchid. Referring to the unusual flowers.

TYPE SPECIES: *Mirandorchis rautaneniana*
(Kraenzlin) Szlachetko & Kras-Lapinska
(*Habenaria rautaneniana* Kraenzlin)

Recognized as belonging to the genus *Habenaria*, *Mirandorchis* was proposed to include three terrestrials found in mid elevation, hill forests, savannas, dune woodlands, marshes or grasslands from Burundi to Zimbabwe growing singly or in small groups. These erect plants have slender, unbranched stems that are leafy throughout. The numerous-flowered inflorescence has green flowers. The outside basal portion of the lip and/or bilobed petals is covered in small protuberances and the broad sepals are dissimilar to each other. The interior lobe of the petals along with the lateral sepals loosely form a hood. The deeply trilobed lip has long, narrow segments and a long cylindrical spur. The flowers have a small, complex column with a trilobed rostellum.

MISCHOBULBON

An orthographic variant introduced in *Orchideen (Schlechter)*, ed 1, 128 (1914). The correct spelling is *Mischobulbum*.

MISCHOBULBUM

Schlechter

Repert. Spec. Nov. Regni Veg. Beih. **1**(2): 98 (1911).

ETYMOLOGY: Greek for stalk and bulb. Descriptive of the pseudobulbs that are conspicuously stalked.

LECTOTYPE: *Mischobulbum scapigerum*
(Hooker f.) Schlechter
(*Nephelaphyllum scapigerum* Hooker f.)

Recognized as belonging to the genus *Tainia*, *Mischobulbum* was previously considered to include fourteen terrestrials found in low to mid elevation, hill to montane evergreen forests and valleys from southern China (Yunnan to Fujian), Taiwan, northern India (Sikkim), Thailand, Vietnam, Malaysia, Indonesia and New Guinea to the Philippines. These plants have clustered, slender pseudobulbs, each with a solitary, heart-shaped, prominently veined leaf. The numerous to few-flowered inflorescence, borne from the base of the pseudobulb, has well-spaced flowers that open simultaneously. The large, long-lasting, showy flowers have exotic coloring of pale yellow with darker colored veins. The lateral sepals are united with column foot. The white, entire or obscurely trilobed lip has a few red to purple spots or blotches, and the yellow-brown to bright yellow midlobe has prominent keels on the upper surface. The flowers have a long, slightly bent, forward column.

MITOPETALUM

Blume

Fl. Javæ **1**: Praef. viii (1828) inv. publ., and *Mus. Bot.* **2**(12): 185 (1856).

ETYMOLOGY: Greek for stalk or string and leaf or petal. Referring to the small floral segments.

TYPE SPECIES: *None designated*

Now recognized as belonging to the genus *Tainia*, *Mitopetalum* was previously considered to include eleven terrestrials found in mid elevation, montane forests from India, Sri Lanka, Thailand, Malaysia to Laos and Indonesia. These creeping plants have slender pseudobulbs, each with a solitary, long, pleated, fleshy leaf. The numerous to few-flowered inflorescence has rather large, olive-yellow to orange-red flowers with tail-like petals that have a broad, crimson streak. The

narrow, lateral sepals (slightly twisted) are joined to the column foot forming a chin-like projection. The yellow, trilobed lip is suffused purple. The flowers have a slender, purple column.

MITOSTIGMA

Blume

Mus. Bot. **2**(12): 189 (1856).

Not *Mitostigma* Decaisne (1844) Asclepiadaceæ.

ETYMOLOGY: Greek for thread or string and stigma. From the two, filament-like stigmatic processes.

TYPE SPECIES: *Mitostigma gracile* Blume

Not validly published because of a prior use of the name, this homonym was replaced by *Amitostigma*.

MITOSTIYMA

An orthographic variant introduced in *Fl. Bras. (Martius)*, **3**(4): 18 (1893). The correct spelling is *Mitostigma*.

MIXIS

(Luer) Luer

Monogr. Syst. Bot. Missouri Bot. Gard. **95**: 258 (2004).

ETYMOLOGY: Latin for mixed up. Refers to the unusual combination of morphological features.

TYPE SPECIES: *Mixis incongrua* (Luer) Luer
(*Pleurothallis incongrua* Luer)

Now recognized as belonging to the genus *Pleurothallis*, *Mixis* was proposed to include one epiphyte found in upper elevation, montane forests of southwestern Colombia (Valle del Cauca). This tufted, small plant, often forming clumps, has slender, erect, clustered stems, subtended by tubular sheaths, each with a solitary, spear-shaped, leathery leaf. The few-flowered inflorescences, borne at the leaf axils, have tiny, translucent flowers speckled with rosy-violet spots. The concave dorsal sepal is veined and the lateral sepals are completely united into a flat lamina or blade. The concave, obscurely trilobed lip has erect, incurved side lobes. The flowers have a short, footless column.

Currently Accepted | Validly Published | Invalidly Published | Published Pre-1753 | Superfluous Usage | Orthographic Variant | Fossil

Orchid Genera • **248**

MOBILABIUM

Rupp

N. Queensland Naturalist **13**(78): 2 (1946).

Epidendroideæ ※ Vandeæ • Aeridinæ

ETYMOLOGY: Latin for loose or movable and lip. Descriptive of the mobile lip.

TYPE SPECIES: *Mobilabium hamatum* Rupp

One uncommon, monopodial epiphyte is found in low elevation, rain forests of north-eastern Australia (Queensland). This small, straggly plant has long stems, each with oblong, leathery leaves that have a distinct hook at the tips. The short, stiff, few-flowered inflorescence has widespreading, pale green-yellow to yellow-green flowers with brown blotches, and a slightly concave dorsal sepal. The deeply pouched, bilobed lip projects downward, is covered with red-brown blotches, and is hinged to the upturned point of the column foot by a short, highly movable claw. The flowers have a short, forward bent column.

MOERENHOUTIA

Blume

Coll. Orchid. 99, *tt. 28, 42* (1859), and
Fl. Javæ Nov. Ser. 83 (1858).

Orchidoideæ ※ Cranichideæ • Goodyerinæ

ETYMOLOGY: Commemorating Jacques Antoine Moerenhout (1797-1879), a Dutchman who served as counsel to the French government in the South Pacific, author of *Voyages Aux Îles ud Grand Océan*. He collected the type species while in Tahiti.

TYPE SPECIES: *Moerenhoutia plantaginea*
(Hooker & Arnott) Blume
(*Pterochilus plantagineus* Hooker & Arnott)

Thirteen uncommon, sympodial terrestrials are found in humid, low to mid elevation, shady rain forests and scrub of eastern Indonesia (Maluku), New Guinea, Samoa, Vanuatu and the southwestern Pacific Archipelago. These erect plants have slender, unbranched stems, each with several, closely spaced leaves, almost in a rosette. The erect, long, slightly hairy, numerous-flowered inflorescence has fleshy, thinly textured, tubular, white flowers not opening fully. The arrowhead-shaped, trilobed lip has an inrolled margin and two small calli on each side at the base. The flowers have a conspicuous, footless column.

MOLLOYBAS

D.L. Jones & M.A. Clements

Orchadian **13**(10): 448 (2002).

ETYMOLOGY: Honoring Brian Peter John Molloy (1930-), a New Zealand botanist, orchidologist and co-author of *Native Orchids of New Zealand*. Latin for basal or on the ground.

TYPE SPECIES: *Molloybas cryptanthus*
(Hatch) D.L. Jones & M.A. Clements
(*Corybas cryptanthus* Hatch)

Recognized as belonging to the genus *Corybas*, *Molloybas* was proposed to include one epiparasite found in humus or moss, low elevation, often completely buried in kanuka or southern beech (*Nothofagus*) of New Zealand. This tiny, leafless plant lacks any chlorophyll even in the scale-like leaves. The solitary, translucent flower is usually flecked with red. The dorsal sepal is hood-like with the thread-like petals being much longer than the lateral sepals. This plant when emerging is leafless. The seed stem doubles over like a sprouting bean, then straightens up when above the surface.

MOMOLYCA

An orthographic variant introduced in *Cat. Orch.-Samml. Schiller*, 69 (1857). The correct spelling is *Mormolyca*.

MONACANTHUS

An orthographic variant introduced in *Paxton's Mag. Bot.*, **2**: 139 (1836). The correct spelling is *Monachanthus*.

MONACHANTHUS

Lindley

Edwards's Bot. Reg. **18**: sub 1538 (1832).

ETYMOLOGY: Greek for a solitary monk and flower. Alluding to the lip that resembles a hood drawn over a little face represented by the column.

TYPE SPECIES: *Monachanthus viridis* Lindley nom. illeg.

Catasetum cernuum (Lindley) Reichenbach f.
(*Myanthus cernuus* Lindley)

Now recognized as belonging to the genus *Catasetum*, *Monachanthus* was previously considered to include seven epiphytes found in low to mid elevation, hill and montane forests of Brazil, the Guianas, Venezuela and Trinidad. These large, stout plants have spindle-shaped, strongly veined or ribbed pseudobulbs, subtended by numerous, distichous sheaths. The several, narrow leaves are arranged in two ranks. The

erect to arching, numerous to few-flowered inflorescence has fragrant, yellow-white, lime to olive-green, heavily mottled, chocolate to maroon, sometime solid maroon (male or female on separate rachis or both on the same rachis) flowers. The female flowers appear less frequently. The large, green, sac-like, trilobed lip has a notched or fringed margin and is spotted brown. The flowers have an erect, footless column.

MONADENA

An orthographic variant introduced in *Flora*, **66**(29): 461 (1883). The correct spelling is *Monadenia*.

MONADENIA

Lindley

Gen. Sp. Orchid. Pl. 356 (1838).

ETYMOLOGY: Greek for one or single and a gland. In reference to the single, pollen gland.

LECTOTYPE: *Monadenia brevicornis* Lindley

Now recognized as belonging to the genus *Disa*, *Monadenia* was previously considered to include thirty terrestrials confined from Zimbabwe to South Africa, but has one naturalized species occurring in Australia. These erect, mostly insignificant plants have slender, unbranched stems, each with a basal rosette of narrow leaves. The long, spike-like inflorescence bears a densely packed, cylindrical arrangement of small, pale green-white flowers tipped with red or red-brown. The dorsal sepal and petals converge, forming a hood over the short, footless column. The bright yellow, narrow, entire lip is lobeless.

MONADENIORCHIS

(H. Perrier) Szlachetko & Kras

Richardiana **6**(4): 178 (2006).

ETYMOLOGY: Latin for single or one, gland and orchid. Refers to the unusual, long rostellum.

TYPE SPECIES: *Monadeniorchis monadenia*
(H. Perrier) Szlachetko & Kras
(*Cynorkis monadenia* H. Perrier)

Recognized as belonging to the genus *Cynorkis*, *Monadeniorchis* was proposed to include one terrestrial found in mid elevation, montane rain forests and rock faces of east central Madagascar (Fianarantsoa). This erect, insignificant plant has unbranched stems, each with several, narrow leaves clasping the stem upward. The few-flowered inflorescence has small, pink to magenta flowers with a concave dorsal sepal, small lateral sepals and spade-shaped petals. The tiny, narrow, entire lip is concave. The flowers have a small column with a horizontal, long rostellum.

MONANTHOCHILUS

R. Rice

Oasis (Dora Creek) **3**(Suppl.): 2 (2004).

ETYMOLOGY: Latin for single or one, flower and lip. Referring to the single flowered, almost sessile inflorescence and the immobile lip.

TYPE SPECIES: *Monanthochilus chrysanthus*
(Schlechter) R. Rice
(*Sarcochilus chrysanthus* Schlechter)

Recognized as belonging to the genus *Sarcochilus*, *Monanthochilus* was previously considered to include three epiphytes found only in upper elevation, montane rain forests of New Guinea. These mostly insignificant plants have stems adorned with narrow, scythe-like, unequal bilobed leaves. The short, solitary-flowered inflorescence, borne from the opposite leaf base, may be bundled or singular. The small, golden yellow, bright yellow to white, often fragrant flower has red to purple markings. The tiny, immobile lip has a deep, distinct spur and rectangular, flattened callus.

NOTE: These species were formerly included in *Pteroceras* and *Sarcochilus*.

MONANTHUS

(Schlechter) Brieger

Orchideen (Schlechter), ed. 3 **1**(11-12): 660 (1981).

ETYMOLOGY: Greek for single and flower. Referring to the solitary flower.

TYPE SPECIES: *Monanthus biloba* (Lindley) Brieger
(*Dendrobium bilobum* Lindley)

Now recognized as belonging to the genus *Dendrobium*, *Monanthus* was previously considered to include twenty-five epiphytes or sometimes lithophytes found in moist, high humidity, low to mid elevation, rain forests of Vanuatu, Fiji and the Solomons with New Guinea being the center of distribution. These clump-forming plants have long, slender, slightly compressed stems, each with several, needle-like, unequally bilobed leaves arranged in two ranks along the stem. The solitary-flowered inflorescence, borne from upper leaf nodes, has a small, cup-shaped, pale yellow, yellow-green or creamy flower not opening widely, lasting several days. The narrow, dark purple, obscurely trilobed lip has a yellow, slightly curved tip. The flowers have a small, slightly curved column.

MONIXUS

Finet

Bull. Soc. Bot. France **54**(9): 15 (1907).

ETYMOLOGY: Greek for single and reed-like or stiff. Referring to the plant's stiff leaves.

LECTOTYPE: *Monixus striatus* (Thouars) Finet
(*Angraecum striatum* Thouars)

Now recognized as belonging to the genus *Angraecum*, *Monixus* was previously considered to include eight epiphytes found in mid elevation, rain forests from Ghana to Zaire, the Mascarene Islands, Réunion and Madagascar. These plants have short stems, each with several, leathery, pale green, rather stiff, prominently veined leaves. The stiff, few-flowered inflorescence, borne from the base of the plant, has tiny, fragrant, white flowers with recurved segments, an obscurely trilobed lip and a cone-shaped spur. The flowers have a green, small, erect column.

MONOCANTHUS

An orthographic variant introduced in *Hort. Reg.*, **4**(45): 98 (1835). The correct spelling is *Monachanthus*.

MONOCHANTHUS

An orthographic variant introduced in *Paxton's Mag. Bot.*, **4**: 71 (1838). The correct spelling is *Monachanthus*.

MONOCHILIS

An orthographic variant introduced in *Icon. Pl. Ind. Orient. (Wight)*, **5**(1): 16 (1852). The correct spelling is *Monochilus*.

MONOCHILUS

Wallich ex Lindley

Gen. Sp. Orchid. Pl. 486 (1840).

Not *Monochilus* Fischer & C.A. Meyer (1835) Verbenaceæ.

ETYMOLOGY: Greek for single and lip. From the large, conspicuous lip that dominates the other segments.

TYPE SPECIES: *None designated*

Not validly published because of a prior use of the name, this homonym was replaced by *Zeuxine*.

MONOCHRIS

An orthographic variant introduced in *Sp. Pl. (Linnaeus)*, ed. 1, **2**: 947 (1753). The correct spelling is *Monorchis*.

MONOGRAPHIS

Thouars

Hist. Orchid. Table 2, sub 3n, *t. 45* (1822).

Not *Monographos* Fuckel (1875) Dothideaceæ.

Name published without a description. Today this name is most often referred to *Graphorkis*.

MONOMERIA

Lindley

Gen. Sp. Orchid. Pl. 61 (1830), and *Numer. List* 54, no. 1978 (1789).

Epidendroideæ ⁄ Dendrobiinæ • Currently unplaced

ETYMOLOGY: Greek for single or one and part. In reference to the incompleteness of the flower itself with its apparent absence of petals.

TYPE SPECIES: *Monomeria barbata* Lindley

Three sympodial epiphytes are found in cool, mid to upper elevation, montane cloud forests of southern China (Xizang to Yunnan), northern India (Sikkim to Assam), Myanmar to Vietnam and Thailand. These plants have roundish to ovoid pseudobulbs, each with a solitary, long, narrow, leathery leaf that is strongly keeled below. The erect or arching, few-flowered inflorescence has attractive flowers with unusual, intricate bright yellow colors. The long, hairy lateral sepals are united for their whole length and differ in color from the minute, triangular, fringed petals covered in red spots. The erect, yellow dorsal sepal is parallel to the column. The mobile, tongue-shaped, purple-red, entire or trilobed lip, joined to the column base, has short, erect side lobes. The midlobe is deeply grooved with a blunt tip. The flowers have a stout, wingless column that is obliquely twisted.

MONOPHYLLORCHIS

Schlechter

Repert. Spec. Nov. Regni Veg. Beih. **7**: 39 (1920).

Epidendroideæ ⁄ Triphoreæ

ETYMOLOGY: Greek for single or one, leaf and orchid. Refers to the solitary leaf borne by these plants.

TYPE SPECIES: *Monophyllorchis colombiana*
Schlechter
This type name is now considered a synonym of
Monophyllorchis microstyloides
(Reichenbach f.) Garay;
basionym
Pogonia microstyloides Reichenbach f.

Three uncommon, sympodial terrestrials are found in wet, low to mid elevation, hill to montane cloud forests ranging from Nicaragua to Ecuador. These slender-stemmed plants, subtended by several sheaths, each with a solitary, large, heart-shaped or

Currently Accepted | Validly Published | Invalidly Published | Published Pre-1753 | Superfluous Usage | Orthographic Variant | Fossil

O r c h i d   G e n e r a   • **250**

ovate, deep green or purple-green leaf, veined dark red on the underside and heavily streaked with silver or white spots above. The short, few-flowered inflorescence has unattractive, small, green to pale purple flowers which do not open fully, are borne in succession and short-lived. The white, entire or trilobed lip has three prominent keels at the base. The flowers have a long, footless column.

MONORCHIDES

An orthographic variant introduced in *Enum. Meth. Stirp. Helv.*, **1**: 269 (1742). The correct spelling is *Monorchidis*.

MONORCHIDIS

Ruppius
Fl. Iene.   301 (1745).

Pre-1753, therefore not validly published in fulfillment of nomenclatural rules; this name is most often referred to *Corallorhiza*.

MONORCHIS

Mentzel ex Ray
Hist. Pl. (Ray)   **2**: 1216 (1688).

Pre-1753, therefore not validly published in fulfillment of nomenclatural rules; this name is most often referred to *Herminium*.

MONORCHIS

Séguier
Pl. Veron.   **3**: 251 (1754).
ETYMOLOGY: Greek for single and orchid. Referring to the single tuber in contrast to paired ones.
TYPE SPECIES: *None designated*

Not validly published, this name is most often referred to *Herminium*.

MONORCHYS

An orthographic variant introduced in *Encycl. (Lamarck)*, **4**: 570 (1797). The correct spelling is *Monorchis*.

MONOSEPALUM

Schlechter
Repert. Spec. Nov. Regni Veg. Beih.
1(9): 682 (1912), and **1**(12): 895 (1913).
ETYMOLOGY: Greek for single and Latin for sepal. Refers to all of the sepals that are united forming a single, split-tubular structure.
TYPE SPECIES: *None designated*

Now recognized as belonging to the genus *Bulbophyllum*, *Monosepalum* was previously considered to include three epiphytes are found in mid elevation, montane rain forests of New Guinea and eastern Indonesia (Sulawesi). These uncommon plants have tiny, ovoid pseudobulbs, well-spaced along the rhizome, each with a solitary, tiny, thick leathery, blue-green leaf which is heavily streaked white on the top and has bright purple undersides. The wiry, erect to hanging, hairy, solitary-flowered inflorescence has a large, tubular, drooping to nodding, white to yellow flower with the long, slightly twisted, unequal sepals united for almost various lengths. The closely and irregularly spotted or blotched, red to maroon petals are slightly wider to anchor-shaped and have numerous, minute hairs. The bizarre, mobile, oblong, entire lip is strongly curved with downward trailing, flat tails, have scattered soft hairs and/or warts scattered on the entire surface, and is flexibly hinged to the column foot. The flowers have a short, stout column.

MONOTRIS

Lindley
Edwards's Bot. Reg.
20: sub 1701, section no. 10 (1834).
Name ICBN rejected vs. *Holothrix* Richard ex Lindley (1835) Orchidaceæ.
ETYMOLOGY: Greek for single and three times. Refers to the shape of the lip that has three lobes.
TYPE SPECIES: *Monotris secunda* Lindley
    This type name is now considered a synonym of
        Holothrix cernua (Burman f.) Schelpe;
                basionym
            Orchis cernua Burman f.

Although validly published this rejected name is referred to *Holothrix*. *Monotris* was previously considered to include one terrestrial found in South Africa's hot, arid, and sandy environments. This tall, wiry plant has erect, unbranched stems, each with two heart-shaped, basal leaves that have a fine, narrow, pale-colored border. The erect, few-flowered, red inflorescence, covered in fine hairs, has tiny flowers. The sepals are a red hue, while the rest of the flower is colored a pale lemon yellow.

MONTOLIVAEA

Reichenbach *filius*
Otia Bot. Hamburg., fasc. 2   107 (1881).
ETYMOLOGY: Named for Mount Olive in Nicaea. This is a classical name used to identify the Iznih area of northwestern Turkey (where the Nicene Creed of Christianity was devised); the area is also famous for its olives.
Or possibly the name given to the collection locality (Debre Tabor, Gonder) in Ethiopia which was made by Georg Wilhelm Schimper (1804-1878) in 1852.
TYPE SPECIES: *Montolivaea elegans* Reichenbach f.

Now recognized as belonging to the genus *Habenaria*, *Montolivaea* was previously considered to include two terrestrials found in dry, cool, mid elevation, montane regions and leafy humus of open scrub and grasslands of Ethiopia and Eritrea. These variable, erect plants have several basal leaves, or the leaves are borne low on the unbranched stem and are usually absent during flowering. The tall, numerous-flowered inflorescence has flowers opening nearly simultaneously. The often tiny, bright green or white flowers have bright yellow anthers and the triangular, erect petals have a marginal fringe of fine hairs. The long spur is usually hidden and not often seen because of the close arrangement of the flowers. The obscurely trilobed lip has two large, fleshy calli. The above type name is now considered a synonym of *Habenaria montolivaea* Kraenzlin ex Engler.

MONUSTES

Rafinesque
Fl. Tellur.   **2**: 87 (1836)[1837].
ETYMOLOGY: Greek Mythology. In honor of *Monuste*, a nymph who was just one of the fifty daughters of Danaus. The sons of Aegyptus, a King of Egypt, demanded to be wedded to the daughters of Danaus. This was an offer Danaus could not refuse. He consented to the marriages and distributed each of his daughters among them, but at the same time he instructed the girls to kill their bridegrooms on their wedding night, which they all did, except for one daughter.
TYPE SPECIES: *Monustes australis*
                (R. Brown) Rafinesque
            (*Neottia australis* R. Brown)
    This type name is now considered a synonym of
            Spiranthes sinensis (Persoon) Ames;
                basionym replaced with
            Neottia sinensis Persoon

Now recognized as belonging to the genus *Spiranthes*, *Monustes* was previously considered to include one terrestrial found in low to upper elevation, meadows, grasslands and bogs from eastern Russia (Yakutiya to Sakhalin), throughout China, Afghanistan, Mongolia, northern India (Kashmir to Assam), Korea, Japan, Malaysia, Mongolia, Myanmar to Vietnam, Malaysia and the Philippines to southern Australia. This tall, erect plant has unbranched stems, subtended by leaf sheaths, each with several, grass-like, basal leaves. The tall, spirally twisted, numerous-flowered inflorescence has tiny, widespreading, rose-magenta flowers with similar, oblong sepals and petals. The sparkling white, concave, entire lip, united to the erect, short column, has a wavy margin toward the recurved tip. This often considered weed is self-pollinating.

MOOREA

Rolfe

Gard. Chron., ser. 3   **8**(2): 7 (1890).

Not *Moorea* Lemaire (1855) Poaceæ.

ETYMOLOGY: In honor of Frederick William Moore (1857-1949), an Irish curator at the Royal Botanical Gardens Glasnevin in Dublin, who flowered the type species.

TYPE SPECIES: *Moorea irrorata* Rolfe

Not validly published because of a prior use of the name, this homonym was replaced by *Neomoorea*.

MORMODES

Lindley

Intr. Nat. Syst. Bot., ed. 2   446 (1836).

Epidendroideæ ⚬ Cymbidieæ • Catasetinæ

ETYMOLOGY: Greek for phantom or frightful object and resembling or likeness. Refers to the unusual lip shape and the relationship of the column to the lip.

TYPE SPECIES: *Mormodes atropurpurea* Lindley

These seventy-eight sympodial epiphytes or rare terrestrials are found in wet, low to mid elevation, hill to montane forests whose range extends from southern Mexico to Brazil, the Guianas and Venezuela. These plants have oblong, slightly compressed, several noded pseudobulbs, each with heavily veined, deciduous, fleshy, pleated leaves. One to several inflorescences, borne from the middle or lower nodes of the pseudobulbs, have several, often polymorphic or functionally bisexual flowers. These large, short-lived, green, red-brown, white, yellow or maroon flowers are highly variable in color, shape, size, sometimes have stripes or spots, and they have a slightly pungent fragrance. The dorsal sepal arches over the column while lateral sepals curve backward. The entire, trilobed or toothed lip is hairy or slightly hairy, usually strongly twisted in two or three sections. The thick, erect, wingless column is twisted to one side and rests on the lip.

NOTE: The stigma will not accept fertilization until the pollen has been removed. After the pollen has been removed, the column straightens and raises back to expose the stigma now ready for pollination.

MORMOLICA

An orthographic variant cited in *Orchideen (Schlechter): Liter. Reg. Band I/A, B, and C*, 51 (2003). The correct spelling is *Mormolyca*.

MORMOLYCA

Fenzl

Denkschr. Kaiserl. Akad. Wiss., Wein Math.-Naturwiss. Kl.   **1**: 253 (1850).

Epidendroideæ ⚬ Cymbidieæ • Maxillariinæ

ETYMOLOGY: Greek for hobgoblin (a grotesque or ugly elf that is mischievous, sometimes evil and malicious). Alluding to the bizarre appearance and coloration of the flower especially when viewed from the side.

TYPE SPECIES: *Mormolyca lineolata* Fenzl

This type name is now considered a synonym of *Mormolyca ringens* (Lindley) Gentil; basionym *Trigonidium ringens* Lindley

Eight unusual small, sympodial epiphytes are found in thick, dry, low to mid elevation, hill and montane forests from southern Mexico to Bolivia and Brazil. These plants have ovoid or elongate, sharply angled, slightly compressed, shiny pseudobulbs, subtended by thin, dry, leaf-bearing sheaths, each with one to four, narrow, leathery leaves. The erect, solitary-flowered inflorescence, borne from the base of the pseudobulb, has a fleshy, lurid yellow to lavender flower that has a unique appearance with unusual color combinations. The broad, concave dorsal sepal and the hanging, slightly overlapping lateral sepals are lined in purple to red. The white, trilobed lip is streaked with lavender or maroon, has minute, erect side lobes, and has a large, decurved midlobe. The flowers have a curved, wingless column.

MORMOLYCE

An orthographic variant introduced in *J. Roy. Hort. Soc.*, **7**(1): 121 (1886). The correct spelling is *Mormolyca*.

MORMOLYZE

An orthographic variant introduced in *Orchideen (Schlechter)*, ed. 1, 436 (1914). The correct spelling is *Mormolyca*.

MORMORDES

An orthographic variant introduced in *Cat. Pl. Trinidad*, 84 (1870). The correct spelling is *Mormodes*.

MRYMECOPHILA

An orthographic variant introduced in *Icon. Pl. Trop.*, ser. 1, sub 1051 (1984). The correct spelling is *Myrmecophila*.

MULUORCHIS

J.J. Wood

Kew Bull.   **39**(1): 73 (1984).

ETYMOLOGY: Named in honor of Gunung Mulu National Park in Sarawak (an eastern Malaysian state located on the island of Borneo), where the type species was collected. And Greek for orchid.

TYPE SPECIES: *Muluorchis ramosa* J.J. Wood

Now recognized as belonging to the genus *Tropidia*, *Muluorchis* was previously considered to include one saprophyte found in low to mid elevation, hill and montane forests of southeastern Malaysia (Sarawak). This erect, small, leafless plant has repeatedly branched, wiry, chestnut brown stems subtended by small, leaf-like sheaths. The erect, few-flowered inflorescence has translucent, creamy-white or pale yellow flowers with similar, narrow sepals and petals. The boat-shaped, entire lip has a strongly decurved surface with a small, pointed tip. The flowers have a small, footless column. The above type name is now considered a synonym of *Tropidia saprophytica* J.J. Smith.

MUSCARELLA

Luer

Monogr. Syst. Bot. Missouri Bot. Gard.   **105**: 94, *f.* 48 (2006).

ETYMOLOGY: Latin for lots of flies and likeness or similar. Refers to the appearance of the racemes to small flies.

TYPE SPECIES: *Muscarella aristata* (Hooker) Luer (*Pleurothallis aristata* Hooker)

Recognized as belonging to the genus *Specklinia*, *Muscarella* was proposed to include fifty epiphytes found in low to mid elevation, hill and montane forests from Mexico to Bolivia and the Antilles. These small to minute plants have slender, erect, short stems, subtended by overlapping, tubular sheaths, each with a solitary, narrow to elliptical, leathery leaf. The erect to creeping, few-flowered inflorescence has yellow, yellow-green, rose, red-purple to pale purple flowers with smooth, finely spiked or a softy hairy texture and blooms successively. The lateral sepals are united for a short length, tapering into long tails, and the translucent, ovate petals are small with some species shortly fringed. The thick, obscurely trilobed to entire lip has inrolled margins and a pair of low calli

Currently Accepted   Validly Published   Invalidly Published   Published Pre-1753   Superfluous Usage   Orthographic Variant   Fossil

Orchid Genera • **252**

or cilia with a shiny, oval patch in the center. The flowers have a small, slender, narrowly winged (if at all) column.

MXILARA

An orthographic variant introduced in *Cat. Orch.-Samml. Schiller*, 11 (1857). The correct spelling is *Maxillaria*.

MYANGIS

An orthographic variant introduced in *Hist. Orchid.*, t. 60 (1822). The correct spelling is *Miangis*.

MYANTHES

An orthographic variant introduced in *Flowers*, ed. 2, 218 (1878). The correct spelling is *Myanthus*.

MYANTHUS

Lindley
Edwards's Bot. Reg. **18**: sub 1538 (1832).
ETYMOLOGY: Greek for fly and flower. The green sepals and petals are covered with red dots resembling flies at rest on the flower's segments.
TYPE SPECIES: *Myanthus cernuus* Lindley

Now recognized as belonging to the genus *Catasetum*, *Myanthus* was previously considered to include one epiphyte found in hot, low elevation, hill forests and scrub from Trinidad and Venezuela to southern Brazil. This stout, dimorphic plant has numerous leaves borne from a spindle-shaped pseudobulb. The long, hanging to arching, few-flowered inflorescence has green, lime-green to olive-green flowers that are heavily mottled brown to maroon and sometimes are solid maroon on both sides of segments. On separate rachis, the male flowers appear more frequently than the smaller female flowers. The male flowers have a fleshy, concave or helmet-shaped lip and the female flowers have a dorsally flattened lip. The large, flat, green, trilobed lip has no pouch, is spotted brown, and has an entire margin. The flowers have a short, stout column.

MYCARANTHES

Blume
Bijdr. Fl. Ned. Ind. **7**: 352, t. 57 (1825).
Epidendroideæ • Podochileæ • Eriinæ
ETYMOLOGY: Greek for bat and flower. The lip when viewed from the side resembles a small bat.
LECTOTYPE: *Mycaranthes lobata* Blume

Nineteen sympodial epiphytes or uncommon terrestrials are found in low to upper elevation, hill to montane moss laden forests and peaty swamps of Malaysia, Indonesia (Java, Sumatra and Borneo) and New Guinea. These tall, wispy plants have long, thick stems with several nodes, each with numerous, long, narrow, irregularly notched leaves. The several, spirally arranged, few to numerous-flowered inflorescences, covered in cottony hair, have tiny, white, green, to yellow flowers sometimes purple spotted and covered with soft hairs on the sepals. The large lateral sepals and small, oblong petals are wide-spreading. The entire or trilobed lip has a bluntly rounded tip and a mid-ridge that usually ends in a large, powdery callus on the midlobe. The flowers have an erect, short, stout, wingless column with a long foot.

MYCARANTHUS

An orthographic variant introduced in *Gen. Pl. (Bentham & Hooker f.)*, **3**: 510 (1883). The correct spelling is *Mycaranthes*.

MYCARIDANTHES

An orthographic variant introduced in *Fl. Javæ*, **1**: Praef vii (1828). The correct spelling is *Mycaranthes*.

MYCROSTYLIS

An orthographic variant introduced in *Rep. Geol. Mineral. Bot. Zool. Massachusetts*, 628 (1833). The correct spelling is *Microstylis*.

MYLOPHILA

An orthographic variant introduced in *Syn. Pl. (D. Dietrich)*, **5**: 18 (1852). The correct spelling is *Hylophila*.

MYOBROMA

Not *Myobroma* Steven (1832) Leguminosæ.
An orthographic variant introduced in *Hort. Suburb. Calcutt.*, 633 (1845). The correct spelling is *Myrobroma*.

MYODA

Lindley
Edwards's Bot. Reg. **19**: sub 1618 (1833), and *Numer. List* 247, no. 7390 (1832).
ETYMOLOGY: Greek for a fly or mouse-like and resembling or likeness. Refers to the flowers which resemble a small insect when in flight.
TYPE SPECIES: *Myoda rufescens* Lindley
This type name is now considered a synonym of *Ludisia discolor* (Ker Gawler) A. Richard; basionym *Goodyera discolor* Ker Gawler

Now recognized as belonging to the genus *Ludisia*, *Myoda* was previously considered to include one terrestrial found in humid, low elevation, evergreen forests and along river banks ranging from southern China, Myanmar, Thailand to Vietnam, the Philippines and Indonesia (Sumatra). This plant is grown mostly for its showy, iridescent, dark colored, velvety maroon foliage with contrasting metallic, red or golden-yellow veins. The erect, hairy, red-brown, numerous-flowered inflorescence has tiny, sparkling white flowers with a strangely twisted, bright yellow, bilobed lip.

MYODES

Gerard
Herb. Gen. Hist. Pl. 214 (1633).
ETYMOLOGY: Greek for like a fly. Refers to the small size of the flowers.
TYPE SPECIES: *None designated*

Pre-1753, therefore not validly published in fulfillment of nomenclatural rules; this name is most often referred to *Ophrys*. *Myodes* was previously considered to include one terrestrial found in mid to upper elevation, open piney woods, grasslands and fens scattered from Sweden to Russia (West Siberia) and Ireland to Yugoslavia. This erect plant has unbranched stems, subtended by narrow leaves. The few-flowered inflorescence has narrow, slightly curved, green sepals with darker colored, narrow, hairy petals. The velvety, dark brown, deeply trilobed lip tinged red or violet, has wide spreading side lobes, and the notched or lobed midlobe has a central blue or violet pattern. The flowers have an arched column with two appendages. This name is usually now considered a synonym of *Ophrys insectifera* Linnaeus.

MYODIA

An orthographic variant cited in *Handb. Orchid.-Namen*, 479 (2005). The correct spelling is *Myoda*.

MYODIUM

Salisbury

Trans. Hort. Soc. London   **1**: 289 (1812).

ETYMOLOGY: Greek for fly and resembling or likeness. The significance of this name is obscure.

TYPE SPECIES: *Myodium araniferum*
(Hudson) Salisbury
(*Ophrys aranifera* Hudson)

Now recognized as belonging to the genus *Ophrys*, *Myodium* was previously considered to include one terrestrial found in low to mid elevation, open woodlands, scrub and nutrient-poor grasslands from Britain to Albania, southern Italy to Greece, Crete to Turkey, northern Iran and Armenia to Azerbaijan. This erect plant has numerous variants in vegetation: stem is short to tall, numerous to few-flowered; the sepals are long to short, and narrow to wide; the petals are long to short; and a lip's margin is entire to wavy. The floral color, red-brown to yellow-green, and even the widely varied, entire, obscurely to deeply trilobed lip has small to large, boldly colored patterns. The lip varies in size from large to small and sometimes the margin has a yellow edge. The above type name is now considered a synonym of *Ophrys sphegodes* Miller.

MYOIDES

An orthographic variant introduced in *Herb. Gen. Hist. Pl.*, 225 (1633). The correct spelling is *Myodes*.

MYOXANTHUS

Poeppig & Endlicher

Nov. Gen. Sp. Pl. (Poeppig & Endlicher)
1(7-10): 50, *t.* 88 (1836).

Epidendroideæ ⚬ Epidendreæ • Pleurothallidinæ

ETYMOLOGY: Greek for muscle, yellow and flower. The meaning is puzzling, perhaps referring to the red-brown flowers and the conspicuously fleshy petals.

TYPE SPECIES: *Myoxanthus monophyllus*
Poeppig & Endlicher

Forty-four unusual sympodial epiphytes, occasional lithophytes or terrestrials are found in low to upper elevation, woodlands, scrub and montane cloud forests from Mexico (Chaipas) and Belize to Bolivia, the Guianas, Venezuela and south-eastern Brazil. These small to large plants have numerous, secondary stems, sometimes swollen at the base, partially subtended by overlapping, tubular sheaths that are densely packed on the lower stem and often covered with short, stiff hairs. The plants have a solitary, narrow to

elliptical, leathery leaf. The several, solitary to few-flowered inflorescences, borne at the leaf axils, have a fly-pollinated flower and bloom successively or simultaneously. The fleshy, thickened petals have knob-like tips and the lateral sepals are united in varying degrees. The thickened, hairy, entire, trilobed or even five-lobed lip is quite variable in size, with or without various minute lobules. The margin may be fringed, ragged or entire and is delicately hinged to the column foot. The flowers have a small, slightly curved, winged or toothed column.

MYRIANGIS

Thouars

Hist. Orchid.   Table 2, sub 3o, *t. 74* (1822).

Name published without a description. Today this name is most often referred to *Angraecum*.

MYRMECHILA

D.L. Jones & M.A. Clements

Orchadian   **15**(1): 36 (2005).

ETYMOLOGY: Greek for ant and lip. Refers to the ant-like arrangement of the lip calli.

TYPE SPECIES: *Myrmechila formicifera*
(Fitzgerald) D.L. Jones & M.A. Clements
(*Chiloglottis formicifera* Fitzgerald)

Recognized as belonging to the genus *Chiloglottis*, *Myrmechila* was proposed to include four terrestrials found in shady, low elevation, open forests and scrub of eastern Australia and New Zealand. These small, colony-forming plants have slender, erect, unbranched stems, each with oblong leaves that have entire or slightly wavy margins. The solitary-flowered, red inflorescence has a small, green flower with brown or purple markings. The erect, hood-shaped dorsal sepal is quite constricted in the lower portion, has long, narrow lateral sepals and the petals are either spreading or curved against the ovary. The green, diamond-shaped, entire lip has prominent, ant-shaped, black calli. The flowers have a long, incurved column with the broad wings forming a hood over the anther.

MYRMECHIS

(Lindley) Blume

Fl. Javæ Nov. Ser.   **1**: 64, *t. 21* (1858), and
Coll. Orchid.   76, *tt.77-78* (1858).

Orchidoideæ ⚬ Cranichideæ • Goodyerinæ

ETYMOLOGY: Greek for ant. Referring to a fanciful resemblance of the small-sized flowers to ants.

TYPE SPECIES: *Myrmechis gracilis* (Blume) Blume
(*Anoectochilus gracilis* Blume)

Six sympodial terrestrials or uncommon epiphytes are found in cool to humid, low to upper elevation, hill and montane evergreen forests from Japan, Taiwan, southern China (Xizang to Fujian), northern India to Myanmar, Malaysia, Indonesia, New Guinea and the Philippines. These tiny plants have short stems, each with several to numerous, tiny, dark green, heart-shaped leaves that have silvery or golden-yellow veins, and are placed along the stem or crowded near the tip. Rarely noticed are the solitary or often paired flowers appearing at the tip of the erect, smooth to slightly hairy inflorescence. The white flowers have a faint brown tinge, barely open, and the dorsal sepal and petals converge, forming a hood. The pale green, trilobed lip is attached for a short length to the lower portion of the broad, short, footless column. The hypochile has a single, entire or bilobed appendage, a smooth to slightly hairy mesochile, and the epichile is bilobed if present.

MYRMECOPHILA

Rolfe

Orchid Rev.   **25**(291): 50 (1917).

Not *Myrmecophila* H. Christ ex Nakai (1929) Polypodiaceæ.

Epidendroideæ ⚬ Epidendreæ • Laeliinæ

ETYMOLOGY: Greek for ant and lover or loving. In reference to the habitation of its old, hollow pseudobulbs by ants.

TYPE SPECIES: *Myrmecophila tibicinis*
(Bateman ex Lindley) Rolfe
(*Epidendrum tibicinis* Bateman ex Lindley)

Ten sympodial epiphytes or subterrestrials are found in seasonally dry to damp, low to mid elevation, deciduous forests, savannas, mangroves, coastal dunes and swamps of the Cayman Islands, Aruba, the Guianas, northern Venezuela (Lara) and Belize to northern Costa Rica with greatest diversity found in Mexico. These large, robust plants' most unusual feature is the hollow, cone-shaped, tapering pseudobulbs that are often hosts to colonies of ants each with several, short, tough to fleshy, leathery leaves. The long, 15 foot (4.5 m), erect or branched, stout, numerous-flowered inflorescence has large,

Currently Accepted   Validly Published   Invalidly Published   Published Pre-1753   Superfluous Usage   Orthographic Variant   Fossil

O r c h i d   G e n e r a • **254**

showy, waxy, long-lived, fragrant flowers with a vast variability in both their bright color and shape. The often wavy sepals and slightly narrower petals are slightly to strongly twisted margins. The entire or obscurely trilobed lip has broad, upcurved sides. The broad, fiddle-shaped center is usually keelless, has a longitudinal callus of ridges, and is attached to or clasps the short, arching, wingless, footless column.

MYRMORCHIS

An orthographic variant introduced in *Orchid Conservation*, 85 (2003). The correct spelling is *Myrmechis*.

MYROBOMA

An orthographic variant introduced in *Index Kew.*, **4**: 1170 (1894). The correct spelling is *Myrobroma*.

MYROBORA

An orthographic variant introduced in *Fl. Bras. (Martius)*, **3**(4): 146 (1893). The correct spelling is *Myrobroma*.

MYROBRAMA

An orthographic variant cited in *Syn. Bot.*, 109 (1870). The correct spelling is *Myrobroma*.

MYROBROMA

Salisbury
Parad. Lond.   **2**: t. 82 (1807).
ETYMOLOGY: Greek for a sweet-smelling oil, perfume or ointment and food. Descriptive of the aromatic fragrance of the fruits.
TYPE SPECIES: *Myrobroma fragrans* Salisbury nom. illeg.
  Vanilla planifolia Jackson ex Andrew
    (*Epidendrum rubrum* Lamarck)

Not validly published, this name is referred to *Vanilla*. *Myrobroma* was previously considered to include one epiphyte found from southern Mexico to Paraguay, Cuba to Trinidad, the Guianas and Venezuela.

MYROMBOMA

An orthographic variant introduced in *Sander's Orch. Guide*, ed. 2, 286 (1927). The correct spelling is *Myrobroma*.

MYROSMODES

Reichenbach *filius*
Xenia Orchid.   **1**: 19, t. 8 (1854).
Orchidoideæ ⚘ Cranicheæ • Cranichidinæ
ETYMOLOGY: Greek for perfume, aromatic oil or fragrant and likeness. Refers to the strong fragrance.
TYPE SPECIES: *Myrosmodes nubigenum* Reichenbach f.

Ten sympodial terrestrials or occasionally epiphytes are found in upper elevation, wet montane grasslands, swamp and along river banks from Venezuela to Ecuador and Argentina. These small, erect plants have slender, unbranched stems, each with a basal rosette of short, narrow, often fleshy leaves not usually present during flowering. The stout, densely packed, numerous-flowered inflorescence has minute to small, creamy to white, smooth-textured flowers. The sepals and small, narrow petals are united at the base, forming an elongate tube. The tubular or flared, entire lip is densely fringed along its margin. The flowers have a short, stout, slightly curved column.

MYSTACIDIUM

Lindley
Compan. Bot. Mag.   **2**(19): 205 (1837).
Epidendroideæ ⚘ Vandeæ • Aerangidinæ
ETYMOLOGY: Greek for moustache. Referring to the papillose, hairy or bearded segments of the trilobed rostellum found on the type species.
TYPE SPECIES: *Mystacidium filicorne* Lindley nom. illeg.
  Mystacidium capense (Linnaeus f.) Schlechter
    (*Epidendrum capense* Linnaeus f.)

Nine monopodial epiphytes are found in deep shade to full sunlight, mid to upper elevation, montane evergreen forests, woodlands, savannas and along river banks of southeastern Africa from Tanzania to South Africa. Most of the species in this genus are superficially similar, often making identification difficult. These small or dwarf plants have short to almost stemless stems, subtended by sheathing leaf-bases, each with rounded or bilobed tipped, distichous leaves borne in clusters. The one to several, spreading to hanging, few-flowered inflorescence has small, showy, star-shaped, white, pale green, pale yellow-green or even creamy flowers with pointed or rounded, spreading sepals. The entire or obscurely trilobed lip has a long, slender spur tapering from a broad mouth at the base, and the midlobe is shorter than the side lobes. The flowers have a short or long, slender, wingless column.

MYSTACIDUM

An orthographic variant introduced in *Rev. Gén. Bot.*, **11**: 413 (1988). The correct spelling is *Mystacidium*.

MYSTACORCHIS

Szlachetko & Margońska
Polish Bot. J.   **46**(2): 117 (2002).
ETYMOLOGY: Greek for moustache and orchid. An allusion to the position of the lateral sepals beneath the nose-like lip.
TYPE SPECIES: *Mystacorchis mystax*
  (Luer) Szlachetko & Margońska
  (*Pleurothallis mystax* Luer)

Recognized as belonging to the genus *Stelis*, *Mystacorchis* was proposed to include one epiphyte found in cool, moist, low to upper elevation, hill and montane forests of Panama (Veraguas). This plant has twig-like stems, subtended by several leaf-like sheaths, each with a solitary, ovate leaf. The several, solitary-flowered inflorescences opening in succession, have a maroon flower that emerges from a conspicuous, spatula-shaped ring on the leaf stem. The dorsal sepal is edged in dark maroon and the narrow lateral sepals are united to the middle, then spread widely and taper to a point. The small, rosy, arrow-shaped petals converge over the rosy, mobile, entire lip, which has a long, channeled claw and a spoon-shaped tip. The flowers have a short, slightly curved, footless column.

36

CENTURIA X MONOCOT.
ORCHIDES or SYNARMIA. This fine Nat. Order of plants shall be continued here; having already given many Genera of it, see 1, 117 to 138, 183 to 186, 204, 214, 220, to 228, 318 to 344, 372 to 377, 382 to 385, 801 to 805. It is now become one of the most interesting and prolific orders, evincing the vast progress of modern Botany. Linneus had only 9 Genera of it, Adanson only 7 although he had *Vanilla* omitted by Linneus, Necker in 1790 had 17 Genera, Jussieu, Swartz, Richard, Thouars had vastly increased them,(Persoon had 30) and now Lindley has over 200 Genera; but 100 have been or will be added by myself. The single Genus *Epidendrum* which was a confuse medley has furnished 30 Genera, and even as reformed lately it contains 10 or 15 more as I have shown. Necker had 3 which I could not ascertain as he gave no typical sp. but I give here their characters that they may be ascertained and restored.
  901. PHADROSANTHUS Neck. 1474. Petalis 4-5patulis ineq. undul. label. basi tubul. quadrato dilatato ad apex, anther. 2. stig. infundib. *Scaposa*—This must include several Dendrobiums, and Necker intimated that like Epidendrum, it had many anomalies.
  902. EUDISANTHEMA Neck. 1475 petalis 5 linear. subeq. Label. basi tubul. columna amplectens, anthera cuculata 4loc. pollinis 8. stylo tubo adnato, stigma infundib. caps. ventricosa contorta. *Caulescens*.—Is it the Octomeria? of late Authors.
  903. ABROCHIS Neck. 1470. diff. *Orchis*, petalis 5 ineq. label. resupinato ad basi galei-

Rafinesque
Flora Telluriana
4: page 36 (1836).

NABALUIA

Ames

Orchidaceæ (Ames) **6**: 70, *t.* 87 (1920).

Epidendroideæ ⬩ Arethuseæ • Coelogyninæ

ETYMOLOGY: Name is derived from Mount Kinabalu (13,455 ft./4,000 m), the tallest mountain in southeast Asia, located on the island of Borneo toward the northern coast of Sabah (Malaysia), where the type species was collected.

TYPE SPECIES: *Nabaluia clemensii* Ames

Three sympodial epiphytes or rare lithophytes are found in mid to upper elevation, montane moss laden forests of Mount Kinabalu of Malaysia (Sabah). These clustered plants have more or less flattened, smooth pseudobulbs, each with two narrow, stiff leaves that are turned to one side on the rhizome. The erect, rigid, flattened, numerous-flowered inflorescence has small, fragrant, yellow, lemon-green to green-yellow flowers arranged in two alternating rows. The rachis continues to elongate during flowering. The white to pink, immobile, trilobed lip has a bilobed, sac-like hypochile with a thick, swollen epichile that is recurved and a horseshoe-shaped basal callus. The flowers have a long, slightly curved footless column.

NAEOTTIA

An orthographic variant introduced in *Atti Soc. Ital. Sci. Nat.*, **16**: 334 (1873). The correct spelling is *Neottia*.

NAGELIELLA

L.O. Williams

Bot. Mus. Leafl. **8**: 144 (1940).

Epidendroideæ ⬩ Epidendreæ • Laeliinæ

ETYMOLOGY: In honor of Otto Nagel (1894-1967), a German painter, printmaker, author and journalist who traveled widely in Mexico. And Latin for diminutive.

TYPE SPECIES: *Nageliella purpurea*
(Lindley) L.O. Williams
(*Hartwegia purpurea* Lindley)

Two tufted, sympodial epiphytes or uncommon terrestrials are found in low to mid elevation, rocky hillsides or montane oak-pine forests from southern Mexico to Costa Rica. These small plants have slender, short stems (pseudobulbous), each with a solitary, tough, purple leaf that sometimes has white to brown-purple mottling. The tall, slender to wiry, numerous to few-flowered inflorescences have small, bell-shaped, bright purple-red, pink to lavender flowers clustered at the ends of the branches. The inflorescence can continuously produce flowers for several years. The sepals converge with the column foot, forming a chin-like projection and the petals have minutely, ciliate margins. The small, sac-like lip is entire or trilobed at its base. The flowers have a slender, slightly curved column.

NANDA

An orthographic variant introduced in *Syn. Pl. (D. Dietrich)*, **5**: 12 (1852). The correct spelling is *Vanda*.

NANERIA

An orthographic variant introduced in *Orchid.-Buch*, 364 (1892). The correct spelling is *Nauenia*.

NANODES

Lindley

Edwards's Bot. Reg. **18**: *t.*1541 (1832).

Epidendroideæ ⬩ Epidendreæ • Laeliinæ

ETYMOLOGY: Greek for dwarfish. Referring to the very small size of both the plant and the flowers.

TYPE SPECIES: *Nanodes discolor* Lindley

Two sympodial epiphytes are found in humid, mid elevation, montane cloud forests from southern Mexico to Peru, Trinidad, Venezuela, the Guianas and northern Brazil. These tufted, arching to hanging plants have clustered, cane-like, leafy stems, completely subtended by compressed, fleshy, gray-green, leaf-like sheaths. The leathery, unequally bilobed leaves are arranged in two ranks and somewhat twisted at the base. The several, short, solitary or paired inflorescences have a fantastic, heavily textured, translucent, green, green-yellow, green-brown or pink-purple flower with narrow sepals and petals. The extraordinarily intricate, frilly, shortly clawed, purple-brown to a rich dark maroon, entire lip is partially fused to the short, stout, footless column.

NARICA

Rafinesque

Fl. Tellur. **2**: 87 (1836)[1837].

ETYMOLOGY: Supposedly named for a nymph but none by this name can be found in the classical literature. "Nymph" is a Greek word meaning young woman. Nymphs were considered an important part of Greek religion.

TYPE SPECIES: *Narica moschata*
(Smith) Rafinesque nom. illeg.
Sarcoglottis acaulis (Smith) Schlechter
(*Neottia acaulis* Smith)

Now recognized as belonging to the genus *Sarcoglottis*, *Narica* was previously considered to include one terrestrial found in low to mid elevation, hill to montane forests from Costa Rica to Peru, Venezuela and the Guianas to northern Brazil. This erect plant has slender to stout, unbranched stems, each with several, deciduous leaves in a basal rosette. The velvety green leaves are streaked white above and a dull green, mottled with white specs below. The tall, hairy, few-flowered inflorescence has flowers that are green on the outside and pale green-white inside. The small dorsal sepal and petals converge, forming a hood over the slender column. The long haired, lateral sepals hang downward or curve forward.

NASONIA

Lindley

Pl. Hartw. 150 (1844).

ETYMOLOGY: Latin for the nose. Refers to the hood of the clinandrium (anther bed) that resembles a nose on the column.

TYPE SPECIES: *Nasonia punctata* Lindley

Now recognized as belonging to the genus *Fernandezia*, *Nasonia* was previously considered to include seven epiphytes or terrestrials found in wet, upper elevation, montane cloud forests from Venezuela to Peru. These small, often hanging plants have branching stems, each with a several, tiny, needle-like leaves. The short, solitary-flowered inflorescence has large, pink to bright vermilion red flowers with small sepals and large, broad petals. The spade-shaped, entire lip has a small, hooded column. The above type name is now considered a synonym of *Fernandezia maculata* Garay & Dunsterville.

NAUENIA

Klotzsch

Allg. Gartenzeitung **21**(25): 193 (1853).

ETYMOLOGY: Dedicated to Charles Nauen (1830-1881), a German factory owner and orchid collector from Berlin, whose head gardener and horticulturist, Friedrich August Hermann Gireoud (1821-1896), received a plant specimen from Josef Warszewicz (1812-1866) and brought it to flower for the first time.

TYPE SPECIES: *Nauenia spectabilis* Klotzsch

Now recognized as belonging to the genus *Lacaena*, *Nauenia* was previously considered to include one epiphyte found in dry, mid elevation, premontane forests and steep embankments from southern Mexico (Chiapas) to Panama. This robust plant has ovate pseudobulbs, subtended by thin, dry, triangular sheaths, each with several, thinly textured, deciduous, pleated leaves. The hanging, numerous-flowered inflorescence has lavender to pink, fragrant flowers covered with darker hued spots. The concave dorsal sepal and small petals converge, forming a hood over the small, wingless column. The darker colored, trilobed lip has upcurved side lobes, and the spreading, triangular midlobe has a raised, basal callus.

NAVENIA

An orthographic variant introduced in *Gen. Pl. (Bentham & Hooker f.)*, **3**: 547 (1883). The correct spelling is *Nauenia*.

NEIPPERGIA

C. Morren

Ann. Soc. Roy. Agric. Gand **5**: 375, *t.* 282 (1849).

ETYMOLOGY: Dedicated to Alfred Karl August Camillus von Neipperg (1807-1865), a German count from Württemberg and a patron of the natural sciences.

TYPE SPECIES: *Neippergia chrysantha* C. Morren

Now recognized as belonging to the genus *Acineta*, *Neippergia* was previously considered to include one epiphyte found in upper elevation, montane rain forests of southeastern Mexico to Panama. This plant has ovoid, somewhat compressed pseudobulbs, subtended with a basal sheath, each with several, thick, pleated leaves. The hanging, numerous-flowered inflorescence has lemon yellow, fragrant, long-lived flowers not opening widely. The cup-shaped sepals enfold the small, red spotted, thinly textured petals, the stout, hairy column, and lip. The shortly clawed, trilobed lip has large, roundish side lobes, and a small, slightly concave midlobe with a deep maroon callus.

NELIS

Rafinesque ex Lindley

Coll. Bot. (Lindley) sub *t.* 25 (1821).

Name published without a description. Today this name is most often referred to *Goodyera*.

NEMACIANTHUS

D.L. Jones & M.A. Clements

Orchadian **13**(10): 440 (2002).

ETYMOLOGY: Greek for thread and *Acianthus*, a genus of orchids. Referring to the long, thread-like extension on the sepals.

TYPE SPECIES: *Nemacianthus caudatus*
(R. Brown) D.L. Jones & M.A. Clements
(*Acianthus caudatus* R. Brown)

Recognized as belonging to the genus *Acianthus*, *Nemacianthus* was proposed to include one small terrestrial found in shady, low elevation, coastal scrub and woodlands of southern Australia. This slender, erect plant has unbranched stems, each with a solitary, heart-shaped, basal leaf that is purple underneath. The erect, few-flowered inflorescence has dark maroon flowers with an unpleasant fragrance. The erect dorsal sepal is bent over the small, slender, slightly curved, wingless column, and tapers to a hair-like point. The narrow, tapering lateral sepals are almost as long as the dorsal. The crimson or dark maroon, entire lip has two tooth-like basal calli.

NEMACOMIA

An orthographic variant introduced in *Fl. Bras. (Martius)*, **3**(5): 9 (1898). The correct spelling is *Nemaconia*.

NEMACONIA

Knowles & Westcott

Fl. Cab. **2**: 127 (1838).

Epidendroideæ • Cymbidieæ • Oncidiinæ

ETYMOLOGY: Greek for thread and dart or javelin. Descriptive of the narrow leaves.

TYPE SPECIES: *Nemaconia graminifolia*
Knowles & Westcott
not *Fernandezia graminifolia* Ruiz & Pavón, fide Dressler

One epiphyte or lithophyte is found in seasonally wet, low to upper elevation, hill scrub to montane rain to evergreen forests from southern Mexico to Honduras. This bamboo-like plant has long, thin, finely ridged stems; mature stems have one to two nodes near the base and others at midpoint with occasional branching at the tip into further nodes. The two to three-flowered inflorescence has small, rather fleshy, white, green or creamy, maroon streaked, lined, dotted or blotched, fragrant flowers. The broad, white to yellow, shortly clawed, entire to obscurely four-lobed lip, sometimes with radiating lines, has a disk with papillose, is flat with warts or without any callus and has an entire margin. The flowers have a short, maroon, wingless column.

NEMATOCERAS

Hooker *filius*

Fl. Nov.-Zel. **1**(4): 249, *t.* 57 (1853).

ETYMOLOGY: Greek for thread and horn. Refers to the sepals and petals that both look like horns.

LECTOTYPE: *Nematoceras macrantha* Hooker f.

Now recognized as belonging to the genus *Corybas*, *Nematoceras* was previously considered to include fourteen terrestrials found in damp, shady, low elevation, scrub of New Zealand and Australia. These small to tiny, erect plants have short, unbranched stems, each with a solitary, heart-shaped, basal leaf that has red veins and wavy margins. The solitary-flowered inflorescence has a relatively large, red to green and purple flower. The concave dorsal sepal forms a hood over the widely expanded lip and tapers to a long, thread-like tail. The minute to tail-like lateral sepals and petals are almost hidden beneath the cone-shaped spur. The boat-shaped, entire lip often has a toothed or fringed margin.

NEMATOCEROS

An orthographic variant introduced in *Sander's Orch. Guide*, ed. 1, 132 (1901). The correct spelling is *Nematoceras*.

NEMURANTHES

Rafinesque

Fl. Tellur. **2**: 61 (1836)[1837].

ETYMOLOGY: Greek for thread, tail and flower. Descriptive of the long, thread-like spur.

TYPE SPECIES: *None designated*

Now recognized as belonging to the genus *Habenaria*, *Nemuranthes* was previously considered to include two terrestrials found in low to mid elevation, deciduous forests and grasslands of southern Florida, Cuba and southern Mexico to the Guianas. These erect plants have unbranched stems, each with a pale green rosette of leaves that lies flush to the ground or has slender leaves clasping the stem upward. The erect, few-flowered inflorescence has striking white and green flowers with the concave dorsal sepal forming a hood over the small column. The petals have long, thread-like extensions sweeping gracefully outward and then downward. Matching them is yet another pair of thread-like extensions springing from either side of the base of the trilobed lip. Trailing behind and down the flower is the extra long, slender spur. One species is now considered a synonym of *Habenaria longicauda* Hooker and the other a synonym of *Habenaria quinqueseta* (Michaux) Swartz.

NEOBARTLETTIA

Schlechter

Repert. Spec. Nov. Regni Veg. **16**: 440 (1920).

Not *Neobartlettia* R.M. King & H. Robinson (1971) Asteraceæ.

ETYMOLOGY: Greek for new and in honor of Albert William Bartlett (1875-1943), a British-born collector, mycologist, superintendent of the Botanical Gardens (established in 1877 with the purchase of the coffee plantation *Vlissingen* from Joseph Bourda) in Georgetown, Guyana.

TYPE SPECIES: *None designated*

Now recognized as belonging to the genus *Palmorchis*, *Neobartlettia* was previously considered to include four terrestrials found in low elevation, scrub of the Guianas, Brazil, Peru and Colombia. These plants, often resembling a seedling palm, have clusters of tall (sometimes several feet in height) reed-like stems, each with several, large, pleated, veined leaves. The long stalked, few-flowered inflorescence, subtended with narrow bracts, has small, white or pale green-white, short-lived flowers. The trilobed lip, attached to the long, footless column, has a hairy basal callus, and the midlobe is blunt or bilobed.

NEOBATHIEA

Schlechter

Repert. Spec. Nov. Regni Veg. Beih. **33**: 369 (1925).

Epidendroideæ ⚘ Vandeæ • Angraecinæ

ETYMOLOGY: Greek for new and in commemoration of Joseph Marie Henri Alfred Perrier de la Bâthie (1873-1958), a French plant collector and botanist who wrote extensively about the orchids of Madagascar.

TYPE SPECIES: *Neobathiea perrieri* (Schlechter) Schlechter (*Aeranthes perrieri* Schlechter)

Five uncommon, monopodial epiphytes are found in humid, mid elevation, tropical forests or mossy rocks of central and western Madagascar and the Comoros Islands. These small plants have short stems, each with several, narrow to oblong, leathery, glossy, unequally bilobed, dark green leaves. The short, solitary to few-flowered inflorescence has pale green to white flowers often changing color as they age. The showy, intricate flower has similar, narrow, lateral sepals and petals which are not attached to the base of the short to stout, fleshy column. The shortly clawed, entire lip is trilobed in the middle, has a heart-shaped base, and has a long, slender spur with a broad, funnel-shaped mouth. The flowers have a short, erect, stout column.

NEOBENNETTIA

Senghas

J. Orchideenfr. **8**(4): 364 (2001).

Epidendroideæ ⚘ Cymbidieæ • Oncidiinæ

ETYMOLOGY: Greek for new and in commemoration of David Edward Bennett (1923-), an American-born Peruvian mushroom farmer, orchidologist and co-author of *Icones Orchidacearum Peruvianrum*.

TYPE SPECIES: *Neobennettia genegeorgei* (D.E. Bennett & Christenson) Senghas (*Lockhartia genegeorgei* D.E. Bennett & Christenson)

One sympodial epiphyte is found in wet, mid elevation, montane forests of central Peru (Huanuco). This tufted plant has small, cone-shaped, strongly flattened pseudobulbs, subtended by overlapping, narrow, leaf sheaths, each with a solitary, narrow leaf folded lengthwise. The erect, branched, few-flowered inflorescence, subtended by several, prominent leaf-like bracts, has small, yellow-orange flowers with a concave dorsal sepal. The prominent trilobed lip has small, lateral side lobes, and a fiddle-shaped, deeply notched midlobe that has orange bands on top of the callus in a crater-like depression. The flowers have a short, erect, yellow, footless column.

NEOBENTHAMIA

Rolfe

Gard. Chron., ser. 3 **10**: 272, f. 33 (1891).

Epidendroideæ ⚘ Vandeæ • Polystachyinæ

ETYMOLOGY: Greek for new and in commemoration of George Bentham (1800-1884), a British taxonomist, systematic botanist, secretary and later president of the Royal Horticultural Society, author of *Handbook of the British Flora*, *Plantas Hartwegianas* and co-author of *Genera Plantarum*.

TYPE SPECIES: *Neobenthamia gracilis* Rolfe

One sympodial epiphyte or lithophyte is found in low to mid elevation, rock faces or moss laden ledges of eastern Tanzania and Zambia usually in full sunlight. This large, grass-like plant has long, brittle stems, each with narrow, thinly textured, alternating leaves. The tall, terminal, head-like, numerous-flowered inflorescence is subtended with narrow, brown bracts and can obtain three feet (1 m) or more in height. The clustered, charming, long-lived, fragrant, cup-shaped white flowers do not open widely and sometimes have soft hairs scattered on both surfaces of the sepals and petals. The white to yellow, obscurely trilobed lip has the center edged in pink or brown-red dots, is slightly hairy, and the midlobe has a notched tip and a ruffled margin. The flowers have a short, almost cone-like column with an obscure foot.

NEOBOLUSIA

Schlechter

Bot. Jahrb. Syst. **20**(Beibl. 50): 5 (1895).

Orchidoideæ ⚘ Orchideæ • Orchidinæ

ETYMOLOGY: Greek for new and in commemoration of Harry Bolus (1834-1911), a British-born South African banker, sheep farmer, stockbroker, amateur botanist and author of *Orchids of South Africa*.

TYPE SPECIES: *Neobolusia tysonii* (Bolus) Schlechter (*Brachycorythis tysonii* Bolus)

Four uncommon, sympodial terrestrials are found in mid elevation, montane grasslands and savannas from Tanzania to South Africa. These small plants are often overlooked because of their inconspicuous and dull color. The tall, erect plants have stout, unbranched stems, each with several, spreading, basal leaves graduating upward into floral bracts. The slender, smooth few-flowered inflorescence has small flowers with green to brown sepals. The slightly hooded dorsal sepal and white to pink petals converge, forming a hood over the short, slender column. The white, clawed, entire or trilobed lip has a dark red-brown stripe down the center of the small

Currently Accepted   Validly Published   Invalidly Published   Published Pre-1753   Superfluous Usage   Orthographic Variant   Fossil

midlobe that has an inrolled margin and a basal callus.

NEOCLEMENSIA

Carr
Gard. Bull. Straits Settlem. **8**: 180 (1935).

Epidendroideæ ⚘ **Gastrodieæ**

ETYMOLOGY: Greek for new and dedicated to Joseph Clemens (1862-1936), a British-born American clergyman, who while stationed in the Philippines as a U.S. army missionary chaplain, and along with his wife, Mary Clemens née Strong (1873-1968), collected the flora on Mount Kinabalu in Borneo.

TYPE SPECIES: *Neoclemensia spathulata* Carr

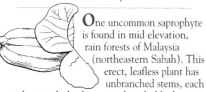

One uncommon saprophyte is found in mid elevation, rain forests of Malaysia (northeastern Sabah). This erect, leafless plant has unbranched stems, each with several, thinly textured, scale-like bracts. The plant somewhat imitates a *Gastrodia*. The erect, solitary-flowered inflorescence has a thinly textured, flower with small, narrow, thread-like, bright orange petals that are united at the base to the white lateral sepals. The large, united sepals form a floral tube shape that has a recurved tip and various papillose. The broad, dull green, shortly clawed, entire lip, united to the base of the small, stout column, has a short, bilobed keel and is suffused olive-brown toward the tip. The claw of the lip is oblong or slightly square, has two calli near the tip and is minutely papillose throughout. The flowers have a long, slender to stout, footless column.

NEOCOGNIAUXIA

Schlechter
Symb. Antill. **7**: 495 (1913).

Epidendroideæ ⚘ **Epidendreæ** • **Pleurothallidinæ**

ETYMOLOGY: Greek for new and in commemoration of Alfred Célestin Cogniaux (1841-1916), a Belgian school teacher, and later a botanist who worked extensively on the orchids of Brazil, the West Indies, and American orchids in general and author of various important orchid monographs including *Dictionnaire Icongraphique des Orchidées*.

TYPE SPECIES: *Neocogniauxia monophylla*
(Grisebach) Schlechter
(*Trigonidium monophyllum* Grisebach)

Two sympodial epiphytes are found in mid elevation, montane forests of Jamaica and Hispaniola. These small plants have short, slender stems, subtended by tubular, leaf sheaths, each with a solitary, narrow to oblong, leathery leaf. The erect to arching, slender solitary-flowered inflorescence, borne from the base of the stem, has a sheath-like, purple spotted bract. The showy flower is brightly hued in various shades of orange. The small, entire or obscurely triloled

---

lip, united to the column, has a ridged disc with a sac-like outgrowth in the center. The flowers have a short, arching, winged, footless, bright orange column.

NEOCRIBBIA

Szlachetko
Ann. Bot. Fenn. **40**(1): 69 (2003).

ETYMOLOGY: Greek for new and in commemoration of Phillip James Cribb (1946-), a British botanist, deputy keeper of the Herbarium at the Royal Botanic Gardens, Kew, and author of numerous books on orchids.

TYPE SPECIES: *Neocribbia wakefieldii*
(Rolfe) Szlachetko
(*Angraecum wakefieldii* Rolfe)

Recognized as belonging to the genus *Solenangis*, *Neocribbia* was proposed to include one epiphyte found in low elevation, coastal scrub of Kenya and Tanzania. This climbing plant has short, bright brown, erect to hanging stems, each with numerous roots all along the branching, flexible stem. The oblong to narrow leaves have unequally bilobed tips. The long, few-flowered inflorescence has small, fragrant, white, well-spaced flowers. The long, narrowly clawed, trilobed lip has long, narrow side lobes, a small, narrow midlobe that tapers to a point, and a long, thread-like, pale green spur with a red-brown tip. The flowers have a short, erect, wingless, footless column.

NEODENTHAMIA

An orthographic variant cited in *Pl. Alkaloids*, 161 (1996). The correct spelling is *Neobenthamia*.

NEODRYAS

Reichenbach *filius*
Bot. Zeitung (Berlin) **10**: 834 (1852).

ETYMOLOGY: Greek for new and wood nymph. Alluding possibly to a woodland habitat.

Greek Mythology. *Dryads* are female nymphs of nature (spirits), who preside over groves and forests. Each nymph is born with a certain tree over which she watches and should the tree perish, then she will die with it.

TYPE SPECIES: *Neodryas rhodoneura* Reichenbach f.

Now recognized as belonging to the genus *Cyrtochilum*, *Neodryas* was previously considered to include two epiphytes or lithophytes found in upper elevation, montane forests of Peru and Bolivia. These plants have ovoid to ovate, sharp-edged pseudobulbs, subtended by two pairs of distichous, overlapping, leaf bearing sheaths, each bearing one to several pairs of distichous,

---

oblong or strap-shaped leaves. The long, branched, numerous-flowered inflorescence has small, cup-shaped, bright red-orange or white flowers not opening fully. The bright yellow to orange-red, trilobed or entire lip is continuous with the short, footless column.

NEODRYES

An orthographic variant introduced in *Hamburger Garten- Blumenzeitung*, **9**: 84 (1853). The correct spelling is *Neodryas*.

NEOESCOBARIA

Garay
Orquideologia **7**(4): 194 (1972).

ETYMOLOGY: Greek for new and to commemorate Gilberto Escobar y Restrepo (1916-1988), a Colombian industrialist, botanist, photographer and orchid enthusiast who collected the type species.

TYPE SPECIES: *Neoescobaria callichroma*
(Reichenbach f.) Garay
(*Trichopilia callichroma* Reichenbach f.)

Now recognized as belonging to the genus *Helcia*, *Neoescobaria* was previously considered to include two epiphytes found in low to mid elevation, hill and montane forests of Colombia and Peru. These plants have clustered, cone-shaped pseudobulbs, partially subtended by overlapping, thin, dry sheaths, each with a solitary, oblong, leathery leaf. The few-flowered inflorescence has showy, yellow-green flowers with bold red blotches. The large, bell-shaped, white, obscurely trilobed lip, enfolding or loosely encircling the short, club-shaped, footless column, is scarcely fused to the base of the column and has purple-brown streaks radiating toward the base.

NEOFINETIA

H.H. Hu
Rhodora **27**: 107 (1925).

Epidendroideæ ⚘ **Vandeæ** • **Aeridinæ**

ETYMOLOGY: Greek for new and in commemoration of Achille Eugène Finet (1862-1913), a French botanist, laboratory assistant, editor of the *Notulae systematicae*, and botanical illustrator who specialized in the orchids of China and Japan.

TYPE SPECIES: *Neofinetia falcata* (Thunberg) Hu
(*Orchis falcata* Thunberg)

Three delightful dwarf, monopodial epiphytes are distributed in mid elevation, montane deciduous forests from Korea, Japan (Honshu, Shikoku, Kyushu and Ryukyu Islands), eastern China (Hubei to Fujian) and Taiwan. These evergreen plants have short, erect stems, each with several, distichous, flat, needle-like, fleshy or leathery leaves arranged in two ranks which gives the plant a fan-shaped appearance. Some clones are highly prized and grown mostly for their variegated foliage. The few-flowered inflorescence, borne from the lower leaf axils, has extremely fragrant, pristine white to pale pink flowers with similarly shaped sepals and petals. The long, slender, trilobed lip has small, erect side lobes, a tongue-shaped, forward bend midlobe, and a long to short, slender, curved spur. The flowers have a short, wingless, footless column.

NOTE: This species has been cultivated by the Japanese warrior class for centuries. At one time anyone who was not a member of the samurai (warrior) class was forbidden even to possess a plant.

NEOGARDNERIA

Schlechter ex Garay

Orquideologia   **8**(1): 32 (1973).

Epidendroideæ ✻ **Cymbidieæ** • **Zygopetalinæ**

ETYMOLOGY: Greek for new and in commemoration of George Gardner (1812-1849), a Scottish author, botanist and explorer who collected the flora of eastern Brazil. He was later superintendent of the Peradeniya Botanic Garden in Sri Lanka.

TYPE SPECIES: *Neogardneria murrayana*
(Gardner ex Hooker) Schlechter ex Garay
(*Zygopetalon murrayanum* Gardner ex Hooker)

One small but attractive sympodial epiphyte is found in humid, mid elevation, evergreen forests of the Serra dos Órgãos in south-eastern Brazil (Rio Janeiro). This plant has clustered, ovoid pseudobulbs, subtended by leaf-bearing sheaths, each with two channeled, deciduous, narrow leaves. The few-flowered inflorescence has large bracts and the large, showy, waxy, fragrant, green to bright green flowers that have similar sepals and petals. The white, clawed, trilobed lip, spotted or striped red, has small, erect, oblong side lobes, and has a horseshoe-shaped, crested callus on the narrow midlobe that is bent outward. The flowers have a small, fleshy, short-footed column.

NEOGYNA

Reichenbach *filius*

Bot. Zeitung (Berlin)   **10**: 931 (1852).

Epidendroideæ ✻ **Arethuseæ** • **Coelogyninæ**

ETYMOLOGY: Greek for new and woman or female. An allusion to the new characters of this genus when compared with *Coelogyne*, an orchid genus.

TYPE SPECIES: *Neogyna gardneriana*
(Lindley) Reichenbach f.
(*Coelogyne gardneriana* Lindley)

One uncommon, sympodial epiphyte or lithophyte is found in upper elevation, montane forests and rocky valleys of northern India (Assam),

Nepal, Bhutan, Myanmar, southwestern China (Yunnan), Thailand and Laos. This small plant has conspicuous, clustered, ovoid to cone-shaped, one-noded pseudobulbs, subtended at the base with fibrous sheaths, each with two large, yellow-green, papery leaves. The hanging, few-flowered inflorescence has large, thinly textured, white flowers, not opening widely, that are somewhat tubular in shape. The long, trilobed lip, attached to the footless column, has a sac-like or flat base with a bright yellow keel. The hypochile has broad, erect side lobes, sac-shaped at the base, and the epichile has semi-orbicular, kidney-shaped, widely notched lobes that remain folded around the rather long, curved column.

NOTE: This species is often included in *Coelogyne*.

NEOGYNE

An orthographic variant introduced in *Cat. Orch.-Samml. Schiller*, ed. 1, 49 (1857). The correct spelling is *Neogyna*.

NEOKOEHLERIA

Schlechter

Repert. Spec. Nov. Regni Veg.   **10**: 390 (1912).

ETYMOLOGY: Greek for new and in commemoration of H. Köhler (*fl.* 1905-1919s), a German botanist who collected some Peruvian orchids for Schlechter.

TYPE SPECIES: *None designated*

Now recognized as belonging to the genus *Scelochilus*, *Neolehmannia* was previously considered to include ten epiphytes found in wet, mid elevation, montane forests from Venezuela to Peru and Bolivia. These tiny, tufted, inconspicuous plants have minute pseudobulbs, each with a solitary, narrow, channeled leaf that is bright green when young, then becomes pale purple as it ages. The simple or branched, few-flowered inflorescence has small, tubular, pale white-yellow to red-violet flowers that barely open and then only in the front. The tongue-like or wedge-shaped, entire lip has a rounded tip with a fringed margin, and has an elongated, swollen spur.

NEOLAUCHAEA

An orthographic variant introduced in *Fragm. Florist. Geobot.*, **3**(Suppl.): 75 (1995). The correct spelling is *Neolauchea*.

NEOLAUCHEA

Kraenzlin

Bull. Herb. Boissier, ser. 1   **5**: 110 (1897).

ETYMOLOGY: Greek for new and in recognition of Friedrich Wilhelm George Lauche (1827-1882), a German-born director for Prince Johannes II (1840-1929) of Liechtenstein gardens. He sent many botanical novelties to Kraenzlin and is the author of *Deutsche Dendrologie*.

TYPE SPECIES: *Neolauchea pulchella* Kraenzlin

Now recognized as belonging to the genus *Isabelia*, *Neolauchea* was previously considered to include three epiphytes found in mid elevation, montane forests of south-eastern Brazil (Rio de Janeiro, São Paulo, Paraná, Santa Catarina and Rio Grande do Sul). These dwarf plants are fragile in all their vegetative parts. They have chains of small, ovoid pseudobulbs, subtended by narrow sheaths, each with a solitary, needle-like, leathery leaf. The short, thread-like, erect or arching, solitary-flowered inflorescences have rather hooded, rosy-red or lilac, widespreading flowers suffused brown toward the base. The concave, oblong, entire lip has two teeth near the base. The flowers have a short column.

NEOLEHMANNIA

Kraenzlin

Bot. Jahrb. Syst.   **26**: 478 (1899).

ETYMOLOGY: Greek for new and in dedication to Friedrich Carl Lehmann (1850-1903), a German consul to Colombia who collected plant specimens in Guatemala, Costa Rica, Colombia and Ecuador.

TYPE SPECIES: *Neolehmannia epidendroides*
Kraenzlin

Now recognized as belonging to the genera *Epidendrum* and *Nanodes*, *Neolehmannia* was previously considered to include fifteen epiphytes found in upper elevation, montane oak-pine forests from Mexico to Peru. These tiny, barely two inches tall (5 cm) plants have erect, cane-like, clustered, branching stems, each with several, narrow, leathery leaves. The solitary-flowered inflorescence, borne from leaf nodes, has an almost beetle-like, pale purple-green flower with narrow lateral sepals and petals. The broad, shiny, recurved, dark red-brown, arrow-head-shaped even to shallowly notched, entire lip has a green, fringed margin and a small spur. The flowers have a short column. The above type name is now considered a synonym of *Epidendrum neolehmannia* Schlechter.

NEOLINDLEYA

Kraenzlin

Orchid. Gen. Sp. **1**: 651 (1899).

ETYMOLOGY: Greek for new and in dedication to John Lindley (1799-1865), a British botanist, horticulturist, professor of botany, a prolific botanical writer and author of *The Genera and Species of Orchidaceous Plants* that later became a landmark for the study of orchids.

TYPE SPECIES: *Neolindleya decipiens*
(Lindley) Kraenzlin nom. illeg.
(*Platanthera decipiens* Lindley nom. illeg.)
This type name is now considered a synonym of
LECTOTYPE: *Platanthera camtschatica* (Chamisso) Soó
(*Orchis camtschatica* Chamisso)

Now recognized as belonging to the genus *Platanthera*, *Neolindleya* was previously considered to include two terrestrials found in low to mid elevation, birch woodlands and thickets of far eastern Russia (Sakha, Kamchatka, Khabarovsk, Kuril Islands), Korea and Japan. These erect plants have unbranched, thick stems, densely subtended with several, fleshy leaves that have entire or wavy margins. The few to numerous-flowered inflorescence has small, rosy-lilac to yellow-green flowers. The dorsal sepal and petals converge, forming a hood over the short column. The lateral sepals are widespreading. The white, broad, but drooping, trilobed lip, covered with spots and splashes of magenta, has oblong side lobes. The short midlobe has a roundish, blunt tip, and a short, incurved spur.

NEOMOOREA

Rolfe

Orchid Rev. **12**(133): 30 (1904).

Epidendroideæ ⚬ Cymbidieæ • Maxillariinæ

ETYMOLOGY: Greek for new and *Moorea*, a genus of orchids.

TYPE SPECIES: *Neomoorea irrorata* (Rolfe) Rolfe
(*Moorea irrorata* Rolfe)
This type name is now considered a synonym of
Neomoorea wallisii (Reichenbach f.) Schlechter;
basionym replaced with
Lueddemannia wallisii Reichenbach f.

One magnificent, sympodial epiphyte or semi-terrestrial is found in low elevation, cloud forests of Colombia and Panama. This large, erect plant has stout, ovoid, compressed pseudobulbs, each with two narrow, strongly veined, slightly leathery leaves borne at the tip. The erect to somewhat arching, few-flowered inflorescence, borne from the pseudobulb base, has showy, waxy, fragrant, red-brown or chestnut flowers banded with brown-purple. The pale yellow, mobile, deeply trilobed lip is heavily banded brown-purple, and attached to the base of the

short column foot. The spreading side lobes are large and the concave, red spotted midlobe has a conspicuous curled, bilobed callus and tapers to a sharp point. The flowers have a slightly curved, club-shaped, wingless column.

NEOMOREA

An orthographic variant introduced in *Etim. Orquidofilos*, 16 (1998). The correct spelling is *Neomoorea*.

NEORUSCHIA

Catharino & V.P. Castro

Richardiana **6**(3): 158 (2006).

Epidendroideæ ⚬ Cymbidieæ • Oncidiinæ

ETYMOLOGY: Greek for new and in commemoration of Augusto Ruschi (1915-1986), a Brazilian naturalist and discoverer of many new orchid species. He created the Santa Lucia Ecological Reserve and is the author of *Orquídeas do Estado do Espírito Santo*.

TYPE SPECIES: *Neoruschia cogniauxiana*
(Schlechter) Catharino & V.P. Castro
(*Oncidium cogniauxianum* Schlechter)

One sympodial epiphyte or occasional lithophyte is found in mid elevation, montane forests of eastern Brazil (Espírito Santo) on moss and lichen-covered branches in full sunlight to partial shade. This dwarf plant has clustered, strongly compressed pseudobulbs, subtended by several, overlapping sheaths, each with one to two, bright green, thinly textured leaves often spotted purple-brown. The erect, numerous-flowered inflorescence has bright yellow flowers. The similar, narrow sepals and petals have a brown-red bar in the center. The obscurely trilobed lip has broad side lobes with small notches along the margins, and the broadly oblong, bilobed midlobe has small, orange, butterfly-like ridges with white tips. The flowers have an erect, winged column.

NEOTAINIOPSIS

Bennett & Raizada

Indian Forester **107**(7): 433 (1981).

ETYMOLOGY: Greek for new and *Tainiopsis*, a genus of orchids. Referring to a relationship to *Tainiopsis*.

TYPE SPECIES: *Neotainiopsis barbata*
(Lindley) Bennett & Raizada
(*Tainia barbata* Lindley)

Now recognized as belonging to the genus *Eriodes*, *Neotainiopsis* was previously considered to include one epiphyte found in upper elevation, montane forests of northeastern India, Bhutan, Myanmar, southern China (Yunnan), Thailand and Vietnam. This large plant has egg-shaped (wrinkled when dry) pseudobulbs,

each with several, veined leaves. The soft, downy-covered inflorescence has an irregular line of flat, brown hairs on one side of the pedicels. The faintly fragrant, yellow flowers are striped brown-purple, maroon or red and have narrow, strongly reflexed sepals and petals. The brown-purple, entire lip, united to the column foot, is strongly veined and recurved.

NEOTIA

An orthographic variant introduced in *Ann. Hist. Nat.*, **4**: 99 (1770). The correct spelling is *Neottia*.

NEOTINEA

Reichenbach *filius*

Tent. Orchidogr. Eur. 29 (1850), and
De Pollin. Orchid. 18, 29 (1852).

Orchidoideæ ⚬ Orchideæ • Orchidinæ

ETYMOLOGY: Greek for new and in dedication to Vincenzo Tineo (1791-1856), a Sicilian professor of botany at the University of Palermo and author of *Plantarum rariorum Siciliæ minus cognitarum*.

TYPE SPECIES: *Neotinea maculata* (Desfontaines) Stern
(*Satyrium maculatum* Desfontaines)

Four sympodial terrestrials are found in low to mid elevation, piney woodlands, nutrient-poor grasslands over limestone from Ireland to Portugal, throughout the Mediterranean region, Isle of Man to Turkey, Lebanon, northern Africa (Morocco to Tunisia), and the Caucasus to Kazakhstan and Turkmenistan. These uncommon but interesting plants have erect stems, each with basal foliage often with purple spots in narrow patterns. The cylindrical, sometimes slightly twisted, densely packed, numerous-flowered inflorescence has small, fragrant flowers in various shades of brown-red, pink, white, green-white to pale yellow, streaked with red veins and often spotted and lined in dark pink or purple. The long, narrow sepals and the smaller petals converge, forming a hood over the small, stout column. The trilobed lip has its midlobe often bilobed with minute papillae, and has a spur that is either long and cylindrical or short and cone-shaped.

NEOTINIA

An orthographic variant introduced in *Hand-List Herb. Pl.*, ed. 2, 777 (1909). The correct spelling is *Neotinea*.

NEOTRACHOMA

J.J. Wood

Nordic J. Bot. **10**(5): 485 (1990).

ETYMOLOGY: Greek for new and rough.

TYPE SPECIES: *Saccolabium quisumbingii* L.O. Williams

Name published without a description. Today this name is most often referred to *Tuberolabium*.

NEOTTIA

Guettard

Hist. Acad. Roy. Sci. Mém. Math. Phys. (Paris) **4**: 374 (1754).

Name ICBN conserved.

Epidendroideæ ⚘ Neottieæ

ETYMOLOGY: Greek for nest building. Referring to the tangled mass of fleshy roots.

LECTOTYPE: *Neottia nidus-avis* (Linnaeus) Richard (*Ophrys nidus-avis* Linnaeus)

Sixty-three saprophytes are widespread in mid to upper elevation, montane grasslands, forests and grassy slopes from throughout Canada, the United States, Britain to across Russia, Scandinavia, France to Turkey, Kazakhstan, Mongolia, Pakistan, India (Kashmir to Assam), Korea, Japan and China (Xizang to Heilongjiang) and Myanmar to Vietnam. These dainty, erect, small, slender leafless plants have unbranched, smooth stems, each with several tubular sheaths below the middle, and all without green chlorophyll. They are completely dependent on certain mycorrhizal fungi for their nutrients. The numerous-flowered, smooth to hairy inflorescence has small, fragrant, yellow-brown, green or brown flowers, The small sepals and petals converge, forming a hood over the small column. The drooping, entire or bilobed lip is much longer or larger than the other floral segments, and sometimes is shallow cup-shaped. The flowers have a slightly to forward curved, long or short column with a footless base that is sometimes slightly swollen.

NEOTTIANANTHE

An orthographic variant introduced in *Orchids India*, ed. 2, 337 (1999). The correct spelling is *Neottianthe*.

NEOTTIANTHE

Reichenbach

Icon. Bot. Pl. Crit. **6**: 26 (1828).

Name published without a description. Today this name is most often referred to *Neottianthe* Schlechter.

NEOTTIANTHE

(Reichenbach) Schlechter

Repert. Spec. Nov. Regni Veg. **16**: 290 (1919).

Orchidoideæ ⚘ Orchideæ • Orchidinæ

ETYMOLOGY: *Neottia*, a genus of orchids and Greek for flower. A reference to a superficial resemblance to some Asiatic species of *Neottia*.

TYPE SPECIES: *Neottianthe cucullata* (Linnaeus) Schlechter (*Orchis cucullata* Linnaeus)

Eight uncommon, sympodial terrestrials are found in low to upper elevation, montane meadows and acid soils of pine forests from Poland to eastern Russia (Amur to Primorye), Korea to Japan, Tibet, southern China (Yunnan, Sichuan and Hebei) and northern India to Nepal. These slender plants have usually erect, unbranched stems, each with several, bladeless bracts and two unspotted basal leaves. The numerous to few-flowered inflorescence has showy magenta or pink flowers. The similar, narrow to wedge-shaped dorsal sepal and petals converge, forming a pointed hood over the small, erect column. The white, drooping, hairy, deeply trilobed lip has short, oblong side lobes. The longer, veined midlobe has magenta spots or blotches near the base, and has a tapering, strongly incurved, cone-shaped spur. The flowers have a small, slightly erect column.

NEOTTIDIDIUM

An orthographic variant introduced in *Fl. Berol. (Schlechtendal)*, **1**(65): 454 (1823). The correct spelling is *Neottidium*.

NEOTTIDIUM

Schlechtendal

Fl. Berol. (Schlechtendal) **1**(65): 454 (1823).

ETYMOLOGY: *Neottia*, a genus of orchids and Greek for diminutive.

TYPE SPECIES: *Neottidium nidus-avis* (Linnaeus) Schlechtendal (*Ophrys nidus-avis* Linnaeus)

Not validly published, this name is referred to *Neottia*. *Neottidium* was previously considered to include one saprophyte found from Denmark to Poland, Spain to Romania, Algeria, central Russia (Altay, Krasnoyarsk), Ukraine to Turkey and Kazakhstan. This small, clump-forming plant has erect, unbranched, leafless stems. The short, numerous-flowered inflorescence has tiny flowers with a boat-shaped, deeply notched lip.

NEO-URBANIA

Fawcett & Rendle

J. Bot. **47**: 125 (1909).

ETYMOLOGY: Greek for new and dedicated to Ignatz Urban (1848-1931), a German botanist, professor at the University of Berlin specializing in the flora of the West Indies, and author/editor of *Symbolæ Antillanæ*.

TYPE SPECIES: *Neo-urbania adendrobium* (Reichenbach f.) Fawcett & Rendle (*Ponera adendrobium* Reichenbach f.)

Now recognized as belonging to the genus *Maxillaria*, *Neo-urbania* was previously considered to include one epiphyte found in mid elevation, rain forests of Jamaica, Cuba, Costa Rica and Panama. This tufted plant has long, leafy, cane-like stems, subtended by leaf sheaths, each with roots appearing along the entire stem. The one- to two-flowered inflorescence has small, white to yellow flowers, subtended by a short bract, clustered in the axils of the leaves. The trilobed lip, rigidly attached to the column foot, has short side lobes, and the large midlobe has a somewhat notched margin. The flowers have a short, erect column.

NEOWILLIAMSIA

Garay

Orchid Digest **41**(1): 20 (1977).

ETYMOLOGY: Greek for new and in honor of Louis Otto Williams (1908-1991), an American botanist, expert on Mexican orchids, second editor of the *American Orchid Society Bulletin*, editor of *Ceiba* and co-author of *The Orchids of Panama*.

TYPE SPECIES: *Neowilliamsia epidendroides* Garay

Now recognized as belonging to the genus *Epidendrum*, *Neowilliamsia* was previously considered to include five epiphytes found from southern Mexico to Panama in wet, mid to upper elevation, montane cloud forests. These plants have slender, flattened stems, each with several, ovate leaves. The branched, few-flowered inflorescence has fairly large, fragrant, yellow-brown or brown flowers suffused maroon toward the base. The green, yellow or white, trilobed lip is deeply fringed, and has a callus with two keel-like lobes. The flowers have a short, footless column.

NEPHALAPHYLLUM

An orthographic variant introduced in *Bot. Mag.*, **88**: sub 5332 (1862). The correct spelling is *Nephelaphyllum*.

Currently Accepted | Validly Published | Invalidly Published | Published Pre-1753 | Superfluous Usage | Orthographic Variant | Fossil

Orchid Genera • **262**

NEPHALOPHYLLUM

An orthographic variant introduced in *Wochenschr. Vereines Beford. Gartenbaues Konigl. Preuss. Staaten*, **6**(38): 303 (1863). The correct spelling is *Nephelaphyllum*.

NEPHAPHYLLUM

An orthographic variant introduced in *Syn. Pl. (D. Dietrich)*, **5**: 33 (1852). The correct spelling is *Nephelaphyllum*.

NEPHELAPHYLLUM

Blume

Bijdr. Fl. Ned. Ind. **8**: 372, t. 22 (1825).

Epidendroideæ ᴗ Collabiinæ • Currently unplaced

ETYMOLOGY: Greek for a cloud and leaf. Referring to the mottled appearance of the upper surface of the leaves.

TYPE SPECIES: *Nephelaphyllum pulchrum* Blume

Twelve seldom seen sympodial terrestrials or uncommon epiphytes are found in low to mid elevation, hill and montane evergreen forests of northeastern India (Assam), southern China (Hainan), Hong Kong, Myanmar to Vietnam and Indonesia to the Philippines. These creeping plants have slender, spindle-shaped pseudobulbs, each with a succulent, wide leaf mottled dark and pale green, and often purple suffused. The erect, few-flowered inflorescence has small, intricate, fragrant flowers brilliantly colored from pale green to pink and veined in purples. Has similar sepals and broad, spathe-shaped petals. The large, white or pale yellow, entire, trilobed or obscurely trilobed lip, broadly attached to column foot, has a bright yellow, three-ridge callus, and has a short, sac-like spur. The flowers have a short, thick, club-shaped column with an obscure foot or is footless.

NEPHELEPHYLLUM

An orthographic variant introduced in *Fl. Javæ*, **1**: Praef. vii (1828). The correct spelling is *Nephelaphyllum*.

NEPHELLAPHYLLUM

An orthographic variant introduced in *Sitzungsber. Königl. Böhm. Ges. Wiss. Prag, Math.-Naturwiss. Cl.*, **31**: 10 (1903). The correct spelling is *Nephelaphyllum*.

NEPHILAPHYLLUM

An orthographic variant introduced in *J. Linn. Soc.*, **31**: 262 (1897). The correct spelling is *Nephelaphyllum*.

NEPHRANGIS

(Schlechter) Summerhayes

Kew Bull. **3**: 301 (1948).

Epidendroideæ ᴗ Vandeæ • Aerangidinæ

ETYMOLOGY: Greek for a kidney and a vessel or cup. Referring to the distinctive shape of the lip lobes.

TYPE SPECIES: *Nephrangis filiformis*
(Kraenzlin) Summerhayes
(*Listrostachys filiformis* Kraenzlin)

Two monopodial epiphytes are found in Liberia, Zambia, Congo, Zaire, Rwanda, Burundi and Uganda to Tanzania in mid elevation, woodland rain forests. These small plants have hanging or erect, usually branched, slender stems, each with widely-spaced, narrow, needle-like, often curved leaves. The short, few-flowered inflorescence, borne from the same nodes in successive years, has tiny, pale brown or brown-green, translucent flowers with the sepals and petals recurving backward. The broad, white, entire lip has two roundish (kidney-shaped) lobes from which a thick, cone-shaped, green spur descends. The flowers have a short, erect or slightly curved, wingless, footless column.

NEPHRANTHA

An orthographic variant introduced in *Orchids Java*, 329 (2002). The correct spelling is *Nephranthera*.

NEPHRANTHERA

Hasskarl

Tijdschr. Natuurl. Gesch. Physiol. **9**: 145 (1842).

ETYMOLOGY: Greek for a kidney and flower. Descriptive of the flowers' kidney-shaped anther.

TYPE SPECIES: *Nephranthera matutina*
(Poiret) Hasskarl
(*Epidendrum matutinum* Poiret)

Now recognized as belonging to the genus *Renanthera*, *Nephranthera* was previously considered to include one epiphyte found in humid, low elevation, fairly exposed forests of Indonesia (Java and Sumatra) and Malaysia. This scrambling plant has quite long, climbing or hanging, stout stems, sometimes branching from the base, each with numerous, thick, stiff, dark green, fleshy leaves. The erect, multibranched, numerous to few-flowered inflorescence has well-spaced, pale to bright crimson flowers with deep crimson spots, especially on the lateral sepals. The flowers change to yellow-orange with age. The small, orange-yellow and white, trilobed lip is also covered with crimson spots, and has short, broad side lobes with rolled margins. The strap-shaped midlobe also has a rolled margin, and a cylindrical spur that is somewhat recurved.

NOTE: Hasskarl originally published the genus *Nephrantera* without the second "h", which is a typographical error for anther. This spelling error was changed by later authors.

NERISSA

Rafinesque

Fl. Tellur. **2**: 89 (1836)[1837].

Not *Nerissa* Salisbury (1866) Amaryllidaceæ.

ETYMOLOGY: Apparently named for a nymph but none by this name can be found in classical literature.

Greek Mythology. A nymph is any member of a large class of female nature spirits, sometimes bound to a particular location, land form, or place of abode. They were considered to be something between gods and mortals, rather than real divinities, but were often related to the great gods.

TYPE SPECIES: *Nerissa glandulosa* (Sims) Rafinesque
(*Neottia glandulosa* Sims)

This type name is now considered a synonym of *Ponthieva racemosa* (Walter) C. Mohr; basionym replaced with *Arethusa racemosa* Walter

Now recognized as belonging to the genus *Ponthieva*, *Nerissa* was previously considered to include two terrestrials found in low to mid elevation, meadows and woodlands from the southern United States (Virginia to eastern Texas), southern Mexico to Colombia, Venezuela to western Brazil, the Bahamas and Cuba to Trinidad. These erect plants have unbranched, stout to slender stems, each with a basal rosette of rich, satiny green leaves that have a silvery hue to their underside. The erect, few-flowered inflorescence has translucent, white flowers with green veins. The uppermost, shortly clawed, entire lip has a deeply concave center with a long, pointed tip. The flowers have a small column.

NERVILIA

Commerson ex **Gaudichaud-Beaupré**

Freycinet's Voy. Uraine, Bot. 421, t. 35 (1826)[1829].

Name ICBN conserved vs. *Stellorkis* Thouars (1809) Orchidaceæ.

Epidendroideæ ᴗ Nervilieæ

ETYMOLOGY: Latin for a vein or nerve. Refers to the fine network of prominent veins that radiate throughout the leaf.

LECTOTYPE: *Nervilia aragoana* Gaudichaud-Beaupré

Sixty-five sympodial terrestrials are found in low to upper elevation, forest litter, grasslands, sandy to nutrient-poor soils from Ethiopia, Togo to South Africa, southwestern Saudi Arabia, Yemen, Oman to Madagascar, northern India, Nepal, eastern coastal China, Japan, Malaysia, Indonesia, the Philippines and northern Australia (Queensland) to the southwestern Pacific Archipelago. These small, erect plants have unbranched stems, each with a solitary, stalked, heart-shaped leaf sometimes borne on a long stalk. The broad, variegated leaf usually withers before the flowers appear and has colored hairs appearing between the veins. The solitary to few-flowered inflorescence has small to large, mostly white, green, yellow, pink, purple to brown, fragrant flowers not opening widely. The entire, trilobed or rare fiddle-shaped lip is with or without radiating red veins and has a basal callus, papillate or with short hairs. The flowers have a long, club-shaped, wingless column.

NERVILLEA

An orthographic variant introduced in *Hort. Universel*, **5**: 58 (1844). The correct spelling is *Nervilia*.

NERVILLIA

An orthographic variant introduced in *Landb. Ind. Archipel*, 740 (1950). The correct spelling is *Nervilia*.

NEUMAYERA

Not *Neumayera* Reichenbach (1841) Caryophyllaceæ.

An orthographic variant introduced in *Flora*, **55**(18): 278 (1872). The correct spelling is *Niemeyera*.

NEUWIDIA

An orthographic variant introduced in *Bot. Centralbl.*, **43**(31): 118 (1903). The correct spelling is *Neuwiedia*.

NEUWIEDIA

Blume

De Nov. Fam. Expos.   12 (1833), and
Tijdschr. Natuurl. Gesch. Physiol.   **1**: 140 (1834).

Apostasioideæ ✿

ETYMOLOGY: Dedicated to Maximilian Alexander Philipp zu Wied-Neuwied (1782-1867), a German prince who explored Central America and Brazil and is the author of *Beiträge zur Flora Brasiliens*.

TYPE SPECIES: *Neuwiedia veratrifolia* Blume

Nine sympodial terrestrials comprise this primitive orchid genus that are found scattered in humid, low elevation forest litter from southern China (Hainan to Hong Kong), Thailand to Vietnam, Indonesia, New Guinea to the Philippines and the southwestern Pacific Archipelago with the greatest diversity found in Indonesia (Borneo). These large, hairy plants have short to tall, erect or ascending

stems, each with spirally arranged, pleated leaves, crowded at the base; then becoming well-spaced, with the lowermost dying off and the uppermost grading into leafy bracts. The few-flowered inflorescence has small, nodding, slightly fragrant, tubular-shaped, white, pale yellow to golden-yellow flowers not opening widely. The long, narrow, entire lip is wider than the petals. The flowers often have a short column with three, fertile stamens.

NOTE: These species, along with the genus *Apostasia*, are considered by some taxonomists not to belong to the Orchid family because they have three, fertile stamens and a poorly developed column.

NEWILIA

An orthographic variant introduced in *Flora*, **55**(18): 276 (1872). The correct spelling is *Nervilia*.

NEZAHUALCOYOTLIA

R. González

Bol. Inst. Bot. (Guadalajara)   **4**(1-3): 67 (1996)[1997].

ETYMOLOGY: Dedicated to Nezahualcoyotl (1403-1473), an Alcohaun (Mexican) prince, poet, philosopher, ruler of the Texcocan (Nahuatl speakers or Nahua) tribe, who devised an exemplary code of laws which created many councils for advice giving; this name means hungry coyote.

TYPE SPECIES: *Nezahualcoyotlia gracilis*
(L.O. Williams) R. González
(*Cranichis gracilis* L.O. Williams)

Now recognized as belonging to the genus *Cranichis*, *Nezahualcoyotlia* was previously considered to include one terrestrial found in mid elevation, scrub of western Mexico (Durango and Jalisco). This plant has small, short stems, each with a few silvery green, basal leaves, strikingly veined dark green, that are smooth underneath and hairy on the top. The long, wiry, few-flowered inflorescence has small flowers with green sepals and white petals. The dorsal sepal has a flattened, blunt tip. The erect, bag-like, obscurely trilobed lip gives an impression of a hood with a rolled margin, has thickened, green nerves and a three-toothed tip.

NEZVILIA

An orthographic variant introduced in *Dict. Univ. Hist. Nat.*, **9**: 172 (1847). The correct spelling is *Nervilia*.

NIDEMA

Britton & Millspaugh

Bahama Fl. (Britton & Millspaugh)   94 (1920).

Epidendroideæ ✿ **Epidendreæ** • **Laeliinæ**

ETYMOLOGY: Anagram of *Dinema*, a related genus of orchids and showing great similarity.

TYPE SPECIES: *Nidema ottonis*
(Reichenbach f.) Britton & Millspaugh
(*Epidendrum ottonis* Reichenbach f.)

Two miniature, sympodial epiphytes are found in moist, low to mid elevation, dense forests and woodlands from the Bahamas, Cuba, Hispaniola, Jamaica, and Mexico to Peru, Surinam, Guyana, and Venezuela and northwestern Brazil. These plants have clustered, sometimes stalked, flattened pseudobulbs, each with one to two, narrow, strap-like, leathery, bilobed leaves. The erect, few-flowered inflorescence (produced from new growth as the leaf develops) has small, long-lasting, fragrant, pale cream, green to yellow flowers with a slight dark green tinge, opening fairly widely, and which have narrow sepals and short petals. The narrow, entire lip, attached to the column base, has a splash of brown-red at the base. The flowers have a long, slender, slightly curved, wingless column.

NIDO

An orthographic variant introduced in *Hist. Pl. (Ray)*, **2**: 1229 (1688). The correct spelling is *Nidus*.

NIDUS

Rivinus

Icon. Pl. Fl. Hexapet. (Rivinus)   t. 7 (1764).

ETYMOLOGY: Latin for nest. Taken from Linnaeus' epithet of *Ophrys nidus-avis*, bird's nest ophrys, because of the appearance of the interwoven roots.

TYPE SPECIES: *Neottia nidus-avis* Richard

Not validly published, this name is referred to *Neottia*. *Nidus* was considered to include one saprophyte widespread from Denmark to Poland, Spain to Romania, Algeria, Ukraine to central Russia (West Siberia to Krasnoyarsk) and Turkey to Kazakhstan.

NIDUS AVIS

Daléchamps

Hist. Gen. Pl.   **1**: 1073 (1586).

Pre-1753, therefore not validly published in fulfillment of nomenclatural rules; this name is most often referred to *Neottia*.

Currently Accepted   Validly Published   Invalidly Published   Published Pre-1753   Superfluous Usage   Orthographic Variant   Fossil

Orchid Genera • **264**

NIDUS-AVIS

Ortega

Tab. Bot. 24 (1773).

ETYMOLOGY: Latin for nest. Taken from Linnaeus' epithet of *Ophrys nidus-avis*, bird's nest ophrys, because of the appearance of the interwoven roots.

TYPE SPECIES: *None designated*

A superfluous name proposed as a substitute for *Neottia*.

NIEMEYARA

An orthographic variant introduced in *Fl. Bhutan*, **3**(3): 18 (2002). The correct spelling is *Niemeyera*.

NIEMEYERA

F. Mueller

Fragm. (Mueller) **6**: 96 (1867).

Name ICBN rejected vs. *Niemeyera* F. Mueller (1870) Sapetaceæ.

ETYMOLOGY: Dedicated to Felix von Niemeyer (1820-1871), a German physician, professor, pathologist and therapy specialist at Tübingen University in Baden-Württemberg, Germany.

TYPE SPECIES: *Niemeyera stylidioides* F. Mueller
  This type name is now considered a synonym of
    Apostasia wallichii R. Brown

Although validly published this rejected name is now referred to *Apostasia*. *Niemeyera* was considered to include one terrestrial found in Malaysia, Indonesia, New Guinea and northern Australia to the Philippines. This distinctive plant has erect, long-lived stems, each with several, narrow, grass-like leaves. The few-flowered inflorescence has small, star-shaped flowers which superficially look like a lily.

NIENOKUEA

A. Chevalier

Compt. Rend. Hebd. Séances Acad. Sci., ser. 3 **220**: 634 (1945).

ETYMOLOGY: Named for a granite massif, Niénokué (396 ft./120 m), located in the southern portion of Côte d'Ivoire's Parc National de Taï, where the type species was collected.

TYPE SPECIES: *Nienokuea microbambusa*
    (Kraenzlin) A. Chevalier
    (*Polystachya microbambusa* Kraenzlin)

Now recognized as belonging to the genus *Polystachya*, *Nienokuea* was previously considered to include three epiphytes found on scattered montane, upper plateaus and granite crevices in Guinea, Sierra Leone, Ivory Coast and Liberia. These erect, simple to branched, bamboo-like plants have slender, red stems, each with several, narrow leaves. The simple to branched, few-flowered inflorescence has rather large, yellow flowers. The uppermost lip protrudes between the lateral sepals. These sepals, together with the extended base of the column, form a small, chin-like protuberance. All these species are now considered as synonyms of *Polystachya microbambusa* Kraenzlin.

NIEUWIEDIA

An orthographic variant introduced in *Iconogr. Orchid. Europe*, 518 (1828). The correct spelling is *Neuwiedia*.

NIEYMERA

An orthographic variant introduced in *J. Linn. Soc.*, **25**: 238 (1890). The correct spelling is *Niemeyera*.

NIGRITELLA

Richard

De Orchid. Eur. 19, 26, 34 (1817).

ETYMOLOGY: Latin for black and diminutive. Refers to the rather black-red color of the flowers.

TYPE SPECIES: *Nigritella angustifolia* Richard
  This type name is now considered a synonym of
    Gymnadenia nigra (Linnaeus) Reichenbach f.;
      basionym
    Satyrium nigrum Linnaeus

Now recognized as belonging to the genus *Gymnadenia*, *Nigritella* was previously considered to include two terrestrials found in mid to upper elevation, montane meadows and scrub of Norway, Sweden, western Russia, Germany to Bulgaria, Romania, Greece and eastern Turkey. These small, erect plants have unbranched stems, each with several, narrow, almost grass-like, minutely notched leaves, arranged in a basal rosette. The short, densely packed, numerous-flowered inflorescence (almost cone-shaped) has dark crimson, bright red, pale blue-pink, orange to yellow flowers. The lateral sepals are wider than the dorsal sepal and petals. The short, blunt, entire or obscurely trilobed lip is subtriangular or saddle-shaped and has a small spur. The flowers are vanilla scented and the smaller the plant, the stronger is the fragrance. The flowers have a small column.

NOTE: Current DNA testing of this genus shows that *Nigritella* is clearly nested within *Gymnadenia*.

NINDEMA

An orthographic variant introduced in *Bot. Orchids*, 371 (2002). The correct spelling is *Nidema*.

NIPHANTHA

Luer

Monogr. Syst. Bot. Missouri Bot. Gard. **112**: 107 (2007).

ETYMOLOGY: Greek for snowflake and flower. Refers to the frosty (white) appearance of the hairy sepals.

TYPE SPECIES: *Niphantha gelida* (Lindley) Luer
    (*Pleurothallis gelida* Lindley)

Recognized as belonging to the genus *Stelis*, *Niphantha* was proposed to include two epiphytes or occasional lithophytes found in wet, low to mid elevation, woodlands and montane rain forests from Nicaragua to Ecuador, Venezuela, Jamaica and the Dominican Republic. These plants have short, erect ramicauls, subtended by dry, red-brown sheaths, each with a large, solitary, oblong, leathery, nerved leaf. The several, hanging, numerous-flowered inflorescence, borne from a spathe at the leaf base, has small, translucent, hairy, pale yellow flowers opening widely. The deeply concave lateral sepals, an erect dorsal sepal and has tiny petals. The tiny, entire lip is wedge-shaped. The flowers have a tiny, winged column.

NIPPONORCHIS

Masamune

Mem. Fac. Sci. Taihoku Imp. Univ. **11**(4): 592 (1934).

ETYMOLOGY: Nippon is an ancient Chinese name for the land of Japan meaning "land of the origin of the sun," thus referring to the origin of the type species. And Greek for orchid.

TYPE SPECIES: *Nipponorchis falcata*
        (Thunberg) Masamune
        (*Orchis falcata* Thunberg)

A superfluous name proposed as a substitute for *Neofinetia*.

NITIDOBULBON

Ojeda, Carnevali & G.A. Romero

Lankesteriana **7**(3): 531 (2007).

ETYMOLOGY: Latin for shining or shimmering and Greek for bulb. Refers to the shiny, smooth pseudobulbs.

TYPE SPECIES: *Nitidobulbon nasutus*
    (Reichenbach f.) Ojeda, Carnevali & G.A. Romero
      (*Maxillaria nasuta* Reichenbach f.)

Not validly published, this name is referred to *Maxillaria*. *Nitidobulbon* was considered to include three epiphytes found from southern Mexico to Peru, Venezuela, the Guianas and southeastern Brazil.

NONADES

An orthographic variant introduced in *Orchids Bolivia*, **2**: 131. (2004). The correct spelling is *Nanodes*.

NORNA

Wahlenberg

Fl. Suec. (Wahlenberg), ed. 2   **1**: 561 (1826).

ETYMOLOGY: Teutonic Mythology. Dedicated to *Norna*, an old Norse god-like pagan giantess who compounded the fates of man and the gods.

Or possibly, a Swedish verb meaning to inform secretly, to twist or twine.

TYPE SPECIES: *Norna borealis*
        (Swartz) Wahlenberg nom. illeg.
        Calypso bulbosa (Linnaeus) Oakes
        (*Cymbidium boreale* Swartz)

Now recognized as belonging to the genus *Calypso*, *Norna* was previously considered to include one terrestrial found in the northern hemisphere's temperate zones. This erect plant has a solitary, heart-shaped, blue-green leaf produced late in the season and lasting through the winter. The erect, solitary-flowered inflorescence has a large, fragrant, showy, purple to pink flower. The slipper-shaped, white or yellow, entire lip has three rows of brown hairs down the center.

NOTHERIA

O'Byrne & J.J. Vermeulen

Gard. Bull. Singapore   **52**(2) 286 (2000).

Epidendroideæ ⚘ Podochileæ • Eriinæ

ETYMOLOGY: Greek for not genuine or false and *Eria*, a genus of orchids. Refers to a likeness of the plant to that of an *Eria* section, but not the flowers.

TYPE SPECIES: *Notheria diaphana*
        O'Byrne & J.J. Vermeulen

One sympodial epiphyte is found in dry, mid elevation, forests of eastern Indonesia (Sulawesi). This miniature, clump-forming plant has small, erect pseudo-bulbs, often subtended by thick, red-brown sheaths, each with two narrow, leathery leaves. The short, hairy, two-flowered inflorescences, one to two spikes per bulb, have relatively large, short-lived, densely hairy, white flowers which opening widely and all simultaneously. The small, entire lip has two distinct calli near the base, leaving only a tiny opening to the distinct spur that has short hairs on the upper wall. The flowers have a short, erect, footless column.

NOTHIUM

Lindley ex Spach

Hist. Nat. Veg. (Spach)   **12**: 177 (1846).

ETYMOLOGY: Latin for not anything.

TYPE SPECIES: *None designated*

Name published without a description. Today this name is most often referred to *Bifrenaria*.

NOTHODORITIS

Z.H. Tsi

Acta Phytotax. Sin.   **27**(1): 58 (1989).

Epidendroideæ ⚘ Vandeæ • Aeridinæ

ETYMOLOGY: Greek for false and *Doritis*, a genus of orchids. Referring to a false alliance to the genus *Doritis*.

TYPE SPECIES: *Nothodoritis zhejiangensis* Z.H. Tsi

One small, monopodial epiphyte is found in mid elevation, coastal forests of eastern China (Zhejiang). This plant has short stems, each with several, oblong, flat, basal leaves whose lower surfaces are sprinkled with dark purple spots. The long, hanging, few-flowered inflorescence has small, thinly textured white to mauve-pink flowers often with horizontal purple stripes and veins. The unusual, long, narrow, trilobed lip has small, erect side lobes. The narrow, boat-shaped midlobe has an erect, trunk-like, white appendage extending outward with a purple tip. The flowers have a long, slender column with a narrow, trunk-like rostellum which has a hooked, slightly bilobed tip.

NOTHOSTELE

Garay

Bot. Mus. Leafl.   **28**(4): 339 (1980)[1982].

Orchidoideæ ⚘ Cranichideæ • Cranichidinæ

ETYMOLOGY: Greek for false and column or pillar. Describing the column that lacks fusion between the filament and style.

TYPE SPECIES: *Nothostele acianthiformis*
        (Reichenbach f. & Warming) Garay
        (*Pelexia acianthiformis* Reichenbach f. & Warming)

One sympodial terrestrial is found in mid elevation, canyon cliffs of eastern Brazil (Minas Gerais). This erect plant has unbranched stems that are leafless during flowering. The erect, few-flowered inflorescence, subtended by sheaths and large floral bracts, has small, pale green to white flowers. The lip and narrow dorsal sepal are united with the long, hanging, curved lateral sepals, forming a short, tube-like protuberance. The tiny, brown to maroon, diamond-shaped, entire lip is wedged-shaped at its base with a thick, strongly curved margin. The flowers have a long, slender, column that is hairy on the front portion and the yellow, pointed rostellum has a hooked viscidium at its tip.

NOTHUM

An orthographic variant introduced in *Fl. Bras.* (Hoehne), **12**(7): 25 (1953). The correct spelling is *Nothium*.

NOTIOPHRYS

Lindley

J. Proc. Linn. Soc., Bot.   **1**(4): 189 (1857).

ETYMOLOGY: Greek for southern and *Ophrys*, a genus of orchids. Refers to its distribution in the southern hemisphere.

TYPE SPECIES: *Notiophrys glandulosa* Lindley

Now recognized as belonging to the genus *Platylepis*, *Notiophrys* was previously considered to include three terrestrials found in shady, low elevation, swamps and along river banks of Uganda, Malawi, Zambia, Mozambique, Zimbabwe, Tanzania and South Africa (Natal). These pencil-thick, soft-stemmed plants, leafy in the lower portion, have a creeping base that then becomes erect. The erect, hairy inflorescence has several, sterile sheaths. The outer surface of the green-white or pink-brown flowers is conspicuously glandular-hairy, and the dorsal sepal and petals converge, forming a hood over the column. The white, deeply concave, entire lip is joined to the long column for half of its length. The above type name is now considered a synonym of *Platylepis glandulosa* (Lindley) Reichenbach f.

NOTYLIA

Lindley

Bot. Reg.   **11**: sub 930 (1825).

Epidendroideæ ⚘ Cymbidieæ • Oncidiinæ

ETYMOLOGY: Greek for back and hump or swelling. A probable reference to the anther being on top of the column.

LECTOTYPE: *Notylia punctata* (Ker Gawler) Lindley
        (*Pleurothallis punctata* Ker Gawler)

Fifty-eight sympodial epiphytes are found in wet, low to mid elevation, hill and montane forests from Mexico to Bolivia and Trinidad to Paraguay. These small plants have compressed, clustered, wrinkled, ovoid pseudobulbs, subtended by leaf-like sheaths, each with a solitary, leathery or fleshy leaf that is sometimes laterally flattened. The pseudobulbs are usually concealed by leaf-bearing sheaths. From the base of the pseudobulb or leaf axils, the long, hanging, numerous to few-flowered inflorescences are borne. The small, delicate, faintly fragrant flowers are found in a wide variety of shades from white, green-white to yellow, and sometimes spotted yellow, green or brown. The flower has oblong to tongue-like sepals; the lateral sepals are variously united and has long, narrow petals. The arrowhead-shaped, clawed, entire or obscurely lobed lip is either with or without a hairy callus. The flowers have a straight, short or long, slender or stout, footless, wingless column with a long rostellum which is slightly hairy.

Currently Accepted   Validly Published   Invalidly Published   Published Pre-1753   Superfluous Usage   Orthographic Variant   Fossil

O r c h i d   G e n e r a   • **266**

NOTYLIOPSIS

P. Ortíz

Orquideologia **20**(2): 184 (1996).

Epidendroideæ ⚹ Cymbidieæ • Oncidiinæ

ETYMOLOGY: *Notylia*, a genus of orchids and Greek for like or appearance. Referring to a similarity of flower parts to *Notylia*.

TYPE SPECIES: *Notyliopsis beatricis* P. Ortíz

One small, sympodial epiphyte is found in mid elevation, montane forests of western Colombia (Choco). This small plant has pear-shaped pseudobulbs, subtended by non leaf-like sheaths, each with a solitary, leathery leaf. The several, long, hanging, numerous-flowered, white, transparent inflorescences lengthen successively; the small, transparent white flowers have an erect, arching dorsal sepal and widespreading, narrow petals. The concave lateral sepals are united nearly to their base. The boat-shaped, obscurely trilobed lip has a callus that is enlarged to a pedestal-like shape and is often suffused violet. The flowers have a long, slender, wingless column.

NUPHALLIS

An orthographic variant introduced in *Revis. Gen. Pl.*, **2**: 649 (1891). The correct spelling is *Nuphylis*.

NUPHYLIS

Thouars

Hist. Orchid.   Table 3, sub 3u, *t. 107* (1822).

Name published without a description. Today this name is most often referred to *Bulbophyllum*.

NUPHYLLIS

An orthographic variant introduced in *Revis. Gen. Pl.*, **2**: 657 (1891). The correct spelling is *Nuphylis*.

NYCHOSMA

An orthographic variant introduced in *Orchideen* (Schlechter), ed. 1, 190 (1914). The correct spelling is *Nyctosma*.

NYCTOSMA

Rafinesque

Fl. Tellur.   **2**: 9 (1836)[1837].

ETYMOLOGY: Greek for night and fragrance. Indicating a characteristic nocturnal fragrance.

TYPE SPECIES: *Nyctosma nocturna*
(Jacquin) Rafinesque
(*Epidendrum nocturnum* Jacquin)

Now recognized as belonging to the genus *Epidendrum, Nyctosma* was previously considered to include one epiphyte widespread in low elevation, hill forests and scrub from the south-eastern United States (southern Florida), Mexico to Bolivia, Cuba to Trinidad, the Guianas, Venezuela and Brazil. This tall, erect to hanging plant has a cluster of reed-like stems, each with rather slender to oblong, stiff, leathery leaves sometimes suffused maroon. The short, solitary to few-flowered inflorescence's large flowers have long, narrow green sepals and yellow petals. The white (turning creamy yellow with age), basal-clawed, deeply trilobed lip, united to the club-shaped column, has narrow to broad side lobes and a long midlobe that tapers to a sharp point. The above type name is now considered a synonym of *Epidendrum angustilobum* Fawcett & Rendle.

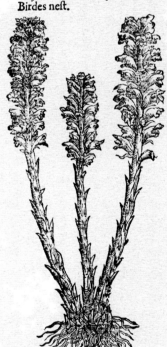

Of Birdes nest.   Chap.106.

Satyrium abortinum, siue nidus auis.
Birdes nest.

❋ The description.

BIrdes nest hath many tangling rootes platted or crossed one ouer another verie intricately, which resembleth a Crowes nest made of stickes : from which riseth vp a thicke soft grosse stalk of a browne colour, set with small short leaues of the colour of a drie oken leafe that hath lien vnder the tree all the winter long : on the top of the stalke groweth a spikie eare or tuft of flowers, in shape like vnto maimed Satyrion, whereof doubtlesse it is a kinde. The whole plant, as well stalkes, leaues, and flowers, are of a parched browne colour.

❋ The place.

This Bastard or vnkindely Satyrion is very seldome seene in these Southerly parts of England. It is reported that it groweth in the North parts of England neer vnto a village called Knaesborough. I found it growing in the middle of a wood in Kent two miles from Graues end, neer vnto a worshipfull gentlemans house called master *VVilliam Swan* of Howcke greene. The wood belongeth to one master *Iohn Sidley* : which plant I did neuer see elsewhere. And bicause it is very rare I am the more willing to giue you all the markes in the wood for your better finding it, bicause it doth growe but in one peece of the wood, that is to say, the ground is couered all ouer in the same place neere about it with the herbe Sanycle, and also the kinde of Orchis called *Hermaphroditica*, or Butter-flie Satyrion.

❋ The time.

It flowreth and flourisheth in Iune and August. The dustie or mealy seede (if it may be called seed) falleth in the end of August, but in my iudgement it is an vnprofitable or barraine dust, and not any seed at all.

❋ The names.

It is called *Satyrium abortiuum*, of some *Nidus auis* : in French *Nid d' ausea* : in English Birdes nest and Goose nest.

❋ The temperature and vertues.

It is not vsed in Phisicke that I can finde in any autoritie, either of the auncient or later writers, but is esteemed as a degenerate kinde of Orchis, and therfore not vsed.

Gerard   *The Herball*   page 176 (1633).

OAKES-AMESIA

C. Schweinfurth & P.H. Allen

Bot. Mus. Leafl. **13**(6): 133, t. 10 (1948).

ETYMOLOGY: In honor of Oakes Ames (1874-1950), an American orchidologist, professor of botany at Harvard University and founder of the Orchid Herbarium of Oakes Ames at Harvard Botanical Museum.

TYPE SPECIES: *Oakes-amesia cryptantha*
C. Schweinfurth & P.H. Allen

Now recognized as belonging to the genus *Ornithocephalus*, Oakes-amesia was previously considered to include one epiphyte found in humid, low elevation, hill forests and woodlands that is restricted to western Panama (Coclé). This inconspicuous, dwarf plant has elongate stems, subtended by leaf-like sheaths, each with long, narrow, fleshy leaves that are arranged in a strong fan shape. The long, erect to hanging, numerous-flowered inflorescence has small, green and white, long-lasting flowers with widespreading sepals and petals. The hairy-glandular, callose, distinctly trilobed lip has large, oblong side lobes, a sac-like midlobe with a fleshy, basal callus. The flowers have a long, slender, winged column.

OATASETUM

An orthographic variant introduced in *Badianus Manuscript*, 309 (1940). The correct spelling is *Catasetum*.

OBERONIA

Lindley

Gen. Sp. Orchid. Pl. 15 (1830).

Name ICBN conserved vs. *Iridorkis* Thouars (1809) Orchidaceæ; and type name conserved.

Epidendroideæ 🌿 Malaxideæ

ETYMOLOGY: Medieval folklore. Named for *Oberon*, the mythical king of the fairies, who lived in hiding and with a spell forced *Titania*, Queen of the fairies, to love a creature who is half man and half donkey. In reference to the insignificance of the flowers that are often hidden in some species.

LECTOTYPE: *Oberonia iridifolia* Lindley nom. illeg.

Oberonia ensiformis (Smith) Lindley
(*Malaxis ensiformis* Smith)

This type name is now considered a synonym of *Oberonia mucronata* (D. Don) Ormerod & Seidenfaden; basionym replaced with *Stelis mucronata* D. Don

A large genus with an estimated three hundred eight sympodial epiphytes, lithophytes or rare terrestrials are widely distributed in shady, humid, low to upper elevation, hill scrub to montane evergreen and moss laden forests from Cameroon to Kenya, south to Zimbabwe, Madagascar to the southwestern Pacific Archipelago, the Philippines, and northern Australia, with the greatest representation in mainland Asia (India to Korea and Japan). These small, clump-forming plants have short to long, clustered stems easily recognized by their broad, flattened fans of fleshy, iris-like leaves. The densely packed, numerous-flowered inflorescence has small to minute (rarely more than 2 mm), purple, yellow, green, brown or white, translucent flowers arranged in flat whorls or in a spiralling pattern and facing in all directions. The first flowers to open are those near the spike's tip and last are those at the bottom. The margins of the petals and lip are irregularly toothed. The variously shaped, lobed or entire lip has small basal ears and the midlobe has a bilobed tip. The flowers have a short, wingless, footless column.

OBERONIAE

An orthographic variant introduced in *Prodr. Fl. Norfolk.*, 31 (1833). The correct spelling is *Oberonia*.

OBERONIOIDES

Szlachetko

Fragm. Florist. Geobot. **3**(Suppl.): 134 (1995).

Epidendroideæ 🌿 Malaxideæ

ETYMOLOGY: *Oberonia*, a genus of orchids and Greek for resembling or likeness. An allusion to the similarity of the flowers to those of *Oberonia*.

TYPE SPECIES: *Oberonioides oberoniiflora*
(Seidenfaden) Szlachetko
(*Malaxis oberoniiflora* Seidenfaden)

Two sympodial terrestrials or lithophytes are found in low elevation, hill forests of Thailand, southern China (Fujian, Jiangxi and Guangdong) and Taiwan. These small, erect plants have clustered, ovoid, fleshy pseudobulbs, each with a solitary, fleshy leaf. The long, slender, often compressed few-flowered inflorescence has tiny, green or yellow flowers almost hidden by the large leaves. The dorsal sepal is ovate to oblong and the narrow petals have one-vein. The trilobed lip has long, narrow or triangular side lobes enfolding the erect, footless column and the larger midlobe has a bilobed tip. The flowers have a short, thick column.

OCAMPOA

A. Richard & Galeotti

Ann. Sci. Nat., Bot., ser. 3 **3**: 31 (1845).

ETYMOLOGY: Honoring Melchor (José Telesforo Nepomuceno) Ocampo (1814-1861), a Mexican statesman, botanist, governor of Michoacán, a friend and supporter of local statesmen and revolutionaries Benito Juárez and Santos Degollado.

TYPE SPECIES: *Ocampoa mexicana*
A. Richard & Galeotti

Now recognized as belonging to the genus *Cranichis*, Ocampoa was previously considered to include one terrestrial found in mid elevation, oak-pine forests of Mexico and Guatemala. This rather stout plant has unbranched stems, each with several, basal leaves. The few-flowered inflorescence has white or pale green flowers that are somewhat hairy on the outer surfaces. The distinctive, entire lip has an S- or C-shaped claw and is parallel with the short column.

Currently Accepted   Validly Published   Invalidly Published   Published Pre-1753   Superfluous Usage   Orthographic Variant   Fossil

OCEOCLADES

An orthographic variant introduced in *Prakt. Stud. Orchid.*, 171 (1854). The correct spelling is *Oeceoclades*.

OCEOCLADUS

An orthographic variant introduced in *Prakt. Stud. Orchid.*, 45, 78 (1854). The correct spelling is *Oeceoclades*.

OCHYRELLA

Szlachetko & R. González

Fragm. Florist. Geobot. **41**(2): 698 (1996).

ETYMOLOGY: Named in honor of Ryszard Ochyra (1949-), a Polish bryologist professor at Jagiellonian University in Kraków and editor of *Fragmenta Floristica et Geobotanica*. And Latin for diminutive.

TYPE SPECIES: *Ochyrella lurida*
(M.N. Corrêa) Szlachetko & R. González
(*Centrogenium luridum* M.N. Corrêa)

Now recognized as belonging to the genus *Pteroglossa*, *Ochyrella* was proposed to include five terrestrials found in low to mid elevation, scrub and grasslands of Brazil, Argentina, Bolivia, Ecuador and Peru. These short, erect plants have unbranched stems, each with a basal rosette of leaves that withers by flowering time. The densely packed, few to numerous-flowered inflorescence has small, inconspicuous flowers. The concave dorsal sepal and the narrow petals converge, forming a hood over the column, and the narrow lateral sepals are recurved. The shortly clawed, obscurely trilobed lip has rounded to pointed side lobes, a small, tongue-shaped midlobe and is constricted near the base. The tapering spur is formed with the basal parts of the lateral sepals that are fused for a short distance.

OCHYRORCHIS

Szlachetko

Richardiana **4**(2): 52 (2004).

ETYMOLOGY: Named in honor of Ryszard Ochyra (1949-). And Greek for orchid.

TYPE SPECIES: *Ochyrorchis multipartita*
(Blume ex Kraenzlin) Szlachetko
(*Habenaria multipartita* Blume ex Kraenzlin)

Recognized as belonging to the genus *Habenaria*, *Ochyrorchis* was proposed to include twenty-three terrestrials found in mid elevation, savannas and grasslands from Pakistan, northern India (Kashmir to Assam), Nepal, Tibet, southern China (Yunnan, Guizhou), Thailand to Vietnam, Indonesia (Java), Ethiopia to Zimbabwe, Cameroon to Nigeria, southern Saudia Arabia and Yemen.

These plants have short, erect, unbranched stems, each with a basal rosette of narrow leaves. The few-flowered inflorescence has large, green or green and white flowers. The dorsal sepal and petals converge, forming a hood over the column. The trilobed lip has thread-like, deeply incised, comb-like lobes, a small, narrow midlobe, and a thread-like spur.

OCTADESMIA

Bentham

J. Linn. Soc., Bot. **18**(110): 311 (1881).

ETYMOLOGY: Greek for eightfold and bond, bundle or connection. Referring to the eight pollen masses.

TYPE SPECIES: *Octadesmia serratifolia*
(Hooker) Bentham
(*Octomeria serratifolia* Hooker)
This type name is now considered a synonym of
Dilomilis montana (Swartz) Summerhayes;
basionym replaced with
Epidendrum montanum Swartz

Now recognized as belonging to the genus *Dilomilis*, *Octadesmia* was previously considered to include seven epiphytes found in mid to upper elevation, montane forests of the greater Antilles (Puerto Rico to Cuba) region. These erect plants have thick stems often reaching heights of over six feet (1.8 m), each with a few thinly textured leaves clasping the stem. The few-flowered inflorescence has small, fragrant, rather long-lived, white to yellow flowers. The trilobed lip, often yellow suffused, has tiny, warty calli along the three nerves. The flowers have a small, purple column.

OCTAMERIA

An orthographic variant introduced in *Bull. Sci. Nat. Geol.*, **22**: 284 (1830). The correct spelling is *Octomeria*.

OCTANDRORCHIS

Brieger

Orchideen (Schlechter), ed. 3 **7**(25-28): 425 (1975), and Validated: *Trab. Congr. Nac. Bot.*, *Rio de Janeiro* **26**: 43 (1977).

ETYMOLOGY: Greek for eightfold, man or stamen and orchid. Descriptive of the eight pollinia.

TYPE SPECIES: *Octandrorchis leptophylla*
(Barbosa Rodrigues) Brieger nom. illeg.
Octomeria leptophylla Barbosa Rodrigues

Not validly published, this name is referred to *Octomeria*. *Octandrorchis* was considered to include one epiphyte found in southeastern Brazil (Minas Gerais).

OCTARRHENA

Thwaites

Enum. Pl. Zeyl. (Thwaites) 305 (1861).

Epidendroideæ ⚘ Podochileæ • Thelasiinæ

ETYMOLOGY: Greek for eightfold and male or stamen. An allusion to the eight free pollinia.

TYPE SPECIES: *Octarrhena parvula* Thwaites

Forty-one seldom encountered, sympodial epiphytes, terrestrials or rare lithophytes are found in low to mid elevation, hill scrub, montane forests, mosses and rocky crevices of Sri Lanka, New Caledonia and the Philippines, but most species are indigenous to New Guinea. These inconspicuous, small plants have elongate stems that are leafy toward the tip, branching from the rooting base and have distichous, pencil-like, or laterally compressed leaves that are jointed at their overlapping sheaths. The short, densely packed, numerous-flowered inflorescences, borne from leaf nodes, have minute, pale green-yellow to white flowers turning orange as they age, with broad, widespreading sepals and small, narrowly pointed petals. The small, concave, entire lip has a disc often with two basal calli. The flowers have a short, footless column that is smooth or hairy.

OCTCMERIA

An orthographic variant cited in *World Checkl. Seed Pl. (Govaerts)*, **1**(2): 10 (1995). The correct spelling is *Octomeria*.

OCTOMERIA

R. Brown

Hortus Kew., ed. 2 **5**: 211 (1813).
Not *Octomeria* Pfeiffer (1874) Rubiaceæ, and not *Octomeris* Naudin (1845) Melastomataceæ.

Epidendroideæ ⚘ Epidendreæ • Pleurothallidinæ

ETYMOLOGY: Greek for eightfold and part. Alluding to the eight pollinia, a mass of fused pollen.

TYPE SPECIES: *Octomeria graminifolia*
(Linnaeus) R. Brown
(*Epidendrum graminifolium* Linnaeus)

An estimated one hundred forty-three sympodial epiphytes or lithophytes are found in low to upper elevation, montane rain forests, woodlands or open sunny meadows from Belize to Panama, Colombia to Bolivia, Uruguay, Paraguay to northern Argentina (Misiones) with the largest diversity found in eastern Brazil. There are a few species scattered from Cuba to Trinidad, the Guianas and Honduras to Costa Rica. These mat-forming plants are poorly known due to their insignificant appearance. The small plants have short or long, secondary stems, subtended by several sheaths, each with a solitary, leathery to fleshy leaf. There are two leaf types: roundish, pencil-shaped leaves or broad, flat leaves. The short, solitary to numerous-flowered inflorescence, borne from the base of the leaves or close to the tip of the stem, has small, dull-colored, translucent flowers with blunt segment points. The short to tiny, entire or usually trilobed lip is attached to the base of the short column.

OCTOMERIA

D. Don

Prodr. Fl. Nepal. 31 (1825).

Etymology: Greek for eight-fold and part. Alluding to the eight pollinia.

Type species: *Octomeria spicata* D. Don

Not validly published, this name is referred to *Eria*. *Octomeria* D. Don was considered to include one epiphyte found in northern India (Sikkim), southern China (Xizang to Yunnan), Myanmar to Vietnam and Thailand.

OCTOMERIS

Not *Octomeris* Naudin (1845) Melastomataceæ.

An orthographic variant introduced in *Fl. Tellur.*, **2**: 85 (1836)[1837]. The correct spelling is *Octomeria*.

ODONECTIS

Rafinesque

Med. Repos., ser. 2 **5**: 357 (1808).

Etymology: Greek for tooth or anything sharp and Latin for to bind or join. Refers to the whorled condition of the sharply pointed leaves that have the appearance of being bonded together.

Type species: *Odonectis verticillata*
(Mühlenberg ex Willdenow) Rafinesque
(*Arethusa verticillata* Mühlenberg ex Willdenow)

Now recognized as belonging to the genus *Isotria*, *Odonectis* was previously considered to include two terrestrials confined in damp to dry, mid elevation, woodlands of the eastern United States (Michigan to Maine, Louisiana to Georgia) and Canada (Ontario). These plants have a unique whorl of five or six leaves, an arrangement unknown in any other orchid genera. The erect, solitary flower, borne from the center of this whorl, has narrow, purple-brown sepals. The small petals converge, forming a hood over the long, slender, slightly curved, footless column. The white to yellow-green, trilobed lip has triangular, inrolled side lobes and the midlobe has a wavy surface.

ODONTHORHYNCHUS

An orthographic variant cited in *Orchideen (Schlechter): Liter. Reg. Band I/A, B, and C,* 168 (2003). The correct spelling is *Odontorrhynchus*.

ODONTOCHILOS

An orthographic variant introduced in *Bot. Centralbl.*, **42**(15): 341 (1903). The correct spelling is *Odontochilus*.

ODONTOCHILUS

Blume

Coll. Orchid. 79 (1858), and
Fl. Javæ Nov. Ser. **1**: 66, *tt.* 29, 36 (1858).

Orchidoideæ ⚬ Cranichideæ • Goodyerinæ

Etymology: Greek for furnished with teeth and a lip. Alluding to the tooth-like margins of the middle segment of the lip.

Type species: *None designated*

Eight interesting, sympodial terrestrials or rarely epiphytes are found in moist, mid to upper elevation, montane moss laden forests from southern China (Guangdong), Malaysia, Thailand to Vietnam, southern Japan and Indonesia to the Fiji Islands. These small plants have erect, slender stems, each with several, green or dull-red, ovate leaves clasping the stem. The erect, short, solitary to few-flowered inflorescence has fairly large, showy, white flowers. The long-clawed, spreading, trilobed lip has a sac-like hypochile enclosed by the lateral sepals. The mesochile is simple or toothed, long to short fringed and the epichile is either unlobed or with a broad, bilobed blade with a small spur. The flowers have a short, thick, footless column.

ODONTOGLOSSUM

Kunth

Nov. Gen. Sp. **1**: 350, *t.* 85 (1815).

Epidendroideæ ⚬ Cymbidieæ • Oncidiinæ

Etymology: Greek for a tooth and a tongue. Refers to the tooth-like projections on the lip of most of the species.

Type species: *Odontoglossum epidendroides* Kunth

Sixty-nine sympodial epiphytes or lithophytes and rare terrestrials, with several thousand manmade hybrids, are found in cool, mid to upper elevation, montane forests from Costa Rica to Panama, Venezuela, the Guianas and Colombia to Bolivia. These evergreen plants

are highly diverse in their vegetative and floral appearance. The plants have variously compressed, ribbed to grooved pseudobulbs, subtended by distichous, overlapping sheaths; the lower are leafless and the upper are leaf-bearing, each with one to three, leathery or fleshy leaves. The exquisite, erect to arching, long to short, sometimes branching inflorescence is borne from the base of flattened pseudobulbs that are subtended by distichous, leaf-bearing sheaths. The usually large to sometimes small, showy, faintly to strongly fragrant flowers have a tremendously wide range of hues and the similar segments are often blotched purple or brown. The entire or trilobed lip has its base parallel to the column or somewhat joined to it and has erect or rolled backward side lobes. The widespreading, recurved midlobe has a wide variety of basal appendages. The flowers have a long, slender, footless column.

NOTE: Some of these species have been moved to other genera including *Otoglossum*, *Rhynchostele*, and *Rossioglossum*.

ODONTOGLOSUM

An orthographic variant introduced in *Nov. Veg. Descr.*, **2**: 33, 35 (1825). The correct spelling is *Odontoglossum*.

ODONTORHYNCHUS

An orthographic variant introduced in *Orchideen (Schlechter)*, ed. 3, **6**(7): 333 (1975). The correct spelling is *Odontorrhynchus*.

ODONTORRHYNCHOS

An orthographic variant introduced in *Phylogeny Classif. Orchid Fam.*, 120, 269 (1993). The correct spelling is *Odontorrhynchus*.

ODONTORRHYNCHUS

M.N. Corrêa

Darwiniana **10**(2): 157 (1953).

Orchidoideæ ⚬ Cranichideæ • Spiranthinæ

Etymology: Greek for a tooth and snout or beak. Descriptive of the protruding three-toothed rostellum.

Type species: *Odontorrhynchus castillonii*
(L. Hauman) M.N. Corrêa
(*Stenorrhynchos castillonii* L. Hauman)

Six nondescript, sympodial terrestrials are found in low to upper elevation, grasslands, woodlands and forest openings of southern Peru to northern Chile and northwestern Argentina often on rocky to pebbly ground. These plants have erect, unbranched stems, each with a

Currently Accepted   Validly Published   Invalidly Published   Published Pre-1753   Superfluous Usage   Orthographic Variant   Fossil

Orchid Genera • 270

basal rosette of narrow leaves and are usually leafless at flowering. The erect, hairy, numerous-flowered inflorescence has small, tubular, pale green flowers not opening widely. The sepals are covered in long, soft hairs, densely so at the base, with nerved segments, and the long, narrow lateral sepals taper to a point. The long, white or yellow, entire or obscurely trilobed lip is with or without green veins and has a wavy margin with a recurved, tapering tip. The flowers have a distinct but short, stout column with a massive, incurved foot.

ODONTOSTELE

Schlechter

Notizbl. Bot. Gart. Berlin-Dahlem
9(88): 585 (1926).
ETYMOLOGY: Greek for tooth-like and column.
TYPE SPECIES: *None designated*

Name published without a description. Today this name is most often referred to *Pleurothallis*.

ODONTOSTYLES

Breda

Gen. Sp. Orchid. Asclep., fasc. I   *t. 4* (Nov. 1828).
Not *Odontostylis* Blume (1828) Orchidaceæ.
ETYMOLOGY: Greek for a tooth and pillar. Descriptive of the tooth-like appendages of the column.
TYPE SPECIES: *None designated*

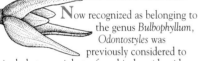

Now recognized as belonging to the genus *Bulbophyllum*, *Odontostyles* was previously considered to include two epiphytes found in humid, mid elevation, montane forests of Indonesia (Sumatra to Borneo) and Malaysia. These small, creeping plants have well-spaced, ovate, somewhat flattened, long, curved, ribbed pseudobulbs, each with a solitary, oblong, leathery leaf. The several, short, wiry, few-flowered inflorescences have tiny, white flowers not opening widely. The long, narrow sepals have pale yellow to bright orange-red tips and the tiny, erect petals have yellow tips. The broad, tongue-shaped, hinged, entire lip is pale orange-buff. The flowers have a short, thick column.

NOTE: Breda originally published the name spelled as *Odontostylis*, but **Hooker f.** (*Gen. Pl.*, 504 (1883)) changed the name to the currently accepted spelling of *Odontostyles*.

ODONTOSTYLIS

Blume

Fl. Javæ   **1**: Praef. vii (Aug. 1828).

Name published without a description. Today this name is most often referred to a section of *Bulbophyllum*.

OECEOCLADES

Lindley

Edwards's Bot. Reg.   **18**: sub 1522 (1832).
Epidendroideæ ⚘ Cymbidieæ • Eulophiinæ
ETYMOLOGY: Greek for a private dwelling or household and a branch or destruction. Possibly alluding to Lindley's separation of certain species from *Angraecum* thus forming a distinct tribe.
LECTOTYPE: *Oeceoclades maculata* (Lindley) Lindley
    (*Angraecum maculatum* Lindley)

Thirty-eight small to large, sympodial terrestrials, rare lithophytes or epiphytes are widespread in dry to damp, low to mid elevation, woodlands, scrub and rocky slopes from Ghana to Uganda, Sudan to Zimbabwe, Madagascar, the Mascarenes, Comoros, Seychelles, India to New Guinea, northern Australia, United States (southern Florida), the Caribbean area, and Mexico to northern Argentina. These plants have clustered, ovoid to spindle-shaped pseudobulbs, each with one to three, dark green leaves that have silver mottling or have an erect, ovoid stem with a solitary leaf. The erect, simple or branched, few-flowered inflorescence, borne from the pseudobulb base, has inconspicuous, rather small, olive-green, cream, green-pink or pale green-yellow, thinly textured flowers that in some cases self-pollinate. The white, deeply trilobed or four-lobed lip has erect side lobes; the midlobe has a bright green, shallowly notched tip with a large, white, basal callus and has a small, curved spur. The flowers have a short, erect to slightly curved column with or without a foot.

OECEOLADES

An orthographic variant introduced in *Syn. Pl. (D. Dietrich)*, **5**: 118 (1852). The correct spelling is *Oeceoclades*.

OECOEOCLADES

An orthographic variant introduced in *Enum. Pl. Jap.*, **2**: 28 (1879). The correct spelling is *Oeceoclades*.

OENIA

An orthographic variant introduced in *Syn. Pl. (D. Dietrich)*, **5**: 13, 121 (1852). The correct spelling is *Oeonia*.

OEONIA

Lindley

Bot. Reg.   **10**: sub 817 (1824), and
Orchid. Scelet.   14 (1826).
Name and orthography ICBN conserved.
Epidendroideæ ⚘ Vandeæ • Angraecinæ
ETYMOLOGY: Greek for bird of prey or a bird of omen. Referring to the spreading perianth parts that along with the trilobed lip, resemble a bird in flight.
LECTOTYPE: *Oeonia aubertii* Lindley nom. illeg.
    This type name is now considered a synonym of
    Oeonia volucris (Thouars) Sprengel;
    basionym
    Epidendrum volucre Thouars

A remarkable genus of six dwarf, monopodial epiphytes are all found in low to mid elevation, moss laden forests of Madagascar except for one species in Réunion. These twig plants have short or slender, almost obsolete, scrambling, climbing or branching, thin stems, each with distichous, long or short, stiff, leathery leaves. The erect, few-flowered inflorescence has large, white, green or yellow-orange flowers with similar sepals and petals. The white, trilobed to six-lobed lip is spotted or blotched bright red or pink at the base, has a kidney-shaped midlobe and a short, tapering spur. The flowers have a short, slightly bent, footless column enfolded at the base by the small side lobes.

OEONIELLA

Schlechter

Beih. Bot. Centralbl.   **33**(2): 439 (1915), and
Beih. Bot. Centralbl.   **36**(2): 176 (1918).
Epidendroideæ ⚘ Vandeæ • Angraecinæ
ETYMOLOGY: *Oeonia*, a genus of orchids and Latin for diminutive. Refers to a similarity to *Oeonia*.
LECTOTYPE: *Oeoniella polystachys*
    (Thouars) Schlechter
    (*Epidendrum polystachys* Thouars)

Two monopodial epiphytes or lithophytes are found in humid, low elevation, coastal forests of eastern Madagascar, and the islands of Comoros, Mascarene and Seychelles. These plants have long, often branched stems, each with narrow, distichous, rigid, leathery, unequal bilobed leaves arranged in two ranks. The several, numerous to few-flowered inflorescences have small, mainly white, pale green-white to creamy-white, fragrant flowers with long, spidery petals and sepals. Quite distinctive is the trumpet-shaped lip that is trilobed at the tip with a short, cone-shaped spur at the base. The side lobes are rounded, and the narrow, spear-shaped midlobe is quite long. The flowers have a short, stout, wingless, footless column.

OERAIA

An orthographic variant introduced in *J. Bombay Nat. Hist. Soc.*, **57**(2): 491 (1960). The correct spelling is *Ceraia*.

OERSTEDELLA

Reichenbach *filius*

Bot. Zeitung (Berlin) **10**: 932 (1852).

ETYMOLOGY: Honoring Anders Sandø Ørsted (1816-1872), a Danish botanist, zoologist, professor of botany at the University of Copenhagen and author of *Centralamericas Gesneraceer, et systematisk, Planteographisk Bidrag til Centralamerikas Flora*, who collected the type species. And Latin for diminutive.

TYPE SPECIES: *None designated*

Now recognized as belonging to the genus *Epidendrum, Oerstedella* was previously considered to include twenty-nine tufted epiphytes, lithophytes or terrestrials found in wet to dry, low to upper elevation, hill scrub, montane evergreen to semi-deciduous forests from Mexico to Bolivia, Cuba and Jamaica. These small, wiry plants have short, sometimes purple, cane-like stems, each with distichous, flat, leathery, narrow leaves. The few to numerous-flowered inflorescence, borne from the leaf sheaths opposite the leaves, often has hoards of small, green-brown, white, yellow to purple, long-lasting, fragrant flowers. The white, red or purple-tinged or streaked, trilobed lip is united at the base to the long, footless column forming a nectary. The oblong side lobes are strongly curved sideways. The large, reflexed midlobe is deeply bilobed with a sharp spine between the lobes and has a yellow, basal callus. The flowers have a short, stout, footless column, but the hooded clinandrium is usually much longer than the column itself.

OERSTEDTELLA

An orthographic variant introduced in *Orchideen (Schlechter)*, ed. 1, 190 (1914). The correct spelling is *Oerstedella*.

OESTLUNDIA

W.E. Higgins

Selbyana **22**(1): 1, *f. 1* (2001).

Epidendroideæ 🌿 Epidendreæ • Laeliinæ

ETYMOLOGY: Honoring Karl Erik Östlund (1857-1938), a Swedish-born chemical engineer, who collected the type species.

TYPE SPECIES: *Oestlundia cyanocolumna* (Ames, Hubbard & C. Schweinfurth) W.E. Higgins (*Epidendrum cyanocolumna* Ames, Hubbard & C. Schweinfurth)

Eleven sympodial epiphytes are found in cool, dry, low to mid elevation, oak-pine forests from Mexico to western Colombia and northern Venezuela. Three of the species are found in Mexico. These plants have clustered or slightly spaced, cone to pear-shaped, ovoid pseudo-bulbs, each with two or three, narrow, grass-like leaves. The simple or branched, few-flowered inflorescence has thinly textured, pale yellow, yellow, orange-yellow, olive-green or green-yellow flowers often suffused purple-brown or brown. The yellow to creamy white, narrow to wedge-shaped, entire lip, attached to the column for a short length, is marked with dull violet or a green stripe. The flowers have a slender column that has a unique, smooth transition between the lip. The midlobe has a roundish mid-tooth and fleshy ridges of papillae that become warty. The column has an ear-like lateral projection more common to *Encyclia*.

OESTLUNDORCHIS

Szlachetko

Fragm. Florist. Geobot. **36**(1): 23 (1991).

ETYMOLOGY: Honoring Karl Erik Magnus Östlund (1857-1938), a Swedish-born Mexican chemical engineer who collected the orchids of Mexico. His vast herbarium collection was donated to the Oakes Ames Orchid Herbarium. And Greek for orchid.

TYPE SPECIES: *Oestlundorchis eriophora* (B.L. Robinson & Greenman) Szlachetko (*Spiranthes eriophora* B.L. Robinson & Greenman)

Now recognized as belonging to the genus *Deiregyne, Oestlundorchis* was proposed to include eleven terrestrials found in mid to upper elevation, oak-pine forests and grasslands from Mexico to Panama. These taxonomically complex plants have erect, stout, unbranched stems, completely subtended by translucent white, brown-veined, leaf-like sheaths, each with several, basal leaves that are usually withered at flowering time. The erect, numerous to few-flowered inflorescence has inconspicuous, small to large, showy, spirally arranged, tubular, pale green and white flowers. The white, diamond-shaped, trilobed

or entire lip has a fine green mid-nerve, papillae at the blunt tip, a scalloped to toothed margin, and some species are fragrant. The flowers have a rather long, erect to curved column that have an obscure foot.

OGYGIA

Luer

Monogr. Syst. Bot. Missouri Bot. Gard. **105**: 252 (2006).

ETYMOLOGY: Greek Mythology. Ogygia was a fabled island controlled by the nymph Calypso. It was a dark, tree-covered, depressing land with cold temperatures and terrifying beasts. Calypso detained Ulysses on Ogygia for seven years as a prisoner.

TYPE SPECIES: *Ogygia unguicallosa* (Ames & C. Schweinfurth) Luer (*Pleurothallis unguicallosa* Ames & C. Schweinfurth)

Recognized as belonging to the genus *Acianthera, Ogygia* was proposed to include one epiphyte found in low elevations of Mexico's Pacific Ocean islands of Revillagigedo. This small plant has slender stems, subtended by a long, tubular sheath, each with a solitary, leathery leaf suffused purple on the underside. The short, few-flowered inflorescence is borne from a small spathe at the base of the leaf. The oblong, concave dorsal sepal is boat-shaped. The narrow lateral sepals, united into an ovate, thin blade, sac-like at the base, have sharply keeled tips. The clawed, entire lip has a fleshy callus and a rounded tip. The flowers have a short, slightly curved column.

OLERONIA

An orthographic variant introduced in *Bot. Centralbl.*, **80**(13): 504 (1899). The correct spelling is *Oberonia*.

OLGASIS

Rafinesque

Fl. Tellur. **2**: 51 (1836)[1837].

ETYMOLOGY: Supposedly named for a nymph, but none exists in classical literature with this name.

TYPE SPECIES: *Olgasis triquetra* (Swartz) Rafinesque (*Epidendrum triquetrum* Swartz)

Now recognized as belonging to the genus *Tolumnia, Olgasis* was previously considered to include one epiphyte found in low elevation, scrub and forests of Jamaica. This tufted plant has inconspicuous pseudobulbs, each with several, narrow, overlapping, leathery leaves that have finely serrated edges and are arranged in a fan shape. The slender, simple to slightly branched, few-flowered inflorescence has showy, long-lived, slightly waxy, bright yellow to brown-yellow flowers strikingly suffused maroon. The white, trilobed lip has small, roundish side lobes, the large, heart-

Currently Accepted   Validly Published   Invalidly Published   Published Pre-1753   Superfluous Usage   Orthographic Variant   Fossil

Orchid Genera • **272**

shaped midlobe is streaked and spotted purple or red-purple and has an orange-yellow basal callus. The flowers have a small, erect column with petal-like wings.

OLIGOCHAETILUS

An orthographic variant cited in *Handb. Orchid.-Namen*, 504 (2005). The correct spelling is *Oligochaetochilus*.

OLIGOCHAETOCHILUS

Szlachetko
Polish Bot. J. **46**(1): 23 (2001).
ETYMOLOGY: Greek for few, bristle and lip. Refers to bristle margins on the short lip.
TYPE SPECIES: *Oligochaetochilus rufus*
(R. Brown) Szlachetko
(*Pterostylis rufa* R. Brown)

Recognized as belonging to the genus *Pterostylis*, *Oligochaetochilus* was proposed to include thirty terrestrials found in low to mid elevation, scrub and open forests of Australia often forming loose colonies. These small, slender, variable plants have erect, unbranched stems, each with a basal rosette of oblong to narrow, dull green leaves. The slender, wiry, few-flowered inflorescence has small, red-brown, red or green flowers. The hood-shaped dorsal sepal projects forward with a narrow opening that rarely reaches the short tip, and the wide lateral sepals gradually taper to a point. The ovate to oblong, red-brown to green, thickened, entire lip has white, bristly hairs along the margin. The flowers have an incurved column with white cilia.

OLIGOPHYTON

H.P. Linder
Kew Bull. **41**(2): 314 (1986).
ETYMOLOGY: Greek for few, small or little and plant. Descriptive of both the plant and the flowers.
TYPE SPECIES: *Oligophyton drummondii*
H.P. Linder & G. Williamson

Now recognized as belonging to the genus *Benthamia*, *Oligophyton* was proposed to include one terrestrial found only in mid elevation, sandy scrub of eastern Zimbabwe's (Manicaland) Chimanimani montane region. This small, erect plant has slender, unbranched stems, each with a basal rosette of ovate, dissimilar leaves. The tall, few-flowered inflorescence has minute, yellow flowers not opening widely. The yellow petals are enclosed by the concave, green-nerved dorsal sepal and lateral sepals. The trilobed lip has blunt side lobes curled up on either side of the small column, a triangular midlobe, and a short, straight or curved spur.

OLIVERIANA

Reichenbach *filius*
Linnaea **41**: 111 (1876).
Epidendroideæ ⚘ Cymbidieæ • Oncidiinæ
ETYMOLOGY: In honor of Daniel Oliver (1830-1916), a British professor of botany at University College in London, keeper of the herbarium at the Royal Botanic Gardens, Kew and editor and co-author of *Flora of Tropical Africa*.
TYPE SPECIES: *Oliveriana egregia* Reichenbach f.

Six sympodial epiphytes or terrestrials are found in extremely wet, mid elevation, montane forests from the Guianas and Colombia to Bolivia. These small plants have elongate rhizomes between the compressed pseudobulbs that are subtended by leaf-like sheaths, each with a solitary, narrow, leathery leaf. The long, often few-flowered inflorescence has rigid, small, dull green-white to green-brown flowers with similar spreading sepals and petals. The small, white to often yellow, entire or trilobed lip, united to the column above the base, has a broad, triangular-shaped side lobe and a small midlobe with a tapering point. The flowers have a small, slightly curved, footless column.

OMAEA

An orthographic variant introduced in *Orchideen (Schlechter)*, ed. 1, 581 (1914). The correct spelling is *Omoea*.

OMARIA

(Yam ex Nyman) Ernst & Stephens
Arditti's Fundamentals Orchid Biol. **1**: 97 (1992).

A fictitious and nomen illegitimum genus (nom. illeg.). This name was published as an example of how to word or credit authors of genera.

OMMATIDIUM

An orthographic variant introduced in *Orchideen (Schlechter)*, ed. 3, **5**(6): 277 (1975). The correct spelling is *Ommatodium*.

OMMATODIUM

Lindley
Gen. Sp. Orchid. Pl. 365 (1838).
ETYMOLOGY: Greek for diminutive of eye. Referring to the eye-like spots located on the lip.
TYPE SPECIES: *Ommatodium volucris*
(Linnaeus f.) Lindley
(*Ophrys volucris* Linnaeus f.)

Now recognized as belonging to the genus *Pterygodium*, *Ommatodium* was previously considered to include one terrestrial found in moist, mid elevation, woodlands and grasslands of the Cape region of South Africa. It will flower only after a fire has swept through the area. This colony forming, erect plant has slender to stout, unbranched stems, each with numerous, oblong to elliptical leaves. The densely packed, numerous-flowered inflorescence has small, rather unpleasantly fragrant, cup-shaped flowers with green sepals and pale yellow-green petals. The dorsal sepal and petals are united, forming a shallow hood. The pale yellow, trilobed lip is wedge-shaped and has a large appendage.

OMOEA

Blume
Bijdr. Fl. Ned. Ind. **8**: 359 (1825).
Epidendroideæ ⚘ Vandeæ • Aeridinæ
ETYMOLOGY: Greek for like or resembling. Referring possibly to the petals or a close similarity to *Ceratochilus*.
TYPE SPECIES: *Omoea micrantha* Blume

Two dwarf, monopodial epiphytes are found in mossy, mid elevation montane forests of Indonesia (Sumatra and Java) and the Philippines (Luzon). These tiny, twig plants have horizontal stems, often downward hanging as they lengthen with age, each with narrow, thick, fleshy leaves arranged in two rows along the stem. The short, solitary-flowered inflorescence, only one to two to a stem, has a small, pale green, yellow or white flower with spreading sepals and narrow petals. The trilobed lip has thickened side lobes, a heart-shaped, fleshy midlobe, and a recurved, sac-like spur. The flowers have a short, broad and obtuse, footless column.

ONCIDIDIUM

An orthographic variant introduced in *Repert. Spec. Nov. Regni Veg. Beih.*, **27**: 111 (1924). The correct spelling is *Oncidium*.

ONCIDIOCHILUS

Falconer

J. Bot. (Hooker) **4**(26): 75 (1842).

ETYMOLOGY: Greek for tumor or swelling and lip. Refers to the projection at the tip of the lip.

TYPE SPECIES: *None designated*

Name published without a description. Today this name is most often referred to *Goodyera*.

ONCIDIUM

Swartz

Kongl. Vetensk. Acad. Nya Handl. **21**: 239 (1800).

Name ICBN conserved, type name also conserved; and not *Oncidium* Nees von Esenbeck (1823) Fungi.

Epidendroideæ ※ Cymbidieæ • Oncidiinæ

ETYMOLOGY: Greek for a tumor or swelling. An allusion to the small, warty calluses found at the base of the lip.

LECTOTYPE: *Oncidium variegatum* Swartz
designated by Garay, *Taxon*, **19**: 444 (1970).

both of the following lectotypes are not validly designated

LECTOTYPE: *Oncidium altissimum* (Jacquin) Swartz
(*Epidendrum alissimum* Jacquin)
by Pfeiffer, *Nomencl. Bot. (Pfeiffer)*, **2**: 497 (1874).

LECTOTYPE: *Oncidium carthagenense* (Jacquin) Swartz
(*Epidendrum carthagenense* Jacquin)
by Britton & Wilson, *Bahama Fl.*, 97 (1920).

A vast group with a traditionally estimated three hundred thirty-six sympodial species growing primarily as epiphytes with a few lithophytes or terrestrials. Their range extends in low to upper elevation, hill woodlands, savannas, sunny grasslands and montane forests from the southeastern United States (southern Florida), the Bahamas, Cuba, Mexico to Panama, then south to Argentina, with the greatest development in Brazil. These evergreen, extremely varied plants range from diminutive, fan-like foliaged plants to large-bulbed and long foliaged plants. The plants have clumped to laxly-spaced pseudobulbs, each with one to three, flat, leathery leaves. A usually solitary inflorescence, borne from the pseudobulb base, is produced from a single growth, but it can be very short or immensely elongate, multi-branched and bearing up to several hundred flowers apiece. The tiny to large, showy, often fragrant, commonly yellow and brown flowers may be found in a vast range of colors, with the petals similar to the dorsal sepal or often larger. The prominent, entire or trilobed lip, commonly borne at a right-angle to the column, has tiny to large side lobes with an often widespreading, large midlobe that has a prominent warty to fringed basal callus. These calluses sometimes have oil producing glands. The flowers have a short, stout, footless column with wings, arms or finger-like projections.

ONCIDUM

An orthographic variant introduced in *Rep. Prog. Zool. Bot.*, 46 (1842). The correct spelling is *Oncidium*.

ONCODIA

Lindley

Fol. Orchid. **4**: *Oncodia*, 1 (1853).

ETYMOLOGY: Greek for pad, mass or bulk. Referring to the bracts which have an anterior hollow tumor; bracts are borne from the top of the ovary.

TYPE SPECIES: *Oncodia glumacea*
(Reichenbach f.) Lindley
(*Brachtia glumacea* Reichenbach f.)

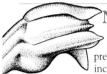

Now recognized as belonging to the genus *Brachtia*, *Oncodia* was previously considered to include two epiphytes found in mid to upper elevation, montane forests of Venezuela and Colombia to Ecuador. These plants have strongly compressed, sharp edged pseudobulbs, completely subtended by leaf-bearing sheaths, each with several, fleshy to papery leaves. The few-flowered inflorescence, slightly asymmetrical, has bright yellow flowers that develop slowly but with all the flowers crowded toward the tip. The immovable, entire lip has a raised segment densely covered in long, coarse white hairs. The flowers have a short, winged column.

ONCOPHYLLUM

D.L. Jones & M.A. Clements

Orchadian **13**(9): 420 (2001).

ETYMOLOGY: Greek for swollen and leaf. Referring to the pseudobulbs, that have an apical cavity containing internal stomata and are more suggestive of a swollen leaf than a swollen stem.

TYPE SPECIES: *Oncophyllum minutissimum*
(F. Mueller) D.L. Jones & M.A. Clements
(*Bulbophyllum minutissimum* F. Mueller)

Recognized as belonging to the genus *Bulbophyllum*, *Oncophyllum* was proposed to include two epiphytes found in wet to dry, low elevation, rocky woodlands, mangroves to along river banks of eastern Australia (Queensland to northern New South Wales). These plants form spreading mats of tiny, ovoid to globose or flattened pseudobulbs, each with a reduced to minute, papery leaf. The solitary-flowered inflorescence, borne from the pseudobulb base, has minute, green, white to creamy white flowers with numerous red-purple veins. The sepals are united at the base; the lateral sepals form a chin-like protuberance with the column foot. The fleshy, curved, entire lip is hinged to the tip of the column foot. The flowers have a short, winged column.

ONDICIUM

An orthographic variant introduced in *Cat. Pl. Cub.*, 266 (1866). The correct spelling is *Oncidium*.

ONEKETTIA

An orthographic variant introduced in *Bot. Centralbl.*, **98**: 102 (1905). The correct spelling is *Quekettia*.

ONKERIPUS

Rafinesque

Fl. Tellur. **4**: 42 (1836)[1837].

ETYMOLOGY: Greek for swollen and foot. In reference to the perianth parts that are basally somewhat bag or pouch-like.

TYPE SPECIES: *Onkeripus pallidus* Rafinesque nom. illeg.
Xylobium pallidiflorum (Hooker) G. Nicholson
(*Maxillaria pallidiflora* Hooker)

Now recognized as belonging to the genus *Xylobium*, *Onkeripus* was previously considered to include one epiphyte found in wet, mid to upper elevation, montane forests from Cuba to Hispaniola, Surinam, Venezuela and Colombia to Peru. This plant has tapered to slender pseudobulbs, subtended by dry sheaths, each with a solitary, thinly textured leaf that has prominent veins on the undersides. The short, erect, few-flowered inflorescence has bell-shaped, yellow to green-yellow flowers with widespreading sepals; the petals provide a hood over the slender, slightly curved column. The white, distinctly trilobed lip is either decorated with or without a few minute warts and has a yellow base.

ONYCHIUM

Blume

Bijdr. Fl. Ned. Ind. **7**: 323, t. 10 (1825).

Not *Onychium* Kaulfuss (1820) Pteridophyta, and not *Onychium* Reinwardt (1825) Polypodiaceæ.

ETYMOLOGY: Greek for a nail or claw. In reference to the bracts that are rather stiff.

TYPE SPECIES: *None designated*

Not validly published because of a prior use of the name, this homonym was replaced by *Dendrobium*.

ONYCHYUM

An orthographic variant cited in *Nomencl. Bot. (Steudel)*, ed. 2, **1**: 489 (1840). The correct spelling is *Onychium*.

Currently Accepted | Validly Published | Invalidly Published | Published Pre-1753 | Superfluous Usage | Orthographic Variant | Fossil

Orchid Genera • **274**

OPHIDION

Luer
Selbyana **7**(1): 79 (1982).

ETYMOLOGY: Greek for like a snake or a little serpent. An allusion to the appearance of the lip's lobes to the head of a viper.

TYPE SPECIES: *Ophidion cymbula* (Luer) Luer (*Cryptophoranthus cymbula* Luer)

Now recognized as belonging to the genus *Phloeophila*, *Ophidion* was previously considered to include four terrestrials or epiphytes found in wet, low elevation, hill forests from Panama to Bolivia. These small plants have erect stems, subtended by overlapping, tubular sheaths, each with a solitary, fleshy leaf. The short, weak, solitary to several-flowered inflorescence has white to green-red flowers. All three sepals are joined in varying degrees at their tips, forming a window view into the interior of the flower. There is a large, rigid, trilobed lip tucked inside that has tiny, rounded side lobes. The flowers have an arching, club-shaped column with a pedestal-like foot.

OPHIOGLOSELLA

An orthographic variant introduced in *Orchideen (Schlechter)*, ed. 3, 2759 (2002). The correct spelling is *Ophioglossella*.

OPHIOGLOSSELLA

Schuiteman & Ormerod
Kew Bull. **53**(3): 742 (1998).

Epidendroideæ Vandeæ • Aeridinæ

ETYMOLOGY: Greek for snake's tongue. In reference to the shape of the rostellum that is especially suggestive in conjunction with the cobra-like appearance of the column.

TYPE SPECIES: *Ophioglossella chrysostoma* Schuiteman & Ormerod

One monopodial epiphyte is found in mid to upper elevation, montane forests of New Guinea. This small, plant has short stems, each with several, leathery, purple suffused leaves that are twisted at the base, and more or less spreading in one plane. The several to few-flowered inflorescence has white, suffused purple flowers, opening a few at a time, then becoming pink with age. The white, strongly concave, trilobed lip, hinged to the tip of the column-foot, has rich purple, rounded side lobes that are connected to the midlobe by two conspicuous, flat scales, and has golden-yellow, basal calli. The flowers have a white, slender, curved column.

OPHRIS

Tournefort
Inst. Rei Herb. 437, *t. 250* (1700).

Pre-1753, therefore not validly published in fulfillment of nomenclatural rules; this name is most often referred to *Ophrys*.

OPHRIS

P. Miller
Gard. Dict. Abr., ed. 4 (1754).

Name published without a description. Today this name is most often referred to *Listera*.

OPHRRYS

An orthographic variant introduced in *Gard. Dict. Abr.*, ed. 8, (1768). The correct spelling is *Ophrys*.

OPHRYDEA

An orthographic variant introduced in *Itin. Pl. Khasyah Mts.*, 95 (1848). The correct spelling is *Ophrys*.

OPHRYDIS

An orthographic variant introduced in *Hist. Stirp. Helv.*, **2**: 134, 147 (1768). The correct spelling is *Ophrys*.

OPHRYOS

An orthographic variant introduced in *Hist. Stirp. Helv.*, **2**: 131, 132 (1768). The correct spelling is *Ophrys*.

OPHRYS

Pliny
Hist. Nat. **XXVI**: 164 (AD 56).

Pre-1753, therefore not validly published in fulfillment of nomenclatural rules; this name is most often referred to *Ophrys* Linnaeus.

OPHRYS

Caesalpinus
Pl. Libri XVI 430 (1583).

Pre-1753, therefore not validly published in fulfillment of nomenclatural rules; this name is most often referred to *Ophrys* Linnaeus.

OPHRYS

Linnaeus
Sp. Pl. (Linnaeus), ed. 1 **2**: 945 (1753), and *Gen. Pl.*, ed 5 406 (1754).

Orchidoideæ Orchideæ • Orchidinæ

ETYMOLOGY: The name of a plant of uncertain identity that was used by Pliny (Gainus Plinius Secundus) the elder (AD 23-79), a Roman naturalist, statesman, and equestrian, who mentions this plant's use to blacken eyebrows or hair in his book *Historia Naturalis*.

Or perhaps, Greek for eyebrow. An allusion to the resemblance of the curved sepals of some species to an arched eyebrow.

LECTOTYPE: *Ophrys insectifera* Linnaeus designated by M.L. Green, *Prop. Brit. Bot.*, 185 (1929); see Jarvis, *Taxon*, **41**: 566 (1992).

There are approximately sixty sympodial terrestrials plus numerous, natural hybrids. These species are found in low to mid elevation, meadows, marshes and montane woodlands from Norway to central Russia (West Siberia), Denmark to Ukraine, Albania to Israel, Morocco to Libya, Turkey and southern Turkmenistan to Iran. These attractive bee orchids are so-named because of their resemblance to the insects that pollinate them, usually each species has a specific bee or wasp pollinator. When not in flower, the various species are difficult to separate as they all have similar leaf rosettes and erect, unbranched stems. The erect, few-flowered inflorescence has green to pink sepals with the petals often smaller than the sepals, that sometimes are antenna-like. The trilobed or obscurely trilobed lip is hairy around the margin with a central shiny area of blue, gray or blue-gray. The flowers have a small, broad, wingless, footless column.

NOTE: These flowers have highly specialized methods for attracting pollinators. The male insects are attracted by floral mimicry or by a fragrance resembling a female insect, and thus are duped into pseudocopulation with the flower. There is wide variation in flower color and shapes mainly due to hybridization, with previously isolated species being brought together.

OPONTOGLOSSUM

An orthographic variant introduced in *Sempervirens*, **21**: 127 (1892). The correct spelling is *Odontoglossum*.

ORBIS

Luer

Monogr. Syst. Bot. Missouri Bot. Gard.
103: 308 (2005).

ETYMOLOGY: Latin for round or circular. Refers to the small, roundish flowers.

TYPE SPECIES: *Orbis truncata* (Lindley) Luer
(*Pleurothallis truncata* Lindley)

Now recognized as belonging to the genus *Pleurothallis*, *Orbis* was proposed to include one epiphyte or occasional lithophyte found in upper elevation, montane forests of Ecuador. This large, creeping plant has erect, slender stems, each with a solitary, leathery leaf. The numerous-flowered inflorescence, borne from the leaf axils, has small, intensely orange flowers shaped like little beads that do not open fully. The successive opening flowers have united lateral sepals forming a deep cup-like shape; the tiny petals have a roundish tip. The tiny, entire lip is usually found inside the barely opened flower. The flowers have a short, footless column.

ORCHEOS

An orthographic variant introduced in *Pinax*, 83 (1623). The correct spelling is *Orchis*.

ORCHIASTRUM

Micheli

Nov. Pl. Gen.   30, *t.* 26 (1729).

Pre-1753, therefore not validly published in fulfillment of nomenclatural rules; this name is most often referred to *Spiranthes*.

ORCHIASTRUM

Séguier

Pl. Veron.   **3**: 252 (1754).

Name ICBN rejected vs. *Spiranthes* Richard (1817), and not *Orchiastrum* Lemaire (1855) Liliaceæ.

ETYMOLOGY: Greek for testicle and Latin for wild or resemblance. Refers to the size and shape of the tuber.

TYPE SPECIES: *None designated*

An invalid name proposed as a substitute for *Spiranthes*.

ORCHIDACITES

Straus

Palaeontogra.   **96B**: 6, *t.* 1 (1954), and
Validated: *Argum. Palaeobot.*   **3**: 167 (1969).

ETYMOLOGY: Greek for testicle and Latin for connection. Implying a connection between this fossil and modern orchid plants.

TYPE SPECIES: *Orchidacites orchidioides* Straus

Three fossils are based on fruit fragments which were thought to resemble various species of Orchids (*Cypripedium*{1} and *Orchis*{2}). These finds are from the recent Pliocene epoch. These fragments, now regarded more or less doubtful as orchidaceous, were found in a clay pit near Willershausen, Germany, which is located in the Hartz Mountains (east of Cologne).

ORCHIDASTRUM

An orthographic variant introduced in *Bot. Gall.*, *pars prima*, ed 2, 448 (1828). The correct spelling is *Orchiastrum*.

ORCHIDEA

Burchell

Cat. Geogr. Pl. (Burchell)
Unpublished, conserved at Kew.   (1860).

ETYMOLOGY: Greek for orchid.

TYPE SPECIES: *None designated*

Not validly published, this name is often referred to a variety of different orchid genera. One is a terrestrial, *Orchidea hispidula* – No.: 6369, found in the southern Cape regions of South Africa. This plant has a pair of thinly textured, basal leaves and an erect, slender, hairy, numerous-flowered inflorescence with tiny, yellow flowers for which you need a magnifying glass to aid in their identification. This name is now often considered a synonym of *Holothrix cernua* (Burman f.) Schelpe.

There could be a few other orchid species listed in this five-volume manuscript that has over some 8700 entries but have listed only the numbers that I know about.

A terrestrial labeled **Orchidea appressa** - No.: 7356 - now often considered a synonym of *Pachites appressa* Lindley. This plant is found only in the western Cape of South Africa.

A terrestrial labeled **Orchidea pectinata** - No.: 6709 - now often considered a synonym of *Holothrix burchellii* (Lindley) Reichenbach f. This unusual little plant is found only in South Africa.

A terrestrial labeled **Orchidea falcicornis** - No.: 5178 - now often considered a synonym of *Habenaria falcicornis* (Lindley) Bolus. This is a

tall, slender plant found in grasslands from western South Africa to Zimbabwe.

A terrestrial labeled **Orchidea pilosa** - No.: 7483 - now often considered a synonym of *Holothrix pilosa* (Burchell ex Lindley) Reichenbach f. This unusual species is found in the extreme southern tip of South Africa.

A terrestrial labeled **Orchidea exillis** - No.: 6738-1 - now often considered a synonym of *Holothrix exilis* Lindley. This species is found in the extreme southern tip of South Africa and has its leaves absent during flowering.

A terrestrial labeled **Orchidea membranaceum** - No.: 6738-2 - often referred to as a synonym of *Satyrium membranaceum* Swartz. This species is found in extreme southern tip of South Africa.

A terrestrial labeled **Orchidea arenaria** - No.: 5654 - now often considered a synonym of *Habenaria arenaria* Lindley. This unusual species is found in the extreme southern tip of South Africa.

These few additional orchid species are found with the following numbers from the same book but I have no idea as to their labels:

No.: 7337 - **Disa glandulosa** Burchell ex Lindley - a terrestrial found in South Africa,

No.: 5841 - **Angraecum pusillum** Lindley - an epiphyte found throughout tropical Africa; and

No.: 7801 - **Disa graminifolia** Ker Gawler ex Sprengel - a terrestrial commonly found in the southern Cape of South Africa.

ORCHIDEA

Griffith

Itin. Pl. Khasyah Mts.   343 (1848).

Name published without a description. Today this name is most often referred to *Orchis*.

ORCHIDEM

An orthographic variant introduced in *Cat. Pl. Angl.*, ed. 2, 228 (1677). The correct spelling is *Orchis*.

ORCHIDES

An orthographic variant introduced in *Sp. Pl.* (Linnaeus), ed 2, **2**: 1275, 1475 (1762). The correct spelling is *Orchis*.

ORCHIDIA

An orthographic variant introduced in *Itin. Pl. Khasyah Mts.*, 65 (1848). The correct spelling is *Orchis*.

ORCHIDIASTRUM

An orthographic variant introduced in *Enum. Pl. Vasc.*, 325 (1855). The correct spelling is *Orchiastrum*.

Currently Accepted   Validly Published   Invalidly Published   Published Pre-1753   Superfluous Usage   Orthographic Variant   Fossil

ORCHIDION

Mitchell

Acta Phys.-Med. Acad. Caes. Leop.-Francisc. Nat. Cur. **8**: 218 (1748), and
Diss. Bot. & Zool. 40 (1769).

Pre-1753, therefore not validly published in fulfillment of nomenclatural rules; this name is most often referred to *Bletia*.

ORCHIDIS

C. Bauhin

Pinax 83 (1623).

Pre-1753, therefore not validly published in fulfillment of nomenclatural rules; this name is most often referred to *Orchis*.

ORCHIDIS

An orthographic variant introduced in *Flora*, **68**(30): 536 (1885). The correct spelling is *Orchis*.

ORCHIDIUM

Swartz

Svensk Bot. Tidskr. **8**: t. 518 (1816), and
Summa Veg. Scand. (Swartz) 32 (1814).

ETYMOLOGY: Diminutive of *Orchis*, a genus of orchids, meaning little testicle. Refers to the small tubers.

TYPE SPECIES: *Orchidium boreale* (Swartz) Swartz
(*Cymbidium boreale* Swartz)
This type name is now considered a synonym of
Calypso bulbosa (Linnaeus) Oakes;
basionym replaced with
Cypripedium bulbosum Linnaeus

Now recognized as belonging to the genus *Calypso*, *Orchidium* was previously considered to include three terrestrials found in the northern hemisphere temperate zone. These tiny, erect plants have unbranched stems, each with a solitary, heart-shaped, blue-green leaf produced late in the season which lasts through the winter. The erect, solitary-flowered inflorescence has a fragrant, showy, purple to pale pink flower. The slipper-shaped, white or yellow, entire lip has three rows of brown hairs.

ORCHIDOFUNCKIA

A. Richard & Galeotti

Ann. Sci. Nat., Bot., ser. 3 **3**: 24 (1845).

ETYMOLOGY: Greek for orchid and in honor of Nicolas Funck (1816-1896), a Luxemburg naturalist, artist, plant collector, a director of the Zoological Gardens in both Brussels and Cologne and orchid collector in Central and South America.

TYPE SPECIES: *Orchidofunckia pallidiflora*
A. Richard & Galeotti

Now recognized as belonging to the genus *Cryptarrhena*, *Orchidofunckia* was previously considered to include one epiphyte found in low to mid elevation, hill to montane rain forests from southern Mexico to Colombia, Peru, Trinidad and Jamaica. This dwarf plant has short, leafy stems, with or without tiny, compressed pseudobulbs, each with numerous, narrow leaves. The few-flowered inflorescence has tiny, yellow-green flowers with a distinct, long, fleshy claw on the four-lobed lip. The above type name is now considered a synonym of *Cryptarrhena lunata* R. Brown.

ORCHIDOFUNKIA

An orthographic variant introduced in *Dict. Univ. Hist. Nat.*, **9**: 171 (1847). The correct spelling is *Orchidofunckia*.

ORCHIDOTYPUS

Kraenzlin

Bot. Jahrb. Syst. **37**: 383 (1906).

ETYMOLOGY: Greek for orchid and model. Most likely alluding to a new genus of orchids.

TYPE SPECIES: *Orchidotypus muscoides* Kraenzlin
This type name is now considered a synonym of
Pachyphyllum hispidulum
(Reichenbach f.) Garay & Dunsterville;
basionym
Aeranthes hispidula Reichenbach f.

Now recognized as belonging to the genus *Pachyphyllum*, *Orchidotypus* was previously considered to include four epiphytes found in upper elevation, montane rain forests of Costa Rica, Panama, Colombia, Ecuador, Peru and Venezuela. These minute plants have short, leafy, branching stems, subtended completely by persistent leaf sheaths, each with distichous, fleshy leaves overlapping at the base. The short, few-flowered inflorescences have minute, bell-shaped, pale green, white or yellow-green flowers. The tiny, entire or somewhat trilobate lip usually has a pair of calli. The flowers have a thick column.

ORCHIDUM

Porta

Phytognomonica 141 (1588).

Pre-1753, therefore not validly published in fulfillment of nomenclatural rules; this name is most often referred to *Orchis*.

ORCHIES

An orthographic variant introduced in *Fl. Coron. Herb. Hist.*, 199 (1578). The correct spelling is *Orchis*.

ORCHIM

Pliny

Hist. Nat. **XXVII**: 65 (AD 56).

Pre-1753, therefore not validly published in fulfillment of nomenclatural rules; this name is most often referred to *Orchis*.

ORCHIN

An orthographic variant introduced in *Fl. Coron. Herb. Hist.*, 212 (1578). The correct spelling is *Orchis*.

ORCHIODES

Trew

Acta Phys.-Med. Acad. Caes. Leop.-Francisc. Nat. Cur. **3**: 409, t. 6, f. 7 (1736).

Pre-1753, therefore not validly published in fulfillment of nomenclatural rules; this name is most often referred to *Goodyera*.

ORCHIODES

Trew ex Kuntze

Revis. Gen. Pl. **2**: 661, 674 (1891).

ETYMOLOGY: Greek for testicle (orchid) and likeness or resembling. Refers to the root tubers.

TYPE SPECIES: *None designated*

Now recognized as belonging to the genus *Goodyera*, *Orchiodes* was previously considered to include thirty-eight terrestrials or uncommon epiphytes widespread in almost all parts of the globe except Africa. These erect plants have unbranched stems, each with numerous, showy, reptile-like, mottled, spirally arranged leaves. The erect, hairy, few-flowered inflorescence has tightly, spirally arranged flowers. The insignificant flowers are often rather small, white, green or pale brown and do not open widely. The large dorsal sepal and petals converge, forming a hood over the short column, and the petals are sometimes united near their tips. The small, tongue-shaped, entire lip is hairy.

ORCHIOIDES

An orthographic variant introduced in *Fl. Lapp. (Linnaeus)*, 315 (1737). The correct spelling is *Orchiodes*.

ORCHION

An orthographic variant introduced in *Fl. Coron. Herb. Hist.*, 200 (1578). The correct spelling is *Orchis*.

ORCHIOS

An orthographic variant introduced in *Hist. Pl. (Dodoens)*, 152 (1557). The correct spelling is *Orchis*.

ORCHIPEDA

Not *Orchipeda* Blume (1826) Apocynaceæ.

An orthographic variant introduced in *Allg. Bot. Z. Syst.*, **7**(7-8): 159 (1901). The correct spelling is *Cordyla*

ORCHIPEDIUM

An orthographic variant introduced in *J. Linn. Soc., Bot.*, **18**(110): 344 (1881). The correct spelling is *Orchipedum*.

ORCHIPEDUM

Breda

Gen. Sp. Orchid. Asclep., fasc. II   *t. 10* (1829).

Orchidoideæ ◊ Cranichideæ • Goodyerinæ

ETYMOLOGY: Greek for orchis (testicle) and slipper or shoe. From the resemblance of the pouch-like spur to a testicle.

TYPE SPECIES: *Orchipedum plantaginifolium* Breda

Two uncommon, sympodial terrestrials are found in low to mid elevation, hill scrub, along river banks and montane forests of Malaysia, Indonesia (Java and Sumatra) and the Philippines. These robust, creeping plants have erect stems, each bearing several leaves that have unequal halves and clasping upward. The long, hairy, numerous-flowered inflorescence has thinly textured, white or green flowers. The concave dorsal sepal and small petals converge, forming a hood over the slender, footless column. Each flower is subtended by a pale red bract that is nearly as long as the flower. The concave, white, trilobed lip is attached to the lower half of the column margins. The hypochile has squarish,

flared side lobes; the mesochile has a short claw; the entire or bilobed epichile is kidney-shaped and has a somewhat sac-like, compressed spur. The flowers have a short, slender, weakly arched column, with the anther and rostellum, subequal to the column and bent at right angles to it.

ORCHIS

Pliny

Hist. Nat.   **XXVI**: 96, 128, 146 (AD 56).

Pre-1753, therefore not validly published in fulfillment of nomenclatural rules; this name is most often referred to *Orchis* Linnaeus.

ORCHIS

Besler

Hort. Eystet.   *tt.* 196, 197 (1613).

Pre-1753, therefore not validly published in fulfillment of nomenclatural rules; this name is most often referred to *Orchis*, *Platanthera* and *Goodyera*.

ORCHIS

Linnaeus

Sp. Pl. (Linnaeus), ed. 1   **2**: 939 (1753), and *Gen. Pl.*, ed 5   405 (1754).

Orchidoideæ ◊ Orchideæ • Orchidinæ

ETYMOLOGY: Greek for testicle. Theophrastus (372-286 BC) a native of the island of Lesbos, who first applied the name *Orchis*, scientifically, which was in reference to the double root tubers of these plants (*Enquiry into Plants*) that often resemble male genitalia. Pliny the Elder (AD 23-79) in *Natural History*, **26**: 62 - mentions the word *Orchis* in reference to a plant that was said to arouse sexual desire. Dioscorides (90-40 BC) wrote describing two orchids (*Materia Media*) while serving in the Roman army, but he named them *Cynorchis*.

Greek Mythology. Orchis was a young son of a nymph and a satyr, who during a feast for Bacchus, attempted the rape of a priestess. As punishment he was torn limb from limb by wild beasts, and the parts were scatted to the winds, but his organs were transformed into a plant's tubers.

This name is also the root of the word orchid and of Orchidaceæ, used to described one plant family.

LECTOTYPE: *Orchis militaris* Linnaeus

There are about twenty-seven sympodial terrestrials, plus numerous natural hybrids whose greatest development is found from Britain to central Russia (West Siberia), and Spain to Ukraine, although some species extend into North America, Morocco to Iran, Mongolia, central China and Japan. These plants are found in low to upper elevation, woodlands and meadows with poor, dry soil and are extremely diverse in their

appearance. The floral structure often varies markedly, even within a given species. The plants rely heavily upon a mycorrhizal association with their own specific fungus. The plants form colonies varying in number from year to year and the foliage, appearing in the spring, forms a basal rosette of (sometimes spotted) leaves with a central floral spike. The few to numerous-flowered inflorescence has showy, white, pink or purple, rare yellow or yellow-green flowers. The sepals and petals converge, forming a hood, or the lateral sepals are spreading and bent outwards. The strongly curved, trilobed or four-lobed lip has margins densely bearded with red or brown hairs, and has narrow side lobes with the longer midlobe roundish or egg-shaped. The long spur (rarely spurless) is thread-like or sac-like. The flowers have a short, wingless, footless column that is blunt at the tip.

NOTE: This name (*Orchis*) was applied by the early herbalists and botanists of the middle ages quite indiscriminately to any type of ground orchid that had a root system of tubers. Currently in Turkey, terrestrial orchid bulbs have been harvested and used since antiquity to produce salep (dried, ground orchid bulbs) which is used as medicine, in drinks, and as binder for ice cream.

ORCHISCON

An orthographic variant introduced in *Pl. Rar. Horti Upsal.*, **4**: 14 (1767). The correct spelling is *Orchis*.

ORCHITES

Schur

Enum. Pl. Transsilv.   942 (1866).

ETYMOLOGY: Greek for orchid and having the nature of. Referring to a similarity to Orchis.

Or possibly named for a type of olive tree which was highly prized during early Roman times as mentioned by Marcus Porcius Cato (234-149 BC) in *De Re Rustica*.

TYPE SPECIES: *Orchites globosa* (Linnaeus) Schur (*Orchis globosa* Linnaeus)

Now recognized as belonging to the genus *Traunsteinera*, *Orchites* was previously considered to include one terrestrial commonly found in mid to upper elevation, montane meadows from Germany to Italy and Poland to coastal Turkey. This erect plant has stout, unbranched stems, each with several, narrow, basal leaves. The flowers are tightly packed into a pyramidal ball. The smallish, usually pale pink-purple to creamy white flowers have long sepals with a swollen, club-shaped tip. The wedge-shaped, dark purple spotted or with no spots, trilobed lip has long, slender spur.

Currently Accepted | Validly Published | Invalidly Published | Published Pre-1753 | Superfluous Usage | Orthographic Variant | Fossil

O r c h i d   G e n e r a   • **278**

ORCHIUM

An orthographic variant introduced in *Fl. Coron. Herb. Hist.*, 215 (1578). The correct spelling is *Orchis*.

ORCHYS

An orthographic variant introduced in *Hist. Pl. (Ray)*, **2**: 1220 (1688). The correct spelling is *Orchis*.

ORCHYS

Ruiz

Unpublished Manuscript **4**: 4, 3, *f. 28* (*c.*1800). Held at the Real Jardín Botánico, Madrid.

ETYMOLOGY: Greek for woman and flower.

TYPE SPECIES: *Orchys - Gynandria Diandria* Ruiz

Not validly published, this name is referred to the genus *Lycaste*. *Orchys* was considered to include one epiphyte found from Costa Rica to Bolivia. This species is now considered a synonym of *Lycaste macrophylla* (Poeppig & Endlicher) Lindley.

NOTE: There is a painting in Madrid, Spain by Jose Gabriel Rivera, entitled *Orchis*, in the Ruiz López and Pavón archives IV, lamina 1255, *t.* 98, and a herbarium specimen (dated 1797) with a label *Gynand. Diand. Orchys …*

OREGURA

Lindley ex **Wittstein**

Etym.-Bot.-Handw.-Buch, ed. 1 637 (1852).

Name published without a description. Today this name is most often referred to as a section of *Disa*.

OREOCLADES

An orthographic variant introduced in *Hamburger Garten- Blumenzeitung*, **19**: 540 (1863). The correct spelling is *Oeceoclades*.

OREORCHIS

Lindley

J. Proc. Linn. Soc., Bot. **3**: 26 (1859).

Epidendroideæ ⚘ Calypsoeæ

ETYMOLOGY: Greek for of a mountain and orchid. Alluding to their native mountainous habitat.

LECTOTYPE: *Oreorchis patens* (Lindley) Lindley
(*Corallorhiza patens* Lindley)

Eighteen insignificant terrestrials or saprophytes are found in mid to upper elevation, woodlands, grasslands and valleys of eastern Russia (Sakha to Kamchatka and Kuril Islands), Korea, Japan and Taiwan with the largest concentration found in China (Xizang to Zhejiang and Helongjiang to Sichuan). These erect plants have small, ovate or oblong pseudobulbs with several internodes or oblong corms usually found underground, each with one to two, narrow, pleated leaves borne at the tip. The tall, numerous to few-flowered inflorescence has minute, yellow-white, red to purple, strongly nerved, spirally arranged flowers. The lateral sepals are similar or slightly smaller and narrower than the petals and are shallowly sac-like at their base. The long-clawed, white, entire, trilobed or slightly notched lip is sprinkled with purple spots and has sickle-shaped, erect side lobes. The roundish midlobe has a shallow notch at the tip. The flowers have a straight or slightly curved, wingless column.

ORESTIAS

Ridley

J. Linn. Soc., Bot. **24**(161): 197 (1887).

Epidendroideæ ⚘ Malaxideæ

ETYMOLOGY: Greek Mythology. Named for a mountain nymph that mostly belongs to the countryside or to a particular river, grove or hill. Referring to the plants' modest habit of growing at upper elevations.

Or Edirne, a city in northwestern Turkey also called *Orestia* by early Byzantine writers, that was founded (*c.* AD 125) by Hadrian (AD 117-138), the Roman emperor.

Or *Orestia* (stories of Agamemnon, the Eumenides, and the Libation Bearers) was a play written by the Greek playwright Aeschylus in 456 BC.

TYPE SPECIES: *Orestias elegans* Ridley

Four sympodial terrestrials are found in shady, low to mid elevation, montane forests on the island of São Tomé, and Principle, Sierra Leone to Kenya and Ethiopia south to Zambia, Mozambique, Zimbabwe and Madagascar. This uninteresting, creeping plant has thin, white bracts spaced up to the erect, unbranched stems' midsection and then has several, large, oval, thinly textured, pleated leaves that are papery when dry. The erect, few-flowered inflorescence has small to minute, pale green or maroon flowers that have an unusual, thin-walled, slender, tubular, curved, footless column. The roundish, entire to obscurely trilobed lip has several, basal warts or hairy callus structures.

NOTE: Ridley originally published the spelling of this genus as *Orestia*, but later in *J. Linn Soc. Bot.*, **24**: 488, *t.* 6 (1888) he changed the spelling.

ORKERIPUS

An orthographic variant introduced in *Fl. Bras. (Martius)*, **3**(5): 467 (1898). The correct spelling is *Onkeripus*.

ORLCANESIA

An orthographic variant introduced in *Index Gen. Phan.*, 404 (1888). The correct spelling is *Orleanesia*.

ORLEANESIA

Barbosa Rodrigues

Gen. Sp. Orchid. **1**: 62, *t. 255* (1877).

Epidendroideæ ⚘ Epidendreæ • Laeliinæ

ETYMOLOGY: In honor of Louis Philippe Marie Ferdinand Gaston d'Orléans (1842-1921), Comte d'Eu, a French-born Brazilian prince, patron of floriculture, supreme commander of allied Brazilian armies and husband to the Princess Isabelia.

TYPE SPECIES: *Orleanesia amazonica*
Barbosa Rodrigues

Nine uncommon, sympodial epiphytes or lithophytes are found in humid, low elevation, pine-oak, scrub forests and grasslands of the eastern Andes of Venezuela, the Guianas, Colombia to Bolivia and northwestern Brazil (Acre, Amazonas and Pará) with Ecuador having the greatest diversity. These relatively insignificant, inconspicuous plants have thick, spindle-shaped stems or pseudobulbs, subtended by overlapping, tubular, leafless sheaths, each with several, fleshy or leathery, distichous leaves. The erect or rarely arching, shortly branched, numerous to few-flowered inflorescence has small, green flowers with similar, broad, widespreading petals and sepals that are variously tinged, suffused or spotted purple, brown, maroon or orange. The hood-like, hinged, entire lip is joined to the base of the broad, stout, arched or rarely straight, with wings or wingless column striped bright purple.

ORLEANISIA

An orthographic variant introduced in *Index Kew.*, **3**: 367 (1894). The correct spelling is *Orleanesia*.

ORMERODIA

Szlachetko

Ann. Bot. Fenn. **40**(1): 68 (2003).

ETYMOLOGY: In honor of Paul Abel Ormerod (1969-), an Australian botanist, orchidologist and author of numerous articles about orchids.

TYPE SPECIES: *Ormerodia belophora*
(Reichenbach f.) Szlachetko
(*Sarcanthus belophorus* Reichenbach f.)
This type name is now considered a synonym of *Cleisostoma linearilobatum*
(Seidenfaden & Smitinand) Garay;
basionym replaced with
Sarcanthus linearilobatus Seidenfaden & Smitinand

Recognized as belonging to the genus *Cleisostoma*, *Ormerodia* was previously considered to include three epiphytes found in mid elevation, montane forests of Thailand. These small plants have short stems, subtended by old leaf sheaths, each with several, narrow, leathery, unequally bilobed leaves. The short, multibranched, hanging, red-brown, numerous-flowered inflorescence has small, lavender to pale yellow-brown flowers with purple veins. The purple, trilobed lip has forward pointing, slightly concave (bladder-like) side lobes; a broad, arrow-shaped midlobe with a white tip, and a short, concave spur. The flowers have a short, stout, wingless column.

ORMOSTEMA

Rafinesque

Fl. Tellur. **4**: 38 (1836)[1837].

ETYMOLOGY: Greek for a chain or necklace and stamen or man. Refers to the rhizome with its bead-like swellings at the joints.

TYPE SPECIES: *None designated*

Now recognized as belonging to the genus *Dendrobium*, *Ormostema* was previously considered to include two epiphytes found in low to upper elevation, hill to montane forests from southeastern China (Guangxi to Fujian), Taiwan, Korea and southern Japan. These small plants have clustered, hanging or erect, spindle-shaped, noded pseudobulbs, each with several rather glossy, deciduous, narrow to oblong leaves. The short, numerous to few-flowered inflorescence has extremely fragrant, showy, pristine white (often suffused pink) to lavender flowers with red-purple specks. The white or yellow-green, tubular, trilobed lip has the side lobes enfolding the short column.

ORMOSTEMMA

An orthographic variant introduced in *Orchideen (Schlechter)*, ed. 1, 249 (1914). The correct spelling is *Ormostema*.

ORNETHOCEPHALUS

An orthographic variant introduced in *Pansey*, 45 (1835). The correct spelling is *Ornithocephalus*.

ORNITHARIUM

Lindley & Paxton

Paxton's Fl. Gard. **1**: 188, *f. 117* (1851).

ETYMOLOGY: Greek for a small bird. The violet stained lip with its round terminal knob give the flower the appearance of concealing within a tiny, white bird with a purple head.

TYPE SPECIES: *Ornitharium striatulum*
Lindley & Paxton

This type name is now considered a synonym of *Pteroceras teres* (Blume) Holttum; basionym *Dendrocolla teres* Blume

Now recognized as belonging to the genus *Pteroceras*, *Ornitharium* was previously considered to include one epiphyte found in mid elevation, secondary growth forests from India, Thailand, Vietnam, and Indonesia to the Philippines. This small plant has short stems, each with narrow, leathery, unevenly bilobed leaves. The several, hanging, few-flowered inflorescences have small, sweetly fragrant, white or yellow flowers lasting only a single day. The dark red, trilobed lip is dominated by a forward pointing spur that is variously twisted as it narrows, is in line with the column foot, and is movably jointed to it. The thick-walled spur is without any inside ornaments.

ORNITHIDIUM

Salisbury

Trans. Hort. Soc. London **1**: 293 (1812).

ETYMOLOGY: Greek for little bird. The small, red flowers give the appearance of a tiny bird's head in the type species.

TYPE SPECIES: *Ornithidium coccineum*
(Jacquin) Salisbury
(*Epidendrum coccineum* Jacquin)

Now recognized as belonging to the genus *Maxillaria*, *Ornithidium* was previously considered to include ninety-two epiphytes found in low to upper elevation, hill scrub, grasslands, roadsides and montane evergreen to deciduous forests from Cuba to Trinidad, the Guianas, Venezuela, Colombia and northern Brazil. These small plants have compressed, bright green pseudobulbs, each with several, leathery leaves. The one to several, solitary-flowered inflorescences have a small, variously colored, fragrant flower with the lateral sepals somewhat united to the erect or curved, stout, wingless column. The petals are usually smaller. The concave, trilobed or entire lip has a disk with an unusually oily or waxy callus.

NOTE: One year later **R. Brown** republished and expanded the genus in *Hortus Kew.*, ed. 2, **5**: 210 (1813).

ORNITHIDUM

An orthographic variant introduced in *Bonplandia* , **4**(20/21): 313 (1856). The correct spelling is *Ornithidium*.

ORNITHOCEPHALUS

Hooker

Exot. Fl. **2**(15): *t. 127* (1824).

Epidendroideæ ▨ Cymbidieæ • Oncidiinæ

ETYMOLOGY: Greek for a bird and head. Descriptive of the curious shape of the column, its appendages and their similarity to a bird's bill.

TYPE SPECIES: *Ornithocephalus gladiatus* Hooker

Forty-four interesting, psygmoid epiphytes are widespread in cool to humid, low to upper elevation, dry savannas and montane forests from southern Mexico to Bolivia and Brazil usually in shady spots on moss covered twigs and branches. These small, densely clumped, twig-like, fan-shaped, fleshy-leafed plants have short stems, each with several, narrow to oblong, overlapping, rigid leaves arranged in a fan shape. Both the short to long-stemmed, erect to hanging, few to numerous-flowered inflorescence and the outside flower surface are sometimes but not always covered with relatively long hairs. These delightful dwarfs have tiny, yet incredibly complex, green, white or green-yellow, sometimes fragrant flowers. The entire or trilobed lip has a thickened basal callus. The flowers have a green, long, hooked-shaped, incurved, wingless, footless column.

ORNITHOCHEILUS

An orthographic variant introduced in *Rep. Bot. Gard. Calcutta*, 11 (1843). The correct spelling is *Ornithochilus*.

ORNITHOCHILUS

(Lindley) Wallich ex Bentham

Gen. Pl. (Bentham & Hooker f.) **3**: 478, 581 (1883), and *J. Linn. Soc., Bot.* **18**(110): 334 (1881).

Epidendroideæ ▨ Vandeæ • Aeridinæ

ETYMOLOGY: Greek for a bird and lip. Descriptive of the bilobed lip that resembles a bird in flight.

TYPE SPECIES: *Ornithochilus fuscus*
Wallich ex Lindley nom. inval.

Ornithochilus difformis (Wallich ex Lindley) Schlechter
(*Aerides difforme* Wallich ex Lindley)

Three uncommon, monopodial epiphytes are found in humid, low to mid elevation, hill and montane deciduous to piney forests from southern China (Yunnan to Guangdong), northern India

Currently Accepted   Validly Published   Invalidly Published   Published Pre-1753   Superfluous Usage   Orthographic Variant   Fossil

O r c h i d   G e n e r a • 280

(Kashmir to Assam), Bhutan, Nepal, Myanmar to Vietnam, Malaysia and Indonesia. These plants, vegetatively similar to *Phalaenopsis*, have short, unbranched stems, subtended by leaf sheaths, each with several, fleshy leaves arranged in two rows. The hanging, simple to branched, numerous-flowered inflorescence has small, insect-like, green-yellow flowers with bold red stripes. The large, dark maroon, immobile, heavily fringed, trilobed lip has yellow markings radiating toward the base; squarish, upturned side lobes, a clawed, fan-shaped, incurved midlobe with slender processes, and has a long, cylindrical, forward curved spur. The flowers have a short, stout, footless column.

ORNITHOCHILUS

Wallich ex **Lindley**
Gen. Sp. Orchid. Pl. 242 (1833).

Originally published as a section name, this name as originally published is referred to *Aerides*.

ORNITHODIUM

An orthographic variant introduced in *Fl. Ned. Ind.*, **3**: 697 (1860). The correct spelling is *Ornithidium*.

ORNITHOPHORA

L'Obel
Icon. Stirp. 183, *f. 2* (1591).

Pre-1753, therefore not validly published in fulfillment of nomenclatural rules; this name is most often referred to *Orchis*.

ORNITHOPHORA

Barbosa Rodrigues
Gen. Sp. Orchid. **2**: 225, t. 264 (1882).
Epidendroideæ ◊ Epidendreæ ◊ Oncidiinæ
ETYMOLOGY: Greek for a bird and bearing. In reference to the column that when viewed from the side resembles a bird.
TYPE SPECIES: *Ornithophora quadricolor*
Barbosa Rodrigues
This type name is now considered a synonym of *Ornithophora radicans* (Reichenbach f.) Garay & Pabst; basionym
Sigmatostalix radicans Reichenbach f.

One sympodial epiphyte is found only in low elevation, montane forests of eastern Brazil (Rio Grande de Sul, Paraná, Espírito Santo, Rio de Janeiro, São Paulo and Santa Catarina). This small, rambling plant has compressed, ovoid, pear-shaped pseudobulbs, subtended by leaf-bearing sheaths, each with two narrow, channeled, grass-like leaves. The erect, few to numerous-flowered inflorescence has small, green-yellow or white-green flowers. The long-clawed, white, trilobed lip has a transversely crescent-shaped, flat plate with a backward pointing appendage. The flowers have an erect, slender column that is over half the length of the lip.

ORNITHOPHORAM

An orthographic variant introduced in *Enum. Meth. Stirp. Helv.*, 266 (1742). The correct spelling is *Ornithophora*.

ORNITHORRHYNCHUM

An orthographic variant introduced in *Gart.-Zeitung (Berlin)*, **2**: 155 (1883). The correct spelling is *Ornithidium*.

OROBANCHE

Plukenet
Alm. Bot. Pl. 278 (1700).
Not *Orobanche* Linnaeus (1753) Orobanchaceæ.
ETYMOLOGY: Latin for parasite or a kind of vetch. Refers to the parasitic habit of the plant.
TYPE SPECIES: *None designated*

Pre-1753, therefore not validly published in fulfillment of nomenclatural rules; this polynomial name is most often referred to at least two different species. This name as published by Plukenet used the above name, and they are now recognized as orchid saprophytes.

One species **Orobanche verna, radice dentatâ** is found in Canada, the United States and from Mexico to Guatemala. This name is now often considered a synonym of *Corallorhiza maculata* (Rafinesque) Rafinesque.

The second species **Orobanche autumnalis Virginiana radice dentatâ** is widespread in Europe, throughout temperate Asia, the Himalayas, Russia to Korea and Japan. This name is now often considered a synonym of *Epipogium aphyllum* Swartz.

ORPHRYS

An orthographic variant introduced in *Mag. Zool. Bot.*, **2**: 167 (1838). The correct spelling is *Ophrys*.

ORSIDICE

Reichenbach *filius*
Bonplandia **2**(7): 93 (1854).
ETYMOLOGY: Possibly named for a nymph but no such name can be found in classical literature.
Or possibly Greek Mythology. *Orsedice* was one of four daughters of Cinyas and Metharme. Because of the wrath of Aphrodite she cohabited with foreigners and died in Egypt.
TYPE SPECIES: *None designated*

Now recognized as belonging to the genus *Thrixspermum*, *Orsidice* was previously considered to include two epiphytes found in low to mid elevation, montane forests and scrub of Thailand, Malaysia, Indonesia, Australia and New Guinea to the Philippines. These often climbing plants have long, pale yellow-green stems often spotted purple, each with several, well-spaced, heart-shaped, olive-green, leathery leaves. The slender, few-flowered inflorescence, conspicuously bracted, has pale lilac to nearly white, short-lived flowers opening widely that bloom in continuous succession. Flowering is often triggered by a sudden drop in temperature. The trilobed lip, flush to the column foot, has a white, fleshy, blunt midlobe with a basal patch of orange-red hairs and crescent-shaped side lobes.

ORSIDYCE

An orthographic variant introduced in *Orchid.-Buch*, 446 (1892). The correct spelling is *Orsidice*.

ORTHOCERAS

R. Brown
Prodr. Fl. Nov. Holland. 316 (1810).
Orchidoideæ ◊ Diurideæ ◊ Diuridinæ
ETYMOLOGY: Greek for straight or upright and a horn. Refers to the conspicuously horn-like lateral sepals.
LECTOTYPE: *Orthoceras strictum* R. Brown

Two uncommon, sympodial terrestrials are found in moist, low elevation, grassy scrub and along clay banks from southeastern Australia (Victoria), Tasmania and New Zealand to New Caledonia. These slender, robust plants have erect, short, unbranched stems, each with several, overlapping, grass-like, basal leaves that are spirally arranged. The terminal, solitary to numerous-flowered inflorescence has small, yellow-brown, green to red, self-pollinating flowers. The flowers have a large, concave, hood-shaped dorsal sepal, the lateral sepals are thread-like, and the small petals, hidden by the dorsal sepal, are bilobed or unequally notched. Each adjacent flower faces a different direction on the floral rachis. The red-brown, distinctly trilobed lip has erect, incurved side lobes flanking the short, winged column, and the flat, recurved midlobe has a yellow callus down the center.

ORTHOCHILUS

Hochstetter ex **A. Richard**

Tent. Fl. Abyss. **2**: 284, *t. 82* (1850).

ETYMOLOGY: Greek for straight or upright and a lip. Referring to the long claw that is attached to the column, thus giving the whole lip a rigid appearance.

TYPE SPECIES: *Orthochilus abyssinicus*
(Reichenbach f.) Hochstetter
(*Eulophia abyssinica* Reichenbach f.)

Now recognized as belonging to the genus *Eulophia*, *Orthochilus* was previously considered to include four terrestrials widespread in dry to marshy, mid elevation, grasslands from Eritrea, Ethiopia, Sudan, Nigeria and Zaire to South Africa. These plants have numerous, grass-like leaves and small pseudobulbs. The short, few-flowered inflorescence has pale brown-yellow flowers, not opening widely, often suffused pale green. The yellow, shortly sac-like, trilobed lip has dark purple blotches on the side lobes, a rounded midlobe and has two fleshy, basal crests. The above type name is now considered a synonym of *Eulophia abyssinica* Reichenbach f.

ORTHOCHYLLUS

An orthographic variant introduced in *Prakt. Stud. Orchid.*, 45 (1854). The correct spelling is *Orthochilus*.

ORTHOGLOTTIS

Breda

Gen. Sp. Orchid. Asclep., fasc. IIII, n.s.   (1830).

ETYMOLOGY: Greek for straight or erect and tongue. Refers to the straight, tongue-like lip of the species.

TYPE SPECIES: *Orthoglottis imbricata* Breda
This type name is now considered a synonym of
Dendrobium aloefolium (Blume) Reichenbach f.;
basionym
Macrostomium aloefolium Blume

Now recognized as belonging to the genus *Dendrobium*, *Orthoglottis* was previously considered to include one epiphyte found in low elevation, hill forests and scrub from Myanmar to Vietnam, Malaysia, Thailand, Indonesia, the Philippines and New Guinea. This compact, tangled plant has clumped stems, each with short, bract-like leaves that overlap in two rows, enclose the long, red stem and are often purple. The plant is erect when young and later becomes hanging with age. The solitary-flowered inflorescence has a minute, white to creamy flower with bent backward

sepals and petals. The trilobed lip has small, oblong side lobes and a notched, flared, bilobed midlobe. The flowers have a small column.

ORTHOPENTHEA

Rolfe

Fl. Cap. (Harvey)   **5**(3): 179 (1912).

ETYMOLOGY: Greek for straight or upright and *Penthea*, a genus of orchids. Alluding to a similarity to *Penthea*.

LECTOTYPE: *Orthopenthea bivalvata*
(Linnaeus f.) Rolfe
(*Ophrys bivalvata* Linnaeus f.)

Now recognized as belonging to the genus *Disa*, *Orthopenthea* was previously considered to include thirteen terrestrials restricted in low elevation, swampy to well-drained scrub of the Cape region of South Africa. These erect plants have numerous, same-sized leaves that ascend the length of the slender, unbranched stem or are clustered at the base. The densely packed, flat-topped, few-flowered inflorescence has tightly bunched flowers with white sepals. Has a shallowly helmet-shaped dorsal sepal and widespreading, oblong lateral sepals that are flat to slightly concave. The red, oblong, curved petals are parallel to or flank the column and are often hood-like. The pale to deep red, narrow, small, entire lip has an upcurved tip. The flowers have a small, stout, fleshy column.

ORTMANNIA

Opiz

Flora   **17**(2): 592 (1834).

ETYMOLOGY: Honoring Anton Ortmann (1801-1861), a German pharmacist, apothecary whose studies in Bohemian flora brought forth several new species and author of *Die Flora Karlsbads und seiner Umgegend*.

TYPE SPECIES: *Ortmannia cernua* (Willdenow) Opiz
(*Malaxis cernua* Willdenow)
This type name is now considered a synonym of
Geodorum densiflorum (Lamarck) Schlechter;
basionym replaced with
Limodorum densiflorum Lamarck

Now recognized as belonging to the genus *Geodorum*, *Ortmannia* was previously considered to include one terrestrial found from Myanmar, Thailand, Malaysia, Indonesia, New Guinea and northern Australia to New Caledonia. This robust plant has subterranean pseudobulbs, each with several, pleated leaves. The long, numerous-flowered inflorescence has waxy, fragrant, pink or white flowers that do not open widely. The obscurely trilobed lip has a wide, bright yellow, ridged-splash down the center. The flowers have a long, rather thick column with a distinct foot.

ORXERA

Rafinesque

Fl. Tellur.   **4**: 37 (1836)[1837].

ETYMOLOGY: Origin and meaning of this name is unknown but could be Greek for sharply pointed. Referring to the stout, hanging spur.

TYPE SPECIES: *Orxera cornuta* (Roxburgh) Rafinesque
(*Aerides cornuta* Roxburgh)

Now recognized as belonging to the genus *Aerides*, *Orxera* was previously considered to include one epiphyte found in low to mid elevation, hill scrub to montane forests of southern China, northern India (Kashmir to Assam), Nepal, Myanmar, Thailand to Vietnam, Malaysia, the Philippines, Indonesia and New Guinea. This highly variable, hanging plant has stout stems, strongly branched in older specimens, subtended by leaf sheaths, each with oblong, leathery, yellow-green, bilobed leaves. The densely packed, numerous-flowered inflorescence has fragrant, pristine white to purple flowers marked with magenta blotches. The trilobed lip almost encloses the short column, and the horn-like, incurved spur is green-yellow at its tip. The above type name is now considered a synonym of *Aerides odorata* Loureiro.

OSIRYCERA

An orthographic variant introduced in *Syn. Pl. (D. Dietrich)*, **5**: 30 (1852). The correct spelling is *Osyricera*.

OSMOGLOSSUM

(Schlechter) Schlechter

Orchis   **10**: 162 (1916).

ETYMOLOGY: Greek for odor or smell and tongue. The type species has a remarkably sweet fragrance.

TYPE SPECIES: *Osmoglossum pulchellum*
(Bateman ex Lindley) Schlechter
(*Odontoglossum pulchellum* Bateman ex Lindley)

Now recognized as belonging to the genus *Cuitlauzina*, *Osmoglossum* was previously considered to include seven epiphytes or sometimes lithophytes are found in wet, humid, upper elevation, montane forests from central Mexico to Ecuador. These plants often form dense clumps, have tall, ovoid or oblong, flattened to compressed, yellow pseudobulbs clustered on short rhizomes, subtended by several, distichous, leaf-like sheaths, each with two grass-like leaves. The numerous to few-flowered inflorescence, borne from the pseudobulb base, usually has small, fleshy, sometimes showy, sweetly fragrant, white or pink flowers often suffused with pink to purple hues. The narrowly clawed, entire lip has a bright yellow

Currently Accepted   Validly Published   Invalidly Published   Published Pre-1753   Superfluous Usage   Orthographic Variant   Fossil

O r c h i d   G e n e r a   • 282

callus spotted red that is twisted 90° or more from the slender to stout, rather short column.

OSMOPHYTUM

Brieger ex **Withner** & **Harding**
Cattleyas & Relatives 28 (2004).

Name published without a description. Today this name is most often referred to *Prosthechea*.

OSSICULUM

P.J. Cribb & **Laan**
Kew Bull. **41**(4): 823 (1986).
Epidendroideæ 🌿 **Vandeæ** • **Angraecinæ**
ETYMOLOGY: Latin for a small bone. In honor of Henk Jaap Beentje (1951-), a Belgian-born botanist, editor of *Curtis's Botanical Magazine*, author of numerous works on African flora and collector of the type species.
TYPE SPECIES: *Ossiculum aurantiacum*
P.J. Cribb & Laan

One monopodial epiphyte is found in low elevation of the Mungo river forest reserves of northern Cameroon. This small plant has erect stems, each with somewhat flattened, thick, oblong, distichous, fleshy leaves but loses the lower leaves with age and the stem also becomes woody with age. The short, spirally arranged, few-flowered inflorescence has small, fleshy flowers with bright orange-red sepals and narrower petals converging over the short column. The yellow, oblong, shell-shaped, entire lip has a fleshy callus on each side at the mouth of the somewhat S-shaped spur. The flowers have a short, erect, wingless, footless column.

OSYRICERA

Blume
Bijdr. Fl. Ned. Ind. **7**: 307, t. 58 (1825).
ETYMOLOGY: Egyptian Mythology. *Osiris* was a legendary ruler of predynastic Egypt, god of the underworld, and brother-husband to Isis. Osiris according to legend was slain by his brother Seth, who cut his body into pieces and spread the parts throughout Egypt. Isis searched for and then buried each piece as a shrine. And Greek for horn.
TYPE SPECIES: *Osyricera crassifolia* Blume

Now recognized as belonging to the genus *Bulbophyllum*, *Osyricera* was previously considered to include six epiphytes found in Indonesia (Java and Sumatra to Borneo) New Guinea, northern Australia (Queensland) and the Philippines. Often, these plants form dense, matted clumps with the tiny pseudobulbs somewhat fattened on the top, each with several, long, narrow, leathery leaves. The long, erect, one- to two-flowered inflorescence

has tiny, deep red or purple flower. The narrow dorsal sepal is held at a right angle to the inflorescence; the slightly wider lateral sepals are parallel to the lip and the small petals are triangular shaped. The orange, strap-shaped, entire lip is uppermost. The flowers have a tiny, footless column. The above type name is now considered a synonym of *Bulbophyllum osyricera* Schlechter.

OSYRICERAS

An orthographic variant cited in *Lex. Gen. Phan.*, 407 (1904). The correct spelling is *Osyricera*.

OTANDRA

Salisbury
Trans. Hort. Soc. London **1**: 298 (1812).
ETYMOLOGY: Greek for ear-shaped and stamen or male. Refers to the column shape.
TYPE SPECIES: *Otandra cernua* (Willdenow) Salisbury
(*Malaxis cernua* Willdenow)
This type name is now considered a synonym of *Geodorum densiflorum* (Lamarck) Schlechter; basionym replaced with *Limodorum densiflorum* Lamarck

Now recognized as belonging to the genus *Geodorum*, *Otandra* was previously considered to include one terrestrial found in low to mid elevation, coastal scrub, savannas and montane forests from southern China (Yunnan to Hainan), northern India (Kashmir to Assam), Myanmar to Vietnam, southern Japan (Ryukyu Islands), Malaysia to the Philippines, Australia and the southwestern Pacific Archipelago. This highly variable, rarely cultivated plant has underground pseudobulbs, each with several, large, thin, pleated leaves. The long, head-like, few to numerous-flowered inflorescence has tubular sheaths and white to pale purple, attractive, waxy flowers not opening widely. The clustered flowers are on the downward side of the strongly curved rachis until fertilization occurs which causes the rachis to straighten out. The broad, slightly concave, entire lip surrounds the footless column at the base.

OTOCHILUS

Lindley
Gen. Sp. Orchid. Pl. 35 (1830).
Epidendroideæ 🌿 **Arethuseæ** • **Coelogyninæ**
ETYMOLOGY: Greek for an ear and lip. Referring to the lip being like or similar to the petals and sepals.
LECTOTYPE: *Otochilus porrectus* Lindley

Five sympodial epiphytes are found in low to upper elevation, hill scrub to montane cloud forests of southern China, (Yunnan) northern India (Kashmir to Assam), Myanmar to Vietnam. These

creeping plants have cylindrical, long to club-shaped pseudobulbs with an unusual habit of growing on top of each other, each with one internode, and each has two narrow to elliptical, pleated leaves borne from the pseudobulb tip. The straight, weakly curved or sometimes zig-zagged, numerous to few-flowered inflorescence has charming chains of translucent, small, pale pink or white flowers often with brown markings and have narrow sepals and petals. The trilobed lip is sac-like at the base with or without callus ridges, has erect side lobes embracing the nearly footless column, and a tongue-shaped midlobe. The flowers have a long, yellow-brown, erect or bent forward column.

OTOGLOSSUM

(**Schlechter**) **Garay** & **Dunsterville**
Venez. Orchid. Ill. **6**: 41 (1976).
Epidendroideæ 🌿 **Cymbidieæ** • **Oncidiinæ**
ETYMOLOGY: Greek for an ear and tongue. Refers to the ear-like side lobes of the lip.
TYPE SPECIES: *Otoglossum hoppii*
(Schlechter) Garay & Dunsterville
(*Odontoglossum hoppii* Schlechter)

Thirteen unusual sympodial epiphytes or terrestrials are found in wet, cool, low to upper elevation, hill scrub to montane forests from Costa Rica to Bolivia. These plants have cylindrical, compressed pseudobulbs, subtended by pairs of leaf-bearing sheaths, each with one to two, ovate, slightly leathery leaves. The long, stiffly erect, few to numerous-flowered inflorescence has large, showy, glossy, chestnut-brown flowers edged in yellow. The yellow, trilobed lip has a brown band across the spoon-shaped center, has small, spreading or erect side lobes, and the wedge-shaped midlobe is bilobed at the tip. The flowers have a small, short, stout column.

OTOPETALUM

F. Lehmann & **Kraenzlin**
Bot. Jahrb. Syst. **26**: 457 (1899).
Not *Otopetalum* Miguel (1857) Apocynaceæ.
ETYMOLOGY: Greek for an ear and petal or leaf. Refers to the petals, which have small, ear-like basal lobes.
TYPE SPECIES: *Otopetalum tunguraguae*
F. Lehmann & Kraenzlin
This type name is now considered a synonym of *Kraenzlinella otopetalum* (Schlechter) Luer; basionym *Pleurothallis otopetalum* Schlechter

Not validly published because of a prior use of the name, this homonym was replaced by *Kraenzlinella*.

OTOSTYLIS

Schlechter

Orchis **12**: 38 (1918).

Epidendroideæ ⚘ Cymbidieæ • Zygopetalinæ

ETYMOLOGY: Greek for an ear and column or pillar. An allusion to the two, rounded, ear-shaped wings of the column that project beyond.

TYPE SPECIES: *None designated*

Four uncommon, sympodial terrestrials are found in mid elevation, montane meadows and grasslands of Venezuela, Peru, the Guianas, Brazil and Trinidad sometimes fully exposed to bright sunlight. These plants have small, ovoid pseudobulbs often tinged dull purple, subtended by several, overlapping sheaths, each with one to several, narrow leaves at the tip. The erect, numerous to few-flowered inflorescence has showy, small, short-lived, white to creamy-yellow flowers. The unique, cup-shaped, white, entire or trilobed lip has small triangular or ear-shaped side lobes. The large, ovate midlobe has green-yellow and pale magenta streaks on the crested disc. The flowers have a short, white column.

OUCIDIUM

An orthographic variant introduced in *Fl. Brit. W.I. (Grisebach)*, 630 (1864). The correct spelling is *Oncidium*.

OVYANTHERA

An orthographic variant introduced in *Bot. Jahrb. Syst.*, **56**: 489 (1921). The correct spelling is *Oxyanthera*.

OXYANTHERA

Brongniart

Duperrey's *Voy. Monde, Bot.* **2**: 197, t. 37b (1834).

ETYMOLOGY: Greek for sharp and anther. Descriptive of the pointed anther.

TYPE SPECIES: *Oxyanthera micrantha* Brongniart

Now recognized as belonging to the genus *Thelasis*, *Oxyanthera* was previously considered to include six insignificant, uncommon epiphytes or lithophytes found in low to mid elevation, hill to montane forests ranging from Malaysia to New Guinea. These small, flattened but erect, tufted plants have short stems, each with several, thinly textured leaves narrowing to a sharp point. The terminal, arching, few-flowered inflorescence has tiny, crisp white to yellow-green, tubular flowers with a pale green to pale brown shade at the base. The often barely opening flowers are self-pollinating and almost all open simultaneously. The long, tapered, entire or obscurely trilobed lip has strongly inrolled sides and a blunt tip. The flowers have an erect, short to obscure, footless column.

OXYGLOSSELLUM

M.A. Clements & D.L. Jones

Orchadian **13**(11): 490 (2002).

ETYMOLOGY: Greek for sharp pointed and tongue. Referring to the small, sharply tapering lip.

TYPE SPECIES: *Oxyglossellum cyanocentrum*
(Schlechter) M.A. Clements & D.L. Jones
(*Dendrobium cyanocentrum* Schlechter)

Recognized as belonging to the genus *Dendrobium*, *Oxyglossellum* was proposed to include thirty-five epiphytes found in mid to upper montane, moss laden forests of eastern Indonesia (Sulawesi and Maluku), New Guinea, New Caledonia, the Solomons and Fiji, often forming small colonies. These small, tufted to loosely branched, twig plants have erect, tiny pseudobulbs, each with several, short, rough textured, twisted, narrow leaves. The short, solitary-flowered inflorescence has a long-lasting, large, glossy-textured flower, borne from the tip of the pseudobulb, has strongly reflexed, blue sepals and petals that are striped bright purple, and some flowers are white. The tiny, green or yellow, sac-like, entire lip tapers to a sharp, downward point. The flowers have a short, blunt column.

OXYSEPALA

Wight

Icon. Pl. Ind. Orient. (Wight) **5**(1): 17 (1851).

ETYMOLOGY: Greek for sharp or pointed and Latin for sepal. Descriptive of the very long sepals.

TYPE SPECIES: *Oxysepala ovalifolium* Wight

Now recognized as belonging to the genus *Bulbophyllum*, *Oxysepala* was previously considered to include nine epiphytes found in low elevation, evergreen forests of Myanmar, Laos, Vietnam, Malaysia, Indonesia, New Guinea, Fiji and the Solomons. These slender, hanging plants often form considerable colonies. The tiny pseudobulbs each have a solitary, fleshy leaf. The short, solitary-flowered inflorescence has a minute, pale yellow or white flower not opening widely with long, narrow sepals and small petals. The tiny, usually rather broad, thick textured, entire lip is yellow-green. The flowers have a short column. The above type name is now considered a synonym of *Bulbophyllum clandestinum* Lindley.

OXYSTOPHYLLUM

Blume

Bijdr. Fl. Ned. Ind. **7**: 335, t. 38 (1825).

Epidendroideæ ⚘ Dendrobiinæ • Currently unplaced

ETYMOLOGY: Greek for sharp and leaf. Referring to the leaf that is stiffly leathery and strict.

LECTOTYPE: *Oxystophyllum rigidum* Blume
This type name is now considered a synonym of *Oxystophyllum carnosum* Blume

Fifteen sympodial epiphytes or lithophytes are found in low to mid elevation, montane rain forests from southern China (Hainan), Myanmar to Vietnam, Indonesia, the Philippines and New Guinea to the Solomon Islands. The flowers are similar to those of the *Dendrobium* section *Aporum* but can be distinguished by a small, conical wart located beneath the tip of the lip. These erect to hanging, clump-forming plants have wiry, long, thin, flexible stems, each with flattened, rigid, sickle-shaped to narrow leaves that are overlapping at the base. The several, short, few-flowered inflorescences have tiny, thick, dull yellow or dark purple flowers with short, pointed petals and dorsal sepal. The tongue-shaped, thick, entire lip, hinged to the tip of the column foot, is sac-like at the base, secretes a sticky liquid at the lip base and also along the grooved upper surface and has a small wart beneath the tip of the lip. The flowers have a short, small column.

OXYTANTHERA

An orthographic variant introduced in *Bot. Centralbl.*, **59**(1/2): 28 (1894). The correct spelling is *Oxyanthera*.

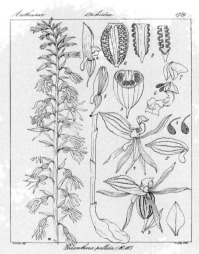

Wight
Icones Plantarum Indiae Orientalis
plate 1759 (1851).

Currently Accepted   Validly Published   Invalidly Published   Published Pre-1753   Superfluous Usage   Orthographic Variant   Fossil

Orchid Genera • 284

PABSTIA

Garay

Bradea   **1**(27): 306 (1973).

Epidendroideæ ⧸ Cymbidieæ • Zygopetalinæ

ETYMOLOGY: Named in honor of Guido João Frederico Pabst (1914-1980), a Brazilian amateur botanist, researcher, director of air traffic for Varig airlines, who founded Herbarium Bradeanum in Rio de Janeiro and was co-author of *Orchidaceæ Brasilienses*.

TYPE SPECIES: *Pabstia viridis* (Lindley) Garay
(*Maxillaria viridis* Lindley)

Six sympodial epiphytes, lithophytes or sometimes terrestrials allied to *Zygopetalum*, are confined to cool, low to mid elevation, hill scrub and montane forests of Brazil (Rio de Janeiro and São Paulo). These plants have densely clustered, compressed to slightly grooved pseudobulbs, each with two, somewhat pleated, leathery leaves at the tip. The erect or arching, solitary to few-flowered inflorescence has large, showy, green, white to creamy, waxy, fragrant flowers with narrowly oblong petals distinctly blotched or spotted deep purple to red; the similar, spreading sepals are broadly oblong. The yellow, purple or white, narrowly to shortly clawed, entire or deeply trilobed lip is blotched and/or spotted rosy-purple, and has a fleshy, slightly hairy, basal callus. The flowers have a stout, club-shaped column that is hairy in the front and bent toward the tip.

PABSTIELLA

Brieger & Senghas

Orchidee (Hamburg)   **27**(5): 195 (1976).

Epidendroideæ ⧸ Epidendreæ • Pleurothallidinæ

ETYMOLOGY: Honoring Guido João Frederico Pabst (1914-1980). And Latin for diminutive.

TYPE SPECIES: *Pabstiella mirabilis*
(Schlechter) Brieger & Senghas
(*Pleurothallis mirabilis* Schlechter)

Seven sympodial epiphytes are found in cool, moist, upper elevation, montane cloud forests and woodlands from Costa Rica to northern Argentina (Misiones). These small, tufted plants have long, wiry stems, subtended by loose, tubular sheaths, each with a solitary, small to large, leathery leaf. The long, few-flowered inflorescence, borne successively and from the leaf axils, has small, white, long-chinned, pink suffused, white to pale brown flowers with a large, slightly concave dorsal sepal and small, incurved petals. The long-clawed, arrowhead-shaped to ovate, hinged, entire lip, joined to the column foot, is strongly bent at a right angle in the middle. The flowers have a swollen, hooded or winged, curved column.

PACHINE

An orthographic variant introduced in *Fortsetz. Allg. Teutsch. Gart.-Mag.*, **7**(4): 165 (1823). The correct spelling is *Pachyne*.

PACHIPHILLUM

An orthographic variant introduced in *Nov. Veg. Descr.*, fasc. 2, 42 (1825). The correct spelling is *Pachyphyllum*.

PACHIRA

An orthographic variant introduced in *Ann. Hort. Bot.*, **5**: 176 (1862). The correct spelling is *Pachyne*.

PACHITES

Lindley

Gen. Sp. Orchid. Pl.   301 (1835).

Orchidoideæ ⧸ Orchideæ • Orchidinæ

ETYMOLOGY: Greek for thick or stout and having the nature of. Descriptive of the rostellum, that is so thick and large as to completely cut off the anther.

TYPE SPECIES: *Pachites appressa* Lindley

Two genuinely rare, primitive sympodial terrestrials are found in dry, low elevation, on sandy, pebbly or rocky montane soils of the western Cape area of South Africa. These robust or slender plants have erect, unbranched stems, each with several, narrow to oblong, softly textured leaves. The dark to pale pink flowers are borne in a tight cluster at the top of a slender, few-flowered inflorescence. They have similar segments and do not open widely. The entire or minutely trilobed lip is similar to the sepals and petals. The flowers have a prominent, erect, footless column. They will bloom in the following year after a veld fire and then appearing only as a single plant or a few widely scattered plants are found.

PACHYCENTRON

Not *Pachycentron* Hasskarl (1884) Melastomataceæ.

An orthographic variant introduced in *Orchideen (Schlechter)*, ed. 1, 18 (1914). The correct spelling is *Pachyplectron*.

PACHYCHILUS

Blume

Fl. Javæ   **1**: Praef. vii (1828).

ETYMOLOGY: Greek for thick or stout and lip. Descriptive of the fleshy lip.

TYPE SPECIES: *None designated*

A superfluous name proposed as a substitute for *Pachystoma*.

PACHYGENIUM

(Schlechter) Szlachetko, R. González & Rutkowski

Polish Bot. J.   **46**(1): 3 (2001).

ETYMOLOGY: Greek for thick or stout and chin. Referring to the shape of the spur.

TYPE SPECIES: *Pachygenium oestriferum*
(Reichenbach f. & Warming)
Szlachetko, R. González & Rutkowski
(*Spiranthes oestrifera* Reichenbach f. & Warming)

Recognized as belonging to the genus *Pelexia*, *Pachygenium* was proposed to include thirty-eight terrestrials found in low elevation, hill rain forests, savannas and prairies from southern Mexico to Panama and Colombia to eastern Brazil. These erect plants have unbranched stems, each with attractive, narrow leaves gathered at the lower part of the stem. The erect, few-flowered inflorescence has small, green flowers with sac-like lateral sepals. The hairy, white, narrow, entire or trilobed lip has a bright yellow base. The narrow, roundish, sac-like spur reaches to the middle of the ovary. The flowers have a short, footless column.

PACHYNA

An orthographic variant introduced in *Dict. Univ. Hist. Nat.*, **9**: 170 (1847). The correct spelling is *Pachyne*.

PACHYNE

Salisbury

Trans. Hort. Soc. London   **1**: 299 (1812).

ETYMOLOGY: Greek for thick or stout. Alluding possibly to the very large inflorescence and the wide, coarsely nerved leaves.

TYPE SPECIES: *Pachyne spectabilis* (Salisbury) Salisbury (*Limodorum spectabile* Salisbury)

This type name is now considered a synonym of *Phaius tankervilleae* (Banks ex L'Héritier) Blume; basionym replaced with *Limodorum tankervilleae* Banks ex L'Héritier

Now recognized as belonging to the genus *Phaius*, *Pachyne* was previously considered to include one terrestrial found in low to mid elevation, hill scrub to montane forests from southern China to Australia. This large, showy plant has ovoid pseudobulbs, each with several, thinly textured leaves. The erect, few-flowered inflorescence has flowers that are white on the outer surfaces and green, rosy to brown on the inside. The tubular, trilobed lip has a wavy, recurved margin. The flowers have a small, club-shaped column.

PACHYONE

An orthographic variant introduced in *Feddes Repert.*, **32**: 239 (1933). The correct spelling is *Pachyne*.

PACHYPHYLLUM

Kunth

Nov. Gen. Sp.   **1**: 338, *t. 77* (1815).

Not *Pachyphyllum* Lesquereux (1854) Fossil, and not *Pachyphyllum* (A. Pomel) G. Saporta (1873) Fossil.

Epidendroideæ 〰 Cymbidieæ • Oncidiinæ

ETYMOLOGY: Greek for thick and leaf. Refers to the thickened, fleshy foliage of the members of this genus.

TYPE SPECIES: *Pachyphyllum distichum* Kunth

Thirty-nine pseudomonopodial epiphytes are found in wet, mid to upper elevation, montane cloud forests and along steep embankments from southern Mexico to Panama and Colombia to Bolivia. Smaller species often manage to be mistaken for moss or lichen, while the larger species often resemble small ferns. These attractive, dwarf

to tiny plants have erect, creeping or hanging stems that have the distichous, fleshy leaves with variously toothed margins. The short, few-flowered inflorescence has tiny, yellow, green or white flowers. The similar sepals are sometimes partially united forming a tube shape, and the petals are often joined to the sepals forming a portion of the cup of the tube. The usually entire or sometimes obscurely trilobed lip has a pair of thick calli. The flowers have a short column.

PACHYPLECTRON

Schlechter

Bot. Jahrb. Syst.   **39**: 51 (1906).

Orchidoideæ 〰 Cranichideæ • Goodyerinæ

ETYMOLOGY: Greek for thick and spur. Referring to the distinct shape of the fleshy spur.

TYPE SPECIES: *None designated*

Three sympodial terrestrials or occasional lithophytes are found in low to mid elevation, hill scrub and montane forests of New Caledonia. These tall plants have variegated, dark red-brown, arrowhead-shaped, basal leaves that have a coppery tint. Some species are leafless. The erect, spiraled, numerous to few-flowered inflorescence has small to tiny, nerved flowers that are difficult to see, do not open widely, and are found in a range of hues from pink, green or cream-colored. The concave dorsal sepal, along with the petals converge, forming a hood over the long, erect, slender to more or less club-shaped, footless column. The spoon-shaped, entire lip is recurved at the blunt tip, and the bilobed spur is hairy inside and lacks thickenings or appendages.

PACHYRHIZANTHE

(Schlechter) Nakai

Bot. Mag. (Tokyo)   **45**: 109 (1931).

ETYMOLOGY: Greek for thick, root and flower. Descriptive of the thickened rhizomes associated with this genus.

TYPE SPECIES: *None designated*

Now recognized as belonging to the genus *Cymbidium*, *Pachyrhizanthe* was previously considered to include five saprophytes found in montane forests and along river banks of northern Pakistan and India, southern China, Nepal, Myanmar, Taiwan and southern Japan (Ryukyu Islands). These erect plants have small, scale-like leaves or are leafless. The slender branches, subtended by overlapping sheaths, originate from white subterranean tubers. The purple-red, few-flowered inflorescence has pale cream or yellow flowers suffused pink. The white, obscurely trilobed lip has purple-red stripes on the erect side lobes and crimson spots on

the triangular, recurved midlobe which has a slightly wavy margin. The two, not flexible, white calli are sometimes stained pink. The flowers have a slightly bent forward column. These species are all now often considered as synonyms of *Cymbidium macrorhizon* Lindley.

PACHYSTELE

Schlechter

Repert. Spec. Nov. Regni Veg. Beih.   **19**: 28 (1923).

Not *Pachystela* Pierre ex Radlkofer (1899) Sapotaceæ.

ETYMOLOGY: Greek for thick, stout or broad and column or pillar. In reference to the short, fleshy column.

LECTOTYPE: *Pachystele jimenezii* (Schlechter) Schlechter (*Scaphyglottis jimenezii* Schlechter)

Not validly published because of a prior use of the name, this homonym was replaced by *Scaphyglottis*.

PACHYSTELIS

Rauschert

Feddes Repert.   **94**(7-8): 456 (1983).

ETYMOLOGY: Greek for thick or stout and column or pillar. Descriptive of the thickened column.

TYPE SPECIES: *Pachystelis jimenezii* (Schlechter) Rauschert (*Scaphyglottis jimenezii* Schlechter)

A superfluous name proposed as a substitute for *Pachystele*.

PACHYSTOMA

Blume

Bijdr. Fl. Ned. Ind.   **8**: 376, *t. 29* (1825).

Epidendroideæ 〰 Collabiinæ • Currently unplaced

ETYMOLOGY: Greek for thick and opening or mouth. Descriptive of the callosities or thickness of the lip and mouth-like appearance of the swollen bases of the lateral sepals.

TYPE SPECIES: *Pachystoma pubescens* Blume

Two sympodial terrestrials are widespread in low to mid elevation, tall grasslands and dry, rice fields that are often subject to periodic fires in southern China (Guangdong, Guangxi, Hainan, Guizhou and Yunnan) northern India, Nepal, Myanmar to Vietnam, Thailand, Malaysia, Indonesia, the Philippines, New Guinea and northern Australia to the south-western Pacific Archipelago. The rhizomes can shrivel and remain dormant underground for several years and will reappear when conditions are again suitable. These erect plants have unbranched stems, each with a solitary, grass-like leaf that withers as the plant begins to flower. The erect, tall, red, numerous-flowered inflorescence, borne separate from

| Currently Accepted | Validly Published | Invalidly Published | Published Pre-1753 | Superfluous Usage | Orthographic Variant | Fossil |

Orchid Genera • 286

the leaf, is filled with small, attractive, hairy flowers that tend to hang downward. The sepals are distinctly swollen at the base and the lateral sepals are attached to the column foot forming a chin-like projection. The outside floral surface and even the column are hairy. The distinctly trilobed lip has a green-yellow blotch at the base, and a wavy, magenta margin. The flowers have a hairy, incurved, club-shaped column with a short foot or which is footless.

PACHYSTOMA

Reichenbach *filius*

Gard. Chron., n.s. **1879**(2): 582 (1879).

ETYMOLOGY: Greek for thick and opening or mouth. Refers to the sac-like lip.

TYPE SPECIES: *Pachystoma thomsonianum* Reichenbach f.

Not validly published, this name is referred to *Ancistrochilus*. *Pachystoma* Reichenbach f. was considered to include one epiphyte found from southern Nigeria, Cameroon, Central African Republic to the Gulf of Guinea Islands.

PACYPHYLLUM

An orthographic variant introduced in J. Roy. Hort. Soc., **7**(1): 125 (1886). The correct spelling is *Pachyphyllum*.

PAGONIA

An orthographic variant introduced in *Phytologist*, **2**: 59 (1845). The correct spelling is *Pogonia*.

PALAENOPSIS

An orthographic variant introduced in *Philipp. J. Sci., C.*, **12**: 249 (1917). The correct spelling is *Phalaenopsis*.

PALAEONOPSIS

An orthographic variant introduced in *Xenia Orchid.*, **2**: 146 (1862). The correct spelling is *Phalaenopsis*.

PALAEOORCHIS

An orthographic variant introduced in *Handb. Palaeont., Paleophyt.*, 388 (1890). The correct spelling is *Palaeorchis*.

PALAEORCHIS

Massalongo

Atti Reale Ist. Veneto Sci. Lett. Arti, ser. 3 **3**: 750 (1858).

ETYMOLOGY: Greek for ancient or prehistoric and orchid.

TYPE SPECIES: *Palaeorchis rhizoma* Massalongo

One fossil orchid is based on a few rhizome pieces (that are dated from the second oldest epoch, 65 million years, of the Cenozoic era that is characterized by the rise of mammals, birds, and flowering plants). These dubious orchidaceous fragments were discovered in the Veronese area of northern Italy.

PALENOPSIS

An orthographic variant introduced in *Hort. Franc.*, ser. 2, **2**: 233 (1860). The correct spelling is *Phalaenopsis*.

PALIRIS

Dumortier

Fl. Belg. (Dumortier) 134 (1827).

ETYMOLOGY: An anagram of *Liparis*, a genus of orchids.

TYPE SPECIES: *Paliris loeselii* (Linnaeus) Dumortier (*Ophrys loeselii* Linnaeus)

Now recognized as belonging to the genus *Liparis*, *Paliris* was previously considered to include one terrestrial found in mid elevation, bogs, fens and swamps from Norway to central Russia (West Siberia), and Britain to Romania. This plant has a new stem borne near the previous year's stem. The small pseudobulbs are subtended by dry, leaf sheaths, each with several, oblong or elliptical, glossy, green leaves. The numerous to few-flowered inflorescence has small, dull pale green to yellow-green flowers with narrow, recurved sepals, and thread-like petals. The small, sickle-shaped, entire lip is folded lengthwise and has a wavy, notched margin. The flowers have a long, arched column.

PALMA

Cordus

Annot. 132 (1561).

Not *Palma* P. Miller (1754) Arecaceæ.

Pre-1753, therefore not validly published in fulfillment of nomenclatural rules; this name is most often referred to *Orchis*.

PALMAM

An orthographic variant introduced in *Fl. Coron. Herb. Hist.*, 219 (1568). The correct spelling is *Palma*.

PALMANGIS

Thouars

Hist. Orchid. Table 2, sub 3o, tt. 68-69 (1822).

Name published without a description. Today this name is most often referred to *Angraecum*.

PALMAS

An orthographic variant introduced in *Stirp. Hist. Pempt.*, 241 (1616). The correct spelling is *Palma*.

PALMATA

An orthographic variant introduced in *Hist. Pl. (Bauhin)*, **2**: 773 (1650). The correct spelling is *Palma*.

PALMATAM

An orthographic variant introduced in *Hist. Pl. (Ray)*, **2**: 1224 (1688). The correct spelling is *Palma*.

PALMOGLOSSUM

Klotzsch ex Reichenbach *filius*

Xenia Orchid. **1**: 174 (1856).

ETYMOLOGY: Greek for palm and tongue. Referring to the similarity shown by the genus to some palms.

TYPE SPECIES: *Palmoglossum crassifolium* Klotzsch
This type name is now considered a synonym of *Anathallis minutalis* (Lindley) Pridgeon & M.W. Chase; basionym *Pleurothallis minutalis* Lindley

Not validly published, this name is referred to *Anathallis*. *Palmoglossum* was considered to include one epiphyte in mid to upper elevation, montane forests ranging from southern Mexico to Peru, Trinidad, Venezuela, the Guianas and Brazil.

PALMORCHIS

Barbosa Rodrigues

Gen. Sp. Orchid. **1**: 169, *t. 316* (1877).

Epidendroideæ ✹ Neottieæ

ETYMOLOGY: Greek for palm or date tree and orchid. Suggesting by the style of its leaves a certain likeness to a palm tree.

LECTOTYPE: *Palmorchis pubescentis*
Barbosa Rodrigues

Twelve unusual, sympodial terrestrials are dispersed in wet, low to mid elevation, hill forests, scrub and along river banks from Nicaragua to Bolivia, Brazil and Trinidad. These primitive plants often resemble a seedling palm or broad leaf grasses. They have clusters of tall (sometimes several feet in height), reed-like stems, each with several, large, thinly textured, pleated, veined, ovate to elliptical leaves. The long-stalked, few-flowered inflorescence, subtended by narrow bracts, has small, white or pale green-white, short-lived flowers. The sepals are spreading or converge; the petals are somewhat smaller, and all are sparsely hairy. The erect, trilobed to obscurely trilobed lip attached to the long, arching, footless column has a hairy basal callus. The erect side lobes are parallel with or enclose the column. The much smaller midlobe's tip is either blunt or bilobed and has a hairy or smooth, basal disc.

PALUMBINA

Reichenbach *filius*

Ann. Bot. Syst. **6**: 699 (1863).

ETYMOLOGY: Latin for belonging to wood pigeon. Perhaps for a fanciful resemblance of the flower to a bird with widespread wings.

TYPE SPECIES: *Palumbina candida*
(Lindley) Reichenbach f.
(*Oncidium candidum* Lindley)

Now recognized as belonging to the genus *Cuitlauzina*, *Palumbina* was previously considered to include one epiphyte found in a small area of moist, mid to upper elevation, montane cloud forests from southern Mexico (Chiapas) to Guatemala. This small plant has clustered, oblong, compressed pseudobulbs, subtended by thin, dry sheaths, each with a solitary, narrow leaf. The erect, slender, dark purple, few-flowered inflorescence has small, pretty, flat-faced, waxy, often long-lived, pristine white, creamy to pale pink, fragrant flowers. The lateral sepals are united, forming an elliptical membrane. The oblong to ovate, blunt, rounded or weakly notched, entire lip has a warty, yellow callus spotted red. The flowers have a short, winged, footless column that is fused to the lip base.

PANARICA

Withner & P.A. Harding

Cattleyas & Relatives **7**(Suppl.): 207 (2004).

ETYMOLOGY: The name is a combination of both Panama and Costa Rica, reflecting the central distribution of these species in Central America.

TYPE SPECIES: *Panarica prismatocarpa*
(Reichenbach f.) Withner & P.A. Harding
(*Epidendrum prismatocarpa* Reichenbach f.)

Now recognized as belonging to the genus *Prosthechea*, *Panarica* was proposed to include six epiphytes found in cool, low elevation, coastal forests of Costa Rica and Panama. These plants have usually yellow, narrowly ovoid pseudobulbs often tapering gradually above the middle and becoming slender at the top. Each pseudobulb has two or rarely three, long, leathery leaves. The erect, numerous to few-flowered inflorescence has fragrant, waxy, long-lasting flowers. Color is somewhat variable, but the narrow sepals and petals are usually sulfur-yellow with dark sepia-brown or dull magenta blotches or spots. The creamy-yellow to rosy-red, trilobed lip has a central callus extending from the base of the lip almost to the often long tapering tip. The flowers have a stout, club-shaped column.

PANISEA

Lindley ex Steudel

Nomencl. Bot, (Steudel), ed. 2 **2**: 265 (1841).

Name published without a description. Today this name is most often referred to *Panisea* Lindley.

PANISEA

(Lindley) Lindley

Fol. Orchid. **5**: *Panisea*, 1 (1854).

Name ICBN conserved vs. *Androgyne* Griffith (1851) Orchidaceæ.

Epidendroideæ ✹ Arethuseæ • Coelogyninæ

ETYMOLOGY: Greek for all and equal. Alluding to the similarity of all the floral segments.

TYPE SPECIES: *Panisea parviflora* (Lindley) Lindley
(*Coelogyne parviflora* Lindley)
This type name is now considered a synonym of *Panisea demissa* (D. Don) Pfitzer; basionym replaced with *Dendrobium demissum* D. Don

Eight uncommon, sympodial epiphytes or lithophytes are found in low to upper elevation, hill scrub and montane forests of northeastern India, Bhutan, Nepal, southern China (Yunnan, Guangxi and Guizhou), Myanmar, Thailand, Cambodia, Laos and Vietnam.

These small plants have ovoid, single noded, congested pseudobulbs, each with one to two, long, narrow, thinly leathery leaves borne at the tip of the pseudobulb. The one to several, solitary to few-flowered inflorescences, produced either before or after the plant has developed a new pseudobulb, have small to medium-sized, translucent, quite showy, yellow-brown, pale green, white or almost orange-pink flowers which do not open fully. The entire, obscurely trilobed or trilobed lip is more or less distinctly clawed and has an S-shaped curve which may be with or without, small side lobes or callus. If side lobes are present, they are usually a darker color. The flowers have a slender, moderately long, incurved column that is footless or has a short, almost obscure foot.

PANISIA

Not *Panisia* Rafinesque (1838) Caesalpiniaceæ.

An orthographic variant introduced in *Ann. Roy. Bot. Gard. Calcutta*, **5**: 19 (1895), and in *Orchids Burma*, 390 (1895). The correct spelling is *Panisea*.

PANMORPHIA

Luer

Monogr. Syst. Bot. Missouri Bot. Gard. **105**: 144, *f. 100* (2006).

ETYMOLOGY: Greek for of all forms. Referring to the diverse morphology of the species.

TYPE SPECIES: *Panmorphia sertularioides* (Swartz) Luer
(*Epidendrum sertularioides* Swartz)

Recognized as belonging to the genus *Anathallis*, *Panmorphia* was proposed to include seventy-three epiphytes, lithophytes or terrestrials found in low to mid elevation, hill to montane forests from southern Mexico to central Argentina and Cuba to Trinidad. These minute to large plants have slender to stout, erect to ascending stems, subtended by overlapping, tubular sheaths, each with a leathery, narrow to ovate leaf. The short to long, solitary, numerous to few-flowered inflorescence has purple, pale red-brown, red-purple, red-yellow, brown to orange flowers suffused purple or brown. The lateral sepals are united, semi-united or broadly spreading; the petals are ciliate or hairy but not fringed. The small, tongue-shaped, entire to obscurely trilobed lip has a callus frequently channeled in the middle, usually with lobules at the corners of the base, and it has a rounded tip. The flowers have a long to short, slender to stout, slightly curved, variously winged column.

| Currently Accepted | Validly Published | Invalidly Published | Published Pre-1753 | Superfluous Usage | Orthographic Variant | Fossil |

Orchid Genera • 288

PANNAMPU

An orthographic variant introduced in *Fl. Medicale*, **6**: 240 (1828). The correct spelling is *Pornampou*.

PANSTREPIS

Rafinesque

Fl. Tellur. **4**: 41 (1836)[1837].

ETYMOLOGY: Greek for all and twisted. Referring to the twisted perianth segments.

TYPE SPECIES: *Panstrepis paradoxa* Rafinesque nom. illeg.
Coryanthes macrantha (Hooker) Hooker
(*Gongora macrantha* Hooker)

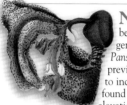

Now recognized as belonging to the genus *Coryanthes*, *Panstrepis* was previously considered to include one epiphyte found in wet, low elevation, rain forests of Venezuela, the Guianas, Trinidad, Colombia to Peru and northern Brazil. This plant has yellow-brown, grooved, ovoid pseudobulbs, each with a solitary, thinly nerved, pleated leaf. The solitary, pale yellow-brown, short-lived, strongly fragrant flower is suffused dark maroon, and hangs downward from the base of the plant. The hanging lip has three sections: a basal, concave, helmet-shaped hypochile which emerges from the slender, tube-like mesochile that then expands into the bucket-shaped epichile. The trilobed epichile has a claw-like midlobe and almost touches the long stout column.

PANTHIEVA

An orthographic variant introduced in *Nat. Syst. Pl.*, 302 (1832). The correct spelling is *Ponthieva*.

PANTLINGIA

Prain

J. Asiat. Soc. Bengal, Pt. 2, *Nat. Hist.* **65**(2): 107 (1896).

ETYMOLOGY: In honor of Robert Pantling (1857-1910), a British public servant who worked in India as deputy-superintendent of a *Cinchona* plantation (source of quinine), was a botanical illustrator, a co-author of *The Orchids of Sikkim-Himalaya*, and who collected the type species.

TYPE SPECIES: *Pantlingia paradoxa* Prain

Now recognized as belonging to the genus *Stigmatodactylus*, *Pantlingia* was previously considered to include twelve terrestrials or sometimes saprophytes scattered in mid elevation, dense, shady forests and woodlands from eastern China (Fujian and Hunan), northern India (Sikkim to Assam) to Indonesia, southern Japan, New Guinea and the Solomon Islands. These small, delicate plants have erect, unbranched stems, each with a solitary, small, oval to heart-shaped leaf located at the mid stem. The few-flowered inflorescence has leafy floral bracts, small, green to pale yellow flowers with small, usually narrow sepals and petals. The lateral sepals lie under and close to the lip. The large, roundish, pale purple, slightly concave, entire lip has a deeply bilobed appendage. The flowers have an erect, slender, curved, prominent, footless column that has a tooth-like protuberance near the base.

PAPHINIA

Lindley

Edwards's Bot. Reg. **29**(Misc.): 14 (1843).

Epidendroideæ • Cymbidieæ • Stanhopeinæ

ETYMOLOGY: A local Cypriot name for Aphrodite for whom the city and early kingdom of Paphos, Cyprus is named. In Greek mythology this area was the site of a famous sanctuary for Aphrodite who by local tradition emerged nearby in the sea-foam.

TYPE SPECIES: *Paphinia cristata* (Lindley) Lindley
(*Maxillaria cristata* Lindley)

Sixteen sympodial epiphytes are found in low to mid elevation, hill to montane forests of Costa Rica to Panama, Venezuela, the Guianas, Trinidad, Colombia to Ecuador and northern Brazil (Amazonas and Pará). These tufted plants have a small vegetative stature but produce large, spectacular flowers. The plants have small, ovoid to roundish, slightly compressed, grooved pseudobulbs, subtended by several, two-ranked, overlapping sheaths, each with two or more, small to large, thinly to softly textured, pleated, prominently nerved leaves. The short, hanging or rarely erect, few-flowered inflorescence, borne from the base of the pseudobulb, has showy, large, white flowers heavily streaked with dark red stripes. The purple to yellow, clawed, deeply trilobed lip, united to the column foot, has erect, oblong, strongly curved side lobes. The variably crested midlobe has glandular hairs, fleshy calli, and the margin is coarsely fringed with hairs. The flowers have a long, slender, curved, club-shaped column.

PAPHIODIPILUM

An orthographic variant introduced in *Cypripedium Monogr.*, 542 (1898). The correct spelling is *Paphiopedilum*.

PAPHIOPEDILUM

Pfitzer

Morph. Stud. Orchideenbl. 11 (1886).

Name ICBN conserved, type name also conserved; vs. *Cordula* Rafinesque (1838) Orchidaceæ, and vs. *Stimagas* Rafinesque (1838) Orchidaceæ.

Cypripedioideæ

ETYMOLOGY: A local Cypriot name for *Aphrodite*, for whom the city of Paphos, Cyprus is named. This western Mediterranean island had a temple dedicated to Aphrodite, who according to a poem by the poet Hesiod (*Theogony* 190), appeared nearby in the sea-foam, but Homer in the *Iliad*, said that she was the daughter of Zeus and Dione. Her name literally means foam-born and the Romans called her Venus. And Greek for slipper.

TYPE SPECIES: *Paphiopedilum insigne*
(Wallich ex Lindley) Pfitzer
(*Cypripedium insigne* Wallich ex Lindley)

Seventy-seven unique, sympodial terrestrials, lithophytes or semi-epiphytes are widespread in shady, moist mid to upper elevation, montane forests, often found on steep limestone cliffs and grassy slopes from southern China (Guangxi, Guizhou and Xizang to Hainan), northeastern India (Sikkim), Nepal, Myanmar to Vietnam, Hong Kong, Indonesia to New Guinea and the Philippines. These popular, colony-forming plants consist of more or less well-developed tufts of ovate or tongue-shaped, distichous, leathery, frequently mottled foliage. The leaves are pale to dark green on the upper surface and often with pale red-purple markings or spots on the underside. The usually solitary to few-flowered, thick-stemmed inflorescence often has a spectacular flower with thick, waxy, either smooth or hairy petals and sepals. The dominating colors are green, brown, white, yellow and pink, and can also be softly blended or patterned in bold stripes and spots. The large, broad dorsal sepal is colorfully marked with distinctive stripes or spots. Tufts of black hairs sprout from the petal margins in some of the species. The deeply pouched and inflated slipper or urn-shaped lip has incurved side lobes. The flowers have a short, often down curved column.

NOTE: In the past *Paphiopedilum*, closely related to the other slipper type orchid genera, *Selenipedium* and *Phragmipedium*, have all been treated in the one genus *Cypripedium*.

PAPHIOPEDIUM

An orthographic variant introduced in *Livre Orchid.*, 453 (1894). The correct spelling is *Paphiopedilum*.

PAPILIONANTHE

Schlechter

Orchis   **9**: 78, *t. 12* (1915).

Epidendroideæ ⚘ Vandeæ • Aeridinæ

ETYMOLOGY: Latin for butterfly and Greek for flower. From a fanciful resemblance of the yellow and purple flower to a butterfly.

TYPE SPECIES: *Papilionanthe teres*
      (Roxburgh) Schlechter
      (*Dendrobium teres* Roxburgh)

Ten vigorous, scrambling monopodial terrestrials, epiphytes or lithophytes are found in low to mid elevation, montane forests and humid swamps usually in full sunlight from the Himalayas, Bhutan, Myanmar, southern China, Laos, Vietnam, Thailand to Malaysia and Indonesia (Sumatra to Borneo). These tall, large plants have long, branched or hanging, but often climbing stems, each with several, pencil-shaped, leathery leaves arranged in two rows. The short, solitary to few-flowered inflorescence has large, showy flat-faced, white to mauve flowers with the petals twisted at the base. The trilobed lip, continuous with the column foot, has erect, upward side lobes. The kidney- to fan-shaped midlobe has a small, basal callus and a funnel-shaped spur. The flowers have a short, fleshy, wingless column. These species were often included in *Vanda*.

PAPILIOPSIS

E. Morren

Pl. Ornem.   **2**: sub *t. 55* (1874), and
Belgique Hort.   **24**: 261, *t. 11* (1874).

ETYMOLOGY: Latin for butterfly and like. Alluding to the butterfly-like appearance of the flowers.

TYPE SPECIES: *Papiliopsis nodosus* E. Morren
   This type name is now considered a synonym of
   Psychopsis krameriana (Reichenbach f.) H.G. Jones;
      basionym
   Oncidium kramerianum Reichenbach f.

Now recognized as belonging to the genus *Psychopsis*, *Papiliopsis* was previously considered to include two epiphytes found in low elevation, hill forests and scrub from Costa Rica to Ecuador. These plants have tightly clustered, strongly compressed, purple or purple-brown pseudobulbs, subtended by overlapping bracts, each with a solitary, rigid, leathery leaf. The erect, few-flowered inflorescence, lasting for several years, has large, rich golden-brown flowers with densely mottled lateral sepals. The narrow, dark red-brown dorsal sepal and petals are spoon-shaped. The large, trilobed lip has small side lobes and the broad, bright yellow midlobe has red or red-brown blotches along its wavy margin. The flowers have a short, erect, footless column.

PAPILLILABIUM

Dockrill

Australasian Sarcanthinæ   31, *t. 7* (1967).

Epidendroideæ ⚘ Vandeæ • Aeridinæ

ETYMOLOGY: Latin for having a nipple or teat and Greek for lip. In reference to the papillae present on the surface of the lip.

TYPE SPECIES: *Papillilabium beckleri*
      (F. Mueller ex Bentham) Dockrill
      (*Cleisostoma beckleri* F. Mueller ex Bentham)

One monopodial epiphyte is found in humid, low elevation, coastal scrub of Australia (southeastern Queensland and New South Wales) on slender bushes to tree limbs close to flowing rivers and creeks. They will often form vast colonies in a small area. This tiny, twig plant has short, rigid stems, each with several, narrow, somewhat purple leaves and numerous, long, zig-zagging roots. The slender, few-flowered inflorescence has sweetly fragrant, pale green flowers with a dense mass of calli extending from the spur to the tip of the lip. The trilobed lip has short, erect side lobes. The midlobe is semi-circular and divided into two, shallow segments or is notched at the tip, and is immovably attached to the prominent column foot. The long, delicate column foot forms the back of the narrow, conical spur. The flowers have a straight, stout, erect column that is nearly parallel to the dorsal sepal.

PAPPERITZIA

Reichenbach *filius*

Bot. Zeitung (Berlin)   **10**: 670 (1852).

Epidendroideæ ⚘ Cymbidieæ • Oncidiinæ

ETYMOLOGY: Dedicated to William (Wilhelm) Papperitz (x-1851), a Prussian botanical collector from Dresden, who collected in Prussia, Germany and Yugoslavia and a friend of Reichenbach's.

TYPE SPECIES: *Papperitzia leiboldii*
      (Reichenbach f.) Reichenbach f.
      (*Leochilus leiboldii* Reichenbach f.)

One uncommon, sympodial epiphyte is found in mid elevation, montane forests of southern Mexico (Oaxaca and Veracruz) usually in full sunlight. This tufted, clump-forming, small plant has clustered, ovate to elliptical, slightly compressed pseudobulbs, completely subtended by distichous, overlapping, leaf-bearing sheaths, each with a solitary, narrow, leathery, red-green leaf borne at the tip. The erect to hanging, several to few-flowered inflorescence has small, intricate, pale green flowers with yellow hairs. The hood-like dorsal sepal is cone shaped like a spur, and the united lateral sepals are shaped like a deeply keeled boat. The white, entire lip, attached to the column base, is funnel-

shaped at the base, forming a sac-like pouch and is covered with hairs that partially enclose the short, footless column.

PAPUAEA

Schlechter

Repert. Spec. Nov. Regni Veg.   **16**: 105 (1919).

Orchidoideæ ⚘ Cranichideæ • Goodyerinæ

ETYMOLOGY: *Papua*, the name of the Kanakas tribe (a local indigenous people) found on the island of New Guinea (this island is found in the southwestern Pacific Ocean just north of Australia).

TYPE SPECIES: *Papuaea reticulata* Schlechter

One uncommon, evergreen sympodial is found in low to mid elevation, rain forests to woodlands of southern New Guinea. This plant is somewhat similar to *Macodes* but these small flowers differ in technical details. The erect plant has unbranched stems, each with several, broad, showy, dark green leaves clasping the stem which has white or yellow netting throughout. The erect, hairy, few-flowered inflorescence has scattered, small, smooth, white flowers with the lateral sepals enclosing the base of the lip and has narrow, horn-like petals. The distinctly concave, obscurely trilobed lip has roundish side lobes; the midlobe has two basal calli and three or four, finger-like appendages at the tip. The flowers have a large, slightly twisted, wingless, footless column.

PAPULIPETALUM

(Schlechter) M.A. Clements & D.L. Jones

Orchadian   **13**(11): 500 (2002).

ETYMOLOGY: Latin for having petals set with blisters. Referring to raised blisters found on the lip.

TYPE SPECIES: *Papulipetalum angustifolium*
      (Schlechter) M.A. Clements & D.L. Jones
      (*Bulbophyllum papulipetalum* Schlechter)

Recognized as belonging to the genus *Bulbophyllum*, *Papulipetalum* was proposed to include two epiphytes found in low elevation, rain forests of New Guinea and northern Australia. These small plants have ovate pseudobulbs, each with a solitary, leathery leaf. The solitary-flowered inflorescence has a small, yellow to creamy colored flower not opening widely and a hood-shaped dorsal sepal sprinkled with large spots. The tiny petals (each furnished at the tip with a distinct, long papillae) are tipped with red-purple and have large, broad lateral sepals. The white, short, thick, arched, trilobed lip is edged with bright red-purple, and the midlobe tapers to a point. The flowers have a short rather than stout, wingless column that has an inflexed column foot.

Currently Accepted   Validly Published   Invalidly Published   Published Pre-1753   Superfluous Usage   Orthographic Variant   Fossil

O r c h i d   G e n e r a   • **290**

PARACALANTHE

Kudô

J. Soc. Trop. Agric. **2**: 235 (1930).

ETYMOLOGY: Greek for beside or near and *Calanthe*, a genus of orchids. Referring to a resemblance to *Calanthe*.

TYPE SPECIES: *Paracalanthe gracilis* (Lindley) Kudô
(*Calanthe gracilis* Lindley)

This type name is now considered a synonym of *Cephalantheropsis obcordata* (Lindley) Ormerod; basionym replaced with *Bletia obcordata* Lindley

Now recognized as belonging to the genera *Cephalantheropsis* and *Calanthe*, *Paracalanthe* was previously considered to include seven terrestrials native in moist, mid elevation, grasslands or montane evergreen forests of southern Japan, eastern China, Taiwan, Hong Kong and Malaysia. These plants have erect stems, somewhat swollen at the base, subtended by overlapping sheaths, each with the pleated leaves confined to the upper stem. The erect, numerous-flowered inflorescence has small, white, pale lilac to yellow flowers. The brightly colored (slightly sac-like at the base), trilobed lip has small side lobes and a kidney-shaped midlobe. The flowers have a short, winged column.

PARACALEANA

Blaxell

Contr. New South Wales Natl. Herb. **4**(5): 280 (1972).

ETYMOLOGY: Greek for beside or near and *Caleana*, a genus of orchids. Referring to a relationship to *Caleana*.

TYPE SPECIES: *Paracaleana minor* (R. Brown) Blaxell
(*Caleana minor* R. Brown)

Now recognized as belonging to the genus *Caleana*, *Paracaleana* was previously considered to include nine terrestrials found in low elevation, thick coastal scrub, rocky crevices, steep slopes and open woodlands of southern Australia, Tasmania and New Zealand. These small, erect plants have unbranched, slender stems, each with a solitary, ground-hugging, narrow leaf (more or less red) that usually withers by flowering time. The long, wiry, few-flowered inflorescence has dull green-red flowers. The column is set at right angles to the ovary. The duckbill-shaped, entire lip is attached to the base of the column by a long, strap-like claw that is extremely sensitive. The center is inflated and hollow with a cavity open below, and a flattened blunt appendage at the other end. The flowers have an incurved column that is much larger than the other segments and broadly winged from the erect anther to the base.

PARADISANTHUS

Reichenbach *filius*

Bot. Zeitung (Berlin) **10**: 930 (1852).

Epidendroideæ ⚘ Cymbidieæ • Zygopetalinæ

ETYMOLOGY: Greek for garden, park or paradise and flower. Referring to the beauty of the flower.

TYPE SPECIES: *Paradisanthus bahiensis* Reichenbach f.

Four uncommon, sympodial terrestrials are restricted to mid elevation, coastal woodlands with year-round rain fall of southeastern Brazil (Bahia, Rio de Janeiro and Paraná). These tiny plants have small, ovoid to oblong, clustered pseudobulbs, subtended by several sheaths, each with one to two, strongly nerved leaves that are highly variable in both size and shape. The erect, simple to branched, few-flowered inflorescence, borne from the tip of the pseudobulb, has small, short-lived, fragile, usually green-yellow to yellow, widespreading flowers that are mottled or barred red or brown-red. The pristine white, spear-shaped, long-clawed, trilobed lip has darker red-brown to purple streaks or bars at the base of the red column. The flowers have a short, slightly curved, club-shaped, winged column.

PARADISIANTHUS

An orthographic variant introduced in *Ill. Hort.*, **30**: 182 (1883). The correct spelling is *Paradisanthus*.

PARAGNATHIS

Sprengel

Syst. Veg. (Sprengel), ed. 16 **3**: 675, 695 (1826).

ETYMOLOGY: Greek for cheek piece of the helmet or tiara. Referring to the large, conspicuous petals that resemble the cheek pieces found on ancient Greek helmets.

TYPE SPECIES: *Paragnathis pulchella* (D. Don) Sprengel
(*Diplomeris pulchella* D. Don)

Now recognized as belonging to the genus *Diplomeris*, *Paragnathis* was previously considered to include two terrestrials found in low to upper elevation, montane slopes and grasslands of northeastern India and Myanmar to Vietnam. These tiny plants lie more or less stretched out along the ground and the short stems each have one to two large, roundish or sword-shaped, hairy or smooth leaves. The arching, one- to two-flowered inflorescence has a comparatively large, roundish, white flower with the large petals much broader than the sepals. The fan-shaped, hanging, entire to minutely trilobed, yellow lip has a slender curved, green spur.

PARAGNATIS

An orthographic variant cited in *Handb. Orchid.-Namen*, 284 (2005). The correct spelling is *Paragnathis*.

PARALOPHIA

P.J. Cribb & J. Hermans

Bot. Mag. **22**(1): 47 (2005).

Orchidoideæ ⚘ Orchideæ • Orchidinæ

ETYMOLOGY: Greek for beside or from the side of and mane or bristly ridge. Referring to the callus ridges found in this genus.

TYPE SPECIES: *Paralophia epiphytica*
(P.J. Cribb, DuPuy & Bosser) P.J. Cribb & J. Hermans
(*Eulophia epiphytica* P.J. Cribb, DuPuy & Bosser)

Two epiphytes are found in southeastern Madagascar and then only on certain species of palms (*Dypsis*, *Elaeis* and *Raphia*). These plants grow near the base trunks of the palms with the long, roundish stems hanging, then curving upward, around the tree trunk. They are subtended by papery sheaths on the lower stem and have narrow, papery leaves. The several, few-flowered inflorescences have fragrant, green or yellow-green flowers that open widely. The white, trilobed lip turns yellow with age, has green side lobes with purple veins, and has a short spur. The base of the midlobe is also covered with purple veins. The flowers have a slender column.

PARANAEA

Dusén

Notizbl. Bot. Gart. Berlin-Dahlem **9**(88): 586 (1926).

ETYMOLOGY: Named in honor of a state (Paraná) in southeastern Brazil.

TYPE SPECIES: *None designated*

Name published without a description. Today this name is most often referred to *Loefgrenianthus*.

PARAPACTIS

W. Zimmermann

Mitt. Bad. Landesvereins Naturk. Naturschutz Freiburg, n.f. **1**: 232 (1922), and *Feddes Repert.* **18**: 283 (1922).

ETYMOLOGY: Greek for beside or near and *Epipactis*, a genus of orchids. Alluding to a relationship to *Epipactis*.

TYPE SPECIES: *Parapactis epipactoides* W. Zimmermann

Now recognized as belonging to the genus *Epipactis*, *Parapactis* was previously considered to include one terrestrial found in mid elevation, open scrub and nutrient-poor grasslands from German to Spain, Italy, Sicily,

Bosnia and Yugoslavia. This erect, slender plant has several leaves, often arranged in two rows, proceeding up the hairy, unbranched stem. The few-flowered inflorescence has nodding, bell-shaped, pale green-yellow flowers. The white, trilobed lip has a brown-red splash in the center. The above type name is now considered a synonym of *Epipactis muelleri* Godfery.

PARAPHALAENOPSIS

A.D. Hawkes

Orquídea (Rio de Janeiro) **25**: 212 (1963), and Validated: *Orchidee (Hamburg)* **17**: 142 (1966).

Epidendroideæ ‡ **Vandeæ** • **Aeridinæ**

ETYMOLOGY: Greek for beside or near and *Phalaenopsis*, a genus of orchids. Refers to a similarity to *Phalaenopsis*.

TYPE SPECIES: *Paraphalaenopsis denevei*
(J.J. Smith) A.D. Hawkes
(*Phalaenopsis denevei* J.J. Smith)

Four monopodial epiphytes are found in low to mid elevation, hill and montane rain forests of Borneo (eastern Indonesia). These plants have short, leafy stems, each with several, channeled, long, narrow, pencil-like, hanging leaves. The short, more or less erect, numerous to few-flowered inflorescence has showy, fleshy, long-lasting, faintly fragrant flowers. These vary both in size and color which can range from pale green-yellow, white to dark yellow-brown. The long-clawed, widespreading petals are turned downward and have twisted tips. The trilobed lip, rigidly attached to the column base, has erect, narrow side lobes. The narrow, spoon-shaped midlobe has a fleshy, squarish, basal callus. The flowers have a long, white, stout, wingless column.

PARAPTEROCERAS

Averyanov

Bot. Zhurn. (Moscow & Leningrad) **75**(5): 723 (1990), and *Vasc. Pl. Syn. Vietnamese Fl.* **1**: 134 (1990).

Epidendroideæ ‡ **Vandeæ** • **Aeridinæ**

ETYMOLOGY: Greek for beside or near and *Pteroceras*, a genus of orchids. Refers probably to the similarity of the two genera.

TYPE SPECIES: *Parapteroceras elobe*
(Seidenfaden) Averyanov
(*Tuberolabium elobe* Seidenfaden)

Five monopodial epiphytes are found in low to mid elevation, woodlands and savanna thickets of southern China (Yunnan to Hainan), Thailand, Laos and Vietnam. These small plants have short to long, erect to hanging stems, each with distichous, leathery or slightly fleshy, pointed or unequally

bilobed leaves. The slender, numerous-flowered inflorescence has green-yellow flowers opening simultaneously and lasting for only a few days. The cone-shaped or bag-like, trilobed lip is laterally compressed, with entire or bilobed side lobes. The slightly fleshy midlobe is reduced, and the cone-shaped, white spur has a red-purple tip. The flowers have a thick, short column with a long, short or obscure foot.

PARASARCOCHILUS

Dockrill

Australasian Sarcanthinæ 22 (1967).

ETYMOLOGY: Greek for beside or near and *Sarcochilus*, a genus of orchids. Alluding to a relationship to *Sarcochilus*.

TYPE SPECIES: *Parasarcochilus spathulatus*
(R.S. Rogers) Dockrill
(*Sarcochilus spathulatus* R.S. Rogers)

Now recognized as belonging to the genus *Sarcochilus*, *Parasarcochilus* was previously considered to include three epiphytes found in wet to dry, low to mid elevation, hill to montane forests and rocky crevices of Australia (Queensland to New South Wales). These small plants have short stems, each with drooping or often spreading, narrow, ovate or oblong leaves arranged in two rows along the stem. The hanging, few-flowered inflorescence has fragrant, green-yellow to yellow-brown flowers opening widely. The cream-colored, obscurely trilobed or trilobed lip is attached to the short column by a short, movable claw and has red, yellow and purple markings.

PARDOGLOSSA

Lindley ex Wittstein
Etym.-Bot.-Handw.-Buch, ed. 1 658 (1852).

Name published without a description. Today this name is most often referred to as a section of *Disa*.

PARHABENARIA

Gagnepain
Bull. Mus. Natl. Hist. Nat., sér. 2 **4**(5): 597 (1932).

Orchidoideæ ‡ **Orchideæ** • **Orchidinæ**

ETYMOLOGY: Greek for similar or near and *Habenaria*, a genus of orchids. Refers to a possible relationship to *Habenaria*.

TYPE SPECIES: *Parhabenaria cambodiana* Gagnepain

Two sympodial terrestrials are found in Cambodia and southern Vietnam. These plants are known only by flower fragments

on an herbarium sheet and some colored drawings; also an illustration by Paul Louis Simond (*t. 92*), which is located at Laboratoire de Phanérogamie du Muséum National d'Histoire Naturelle de Paris. This erect plant has a solitary, flat-faced flower with a large, trilobed lip that has broad, roundish side lobes, a small, oblong midlobe and a long, strongly hooked spur.

PARLATOREA

Barbosa Rodrigues
Gen. Sp. Orchid. **1**: 141, *t.* 356 (1877).
Not *Parlatoria* Boissier (1842) Brassicaceæ.

ETYMOLOGY: Dedicated to Filippo Parlatore (1816-1877), an Italian physician, botanical explorer and director of the Institute of Natural Sciences in Florence who did much to popularize the studies of Barbosa Rodrigues.

TYPE SPECIES: *Parlatorea discolor* Barbosa Rodrigues

Not validly published because of a prior use of the name, this homonym was replaced by *Sanderella*.

PATTONIA

Wight
Icon. Pl. Ind. Orient. (Wight) **5**(1): 20, *t.* 1750. (1851).

ETYMOLOGY: Dedicated to a Mrs. A.W. Walker née Paton (*fl.* 1820-40s), an Englishwoman who provided illustrations for Robert Wight's (1796-1872) book *Flora of Ceylon*. She, along with her husband George Warren Walker (x-1844), a colonel in the British army, collected the flora of Ceylon for twenty years.

TYPE SPECIES: *Pattonia macrantha* Wight

Now recognized as belonging to the genus *Grammatophyllum*, *Pattonia* was previously considered to include one epiphyte found in low to mid elevation, scrub and along river banks of Laos, Myanmar, Thailand, Malaysia, Vietnam, Indonesia, the Philippines and New Guinea. This is the largest plant of the pseudo-bulbous orchids that can average nine to ten feet (2.7-3 m) in height. These plants have short, thick, clustered, yellowing pseudobulbs that get very long with age. They are not subtended by leaf bases and each has several, distichous, thinly textured leaves toward the tip. The several, numerous-flowered inflorescences have heavily textured, long-lasting, fragrant, yellow or green-yellow flowers spotted and blotched red-brown. The flowers located on the upper spike are clustered and perfect; those found closer to the base are distant and abnormal. The small trilobed lip has tiny, yellow side lobes striped with brown, while the midlobe is marked with fine red lines. The flowers have a short column that is pale green above, then white and spotted with purple below. The above type name is now considered a synonym of *Grammatophyllum speciosum* Blume.

Currently Accepted   Validly Published   Invalidly Published   Published Pre-1753   Superfluous Usage   Orthographic Variant   Fossil

ORCHID GENERA • 292

PAXTONIA

Lindley

Edwards's Bot. Reg.
24(Misc): 61, section no. 113 (1838).

ETYMOLOGY: Dedicated to Joseph Paxton (1803-1865), a British architect, designer, estate manager, head gardener for the Duke of Devonshire, botanical editor, writer and publisher of *Magazine of Botany*, and author of *Paxton's Botanical Dictionary*.

TYPE SPECIES: *Paxtonia rosea* Lindley

Now recognized as belonging to the genus *Spathoglottis*, *Paxtonia* was previously considered to include one terrestrial found in low elevation, grassy, semi-deciduous and dry, deciduous forests, savanna-like woodlands from Bangladesh, Andaman Islands, Myanmar to Vietnam, Indonesia, Taiwan, the Philippines, Malaysia, Indonesia, New Guinea and northern Australia to the southwestern Archipelago. It also has it become an invasive species in tropical and semitropical areas of the United States (Hawaii and Florida) and the Caribbean. This plant has tightly clustered, strongly ringed pseudobulbs, each with several, long, bright green, pleated leaves. The erect, thin, numerous to few-flowered inflorescence has violet-red to pink flowers opening successively over a long period. The trilobed lip has bright yellow calli between the side lobes. The above type name is now considered a synonym of *Spathoglottis plicata* Blume.

PECTANGIS

Thouars
Hist. Orchid.   Table 2, sub 3o, t. 51 (1822).

Name published without a description. Today this name is most often referred to *Mystacidium*.

PECTEILIS

Rafinesque
Fl. Tellur.   **2**: 37 (1836)[1837].

Orchidoideæ ⚘ Orchideæ • Orchidinæ

ETYMOLOGY: Greek for to comb. Descriptive of the much divided, lateral side lobes of the lip.

LECTOTYPE: *Pecteilis susannae* (Linnaeus) Rafinesque
(*Orchis susannae* Linnaeus)

Four spectacular sympodial terrestrials are found in low to upper elevation, hill scrub, grassy slopes and montane forests from Pakistan, northern India (Kashmir to Assam), Nepal, southern China (Yunnan to Jiangxi), Japan, Myanmar to Vietnam, Thailand and Indonesia. These erect plants have stout, unbranched stems that are leafy throughout or with a basal rosette. The numerous to few-flowered inflorescence bears large, usually white, yellow or pale green flowers with small, narrow petals and sepals that converge, forming a hood over the erect column. These attractive, showy, nocturnally fragrant flowers have a distinct trilobed lip with extravagantly fringed or minutely toothed (rarely entire) side lobes. The long, much smaller midlobe is entire and bears a long, slightly curved spur. The flowers have a broad, erect column.

PECTINARIA

(Bentham) Cordemoy
Rev. Gén. Bot.   **11**: 412 (1899).

Not *Pectinaria* Bernhardi (1800) Apiaceæ, not *Pectinaria* Haworth (1819) Asclepiadaceæ, and not *Pectinaria* (Bentham) Hackel (1887) Poaceæ.

ETYMOLOGY: Greek for comb. Refers to the leaves whose arrangement resembles the teeth of a comb.

TYPE SPECIES: *Pectinaria thouarsii*
(Thouars) Cordemoy nom. illeg.
(*Angraecum pectinatum* Thouars)

This type name is now considered a synonym of *Angraecum pectinatum* Thouars

Not validly published because of a prior use of the name, this homonym was replaced by *Angraecum*.

PEDILEA

Lindley
Orchid. Scelet.   17, 21, 27 (1826), and
Exot. Fl.   **2**(13): sub 115 (1824).

ETYMOLOGY: Greek for shoe or slipper. Referring to the descriptive shape of the lip.

TYPE SPECIES: *Pedilea myurus* Lindley

Now recognized as belonging to the genus *Dienia*, *Pedilea* was previously considered to include one terrestrial found in upper elevation, montane forests of central Mexico (Michoacán). This stout, inconspicuous plant has thinly textured, deciduous leaves borne from a pseudobulbous base. The tall, erect, densely packed, few-flowered inflorescence has minute, yellow-green flowers with thinly textured, thread-like, lateral sepals. The dorsal sepal and petals converge, forming a hood over the short column and the lateral sepals are thread-like. The tongue-shaped, entire lip is tiny.

PEDILIA

An orthographic variant introduced in *Sander's Orch. Guide*, ed. 4, 365 (1927). The correct spelling is *Pedilea*.

PEDILOCHILUS

Schlechter
Nachtr. Fl. Schutzgeb. Südsee   218 (1905).

Epidendroideæ ⚘ Dendrobiinæ • Currently unplaced

ETYMOLOGY: Greek for shoe or slipper and lip. In reference to the slipper-shaped lip.

TYPE SPECIES: *Pedilochilus papuanum* Schlechter

Thirty-five epiphytes are found in misty, mid to upper elevation, montane moss laden forests of New Guinea, Indonesia (Sulawesi) to Vanuatu and neighboring islands. These small plants have tiny, ovate, ribbed pseudobulbs, each with a solitary, narrow, erect, ovate to obtuse leaf, and they vegetatively resemble *Bulbophyllum*. The several, solitary-flowered inflorescences, borne from the base of the pseudobulb, have small to medium-sized, pale yellow, yellow-green or maroon flowers with white or pale brown nerves. The flowers have tiny, clawed petals slightly curved or S-shaped, and the lateral sepals are fringed with small hairs. The distinct, pouch-like lip has a thick callus with keeled midveins and thickened margins. The flowers have a short column with a short foot and a long stylidia.

PEDILONIUM

An orthographic variant introduced in *Gen. Pl.* (Endlicher), 193 (1836). The correct spelling is *Pedilonum*.

PEDILONUM

Blume
Bijdr. Fl. Ned. Ind.   **7**: 320, t. 36 (1825).

ETYMOLOGY: Greek for shoe or slipper. Descriptive of the lateral sepals that form an elongated sac.

TYPE SPECIES: *None designated*

Now recognized as belonging to the genus *Dendrobium* as a section, *Pedilonum* was previously considered to include twenty-two epiphytes or occasional lithophytes found in low to upper elevation, hill scrub to dense, montane moss laden forests from India, Malaysia, Indonesia and New Guinea to the Philippines. These small, creeping plants have long, slender stems usually forming pseudobulbs, each with several, well-spaced, fleshy leaves arranged in two ranks. The drooping, hanging or erect, short, numerous-flowered inflorescence is usually borne from leafless, older stems. The long, large to small, white, yellow or mauve flowers do not open widely. The clawed, entire lip has its margins attached to the long, flat column foot for some length which forms a long, chin-like protuberance.

PEDOCHELUS

An orthographic variant introduced in *Icon. Pl. Ind. Orient. (Wight)*, **5**: *t. 1748, f. 2* (1851). The correct spelling is *Podochilus*.

PEGONIA

An orthographic variant introduced in *Arch. Pharm.*, **19**: 230 (1869). The correct spelling is *Pogonia*.

PEIRARDIA

An orthographic variant introduced in *Telopea*, **10**(1): 282 (2003). The correct spelling is *Pierardia*.

PELATANTHERIA

Ridley

J. Linn. Soc., Bot.   **32**: 371 (1896).

Epidendroideæ ⚘ Vandeæ • Aeridinæ

ETYMOLOGY: Greek for approaching or a neighbor and anther. Refers to the relationship between the column and anther cap.

LECTOTYPE: *Pelatantheria ctenoglossum* Ridley

Seven uncommon, monopodial epiphytes or lithophytes are found in low to mid elevation, evergreen to deciduous forests and savanna-like woodlands of southern China (Yunnan and Guangxi), northern India (Kashmir to Assam), Myanmar to Vietnam, Japan, Cambodia and Malaysia to Indonesia (Sumatra). These robust plants have long, climbing stems, each with several, stiff, oblong, unequally bilobed leaves. The roots are found along the whole length of the stem. The short, few-flowered inflorescence has small, sweetly fragrant, pale yellow to white flowers closely veined red-brown with heavily red-striped petals and sepals. The white, trilobed lip has pink markings with a green, distinctly pointed midlobe and erect side lobes that have narrow, downward pointed margins and a small, cone-like spur. The flowers have a broad, stout, footless column. These fleshy flowers are often virtually indistinguishable from those of *Cleisostoma*.

PELEXIA

Poiteau

Nouv. Dict. Hist. Nat.   **25**: 136 (1817).

Name published without a description. Today this name is most often referred to *Pelexia* Lindley.

PELEXIA

Poiteau ex Lindley

Bot. Reg.   **12**: sub 985 (1826).

Name ICBN conserved vs. *Collea* Lindley (1823) Orchidaceæ.

Orchidoideæ ⚘ Cranichideæ • Spiranthinæ

ETYMOLOGY: Greek for helmet or crest. Refers to the helmet-like, narrow hood formed by the dorsal sepal and petals.

TYPE SPECIES: *Pelexia spiranthoides* Lindley nom. illeg.
This type name is now considered a synonym of
LECTOTYPE: *Pelexia adnata* (Swartz) Poiteau ex Richard (*Satyrium adnatum* Swartz)

A genus of seventy-seven sympodial terrestrials, occasional lithophytes or epiphytes, widespread in wet, low to upper elevation, evergreen, semi-deciduous to oak-pine forests, boggy grasslands and savannas from Cuba to Trinidad, the Guianas, Venezuela, southeastern Mexico to Paraguay and northern Argentina with the greatest development found in Brazil. These erect, slender plants have short, unbranched stems, each with a basal rosette of dark green leaves that are sometimes spotted, variegated or splashed silver. The fairly long, stout to delicate, numerous-flowered inflorescence has deeply concave, hairy, tubular, dark green flowers fading to pale green toward their bases. The dorsal sepal and petals (often with ciliate margins) converge, forming a narrow hood over the short, erect to slightly curved column. The narrow lateral sepals are extended, forming a distinct (sepaline sac) spur that is fused to the ovary for a major portion and has a blunt or pointed tip. The minutely hairy, white, narrow, clawed, entire or obscurely trilobed lip, attached to the sepaline sac, has a bright yellow base and is abruptly bent toward the recurved tip.

PELLORCHIS

An orthographic variant introduced in *Orchids Madagascar*, 82 (1992). The correct spelling is *Phyllorkis*.

PELMA

Finet

Notul. Syst. (Paris)   **1**: 112 (1909).

ETYMOLOGY: Greek for sole of a foot or sole of a sandal. An allusion to the long, flat, and apically bent column foot.

TYPE SPECIES: *None designated*

Now recognized as belonging to the genus *Bulbophyllum* as a section, *Pelma* was previously considered to include two epiphytes found growing in deep shade, mid elevation, montane forests from eastern Indonesia (Sumatra, Java

and Bali) to New Guinea and Vanuatu. These small, creeping plants have conspicuous, pale green, ribbed, cone-shaped pseudobulbs borne in chains; they are subtended by dry sheaths, each with a solitary, fleshy leaf. The short, solitary-flowered inflorescence, borne from the pseudobulb base, has a tiny, fleshy, white to pale green flower with broad sepals that have long tails. The flowers have a tiny, trilobed lip.

PELTANATHERIA

An orthographic variant cited in *Dict. Fl. Pl.*, ed. 7, 843 (1966). The correct spelling is *Pelatantheria*.

PELTANTHERIA

An orthographic variant cited in *Lex. Gen. Phan.*, 420 (1904). The correct spelling is *Pelatantheria*.

PELTOPUS

Szlachetko & Margońska

Polish Bot. J.   **46**(2): 114 (2002).

ETYMOLOGY: Greek for shield shaped. Referring to the shape of the column foot.

TYPE SPECIES: *Peltopus greuterianus* (Schlechter) Szlachetko & Margońska (*Bulbophyllum peltopus* Schlechter)

Recognized as belonging to the genus *Bulbophyllum*, *Peltopus* was proposed to include thirty-four epiphytes or lithophytes found in misty, low to mid elevation, hill and montane forests of New Guinea. These small to minute plants have tiny, ovoid pseudobulbs, each with a solitary, oblong, leathery leaf. The wiry, solitary-flowered inflorescence, borne from the pseudobulb base, has a pristine white to yellow flower which opens widely and has pink or purple veins. The narrow sepals are quite long and the tiny petals are rather thinly textured. The bright magenta to white, spoon-shaped, rather thick, entire lip has a deep slit half way up and a widely concave, roundish tip. The flowers have a tiny, white column.

PENDIPHYLIS

Thouars

Hist. Orchid.   Table 3, sub 3u (1822).

Name published without a description. Today this name is most often referred to *Bulbophyllum*.

Currently Accepted   Validly Published   Invalidly Published   Published Pre-1753   Superfluous Usage   Orthographic Variant   Fossil

O r c h i d   G e n e r a • **294**

PENDIPHYLLIS

An orthographic variant introduced in *Hist. Orchid.*, t. 104 (1822). The correct spelling is *Pendiphylis*.

PENKIMIA

Phukan & Odyuo

Orchid Rev. **114**(1272): 330 (2006).

ETYMOLOGY: Named for the village of Penkimia where the type species was found.

TYPE SPECIES: *Penkimia nagalandensis*
Phukan & Odyuo

This genus was proposed to include one epiphyte found in mid elevation, montane pine forests of northeastern India (Nagaland). This small, fan-shaped plant has short stems, subtended by purple leaf bracts, each with narrow, distichous, grooved leaves. The erect, purple, few-flowered inflorescence has small, dull brown-yellow flowers suffused purple on the outside and which have thick, similar sepals and petals. The concave, pale yellow, trilobed lip has small side lobes; the midlobe is shallowly notched at the tip, dotted with glands and has a small, purple, cone-shaped spur. The flowers have a short, stout, club-shaped, footless column.

PENNILABIUM

J.J. Smith

Bull. Jard. Bot. Buitenzorg, sér. 2 **13**: 47 (1914), and *Bull. Jard. Bot. Buitenzorg*, sér. 2 **14**: 43 (1914).

Epidendroideæ ● Vandeæ ● Aeridinæ

ETYMOLOGY: Latin for a feather and a lip. Descriptive of the fringed margin on the lobes of the lip.

LECTOTYPE: *Pennilabium angraecum*
(Ridley) J.J. Smith
(*Saccolabium angraecum* Ridley)

Ten dwarf, scrambling monopodial epiphytes are found in low to mid elevation, hill scrub to montane forests from northeastern India (Assam), southern China (Yunnan), Thailand and Malaysia to the Philippines. These plants have short stems, each with a few clustered, fleshy, narrow, unequally bilobed leaves often twisted at the base. The short, flattened, few-flowered inflorescence has small, short-lived, yellow, cream, orange or white flowers, opening in succession, and are often red spotted. The petals are sometimes slightly toothed. The immobile, trilobed lip has large to small, thinly textured side lobes, that when present, are toothed or have minutely fringed edges. The smaller, fleshy midlobe forms a conspicuous, solid structure and has a thin, long, slender spur with raised edges at the mouth. The flowers have a short to long, erect, footless column.

PENSTYLUS

An orthographic variant introduced in *Hist. Phys. Pl. Europ.*, **4**: 246 (1841). The correct spelling is *Peristylus*.

PENTHEA

Lindley

Gen. Sp. Orchid. Pl. 360 (Dec.1838), and *Intr. Nat. Syst. Bot.*, ed. 2 446 (1836).
Not *Penthea* (D. Don) Spach (1841) Asteraceæ.

ETYMOLOGY: Greek for grief or sorrow. In reference to the drab, dark color of the flowers often covered with darker veins and spots.

LECTOTYPE: *Penthea patens* (Linnaeus f.) Lindley
(*Ophrys patens* Linnaeus f.)

Now recognized as belonging to the genus *Disa*, *Penthea* was previously considered to include eleven terrestrials found in low elevation, grasslands from Ivory Coast to Nigeria with most found in the Cape area of South Africa. These erect plants, often growing in colonies, have several, narrow leaves clasping the stout, unbranched stem that is subtended by sheathing bracts. The few-flowered inflorescence has widely opening, pink to bright yellow flowers often with spotted segments. The spurred dorsal sepal forms a hood over the short column, and the spur is reduced to an obsolete sac. These plants bloom only after a fire has swept through the area. The above type name is now considered a synonym of *Disa tenuifolia* Swartz.

PENTHIA

An orthographic variant introduced in *Syn. Pl.* (D. Dietrich), **5**: 17 (1852). The correct spelling is *Penthea*.

PENTISEA

(Lindley) Szlachetko

Polish Bot. J. **46**(1): 19 (2001).

ETYMOLOGY: Greek for five and equal. Refers to the floral segments being of equal size.

TYPE SPECIES: *Pentisea gemmata* (Lindley) Szlachetko
(*Caladenia gemmata* Lindley)

Recognized as belonging to the genus *Cyanicula*, *Pentisea* was proposed to include ten terrestrials found in a wide variety of low elevation, forests, swamps, woodlands and rock crevices of southwestern Australia with two species found in the eastern regions. These small, clump-forming plants (heat sensitive) have erect, unbranched stems, each with a distinctive solitary, long, narrow, hairy leaf that is purple underneath. The erect, hairy, few-flowered inflorescence has brightly

colored, usually blue flowers. The nearly equal, spreading sepals and petals are almost clawed at the base. The small, entire lip is densely packed with club-shaped calli and recurved at the tip. The flowers have a short column.

PENTULOPS

Rafinesque

Fl. Tellur. **4**: 42 (1836)[1837].

ETYMOLOGY: Greek for five, lump or knob and like. Referring to the five, parallel, wart-like calluses on the lip.

TYPE SPECIES: *Pentulops discolor* Rafinesque nom. illeg.
Maxillaria palmifolia (Swartz) Lindley
(*Epidendrum palmifolium* Swartz)

Now recognized as belonging to the genus *Maxillaria*, *Pentulops* was previously considered to include one epiphyte found in Cuba, Hispaniola, Jamaica, Trinidad and the Guianas. This plant has ovoid, compressed pseudobulbs, each with a solitary, large leaf. The numerous to few-flowered inflorescence has unpleasantly fragrant, white to yellow-white flowers that have a narrow dorsal sepal, widespreading lateral sepals, small, curved petals and an obscurely trilobed lip. The flowers have an erect column.

PERAMIUM

Salisbury

Trans. Hort. Soc. London **1**: 301 (1812).

ETYMOLOGY: Greek for a pouch or little wallet. An allusion to the sac-like basal portion of the lip.

TYPE SPECIES: *Peramium repens* (Linnaeus) Salisbury
(*Satyrium repens* Linnaeus)

Now recognized as belonging to the genera *Epipactis* and *Goodyera*, *Peramium* was previously considered to include thirty-two terrestrials widespread in low to upper elevation, forests slopes and grasslands from Canada, the United States (Alaska, Montana to New Mexico and Maine to western North Carolina), then from Scandinavia, Europe to Kazakhstan, eastern Russia (Sakha to Kamchatka), China, Korea, Japan (Hokkaido to Honshu), Mongolia, Pakistan to Vietnam and Indonesia to northern Australia. This erect plant has hairy, unbranched stems, each with several, dark green leaves, sometimes obscurely veined silvery white, in a basal rosette. The slightly hairy, one sided, few-flowered inflorescence has small, white flowers suffused green or pale brown-pink. The concave dorsal sepal and oblong petals converge, forming a hood over the short column.

PERAMUM

An orthographic variant introduced in *Hort. Thenensis*, 186 (1895). The correct spelling is *Peramium*.

PERESTERIA

An orthographic variant introduced in *Floric. Cab. & Florist's Mag.*, **24**: 291 (1856). The correct spelling is *Peristeria*.

PERESTYLUS

An orthographic variant introduced in *Ann. Hort. Bot.*, **5**: 160 (1862). The correct spelling is *Peristylus*.

PERFOLIATA

Brunfels
Herb. (Brunfels) **1**: 182 (1532).

Pre-1753, therefore not validly published in fulfillment of nomenclatural rules; this name is most often referred to *Platanthera*.

PERGAMENA

Finet
Bull. Soc. Bot. France **47**(7): 263, t. 8 (1900).
ETYMOLOGY: Latin for parchment. Descriptive of the leaf texture.
TYPE SPECIES: *Pergamena uniflora* Finet

Now recognized as belonging to the genus *Dactylostalix*, *Pergamena* was previously considered to include one terrestrial found in cold, mid elevation, montane forests of northern Japan (Hokkaido) and eastern Russia (Sakha and Kuril Islands) and found only on a few occasions. This small plant somewhat resembles *Calypso bulbosa* but has a solitary-flowered inflorescence with a delicate, slightly nodding flower that is quite large for the size of the plant. These pretty, pale green flowers are spotted purple on their basal segments. The fairly large, white, trilobed lip has erect side lobes; the wedge-shaped midlobe has a few purple spots and a wavy margin. The above type name is now considered a synonym of *Dactylostalix ringens* Reichenbach f.

PERGAMENEA

An orthographic variant introduced in *Nat. Pflanzenfam. Nachtr.*, **2/3**: 88 (1908). The correct spelling is *Pergamena*.

PERISTERA

Not *Peristera* (A.P. de Candolle) Ecklon & Zeyher (1835) Geraniaceæ.

An orthographic variant introduced in *Gen. Pl. (Endlicher)*, 199 (1837). The correct spelling is *Peristeria*.

PERISTERANTHUS

T.E. Hunt
Queensland Naturalist **15**: 17 (1954).

Epidendroideæ 🌿 Vandeæ • Aeridinæ

ETYMOLOGY: Greek for pigeon or dove and flower. Referring to the anther cap that fancifully resembles the head of a bird.

TYPE SPECIES: *Peristeranthus hillii* (F. Mueller) T.E. Hunt (*Saccolabium hillii* F. Mueller)

One monopodial epiphyte is found in hot, low elevation, hill forests and woodlands of northeastern Australia (Queensland and New South Wales). This semi-hanging, rigid plant has stout stems, subtended by the deeply ribbed bases of fallen leaves, each with pale colored, drooping, prominently nerved leaves. The hanging, numerous-flowered inflorescence has small, fragrant, green flowers spotted and blotched red or red-brown. The floral segments are similar and the lateral sepals are joined to the column foot. The sac-like, bilobed lip has a finger-like callus, and a short, broad, but hollow spur at the base. The flowers have a short, erect, stout, wingless column.

PERISTERIA

Hooker
Bot. Mag. **58**: t. 3116 (1831).

Epidendroideæ 🌿 Cymbidieæ • Coelioposidinæ

ETYMOLOGY: Greek for little pigeon or dove. For the column and beaked anther found within the erect lateral lobes of the lip, giving the flower a fanciful likeness to a dove.

TYPE SPECIES: *Peristeria elata* Hooker

Eleven attractive, sympodial epiphytes or terrestrials are found in shady, low to mid elevation, grassy margins, stony outcrops in tropical wet forests ranging from Costa Rica to Panama, the Guianas, and Brazil to Peru. These plants have clustered, large, ovoid, fleshy pseudobulbs, subtended by overlapping, papery sheaths, each with one to several, long, pleated leaves. The basal, erect or curved, few to several-flowered inflorescence has waxy, strongly fragrant flowers opening in succession over a long period. The cup-shaped flowers vary in color but are generally pale green-white on the outside, white to red-purple on the inside, and sprinkled with fine to minute, red spots. The white, yellow or red, spotted purple, trilobed lip is continuous with the short, footless column and has erect side lobes. The tongue or diamond-shaped, recurved midlobe is transversed by a large callus.

PERISTYLES

An orthographic variant introduced in *Icon. Pl. Ind. Orient. (Wight)*, **5**(1): 13 (1852). The correct spelling is *Peristylus*.

PERISTYLIS

An orthographic variant introduced in *Tab. Pl. Jav. Orchid.*, t. 30 (1825). The correct spelling is *Peristylus*.

PERISTYLUS

Blume
Bijdr. Fl. Ned. Ind. **8**: 404, t. 30 (1825).
Name ICBN conserved vs. *Glossula* Lindley (1825) Orchidaceæ.

Orchidoideæ 🌿 Orchideæ • Orchidinæ

ETYMOLOGY: Greek for near or around and a column or style. Alluding to the glands found on each side of the column.

LECTOTYPE: *Peristylus grandis* Blume

Over one hundred sympodial terrestrials are widely dispersed in damp, low to upper elevation, evergreen forests, grasslands, sandy to gravelly river banks and roadside scrub from the Mascarene Islands, southern China (Xizang to Fujian), Mongolia, southern Japan (Ryukyu Islands), Taiwan, northern India (Kashmir to Assam), Bhutan, Nepal, Myanmar to Vietnam, Indonesia to the Philippines, New Guinea, northeastern Australia (Queensland) to the southern Pacific Archipelago and Hawaii (US). These plants are usually leafless on the lower third of the unbranched stems; narrow to oblong, thinly textured leaves can be spirally spaced along the stem but are most often grouped near the center. The erect, few to numerous-flowered inflorescence has small, spirally arranged, short-lived, often hairy, green or yellow-green flowers. The unique, short column has two widely separated, cushion-shaped lobes fused to the base of the trilobed or entire lip that has a short, swollen, sac-like spur.

Currently Accepted | Validly Published | Invalidly Published | Published Pre-1753 | Superfluous Usage | Orthographic Variant | Fossil

Orchid Genera • **296**

PERISTYULS

An orthographic variant introduced in *Orchid. Nepal*, 19 (1978). The correct spelling is *Peristylus*.

PEROMERIA

An orthographic variant introduced in *Bull. Fed. Soc. Hort. Belgique*, **5**: 139 (1864). The correct spelling is *Pesomeria*.

PERRIERELLA

An orthographic variant introduced in *Phylogeny Classif. Orchid Fam.*, 208 (1993). The correct spelling is *Perrieriella*.

PERRIERIELLA

Schlechter

Repert. Spec. Nov. Regni Veg. Beih. **33**: 365 (1925).
Etymology: Dedicated to Joseph Marie Henri Perrier de la Bâthie (1873-1958), a French botanist and explorer who collected the flora of Madagascar and author of *Flore de Madagascar*. And Latin for diminutive.
Type species: *Perrieriella madagascariensis* Schlechter

Now recognized as belonging to the genus *Oeonia*, *Perrieriella* was previously considered to include one small epiphyte found in humid, low to mid elevation, moss laden and lichen-covered forests of Madagascar. This tiny, fleshy plant has thin, branched stems with numerous, small, narrow leaves. The few-flowered inflorescence has small, inverted, green flowers with the concave, trilobed lip almost obscuring the flower. The flowers have a thick column.

PERULARIA

Lindley

Gen. Sp. Orchid. Pl. 281 (1835), and *Edwards's Bot. Reg.* **20**: sub 1701, section no. 32 (1835).
Etymology: Latin for a little pocket or wallet and to bear or carry. Referring possibly to cavities on the stigmatic surfaces.
Type species: *Perularia fuscescens* (Linnaeus) Lindley (*Orchis fuscescens* Linnaeus)

Now recognized as belonging to the genus *Platanthera*, *Perularia* was previously considered to include nine terrestrials found in low elevation, woodlands, wet forests, swamps and coastal plains of the United States (Minnesota to Maine and Illinois to western North Carolina), Canada (southern Ontario, New Brunswick and Nova Scotia), eastern Russia (Krasnoyarsk, Primorye to Sakhalin) and Korea. These erect plants have short to tall, unbranched stems, each

with dark green, narrow leaves that sheath the stem below and then become bracts above. The erect, numerous to few-flowered inflorescence has small, yellow-green to yellow flowers. The trilobed lip has a tiny disc, a wavy margin, and a long, slender spur. The flowers have a small column.

PERYSTYLUS

An orthographic variant cited in *Nomencl. Bot. (Steudel)*, ed. 2, **1**: 752 (1840). The correct spelling is *Peristylus*.

PERYSTYLUS

An orthographic variant introduced in *Atti Soc. Ital. Sci. Nat.*, **16**: 334 (1873). The correct spelling is *Peristylus*.

PESCATEREA

An orthographic variant introduced in *Neubert's Deutsch. Gart.-Mag.*, **36**: 44 (1883). The correct spelling is *Pescatoria*.

PESCATOREA

An orthographic variant introduced in *Treas. Bot.*, **2**: 867 (1866). The correct spelling is *Pescatoria*.

PESCATOREI

An orthographic variant introduced in *J. Roy. Hort. Soc.*, **7**(1): 85 (1886). The correct spelling is *Pescatoria*.

PESCATORIA

Reichenbach *filius*

Bot. Zeitung (Berlin) **10**: 667 (1852).
Epidendroideæ ⚬ Cymbidieæ ⚬ Zygopetalinæ
Etymology: Dedicated to Jean Pierre Pescatore (1792-1855), a Luxembourg-born Paris banker and an orchidophile who maintained an extensive orchid collection at Chateau Celle St. Cloud in northern France.
Type species: *Pescatoria cerina* (Lindley & Paxton) Reichenbach f. (*Huntleya cerina* Lindley & Paxton)

Sixteen spectacular epiphytes range in wet, low to mid elevation, hill to montane forests from Costa Rica to Colombia and Ecuador. These erect, tufted plants have short stems, each with distichous, pleated, narrow, lightly veined leaves arranged in an open fan shape. The short, erect to arching, solitary-flowered inflorescence, borne from the axils of leaf-like

basal sheaths, has relatively large, waxy, long-lived, white or blue-violet, fragrant flowers blotched green-yellow at the base. The white or purple, fleshy, clawed, trilobed lip is marked from red to purple-brown on the callus, has sickle-shaped side lobes resting against the base of the white, short, stout column, and has a concave midlobe with an incurved margin.

PESOMERIA

Lindley

Edwards's Bot. Reg. **24**(Misc.): 4, section no. 6 (1838).
Etymology: Greek for to fall off and part. Alluding to the sepals that are spontaneously thrown off the flower shortly after the flower has opened.
Type species: *Pesomeria tetragona* (Thouars) Lindley (*Epidendrum tetragonum* Thouars)

Now recognized as belonging to the genus *Phaius*, *Pesomeria* was previously considered to include one terrestrial found in low to mid elevation, rain forests of Sri Lanka and Mauritius. This plant has long, thin, four-angled stems, each with several, pleated, narrow leaves. The few to numerous-flowered inflorescence has large, maroon flowers suffused yellow-green above and below. The tubular-shaped, orange-red to yellow, obscurely trilobed lip has the side lobes embracing the long column, and has a sac-like spur.

PETALANTHERIA

An orthographic variant introduced in *Nat. Pflanzenfam. Nachtr.*, **2**: 16 (1900). The correct spelling is *Pelatantheria*.

PETALOCENTRUM

Schlechter

Repert. Spec. Nov. Regni Veg. **15**: 144 (1918).
Etymology: Greek for petal or leaf and spur. Refers to the long, spurred petals.
Type species: *Petalocentrum pusillum* (Schlechter) Schlechter (*Sigmatostalix pusilla* Schlechter)
This type name is now considered a synonym of *Sigmatostalix graminea* (Poeppig & Endlicher) Reichenbach f.; basionym replaced with *Specklinia graminea* Poeppig & Endlicher

Now recognized as belonging to the genus *Sigmatostalix*, *Petalocentrum* was previously considered to include two epiphytes found in mid elevation, montane cloud forests from Ecuador to Bolivia. These tiny plants have clustered, nearly ovoid, compressed pseudobulbs, each with several, narrow, bilobed leaves. The few-flowered inflorescence has thinly textured, minute, widespreading, pale yellow flowers with a deep purple, spur-like horn near the base of each petal. The broad, long-clawed, entire to trilobed lip has front margins with short hairs and is bilobed at the tip. The flowers have a long, slender, club-shaped column.

PETALOCHILUS

R.S. Rogers

J. Bot.   **62**: 65 (1924).

ETYMOLOGY: Greek for petal or leaf and a lip. In reference to the irregular form and undeveloped petal-lip of the type species.

LECTOTYPE: *Petalochilus calyciformis* R.S. Rogers

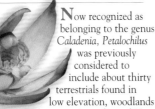

Now recognized as belonging to the genus *Caladenia*, *Petalochilus* was previously considered to include about thirty terrestrials found in low elevation, woodlands and grasslands southeastern Australia and New Zealand. These tall, tiny, wispy plants have slender, unbranched stems, each with a solitary, thread-like leaf. The solitary-flowered inflorescence has a green, bright pink or white flower with a broad, stiff, trilobed lip that is barred red, and has two rows of yellow calli. The heads of individual calli are enlarged with the larger, basal callus usually a different color. The slender, curved, winged column is usually ornamented with red transverse bars.

PETALODON

Luer

Monogr. Syst. Bot. Missouri Bot. Gard. **105**: 11 (2006).

ETYMOLOGY: Greek for petal and toothed. Refers to the edges or margin of the small petals.

TYPE SPECIES: *Petalodon collinus* (L.O. Williams) Luer (*Masdevallia collina* L.O. Williams)

Recognized as belonging to the genus *Masdevallia*, *Petalodon* was proposed to include four epiphytes found in low to mid elevation, hill scrub and montane forests from eastern Panama (Coclé) to Colombia. These small plants have short stems, each with a broad, leathery, nerved leaf. The one- to two-flowered inflorescence has minute, deep maroon-purple flowers; the sepals are united for about half their length into an abruptly bent, sepaline cup and extended into long, pale yellow tails. The small, hard, tough petals have an elongate, basal callus. The oblong, entire lip has a rounded tip that has a fringe of soft hairs. The flowers have a small, more or less club-shaped column.

PETOCHELUS

An orthographic variant introduced in *Prakt. Stud. Orchid.*, 296 (1854). The correct spelling is *Podochilus*.

PETOCHILUS

An orthographic variant introduced in *Prakt. Stud. Orchid.*, 44 (1854). The correct spelling is *Podochilus*.

PETRONIA

Barbosa Rodrigues

Gen. Sp. Orchid.   **1**: 106, t. 299 (1877).

Not *Petronia* Junghuhn (1845) Asteraceæ.

ETYMOLOGY: In homage to Pedro II de Alcântara, João Carlos Leopoldo Salvador Bibiano Francisco Xavier de Paula Leocádio Miguel Gabriel Rafael Gonzaga de Bragança e Habsburgo (1825-1891), Emperor of Brazil (1831-1889), a patron of the sciences, whose long reign was characterized by great social change and material progress in Brazil.

TYPE SPECIES: *Petronia regia* Barbosa Rodrigues

Not validly published because of a prior use of the name, this homonym was replaced by *Batemannia*. The above type name is now considered a synonym of *Batemannia colleyi*.

PETRORCHIS

D.L. Jones & M.A. Clements

Austral. Orchid Res.   **4**: 78 (2002).

ETYMOLOGY: Greek for rocks and orchid. Referring to the plant's preferred habit of growing on rock ledges.

TYPE SPECIES: *Petrorchis bicornis* (D.L. Jones & M.A. Clements) D.L. Jones & M.A. Clements (*Pterostylis bicornis* D.L. Jones & M.A. Clements)

Recognized as belonging to the genus *Pterostylis*, *Petrorchis* was proposed to include one terrestrial found in low elevation, small pockets on bare rocks in the Mount Maroon region of southeastern Australia (Queensland). This erect plant has a basal rosette (on sterile, non blooming plants only) of heart-shaped, pointed leaves. The slender, flowering stems, subtended by several, sheathing bracts, has a solitary to few-flowered inflorescence of dark green and white flowers. The erect, hood-shaped dorsal sepal curves forward in a semicircle; the protruding petals' tips form conspicuous horn-like points, and the lateral sepals closely embrace and just exceed the hood. The oblong, curved, entire lip is constricted near the tip and is not visible from the outside.

PETROSTYLIS

An orthographic variant introduced in *Icon. Bot. Index*, **1**: 828 (1855). The correct spelling is *Pterostylis*.

PFITZERIA

Senghas

J. Orchideenfr.   **5**(1): 30 (1998).

Epidendroideæ 🌿 Cymbidieæ • Oncidiinæ

ETYMOLOGY: Named in honor of Ernst Hugo Heinrich Pfitzer (1846-1906), a German professor of botany, Director of the Heidelberg Botanic Gardens and whose main interest was the development of a new system of classification for the Orchidaceæ.

TYPE SPECIES: *Pfitzeria schaeferi* Senghas

One sympodial epiphyte is found in mid elevation, coffee trees of northeastern Peru (Amazonas). This small plant has tiny, ovate pseudobulbs, subtended by leafy sheaths, each with several, slightly pencil-like leaves that are arranged in a fan shape. The erect, few-flowered inflorescence has globular, bright yellow flowers that do not open widely. The white, trilobed lip is boat-shaped. The flowers have a short column with a few soft hairs.

PHADROSANTHES

An orthographic variant introduced in *Hort. Donat.*, 203 (1858). The correct spelling is *Phaedrosanthus*.

PHAEDROSANTHUS

Necker

Elem. Bot. (Necker)   **3**: 133 (1790).

ETYMOLOGY: Greek for shining or gay and flower. Refers to the rather waxy floral segments.

TYPE SPECIES: *None designated*

Not validly published, this name is referred to *Epidendrum*. *Phaedrosanthus*'s original description was so vague that when Rafinesque (*Fl. Tellur.*, **4**: 36 (1836)[1837]) looked at the description, he could only conclude that it might belong with *Dendrobium*. But Govaerts (1995) thinks that the species belongs with *Epidendrum*.

PHAEDROSANTHUS

An orthographic variant cited in *Lex. Gen. Phan.*, 428 (1904). The correct spelling is *Phaedrosanthus*.

PHAEUS

An orthographic variant cited in *Lex. Gen. Phan.*, 268, 429 (1904). The correct spelling is *Phaius*.

PHAGUS

An orthographic variant introduced in *Hort. Spaarn-Berg.*, 26 (1839). The correct spelling is *Phaius*.

Currently Accepted   Validly Published   Invalidly Published   Published Pre-1753   Superfluous Usage   Orthographic Variant   Fossil

O r c h i d   G e n e r a   •   **298**

PHAIOS

An orthographic variant cited in *Etym.-Bot.-Handw.-Buch*, ed. 1, 677 (1852). The correct spelling is *Phaius*.

PHAIUS

Loureiro

Fl. Cochinch. **2**: 517, 529 (1790).

Epidendroideæ ⚭ Collabiinæ • Currently unplaced

ETYMOLOGY: Greek for gray, swarthy, dusky or dark. From the predominantly dark hue of the flowers.

TYPE SPECIES: *Phaius grandifolius* Loureiro

This type name is now considered a synonym of *Phaius tankervilleae* (Banks ex L'Héritier) Blume; basionym *Limodorum tankervilleae* Banks ex L'Héritier

Forty-eight sympodial terrestrials or epiphytes are found in low to upper elevation, hill to montane scrub and grasslands from Gabon to Zaire, Madagascar, Réunion, Sri Lanka, northern India (Kashmir to Assam) to southern China (Xizang to Fujian), Taiwan, southern Japan, Myanmar to Vietnam, Indonesia, New Guinea, and eastern Australia to the southwestern Pacific Archipelago. These plants have clustered stems, with or without pseudobulbs that are sometimes cylindrical and rather cane-like, each with large, pleated, thinly textured leaves. The erect, numerous-flowered inflorescence has large, showy flowers opening successively so that the plant remains in bloom for extended periods. The similar, narrow sepals and petals are dark red, yellow, white to purple-brown in color. The white or pink, distinct tubular, short, entire or lobed lip has a wavy, recurved front margin speckled purple. The fleshy, rather long to short column is largely free from the entire or trilobed lip that partly encloses the footless column. The spurless or long to short, narrow to cone-shaped, often yellow spur has a forked tip. These flowers have a variety of unusual, unique, and often spectacular color combinations. The species found in Africa are often included in *Gastrorchis*.

PHAJAS

An orthographic variant introduced in *Icon. Pl. Ind. Orient. (Wight)*, **3**: 8, *t. 1659-60* (1851). The correct spelling is *Phaius*.

PHAJUS

An orthographic variant introduced in *Ist. Bot.*, **3**: 226 (1813). The correct spelling is *Phaius*.

PHALAENOPSIS

Blume

Bijdr. Fl. Ned. Ind. **7**: 294, *t. 44* (1825).

Epidendroideæ ⚭ Vandeæ • Aeridinæ

ETYMOLOGY: Greek for a moth and appearance or like. Referring to the supposed likeness of the flower of the type species to certain tropical moths.

TYPE SPECIES: *Phalaenopsis amabilis* (Linnaeus) Blume (*Epidendrum amabile* Linnaeus)

Sixty-two monopodial epiphytes or sometimes lithophytes are better known as moth orchids. They grow in dense, shady, steamy, low elevation, hill forests with a few species found in cool, upper elevation, montane forests from southern China (Xizang to Hainan), Taiwan, India, Sri Lanka, Myanmar to Vietnam, Thailand, Indonesia, the Philippines and New Guinea to northern Australia. These plants have short, leafy stems, each with several, broad, usually drooping, leathery, closely clustered leaves. There are a few species with attractive patterned leaves. The short or long, solitary to numerous-flowered inflorescence has exquisitely fragrant or not fragrant, often large, colorful flowers lasting for several months. The sepals and petals range from large and roundish to long and narrow. The petals, usually larger than the sepals, give the flower a gracefully rounded appearance. The trilobed lip has erect side lobes; the midlobe has a fleshy ridge of calli and is often tipped with a pair of appendages that resemble antennae and are with or without a spur. The flowers have an erect to slightly curved, wingless column that is parallel with the lip.

PHALAEONOPSIS

An orthographic variant introduced in *Xenia Orchid.*, **2**: 146 (1862). The correct spelling is *Phalaenopsis*.

PHALANOPSIS

An orthographic variant introduced in *Hort. Franc.*, **1**: 112 (1852). The correct spelling is *Phalaenopsis*.

PHALENOPSIS

An orthographic variant introduced in *Floric. Cab. & Florist's Mag.*, **25**: 143 (1857). The correct spelling is *Phalaenopsis*.

PHALOENOPSIS

An orthographic variant introduced in *Rev. Hort. Belge Étrangère*, **30**: 163 (1904). The correct spelling is *Phalaenopsis*.

PHANIASIA

Blume ex Miquel

Ann. Mus. Bot. Lugduno-Batavi **2**: 206 (1866).

ETYMOLOGY: Greek for visible, bright or evident and muddy. Refers to the brightly colored flowers usually found growing in a muddy habitat.

TYPE SPECIES: *Phaniasia pulchella* Blume ex Miquel

Not validly published, this name is referred to *Ponerorchis*. *Phaniasia* was considered to include one, tiny terrestrial found in mid elevation, montane rocky forests of Korea and northern Japan. The above type name is now considered a synonym of *Ponerorchis graminifolia* Reichenbach f.

PHAPHIOPEDILUM

An orthographic variant introduced in *Proc. Indian Natl. Sci. Acad.*, **36**: 363 (1970). The correct spelling is *Paphiopedilum*.

PHAROCHILUM

D.L. Jones & M.A. Clements

Austral. Orchid Res. **4**: 80 (2002).

ETYMOLOGY: Greek for cloak or mantle and lip. Referring to the large lateral lobes of the lip that appear to hide the midlobe.

TYPE SPECIES: *Pharochilum daintreanum* (F. Mueller ex Bentham) D.L. Jones & M.A. Clements (*Pterostylis daintreana* F. Mueller ex Bentham)

Recognized as belonging to the genus *Pterostylis*, *Pharochilum* was proposed to include one terrestrial found in low elevation, coastal woodlands and rocky crevices of eastern Australia (New South Wales). This small, erect plant, often forming extensive colonies, has one to several basal rosettes (appearing as tufts) that have numerous, overlapping, pale green leaves with wavy margins. The few-flowered inflorescence has small, shiny, white flowers with an incurved hood (tapering to a thin tip) that has fine green stripes and markings. The lateral sepals are joined at their base and then taper to a thread-like tip. The long, narrow, obscurely trilobed lip has dark red-brown side lobes and an entire, channeled midlobe that tapers to a blunt tip.

PHELADENIA

D.L. Jones & M.A. Clements
Orchadian   **13**(9): 411 (2001).

Orchidoideæ 🌿 Diurideæ • Caladeniinæ

ETYMOLOGY: Greek for false and gland. Referring to the distinctive calli on the lip.

TYPE SPECIES: *Pheladenia deformis*
(R. Brown) D.L. Jones & M.A. Clements
(*Caladenia deformis* R. Brown)

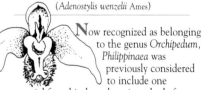

One small, sympodial terrestrial is found in damp, shady, low elevation, coastal woodlands of southern Australia and they often form small colonies. This plant's tubers are fully enclosed by a multilayered tunic and the solitary, bright green, narrow leaf is sparsely hairy. The solitary or rarely two-flowered inflorescence has a bright blue or rare pink flower with the segments colored and sprinkled with minute, purple specks. The dark purple, obscurely trilobed lip has a pale yellow to blue midlobe with curved, congested, fringed calli that are slightly club-like in four or more rows which extend to the tip of the midlobe. In addition, the erect side lobes have margins with short calli.

PHILIPPINAEA

Schlechter & Ames
Orchidaceæ (Ames)   **6**: 278, t. 100 (1920).

ETYMOLOGY: Named to honor the Republic of the Philippines (the second largest archipelago with over 7,000 islands located between the South China Sea and the southwestern Pacific Ocean) where the type species was collected.

TYPE SPECIES: *Philippinaea wenzelii*
(Ames) Schlechter & Ames
(*Adenostylis wenzelii* Ames)

Now recognized as belonging to the genus *Orchipedum*, *Philippinaea* was previously considered to include one terrestrial found in low elevation, shady forests of central Indonesia (Java), Malaysia and the Philippines. This erect plant has non-branching succulent stems, subtended by loose sheaths that are leafy below the middle and with several bracts above. The tall, numerous-flowered inflorescence has well-spaced, glandular, hairy, white flowers. The concave dorsal sepal and small petals converge, forming a hood over the column. The sac-like, bilobed lip has a comb-like basal portion and a long, two-lobed claw.

PHILOCNEMA

An orthographic variant introduced in *Nat. Pflanzen-Syst.*, 197 (1829). The correct spelling is *Ptilocnema*.

PHILODOTA

An orthographic variant cited in *Lex. Gen. Phan.*, 2 (1904). The correct spelling is *Pholidota*.

PHLEBIDIA

Lindley ex Wittstein
Etym.-Bot.-Handw.-Buch, ed. 1   682 (1852).

Name published without a description. Today this name is most often referred to as a section of *Disa*.

PHLEBOCHILUS

(Bentham) Szlachetko
Polish Bot. J.   **46**(1): 14 (2001).

ETYMOLOGY: Greek for veined and lip. Referring to the lip with its red-brown nerves.

TYPE SPECIES: *None designated*

Not validly published, this name is referred to *Caladenia*. *Phlebochilus* was proposed to include twenty terrestrials found in low to mid elevation, open sandy forests and scrub of southern Australia.

PHLEOPHILA

An orthographic variant cited in *Handb. Orchid.-Namen*, 592 (2005). The correct spelling is *Phloeophila*.

PHLOEOPHILA

Hoehne & Schlechter
Arch. Bot. São Paulo   **1**(3): 199 (1926).

Epidendroideæ 🌿 Epidendreæ • Pleurothallidinæ

ETYMOLOGY: Greek for bark of trees and loving or lover. Referring to its creeping, appressed growth habit on the bark of trees.

LECTOTYPE: *Phloeophila paulensis*
Hoehne & Schlechter
This type name is now considered a synonym of
Phloeophila nummularia (Reichenbach f.) Garay;
basionym
Pleurothallis nummularia Reichenbach f.

Ten tufted, sympodial epiphytes to lithophytes are found in cool, low to mid elevation, hill scrub to montane cloud forests from Cuba, Belize to Bolivia, Venezuela to eastern Brazil and northern Argentina. These small, creeping plants, often producing dense mats, have small, roundish, strongly dimpled, flat pseudobulbs, each with a solitary leaf. The tiny bulbs are found hugging tree bark. The several, erect, short, solitary-flowered inflorescences, borne from the leaf axils, have a tiny, widely opening, red to yellow flower covered in fine hairs. The sepals are united usually to the middle, often with their tips forming a concave synsepal with the flower has tiny, oblong petals. The tiny, ovate to oblong, entire or trilobed lip is attached directly to the column base or is hinged to the column foot. The flowers have a short, slightly club-shaped, curved column.

PHODROSANTHUS

An orthographic variant introduced in *Fl. Bras. (Martius)*, **3**(5): 31 (1893). The correct spelling is *Phaedrosanthus*.

PHOLIAOTA

An orthographic variant introduced in *Beih. Bot. Centralbl.*, **8**(4-5): 312 (1899). The correct spelling is *Pholidota*.

PHOLIDOTA

Lindley ex Hooker
Exot. Fl.   **2**(18): t. 138 (1825).

Epidendroideæ 🌿 Arethuseæ • Coelogyninæ

ETYMOLOGY: Greek for clad in scales or scaly. Refers to the prominent, overlapping flower bracts that are distinct before flowering, giving the inflorescence a scaly, snakeskin-like appearance.

LECTOTYPE: *Pholidota imbricata* Hooker

Forty-three mostly insignificant, sympodial epiphytes, rare lithophytes or terrestrials are found in low to upper elevation, hill scrub and montane evergreen to semi-deciduous forests on rocky crevices, steep moss laden slopes and along river banks from northern India (Sikkim), southern China (Xizang to Jiangxi), Taiwan, Myanmar to Vietnam, Malaysia, Indonesia to New Guinea, northern Australia (Queensland) and the Philippines to the southwestern Pacific Archipelago. These hanging or erect, often clump-forming plants have large or small, thick, wrinkled or sunken, clustered or widely spaced pseudobulbs, or slender, well-spaced pseudobulbs, each with one to two, large, oblong to narrow, rolled or twisted together leaves. A new pseudobulb is borne from the tip of last year's mature pseudobulb. The erect or arching, often zig-zagged, few to numerous-flowered inflorescence has small to tiny, fleshy, dull white, yellow to green, musky fragrant flowers not opening fully but opening simulta-neously. They are subtended by large, papery bracts that are arranged in two alternating rows. The flowers, arranged in two ranks, give the appearance of a string of pearls, with the petals smaller than the sepals. The short, boat-shaped or concave, trilobed lip has erect to

| Currently Accepted | Validly Published | Invalidly Published | Published Pre-1753 | Superfluous Usage | Orthographic Variant | Fossil |

Orchid Genera • **300**

downward turned side lobes; the midlobe has a cup-like basal part, and the disc sometimes has thick veins or lamella. The flowers have a short, compact, footless column.

PHORINGOPSIS

D.L. Jones & M.A. Clements
Orchadian   **13**(10): 457 (2002).
ETYMOLOGY: Greek for truffles and resemblance. In reference to the fungoid-like callus on the lip.
TYPE SPECIES: *Phoringopsis byrnesii*
(Blaxell) D.L. Jones & M.A. Clements
(*Arthrochilus byrnesii* Blaxell)

Recognized as belonging to the genus *Arthrochilus*, *Phoringopsis* was proposed to include two terrestrials found in low elevation, woodlands of northeastern Australia (Queensland) and southern New Guinea. These small, erect plants have unbranched stems, each with one to two, narrow, distichous leaves arranged under the leaf-like sheathing of the few-flowered inflorescence. The widely-spaced, insect-like, green flowers have long, narrow segments. The oblong, entire lip lacks a supporting stalk and has a prominent mushroom-shaped callus on the upper surface which is covered with hairy cilia. The flowers have a long, slender, incurved column with the column foot set at a right angle to the base.

PHORMANGIS

Schlechter
Beih. Bot. Centralbl.   **36**(2): 103 (1918).
ETYMOLOGY: Greek for mat and a vessel or cup. Descriptive of the cylindrical spur of the lip.
TYPE SPECIES: *Phormangis schumannii*
(Kraenzlin) Schlechter
(*Angraecum schumannii* Kraenzlin)

Now recognized as belonging to the genus *Ancistrorhynchus*, *Phormangis* was previously considered to include one epiphyte found in deeply shady, low to mid elevation, evergreen forests of Nigeria, Gabon, the Congo and Zaire. This plant has short, thick stems and overlapping, narrow, unequally bilobed leaves with notched tips. The short, numerous to few-flowered inflorescence has small, white flowers with similar segments. The trilobed lip has a wide mouth, and a long, slightly swollen spur. The flowers have a short column.

PHOSCATIA

An orthographic variant introduced in *Beih. Bot. Centralbl.*, **8**(4-5): 312 (1899). The correct spelling is *Phreatia*.

PHRAGMIPEDILUM

An orthographic variant introduced in *Bot. Jahrb. Syst.*, **25**: 527 (1898). The correct spelling is *Phragmipedium*.

PHRAGMIPEDIUM

Rolfe
Orchid Rev.   **4**(47): 330, 331 (1896).
Name ICBN conserved, also type name conserved; vs. *Uropedium* Lindley (1846) Orchidaceæ.

Cypripedioideæ
ETYMOLOGY: Greek for partition or division and a slipper or shoe. An allusion to the three chamber-like divisions of the ovary and the slipper-shaped lip.
TYPE SPECIES: *Phragmipedium caudatum*
(Lindley) Rolfe
(*Cypripedium caudatum* Lindley)

Twenty-one sympodial terrestrials, lithophytes or less commonly epiphytes are found in low to upper elevation, hill to montane forests, grasslands and cliff faces from southern Mexico (Chiapas) to Bolivia and western Brazil. These plants have short, erect stems, each with gracefully arching, grooved, narrow, leathery leaves. The entire to sometimes branching, solitary to few-flowered inflorescence has a few species with flowers that have extremely long, slender petals with some over 2¹/₂ feet (6.5 m) in length and extremely twisted. These petals were originally thought to serve as ladders for the pollinating insects. Most of the species have similar spreading petals and dorsal sepal; the lateral sepals are united for their entire length forming a synsepalum. The trilobed lip has incurved side lobes and the midlobe is inflated and pouch-like. The flowers have a short, stout column and a shield-shaped triangular to elliptic staminode. The typically brown and green flowers last about a month and will suddenly drop off, still in pristine condition.

PHRAGMOPEDILUM

An orthographic variant introduced in *Bot. Jahrb. Syst.*, **19**: 41 (1894). The correct spelling is *Phragmipedium*.

PHRAGMOPEDIUM

An orthographic variant introduced in *Orchidaceae (Ames)*, **5**: 9 (1915). The correct spelling is *Phragmipedium*.

PHRAGMORCHIS

L.O. Williams
Bot. Mus. Leafl.   **6**(3): 52 (1938).
Epidendroideæ • Vandeæ • Aeridinæ
ETYMOLOGY: *Phragmites*, a genus of reed-like grasses and Greek for orchid. Alluding to the reed-like plant stems.
TYPE SPECIES: *Phragmorchis teretifolia* L.O. Williams

One uncommon, monopodial epiphyte is found in low elevation, hill scrub of the northern Philippines (Luzon). This tall plant has erect, slender stems, each with several, well-spaced, strap-like leaves. The solitary to few-flowered inflorescence, borne from the leaf sheaths, has minute, white flowers. The concave dorsal sepal and the petals converge to form a hood over the column. The yellow, trilobed lip has small, erect side lobes, and a broadly ovate midlobe. The large, bag-like spur has two slender calli inside. The flowers have a short, fleshy, nearly footless column.

PHREATEA

An orthographic variant introduced in *Icon. Pl. Ind. Orient. (Wight)*, **5**(1): 17 (1851). The correct spelling is *Phreatia*.

PHREATIA

Lindley
Gen. Sp. Orchid. Pl.   63 (1830).
Epidendroideæ • Podochileæ • Thelasiinæ
ETYMOLOGY: Greek for a well or cistern. Referring probably to the well-like structure formed by the lateral sepals and the lip.
TYPE SPECIES: *Phreatia elegans* Lindley

A remarkable genus comprised of more than two hundred typically tiny, tufted, monopodial or sympodial epiphytes or lithophytes with many diverse shapes. They are found growing in full sunlight to shady, low to upper elevation, montane to swamp forests from northern India (Assam) to Samoa with a vast number found in New Guinea. These plants have a rather diverse number of growth forms. Some species are without a well-developed stem or pseudobulb and produce a fan of overlapping leaves. Other species have small pseudobulbs or leafy stems. These often inconspicuous plants form dense mats resembling patches of moss. The long, numerous to few-flowered inflorescence has tiny to minute, intricate, usually pale green to white flowers which do not open widely. The concave, usually clawed, entire or obscurely trilobed lip is usually spurless. The flowers have an obscure to short, wingless column.

PHYLLOMPHAX

Schlechter

Repert. Spec. Nov. Regni Veg. Beih. **4**: 118 (1919).

ETYMOLOGY: Greek for leaf and unripe fruit, sour or bitter. Refers to the bracts that have the appearance of juvenile or young leaves.

TYPE SPECIES: *None designated*

Now recognized as belonging to the genus *Brachycorythis*, *Phyllomphax* was previously considered to include thirteen terrestrials found in low to upper elevation, sandy grasslands and montane forests from Africa (Guinea to Nigeria) and northern India (Assam) to southern China (Yunnan) and Myanmar to Vietnam. These tall, leafy plants have erect, unbranched stems, each with numerous leaves decreasing in size up the stem and graduating into large, leaf-like bracts that almost obscure the lowermost flowers. The few-flowered inflorescence has pink, purple or green flowers. The boat-shaped, entire or obscurely trilobed lip has small, erect side lobes and with a base that is sometimes sac-like or with a cone-like spur. The lip can sometimes flatten out becoming kidney-shaped or even trilobed. The flowers have a small to large, stout column.

PHYLLORCHIS

An orthographic variant introduced in *Hist. Orchid.*, Table 3, sub 3u (1822). The correct spelling is *Phyllorkis*.

PHYLLORKIS

Thouars

Nouv. Bull. Sci. Soc. Philom. Paris **1**(19): 319 (1809).

Name ICBN rejected vs. *Bulbophyllum* Thouars (1822) Orchidaceæ.

ETYMOLOGY: Greek for leaf and orchid. From the prominent floral bracts.

TYPE SPECIES: *None designated*

Although validly published this rejected name is now referred to *Bulbophyllum*. *Phyllorkis* was considered to include two hundred sixty-seven epiphytes found in both the New and Old Worlds in various types of habitats. This diverse group of plants have drooping to erect inflorescences with usually tiny flowers in a wide range of colors and combinations of colors. The flowers do not open widely and are often spotted, splashed or blotched on their outer surfaces.

PHYLLOSTACHYA

E. Goeze

Hamburger Garten- Blumenzeitung **40**: 155 (1884).

ETYMOLOGY: Greek for having a leaf-like flower spike.

TYPE SPECIES: *None designated*

Name published without a description. Today this name is most often referred to *Pseudorchis*.

PHYLOMPAX

An orthographic variant introduced in *Bull. Fan Mem. Inst. Biol. Bot.*, **10**: 27 (1940). The correct spelling is *Phyllomphax*.

PHYLORCHIS

An orthographic variant introduced in *Hist. Orchid.*, Table 4, sub 3 (1822). The correct spelling is *Phyllorchis*.

PHYMATIDIOPSIS

Szlachetko

Polish Bot. J. **51**(1): 37 (2006)[2007].

ETYMOLOGY: *Phymatidium*, a genus of orchids, and Greek for like or appearance.

TYPE SPECIES: *Phymatidiopsis mellobarretoi*
(L.O. Williams & Hoehne) Szlachetko
(*Phymatidium mellobarretoi* L.O. Williams & Hoehne)

Recognized as belonging to the genus *Phymatidium*, *Phymatidiopsis* was proposed to include one epiphyte found in wet, mid elevation, montane forests of southeastern Brazil (Minas Gerais and Rio de Janeiro). This tiny plant a few narrow leaves with numerous roots. The long, few-flowered inflorescence has small, semi-transparent, white flowers with spreading sepals and narrow petals. The broadly clawed, entire lip is attached to the column base. The flowers have a slender, winged column.

PHYMATIDIUM

Lindley

Gen. Sp. Orchid. Pl. 209 (1833).

Epidendroideæ ※ Cymbidieæ • Oncidiinæ

ETYMOLOGY: Greek for a swelling or full of tumors and diminutive. In reference to the often thick, swollen base of the column.

LECTOTYPE: *Phymatidium delicatum* Lindley

Eight tiny, monopodial epiphytes are found in humid, low to mid elevation, rain forests of southeastern Brazil (Rio de Janeiro to Rio Grande do Sul). These plants have short stems, subtended by persistent leaf sheaths, each with small, grass-like, spirally arranged or fan-shaped, distichous, narrow leaves. Some species have the appearance of a *Tillandsia* with their delicate, pale green, pin-like, recurved leaves. The tall, slender, simple to slightly zig-zagged, numerous to few-flowered inflorescence has minute, white or pale-colored, semi-translucent flowers. They are extremely complex for their tiny size with similar, oblong to narrow sepals and petals. The broadly clawed, ovate, entire lip, attached to the column base, has a large, fleshy callus, a blunt tip and a notched margin. The flowers have a long, slender, incurved, sometimes winged column.

PHYMATOCHILUM

Christenson

Richardiana **5**(4): 195 (2005).

ETYMOLOGY: Greek for growth or swelling and a lip. Refers to the fleshy keels or teeth.

TYPE SPECIES: *Phymatochilum brasiliense*
(Lindley) Christenson
(*Oncidium phymatochilum* Lindley)

Recognized as belonging to the genus *Miltonia*, *Phymatochilum* was proposed to include one epiphyte found in low to mid elevation, hill and montane forests of southeastern Brazil (Bahia, Espírito Santo, Rio de Janeiro and São Paulo). These tufted plants have small, dense clumps of strongly compressed, ovoid pseudobulbs suffused red-brown, subtended by overlapping sheaths, each with a solitary, leathery, red speckled leaf. The long, hanging, branched, numerous-flowered inflorescence has spidery, white to pale yellow, fragrant flowers with twisted, wavy segments. The narrow sepals and petals are covered with pale brown to maroon bars. The white, trilobed lip has ear-like, spreading side lobes; the long-clawed, fiddle-shaped, midlobe has a fleshy, yellow callus sprinkled with red-brown spots. The flowers have an erect, club-shaped, strongly winged column.

PHYSANTHERA

Bertero ex Steudel

Nomencl. Bot. (Steudel), ed. 2 **2**: 330, 463 (1841).

ETYMOLOGY: Greek for visible, bright or evident and muddy. Referring to the habit of this orchid that is located in crevices or on rocks.

TYPE SPECIES: *Physanthera callistachys*
Bertero ex Steudel
This type name is now considered a synonym of
Gomesa stricta Sprengel

Not validly published, this name is referred to *Gomesa*. *Physanthera* was considered to include one epiphyte found in low to upper elevation, hill to montane forests of Jamaica.

Currently Accepted   Validly Published   Invalidly Published   Published Pre-1753   Superfluous Usage   Orthographic Variant   Fossil

Orchid Genera • 302

PHYSARUS

An orthographic variant cited in *Nomencl. Bot. (Steudel)*, ed. 2, **2**: 330 (1841). The correct spelling is *Physurus*.

PHYSINGA

Lindley

Edwards's Bot. Reg.
24(Misc.): 32, section no. 45 (1838).

ETYMOLOGY: Greek for blister or a kind of garlic. Alluding to the bladder-like pouch or spur at the base of the lip.

TYPE SPECIES: *Physinga prostrata* Lindley

Now recognized as belonging to the genus *Epidendrum*, *Physinga* was previously considered to include five epiphytes found in wet, low elevation, forests and woodlands of northern Brazil, Ecuador, Peru and the Guianas. These plants have leafy stems, subtended by overlapping, leaf sheaths, each with several, thick, leathery, mid-nerved leaves borne in two rows. The long, solitary to few-flowered inflorescence has small, somewhat bell-shaped, nerved, creamy colored flowers. The bilobed lip, attached to the base of the small column, has sides inrolled with three, pink calli.

PHYSINGIA

An orthographic variant introduced in *Hort. Brit. (Sweet)*, 640 (1839). The correct spelling is *Physinga*.

PHYSOCERAS

Schlechter

Repert. Spec. Nov. Regni Veg. Beih. **33**: 78 (1924).

Orchidoideæ ⚬ Orchideæ • Orchidinæ

ETYMOLOGY: Greek for bladder and horn. Referring to the spur of the lip.

LECTOTYPE: *Physoceras bellum* Schlechter

Eleven sympodial epiphytes, lithophytes or terrestrials are found in low to upper elevation, moss laden and lichen covered scrub, along river banks and montane evergreen forests of north central Madagascar (Antsiranana to Antananarivo) with one species in Réunion (Cilaos) and Mauritius. These spreading or erect plants have one to two stems; the solitary leaf is borne in the middle of the stem, and each is enclosed at the base by brown or black sheaths. The erect, few-flowered inflorescence has showy, large, white, pink, lilac or rosy-purple flowers. The erect dorsal sepal and small petals converge, forming a hood over the tiny, erect column. The trilobed lip has spreading side lobes; the large midlobe has a small, notched tip, and has a long, hanging or

incurved spur. The flowers have a small, club-shaped column.

PHYSOGYNE

Garay

Bot. Mus. Leafl. **28**(4): 346 (1980)[1982].

ETYMOLOGY: Greek for bladder or to inflate and female or woman. In reference to the column that is ballooned outward in the front.

TYPE SPECIES: *Physogyne gonzalesii*
(L.O. Williams) Garay
(*Spiranthes gonzalesii* L.O. Williams)

Now recognized as belonging to the genus *Pseudogoodyera*, *Physogyne* was previously considered to include three terrestrials or lithophytes found in low to mid elevation, roadsides and along river banks, deciduous and oak-pine forests of south central and western Mexico (Colima, Jalisco to Morelos). These erect plants have slender, unbranched stems, densely covered with minute hairs and subtended by overlapping, thin, sheathing bracts. The basal rosette is often withered at flowering. The erect, weak to delicate, numerous to few-flowered inflorescence has tiny, inconspicuous, dull white, nerved flowers. The dorsal sepal is concave near its base and strongly recurved near the middle with the lateral sepals widespreading. The pale yellow, nerved, minute, shortly clawed (united with the lateral sepals), trilobed lip is bent backward, concave, and sparsely covered with small, soft protuberances. The flowers have a curved, slender, club-shaped column with a narrow, sharply pointed rostellum.

PHYSOSIPHON

Lindley

Edwards's Bot. Reg. **21**: sub 1797 (1835).

ETYMOLOGY: Greek for bellows or bladder and tube. Referring to the basally inflated tube formed by the united sepals.

LECTOTYPE: *Physosiphon loddigesii* Lindley nom. illeg.
This type name is now considered a synonym of
Stelis tubata Loddiges

Now recognized as belonging to the genus *Stelis*, *Physosiphon* was previously considered to include thirty-one epiphytes widespread in mid to upper elevation, oak-pine forests from southern Mexico to Brazil. These often yellow-green plants have erect stems, subtended by tubular sheaths, each with a solitary, fleshy or leathery leaf. The several, long, few-flowered inflorescences have small flowers ranging from green-yellow to brick-red. The sepals are joined for more than half of their length, forming an inflated tube that is spreading or constricted at the mouth. The minute petals are enclosed within. The tiny, entire or trilobed lip is joined to the base of the column or column foot. The flowers have a small, erect or slightly curved column.

PHYSOSYPHON

An orthographic variant introduced in *Bot. Centralbl.*, **70**(19-20): 216 (1897). The correct spelling is *Physosiphon*.

PHYSOTHALLIS

Garay

Svensk Bot. Tidskr. **47**: 199 (1953).

ETYMOLOGY: A combination of the orchid genera names of *Physosiphon* and *Pleurothallis*. Refers to the combined characteristics of this species.

TYPE SPECIES: *Physothallis harlingii* Garay

Now recognized as belonging to the genera *Stelis* and *Pleurothallis*, *Physothallis* was previously considered to include three terrestrials or epiphytes found in upper elevation, montane cloud forests of southern Ecuador. These small, creeping plants have erect stems, subtended by tubular sheaths, each with a solitary, thickly textured, leathery leaf. The whip-like, few-flowered inflorescence has small, hard, waxy, yellow or purple flowers opening in succession. The dorsal sepal is united with lateral sepals at the base for two thirds of their length, and the tiny petals are tucked inside this cup. The green, fleshy, minute lip has a rounded tip. The flowers have a straight, club-shaped column.

PHYSURNS

An orthographic variant introduced in *Orchid.-Buch*, 77 (1892). The correct spelling is *Physurus*.

PHYSURUS

Richard

De Orchid. Eur. 33 (1817).

Name published without a description. Today this name is most often referred to *Erythrodes*.

PHYSURUS

Richard ex Lindley

Gen. Sp. Orchid. Pl. 501 (1840).

ETYMOLOGY: Greek for a bladder and tail. Refers to the long, bladder-like, swollen spur of the type species.

LECTOTYPE: *Physurus plantagineus*
(Linnaeus) Lindley
(*Satyrium plantagineum* Linnaeus)

Now recognized as belonging to the genera *Erythrodes* and *Microchilus*. *Physurus* was previously considered to include one hundred sixteen terrestrials found from Mexico to Panama and northern Brazil, northern India to southern

China and New Guinea to the southwestern Pacific Archipelago. These tall, stout plants have erect, unbranched stems with narrow to ovate, bright green leaves that are silver veined. The numerous-flowered inflorescence has small flowers with a concave dorsal sepal and widespreading lateral sepals. The entire or trilobed lip has a tubular spur with the tip shallowly bilobed.

PHYURUS

An orthographic variant introduced in *Enum. Phan. Born.*, 185 (1942). The correct spelling is *Physurus*.

PIERARDIA

Rafinesque
Fl. Tellur. **4**: 41 (1836)[1837].
Not *Pierardia* Roxburgh (1814) Euphorbiaceæ.

ETYMOLOGY: Named in honor of Francis Pierard (1763-1841), a British civil servant working in Chittagong, India who sent the type species to the Royal Botanic Garden in Calcutta, India.
TYPE SPECIES: *Pierardia bicolor* (Roxburgh) Rafinesque
(*Limodorum aphyllum* Roxburgh)
This type name is now considered a synonym of *Dendrobium aphyllum* (Roxburgh) C.E.C. Fischer; basionym
Limodorum aphyllum Roxburgh

Not validly published because of a prior use of the name, this homonym was replaced by *Dendrobium*.

PILEARIA

Lindley ex d'Orbigny
Dict. Univ. Hist. Nat. **9**: 170 (1847).

Name published without a description. Today this name is most often referred to as a section of *Aerides*.

PILOPHYLLUM

Schlechter
Orchideen (Schlechter), ed. 1 131 (1914).
ETYMOLOGY: Greek for felt or hairy and leaf. Descriptive of the felt-like or densely hairy surface texture of the leaves.
TYPE SPECIES: *Pilophyllum villosum*
(Blume) Schlechter
(*Chrysoglossum villosum* Blume)

Now generally recognized as belonging to the genus *Chrysoglossum*, *Pilophyllum* was previously considered to include two terrestrials found in dense, low to mid elevation, woodlands and montane forests of Malaysia, Indonesia (Java and Borneo), New Guinea, the Philippines and the Solomon

Islands. These large plants have above-ground pseudobulbs, each with a solitary, large leaf that is densely covered in soft hairs, giving it the appearance of a golden velvety sheen. The dark red, numerous-flowered inflorescence, also covered in woolly brown hairs, has golden-yellow flowers with dark purple and crimson markings in the center of the petals and sepals. The white, purple spotted, mobile, trilobed lip has narrow side lobes, and the midlobe has two keels with a rounded tip. The flowers have an erect, forward curved, slender, winged column.

PILUMNA

Lindley
Edwards's Bot. Reg.
30(Misc.): 73, section no. 74 (1844).
ETYMOLOGY: Latin for pestle or pounder. Referring to the pestle shaped column.
Or possibly in reference to Pilum, a military javelin with a thin metal shank which allowed it to penetrate shields.
TYPE SPECIES: *None designated*

Now recognized as belonging to the genus *Trichopilia*, *Pilumna* was previously considered to include five epiphytes or terrestrials found in wet, mid elevation, montane forests of Hispaniola, Cuba, the Guianas, Venezuela and Colombia to Bolivia. These plants have clustered, slightly compressed pseudobulbs, each with a solitary, leathery leaf. The long, hanging, solitary to few-flowered inflorescence has pale green, red-brown spotted floral bracts, and pale green to creamy colored, waxy, fragrant, long-lasting flowers. The large, white, trilobed or obscurely trilobed lip has a basal margin upturned around the column and a pale yellow or orange, central splash.

PINALIA

Buchanan-Hamilton ex D. Don
Prodr. Fl. Nepal. 31 (1825).

Name published without a description. Today this name is most often referred to *Eria*.

PINALIA

Buchanan-Hamilton ex Lindley
Orchid. Scelet. 14, 21, 23, *t. 71* (1826).
Not *Pinalia* D. Don (1825) Orchidaceae, and not *Pinelia* Lindley (1853) Orchidaceae.
ETYMOLOGY: Latin for pine. Referring to the narrow, shaped sepals and petals.
TYPE SPECIES: *None designated*

Not validly published because of a prior use of the name, this homonym was replaced by the genus *Eria* as a section.

PINELEA

Willis
Man. Dict. Fl. Pl., ed. 4 513 (1914).

Name published without a description. Today this name is most often referred to *Restrepia*.

PINELIA

Lindley
Fol. Orchid. **4**: Pinelia, 1 (1853).
Not *Pinellia* Tenore (1839) Araceæ.
ETYMOLOGY: Dedicated to Chevalier Pinel (*fl.* 1850s), a French merchant based in Rio de Janeiro, who collected orchids and other plants in the Cantagalo region of southeastern Brazil for French florists.
TYPE SPECIES: *Pinelia hypolepta* Lindley

Now recognized as belonging to the genus *Homalopetalum*, *Pinelia* was previously considered to include four epiphytes found in mid elevation, montane forests from Cuba, Hispaniola, southern Venezuela (Bolivar) to southeastern, coastal Brazil (Rio de Janeiro to São Paulo). These whole, minute plants seldom exceed one-half inch (1 cm) in height. The minute, roundish to ovate pseudobulbs each have a solitary, fleshy leaf but bear proportionately large-sized flowers for their small stature. The thin, wiry, solitary-flowered inflorescence has a white, pale yellow to green-yellow flower, which does not open widely, with usually slightly narrow petals and sepals. The entire to trilobed lip is adorned with calli near the base. The flowers have a short, fleshy, broadly winged column.

PINELIANTHE

Rauschert
Feddes Repert. **94**(7-8) 465 (1983).
ETYMOLOGY: *Pinelia*, a genus of orchids, and Greek for flower. Referring to a resemblance to *Pinelia*.
TYPE SPECIES: *Pinelianthe hypolepta*
(Lindley) Rauschert
(*Pinelia hypolepta* Lindley)

A superfluous name proposed as a substitute for these species, which are now included in *Homalopetalum*.

| Currently Accepted | Validly Published | Invalidly Published | Published Pre-1753 | Superfluous Usage | Orthographic Variant | Fossil |

O r c h i d   G e n e r a   • **304**

PIPERIA

Rydberg

Bull. Torrey Bot. Club **28**: 269, 632 (1901).

Orchidoideæ ✤ Orchideæ • Orchidinæ

ETYMOLOGY: Dedicated to Charles Vancouver Piper (1867-1926), a Canadian-born American taxonomist, agronomist, researcher at the Agricultural Experiment Station in Pullman, Washington and author of *Flora of the Northwest Coast Including the Areas West of the Cascade Mountains.*

LECTOTYPE: *Piperia elegans* (Lindley) Rydberg
(*Planthera elegans* Lindley)

Ten sympodial terrestrials are found in low to mid elevation, open forests and grasslands of the far eastern coastal regions Russia (Kamchatka), Aleutian Islands (Alaska), western Canada (British Colombia to Alberta), and the western United States (Washington, Idaho, Montana, Oregon to California) to northwestern Mexico (Baja California). These small plants form new tubers annually, producing a few bract-like leaves that fade long before the flower spike reaches maturity. These plants are taxonomically complex. The erect, tall or short, numerous to few-flowered inflorescence has small, green, green-white to yellow-green flowers often opening simultaneously. The lateral sepals are partly united to the base of the fleshy, entire lip which is united to the column. The swollen, thread-like to club-shaped spur is often longer than the lip but is not easily seen due to the close overlapping of the flowers. The flowers have a short, footless, and wingless column.

PISCATORIA

Norich & Tangor

Orchid. Cult. Protect. **34**(2): 12 (1998).

ETYMOLOGY: Greek for fish and twisted. Referring to this being a twisted tale.

TYPE SPECIES: *Piscatoria aprilensis* Norich & Tangor

Not validly published in fulfillment
of nomenclatural rules.
This was published as an April fool's spoof.

One terrestrial found in the eastern (Gulf) coastal forests of Mexico (Veracruz).

PITLOCNEMA

An orthographic variant introduced in *Orchid. Nepal,* 74 (1978). The correct spelling is *Ptilocnema.*

PITTIERELLA

Schlechter

Repert. Spec. Nov. Regni Veg. **3**: 80 (1906).

ETYMOLOGY: Dedicated to Henry François Pittier di Fábrega (1857-1905), a Swiss geographer and ethnologist, a botanical authority on tropical American flora, and author of numerous books on the flora of Costa Rica and Venezuela. And Latin for diminutive.

TYPE SPECIES: *Pittierella calcarata* Schlechter

Now recognized as belonging to the genus *Cryptocentrum,* *Pittierella* was previously considered to include one epiphyte common in mid elevation, montane cloud forests from Costa Rica to Panama. This plant has short stems, subtended by leaf bearing sheaths, each with several, distichous, narrow, leathery leaves. The wiry, solitary-flowered inflorescence, borne from the leaf axils, has a small, green-yellow, nocturnally fragrant flower with long, narrow sepals and tiny, blunt petals. The tiny, sharply pointed, entire or obscurely trilobed lip is united with the column foot, forming a small spur.

PITYPHYLLUM

Schlechter

Repert. Spec. Nov. Regni Veg. Beih. **7**: 162 (1920).

Epidendroideæ ✤ Cymbidieæ • Maxillariinæ

ETYMOLOGY: Greek for pine or fir tree and leaf. Refers to the tufted, little leaves that resemble pine needles.

Greek Mythology. Pitus was a nymph beloved by Pan. She fled to escape him and was transformed into a fir tree.

LECTOTYPE: *Pityphyllum antioquiense* Schlechter

Five uncommon, sympodial epiphytes are found in low to upper elevation, hill woodlands and montane forests from Venezuela and Colombia to Peru. These small plants have hanging, branching stems with large, shiny, dark green to brown, ribbed pseudobulbs, each with numerous, tiny, short, stiff, needle-like leaves. The pseudobulbs are completely subtended by brown sheaths that are fused to the bulb for most of its length and it has a hole at the tip through which the leaves emerge. The short, solitary-flowered inflorescence, borne between the bracts along the rhizome, has a tiny, white, pale cream, yellow to salmon-colored flower not opening widely with similar sepals, and tiny, sharply pointed petals. The small, entire lip is wedge to spear-shaped. The flowers have a short, straight to slightly curved, club-shaped, wingless, footless column.

PLACOSTIGMA

Blume

Fl. Javæ **1**: Praef. viii (1828).

ETYMOLOGY: Greek for flat, a plain or broad surface and point. Referring to the broad, pointed stigma.

TYPE SPECIES: *None designated*

Name published without a description. Today this name is most often referred to *Podochilus.*

PLAJUS

An orthographic variant introduced in *Syn. Pl. (D. Dietrich),* **5**: 74 (1852). The correct spelling is *Phaius.*

PLALANTHERA

An orthographic variant introduced in *Icon. Pl. Ind. Orient. (Wight),* **5**(1): 11 (1851). The correct spelling is *Platanthera.*

PLANTAGINIS

Dodoens

Fl. Coron. Herb. Hist. 210 (1578).

Pre-1753, therefore not validly published in fulfillment of nomenclatural rules; this name is most often referred to *Ophrys* or *Orchis.*

PLANTAGINORCHIS

Szlachetko

Richardiana **4**(2): 61 (2004).

ETYMOLOGY: *Plantago,* the genus of plantains, and Greek for orchid. Referring to both genera's love of growing near water.

TYPE SPECIES: *Plantaginorchis plantaginea*
(Lindley) Szlachetko
(*Habenaria plantaginea* Lindley)

Now recognized as belonging to the genus *Habenaria,* *Plantaginorchis* was proposed to include fifteen terrestrials found in damp to slightly boggy, low to mid elevation, open forest undergrowth, savannas and woodlands from Guinea to Cameroon, India, Sri Lanka, Bangladesh to southern China (Yunnan to Zhejiang), eastern Russia (Primorye), Korea, Japan, Indonesia (Sulawesi) and New Guinea. These often stout plants have erect, unbranched stems, each with several, large, deciduous, basal rosette leaves. The terminal, few-flowered inflorescence has small, dull green, pale green to white flowers. The broad, trilobed lip has notched side lobes that vary widely in shape, a small, narrow, pointed midlobe, and a long, curved spur.

PLANTANTHERA

An orthographic variant introduced in *Icon. Pl. Ind. Orient. (Wight)*, **2**: *tt. 919-920* (1851). The correct spelling is *Platanthera*.

PLANTENTHERA

An orthographic variant introduced in *Orchids India*, ed. 2, 278 (1999). The correct spelling is *Platanthera*.

PLANTHERA

An orthographic variant introduced in *Gazetteer Bombay*, 445 (1883). The correct spelling is *Platanthera*.

PLATANTERA

An orthographic variant introduced in *Deutsch. Mag. Garten- Blumenk.*, 85 (1864). The correct spelling is *Platanthera*.

PLATANTHERA

Richard

De Orchid. Eur. 20, 26, 35 (1817).
Name ICBN conserved.

Orchidoideæ ⚘ Orchideæ • Orchidinæ

ETYMOLOGY: Greek for broad or wide and anther. Refers to the unusually broad anther-bed or column.

LECTOTYPE: *Platanthera bifolia* (Linnaeus) Richard
(*Orchis bifolia* Linnaeus)

One hundred thirty-five sympodial terrestrials inhabit the northern temperate zones with a few species found in the western Pacific Archipelago tropics and even northern Africa (Morocco to Tunisia) but most species are found in low to upper elevation, woodlands, meadows, swamps to peat bogs and montane forests of Greenland, Canada and the United States to northern Mexico. These variable, small to large-sized plants have an erect to decumbent, leafless or leafy stems, each with numerous, narrow leaves. The erect, usually sparse to densely arranged, numerous to few-flowered inflorescence often has fragrant, pale green-white, green, bright orange, purple to yellow flowers varying considerably in size. The dorsal sepal and small petals usually converge, forming a hood over the broad, erect, short column. The broad, entire or obscurely trilobed lip ranges from beautifully fringed to having a simple or entire margin. The usually long to short, cylindrical to thread-like spur is sometimes club shaped above the middle, and curves downward.

NOTE: Most of the species are pollinated by hawk moths, but some species are self pollinating.

PLATANTHEROIDES

Szlachetko

Richardiana 4(3): 103 (2004).

ETYMOLOGY: *Platanthera*, a genus of orchids and Greek for being like. Referring to these species formerly being part of *Platanthera*.

TYPE SPECIES: *Platantheroides obtusa*
(Lindley) Szlachetko
(*Habenaria obtusa* Lindley)

Now recognized as belonging to the genus *Habenaria*, *Platantheroides* was proposed to include thirty-five terrestrials widespread in low to upper elevation, hill grasslands, montane forests, valleys and slopes from Ethiopia to South Africa, Ghana to Zambia, Madagascar, Pakistan, India (Kashmir to Arunachal Pradesh), Nepal, southern China (Xizang to Hainan), Myanmar to Vietnam, Taiwan, and the southeastern United States (south Florida), the Bahamas, Jamaica to Cuba, Venezuela and southern Mexico to northern Argentina. These often stout plants have erect, unbranched stems with a basal rosette of several, large leaves. The terminal, few to numerous-flowered inflorescence has small, dull green, yellow-green to white flowers with a concave dorsal sepal and deeply recurved lateral sepals forming a hood over the short, stout column. The broad, trilobed lip has notched side lobes that vary widely in shape and size, a small, narrow, pointed midlobe, which has a long, thin, curved spur.

PLATHANTHERA

An orthographic variant introduced in *Bull. Soc. Roy. Bot. Belgique*, **15**: 437 (1876). The correct spelling is *Platanthera*.

PLATYCLINIS

Bentham

J. Linn. Soc., Bot. **18**(110): 295 (1881).

ETYMOLOGY: Greek for broad or flat and a bed. Refers to the broad anther bed or clinandrium.

LECTOTYPE: *Platyclinis abbreviata*
(Blume) Bentham ex Hemsley
(*Dendrochilum abbreviatum* Blume)

Now recognized as belonging to the genus *Dendrochilum*, *Platyclinis* was previously considered to include thirty-eight epiphytes or lithophytes found in low to upper elevation, hill to montane forests of Malaysia, Thailand and Indonesia to the Philippines. These dainty, tufted plants have ovoid to oblong pseudobulbs, subtended by thin to papery, brown to green bracts, each with a solitary, narrow leaf. The plant often looks more like a clump of grass than an orchid. The long, draping, densely packed, numerous-flowered inflorescence has attractive, small, pale green-brown, green-yellow, pale red to white, fragrant flowers arranged in two distinct rows and has narrow sepals and petals. The trilobed or obscurely trilobed lip is often colored in a darker hue. The flowers have a short, slightly arched or curved column.

PLATYCLNIS

An orthographic variant introduced in *Enum. Phan. Born.*, 169 (1942). The correct spelling is *Platyclinis*.

PLATYCORYNE

Reichenbach *filius*

Bonplandia 3(15-16): 212 (1855).

Orchidoideæ ⚘ Orchideæ • Orchidinæ

ETYMOLOGY: Greek for broad or flat and a club. Refers to the broad, thickened rostellum.

TYPE SPECIES: *Platycoryne pervillei* Reichenbach f.

Seventeen sympodial terrestrials are found in seasonally wet, low to mid elevation, grasslands and marshes of western Ethiopia, Malawi, Zambia, Mozambique and Zimbabwe with a single species occurring in Madagascar. These showy, small, erect, colony-forming plants have stout, unbranched stems, each with grass-like leaves; the lower leaves are most often clustered, and those above are smaller, grading into bracts. The slender, solitary to few-flowered inflorescence usually has bright orange, yellow, green or rare white flowers bundled close together. The small, erect petals and concave dorsal sepal converge, forming a shallow hood. The small, hanging, tongue-like, entire to trilobed lip has entire or short side lobes, and a long, slender, tapering spur with a swollen tip that is usually tucked into the bracts. The flowers have a small, erect, club-shaped column.

PLATYCORYNOIDES

Szlachetko

Orchidee (Hamburg) **56**(2): 205 (2005).

ETYMOLOGY: Greek for broad or flat, a club and for being like or similar. Refers to a similarity to *Platycoryne*, an orchid genus.

TYPE SPECIES: *Platycorynoides hircina*
(Reichenbach f.) Szlachetko
(*Habenaria hircina* Reichenbach f.)

Recognized as belonging to the genus *Habenaria*, *Platycorynoides* was proposed to include six terrestrials found in low elevation, coastal woodlands, savannas, marshy

Currently Accepted   Validly Published   Invalidly Published   Published Pre-1753   Superfluous Usage   Orthographic Variant   Fossil

O r c h i d   G e n e r a   • **306**

grasslands or rocky slopes from Ethiopia, Rwanda, Angola, Kenya, Tanzania, Uganda and Namibia to eastern South Africa. These erect, stout plants have ovate to narrow leaves clasping the lower, unbranched stem. The long, densely packed, numerous-flowered inflorescence has rather small, green flowers with downward hanging, spreading or curved lateral sepals. The shallowly concave dorsal sepal and rounded, simple petals converge, forming a hood over the short, massive, cone-like column. The white, tongue-shaped, trilobed lip has tiny, narrow side lobes, a long, narrow midlobe, and a long, hanging spur with a distinctly swollen, knob-like tip. The above type name is now considered a synonym of *Habenaria epipactidea* Reichenbach f.

PLATYGLOTTIS

L.O. Williams

Ann. Missouri Bot. Gard. **29**: 345, *t. 34* (1942).

ETYMOLOGY: Greek for broad and tongue. Referring to the size of the lip.

TYPE SPECIES: *Platyglottis coriacea* L.O. Williams

Now recognized as belonging to the genus *Scaphyglottis*, *Platyglottis* was previously considered to include one epiphyte or terrestrial with a limited range in mid elevation, montane forests of western Panama (Coclé). This rather large, hanging plant has unbranched stems, subtended by leaf-sheaths, each with alternating, distichous, leathery leaves. The short, few-flowered inflorescence has nerved, green flowers. The concave dorsal sepal tapers to a point, and along with the smaller petals converge, forming a hood over the column. The broad, entire lip, attached to the tip of the column foot, has a wavy, green to pale pink margin, and a hairy callus.

PLATYLEPIS

A. Richard

Mém. Soc. Hist. Nat. Paris **4**: 34, *t. 6* (1828), and *Monogr. Orchid. Bourbon* 39, *t. 6* (1828).

Name ICBN conserved vs. *Erporkis* Thouars (1809); not *Platylepis* Kunth (1837) Cyperaceæ, and not *Platylepis* Saporta (1874) Fossil.

Orchidoideæ ◊ Cranichideæ • Goodyerinæ

ETYMOLOGY: Greek for broad or flat and a scale. Descriptive of the large, floral bracts.

LECTOTYPE: *Platylepis goodyeroides* A. Richard nom. illeg.
Platylepis occulta (Thouars) Reichenbach f.
(*Goodyera occulta* Thouars)

Ten insignificant, sympodial terrestrials or occasional lithophytes are found in shady, low to mid elevation, rain forests and humus-covered rocks from Ethiopia to South Africa, Madagascar, Comoros Islands, the Seychelles,

and New Guinea to Samoa and Tahiti. These erect plants have unbranched stems, usually creeping at the base, each with several, shiny, subrosulate or scattered leaves. The thick, hairy, numerous to few-flowered inflorescence has tiny, white flowers suffused pink or brown which usually do not open widely. The petals have a thinly textured appearance, and the dorsal sepal is somewhat hooded. The deeply concave to semi-tubular, trilobed lip, attached for a short length to the column margins, has long side lobes; the midlobe has one to two, irregularly curved appendages and has a rounded, recurved tip. The flowers have a long, slender column.

PLATYPUS

Small & Nash

Fl. S.E. U.S. 329, 1329 (1903).

ETYMOLOGY: Greek for broad and a foot. Referring to the broad shape of the column foot.

TYPE SPECIES: *Platypus papilliferus* Small
This type name is now considered a synonym of *Eulophia alta* (Linnaeus) Fawcett & Rendle;
basionym
Limodorum altum Linnaeus

Now recognized as belonging to the genus *Eulophia*, *Platypus* was previously considered to include two terrestrials found in low to mid elevation, marshes and roadsides from the south-eastern United States (Georgia to Florida), the Bahamas, Cuba to Trinidad, the Guianas, Venezuela, Mexico to Peru, Brazil to northern Argentina and even to tropical Africa. These tall plants, often up to six feet (2 m), have several, narrow, strongly veined, yellow-green, pleated leaves, borne from fleshy corms. The erect inflorescence, subtended by dry sheaths, has fragrant flowers that are extremely variable in color. The trilobed lip, hinged to the base of the short, erect, slightly curved column, is any shade of purple to green and white, and has a concave, sac-like base. The oblong side lobes curve upward and the midlobe curves downward with a wavy margin.

PLATYRHIZA

Barbosa Rodrigues

Gen. Sp. Orchid. **2**: 230, *t. 679* (1881).

Epidendroideæ ◊ Cymbidieæ • Oncidiinæ

ETYMOLOGY: Greek for broad and root. Referring to the broad, flattened roots.

TYPE SPECIES: *Platyrhiza quadricolor*
Barbosa Rodrigues

One uncommon, sympodial epiphyte is found in mid elevation, montane Atlantic rain forests of southeastern Brazil (São Paulo and Rio Grande do Sul) and are usually found sprinkled among the tree limb

mosses. These dwarf to minute, attractive, short-stemmed plants have flattened leaves with the bases subtended by overlapping leaf sheaths. The short, often hanging, few-flowered inflorescence has thinly textured, brightly colored, green-yellow, tiny flowers with equal sized and shaped segments. The bright yellow, trilobed lip has narrow, upward pointed side lobes, a broad, roundish midlobe with a tiny, recurved tip, and a small, sac-like spur. The flowers have a large, somewhat trumpet-shaped column that has a short foot with a pair of erect teeth.

PLATYRRHIZA

An orthographic variant introduced in *Nat. Pflanzenfam.*, **2**(6): 220 (1888). The correct spelling is *Platyrhiza*.

PLATYSMA

Blume

Bijdr. Fl. Ned. Ind. **7**: 295, *t. 43* (1825).

Not *Platysma* Nylander (1855) Lichens.

ETYMOLOGY: Greek for a flat object, plate or flat cake. Descriptive of the flat lip.

TYPE SPECIES: *Platysma gracile* Blume

Now recognized as belonging to the genus *Podochilus*, *Platysma* was previously considered to include one epiphyte found in moist, low to mid elevation, forests of Indonesia (Sumatra, Java, Bali and Borneo). This small, moss-like plant has long, branching stems, each with several, green or pale red, small leaves. The tiny, broad, pale rosy-red flower opens widely and is usually cross-shaped. The oblong, pointed petals spread out at right angles to the erect dorsal sepal with the lateral sepals converging at the bottom. The flowers have a tongue-shaped, entire lip with a brightly colored tip.

PLATYSTELE

Schlechter

Repert. Spec. Nov. Regni Veg. **8**: 565 (1910).

Epidendroideæ ◊ Epidendreæ • Pleurothallidinæ

ETYMOLOGY: Greek for broad or flat and column or style. Descriptive of the short, wide column that is dilated above.

TYPE SPECIES: *Platystele bulbinella* Schlechter
This type name is now considered a synonym of *Platystele compacta* (Ames) Ames;
basionym
Stelis compacta Ames

Ninety-one, small to minute, sympodial epiphytes, lithophytes or terrestrials are found in cool to wet, low to upper elevation, hill scrub and montane forests from southern Mexico, Belize to Bolivia, Venezuela,

Trinidad, the Guianas to southern Brazil and Cuba. These tufted, short-stemmed plants have a solitary, leathery leaf, each with several, tiny, white sheaths folded face to face at the base forming a conspicuous stalk. The tiny to small flowers appear in succession over a long period on a lengthening, numerous-flowered inflorescence. The thin, yellow-brown to red flowers are usually spotted and have a dark colored lip with a white to yellow, marginal fringe. The small to minute, entire, ovate or obscurely trilobed lip has a broad, dense callus and a sharp pointed tip. The flowers have a short to obscure, broad, winged or hooded column with a short foot.

PLATYSTYLIPARIS

Margońska

Richardiana   **7**(1): 35 (2007).

ETYMOLOGY: Greek for broad, column and *Liparis*, a genus of orchids. Refers to a similarity to *Liparis*.

TYPE SPECIES: *Platystyliparis decurrens*
(Blume) Margońska
(*Malaxis decurrens* Blume)

Recognized as belonging to the genus *Liparis*, *Platystyliparis* was proposed to include sixteen terrestrials found in mid to upper elevation, wet montane forests from India, Thailand to Malaysia, Indonesia to southern China (Yunnan), Korea, Japan and Taiwan. The small, erect plant has clustered, pear-shaped pseudobulbs, subtended by a few thin, dry sheaths, each with two fleshy leaves. The erect, few-flowered inflorescence has small, green flowers with broad sepals and narrow petals. The obscurely trilobed lip has small, rounded side lobes and a oblong midlobe. The flowers have a small, slightly curved column.

PLATYSTYLIS

Lindley

Gen. Sp. Orchid. Pl.   18 (1830).
Not *Platystylis* Sweet (1828) Fabaceæ.

ETYMOLOGY: Greek for broad or flat and pillar or style. Alluding to the margin of the column that is widened or expanded.

TYPE SPECIES: *None designated*

Not validly published because of a prior use of the name, this homonym was replaced by *Liparis*.

PLATYTHELIS

An orthographic variant introduced in *Cat. Pl. Vasc. Rep. Argentina*, **1**: 263 (1996). The correct spelling is *Platythelys*.

PLATYTHELYS

Garay

Bradea   **2**(28): 196 (1977).

Orchidoideæ ༖ Cranichideæ • Goodyerinæ

ETYMOLOGY: Greek for broad or flat and pertaining to a woman. In reference to the broad, flat rostellum.

TYPE SPECIES: *Platythelys querceticola* (Lindley) Garay
(*Physurus querceticola* Lindley)

Twelve rather small, sympodial terrestrials, semi-epiphytes or uncommon saprophytes are found in damp, low to mid elevation, swampy forests, along river banks, dense woodlands and limestone cliffs from the United States (south Florida to eastern Texas), the Bahamas, Cuba to Trinidad, Mexico to Bolivia, Venezuela, Brazil and northern Argentina. These small, creeping plants have rising upward or erect stems, each with several, small, yellow-green, silver-spotted leaves gradually reducing in size up the stem. The numerous to few-flowered inflorescence has fleshy, translucent, tiny, somewhat tubular, white to pale green flowers. The dorsal sepal and petals converge over the wedge-shaped, footless column. The white, concave, bilobed lip is more or less trilobed at the tip and has a sac-like, unequally swollen spur at the base.

PLECTORHIZA

An orthographic variant introduced in *Orchideen (Schlechter)*, ed. 3, **21**: 1283 (1988). The correct spelling is *Plectorrhiza*.

PLECTORRHIZA

Dockrill

Australasian Sarcanthinæ   27 (1967).

Epidendroideæ ༖ Vandeæ • Aeridinæ

ETYMOLOGY: Greek for plaited or twisted and a root. Descriptive of the distinctive appearance of the twisted tangle of crooked, wiry roots.

TYPE SPECIES: *Plectorrhiza tridentata* (Lindley) Dockrill
(*Cleisostoma tridentatum* Lindley)

Three monopodial epiphytes are found in low to mid elevation, coastal forests of eastern Australia (Queensland to Victoria) and Lord Howe Island, often found near running water. These hanging plants have numerous, tangled roots, and have narrow, sickle-shaped leaves spaced along the long, wiry stem. The lengthy, hanging, few-flowered inflorescence have small, fragrant, long-lasting, green, olive-green to dark brown flowers marked red-brown, The erect, narrow, forward curved dorsal sepal forms a hood over the short, erect, wingless column. The white, trilobed lip has long, narrow side lobes; the

wide midlobe has a blotch of green, is set at right angles to the column, and has a short, broad spur.

PLECTOSTYLIS

An orthographic variant cited in *Syn. Bot.*, 108 (1870). The correct spelling is *Pterostylis*.

PLECTRELMINTHES

An orthographic variant cited in *Index Raf.*, 104 (1949). The correct spelling is *Plectrelminthus*.

PLECTRELMINTHUS

Rafinesque

Fl. Tellur.   **4**: 42 (1836)[1837].

Epidendroideæ ༖ Vandeæ • Aerangidinæ

ETYMOLOGY: Greek for a spur and worm. Descriptive of the long, twisted, worm-shaped spur.

TYPE SPECIES: *Plectrelminthus bicolor*
Rafinesque nom. illeg.

Plectrelminthus caudatus (Lindley) Summerhayes
(*Angraecum caudatum* Lindley)

One short-stemmed, monopodial epiphyte is widespread in low elevation, woodlands from Guinea to the Cameroons usually in full sunlight. This showy plant has short, leafy (almost woody) stems, each with numerous, leathery, strap-shaped, distichous, close-set, bilobed leaves. The zig-zagged, hanging inflorescence, borne from the lower leaf axils, has distinctive, heavily textured, long-lived, fragrant, olive-green flowers suffused pale brown. The cream-colored, fan-shaped, entire lip is tipped pale green at the end of the long, tapering point. The long, twisted, coiled to cork-screwed, cylindrical spur is yellow-green. The flowers have a short, stout column.

PLECTROPHORA

H. Focke

Tijdschr. Wis-Natuurk. Wetensch. Eerste Kl. Kon. Ned. Inst. Wetensch.   **1**: 212 (1848).

Epidendroideæ ༖ Cymbidieæ • Oncidiinæ

ETYMOLOGY: Greek for a spur or spear point and to carry or bear. Referring to the long, tubular spur of the type species.

TYPE SPECIES: *Plectrophora iridifolia*
(Loddiges ex Lindley) H. Focke
(*Trichocentrum iridifolium* Loddiges ex Lindley)

Ten small, sympodial epiphytes are found in shady, low to mid elevation, hill scrub to montane forests ranging from Costa Rica to Bolivia, Venezuela,

Currently Accepted   Validly Published   Invalidly Published   Published Pre-1753   Superfluous Usage   Orthographic Variant   Fossil

Orchid Genera • **308**

the Guianas and Brazil. These plants have small, rounded pseudobulbs, subtended by pleated, leaf-like sheaths, each with a solitary, fleshy, dagger-shaped leaf. The several, solitary to few-flowered inflorescences, blooming in rapid succession, have large, attractive, white or yellow flowers with pale orange stripes. The large, bell-shaped, white, entire lip, sprinkled with red-brown spots, has radiating, red-gold lines with a splash of bright yellow inside, and a conspicuous, long, thick, tubular spur. The flowers have a small, stout, wingless, footless column.

PLECTRURUS

Rafinesque

Neogenyton   4 (1825).

ETYMOLOGY: Greek for twisted and tail. Referring to the long, slender, strongly upcurved spur of the lip.

TYPE SPECIES: *Plectrurus discolor* (Pursh) Rafinesque
(*Orchis discolor* Pursh)

Now recognized as belonging to the genus *Tipularia*, *Plectrurus* was previously considered to include one terrestrial found in low to mid elevation, hill scrub and montane deciduous forests of the eastern United States (New York to northern Florida and Ohio to eastern Texas). This erect plant has a solitary, velvety green leaf whose underside is a satiny purple. The leaf appears in the fall; in the spring it turns a dull red just before it withers. During the summer, a tall, erect, few-flowered inflorescence appears. The flimsy, purple-green flowers have a white, trilobed lip with small, rounded side lobes. The long, narrow midlobe spreads toward the notched tip, and has a long, slender spur.

PLECTURUS

An orthographic variant introduced in *Herb. Raf.*, 73 (1833). The correct spelling is *Plectrurus*.

PLEIONE

D. Don

Prodr. Fl. Nepal.   36 (1825).

Epidendroideæ ☙ Arethuseæ • Coelogyninæ

ETYMOLOGY: Greek for annual. Refers to the annual production of pseudobulbs, leaves and flowers.

Or Greek Mythology. Dedicated to *Pleione*, beloved by Atlas and the mother of his seven daughters known as the Pleiades. Orion, a giant hunter, pursued *Pleione* and her daughters as they were traveling across the desert. They prayed to the gods for rescue; their prayers were answered, and they were changed into doves. Later Zeus placed them in the sky as stars in the constellation Taurus and are often referred to as the seven sisters.

LECTOTYPE: *Pleione praecox* (Smith) D. Don
(*Epidendrum praecox* Smith)

Twenty cool-growing, dwarf sympodial terrestrials, epiphytes or lithophytes are found in mid to upper elevation, montane cloud forests, cliff faces and woodland margins with high rainfall from northern India (Kashmir to Assam) and Nepal with a few species extending into Taiwan, Myanmar to Vietnam and Thailand. The largest number of species are found in China (Xizang to Guangdong and Gansu to Hubei). These small, deciduous plants have clustered, rounded, cone or barrel-shaped pseudobulbous stems, each with one to two, narrowly oval, ribbed, pleated, deciduous leaves, borne at the tips of the bulbs which are usually withered by flowering time. The solitary or rarely two-flowered inflorescence, only one to two per bulb, has a short-lived, sometimes fragrant flower in a wide range of hues from bright rose, crisp white, clear yellow to pink with similar, narrow sepals and petals. The pale white to pink, somewhat trumpet-shaped, entire or obscurely trilobed lip, marked with dark colors, has a white, showy, callus ridge that is ornately frilled. The basal portion of the lip clasps the long, slender, arched, footless column.

PLEJONE

An orthographic variant cited in *Cat. Pl. (Warszewicz)*, 59 (1864). The correct spelling is *Pleione*.

PLEURANTHIUM

(Reichenbach f.) Bentham

J. Linn. Soc., Bot.   **18**(110): 312-313 (1881).

ETYMOLOGY: Greek for rib or side and a flower. Alluding to the placement of the flowers in the axis of the leaves.

LECTOTYPE: *Pleuranthium dendrobii*
(Reichenbach f.) Bentham & Hooker f.
(*Epidendrum dendrobii* Reichenbach f.)

Now recognized as belonging to the genera *Epidendrum* and *Maxillaria*, *Pleuranthium* was previously considered to include six epiphytes found from Cuba to Jamaica, the Guianas, Colombia and northern Brazil to Bolivia. These plants have long, slightly zig-zagged, erect stems that are leafy throughout, each with several, long, narrow leaves. The short, solitary-flowered inflorescence, borne from the leaf node, has a pink to white, small flower with widespreading, similar, narrow sepals and petals. The broad, trilobed lip, attached to the long column, has small, erect side lobes and a spear-shaped midlobe with a magenta basal splash.

PLEURANTHUS

An orthographic variant introduced in *Bot. Mitt. Tropen*, **2**: 13 (1888). The correct spelling is *Pleuranthium*.

PLEURETHALLIS

An orthographic variant introduced in *Cat. Descr. Orquid., Estac. Exp. Agron. Santiago, Cuba*, **60**: 122 (1938). The correct spelling is *Pleurothallis*.

PLEUROBLEPHARON

Kunze ex Reichenbach

Consp. Regn. Veg.   212a, 279 (1828).

ETYMOLOGY: Greek for rib or side and fringed.

TYPE SPECIES: *None designated*

Name published without a description. Today this name is most often referred to *Disa*.

PLEUROBLEPHARUM

An orthographic variant cited in *Etym.-Bot.-Handw.-Buch*, ed. 1, 706 (1852). The correct spelling is *Pleuroblepharon*.

PLEUROBOTRIUM

An orthographic variant introduced in *Dic. Etim. Orquid. Brasil.*, ed. 3, 180 (2005). The correct spelling is *Pleurobotryum*.

PLEUROBOTRYUM

Barbosa Rodrigues

Gen. Sp. Orchid.   **1**: 20, *t.* 98 (1877).

ETYMOLOGY: Greek for rib or side and bunch or cluster of grapes. Descriptive of the disposition of the flowers.

TYPE SPECIES: *Pleurobotryum atropurpureum*
Barbosa Rodrigues

Now recognized as belonging to the genus *Pleurothallis*, *Pleurobotryum* was previously considered to include seven epiphytes found in mid elevation, montane forests from southeastern Brazil to northern Argentina. These small, wiry plants have erect stems, subtended by compressed sheaths, each with a solitary, narrow, pencil-like, green to red leaf. The several, arching, solitary to few-flowered inflorescences, borne from the leaf axils, have intricate, dark purple to yellow flowers which do not open fully and are reminiscent of a bunch of hanging grapes. The above type name is now considered a synonym of *Pleurothallis teretifolia* Rolfe.

PLEUROPETALUM

Sprague

Bull. Misc. Inform. Kew **9**: 339 (1928).

Not *Pleuropetalum* J.D. Hooker (1846) Amaranthaceæ and not *Pleuropetalum* Sprague (1928) Asclepiadaceæ.

Name published without a description. This name was cited as belong to Orchidaceæ.

PLEUROPHALLIS

An orthographic variant introduced in *Bot. Centralbl.*, **70**(19-20): 216 (1897). The correct spelling is *Pleurothallis*.

PLEUROTALYS

An orthographic variant introduced in *Prakt. Stud. Orchid.*, 32 (1854). The correct spelling is *Pleurothallis*.

PLEUROTHALIS

An orthographic variant introduced in *J. Gener. Litter.*, 34 (1830). The correct spelling is *Pleurothallis*.

PLEUROTHALLIS

R. Brown

Hortus Kew., ed. 2   **5**: 211 (1813).

Epidendroideæ ❦ Epidendreæ • Pleurothallidinæ

ETYMOLOGY: Greek for side or rib and blossom or branch. Perhaps in reference to the many, rib-like stems that arise in dense tufts in most of the species.

TYPE SPECIES: *Pleurothallis ruscifolia*
(Jacquin) R. Brown
(*Epidendrum ruscifolium* Jacquin)

Without a doubt the largest orchid genus in the New World, it is estimated to be in excess of eight hundred, sympodial epiphytes, lithophytes or terrestrials. These species are extremely diverse in their vegetative habit and it is not uncommon to encounter a dozen or more different species on just a single tree trunk. They are found in low to upper elevation, hill woodlands and montane forests from the southeastern United States (southern Florida), southern Mexico to Panama, Venezuela, and Colombia to Bolivia, Brazil and Paraguay to northern Argentina with a few species scattered in the Caribbean basin. These plants range from minute, moss-like, erect plants to bushy structures, three feet (0.9 m) in height and have narrow, rib-like, solitary-leafed stems that tend to grow in dense clusters. The stems are subtended by tubular sheaths. The numerous, short to sometimes long, solitary to few-flowered inflorescence, borne from the leaf axils, has tiny flowers for the most part with extremely diverse colors and shapes. The sepals are usually larger than the petals. The small, entire, trilobed to five-lobed lip, attached to the base of the column, is tongue-shaped to ovate and has a pointed to rounded tip. The flowers have an erect to curved, slender to stout, winged to wingless column that is with or without a foot, whose anther can be exposed or hooded. The footed column can have a knob-like, stout foot. But the whole flower in most instances must be seen under magnification to be studied and appreciated.

NOTE: The boundaries of this huge and complex Pleurothallidinæ group are being been redefined using current DNA testing to reassess the numerous morphological characteristics into better organized clades.

PLEUROTHALLOPSIS

Porto & Brade

Arq. Inst. Biol. Veg.   **3**: 133 (1937).

Epidendroideæ ❦ Epidendreæ • Pleurothallidinæ

ETYMOLOGY: *Pleurothallis*, a genus of orchids and Greek for resemblance or likeness.

TYPE SPECIES: *Pleurothallopsis nemorosa*
(Barbosa Rodrigues) Porto & Brade
(*Lepanthes nemorosa* Barbosa Rodrigues)

Sixteen sympodial epiphytes, lithophytes or terrestrials are found in cool to warm, low to upper elevation, hill scrub to montane cloud forests from Guatemala to Bolivia, Venezuela and two small areas in southeastern Brazil. These small plants have erect stems, subtended by overlapping, red-brown sheaths, each with a solitary, leathery leaf. The several, solitary-flowered inflorescences have a creamy-white to red-brown, translucent flower which does not open fully. It has purple veins, and the small petals are not as large as the brown-red long, narrow lateral sepals. The tiny, pale colored, trilobed lip has a squarish tip with a triangular callus from the base to midway between midlobe with two slightly raised, basal calli. The flowers have a small, wingless, footless column.

PLEUROTHALLUS

An orthographic variant introduced in *Trimehri*, **1**: 60 (1882). The correct spelling is *Pleurothallis*.

PLEXAURA

An orthographic variant cited in *Etym.-Bot.-Handw.-Buch*, ed. 1, 707 (1852). The correct spelling is *Plexaure*.

PLEXAURE

Endlicher

Prodr. Fl. Norfolk.   30 (1833).

ETYMOLOGY: Latin for braided, plaited or twining and ear. Descriptive of the long, braided inflorescences.

TYPE SPECIES: *Plexaure limenophylax* Endlicher

Now recognized as belonging to the genera *Phreatia* and *Octarrhena*, *Plexaure* was previously considered to include five epiphytes found in low to mid elevation, hill forests of New Guinea, north-eastern Australia (Queensland), the Solomons, Christmas Island, Norfolk Island, Caroline Island, Wallis & Futuna and Vanuatu. These tiny, monopodial plants form small, tufted mats of well developed, but simple pseudo-bulbous stems, each with several, thinly textured, fleshy leaves arranged in a fan shape. The erect, numerous-flowered inflorescence has small, pale green to white flowers that open simultaneously but rarely widely. The flowers have a concave dorsal sepal, small petals, and widespreading lateral sepals. The flowers have a short, wingless, footed column.

PLICANGIS

Thouars

Hist. Orchid.   Table 2, sub 3o, t. 58 (1822).

Name published without a description. Today this name is most often referred to *Angraecum*.

PLIEONE

An orthographic variant introduced in *Orchids Sumatra*, 323 (2002). The correct spelling is *Pleione*.

PLOCAGLOTTIS

An orthographic variant cited in *Nomencl. Bot. (Steudel)*, ed. 2, **2**: 356 (1841). The correct spelling is *Plocoglottis*.

PLOCOGLOTTIS

Blume

Bijdr. Fl. Ned. Ind.   **8**: 380, t. 21 (1825).

Epidendroideæ ❦ Collabiinæ • Currently unplaced

ETYMOLOGY: Greek for binding, enfold or fastening and tongue. Alluding to the thin membrane that connects the lip to the base of the column.

TYPE SPECIES: *Plocoglottis javanica* Blume

Thirty-nine uncommon, sympodial terrestrials or rare epiphytes are found in shady, low to mid elevation, hill woodlands to montane forests and along river banks from the

Andaman Islands (India), Thailand to Cambodia, Malaysia to Indonesia, New Guinea and the Solomons to the Philippines. These attractive plants have narrow, roundish pseudobulbs, each with a solitary, stalked, pleated leaf or stem-like pseudobulbs. The pleated leaves are often mottled yellow or sometimes variegated with silver lines. The long, few-flowered, finely hairy inflorescence, borne from the base of the pseudobulb or stem, has well-spaced, small, yellow to orange flowers covered with red spots, opening widely, in succession over a long period of time, and often lasting for over four weeks. It is a highly distinctive genus that is easily recognized by the small, sensitive, hinged, entire lip that is attached to the sides and tip of the column foot forming a small sac at the base. This lip snaps upward against the rather short, erect, wingless column when touched and never returns to its original position unless forced.

PLOCOSTIGMA

Bentham

J. Linn. Soc., Bot. **18**(110): 338 (1881).

ETYMOLOGY: Latin for wicker work and and column. Refers to the erect column.

TYPE SPECIES: *None designated*

A superfluous name proposed as a substitute for *Podochilus*.

PLUMATICHILOS

Szlachetko

Polish Bot. J. **46**(1): 22 (2001).

ETYMOLOGY: Latin for feathered and Greek for a lip. An allusion to the wildly feathered lip that is characteristic of these species.

TYPE SPECIES: *Plumatichilos barbatus*
(Lindley) Szlachetko
(*Pterostylis barbata* Lindley)

Recognized as belonging to the genus *Pterostylis*, *Plumatichilos* was proposed to include four terrestrials found in sandy, low elevation, open forests of southwestern and extreme southeastern Australia, Tasmania and New Zealand. These tiny, erect plants have short, unbranched stems, each with a basal rosette of pale green or yellow leaves that have variegated, darker colored veins. The erect, wiry, solitary-flowered inflorescence has a translucent, pale green flower with dark green markings. The petals and lateral sepals are suffused purple-brown. The long, thread-like, entire lip is sparsely fringed with long, coarse, yellow hairs and has a club-shaped tip.

PLUMATICHILUS

An orthographic variant cited in *Orchideen (Schlechter): Liter. Reg. Band I/A, B, and C,* 169 (2003). The correct spelling is *Plumatichilos*.

PLUMATOCHILOS

An orthographic variant cited in *Handb. Orchid.-Namen*, 610 (2005). The correct spelling is *Plumatichilos*.

POAEPHYLLUM

Ridley

Mat. Fl. Malay. Penins. **1**: 108 (1907).

Epidendroideæ ⚘ Podochileæ • Podochilinæ

ETYMOLOGY: Greek for grass or pasture grass and leaf. Descriptive of the narrow, grass-like leaves.

TYPE SPECIES: *Poaephyllum pauciflorum*
(Hooker f.) Ridley
(*Agrostophyllum pauciflorum* Hooker f.)

Six uncommon, sympodial epiphytes, occasional lithophytes or terrestrials are found in misty, low to mid elevation, hill and montane forests, peaty swamps and along river banks of Malaysia, Indonesia and New Guinea. These plants vegetatively resemble some species of *Appendicula*. These tall plants have a creeping rhizome from which emerge large, slender, stiff stems that have narrow, distichous, pale green leaves with notched tips, and are arranged in two rows up the stem. The several, short, hairy, few-flowered inflorescences have minute to small, pale green, red, brown to white flowers not opening widely but in succession. The lateral sepals are united at the base forming a chin-like projection. The small, pale green sepals are similar and the sharply pointed petals have their tips turned backward. The white, fleshy, long-clawed, usually entire or trilobed lip, united to the column foot nearly all along its edges, has a sac-like base. The flowers have a short, dorsally flattened column.

PODANDRIA

Rolfe

Fl. Trop. Afr. **7**: 205 (1898).

Not *Podandra* Baillon (1890) Asclepiadaceæ.

ETYMOLOGY: Greek for a foot and man or stamen. An allusion to the elongate, stake-shaped anther.

TYPE SPECIES: *Podandria macrandra* (Lindley) Rolfe
(*Habenaria macrandra* Lindley)

Not validly published because of a prior use of the name, this homonym was replaced by *Podandriella*.

PODANDRIELLA

Szlachetko

Fl. Cameroun **34**: 194 (1998).

ETYMOLOGY: *Podandria*, a genus of orchids and Latin for diminutive.

TYPE SPECIES: *Podandriella macrandra*
(Lindley) Szlachetko & Olszewski
(*Habenaria macrandra* Lindley)

Now recognized as belonging to the genus *Habenaria*, *Podandriella* was proposed to include five terrestrials with one species widely distributed in low to mid elevation, evergreen forests and along river banks of Tanzania, Uganda, Malawi, Zaire, Mozambique and Zimbabwe. Other species are restricted to small areas of São Tomé and Principe, Cameroon and the Congo. These erect plants have short, unbranched stems, each with a basal rosette of narrow leaves. The few-flowered inflorescence has large, showy, pale green or green and white flowers opening widely. The erect, narrow dorsal sepal and narrow to thread-like petals converge, forming a hood. The trilobed lip, united to the column base, has thread-like side lobes that are incised deeply like a comb, and it has a green, thread-like, yellow tipped spur that either points downward or has a backward curl.

PODANGIS

Schlechter

Beih. Bot. Centralbl. **36**(2): 82 (1918).

Epidendroideæ ⚘ Vandeæ • Aerangidinæ

ETYMOLOGY: Greek for a foot and a vessel or cup. In reference to the foot-like spur of the lip.

TYPE SPECIES: *Podangis dactyloceras*
(Reichenbach f.) Schlechter
(*Listrostachys dactyloceras* Reichenbach f.)

One uncommon, monopodial epiphyte or occasional lithophyte is found in low to mid elevation, evergreen rain forests often near waterfalls or rivers and seems to be rather widespread from Guinea to Angola and Tanzania. This interesting plant has short, sometimes branching stems, subtended completely by folded leaf bases, each with several, stiff, brittle, flattened, distichous, sickle-shaped, fleshy leaves arranged in a fan-like shape. The densely packed, few-flowered inflorescence has powder-puff bunches of translucent, glistening white, long-lasting, cup-shaped flowers. The concave, entire lip is swollen at the bilobed tip and has a long, nearly straight spur with a broad mouth that is often lobed at the tip. The flowers have a short, erect, wingless, footless column.

PODANTHERA

Wight

Icon. Pl. Ind. Orient. (Wight) **5**(1): 22, *t. 1759* (1851).

ETYMOLOGY: Greek for a foot and anther. Descriptive of the arched crest-like foot of the anther.

TYPE SPECIES: *Podanthera pallida* Wight

This type name is now considered a synonym of
Epipogium roseum (D. Don) Lindley;
basionym
Limodorum roseum D. Don

Now recognized as belonging to the genus *Epipogium*, *Podanthera* was previously considered to include one saprophyte found in low to mid elevation, moist, shady woodlands from Ghana to Angola, northern India, southern China, Japan, Taiwan, Thailand to Indonesia, the Philippines, eastern Australia (Queensland to New South Wales) and the southwestern Pacific Archipelago. This erect plant has thick, scaly, leafless, unbranched stems. The few to numerous-flowered, pale pink inflorescence has variable, large, white or pale green, delicate flowers sometimes pink flushed or with several, purple-brown markings and spots. The upturned, entire lip has two rows of minute warts down the center and has a notched margin, and a small, cone-like spur.

PODOCHILOPSIS

Guillaumin

Bull. Mus. Hist. Nat. (Paris), sér. 2
34(5): 478 (1963).

ETYMOLOGY: *Podochilus*, a genus of orchids and Greek for resemblance or likeness.

TYPE SPECIES: *Podochilopsis dalatensis* Guillaumin

Now recognized as belonging to the genus *Adenoncos*, *Podochilopsis* was previously considered to include one epiphyte found in dry, low elevation, semi-deciduous, deciduous forests and woodlands of Thailand, Vietnam and Malaysia. This small, erect plant has short, rigid, unbranched stems, each with several, small to minute, oblong, fleshy leaves. The short, solitary to few-flowered inflorescence has equally small, pale green, yellow to yellow-green flowers with widespreading sepals and petals. The broad, concave, entire lip is immovability attached to the short, footless column, and has an inward curved margin. The above type name is now considered a synonym of *Adenoncos vesiculosa* Carr.

PODOCHILUS

Blume

Bijdr. Fl. Ned. Ind. **7**: 295, *t. 12* (1825).

Epidendroideæ ⚬ Podochileæ • Podochilinæ

ETYMOLOGY: Greek for a foot and lip. In reference to the two appendages at the base of the lip.

TYPE SPECIES: *Podochilus lucescens* Blume

About sixty small, mostly moss-like, sympodial epiphytes, lithophytes or uncommon terrestrials are found in humid, low elevation, evergreen scrub and forests with a widespread range from Sri Lanka, India and New Guinea to the southwestern Pacific Archipelago. These creeping plants often form dense mats on trees or rocks. The long, thin, tufted, leafy, simple or branching stems are completely subtended by leaf sheaths. The numerous, short, distichous leaves are arranged in two rows that are flat or sometimes laterally incurved, often twisted at the base. The short, numerous to few-flowered inflorescence has flowers produced in rapid succession over a period of many months. The tiny, tubular, white or green flowers, not opening fully, have purple blotches, and turn yellow as they age. The narrow, entire or obscurely trilobed lip has a basal disc with a simple or bilobed appendage. The flowers have a short to obscure, footless column that is laterally united to the lateral sepals forming a spur-like protuberance.

PODOCHYLUS

An orthographic variant introduced in *Gen. Pl., Suppl. 3 (Endlicher)*, 62 (1843). The correct spelling is *Podochilus*.

POGOCHILUS

Falconer

J. Bot. (Hooker) **4**(26): 73 (1842).

ETYMOLOGY: Greek for beard and lip. Referring to the soft flexible hairs commonly found on the lip.

TYPE SPECIES: *None designated*

Name published without a description. Today this name is most often referred to *Galeola*.

POGOINA

An orthographic variant introduced in *Orchids Burma*, 355 (1895). The correct spelling is *Pogonia*.

POGONIA

Jussieu

Gen. Pl. (Jussieu) 65 (1789).

Not *Pogonia* Andrews (1802) Myoporaceæ.

Vanilloideæ ⚬ Pogoniieæ

ETYMOLOGY: Greek for bearded. In reference to the prominent, hair-like crest of the lip.

LECTOTYPE: *Pogonia ophioglossoides*
(Linnaeus) Ker Gawler
(*Arethusa ophioglossoides* Linnaeus)

Seven small, sympodial terrestrials are found in low to upper elevation, wet meadows, scrub, swampy bogs and prairies of Canada (Ontario and Quebec to Newfoundland) and the eastern United States (Maine to eastern Texas), eastern Russia (Amur to the Kuril Islands) Mongolia, China (Heilongjiang to Sichuan and Xizang to Jiangxi), Taiwan, Korea, Japan and eastern Indonesia (Maluku). These erect, unbranched plants, often forming large colonies, have small, ovate leaves placed midway on the purple-green, fragile stem or a solitary leaf produced by the underground shoots. The slender, hollow, solitary to few-flowered inflorescence has showy, rose, white or green-pink, fragrant flowers opening widely and lasting for just a few days. The floral color and shape vary greatly from colony to colony. The sepals are widespreading and the similarly shaped petals curve inward over the long, wingless, footless column. The oblong, rose to white, erect, entire or trilobed lip, inrolled around the long column, has its margin irregularly and deeply notched. There are short, yellow-white bristles along the three, central veins, and it has a large mass of deep rose bristles or fringes toward the tip.

POGONIOPSIS

Reichenbach *filius*

Otia Bot. Hamburg., fasc. 1 82 (1881).

Vanilloideæ ⚬ Pogoniieæ

ETYMOLOGY: *Pogonia*, a genus of orchids and Greek for resemblance or likeness. Referring to a similarity to *Pogonia*.

TYPE SPECIES: *Pogoniopsis nidus-avis* Reichenbach f.

Two uncommon, sympodial terrestrials are found in low to mid elevation, Atlantic coastal forests, scrub and along river banks of southeastern Brazil (São Paulo, Rio de Janeiro and Minas Gerais) in decaying leaf litter. These dwarf, leafless plants have thick, red-brown to yellow stems, each with several, scale-like, golden-brown bracts. The erect, congested, few-flowered inflorescence has medium-sized, green-white to pale yellow-brown flowers, each subtended by large, yellow

Currently Accepted   Validly Published   Invalidly Published   Published Pre-1753   Superfluous Usage   Orthographic Variant   Fossil

O r c h i d   G e n e r a • **312**

bracts. The white petals converge, forming a hood over the short, slightly dilated, winged column. The white, trilobed lip has orange grooves or lines, erect side lobes, and the long midlobe is lacerated along its margin.

POICILANTHE

Schlechter

Notizbl. Bot. Gart. Berlin-Dahlem **9**(88): 588 (1926).

ETYMOLOGY: Latin for colorful and flower. Refers to the variously colored flowers.

TYPE SPECIES: *None designated*

Name published without a description. Today this name is most often referred to *Cymbidium*.

POLCYCNIS

An orthographic variant introduced in *Cat. Samm. Ausstell.*, 120 (1869). The correct spelling is *Polycycnis*.

POLIDOTA

An orthographic variant introduced in *Hort. Universel*, **1**(2): 39 (1847). The correct spelling is *Pholidota*.

POLINIRHIZA

An orthographic variant introduced in *Orchideen (Schlechter)*, ed. 1, 95 (1914). The correct spelling is *Pollinirhiza*.

POLISTACHIA

An orthographic variant introduced in *Prakt. Stud. Orchid.*, 52 (1854). The correct spelling is *Polystachya*.

POLISTECKIA

An orthographic variant introduced in *Jorn. Sci. Math. Phys. Nat.*, **4**(14): 184 (1873). The correct spelling is *Polystachya*.

POLLARDIA

Withner & P.A. Harding

Cattleyas & Relatives **7**(Suppl.): 217 (2004).

ETYMOLOGY: Honoring Glenn E. Pollard (1901-1976), an American-born steel strapping manager who retired to Mexico, collected the flora of Mexico extensively and was a co-author of *The Genus Encyclia in Mexico* with Robert Louis Dressler.

TYPE SPECIES: *Pollardia livida*
(Lindley) Withner & P.A. Harding
(*Epidendrum lividum* Lindley)

Now recognized as belonging to the genus *Prosthechea*, *Pollardia* was proposed to include sixteen epiphytes found in humid to seasonally dry, low to mid elevation, oak-pine forests, cacti and scrub from central Mexico to Peru and Venezuela. These small to tiny plants form mats on cacti, trees or rocks in semi-shade to full sunlight. These plants have small, oblong to spindle-shaped, clustered, slightly compressed pseudobulbs, partially subtended by thin, dry sheaths or papery bracts, each with two minutely bilobed to sharply pointed, thinly textured leaves. The occasionally branched, few-flowered inflorescence, borne from a mature pseudobulb, has pale green to yellow flowers heavily suffused with brown. The trilobed lip has red-brown veins, the side lobes partially clasping the short column, and the creamy midlobe has a wavy margin.

NOTE: These species were formerly included in *Encyclia, Epidendrum* and *Anacheilium*.

POLLINIRHIZA

Dulac

Fl. Hautes-Pyrénées 120 (1867).

ETYMOLOGY: *Pollinia*, a genus of grasses and Greek for root. Referring to the roots being similar to *Pollinia*.

Or possibly dedicated to Ciro Pollini (1782-1833), an Italian professor of botany at Verona and author of several works on northern Italy's flora.

TYPE SPECIES: *None designated*

Now recognized as belonging to the genus *Neottia*, *Pollinirhiza* was previously considered to include two terrestrials widely distributed in low to mid elevations of the northern hemisphere from Greenland, Iceland, Norway to throughout Russia, Denmark to France, Romania to Kazakhstan, Japan to Alaska (US), Canada (British Colombia to Nova Scotia) and the United States (Maine to western North Carolina and Washington to central Colorado). These small plants are mostly found in wet, spongy, sphagnum bogs, woodlands, scrub or fens. The erect plants have slender, unbranched stems, each with two ovate leaves opposite each other, midway up the stem. The few-flowered inflorescence has tiny, green to red-brown flowers with small segments bent forward. The

long, bilobed to trilobed lip has a grooved nectary down the center.

POLYBACTRUM

Salisbury

Monthly Rev. **75**: 80 (1814).

ETYMOLOGY: Greek for many and a cane or walking staff. Refers to the numerous, small flowers that are reminiscent of walking sticks.

TYPE SPECIES: *None designated*

A superfluous name proposed as a substitute for *Pseudorchis*.

POLYCHILOS

Breda

Gen. Sp. Orchid. Asclep., fasc. I   t. 1 (1828).

ETYMOLOGY: Greek for many and a lip. In reference to the conspicuously lobed lip and the appendage, thus giving an appearance of having several lips.

TYPE SPECIES: *Polychilos cornu-cervi* Breda

Now recognized as belonging to the genus *Phalaenopsis*, *Polychilos* was previously considered to include forty epiphytes found in heavy dewed, low elevation, exposed forests ranging from India, Myanmar and Thailand to Indonesia (Borneo). These plants have short stems, subtended by overlapping leaf bases, each with several, semi-deciduous, oblong leaves. The simple or branched inflorescences are laterally compressed. The small, fleshy, waxy, long-lasting, fragrant, yellow-green, red-purple to magenta flowers are often heavily marked with red-brown bars, spots and blotches. The shortly clawed, white, yellow or magenta, trilobed lip has oblong, spreading side lobes, and the wedge-shaped midlobe has a central ridge merging into a rounded callus at the tip. The flowers have a fleshy, curved, wingless column.

POLYCHILUS

An orthographic variant introduced in *Hort. Franc.*, ser. 2, **6**: 95 (1864). The correct spelling is *Polychilos*.

POLYCICNIS

An orthographic variant introduced in *Cat. Samm. Ausstell.*, 173 (1869). The correct spelling is *Polycycnis*.

POLYCYCCNIS

An orthographic variant introduced in *Fl. Analítica Fitogeogr. Estado São Paulo*, **6**: 1260 (1973). The correct spelling is *Polycycnis*.

POLYCYCNIS

Reichenbach *filius*

Bonplandia **3**(15-16): 218 (1855).

Epidendroideæ ◊ Cymbidieæ • Stanhopeinæ

ETYMOLOGY: Greek for many and a swan. Alluding to a fanciful resemblance of the flower to a small swan.

TYPE SPECIES: *None designated*

Seventeen uncommon, variable species make up this oddly interesting genus of sympodial epiphytes or sometime terrestrials found in humid, densely shaded, low to mid elevation, hill scrub, roadside banks and montane forests from Costa Rica to Bolivia and Brazil. These plants have short, fleshy, subcylindrical to ovoid pseudobulbs, subtended by overlapping, basal sheaths, each with a solitary or several, large leaves borne at the tip. The erect to hanging, numerous to few-flowered inflorescence, borne from the pseudobulb base, has short-lived, fragrant, translucent, brown-red, often densely spotted flowers that are hairy on the outer surfaces. The white to green, obscurely to deeply trilobed lip, attached to the base of the column, has narrow, rounded side lobes. The diamond-shaped to narrow midlobe has a central, fleshy callus. The flowers have a long, slender, arched, footless, sometimes winged column.

POLYCYNIS

An orthographic variant introduced in *Orquideologia*, **10**(2): 181 (1975). The correct spelling is *Polycycnis*.

POLYCYCNOPSIS

Szlachetko

Polish Bot. J. **51**(1): 34 (2006)[2007].

ETYMOLOGY: *Polycycnis*, a genus of orchids, and Greek for like or appearance.

TYPE SPECIES: *Polycycnopsis aurita*
(Dressler) Szlachetko
(*Polycycnis aurita* Dressler)

Recognized as belonging to the genus *Polycycnis*, *Polycycnopsis* was proposed to include four epiphytes found in humid, low to mid elevation, hill to montane forests of Surinam, Venezuela, Colombia (Chocó), Ecuador and western Panama. These plants have fleshy, ovoid pseudobulbs, subtended by papery bracts, each with a solitary (rarely three), narrow, pleated leaf. The hairy, hanging, few-flowered inflorescence has small, pale red-brown, yellow to buff, fragrant flowers spotted to barred red-brown or dark pink. The trilobed lip, united to the base of the column, has narrow, ear-like side lobes, the narrow, pointed to tapering midlobe is entire or obscurely trilobed has has a narrow, basal callus. The flowers have a long, slender, arched, footless column.

POLYDENDRIS

Thouars

Hist. Orchid. Table 3, sub 3q, *t.* 85 (1822).

Name published without a description. Today this name is most often referred to *Polystachya*.

POLYEYENIS

An orthographic variant cited in *Orchid. Lex.*, ed. 1, 3 (1969). The correct spelling is *Polycycnis*.

POLYOTIDIUM

Garay

Bot. Mus. Leafl. **18**: 105 (1958).

Epidendroideæ ◊ Cymbidieæ • Oncidiinæ

ETYMOLOGY: Greek for many and small ear. An allusion to the several, ear-like appendages on the column.

TYPE SPECIES: *Polyotidium huebneri* (Mansfeld) Garay
(*Hybochilus huebneri* Mansfeld)

One uncommon epiphyte is found in low elevations of the Amazon River basins of Venezuela, Colombia, Ecuador and northwestern Brazil (Amazonas). This dwarf plant has small, ovoid, somewhat elongate pseudobulbs, completely subtended by thin, dry, tapering sheaths, each topped by a long, dark green, narrow, leathery leaf flecked with shades of even darker green. The long, few-flowered inflorescence, borne from the pseudobulb tip, has small, bright orange or red, nondescript flowers. The strongly concave dorsal sepal tapers to a blunt point and covers the small, club-shaped, winged column. The partially united lateral sepals form a chin-like protuberance at the base. The long, trilobed lip is notched at the tip and has a large, erect tooth in the middle.

POLYRADICION

Garay

J. Arnold Arbor. **50**(3): 466 (1969).

ETYMOLOGY: Latin for many or numerous and slim roots. Referring to the numerous roots, originating from a central point of this leafless plant.

TYPE SPECIES: *Polyradicion lindenii* (Lindley) Garay
(*Angraecum lindenii* Lindley)

Now recognized as belonging to the genus *Dendrophylax*, *Polyradicion* was previously considered to include three unique, leafless epiphytes found in low elevation, dense, swampy forests ranging from the United States (southern Florida), the Bahamas, Cuba and Hispaniola. These plants have short stems, each with numerous, long, chlorophyllous, green roots that radiate out from a central hub. The solitary or rarely two large, striking white flowers suffused green, are produced in succession on long, wiry inflorescences. The long, narrow sepals and petals are similarly shaped and widespreading. The trilobed lip has a long, arching spur, small side lobes, and a triangular midlobe with two deeply bilobed, lateral, tapering, twisted tails. The flowers have a short, thick, white column.

POLYRHIZA

An orthographic variant cited in *Lex. Gen. Phan.*, 455 (1904). The correct spelling is *Polyrrhiza*.

POLYRRHIZA

Pfitzer

Nat. Pflanzenfam. **2**(6): 208, 215 (1889).

ETYMOLOGY: Greek for many and root. In reference to the quite extensive and conspicuous roots.

TYPE SPECIES: *Polyrrhiza funalis* (Lindley) Pfitzer
(*Angraecum funale* Lindley)

Not validly published, this name is most often referred to *Dendrophylax*.

POLYSTACHA

An orthographic variant introduced in *Hamburger Garten- Blumenzeitung*, **4**: 214 (1858). The correct spelling is *Polystachya*.

POLYSTACHIA

An orthographic variant introduced in *Nat. Pflanzen-Syst.*, 197 (1829). The correct spelling is *Polystachya*.

Currently Accepted | Validly Published | Invalidly Published | Published Pre-1753 | Superfluous Usage | Orthographic Variant | Fossil

Orchid Genera • **314**

POLYSTACHYA

Hooker

Exot. Fl. **2**(10): *t. 103* (1824).

Name ICBN conserved vs. *Dendrorkis* Thouars (1809) Orchidaceæ.

Epidendroideæ 🌿 Vandeæ • Polystachyinæ

ETYMOLOGY: Greek for many and ear of grain or spike. From the many branchlets that make up the inflorescence in some species and which may resemble spikes of wheat.

LECTOTYPE: *Polystachya luteola* Hooker nom. illeg.

Epidendrum minutum Aublet

This type name is now considered a synonym of *Polystachya concreta* (Jacquin) Garay & H.R. Sweet; basionym *Epidendrum concretum* Jacquin

More than two hundred twenty-four sympodial epiphytes, lithophytes or rare terrestrials are found in low to upper elevation, evergreen rain forests, montane meadows, woodlands and grasslands. Their highly diverse distribution has the vast majority of the species found in tropical Africa (Guinea to Zimbabwe), Madagascar, Réunion and the Seychelles. Several species even extend into the Americas from the United States (southern Florida), Cuba, Hispaniola, Mexico southward to Brazil and northern Argentina with a few species also found from Thailand to Vietnam, Indonesia and the Philippines. These small to large, clump-forming plants have erect stems that are often pseudobulbous or have spindle-shaped, long or flattened, erect to hanging pseudobulbs. The few to several, usually thinly textured, leathery to fleshy leaves are found at the tip. They are often distichous and are narrow to oblong with shallowly notched tips. The erect, arching to hanging, simple to branched, few to numerous-flowered inflorescence has diversely shaped bracts. The fairly large to minute, but generally small, rarely showy white, green, yellow, orange, purple, pink or uncommon red flowers are usually hairy on the outside with petals smaller than the sepals. The entire or trilobed lip, usually uppermost, is united to the column foot, is with or without a small to large, hairy basal callus that is often fleshy and recurved. The flowers have a short, stout column with a more or less elongated foot.

NOTE: This genus has numerous diverse vegetative forms ranging from small to medium-sized and inverted, hood-shaped flowers.

POLYSTACHYIA

An orthographic variant cited in *Hist. Nat. Veg. (Spach)*, **12**: 176 (1846). The correct spelling is *Polystachya*.

POLYSTEPIS

Thouars

Hist. Orchid. Table 3, sub 3p, *t. 82* (1822).

Name published without a description. Today this name is most often referred to *Oeoniella*.

POLYSTYLUS

Hasselt ex Hasskarl

Retzia **1**: 3 (1855).

ETYMOLOGY: Greek for many and column. An allusion to the appendaged lip which has the appearance of having numerous segments.

TYPE SPECIES: *Polystylus cornu-cervi*
(Breda) Hasselt ex Hasskarl
(*Polychilos cornu-cervi* Breda)

Now recognized as belonging to the genus *Phalaenopsis*, *Polystylus* was previously considered to include one epiphyte found in low elevation, dense, open or exposed forests with heavy dew from India, Myanmar and Thailand to Indonesia (Borneo). This plant has short stems, subtended by overlapping leaf bases, each with several, distichous, broad or oval, often drooping, olive-green leaves shallowly bilobed at the tip. The long, branched or simple, flattened, few-flowered inflorescence has small, fleshy, waxy, long-lasting, yellow-green to yellow, fragrant flowers marked with red-brown bars, spots and blotches. The fleshy, white, trilobed lip has almost square side lobes, and the anchor-shaped midlobe has hook-like projections, and red-brown to cinnamon spots.

POLYTOMA

Loureiro ex Gomes

Mem. Acad. Real Sci. Lisboa, 2 Cl. Sci. Moraes, n.s. **4**(1): 30 (1868), and
Merrill's *Trans. Amer. Philos. Soc., n.s.* **24**(2): 18, 123 (1935).

Not *Polytoma* Ehrenberg (1831) Chlamydomonadaceæ.

ETYMOLOGY: Greek for numerous or many and division or section. Refers to the crested lip.

TYPE SPECIES: *None designated*

Not validly published because of a prior use of the name, this homonym was replaced by the genera *Bletilla* or *Aerides*.

POMATOCALPA

Breda, Kuhl & Hasselt

Gen. Sp. Orchid. Asclep., fasc. III *t. 15* (1829).

Epidendroideæ 🌿 Vandeæ • Aeridinæ

ETYMOLOGY: Greek for a lid or cover and a pitcher, jug or urn. In reference to the flask-like structure of the lip.

TYPE SPECIES: *Pomatocalpa spicatum* Breda

Twenty-eight monopodial epiphytes are found in low elevation, rain forests from Sri Lanka, India, southern China (Hainan), Taiwan, Myanmar to Vietnam, Indonesia, New Guinea, the Philippines and northeastern Australia to the southwestern Pacific Archipelago usually in fairly exposed areas. These small to fairly large plants have slender stems, each with numerous to several, thickly textured, strap-like leaves arranged in two rows. The simple or usually branched, long or short, erect or hanging, numerous-flowered inflorescence has small, pale yellow, yellow-brown to dull brown, cup-shaped flowers speckled or edged in maroon. The white to pale yellow, trilobed lip has pink markings, and small side lobes, a straight or downward curved midlobe, and a rounded, sac-like spur. A tongue-like callus projects from the back wall and is fused to the short, broad, wingless, footless column.

POMATOCALYX

An orthographic variant introduced in *J. Linn. Soc., Bot.*, **18**(110): 335 (1881). The correct spelling is *Pomatocalpa*.

PONERA

Lindley

Gen. Sp. Orchid. Pl. 113 (1831).

Epidendroideæ 🌿 Epidendreæ • Ponerinæ

ETYMOLOGY: Greek for miserable or good for nothing. Descriptive of this plant's small flowers.

TYPE SPECIES: *Ponera juncifolia* Lindley

Eight scrambling, sympodial epiphytes or lithophytes are found in wet to dry, mid to upper elevation, montane pine-oak and evergreen cloud forests from southern Mexico to Guatemala and El Salvador. These erect to hanging plants, often forming dense colonies, have robust, wiry to thick, cane-like, leafy stems widely spaced along the rhizome. The stems are subtended completely by tubular, minutely warty sheaths, each with several, flat, distichous leaves scattered along the stem. The short, solitary to few-flowered inflorescence has small to minute, almost insignificant, short-lived, dull-colored flowers opening widely and in succession. The pale green to white sepals and smaller petals have lavender or red-brown stripes. The white, fleshy, entire lip is curved like a bow, has several, lavender stripes, is bilobed at the tip, and attached at the base to the short, slender, thick, wingless column.

PONERORCHIS

Reichenbach *filius*

Linnaea **25**: 227 (1852).

Orchidoideæ ◊ Orchideæ • Orchidinæ

ETYMOLOGY: Greek for worthless or miserable and orchid. An allusion to the small size of the orchid.

TYPE SPECIES: *Ponerorchis graminifolia* Reichenbach f.

Eighteen sympodial terrestrials are found primarily in low to upper elevation, grasslands and open woodlands of eastern Russia (Amur to Primorye), Japan, Taiwan, Korea, China (Heilongjiang to Yunnan), northern India (Kashmir to Assam) and Myanmar. These erect plants have slender, unbranched stems, each with one to two, usually basal leaves that can appear grass-like or found midway up the stem. The few-flowered inflorescence has showy, white, pink, magenta to red-purple flowers, rather large for the plant size, usually marked or blotched with purple especially on the lip. The concave dorsal sepal often united with the small petals converge, forming a hood over the short, stout column. The trilobed lip has widespreading lobes and an elongate spur.

NOTE: These species are often included in *Gymnadenia*.

PONGONIA

An orthographic variant introduced in *Orchids Burma*, 351 (1895). The correct spelling is *Pogonia*.

PONNAM

An orthographic variant introduced in *Hist. Pl. (Ray)*, **3**: 589 (1704) The correct spelling is *Ponnampou*.

PONNAMPOU-maravara

Rheede

Hort. Malab. **12**: 7-8, t. 3 (1693).

ETYMOLOGY: A local Malayalam word for gold and flower. Referring to the color of the flowers.

TYPE SPECIES: *Ponnampou-maravara* Rheede

Pre-1753, therefore not validly published in fulfillment of nomenclatural rules; this binomial name is most often referred to *Vanda*. Ponnampou was previously considered to include one epiphyte found in exposed, low elevation, dry hill forests of southern India (Kerala and Tamil Nadu) and Sri Lanka. This plant has stout, erect stems with a cluster of channeled, leathery leaves near the tip. The erect, few-flowered inflorescence has fragrant, pale creamy yellow flowers opening widely. The trilobed lip has erect side lobes, a long midlobe with several, raised keels, and a small spur. The flowers have a short, footless column. This name is usually now considered as synonym of *Vanda spathulata* (Linnaeus) Sprengel.

PONNAMPU

An orthographic variant introduced in *Pl. Amer.*, 175 (1755). The correct spelling is *Ponnampou*.

PONTHIAEVA

An orthographic variant introduced in *Hamburger Garten- Blumenzeitung*, **27**: 218 (1871). The correct spelling is *Ponthieva*.

PONTHIAEVA

An orthographic variant introduced in *Traité Gén. Bot.*, 563 (1876). The correct spelling is *Ponthieva*.

PONTHIEA

An orthographic variant introduced in *Repert. Spec. Nov. Regni Veg.*, **3**: 47 (1906). The correct spelling is *Ponthieva*.

PONTHIENA

An orthographic variant introduced in *Pl. Hartw.*, **2**: 258 (1846). The correct spelling is *Ponthieva*.

PONTHIERA

An orthographic variant introduced in *Dict. Sci. Nat.*, **36**: 304 (1825). The correct spelling is *Ponthieva*.

PONTHIEUA

An orthographic variant cited in *Nom. Bot. Hort.*, 647 (1840). The correct spelling is *Ponthieva*.

PONTHIEVA

R. Brown

Hortus Kew., ed. 2 **5**: 199 (1813).

Orchidoideæ ◊ Cranichideæ • Cranichidinæ

ETYMOLOGY: In commemoration of Henri de Ponthieu (*fl.* 1773-1791), a French-born merchant in the West Indies who sent plant collections to Joseph Banks (1743-1820), a British botanist. Though Banks conducted little research, he was influential in promoting scientific investigations.

TYPE SPECIES: *Ponthieva glandulosa* (Sims) R. Brown (*Neottia glandulosa* Sims)

This type name is now considered a synonym of *Ponthieva racemosa* (Walter) C. Mohr; basionym replaced by *Arethusa racemosa* Walter

Fifty-seven sympodial terrestrials are widespread in damp, low to upper elevation, shady woodlands, swamps, along river banks and montane forests from the south-eastern United States (eastern Virginia to eastern Texas and Florida), Cuba to Trinidad, the Guianas, Venezuela, southern Mexico to Chile and Brazil to northern Argentina and Paraguay with the largest group occurring in Ecuador where they often form large colonies. These small, erect plants have short to long, unbranched stems, each with a dark green basal rosette, although a few species have hairy leaves. The numerous to few-flowered, sometimes hairy inflorescence has small to tiny, delicate, pale white-green to white flowers usually veined in dark hues or heavily spotted. The small, concave, upper-most, entire or trilobed lip has contrasting colored stripes and is united to the short, massive, slightly winged, footless column.

POOEPHYLLUM

An orthographic variant introduced in *Bot. Centralbl.*, **107**(20): 527 (1908). The correct spelling is *Poaephyllum*.

POROGLOSSUM

An orthographic variant introduced in *Cattleya Relatives*, **5**: 8 (2000). The correct spelling is *Porroglossum*.

| Currently Accepted | Validly Published | Invalidly Published | Published Pre-1753 | Superfluous Usage | Orthographic Variant | Fossil |

Orchid Genera • 316

POROLABIUM

T. Tang & F.T. Wang

Bull. Fan Mem. Inst. Biol. Bot., ser. 1
10: 36 (1940).

Orchidoideæ ⚬ Orchideæ • Orchidinæ

ETYMOLOGY: Greek for a pore or hole and Latin for a lip. Descriptive of the two pores located near the base of the lip.

TYPE SPECIES: *Porolabium biporosum*
(Maximowicz) T. Tang & F.T. Wang
(*Herminium biporosum* Maximowicz)

One uncommon, small sympodial terrestrial is found in upper elevation, grassy montane valleys, slopes and lake banks of northeastern China (Shanxi and Qinghai) and Mongolia. This short plant has slender, unbranched stems, subtended by two or three, leaf-like, sheathing bracts, each with a solitary, oblong to narrow, basal leaf. The terminal, few-flowered inflorescence has small, pale green to yellow flowers which do not open fully. The broadly blunt, erect dorsal sepal and ovate, veined petals converge, forming a hood over the short column. The tongue-shaped, entire lip has two pore-like glands near the base. The flowers have a small, footless column.

PORPAX

Lindley

Edwards's Bot. Reg.
31(Misc): 62, section no. 66 (1845).

Not *Porpax* T. Evans ex R.A. Salisbury (1866) Liliaceæ.

Epidendroideæ ⚬ Podochileæ • Eriinæ

ETYMOLOGY: Greek for handle of a shield. Alluding to the pair of small, oblong leaves that arise from the pseudobulbs, which are recurved at their points.

TYPE SPECIES: *Porpax reticulata* Lindley

Thirteen dwarf, sympodial epiphytes or lithophytes are found in mid elevation, evergreen forests often growing unnoticed on tree trunks and cliff faces of northern India (Assam), Myanmar to Vietnam, Thailand, southern China (Yunnan), Malaysia and Indonesia (Borneo). These tiny, clump forming plants have clustered, flattened, roundish to disc-like pseudobulbs subtended by net veined sheaths. Each has two oblong, minute to small, deciduous, hairy to hairless leaves, or the plants are leafless at flowering, and sometimes appear after the flowers. The short, solitary-flowered inflorescence borne from a sheath tip or from the base of pseudobulb appears attached directly to the pseudobulb. The dull brown to orange-red, thinly textured, strongly tubular flower never fully opens. The minute, blunt, entire or obscurely trilobed lip is smooth or slightly toothed. The flowers have a minute, massive column with a long, slightly curved to abruptly upcurved foot.

PORPHYRODESME

Schlechter

Repert. Spec. Nov. Regni Veg. Beih.
1(13): 982 (1913).

Epidendroideæ ⚬ Vandeæ • Aeridinæ

ETYMOLOGY: Greek for purple and bundle. Refers to the branched red inflorescence with its red flowers.

TYPE SPECIES: *Porphyrodesme papuana* Schlechter
(*Saccolabium porphyrodesme* Schlechter)

Three monopodial epiphytes are found in low to mid elevation, hill forests of Indonesia, New Guinea and the Philippines. These large, scrambling plants have fragile, often branched stems, each with narrow, slightly twisted, slightly channeled, thick, fleshy, shiny red-green leaves borne on the upper third of the stem. The short, numerous-flowered, red inflorescence has tiny, yellow or orange-red flowers flecked with red spots throughout. The small, bucket-shaped, immobile, trilobed lip (firmly attached to the column base) has bow-shaped side lobes that converge, leaving a narrow slit for the entrance to the laterally compressed, flattened spur. The flowers have a short, broad, red, footless column.

PORPHYROGLOTTIS

Ridley

J. Linn. Soc., Bot. **31**(215): 290, t. 5 (1896).

Epidendroideæ ⚬ Cymbidieæ • Cymbidiinæ

ETYMOLOGY: Greek for purple and tongue or mouth. Descriptive of the dark purple lip of the type species.

TYPE SPECIES: *Porphyroglottis maxwelliae* Ridley

One uncommon, extraordinary, sympodial epiphyte is found low elevation, open, dwarf woodlands and forests native to Indonesia (Sumatra and Borneo) and southern Malaysia. This plant has long, clustered stems with numerous nodes, each with narrow, grass-like leaves that are shiny above and pale green on the undersides. Vegetatively, the plant resembles *Grammatophyllum speciosum* Blume, but the flower structure is quite different. The arching, occasionally branching, zig-zagging and slowly lengthening to over 5 feet (1.5 m), numerous to few-flowered inflorescence has small, dull-pink flowers borne in succession with only a few open at a time. The insect-like flowers have a glossy, maroon and yellow, hairy lip mimicking the body of a bee. The narrow sepals and petals on opening turn backward along the ovary and then the following day return to a widespreading position. The mobile, entire lip is attached to the short, massive column foot by a strap-like hinge. The flowers have a long, slender, curved, winged column.

PORPHYROSTACHYS

Reichenbach *filius*

Xenia Orchid. **1**: 18 (1854).

Orchidoideæ ⚬ Cranichideæ • Cranichidinæ

ETYMOLOGY: Greek for purple and ear of wheat or a spike. Alluding to the resemblance of the inflorescences to an ear of wheat.

TYPE SPECIES: *Porphyrostachys pilifera*
(Kunth) Reichenbach f.
(*Altensteinia pilifera* Kunth)

Two sympodial terrestrials are found in mid to upper elevation, hill to montane scrub, in sandy, gravelly or rocky soil of Ecuador and Peru usually in full sunlight. These spectacular, erect, plants can attain heights of over two feet (60 cm), each with oblong, basal leaves that are usually withered by flowering time. The erect, few-flowered inflorescence has papery bracts and showy, brilliant scarlet to green, somewhat intricate flowers. Each is subtended by a floral bract and have quite a distinctive structure with their tightly curled (reflexed or spirally recurved) floral segments. The spoon-shaped, concave, clawed, entire or obscurely trilobed lip extends down the long column foot, and together with the lateral sepals form a nectary or a short, tube-like structure. The flowers have a short to long, slender column.

PORRHORCHAIS

An orthographic variant introduced in *Bot. Mus. Leafl.*, **23**(4): 191 (1972). The correct spelling is *Porrorhachis*.

PORRHORHACHIS

An orthographic variant introduced in *Orchideen* (Schlechter), ed. 3, **3**, **19-20**: 1156 (1988). The correct spelling is *Porrorhachis*.

PORROGLOSSUM

Schlechter

Repert. Spec. Nov. Regni Veg. Beih. **7**: 82 (1920).

Epidendroideæ ⚬ Epidendreæ • Pleurothallidinæ

ETYMOLOGY: Greek for forward or onward and tongue. Refers to the characteristic, sensitive lip that projects far forward on a long, narrow column foot.

TYPE SPECIES: *Porroglossum colombianum*
Schlechter
This type name is now considered a synonym of
Porroglossum mordax (Reichenbach f.) H.R. Sweet;
basionym
Masdevallia mordax Reichenbach f.

Thirty-four sympodial epiphytes or sometimes lithophytes are found in mid to upper elevation, montane cloud forests from Colombia to Bolivia and Venezuela usually growing on moss laden tree trunks and branches. These erect plants have short stems, subtended by overlapping sheaths, each with several, erect, smooth to warty, leathery leaves. The long, few-flowered inflorescence, covered with long hairs, has small, thinly textured to fleshy flowers, opening one at a time, ranging in shades from yellow to rose with the veins colored in darker shades. The long, lateral sepals have slender, reflexed tails, and the small petals are narrow or oblong, rounded or blunt. The sensitive, spoon-shaped, smooth or hairy, triangular or ovate, entire lip, hinged to the tip of the long, curved column foot, has a long, slender claw that curves around the tip of the column foot and has a longitudinal or a short transverse callus at the base. The lip hangs downward when open, but when the center callus is touched, the lip raises up against the petals forming a chamber for the trapped insect. The lip closes at night and will reopen at dawn. The flowers have a short, winged column with a prominent, curved foot.

PORRORHACHIS

Garay

Bot. Mus. Leafl.   **23**(4): 191 (1972).

ETYMOLOGY: Greek for forward or onward and Latin for inflorescence. In reference to the position of the inflorescences that are inserted at a right angle to the main stem.

TYPE SPECIES: *Porrorhachis galbina* (J.J. Smith) Garay
(*Saccolabium galbinum* J.J. Smith)

Two monopodial epiphytes are found in mid elevation, montane forests of Indonesia (Java, northern Borneo and Sulawesi). These tiny, stout-stemmed plants have several, small, narrow, rigid, thick, channeled, fleshy leaves. The long, wiry, few-flowered inflorescence has tiny, well-spaced, green or yellow flowers that turn a shiny yellow as they age but do not open widely. The fleshy, compressed, sac-like, rigid, entire lip has a spur-like, tubular sac at the tip and is without any internal calli. The flowers have a short, stout, wingless, footless column.

PORTILLIA

Königer

Arcula   **6**: 154 (1996).

ETYMOLOGY: Named in honor of José 'Pepe' Portilla y Andrade (1966-), an Ecuadorian who along with his family has a large orchid nursery (Ecuagenera) near Cuenca.

TYPE SPECIES: *Portillia popowiana*
Königer & J. Portilla
not *Masdevallia popowiana* Königer

Now recognized as belonging to the genus *Masdevallia*, *Portillia* was previously considered to include one epiphyte found in low elevation, hill forests of

southeastern Ecuador (Morona-Santiago). This small plant has stout, erect stems, subtended by tubular sheaths, each with a solitary, narrow leaf. The several, long, wiry, solitary-flowered inflorescences are densely covered in soft hairs, have a brown-purple flower with a yellow veined inner surface, and are purple on the outside with yellow veins dotted purple. The large sepals have lengthy tails. The purple, entire lip has a yellow-green interior and is shallowly bilobed at the tip. The above type name is now considered a synonym of *Masdevallia bicornis* Luer.

POTOSIA

(Schlechter) R. González & Szlachetko
ex Mytnik

Genus   **14**(Suppl.): 59 (2003).

ETYMOLOGY: Named in honor of the northeastern Mexican state of San Luis Potosí where the type species was collected by Johann Wilhelm Schaffner (1830-1882), a German-born Mexican doctor, pharmacist and plant collector in San Louis Potosi.

TYPE SPECIES: *Potosia schaffneri*
(Reichenbach f.) R. González & Szlachetko ex Mytnik
(*Pelexia schaffneri* Reichenbach f.)

Recognized as belonging to the genus *Sarcoglottis*, *Potosia* was proposed to include five terrestrials found in deep humus, mid to upper elevation, montane forests of northeastern Mexico and Guatemala to El Salvador. These tall, stout plants have a yellow or red-brown, unbranched, hairy stem whose basal rosette of leaves are withered or absent by flowering time. The hairy, few-flowered inflorescence has rather small, brown-pink or green, tubular flowers. In some species the flowers all face in one direction and in other species the flowers appear on all sides, but all have reflexed lateral sepals. The white, trough-shaped, clawed, trilobed lip has a wavy margin, and there are two tiny, narrow appendages located at the hairy base. The spur is completely attached to the ovary. The flowers have a rather short, massive column. These species were formerly treated as a section in *Pelexia*.

PRAECOXANTHUS

Hopper & A.P. Brown

Lindleyana   **15**(2): 124 (2000).

Orchidoideæ 🌿 Diurideæ • Caladeniinæ

ETYMOLOGY: Latin for developing early and Greek for flower. Alluding to its early appearance in the fall.

TYPE SPECIES: *Praecoxanthus aphyllus*
(Bentham) Hopper & A.P. Brown
(*Caladenia aphyllus* Bentham)

One sympodial terrestrial is found in low elevation, coastal scrub and woodlands of south-western Australia. This slender, erect plant has short, unbranched stems, each with several, minute, shiny leaves that wither before flowering. The erect, wiry, solitary-flowered inflorescence has a creamy white, highly fragrant, fan-shaped flower. The showy, yellow-white, strongly trilobed lip is longer than the sepals and is often mottled with red-brown. The longer midlobe has a recurved, yellow tip with a wavy margin, and the long, mauve calli are arranged in two rows which have yellow tips. The flowers have a slender, footless column.

PRASOPHYLLUM

R. Brown

Prodr. Fl. Nov. Holland.   317 (1810).

Orchidoideæ 🌿 Diurideæ • Prasophyllinæ

ETYMOLOGY: Greek for a leek and a leaf or petal. Referring to the hollow, terete leaves that are reminiscent of those of onions or leeks.

LECTOTYPE: *Prasophyllum australe* R. Brown

One hundred taxonomically confusing, sympodial terrestrials are found in low elevation, hill scrub, swamps, open woodlands and grasslands with nearly all the species restricted to Australia and Tasmania, but a few species are found in New Zealand. These erect plants have hollow, unbranched stems, each with a solitary, cylindrical, basal leaf that is subtended by a bract-like sheath. The plants reproduce solely from seed. The wiry to stout, sometimes wavy and slender, numerous to few-flowered inflorescence has sweetly fragrant flowers usually inconspicuous that are dull-colored green, purple or white and suffused or streaked with pink or green. The flower layout is reversed with the dorsal sepal uppermost and has narrow lateral sepals and petals. The broad, mobile lip is attached to a projection at the column base. The shortly clawed, rigid, entire lip has a wavy or comb-like margin. The flowers have a small, very short, footless column.

NOTE: Many of the species are stimulated to flower only following summer fires.

Currently Accepted   Validly Published   Invalidly Published   Published Pre-1753   Superfluous Usage   Orthographic Variant   Fossil

Orchid Genera • **318**

PRECOTIA

An orthographic variant introduced in *Neues Allg. Gart.-Mag.*, **6**(4): 299 (1826). The correct spelling is *Prescottia*.

PREPTANTHE

Reichenbach *filius*

Fl. Serres Jard. Eur., ser. 1   **8**: 245 (1853).

ETYMOLOGY: Greek for to be distinguished or eminent and flower. In reference to the attractive flowers.

TYPE SPECIES: *Preptanthe vestita*
(Wallich ex Lindley) Reichenbach f.
(*Calanthe vestita* Wallich ex Lindley)

Now recognized as belonging to the genus *Calanthe*, *Preptanthe* was previously considered to include four terrestrials or occasional lithophytes found in hot to cool, low to mid elevation, hill and montane forests from Myanmar to Thailand and eastern Indonesia (Borneo and Sulawesi). These stout, leafless plants, flowering during the dry season, have silvery to green-gray, ovoid pseudobulbs, each with broad, prominently ribbed underneath, deciduous leaves borne on a slender stalk which wither before flowering. The arching, hairy, few-flowered inflorescence has large, fragile, long-lived, white flowers with similar sepals and petals that are shortly hairy on their outside surfaces. The white to bright magenta, trilobed lip has a dark yellow patch at its base and small, roundish side lobes. The bilobed midlobe widens from a narrow base, and has a pale yellow to cream colored spur.

PRESCOTHIA

An orthographic variant introduced in *Repert. Spec. Nov. Regni Veg. Beih.*, **59**(2): 7 (1931). The correct spelling is *Prescottia*.

PRESCOTIA

An orthographic variant introduced in *Bot. Reg.*, **10**: sub 825 (1824). The correct spelling is *Prescottia*.

PRESCOTTIA

Lindley

Exot. Fl.   **2**(13): t. 115 (1824).

Name ICBN conserved vs. *Prescotia* Lindley (Orchidaceæ).

Orchidoideæ ⚘ Cranichideæ • Cranichidinæ

ETYMOLOGY: Honoring John D. Prescott (x-1837), a British merchant who lived in Saint Petersburg and as an amateur botanist traveled and collected widely in Russia, northern Asia, Labrador and Greenland. He was a cousin of William Cattley and ran the Saint Petersburg family firm involved in the 'Russia Trade.'

TYPE SPECIES: *Prescottia plantaginea* Lindley

Thirty-one sympodial terrestrials are widespread in damp, low to upper elevation, woodlands, scrub and grasslands from the southern United States (Florida), Cuba to Trinidad, the Guianas, Venezuela, southern Mexico to Peru, Brazil, Argentina and Paraguay. These small plants have erect, unbranched stems, each with delicate, soft satiny, blue-green rosettes that are often withered by flowering time. The leaves are narrow to heart-shaped. The slender, densely packed, numerous to few-flowered inflorescence is covered by numerous, thinly textured sheaths. The usually roundish, strongly fragrant, tiny, green flowers are sometimes suffused pink or red-brown. The spreading or reflexed sepals are united at the base forming a cup-like (sepaline) shape, and the tiny, narrow thinly textured petals are frequently strongly recurved. The darker hued, deeply concave, helmet-like or spoon-shaped, clawed, entire or obscurely trilobed lip is uppermost, has a narrow, slit-like mouth and surrounds the short, blunt, thick, footless column.

PRISMOPHYLIS

Thouars

Hist. Orchid.   Table 3, sub 3u, t. 109 (1822).

Name published without a description. Today this name is most often referred to *Bulbophyllum*.

PRISTIGLOTTIS

Cretzoiu & J.J. Smith

Acta Fauna Fl. Universali, ser. 2, Bot. **1**(14): 4 (1934).

Orchidoideæ ⚘ Cranichideæ • Goodyerinæ

ETYMOLOGY: Greek for a saw and tongue. An allusion to the margin of the lip.

LECTOTYPE: *Pristiglottis uniflora*
(Blume) Cretzoiu & J.J. Smith
(*Cystopus uniflorus* Blume)

Twenty-one sympodial terrestrials or uncommon epiphytes are found in low to mid elevation, montane evergreen forests from northern India (Assam), Thailand, southern Japan (Ryukyu Islands), Indonesia and New Guinea

to the southwestern Pacific Archipelago. These small, erect plants have short stems, each with rather small, mottled or variegated, distichous leaves. The short, stout, numerous to few-flowered inflorescence has relatively large, tube-shaped, white to pale blue flowers. The long-clawed, bilobed lip has a sac-like base, with or usually without a spur, often has a toothed or fringed margin, and forms a bilobed blade. The flowers have a short, footless column.

NOTE: The *Pristiglottis* flowers are similar to *Anoectochilus* but their stigmatic surface is not divided into two, separate lobes.

PROCTORIA

Luer

Monogr. Syst. Bot. Missouri Bot. Gard. **95**: 258 (2004).

ETYMOLOGY: Named for George 'Swampy' Richardson Proctor (1920-), an American who worked at the Institute of Jamaica, wrote numerous articles on the local flora and ferns and collected this type species.

TYPE SPECIES: *Proctoria caymanensis*
(C.D. Adams) Luer
(*Pleurothallis caymanensis* C.D. Adams)

Recognized as belonging to the genus *Pleurothallis*, *Proctoria* was proposed to include one epiphyte found in low elevation, scrub of the Cayman Islands (Grand) and western Cuba (Pinar del Río). This small, tufted, mat-forming plant has creeping rhizomes with small swellings at intervals. The stout, erect stem, subtended by thin, tubular sheaths, has a solitary, slender, thick, leathery leaf. The several, thin, solitary-flowered inflorescences, borne successively from the leaf axils, have a thinly textured, pale yellow-green flower with purple veins. The lateral sepals are united into a bifid synsepal with minutely notched margins and the white, small petals have a deep red dot at the tip. The tiny, spear-shaped, trilobed lip has a disc with a shallow channel between a pair of calli. The flowers have a short, curved column.

PROMENAEA

Lindley

Edwards's Bot. Reg.   **29**(Misc): 13 (1843).

Epidendroideæ ⚘ Cymbidieæ • Zygopetalinæ

ETYMOLOGY: Greek for moon or crescent moon. Refers to the shape of the viscidium.

LECTOTYPE: *Promenaea lentiginosa* (Lindley) Lindley
(*Maxillaria lentiginosa* Lindley)

Nineteen sympodial epiphytes or lithophytes are found in cool to damp, low to mid elevation, hill to montane forests and rocky crevices of southeastern to southern Brazil. These variable, often dwarf plants form dense clumps, and have distinct ovoid, slightly four-angled, compressed pseudobulbs, each with one to three, small, softly textured, slightly pleated leaves at the tip. The short, arching to hanging, thin, solitary-flowered inflorescence has a large, showy, waxy, bright white to yellow, often very fragrant, slightly cup-shaped flower. The lateral sepals are obliquely inserted on the short column foot forming a small, chin-like protuberance. The mobile, distinctly trilobed lip, attached to the tip of the column foot, has narrow, erect side lobes; the spreading midlobe has dull-colored blotches and a fleshy disk with lobed or crested tubercles or warts. The flowers have a stout, slightly incurved, wingless column.

PROMENAEX

An orthographic variant introduced in *Cat. Orch.-Samml. Schiller*, ed. 1, 46 (1857). The correct spelling is *Promenaea*.

PROMENEA

An orthographic variant introduced in *Wochenschr. Vereines Beford. Gartenbaues Konigl. Preuss. Staaten*, **6**(48): 384 (1863). The correct spelling is *Promenaea*.

PROMOENOEA

An orthographic variant introduced in *Florist Hort. J.*, **2**: 249 (1853). The correct spelling is *Promenaea*.

PROSCHISIA

Richard
De Orchid. Eur.   23 (1817).
ETYMOLOGY: Greek for extended and Latin for cleft or split. Refers to the split that occurs in the ovary.
TYPE SPECIES: *Neottia picta* (Anderson) R. Brown
(*Arethusa picta* Anderson)
This type name is now considered a synonym of *Sarcoglottis acaulis* (Smith) Schlechter; basionym replaced with *Neottia acaulis* Smith

Not validly published, this name is referred to *Sarcoglottis*. *Proschisia* was considered to include one terrestrial found from southern Mexico to Argentina.

PROSTECHEA

An orthographic variant introduced in *Orchideen (Schlechter)*, ed. 1, 190 (1915). The correct spelling is *Prosthechea*.

PROSTHECHEA

Knowles & Westcott
Fl. Cab.   **2**: 111 (1838).
Epidendroideæ • Epidendreæ • Laeliinæ
ETYMOLOGY: Greek for appendage or addition. In reference to the appendage of tissue located on the back of the column.
TYPE SPECIES: *Prosthechea glauca* Knowles & Westcott

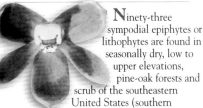

Ninety-three sympodial epiphytes or lithophytes are found in seasonally dry, low to upper elevations, pine-oak forests and scrub of the southeastern United States (southern Florida), the Bahamas, Cuba to Trinidad, the Guianas, Venezuela, southern Mexico to Bolivia and Brazil. These plants have flattened, spindle-shaped, clustered to well-spaced, compressed, ovoid, distinctly grooved pseudobulbs, each with a solitary to several, thinly leathery, strap-like leaves. The short, simple to branched, numerous to few-flowered inflorescence, subtended by a leaf bract at the base, has green-yellow to green, rigid, long-lived, sometimes fragrant flowers with similar sepals and petals. The cup-shaped, trilobed lip, joined to about half of the column, is usually uppermost, and has a thick, basal callus. The flowers have a short, wingless, footless column.
NOTE: Most of these species were formerly included in the genera *Encyclia* and *Epidendrum*.

PROSTHECIA

An orthographic variant introduced in *Edwards's Bot. Reg.*, **25**(Misc.): 16 (1839). The correct spelling is *Prosthechea*.

PROTEROCERAS

J. Joseph & Vajravelu
J. Indian Bot. Soc.   **53**(3-4): 189, t. 1-6 (1974).
ETYMOLOGY: Greek for earlier or first and horn. Refers to the lip with an up curved spur appearing as if a horn is projecting in the front.
TYPE SPECIES: *Proteroceras holttumii*
J. Joseph & Vajravelu
This type name is now considered a synonym of *Pteroceras leopardinum*
(C.S.P. Parish & Reichenbach f.) Seidenfaden & Smitinand; basionym
Thrixspermum leopardinum C.S.P. Parish & Reichenbach f.

Not validly published, this name is referred to *Pteroceras*. *Proteroceras* was considered to include one epiphyte found in evergreen forests from southern India, China (Yunnan), Indonesia (Sumatra and Borneo), Myanmar to Vietnam and the Philippines.

PROTORCHIS

Massalongo
Atti Reale Ist. Veneto Sci. Lett. Arti, ser. 3
3: 749 (1858).
ETYMOLOGY: Greek for extended and orchid. Refers to the orchid-like leaf fragments.
TYPE SPECIES: *Protorchis monorchis* Massalongo

Two fossil orchids are based on leaf fragments dated from the Eocene epoch (lasted from 56.5 million to 35.4 million years ago), the second period of the Cenozoic era. These dubious orchidaceous pieces were discovered at Monte Bolca in the calcareous deposits of northeastern Italy. The specimens were originally listed without the benefit of a description or an illustration but Massalongo later published a more complete description and a photograph.

PSEUDACORIDIUM

Ames
Orchidaceæ (Ames)   **7**: 79 (1922).
ETYMOLOGY: Greek for false and *Acoridium*, a genus of orchids. Referring to a false resemblance to *Acoridium*.
TYPE SPECIES: *Pseudacoridium woodianum*
(Ames) Ames
(*Dendrochilum woodianum* Ames)

Now recognized as as belonging to the genus *Dendrochilum*, *Pseudacoridium* was proposed to include six epiphytes found in mid elevation, scrubby forests of the Philippines (Luzon, Leyte and Bukidnon). These attractive plants, growing in dense patches, have densely clustered, pear-shaped to tapered pseudobulbs, subtended by several, thin, brown bracts, each with a solitary, small, leathery, grass-like leaf. The tall, terminal, numerous-flowered inflorescence, crowded with rigid, floral bracts, has tiny, dark orange, dark red or green-yellow flowers arranged in two ranks and which do not open fully. The small, sac-like, bilobed lip has erect, shell-shaped side lobes both with a small callus. These small lobes converge, forming a hood over the tiny, erect, winged column.

Currently Accepted   Validly Published   Invalidly Published   Published Pre-1753   Superfluous Usage   Orthographic Variant   Fossil

PSEUDELLEANTHUS

Brieger

Orchideen (Schlechter), ed. 3   **1**(13): 794 (1983).

ETYMOLOGY: Greek for false and *Elleanthus*, a genus of orchids. Referring to a false resemblance to *Elleanthus*.

TYPE SPECIES: *Pseudelleanthus virgatus*
(Reichenbach f.) Brieger
(*Sertifera virgata* Reichenbach f.)

 **N**ow recognized as belonging to the genus *Sertifera, Pseudelleanthus* was previously considered to include one epiphyte or terrestrial found in very wet, upper elevation, montane cloud forests from Venezuela, Colombia to Peru and Brazil. This plant has a dark purple-brown stems, subtended by persistent, gray, tubular sheaths, each with several, narrow, pleated, veined leaves. The erect, few-flowered inflorescence has white flowers suffused rosy-pink. The thinly textured, entire lip has two, white, wall-like calli located at the base, and a lacerated or notched margin.

PSEUDENCYCLIA

Chiron & V.P. Castro

Richardiana   **4**(1): 31 (2003).

ETYMOLOGY: Greek for false and *Encyclia*, a genus of orchids. Referring to a false resemblance to *Encyclia*.

TYPE SPECIES: *Pseudencyclia michuacana*
(Lexarza) Chiron & V.P. Castro
(*Epidendrum michuacanum* Lexarza)

Recognized as belonging to the genus *Prosthechea, Pseudencyclia* was previously considered to include twenty epiphytes found in seasonally dry, mid to upper elevation, pine-oak forests of central Mexico, then southward to Guatemala and Honduras. These plants have clustered, ovoid to pear-shaped pseudobulbs, partially subtended by thin, dry sheaths, each with several, narrow leaves. The often branched, numerous to few-flowered inflorescence has fleshy, long-lived, mostly red-brown to green-brown flowers with narrow to oblong sepals and petals. The creamy to pale yellow, often spotted purple, trilobed lip has oblong side lobes and a nearly circular to triangular midlobe with a fleshy callus. The flowers have a short, straight column.

PSEUDEPIDENDRUM

Reichenbach *filius*

Bot. Zeitung (Berlin)   **10**: 733 (1852).

ETYMOLOGY: Greek for false and *Epidendrum*, a genus of orchids. Referring to a false resemblance to *Epidendrum*.

TYPE SPECIES: *Pseudepidendrum spectabile*
Reichenbach f.

Now recognized as belonging to the genus *Epidendrum, Pseudepidendrum* was previously considered to include one epiphyte found in low to mid elevation, rain forests of Costa Rica and Panama. This robust plant has simple, clustered stems, often more than three feet (1 m) tall, subtended by tubular, thin, dry sheaths, each with two ranked, deep green leaves that are deeply keeled in the upper portion. The few-flowered inflorescence has fragrant, bright apple-green flowers with narrow sepals that flare at the tips and have narrow petals. The large, widely flared, orange-red or orange, long-clawed, entire lip has a wavy surfaced, notched margin, and has five thick, yellow, basal keels. The flowers have a thick, orange column. The above type name is now considered a synonym of *Epidendrum pseudepidendrum* Reichenbach f.

PSEUDERIA

Schlechter

Repert. Spec. Nov. Regni Veg. Beih.
1(9): 643 (1912).

Epidendroideæ • Podochileæ • Eriinæ

ETYMOLOGY: Greek for false and *Eria*, a genus of orchids. Referring to a false resemblance to *Eria*.

TYPE SPECIES: *None designated*

Nineteen unusual, climbing or scrub-like, sympodial terrestrials are found in humid, low elevation, rain forests of New Guinea with a few species also in eastern Indonesia (Maluku), Samoa and Fiji. These woody-stemmed, branched plants are seldom recognized as orchids due to their creeping or climbing habit. They often will cover a wide area. The several, short, few-flowered inflorescences have inconspicuous, small flowers in a variety of colors ranging from pale yellow-green with red to purple spots and yellow patches. These are usually small and insignificantly colored flowers. The large sepals are widespreading, and the tiny, narrow, upright petals surround the bent, slender, footless column. The small, white, entire lip has a blunt, roundish tip.

PSEUDERIOPSIS

Reichenbach *filius*

Linnaea   **22**: 852 (1850).

ETYMOLOGY: Greek for false and *Eriopsis*, a genus of orchids. Referring to a false resemblance to *Eriopsis*.

LECTOTYPE: *Pseuderiopsis schomburgkii*
Reichenbach f.

Now recognized as belonging to the genus *Eriopsis, Pseuderiopsis* was previously considered to include one terrestrial or occasional epiphyte widely distributed in wet, low to mid elevation, hill to montane forests and rocky or clay slopes of Costa Rica to Peru, Venezuela, the Guianas and northern Brazil. This plant has extremely variable pseudobulbs ranging from tall and slender, to stout and compressed. The several, rigid or thinly textured, narrow leaves are borne from the tip of the pseudobulb. The erect to arching, numerous-flowered inflorescence has yellow or brown-yellow, waxy, fragrant flowers suffused with varying degrees of maroon. The variously trilobed lip has spreading, oblong, purple-brown side lobes and a small, white midlobe covered with dark purple spots. The flowers have a green, short, slender, curved column. The above type name is now considered a synonym of *Eriopsis biloba* Lindley.

PSEUDOCENTRUM

Lindley

J. Proc. Linn. Soc., Bot.   **3**: 63, 64 (1859).

Orchidoideæ • Cranichideæ • Cranichidinæ

ETYMOLOGY: Greek for false and spur. Referring to the lateral sepals that are excessively produced at their base, forming a bag around the lip.

TYPE SPECIES: *Pseudocentrum macrostachyum*
Lindley

Seven sympodial terrestrials are found in deep shade, mid to upper elevation, montane forests from Costa Rica to Peru, Dominican Republic to Jamaica and Guadeloupe. These tall plants have erect, unbranched stems, each with a basal rosette of softly textured leaves. The long, numerous-flowered inflorescence has large to medium-sized, pale green to yellow flowers that are hairy on the outside. The dorsal sepal is hood-shaped, the lateral sepals are united at their base forming a long, cylindrical, deeply sac-like, hanging, short spur. The small, entire petals are spreading. The white to yellow, trilobed lip turns upward, forms a long, narrow, channeled protuberance. It has two, thread-like appendages with the small side lobes almost touching each other, and the long, narrow midlobe is tightly folded over. The flowers have a short, massive, footless column.

PSEUDOCOELOGLOSSUM

(Szlachetko & Olszewski) Szlachetko

Orchidee (Hamburg)   **54**(3): 334 (2003).

ETYMOLOGY: Greek for false and *Coeloglossum*, a genus of orchids. Referring to a false resemblance to *Coeloglossum*.

TYPE SPECIES: *Pseudocoeloglossum coeloglossoides*
(Summerhayes) Szlachetko
(*Habenaria coeloglossoides* Summerhayes)

Recognized as belonging to the genus *Habenaria*, *Pseudocoeloglossum* was proposed to include four terrestrials found growing in low elevation, marshes and rocky grasslands from Ethiopia to Zambia. These small plants have slender, erect stems that are leafy throughout with the lower most, narrow leaves reduced to sheaths and the upper most and leafy bracts. The numerous to few-flowered inflorescence has showy, fragrant, pale green and white to yellow-green flowers with an almost hood-shaped dorsal sepal. The trilobed lip, narrow at the base, has widespreading, triangular to narrow, bilobed side lobes, a small, narrow midlobe, and a cylindrical spur that is as long as the ovary.

PSEUDOCRANICHIS

Garay

Bot. Mus. Leafl.   **28**(4): 347 (1980)[1982].

Orchidoideæ ◊ Cranichideæ • Cranichidinæ

ETYMOLOGY: Greek for false and *Cranichis*, a genus of orchids. Refers to a false resemblance to *Cranichis*, a mistaken assignment of the type species.

TYPE SPECIES: *Pseudocranichis thysanochila*
(B.L. Robinson & Greenman) Garay
(*Cranichis thysanochila* B.L. Robinson & Greenman)

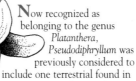

One sympodial terrestrial is found in mid elevation, canyon cliffs of Mexico (Oaxaca). This erect plant has unbranched stems, each with a few basal leaves usually present during flowering. The slender, numerous-flowered inflorescence has leafy bracts and small, white flowers. The uppermost, clawed, trilobed lip has calli near the tip of the short, fleshy, slender, wingless column which has a long slit in the stigma. The dorsal sepal is united to the obscure to footless column base. The broad, oblong lateral sepals are fused with the lip claw forming a rounded sac. The narrow petals are irregularly notched. The arrowhead-shaped, entire lip is coarsely lacerated or notched and multilobed at the tip.

PSEUDOCTOMERIA

Kraenzlin

Bull. Misc. Inform. Kew   **1925**: 116 (1925).

ETYMOLOGY: Greek for false and *Octomeria*, a genus of orchids. Referring to a false resemblance to *Octomeria*.

TYPE SPECIES: *Pseudoctomeria lentiginosa*
(F. Lehmann & Kraenzlin) Kraenzlin
(*Pleurothallis lentiginosa* F. Lehmann & Kraenzlin)

Now recognized as belonging to the genus *Specklinia*, *Pseudoctomeria* was previously considered to include one epiphyte found in upper elevation, montane forests of Costa Rica. This tiny, erect plant has long, slender stems, subtended by tubular sheaths, each with a solitary, oblong leaf. The solitary-flowered inflorescence has a pale yellow-orange flower. The flowers have an externally warty surface with the sepals united for most of their length. The tiny petals and fleshy, clawed, entire lip are found tucked inside this tubular-shaped flower. The flowers have a slender, curved column.

PSEUDODIPHRYLLUM

Nevski

Komarov's *Fl. URSS*   **4**: 494, 573 (1935).

ETYMOLOGY: Greek for false and *Diphryllum*, a genus of orchids. Referring to a false resemblance to *Diphryllum*.

TYPE SPECIES: *Pseudodiphryllum chorisianum*
(Chamisso) Nevski
(*Habenaria chorisiana* Chamisso)

Now recognized as belonging to the genus *Platanthera*, *Pseudodiphryllum* was previously considered to include one terrestrial found in upper elevation, montane meadows and grasslands of eastern Russia (Kamchatka, Kuril Islands and Sakhalin), Japan, and the Aleutian Islands (United States) to British Colombia (Canada). This miniature plant is so small that it lies hidden in grasses and mossy turf. The erect plant has several, glossy, green leaves sheathing the unbranched stem below and has a solitary, narrow bract above. The numerous-flowered inflorescence, bent to one side, has tiny, green-yellow flowers. The rounded, drooping, cup-shaped, entire lip has a short, blunt, sometimes bilobed spur. The flowers have a short, wingless column.

PSEUDOERIOPSIS

An orthographic variant introduced in *Harvard Pap. Bot.*, **10**(2): 245 (2005). The correct spelling is *Pseuderiopsis*.

PSEUDOEURYSTYLES

Hoehne

Arq. Bot. Estado São Paulo, n.s.   **1**(6): 129 (1944).

ETYMOLOGY: Greek for false and *Eurystyles*, a genus of orchids. Referring to a false resemblance to *Eurystyles*.

LECTOTYPE: *Pseudoeurystyles lorenzii*
(Cogniaux) Hoehne
(*Stenoptera lorenzii* Cogniaux)

Now recognized as belonging to the genus *Eurystyles*, *Pseudoeurystyles* was previously considered to include four epiphytes found in damp, low elevation, coastal forests of southern Brazil (Minas Gerais, São Paulo and Paraná). These small plants have short stems, each with a basal rosette of narrow, translucent gray-green, waxy leaves; the roots are covered with felt-like hairs. The long, erect, few-flowered inflorescence has small, pale white-green, fleshy flowers with the lateral sepals united forming a synsepalum. The inflated, floral bracts are covered with soft, slender hairs. The entire lip has a channeled, concave groove and is parallel with the slender, semi-terete column that has an oblong anther cap.

PSEUDOGOODYERA

Schlechter

Beih. Bot. Centralbl.   **37**(2): 369 (1920).

Orchidoideæ ◊ Cranichideæ • Spiranthinæ

ETYMOLOGY: Greek for false and *Goodyera*, a genus of orchids. Refers to a superficial similarity to *Goodyera*.

LECTOTYPE: *Pseudogoodyera wrightii*
(Reichenbach f.) Schlechter
(*Goodyera wrightii* Reichenbach f.)

Two sympodial terrestrials or lithophytes are found in low to mid elevation, tropical evergreen and semi-deciduous forests from Mexico (Hidalgo), Belize to Guatemala and Cuba. These small, erect plants have unbranched stems, each with a basal rosette of dark green leaves that sometimes have silvery veins or markings. The tall, dark green-red, delicate, spirally arranged, densely packed, numerous-flowered inflorescence is enclosed with a number of sheaths. The minute, compact flowers have narrow, dark green sepals and gray-red petals that are single nerved. The small, triangular, white to red, rather fleshy, erect, shortly clawed, entire lip has an orange blotch of color at the tip and a wavy margin. The flowers have a tiny, curved, club-shaped column.

Currently Accepted   Validly Published   Invalidly Published   Published Pre-1753   Superfluous Usage   Orthographic Variant   Fossil

Orchid Genera • **322**

PSEUDOHEMIPILIA

Szlachetko

Orchidee (Hamburg) **54**(2): 214 (2003).

ETYMOLOGY: Greek for false and *Hemipilia*, a genus of orchids. Refers to a resemblance of its gynostemium structure to that of *Hemipilia*.

TYPE SPECIES: *Pseudohemipilia hirsutissima*
(Summerhayes) Szlachetko
(*Habenaria hirsutissima* Summerhayes)

Recognized as belonging to the genus *Habenaria*, *Pseudohemipilia* was proposed to include eight terrestrials found in low to mid elevation, forests, savannas, dune woodlands, marshes or grasslands from Ethiopia to Angola, Zimbabwe to Mozambique, Togo to Cameroon, Oman and Yemen usually growing in small groups. These small, erect plants have short, unbranched stems, each with a ground hugging, heart-shaped, basal leaf that has slightly hairy, wavy margins. The hairy, numerous-flowered inflorescence has small, green flowers with a shell-shaped dorsal sepal. The lateral sepals are recurved and the bilobed petals are unequal in size and are not always hairy. The trilobed lip has dissimilar, non-hairy lobes, and a long, slightly swollen, cylindrical spur. The flowers have a short, massive column.

PSEUDOHEXADESMIA

Brieger

Orchideen (Schlechter), ed. 3 **8**(29-32): 488 (1976).

ETYMOLOGY: Greek for false and *Hexadesmia*, a genus of orchids. Referring to its false resemblance to *Hexadesmia*.

TYPE SPECIES: *Pseudohexadesmia micrantha*
(Lindley) Brieger
(*Hexadesmia micrantha* Lindley)

Not validly published, this name is referred to *Scaphyglottis*. *Pseudohexadesmia* was considered to include one epiphyte found in forests and scrub from Guatemala to Panama.

PSEUDOLAELIA

Porto & Brade

Arq. Inst. Biol. Veg. **2**(2): 209 (1935).

Epidendroideæ ◊ Epidendreæ • Laeliinæ

ETYMOLOGY: Greek for false and *Laelia*, a genus of orchids. Refers to its false resemblance to *Laelia* that also bears eight pollinia.

TYPE SPECIES: *Pseudolaelia corcovadensis*
Porto & Brade

Eleven uncommon, rambling, sympodial epiphytes or lithophytes are found in low to mid elevation, coastal scrub to rocky granite outcropping of eastern Brazil (Minas Gerais, Rio de Janeiro, Bahia and Espírito Santo) usually growing exclusively on stunted *Vellozia* scrub. These erect plants have slender stems, each

with several, narrow, thinly textured or leathery, deciduous leaves spaced along the basal portion and narrow, leaf-like bracts proceeding upward or have spindle-shaped, noded pseudobulbs, each with several, narrow, thin to leathery leaves that are sometimes suffused dark pink. The long, wiry, erect to arching, simple or branched, numerous to few-flowered inflorescence has showy, pale to dark mauve-pink or even yellow flowers with either wide or narrow segments. Several species have creamy yellow keels (or none) radiating out from the base of the deeply lobed, heavily veined, trilobed lip that has colored margins. The flowers have a short, brown-green column that is laterally extended at the tip as arm-like wings.

PSEUDOLEIMODORON

Clusius

Rar. Pl. Hist. 270 (1601).

Pre-1753, therefore not validly published in fulfillment of nomenclatural rules; this name is most often referred to *Neottia*.

PSEUDOLEPANTHES

(Luer & R. Escobar) Archila

Revista Guatemal. **3**(1): 76 (2000).

ETYMOLOGY: Greek for false and *Lepanthes*, a genus of orchids. Referring to its deceptive appearance to *Lepanthes*.

TYPE SPECIES: *Pseudolepanthes colombiae*
(Luer & R. Escobar) Archila
(*Trichosalpinx pseudolepanthes* Luer & R. Escobar)

Recognized as belonging to the genus *Trichosalpinx*, *Pseudolepanthes* was previously considered to include ten epiphytes found in mid to upper elevation, montane cloud forests from western Colombia to Ecuador. These small plants have slender, erect stems, subtended by sheaths, each with an erect, solitary leaf suffused purple on the underside. The zig-zagged, few-flowered inflorescence has small, pale yellow to purple flowers. The concave dorsal and lateral sepals have long, spike-like hairs on the outside surfaces and the flowers have smaller petals. The entire lip has a large, conspicuous disc with callus. The flowers have a short, footless column.

PSEUDOLIMODORON

An orthographic variant introduced in *Pinax*, 86 (1623). The correct spelling is *Pseudoleimodoron*.

PSEUDO-LIMODORUM

An orthographic variant introduced in *Summa Pl.*, **5**: 218 (1791). The correct spelling is *Pseudoleimodoron*.

PSEUDOLIPARIS

Finet

Bull. Soc. Bot. France **54**(9): 536 (1907).

ETYMOLOGY: Greek for false and *Liparis*, a genus of orchids. Referring to its false resemblance to *Liparis*.

TYPE SPECIES: *Pseudoliparis epiphytica*
(Schlechter) Finet
(*Microstylis epiphytica* Schlechter)

Now recognized as belonging to the genus *Malaxis*, *Pseudoliparis* was previously considered to include forty epiphytes found in New Guinea and the southwestern Pacific Archipelago region. These plants have slender pseudobulbs, each with several, thinly textured leaves. The long, few-flowered inflorescence has small flowers with the sepals and petals similar in size and form. The flowers have a thin, plate-like, elevation located at the base of the flat, obscurely trilobed lip. The above type name is now considered a synonym of *Malaxis pseudoliparis* P.F. Hunt.

PSEUDOMACODES

Rolfe

Bull. Misc. Inform. Kew **1892**: 127 (1892).

ETYMOLOGY: Greek for false and *Macodes*, a genus of orchids. Referring to its false resemblance to *Macodes*.

TYPE SPECIES: *Pseudomacodes cominsii* Rolfe

Now recognized as belonging to the genus *Macodes*, *Pseudomacodes* was previously considered to include one terrestrial found in low elevation, rain forests of the Solomon Islands. The olive-green leaves of this evergreen plant have wavy margins and pale green veins. The numerous-flowered, red inflorescence is covered with red-brown hairs and the flowers, opening widely, have red-brown sepals and white petals. The uppermost, trilobed lip, small spur, and the short column are colored a dull orange.

PSEUDOMAXILLARIA

Hoehne

Arq. Bot. Estado São Paulo, n.s. **2**(4): 71 (1947).

ETYMOLOGY: Greek for false and *Maxillaria*, a genus of orchids. Referring to its false resemblance to *Maxillaria*.

TYPE SPECIES: *Pseudomaxillaria chloroleuca*
(Barbosa Rodrigues) Hoehne
(*Ornithidium chloroleucum* Barbosa Rodrigues)

This type name is now considered a synonym of *Maxillaria parviflora* (Poeppig & Endlicher) Garay; basionym replaced with *Scaphyglottis parviflora* Poeppig & Endlicher

Now recognized as belonging to the genera *Maxillaria* or *Ornithidium*, *Pseudomaxillaria* was previously considered to include seven epiphytes found in wet, low to mid elevation, hill forests and scrub from the southeastern United States (Florida), Cuba to Trinidad, the Guianas, Venezuela and Mexico south to Brazil. These plants have well-spaced, strongly grooved with age, pseudobulbs, subtended by a pair of dry sheaths; each with a solitary, oblong, leathery leaf borne from the tip of a mature pseudobulb. The clustered, small, green to yellow-white flowers do not open fully. The yellow-green or yellow, trilobed lip has erect side lobes and a spear-shaped midlobe.

PSEUDOOCHRIS

An orthographic variant introduced in *Sp. Pl.* (*Linnaeus*), ed. 1, **2**: 947 (1753). The correct spelling is *Pseudoorchis*.

PSEUDOORCHIS

Dodoens

Fl. Coron. Herb. Hist. 220 (1578).

Pre-1753, therefore not validly published in fulfillment of nomenclatural rules; this name is most often referred to *Ophrys*.

PSEUDO-ORCHIS

An orthographic variant introduced in *Nov. Pl. Gen.*, 30, t. 26 (1729). The correct spelling is *Pseudorchis*.

PSEUDO-ORCHYS

An orthographic variant introduced in *Encycl.* (*Lamarck*), **4**: 570 (1797). The correct spelling is *Pseudorchis*.

PSEUDOORLEANESIA

An orthographic variant introduced in *Feddes Repert.*, **94**(7-8): 465 (1983). The correct spelling is *Pseudorleanesia*.

PSEUDOPERISTYLUS

(P.F. Hunt) Szlachetko & Olszewski

Fl. Cameroun **34**(1): 210 (1998).

ETYMOLOGY: Greek for false and *Peristylus*, a genus of orchids. Referring to its false resemblance to *Peristylus*.

TYPE SPECIES: *Pseudoperistylus petitianus* (A. Richard) Szlachetko & Olszewski (*Peristylus petitianus* A. Richard)

Now recognized as belonging to the genus *Habenaria*, *Pseudoperistylus* was proposed to include ten terrestrials found from Cameroon to Eritrea, Ethiopia to

Zimbabwe and Yemen. These plants have erect, unbranched stems that are leafy throughout their length, each with several, ovate to narrow leaves. The multi-flowered, long, spirally arranged inflorescence has small, inconspicuous, green-white flowers. The concave dorsal sepal and erect, narrow petals converge, forming a hood over the small column. The distinctly trilobed lip has hanging to spreading, narrow lobes, and the usually thread-like spur varies in length.

PSEUDOPONERA

Brieger

Orchideen (*Schlechter*), ed. 3 **8**(29-32): 475 (1976).

ETYMOLOGY: Greek for false and *Ponera*, a genus of orchids. Referring to its false resemblance to *Ponera*.

TYPE SPECIES: *None designated*

Not validly published, this name is referred to a variety of genera including *Ponera*, *Scaphyglottis* and *Helleriella*. *Pseudoponera* was considered to include three epiphytes found from Mexico to Bolivia, Venezuela and the Leeward Islands to Puerto Rico.

PSEUDORCHIS

Clusius

Rar. Pl. Hist. 269 (1601).

Pre-1753, therefore not validly published in fulfillment of nomenclatural rules; this name is most often referred to *Ophrys* or *Satyrium*.

PSEUDORCHIS

Séguier

Pl. Veron. **3**: 254 (1754).

Orchidoideæ • Orchideæ • Orchidinæ

ETYMOLOGY: Greek for false and *Orchis*, a genus of orchids. Referring to the genus as being non-orchid like.

TYPE SPECIES: *Pseudorchis albida* (Linnaeus) Séguier replaced basionym *Pseudorchis albidus* (Linnaeus) designated by Á. Löve & D. Löve, *Taxon*, **18**: 312 (1969). (*Satyrium albidum* Linnaeus)

One small, sympodial terrestrial or uncommon saprophyte is found in low to upper elevation, rough meadows, pastures, wet to rather dry tundra, nutrient-poor grasslands and limestone barrens from Greenland, eastern Canada (Newfoundland to Quebec), Iceland, Norway to Ukraine, France to Yugoslavia and Kazakhstan to eastern Russian (Kamchatka to Sakhalin) usually growing in full sunlight. The plant is quite common locally. This small, erect plant has unbranched stems, each with several, narrow leaves near the base. The densely packed, numerous to few-flowered

inflorescence has small, dull green, pale yellow to white, sweetly fragrant flowers. The widespreading sepals and narrow, ovate petals converge, forming a hood over the tiny, wingless column. The equally tiny, trilobed lip has narrow to slightly curved side lobes, an oblong midlobe and a tiny, short spur.

PSEUDORCHIS

Gray

Nat. Arr. Brit. Pl. **2**: 199, 213 (1821).

Not *Pseudorchis* Séguier (1754) Orchidaceæ.

ETYMOLOGY: Greek for false and *Orchis*, a genus of orchids. Referring to its false resemblance to *Orchis*.

TYPE SPECIES: *Pseudorchis loeselii* (Linnaeus) Gray (*Ophrys loeselii* Linnaeus)

Not validly published because of a prior use of the name, this homonym was replaced by *Liparis*.

PSEUDORLEANESIA

Rauschert

Feddes Repert. **94**(7-8): 465 (1983).

ETYMOLOGY: Greek for false and *Orleanesia*, a genus of orchids. Referring to its false resemblance to *Orleanesia*.

TYPE SPECIES: *Pseudorleanesia yauaperyensis* (Barbosa Rodrigues) Rauschert (*Orleanesia yauaperyensis* Barbosa Rodrigues)

A superfluous name proposed as a substitute for *Orleanesia*.

PSEUDOSTELIS

Schlechter

Anexos Mem. Inst. Butantan, Secç. Bot. 1(4): 36 (1922).

ETYMOLOGY: Greek for false and *Stelis*, a genus of orchids. Referring to its false resemblance to *Stelis*.

LECTOTYPE: *Pseudostelis spiralis* (Lindley) Schlechter (*Physosiphon spiralis* Lindley) designated by Garay, *Orquideologia*, **9**: 118 (1974).

LECTOTYPE: *Stelis deregularis* Barbosa Rodrigues designated superfluously by Luer, *Monogr. Syst. Bot. Missouri Bot. Gard.*, **20**: 36 (1986).

Now recognized as belonging to the genus *Stelis*, *Pseudostelis* was previously considered to include five epiphytes found in low elevation, forests and woodlands from Honduras to Peru and Brazil. These small, creeping plants have erect stems, subtended by several, loose sheaths, each with a solitary, fleshy leaf. The several (two branched), long, numerous to few-flowered inflorescences have tiny, purple to pale green flowers with the lateral sepals united forming a synsepal and have narrow, thread-like petals. The minute, yellow, trilobed lip is heart-shaped. The above second lectotype name is now considered a synonym of *Stelis deregularis* Barbosa Rodrigues.

Currently Accepted   Validly Published   Invalidly Published   Published Pre-1753   Superfluous Usage   Orthographic Variant   Fossil

Orchid Genera • 324

PSEUDOVANDA

Lindley ex d'Orbigny
Dict. Univ. Hist. Nat. **9**: 170 (1847).

Name published without a description. Today this name is most often referred to *Vanda*.

PSEUDOVANILLA

Garay
Bot. Mus. Leafl. **30**(4): 234 (1986).

Vanilloideæ ᴠ **Vanillineæ**

ETYMOLOGY: Greek for false and *Vanilla*, a genus of orchids. Referring to its similarity of these plants to the habit of the climbing *Vanilla*.

TYPE SPECIES: *Pseudovanilla foliata* (F. Mueller) Garay
(*Ledgeria foliata* F. Mueller)

Eight leafless, vining saprophytes are found in very wet, mid elevation, dense rain forests of Indonesia (Java and Maluku), New Guinea, eastern Australia (Queensland to New South Wales), the Philippines, Fiji and the Solomon Islands usually near rivers and waterfalls. These large, spectacular plants have long, climbing to vining, stout stems (orange or yellow when young becoming green with age) and have tiny, triangular scales at each node. The plants often attain heights in excess of ten feet (3 m) The multibranched inflorescence has literally hundreds of widespreading, honey scented, short-lived, pale yellow to orange, conspicuous flowers with narrow sepals and petals. The broad, bright crimson-red, obscurely trilobed lip has a yellow, orange or white, wavy margin, and has two raised crimson lines along its center with numerous, warty calli, and the surface on either side is smooth. The flowers have a slender, curved, footless column.

PSILANTHEMUM

Klotzsch ex **Planchon**
Hort. Donat, 160 (1858).

Name published without a description. Today this name is most often referred to as a section of *Epidendrum*.

PSILOCHILUS

Barbosa Rodrigues
Gen. Sp. Orchid. **2**: 272, *t.* 628 (1882).

Epidendroideæ ᴠ **Triphoreæ**

ETYMOLOGY: Greek for bare and lip. Referring to the smooth texture of the lip of the type species.

TYPE SPECIES: *Psilochilus modestus* Barbosa Rodrigues

Seven uncommon, sympodial terrestrials are widespread in wet, low to mid elevation, hill scrub and montane forests from southern Mexico to Ecuador, Cuba to Trinidad, the Guianas, Venezuela and Brazil. These erect plants have short, purple-green stems, each with the narrow leaves that have a pale to dark green upper surface and a rich magenta-purple color on the undersides. The short, purple, few-flowered inflorescence has dark green-purple to green-yellow, nerved flowers opening in succession with the smaller petals converging over the long, slender, curved, winged column. The pale green-yellow or white, trilobed (above the middle) lip has a raised callus with purple to green stripes along the mid-nerve, a notched purple margin, and the midlobe has a fringed or scalloped margin.

PSITTACOGLOSSUM

Lexarza
Nov. Veg. Descr. **2**: 29 (1825).

ETYMOLOGY: Greek for parrot and tongue. From the thick, fleshy lip that resembles the tongue of a parrot.

TYPE SPECIES: *Psittacoglossum atratum* Lexarza

Now recognized as belonging to the genus *Maxillaria*, *Psittacoglossum* was previously considered to include one epiphyte, lithophyte or terrestrial found in mid to upper elevation, montane cloud forests and meadows from Mexico to Costa Rica. This variable plant has ovoid, compressed pseudobulbs, subtended almost completely by thin, dry sheaths, each with two, narrow to oblong, leathery leaves. The several, solitary-flowered inflorescences, borne from mature pseudobulbs, has a yellow to green-yellow flower spotted or striped red. The erect dorsal sepal and small petals converge, forming a hood over the stout column. The lateral sepals form a short, chin-like protuberance with the column foot. The dark purple, trilobed (above the middle) lip has short, blunt side lobes with a red-spotted callus between, and the yellow, oblong midlobe is distinctly pointed at the tip. The above type name is now considered a synonym of *Maxillaria exarzana* Soto Arenas & F. Chiang.

PSITTAGLOSSUM

An orthographic variant introduced in *Syn. Pl.* (D. Dietrich), **5**: 83 (1852). The correct spelling is *Psittacoglossum*.

PSYCHECHILOS

Breda
Gen. Sp. Orchid. Asclep., fasc. II   *t.* 9 (1829).

ETYMOLOGY: Greek for butterfly and a lip. Descriptive of the conspicuously bilobed lip that fancifully resembles a butterfly's wings.

TYPE SPECIES: *Psychechilos gracilis* Breda

Now recognized as belonging to the genus *Zeuxine*, *Psychechilos* was previously considered to include one terrestrial found in low to mid elevation, open forests of southern China, northern India (Assam), Indonesia (Sumatra to Borneo) and Malaysia. This creeping (at the base) plant has thin leaves (middle section graduating in size) that are withered by flowering time with a few sterile, hairy bracts. The long, hairy, numerous to few-flowered inflorescence has small to tiny, green flowers with hairy sepals. The small, green petals have white tips. The sepals and petals converge, forming a hood over the short, curved column. The yellow (at the base), shortly clawed, bilobed lip has a tiny, sac-like base with two oblong lobes that are at a right angle to the base of the lip.

PSYCHECHILUS

An orthographic variant introduced in *Gen. Pl.* (Bentham & Hooker f.), **3**: 599 (1883). The correct spelling is *Psychechilos*.

PSYCHILIS

Rafinesque
Fl. Tellur. **4**: 40 (1836)[1837].

Epidendroideæ ᴠ **Epidendreæ** • **Laeliinæ**

ETYMOLOGY: Ancient Greek for butterfly, later meaning soul or breath and in modern Greek for mind.

TYPE SPECIES: *Psychilis amena* Rafinesque nom. illeg.
Psychilis bifida (Aublet) Sauleda
(*Epidendrum bifidum* Aublet)

Fifteen sympodial epiphytes, lithophytes or sometimes terrestrials are found in low to mid elevation, coastal to hill oak-pine forests, thorn scrub and cactus of Hispaniola, Leeward Islands and Puerto Rico usually growing in full sunlight. These plants have pear-shaped, spindle-shaped or cylindrical, transversely ringed pseudobulbs, each with sheath scars, internodes evenly sized or spaced, and each with several, rigid, leathery leaves that have serrated margins. The arching to erect, slightly branched, few-flowered inflorescence produces one to two at a time, showy flowers whose color varies among the species but includes lavender, magenta, green-yellow and yellow. The contrastingly colored, short-clawed, trilobed lip, joined to the column at the base, has two roundish, erect side lobes embracing the column, and the entire or bilobed midlobe has a channeled callus. The flowers have a short, fleshy, footless column.

PSYCHILUS

An orthographic variant introduced in *Phylogeny Classif. Orchid Fam.*, 193, 275 (1993). The correct spelling is *Psychilis*.

PSYCHOCHEILOS

An orthographic variant introduced in *Fl. Ned. Ind.*, **3**: 746 (1860). The correct spelling is *Psychechilos*.

PSYCHOCHEILUS

An orthographic variant introduced in *Coll. Orchid.*, 105 (1858). The correct spelling is *Psychechilos*.

PSYCHOCHILUS

An orthographic variant cited in *Lex. Gen. Phan.*, 467 (1904). The correct spelling is *Psychechilos*.

PSYCHOPSIELLA

Lückel & Braem

Orchidee (Hamburg)   **33**(1): 7 (1982).

Epidendroideæ ≀ Cymbidieæ • Oncidiinæ

ETYMOLOGY: *Psychopsis*, a genus of orchids and Latin for diminutive. Indicating its relationship to *Psychopsis*.

TYPE SPECIES: *Psychopsiella limminghei*
(E. Morren ex Lindley) Lückel & Braem
(*Oncidium limminghei* E. Morren ex Lindley)

One sympodial epiphyte is found in low elevation, hill woodlands of southeastern Brazil (Rio de Janeiro) and northern Venezuela. This dwarf plant has compressed, small, ovoid to heart-shaped pseudobulbs, subtended by white, prominently nerved sheaths that soon wither, each with a solitary leaf that has backward curled margins. The pale brown-green leaves are mottled, dull green-maroon and borne at the tip of the pseudobulb. The erect, wiry, solitary-flowered inflorescence, borne from the base of a new pseudobulb, has comparatively large, striking,

dark red-brown flowers with faint yellow banding. The egg-shaped lateral sepals are not as brightly colored. The rachis continues to lengthen, and a new flower blooms after the older one has have fallen off. The bright yellow, trilobed lip is covered with orange-brown to red-brown spots, and has oblong, erect side lobes; the broad, kidney-shaped midlobe has a broad depression, and a three ridged callus. The flowers have a short, erect, winged column.

PSYCHOPSIS

Rafinesque

Fl. Tellur.   **4**: 40 (1836)[1837].

Epidendroideæ ≀ Cymbidieæ • Oncidiinæ

ETYMOLOGY: Ancient Greek for butterfly, later meaning soul or breath and in modern Greek for mind. Refers to the striking resemblance of the flowers to certain tropical butterflies.

TYPE SPECIES: *Psychopsis picta* Rafinesque nom. illeg.
Psychopsis papilio (Lindley) H.G. Jones
(*Oncidium papilio* Lindley)

Four butterfly-like, sympodial epiphytes are found in wet, low to mid elevation, hill and montane forests from Costa Rica to Peru, Trinidad, the Guianas, Venezuela and northern Brazil. These clustered plants have strongly compressed pseudobulbs, subtended by distichous sheaths, each with a solitary, leathery leaf that is sometimes mottled or spotted red or green. The spectacular, exceptionally large, yellow flowers, borne on a long, graceful inflorescence, are tiger-striped in brick-red and emerge one at a time over an extended period. The flowers have erect, long, very narrow dorsal sepal and petals. The widespreading, hanging lateral sepals have wavy margins. The heavily striped, yellow, trilobed lip has small, rounded side lobes, and the broadly clawed midlobe has a wavy margin. The flowers have an erect, footless column.

PSYGMAEORCHIS

An orthographic variant cited in *Handb. Orchid.-Namen*, 628 (2005). The correct spelling is *Pygmaeorchis*.

PSYGMORCHIS

Dodson & Dressler

Phytologia   **24**(4): 288 (1972).

ETYMOLOGY: Greek for S-shape or a fan and orchid. In reference to the plant's fan-shaped growth habit.

TYPE SPECIES: *Psygmorchis pusilla*
(Linnaeus) Dodson & Dressler
(*Epidendrum pusillum* Linnaeus)

Now recognized as belonging to the genus *Erycina*, *Psygmorchis* was previously considered to include eight epiphytes found in humid, low to mid elevation, hill to montane forests, grasslands and canyons from southern Mexico to Bolivia and Brazil. These short-lived plants have short stems with the fleshy, distichous leaves arranged in a flat, fan shape. The short, one- to two-flowered inflorescence has proportionately large, yellow flowers with red bars at the base. The yellow, four-lobed lip, held at right angles to the short, winged column, has red-brown bars at the base and on the callus. The shortly clawed, trilobed lip has small, rounded, clawed side lobes. The large, broadly clawed midlobe has four roundish lobules, with the middle two lobes larger than the outer lobes.

PTALYLEPIS

An orthographic variant introduced in *Gen. Pl., Suppl. 1 (Endlicher)*, 1366 (1840). The correct spelling is *Platylepis*.

PTEREGLOSSAPSIS

An orthographic variant introduced in *Cat. Descr. Orquid., Estac. Exp. Agron. Santiago, Cuba*, **60**: 160 (1938). The correct spelling is *Pteroglossaspis*.

PTERICHIS

Lindley

Gen. Sp. Orchid. Pl.   444 (1840).

Orchidoideæ ≀ Cranichideæ • Cranichidinæ

ETYMOLOGY: Greek for wing, feather or fern and orchid. Refers to the large lip that looks like the spread wings of birds in flight or to the radiating dark nerves that resemble a feathery or leafy fern frond.

TYPE SPECIES: *Pterichis galeata* Lindley

Twenty uncommon, sympodial terrestrials are found in damp to wet, mid to upper elevation, montane forests, grassy meadows, scrub and stony hillsides from Costa Rica to Bolivia, Jamaica and northwestern Argentina. These erect, small, slightly to densely hairy plants have unbranched stems, each with either a solitary, ground hugging leaf

Currently Accepted   Validly Published   Invalidly Published   Published Pre-1753   Superfluous Usage   Orthographic Variant   Fossil

Orchid Genera • 326

or several, basal leaves that are usually withered by flowering time. The erect, rigid, few-flowered inflorescence has intricate, small, white, yellow or red, fleshy textured flowers. The minute, roundish or heart-shaped, white, entire lip is uppermost, has a wavy margin with radiating brightly colored veins, and upturned sides that enclose the short, stout to massive, footless column.

PTERIGODIUM

An orthographic variant introduced in *Nouv. Dict. Hist. Nat.*, **18**: 558 (1803). The correct spelling is *Pterygodium*.

PTEROCERAS

Hasselt ex **Hasskarl**
Flora **25**(2 Beibl.): 6 (1842), and
Tijdschr. Natuur. Gesch. Physiol. **9**: 142 (1842).
Not *Pteroceras* Kuetzing (1849) Ceramiaceæ.

Epidendroideæ ⚘ **Vandeæ • Aeridinæ**

ETYMOLOGY: Greek for wing and a horn. Descriptive of the two, wing-like appendages at the base of the spurred lip.

TYPE SPECIES: *Pteroceras radicans* Hasskarl
This type name is now considered a synonym of
Pteroceras teres (Blume) Holttum;
basionym
Dendrocolla teres Blume

Twenty-four monopodial epiphytes are found mainly from low to mid elevation, tropical rain forests of India, southern China (Yunnan), Myanmar to Vietnam and Indonesia to the Philippines. These small plants have short to long stems, each with a few to several leaves that have unequally bilobed tips and are arranged in two rows. The long, flattened, numerous to few-flowered inflorescence has short-lived, green-yellow to yellow, fragrant, small flowers with brown markings. The mobile, trilobed lip, hinged to the long column foot, has a short midlobe with small protuberances, and the spur may be sac-like, funnel-shaped or only a small excavation. The flowers have a short, stout, wingless column.

NOTE: These plants typically resemble a miniature *Phalaenopsis* vegetatively.

PTEROCHILUS

Hooker & Arnott
Bot. Beechey Voy. 71, t. 17 (1832).
ETYMOLOGY: Greek for feather or wing and lip. From the lip found above the two ovate rings.
TYPE SPECIES: *Pterochilus plantaginea*
Hooker & Arnott
This type name is now considered a synonym of
Malaxis resupinata (G. Forster) Kuntze;
basionym
Epidendrum resupinatum G. Forster

Now recognized as belonging to the genus *Malaxis*, *Pterochilus* was previously considered to include one terrestrial found in low elevation, tropical rain forests of the southwestern Pacific Archipelago. This erect plant has a multitude of ascending leaves and a numerous-flowered inflorescence. The tiny, maroon to green-yellow flowers have an arrow-shaped, entire lip that is minutely toothed. The flowers have a small column with a yellow anther cap.

PTEROCILUS

An orthographic variant cited in *Handb. Orchid.-Namen*, 630 (2005). The correct spelling is *Ptychochilus*.

PTEROCOCCUS

Not *Pterococcus* Pallas (1773) Polygonaceæ, not *Pterococcus* Hasskarl (1842) Euphorbiaceæ, and not *Pterococcus* Lohmann (1904) Pterospermataceæ.

An orthographic variant introduced in *Orchid.-Buch*, 543 (1892). The correct spelling is *Pteroceras*.

PTEROGLOSSA

Schlechter
Beih. Bot. Centralbl. **37**(2): 450 (1920).
Orchidoideæ ⚘ **Cranichideæ • Spiranthinæ**
ETYMOLOGY: Greek for wing and tongue. Alluding to the wing-like lateral lobes of the lip in the species originally assigned to this genus.
LECTOTYPE: *Pteroglossa macrantha*
(Reichenbach f.) Schlechter
(*Spiranthes macrantha* Reichenbach f.)

Eleven sympodial terrestrials are found in dark, damp, low elevation, hill forests and woodlands from southern Mexico to Costa Rica, Colombia to Bolivia, Brazil, Paraguay and northern Argentina usually in sandy soil. These erect plants have short stems, each with a basal rosette usually present but sometimes withered by flowering time. These bright green to olive-green leaves are irregularly spotted white and have red-purple or silvery veins and margins. The terminal, several-flowered inflorescence, partially subtended by smooth, green to red-purple sheaths, has large, showy, green-white flowers with purple veins. The long-clawed, obscurely trilobed lip has blunt side lobes; the heart-shaped midlobe is attached at the base to the lateral sepals and has a wavy margin with a recurved tip. The flowers have a stout, smooth to hairy, channeled column.

PTEROGLOSSASPIS

Reichenbach *filius*
Otia Bot. Hamburg., fasc. 2   67 (1878).
ETYMOLOGY: Greek for wing, lip or tongue and shield. Referring to the shield-like wings of the column.
TYPE SPECIES: *Pteroglossaspis eustachya*
Reichenbach f.

Now recognized as belonging to the genus *Eulophia*, *Pteroglossaspis* was previously considered to include five terrestrials widespread in mostly dry, low to mid elevation, open forests, woodlands and meadows from western Ethiopia to Rwanda, South Africa, the United States (southern Louisiana to Florida and the eastern Carolinas), Cuba, eastern Brazil to northern Argentina. These erect plants have a few grass-like, basal leaves usually wilted at the end of each growing season. The strongly twisted, extremely tall, numerous-flowered inflorescence has nodding, green, dull brown, dark purple or purple-maroon flowers suffused purple or maroon, with all blooming at once, but then lasting for only a few days. The dorsal sepals and petals converge, forming a hood over the short, stout, erect, wingless column that is either footless or has an obscure foot. The deeply trilobed or rare entire lip has small, pale yellow, recurved side lobes with dark purple-red veins, and the flat, downward hanging, dark purple or red, roundish midlobe has a point at the tip. The basal, dark velvety textured callus is strongly veined, or the nerves are variously covered with small warts or is irregularly keeled. The above type name is now considered a synonym of *Eulophia eustachya* (Reichenbach f.) Geerinck.

PTEROGODIUM

An orthographic variant introduced in *Gen. S. Afr. Pl.*, 319, 325 (1838). The correct spelling is *Pterygodium*.

PTEROON

Luer
Monogr. Syst. Bot. Missouri Bot. Gard.
105: 12 (2006).
ETYMOLOGY: Greek for winged and egg. Referring to the texture of the thin, flat scales on the ovary.
TYPE SPECIES: *Pteroon hoeijeri* (Luer & Hirtz) Luer
(*Masdevallia hoeijeri* Luer & Hirtz)

Recognized as belonging to the genus *Diodonopsis*, *Pteroon* was proposed to include two epiphytes or lithophytes found in wet, upper elevation, montane forests from Colombia to southeastern Ecuador. These minute, tufted plants, often forming dense clumps, have short, erect stems, subtended by thinly textured, tubular sheaths, each with a solitary, oblong, leathery leaf. The slender, solitary-flowered inflorescence has a small, pale yellow to pale brown flower striped or veined red-brown. The sepals are united for a short length forming a cylindrical tube, each with short, thick, yellow tails. The flowers have small, oblong, translucent white petals. The tiny, red-brown, oblong, thick, entire lip has a rounded, minutely warty tip. The flowers have a small, club-shaped column and crested ovaries.

PTEROSERAS

An orthographic variant introduced in *Syn. Pl. (D. Dietrich)*, **5**: 104 (1852). The correct spelling is *Pteroceras*.

PTEROSTELMA

Not *Pterostelma* Wight (1834) Asclepiadaceæ.

An orthographic variant cited in *Lex. Gen. Phan.*, 469 (1904). The correct spelling is *Pterostemma*.

PTEROSTEMMA

Kraenzlin

Bot. Jahrb. Syst. **26**: 489 (1899).

Epidendroideæ ⚘ Cymbidieæ • Oncidiinæ

ETYMOLOGY: Greek for wing or feather and garland or wreath. Descriptive of the leaves that gives the plant a wing-like appearance.

TYPE SPECIES: *Pterostemma antioquiense*
F. Lehmann & Kraenzlin

One uncommon, psygmoid epiphyte is found in cool, upper elevation, montane forests of Colombia (Antioquia), Ecuador (Loja) and northwestern Brazil (Rondônia). This small plant has short stems, each with the several, green-red leaves heavily suffused purple, arranged in an overlapping, fan shape and covered with red hairs. The several, short, thick, few-flowered inflorescences have small, bright yellow flowers not opening widely. The lateral sepals are united for most of their length, and the small, narrow petals are found inside. The tiny, entire lip is without any adornment. The flowers have a small, straight or curved, winged column with a triponged tip.

PTEROSTILIS

An orthographic variant introduced in *Prakt. Stud. Orchid.*, 32, 113 (1854). The correct spelling is *Pterostylis*.

PTEROSTYLIS

R. Brown

Prodr. Fl. Nov. Holland. 326 (1810).

Name ICBN conserved, type name also conserved; vs. *Diplodium* Swartz (1810) Orchidaceæ.

Orchidoideæ ⚘ Cranichideæ • Pterostylidinæ

ETYMOLOGY: Greek for winged and style or column. Referring to the broad wings found on the upper half of the column.

LECTOTYPE: *Pterostylis curta* R. Brown

More than one hundred sixty, cool-growing, sympodial terrestrials are found in cool, moist to dry, low to upper elevation, grasslands and woodlands. The majority of the species are native to Australia with a few species found in New Zealand, central New Guinea, New Caledonia and eastern Indonesia (Maluku-Ceram). These tiny, often colony-forming plants have thin, unbranched stems. The leaves are borne along the stem and have crisp or wavy margins; or have a basal rosette that is either at the base of the flowering shoot or on a separate sterile shoot. The solitary to few-flowered inflorescence has drab-colored flowers seldom showy even when in full bloom; they are somewhat tubular in shape. The concave dorsal sepal forms a helmet-shaped hood with the petals. The lateral sepals are fused in the basal part and have long to short, erect tails borne at the top. The mobile, shortly clawed, entire or trilobed lip, more or less hidden in the flower, is hinged to the column by a long or short, elastic strap and springs toward the downward curved, footless or small footed column when touched.

PTERYGODIUM

Swartz

Kongl. Vetensk. Acad. Nya Handl., ser. 2
21: 217, t. 3e (1800).

Orchidoideæ ⚘ Orchideæ • Disinæ

ETYMOLOGY: Greek for a wing and denoting likeness. Descriptive of the dorsal sepal and petals that are united into an erect, hood shaped segment.

LECTOTYPE: *Pterygodium alatum* (Thunberg) Swartz
(*Ophrys alata* Thunberg)

Eighteen sympodial terrestrials are native in cool, low elevation, sandy hill grasslands of South Africa and Tanzania. These showy, robust plants have erect, unbranched stems, each with few to numerous, narrow, deciduous leaves clustered near the base. The erect, numerous to few-flowered inflorescence has pale green, yellow or rare white flowers generally with a shallow hood (formed by the united sepals and petals) and which sometimes

are suffused red or purple. The dorsal sepal is somewhat hooded. The flowers produce an extraordinarily strong scent, somewhat musky sweet that can often be pungent. The diversely shaped, rarely fringed, trilobed or bilobed lip is without or with a long, unlobed, funnel-shaped base, has a hollow, oblong, ovate or trilobed appendage, and a somewhat sac-like spur. The lip is united with the broad gynostemium which forms a massive structure.

PTERYPODIUM

An orthographic variant introduced in *Flora*, **50**(7): 117 (1867). The correct spelling is *Pterygodium*.

PTICHOCHILUS

An orthographic variant introduced in *J. Linn. Soc., Bot.*, **18**(110): 341 (1881). The correct spelling is *Ptychochilus*.

PTILOCNEMA

D. Don

Prodr. Fl. Nepal. 33 (1825).

ETYMOLOGY: Greek for feather and limb or leg. Refers to the plume-like stalk that bears the inflorescence.

TYPE SPECIES: *Ptilocnema bracteatum* D. Don

Now recognized as belonging to the genus *Pholidota*, *Ptilocnema* was previously considered to include one epiphyte, lithophyte or terrestrial found in mid to upper elevation, tropical, sub-tropical and evergreen forests from southern China (Xizang to Sichuan), northern India (Kashmir to Assam), Myanmar to Vietnam, Sri Lanka, Indonesia, New Guinea and northeastern Australia to the Philippines. This plant has gray-green, wrinkled or shrunken pseudobulbs, each with a solitary, oblong to narrow, leathery, dark green, prominently veined leaf that has a pale underside sprinkled with red spots. The drooping, zig-zagging, numerous-flowered inflorescence has brown bracts almost hiding the fragrant flowers that do not open fully. The flowers are arranged spirally around the rachis. The veined dorsal sepal and petals converge, forming a hood. The tiny, tan to pale pink flower has a yellow spot on the midlobe of the lip. The broadly trilobed lip has erect, triangular side lobes, and the deeply bilobed midlobe is shallowly notched in the front. The above type name is now considered a synonym of *Pholidota imbricata* Lindley.

Currently Accepted   Validly Published   Invalidly Published   Published Pre-1753   Superfluous Usage   Orthographic Variant   Fossil

Orchid Genera • **328**

PTYCHOCHILUS

Schauer

Nov. Actorum Acad. Caes. Leop.-Carol. German. Nat. Cur., ser. 3 **19**(Suppl. 1): 431, t. 12B (1843), or *Observ. Bot.* **16**(Suppl. 2): 431, t. 12B (1843).

ETYMOLOGY: Greek for a fold and lip. Descriptive of the lip that encloses the column within its folds.

TYPE SPECIES: *Ptychochilus septemnervis* Schauer

Now recognized as belonging to the genus *Tropidia*, *Ptychochilus* was previously considered to include one terrestrial found in low to mid elevation, forested slopes of the Philippines. This low growing plant has thin stems with long, tubular, nearly pointed bracts, each with numerous, pleated, distichous leaves. The branched, numerous-flowered inflorescence has tiny, green-white, fragrant flowers with similar sepals and petals. The boat-shaped, strongly pointed, entire lip has a thick mid-vein. The above type name is now considered a synonym of *Tropidia septemnervis* (Schauer) Reichenbach f.

PTYCHOGYNE

Pfitzer

Pflanzenr. (Engler) **IV.50**(II.B.7): 18 (1907).

ETYMOLOGY: Greek for a fold and woman or female. An allusion to the prominent S-shaped fold at the base of the lip.

TYPE SPECIES: *Ptychogyne flexuosa* (Rolfe) Pfitzer (*Coelogyne flexuosa* Rolfe)

Now recognized as belonging to the genus *Coelogyne*, *Ptychogyne* was previously considered to include two epiphytes found in low to mid elevation, hill and montane forests of Indonesia (Sumatra, Bali and Java) and Malaysia. These erect plants have clustered, ovoid, ridged pseudobulbs, each with two narrow, rather leathery leaves that have slightly wavy margins. The tall, erect then becoming arched, zig-zagged, few-flowered inflorescence, borne from a mature pseudobulb, has short-lived, sweetly fragrant, white flowers which open simultaneously but never fully open. The flowers are arranged in two rows along the rachis. The trilobed lip has a yellow spot in the center of the midlobe, continuing to the back base of the erect side lobes. The long midlobe has a wavy margin.

PURPURABENIS

Thouars

Hist. Orchid. Table 1, sub 1e, t. 17 (1822).

Name published without a description. Today this name is most often referred to *Cynorkis*.

PURPUROCYNIS

Thouars

Hist. Orchid. t. 15 (1822).

Name published without a description. Today this name is most often referred to *Cynorkis*.

PURPUROLEPTIS

Thouars

Hist. Orchid. Table 1, sub 1e, tt. 26-27 (1822).

Name published without a description. Today this name is most often referred to *Malaxis*.

PUSIPHYLIS

Thouars

Hist. Orchid. Table 2, sub 3u, t. 102 (1822).

Name published without a description. Today this name is most often referred to *Bulbophyllum*.

PYGMAEORCHIS

Brade

Arq. Serv. Florest. **1**(1): 42 (1939).

Epidendroideæ ◊ Epidendreæ • Laeliinæ

ETYMOLOGY: Greek for miniature or dwarf and orchid. Refers to the plant's extremely small stature.

TYPE SPECIES: *Pygmaeorchis brasiliensis* Brade

Two uncommon, sympodial epiphytes are found in cool, mid elevation, coastal to montane rain forests, savannas and prairies of southeastern Brazil (Minas Gerais to São Paulo) and are usually found growing on *Vellozia* trees. These tiny plants have minute, ovate to roundish pseudobulbs, each with one to two oblong, leathery, recurved leaves. The erect, short, solitary-flowered inflorescence, borne between the leaves, has a diminutive, purple or green-yellow flower suffused green at the base, The flower never fully opens and has elliptical sepals and narrowly ovate petals. The tiny, entire lip is fused to the column foot for a portion of its length. The flowers have a tiny, stout, footless column.

PYROLA

Linnaeus

Sp. Pl. (Linnaeus), ed. 1 **1**: 396 (1753).

ETYMOLOGY: Latin for a diminutive of *Pyrus*, a genus of pears. Refers to the outline image of the pear-shaped leaves.

TYPE SPECIES: *Not Orchidaceæ*

Linnaeus did not include this genus in Orchidaceæ. However in 1703, there was one species originally placed in this pre-Linnaeus named genus by Loesel. This terrestrial species is now recognized as belonging to *Goodyera* which is found from Scandinavia, Britain to eastern Russia (Amur to Kamchatka), and Turkey to China, Korea, Japan and Alaska (United States) to across Canada. This plant has erect, unbranched stems, each with a basal rosette. The few-flowered inflorescence has white to creamy, fragrant flowers that are hairy on the outer surfaces. The small, trilobed lip is spear-shaped. The species (*Pyrola angustifolia polyanthos, radice geniculata*, Loesel, *Fl. Prussica*, 210, t. 68 (1703)) was mistakenly included in the Pyrolaceæ (Indian Pipe) family, but the name should now be correctly identified as a synonym of *Goodyera repens* (Linnaeus) R. Brown *Hortus Kew.*, **5**: 198 (1813).

PYRORCHIS

D.L. Jones & M.A. Clements

Phytologia **77**(6): 448 (1995).

Orchidoideæ ◊ Diurideæ • Thelymitrinæ

ETYMOLOGY: Greek for fire and orchid. Referring to the habit of the plant's flowering only after a fire or a disturbance such as mowing.

TYPE SPECIES: *Pyrorchis nigricans* (R. Brown) D.L. Jones & M.A. Clements (*Lyperanthus nigricans* R. Brown)

Two sympodial terrestrials are found in low elevation, coastal scrub, rocky crevices and swamp margins from southern Australia (New South Wales to Western Australia and Tasmania) often forming loose, extensive colonies. These small, stout, fleshy plants have erect, unbranched stems, each with several, ground hugging, wide, roundish leaves that have both surfaces minutely papillate. The few-flowered inflorescence has dull brown, mildly fragrant, large flowers with dark red-brown lateral sepals. The usually broad dorsal sepal is incurved over the column. The white, trilobed lip has purple veins and purple markings on the blunt tip. The erect side lobes clasp the erect, incurved, narrowly winged column, and the midlobe has a plate-like ridge of small calli scattered over the surface between the side lobes.

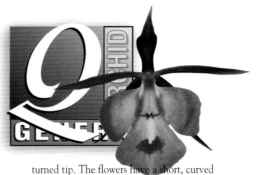

QUECKETTIA

An orthographic variant introduced in *Hamburger Garten- Blumenzeitung*, **8**: 574 (1852). The correct spelling is *Quekettia*.

QUEKETTIA

Lindley

Edwards's Bot. Reg.
25(Misc.): 3, section no. 6 (1839).

Epidendroideæ ⚘ **Cymbidieæ • Oncidiinæ**

ETYMOLOGY: Honoring Edwin John Quekett (1808-1847), a British microscopist, surgeon, professor, botanist and author of numerous articles on the use of the microscope.

TYPE SPECIES: *Quekettia microscopica* Lindley

Seven uncommon, sympodial epiphytes are found in misty, mid elevation, forests and canyon edges of eastern Brazil (Pará to Rio Grande do Sul), Venezuela, the Guianas and Trinidad. These dwarf to minute plants have oblong, flattened to somewhat compressed pseudobulbs, subtended by two leaf-like sheaths, each with a solitary to two, narrow fleshy to leathery, gray-green leaves. The erect, simple or branched, solitary to few-flowered inflorescence has minute, white to yellow-green flowers with narrow, similar sepals and petals. The slender to broad, pale yellow, entire lip has a concave midsection with a downward

turned tip. The flowers have a short, curved column.

QUEKKETTIA

An orthographic variant introduced in *J. Roy. Hort. Soc.*, **7**(1): 130 (1886). The correct spelling is *Quekettia*.

QUENETTIA

An orthographic variant introduced in *Syn. Pl. (D. Dietrich)*, **5**: 11, 97 (1852). The correct spelling is *Quekettia*.

QUETELETIA

Blume

Coll. Orchid. 117 (1859), and
Fl. Javæ Nov. Ser. **1**: 99, *t. 37* (1858).

ETYMOLOGY: Honoring Lambert Adolphe Jacques Quételet (1796-1874), a Belgian physician, botanist, statistician, mathematician, historian, astronomer and author of *A Treatise on Man*. This book established guidelines still used today in modern census taking.

TYPE SPECIES: *Queteletia plantaginifolia*
(Breda) Blume
(*Orchipedum plantaginifolium* Breda)

A superfluous name proposed as a substitute for *Orchipedum* Breda 1829, not *Orchipeda* Blume 1826.

QUISQUEIA

An orthographic variant cited in *Orchideen (Schlechter): Liter. Reg. Band I/A, B, and C*, 170 (2003). The correct spelling is *Quisqueya*.

QUISQUEYA

Dod

Amer. Orchid Soc. Bull. **48**(2): 142 (1979).

Epidendroideæ ⚘ **Epidendreæ • Laeliinæ**

ETYMOLOGY: A pre-Colombian (Taíno) name used for the island of Hispaniola, meaning "mother of the earth." Now used by Dominicans as part of their country's national anthem.

TYPE SPECIES: *Quisqueya karstii* Dod

Four sympodial epiphytes, lithophytes or terrestrials are found in wet, low elevation, pine forest and valley slopes on the island of Hispaniola. These small plants have erect to nodding stems, each with narrow, sword-shaped to grass-like, leathery to rigid leaves with finely notched margins. The long, solitary to few-flowered inflorescence has strikingly attractive, delicate, deep magenta, pink to white flowers suffused pale brown and are borne at the tip of the floral spike. The spreading petals are smooth, of thinner texture and are narrower than the sepals. The clawed, deeply trilobed lip has a splash of color in the center that ranges from golden-yellow to magenta. The flowers have an erect, stout, footless column.

Tlilxochitl	Mecaxochitl	Coatzontecomaxochitl

Sahagún *General History of the Things of New Spain* Book 11 - Earthly Things (1590).

Currently Accepted   Validly Published   Invalidly Published   Published Pre-1753   Superfluous Usage   Orthographic Variant   Fossil

RACIBORSCANTHUS

An orthographic variant cited in *Orchideen (Schlechter): Liter. Reg. Band I/A, B, and C,* 170, 250 (2003). The correct spelling is *Raciborskanthos*.

RACIBORSKANTHOS

Szlachetko

Fragm. Florist. Geobot. **3**(Suppl.): 135 (1995).

ETYMOLOGY: Honoring Marjan Rachiborski (1863-1917), a Polish professor and botanist who collected and studied the flora of the Indonesian island of Java and a pioneer of nature protection in Poland. And Greek for flower.

TYPE SPECIES: *Raciborskanthos capricornis*
(Ridley) Szlachetko
(*Ascochilus capricornis* Ridley)

Now recognized as belonging to the genus *Cleisostoma*, *Raciborskanthos* was proposed to include three epiphytes found in mid elevation, montane forests of northern India (Assam), southern China (Hainan), Thailand to Vietnam, Malaysia and Indonesia (Java, Sumatra and Borneo). These plants have long, erect or hanging, branching stems, each with strongly recurved, pencil-like leaves at the tip. The long, wiry, few-flowered inflorescence, borne from old leaf nodes, has tiny, yellow to magenta flowers. The dorsal sepal is concave; the lateral sepals are recurved, and the oblong petals project forward. The trilobed lip has wing-like parts; the roundish side lobes are incurved, and the narrow midlobe tapers to a roundish tip, has short hairs at the mouth of the spur and a T-shaped flap at the back wall. The flowers have a short, wingless column.

RADINOCION

Ridley

Bol. Soc. Brot. **5**(2): 200 (1887).

ETYMOLOGY: Greek for delicate or slender and a column. Descriptive of the slender column.

TYPE SPECIES: *Radinocion flexuosa* Ridley

Now recognized as belonging to the genus *Aerangis*, *Radinocion* was previously considered to include one epiphyte found in warm, humid, low elevation, evergreen forests of São Tomé. This plant has erect, woody stems, each with several, fleshy leaves that have unequally bilobed tips. The hanging, slightly zig-zagged, few-flowered inflorescence has small, white flowers with similarly shaped sepals and petals. The long, narrow, entire lip has a wide-mouthed, cylindrical spur tapering to a slender tip. The flowers have a long, slender column.

RAMANGIS

Thouars

Hist. Orchid. Table 2, sub 3o, t. 59 (1822).

Name published without a description. Today this name is most often referred to *Angraecum*.

RAMONIA

Schlechter

Repert. Spec. Nov. Regni Veg. Beih. **19**: 294 (1923). Not *Ramonia* Stizenberger (1862) Lichenes.

ETYMOLOGY: Named in honor for the city of San Ramón, located in western central Costa Rica where the type species was collected.

TYPE SPECIES: *Ramonia pulchella* Schlechter

Now recognized as belonging to the genus *Scaphyglottis*, *Ramonia* was previously considered to include one epiphyte found in low to mid elevation, hill scrub to montane rain forests of western Panama to Costa Rica. This plant has distinctly thickened, long, spindle-shaped pseudobulbs, subtended when new by several, thin, dry bracts, each with one to two, narrow, slightly leathery leaves. The short, hanging, solitary to few-flowered inflorescence has a large, cream or pale green flower borne successively. The broad, oblong, entire lip, united to the short column base by a narrow claw, often has a pale purple tinge or lines, and has a smooth margin.

RAMPHIDIA

An orthographic variant introduced in *Fl. Ind. Batav.*, or alternate title *Fl. Ned. Ind.*, **3**: 730 (1859). The correct spelling is *Rhamphidia*.

RAN

Jo-an Matsuoka

Igansai-ranpin (1728).

ETYMOLOGY: The local Japanese and Korean name used for an orchid plant.

TYPE SPECIES: *None designated*

The first Japanese published book on orchids, it contained six orchid species, all with the same name of Ran and each including descriptions and illustrations. Orchid plants were highly prized as living gems for centuries among the various Japanese social orders. This wood-block illustrated book has gone through several editions throughout the years, each with more details, and is beautifully produced.

RAN

Kaempfer

Am. Exot. t. 863 (1712).

ETYMOLOGY: A local Japanese vernacular name for orchid.

TYPE SPECIES: *Ran vulgo et litteratis* Kaempfer

Pre-1753, therefore not validly published in fulfillment of nomenclatural rules; this polynomial name is most often referred to *Cymbidium*. *Ran* was previously considered to include one terrestrial or lithophyte found in low to mid elevation, evergreen forests with damp soil or moss laden limestone rocks ranging from Sri Lanka, India, Thailand, Malaysia, southern China (Yunnan to Jiangxi), southern Japan and Indonesia to New Guinea. This plant has small pseudo-bulbs, subtended completely by overlapping, leaf-bearing sheaths, each with several, stiff, erect, strap-shaped, attractive leaves that are sometimes variegated. The erect, few to numerous-flowered inflorescence has long-lasting, fragrant, highly variable in color, usually pale yellow-green, pale brown to green flowers spotted purple. The sepals and petals have several, red lines. The pale yellow or green, trilobed lip has small, erect side lobes and a tightly inrolled midlobe. This name is now usually considered a synonym of *Cymbidium ensifolium*.

RANGAERIS

(Schlechter) Summerhayes

Kew Bull. **1936**: 227 (1936), and
Fl. W. Trop. Afr. **2**: 404 (1936).

Epidendroideæ ⚏ Vandeæ • Aerangidinæ

ETYMOLOGY: A near anagram of *Aerangis*, a genus of orchids.

TYPE SPECIES: *Rangaeris muscicola*
(Reichenbach f.) Summerhayes
(*Aeranthes muscicola* Reichenbach f.)

Seven monopodial epiphytes, occasional lithophytes or terrestrials are indigenous in dry and wet, low to upper elevation, evergreen forests, scrub and rocky crevices from Sierra Leone and Senegal to Kenya, Ethiopia, Eritrea, then south to Zimbabwe and South Africa. These plants, often forming large clumps on tree branches, have short to long, stout stems, each with leathery, pleated, narrow to oblong, distichous, unequally bilobed leaves arranged in a fan shape. The erect to hanging, numerous to few-flowered inflorescence has two ranks of black bracts. The small to large, mostly white or yellow, star-shaped flowers often fade to pale orange as they age and are sweetly fragrant particularly in the evening. The entire or obscurely trilobed lip has a long, slender, hanging spur with a narrow mouth. The flowers have a short to long, smooth to hairy, wingless, footless column.

RANORCHIS

D.L. Jones & M.A. Clements

Austral. Orchid Res. **4**: 82 (2002).

ETYMOLOGY: Latin for frog and orchid. Referring to the common name of this species "frog greenhood."

TYPE SPECIES: *Ranorchis sargentii*
(C.R.P. Andrews) D.L. Jones & M.A. Clements
(*Pterostylis sargentii* C.R.P. Andrews)

Recognized as belonging to the genus *Pterostylis*, *Ranorchis* was proposed to include one terrestrial widespread in low elevation, moist woodlands of western Australia. This small, erect plant has a basal rosette appearing separately from the flowering stem. The solitary to few-flowered inflorescence has narrow, alternating, clasping leaves that are reduced to scales near the base. The small, green and white flowers have dark brown markings and an incurved hood which tapers to a thin tip. The petals are shortly joined at their base, then each shortly tapers to a point. The tiny, broadly clawed, entire lip has horn-shaped, recurved, non-hairy side lobes, and the large, front, black lobes are quite hairy.

RAPHIDORHYNCHUS

An orthographic variant introduced in *Orchideen (Schlechter)*, ed. 3, 1049 (1986). The correct spelling is *Rhaphidorhynchus*.

RAPHIDORRHYNCHUS

An orthographic variant introduced in *Orchideen (Schlechter)*, ed. 1, 591 (1914). The correct spelling is *Rhaphidorhynchus*.

RAUHIELLA

Pabst & Braga

Bot. Jahrb. Syst. **99**(23): 143 (1978).

Epidendroideæ ⚏ Cymbidieæ • Oncidiinæ

ETYMOLOGY: In honor of Werner Rauh (1913-2000), a German professor of botany at the University of Heidelberg, a specialist on the flora of Madagascar and author of numerous books on bromeliads. And Latin for diminutive.

TYPE SPECIES: *Rauhiella brasiliensis* Pabst & Braga

Three dwarf, sympodial epiphytes are restricted in low elevation, coastal forests of Brazil (eastern Bahia to Rio de Janeiro). These plants have small, pale green, ovoid pseudobulbs, subtended at the base by sheathing leaves, each with a solitary, narrow, rigid leaf. The spreading to hanging, few-flowered inflorescence has small, white flowers with the lateral sepals slightly longer than the dorsal sepal. The somewhat twisted, entire lip has necklace-like, orange bands of papillae across the middle, is hairy toward the base, shortly notched at the tip, and the margin is irregularly notched. The flowers have a footless column.

RAURANITA

Grélet

Monde Pl. Rev. Mens. Bot. **6**: 161 (1897), and
Bull. Soc. Bot. Deux-Sevres **36** (1894).

ETYMOLOGY: Greek for rough. The description and meaning are unknown.

TYPE SPECIES: *Rauranita paludosa* Grélet

Not validly published, this name is referred to *Malaxis*. *Rauranita* was considered to include one terrestrial widely scattered with circum-polar distribution from Scandinavia to eastern Russia (Kamchatka to Sakhalin), Denmark to France, Italy to Ukraine, northwestern United States (Alaska) and western Canada (Yukon Territory).

RAYCADENCO

Dodson

Icon. Pl. Trop., ser. 2 **6**: t. 577 (1989).

Epidendroideæ ⚏ Cymbidieæ • Oncidiinæ

ETYMOLOGY: A composite word made from the collectors names, Raymond McCullough (1912-1996), Carl Leslie Withner (1918-), Dennis D'Alessandro (1951-1989) and Cordelia Head (1949-).

TYPE SPECIES: *Raycadenco ecuadorensis* Dodson

One monopodial epiphyte is found in misty, upper elevation, Andean forests of southeastern Ecuador (Zamora-Chinchipe). This small plant has short stems, subtended by distichous, overlapping sheaths, each with several, thick, oblong leaves. The short, one- to two-flowered inflorescence, borne from the leaf axils, has a bright yellow flower blotched red-brown on the petals and callus. The four-lobed lip has heart-shaped side lobes, and the deeply notched, squared midlobe has a series of warty, hair-like projections. The flowers have a small, erect column with a broad, hood-like extension over the anther.

RECTANGIS

Thouars

Hist. Orchid. Table 2, sub 3o, t. 55 (1822).

Name published without a description. Today this name is most often referred to *Jumellea*.

RECTOPHYLIS

Thouars

Hist. Orchid. Table 3, sub 3u, t. 96 (1822).

Name published without a description. Today this name is most often referred to *Bulbophyllum*.

REGALIA

Luer

Monogr. Syst. Bot. Missouri Bot. Gard. **105**: 12 (2006).

ETYMOLOGY: Latin for royal or of outstanding merit. Refers to a regal status among the Pleurothallidineæ for these species.

TYPE SPECIES: *Regalia dura* (Luer) Luer
(*Masdevallia dura* Luer)

Recognized as belonging to the genus *Masdevallia*, *Regalia* was proposed to include ten epiphytes or lithophytes found in upper elevation, montane forests of Panama, Peru and Ecuador. These large to small, tufted plants, often forming dense clumps, have stout, erect stems,

Currently Accepted   Validly Published   Invalidly Published   Published Pre-1753   Superfluous Usage   Orthographic Variant   Fossil

Orchid Genera • 332

subtended by loose, tubular sheaths, each with a solitary, narrow, thick, leathery leaf. The few-flowered inflorescence has large, rigid, fleshy, long-lasting, red flowers blooming successively. They have united, fleshy, thick, rigid sepals tapering into long tails that are densely spotted purple and warty. The small, thick, fleshy petals are paddle-shaped. The oblong, thick, entire lip has a pair of cavities at the base. The flowers have a small, slightly curved column with a thick foot.

REGNELLIA

Barbosa Rodrigues

Gen. Sp. Orchid. **1**: 81, t. 376 (1877).

ETYMOLOGY: Dedicated to Andrés Frederick Regnell (1807-1884), a Swedish physician, explorer and botanist who discovered numerous new flora and fauna species in Brazil.

TYPE SPECIES: *Regnellia purpurea* Barbosa Rodrigues

Now recognized as belonging to the genus *Bletia*, *Regnellia* was previously considered to include one terrestrial found in wet, mid to upper elevation, montane forests, savannas, embankments and open clearings from Colombia to Ecuador and Brazil. This large plant has small, tightly clustered, ovoid pseudobulbs or corms, subtended with leaf-like sheaths, each with several, fairly large, narrow, deciduous leaves. The erect to arching, few-flowered inflorescence, borne from the top of a mature pseudobulb, has white flowers at its base graduating to pink-purple toward the tips. The purple, deeply trilobed lip has erect, large side lobes, and the dark purple, kidney-shaped midlobe has a disk with three to five, thickened, yellow nerves and a wavy margin. The above type name is now considered a synonym of *Bletia catenulata* Ruiz & Pavón.

REICHANTHA

Luer

Monogr. Syst. Bot. Missouri Bot. Gard.
105: 13 (2006).

ETYMOLOGY: Honoring Heinrich Gustav Reichenbach (1823-1889), a German orchidologist and professor of botany at the University of Hamburg.

TYPE SPECIES: *Reichantha schroederiana*
(Sander ex H.J. Veitch) Luer
(*Masdevallia schroederiana* Sander ex H.J. Veitch)

Recognized as belonging to the genus *Masdevallia*, *Reichantha* was proposed to include eighteen epiphytes or lithophytes found in upper elevation, montane forests from Costa Rica to Colombia, Ecuador, the Guianas, Peru and western Brazil. These small to minute, densely tufted plants have erect, stout stems, subtended by loose, tubular sheaths, each with a solitary, oblong to narrow, leathery leaf. The erect, solitary-flowered

inflorescence has a rich orange, yellow-orange, white to pale pink flower. The sepals are united for a short length forming a tube or cup shape and then taper into long tails that arch backward. The plant has small, oblong petals with wavy margins. The oblong, entire lip has a pair of calli on the middle third and a recurved tip. The flowers have an elongate, club-shaped column.

REICHEMBACHANTHUS

An orthographic variant introduced in *Gen. Sp. Orchid.*, **2**: 164 (1882). The corrected spelling is *Reichenbachanthus*.

REICHENBACHANTHUS

Barbosa Rodrigues

Gen. Sp. Orchid. **2**: 164 (1882).

ETYMOLOGY: Dedicated to Heinrich Gustav Reichenbach (1824-1889), a German professor of natural history, orchidologist, director of the Botanic Garden at Hamburg and founder of the Reichenbach Herbarium in Vienna. Latin for flower.

TYPE SPECIES: *Reichenbachanthus modestus*
Barbosa Rodrigues
not *Scaphyglottis modesta* (Reichenbach f.) Schlechter

Now recognized as belonging to the genus *Scaphyglottis*, *Reichenbachanthus* was previously considered to include five uncommon epiphytes found in wet, low to mid elevation, hill and montane forests from Trinidad, the Guianas, Venezuela, Costa Rica to Bolivia and northern Brazil (Rondônia and Amazonas to Amapá). These erect to hanging plants have branching, cane-like stems, each with long, pencil-like, deeply grooved leaves. The short, solitary-flowered inflorescence has an inconspicuous, small, pale green flower with several, purple markings. Though complex, they are of no great beauty. The sepals open, then turn backward along with the smaller petals. The entire lip is fleshy in the center, thin at the lateral margins, has a green, recurved tip, and has a yellow splash in the center with longitudinal red stripes. The thickened base of the lip, along with the bases of the lateral sepals and column foot form a nectary. The flowers have a small, slender, wingless column. The above type name is now considered a synonym of *Scaphyglottis reflexa* Lindley.

NOTE: Barbosa Rodrigues originally published the genus Reichembachanthus with an 'm', which is his typographical error. This spelling error was later changed by Pfitzer in *Nat. Pflanzenfam. Nachtr.*, **1**: 106 (1897).

RENANTHERA

Loureiro

Fl. Cochinch. **2**: 516, 521 (1790).

Epidendroideæ ☙ Vandeæ • Aeridinæ

ETYMOLOGY: Latin for kidney and Greek for anther. An allusion to the kidney shaped pollinia of the original species.

TYPE SPECIES: *Renanthera coccinea* Loureiro

Seventeen monopodial epiphytes, lithophytes or rare terrestrials are found in hot, steamy, low to mid elevation, hill forests ranging from southern China (Yunnan to Hainan), northern India (Assam), Myanmar to Vietnam, Thailand, Indonesia and New Guinea to the Philippines usually in bright or full sunlight. These robust, climbing plants have long, scrambling stems, each with several, leathery leaves, often bilobed at the tip, that are arranged in two rows; the roots are arranged along the entire length. The often huge, numerous-flowered inflorescences are horizontally branched. The showy, flat-faced, usually scarlet, orange or crimson flowers, opening widely, are netted or spotted in darker colors and long-lasting. The trilobed lip is much smaller than are the other segments, has erect side lobes, a recurved midlobe, and a short or sac-like spur. The flowers have a short, stout, wingless column.

RENANTHERELLA

Ridley

J. Linn. Soc., Bot. **32**: 354 (1896).

ETYMOLOGY: *Renanthera*, a genus of orchids and Latin for diminutive. Implying a relationship with *Renanthera*.

TYPE SPECIES: *Renantherella histrionica*
(Reichenbach f.) Ridley
(*Renanthera histrionica* Reichenbach f.)

Now recognized as belonging to the genus *Renanthera*, *Renantherella* was previously considered to include two uncommon epiphytes found in shady, low to mid elevation, rocky forests and mangroves from Thailand to Malaysia. These small, scrambling plants have long, slender, leafy, branching stems, each with several, sharp, narrow, tapering, channeled, fleshy leaves. The long, several to few-flowered inflorescence has showy, inverted, small, lemon yellow flowers covered with small, crimson spots. Only one or two are open at any one time. The shorter lateral sepals curl backward forming a half circle. The sac-shaped, trilobed lip has long erect side lobes and a bent downward midlobe. The flowers have a long, slender column with an obscure foot.

RENATA

Ruschi

Orquid. Nov. Estad. Espirito Santo   5 (1946).

Epidendroideæ ☙ **Epidendreæ** • **Laeliinæ**

ETYMOLOGY: Dedicated to Renata Aurelia Ruschi e Cainargo (1926-), a Brazilian cousin of Augusto Ruschi (1915-1986), who was an agronomist engineer, a botanist specialist on Brazil's hummingbirds, a professor at the Rio de Janeiro Federal University and author of *Orquideas do Estado do Espírito Santo*.

TYPE SPECIES: *Renata canaanensis* Ruschi

One sympodial epiphyte or lithophyte is found in low elevation, coastal and hill forests of eastern Brazil (Espírito Santo). This tall, erect, large plant has stout, pear-shaped, noded pseudobulbs, each with numerous, overlapping, narrow, but rather large, fleshy, deciduous leaves borne toward the tip. The wiry, multibranched, numerous-flowered inflorescence, borne from the upper leaf axils, has small, yellow, fragrant flowers. The broad, long-clawed (longer than the length of the column), spade-shaped, entire lip has a wavy margin toward the tip. The flowers have a stout, wingless, footless column. This hard to find species is sometimes included in *Pseudolaelia*.

RENNATHERA

An orthographic variant introduced in *Mém. Acad. Sci. Toulouse*, ser. 8, **5**(2): 241 (1883). The correct spelling is *Renanthera*.

RENZORCHIS

Szlachetko & Olszewski

Adansonia, sér. 3   **20**(2): 324 (1998).

ETYMOLOGY: In honor of Jany Renz (1907-1999), a Greek-born Swiss research chemist and an orchidologist who wrote numerous works on the orchids of Iran, Turkey, Bhutan and Pakistan. And Greek for orchid.

TYPE SPECIES: *Renzorchis pseudoplatycoryne*
Szlachetko & Olszewski

Now recognized as belonging to the genus *Habenaria*, *Renzorchis* was proposed to include two terrestrials found in Gabon and Zimbabwe. This tall, erect plant has unbranched stems, each with several, narrow leaves distributed on the lower third of the stem. The few-flowered inflorescence has small, three-veined flowers that are densely glandular along the margins. The dorsal sepal is helmet-shaped, and the petals have two unequal parts. The trilobed lip has thread-like side lobes, and the narrow midlobe has three nerves with a cylindrical, club-shaped spur.

REPANDRA

Lindley

Orchid. Scelet.   12 (1826).

Name published without a description. Today this name is most often referred to *Disa*.

REPHOSTEMON

An orthographic variant introduced in *Orchids Bombay*, 125 (1966). The correct spelling is *Rophostemon*.

RESTREPI

An orthographic variant introduced in *Rad. Jugoslav. Akad. Znan.*, **21**: 129 (1872). The correct spelling is *Restrepia*.

RESTREPHIA

An orthographic variant introduced in *Bot. Reg.*, **10**: sub 825 (1824). The correct spelling is *Restrepia*.

RESTREPIA

Kunth

Nov. Gen. Sp.   **1**: 366, *t.* 94 (1816).

Epidendroideæ ☙ **Epidendreæ** • **Pleurothallidinæ**

ETYMOLOGY: Dedicated to José Manuel Restrepo (1782-1863), a Colombian lawyer, governor, cabinet secretary, mint director and historian who investigated the geography and natural history of the Antioquian Andes in Colombia.

TYPE SPECIES: *Restrepia antennifera* Kunth

Forty-eight dainty, sympodial epiphytes are found in low to upper elevation, hill scrub to montane cloud forests from southern Mexico (Chiapas) to Bolivia and Venezuela, with the center of diversity in Colombia, Ecuador and Peru. These small, clump-forming plants have short, tufted stems, subtended by papery bracts, each with a solitary, blunt or rounded, fleshy or leathery leaf. The several, short, solitary to few-flowered inflorescence, barely clearing the leaf surface, have translucent flowers varying in size. The narrow, colorful flowers have a variety of hues ranging from cream, yellow-green, buff to red and are suffused, speckled or striped in red. The long to short lateral sepals are united, forming a synsepal. The slender, small, oblong or trilobed lip has small, bristly side lobes, and the fiddle-shaped midlobe is oblong. The flowers have a slender, erect to curved, club-shaped column that is footless or has an obscure foot. These species are often included in *Pleurothallis*.

RESTREPIELLA

Garay & Dunsterville

Venez. Orchid. Ill.   **4**: 266 (1966).

Epidendroideæ ☙ **Epidendreæ** • **Pleurothallidinæ**

ETYMOLOGY: *Restrepia*, a genus of orchids and Latin for diminutive. Implying a similarity to *Restrepia*.

TYPE SPECIES: *Restrepiella ophiocephala*
(Lindley) Garay & Dunsterville
(*Pleurothallis ophiocephala* Lindley)

One sympodial epiphyte is found in low to mid elevation, riverside forests, swamps and canyons from the United States (southern Florida) and southern Mexico to Costa Rica and Colombia. This tiny plant, often forming dense clumps, has slender, clustered stems, subtended by tubular bracts, each with a solitary, leathery leaf. The several, short, solitary or rarely two-flowered inflorescences are borne near the axils of the leaf. The small, strongly fragrant, dull yellow, yellow-white or pink flowers are often variously blotched or spotted red-purple. The oblong dorsal sepal is fused at the base with the tiny petals and has a hairy margin. The tiny, mobile, oblong to elliptical, entire lip has two ridge-like calli, is attached to the long column foot, and has a notched tip. The flowers have a small, winged, hooded column.

RESTREPIOPSIS

Luer

Selbyana   **2**(2-3): 199 (1978).

Epidendroideæ ☙ **Epidendreæ** • **Pleurothallidinæ**

ETYMOLOGY: *Restrepia*, a genus of orchids and Greek for like or appearance. Referring to a similarity to *Restrepia*.

TYPE SPECIES: *Restrepiopsis ujarensis*
(Reichenbach f.) Luer
(*Restrepia ujarensis* Reichenbach f.)

Fifteen sympodial epiphytes are found in mid to upper elevation, montane cloud forests and scrub from Costa Rica to Colombia, Venezuela and northern Ecuador. These small, erect plants have secondary stems, subtended by overlapping, ribbed tubular sheaths, each with a solitary, thin to thick leathery leaf sometimes suffused purple. The erect, solitary-flowered inflorescence has a creamy-white to white, translucent flower, often not opening fully, has purple veins, and the small petals are not as large as the long, narrow lateral sepals. The tiny, pale-colored, trilobed lip has a squarish tip with a triangular callus from the base to midway between midlobe. The flowers have a slender, erect, slightly curved column that has a short foot with a massive, knob-like base.

Currently Accepted   Validly Published   Invalidly Published   Published Pre-1753   Superfluous Usage   Orthographic Variant   Fossil

Orchid Genera • **334**

REUNANTHERA

An orthographic variant introduced in *Tijdschr. Natuurl. Gesch. Physiol.*, **6**: 78 (1839). The correct spelling is *Renanthera*.

REYMONDIA

An orthographic variant introduced in *Bot. Zeitung (Berlin)*, **6**: 398 (1848). The correct spelling is *Dubois-Reymondia*.

RHAESTERIA

Summerhayes
Kew Bull. **20**: 191 (1966).

Epidendroideæ ⚘ Vandeæ • Aerangidinæ

ETYMOLOGY: Greek for hammer. In reference to the rostellum that is hammer shaped.

TYPE SPECIES: *Rhaesteria eggelingii* Summerhayes

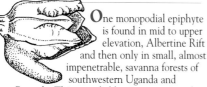

One monopodial epiphyte is found in mid to upper elevation, Albertine Rift and then only in small, almost impenetrable, savanna forests of southwestern Uganda and Rwanda. This remarkable, tiny, creeping plant has short, spreading or hanging stems, each with ovate, fleshy, minutely bilobed leaves that have a tangle of gray-green roots. The few-flowered inflorescence has small, cup-shaped, yellow flowers not opening fully. The narrow sepals and oblong petals are united along their lower segments. The broad, cup-shaped or boat-shaped, entire lip embraces the tiny, short, erect, wingless, footless column. The elongate rostellum somewhat resembles a hammer and has a large, forward curved, stout spur.

RHAMBODIA

An orthographic variant cited in *Orchideen (Schlechter): Liter. Reg. Band I/A, B, and C*, 170, 250 (2003). The correct spelling is *Rhomboda*.

RHAMPHIDIA

(Lindley) Lindley
J. Proc. Linn. Soc., Bot. **1**(4): 181 (1857).

ETYMOLOGY: Greek for crooked beak. Referring to the bent, beak-like lip.

TYPE SPECIES: *Rhamphidia elongata* (Lindley) Lindley
(*Goodyera elongata* Lindley)

Now recognized as belonging to the genus *Hetaeria*, *Rhamphidia* was previously considered to include thirteen terrestrials found in low elevation, rain forests from Sri Lanka to Vietnam and the southwestern Pacific Archipelago. These small, creeping plants have erect, unbranched stems, each with several, broad leaves, distinctly stalked above the sheathing base. The terminal, hairy, numerous-flowered inflorescence has small, white, creamy-white or pink flowers that do not open fully. The outside floral surfaces are covered with fine hairs. The thinly textured, veined dorsal sepal and petals converge, forming a broad hood over the small, short, winged column. The strongly concave, uppermost, entire lip has small growths located near the tip and inrolled side margins. The above type name is now considered a synonym of *Hetaeria finlaysoniana* Seidenfaden.

RHAMPHORHYNCHUS

Garay
Bradea **2**(28): 196 (1977).

Orchidoideæ ⚘ Cranichideæ • Goodyerinæ

ETYMOLOGY: Greek for a curved beak and nose or snout. Referring to the elongate, folded lengthwise rostellum that is refolded upon itself and therefore projects forward.

TYPE SPECIES: *Rhamphorhynchus mendoncae*
(Brade & Pabst) Garay
(*Erythrodes mendoncae* Brade & Pabst)

One small, sympodial terrestrial is found in low elevation, coastal and hill forests of eastern Brazil (southern Bahia). This small plant has leafy stems, each with several, broad, oblong leaves sheathing the base. The short, hairy to smooth, solitary to few-flowered inflorescence has large, white flowers with dissimilar lateral sepals and petals. The deeply concave, almost helmet-shaped, nerved dorsal sepal is difficult to expand. The nerved, trilobed lip has erect, blunt side lobes with a basal callus; the arrowhead-shaped midlobe has an inrolled margin at the tip with a long, swollen spur. The flowers have a short to long, wingless, footless column.

RHAMPIDIA

An orthographic variant introduced in *Orchid. Philipp.*, **1**: 226 (1984). The correct spelling is *Rhamphidia*.

RHAPHIDORHYNCHUS

Finet
Bull. Soc. Bot. France **54**(9): 32 (1907).

ETYMOLOGY: Greek for needle and snout or horn. Descriptive of the greatly elongated rostellum.

TYPE SPECIES: *None designated*

Now recognized as belonging to the genera *Microcoelia* and *Aerangis*, *Rhaphidorhynchus* was previously considered to include twenty-six epiphytes found in low elevation, coastal forests and valleys from Senegal to Sudan, Eritrea to Mozambique and Madagascar. These plants have narrow, compressed, woody stems, each with several, thinly textured leaves and masses of entangled, silvery roots. The small, but several, inflorescences have loosely arranged, small, white flowers not opening fully. The almost entire lip has a thread-like or roundish spur. The flowers have a short column.

RHAPHIDORRHYNCHUS

An orthographic variant introduced in *Beih. Bot. Centralbl.*, **33**(2): 426 (1915). The correct spelling is *Rhaphidorhynchus*.

RHENANTHERA

An orthographic variant introduced in *Syn. Pl. (D. Dietrich)*, **5**: 12, 112 (1852). The correct spelling is *Renanthera*.

RHEPANDRA

An orthographic variant introduced in *Ann. erd, Völk. Staat.*, **10**(1): 37 (1840). The correct spelling is *Repandra*.

RHETINANTHA

M.A. Blanco
Lankesteriana **7**(3): 534 (2007).

ETYMOLOGY: Greek for resin and flower. Refers to the flowers which secrete resin (of most species) on the lip and occasionally on the petals.

TYPE SPECIES: *Rhetinantha acuminata*
(Lindley) M.A. Blanco
(*Maxillaria acuminata* Lindley)

Recognized as belonging to the genus *Maxillaria*, *Rhetinantha* was proposed to include fifteen epiphytes found in wet, low low to upper elevation, hill to montane forests from southern Mexico to Bolivia and northern Brazil. These small plants have well-spaced, ovate, flattened pseudobulbs, subtended by distichous, overlapping sheaths, each with narrowly oblong, thinly textured leaves. The several, wiry, solitary-flowered inflorescence has a bell-shaped, yellow-green to orange-yellow flower with widespreading, narrow to oblong sepals and slightly smaller, erect petals. The trilobed lip has small, erect side lobes and a tongue-like midlobe with a thickened, basal callus. The lip secretes a sticky, resinous substance in most of the species. The flowers have a small, slightly curved, erect column.

RHINERRHIZA

Rupp

Vict. Naturalist **67**: 206 (1951).

Epidendroideæ ✿ **Vandeæ** • **Aeridinæ**

ETYMOLOGY: Greek for to file or rasp and a root. Referring to the roughened appearance and warty outer surface of the strongly flattened roots.

TYPE SPECIES: *Rhinerrhiza divitiflora*
(F. Mueller ex Bentham) Rupp
(*Sarcochilus divitiflorus* F. Mueller ex Bentham)

One monopodial epiphyte is found in low to mid elevation, coastal and montane forest canopies of northeastern Australia and New Guinea. This large, unique plant has thick, raspy roots, long, flat stems, each with coarse, rigid, leathery leaves. The large, spider-like flowers open in the evening. The several, long, hanging, numerous-flowered inflorescences have bright orange or yellow flowers which last for a day or two. They have long, narrow sepals and petals tapering to a hair-like point and are often densely covered with red spots. The small, narrowly clawed, white, trilobed lip has large, erect, incurved side lobes, and a small midlobe. The flowers have a short, stout, wingless column with a long, upcurved foot.

RHINERRHIZOPSIS

Ormerod

Oasis (Dora Creek) **1**(Suppl.): 2 (2001).

Epidendroideæ ✿ **Vandeæ** • **Aeridinæ**

ETYMOLOGY: *Rhinerrhiza*, a genus of orchids and Greek for like or appearance.

TYPE SPECIES: *Rhinerrhizopsis moorei*
(Reichenbach f.) Ormerod
(*Thrixspermum moorei* Reichenbach f.)

One monopodial epiphyte is found in hot, low to mid elevation, coastal forests, rain to semi-deciduous forests and savannas from New Guinea, Aru Islands, northeastern Australia and the Solomon Islands. This plant has short to slightly elongate stems, each with a few to several, smooth, glossy, pencil-like

leaves. The erect, laxly arranged, numerous-flowered inflorescence, emerging from nodes through the base of the leaf sheaths, has fragrant, yellow flowers sprinkled with red spots which often last up to three days. The trilobed lip, flexibly attached to the short, slightly upcurved column foot, has a simple, low callus with long, soft hairs, is free from the side lobes, and has a club-shaped spur that is unadorned internally. The flowers have an erect, short, wingless column.

RHINOCEROTIDIUM

Szlachetko

Polish Bot. J. **51**(1): 40 (2006)[2007].

ETYMOLOGY: Greek for rhinoceros and diminutive. An allusion to the shape of the lip callus, which reminds one of the horn of a rhinoceros.

TYPE SPECIES: *Rhinocerotidium rhinoceros*
(Reichenbach f.) Szlachetko
(*Oncidium rhinoceros* Reichenbach f.)

Recognized as belonging to the genus *Oncidium*, *Rhinocerotidium* was proposed to include three epiphytes found in shady, humid, mid elevation, montane forests of eastern Brazil (Minas Gerais to Rio Grande do Sul, northern Argentina and Paraguay). These plants have oblong to cone-shaped, ridged, slightly compressed pseudobulbs, subtended by overlapping, leaf-bearing sheaths, each with one to two, narrow leaves borne at the tip. The long, branching, few to numerous-flowered inflorescence has small, dull yellow, pale green or red-brown flowers. The trilobed lip has oblong side lobes with recurved margins and a fan-shaped midlobe with a red callus that has a long, incurved horn. The flowers have a slender, slightly curved, wingless column. The above type name is now considered a synonym of *Oncidium longicornu* Mutel.

RHINOCIDIUM

Baptista

Colet. Orquídeas Brasil. **3**: 93 (2006).

ETYMOLOGY: Latin for horn and *Oncidium*, a genus of orchids. Refers to the horn-like tooth of the callus.

TYPE SPECIES: *Rhinocidium longicornu*
(Mutel) D.H. Baptista
(*Oncidium longicornu* Mutel)

Recognized as belonging to the genus *Oncidium*, *Rhinocidium* was proposed to include two epiphytes found in mid elevation, Atlantic forests from southeastern Brazil to northern Argentina. These plants have clustered, cone-like, slightly compressed, ribbed pseudobulbs, each with several, deep green, oblong, leathery leaves. The loose hanging, few-flowered inflorescence, borne from the pseudobulb base, has small, bright yellow-green to red-brown flowers with

the lateral sepals joined for about half their length. The bright yellow (pale red on the underside), trilobed lip has large side lobes, a broad, clawed, notched midlobe with a long, recurved, horn-like appendage. These flowers have a small, slightly curved, club-shaped, wingless column.

RHIPIDOGLOSSUM

Schlechter

Beih. Bot. Centralbl. **36**(2): 80 (1918).

Epidendroideæ ✿ **Vandeæ** • **Aerangidinæ**

ETYMOLOGY: Greek for bellows or a fan and tongue. Referring to the fan shape of the lip.

LECTOTYPE: *Rhipidoglossum xanthopollinium*
(Reichenbach f.) Schlechter
(*Aeranthes xanthopollinius* Reichenbach f.)

Thirty-seven monopodial epiphytes are found in warm, humid, low elevation, hill and river forests of Angola, Kenya, Tanzania, Malawi, Mozambique to eastern South Africa, Uganda, Zaire, Zambia and Zimbabwe. These quite variable plants have short or long, erect to hanging, slender to stout stems. The numerous, narrow to tongue-shaped, leathery, equally bilobed leaves are often suffused purple and well-spaced along the stem. The short, numerous-flowered inflorescences produce vast quantities of attractive, small, lightly fragrant, translucent to pale yellow, pale green or white flowers that are often suffused green or orange. The tiny, broad, fan-shaped, usually entire lip is sometimes bilobed at the tip with the lower margin rolled backward, and a long to short, curved spur. The flowers have a short, erect, wingless column.

RHIPIDORCHIS

D.L. Jones & M.A. Clements

Orchadian **14**(8: Sci. Suppl.): xiv (2004).

ETYMOLOGY: Greek for fan and orchid. Refers to the arrangement of the distichous leaves.

TYPE SPECIES: *Rhipidorchis micrantha*
(A. Richard) D.L. Jones & M.A. Clements
(*Oberonia micrantha* A. Richard)

Recognized as belonging to the genus *Phreatia*, *Rhipidorchis* was proposed to include one epiphyte found in low to mid elevation, seasonally dry forests from northern Australia (Queensland) to New Guinea and the southwestern Pacific Archipelago. This small, fan-shaped plant has its fleshy, yellow-green, overlapping leaves arranged in two ranks. The erect, numerous-flowered inflorescence, borne from the leaf axils, has minute, green-yellow to white flowers each with an ovate bract. The rachis blooms successively, opening from the base and moving upward. The tiny, entire lip is ovate. The flowers have a short, broad column.

Currently Accepted   Validly Published   Invalidly Published   Published Pre-1753   Superfluous Usage   Orthographic Variant   Fossil

Orchid Genera • **336**

RHIZANTHELLA

R.S. Rogers

J. Roy. Soc. Western Australia **15**: 1, *tt. I-II* (1928).

Orchidoideæ ⚘ Diurideæ • Rhizanthellinæ

ETYMOLOGY: Greek for root (*Rhizanthes* Dumortier, a saprophyte - Rafflesiaceæ), flower and Latin for like or diminutive. Refers to its saprophyte characteristics and its almost wholly underground growth.

TYPE SPECIES: *Rhizanthella gardneri* R.S. Rogers

Two very extraordinary, subterranean saprophytes without any chlorophyll. These species are found in southwestern and southeastern coastal scrub areas of Australia in association with the broom honey myrtle. This *Melaleuca* species provides all the essential sugars and nutrients for its growth. It usually is found growing in nutrient-poor soils. These unusual, remarkable plants spend most of their life underground. The widespreading, rootless rhizomes have a dense, daisy-like head of flowers, borne at or near the surface of the soil, with all the leaves reduced to mere scales. Although never seeing the light of day, these plants depend on ants and other terrestrial insects to pollinate the flowers. The numerous, small, spirally arranged, inward facing flowers are dark purple to red. The petals and sepals are united, forming a tube-like structure with only the curved tips free. The tiny, entire lip is uniquely hinged. The flowers have a slightly curved, footless column.

RHIZOCORALLON

Haller

Ruppius' Fl. Jen., ed. 3   301 (1745).

ETYMOLOGY: Greek for root and coral. Descriptive of the often brittle, coral-like appearance or texture of the roots.

TYPE SPECIES: *None designated*

Pre-1753, therefore not validly published in fulfillment of nomenclatural rules; this name is most often referred to *Corallorhiza*. *Rhizocorallon* was considered to include one terrestrial often found growing in clusters, in dark or deeply shady woodlands, tundra or dunes from Norway to eastern Russia (Kamchatka) and Germany to Greece. This odd, slender, leafless plant has an erect, unbranched, green to brown stem. The few-flowered inflorescence has small flowers varying in color. The color depends upon the degree of light received during the usually short growing season. The dorsal sepal and petals converge, forming a hood over the small column. The triloled lip has small, white or spotted dark purple side lobes. The oblong midlobe has a basal callus and a scalloped or wavy margin. This name is now usually considered a synonym of *Corallorhiza trifida* Châtelain.

RHIZOCORALLON

Haller ex Gagnebin

Acta Helv. Phys.-Math.   **2**: 61 (1755).

ETYMOLOGY: Greek for root and coral. Descriptive of the often brittle, coral-like appearance or texture of the roots.

TYPE SPECIES: *None designated*

A superfluous name proposed as a substitute for *Corallorhiza*.

RHIZONIUM

Corda

Beitr. Fl. Vorwelt   46, *t.* 27 (1845).

ETYMOLOGY: Greek for root stock. Refers to the hair-like roots found in the fossilized rock.

TYPE SPECIES: *Rhizonium orchideiforme* Corda

One fossilized stem and a few structurally preserved, hair-like roots, which were originally found in Hungary and determined to belong to the orchid family. These pieces date from the Miocene Epoch which lasted from 23.3 million to 5.2 million years ago; this epoch of the Tertiary Period was between the Oligocene and Pliocene epochs.

RHIZONIUM

Lindley

Veg. Kingd., ed. 3   890 (1853).

Not *Rhizonium* Corda (1845) Fossil.

Name published without a description. Today this name is most often referred to *Dockrillia*.

RHOMBODA

Lindley

J. Proc. Linn. Soc., Bot.   **1**(4): 181 (1857).

Orchidoideæ ⚘ Cranichideæ • Goodyerinæ

ETYMOLOGY: Greek for spinning top. Referring to the two, diamond-shaped appendages borne near the base of the lip of the type species.

TYPE SPECIES: *Rhomboda longifolia* Lindley

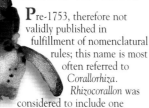

Nineteen sympodial terrestrials or uncommon epiphytes are found in shady, low to upper elevation, rain forests and valley slopes from northern India (Assam), Nepal, Bhutan, Myanmar to Vietnam, southern China (Guangxi to Hainan), southern Japan (Ryukyu Islands) to the Philippines, Indonesia, New Guinea, and northern Australia (Queensland) to the southwestern Pacific Archipelago. These tall, robust plants have erect stems with a few internodes of equal length, each with several, large, narrow, green-red leaves suffused bronze that have a median line often striped white-red. The erect, long, numerous to few-flowered inflorescence (sparsely hairy) has tiny, translucent white flowers. The triloled to four-lobed lip has small, inrolled side lobes, and the midlobe has two solitary warts. The flowers have an unusual, club-shaped, winged column and the funnel-shaped anther base is uppermost at an angle. These species were often included in *Hetaeria* or *Anoectochilus*.

RHOPALORRHACHIS

Klotzsch ex Reichenbach *filius*

Cat. Orch.-Samml. Schiller, ed. 1   62 (1857).

ETYMOLOGY: Greek for a rod-like inflorescence.

TYPE SPECIES: *None designated*

Name published without a description. Today this name is most often referred to *Polystachya*.

RHOPHOSTEMON

An orthographic variant cited in *Etym.-Bot.-Handw.-Buch*, ed. 1, 763 (1852). The correct spelling is *Roptrostemon*.

RHYCANTHERA

An orthographic variant introduced in *Orchids S. Ryukyu Islands*, 93 (1974). The correct spelling is *Rhynchanthera*.

RHYNCADENIA

An orthographic variant introduced in *Fl. Jamaica (Fawcett & Rendle)*, **1**: 124 (1910). The correct spelling is *Rhynchadenia*.

RHYNCANTHERA

An orthographic variant introduced in *Nat. Syst. Bot.*, ed. 2, 342 (1836). The correct spelling is *Rhynchanthera*.

RHYNCHADENIA

A. Richard

Hist. Fis. Cuba, Bot.   **11**: 248, *t.* 85 (1850).

ETYMOLOGY: Greek for beak and gland. Refers to the long rostellum that is terminated with an elliptic gland.

TYPE SPECIES: *Rhynchadenia cubensis* A. Richard

Now recognized as belonging to the genus *Macradenia*, *Rhynchadenia* was previously considered to include one epiphyte found in wet, low elevation, hill forests and scrub of the United States (southern Florida), Cuba, Trinidad, the Guianas, Venezuela and Colombia. This small plant has narrow, compressed pseudobulbs, subtended by white sheaths, each with a solitary, oblong, leathery leaf. The hanging, numerous to few-flowered inflorescence has yellow-green flowers. The sepals are purple-brown on their inner surfaces. The white, trilobed lip has heart-shaped side lobes that are pointed near their tips, and the narrow midlobe has a rolled margin. The flowers have a slender, wingless, footless column. The above type name is now considered a synonym of *Macradenia lutescens* R. Brown.

RHYNCHANDRA

Reichenbach

Deut. Bot. Herb.-Buch. 56 (1841).
Name rejected *Rynchanthera* Blume (1825) Orchidaceæ.
ETYMOLOGY: Greek for snout or beak and flower.
TYPE SPECIES: *None designated*

Name published without a description. Today this name is most often referred to *Corymborkis*.

RHYNCHANTHERA

Blume

Tab. Pl. Jav. Orchid. f. 78 (1826).
Not *Rhynchanthera* A.P. de Candolle (1828) Melastomataceæ and not *Rhynchanthera* Bentham (1868) Asclepiadaceæ.
ETYMOLOGY: Greek for snout or beak and flower.
TYPE SPECIES: *Rhynchanthera paniculata* Blume

Name published without a description. Today this name is most often referred to *Corymborkis*.

RHYNCHOGYNA

Seidenfaden & Garay

Bot. Tidsskr. 68(1): 88 (1973).
Epidendroideæ ◆ Vandeæ • Aeridinæ
ETYMOLOGY: Greek for snout or beak and woman or female. In reference to the rostellum that is extended forward, beak-like.
TYPE SPECIES: *Rhynchogyna luisifolia*
(Ridley) Seidenfaden & Garay
(*Saccolabium luisifolium* Ridley)

Three monopodial epiphytes are found in low elevation, hill forests of Thailand, Malaysia, Laos and Vietnam. These plants have long, hanging stems, each with numerous, purple, pencil-like leaves arranged in two rows along the stem. The simple to branching, numerous-flowered inflorescences have small, green flowers sprinkled with purple dots. The dorsal sepal is hood-shaped with the lateral sepals fused to the column foot and it has small, erect petals. The fleshy, trilobed or sac-like lip has an arrow-shaped midlobe; the raised side lobes have inrolled, forward margins. The spur has varying ornaments or appendages near the entrance but no partition, and its entrance is nearly closed by a large callus. The flowers have a slender, wingless column.

RHYNCHOLAELIA

Schlechter

Beih. Bot. Centralbl. 36(2): 477 (1918).
Epidendroideæ ◆ Epidendreæ • Laeliinæ
ETYMOLOGY: Greek for snout or horn and *Laelia*, a genus of orchids. Refers to the prominent beak separating the ovary from the rest of the flower.
TYPE SPECIES: *None designated*

Two sympodial epiphytes or sometimes terrestrials, often labeled as *Brassavola* where they were formerly placed. These plants are found in hot, seasonally dry, low to mid elevation, hill forests, thorn bushes and cacti of southern Mexico, Guatemala, Honduras and Belize to Nicaragua. These large plants have long, compressed, club-shaped pseudobulbs, subtended by off-white sheaths, each with a solitary, long, oblong, leathery to fleshy leaf. The plants have fat sheaths often containing a solitary, extremely showy flower with a strong, almost overpowering fragrance. The flowers have a short, erect, footless column. They differ from *Brassavola* by their broad, flat leaves and much larger flowers. The species *Rhyncholaelia glauca* (Lindley) Schlechter (found from southern Mexico to Nicaragua) has small, pale green, white or lavender flowers with a plain, non fringed, white or creamy lip that has a purple mark at the base and purple stripes in the throat. The second species *Rhyncholaelia digbyana* (Lindley) Schlechter has robust, fragrant, creamy, green, olive-green or yellow-green flowers with exceedingly large, spectacular and extremely frilly, obscurely trilobed lip.

RHYNCHOPERA

Klotzsch

Icon. Pl. Rar. (Link) 2: 103, t. 41 (1844).
Not *Rhynchopera* Börner (1912) Cyperaceæ.
ETYMOLOGY: Greek for a horn or snout and a pouch. Perhaps an allusion to the column shape and the lip which is basally concave.
TYPE SPECIES: *Rhynchopera pedunculata* Klotzsch
This type name is now considered a synonym of
Stelis lanceolata (Ruiz & Pavón) Willdenow;
basionym
Humboldtia lanceolata Ruiz & Pavón

Now recognized as belonging to the genus *Pleurothallis*, *Rhynchopera* was previously considered to include seven epiphytes found in cool, misty, upper elevation, montane forests from Colombia to Peru and Venezuela. These minute plants have well developed, twig-like stems, subtended by leaf-like sheaths, each with a solitary, ovate leaf that have a long, twisted stem. The

solitary-flowered inflorescence emerges from a conspicuous, spatula-shaped ring on the leaf base. The pale brown flower has spotted, joined, lateral sepals suffused maroon. The narrow petals are tail-like, and the immobile, arrow-shaped, brown, entire lip tapers. The flowers have a slender, footless column.

RHYNCHOPHREATIA

Schlechter

Bot. Jahrb. Syst. 56: 488 (1921).
ETYMOLOGY: Greek for snout or beak and *Phreatia*, a genus of orchids. In reference to the prominent beak on the rostellum of this genus, thus allowing it to be easily distinguished from *Phreatia*.
TYPE SPECIES: *Rhynchophreatia palawensis*
Schlechter

Now recognized as belonging to the genera *Thelasis* and *Phreatia*, *Rhynchophreatia* was previously considered to include ten epiphytes found in warm, low to mid elevation, dry hill and montane rain forests from Indonesia and northern Australia to the Solomons with most species found in New Guinea. These plants have tiny pseudobulbs, almost completely subtended by small, leaf-like sheaths, each with one to two, narrow, leathery, bilobed leaves. The erect, long, wiry, arching or slightly arching, numerous-flowered inflorescence is borne from the base of the pseudobulb. The tiny, cup-shaped, yellow-brown, yellow or white flowers, borne on the upper two-thirds of the stem, rarely open widely. The entire lip has a broad wedge-shaped base. The flowers have an extremely short, wingless column with a short, stout foot. The above type name is now considered a synonym of *Phreatia palawensis* (Schlechter) Tuyama.

RHYNCHOSTELE

Reichenbach *filius*

Bot. Zeitung (Berlin) 10: 770 (1852).
Epidendroideæ ◆ Cymbidieæ • Oncidiinæ
ETYMOLOGY: Greek for snout or horn and stalk or pillar. Descriptive probably of the elongate rostellum.
TYPE SPECIES: *Rhynchostele pygmaea*
(Lindley) Reichenbach f.
(*Odontoglossum pygmaeum* Lindley)

Sixteen sympodial epiphytes, lithophytes or terrestrials make up this genus. Many of these fancy plants are found in cool, upper elevation montane forests from Mexico to Panama and northwestern Venezuela. These plants have clustered, egg-shaped, somewhat flattened pseudobulbs, subtended by distichous, leaf-like sheaths, each with a solitary, thinly textured, narrow, strap-

Currently Accepted | Validly Published | Invalidly Published | Published Pre-1753 | Superfluous Usage | Orthographic Variant | Fossil

like leaf. The erect to arching, long to short, simple to branched, numerous to few-flowered inflorescence has small, showy, fragrant flowers heavily barred or spotted dark red or brown. The heart-shaped, white or pink, trilobed lip has small, united side lobes forming a small saddle with a tiny, grooved callus in the center, and a large, thinly textured midlobe with a wavy margin. The flowers have a long, slender, footless column.

RHYNCHOSTELIS

An orthographic variant introduced in *Beih. Bot. Centralbl.*, **36**(2): 509 (1918). The correct spelling is *Rhynchostylis*.

RHYNCHOSTYLES

An orthographic variant introduced in *Edwards's Bot. Reg.*, **27**(Misc.): 55, section no. 115 (1841). The correct spelling is *Rhynchostylis*.

RHYNCHOSTYLIS

Blume

Bijdr. Fl. Ned. Ind.   **7**: 285, *t.* 49 (1825), and
Tab. Pl. Jav. Orchid.   *t.* 5 (1825).

Not *Rhynchostylis* Tausch (1834) Apiaceæ.

Epidendroideæ ◊ **Vandeæ** • **Aeridinæ**

ETYMOLOGY: Greek for beak or nose and column or style. Refers to the beaked column on the flowers of the type species.

TYPE SPECIES: *None designated*

Three monopodial epiphytes are found in low to mid elevation, hill woodlands and montane forests of southern China (Yunnan and Guizhou), northern India (Kashmir to Assam), Nepal, Myanmar to Vietnam, Thailand, Indonesia and extending to the Philippines. Often erroneously classified under the genera *Saccolabium* or *Anota*, these plants have short, stout stems, each with thick, channeled, distichous, pale green lined, unequally bilobed leaves (often tape-like) that are arranged in two ranks along the stem. A single plant might easily bear 200 waxy, spicy fragrant, mainly white flowers marked red, purple or pale blue and are often sprinkled with several, purple or pink spots on erect or arching, densely packed inflorescences. The dark colored, entire, trilobed or obscurely trilobed lip has bright purple lobes (not hinged) that are united to the base of the short, stout, wingless column, and has a deeply sac-like or backward pointing, flattened spur.

NOTE: Blume originally spelled this genus without the first 'h' in the *Bijdr.* but he later added the second 'h' in the *Tab. Pl. Jav. Orchid.* illustration spelling (*t.* 49).

RHYNCOPERA

An orthographic variant introduced in *Ann. Hort.*, **5**: 232 (1850). The correct spelling is *Rhynchopera*.

RHYNCOSTYLIS

An orthographic variant introduced in *Bot. Reg.*, **18**: sub 1552 (1832). The correct spelling is *Rhynchostylis*.

RHYTIONANTHES

An orthographic variant cited in *Handb. Orchid.-Namen*, 642 (2005). The correct spelling is *Rhytionanthos*.

RHYTIONANTHOS

Garay, Hamer & Siegerist

Nordic J. Bot.   **14**(6): 637 (1994).

ETYMOLOGY: Greek for small drinking horn and flower. An allusion to the shape of the lateral sepals.

TYPE SPECIES: *Rhytionanthos cornutum*
            (Lindley) Garay, Hamer & Siegerist
            (*Cirrhopetalum cornutum* Lindley)

This type name is now considered a synonym of *Bulbophyllum helenae* (Kuntze) J.J. Smith; basionym replaced with *Phyllorkis helenae* Kuntze

Now recognized as belonging to the genus *Bulbophyllum*, *Rhytionanthos* was proposed include ten epiphytes or lithophytes found in low to mid elevation, hill scrub and montane forests from southern China (Yunnan), northern India (Sikkim), Nepal, Myanmar, Thailand, Malaysia and Indonesia to the Philippines. These small, creeping plants form huge colonies, and their tiny, stout pseudobulbs, each with a solitary, strongly channeled leaf. The long, few-flowered inflorescence has pink to magenta, brown-orange to yellow, foul odor flowers with a few faint purple lines or dots. The long lateral sepals are firmly united along both margins forming a small pouch; the small, ovate petals are hairy. The mobile, fleshy, recurved, entire lip is a pale yellow. The flowers have a short, stout, wingless column with a strongly incurved foot that completes a 180° turn.

RIDLEYA

Hooker *filius*

Fl. Brit. India   **6**: 33, 42 (1894).

Not validly published, this name is referred to *Thrixspermum*.

RIDLEYA

(Hooker *filius*) **Pfitzer**

Nat. Pflanzenfam. Nachtr.   **2**: 16 (1900).

ETYMOLOGY: Dedicated to Henry Nicholas Ridley (1855-1956), a British explorer, collector and botanist who developed a method of tapping rubber trees for their latex sap, the first scientific director of Singapore Botanic Gardens and author of *Flora of the Malayan Peninsula*.

TYPE SPECIES: *Ridleya notabilis* (Hooker f.) Pfitzer
            (*Sarcochilus notabilis* Hooker f.)

This type name is now considered a synonym of *Thrixspermum acuminatissimum* (Blume) Reichenbach f.; basionym replaced with *Dendrocolla acuminatissima* Blume

Now recognized as belonging to the genus *Thrixspermum*, *Ridleya* was previously considered to include one epiphyte found in moist, low elevation, woodlands and sandy forests of Indonesia (Java to Borneo), Malaysia, Thailand, Cambodia and the Philippines. This plant has short, flattened stems, each with small, leathery, two-ranked, green or deep purple leaves. The short to long, few-flowered inflorescence has short-lived, pale yellow flowers suffused red at the base and they open simultaneously. The similar, long, narrow sepals and petals taper to sharp points. The pale yellow, red-orange spotted, sac-like, trilobed lip, united with the column foot, has a long, thread-like, white tipped midlobe. The flowers have a tiny column.

RIDLEYELLA

Schlechter

Repert. Spec. Nov. Regni Veg. Beih.
1(12): 948 (1913).

Epidendroideæ ◊ **Podochileæ** • **Thelasinæ**

ETYMOLOGY: Honoring Henry Nicholas Ridley (1855-1956). And Latin for diminutive.

TYPE SPECIES: *Ridleyella paniculata*
            (Ridley) Schlechter
            (*Bulbophyllum paniculatum* Ridley)

One uncommon, sympodial epiphyte is found along the edge of low to mid elevation, hill and montane rain forests in New Guinea with plenty of sunlight. This small plant has oblong to spindle-shaped pseudobulbs, which are always subtended by a slimy substance, each with two long, narrow, slightly leathery leaves. The several, multibranched, numerous-flowered inflorescence has tiny, dark purple-blue flowers not opening widely that have a concave dorsal sepal. The floral segments are off white on their outside surfaces. The white, shortly clawed, trilobed lip has a spear-shaped or shallowly trilobed midlobe. The flowers have a short, thick column.

NOTE: Vegetatively and florally this species simulates the genus *Acriopsis*, especially when the plant is not in flower.

An orthographic variant introduced in *Beih. Bot. Centralbl.*, **42**(2): 129 (1925). The correct spelling is *Bifrenaria*.

RIMACOLA

Rupp

Vict. Naturalist   **58**: 188 (1942).

Orchidoideæ ⚘ Diurideæ • Thelymitrinæ

ETYMOLOGY: Latin for cleft or crack and an inhabitant. In reference to the habitat, wet crevices and damp, sandstone cliff ledges favored by this genus.

TYPE SPECIES: *Rimacola elliptica* (R. Brown) Rupp (*Lyperanthus ellipticus* R. Brown)

One uncommon, sympodial terrestrial or lithophyte is found in moist, low elevation, sandstone cliffs with a constant water supply of the Sydney coastal basin of eastern Australia (New South Wales). This small, erect plant has short, unbranched stems, each with several, narrow, arching to hanging leaves per shoot. The wiry, few-flowered inflorescence has small, drooping, pale green to yellow, long-lasting flowers with brown or red markings. The dorsal sepal is helmet-shaped over the erect, slender, narrowly winged, footless column. The long floral segments are drawn out to fine points. The white, obscurely trilobed or entire lip has small side lobes, and the midlobe has veined, irregular raised papillae at the base and bold, radiating, red streaks.

RISLEYA

King & Pantling

Ann. Roy. Bot. Gard. (Calcutta) **8**: 246, *t. 328* (1898).

Epidendroideæ ⚘ Malaxideæ

ETYMOLOGY: Dedicated to Herbert Hope Risley (1851-1911), a British-born secretary to the Indian Government of Bengal, ethnologist, commissioner of the 1901 census who used the caste system in census taking, and author of *The Tribes and Castes of Bengal* and *The People of India*.

TYPE SPECIES: *Risleya atropurpurea* King & Pantling

One uncommon, sympodial, terrestrial or saprophyte is found in upper elevation, montane forests and bogs of northeastern India (Sikkim), Nepal, Bhutan, Myanmar and southwestern China (Yunnan and Sichuan). This small, leafless, purple plant, barely three inches (7 cm) in height, has neither tubers nor pseudobulbs but has erect, unbranched smooth, ridged stems, each with several, clasping sheaths at the base. The terminal, densely packed, numerous-flowered inflorescence has minute, flat-faced, deep black-purple flowers with similar, spreading sepals and shorter, narrow petals. The concave, fleshy, erect, entire lip, united to the column base, has a small to short, upturned tip and is slightly scalloped near the base. The flowers have a short, erect, club-shaped column.

An orthographic variant introduced in *Schriften Ges. Beförd. Gesammten Nauturwiss. Marburg*, **2**: 125 (1831). The correct spelling is *Restrepia*.

RITAIA

King & Pantling

Ann. Roy. Bot. Gard. (Calcutta) **8**: 156, *t. 214* (1898).

ETYMOLOGY: Dedicated to a Mr. S.E. (or G.) Rita (*fl.* 1890s), an Indian of the Khasia Commission and an avid collector of the flora and fauna from the northeastern Indian region of Assam.

TYPE SPECIES: *Ritaia himalaica* (Hooker f.) King & Pantling (*Ceratostylis himalaica* Hooker f.)

Now recognized as belonging to the genus *Ceratostylis*, *Ritaia* was previously considered to include one terrestrial or lithophyte found in low to mid elevation, forests of southwestern China (Xizang and Yunnan), northeastern India (Assam), Nepal, Bhutan, and Myanmar to Vietnam. This hanging plant, often forming large clumps, has numerous, tufted, equally branching stems, subtended by overlapping, thin sheaths. Each stem has a solitary, strongly veined, narrow leaf. The short, thick, solitary to few-flowered inflorescence has externally hairy, purple veined, pale green-yellow to white flowers spotted purple-red and do not open widely. The bright yellow, concave, hairy, oblong, entire lip is attached to the small, short column forming a chin-like protuberance, and tapers to a point.

An orthographic variant introduced in *Heidelberger Jahrb. Lit.*, **24**: 263 (1831). The correct spelling is *Rodriguezia*.

ROBIQUETIA

Gaudichaud-Beaupré

Freycinet's Voy. Uranie, Bot.   426, *t. 34* (1826)[1829].

Epidendroideæ ⚘ Vandeæ • Aeridinæ

ETYMOLOGY: In honor of Pierre-Jean Robiquet (1780-1832), a French scientist, chemist, pharmacist and a co-discoverer of both asparagine (caffeine) from *Asparagus* and codeine (morphine) from *Papaver*.

TYPE SPECIES: *Robiquetia ascendens* Gaudichaud-Beaupré

Thirty-eight monopodial epiphytes are found in shady, low to mid elevation, open forests and cliff faces over a region extending from southern China (Yunnan to Fujian and Hong Kong) Sri Lanka, India, Andaman Island, Myanmar to Vietnam, Malaysia, Indonesia, the Philippines, New Guinea and northeastern Australia (Queensland) to the southwestern Pacific Archipelago. These rather robust plants have long, hanging stems, each with several to numerous, broad to narrow, flat, leathery, unequally bilobed leaves that are arranged in two rows. The thick, hanging, simple or branched, densely packed, numerous-flowered inflorescence has small to tiny, bright yellow to red-orange flowers, not opening widely, which are heavily marked or spotted red, brown, purple-red or pink including the spur. The dorsal sepal is helmet-shaped. The immobile, trilobed lip, fused to the white, short, stout, wingless, footless column, has small, erect, thickened side lobes, and the small, concave midlobe is long or tapering. The small spur is rather long, cylindrical, often bent and flattened.

An orthographic variant introduced in *Hort. Donat.*, 208 (1858). The correct spelling is *Robiquetia*.

An orthographic variant introduced in *Bot. Reg.*, **10**: sub 832 (1824). The correct spelling is *Rodriguezia*.

Currently Accepted   Validly Published   Invalidly Published   Published Pre-1753   Superfluous Usage   Orthographic Variant   Fossil

O r c h i d   G e n e r a • 340

RODRIGNETZIA

An orthographic variant introduced in *Prakt. Stud. Orchid.*, 302 (1854). The correct spelling is *Rodriguezia*.

RODRIGOA

Braas

Orchidee (Hamburg) **30**(5): 203 (1979).

ETYMOLOGY: Dedicated to Rodrigo Escobar y Restrepo (1935-), a Colombian orchidologist, author of *Native Colombian Orchids*, editor of *Orquideología* and curator at Jardin Botanico Joaquin in Medellín.

TYPE SPECIES: *Rodrigoa meleagris* (Lindley) Braas
(*Masdevallia meleagris* Lindley)

Now recognized as belonging to the genus *Masdevallia*, *Rodrigoa* was previously considered to include twelve epiphytes found in upper elevation, montane forests of western and central Colombia, and Ecuador to Bolivia. These small, tufted, often clump-forming plants have short, tiny stems, subtended by tubular sheaths, each with a solitary, thinly leathery leaf tapering to a point. The several, solitary to few-flowered inflorescences have showy, pale lavender to magenta flowers (borne successively) that have tiny petals. The broad to long (narrow), spotted to barred brown-red to purple sepals taper into long, thin, brown to yellow tails. The lateral sepals are united with the base of the small, entire lip forming a chin-like projection and also taper into long tails. The flowers have a short, erect column.

RODRIGUESIA

An orthographic variant introduced in *Bot. Reg.*, **23**: sub 1929 (1837). The correct spelling is *Rodriguezia*.

RODRIGUESIA

Kraenzlin

Kongl. Svenska Vetensk. Acad. Handl. **46**(10): 75 (1911).

ETYMOLOGY: In honor of João Barbosa Rodrigues (1842-1909).

TYPE SPECIES: *Rodriguesia lindmanii* Kraenzlin
This type name is now considered a synonym of
Solenidium lunatum (Lindley) Schlechter;
basionym
Oncidium lunatum Lindley

Not validly published, this name is referred to *Solenidium*. *Rodriguesia* was considered to include one epiphyte found from the Guianas, Venezuela, Colombia to Peru and Brazil.

RODRIGUEZA

An orthographic variant introduced in *Anal. Fam. Pl.*, 57 (1829). The correct spelling is *Rodriguezia*.

RODRIGUEZIA

Ruiz & Pavón

Fl. Peruv. Prodr. 115, t. 25 (1794).

Epidendroideæ ⚘ Cymbidieæ • Oncidiinæ

ETYMOLOGY: In commemoration of Manuel (Emanuel) Rodríguez (fl. 1780s-1790s), a Spanish botanist, royal apothecary and a contemporary of Ruiz & Pavón.

LECTOTYPE: *Rodriguezia lanceolata* Ruiz & Pavón

Forty-eight sympodial epiphytes are found in wet, low to upper elevation, hill scrub and montane forests of the American tropics from Mexico to Peru with the greatest concentration found in Brazil. These attractive, twig plants have prominent, small, flattened pseudobulbs, clustered or borne at considerable intervals from each other, subtended by overlapping, leaf-bearing sheaths, each with one to two, leathery leaves at the tip. The erect or arching, few to numerous-flowered inflorescence, borne from the axils of the bracts at the base of the pseudobulb, has rather large to small, showy, white or yellow, to magenta or scarlet flowers. The white or creamy, deeply notched, entire lip, united to the slender, footless column base, has radiating veins, a ridged callus, a wavy margin, and is either spurless or has a short spur.

RODRIGUEZIELLA

Kuntze

Revis. Gen. Pl. **2**: 649 (1891).

Not *Rodriguezella* Schmitz (1895) Rhodomelaceæ.

Epidendroideæ ⚘ Cymbidieæ • Oncidiinæ

ETYMOLOGY: In honor of João Barbosa Rodrigues (1842-1909), a Brazilian naturalist, explorer, publisher, artist and a director of Jardím Botânico in Rio de Janeiro. And Latin for diminutive.

TYPE SPECIES: *Rodrigueziella gomezoides*
(Barbosa Rodrigues) Kuntze
(*Theodorea gomezoides* Barbosa Rodrigues)

Six sympodial epiphytes are found in low elevation, coastal woodlands of Brazil (Rio de Janeiro to São Paulo). These small plants have clustered, elongate pseudobulbs, subtended by large, leaf-like sheaths, each with one to two, long, narrow leaves borne at the tip. The erect to arching, stiff, slightly zig-zagged, numerous to few-flowered inflorescence has small, green-yellow to green-brown, sweetly fragrant flowers that are widespreading and/or drooping. Each flower is subtended by a large, narrow bract, and all appear on one side of the floral rachis. The yellow-white or white, shortly clawed, entire lip has hairy, bright yellow or orange calli. The flowers have a short, erect column.

RODRIGUEZIOPSIS

Schlechter

Repert. Spec. Nov. Regni Veg. **16**: 427 (1920).

Epidendroideæ ⚘ Cymbidieæ • Oncidiinæ

ETYMOLOGY: *Rodriguezia*, a genus of orchids and Greek for resemblance. Referring to a similarity to *Rodriguezia*.

LECTOTYPE: *Rodrigueziopsis eleutherosepala*
(Barbosa Rodrigues) Schlechter
(*Rodriguezia eleutherosepala* Barbosa Rodrigues)

Two scarce, miniature sympodial epiphytes are found in humid, low elevation, hill forests of southeastern and southern Brazil (Paraná and Santa Catarina). These plants have small pseudobulbs, subtended by overlapping sheaths, each with several, tiny, sickle-shaped leaves. The unusual, clambering rhizomes propagate the plant by sending out a long, wiry stem with new plantlets at the end. The numerous-flowered inflorescence has small, attractive, green-yellow flowers with equally narrow segments. The broad, white, trilobed lip has a delicate yellow edge, purple basal blotches and specks; small, spreading side lobes, and a broad midlobe with a small, center notch. The flowers have a recurved column that does not widen at the base.

RODRIGUFZIA

An orthographic variant introduced in *Cat. Pl. Horti Paris.*, ed. 3, 61 (1829). The correct spelling is *Rodriguezia*.

ROEPAROCHARIS

An orthographic variant cited in *Lex. Gen. Phan.*, 488 (1904). The correct spelling is *Roeperocharis*.

ROEPEROCHARIS

Reichenbach *filius*

Otia Bot. Hamburg., fasc. 2 104 (1881).

Orchidoideæ ⚘ Orchideæ • Orchidinæ

ETYMOLOGY: Dedicated to Johannes August Christian Roeper (1801-1885), a German physician, botanist, professor, and author of *Zur Flora Mecklenburgs*. And Greek for grace or honor.

LECTOTYPE: *Roeperocharis bennettiana* Reichenbach f.

Five uncommon, sympodial terrestrials are scattered in mid to upper elevation, montane grasslands and bogs from Ethiopia to Malawi and the Cameroons. These large, robust to rather slender plants have long, leafy, unbranched stems, each with the usually erect, narrow leaves scattered along the stem, but not clustered. The two lowermost leaves are black and have sheathing at the base. The terminal, numerous to few-flowered inflorescence has small, green or yellow-green flowers and will continue to bloom over an extended period. The erect dorsal sepal and erect petals converge, forming a hood over the small, erect column. The twisted, narrow, fleshy petals are folded in the middle and have a distinctly sharp tip or are toothed. The trilobed or rare entire lip has upward curved side lobes, a long midlobe, and a thick, cylindrical, downward hanging spur with a slightly bilobed tip. The flowers have a small, curved, wingless column.

ROEZLIELLA

Schlechter

Repert. Spec. Nov. Regni Veg. **15**: 146 (1918).
Etymology: Dedicated to Benedikt Roezl (1824-1885), a Czech botanical explorer who traveled in Canada, the western United States, Mexico, Cuba and South America collecting seeds, bulbs and plants. He published a series of articles expanding the knowledge of the flora in the new world. And Latin for diminutive.

Type species: *None designated*

Now recognized as belonging to the genus *Sigmatostalix*, *Roezliella* was previously considered to include seven epiphytes found in wet, low to mid elevation, hill and montane cloud forests of Colombia. These small plants have clustered, compressed, egg-shaped to oblong pseudobulbs, subtended by distichous, overlapping, folded bracts, each with a solitary or rarely two leaves. The erect, few-flowered inflorescence has small, green flowers with the free sepals bent backward, but the sepals and petals are similar in shape. The long-clawed, entire or trilobed lip bears a prominent callus or has a series of calli that can be hollowed out and contain a thick liquid. The flowers have a slender, strongly arched column.

ROLFEA

Zahlbruckner

J. Bot. **36**: 493 (1898).
Etymology: In honor of Robert Allen Rolfe (1855-1920), a British botanist, orchidologist, curator, gardener and herbarium keeper at Kew. He was the founder and first editor of *The Orchid Review*.

Type species: *Rolfea elata* (Rolfe) Zahlbruckner
(*Jenmania elata* Rolfe)

Now recognized as belonging to *Palmorchis*, *Rolfea* was previously considered to include two terrestrials found in low elevation, woodlands of Colombia, Venezuela, the Guianas, Costa Rica to Panama and Trinidad. These tall robust, clump-forming plants are not showy,

often resembling a seedling palm. They have slender, reed-like stems, each with several, long, strongly veined leaves. The few-flowered inflorescence has small, white, sparsely hairy flowers. The long, trilobed lip has a notched margin. The flowers have a long, slender, curved, footless column. The above type name is now considered a synonym of *Palmorchis pubescentis* Barbosa Rodrigues.

ROLFEELLA

Schlechter

Repert. Spec. Nov. Regni Veg. Beih. **33**: 18 (1924).
Etymology: Honoring Robert Allen Rolfe (1855-1920). And Latin for diminutive.

Type species: *Rolfeella glaberrima* (Ridley) Schlechter
(*Holothrix glaberrima* Ridley)

Now recognized as belonging to genus *Benthamia*, *Rolfeella* was previously considered to include one terrestrial found in cool, mid to upper elevation, montane forests of Madagascar. This tall, slender plant has erect, unbranched stems, each with a solitary, grass-like, basal leaf, and has several, narrow bracts clasping the stem upward. The few-flowered inflorescence has long bracts and small, bright golden-yellow flowers. The trilobed lip has small, erect side lobes, the oblong midlobe has a ruffled margin and a long, roundish spur. The flowers have a small, wingless column.

ROMBODA

An orthographic variant cited in *Lex. Gen. Phan.*, 276, 484 (1904). The correct spelling is *Rhomboda*.

RONALDELLA

Luer

Monogr. Syst. Bot. Missouri Bot. Gard. **105**: 195, *f. 153* (2006).
Etymology: Named for Ronald Oskar Determann (1957-), an American botanist and Fuqua Conservatory superintendent at the Atlanta Botanical Garden in Georgia. And Latin for diminutive.

Type species: *Ronaldella determannii* (Luer) Luer
(*Pleurothallis determannii* Luer)

Recognized as belonging to the genus *Pabstiella*, *Ronaldella* was proposed to include two epiphytes found in low elevation, forests and woodlands from the Guianas, Costa Rica and Colombia to Bolivia. These minute plants have short, stout stems, subtended by two thinly textured, tubular sheaths, each with a solitary, oblong, leathery leaf that often is reclining. The sometimes arched, solitary-flowered inflores-

cence has a large, yellow-green flower with a narrow, concave dorsal sepal and small, oblong petals. The uppermost, cup-like, lateral sepals are united, forming a synsepal covered with short hairs on the inside. The wedge-shaped, small, entire lip has a hairy callus. The flowers have a slender, slightly curved column.

ROPHOSTEMON

An orthographic variant introduced in *Gen. Pl. (Endlicher)*, 216 (1837). The correct spelling is *Roptrostemon*.

ROPHOSTEMON

Blume

Coll. Orchid. 153 (1858)[1859].
Etymology: Latin for red and diminutive. Refers to the small habit and the size of the little, red flower.

Type species: *None designated*

Now recognized as belonging to the genus *Nervilia*, *Rophostemon* was proposed to include two terrestrials found in Indonesia, Malaysia, Myanmar, Thailand, New Guinea and Australia. These small plants have a dark colored, heart-shaped leaf blade, sitting just above the ground, that has numerous, raised veins and is hairy on both sides of the leaf. The erect, two-flowered inflorescence has pale olive-green to dull purple flowers with long, narrow sepals and petals that are sharply pointed. The entire or obscurely trilobed lip is white at the base with a raised, yellow median band and purple veins. The flowers have a long, club-shaped column.

ROPHOSTEMUM

An orthographic variant cited in *Deut. Bot. Herb.-Buch*, 55 (1841). The correct spelling is *Roptrostemon*.

ROPTROSTEMON

Blume

Fl. Javæ **1**: Praef vi (1828).

Name published without a description. Today this name is most often referred to *Nervilia*.

ROSSATIS

Thouars

Hist. Orchid. Table 1, sub 1c, *t. 8, t. 12d* (1822).

Name published without a description. Today this name is most often referred to *Cynorkis*.

| Currently Accepted | Validly Published | Invalidly Published | Published Pre-1753 | Superfluous Usage | Orthographic Variant | Fossil |

Orchid Genera • 342

ROSSIOGLOSSUM

(Schlechter) Garay & G.C. Kennedy
Orchid Digest **40**(4): 139 (1976).

Epidendroideæ ⫽ Cymbidieæ • Oncidiinæ

ETYMOLOGY: In honor of John Ross (1777-1856), a minster, who collected in central Mexico mainly for George Barker (1776-1845) of England and later in northern China (Manchuria). And Latin for tongue or lip.

TYPE SPECIES: *Rossioglossum grande*
(Lindley) Garay & G.C. Kennedy
(*Odontoglossum grande* Lindley)

Six sympodial epiphytes are found in dense, moist to wet, mid to upper elevation, montane deciduous, rain forests from southern Mexico to Panama. These species were once considered as a section in the genus *Odontoglossum* but are readily distinguished by their free lip that forms at a right-angle with the column. These evergreen plants have dark green to gray-green, ovoid, somewhat compressed pseudobulbs, each with two to three, narrow to broad leaves becoming peppered with brown specks (an unusual feature often mistaken for insect infestation) and wrinkled as they age. The long, erect or bowed, few-flowered inflorescence has large, extremely showy, waxy, long-lasting, yellow flowers barred and/or flecked with red. The creamy, shortly clawed, fiddle-shaped or unequally trilobed lip and bilobed callus are flecked red-brown. The small side lobes are ear-like and the large midlobe has a prominent callus. The flowers have an erect, long, slightly curved column.

NOTE: The species of this genus do not hybridize or cross with the species of any other genus.

RUBELLIA

(Luer) Luer
Monogr. Syst. Bot. Missouri Bot. Gard.
95: 258 (2004).

ETYMOLOGY: Latin for red and diminutive. Refers to the small habit and the size of the little, red flower.

TYPE SPECIES: *Rubellia rubella* (Luer) Luer
(*Pleurothallis rubella* Luer)

Now recognized as belonging to the genus *Pleurothallis*, *Rubellia* was proposed to include one epiphyte found in mid elevation, montane forests from Panama to Ecuador. This small, tufted, often clump-forming plant has several, slender, clustered stems, each with a solitary, narrow, leathery leaf. The several, few-flowered inflorescences have tiny, translucent, bright red, yellow-orange or yellow flowers borne successively. The thinly textured, dorsal sepal is concave, the lateral sepals united for most of their length, and the tiny, paddle-shaped petals have hairy tips. The spear-shaped, red-purple, entire lip has a rounded, concave, hairy, basal callus with a shallow channel in the upper portion. The flowers have an erect, short, blunt column with or without a foot.

RUDOLFIELLA

Hoehne
Arq. Bot. Estado São Paulo, n.s., f.m. **2**: 14 (1944).

Epidendroideæ ⫽ Cymbidieæ • Maxillariinæ

ETYMOLOGY: Dedicated to Friedrich Richard Rudolf Schlechter (1872-1925), a German orchidologist, botanical explorer of Africa, Indonesia, New Guinea, and Australia and the author of numerous articles and books on orchids. And Latin for diminutive.

TYPE SPECIES: *Rudolfiella aurantiaca* (Lindley) Hoehne
(*Bifrenaria aurantiaca* Lindley)

Six uncommon, sympodial epiphytes are found in warm, humid, low elevation, tropical forests of Brazil with a few species found from the Guianas, Trinidad, Venezuela and Panama to Bolivia. These small plants have ovoid, compressed, dark green pseudobulbs, each with a solitary, pleated leaf that has prominent veining on the underside. The erect, long, several-flowered inflorescence has small to medium-sized, showy, vividly colored flowers often brown spotted. The lateral sepals, attached at the base of the column foot, form a triangular chin-like projection. The narrowly clawed, trilobed lip has a strongly thickened midlobe with a short, abrupt soft tip and has a fleshy, hairy callus. The flowers have a small, slightly hairy, wingless column.

RUMPHIA

Blume ex Planchon
Hort. Donat. 220 (1858).
Not *Rumphia* Linnaeus (1753) Anacardiaceæ.

Name published without a description. Today this name is most often referred to *Vanda*.

RUSBYELLA

Rolfe
Mem. Torrey Bot. Club **6**(1): 122 (1896).

ETYMOLOGY: Commemorating Henry Hurd Rusby (1855-1940), an American medical botanist, and professor of botany at Columbia University who made numerous collecting trips to Bolivia and Brazil. And Latin for diminutive.

TYPE SPECIES: *Rusbyella caespitosa* Rolfe

Now recognized as belonging to the genus *Cyrtochilum*, *Rusbyella* was previously considered to include two epiphytes found in low to mid elevation, hill and montane cloud forests from Ecuador to Bolivia. These small plants have smooth, compressed pseudobulbs, each with a solitary, slender leaf. The erect, dark maroon, few-flowered inflorescence has large, clear yellow to green flowers with narrow, spoon-shaped dorsal sepal and petals. The lateral sepals are united nearly to their tips. The short, squat, white, long-clawed, entire lip has a few maroon spots in the midsection which is grooved and strongly curves under. The flowers have an erect, slender, wingless column.

RUSCUS

Plumier
Pl. Amer. 171, 172 (1758).

ETYMOLOGY: Latin for kettle-shaped.

TYPE SPECIES: *None designated*

Although validly published this rejected name is now referred to *Pleurothallis* and *Stelis*. *Ruscus* was considered to include at least two different orchid species that used the same first name: ***Ruscus foliis solitariis, petiolatis, lanceolato-ovatis, basi racemiseris*** (171, *t. 176, f. 2*) an epiphyte widespread from Cuba to Trinidad, Mexico to Peru and northern Brazil. This small plant has a solitary, leathery leaf and several inflorescences with small flowers. This name is now usually considered as a synonym of *Pleurothallis ruscifolia* (Jacquin) R. Brown. ***Ruscus foliis ovatis, petiolatis, basi spiciseris*** (172, *t. 176, f. 3*) an epiphyte widespread from Cuba to Trinidad, the Guianas and Venezuela. This small plant has erect stems, each with a solitary, leathery leaf. The several, solitary-flowered inflorescences have tiny flowers. This name is now usually considered as a synonym of *Stelis ophioglossoides* (Jacquin) Swartz.

RYNCHADENIA

An orthographic variant cited in *Lex. Gen. Phan.*, 484, 492 (1904). The correct spelling is *Rhynchadenia*.

RYNCHANDRA

An orthographic variant cited in *Lex. Gen. Phan.*, 484, 492 (1904). The correct spelling is *Rhynchandra*.

RYNCHANTHERA

Blume
Tab. Pl. Jav. Orchid. f. 78 (1825).

ETYMOLOGY: Greek for beak and flower. Refers to the lip that looks like a bird's beak.

TYPE SPECIES: *Rynchanthera paniculata* Blume
This type name is now considered a synonym of *Corymborkis veratrifolia* (Reinwardt) Blume; basionym *Hysteria veratrifolia* Reinwardt

Not validly published, this name is referred to *Corymborkis*. *Rynchanthera* was considered to include one terrestrial found from India to the western Pacific Archipelago.

RYNCHOPERA

An orthographic variant cited in *Lex. Gen. Phan.*, 484, 493 (1904). The correct spelling is *Rhynchopera*.

RYNCHOSTELE

An orthographic variant cited in *Lex. Gen. Phan.*, 484, 493 (1904). The correct spelling is *Rhynchostele*.

RYNCHOSTELIS

An orthographic variant introduced in *Bijdr. Fl. Ned. Ind.*, **8**: 434 (1825). The correct spelling is *Rhynchostylis*.

RYNCHOSTYLIS

An orthographic variant introduced in *Bijdr. Fl. Ned. Ind.*, **7**: 285 (1825). The correct spelling is *Rhynchostylis*.

RYNCHOSTYLIS

An orthographic variant cited in *Lex. Gen. Phan.*, 484, 493 (1904). The correct spelling is *Rhynchostylis*.

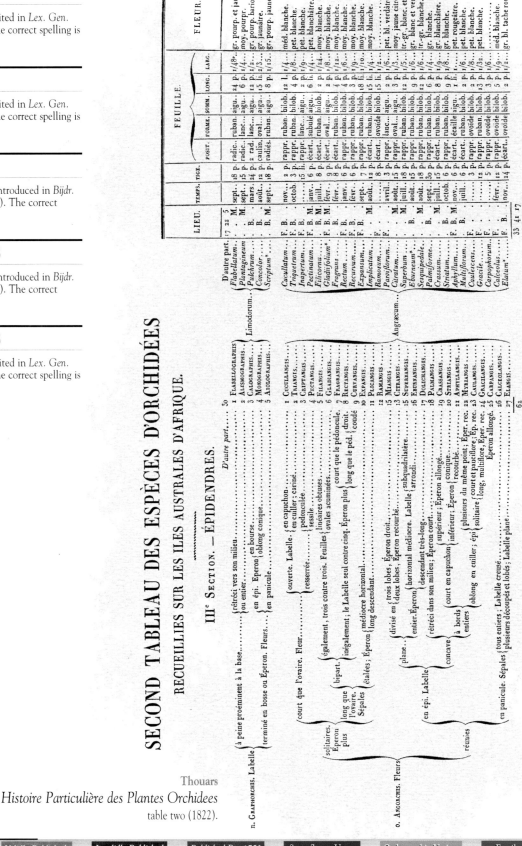

Thouars
Histoire Particulière des Plantes Orchidees
table two (1822).

Currently Accepted Validly Published Invalidly Published Published Pre-1753 Superfluous Usage Orthographic Variant Fossil

SABOT

Redouté

Liliac. (Redouté) **1**: *t. 19* (1802).

ETYMOLOGY: French for a wooden shoe worn in some European countries. A sandal or shoe having a band of leather or other material across the instep. The word is probably of Turkish or Arabic origin.

TYPE SPECIES: *None designated*

Not validly published, this name is referred to *Cypripedium*. *Sabot* was considered to include two terrestrials found in cool, low to upper elevation, swamps and bogs widespread from Britain to Russia, Japan, Canada and the northern United States. These erect, densely hairy, small plants have short, unbranched stems, each with several, oblong, prominently veined leaves. The usually solitary-flowered inflorescence has a showy, yellow flower with a strongly inflated lip (united lateral sepals). The long, narrow, brown-red dorsal sepal and petals are often tightly twisted.

SABRALIA

An orthographic variant introduced in *Rev. Hort. (Paris)*, ser. 2, **3**: 164 (1845). The correct spelling is *Sobralia*.

SACCALABIUM

An orthographic variant introduced in *Cat. Pl. Trinidad*, 82 (1870). The correct spelling is *Saccolabium*.

SACCALOBIUM

An orthographic variant introduced in *Paxton's Mag. Bot.*, **2**: 131 (1836). The correct spelling is *Saccolabium*.

SACCANTHUS

Not *Saccanthus* Herzog (1916) Scrophulariaceæ.

An orthographic variant introduced in *Exot. Fl.*, **3**(29): sub 187 (1825). The correct spelling is *Sarcanthus*.

SACCIDIUM

Lindley

Gen. Sp. Orchid. Pl. 258, 301 (1835).
Name ICBN rejected vs. *Holothrix* Richard ex Lindley (1835) Orchidaceæ.

ETYMOLOGY: Greek for bag or sack. Referring to the bag or pouch-like lateral sepals.

TYPE SPECIES: *Saccidium pilosum* Lindley

Although validly published this rejected name is now referred to *Holothrix*. *Saccidium* was considered to include one terrestrial found on the rocky slopes and ledges of the South African Cape area. This deciduous, fairly robust plant has erect, unbranched stems, each with a few appressed to ground leaves that are hairy on the topside and densely hairy underneath. The hairy, few to numerous-flowered inflorescence has small flowers. The prominent lip has five or more lobes which may be hair-like thin and it has a tiny spur.

SACCILABIUM

An orthographic variant cited in *Lex. Gen. Phan.*, 494 (1904). The correct spelling is *Saccolabium*.

SACCOCHILUS

Blume

Fl. Javæ **1**: Praef. viii (1828).

ETYMOLOGY: Greek for bag and lip. Descriptive of the bag-like lip.

TYPE SPECIES: *None designated*

A superfluous name proposed as a substitute for *Thrixspermum*.

SACCOGLOSSUM

Schlechter

Repert. Spec. Nov. Regni Veg. Beih.
1(9): 683 (1912).

Epidendroideæ ⚜ Dendrobiinæ • Currently unplaced

ETYMOLOGY: Greek for sac or bag and tongue. Emphasizing the bag-like lip.

TYPE SPECIES: *None designated*

Five uncommon, monopodial or sympodial epiphytes are found in misty, mid elevation, montane forests of New Guinea. These small plants have tiny, ovoid pseudobulbs, each with a solitary, broad, leathery, red-green leaf that vegetatively resembles a *Bulbophyllum*. The charming, wiry, solitary-flowered inflorescence has a small, white to creamy-yellow flower not opening widely. The erect, recurved, pale brown petals are covered with red-brown blotches or spotted pink. The erect, dark red-brown dorsal sepal curves forward over the slender, recurved column that has two hanging, horn-like appendages at the tip. The white to orange-red, cup-shaped lip has red streaks inside at the base and is movably attached to the footless column.

SACCOLABIOPSIS

J.J. Smith

Bull. Jard. Bot. Buitenzorg, sér. 2 **26**: 93 (1918).

Epidendroideæ ⚜ Vandeæ • Aeridinæ

ETYMOLOGY: *Saccolabium*, a genus of orchids and Greek for resemblance. Referring to a similarity to *Saccolabium*.

TYPE SPECIES: *Saccolabiopsis bakhuizenii* J.J. Smith

Thirteen uncommon, monopodial epiphytes are found in humid, low elevation, woodlands from northern India, Thailand to Malaysia, Indonesia, New Guinea, northern Australia and the Philippines to Fiji. These tiny, slender plants have short stems, each with several, flat, pale green leaves arranged in two rows and are suffused red when exposed to bright sunlight. The long to short, numerous-flowered inflorescence has tiny to minute, downward-facing, thinly textured, pale green to green-yellow flowers that turn yellow as they age and do not open fully. The white, sac-like to cup-shaped, obscurely trilobed lip has a red tinge, is fused to the small, footless column, and has a long, swollen spur.

SACCOLABIUM

Blume

Bijdr. Fl. Ned. Ind. **7**: 292, *t. 50* (1825).
Name ICBN conserved vs. *Gastrochilus* D. Don (1825)
Orchidaceæ.

Epidendroideæ ⚬ Vandeæ • Aeridinæ

ETYMOLOGY: Latin for sac or bag and lip. Referring
to the prominent bag-like spur of the lip.

LECTOTYPE: *Saccolabium pusillum* Blume

Five small, monopodial epiphytes are found in low elevation, hill forests from southern India to western Indonesia (Sumatra and Java). These tiny plants have short to long, semi-hanging stems, subtended by old leaf bases, each with several, fleshy, strap-like leaves arranged in two rows. The short, solitary-flowered inflorescence has a short-lived, white flower not opening widely, suffused pale pink at the base and covered with maroon blotches. The trilobed lip has a large, long to short, swollen spur. The flowers have a small, short, stout, footless column.

NOTE: Originally this genus was more broadly defined and contained over 100 species.

SACCOLABUM

An orthographic variant introduced in *Not. Pl. Asiat.*, **3**: 358 (1851). The correct spelling is *Saccolabium*.

SACCOLOBIUM

An orthographic variant introduced in *Paxton's Mag. Bot.*, **2**: 141 (1836). The correct spelling is *Saccolabium*.

SACCULOBIUM

An orthographic variant introduced in *Paxton's Mag. Bot.*, **2**: 130 (1836). The correct spelling is *Saccolabium*.

SACODON

Rafinesque

Fl. Tellur. **4**: 45 (1836)[1837].

ETYMOLOGY: Greek for bag or pouch and a tooth. Descriptive of the sac-like lip's mouth that is toothed.

TYPE SPECIES: *None designated*

Now recognized as belonging to the genus *Cypripedium*, *Sacodon* was previously considered to include two terrestrials found in low to upper elevation, hill woodlands, montane forests and grassy slopes from Belarus to eastern Russia (Yakutiya

to Kamchatka), northern China (Heilongjiang to Nei Mongol and Hebei to Shandong), Mongolia, Korea, Japan and Taiwan. These small, stout, erect plants have short, unbranched stems covered in soft hairs, each with ovate, bright green leaves that have wavy margins. The erect, solitary to two-flowered inflorescence has rosy-purple to pink flowers, mottled dark purple, and the drooping petals are not twisted. The lateral sepals are united behind the sac or bag-like lip that has an inrolled margin.

SACOILA

Rafinesque

Fl. Tellur. **2**: 86 (1836)[1837].

Orchidoideæ ⚬ Cranichideæ • Spiranthinæ

ETYMOLOGY: Greek for bag or sack and hollow. Refers to the hollow, sac-like spur formed by the sepals.

TYPE SPECIES: *Sacoila lurida* Rafinesque nom. illeg.

Sacoila lanceolata (Aublet) Garay
(*Limodorum lanceolatum* Aublet)

Five sympodial terrestrials are found in low to mid elevation, gravelly clay or sandy grasslands, dry woodlands, savannas and deciduous to semi-evergreen tropical forests from the southeastern United States (Florida), the Bahamas, Cuba to Trinidad, the Guianas, Venezuela, Mexico to northeastern Argentina and Paraguay. These erect plants have unbranched, slender or stout stems, each with a basal rosette of thinly textured leaves that are reduced to sheaths above and are usually withered by flowering time. The tall, erect, hairy, numerous-flowered inflorescence has showy, large, coral-red, pale green, yellow-tan, pink or brick-red, tubular flowers not opening fully. The long, often narrow, deeply grooved, distinctly clawed, entire lip envelopes and adheres to the sides of the small, stout, massive column below, and often has a hairy disc. The short, blunt, sac-like or cone-shaped spur is formed by the united, long, backward extending column foot. It is also united with the bases of lip and lateral sepals.

SACOLABIUM

An orthographic variant introduced in *Pansey*, 45 (1835). The correct spelling is *Saccolabium*.

SACOOCHILUS

An orthographic variant introduced in *Bibliogr. Bot. Handbuch*, 284 (1841). The correct spelling is *Saccochilus*.

SAECANTHUS

Ridley

J. Linn. Soc., Bot. **32**: 370 (1896).

ETYMOLOGY: Greek for flesh and flower. Suggestive of the texture of the flowers.

TYPE SPECIES: *Saecanthus bracteatus* Ridley
(*Saccolabium bracteatum* (Ridley) Ridley)

Not validly published, this name is referred to *Cleisomeria*. *Saecanthus* was considered to include two epiphytes found in southern Myanmar, Thailand, Laos, Vietnam and Malaysia. The above type name species is currently unplaced, but the second species is now considered a synonym of *Cleisomeria lanatum* (Lindley) Lindley ex G. Don, according to Seidenfaden.

SALACISTIS

Reichenbach *filius*

Xenia Orchid. **1**: 214, *t. 87a* (1856), and
Bonplandia **5**(3): 36 (1857).

ETYMOLOGY: Named for a volcano Gunung Salak (2,200 ft./650 m), located southeast of the city of Bogor, Indonesia. This volcano last erupted in 1938 and today is the site of a geothermal power generating plant on the Indonesian island of Java.

TYPE SPECIES: *Salacistis novembrilis* Reichenbach f.

Now recognized as belonging to the genus *Goodyera*, *Salacistis* was previously considered to include one terrestrial found in Indonesia (Java and Sumatra). This erect plant has tall, slender, unbranched stems, each with several, pale green, oblong leaves that have dark green veining. The hairy, few-flowered inflorescence has small, tubular, yellow flowers which do not open fully and are also hairy on their outer surfaces. The lateral sepals are suffused green-brown and have a small, entire lip. The flowers have a small, footless column. The above type name is now considered a synonym of *Goodyera novembrilis* (Reichenbach f.) Ormerod.

SALPINARIA

An orthographic variant introduced in *Nat. Pflanzenfam.*, **2**(6): 139 (1888). The correct spelling is *Talpinaria*.

SALPINGARIA

An orthographic variant introduced in *Allg. Bot. Z. Syst.*, **7**(7-8): 161 (1901). The correct spelling is *Talpinaria*.

| Currently Accepted | Validly Published | Invalidly Published | Published Pre-1753 | Superfluous Usage | Orthographic Variant | Fossil |

O r c h i d   G e n e r a • **346**

SALPISTELE

Dressler

Orquideologia **14**(1): 6 (1979).

ETYMOLOGY: Greek for trumpet, trunk or central part of stem and column or style. Refers to the shape of the column's tip.

TYPE SPECIES: *Salpistele brunnea* Dressler

Now recognized as belonging to the genus *Stelis*, *Salpistele* was previously considered to include six epiphytes or terrestrials found in wet, low to mid elevation, hill scrub and montane forests of Costa Rica and Panama with two species also in Ecuador. These tiny, clustered plants have hanging stems (lengthen with age), subtended by tubular sheaths, each joint has a solitary, narrow, leathery leaf. The often hanging, few-flowered inflorescence has only one flower open at a time. The strikingly, long-lasting, red-brown flower is either marked, flecked or striped in brown or yellow; the erect dorsal sepal is concave and has very narrow petals, and the lateral sepals are united for their whole length. The cup-shaped or concave, trilobed lip has erect, often ear-like side lobes that clasp the prominent trumpet-shaped column.

SANDERELLA

Kuntze

Revis. Gen. Pl. **2**: 649 (1891).

Epidendroideæ ⚘ Cymbieæ • Oncidiinæ

ETYMOLOGY: Commemorating Henry Frederick Conrad Sander (1847-1920), a German-born British horticulturist; gardner who developed the *List of Hybrid Names* and *Sander's List of Orchid Hybrids*, and wrote the folios for *Reichenbachia*; and founder of a nursery in both St. Albans, England and St. Andre, Belgium. And Latin for diminutive.

TYPE SPECIES: *Sanderella discolor*
(Barbosa Rodrigues) Cogniaux
(*Parlatorea discolor* Barbosa Rodrigues)

Two uncommon sympodial epiphytes are found in cool, mid elevation, montane coastal forests of southeastern Brazil and northeastern Argentina (Misiones and Salta). These small plants have ovoid, sharply angled pseudobulbs, subtended by leaf-like sheaths, each with a solitary, leathery leaf. The long, whip-like, few-flowered inflorescence has tiny, pale lilac flowers not opening widely, that are creamy colored at the base. The lateral sepals are joined for most of their length and has a concave dorsal sepal. The entire lip has two long, basal calli. The flowers have a very short, broad column.

SANOPODIUM

An orthographic variant introduced in *Flora*, **71**(10): 156 (1888). The correct spelling is *Sarcopodium*.

SARCADENIA

Brongniart

Enum. Pl. Mus. Paris 74 (1843).

Name published without a description. Today this name is most often referred to *Epidendrum*.

SARCADENIA

Reichenbach *filius*

Cat. Orch.-Samml. Schiller, ed. 1 64 (1857).
Not *Sarcadenia* Brongniart (1843) Orchidaceæ.

ETYMOLOGY: Greek for flesh and gland.

TYPE SPECIES: *Sarcadenia gracilis* Reichenbach f.

Not validly published, this name is referred to *Epidendrum*. *Sarcadenia* was considered to include one epiphyte or terrestrial found from Ecuador, Peru, Bolivia to Brazil and Mexico.

SARCANTHOPSIS

Garay

Bot. Mus. Leafl. **23**(4): 198 (1972).

Epidendroideæ ⚘ Vandeæ • Aeridinæ

ETYMOLOGY: *Sarcanthus*, a genus of orchids and Greek for like or resemblance. Refers to a likeness of the flowers of *Sarcanthus*.

TYPE SPECIES: *Sarcanthopsis nagarensis*
(Reichenbach f.) Garay
(*Sarcanthus nagarensis* Reichenbach f.)

Five large, sympodial epiphytes or rare lithophytes are found in low to mid elevation, grasslands, rocky scrub and cliff faces from New Guinea, the Solomons, Vanuatu and the Fiji Islands to the Philippines, usually exposed to bright sunlight. These large, erect plants have stout, leafy stems, often growing in excess of 13 feet (4 m) in height, each with several, narrow leaves. The spreading or branched, few to numerous-flowered inflorescence has small, fleshy, slightly fragrant, yellow flowers spotted red-brown inside and are a solid brown-red outside. The pale yellow, rigid, trilobed lip, fused to the column foot, has purple markings and lines, is almost sac-like at its base, bilaterally flattened, and has a keel-like, fleshy callus. The flowers have a short, stout, wingless column with a small projection in front at its base.

SARCANTHUS

Lindley

Bot. Reg. **10**: sub 817 (1824).
Name ICBN rejected vs. *Acampe* Lindley (1853) Orchidaceæ.

ETYMOLOGY: Greek for flesh and flower. Suggestive of the fleshy texture of the flower.

TYPE SPECIES: *Sarcanthus praemorsus*
(Roxburgh) Lindley ex Sprengel
(*Epidendrum praemorsum* Roxburgh)
This type name is now considered a synonym of
Acampe praemorsa (Roxburgh) Blatter & McCann;
basionym
Epidendrum praemorsum Roxburgh

Although validly published this rejected name is now referred to *Acampe*. *Sarcanthus* was considered to include one epiphyte found in the Seychelles, southern India and Sri Lanka. This rather coarse plant often has branched stems, each with overlapping, strap-shaped, thick, fleshy, bilobed leaves. The short, branched, few-flowered inflorescence has flowers with an entire lip and a short, cone-shaped spur.

SARCANTHUS

Lindley

Coll. Bot. (Lindley) t. 39B (1826).
Not *Sarcanthus* Lindley (1824) Orchidaceæ, and not *Sarcanthus* Andersson (1855) Boraginaceæ.

ETYMOLOGY: Greek for flesh and flower. Suggestive of the texture of the flowers.

TYPE SPECIES: *Sarcanthus rostratus* Lindley
This type name is now considered a synonym of
Cleisostoma recurvum (Hooker) Hooker ined.;
basionym
Vanda recurva Hooker

Not validly published because of a prior use of the name, this homonym was replaced by *Cleisostoma*.

SARCHANTUS

An orthographic variant introduced in *Remarques Fl. Polynésie*, 33 (1890). The correct spelling is *Sarcanthus*.

SARCHOCHILUS

An orthographic variant introduced in *Contr. Fl. Austral.*, 18, 192 (1867). The correct spelling is *Sarcochilus*.

SARCINULA

Luer

Monogr. Syst. Bot. Missouri Bot. Gard.
105: 201, *f. 155* (2006).

ETYMOLOGY: Latin for a little bundle. Refers to the cluster or bundle of stalks or stalk-like ovary.

TYPE SPECIES: *Sarcinula acicularis*
(Ames & C. Schweinfurth) Luer
(*Pleurothallis acicularis* Ames & C. Schweinfurth)

Recognized as belonging to the genus *Specklinia*, *Sarcinula* was proposed to include twenty-five epiphytes found in low to mid elevation, hill scrub to montane forests ranging from southern Mexico to Bolivia, with a few species found in the Antilles and Brazil. These tiny, tufted plants often forming clusters, have erect, slender stems, subtended by overlapping, tubular sheaths, each with a solitary, narrow, leathery leaf. The densely packed, numerous to few-flowered inflorescence has thinly textured, red, purple, green, yellow-green, yellow-orange to pale brown flowers often suffused or mottled purple. The oblong, concave dorsal sepal has a sharp point and the lateral sepals are united nearly to their tips. The small, thick petals taper to a sharp point or have blunt tips. The fleshy, oblong to elliptical, entire lip is covered with warts, has variable margins and delicately hinged to the column foot. The basal disc is shallowly channeled between low calli which are often obscure. The flowers have a slender to stout, slightly arched column.

SARCOBODIUM

Beer

Prakt. Stud. Orchid. 306 (1854).

ETYMOLOGY: Greek for flesh and a little ox. The origin and the meaning as applied here is unknown.

TYPE SPECIES: *Sarcobodium lobbii* (Lindley) Beer
(*Bulbophyllum lobbii* Lindley)

Now recognized as belonging to the genus *Bulbophyllum*, *Sarcobodium* was previously considered to include one epiphyte found in low to mid elevation, hill and montane forests from India (Arunachal Pradesh) to Malaysia and Indonesia. This small to medium-sized plant has ovoid pseudobulbs well-spaced on stout rhizomes; smooth when young then with remote pale green, netted veins as they age, each with a solitary, leathery leaf. The short, solitary-flowered inflorescence has a widespreading, fragrant, large, buff to yellow flower with purple lines on the strongly curved lateral sepals and petals. The short, broadly ovate, entire lip, joined to the column by a thin hinge, is quite mobile. When a pollinator climbs over the lip,

it is immediately thrown onto the short, broad column. The above type name is now considered a synonym of *Bulbophyllum lobbii* Lindley.

SARCOCADETIA

M.A. Clements & D.L. Jones

Orchadian **13**(11): 490 (2002).

ETYMOLOGY: Greek for flesh and *Cadetia*, a genus of orchids. Refers to the texture of the stems.

TYPE SPECIES: *Sarcocadetia funiformis*
(Blume) M.A. Clements & D.L. Jones
(*Dendrobium funiforme* Blume)

Recognized as belonging to the genus *Cadetia*, *Sarcocadetia* was proposed to include two epiphytes found in shady, low elevation, rain forests of New Guinea. These tufted or small, clumped plants have several nodes with fleshy, three-edged stems, each with a solitary, flat leaf at the tip. The solitary or rare two at a time, white flowers, borne at the leaf axils, have several, yellow patches. The petals are narrower than the sepals, and the lateral sepals are joined at the base to form a spur. The trilobed lip has patches of lavender, rose or purple, is joined to the tip of the column foot. The sides form a distinct, chin-like projection and has a hairy midlobe.

SARCOCHILOS

An orthographic variant introduced in *Syst. Veg. (Sprengel)*, ed. 16, **3**: 679, 721 (1826). The correct spelling is *Sarcochilus*.

SARCOCHILUS

R. Brown

Prodr. Fl. Nov. Holland. 332 (1810).

Epidendroideæ ⁄ **Vandeæ** • **Aeridinæ**

ETYMOLOGY: Greek for flesh and a lip. Suggestive of the fleshy texture of the lip found in most species of this genus.

LECTOTYPE: *Sarcochilus falcatus* R. Brown

Twenty-five monopodial epiphytes or lithophytes are found in shady, low elevation, hill scrub and cliff faces of eastern Australia, Tasmania, New Caledonia and New Zealand. These small, often clump-forming, slender plants have short stems, each with semi-rigid leaves arranged in a flat, fan shape and usually have sunken midveins. The short, arching to hanging, numerous to few-flowered inflorescence has moderately short-lived, often fragrant, relatively large flowers (facing all directions or two-ranked) occurring in a variety of attractive colors and shapes. The lateral sepals are completely or partially fused to the column base. The mobile, sac-like, small to large,

trilobed lip is hinged to the tip of the column foot and has large, erect, curved side lobes. The small, fleshy midlobe has a basal sac almost filled by a callus and a short, tubular-shaped, poorly developed spur. The flowers have an erect, short, wingless column with an upcurved foot.

SARCOCHYLLUS

An orthographic variant introduced in *Prakt. Stud. Orchid.*, 46, 171 (1854). The correct spelling is *Sarcochilus*.

SARCOCHYLUS

An orthographic variant introduced in *Prakt. Stud. Orchid.*, 77, 305 (1854). The correct spelling is *Sarcochilus*.

SARCOGLOSSUM

Beer

Prakt. Stud. Orchid. 306 (1854).

ETYMOLOGY: Greek for flesh and tongue. Refers to the thick, succulent lip.

TYPE SPECIES: *Sarcoglossum suaveolens* Beer
This type name is now considered a synonym of
Cirrhaea dependens (Loddiges) Loudon;
basionym
Cymbidium dependens Loddiges

Not validly published, this name is referred to *Cirrhaea*. *Sarcoglossum* was considered to include one epiphyte found in eastern Brazil (Rio de Janeiro to Paraná).

SARCOGLOTTIS

C. Presl

Reliq. Haenk. **1**: 95, *t. 15* (1827).

Orchidoideæ ⁄ **Cranichideæ** • **Spiranthinæ**

ETYMOLOGY: Greek for flesh and tongue. Referring to the fleshy texture of the lip.

TYPE SPECIES: *Sarcoglottis speciosa* C. Presl
This type name is now considered a synonym of
Sarcoglottis acaulis (Smith) Schlechter;
basionym
Neottia acaulis Smith

Forty-one sympodial terrestrials or uncommon epiphytes are found in dry to very wet, low to upper elevation, hill scrub, montane evergreen, pine-oak to deciduous forests and rocky grasslands from Trinidad, the Guianas, Venezuela, Mexico to Bolivia, Brazil and northern Argentina. These erect plants have slender, unbranched stems, each with a basal rosette. The blue-green, deciduous leaves are often variegated with silvery stripes or spots and usually appear after flowering time. The erect, hairy, few to numerous-flowered inflores-

Currently Accepted   Validly Published   Invalidly Published   Published Pre-1753   Superfluous Usage   Orthographic Variant   Fossil

Orchid Genera • **348**

cence, subtended by long, narrow bracts, has small to large, rare showy flowers that are pleasantly or nauseatingly fragrant. The color varies from pale green-yellow, green to white. The dorsal sepal and petals converge, forming a hood over the short to long, straight to curved column with a long foot. The narrow, recurved lateral sepals, united in the basal portion, are sickle-shaped and enclose the lip base. The narrow, concave, distinctly clawed, entire or more often, divided into hypochile and epichile lip forms a narrow, tunnel-like entrance to the nectary, has an uprolled margin and is trilobed toward the tip. The flattened spur is completely fused with the ovary.

SARCOGLYPHIS

Garay
Bot. Mus. Leafl. **23**(4): 200 (1972).

Epidendroideæ ⚘ Vandeæ • Aeridinæ

ETYMOLOGY: Greek for flesh and to carve or engrave. In reference to the prominent, fleshy rostellum that sits on top of the clinandrium like a carved ornament.

TYPE SPECIES: *Sarcoglyphis mirabilis*
(Reichenbach f.) Garay
(*Sarcanthus mirabilis* Reichenbach f.)

Twelve monopodial epiphytes are distributed in low elevation, evergreen forests and along river banks from south central China (Yunnan), eastern Himalayas, Myanmar to Vietnam and Indonesia (Sumatra, Java and Borneo). These smallish plants, often resembling *Cleisostoma*, have short, stout, hanging stems, each with several, narrow, strapped to V-shaped, tough, leathery to slightly fleshy, unequally bilobed leaves. The often long, branched, numerous-flowered inflorescence has small, yellow-green to dull olive-green, long-lived flowers sometimes suffused purple, maroon to brown or has lilac markings. The bright pink, arrowhead-shaped, trilobed lip tapers to a sharp point, is fused to a short, stout, footless column that has a highly compressed rostellum and has a small, cylindrical, downward curved spur.

SARCOGLYPSIS

An orthographic variant introduced in *Opera Bot.*, **114**: 382 (1992). The correct spelling is *Sarcoglyphis*.

SARCOPHYTON

Garay
Bot. Mus. Leafl. **23**(4): 201 (1972).

Epidendroideæ ⚘ Vandeæ • Aeridinæ

ETYMOLOGY: Greek for flesh and a plant. In reference to the excessively fleshy nature of the plants in all their segments.

TYPE SPECIES: *Sarcophyton crassifolium*
(Lindley & Paxton) Garay
(*Cleisostoma crassifolium* Lindley & Paxton)

Three robust, monopodial epiphytes are found in humid, low elevation, deciduous hill and pine forests, river valleys and cliff faces of Taiwan, Myanmar and the Philippines. These stout, erect plants have unbranched stems, each with several to numerous, tough, leathery or fleshy, unequally bilobed leaves. The rigid, branched, numerous-flowered inflorescence has small, yellow-green, yellow or white, widespreading, faintly fragrant flowers. The rosy or violet, slightly trilobed lip, fused to the column, has erect, toothed side lobes, the thick midlobe is recurved and has a hanging, blunt, oblong, honey-filled spur. The flowers have a short, footless column with a blunt tooth that partly closes the spur opening.

SARCOPODIUM

Lindley & Paxton
Paxton's Fl. Gard. **1**: 155 (1850).
Not *Sarcopodium* Ehrenberg ex Brongniart (1824) Fungi.

ETYMOLOGY: Greek for flesh and a little foot. Refers to the fleshy, foot-like development at the base of the column.

TYPE SPECIES: *None designated*

Not validly published because of a prior use of the name, this homonym was replaced by *Epigeneium* and *Bulbophyllum*.

SARCORHYNCHUS

Schlechter
Beih. Bot. Centralbl. **36**(2): 104 (1918).

ETYMOLOGY: Greek for flesh and snout or horn. Refers to the fleshy rostellum.

TYPE SPECIES: *None designated*

Now recognized as belonging to the genus *Rhipidoglossum*, *Sarcorhynchus* was previously considered to include four attractive epiphytes or rare lithophytes found in humid, low to mid elevation, evergreen forests from the Gulf of Guinea, Cameroon and Burundi to Uganda. These often straggly plants have long stems, each with narrow, unequally bilobed leaves. The numerous roots have distinct, white streaks when wet. The short, numerous-flowered inflorescence has

small, green, white or pale yellow flowers with oblong petals. The oblong, broad, entire lip has a short, swollen spur. The flowers have a short, erect, wingless, column.

SARCOSTOMA

Blume
Bijdr. Fl. Ned. Ind. **7**: 339, t. 45 (1825).

Epidendroideæ ⚘ Podochileæ • Eriinæ

ETYMOLOGY: Greek for flesh and mouth. An allusion to the fleshy midlobe of the lip.

TYPE SPECIES: *Sarcostoma javanica* Blume

Five sympodial epiphytes are found in low to mid elevation, hill woodlands and montane forests of Malaysia and Cambodia to Indonesia (Sumatra, Java and Borneo). These small tufted plants, vegetatively different from *Ceratostylis*, have short stems, subtended by withered sheaths, each with one to three, narrow, thick, fleshy, unequally bilobed leaves. The several, extremely short inflorescences are borne one at a time from a cluster of buds between the leaves. The solitary-flowered inflorescence has a small, cup-shaped, pure white, small flower with bright purple margins, which opens widely and lasts for only a day. The creamy, trilobed lip is narrow at the base with the tip thickened, and has a disk with two hairy ridges. The flowers have a club-shaped column with a short foot.

SARMENTICOLA

Senghas & Garay
Willdenowia **25**(2): 657 (1996).

Epidendroideæ ⚘ Cymbidieæ • Oncidiinæ

ETYMOLOGY: Greek for branch or having runners and inhabiting. Referring to the natural growing habit of being found on thin twigs.

TYPE SPECIES: *Sarmenticola calceolaris*
(Garay) Senghas & Garay
(*Pterostemma calceolare* Garay)

One dwarf, sympodial epiphyte is found in low elevation along the Amazon River basin of northern Peru (Loreto) and northwestern Brazil (Amazonas). This twig plant has short stems, subtended by overlapping, basal sheaths, each with several, narrow, fan-shaped leaves. The few-flowered inflorescence, borne from the leaf axils, has tiny, purple flowers that open in succession but last for only a day, and have narrow lateral sepals and petals. The broad, obscurely trilobed lip, united to the column base, has incurved side lobes; and the downward hanging, triangular midlobe has a sharp point and a raised, erect, callus. The flowers have a short, stout column. This species was formerly included in *Notylia*.

SAROTHROCHILUS

Schlechter

Repert. Spec. Nov. Regni Veg. **3**: 50 (1906).

ETYMOLOGY: Greek for a broom and lip. Refers to the dense reddish beard of rigid hairs found on the lip.

TYPE SPECIES: *Sarothrochilus dawsonianus*
(Reichenbach f.) Schlechter
(*Trichoglottis dawsoniana* Reichenbach f.)

Now recognized as belonging to the genus *Trichoglottis*, *Sarothrochilus* was previously considered to include one epiphyte found in hot, humid, low elevation, forest margins of southern China (Yunnan), Myanmar, Thailand and Laos. This small, climbing plant has short, stout, sometimes branching stems, each with several, slightly fleshy, unequally bilobed leaves. The several, branched, few-flowered inflorescences have small, fleshy flowers. The green, yellow-green or pale yellow flowers are heavily spotted or banded brown-red and are a pale yellow on the backside. The deep yellow to white, trilobed lip is blotched or streaked brown or red, has oblong side lobes. The midlobe has terminal, thickly fleshy lobelets, has numerous, brown hairs in the center and a small, thickly cone-like spur. The flowers have a short, stout, footless column.

SARRACENELLA

Luer

Selbyana **5**(3-4): 388 (1981).

ETYMOLOGY: *Sarracenia*, a genus of pitcher plants and Latin for diminutive. Refers to the similarity of the sepaline tube to the leaves of *Sarracenia*.
Or Michel Sarrasin (1659-1734), a French-born Canadian physician, scientist and early botanist. And Latin for diminutive.

TYPE SPECIES: *Sarracenella pubescens*
(Barbosa Rodrigues) Luer
(*Physosiphon pubescens* Barbosa Rodrigues)
This type name is now considered a synonym of
Acianthera bragae (Ruschi) F. Barros;
basionym replaced with
Physosiphon bragae Ruschi

Now recognized as belonging to the genus *Acianthera*, *Sarracenella* was previously considered to include two epiphytes found in shady, humid to cool, misty, mid elevation, montane forests of southeastern Brazil's coastal regions. These tiny, clump-forming plants have short, thick stems, each with several, succulent, boat-shaped green-yellow leaves set on creeping rhizomes. The unusual, slug-like, dark red-purple flowers (always borne in pairs) have the sepals joined forming a long, curved tube with the petals and tiny lip hidden deep inside.

SARRANTHUS

An orthographic variant introduced in *Refug. Bot.*, **2**(1): t. 109 (1872). The correct spelling is *Sarcanthus*.

SATIRIO

An orthographic variant introduced in *Pl. Effigies*, 316-322 (1551). The correct spelling is *Satyrion*.

SATIRION

Schöffer

Herbarius 128 (1484).

Pre-1753, therefore not validly published in fulfillment of nomenclatural rules; this name is most often referred to *Orchis*.

SATIRIUM

An orthographic variant introduced in *Delic. Gallo-Belg.*, **2**: 372 (1768). The correct spelling is *Satyrium*.

SATORCHIS

An orthographic variant introduced in *Hist. Orchid.*, t. 12 (1822). The correct spelling is *Satorkis*.

SATORKIS

Thouars

Nouv. Bull. Sci. Soc. Philom. Paris **1**(19): 316 (1809).

ETYMOLOGY: *Satyrium*, a genus of orchids and Greek for orchid. Alluding to a relationship with *Satyrium*.

TYPE SPECIES: *None designated*

A superfluous name proposed as a substitute for *Dactylorhiza*.

SATURION

An orthographic variant introduced in *Fam. Pl.*, **2**: 502 (1763). The correct spelling is *Satyrion*.

SATYRIA

Not *Satyria* Klotzsch (1851) Vacciniaceæ/Ericaceæ.

An orthographic variant introduced in *Fl. Coron. Herb. Hist.*, 199 (1578). The correct spelling is *Satyrion*.

SATYRICUM

An orthographic variant introduced in *Fl. Suec.* (*Linnaeus*), 263 (1745). The correct spelling is *Satyrium*.

SATYRIDIUM

Lindley

Gen. Sp. Orchid. Pl. 345 (1838).

ETYMOLOGY: *Satyrium*, a genus of orchids and Greek for diminutive. Referring to a likeness to *Satyrium*.

TYPE SPECIES: *Satyridium rostratum* Lindley

Now recognized as belonging to the genus *Satyrium*, *Satyridium* was previously considered to include one uncommon terrestrial found in misty, low elevation, rocky fields and meadows in the southwestern Cape regions of South Africa. This erect plant has unbranched, flowering stems that are always leafy, each with several, basal leaves graduating upward into open sheathing bracts. The densely packed, numerous-flowered inflorescence has small, fleshy, strongly fragrant, lilac to pink flowers spotted purple. The slightly hooded, entire lip has two spurs located at the base. The flowers have a long, erect column which is found inside the hooded lip. The above type name is now considered a synonym of *Satyrium rhynchanthum* Bolus.

SATYRII

Pliny

Hist. Nat. **XXVI**: 97 (AD 56).

Pre-1753, therefore not validly published in fulfillment of nomenclatural rules; this name is most often referred to *Orchis*.

SATYRIJ

An orthographic variant introduced in *Fl. Coron. Herb. Hist.*, 199 (1578). The correct spelling is *Satyrion*.

SATYRIO

An orthographic variant introduced in *Herb.* (*Brunfels*), **1**: 107 (1532). The correct spelling is *Satyrion*.

Currently Accepted Validly Published Invalidly Published Published Pre-1753 Superfluous Usage Orthographic Variant Fossil

O r c h i d   G e n e r a   •   **350**

SATYRION

Pliny

Hist. Nat. **XXV**: 98 (AD 56), and
Hist. Nat. **XXVI**: 96, 97, 99 (AD 56).

Pre-1753, therefore not validly published in fulfillment of nomenclatural rules; this name is most often referred to *Satyrium*.

SATYRION

An orthographic variant introduced in *Gard. Dict.*, ed. 2, **2**: (1735). The correct spelling is *Satyrium*.

SATYRIONIS

An orthographic variant introduced in *Herb. (Brunfels)*, **1** 109 (1532). The correct spelling is *Satyrium*.

SATYRIOS

Pliny

Hist. Nat. **XXVI**: 96 (AD 56).

Pre-1753, therefore not validly published in fulfillment of nomenclatural rules; this name is most often referred to *Orchis*.

SATYRIUM

Fuchs

Pl. Effigies 316-322 (1551).

Pre-1753, therefore not validly published in fulfillment of nomenclatural rules; this name is most often referred to *Ophrys*.

SATYRIUM

Linnaeus

Sp. Pl. (Linnaeus), ed. 1 **2**: 944 (1753), and
Gen. Pl., ed 5 405 (1754).

Name officially rejected vs. *Satyrium* Swartz (1800).

ETYMOLOGY: Roman Mythology. *Sylvan* was the god of woods and trees, a deity or spirit frequenting groves or the woods, or is referring to its growth habit.

LECTOTYPE: *Satyrium viride* Linnaeus

Although validly published this rejected name is referred to the genera *Coeloglossum*, *Habenaria*, and *Spiranthes*.

SATYRIUM

Swartz

Kongl. Vetensk. Acad. Nya Handl., ser. 2
21: 214 (1800).

Name ICBN conserved, the type name also conserved; vs. *Satyrium* Linnaeus (1753) Orchidaceæ.

Orchidoideæ Diseæ • Satyriinæ

ETYMOLOGY: In the Greek herbals of both Dioscorides and Pliny, satyrion refers to *Aceras anthropophorum*, commonly known as the man orchid. It is a name used by both Pedanius Dioscorides (90-40 BC), a Greek physician who wrote on medical drugs in *Materia Medica* and Pliny (Gaius Plinius Secundus) the elder (79-23 BC), a Roman historian who wrote *Naturalis Historia*.

Greek Mythology. The Satyri are imaginary male inhabitants (gods) of wild areas (mountains and woods) that are half human and half beast with usually a goat's tail, flanks, and hooves. While the upper part of the body is that of a human, the heads also have the horns of a goat. They are companions of Dionysus, the god of wine, and they spent their time drinking, dancing, and mischievously chasing nymphs. It also refers to the reputed aphrodisiac properties of the orchid that were thought to be contained in the roots or tubers.

TYPE SPECIES: *Satyrium bicorne* (Linnaeus) Thunberg (*Orchis bicornis* Linnaeus)

Approximately eighty-two sympodial terrestrials are found in moist, low to upper elevation, rocky meadows and grassy slopes from Ethiopia to South Africa with a few species scattered in Yemen, Madagascar, the Mascarenes Islands, Indonesia (Java), southern China (Xizang to Hunan), northern India (Kashmir to Assam), Nepal, Sri Lanka and Myanmar. These slender, robust plants have erect, unbranched, succulent stems, each with white or transparent leaf sheaths below the foliage leaves. The upper part (those above the foliage leaves) has sheaths grading into bracts with one to few, soft to stiff, narrow to ovate, basal leaves. Some species have their leaves on separate non-flowering stems. The terminal, numerous to few-flowered inflorescence has showy, fragrant, often brightly colored flowers (some species have functionally unisexual flowers) with hues ranging through white, green, yellow, pink, red or purple. The small petals and sepals are fused at the base. The uppermost, helmet-shaped lip has two long to short or sac-like spurs at the back. The flowers have a long to short, curved, footless column that is located inside the hooded lip, and is usually bent backward.

SATYRUM

An orthographic variant introduced in *Fl. Brit. Ind.*, **6**: 160 (1890). The correct spelling is *Satyrium*.

SAUNDERSIA

Reichenbach *filius*

Bot. Congr. London 120 (1866), and
Beitr. Orchid.-K. 17, t. 6 (1869).

Epidendroideæ Cymbideæ • Oncidiinæ

ETYMOLOGY: Honoring William Wilson Saunders (1809-1879), a British insurance underwriter, entomologist, horticulturist, ardent orchid enthusiast and editor of *Refugium Botanicum or figures & description from living specimens of little known or New Plants of botanical interest.*

TYPE SPECIES: *Saundersia mirabilis* Reichenbach f.

Three uncommon, sympodial epiphytes are found in low to mid elevation, montane rain forests of southeastern Brazil (Minas Gerais to São Paulo). These tiny plants have erect to slightly curved stems, subtended by overlapping sheaths, each with a solitary, strap-shaped leaf. The short, simple to branched inflorescence is tightly bound with brown floral bracts. The brown to red-yellow flowers have similar, small sepals and petals barred red-brown. The bright white, long-clawed, entire lip has a large, bilobed tip. The flowers have a minute to small column. The plant's roots, inflorescence, and outside floral surfaces are covered with short brown hairs.

SAUNDRSIA

An orthographic variant cited in *Dict. Gen. Names Seed Pl.*, 60 (1995). The correct spelling is *Saundersia*.

SAUROGLOSSUM

Lindley

Edwards's Bot. Reg. **19**: t. 1618 (1833).

Orchidoideæ Cranichideæ • Spiranthinæ

ETYMOLOGY: Greek for lizard and tongue. Parts of this plant have a likeness to the tongue of some types of reptiles.

TYPE SPECIES: *Sauroglossum elatum* Lindley
This type name is now considered a synonym of *Sauroglossum nitidum* (Vellozo) Schlechter;
basionym
Serapias nitida Vellozo

Twelve sympodial epiphytes are found in moist to dry, low to upper elevation, hill scrub and montane cloud forests, grassy to rocky fields from Ecuador to central Bolivia and Brazil to northwestern Argentina. These tall, erect plants have unbranched stems, each with a basal rosette; the leaves may be present at flowering. The terminal, numerous-flowered inflorescence has small, green and white, yellow, orange or brick-red, tubular flowers, not opening widely. The long, narrow, sparsely to densely hairy lateral sepals have a fleshy protuberance located at the tip, and the small petals are smooth or slightly hairy along their outer margins. The shortly clawed, trilobed lip has a strongly concave hypochile with a thick, fleshy crest; the epichile has wing-like lobules with thick margins and a small spur. The flowers have a small, slender, club-shaped, wingless column that is often arched at the tip of the footless column.

SAUROLOPHORKIS

Margońska & Szlachetko

Polish Bot. J.   **46**(1): 7 (2001).

Epidendroideæ 〜 Malaxideæ

ETYMOLOGY: *Parasaurolophus*, a genus of dinosaur and Greek for orchid. An allusion to the column's dorsal projection located at the top, similar to a dinosaur's head.

TYPE SPECIES: *Saurolophorkis cordanthemon*
Margońska & Szlachetko

Two small, sympodial terrestrials are found in New Guinea. These plants have oblong to cone-shaped pseudobulbs, each with several, ovate, pleated leaves. The elongate, densely packed, numerous-flowered inflorescence has green, apple-green to pale brown flowers. The dorsal sepal is concave, the lateral sepals have green nerves and are almost completed fused together; the small, narrow petals are tightly curled. The small, obscurely trilobed lip has numerous, dark green to blue-green calli on the margin. The flowers have an erect, stout, footless column.

SAUVETREA

Szlachetko

Richardiana   **7**(1): 28 (2007).

ETYMOLOGY: Named in honor of Pascal Sauvêtre (1966-), a French horticulturist with the Jardin de Luxemburg in Paris.

TYPE SPECIES: *Sauvetrea alpestris* (Lindley) Szlachetko
(*Maxillaria alpestris* Lindley)

Recognized as belonging to the genus *Maxillaria*, *Sauvetrea* was proposed to include sixteen epiphytes found in wet, low to upper elevation, hill to montane forests and along river banks from northwestern Venezuela and Colombia to Bolivia. These small, creeping plants have ovate, flattened, wrinkled pseudobulbs, subtended by overlapping, distichous, thin, dry sheaths, each with a solitary, narrow, leathery leaf. The erect, solitary-flowered inflorescence has a pink-brown, pale brown-yellow to green-yellow flower with wide-spreading sepals and small, erect petals. The entire to obscurely trilobed lip has erect side lobes, a tongue-shaped midlobe with a narrow, strap-shaped callus. Each mature pseudobulb can have several inflorescences over a period of time.

SAYERA

An orthographic variant cited in *Lex. Gen. Phan.*, 502 (1904). The correct spelling is *Sayeria*.

SAYERIA

Kraenzlin

Oesterr. Bot. Z.   **44**: 257, 298 (1894).

ETYMOLOGY: Dedicated to a Mr. W.A. Sayer (*fl.* 1886-1897), an Australian naturalist who collected the type species while exploring New Guinea with the Cuthbertson expedition.

TYPE SPECIES: *Sayeria paradoxa* Kraenzlin

Now recognized as belonging to the genus *Dendrobium*, *Sayeria* was previously considered to include fifty-three epiphytes or lithophytes found in mid to upper elevation, montane forests and woodlands from Indonesia to the Solomons. These plants, often growing in large masses, have stout, cane-like pseudobulbs, each with several leaves borne at the tip. The erect, long, numerous to few-flowered inflorescence has closely-spaced, green-brown, white or yellow flowers with a few species that are heavily spotted red or have purple stripes or spots. The entire or trilobed lip has a strongly, irregularly wavy margin, erect side lobes, a spear-shaped midlobe decorated with numerous yellow strips, and has a basal callus. The above type name is now considered a synonym of *Dendrobium cruttwellii* T.M. Reeve.

SCANDEDERIS

Thouars

Hist. Orchid.   Table 3, sub 3s, t. 91 (1822).

ETYMOLOGY: Latin for climbing vine. Refers to the climbing growth habit of the plant.

TYPE SPECIES: *Scandederis scandens* Thouars

Now recognized as belonging to the genus *Hederorkis*, *Scandederis* was previously considered to include one saprophyte found in the islands of Mauritius. This plant has fleshy stems, each with the leaves reduced to tiny, sheathing scales. The fairly complex, dull brown to purple-brown flowers have similar sepals and petals. The swollen, sac-like, entire lip has a deep cleft at the tip.

SCAPHIGLOTTIS

An orthographic variant introduced in *Enum. Pl. Mus. Paris*, ed. 2, 75 (1850). The correct spelling is *Scaphyglottis*.

SCAPHOGLOTTIS

An orthographic variant introduced in *J. Roy. Hort. Soc.*, **7**(1): 131 (1886). The correct spelling is *Scaphyglottis*.

SCAPHOSEPALUM

Pfitzer

Nat. Pflanzenfam.   **2**(6): 136, 139 (1889).

Epidendroideæ 〜 Epidendreæ • Pleurothallidinæ

ETYMOLOGY: Greek for bowl or boat and for sepal. Refers to the partially fused lateral sepals that form a bowl-shaped segment.

LECTOTYPE: *Scaphosepalum ochthodes*
(Reichenbach f.) Pfitzer
(*Masdevallia ochthodes* Reichenbach f.)

This type name is now considered a synonym of *Scaphosepalum verrucosum* (Reichenbach f.) Pfitzer; basionym replaced with *Masdevallia verrucosa* Reichenbach f.

Forty-one small, sympodial epiphytes, sometimes lithophytes or terrestrials are found in low to upper elevation, hill to montane cloud forests from southern Mexico to Bolivia and the Guianas. These creeping or tufted, clump-forming plants range from tiny to large, have long stems, subtended by overlapping sheaths, each with a solitary, leathery, narrow leaf. The several, erect to hanging, numerous to few-flowered inflorescences have small, yellow flowers, opening in succession, with some strange and exotic shapes. The fleshy flowers are lined or marked in darker hues, and the spreading sepals are furnished with a tail at their tips. The lateral sepals are united almost to their tips forming a concave blade and each has a fleshy callus pad. The tiny petals are inconspicuous. The uppermost, small to tiny, trilobed, oblong or fiddle-shaped lip has a disc with longitudinal thin, flat scales. The flowers have an incurved, long, winged, hooded column with the base often bilobed and hinged to the column foot.

SCAPHOSPALEUM

An orthographic variant introduced in *Orchideen (Schlechter)*, ed. 1, 164 (1914). The correct spelling is *Scaphosepalum*.

SCAPHYCLOTIS

An orthographic variant introduced in *Beitr. Morph. Biol. Orchid.*, 15 (1863). The correct spelling is *Scaphyglottis*.

| Currently Accepted | Validly Published | Invalidly Published | Published Pre-1753 | Superfluous Usage | Orthographic Variant | Fossil |

SCAPHYGLOSSIS

An orthographic variant introduced in *Bot. Mitt. Tropen*, **2**: 13 (1888). The correct spelling is *Scaphyglottis*.

SCAPHYGLOTTIS

Poeppig & Endlicher

Nov. Gen. Sp. Pl. (Poeppig & Endlicher) **1**(7-10): 58, *tt.* 97-100 (1836).

Name ICBN conserved vs. *Hexisea* Lindley (1834) Orchidaceæ.

Epidendroideæ ⚘ Epidendreæ • Laeliinæ

ETYMOLOGY: Greek for bowl, cupped or hollowed out and tongue. Refers to the shape of the concave lip.

LECTOTYPE: *Scaphyglottis graminifolia*
(Ruiz & Pavón) Poeppig & Endlicher
(*Fernandezia graminifolia* Ruiz & Pavón)
not *Nemaconia graminifolia* Knowles & Westcott
designated by both Dressler, *Taxon*, **9**: 214 (1960), and
Garay & H.R. Sweet, *J. Arnold. Arbor.*, **53**: 528 (1972).

LECTOTYPE: *Scaphyglottis parviflora*
Poeppig & Endlicher
designated by Pfeiffer, *Nomencl. Bot. (Pfeiffer)*,
2(2): 1068 (1874).

Sixty-three sympodial epiphytes or lithophytes are found in wet to seasonally dry, low to upper elevation, hill woodlands to montane cloud forests ranging from Cuba to Trinidad, the Guianas, Venezuela, southern Mexico to Bolivia and central Brazil with the greatest diversity found in Costa Rica. These small, densely clustered, densely branched plants are highly variable in their leaf habit, from thin, grass-like to oblong or ovate, broadly fleshy, leathery to papery. The spindle-shaped to slightly swollen pseudobulbs are often produced in an upward series with the new growth borne at the tip of the old pseudobulb. The short, few-flowered inflorescence has tiny, attractive, white to magenta flowers, borne in the axils of the leaves, often produced in great profusion. The tiny, wedge-shaped, entire, trilobed or notched lip, joined to the column foot or rarely firmly united, has a scalloped margin. The flowers have a short, winged to wingless column.

SCAPPHYGLOTTIS

An orthographic variant introduced in *Hist. Br. Guiana.*, **2**: 230 (1855). The correct spelling is *Scaphyglottis*.

SCAREDEDERIS

An orthographic variant introduced in *Hist. Orchid.*, *t.* 90 (1822). The correct spelling is *Scandederis*.

SCELOCHILOIDES

Dodson & M.W. Chase

Icon. Pl. Trop., ser. 2 **3**: *t.* 293 (1989).

Epidendroideæ ⚘ Cymbidieæ • Oncidiinæ

ETYMOLOGY: *Scelochilus*, a genus of orchids and Greek for resembling. Refers to its similarity to *Scelochilus*.

TYPE SPECIES: *Scelochiloides vasquezii*
Dodson & M.W. Chase

Three sympodial epiphytes are found in wet, mid elevation, montane cloud forests of central Bolivia (Cochabamba and Santa Cruz). These small plants have ovoid pseudobulbs, subtended by overlapping, leaf-like sheaths, each with a solitary leaf. The long, hanging, few-flowered inflorescence has small, yellow to orange flowers sprinkled with a few red spots or stripes. The concave dorsal sepal converges with the petals surrounding the straight, wingless, footless column; the lateral sepals are joined to their tips, with the base extended forming a scrotum-like spur. The white, spoon-shaped, entire lip has pink spots; the roundish midlobe has a few spines on the disc, a three hook-shaped calli, and the base is extended to a single, coiled spur.

SCELOCHILOPSIS

Dodson & M.W. Chase

Orquideologia **21**(1): 61 (1998).

Epidendroideæ ⚘ Cymbidieæ • Oncidiinæ

ETYMOLOGY: *Scelochilus*, a genus of orchids and Greek for resemblance or likeness. Refers to a similarity to *Scelochilus*.

TYPE SPECIES: *Scelochilopsis ecalcarata*
(Determann) Dodson & M.W. Chase
(*Scelochilus ecalcaratus* Determann)

One nondescript sympodial epiphyte is found in low elevation, hill scrub and river forests from French Guiana and northern Peru (Loreto) to northern Brazil (Pará). This small, hanging plant has narrow, ovoid pseudobulbs, subtended by distichous, leaf-like sheaths, each with a solitary, leathery, leaf borne from the tip. The hanging, few-flowered inflorescence has a half-closed, yellow flower whose most distinguishing feature is the rigid, spoon-shaped, entire lip that has a pair of elongate, thin, scale-like calli. The lateral sepals are united at their base forming a small, chin-like projection, and the small petals are pressed against the dorsal sepal. The flowers have a slender, wingless column.

SCELOCHILUS

Klotzsch

Allg. Gartenzeitung **9**(33): 261 (1841).

Epidendroideæ ⚘ Cymbidieæ • Oncidiinæ

ETYMOLOGY: Greek for leg and lip. In reference to the two, small horn-like structures located at the base of the lip.

TYPE SPECIES: *Scelochilus ottonis* Klotzsch

Forty-eight sympodial epiphytes are found in low to mid elevation, montane forests from southern Mexico, Guatemala to Peru and the Guianas. These small plants have clustered, flattened ovoid, one-noded pseudobulbs, subtended by distichous sheaths, each with a solitary, leathery leaf. The numerous to few-flowered inflorescence has bright yellow flowers, not opening fully, with pale green veins. The rigid, green-yellow to purple, trilobed lip is attached to the long, club-shaped, footless column that is with or without wings. The extended lip base has two narrowly separated spurs entirely concealed in the sac-like structure of the lateral sepals.

SCHAENOMORPHUS

An orthographic variant introduced in *Bull. Soc. Bot. France*, **80**: 351, 352 (1933). The correct spelling is *Schoenomorphus*.

SCHAMBURGKIA

An orthographic variant introduced in *Flora*, **66**(33): 519 (1883). The correct spelling is *Schomburgkia*.

SCHELOCHILUS

An orthographic variant introduced in *Sander's Orch. Guide*, ed. 4, 403 (1927). The correct spelling is *Scelochilus*.

SCHIDORHYNCHOS

Szlachetko

Fragm. Florist. Geobot. **38**(2): 469 (1993).

ETYMOLOGY: Greek for split, tooth and snout. In reference to the shape of the rostellum remnant.

TYPE SPECIES: *Schidorhynchos andinum*
(Hauman) Szlachetko
(*Spiranthes nitida* var. *andina* Hauman)

Now recognized as belonging to the genus *Sauroglossum*, *Schidorhynchos* was proposed to include two terrestrials found in mid to upper elevation, montane forests and grasslands of northwestern Argentina (Salta, Catamarca and La Rioja). These plants have erect, long, unbranched stems, each with a rosette of rather broad leaves. The long, numerous-flowered inflorescence has small, thinly textured, nerved, green flowers. The dorsal sepal is oblong; the spoon-shaped lateral sepals are slightly asymmetric, and the slightly spoon-shaped petals are semi-transparent. The trilobed lip has tree-like venation; the long hypochile has margins rolled outwards, and the forward bent epichile is heart-shaped.

SCHIDORRHYNCHOS

An orthographic variant introduced in *Cat. Pl. Vasc. Rep. Argentina*, **1**: 267 (1966). The correct spelling is *Schidorhynchos*.

SCHIEDEELLA

Schlechter

Beih. Bot. Centralbl. **37**(2): 379 (1920).

Orchidoideæ ◊ Cranichideæ • Spiranthinæ

ETYMOLOGY: Honoring Christian Julius Wilhelm Schiede (1798-1836), a German-born Mexican physician, naturalist and botanist who collected throughout Central America. And Latin for diminutive.

LECTOTYPE: *Schiedeella saltensis* (Ames) Schlechter
(*Spiranthes saltensis* Ames) nom. illeg.
designated by Burns-Balogh, *Amer. J. Bot.*, **69**(7): 1131 (1982).

LECTOTYPE: *Schiedeella transversalis*
(A. Richard & Galeotti) Schlechter
(*Spiranthes transversalis* A. Richard & Galeotti)
designated by Garay, *Bot. Mus. Leafl.*, **8**: 357 (1982).

Twenty-one sympodial terrestrials are found in low to upper elevation, hillsides, rocky meadows, pine-oak forests from the southwestern United States (Arizona, New Mexico and southern Texas), Mexico to Costa Rica, eastern Cuba and Hispaniola. These small plants have erect, unbranched stems, each with a solitary to several, soft textured, variegated leaves forming a basal rosette. The leaves are usually withered by flowering time. The slender, spirally arranged, numerous to few-flowered inflorescence has inconspicuous, minute, creamy green, white, pink to purple-red, tubular, delicately fragrant flowers not opening fully with similar sepals and petals. The white, oblong, distinctly clawed, obscurely trilobed lip is usually sprinkled with red, olive-brown or green spots. The flowers have a slender, straight or slightly recurved, club-shaped column. The second above lectotype name *Schiedeella transversalis* (A. Richard & Galeotti) Schlechter is now considered a synonym of *Schiedeella llaveana* (Lindley) Schlechter.

SCHISMACERAS

An orthographic variant cited in *Lex. Gen. Phan.*, 504 (1904). The correct spelling is *Schismoceras*.

SCHISMATOCERAS

An orthographic variant introduced in *Contr. Bot. Dept. Nebraska Univ.*, **3**(1): 53 (1902). The correct spelling is *Schismoceras*.

SCHISMOCERAS

C. Presl

Reliq. Haenk. **1**(2): 96, *t. 13, f. 2* (1827).

ETYMOLOGY: Greek for cleavage or division and a horn. Refers to the fleshy, distinctly pointed sepals that stand erect like small horns.

TYPE SPECIES: *Schismoceras disticha* C. Presl

Now recognized as belonging to the genus *Dendrobium*, *Schismoceras* was previously considered to include one epiphyte found in low elevation, swamps and among mangroves throughout the Philippines. This tufted, semi-hanging plant has flattened stems, each with triangular-shaped, rigid, overlapping leaves arranged in two ranks along the stem. The short, few-flowered inflorescence, borne at the tip of the stem, has lovely, small, slightly fragrant, green-yellow flowers, lined or striped lavender or bright red. The creamy white, entire lip has a large callus and an inrolled margin with a sharp tip. The flowers have a short, erect column. The above type name is now considered a synonym of *Dendrobium distichum* (C.Presl) Reichenbach f.

SCHISMOCERUS

An orthographic variant cited in *Nomencl. Bot. (Steudel)*, ed. 2, **2**: 530 (1840). The correct spelling is *Schismoceras*.

SCHISTOSTYLUS

An orthographic variant introduced in *Australasian Sarcanthinæ*, 30, *t. 43* (1967). The correct spelling is *Schistotylus*.

SCHISTOTYLUS

Dockrill

Australasian Sarcanthinæ 29, *t. 43* (1967).

Epidendroideæ ◊ Vandeæ • Aeridinæ

ETYMOLOGY: Latin for separated, to split or lump and stylis or pillar. Refers to the notched callus located on the midlobe of the lip.

TYPE SPECIES: *Schistotylus purpuratus* (Rupp) Dockrill
(*Cleisostoma purpuratum* Rupp)

One monopodial epiphyte is found in low elevation, coastal scrub, swamps and along river banks of eastern Australia. This dwarf, twig-like plant,

often forming dense colonies, has short stems, each with narrow, purple spotted, fleshy leaves arranged in two ranks and has numerous, zig-zagged, gray roots. The short, few-flowered inflorescence has pale green flowers with purple margins and a purple median line on the backside of the ovate petals. The thick, white, trilobed lip has small, erect side lobes; the recurved midlobe has large spots, and the long, white spur has a hairy callus inside the mouth. The flowers have a short, bright purple to orange, wingless, footless column.

SCHIZOCHILUS

Sonder

Linnaea **19**: 78 (1847).

Orchidoideæ ◊ Orchideæ • Orchidinæ

ETYMOLOGY: Greek for to split or divide and lip. Alluding to the divided condition of the lip.

TYPE SPECIES: *Schizochilus zeyheri* Sonder

Eleven sympodial terrestrials are found in mid to upper elevation, rocky to marshy grasslands with high rainfall of Tanzania, the Cape and central areas of South Africa. These small, erect plants have unbranched stems, each with several, grass-like leaves often clustered at the base, graduating into floral bracts upward. The terminal, wiry, few-flowered inflorescence is sharply bent over just below the lowest flower. The small to minute, pretty, bell-shaped, white, white and yellow, bright yellow or white flowers are suffused mauve or pink. The narrow, oblong to roundish dorsal sepal is shallowly helmet-shaped. The wedge-shaped, obscurely trilobed or trilobed lip has the concave hypochile leading to the slightly curved spur, frequently with calli found between the hypochile and epichile. The slender to club-shaped or cylindrical to deeply cleft spur is always shorter than the lip. The flowers have a very short column.

SCHIZODIUM

Lindley

Gen. Sp. Orchid. Pl. 358 (1838).

Orchidoideæ ◊ Diseæ • Disinæ

ETYMOLOGY: Greek for to split or divide and resemblance. Descriptive of the bilobed petals.

TYPE SPECIES: *None designated*

Six almost leafless, sympodial terrestrials are found in low elevation, open meadows with sandy, gravelly or clay soils of the southwestern Cape region of South Africa. These erect plants have unbranched, often zig-zagging stems, each with a basal rosette of tiny, net-veined leaves. The tall, wiry, few-flowered inflorescence has small, but not showy, mostly

Currently Accepted   Validly Published   Invalidly Published   Published Pre-1753   Superfluous Usage   Orthographic Variant   Fossil

Orchid Genera • **354**

pale to dark pink, white or yellow flowers that are densely spotted. The helmet-shaped dorsal sepal is spurred; this swollen spur is straight or curves either upward or downward. The petals have obscure to prominent basal lobes. The fiddle-shaped, entire lip often has dark spots and has a small tooth at the usually darker colored tip. The flowers have a short, stout, bilobed, wingless, footless column.

NOTE: Current DNA testing shows that *Schizodium* is deeply embedded within the genus *Disa* and should be reduced to a section of *Disa*.

SCHIZOPEDIUM

Salisbury

Monthly Rev. **75**: 81 (1814).

ETYMOLOGY: Greek for split and slipper. Refers to the bag-like pouch of the lip.

TYPE SPECIES: *None designated*

A superfluous name proposed as a substitute for *Cypripedium*.

SCHLECHTERELLA

Hoehne

Arq. Bot. Estado São Paulo, n.s., f.m. **2**: 13 (1944).
Not *Schlechterella* K. Schumann (1899) Asclepiadaceæ.

ETYMOLOGY: Dedicated to the memory of Friedrich Richard Rudolf Schlechter (1872-1925), a German taxonomist, botanist and author of numerous taxonomical works on orchids. And Latin for diminutive.

TYPE SPECIES: *Schlechterella aurantiaca*
(Lindley) Hoehne
(*Bifrenaria aurantiaca* Lindley)

Not validly published because of a prior use of the name, this homonym was replaced by *Rudolfiella*.

SCHLECHTERORCHIS

Szlachetko

Orchidee (Hamburg) **54**(2): 217 (2003).

ETYMOLOGY: Honoring Friedrich Richard Rudolf Schlechter (1872-1925). And Greek for orchid.

TYPE SPECIES: *Schlechterorchis occidentalis*
(Lindley) Szlachetko
(*Amphorchis occidentalis* Lindley)

Recognized as belonging to the genus *Habenaria*, *Schlechterorchis* was proposed to include four terrestrials with small groups found in low elevation, savannas, dune scrub, marshes or grasslands from Ivory Coast to Uganda and Tanzania to Zimbabwe. These small plants have short, erect, unbranched stems, each with a solitary, heart-shaped, ground hugging basal leaf that is often hairy along its margins. The wiry, hairy inflorescence has an unattractive small flower. The sepals and petals are widest at their tips and have wavy margins. The uppermost, trilobed lip has long, shallowly notched side lobes, a short, notched midlobe with a tapering point, and a long tapering, cylindrical spur. The flowers have a short, erect column.

SCHLIMIA

Not *Schlimia* Regel (1875) Gentianaceæ.

An orthographic variant introduced in *Ann. Bot. Syst.*, **6**(1): 614 (1861). The correct spelling is *Schlimmia*.

SCHLIMMIA

Planchon & Linden

Linden's *Prix-Courant Cat.* 7   *f.* 287 (1852),
Jard. Fleur.   **3**(Misc.): 113 (1853), and
Paxton's Fl. Gard.   **3**: 115 (1853).

Epidendroideæ ⚮ Cymbidieæ • Stanhopeinæ

ETYMOLOGY: Honoring Louis Joseph Schlim (*fl.* 1840s-1850s), a Belgian who collected plants in Colombia and Venezuela for his cousin Jean Jules Linden (1817-1898), a Luxemburg-born Belgian who explored mostly Venezuela with Nicolas Funck, established a Horticulture Internationale nursery in Brussels and was the author of *Pescatorea*.

TYPE SPECIES: *Schlimmia jasminodora*
Planchon & Linden

Eight exquisite, sympodial epiphytes are found in mid elevation, montane forests from Costa Rica to Peru and Venezuela. These plants have clustered, ovoid pseudobulbs, subtended by overlapping, distichous sheaths, each with a solitary, pleated, heavily veined leaf. The arching, few-flowered inflorescence has small, bell-shaped, fragrant, waxy, creamy-green to white flowers. The purple spotted, fused lateral sepals form a large, sac-like protuberance that contains the short, pale green, winged column. The small, short, tongue-shaped, entire lip has a broad, trilobed-like hypochile in front with two yellow swellings and a small, heart-shaped epichile.

SCHLUCKEBIERIA

(Pabst) Braem

Richardiana   **4**(2): 49 (2004).

ETYMOLOGY: Named in honor of Gudrun Braem née Schluckebier (1951-), the German-born wife from Mengeringhausen, of Guido Braem (1944-), a Belgian art historian, orchidologist and author of numerous books on Cattleyas and Paphiopedilums.

TYPE SPECIES: *Schluckebieria araguaiensis*
(Pabst) Braem
(*Cattleya araguaiensis* Pabst)

A superfluous name proposed as a substitute for *Cattleyella*.

SCHOENLEINIA

Klotzsch ex **Lindley**

Veg. Kingd., ed. 2   182 (1847).

ETYMOLOGY: Latin for reed-shaped and smooth.

TYPE SPECIES: *None designated*

Name published without a description. Today this name is most often referred to *Ponthieva*.

SCHOENLEINLIA

An orthographic variant introduced in *Orchideen (Schlechter)*, ed. 3, **5**(6): 316 (1974). The correct spelling is *Schoenleinia*.

SCHOENLEMLIA

An orthographic variant cited in *Orchideen (Schlechter): Liter. Reg. Band I/A, B, and C,* 254 (2003). The correct spelling is *Schoenleinia*.

SCHOENOMORPHIS

An orthographic variant introduced in *Bull. Soc. Bot. France*, **80**: 351 (1933). The correct spelling is *Schoenomorphus*.

SCHOENOMORPHUS

Thorel ex **Gagnepain**

Bull. Soc. Bot. France   **80**: 351, 352 (1933).

ETYMOLOGY: Greek for reed or rush and shaped. From the plant's rush-like habitat.

TYPE SPECIES: *Schoenomorphus capitatus*
Thorel ex Gagnepain

Now recognized as belonging to the genus *Tropidia*, *Schoenomorphus* was previously considered to include one terrestrial found in low elevation, woodlands and along river banks of Thailand, Laos, Malaysia and Indonesia. This tall plant has numerous, tough leaves on its elongated stems. The few-flowered inflorescence, borne at the tip of the stem, has white flowers not opening widely but simultaneously. The broad, entire lip has a short, broad spur, often with a downward turned tip. The flowers have a short column. The above type name is currently unplaced at this time.

SCHOENORCHIS

Reinwardt

Cat. Gew. Buitenzorg   100 (1823).

Name published without a description. Today this name is most often referred to *Schoenorchis* Blume.

SCHOENORCHIS

Reinwardt ex **Blume**

Bijdr. Fl. Ned. Ind. **8**: 361 (1825), and
Hornschuh's *Syll. Pl. Nov.* **2**: 4 (1825).

Epidendroideæ ⚬ **Vandeæ** • **Aeridinæ**

ETYMOLOGY: Greek for reed or rush and orchid.
Alluding to the rush-like leaves.

LECTOTYPE: *Schoenorchis juncifolia*
Reinwardt ex Blume

Twenty-six uncommon,
monopodial epiphytes are
found in low to mid elevation,
hill to montane forests from
southern China (Xizang to Hong
Kong), Taiwan, northeastern India
(Assam), Nepal, Sri Lanka, Myanmar
to Vietnam, Malaysia, New Guinea
and northern Australia (Queensland)
to the southwestern Pacific Archipelago.
These small, erect or hanging plants have
stems (sometimes branching) with condensed
or long internodes, each with broad or slender,
flat or pencil-like, shallowly lobed leaves. The
several, simple or branched, usually drooping,
long or short, numerous-flowered inflorescence
has minute, white, blue or red-purple flowers
not opening widely. What these showy,
fragrant flowers lack in size is overcome by
sheer numbers and their bright colors. The
trilobed lip has a straight midlobe; the erect
side lobes clasp the column and has an
elongate or helmet-like, twisted spur. The
flowers have a short, wingless, footless column.

SCHOMBURGKIA

Lindley

Sert. Orchid. tt. 10, 13 (1838).

Not *Schomburghia* A.P. de Candolle (1838) Asteraceæ.

ETYMOLOGY: Dedicated to Robert Hermann
Schomburgk (1804-1865), a Prussian-born British
surveyor of the Guyana regions for the Royal
Geographical Society, collector of extensive
botanical materials, and later served as a British
consul for Santo Domingo and later Bangkok.

TYPE SPECIES: *Schomburgkia crispa* Lindley

This type name is now considered a synonym of
Laelia gloriosa (Reichenbach f.) L.O. Williams;
basionym
Schomburgkia gloriosa Reichenbach f.

Now recognized as
belonging to the genus
Laelia, *Schomburgkia* was
previously considered to
include fifteen epiphytes
or lithophytes scattered
from dry or damp, low to
mid elevation, open forests
and valleys throughout southern Mexico
(Guerrero, Jalisco and Michoacán) to Peru,
Cuba, Jamaica, Venezuela and the Guianas.
These large plants have long, spindle-shaped
or cylindrical pseudobulbs of several nodes,
sometimes hollow, each with two or three,

oblong, leathery leaves borne at the tip. The
more or less erect, sometimes up to four foot
(1.2 m), numerous to few-flowered inflorescence has showy, often waxy, short-lived, pale
honey-brown to purple flowers with narrow
petals and sepals that are often slightly to
strongly curled. The white, pink to magenta,
trilobed lip has golden-brown margins, erect
side lobes, and a widespreading midlobe with a
recurved tip. The flowers have a curved, short,
stout, footless column.

SCHONLEINIA

An orthographic variant introduced in *Veg.
Kingd.*, ed. 2, 182 (1847). The correct spelling
is *Schoenleinia*.

SCHUITEMANIA

Ormerod

Lindleyana **17**(4): 228 (2002).

Orchidoideæ ⚬ **Cranichideæ** • **Goodyerinæ**

ETYMOLOGY: Dedicated to André Schuiteman
(1960-), a Belgian orchidologist at Rijksherbarium in
Leiden and author of *Orchid Genera of Thailand,
Laos, Cambodia and Vietnam.*

TYPE SPECIES: *Schuitemania merrillii* (Ames) Ormerod
(*Herpysma merrillii* Ames)

One sympodial
terrestrial is found in
deep shade or damp areas in low elevation,
hill forests of the Philippines (Mindoro). This
small, creeping plant has slender, erect stems,
each with several, basal leaves. The hairy, few-
flowered inflorescence has tubular, white
flowers with thinly textured, narrow segments
that do not open fully. The trilobed lip,
attached to the lower half of the column, has
a roundish hypochile; the mesochile is formed
by the lip margin; the epichile is entire or
bilobed and has a small spur. The flowers have
a long, club-shaped column. This species was
formerly included in *Kuhlhasseltia*.

SCHUNKEA

Senghas

Palmengarten **58**(2): 128 (1994).

Epidendroideæ ⚬ **Cymbidieæ** • **Stanhopeinæ**

ETYMOLOGY: In honor of Vital Joaquim Schunk
(1951-), a Brazilian orchid nursery owner in Minas
Gerais who collected the type species along with
Gerhard Pfister (1940-2000), a German collector.

TYPE SPECIES: *Schunkea vierlingii* Senghas

One sympodial epiphyte is found
in mid elevation, montane forests
of eastern Brazil (Espírito
Santo). This small plant has
slender, tapered pseudobulbs,
each with a solitary, thick,
narrow leaf. The short,
hanging, few-flowered inflores-
cence has small, brown-red flowers with wide

pale yellow margins. The sepals and petals are
all similarity shaped. The heart-shaped, entire
lip has a red center and yellow margin with a
raised, slightly hairy, basal calli. The flowers
have a short, erect, stout column.

SCHWARTZKOPFIA

An orthographic variant cited in *Handb.
Orchid.-Namen*, 666 (2005). The correct
spelling is *Schwartzkopffia.*

SCHWARTZKOPFFIA

Kraenzlin

Bot. Jahrb. Syst. **28**: 177 (1900).

ETYMOLOGY: Dedicated to two brothers, Paul
Schwartzkopff (1849-1920), a German professor of
Theology and author of *Das Leben im Traum*, and
Ernest Schwartzkopff, who were friends of Kraenzlin
from Leipzig.

TYPE SPECIES: *Schwartzkopffia buettneriana*
Kraenzlin

This type name is now considered a synonym of
Brachycorythis pumilio (Lindley) Reichenbach f.;
basionym
Penthea pumilio Lindley

Now recognized as
belonging to the genus
Brachycorythis,
Schwartzkopffia was
previously considered to include two terrestrials
or sometimes saprophytes found in low to mid
elevation, swampy grasslands of Angola,
Tanzania, Malawi, Zimbabwe, Zambia and
Mozambique. These small, erect plants, often
found in clusters, have short, unbranched,
stout, leafless stems, subtended by several,
large, dark brown, leaf-like bracts. The few-
flowered inflorescence has white or mauve,
strongly fragrant flowers suffused pink or
purple and borne in a tight bundle toward the
tip of the stem. The smaller petals are joined
to the slender column and converge, forming a
hood over the wedge-shaped, bright magenta,
trilobed lip that has slightly curved sides.

SCHWARZKOPFFIA

An orthographic variant introduced in
Notizbl. Bot. Gart. Berlin-Dahlem, **9**(88): 582
(1926). The correct spelling is *Schwartzkopffia.*

SCIAPHYGLOTTIS

An orthographic variant introduced in *Bot.
Centralbl.*, **76**(49): 345 (1898). The correct
spelling is *Scaphyglottis.*

Currently Accepted   Validly Published   Invalidly Published   Published Pre-1753   Superfluous Usage   Orthographic Variant   Fossil

Orchid Genera • 356

SCLEROCHILUS

An orthographic variant introduced in *Ceiba*, **5**(4): 214 (1956). The correct spelling is *Scelochilus*.

SCLEROPTERIS

Scheidweiler

Allg. Gartenzeitung **7**(51): 407 (1839).

Not *Scleropteris* H.N. Andrews (1942) Fossil, and not *Scleropteris* G. Saporta (1872) Fossil.

ETYMOLOGY: Greek for dry, hash or hard and a wing. Referring to the flat, dry stigma.

TYPE SPECIES: *Scleropteris flava* Scheidweiler

Now recognized as belonging to the genus *Cirrhaea*, *Scleropteris* was previously considered to include one epiphyte found in cool, low elevation, hill scrub and forests of southeastern Brazil (São Paulo). This plant has clustered, ovoid, dark green to yellow, ridged pseudobulbs, each with a solitary, dark green, obscurely pleated leaf. The hanging, numerous-flowered inflorescence has small, red-brown to green, fragrant flowers with widespreading sepals and petals. The shortly clawed, trilobed lip has a broad, shell-shaped, midlobe. The flowers have a slender, club-shaped column. The above type name is now a synonym of *Cirrhaea fuscolutea* Lindley.

SCOLIOCHILUS

Reichenbach *filius*

Xenia Orchid. **2**: 118 (1867).

ETYMOLOGY: Greek for curved, bent or crooked and lip. Alluding to the callus on the lip.

TYPE SPECIES: *Scoliochilus rhodiola*
(Reichenbach f.) Reichenbach f.
(*Appendicula rhodiola* Reichenbach f.)

Now recognized as belonging to the genus *Appendicula*, *Scoliochilus* was previously considered to include one epiphyte found in low to mid elevation, hill scrub, roadsides to montane ridges and oak-laurel forests of Malaysia and Indonesia (Java, Sumatra and Borneo). This small plant has stems with flattened internodes, each with small, overlapping, oblong, unevenly bilobed leaves that are arranged in two ranks and held at right angles to the stem. The few-flowered inflorescence has tiny, yellow flowers, arranged in two rows, hardly visible between large, pale purple bracts. The entire lip has a grooved, basal section with a deeply notched, twisted tip. The above type name is now considered a synonym of *Appendicula torta* Blume.

SCOPULARIA

Lindley

Edwards's Bot. Reg. **20**: sub 1701 (1835), and
Gen. Sp. Orchid. Pl. 303 (1835).

Name ICBN rejected vs. *Holothrix* Richard ex Lindley (1835) Orchidaceæ; not *Scopularia* Preuss (1851) Fungi, and not *Scopularia* Chauvin (1842) Chlorophyceæ-Siphonocladaceæ.

ETYMOLOGY: Latin for a little broom. Referring to the finely lacerated tip of the lip.

TYPE SPECIES: *Scopularia burchellii* Lindley

Although validly published this rejected name is now referred to *Holothrix*. *Scopularia* was considered to include three terrestrials found in Malawi, Tanzania and South Africa. These erect plants have unbranched stems, each with two roundish leaves that have silvery-white venation and hug the ground. The tall, few-flowered, purple inflorescence has small, crowded flowers with a wedge-shaped lip and a small, tightly curled spur. These dimorphic flowers are much smaller on the upper portion of the rachis.

SCORPAENA

Noroña

Verh. Batav. Genootsch. Kunsten, ed. 1 **5**(4): 3 (1790).

Name published without a description. Today this name is most often referred to *Dendrobium*.

SCRAPIUS

An orthographic variant introduced in *Enum. Pl. Transsilv.*, 649 (1885). The correct spelling is *Serapias*.

SCROTELLA

(Lindley) Carlsward & Whitten

Int. J. Pl. Sci. **164**(1): 47 (2003).

Name published without a description. Today this name is most often referred to *Harrisella*.

SCUTICARIA

Lindley

Edwards's Bot. Reg. **29**(Misc.): 14 (1843).

Epidendroideæ ‡ Cymbidieæ • Maxillariinæ

ETYMOLOGY: Latin for a lash or whip. Refers to the unusual shape of the long, rounded, hanging leaves in most of the species that resemble a whip or lash.

TYPE SPECIES: *Scuticaria steelei* (Hooker) Lindley
(*Maxillaria steelei* Hooker)

Eight sympodial epiphytes are found in cool, mid elevation, montane forests of Brazil, the Guianas, Venezuela and Colombia to Peru.

These interesting plants have short to long, knotty, ash-brown pseudobulbs, subtended by tubular, overlapping sheaths, each with a solitary, long, whip-like, strictly hanging, deep green leaf. The one- to two-flowered inflorescence has an exceedingly large, showy, long-lasting, fragrant, yellow flower sometimes covered with bold, chestnut brown blotches. The lateral sepals are joined to the column foot forming a chin-like protuberance. The yellow or white, concave, deeply trilobed lip is blotched or spotted magenta, has large, erect side lobes, and a small, notched midlobe. The flowers have an erect, wingless, purple spotted column.

SCYPHYGLOTTIS

An orthographic variant introduced in *Icon. Bot. Index*, **1**: 1012 (1855). The correct spelling is *Scaphyglottis*.

SEDIREA

Garay & H.R. Sweet

Orchids S. Ryukyu Islands 149 (1974).

Epidendroideæ ‡ Vandeæ • Aeridinæ

ETYMOLOGY: An anagram of *Aerides*, a genus of orchids. *Aerides* is spelled backward.

TYPE SPECIES: *Sedirea japonica*
(Linden & Reichenbach f.) Garay & H.R. Sweet
(*Aerides japonica* Linden & Reichenbach f.)

Two monopodial epiphytes are found in low to mid elevation, forest slopes and cliff faces of southern Japan (Ryukyu Islands), eastern China (Sichuan to Zhejiang) and Korea. These small plants have short leafy stems, subtended by leafy bases, each with several, distichous, leathery, slightly unequally bilobed leaves that are arranged alternately. The erect to hanging, few-flowered inflorescence, borne from leaf axils, has white or green, delightfully fragrant flowers. The lateral sepals are blotched with red-purple bars toward the base. The white, fleshy, obscurely trilobed lip is covered with magenta spots. The incurved side lobes are tiny; the spoon-shaped midlobe has a wavy margin, that has a strongly incurved, yellow, funnel-shaped spur. The flowers have a long, slender, forward-bent, wingless column that is footless or with a short foot.

SEEGERIELLA

Senghas

J. Orchideenfr. **4**(4): 190 (1997).

Epidendroideæ ⚘ Cymbidieæ • Oncidiinæ

ETYMOLOGY: Named in honor of Hans Gerhardt Seeger, (1939-) a German head horticulturist for the Heidelberg Botanic Gardens who brought the type species to flower. And Latin for diminutive.

TYPE SPECIES: *Seegeriella pinifolia* Senghas

One sympodial, twig epiphyte is found in wet, mid elevation, montane moss laden forests of Bolivia. This charming, dwarf plant has tiny pseudobulbs, each with several, stiff, needle-like leaves. The short, hanging, few-flowered inflorescence, born from the base of the pseudobulb, has translucent, pristine white to pale green flowers in a tight cluster at the tip. The long-clawed, green-white, trilobed lip has long, recurved side lobes, a tiny midlobe (forming an anchor shape), and is fused to the base of the slender, club-shaped column.

SEIDENFADENIA

Garay

Bot. Mus. Leafl. **23**(4): 203 (1972).

Epidendroideæ ⚘ Vandeæ • Aeridinæ

ETYMOLOGY: In honor of Gunnar Seidenfaden (1908-2001), a Danish diplomat, politician, explorer, naturalist, expert on tropical Asiatic orchids, author of numerous articles on Thai orchids and co-author of *The Orchids of Peninsular Malaysia and Singapore*.

TYPE SPECIES: *Seidenfadenia mitrata*
(Reichenbach f.) Garay
(*Aerides mitrata* Reichenbach f.)

One monopodial epiphyte is found in low to mid elevation, hill and montane forests of Myanmar and Thailand with heavy seasonal rainfall. This plant has short stems, each with several, long (20 inches/ 50 cm), hanging, channeled, pencil-like leaves arranged in two rows. The leaves turn red when exposed to bright sunlight. The erect, densely packed, numerous to few-flowered inflorescence, borne from the axils of the leaves, has attractive but small, pale pink, white to red-magenta flowers with a strong candy fragrance. The white to mauve, lobed lip has pink spots, minute horn-like side lobes, a flat, prominent midlobe with a yellow stripe. There is a strongly compressed, downward pointing, yellow spur. The flowers have a short, wingless column with a short foot.

SEIDENFADENIELLA

C.S. Kumar

Cat. Indian Orchids 43 (1994).

Epidendroideæ ⚘ Vandeæ • Aeridinæ

ETYMOLOGY: Honoring Gunnar Seidenfaden (1908-2001) a Danish arctic explorer, ambassador and orchidologist. And Latin for diminutive.

TYPE SPECIES: *Seidenfadeniella rosea*
(Wight) C.S. Kumar
(*Sarcanthus rosea* Wight)

Two monopodial epiphytes are found in mid elevation, montane forests of southern India (Kerala and Tamil Nadu) and Sri Lanka. These species are similar to *Cleisostomopsis* and *Schoenorchis* but differ on technical details. These often, hanging plants have short, stiff stems, each with several, leathery, pencil-like leaves. The multibranched, numerous-flowered, stiffly erect inflorescence has tiny, bright orange, pale pink, purple-violet to rosy flowers not fully opening. The trilobed lip has small, rounded side lobes, a bent-downward midlobe, and a broad, curled spur. The flowers have a short, wingless, footless column.

SEIDENFIA

Szlachetko

Fragm. Florist. Geobot. **3**(Suppl.): 122 (1995).

ETYMOLOGY: Honoring Gunnar Seidenfaden (1908-2001).

TYPE SPECIES: *Seidenfia rheedei* (Swartz) Szlachetko
(*Malaxis rheedei* Swartz) nom. illeg.
This type name is now considered a synonym of
Malaxis resupinata (G. Forster) Kuntze;
basionym replaced with
Epidendrum resupinatum G. Forster

Recognized as belonging to the genus *Malaxis*, *Seidenfia* was proposed to include nine terrestrials or uncommon epiphytes found in mid elevation, forest thickets and woodlands from southern India (Karnataka, Kerala and Tamil Nadu) to Sri Lanka with one species found in the Seychelles. These plants have spindle-shaped to ovate pseudobulbs, subtended by tubular, papery sheaths, each with several, veined, wavy margined leaves. The tall, densely packed, numerous-flowered inflorescence (increasing in length with age) has tiny, yellow, green-yellow, orange, red or purple flowers (color varies, depending on age and light intensity). The wedge-shaped, obscurely trilobed lip has side lobes with toothed margins and the fan-shaped midlobe has a scalloped margin. The flowers have a short, stout, slightly curved, footless column.

SEIDENFORCHIS

Margońska

Acta Soc. Bot. Poloniae **75**(4): 302 (2006).

ETYMOLOGY: Honoring Gunnar Seidenfaden (1908-2001).

TYPE SPECIES: *Seidenforchis propinqua*
(Ames) Margońska
(*Malaxis propinqua* Ames)

Recognized as belonging to the genus *Malaxis*, *Seidenforchis* was proposed to include three terrestrials found in moist, low to mid elevation, hill scrub to montane deciduous forests and cliff faces from central China (Yunnan), northwestern India, Bangladesh, Myanmar, northern Thailand and the Philippines (Luzon). These small plants have underground, compressed pseudobulbs, each with two slightly fleshy, ovate, flattened, ground hugging leaves. The tall, numerous-flowered inflorescence, that elongates with age, has tiny, pink-violet, red-purple, yellow, yellow-green to white flowers. The wedge-shaped, shortly clawed, trilobed lip has small, ear-like side lobes, the ovate midlobe has a notched tip. The flowers have a short, stout, erect column.

SELENIPEDIA

An orthographic variant introduced in *J. Linn. Soc.*, **42**: 161 (1914). The correct spelling is *Selenipedium*.

SELENIPEDILUM

An orthographic variant introduced in *Morph. Stud. Orchideenbl.*, 16 (1886). The correct spelling is *Selenipedium*.

SELENIPEDIUM

Reichenbach *filius*

Xenia Orchid. **1**: 3, *t. 2, f. 1, 1-5* (1854), and *Bonplandia* **2**(9): 116 (1854).

Cypripedioideæ ⚘

ETYMOLOGY: Greek for moon or crescent and sandal or shoe. Referring to the lunar-crescent shape of the curled over edge of the lip.

Greek Mythology: *Selene* was a daughter of the Titans Hyperion and Thea. She was the goddess of the moon, who bore Zeus two daughters, but she really loved Endymion with whom it is said that she had fifty daughters.

LECTOTYPE: *Selenipedium chica* Reichenbach f.

Five sympodial epiphytes are found in low to mid elevation, hill to montane forests and grassy slopes from Panama to Peru, Venezuela, northern Brazil, the Guianas and Trinidad. These tall, erect plants have often branching, rather woody, clustered or well-spaced, hairy stems,

Currently Accepted   Validly Published   Invalidly Published   Published Pre-1753   Superfluous Usage   Orthographic Variant   Fossil

O r c h i d   G e n e r a   • **358**

subtended by sheathing bracts below, each with numerous, broad to narrow, veined, pleated, sparsely hairy leaves. The terminal, erect or branching, few-flowered inflorescence has small, yellow to red flowers covered with spots. The dorsal sepal is erect to hooded over the lip; the lateral sepals are joined for two-thirds of their length, and the narrow petals have wavy margins. The pale yellow, trilobed lip has obscure but entire side lobes. The slipper-shaped midlobe is incurved on the front margin and is hairy within.

NOTE: In the past *Selenipedium*, closely related to the other slipper type orchid genera, *Paphiopedilum* and *Phragmipedium*, have usually all been treated in the one genus *Cypripedium*.

SEMIPHAIUS

An orthographic variant cited in *Handb. Orchid.-Namen*, 339 (2005). The correct spelling is *Semiphajus*.

SEMIPHAJUS

Gagnepain

Bull. Mus. Natl. Hist. Nat., sér. 2 **4**(5): 598 (1932).

ETYMOLOGY: Latin for half and *Phaius*, a genus of orchids. Alluding to the number of pollinia, which is half that of *Phaius*.

TYPE SPECIES: *None designated*

Now recognized as belonging to the genera *Cymbidium* and *Eulophia*, *Semiphajus* was previously considered to include two terrestrials usually found in humid, low elevation, rocky crevices, woodlands and bamboo thickets from India, Sri Lanka, Bangladesh, Myanmar to Vietnam and southeastern China (Yunnan to Jiangxi) to the southwestern Pacific Archipelago. These erect plants (based on poor herbarium sheets) lack pseudobulbs and the grass-like leaves wither before flowering. The elongate, thin to thick, few-flowered inflorescence has relatively attractive, rose to green-purple flowers.

SENELIPEDIUM

An orthographic variant introduced in *Hort. Franc.*, **8**: 68 (1858). The correct spelling is *Selenipedium*.

SENGHASIA

Szlachetko

J. Orchideenfr. **10**(4): 335 (2003).

ETYMOLOGY: Honoring Karlheinz Senghas (1928-2004).

TYPE SPECIES: *Senghasia wercklei* (Schlechter) Szlachetko (*Kefersteinia wercklei* Schlechter)

Recognized as belonging to the genus *Kefersteinia*, *Senghasia* was proposed to include twelve epiphytes found in mid elevation, montane cloud forests from southern Mexico to Panama. These plants have a fan-shaped arrangement of strap-shaped leaves that are basally overlapping. The short, solitary-flowered inflorescence, borne from the leaf axils or base of the leaf fan, has a small, white to yellow flower often spotted rose to maroon especially on the lip. It has narrow sepals and petals. The entire or obscurely trilobed lip has a sac-like base, a large, circular basal callus, and an entire to notched margin. The flowers have a short column.

SENGHASIELLA

Szlachetko

J. Orchideenfr. **8**(4): 365 (2001).

Orchidoideæ • Orchideæ • Orchidinæ

ETYMOLOGY: Named in honor of Karlheinz Senghas (1928-2004) a German botanist, researcher, curator and scientific director at Heidelberg University Botanical Gardens, orchidologist, and author of numerous articles and books on orchids. And Latin for diminutive.

TYPE SPECIES: *Senghasiella glaucifolia* (Bureau & Franchet) Szlachetko (*Habenaria glaucifolia* Bureau & Franchet)

Two uncommon, sympodial terrestrials are found in upper elevation, montane grasslands of southern China (Xizang to Shaanxi, Gansu and Sichuan). These erect plants have unbranched stems, each with two broad, ovate leaves tightly pressed against the ground forming a basal rosette. The few-flowered inflorescence has large, fragrant, unusually shaped, white or green flowers. The dorsal sepal and petals converge, forming a hood over the column, and the lateral sepals are widespread. The unusual trilobed lip has thread-like side lobes that are tightly curled at the tips; the long midlobe is spear-shaped, and the slender spur is swollen toward the tip.

SEPALAUCCUS

An orthographic variant introduced in *Repert. Spec. Nov. Regni Veg. Beih.*, **59**(2): 8 (1931). The correct spelling is *Sepalosaccus*.

SEPALOSACCUS

Schlechter

Repert. Spec. Nov. Regni Veg. Beih. **19**: 245 (1923).

ETYMOLOGY: Latin for sepal and sac or bag. From the lateral sepals that are sac-shaped and found at the base of the lip.

LECTOTYPE: *Sepalosaccus humilis* Schlechter This type name is now considered a synonym of *Maxillaria strumata* (Endres & Reichenbach f.) Ames & Correll; basionym *Ornithidium strumatum* Endres & Reichenbach f.

Now recognized as belonging to the genus *Maxillaria*, *Sepalosaccus* was previously considered to include two epiphytes found in humid, mid elevation, montane forests of Guatemala and Costa Rica to western Panama. These small plants, often forming dense colonies, have oblong pseudobulbs, each with a solitary, leathery leaf. The erect, short, solitary-flowered inflorescence, borne from the pseudobulb base, has a tiny, drooping, creamy flower with the broad, partially united lateral sepals joined to the column foot. The small, cup-shaped, entire lip tapers to a sharp or rounded point and has a short, swollen spur. The flowers have a short, wingless column with a dark purple anther cap.

SEPALOSIPHON

Schlechter

Repert. Spec. Nov. Regni Veg. Beih. **1**: 317 (1912).

ETYMOLOGY: Latin for sepal and siphon or tube. Referring to the elongated lateral sepals that are closely united with the fleshy claw of the lip.

TYPE SPECIES: *Sepalosiphon papuanum* Schlechter This type name is now considered a synonym of *Glomera sepalosiphon* Schuiteman & de Vogel

Now recognized as belonging to the genus *Glomera*, *Sepalosiphon* was previously considered to include one uncommon epiphyte found in misty, upper elevation, montane (Kani Range) forests of New Guinea on mossy covered tree limbs. This rather small, erect plant has branched stems completely sheathed by several, short fleshy, leathery, spreading leaves. The solitary-flowered inflorescence has a dark olive-green flower. The obscurely trilobed lip has two basal calli. The long, thread-like spur is formed by the fusion of the lateral sepals and is closely united with the fleshy, claw of the lip. The flowers have a short, wingless, footless column.

SEPTOTES

An orthographic variant cited in *Pl. Vasc. Gen. (Meisner)*, **1**: 279 (1837). The correct spelling is *Leptotes*.

SERAPHYTA

Fischer & C.A. Meyer

Bull. Sci. Acad. Imp. Sci. Saint-Pétersbourg **8**: 24 (1840).

ETYMOLOGY: Greek for rope and plant. Suggesting that the white rhizomes look like long strings or slender ropes.

TYPE SPECIES: *Seraphyta multiflora*
    Fischer & C.A. Meyer nom. illeg.
    Epidendrum diffusum Swartz

Now recognized as belonging to the genus *Epidendrum*, *Seraphyta* was previously considered to include two epiphytes found in low to mid elevation, woodlands from Cuba to Jamaica, southern Mexico to Colombia, Guyana and Venezuela. These highly variable plants have somewhat compressed, often red-suffused stems, each with several, rigid leaves suffused purple or purple-red. The multibranched, arching or erect, numerous-flowered inflorescence has small, red-brown to green-red, translucent flowers with narrow sepals and petals. The large, heart-shaped, entire lip tapers to a point at the tip. The flowers have an erect, footless column that is united with the lip at its tip. Both species are now considered as synonyms of *Epidendrum diffusum* Swartz.

SERAPIA

An orthographic variant introduced in *Mant. Pl. Altera*, 293 (1771). The correct spelling is *Serapias*.

SERAPIAS

Pliny

Hist. Nat. **XXVI**: 95 (AD 56).

Pre-1753, therefore not validly published in fulfillment of nomenclatural rules; this name is most often referred to *Orchis*.

SERAPIAS

Brunfels

Herb. (Brunfels) 107 (1532).

Pre-1753, therefore not validly published in fulfillment of nomenclatural rules; this name is most often referred to *Serapias*.

SERAPIAS

Linnaeus

Sp. Pl. (Linnaeus), ed. 1 **2**: 949, 950 (1753), and *Gen. Pl.*, ed 5 406 (1754).

Name and type ICBN conserved.

Orchidoideæ • Orchideæ • Orchidinæ

ETYMOLOGY: Egyptian Mythology. *Serapia* was an Egyptian god known for his lack of sexual restraint. His cult rose to its greatest significance in the city of Alexandria during the reign of Ptolemy I (323-285 BC); this cult later died out after the destruction of the Alexandrian temple in AD 391.

Greek Mythology: *Serapis* was the goddess of fertility, medicine and ruler of the dead. Referring to the supposed aphrodisiac qualities of the roots.

LECTOTYPE: *Serapias lingua* Linnaeus

Fourteen sympodial terrestrials are found in low to mid elevation, cold to cool, sand dunes, wet marshes, damp meadows and open fields from Britain to Italy, Sardinia, Corsica to Crete, Greece, Morocco to Tunisia, the Canary Islands and extending into Turkey, Syria, Iraq, Armenia and the Republic of Georgia. These small plants have erect, short to long, slender to stout, smooth, unbranched stems, each with narrow, erect or sometimes folded and curved leaves that have spotted or unspotted sheathing bases. The few-flowered inflorescence has large, leafy, gray floral bracts often exceeding the gray-purple flowers. The narrow sepals and petals converge, forming a sharply pointed to tapering hood, heavily veined in dark purple. The purple suffused, prominent, trilobed lip has a one to two lobed, densely hairy callus located between the erect side lobes, and has a hanging, tongue-shaped midlobe. The flowers have a long, erect, mealy column.

SERAPIAS

Persoon

Syn. Pl. (Persoon) **2**: 512 (1807).

Not *Serapias* Linnaeus (1753) Orchidaceæ.

ETYMOLOGY: Egyptian Mythology. *Serapia* was an Egyptian god known for his lack of sexual restraint. His cult rose to its greatest significance in the city of Alexandria during the reign of Ptolemy I (323-285 BC). Referring to the supposed aphrodisiac qualities of the roots.

TYPE SPECIES: *None designated*

A superfluous name proposed as a substitute for *Epipactis*.

SERAPIASTRUM

Kuntze

Revis. Gen. Pl. **3**(2): 141 (1898).

Name published without a description. Today this name is most often referred to *Serapias*.

SERAPIASTRUM

Kuntze ex **A.A. Eaton**

Proc. Biol. Soc. Wash. **21**: 67 (1908).

ETYMOLOGY: *Serapias*, a genus of orchids and Latin for a kind of. Indicating a relationship with *Serapias*.

TYPE SPECIES: *None designated*

Now recognized as belonging to the genus *Serapias*, *Serapiastrum* was previously considered to include five terrestrials found in low to mid elevation, meadows, grasslands and marshes from France to Bulgaria and Turkey. These small, erect plants have scale-like basal leaves with several, narrow leaves clasping the unbranched stem upward. The few-flowered inflorescence has gray-lilac flowers with the sepals and petals converge, forming a hood over the small column. The long, brown-red to black-purple, roundish to violin-shaped, trilobed lip has sparse, variously colored hairs in the center.

SERAPIUS

An orthographic variant introduced in *Enum. Pl. Transsilv.*, 649 (1885). The correct spelling is *Serapias*.

SERASTYLIS

An orthographic variant introduced in *Repert. Spec. Nov. Regni Veg. Beih.*, **7**: 277 (1920). The correct spelling is *Serrastylis*.

SERPENTICAULIS

M.A. Clements & D.L. Jones

Orchadian **13**(11): 500 (2002).

ETYMOLOGY: Latin for small snake or to creep and stem. Refers to the long, snake-like rhizome.

TYPE SPECIES: *Serpenticaulis bowkettiae*
    (F.M. Bailey) M.A. Clements & D.L. Jones
    (*Bulbophyllum bowkettiae* F.M. Bailey)

Recognized as belonging to the genus *Bulbophyllum*, *Serpenticaulis* was proposed to include six epiphytes found in low elevation, woodlands of northern Australia (Queensland), often forming dense clumps. These small plants have creeping rhizomes with ovate, oblong, compressed, bluntly ribbed pseudobulbs (spaced along the rhizome), each with a solitary, small, dark green leaf. The short, solitary-flowered inflorescence has a white to creamy flower heavily striped dark red-purple. The lateral sepals are united at the base forming a short spur, and the small, ear-like petals each have one, central dark colored stripe. The small, thick, oblong, entire lip has

Currently Accepted   Validly Published   Invalidly Published   Published Pre-1753   Superfluous Usage   Orthographic Variant   Fossil

Orchid Genera • **360**

red or purple-red blotches, a narrow groove on the upper surface, and a pale colored margin.

SERRAPYLIS

An orthographic variant introduced in *Nat. Pflanzenfam. Nachtr.*, **2**(4): 462 (1897). The correct spelling is *Serrastylis*.

SERRASTYLIS

Rolfe

Bull. Misc. Inform. Kew **1894**: 158 (1894), and *Gard. Chron.* **16**: 726, *f*. 91 (1894).

ETYMOLOGY: Latin for saw and Greek for column or style. Descriptive of the fringed-toothed clinandrium.

TYPE SPECIES: *Serrastylis modesta* Rolfe

Now recognized as belonging to the genus *Macradenia*, *Serrastylis* was previously considered to include one epiphyte found in wet, low to mid elevation, hill scrub and montane forests from Mexico to Ecuador and Venezuela. This plant has clustered, moderately compressed, pear-shaped pseudobulbs, each with a solitary, oblong to narrow, slightly leathery leaf. The hanging, numerous-flowered inflorescence has dark red-maroon, faintly fragrant flowers whose segments have a narrow but sharply marked yellow border. The white, trilobed lip has maroon marks on a narrow, central keel, short side lobes, and the narrow midlobe is sharply twisted to one side. The above type name is now considered a synonym of *Macradenia brassavolae* Reichenbach f.

SERTIFERA

Lindley & Reichenbach *filius*

Linnaea **41**: 63 (1877).

Epidendroideæ ◊ **Sobralieæ**

ETYMOLOGY: Latin for wreath or garland and to bear or carry. Perhaps alluding to the several inflorescences that adorn the plant like a floral wreath.

TYPE SPECIES: *None designated*

Eight sympodial terrestrials are found in mid to upper elevation, montane or scrub forests and along embankments of Venezuela, Colombia and Ecuador. These erect plants have slender, cane-like stems, each with thinly textured, usually dark green leaves that have maroon veins on their undersides. The short, few-flowered inflorescence has small to tiny, bright rose to purple, fleshy flowers that are deeply concave. The lateral sepals are united at the base forming a projection. The broad, folded, entire lip cannot spread widely because of its fusion to the sides of the flower base and has a high,

wall-like callus. The flowers have a long, slender, winged, footless column.

NOTE: These species differ from the genus *Elleanthus* especially by their lateral inflorescences.

SESSILIBULBUM

Brieger

Orchideen (Schlechter), ed. 3 **8**(29-32): 486 (1976).

ETYMOLOGY: Latin for stalkless and a bulb. Referring to the pseudobulbs that often sit atop one another.

TYPE SPECIES: *None designated*

Not validly published, this name is referred to *Scaphyglottis*. *Sessilibulbum* was considered to include four epiphytes ranging from southern Mexico to Colombia and Brazil.

SESTOCHILOS

Breda

Gen. Sp. Orchid. Asclep., fasc. I *t*. 3 (1828).

ETYMOLOGY: Greek for to sift or to shake with a quivering motion and lip. Refers to the long-clawed lip that easily moves on its slender, narrow claw.

TYPE SPECIES: *Sestochilos uniflorum* Breda

Now recognized as belonging to a section of the genus *Bulbophyllum*, *Sestochilos* was previously considered to include one epiphyte found in low to mid elevation, hill thickets and montane forests of northeastern India, (Arunachal Pradesh to Assam) Myanmar, Thailand, Malaysia and Indonesia to the Philippines. This creeping plant has egg-shaped, yellow-green pseudobulbs, each with a solitary, leathery leaf. The rhizomes and pseudobulbs are encased in long, stiff bristles. The solitary-flowered inflorescence, borne from the base of the pseudobulb, has a large, predominately yellow, foul smelling flower variously spotted or streaked red, maroon or purple, and the petals are much smaller than the sepals. The strongly curved, purple spotted, entire lip has a small, orange splash at the base and a recurved tip. The above type name is now considered a synonym of *Bulbophyllum lobbii* Lindley.

SESTOCHILUS

Hooker ex **Lindley**

Edwards's Bot. Reg. **33**: sub 29 (1847).

Name published without a description. Today this name is most often referred to *Bulbophyllum*.

SESTOCHILUS

An orthographic variant introduced in *Fl. Javæ*, **1**: Praef. vii (1828). The correct spelling is *Sestochilos*.

SHOMBURGKIA

An orthographic variant introduced in *Orchid. Mexico Guatemala*, 16 (1837). The correct spelling is *Schomburgkia*.

SIAGNANTHUS

An orthographic variant introduced in *Syn. Pl. (D. Dietrich)*, **5**: 8, 82 (1852). The correct spelling is *Siagonanthus*.

SIAGONANTHUS

Poeppig & Endlicher

Nov. Gen. Sp. Pl. (Poeppig & Endlicher) **1**(7-10): 40, *t*. 69 (1836).

ETYMOLOGY: Greek for a jawbone and flower. Refers to the resemblance of the gaping flower when viewed from the side as if having an open jaw.

TYPE SPECIES: *Siagonanthus multicaulis* Poeppig & Endlicher

Now recognized as belonging to the genus *Maxillaria*, *Siagonanthus* was previously considered to include one epiphyte found in low to mid elevation, hill and montane forests from Colombia to Peru and Venezuela. This plant has smooth, ovoid pseudobulbs, subtended by thin, dry sheaths, each with an oblong, curved leaf. The short, solitary-flowered inflorescence has a pale creamy-brown flower moderately to strongly suffused brown-maroon or pink. It has similar sepals and the small, erect petals curve over the small column. The yellow-brown, entire lip, suffused with various amounts of maroon, has a stubble of minute hairs along the margin.

SIAPHYGLOTTIS

An orthographic variant cited in *Deut. Bot. Herb.-Buch*, 53 (1841). The correct spelling is *Scaphyglottis*.

SIBERIA

An orthographic variant introduced in *Orchideen (Schlechter)*, ed. 1, 68 (1915). The correct spelling is *Sieberia*.

SIEBERA

Not *Siebera* Reichenbach (1828) Apiaceæ, not *Siebera* Hoppe (1819) Caryophyllaceæ, and not *Siebera* J. Gay (1827) Asteraceæ.

An orthographic variant cited in *Lex. Gen. Phan.*, 519 (1904). The correct spelling is *Sieberia*.

SIEBERIA

Sprengel

Anleit. Kenntn. Gew., ed. 2   **2**(1): 282 (1817).
Not *Siebera* J. Gay (1827) Asteraceæ.

ETYMOLOGY: Dedicated to Franz Wilhelm Sieber (1789-1844), a Czech (Bohemian) who traveled and collected plants in many parts of the world; he published on the floras of Turkey, Crete and Egypt and later died in a psychiatric asylum.

TYPE SPECIES: *None designated*

Now recognized as belonging to the genera *Platanthera, Gymnadenia, Dactylorhiza* and *Pseudorchis, Sieberia* was previously considered to include four, widely varied terrestrials found in low to upper elevation, open woodlands, scrub and nutrient-poor meadows throughout Europe (Norway to Spain and Britain to far eastern Russia), Greenland, Turkey, Morocco to Tunisia and Canada. These erect plants have unbranched stems, each with several, basal leaves. The tall, erect, few-flowered inflorescence has sweetly fragrant, white, hooded flowers with a heart-shaped dorsal sepal and widespreading lateral sepals. The long, tongue-shaped, entire lip has a long, upcurved, green spur.

SIEDENFIA

An orthographic variant introduced in *Acta Soc. Bot. Poloniae*, **75**(3): 229 (2006). The correct spelling is *Seidenfia*.

SIEDENFORCHIS

An orthographic variant introduced in *Acta Soc. Bot. Poloniae*, **75**(3): 229 (2006). The correct spelling is *Seidenforchis*.

SIEDERELLA

Szlachetko, Mytnik, Górniak & Romowicz

Biodivers. Res. Conservation   **1-2**: 4 (2006).

ETYMOLOGY: Dedication to Anton Sieder (1962-), an Austrian curator of the living orchid collection at the Botanical Garden at the University of Vienna. And Latin for diminutive.

TYPE SPECIES: *Siederella aurea*
     (Lindley) Szlachetko, Mytnik, Górniak & Romowicz
       (*Oncidium aureum* Lindley)

Recognized as belonging to the genus *Cyrtochilum, Siederella* was proposed to include one terrestrial or occasional epiphyte found in mid to upper elevation, montane slopes, brush and grasslands from Ecuador to Peru. These plants have oval pseudobulbs, subtended by distichous, overlapping, leaf-like bracts, each with narrow, central veined leaves. The erect, few-flowered inflorescence, borne from

mature pseudobulbs that emerge through the axil of the leaf sheath, has showy, red-brown to orange-yellow flowers with spreading sepals and slightly smaller petals. The bright yellow, broad, clawed, entire lip has a wavy margin with a small notched tip. The flowers have a short, erect column.

SIEVEKINGIA

Lindley ex **Reichenbach** *filius*

Beitr. Syst. Pflanzenk.   3 (1871).

Epidendroideæ Cymbidieæ • Stanhopeinæ

ETYMOLOGY: Commemorating Friedrich Sieveking (1798-1872), a German physician, Bürgermeister (mayor) of Hamburg and a friend of Reichenbach.

TYPE SPECIES: *Sievekingia suavis* Reichenbach f.

Sixteen dwarf, sympodial epiphytes or lithophytes are extremely scarce in their native habitats of moist, low elevation, hill forests rom Costa Rica to Bolivia. These plants have clustered, ovoid or semi-cylindrical, deeply grooved, one-noded pseudobulbs, subtended by papery bracts, each with a solitary, pleated, heavily veined leaf. The hanging, few-flowered inflorescence, borne from the base of a mature pseudobulb, has attractive, thinly textured, yellow to orange-yellow flowers. The smaller petals are entire to deeply fringed and the concave dorsal sepal is sharply pointed. The white or yellow, diamond-shaped, entire or trilobed lip, united to the column base, has either an entire or a torn-fringed margin and has a small, hairy callus of upturned teeth located near the base. The flowers have a curved, club-shaped or broadly winged column.

SIEVKINGIA

An orthographic variant introduced in *Sander's Orch. Guide*, ed. 4, 407 (1927). The correct spelling is *Sievekingia*.

SIGILLABENIS

Thouars

Hist. Orchid.   Table 1, sub 1e (1822).

Name published without a description. Today this name is most often referred to *Habenaria*.

SIGILLAHENIS

An orthographic variant introduced in *Hist. Orchid.*, t. 20 (1822). The correct spelling is *Sigillabenis*.

SIGILLUM

Caesalpinus

Pl. Libri XVI   431 (1583).

Pre-1753, therefore not validly published in fulfillment of nomenclatural rules; this name is most often referred to *Serapias*.

SIGMATOCHILUS

Rolfe

J. Linn. Soc., Bot.   **42**(285): 155 (1914).

ETYMOLOGY: Greek for S-shaped and a lip. Referring to the deep sac-like lip.

TYPE SPECIES: *Sigmatochilus kinabaluensis* Rolfe

Now recognized as belonging to the genus *Chelonistele, Sigmatochilus* was previously considered to include one epiphyte found in upper elevation, thick, moss laden, montane forests (Mt. Kinabalu) of southern Malaysia (northern Sabah). This plant has rather slender, oblong pseudobulbs, subtended by dried sheaths, each with a solitary, thick leaf. The erect, few-flowered inflorescence has white to creamy flowers not opening widely and all are turned to one side; the concave dorsal sepal is nerved. The entire lip has a boat-shaped hypochile that is somewhat compressed, without side lobes, and the folded upward epichile is somewhat swollen. The flowers have a small, club-shaped column.

SIGMATOGYNE

Pfitzer

Pflanzenr. (Engler)   **IV.50**(II.B.7): 133 (1907).

ETYMOLOGY: Greek for S-shaped and woman or female. An allusion to the slender S-shaped column.

TYPE SPECIES: *Sigmatogyne tricallosa* (Rolfe) Pfitzer
     (*Panisea tricallosa* Rolfe)

Now recognized as belonging to the genus *Panisea, Sigmatogyne* was previously considered to include two epiphytes found in mid elevation, montane forests from northern India (Sikkim to Assam), Nepal, Bhutan, southern China (Yunnan and Hainan) and Laos to Vietnam. These small plants have ovoid pseudobulbs, subtended by leaf-like sheaths, each with a solitary, fleshy leaf. The solitary to few-flowered inflorescence has tiny, pale brown-white, pale yellow to pale green-yellow flowers not opening fully. The oblong, obscurely trilobed lip has three, dull brown to orange calli with thick veins and a prominent S-shaped claw. The flowers have a long, winged column.

Currently Accepted   Validly Published   Invalidly Published   Published Pre-1753   Superfluous Usage   Orthographic Variant   Fossil

O r c h i d   G e n e r a   •   **362**

SIGMATOSTALIX

Reichenbach *filius*

Bot. Zeitung (Berlin)   **10**: 769 (1852).

Epidendroideæ ◊ **Cymbidieæ** ● **Oncidiinæ**

ETYMOLOGY: Greek for stigma, S-shaped and a stake. An allusion to the elongate, slender column that is often so bow-shaped it assumes the shape of an S.

TYPE SPECIES: *Sigmatostalix graminea*
(Poeppig & Endlicher) Reichenbach f.
(*Specklinia graminea* Poeppig & Endlicher)

Fifty-six unusual, sympodial epiphytes are found in wet, low to upper elevation, hill scrub and montane forests from southern Mexico to Bolivia, the Guianas, Venezuela and northern Brazil. These small plants have clustered, two-edged pseudobulbs, subtended by distichous sheaths, each with one to two, narrow, bilobed leaves. The few-flowered inflorescence, which usually reflowers, is longer than the leaves and is borne from the base of the pseudobulb. The small, thinly textured, green-yellow to pale yellow flowers are barred purple or red-brown, and are often concealed by several bracts. The narrow, long-clawed, entire or trilobed lip has a front margin filled with short hairs, is bilobed at the tip, and has a huge, oil-bearing callus. The flowers have an erect, slender column that abruptly curves inward and then expands near the tip.

SIGMATOSTALYX

An orthographic variant introduced in *Hamburger Garten- Blumenzeitung*, **9**: 122 (1853). The correct spelling is *Sigmatostalix*.

SILIQUA

Sloane

Cat. Pl. Jamaica   70 (1696).

Pre-1753, therefore not validly published in fulfillment of nomenclatural rules; this name is most often referred to *Vanilla*.

SILVALISIMIS

An orthographic variant introduced in *Hist. Orchid.*, Table 1, sub 2l (1822). The correct spelling is *Sylvalismis*.

SILVORCHIS

J.J. Smith

Bull. Dépt. Agric. Indes Néerl.   **13**: 2 (1907), and
Repert. Spec. Nov. Regni Veg.   **5**: 289 (1908).

Epidendroideæ ◊ **Nervilieæ**

ETYMOLOGY: Latin for forest or woodland and Greek for orchid. Descriptive of its preferred humus habitat in thick forests.

TYPE SPECIES: *Silvorchis colorata* J.J. Smith

One saprophyte is found in mid elevation, montane forests of Indonesia (western Java) and Vietnam, found only a few occasions. This leafless, erect plant has stout, unbranched stems, subtended by fairly large, overlapping bracts. The erect, solitary to few-flowered inflorescence, subtended by smooth, oblong, white bracts, has large, white flowers covered with pale purple spots and streaks. The dorsal sepal is erect; the widespread lateral sepals have irregular, purple margins and the tiny petals curve over the small, footless column. The flat, purple spotted, trilobed lip has a yellow, basal spot, and large, oblong side lobes that curve downward and have rounded tips. The short, triangular midlobe tapers to a sharp point and curls upward. The flowers have a compressed column with a large stigma.

SIMPLIGLOTTIS

Szlachetko

Polish Bot. J.   **46**(1): 13 (2001).

ETYMOLOGY: Latin for simple and Greek for tongue. In reference to the simple callus on the lip surface.

TYPE SPECIES: *Simpliglottis valida*
(D.L. Jones) Szlachetko
(*Chiloglottis valida* D.L. Jones)

Recognized as belonging to the genus *Chiloglottis*, *Simpliglottis* was proposed to include six terrestrials found in low to mid elevation, open pine, birch and montane forests of southeastern Australia, Tasmania and New Zealand. These erect, robust plants have unbranched stems, each with several, broad, heavily veined, dark green leaves. The erect, solitary-flowered inflorescence has a green or green-purple flower which darkens to purple-brown as it ages. The dorsal sepal is broad, has narrow lateral sepals tapering downward. The petals are fan-shaped. The heart-shaped, entire lip has numerous, black tipped calli sometimes on short stalks, and one, tall, dark columnar gland in the center at the base. These species are now considered as a subgenus of *Chiloglottis*.

SINGULARYBAS

Molloy, D.L. Jones & M.A. Clements

Orchadian   **13**(10): 449 (2002).

ETYMOLOGY: Latin for solitary, different and the last portion of *Corybas*, a genus of orchids.

TYPE SPECIES: *Singularybas oblongus*
(Hooker f.) Molloy, D.L. Jones & M.A. Clements
(*Nematoceras oblongum* Hooker f.)

Recognized as belonging to the genus *Corybas*, *Singularybas* was proposed to include three terrestrials found in low elevation, clay banks and sandstone or limestone cliffs from New Zealand, Stewart, Auckland and Chatham Islands. These tiny, erect plants have short stems, subtended by a solitary, narrow, wavy bract, each with a solitary, thinly textured, wavy to smooth edged leaf, varying from green to red veined. The solitary-flowered inflorescence has a pale to dark crimson, tubular-shaped, entire lip with hairy margins. The dorsal sepal forms a hood over the lip with dissimilar, long, thread-like sepals and petals.

SINORCHIS

S.C. Chen

Acta Phytotax. Sin.   **16**(4): 82 (1978).

ETYMOLOGY: Greek for China (a geographical reference to the People's Republic of China that occupies a vast area in eastern Asia) and orchid.

TYPE SPECIES: *Sinorchis simplex*
(T. Tang & F.T. Wang) S.C. Chen
(*Aphyllorchis simplex* T. Tang & F.T. Wang)

Now recognized as belonging to the genus *Aphyllorchis*, *Sinorchis* was previously considered to include one saprophyte found in low elevation, rocky coastal slopes of Meizhou Shi, southeastern China (northeastern Guangdong). This tall, erect plant has slender, unbranched, leafless stems, subtended by several, sheaths on the lower section. The few-flowered inflorescence, subtended by hanging, floral bracts, has primitively structured, creamy colored flowers not opening widely. The thinly textured sepals and petals are similar to each other. There is no modified lip, but the slightly swollen column has four, silver colored staminodes on each side of the two clinandria and has a narrow appendage on the front, near the tip.

SIPARIS

An orthographic variant introduced in *J. Straits Branch Roy. Asiat. Soc.*, **49**: 27 (1907). The correct spelling is *Liparis*.

SIRHOOKERA

Kuntze

Revis. Gen. Pl.   **2**: 681 (1891).

Epidendroideæ ❦ Agrostophyllinæ • Currently unplaced

ETYMOLOGY: Commemorating Joseph Dalton Hooker (1871-1911), a British explorer, director of the Royal Botanic Gardens at Kew, one of the most important botanists of the 19th century and author of *Flora of British India, Orchideæ*. J.D. Hooker *filius*, was the son of W.J. Hooker (1785-1865).

TYPE SPECIES: *Sirhookera lanceolata* (Wight) Kuntze
(*Josephia lanceolata* Wight)

Two sympodial epiphytes are found in wet, low to mid elevation, hill thickets and montane forests of southern India (Kerala, Karnataka and Tamil Nadu) and Sri Lanka. These small, tufted plants have short stems, subtended by papery sheaths, each with one to two, leathery leaves that are purple-spotted or blotched on the underside. The erect, multibranched, few-flowered inflorescence has minute, off-white to yellow flowers often suffused purple or pink and borne at the tip of the rachis. This persistent rachis blooms repeatedly, becoming more and more branched with each flowering season. The concave to blunt, trilobed lip, jointed to the column base, has incurving side lobes and the smaller midlobe has a basal callus uniting the side lobes. The flowers have a small, footless, bright magenta column.

SIRINDHORNIA

H.A. Pedersen & Suksathan

Nordic J. Bot.   **22**(4): 393 (2002)[2003].

Orchidoideæ ❦ Orchideæ • Orchidinæ

ETYMOLOGY: Named in honor of Maha Chakri Sirindhorn (1955-), a Thai princess, for her work in plant conservation; she also holds doctorates in educational development and administration.

TYPE SPECIES: *Sirindhornia monophylla*
(Collett & Hemsley) H.A. Pedersen & Suksathan
(*Habenaria monophylla* Collett & Hemsley)

Three sympodial terrestrials are found in low to mid elevation, hill to montane grasslands, limestone slopes and rocky crevices of northern Thailand (Chiang Mai and Tak), north-eastern Myanmar (Shan) and southwestern China (Yunnan). These erect, stout plants have short unbranched, usually slightly hairy stems, each with several, narrow, basal leaves sometimes spotted purple on the upper surface and mottled purple-green on the underside. The erect, numerous to few-flowered inflorescence has pink to purple-red flowers. The dorsal sepal is veined; the often spotted, concave lateral sepals and petals converge, forming a hood over the small, club-shaped column. The

variable sized, trilobed lip has deeper colored spots on the midlobe but none on the smaller side lobes which have purple spots or tufts. The lip has a small, incurved or straight spur.

SKEPTROSTACHYS

Garay

Bot. Mus. Leafl.   **28**(4): 358 (1980)[1982].

Orchidoideæ ❦ Cranichideæ • Spiranthinæ

ETYMOLOGY: Greek for baton or royal staff and a spike. An allusion of the appearance of the inflorescence in most of the species.

TYPE SPECIES: *Skeptrostachys rupestris* (Lindley) Garay
(*Spiranthes rupestris* Lindley)

Twelve sympodial terrestrials are found in low to mid elevation, open meadows, rocky fields, sandy soils and areas subject to periodic fires in Paraguay, Uruguay and northern Argentina (Corrientes) with the center of distribution in eastern Brazil. These tall plants have erect, unbranched stems, each with either a basal rosette of leaves withering by flowering time, or has long, narrow to elliptical leaves distributed along the rachis. The densely hairy (above), numerous-flowered, spirally arranged inflorescence (nearly subtended by sheaths) has small, hairy, tubular, showy, white, pale yellow, green-yellow, brown-orange, brick-red to bright red, strongly nerved flowers. They are hairy on their outer surfaces and have slender, long-tapering petals. The somewhat diamond-shaped, entire to obscurely trilobed lip has roundish, concave side lobes; an oblong midlobe that tapers to a point and has a wavy margin. The flowers have a short, small column with a backward-pointing foot.

SMALLIA

Nieuwland

Amer. Midl. Naturalist   **3**(5-6): 158 (1913).

ETYMOLOGY: Dedicated to James Kunkel Small (1869-1938), an American botanist, curator at Columbia College and the New York Botanical Garden, and author of many books and articles on the flora of southeastern United States.

TYPE SPECIES: *Smallia ecristata* (Small) Nieuwland
(*Triorchos ecristatus* Small)

A superfluous name proposed as a substitute for *Pteroglossaspis*, which is now considered a synonym of *Eulophia*.

SMITHANTHE

Szlachetko & Margońska

Orchidee (Hamburg)   **55**(2): 172 (2004).

ETYMOLOGY: Dedicated to Johannes Jacobus Smith (1867-1947), a Belgian-born botanist and director of the Buitenzorg (now called Bogor) Botanic Gardens, who wrote about the orchids of Indonesia and New Guinea. And Greek for flower.

TYPE SPECIES: *Smithanthe rhodocheila*
(Hance) Szlachetko & Margońska
(*Habenaria rhodocheila* Hance)

Recognized as belonging to the genus *Habenaria*, *Smithanthe* was proposed to include four terrestrials found in low to mid elevation, forest or valley slopes and shady, rocky woodlands of southeastern China (Guangxi, Hainan to Fujian, Laos to Vietnam, and Malaysia to the Philippines). These tall, erect plants have unbranched stems, each with several, green or red suffused, basal leaves that have a network of darker veins. The few-flowered inflorescence has showy, green-brown flowers. The small, green dorsal sepal and petals converge, forming a hood over the short column. The narrow, widespreading lateral sepals are reflexed or twisted. The bright orange, yellow or scarlet, deeply trilobed lip has roundish side lobes with the midlobe bilobed at the tip and a long, slender spur.

SMITHORCHIS

T. Tang & F.T. Wang

Bull. Fan Mem. Inst. Biol. Bot.   **7**: 139 (1936).

Orchidoideæ ❦ Orchideæ • Orchidinæ

ETYMOLOGY: Honoring William Wright Smith (1875-1956), a Scottish systematic botanist, who as a keeper at the Royal Botanic Gardens in Edinburgh and Calcutta gathered numerous important studies on the flora of China and the Himalayas. And Greek for orchid.

TYPE SPECIES: *Smithorchis calceoliformis*
(W.W. Smith) T. Tang & F.T. Wang
(*Herminium calceoliforme* W.W. Smith)

One uncommon, sympodial terrestrial is found in upper elevation, stony pastures and grasslands of southern China (northwestern Yunnan). This small, erect, plant has slender, unbranched stems, each with two small, narrow leaves located on the lower stem. The terminal, whip-like, few-flowered inflorescence has small, fragrant, orange-red flowers with thinly textured, similar-shaped sepals and tiny, wide-spreading, yellow petals. The uppermost, deeply cup-shaped, entire lip forms a hood or slipper-shaped structure over the small, erect column and has a broad, short spur.

Currently Accepted   Validly Published   Invalidly Published   Published Pre-1753   Superfluous Usage   Orthographic Variant   Fossil

Orchid Genera • **364**

SMITHSONIA

C.J. Saldanha

J. Bombay Nat. Hist. Soc. **71**(1): 73 (1974).

Epidendroideæ 🍃 Vandeæ • Aeridinæ

ETYMOLOGY: Honoring James Smithson (1765-1825), a British scientist who bequeathed his fortune to the U.S. for the increase and diffusion of knowledge among men. This philanthropic gift led to the establishment of the Smithsonian Institution in Washington, D.C.

TYPE SPECIES: *Smithsonia straminea* C.J. Saldanha

Three monopodial epiphytes are found in mid elevation, montane forests of southern India (Karnataka, Kerala and Tamil Nadu). These tiny plants have stems with numerous roots and a stiff, numerous to few-flowered inflorescence. The yellow to creamy flowers have a red blotch in the center of the similar sepals and petals. The immobile, white, trilobed lip has small, erect side lobes, a curved, triangular midlobe, and a short, usually bent forward, white to pink pointed spur. The flowers have a short, footless column.

SMITINANDIA

Holttum

Gard. Bull. Singapore **25**: 105 (1969).

Epidendroideæ 🍃 Vandeæ • Aeridinæ

ETYMOLOGY: Honoring Tem Smitinand (1920-1995), a Thai orchid botanist, taxonomist, director of the Royal Thailand Department of Forestry and a co-author of *Orchids of Thailand*.

TYPE SPECIES: *Smitinandia micrantha*
(Lindley) Holttum
(*Saccolabium micranthum* Lindley)

Three monopodial epiphytes are found in low to mid elevation, forests and along river banks from southern China (western Yunnan), northern India (Kashmir to Assam), Nepal, Myanmar to Vietnam and Laos to Indonesia (Sulawesi and Borneo). These plants have slender, short to long, branching stems, each with several, distichous, flat, leathery or slightly fleshy, unequally bilobed leaves. The erect to hanging, stout, numerous-flowered inflorescence has spirally arranged, small, fleshy, sparkling white to pale pink flowers that are sometimes purple spotted. The unusual rose-purple, sac-like, trilobed lip has a spur without any ornamentation, but the mouth is almost closed by a fleshy, wall-like callus at the base of the lip. The trilobed lip has small, roundish side lobes, and the strap-shaped midlobe has a basal ridge. The flowers have a short, erect, wingless, footless column.

SOBENNIKOFFIA

Schlechter

Repert. Spec. Nov. Regni Veg. Beih. **33**: 361 (1925).

Epidendroideæ 🍃 Vandeæ • Angraecinæ

ETYMOLOGY: In honor of Alexandra Schlechter née Sobennikoff (1886-x), the Russian-born wife of German botanist and orchidologist Rudolf Schlechter (1872-1925).

LECTOTYPE: *Sobennikoffia robusta*
(Schlechter) Schlechter
(*Oeonia robusta* Schlechter)

Four uncommon, monopodial terrestrials, lithophytes or sometimes epiphytes are found in seasonally dry, mid elevation, shady forests of northern Madagascar. These erect, robust plants have short to long stems, each with several, distichous, leathery to fleshy, unequally bilobed leaves. The spreading to erect, few-flowered inflorescence has showy, often large, white to green-white flowers turning yellow-orange as they age. The large, concave, trilobed lip has a dark green blotch in the center, a narrow midlobe with a longitudinal callus, and a green spur that tapers from a broad mouth which is upturned in the front half. The flowers have a short, slightly bent, footless column.

SOBRALIA

Ruiz & Pavón

Fl. Peruv. Prodr. 120, *t.* 26 (1794).

Epidendroideæ 🍃 Sobralieæ

ETYMOLOGY: In honor of Francisco Martínez Sobral (x-1799), a Spanish physician for King Charles IV of Spain, promoter of botany, and a contemporary and friend of Ruiz and Pavón.

LECTOTYPE: *Sobralia dichotoma* Ruiz & Pavón

A complex, often misunderstood, genus of over one hundred sympodial terrestrials, sometimes epiphytes or lithophytes are widespread in low to upper elevation, hill woodlands and montane forests from central Mexico, Belize to Bolivia, the Guianas, Venezuela and northern Brazil (Acre to Amapá and Maranhão) with the largest diversity found in Colombia. These mostly large, simple to branched plants, forming dense thickets, have reedy, short to long, clustered stems, subtended by long, tubular sheaths, each with several, strongly nerved, leathery, rigid leaves. The spectacular, showy flowers, in many instances, simulate or even excel in beauty those of the *Cattleya*. The short, solitary or few-flowered inflorescence has large, fragrant flowers, opening one at a time, but most seldom last more than a day or two; and are produced in succession with a wide range of colors. The entire or obscurely trilobed lip is tubular toward the base and spreading above.

The pale purple, lavender to red disc comes in every color but blue, it has a smooth, lamellate or crested callus and has an inrolled margin. The lip is united to the long, stout, footless column at the base.

SOBRALLIA

An orthographic variant introduced in *Syn. Pl. (D. Dietrich),* **5**: 187 (1852). The correct spelling is *Sobralia*.

SODIROELLA

Schlechter

Repert. Spec. Nov. Regni Veg. Beih. **8**: 107 (1921).

ETYMOLOGY: Dedicated to Aloyusius (Luis) Sodiro (1836-1909), an Italian-born Ecuadorian scientist, a Jesuit priest, who ministered from the monastery at Cotocallao, explored most of the area around Quito, and was a professor of botany at Escuela Politécnia and the Central University of Quito. And Latin for diminutive.

TYPE SPECIES: *Sodiroella ecuadorensis* Schlechter

Recognized as belonging to the genus *Telipogon*, *Sodiroella* was previously considered to include one twig epiphyte found in mid to upper elevation, montane cloud forests of northern Ecuador. This small, short-lived, short-stemmed plant has deciduous leaves arranged in a fan shape. The long, arching, few-flowered inflorescence has inverted, fragile, yellow flowers and has a yellow, entire lip. The flowers have a short column with white spines located on the side. The above type name is now considered a synonym of *Telipogon pogonostalix* Reichenbach f.

SOLENANGIS

Schlechter

Beih. Bot. Centralbl. **36**(2): 133 (1918).

Epidendroideæ 🍃 Vandeæ • Aerangidinæ

ETYMOLOGY: Greek for pipe or tube and a vessel or cup. Referring to the shape of the lip that consists almost entirely of a spur.

TYPE SPECIES: *None designated*

Five unusual, monopodial epiphytes are distributed in wet, humid, low to upper elevation, coastal woodlands thickets and montane forests, from Equatorial Guinea, Kenya to Mozambique, Madagascar, the Comoros and Mascarenes Islands. These miniature plants have long, somewhat scrambling stems with numerous roots, but the narrow to needle-like leaves are borne near the tip of the stem and are either small or even totally absent. The usually several, few-flowered inflorescences have small, white, pale pink, green to green-yellow, nocturnally fragrant flowers that are either insignificant or quite attractive. In some species all the floral segments are so small that the flower appears to consist only of a long spur. The tiny, entire or obscurely trilobed lip is concave with a wide opening to the curved, stout spur. The flowers have a short, stout, wingless, footless column.

SOLENIDIOPSIS

Senghas

Orchidee (Hamburg) **37**(6): 274 (1986).

Epidendroideæ ᴠ Cymbidieæ • Oncidiinæ

ETYMOLOGY: *Solenidium*, a genus of orchids and Greek for resemblance. Referring to a similarity to *Solenidium*.

TYPE SPECIES: *Solenidiopsis tigroides*
(C. Schweinfurth) Senghas
(*Odontoglossum tigroides* C. Schweinfurth)

Four sympodial epiphytes are found in mid to upper elevation, montane cloud forests of Peru. These small plants have pear-shaped to ovoid pseudobulbs, subtended by distichous, overlapping sheaths (the lower being leafless and the uppermost leaf-bearing), each with one to two, oblong, leathery leaves, borne at the tip of the pseudobulb. The long, few-flowered inflorescence, borne from the pseudobulb base, has small, yellow-white, fragrant flowers. The floral segments have one to two broad, widespreading, brown-red bands. The white or yellow, entire or trilobed lip has broad side lobes, a small, narrow to broad midlobe with a bilobed or sharply pointed tip, and a darker colored spot on the callus. The flowers have an erect, club-shaped column.

SOLENIDIUM

Lindley

Orchid. Linden. 15 (1846).

Epidendroideæ ᴠ Cymbidieæ • Oncidiinæ

ETYMOLOGY: Greek for a small canal or tube. In reference to the supposed channeled claw of the lip.

TYPE SPECIES: *Solenidium racemosum* Lindley

Two uncommon, sympodial epiphytes found in wet, low to mid elevation, hill scrub to montane forests of Colombia, Venezuela, the Guianas, Peru and Brazil (Amazonas, Pará, Maranhaõ and Mato Grosso). These plants have clustered, compressed, heavily grooved pseudobulbs (usually a shiny pale brown), subtended by short-lived sheaths, each with several, thinly textured, wavy leaves. The erect to arching, numerous to few-flowered inflorescence has yellow to pale green flowers with the petals and sepals heavily marked chestnut brown. The narrowly clawed, entire lip is joined to the column foot and is held at a right angle to

it. The entire lip has two white, downy calli along its length, is shallowly notched, and sometimes has a pair of small, basal lobes. The flowers have an erect to downward-curved column.

SOLENOCENTRUM

Schlechter

Repert. Spec. Nov. Regni Veg. **9**: 163 (1911).

Orchidoideæ ᴠ Cranichideæ • Cranichidinæ

ETYMOLOGY: Greek for tube or pipe and a spur. In reference to the shape of the tube-like spur formed by the bases of the lateral sepals.

TYPE SPECIES: *Solenocentrum costaricense*
Schlechter

Four sympodial epiphytes or rare terrestrials are found in damp, mid to upper elevation, montane forests from Costa Rica to Panama, Ecuador (Napo) and northern Bolivia (Cochabamba). These plants have short, creeping, unbranched stems, each with a basal rosette of soft nerved leaves. The erect, terminal, numerous-flowered inflorescence has rather bizarre shaped, green to green-yellow, fragrant flowers. The dorsal sepal is quite narrow with thin, slightly larger, hairy lateral sepals which enclose the long, narrow spur, and has tiny, triangular-shaped to bilobed petals. The small, concave, triangular-shaped, entire lip is attached in the basal part to the short, erect, footless column.

SOPHRONIA

Lindley

Bot. Reg. **13**: t. 1129 (1828).

Not *Sophronia* Roemer & Schultes (1817) Iridaceæ, and not *Sophronia* Persoon (1827) Gasteromycetes-Phallales.

ETYMOLOGY: Greek for discreet, chaste or modest. Alluding to the inconspicuous habit of the plant.

TYPE SPECIES: *Sophronia cernua* Lindley

Not validly published because of a prior use of the name, this homonym was replaced by *Sophronitis*.

SOPHRONITELLA

Schlechter

Repert. Spec. Nov. Regni Veg. Beih. **35**: 76 (1925).

ETYMOLOGY: *Sophronitis*, a genus of orchids and Latin for diminutive. Implying a likeness to *Sophronitis*.

TYPE SPECIES: *Sophronitella violacea*
(Lindley) Schlechter
(*Sophronitis violacea* Lindley)

Now recognized as belonging to the genus *Isabelia*, *Sophronitella* was previously considered to include one epiphyte or lithophyte found in

cool, seasonally dry, mid elevation, montane forests of eastern Brazil (Espírito Santo to Rio Grande do Sul) exposed to fairly strong sunlight. This small, creeping plant has densely clustered, fluted to spindle-shaped, strongly ribbed pseudobulbs suffused purple and are subtended by several, white sheaths. Each has a solitary or rarely two, narrow, grass-like leaf that is pleated along the axis. The several, short, one- to two-flowered inflorescence have a large, showy, violet-purple flower often paler toward the center, and the narrow sepals have edges that are curled upward. The broad, oblong or ovate, entire lip, fused to the column base, is broader than the other segments and has an obscure, bilobed, basal callus. The flowers have a short, stout, club-shaped, footless column.

SOPHRONITES

An orthographic variant introduced in *Hort. Donat.*, 213 (1858). The correct spelling is *Sophronitis*.

SOPHRONITIS

Lindley

Bot. Reg. **14**: sub 1147 (1828).

Epidendroideæ ᴠ Epidendreæ • Laeliinæ

ETYMOLOGY: *Sophronia*, a genus of orchids. Implying to a likeness of *Sophronia*.

TYPE SPECIES: *Sophronitis cernua* (Lindley) Lindley
(*Sophronia cernua* Lindley)

Fifty-seven sympodial epiphytes or rare terrestrials are confined to coastal, low elevation, mangrove hammocks and dry savannas on exposed rock faces with lots of fog and high humidity of southeastern Brazil (Espírito Santo to São Paulo), Paraguay and northern Argentina usually in full sunlight. These exquisite, dwarf plants, often forming large colonies, have flattened, tiny, densely clustered pseudobulbs with several, basal nodes. They varying in appearance from club-like to spindle-shaped, each with an ovate to minute, solitary, leathery to fleshy, erect or spreading, gray-green leaf that is sometimes suffused dark pink. The short, erect, solitary or few-flowered inflorescence has small, showy, vivid red, purple, orange-red, violet or yellow, fragrant flowers. The small, flat, spreading, yellow to pale red, entire or trilobed lip is united to the base of the white or pink, short, club-shaped, footless column.

NOTE: These species, especially *Sophronitis coccinea* (Lindley) Reichenbach f., are used extensively in hybridization for their vivid scarlet coloring. Many of the former *Laelia* species have now been included in this genus.

Currently Accepted   Validly Published   Invalidly Published   Published Pre-1753   Superfluous Usage   Orthographic Variant   Fossil

O r c h i d   G e n e r a • **366**

SOTEROSANTHUS

F. Lehmann ex **Jenny**

Orchidee (Hamburg) **37**(2): 73 (1986).

Epidendroideæ ⚘ **Cymbidieæ** • **Stanhopeinæ**

ETYMOLOGY: Greek for savior and flower. Meaning flower of the savior; we have no idea why Lehmann used this name.

Or possibly honoring Saint Soter (x-174), an Italian-born 12th bishop of Rome from the Campagna area, who was elected pope in 166, and is known as the pope of charity; he was martyred on the Appian Way.

TYPE SPECIES: *Soterosanthus shepheardii*
(Rolfe) Jenny
(*Sievekingia shepheardii* Rolfe)

One uncommon, sympodial epiphyte is found in low elevation, Pacific coastal forests of western Colombia (Chocó) to northeastern Ecuador (Esmeraldas). This dwarf plant has roundish, four-angled pseudobulbs, each with two gray-green, leathery, semi-deciduous leaves that have red undersides. The erect, minutely bristly to downy covered, few-flowered inflorescence, borne from the pseudobulb base and is often larger than the plant. The white, yellow-green or yellow, distinctly fragrant flowers have similar widespreading sepals and smaller, rounded petals. The deeply sac-like, entire lip has evenly distributed deep yellow to red spots. The flowers have an erect, bright green column-like callus with hairs.

SPAHOGLOTTIS

An orthographic variant introduced in *Orchid. Nepal*, 107 (1978). The correct spelling is *Spathoglottis*.

SPATHIGER

Small

Fl. Miami   55 (1913).

ETYMOLOGY: Latin for a spathe or blade. An allusion to the numerous, spathe-like floral bracts.

TYPE SPECIES: *Spathiger rigidus* (Jacquin) Small
(*Epidendrum rigidum* Jacquin)

Now recognized as belonging to the genus *Epidendrum*, *Spathiger* was previously considered to include ten epiphytes found in low to mid elevation, tropical rain forests, semi-deciduous forests as well as mangroves of the United States (southern Florida), Cuba to Trinidad, southern Mexico to Bolivia, the Guianas, Venezuela and northern Brazil. These small, creeping, stiff-stemmed plants have reed-like stems, subtended by overlapping, thin, dry sheaths, each with several, leathery, roundish, unequally bilobed leaves. The laterally compressed, few-flowered inflorescences have

well-spaced, insignificant, tiny to minute, green flowers borne in the axils of the clasping bracts. The uppermost, ovate, shortly clawed, entire lip has a flat disk with a pair of solid protuberances. The flowers have a finely toothed, large column.

SPATHIGLOTTIS

An orthographic variant introduced in *Hamburger Garten- Blumenzeitung*, **40**: 158, 163 (1884). The correct spelling is *Spathoglottis*.

SPATHIUM

Lindley ex **Wittstein**

Etym.-Bot.-Handw.-Buch, ed. 1   825 (1852).

Not *Spathium* Loureiro (1790) Saururaceæ; and not *Spathium* Edgeworth (1842) Sponogetonaceæ.

Not validly published this name is referred to as a section of *Epidendrum*.

SPATHOGLOTIS

An orthographic variant introduced in *Not. Pl. Asiat.*, 323, *t. 311* (1851). The correct spelling is *Spathoglottis*.

SPATHOGLOTTIS

Blume

Bijdr. Fl. Ned. Ind.   **8**: 400, *t. 76* (1825).

Epidendroideæ ⚘ **Collabiinæ** • **Currently unplaced**

ETYMOLOGY: Greek for spathe and tongue. An allusion to the unusually broad midlobe of the lip.

TYPE SPECIES: *Spathoglottis plicata* Blume

Forty-five sympodial terrestrials are widespread in low to mid elevation, forests, scrub and grassy slopes from India, southern China (Xizang to Jiangxi), southern Japan (Ryukyu Islands), Taiwan, Myanmar to Vietnam, Malaysia, Indonesia, New Caledonia to Samoa and the Philippines with the center of development in New Guinea. In some areas of the United States (Hawaii and Florida) they are considered as weeds. These plants have distinctive, corm-like, cone-shaped to ovoid, sometimes depressed pseudobulbs or clustered, pseudobulbous stems (located on or just below the surface of the soil), subtended by dried sheaths, each with one to two, large, broad, pleated leaves. The thin, erect, numerous to few-flowered inflorescence bears a succession of small to large, showy, pink, white, yellow or purple flowers over a period of many months. The trilobed (at the base) lip has oblong side lobes with a hairy, yellow callus mound in the center and a long-clawed, narrow, wedge-shaped midlobe. The flowers have an erect to incurved, club-shaped, footless column.

SPATOGLOTTIS

An orthographic variant cited in *Nomencl. Bot. (Steudel)*, ed. 2, **2**: 616 (1841). The correct spelling is *Spathoglottis*.

SPECKLIANIA

An orthographic variant introduced in *Repert. Spec. Nov. Regni Veg. Beih.*, **7**: 234 (1920). The correct spelling is *Specklinia*.

SPECKLINIA

Lindley

Gen. Sp. Orchid. Pl.   8 (1830).

Epidendroideæ ⚘ **Epidendreæ** • **Pleurothallidinæ**

ETYMOLOGY: Honoring Veit Rudolf Speckle (x-1550), a German wood sculptor/engraver who prepared the woodcuts for Fuchs's *De Historia Stirpium commentarii insignes*. Leonhard Fuchs (1501-1566), a German physician and botanist represents the transition between medieval and modern botany.

LECTOTYPE: *Specklinia lanceola* (Swartz) Lindley
(*Epidendrum lanceola* Swartz)

Three hundred sixty-five, sympodial epiphytes, lithophytes or terrestrials are distributed in low to upper elevation, hill woodlands to montane cloud forests from the southeastern United States (Florida), Cuba to Trinidad, the Guianas, Venezuela, Mexico to Bolivia and southeastern Brazil to northern Argentina. These tufted, rib-like, short-stemmed plants are exceedingly and exasperating variable, often growing in dense clusters. They ranging in size from small to relatively large, each with a solitary leaf often suffused purple with age. The several, solitary to few-flowered inflorescences, borne from the leaf axils, have small to tiny flowers in a wide range of color combinations. The thinly textured lateral sepals and petals are joined or united for various lengths. The entire, trilobed or rare cleaved lip is small to minute (pear-shaped to elliptical, almost straight to rounded, and sometimes bordered with a fringe of slender ciliate) with the base usually hinged to the column foot. The flowers have a long, slender or club-shaped, usually winged column that is footless or with a short foot. These species are often included in *Pleurothallis*.

SPECLINIA

An orthographic variant introduced in *Syn. Pl. (D. Dietrich)*, **5**: 1, 29 (1852). The correct spelling is *Specklinia*.

SPECTACULUM

Luer

Monogr. Syst. Bot. Missouri Bot. Gard.
105: 14 (2006).

ETYMOLOGY: Latin for grand or outstanding. Refers to the grandeur or uniqueness of the species.

TYPE SPECIES: *Spectaculum racemosum*
(Lindley) Luer
(*Masdevallia racemosa* Lindley)

Recognized as belonging to the genus *Masdevallia*, *Spectaculum* was proposed to include one terrestrial or epiphyte found in mid to upper elevation, montane forests of southern Colombia. This creeping plant has stout, erect to ascending stems borne at intervals from the rhizome, subtended by tubular sheaths, each with a solitary, oblong to ovate, leathery leaf. The erect to arching, slender, purple, few-flowered inflorescence has showy, orange-red flowers with vermilion nerves and margins. The small dorsal sepal is united with the much larger, heart-shaped lateral sepals forming a short tube and the small, pale yellow petals are narrowly clawed. The oblong, white, entire lip has a rounded tip. The flowers have an elongate, more or less club-shaped column.

SPECULANTHA

D.L. Jones & M.A. Clements

Austral. Orchid Res. **4**: 82 (2002).

ETYMOLOGY: Greek for mirror-like or a shiny spot and flower. Refers to the flowers facing inward toward the scape.

TYPE SPECIES: *Speculantha parviflora*
(R. Brown) D.L. Jones & M.A. Clements
(*Pterostylis parviflora* R. Brown)

Recognized as belonging to the genus *Pterostylis*, *Speculantha* was proposed to include five terrestrials found in dry, low elevation, forests, grasslands and woodlands of southeastern Australia and Tasmania. This inconspicuous, erect plant has slender to stout, unbranched stems, each with several, ovate leaves in a tiny, ground-hugging rosette. The few-flowered inflorescence has small to tiny, green to pale green flowers, borne in the axils of a small bract, not opening widely. The lateral sepals are united for most of their length and have a distinct hump, just before they diverge sharply forming two upright tips. The dorsal sepal and petals converge, forming a hood over the small, winged column. The oblong, red-brown, entire lip has a mobile claw and a prominent raised, central ridge.

SPEGLYNIA

An orthographic variant introduced in *Prakt. Stud. Orchid.*, 33 (1854). The correct spelling is *Specklinia*.

SPEIRANTHES

Hasskarl

Cat. Hort. Bot. Bogor. (Hasskarl) 47 (1844).

ETYMOLOGY: Greek for coil or twisted and flower. Refers to the twisted inflorescence.

TYPE SPECIES: *None designated*

Not validly published, this name is referred to *Goodyera*. *Speiranthes* was considered to include four terrestrials found from Taiwan, Indonesia, New Guinea, northern Australia and the Philippines to the southwestern Pacific Archipelago.

SPEKLINIA

An orthographic variant introduced in *Orchideen (Schlechter)*, ed. 3, **7**: 426 (1975). The correct spelling is *Specklinia*.

SPHYRARHYNCHUS

Mansfeld

Notizbl. Bot. Gart. Berlin-Dahlem **12**: 706 (1935).

Epidendroideæ ◊ Vandeæ • Aerangidinæ

ETYMOLOGY: Greek for a hammer and snout or horn. An allusion to the hammer shape expansion of the rostellum.

TYPE SPECIES: *Sphyrarhynchus schliebenii* Mansfeld

One truly miniature, monopodial epiphyte found in mid elevation, montane forests of Tanzania and central Kenya with cool nights. This tiny, charming plant has short stems, each with several, small, fleshy, narrow, gray-green, curved, unequally bilobed, tapered leaves and with a mass of gray-green, flattened roots. The several, short, few-flowered inflorescences have glistening white flowers varying in size with the larger flowers found at the tip. The oblong, hanging, entire lip has a splash of bright green in the center and a short, nectar-filled, club-shaped spur. The flowers have a very short, wingless, footless column.

SPHYRARHYNCUS

An orthographic variant introduced in *Bot. Orchids*, 541 (2002). The correct spelling is *Sphyrarhynchus*.

SPHYRARRHYNCHOS

An orthographic variant introduced in *Fragm. Florist. Geobot.*, **3**(Suppl.): 92 (1995). The correct spelling is *Sphyrarhynchus*.

SPHYRASTYLIS

Schlechter

Repert. Spec. Nov. Regni Veg. Beih. **7**: 194 (1920).

ETYMOLOGY: Greek for hammer and column or style. Descriptive of the hammer-shape swelling of the tip of the column.

TYPE SPECIES: *Sphyrastylis oberonioides* Schlechter

Now recognized as belonging to the genus *Ornithocephalus* as a section, *Sphyrastylis* was previously considered to include seven psygmoid epiphytes found in mid to upper elevation, montane cloud forests of Panama, Colombia, Ecuador and Peru. These small, usually hanging plants have elongated stems with the leaves arranged in a fan shape. The erect, densely congested, numerous-flowered inflorescence, borne from the leaf axils, has small, roundish, green-yellow flowers opening together along the rachis in two ranks. The erect, broad, roundish petals are semi-hood-shaped around the column and the base of the lip. The green, oblong, fiddle-shaped, entire or trilobed lip is heart shaped at the base, bilobed or shallowly notched at the tip, and with or without a basal callus. The flowers have an unusual hammer-shaped column with a proportionately large anther cap.

SPICULAEA

Lindley

Sketch Veg. Swan R. **Appendix**: 56 (1840).

Orchidoideæ ◊ Diurideæ • Thelymitrinæ

ETYMOLOGY: Latin for sharp point, tip or sting. The interpretation of this generic name is uncertain, but it may refer to the lip that has the appearance of an insect with a large stinger.

TYPE SPECIES: *Spiculaea ciliata* Lindley

One uncommon, sympodial terrestrial is found in seasonally dry, low elevation, sandy arid scrub of south-western Australia. This erect plant has short, unbranched stems, each with a solitary basal leaf usually absent at flowering. The wiry, numerous to few-flowered inflorescence withers upward as flowering proceeds. This unusual, fleshy stem is able to store water and nutrients, thus enabling the pale brown-yellow flower to continue blooming during the hot, dry summer. The uppermost, entire lip, appearing as an insect lure, is hinged to the long, slender column by a short claw that allows movement in the slightest breeze and

Currently Accepted   Validly Published   Invalidly Published   Published Pre-1753   Superfluous Usage   Orthographic Variant   Fossil

Orchid Genera • 368

is ornamented with numerous, ciliate or club-shaped hairs.

SPILORCHIS

D.L. Jones & M.A. Clements
Orchadian   **15**(1): 37 (2005).
ETYMOLOGY: Greek for spotted, stained or mark and orchid. Refers to the prominent floral markings.
TYPE SPECIES: *Spilorchis weinthalii*
(R.S. Rodgers) D.L. Jones & M.A. Clements
(*Bulbophyllum weinthalii* R.S. Rodgers)

Recognized as belonging to the genus *Bulbophyllum*, *Spilorchis* was proposed to include one epiphyte found in humid, low elevation, hill rain forests of eastern Australia (Queensland and New South Wales) and appears restricted to the local Hoop Pine (*Araucaria cunninghamii*) as a host. These small, clump-forming plants have small, wrinkled pseudobulbs, each with a solitary, rather flat, thinly textured, dark green leaf. The weak, solitary-flowered inflorescence has a relatively large, white or pale green, thick, fragrant flower heavily sprinkled red-brown or magenta splashes, spots and/or suffused. The concave, erect dorsal sepal is incurved over the short, stout column. The mobile, thick, fleshy, trilobed lip, attached to the lip of the column foot, has minute, notched side lobes and the midlobe has a blunt tip and an inrolled margin.

SPILOTANTHA

Luer
Monogr. Syst. Bot. Missouri Bot. Gard.
105: 15 (2006).
ETYMOLOGY: Latin for spotted or flecked and flower. Referring to the various decorations or patterns on the flowers.
TYPE SPECIES: *Spilotantha amanda*
(Reichenbach f. & Warszewicz) Luer
(*Masdevallia amanda* Reichenbach f. & Warszewicz)

Recognized as belonging to the genus *Masdevallia*, *Spilotantha* was proposed to include thirty-two epiphytes or lithophytes found in mid to upper elevation, montane forests from Costa Rica and Panama to Ecuador. These large to small plants have short stems, each with several, leathery leaves. The long, brown, few-flowered inflorescence has more or less inflated, floral bracts and the white to pale yellow flowers are heavily sprinkled with dark red-brown spots or bars. The sepals are usually united into a shallow cup or arched tube. Each tapers into a long tail and has small, keeled petals that are minutely tooted or notched. The entire lip has a rounded tip. The flowers have a small, slightly arched, more or less club-shaped column.

SPIORANTHES

An orthographic variant cited in *Dict. Gen. Names Seed Pl.*, 142 (1995). The correct spelling is *Spiranthes*.

SPIRANTHERA

D. Dietrich
Syn. Pl. (D. Dietrich)   **5**: 17 (1852).

Not validly published this name is referred to *Spiranthes*.

SPIRANTHES

Richard
De Orchid. Eur.   20, 28, 36 (1817).
Name ICBN conserved, the type name also conserved; vs. *Orchiastrum* Séguier (1754) Orchidaceæ.

Orchidoideæ ⚬ Cranichideæ • Spiranthinæ
ETYMOLOGY: Greek for a coil or twisted and flower. From the twisted or spirally arranged inflorescence found in many of the species. Thought to resemble a lady's twisted or braided hair, this gave rise to the common name applied to these orchids.
LECTOTYPE: *Spiranthes autumnalis* (Balbis) Richard
(*Ophrys autumnalis* Balbis)
not validly designated by Correll, *Fl. Texas*, **3**(3): 169 (1944).
The above type name is now considered a synonym of
LECTOTYPE: *Spiranthes spiralis* (Linnaeus) Chevallier
(*Ophrys spiralis* Linnaeus)
designated by M.L. Green, *Prop. Brit. Bot.*, 100 (1929), and Pfeiffer, *Nomencl. Bot. (Pfeiffer)*, **2**(2): 1238 (1874).

When treated in the newer sense, there are twenty-four sympodial terrestrials in this genus that can be the most exasperatingly complex and technical of the whole orchid family. The species are found in all the temperate zones. These erect, unbranched plants often form huge colonies in moist to dry, low to upper elevation, hill and montane meadows, lake shores, roadside ditches and nutrient-poor grasslands. The greatest development is in eastern North America with a few species found from Mexico to Nicaragua, Cuba to Trinidad, Ireland to Spain, Germany to Italy, Morocco to Algeria, Afghanistan, across Russia, Mongolia, throughout China, Myanmar to Vietnam, Thailand to Indonesia, Australia and the Philippines to the Pacific Archipelago. The plants have variably variably shaped leaves often arranged in a basal rosette that are usually present during flowering. The tremendously variable flowers are borne on long, hairy to smooth, numerous-flowered inflorescences in tightly to loosely, spiraling arrangements. These fragrant, tubular flowers are usually rather small, do not open widely, are found in various shades of white, pale yellow, green or rare pink. The erect dorsal sepal and petals converge, forming a hood over the small, short, roundish column. The clawed, entire or lobed lip, enveloping the column at its base, has side lobes that are parallel with the column; the midlobe or tip bends downward and has a wavy margin.

SPIRANTHIS

An orthographic variant introduced in *Itin. Pl. Khasyah Mts.*, 189 (1848). The correct spelling is *Spiranthes*.

SPIRANTHOS

An orthographic variant cited in *Nomencl. Bot. (Steudel)*, ed. 2, **1**: 717 (1840). The correct spelling is *Spiranthes*.

SPIRATHES

An orthographic variant introduced in *Itin. Pl. Khasyah Mts.*, 192 (1848). The correct spelling is *Spiranthes*.

SPIRANTHUS

An orthographic variant introduced in *Hort. Universel*, ser. 2, **1**: 23 (1846). The correct spelling is *Spiranthes*.

SPIROSATIS

Thouars
Hist. Orchid.   Table 1, sub 1c, *t. 9*, *t. 12b* (1822).

Name published without a description. Today this name is most often referred to *Benthamia*.

SPITZELII

Kraenzlin
Orchid. Gen. Sp.   **6**: 137 (1901).

Name published without a description. Today this name is most often referred to *Orchis*.

SPLECKLINIA

An orthographic variant introduced in *Field Guide Orchids Serr. Sao Jose*, 138 (1991). The correct spelling is *Specklinia*.

SPONGIOLA

J.J. Wood & A. Lamb
Orchids Borneo   **1**: 283 (1994).
Epidendroideæ ⚬ Vandeæ • Aeridinæ
ETYMOLOGY: Latin for a little sponge. Refers to the texture of the midlobe lip.
TYPE SPECIES: *Spongiola lohokii* J.J. Wood & A. Lamb

One monopodial epiphyte is found in damp, shady, mid elevation, limestone and sandstone ridges of southern Malaysia (northeastern Sabah). This small plant has short stems, subtended by leafy sheaths, each with several, leathery leaves. The long, hanging, few-flowered inflorescence has small, short-lived, semi-transparent, pale yellow-green to pale yellow flowers with white segment tips. The white, pouch-like, immobile, trilobed lip has tiny side lobes. The midlobe resembles a small, spongy pouch sprinkled with purple spots, and is hollow near the mouth of the pale yellow spur. The flowers have a short, footless column.

SPRECKLINIA

An orthographic variant introduced in *Cat. Descr. Orquid., Estac. Exp. Agron. Santiago, Cuba*, **60**: 115 (1938). The correct spelling is *Specklinia*.

SPURICIANTHUS

Szlachetko & Margońska
Polish Bot. J. **46**(1): 29 (2001).
ETYMOLOGY: Latin for false and *Acianthus*, a genus of orchids. Refers to the appearance of the lip's midlobe.
TYPE SPECIES: *Spuricianthus atepalus*
    (Reichenbach f.) Szlachetko & Margońska
    (*Acianthus atepalus* Reichenbach f.)

Recognized as belonging to the genus *Acianthus*, *Spuricianthus* was proposed to include one terrestrial found in New Caledonia. This small plant has a solitary, heavily veined leaf clasping the midway up the stem. The erect, few-flowered inflorescence has medium-sized, green flowers not opening fully. The long sepals are hair-like and has completely reduced petals. The concave, entire lip has marginal calli and the pollinia lack a sticky glue.

SPYRANTHES

An orthographic variant introduced in *Cat. Veg. Alger*, 52 (1850). The correct spelling is *Spiranthes*.

STACHOBIUM

An orthographic variant introduced in *Orchids India*, ed. 2, 35 (1999). The correct spelling is *Stachyobium*.

STACHYANTHUS

Engler
Nat. Pflanzenfam. **1**: 227 (1897).
Not *Stachyanthus* A.P. de Candolle (1836) Asteraceæ, and not *Stachyanthus* Engler (1897) Olacaceæ.
ETYMOLOGY: Greek for ear of corn and flower.
TYPE SPECIES: *None designated*

Name published without a description. Today this name is most often referred to *Bulbophyllum*.

STACHYBIUM

An orthographic variant cited in *Lex. Gen. Phan.*, 531 (1904). The correct spelling is *Stachyobium*.

STACHYOBIUM

Reichenbach *filius*
Gard. Chron., ser. 1 **28**: 785 (1869).
ETYMOLOGY: Greek for ear of corn, hence a spike and life. Refers to the cylindrical stems that spring to life with a flowing cascade of flowers
TYPE SPECIES: *Stachyobium aureum* Reichenbach f.

Recognized as belonging to a section of *Dendrobium*, *Stachyobium* was previously considered to include one epiphyte or lithophyte found in mid elevation, montane forests of Laos and Malaysia. This plant has long, cylindrical, erect pseudobulbs, becoming hanging with age, each with several leaves arranged in two ranks along the upper portion of the stem. The several, few-flowered inflorescences are borne from the upper part of the leafless stem. The large, showy, fragrant, bright yellow flowers have an entire lip that is heavily fringed along the margins and has two dark purple blotches on the hairy disc. The above type name is now considered a synonym of *Dendrobium binoculare* Reichenbach f.

STACYELLA

Szlachetko
Polish Bot. J. **51**(1): 40 (2006)[2007].
ETYMOLOGY: Dedicated to John E. Stacy (1919-1992), an American aeronautical engineer and horticulturalist who contributed to the knowledge of the *Oncidium* alliance, and author of *Studies in the Genus Oncidium*. And Latin for diminutive.
TYPE SPECIES: *Stacyella crista-galli*
    (Reichenbach f.) Szlachetko
    (*Oncidium crista-galli* Reichenbach f.)

Recognized as belonging to the genus *Erycina*, *Stacyella* was proposed to include one epiphyte found in low to mid elevation, hill to montane rain forests and coffee plantations from southern Mexico to Peru. This dwarf plant has tiny, ovoid, compressed pseudobulbs, subtended by distichous, leafy sheaths, each with several, narrow leaves arranged in a fan shape. The erect to arching, few-flowered inflorescence has showy, large, green-yellow to yellow flowers with the petals barred red-brown. The trilobed lip has roundish side lobes with slightly wavy margins; the broad midlobe has four, often overlapping

lobes and a bright yellow callus with orange spots. The flowers have a short column.

STALKYA

Garay
Bot. Mus. Leafl. **28**(4): 371 (1980)[1982].
Orchidoideæ ※ Cranichideæ · Spiranthinæ
ETYMOLOGY: The nickname for Galfrid Charles Kenneth Dunsterville (1905-1988), a British-born Venezuelan oil petroleum engineer and botanist who specialized in collecting, describing, and illustrating the orchids of Venezuela and co-author of the series *Venezuelan Orchids Illustrated*.
TYPE SPECIES: *Stalkya muscicola*
    (Garay & Dunsterville) Garay
    (*Spiranthes muscicola* Garay & Dunsterville)

One very interesting, sympodial terrestrial or epiphyte is found in upper elevation, montane forests of western Venezuela (Mérida). This erect, slender, unbranched plant is found growing among the mosses on tree trunk canopies. The basal rosette of several, pale green leaves is absent or almost withered by flowering time. The tall, few-flowered inflorescence has small, pale creamy green to green flowers at its base with dark green nerves, not opening fully. The erect, tiny, more or less ovate, entire lip has dark green nerves and clings to the sides of the small, short, stout, footless column.

STAMNORCHIS

D.L. Jones & M.A. Clements
Austral. Orchid Res. **4**: 83 (2002).
ETYMOLOGY: Greek for earthen jar or bottle and orchid. Refers to the common name of this species, jug orchid.
TYPE SPECIES: *Stamnorchis recurva*
    (Bentham) D.L. Jones & M.A. Clements
    (*Pterostylis recurva* Bentham)

Recognized as belonging to the genus *Pterostylis*, *Stamnorchis* was proposed to include one terrestrial found in low elevation, coastal scrub of western Australia. This small, slender to stout plant has ovate leaves in a tiny rosette usually withered by flowering. The erect, solitary to three-flowered inflorescence has a small, jug-shaped, white flower with prominent green and red-brown or gray stripes. The barely recurved hood is somewhat funnel-shaped at the tip. The dorsal sepal and petals end in short, recurved tips, and the lateral sepals are decurved. The shortly clawed, concave, entire lip has a short, hairy margin, tapers to a long narrow point, and has a narrow, raised center line. The flowers have an erect column.

Currently Accepted   Validly Published   Invalidly Published   Published Pre-1753   Superfluous Usage   Orthographic Variant   Fossil

STANHOPEA

J. Frost ex Hooker

Bot. Mag.　　**56**: *tt. 2948-2949* (1829).

Epidendroideæ ⚘ **Cymbidieæ** • **Stanhopeinæ**

ETYMOLOGY: Honoring Philip Henry (1781-1855), a British lord and the 4th Earl of Stanhope and a past president of the London Medico-Botanical Society during the 1830s. The word stanhope means stony and hollow.

TYPE SPECIES: *Stanhopea insignis* J. Frost ex Hooker

Fifty-five sympodial epiphytes, lithophytes or uncommon terrestrials are found in low to upper elevation, evergreen forests from southern Mexico to Peru and Brazil. This is a difficult genus taxonomically because of the similarity of the various species. These plants have densely clustered, stout, ovoid to egg-shaped, ribbed pseudobulbs (ranging from small to quite large), each with a solitary, large, semi-rigid, dark green leaf. Has an extensive aerial root system forming a dense protective mass around the base of the plant. The few-flowered inflorescence hangs sharply downward and has fascinating flowers that are notably variable in color and floral shape, even within a single species. The large, waxy flowers open simultaneously, rarely persist for more than three days, have highly pungent to pleasant scents and are pollinated by fragrance collecting male euglossine bees. The complex, thick lip has a basal portion (hypochile) that is slipper-shaped; the intermediate (mesochile) portion, if present, is entire or divided and often two-horned, and the terminal (epichile) portion is trilobed or entire. The flowers have a long, erect to slightly curved, club-shaped, winged or wingless column.

STANHOPEASTRUM

Reichenbach *filius*

Bot. Zeitung (Berlin)　　**10**: 927 (1852).

ETYMOLOGY: *Stanhopea*, a genus of orchids and Latin for a kind of. Refers to a relationship with *Stanhopea*.

TYPE SPECIES: *Stanhopeastrum ecornutum*
　　　　(Lemaire) Reichenbach f.
　　　　(*Stanhopea ecornuta* Lemaire)

Now recognized as belonging to the genus *Stanhopea*, *Stanhopeastrum* was previously considered to include one epiphyte found in low to mid elevation, evergreen forests and scrub from Guatemala to western Panama. This plant has densely clustered, grooved pseudobulbs, each with a solitary, rigid leaf. The few-flowered inflorescence has fragrant, waxy, creamy-white flowers sprinkled with purple spots. The unusual cup-shaped or squat, yellow, trilobed lip is orange-yellow at the base; the enlarged hypochile is

strongly sac-like; the mesochile lacks horns, and the short epichile has protuberances.

STANHOPHEA

An orthographic variant introduced in *Pansey*, 45 (1835). The correct spelling is *Stanhopea*.

STANHOPIA

An orthographic variant introduced in *Amer. Fl. Gard. Directory*, ed. 2, 207 (1839). The correct spelling is *Stanhopea*.

STANROPSIS

An orthographic variant introduced in *Hamburger Garten- Blumenzeitung*, **40**: 157 (1884). The correct spelling is *Stauropsis*.

STATEUMATICA

J. Bauhin

Hist. Pl. (Bauhin)　　**2**: 758 (1651).

Pre-1753, therefore not validly published in fulfillment of nomenclatural rules; this name is most often referred to *Orchis*.

STAURITIS

Reichenbach *filius*

Hamburger Garten-Blumenzeitung　　**18**: 34 (1862).

ETYMOLOGY: Greek for cross. Refers to the position of the right angle of the side lobes to the midlobe thus forming a cross.

TYPE SPECIES: *Stauritis violacea*
　　　　(H. Witte) Reichenbach f.
　　　　(*Phalaenopsis violaceae* H. Witte)

Now recognized as belonging to the genus *Phalaenopsis*, *Stauritis* was previously considered to include one epiphyte found in humid, low elevation, scrub, woodlands and thickets from Malaysia to western Indonesia (Sumatra). This robust plant has short stems, subtended by leaf sheaths, each with several, leathery, waxy, dark green leaves. The few-flowered inflorescence has faintly to strongly fragrant, white to creamy yellow flowers opening a few at a time. The slightly incurved lateral sepals are almost covered by a large, purple blotch. The trilobed lip has an oblong midlobe with a central keel tipped with white hairs and short, erect, yellow side lobes. The flowers have a white or purple, fleshy, small, slightly curved column.

STAUROCHILUS

Ridley

J. Linn. Soc., Bot.　　**32**: 351 (1896).

Epidendroideæ ⚘ **Vandeæ** • **Aeridinæ**

ETYMOLOGY: Greek for a cross and lip. In reference to the close, parallel lobes of the lip that give the appearance of a cross to the viewer.

TYPE SPECIES: *Staurochilus fasciatus*
　　　　(Reichenbach f.) Ridley
　　　　(*Trichoglottis fasciata* Reichenbach f.)

Fourteen monopodial epiphytes are found in low to mid elevation, hill to montane forests from Thailand to Malaysia with the center of distribution in the Philippines. These species are closely related to *Trichoglottis*. These large, climbing plants have short to long, erect to hanging, stiff stems, subtended by persistent sheaths, each with spreading, leathery, strap-like leaves that are unequally bilobed at the tip and arranged in two ranks. The erect, simple or branched (somewhat zig-zagged), numerous to few-flowered inflorescence has showy, long-lived, fleshy, flat-faced, highly fragrant, creamy, green or pale yellow flowers with transverse brown bands and spots of red. The fleshy, yellow or white, immobile, trilobed lip, attached to the short, broad, footless column, has a green-yellow tip. The cylindrical, curved spur is hairy within and at its entrance.

STAUROGLOTTIS

Schauer

Nov. Actorum Acad. Caes. Leop.-Carol. German. Nat. Cur., ser. 3　　**19**(Suppl. 1): 432 (1843), or
Observ. Bot.　　**16**(Suppl. 2): 432 (1843).

ETYMOLOGY: Greek for a cross and tongue. Alluding to the lip with its lateral lobes forming a cross.

TYPE SPECIES: *Stauroglottis equestris* Schauer

Now recognized as belonging to the genus *Phalaenopsis*, *Stauroglottis* was previously considered to include two epiphytes found in low elevation, woodlands and along river banks of the Philippines to Taiwan. These compact dwarf plants have short stems, subtended by overlapping leaf bases, each with several, oblong, fleshy, recurved leaves that have slightly unequally bilobed tips. The simple or branched, numerous to few-flowered inflorescence, borne from base of the stem, can produce keikis (plantlets formed on the inflorescence), reflower off of old spikes, and continue to send off new branches. The normally magenta to pink flowers, opening successively, have a darker pink center but can range in color from pure white to deep rose. The shortly clawed, trilobed lip has oblong, erect side lobes with roundish tips, and a midlobe with a concave center. The flowers have a small, slender, bent-forward column.

STAUROPSIS

Reichenbach *filius*

Hamburger Garten-Blumenzeitung **16**: 117 (1860).
Not *Stauropsis* Meunier (1907) Bacillariophyta.

ETYMOLOGY: Greek for a cross and appearance or likeness. Descriptive of the unusual cross-shaped lip.

LECTOTYPE: *Stauropsis philippinensis*
(Lindley) Reichenbach f.
(*Trichoglottis philippinensis* Lindley)

Now recognized as belonging to the genus *Trichoglottis*, *Stauropsis* was previously considered to include twenty-five epiphytes ranging in low to mid elevation, coastal scrub and montane forests from northern India to the southwestern Pacific Archipelago with the center of development in the Philippines. These erect or hanging, long-stemmed plants have glossy, flattened leaves. The few-flowered inflorescence has fragrant, long-lived, dull red-brown, yellow-green to yellow flowers with broad, yellow or white margins. The narrow, white, trilobed lip, fused to the column foot, has a laterally compressed midlobe and narrow, triangular side lobes. The flowers have a short column with hairy or papillose projections.

STEGOSTYLA

D.L. Jones & M.A. Clements
Orchadian **13**(9): 411 (2001).

ETYMOLOGY: Greek for cover or roof and column or style. In reference to the strongly incurved, cap-like dorsal sepal that covers the column.

TYPE SPECIES: *Stegostyla gracilis*
(R. Brown) D.L. Jones & M.A. Clements
(*Caladenia gracilis* R. Brown)

Recognized as belonging to the genus *Caladenia*, *Stegostyla* was proposed to include fifteen terrestrials found in open, dry, low elevation, scrub, forests and woodlands of south-eastern Australia, Tasmania and New Zealand. These often abundant, colorful, small, hairy plants have a solitary, narrow leaf, often red at the base, and form loose colonies. The erect, wiry, few-flowered inflorescence has small, white to pale pink or pale green flowers with a strong, musky fragrance. The cap-like dorsal sepal is strongly arched over the slender, incurved, winged column. The obscurely trilobed lip has four rows of club-shaped calli that extend nearly to the tip of the midlobe, which has a serrated margin in contrast to the erect side lobes which have entire margins. The external surfaces of the petals and sepals are usually adorned with stalkless glands.

STELBOPHYLLUM

An orthographic variant introduced in *Orchadian*, **13**(11): 490 (2002). The correct spelling is *Stilbophyllum*.

STELEOCORYS

Endlicher ex d'Orbigny
Dict. Univ. Hist. Nat. **4**: 264 (1844).

Name published without a description. Today this name is most often referred to *Corysanthes*.

STELIOPSIS

Brieger
Orchideen (Schlechter), ed. 3 **7**(29-32): 457 (1976).
Not *Steliopsis* Swartz ex Quattrocchi (2000) Pleurothallidinæ.

ETYMOLOGY: Greek for little pillar and like. Refers to the tiny column.

TYPE SPECIES: *Steliopsis anneliesae* Brieger

Not validly published, this name is referred to *Stelis*. *Steliopsis* was considered to include one epiphyte found from Costa Rica to Panama, Ecuador and Peru. The above type name is now considered a synonym of *Stelis maxima* Lindley.

STELIS

Swartz
J. Bot. (Schrader) **2**(4): 239 (1799)[1800].
Name ICBN conserved, the type name conserved.

Epidendroideæ ▧ Epidendreæ ● Pleurothallidinæ

ETYMOLOGY: Greek for little pillar or mistletoe. A term used by the ancient Greeks for mistletoe, which has a similar tree growing habit as this genus.

LECTOTYPE: *Stelis purpurea* (Ruiz & Pavón) Willdenow
(*Humboldtia purpurea* Ruiz & Pavón)
designated by Garay & H.R. Sweet, *J. Arnold Arbor.*, **53**: 528 (1972).

LECTOTYPE: *Stelis ophioglossoides*
(Jacquin) Swartz nom. illeg.
(*Epidendrum ophioglossoides* Jacquin)
not validly designated by Pridgeon, *Gen. Orch.*, **4**: 405 (2005), nor M.L. Green, *Prop. Brit. Bot.*, 100 (1929).

Over five hundred sympodial epiphytes, lithophytes or terrestrials are found in low to upper elevation, hill scrub, swamps and montane cloud forests, distributed from the southeastern United States (Florida), Cuba to Trinidad, the Guianas, Venezuela, Mexico to Bolivia, Brazil and Argentina with the greatest diversity found in moist habitats of the upper Andes. These species are some of the most taxonomically complex of all the orchids but are of little horticultural merit because of the customarily small or minute, flat-faced, usually translucent, often dull-colored flowers in shades of white, green or purple. Many species are light-sensitive, opening only when exposed to the right amount of sunlight, and then closing tightly during the night. These small plants have tufted stems have horizontal creeping rhizomes (the primary stem), and erect, slender stems, each with a solitary, elliptical to oblong, fleshy to leathery leaf. The several, slender, few to numerous-flowered inflorescences have minute to small flowers. There are some strictly nocturnal blooming species that close during the day. The usually spreading dorsal sepal is the most prominent segment. The minute petals and tiny, entire or trilobed lip (fleshy, often hairy) surround the short, stout to slender, erect, footless column (sometimes the column itself is obscure), and some species have segments with hairy margins. The lip is hinged to the column base or the lip base is attached to the base of column foot sometimes by a thin strap.

STELIS

Smith
Cycl. (Rees) **34**: See *Stelis* item #12 (1816).

ETYMOLOGY: Greek for little pillar. Referring to the tongue-like shape of the lip.

TYPE SPECIES: *Stelis odoratissima* Smith
This type name is now considered a synonym of *Bulbophyllum odoratissimum* (Smith) Lindley ex Hooker f.; basionym
Stelis odoratissima Smith

Not validly published, this name is referred to *Bulbophyllum*. *Stelis* Smith was considered to include one epiphyte found from southern China, northeastern India, Myanmar to Vietnam and Thailand.

STELLILABIUM

Schlechter
Orchideen (Schlechter), ed. 1 530 (1914).

Epidendroideæ ▧ Cymbidieæ ● Oncidiinæ

ETYMOLOGY: Latin for a star or starry and a lip. Descriptive of the hairy or bristly ornamentation on the lip.

TYPE SPECIES: *Stellilabium astroglossum*
(Reichenbach f.) Schlechter
(*Telipogon astroglossus* Reichenbach f.)

Thirty-four uncommon, twig, sympodial epiphytes are restricted to upper elevation, montane forests from Mexico to Panama and Venezuela to Peru. These small, short-lived plants last only one to three years. The short stems are usually sheathed by distichous leaves with some species being seasonally leafless. Most of the plants are so tiny that they are rarely seen or noticed. The short, few-flowered, inflorescence normally has only one small, yellow-green flower open at a time. The spoon-shaped petals

Currently Accepted   Validly Published   Invalidly Published   Published Pre-1753   Superfluous Usage   Orthographic Variant   Fossil

O r c h i d   G e n e r a • **372**

are broadly oval. The rather thick, ovate pale brown-yellow to dark maroon, entire or trilobed lip has a round or heart-shaped, spiny pad at the base, and has a hairy or ciliate margin. The flowers have a short, stout column that protrudes onto the lip, then expands upward forming lateral, swollen, long spiny wings.

STELLIS

An orthographic variant introduced in *Nouv. Dict. Hist. Nat.*, **24**: 4 (1818). The correct spelling is *Stelis*.

STELLORCHIS

An orthographic variant introduced in *Hist. Orchid.*, Table 1, sub 2g, *t.* 24 (1822). The correct spelling is *Stellorkis*.

STELLORKIS

Thouars
Nouv. Bull. Sci. Soc. Philom. Paris, prem. table **1**(19): 317 (1809).
Name ICBN rejected vs. *Nervilia* Commerson ex Gaudichaud-Beaupré (1829) Orchidaceæ.
ETYMOLOGY: Latin for star and Greek for orchid. Descriptive of the star-like position of the segments.
TYPE SPECIES: *Stellorkis aplostellis*
　　　　(Thouars) Thouars nom. illeg.
　　　　(*Arethusa simplex* Thouars)
　　Nervilia petraea (Afzelius ex Swartz) Summerhayes
　　　　(*Arethusa petraea* Afzelius ex Swartz)

Although validly published this rejected name is now referred to *Nervilia. Stellorkis* was considered to include one terrestrial found in low elevation, grasslands and woodlands of Ghana, Gabon to Tanzania, Mozambique and Madagascar to the Seychelles Islands. This small, erect plant has unbranched stems, each with a solitary, dark olive-green leaf that has silvery nerves and purple undersides. The solitary-flowered inflorescence has a tiny, brown-green flower opening for just a few hours. The white, trilobed lip has a bright yellow center with numerous, thin tufts of outgrowths.

STENIA

Lindley
Edwards's Bot. Reg. **23**: sub 1991 (1837).
Epidendroideæ ⚬ Cymbidieæ • Zygopetalinæ
ETYMOLOGY: Greek for narrow. In reference to the slender pollinia that are characteristic of this genus.
TYPE SPECIES: *Stenia pallida* Lindley

Eighteen sympodial epiphytes are found in wet, mid to upper elevation, montane forests of Trinidad, Colombia, Venezuela, the Guianas, Ecuador, Peru, Bolivia and Brazil. These plants

have clustered stems composed of a folded series of short, thinly textured, rigid leaves arranged in a loose fan shape. The short, solitary-flowered inflorescence has a large, showy, short-lived, waxy flower ranging in color from pale lemon yellow to bright yellow green and is sometimes spotted with darker hues. The fleshy, concave to deeply pouch-shaped, obscurely trilobed lip has small, intensely yellow side lobes sprinkled with small, red dots, and the pale yellow midlobe has toothed, crested keels faintly spotted pale rose. The flowers have a long, erect, stout, somewhat club-shaped, wingless column that is obscurely angled or ridged on each side.

STENOCARPA

Lindley ex **Wittstein**
Etym.-Bot.-Handw.-Buch, ed. 1　　841 (1852).

Name published without a description. Today this name is most often referred to as a section of *Disa*.

STENOCORYNE

Lindley
Edwards's Bot. Reg. **29**(Misc.): 53, section no. 68 (1843).
ETYMOLOGY: Greek for narrow and club. Descriptive of the long spur formed by the column foot.
TYPE SPECIES: *Stenocoryne longicornis*
　　　　(Lindley) Lindley
　　(*Bifrenaria longicornis* Lindley)

Now recognized as belonging to the genus *Bifrenaria, Stenocoryne* was previously considered to include fourteen epiphytes or uncommon lithophytes found in cool, low elevation, woodlands of northwestern Brazil (Amazonas), Venezuela, the Guianas and Colombia to Peru. These attractive plants have clustered, narrowly ovate to egg-shaped pseudobulbs, each with an obscurely folded to pleated, leathery leaf. The erect to arching, few-flowered inflorescence, borne from the base of the pseudobulb, has showy, waxy, faintly fragrant, small, rose to rich red-yellow flowers marked dark red. The ivory to pale orange, trilobed lip, edged with pale rose, has erect side lobes; the midlobe has a wavy margin and is fused at the base forming a small pseudospur.

STENOCOYNA

An orthographic variant cited in *Lex. Gen. Phan.*, 535 (1904). The correct spelling is *Stenocoryne*.

STENOGLOSSUM

Kunth
Nov. Gen. Sp. 　　**1**: 355, *t.* 87 (1816).
ETYMOLOGY: Greek for narrow and tongue. Referring to the linear shape of the free section of the lip.
TYPE SPECIES: *Stenoglossum coryophorum* Kunth

Now recognized as belonging to the genus *Epidendrum, Stenoglossum* was previously considered to include five epiphytes or terrestrials found on steep slopes in upper elevation, montane cloud forests of Ecuador and Colombia. These plants have creeping, cane-like stems, subtended by several sheaths, each with a solitary, thick, leathery leaf at the tip. The red, drooping, numerous-flowered inflorescence, borne from the leaf terminal, has small, dark red to maroon flowers with white to yellow-green tips. The long, narrow, spear-like, straight to tightly curled, entire lip is uppermost. The flowers have a short column.

STENOGLOTIS

An orthographic variant introduced in *Jorn. Sci. Math. Phys. Nat.*, **4**(14): 184 (1873). The correct spelling is *Stenoglottis*.

STENOGLOTTIS

Lindley
Compan. Bot. Mag. 　　**2**(19): 209 (1836)[1837].
Orchidoideæ ⚬ Orchideæ • Orchidinæ
ETYMOLOGY: Greek for narrow and tongue. Referring to the linear shape of the free midlobe of the lip.
TYPE SPECIES: *Stenoglottis fimbriata* Lindley

Four sympodial terrestrials, lithophytes or uncommon epiphytes are thinly distributed in low to upper elevation, coastal scrub, moss-covered rocks and rocky cliff crevices along the eastern coast of South Africa and areas around Lake Nyasa in southeastern Tanzania and Malawi. These erect plants have short, unbranched stems, each with a basal rosette of narrow leaves. The large bracts often have a wavy margin and are variously spotted purple. The erect, tall, numerous-flowered inflorescence has small, attractive, pink, lilac-mauve or rare white flowers sprinkled with a few dark purple spots. The broad sepals are united to the column base and lip, and the erect, minute petals curve forward forming a hood over the white, short, stout, broad column. The large, wedge-shaped lip, united with the column, is deeply trilobed to even five-lobed about midway, is often fringed and has either a short spur or is spurless.

STENOPOLEN

Rafinesque

Fl. Tellur.   **4**: 49 (1836)[1837].

ETYMOLOGY: Greek for narrow and a corruption of Latin for pollen or fine dust. Referring to the narrow pollinia.

TYPE SPECIES: *None designated*

A superfluous name proposed as a substitute for *Stenia*.

STENOPTERA

C. Presl

Reliq. Haenk.   **1**(2): 95, *t. 14* (1827).
Not *Stenoptera* Endlicher (1841) Burmanniaceæ.

Orchidoideæ ⚬ Cranichideæ • Cranichidinæ

ETYMOLOGY: Greek for narrow or tight and wing. Referring to the narrow, forward-pointing petals.

TYPE SPECIES: *Stenoptera peruviana* C. Presl

Seven robust, sympodial terrestrials are found in low to upper elevation, open woodlands, montane cloud forests and rocky slopes of Cuba, Jamaica, Costa Rica, northern Brazil, Ecuador and Bolivia with the largest concentration found in Peru. These erect plants have short, unbranched stems, each with a basal rosette of leathery leaves that soon wither. The tall, erect, hairy, few-flowered inflorescence has numerous loose sheaths and small, white to pale yellow flowers not opening fully. The sepals are united, forming a rather slender tube with gaping, spreading tips whose outer surfaces are covered in soft, fine, white hairs. The narrow petals are bilobed. The helmet-shaped, thinly textured, entire lip envelopes the large, curved, footless column.

STENORHYNCHUS

An orthographic variant introduced in *Bot. Reg.*, **10**: sub 823 (1824). The correct spelling is *Stenorrhynchos*.

STENORHYNCHUS

An orthographic variant introduced in *Mém. Mus. Hist. Nat.*, **4**: 59 (1818). The correct spelling is *Stenorrhynchos*.

STENORRHYACHUS

An orthographic variant introduced in *Verh. Vereins Beford. Gartenbaues Konigl. Preuss. Staaten*, **25**: 57 (1849). The correct spelling is *Stenorrhynchos*.

STENORRHYNCHIS

An orthographic variant introduced in *Linnaea*, **22**: 815 (1849). The correct spelling is *Stenorrhynchos*.

STENORRHYNCHIUM

An orthographic variant cited in *Dict. Fl. Pl.*, ed. 8, 1073 (1973). The correct spelling is *Stenorrhynchos*.

STENORRHYNCHOS

Richard ex **Sprengel**

Syst. Veg. (Sprengel), ed. 16   **3**: 677 (1826).

Orchidoideæ ⚬ Cranichideæ • Spiranthinæ

ETYMOLOGY: Greek for narrow and snout, horn or beak. Refers to the typically narrow and slender rostellum on the column.

LECTOTYPE: *Stenorrhynchos speciosum*
(Jacquin) Richard ex Sprengel
(*Neottia speciosa* Jacquin)
designated by Britton & Millspaugh, *Bahama Fl.*, 86 (1920).

LECTOTYPE: *Stenorrhynchos orchioides*
(Swartz) Richard
(*Satyrium orchioides* Swartz)
designated by M.N. Correa, *Darwiniana*, **11**: 70 (1955) but this type name is now considered a synonym of *Sacoila lanceolata* (Aublet) Garay

Some seven attractive sympodial terrestrials or epiphytes are found in seasonally dry, low to upper elevation, moist meadows, semi-deciduous forests, woodlands and along steep embankments from the southeastern United States (Arizona to Texas), Cuba to Trinidad, Mexico to Panama, Venezuela and central Colombia to Peru. These tall, erect plants have unbranched, stout stems with dark to pale green leaves that are spotted or lined silver and often in a low rosette. The leaves are usually present during flowering. The erect, smooth, stout, densely packed, numerous to few-flowered inflorescence, almost completely concealed by prominent bracts, has small to fairly large, rather showy, tubular flowers (subtended by narrow bracts) ranging from brick-red, crimson to salmon. The erect dorsal sepal and petals converge, forming a hood over the short, straight column and have recurved tips. The distinctly clawed, entire, trilobed or obscurely trilobed lip envelopes and adheres to the sides of the column and is basally sac-like. The lip has rounded side lobes and an oblong, rolled inward midlobe, and a hairy disc. The flowers have a short, straight to slightly curved, club-shaped column covered with soft hairs.
NOTE: These species differ from *Spiranthes* by their non-spiraling inflorescences and brightly colored flowers.

STENORRHYNCHUM

An orthographic variant introduced in *Flora*, **66**(1): 16 (1883). The correct spelling is *Stenorrhynchos*.

STENORRHYNCHUS

An orthographic variant introduced in *Dict. Class. Hist. Nat.*, **12**: 309 (1827). The correct spelling is *Stenorrhynchos*.

STENORRHYNCUS

An orthographic variant introduced in *Pl. Hartw.*, 92 (1842). The correct spelling is *Stenorrhynchos*.

STENORYNCHOS

An orthographic variant introduced in *The Lilies*, 398 (2000). The correct spelling is *Stenorrhynchos*.

STENORYNCHUS

An orthographic variant introduced in *Dict. Class. Hist. Nat.*, **11**: 515 (1827). The correct spelling is *Stenorrhynchos*.

STENORYNCHUS

Richard

De Orchid. Eur.   37 (1817).

Name published without a description. Today this name is most often referred to *Stenorrhynchos*.

STENOTYLA

Dressler

Lankesteriana   **5**(2): 96 (2005).

Epidendroideæ ⚬ Cymbidieæ • Zygopetalinæ

ETYMOLOGY: Greek for narrow and callus. Refers to the shape of the lip callus.

TYPE SPECIES: *Stenotyla lendyana*
(Reichenbach f.) Dressler
(*Chondrorhyncha lendyana* Reichenbach f.)

Three sympodial epiphytes are found in humid, low to mid elevation, hill scrub to montane cloud forests from southern Mexico (Chiapas and Oaxaca) to Panama. These fan-shaped plants have small, distinct pseudobulbs, subtended by overlapping, strap-shaped leaf bases, each with several, delicate, long, narrow leaves. The erect, solitary-flowered inflorescence has a

Currently Accepted   Validly Published   Invalidly Published   Published Pre-1753   Superfluous Usage   Orthographic Variant   Fossil

O r c h i d   G e n e r a   • **374**

lemon-yellow flower with narrow, recurved sepals and short, broad petals. The pale yellow, tubular, entire lip has a narrow, two or four-toothed, basal callus, deep maroon basal splash, a short chin, a recurved tip and a wavy margin. The flowers have a white, slightly curved column.

STENOROPSIS

An orthographic variant introduced in *Beih. Bot. Centralbl.*, **8**(4-5): 312 (1899). The correct spelling is *Stauropsis*.

STEPHANOTHELYS

Garay
Bradea   **2**(28): 199 (1977).

Orchidoideæ ⸱ Cranichideæ • Goodyerinæ

ETYMOLOGY: Greek for a crown or diadem and pertaining to woman. In reference to the prominent, trilobed rostellum that terminates the column as if it were a tiara.

TYPE SPECIES: *Stephanothelys xystophylloides*
(Garay) Garay
(*Erythrodes xystophylloides* Garay)

Three small, sympodial terrestrials are found in low to upper elevation, hill scrub to montane forests in the Andes of Colombia, Ecuador, Peru and Bolivia. These tall plants have secondary stems, each with several, well-spaced, narrow, dark green leaves that have a silver midvein. The erect, slender, smooth to hairy, few-flowered inflorescence has small, gray-yellow to pale yellow-white flowers. The trilobed lip has long, oblong side lobes; the small, arrow-head-shaped midlobe has a prominent notch at the tip, and strongly recurved tips. The long, cylindrical spur is slightly incurved. The flowers have a long, slender column.

STEREOCHILUS

Lindley
J. Proc. Linn. Soc., Bot.   **3**: 38 (1859).

Epidendroideæ ⸱ Vandeæ • Aeridinæ

ETYMOLOGY: Greek for solid, firm or tight and lip. Describing the texture of the bag-shaped lip.

TYPE SPECIES: *Stereochilus hirtus* Lindley

Seven monopodial epiphytes are found in low to mid elevation, hill woodlands and montane forests of northern India (Assam), Bhutan, Nepal to Myanmar and Thailand to Vietnam. These small plants have short stems, each with narrow, fleshy to leathery, bilobed leaves arranged in two ranks. The erect to hanging, few to numerous-flowered inflorescence has tiny, fleshy, drooping, short-lived, creamy-white to yellow, faintly fragrant flowers suffused with rose, and have a blotch of color at the tip of each segment. The flowers

are quite hairy on the outside surfaces and the bag-shaped, white, trilobed lip, attached to the column base, is often as long as the sepals and has a short, sac-like spur. The flowers have a long or short, erect, wingless, footless column.

STEREOSANDRA

Blume
Mus. Bot.   **2**(11): 176 (1856).

Epidendroideæ ⸱ Nervilieæ

ETYMOLOGY: Greek for solid or firm and stamen or male. Alluding to the firm texture of the anthers.

TYPE SPECIES: *Stereosandra javanica* Blume

One tiny, leafless, saprophyte is found in shady, humid, low to mid elevation, hill to montane evergreen forests from the eastern Himalayas to southern China (Yunnan), Taiwan, southern Japan (Ryukyu Islands), Thailand to Vietnam, Malaysia, Indonesia (Sumatra, Java and Borneo), New Guinea and the Solomons. This small, erect plant only grows to a height of 1¹/₂ inches (4 cm). The thin, pale yellow-white stem has purple streaks along its whole length and several, scale-like sheaths. The numerous to few-flowered inflorescence has downward hanging, white, violet or yellow flowers with similar, narrow sepals and petals and do not open fully. The white, purple tinged, deeply concave, entire lip has two warts located at the base, and has a wavy margin. The flowers have a short, club-shaped, footless column.

STETIS

An orthographic variant introduced in *Exot. Fl.*, **2**(22): t. 158 (1825). The correct spelling is *Stelis*.

STEVENIELLA

Schlechter
Repert. Spec. Nov. Regni Veg.   **15**: 292, 295 (1918).

Orchidoideæ ⸱ Orchideæ • Orchidinæ

ETYMOLOGY: Dedicated to Christian von Steven (1781-1863), a Finnish physician and botanist who collected flora from the Caucasus region of present day Russia and the Republic of Georgia. And Latin for diminutive.

TYPE SPECIES: *Steveniella satyrioides*
(Sprengel) Schlechter
(*Himantoglossum satyrioides* Sprengel)

One uncommon, sympodial terrestrial with a very restricted range is found in low to mid elevation, open piney woodlands and meadows bordering the eastern Black Sea from southern Ukraine (Krym), Ingushetiya, Georgia, Armenia and northern Turkey to northern Iran. This small, erect plant has brown-purple, unbranched

stems, each with one green leaf and two red, sheathing leafs at the stem base. The numerous-flowered inflorescence has small, dull green to green-yellow flowers splashed or suffused with purple. The small sepals and petals converge, forming a closed hood over the small, short, erect column. The green, tongue-shaped, trilobed lip, suffused pale brown, has short, rounded side lobes; the midlobe base is covered with fine red hairs and has a short, cone-shaped spur with a cleft tip.

STEVENORCHIS

Wankow & Kraenzlin
Repert. Spec. Nov. Regni Veg. Beih.   **65**: 45 (1931).

ETYMOLOGY: Dedicated to Christian von Steven (1781-1863). And Greek for orchid.

TYPE SPECIES: *Stevenorchis satyrioides*
(Sprengel) Wankow & Kraenzlin
(*Himantoglossum satyrioides* Sprengel)

A superfluous name proposed as a substitute for *Steveniella*.

STICHORCHIS

An orthographic variant introduced in *Hist. Orchid.*, Table 3, sub 3r, t. 88 (1822). The correct spelling is *Stichorkis*.

STICHORCKIS

An orthographic variant introduced in *Nomencl. Bot. (Pfeiffer)*, **2**(2): 1285 (1874). The correct spelling is *Stichorkis*.

STICHORKIS

Thouars
Nouv. Bull. Sci. Soc. Philom. Paris
1(19): 318 (1809).

Epidendroideæ ⸱ Malaxideæ

ETYMOLOGY: Greek for a row or rank and orchid. Refers to the two, distichous rows of bracts that characterize this genus.

LECTOTYPE: *Stichorkis disticha* (Thouars) Pfitzer
(*Malaxis disticha* Thouars)

Thirty-eight sympodial epiphytes, uncommon terrestrials or lithophytes are often found in low to upper elevation, dense to open montane rain forests and cliff faces of the Comoros Islands, Mauritius, Réunion, India, Myanmar, Sri Lanka, Indonesia and the Philippines. These plants have erect, pseudobulbous, one-noded stems, each with a solitary, long, narrow leaf. The erect, few-flowered inflorescence, subtended by several, distichous, overlapping bracts, has yellow, green or orange often translucent flowers. The flowers open in succession and have recurved sepals, with the lateral sepals united for part or all of their length. The erect petals are often narrow. The large, broad, flat, red-yellow, entire or lobed lip has a finely toothed or notched margin and a concave base. The flowers have a small, incurved or arching, slender, winged column.

STICTOPHYLLORCHIS

Dodson & Carnevali
Lindleyana   **8**(2): 101 (1993).
Epidendroideæ ⚬ Cymbidieæ • Oncidiinæ
ETYMOLOGY: *Stictophyllum*, a genus of orchids and Greek for orchid.
TYPE SPECIES: *Stictophyllorchis pygmaea*
       (Cogniaux) Dodson & Carnevali
       (*Ionopsis pygmaea* Cogniaux)

Two interesting, sympodial epiphytes are widespread in low elevation, rain forests from Trinidad, Venezuela, Ecuador (Napo) and Peru (Loreto) to northwestern Brazil. These minute, twig-like, fan-shaped plants have insignificant pseudobulbs, subtended by overlapping, distichous sheaths (upper two leaf-like, the lower thin and stiff), each with several, flat, pale green leaves spotted brown-red. The thread-like, branched, numerous-flowered inflorescence has tiny, tubular, white flowers not opening widely. The lateral sepals are united almost to their tips. The yellow, broad, trilobed lip has erect side lobes and a small, roundish midlobe. The flowers have a long, slightly curved, swollen in the middle, club-shaped, wingless column.

STICTOPHYLLUM

Dodson & M.W. Chase
Icon. Pl. Trop., ser. 2   **6**: 584 (1989).
Not *Stictophyllum* Edgewater (1845) Asteraceæ, not *Stictophyllum* Kutzing (1847) Algae, and not *Stictophyllum* Philippi (1860) Caryophyllaceæ.
ETYMOLOGY: Latin for spotted or punctured and leaf. In reference to the red spots on the tiny leaves.
TYPE SPECIES: *Stictophyllum pygmaeum*
       (Cogniaux) Dodson & M.W. Chase
       (*Ionopsis pygmaea* Cogniaux)

Not validly published because of a prior use of the name, this homonym was replaced by *Stictophyllorchis*.

STIGMATOCALYX

An orthographic variant introduced in *Handb. Syst. Bot.*, 913 (1924). The correct spelling is *Sigmatostalix*.

STIGMATARTHOS

An orthographic variant introduced in *Fragm. Florist. Geobot.*, **3**(Suppl.): 104 (1995). The correct spelling is *Stigmatorthos*.

STIGMATODACTYLUS

Maximowicz ex Makino
Ill. Fl. Jap.   **1**: *t. 43* (1891).
Orchidoideæ ⚬ Diurideæ • Acianthinæ
ETYMOLOGY: Greek for mark or spot and a finger. In reference to the finger-like projection in front of the column.
TYPE SPECIES: *Stigmatodactylus sikokianus*
       Maximowicz ex Makino

Eleven sympodial terrestrials are native in mid to upper elevation, moss laden rain forests of northeastern India (Assam), southern China (Hunan and Fujian), southern Japan, Taiwan, Indonesia (Borneo, Sulawesi and Maluku), Palau, central New Guinea and the Solomon Islands (Bougainville and Guadalcanal). The plants reproduce solely from seed. These uncommon, inconspicuous, minute plants have erect, unbranched stems, each with a solitary, tiny, ovate, veined leaf located midway up the stem and have a tiny, scale-like sheath at the base. The large, dark green, heart-shaped leaf has scalloped margins and is held well above the ground. The solitary to few-flowered inflorescence has small, dull white to pale green flowers with narrow petals and sepals. The broad, pale purple, entire lip has a large, entire to trilobed, basal callus ridge and keels, a deeply bilobed appendage and a notched margin. The flowers have an erect, footless column.

STIGMATORTHOS

M.W. Chase & D.E. Bennett
Lindleyana   **8**(1): 4 (1993).
Epidendroideæ ⚬ Cymbidieæ • Oncidiinæ
ETYMOLOGY: Greek for sign or mark and straight or erect. In reference to its narrow, slit-like shaped stigmatic cavity.
TYPE SPECIES: *Stigmatorthos peruviana*
       M.W. Chase & D.E. Bennett

One sympodial epiphyte is found in low elevation, rain forests of central Peru (Pasco). This small plant has clustered, ovoid pseudobulbs, subtended by sheathing bracts, each with a solitary, leathery leaf. The erect, branched, numerous-flowered inflorescence, has small, dark yellow-green flowers with continuous, pale brown lines. The fused lateral sepals form a nectary, are shortly attached to the lip base, and the petals are folded backward. The yellow-white, pencil-like, entire lip is more or less parallel to the long, slit-like stigma that is swollen near the base. The flowers have a straight column with a long foot that contributes to the nectar cavity.

STIGMATOSEMA

Garay
Bot. Mus. Leafl.   **28**(4): 376 (1980)[1982].
Orchidoideæ ⚬ Cranichideæ • Spiranthinæ
ETYMOLOGY: Greek for stigma or male and marking or standard. In reference to the large, flared rostellum.
TYPE SPECIES: *Stigmatosema hatschbachii*
       (Pabst) Garay
       (*Brachystele hatschbachii* Pabst)

Twelve small, inconspicuous, sympodial terrestrials or epiphytes are found in mid elevation, semi-deciduous, broad-leaved forests of Venezuela, eastern Brazil and Paraguay to northern Argentina (Misiones and Corrientes). These erect plants have delicate, unbranched stems, each with a basal rosette. The tall, slender, pale brown-red, hairy, numerous to few-flowered inflorescence has tiny to small, thinly textured, red to pale green flowers, subtended by narrow floral bracts, and the narrow sepals and petals are variously nerved. The white, shortly clawed to stalkless, obscurely trilobed lip has rounded side lobes and a triangular-shaped midlobe with two horn-like, fleshy, basal projections. The flowers have a short, straight, rather massive column with an obscure foot.

STILBOPHYLLUM

D.L. Jones & M.A. Clements
Orchadian   **14**(8: Sci. Suppl.): xv (2004).
ETYMOLOGY: Greek for glitter or glisten and leaf or petal. Refers to the appearance, texture, and shape of the tiny leaves.
TYPE SPECIES: *Stilbophyllum toressae*
       (F.M. Bailey) D.L. Jones & M.A. Clements
       (*Bulbophyllum toressae* F.M. Bailey)

Recognized as belonging to the genus *Dendrobium*, *Stilbophyllum* was proposed to include one epiphyte or lithophyte found in humid, low elevation, coastal gorges and tablelands of northeastern Australia (Queensland). This minute plant often forms dense mats with its creeping rhizomes adhering to trees or rocks. The small, distichous, ovate to narrow leaves (about the size and shape of a grain of wheat) are quite concave with a solitary, nearly yellow-white flower borne at the base. The translucent, red-tinged flower is subtended by a large bract. The lateral sepals are joined to the column foot, forming a short, blunt, almost squarish spur. The bright yellow, obscurely trilobed lip has a wide, red-marked, channel between the side lobes and the short, blunt midlobe is quite thick at the tip. The flowers have a very short, yellow, winged column. This species was formerly included in *Dendrobium*.

Currently Accepted   Validly Published   Invalidly Published   Published Pre-1753   Superfluous Usage   Orthographic Variant   Fossil

O r c h i d   G e n e r a   • **376**

STILIFOLIUM

Königer & Pongratz

Arcula **7**: 186 (1997).

ETYMOLOGY: Latin for pencil and leaf-like. Referring to the terete leaves of the type species.

TYPE SPECIES: *Stilifolium cebolleta*
(Jacquin) Königer & Pongratz
(*Epidendrum cebolleta* Jacquin)

Now recognized as belonging to the genus *Trichocentrum*, *Stilifolium* was previously considered to include nine epiphytes widespread in hot, low to mid elevation, grasslands and forests with a fairly long, dry period from the southeastern United States (Florida) to Mexico, Panama to Brazil and Paraguay. These often hanging plants have small, short, squatty to tubular pseudobulbs, subtended by large, white sheaths, each with several, long, narrow, dull gray-green, fleshy leaves. The simple to short branched, numerous-flowered inflorescence has brown-yellow to yellow flowers with dark brown markings. The bright yellow, trilobed lip has widespreading side lobes varying in size, and the broad midlobe has small, oblong lobes often overlapping with a ridged callus. The flowers have a short, erect column.

STIGMEGAS

Rafinesque

Fl. Tellur. **4**: 45 (1836)[1837].

Name ICBN rejected vs. *Paphiopedilum* Pfitzer (1886) Orchidaceæ.

ETYMOLOGY: A blend or mix of Greek for stigma and large. Descriptive of the swollen tip of the column with the trilobed stigma.

TYPE SPECIES: *Stimegas venustum*
(Wallich ex Sims) Rafinesque
(*Cypripedium venustum* Wallich ex Sims)

Although validly published this rejected name is now referred to *Paphiopedilum*. *Stimegas* was considered to include one epiphyte found in northern India, Nepal, Bangladesh and Myanmar. This plant has short stems, each with several, broad, dull to almost rough leaves mottled dark and pale green on top and densely spotted purple underneath. The tall, solitary-flowered inflorescence has a most unusual, variable-colored, waxy flower. The broad, white dorsal sepal is lined with green; the widespreading petals are green at their base fading to pink toward the tips and are lined dark green, sprinkled with black to maroon spots or hairy warts. The green-bronze to yellow, pouch-shaped (synsepal) lip is suffused purple and veined dark green.

STNORHYNCHUS

An orthographic variant introduced in *Séance Publique Soc. Argic.*, 194 (1852). The correct spelling is *Stenorhynchus*.

STOLZIA

Schlechter

Bot. Jahrb. Syst. **53**: 564 (1915).

Epidendroideæ ❦ Podochileæ • Eriinæ

ETYMOLOGY: In honor of Adolf Ferdinand Stolz (1871-1917), a South African who worked as a clerk in a German East-Africa mission (Kyimbila), plantation manager, and botanist who lived, worked and collected flora in present day Tanzania (Nyassaland).

TYPE SPECIES: *Stolzia nyassana* Schlechter

Fifteen sympodial epiphytes or rare lithophytes are found in very restricted, mid elevation, montane evergreen forests and woodlands of Ethiopia, Uganda, Malawi, Tanzania and Zimbabwe. These species may often resemble small *Bulbophyllums*. These tiny, creeping plants resemble a mossy carpet (forming extensive mats which sometimes cover entire tree trunks and branches) and have ovoid, club or spindled-shaped pseudobulbous stems, each with one or two, fleshy or thinly leathery, spreading or erect, oval to tongue-shaped leaves. The solitary to few-flowered inflorescence has a bell-shaped, yellow-green, green-yellow, yellow, bright orange or red flower not widely opening and striped red or brown. The large lateral sepals are more or less united in the basal part, forming a distinct, chin-like protuberance with the long, incurved column foot. The fleshy, curved, V-shaped, entire lip is enclosed within the lateral sepals and often has soft protuberances. The flowers have a short, fleshy, wingless column.

STRATEUMA

Salisbury

Trans. Hort. Soc. London **1**: 290 (1812).

ETYMOLOGY: Greek for army, military company or campaign. Taken from the name of the type species *Orchis militaris* Linnaeus.

TYPE SPECIES: *None designated*

Now recognized as belonging to the genus *Orchis*, *Strateuma* Salisbury was previously considered to include two terrestrials found from Britain to Poland, Spain to Romania, and Sweden to central Russia (West Siberia). This erect plant has unbranched stems, each with several, leaves forming a basal rosette. The erect, densely packed, few-flowered inflorescence has pale lilac to purple flowers with darker colored veins. The dorsal sepal and tongue-shaped petals converge, forming a hood over the small column. The pink to purple, deeply trilobed lip has dark hairs at the base and has a long, club-shaped spur.

STRATEUMA

Rafinesque

Fl. Tellur. **2**: 89 (1836)[1837].

Not *Strateuma* Salisbury (1812) Orchidaceæ.

ETYMOLOGY: Greek for army or military company. Taken from the name of the type species, *Orchis strateumatica*. In reference to the habit that fancifully gives it the appearance of marching men.

TYPE SPECIES: *Strateuma zeylanica* Rafinesque nom. illeg.
Zeuxine strateumatica (Linnaeus) Schlechter
(*Orchis strateumatica* Linnaeus)

Not validly published because of a prior use of the name, this homonym was replaced by *Zeuxine*.

STREPHOGYNE

An orthographic variant introduced in *Handb. Gewachsk.*, ed. 2, **2**(2): 1563 (1829). The correct spelling is *Streptogyne*.

STREPTOGYNE

(Reichenbach) Reichenbach

Deut. Bot. Herb.-Buch 50 (1841).

Not *Streptogyne* Poiret (1827) Poaceæ.

ETYMOLOGY: Greek for twisted and woman or female. Refers to the shape of the twisted ovary.

TYPE SPECIES: *None designated*

Not validly published because of a prior use of the name, this homonym was replaced by *Dactylorhiza*.

STREPTOURA

Luer

Monogr. Syst. Bot. Missouri Bot. Gard. **105**: 16 (2006).

ETYMOLOGY: Greek for twisted and brightly colored. Refers to the thick, twisted, corkscrew-like sepal tails.

TYPE SPECIES: *Streptoura caudivolvula*
(Kraenzlin) Luer
(*Masdevallia caudivolvula* Kraenzlin)

Recognized as belonging to the genus *Masdevallia*, *Streptoura* was proposed to include one epiphyte or lithophyte found in mid elevation, montane forests of central Colombia (Antioquia). This tufted, erect plant, often forming clumps, has short, erect, black stems, subtended by thin, tubular sheaths, each with a solitary, oblong, leathery leaf. The long, solitary-flowered inflorescence has a brown, cup-shaped flower with the long sepals markedly thickened along the veins on the inner surfaces, tapering into thick, rigid, twisted tails, and the callous, minute, white petals lack a tooth. The small, white, tiny hinged, entire lip is divided by lateral folds into a hypochile, a smooth to minutely notched epichile and is purple-dotted. The flowers have a stout, slightly curved, more or less club-shaped column with a long foot.

STRIANGIS

Thouars

Hist. Orchid.   Table 2, sub 3o, *t. 72* (1822).

Name published without a description. Today this name is most often referred to *Angraecum.*

STROBELIA

Senghas

Orchideen (Schlechter), ed. 3   **1/B**(29): 1778 (1994).

ETYMOLOGY: Named for James W. Strobel (1933-), an American horticultural expert at the universities of North Carolina and Florida, President at Mississippi University for Women and University of South Carolina, and an avid orchid collector.

TYPE SPECIES: *Strobelia elegans* Senghas

This type name is now considered a synonym of *Maxillaria pulla* Linden & Reichenbach f.

Not validly published, this name is referred to *Maxillaria. Strobelia* was proposed to include one epiphyte found from Colombia to Bolivia.

SYRONGYLERIA

An orthographic variant introduced in *Orchid.-Buch*, 570 (1892). The correct spelling is *Eria.*

STURMIA

Reichenbach

Iconogr. Bot. Pl. Crit.   **4**: 39 (1826).

Not *Sturmia* Hoppe (1799) Poaceæ, and not
    Sturmia C.F. Gaertner (1823) Rubiaceæ.

ETYMOLOGY: Probably commemorating Jakob Strum (1771-1848), a German botanical artist and engraver from Nürnberg who produced thousands of plates and drawings of German flora and fauna.

TYPE SPECIES: *Sturmia loeselii* (Linnaeus) Reichenbach
    (*Ophrys loeselii* Linnaeus)

Not validly published because of a prior use of the name, this homonym was replaced by *Liparis.*

STYLOGLOSSUM

Breda

Gen. Sp. Orchid. Asclep., fasc. II   *t. 7* (1829).

ETYMOLOGY: Greek for pillar or column and tongue. Alluding to the attachment of the lip to the column.

TYPE SPECIES: *Styloglossum nervosa* Breda
    This type name is now considered a synonym of
        Calanthe pulchra (Blume) Lindley;
            basionym
        Amblyglottis pulchra Blume

Now recognized as belonging to the genus *Calanthe, Styloglossum* was previously considered to include one terrestrial found in humid, low to mid elevation, hill scrub and montane forests of southern India, Indonesia and Malaysia to the Philippines. The plants have clustered, small to almost absent pseudobulbs, subtended by leaf sheaths, each with several, narrow to broad, pleated leaves. The erect, numerous-flowered inflorescence has pale yellow, orange to pale pink flowers not opening widely. The trilobed lip has a fan-shaped midlobe, has small, oblong side lobes, and a short, curved spur that is hook-like. The flowers have a small, fleshy, blunt column.

STYLOGLOTTIS

An orthographic variant introduced in *Fl. Ned. Ind.*, **3**: 709 (1860). The correct spelling is *Styloglossum.*

STYRIUM

An orthographic variant introduced in *Fl. Taiwan*, **5**: 930 (1978). The correct spelling is *Satyrium.*

SU

Kaempfer

Am. Exot.   *t. 864* (1712).

ETYMOLOGY: A local, Japanese vernacular name for this type of orchid.

TYPE SPECIES: *Su ran* Kaempfer

Pre-1753, therefore not validly published in fulfillment of nomenclatural rules; this binomial name is most often referred to *Epipactis. Su* was previously considered to include one terrestrial found in damp, mid elevation, meadows, grasslands and along river banks from eastern Russia (Primorye), Korea, Japan and northern China (Heilongjiang). This erect, tall plant, often forming large clumps, has several, well-spaced, narrow, deeply furrowed, pale green leaves clasping the unbranched, rigid stem. The few-flowered inflorescence has each solitary, drooping, showy, yellow flower well-spaced along the rachis. The white, trilobed lip is spotted or speckled red-purple and has an inrolled margin. This name is now usually considered as a synonym of *Epipactis thunbergii* A. Gray.

SUAREZIA

Dodson

Icon. Pl. Trop., ser. 2   **6**: *t. 585* (1989).

Epidendroideæ • Cymbidieæ • Oncidiinæ

ETYMOLOGY: Dedicated to Carola Alejandro Suarez née Lindberg (1955-), an Ecuadorian illustrator of the local flora and people, and plant collector.

TYPE SPECIES: *Suarezia ecuadorana* Dodson

One sympodial epiphyte is found in wet, low elevation, forests and scrub of eastern Ecuador (Napo and Morona-Santiago). This small, tufted, fan-shaped plant has clustered, ovate pseudobulbs, subtended by overlapping, leaf sheaths, each with a solitary, narrow leaf. The long, solitary to few-flowered inflorescence has small, yellow-green, cup-shaped flowers with widespreading lateral sepals. The obscurely trilobed lip has erect, shallowly triangular side lobes. The blunt, triangular midlobe is slightly recurved and has flattened calli channeled down the center. The flowers have an erect, curved column with a horn on each side of the stigma.

SULLIVANIA

F. Mueller

J. Proc. Roy. Soc. New South Wales   **15**: 229 (1882).

Not *Sullivania* O. Varol (1992) Fossil.

ETYMOLOGY: Dedicated to David Sullivan (1836-1895), an Australian school master and naturalist who collected the flora of Victoria and Tasmania.

LECTOTYPE: *Caleya sullivanii* F. Mueller

Not validly published, this name is referred to *Caleana. Sullivania* was considered to include one terrestrial found in southwestern Australia (Victoria).

Currently Accepted   Validly Published   Invalidly Published   Published Pre-1753   Superfluous Usage   Orthographic Variant   Fossil

Orchid Genera • **378**

SULPITIA

Rafinesque

Fl. Tellur. **4**: 37 (1836)[1837].

ETYMOLOGY: Named for *Sulpicia* (AD 69-96), a Roman poet who was the daughter of Servius Sulpicius Rufus and ward of Valerius Messalla Corvinus. She wrote six short love elegies that have survived from the classical period; these poems were long thought to have been written by Tibellus.

TYPE SPECIES: *Sulpitia odorata* Rafinesque nom. illeg.
Encyclia patens Hooker

Now recognized as belonging to the genus *Encyclia*, *Sulpitia* was previously considered to include one epiphyte found in cool, low to mid elevation, hill scrub and montane forests of southeastern Brazil (Rio Grande do Sul, Bahia and Minas Gerais). This plant has clustered, pseudobulbous stems, each with several, strap-like, leathery leaves. The hanging, numerous to few-flowered inflorescence has fragrant, long-lived flowers with widespreading, green petals that are with or without brown streaks. The creamy white, trilobed lip, attached to the column tip, has a green base with streaks of red, has roundish side lobes; and has an ovate midlobe that is sometimes bilobed at the tip. The flowers have a slender, straight, club-shaped column.

SUMMERHAYESIA

P.J. Cribb

Kew Bull. **32**(1): 184 (1977).

Epidendroideæ ⬙ Vandeæ • Aerangidinæ

ETYMOLOGY: In honor of Victor Samuel Summerhayes (1897-1974), a British chemist, curator at the Royal Botanic Gardens at Kew, an expert on African flora, and author of *Wild Orchids of Britain*.

TYPE SPECIES: *Summerhayesia laurentii*
(De Wildeman) P.J. Cribb
(*Angraecum laurentii* De Wildeman)

Two monopodial epiphytes or occasionally lithophytes are found in low elevation, woodlands and evergreen forests of tropical Africa from Liberia to Zaire and Rwanda, Malawi, Zambia, Tanzania to Zimbabwe. These small plants have short, leafy stems, each with distichous, leathery to fleshy leaves. The leaves have unequally bilobed tips, are arranged in two rows along the stem and have numerous, aerial roots. The erect or arching, few-flowered inflorescence, borne from the leaf axils, has large bracts and bold, striking white, creamy to pale yellow, fleshy flowers. Outside floral segments have scattered, sparse, short, rust-colored hairs. The ovate lateral sepals are joined at the base enclosing the spur. The concave, boat-shaped, hooded, uppermost, entire lip has a slender, long, cylindrical spur. The flowers have a short, stout, footless column.

SUNIPIA

Buchanan-Hamilton ex Smith

Cycl. (Rees) **34**: See *Stelis* items #11 & 13 (1816).

Epidendroideæ ⬙ Dendrobiinæ • Currently unplaced

ETYMOLOGY: Sunipiang is a local vernacular name used for the plant in Nepal (a kingdom located on the northeastern border of India).

TYPE SPECIES: *None designated*

Twenty-two sympodial epiphytes are found in cool, mid to upper elevation, montane forests from northern India (Sikkim), Nepal, Bhutan, southern China (Yunnan), Myanmar to Vietnam and Taiwan. These plants have well-spaced or clustered, ovoid pseudobulbs, each with a solitary, oblong, leathery leaf. The short or long, numerous to few-flowered inflorescence has small to medium-sized, pale green to creamy flowers, usually not showy, with purple veins. The lateral sepals are free or more or less variously united. The purple to yellow-green, tongue-shaped, obscurely trilobed or entire lip has papillae and is with or without a basal callus. The flowers have a short, fleshy, footless column. These species superficially resemble *Bulbophyllum* in both their habit and flowers, but are easily distinguished by the unusual structure of their pollinia being held in pairs.

NOTE: These species have been variously shuttled between the genera *Sunipia*, *Ione* and *Bulbophyllum*.

SUPERBANGIS

Thouars

Hist. Orchid. Table 2, sub 3o, tt. 62-64 (1822).

Name published without a description. Today this name is most often referred to *Angraecum*.

SURIPIA

An orthographic variant introduced in *Syn. Pl. (D. Dietrich)*, **5**: 91 (1852). The correct spelling is *Sunipia*.

SUTRINA

Lindley

Ann. Mag. Nat. Hist. **10**: 184 (1842).

Epidendroideæ ⬙ Cymbidieæ • Oncidiinæ

ETYMOLOGY: Greek for belonging to a cobbler's shop. Descriptive of the gland that resembles a long bristle and projects beyond the column.

TYPE SPECIES: *Sutrina bicolor* Lindley

Two quite small, inconspicuous sympodial epiphytes are found in mid elevation, montane forests of Peru and Bolivia. These plants have tiny pseudobulbs, subtended by overlapping, leaf-bearing sheaths, each with one to two, leathery leaves at the tip. The short, numerous-flowered inflorescence has tiny, green-yellow, tubular flowers not opening fully. The lateral sepals are joined at the base forming a chin-like protuberance. The lemon-yellow, boat-shaped, flared, entire lip is streaked with red-brown veins and has a finely serrated margin. The flowers have a short, arching, wingless, footless column.

SUTRINIA

An orthographic variant introduced in *Syn. Pl. (D. Dietrich)*, **5**: 12, 111 (1852). The correct spelling is *Sutrina*.

SVENKOELTZIA

Burns-Balogh

Orchidee (Hamburg) **40**(1): 12 (1989).

Orchidoideæ ⬙ Cranichideæ • Spiranthinæ

ETYMOLOGY: Named in honor of Sven Koeltz (1941-), a German publisher of botanical books and classic reprints in the fields of botany and zoology.

TYPE SPECIES: *Svenkoeltzia congestiflora*
(L.O. Williams) Burns-Balogh
(*Spiranthes congestiflora* L.O. Williams)

Three sympodial terrestrials or lithophytes are found in humid, mid to upper elevation, montane cloud, pine-oak and semi-forested canyons of western Mexico (Michoacán and Jalisco). These erect plants have unbranched stems, each with a basal rosette of leaves usually absent at the time of flowering. The leaves usually develop after flowering. The erect, head-like to long, yellow-green, numerous to few-flowered inflorescence has large, bright yellow, slightly hairy, tubular, yellow flowers that are nerved and subtended by long, narrow, hairy bracts. The congested flowers all face the same direction on the rachis. The oblong, spoon-like, obscurely trilobed lip has a central hairy disc with a curled, under tip, and has a small spur. The flowers have a straight, slightly club-shaped, smooth or hairy, winged, rather massive column that is dilated at the base. These species are often included in *Funkiella*.

SYCHMATOSTALIX

An orthographic variant introduced in *Gart.-Zeitung*, **1**: 464 (1882). The correct spelling is *Sigmatostalix*.

SYLCALISMIS

An orthographic variant introduced in *Revis. Gen. Pl.*, **2**: 650 (1891). The correct spelling is *Slyvalismis*.

SYLOBIUM

An orthographic variant introduced in *Bot. Centralbl.*, **80**(13): 505 (1899). The correct spelling is *Xylobium*.

SYLPHIA

Luer

Monogr. Syst. Bot. Missouri Bot. Gard. **105**: 227, f. 179 (2006).

ETYMOLOGY: Latin for spirit or graceful nymphs. The term originated with Paracelsus (Theophrastus Philippus Aureolus Bombastus von Hohenheim) (1493-1541), an early Swiss physician and chemist who described sylphs as invisible beings of the air.

TYPE SPECIES: *Sylphia turrialbae* (Luer) Luer (*Pleurothallis turrialbae* Luer)

Recognized as belonging to the genus *Specklinia*, *Sylphia* was proposed to include four epiphytes found in mid elevation, montane forests from Honduras to Colombia. These tiny, tufted plants, often forming dense clumps, have short stems, subtended by thin, ribbed, tubular sheaths, each with a solitary, narrow, leathery leaf. The wiry, zig-zagging, solitary-flowered inflorescence, blooming successively, has a yellow to yellow-green flower mottled and suffused with purple. The long, yellow, tailed sepals are united for a short distance and has small petals. The purple, oblong, trilobed lip has erect side lobes, a small, recurved midlobe with an orange tip, covered with warts and has a rounded tip. The flowers have a long to short, slightly curved, winged column.

SYLVALISIMIS

An orthographic variant introduced in *Hist. Orchid.*, Table 1, sub 2l (1822). The correct spelling is *Sylvalismis*.

SYLVALISMIS

Thouars

Hist. Orchid. Table 1, sub 2l, tt. 35-36 (1822).

Name published without a description. Today this name is most often referred to *Phaius*.

SYLVALISMUS

An orthographic variant cited in *Lex. Gen. Phan.*, 544 (1904). The correct spelling is *Sylvalismis*.

SYLVORCHIS

An orthographic variant introduced in *Repert. Spec. Nov. Regni Veg.*, **1**(1): xvii (1914). The correct spelling is *Silvorchis*.

SYMMERIA

Not *Symmeria* Bentham & Hooker f. (1845) Polygonaceæ.

An orthographic variant introduced in *Fl. Brit. Ind.*, **6**: 142 (1890). The correct spelling is *Synmeria*.

SYMPHYGLOSSUM

Schlechter

Orchis **13**: 8 (1919).

Name ICBN conserved vs. *Symphyoglossum* Turczaninow (1848) Asclepiadaceæ.

ETYMOLOGY: Greek for to grown together and tongue. Alluding to the strong attachment of the lip to the column.

TYPE SPECIES: *Symphyglossum sanguineum* (Reichenbach f.) Schlechter (*Mesospinidium sanguineum* Reichenbach f.)

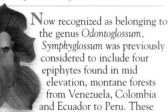

Now recognized as belonging to the genus *Odontoglossum*, *Symphyglossum* was previously considered to include four epiphytes found in mid elevation, montane forests from Venezuela, Colombia and Ecuador to Peru. These plants, often forming dense clumps, have tightly clustered, ovoid to oblong, compressed, gray-green pseudobulbs, subtended by distichous, leaf sheaths, each with one to two leaves at the tip. The variable, simple or few-branched, arching to hanging, numerous-flowered inflorescence has showy, long-lived, crimson, rosy-purple, yellow-brown or pale green flowers with a concave dorsal sepal. The lateral sepals are joined from the base to just beyond the middle. The small, white to pale colored, shortly clawed, entire lip has a white callus. The flowers have a tiny, white, straight, winged, footless column.

SYMPHYOGLOSSUM

Not *Symphyoglossum* Turczaninow (1848) Asclepiadaceæ.

An orthographic variant cited in *Pl. Alkaloids*, 163 (1996). The correct spelling is *Symphyglossum*.

SYMPHYOSEPALUM

Handel-Mazzetti

Symb. Sin. **7**(4-5): 1327 (1936).

ETYMOLOGY: Greek for to grow together and Latin for sepal. In reference to the sepals that are connected for a third of their length.

TYPE SPECIES: *Symphyosepalum gymnadenioides* Handel-Mazzetti

Now recognized as belonging to the genus *Neottianthe*, *Symphyosepalum* was previously considered to include one terrestrial found in upper elevation, montane bamboo forests of southern China (Guangdong, Sichuan, Xizang and Yunnan). This uncommon, small, erect plant has unbranched stems, each with two narrow leaves grouped above the base. The tall, numerous-flowered inflorescence has purple-red or pink flowers not opening widely. The sepals are joined for a third of their length, and the short, narrow petals have margins with minute hairs. The drooping, trilobed, entire or bilobed lip has a broad, tapering, cone-shaped to cylindrical spur with a horseshoe-shaped swelling at the mouth that has numerous, soft glands at the base. The flowers have a short, broad, wingless column.

SYMPTERA

An orthographic variant introduced in *Orchid.-Buch*, 570 (1892). The correct spelling is *Synptera*.

SYNADENA

Rafinesque

Fl. Tellur. **4**: 9 (1836)[1837].

ETYMOLOGY: Greek for united or with and gland. Alluding to the large callus which is undivided.

TYPE SPECIES: *Synadena amabilis* (Linnaeus) Rafinesque (*Epidendrum amabile* Linnaeus)

Now recognized as belonging to the genus *Phalaenopsis*, *Synadena* was previously considered to include one epiphyte widespread from western Indonesia, New Guinea and northern Australia to the Philippines. This plant has short, robust stems, each with a few leathery or fleshy leaves that have a slightly red cast. The arching, numerous to few-flowered inflorescence has showy, large, fragrant, pristine white flowers sometimes suffused pale pink. The trilobed (in the basal half) lip with variable yellow and red markings has erect side lobes, and the cross-shaped midlobe has two, whip-like tendrils. The flowers have an erect, short, cylindrical, wingless column.

Currently Accepted   Validly Published   Invalidly Published   Published Pre-1753   Superfluous Usage   Orthographic Variant   Fossil

Orchid Genera • **380**

SYNANDENA

An orthographic variant introduced in *Malayan Nat. J.*, **36**(1): 18 (1982). The correct spelling is *Synadena*.

SYNANTHES

Burns-Balogh, H. Robinson & Merc.S. Foster

Brittonia **37**(1): 158 (1985).

Orchidoideæ ※ Cranichideæ • Spiranthinæ

ETYMOLOGY: Greek for together and flower. In reference to the tightly packed group of flowers and the column structure.

TYPE SPECIES: *Synanthes bertonii*
Burns-Balogh, H. Robinson & Merc.S. Foster

Two sympodial terrestrials are found in mid elevation, temperate forests from Paraguay and Mexico (Chiapas), Belize to Nicaragua usually growing in dense mosses. These plants have short, erect, unbranched stems, each with a basal rosette of large leaves (often obscured by the moss). These leaves have water-filled cells, warty undersides and hairy outer margins. The head-like, tightly packed, numerous-flowered inflorescence has narrow, tubular, green flowers which face toward the center of the inflorescence. The slightly sickle-shaped lateral sepals are joined at the base, and the oblong, clawed, entire lip has a fleshy tip. These species are mosquito-pollinated. The flowers have a long, slender column.

SYNARMOSEPALUM

Garay, Hamer & Siegerist

Nordic J. Bot. **14**(6): 639 (1994).

ETYMOLOGY: Greek for to join together and sepals. In reference to the three fused sepals.

TYPE SPECIES: *Synarmosepalum kittredgei*
Garay, Hamer & Siegerist

Now recognized as belonging to the genus *Bulbophyllum*, *Synarmosepalum* was proposed to include two epiphytes found in mid to upper elevation, montane tree mosses of southern Malaysia (Sabah) and southern Philippines. These small, usually hanging plants have small to tiny, ovoid pseudobulbs, each with a solitary, rather large, thick, dark green leaf suffused purple or red on the underside. The short, numerous to few-flowered inflorescence, nestled under the leaves, has conspicuous, deep purple, cup-shaped flowers not opening widely with tiny petals. The small sepals are fused for a short distance or are united almost to their sharp tips. The tiny to minute, recurved, entire lip is found tucked inside the united sepals. The flowers have a short, footless column.

SYNASSA

Lindley

Edwards's Bot. Reg. **19**: sub 1618 (1833).

ETYMOLOGY: Greek for together and nearer. Refers to the closeness of the petals and dorsal sepals.

TYPE SPECIES: *Synassa corymbosa* Lindley

Now recognized as belonging to the genus *Sauroglossum*, *Synassa* was previously considered to include two terrestrials found in mid to upper elevation, montane forests and woodlands of Peru and Bolivia. These erect, tall, slender plants have unbranched stems, each with several, narrow, basal leaves. The long, whip-like, terminal, numerous-flowered inflorescence has small, golden-yellow to orange-yellow flowers do not open fully and whose outside segments are covered with fine hairs. The shortly clawed, trilobed lip has thick, wing-like lobes and has a sac-like spur. The flowers have a long, slender, slightly curved column.

SYNMERIA

Nimmo

Graham's *Cat. Pl. Bombay* addenda, page sine numero (1839).

ETYMOLOGY: Greek for together and part. Refers to the two petals that are united with the dorsal sepal forming a helmet-shaped hood.

TYPE SPECIES: *Synmeria schizochilus* (Nimmo) Nimmo
(*Habenaria schizochilus* Nimmo)

Now recognized as belonging to the genus *Habenaria*, *Synmeria* was previously considered to include one terrestrial found in seasonally dry, mid elevation, deciduous to evergreen forests from Bhutan, India and Sri Lanka. This leafy, erect plant has unbranched stems, each with a few-flowered inflorescence borne at the tip of the stem. The showy, white flowers have small sepals and petals that converge, forming a hood over the tiny column. The conspicuous four-lobed lip is longer than the sepals with widespreading, curved side lobes forming long tails. The shortly clawed, bilobed midlobe has widespreading lobes with long tails, and the slender, curved spur is longer than the sepals. The above type name is now considered a synonym of *Habenaria crinifera* Lindley.

SYNOPLECTRIS

Rafinesque

Fl. Tellur. **2**: 89 (1836)[1837].

ETYMOLOGY: Greek for united or with and a spur. Referring to the tube-like spur formed by the lateral sepals.

LECTOTYPE: *Synoplectris viridis* Rafinesque nom. illeg.
Sarcoglottis grandiflora (Hooker) Klotzsch
(*Neottia grandiflora* Hooker)

Now recognized as belonging to the genus *Sarcoglottis*, *Synoplectris* was previously considered to include two terrestrials found in seasonally dry, low to mid elevation, hill scrub and montane forests of El Salvador, Costa Rica, Venezuela, the Guianas, Brazil, Ecuador, Peru and Argentina (Corrientes and Misiones). These erect plants have unbranched stems, each with several leaves in a basal rosette that remain during flowering. The erect, few-flowered inflorescence has flowers with green to pale yellow-green sepals and white to yellow petals. The strongly recurved, shortly clawed, entire lip has green nerves.

SYNOSSA

An orthographic variant cited in *Hist. Nat. Veg.* (*Spach*), **12**: 181 (1846). The correct spelling is *Synassa*.

SYNPHYGLOSSUM

An orthographic variant introduced in *Orchis*, **13**: 8 (1919). The correct spelling is *Symphyglossum*.

SYNPTERA

Llanos

Fragm. Pl. Filip. 98 (1851).

ETYMOLOGY: Greek for together and wing. Refers to the swollen base of the lateral sepals.

TYPE SPECIES: *Synptera subviolacea* Llanos
This type name is now considered a synonym of *Trichoglottis subviolacea* (Llanos) Merrill;
basionym
Synptera subviolacea Llanos

Now recognized as belonging to the genus *Trichoglottis*, *Synptera* was previously considered to include one epiphyte found in low elevation, coastal woodlands of the Philippines. This slender, hanging plant has slender stems, each with several, narrow, leathery leaves. The short, few-flowered inflorescence, borne from the leaf axils, has small, fragrant, yellow flowers sprinkled with brown spots. The trilobed lip has small side lobes, the heart-shaped, flat midlobe has a slightly hairy, basal callus and a sac-like spur.

SYSTELOGLOSSUM

Schlechter

Repert. Spec. Nov. Regni Veg. Beih. **19**: 252 (1923).

Epidendroideæ ⁜ Cymbidieæ • Oncidiinæ

ETYMOLOGY: Greek for to draw together and tongue. Alluding to the margins of the lip, which are united with the column.

TYPE SPECIES: *Systeloglossum costaricense* Schlechter

Five uncommon, sympodial epiphytes are found in wet, low to mid elevation, rain forests from Costa Rica to Peru. These plants have elliptical to ovoid, smooth, laterally compressed pseudobulbs, subtended by leaf-like bracts, each with a solitary, oblong leaf. The erect, few-flowered inflorescence produces flowers one by one in slow succession. The somewhat fleshy, small flowers are found in shades of green or bronzy-green. The blunt dorsal sepal is joined to the base of the petals, and the lateral sepals are united, forming a two-keeled, ovate, shallowly notched synsepal. The keeled petals are joined to the base of the column and are lightly turned backward. The arched, long-clawed, entire lip is slightly notched at the tip and has two, rounded, soft, green protuberances. The flowers have a short, straight column with a conspicuous hood.

SZLACHETKOELLA

Mytnik

Richardiana **7**(2): 57 (2007).

ETYMOLOGY: Named for Dariusz Lucjan Szlachetko (1961-) a Polish botanist and professor of plant taxonomy and nature conservation at the Gdansk University. And Latin for diminutive.

TYPE SPECIES: *Szlachetkoella mystacioides*
(De Wildeman) Mytnik
(*Polystachya mystacioides* De Wildeman)

Recognized as belonging to the genus *Polystachya*, *Szlachetkoella* was proposed to include one epiphyte or terrestrial found in humid, low to mid elevation, savannas and scrub from Ivory Coast to Rwanda. These small, creeping or hanging plants have small pseudobulbs, each with numerous, fleshy, ovate leaves. The solitary-flowered inflorescence has a white flower suffused red or purple with hairy sepals and smaller, triangular petals. The large, obscurely trilobed lip has small side lobes and an oblong midlobe. The trilobed lip has small side lobes and an oblong, shallowly notched midlobe. The flowers have a long column.

Thouars
Histoire Particulière des Plantes Orchidees
table three (1822).

TROISIÈME TABLEAU DES ESPÈCES D'ORCHIDÉES
RECUEILLIES SUR LES ILES AUSTRALES D'AFRIQUE.

Espèce	LIEU	TEMPS	TIGE	POSIT.	FORME	SOMM.	LONG.	LARG.	FLEUR.
1 Volucre	B. M.	juin.	18 p.	écart.	ovoid.	aigu.	1 p.	1/2.	gr. blanche.
2 Polystachion	B. M.	juill.	18 p.	écart.	ruban	bilob.	2 p.	1/6.	moy. blanc.
3 Macrostachion	B.		12 p.	rappr.	rub.	bil.	3 p.	1/8.	moy. blanc.
4 Brachistachion	F.		6 p.	rappr.	rub.	bil.	4 p.	1/8.	gr. blanc.
1 Polystachion, Sw.	F. B.		2 p.	rappr.	ovoid.	bil.	18 p.	1/6.	pet. purp. jaunâtre.
2 Fusiforme	F. B.	sept.	6 p.	biné.	oblon.	bil.	8 li.	1/5.	moy. blanc. taché.
3 Cultriforme	F. B.	sept.	6 p.	uniq.	ovoid.	bil.	5 li.	1/6.	moy. blanc.
Arachnites	F. B.	févr.	4 p.	rap.	rub.	bil.	4 p.	1/6.	gr. blanc jaunâtre.
1 Disticha	F. B.	mars.	5 p.	uniq.	oval.	aigu.	4 p.	1/6.	pet. verd.
2 Caespitosa	F. B. M.		2-3 p.	unig.	oval.	bil.	18 li.	1/4.	moy. pourp. obscur.
1 Scandens	F. B. M.	nov.	5 p.	biné.	oval.	bil.	3 p.	1/6.	très-pet. verd.
1 Equitans	M.		4 p.	unig.	oval.	bil.	5 li.	1/4.	pet. rouge obscur.
1 Occultum		avril.	6 p.	biné.	rub.	bil.	2 p.	1/6.	pet. jaunâtre.
2 Erectum	M.	avril.	7-8 p.	unig.	oval.	bil.		1/4.	pet. obscur.
3 Commersonis	M.	mai.	7 p.	unig.	oval.	bil.	5 p.	1/4.	tr.-long.-rouge obsc.
4 Longiflorum	M.	juin.	4 p.	biné.	rub.	bil.	5 li.	1/4.	pet. roug.
5 Commersonis	F.		6 p.	biné.	rub.	bil.	5 li.	1/12.	pet. roug.
6 Clavatum	F.		12 p.	biné.	rub.	bil.	5 li.	2/3.	pet. verdâtre.
7 Conicum	F.	sept.	2 p.	uniq.	oval.	bil.	15 li.	1/5.	pet. verd.
8 Gracile	B.		15 li.	biné.	rub.	bil.	12 p.	2/3.	moy. jaunâtre.
9 Pusillum		octob.	9 p.	biné.	rub.	bil.	2 p.	1/15.	moy. rouge barriol.
10 Caespitosum	F. B. M.	avril.	2-3 p.	biné.	oval.	bil.	3 p.	1/3.	moy. pourp. jaun.
11 Pendulum, Sw.	B.		5 p.	biné.	rub.	bil.	5 p.	1/6.	pet. rougeâtre.
12 Variegatum	F. B. M.		4 p.	biné.	oval.	bil.	27 li.	1/2.	pet. rougeâtre.
13 Nutans									pet.
14 Densum	M.	sept.	4 p.				4 li.		gr.
15 Prismaticum	B.								
16 Minutum									

91 espèces.

Lles { de France...52
{ de Bourbon...55 }
de Madagascar...26

p. EPIDONCHIS. Fleurs en épis { en petit nombre, éparses......
nombreux, Sépales étroites et acuminées......
peu nombreux { beaucoup plus longs que les feuilles......
{ à peine aussi longs......

q. DENDRONCHIS. Fleurs { réunies en plusieurs épis séparé......
en une seule panicule; feuilles, { Plusieurs caulinaires......
{ Une seule radicale......
solitaires......

r. STICHONCHIS. Fleurs { sur deux rangs, s'épanouissant une à une par année......
en épi. { Eparses, s'épanouissant dans la même année......

s. HEDRONCHIS. Fleurs en épi latéral......
t. IRIDONCHIS. Fleurs en épi terminal......

{ Labelle cilié. Ginostème { appendiculé. Fleurs { à nu......
{ cachés......
{ Quelques-unes ciliées. { nu......
{ Manteau cilié......

u. PHYLONCHIS. Sépales { logées dans leur épi. Hampe { plus longue que les feuilles { binées, Épi { renflé { conique......
{ grêle......
{ unique......
{ plus courte que les feuilles. Fleurs { écartées en petit nombre......
{ écartées en petit nombre, Fleurs { rapprochées, nombreuses......
Toutes nues. Fleurs { Libres, Épi { moins long que les feuilles......
{ plus long que les feuilles......
{ Courbé, pressées......
{ Droit. Fleurs { écartées. Bulbe { prismatique......
{ arrondi......

v. COMMERSORCHIS: La Fleur seule est connue......

1 COMMERSIS......

Currently Accepted · Validly Published · Invalidly Published · Published Pre-1753 · Superfluous Usage · Orthographic Variant · Fossil

TACHYPHYLLUM

An orthographic variant introduced in *Nat. Pflanzen-Syst.*, 196 (1829). The correct spelling is *Pachyphyllum*.

TADEASTRUM

Szlachetko

Richardiana **7**(2): 47 (2007).

ETYMOLOGY: In honor of Tadeusz Wladyslaw Kusibab (1957-), a Polish nurseryman and photographer from Cracovie, who specializes in ericaceous plants, *Catasetinæ, Dracula* and *Stanhopeinæ.*

TYPE SPECIES: *Tadeastrum candidum*
(Barbosa Rodrigues) Szlachetko
(*Stanhopea candida* Barbosa Rodrigues)

Recognized as belonging to the genus *Stanhopea*, *Tadeastrum* was proposed to include three epiphytes distributed in wet, mid elevation, montane forests from Trinidad, the Guianas, Venezuela, Colombia to Bolivia and northern Brazil (Amazonas and Pará). These plants have ovoid, deeply grooved pseudobulbs, subtended by overlapping, thin, papery bracts, each with a solitary, stiff, channeled, slender leaf borne at the tip. The hanging, numerous to few-flowered inflorescence, borne from a mature pseudobulb, has showy, fragrant, creamy-white flowers with a rough, brown, finely scaled covering with spreading to reflexed sepals and petals. The complex, fleshy, trilobed lip has a thick, concave hypochile, and the mesochile has two sickle-shaped horns curving over the broad epichile. The flowers have a long, slender, broadly winged column.

TAENIA

Schlechter

Repert. Spec. Nov. Regni Veg. **9**: 282 (1911).

ETYMOLOGY: Latin for head band, ribbon or tapeworm. Refers to the thin, wiry inflorescence.

TYPE SPECIES: *Taenia fauriei* Schlechter

Not validly published, this name is referred to *Tainia*. *Taenia* was considered to include one terrestrial found in Taiwan, Vietnam and southeastern China (Guangxi and Guangdong). The above type name is now considered a synonym of *Tainia cordifolia* Hooker f.

TAENIA

An orthographic variant cited in *Lex. Gen. Phan.*, 548 (1904). The correct spelling is *Tainia*.

TAENIOPHYLLUM

Blume

Bijdr. Fl. Ned. Ind. **8**: 355, t. 70 (1825).

Not *Taeniophyllum* Pomel (1849) Fossil, and not *Taeniophyllum* Lesquereux (1878) Fossil.

Epidendroideæ ⚜ Vandeæ • Aeridinæ

ETYMOLOGY: Latin for ribbon, tapeworm and leaf. A reference to the flattened, green, ribbon-like roots of the plants in this genus.

LECTOTYPE: *Taeniophyllum obtusum* Blume
This type name is now considered a synonym of
Taeniophyllum pusillum
(Willdenow) Seidenfaden & Ormerod;
basionym
Limodorum pusillum Willdenow

A remarkable group with approximately one hundred eighty-five monopodial, twig epiphytes or lithophytes are found in low to mid elevation, semi-deciduous and evergreen forest margins of northeastern India (Assam), southern China (Yunnan to Guangdong), Taiwan, Thailand, Vietnam, Japan, Indonesia, Tahiti, northern Australia and even Africa (Ghana to Zimbabwe) with the most species found in New Guinea. This is a taxonomically difficult genus, as these small, evergreen plants are seldom common and can be difficult to find. These plants are leafless or have their leaves reduced to tiny, brown scales. The numerous, pale green to gray roots may be terete and spaghetti-like or flattened and tape-worm-like. These plants have several, minute, flat or erect stems while some species have several, minute leaves or are scaly. The short, slowly elongating, numerous-flowered inflorescence has minute, pale yellow to green-white flowers, not opening widely, are borne in succession, and lasting for a few hours to a few days. The sepals and petals are free or united into a tube-like structure below the middle. The spurless, spurred or sac-like, entire or trilobed lip (often larger than the other segments) has a tooth or bristle appendage at the tip and is attached to the base of a short, stout, footless column.

TAENIOPSIS

Not *Taeniopsis* J. Smith (1841) Pteridophyta.

An orthographic variant introduced in *Notizbl. Bot. Gart. Berlin-Dahlem*, **9**(88): 587 (1926). The correct spelling is *Tainiopsis*.

TAENIORHIZA

An orthographic variant introduced in *Phylogeny Classif. Orchid Fam.*, 278 (1993). The correct spelling is *Taeniorrhiza*.

TAENIORRHIZA

Summerhayes

Bot. Mus. Leafl. **11**: 166 (1943).

Epidendroideæ ⚜ Vandeæ • Aerangidinæ

ETYMOLOGY: Greek for a fillet or ribbon and root. Alluding to the ribbon-like roots.

TYPE SPECIES: *Taeniorrhiza gabonensis* Summerhayes

One remarkable, monopodial epiphyte is found in Gabon, Congo and Zaire. This tiny, leafless plant has short stems, each with numerous, flattened, green roots. The short inflorescence has dense clusters of rather small, complicated, pale brown to white flowers. The broad, oval, shortly clawed, lilac, entire lip has numerous, thickened, branching veins. The flowers have an unusual erect, stout, footless column that has its sides in the form of wings that are carried down onto the swollen, cone-shaped spur where they are joined to the margins of the spur's wide mouthed opening.

TAINIA

Blume

Bijdr. Fl. Ned. Ind. **7**: 354, t. 48 (1825).

Epidendroideæ ⚜ Collabiinæ • Currently unplaced

ETYMOLOGY: Latin for head band or ribbon. Refers possibly to the long, narrow petals.

TYPE SPECIES: *Tainia speciosa* Blume

Twenty-nine, sympodial terrestrials or rare epiphytes are found in low to mid elevation, hill forests and rocky limestone scrub from northern India (Assam), Bangladesh, Myanmar to Vietnam, Malaysia, Taiwan,

Indonesia and New Guinea to northeastern Australia with the largest group found in China (Yunnan to Guangdong). These creeping plants have thin, cylindrical, slightly ovoid to tapering, green to red-brown pseudobulbs usually with one to two internodes, subtended by thinly textured sheaths, each with a solitary, large, papery, ridged leaf. The several, long, few-flowered inflorescences, borne from the basal portion of the terminal internode, have fairly large, showy, long-lasting, fragrant, yellow to brown flowers striped brown which open simultaneously. The slightly sac-like, yellow, entire lip, attached to the column foot, has erect side lobes embracing the slender, slightly curved, winged column. The midlobe (front portion trilobed) has smooth keels and sprinkled with red to red-brown spots. Is with a short, red spur or is spurless.

TAINIOPSIS

Hayata

Icon. Pl. Formosan. **4**: 63 (1914).

ETYMOLOGY: *Tainia*, a genus of orchids and Greek for resemblance. Alluding to a relationship with *Tainia*.

TYPE SPECIES: *Tainiopsis unguiculata* (Hayata) Hayata
(*Tainia unguiculata* Hayata)

Now recognized as belonging to the genus *Acanthephippium, Tainiopsis* Hayata was previously considered to include one terrestrial found in mid elevation, montane forests from southeastern China (Yunnan), Taiwan, northern India (Sikkim), Nepal, Thailand to Vietnam. This slender plant has short, erect pseudobulbs, subtended by violet streaked sheaths, each with two short-stalked, tapering, pleated leaves. The short, few-flowered inflorescence has faintly fragrant, cup-like, pale yellow to white flowers striped brown-purple. The mobile, pale brown to white, saddle-shaped, trilobed lip has erect, side lobes, and basal, red-purple calli. The above type name is now considered a synonym of *Acanthephippium striatum* Lindley.

TAINIOPSIS

Schlechter

Orchis **9**: 10 (1915).

Not *Tainiopsis* Hayata (1914) Orchidaceæ.

ETYMOLOGY: *Tainia*, a genus of orchids, and Greek for resemblance.

TYPE SPECIES: *Tainiopsis barbata* Schlechter

Not validly published because of a prior use of the name, this homonym was replaced by *Eriodes*.

TAKULUMENA

Szlachetko

Orchidee (Hamburg) **57**(3): 326 (2006).

ETYMOLOGY: A composite word made from the collectors' names, Tadeusz Kusibab (1957-) and Luis Mendoza y Cabrera (1960-), an Ecuadorian guide.

TYPE SPECIES: *Takulumena sophronitoides*
(F. Lehmann & Kraenzlin) Szlachetko
(*Epidendrum sophronitoides* F. Lehmann & Kraenzlin)

Now recognized as belonging to the genus *Epidendrum, Takulumena* was proposed to include two monopodial epiphytes found in low to upper elevation, hill to montane forests of northern Colombia and Ecuador. These small, tufted, occasionally branching plants have slender stems, each with the several, narrow, stiff, leathery leaves arranged in two ranks. The few-flowered inflorescence, completely subtended by thin, dry bracts, has a bronze-pink to bright magenta flower with spreading sepals and slightly narrower petals that are densely hairy on the lower surfaces. The flowers open in succession. The sea shell-shaped to elliptical, entire lip has a slightly infolded and hairy margin. The flowers have a small column.

TALPINARIA

H. Karsten

Fl. Columb. (H. Karsten) **1**(4): 153, *t.* 76 (1861).

ETYMOLOGY: Latin for mole-like. Alluding to the shape of the lobes that when viewed from the side resemble a mole in the burrowing position.

TYPE SPECIES: *Talpinaria bivalvis* H. Karsten

Now recognized as belonging to the genus *Pleurothallis, Talpinaria* was previously considered to include one epiphyte found in damp, low to upper elevation, hill scrub and montane forests from Colombia to Peru and Venezuela. This small, erect plant has slender stems, subtended by tubular sheaths, each with a solitary, brown-green, leathery leaf. The inflorescence arises from below the leaf lamina with each large, sheath being untidy. The pale creamy green flowers are flecked with pale pink to red-brown. The wide, white, trilobed lip is suffused red-brown, bordered with a fringe of slender processes at the middle, has basally bilobed, rounded side lobes, and then has an entire, trilobed front lobe. The above type name is now considered a synonym of *Pleurothallis talpinaria* Reichenbach f.

TAMAYORKIS

Szlachetko

Fragm. Florist. Geobot. **3**(Suppl.): 121 (1995).

ETYMOLOGY: Named in honor of Roberto González-Tamayo (1940-), a Mexican botanist who specializes in the orchids of the Jalisco region of Mexico. And Greek for orchid.

TYPE SPECIES: *Tamayorkis platyglossa*
(B.L. Robertson & Greenman) Szlachetko
(*Microstylis platyglossa* B.L. Robertson & Greenman)
This type name is now considered a synonym of *Malaxis ehrenbergii* (Reichenbach f.) Kuntze; basionym replaced with *Microstylis ehrenbergii* Reichenbach f.

Now recognized as belonging to the genus *Malaxis, Tamayorkis* was proposed to include four terrestrials found in mid elevation, montane pine-oak forests of the southwestern United States (Arizona) and Mexico to Guatemala. These plants, often withstanding severe weather conditions, have ovoid pseudobulbs, subtended by leaf-like sheaths, each with a solitary leaf that has rolled up edges. The erect, long, few-flowered inflorescence has small, green or purple flowers. The obscurely trilobed or entire lip is attached to the base of the short, stout, footless column.

TANGTSINIA

S.C. Chen

Acta Phytotax. Sin. **10**(3): 194 (1965).

ETYMOLOGY: In honor of T. (Chin) Tang (1897-1984), a Chinese orchidologist who collected in the northeastern Chinese provinces of Shaanxi, Sichuan and Jiangsu. And Latin for China.

TYPE SPECIES: *Tangtsinia nanchuanica* S.C. Chen

Now recognized as belonging to the genus *Cephalanthera, Tangtsinia* was previously considered to include one terrestrial found in low to upper elevation, scrub margins and grassy slopes of south central China (Sichuan and Guizhou) in the Jiafoshan Mountains. This erect plant has slender stems, subtended by basal sheaths, each with oblong, thinly textured to papery leaves alternating up the stem. The few-flowered inflorescence has primitively structured, bright yellow flowers not fully opening. The non-modified lip is similar to the sepals and petals and has a conspicuously clawed base. The flowers have an erect, long, yellow-green column that has neither a clinandrium nor a rostellum but has a relatively long tip with a concave stigma.

TANKARVILLIA

An orthographic variant cited in *Pl. Vasc. Gen. (Meisner),* **1**: 279 (1837). The correct spelling is *Tankervillia.*

| Currently Accepted | Validly Published | Invalidly Published | Published Pre-1753 | Superfluous Usage | Orthographic Variant | Fossil |

O r c h i d   G e n e r a • **384**

TANKERVILLEA

An orthographic variant introduced in *Hort. Donat.*, 222 (1858). The correct spelling is *Tankervillia*.

TANKERVILLIA

Link

Handbuch (Link) **1**: 251 (1829).

ETYMOLOGY: Named in honor of Emma Bennet (x-1836), wife of Charles Bennet (1743-1822), the 4th Earl of Tankerville. The Duchess was an ardent orchid enthusiast. This title is derived from the earldom of Tancarville in Normandy, created in 1419 for John Grey (1384-1421).

TYPE SPECIES: *Tankervillia cantonensis* Link

This type name is now considered a synonym of *Phaius tankervilleae* (Banks ex L'Héritier) Blume;
basionym
Limodorum tankervilleae Banks ex L'Héritier

Now recognized as belonging to the genus *Phaius*, *Tankervillia* was previously considered to include one terrestrial found in low to mid elevation, hill grasslands, scrub and montane forests ranging from northern India, southern China and Australia to the southwestern Pacific Archipelago. This large plant has short, thick, ovoid to cone-shaped pseudobulbs, subtended by leaf bearing sheaths, each with several, thinly textured, pleated leaves. The erect, few-flowered inflorescence, often up to four foot (1.2 m) tall, has large, pleasantly fragrant, widespreading, brown flowers with similar sepals and petals. The large, trumpet-shaped, trilobed lip is white on the outside, purple at the tip, and dark wine-red toward the base.

TAPEINOGLOSSUM

Schlechter

Repert. Spec. Nov. Regni Veg. Beih. **1**(12): 892 (1913).

ETYMOLOGY: Greek for low, humble or modest and tongue. Refers to the minute size of the lip.

TYPE SPECIES: *None designated*

Now recognized as belonging to the genus *Bulbophyllum*, *Tapeinoglossum* was previously considered to include two epiphytes found in open, low to upper elevation, hill scrub and montane rain forests of New Guinea. These plants have small, olive-green pseudobulbs, spaced along a creeping rhizome, each with a solitary, leathery leaf. The short, thick, solitary-flowered inflorescences, borne from the base of the pseudobulb, have a uniquely structured, delightful, white or yellow flower which is heavily veined and suffused dark red or brown-red. The large, concave dorsal sepal forms a hood, and the lateral sepals are joined forming a cup shape under the mobile, entire lip. The inside surface of the flower segments are covered with short, white hairs, but the hairs found inside the small, cup-shaped lip are much longer. The lip has two stiffly, hairy keels. The flowers have a small, yellow column with a strong S-shape.

TAPROBANEA

Christenson

Lindleyana **7**(2): 90 (1992).

ETYMOLOGY: Latin for copper color. Refers to the color of the flowers.

Or possibly an ancient Greek word for the island known today as the Democratic Socialist Republic of Sri Lanka, located off the southern tip of India in the Indian Ocean.

TYPE SPECIES: *Taprobanea spathulata* (Linnaeus) Christenson (*Epidendrum spathulatum* Linnaeus)

Now recognized as belonging to the genus *Vanda*, *Taprobanea* was proposed to include one epiphyte found in low elevation, rocky coastal scrub of southern India (Kerala and Tamil Nadu) and Sri Lanka. This scrambling, climbing or erect plant has slender stems, each with flat, strap-shaped leaves arranged in two opposing ranks with the older portions leafless. The few-flowered inflorescence, borne from leaf axils, has showy, flat-faced, fragrant, bright yellow flowers opening successively over a long period. The obscurely trilobed lip (fused to the column base) has roundish side lobes not continuous with the midlobe, thus creating a tall, narrow tunnel to the spur entrance. The broad, clawed midlobe has radiating red veins. The flowers have a short, curved, wingless column.

TARTARINORCHIS

Kraenzlin ex N. Hallé

Fl. Nouvelle Caledonie & Depend. **8**: 534 (1977).

ETYMOLOGY: Name for a group of people, the Tartars, who were conquered by Genghis Khan (1162-1227) when he overran much of central and western Asia. And Greek for orchid.

TYPE SPECIES: *Tartarinorchis daudetii* Kraenzlin ex N. Hallé

This type name is now considered a synonym of *Goodyera scripta* (Reichenbach f.) Schlechter;
basionym
Rhamphidia scripta Reichenbach f.

Not validly published, this name is referred to *Goodyera*. *Tartarinorchis* was considered to include one terrestrial found on New Caledonia.

TAURANTHA

D.L. Jones & M.A. Clements

Austral. Orchid Res. **4**: 85 (2002).

ETYMOLOGY: Latin for bull and flower. Refers to the lateral sepals for having a horn-like appearance.

TYPE SPECIES: *Taurantha ophioglossa* (R. Brown) D.L. Jones & M.A. Clements (*Pterostylis ophioglossa* R. Brown)

Recognized as belonging to the genus *Pterostylis*, *Taurantha* was proposed to include six terrestrials found in low elevation, coastal woodlands of eastern Australia. This small, erect plant has unbranched, slender stems, each with a basal rosette; these gray-green leaves (shiny on the underside) have wavy margins. The erect, solitary to rarely two-flowered inflorescence has a green-yellow flower with darker green, longitudinal stripes and heavily suffused and striped red-brown. The dorsal sepal and petals converge, forming a hood over the erect column. The lateral sepals taper to thread-like, red-brown tips held high above the hood. The narrowly clawed, green, bilobed lip has a wide space between the lobes.

TAUROSTALIX

Reichenbach *filius*

Bot. Zeitung (Berlin) **10**: 933 (1852).

ETYMOLOGY: Greek for bull and a stake. Possibly in reference to the anterior teeth on the column that are larger than the column itself, fancifully giving the appearance of a bull's horns.

TYPE SPECIES: *Taurostalix herminiostachys* Reichenbach f.

This type name is now considered a synonym of *Genyorchis pumila* (Swartz) Schlechter;
basionym
Dendrobium pumilum Swartz

Now recognized as belonging to the genus *Genyorchis*, *Taurostalix* was previously considered to include one epiphyte found in low to mid elevation, hill scrub, mangroves, savannas and montane of Ghana, Cameroon and Gabon to Uganda. These tiny plants have narrow, compressed, ovoid to oblong pseudobulbs, each with two leathery leaves borne at the tip of the pseudo-bulb. The leaves are often heavily suffused purple. The long, wiry, yellow-brown, few to numerous-flowered inflorescence has tiny, yellow-white flowers with many opening simultaneously, but the individual flowers do not fully open. The narrow, white, creamy or green sepals are often suffused purple-red, and usually have white petals. The small lip is trilobed. The flowers have a short, long-footed column.

TAUROSTALYX

An orthographic variant introduced in *Hamburger Garten- Blumenzeitung*, **9**: 122 (1853). The correct spelling is *Taurostalix*.

TEAGUEIA

(Luer) Luer
Monogr. Syst. Bot. Missouri Bot. Gard.
39: 140 (1991).

Epidendroideæ ◊ **Epidendreæ** • **Pleurothallidinæ**
ETYMOLOGY: In honor of Walter Teague (1926-), an Ecuadorian-born American flight attendant who collected flora worldwide and gathered the type species while exploring in Ecuador.
TYPE SPECIES: *Teagueia teaguei* (Luer) Luer
(*Platystele teaguei* Luer)

Twenty-one sympodial epiphytes or uncommon terrestrials are found in upper elevation, montane cloud forests in restricted areas of the Andes from Colombia to Ecuador. These small to medium-sized, fragile, creeping plants have a solitary, ovate, thinly leathery, basal leaf per growth that has red to purple veins. The few-flowered inflorescence has showy, pale yellow, purple, bright to dark red (almost black) flowers opening simultaneously. The flowers have narrow to tiny, inconspicuous, long petals and the sepals of some species have long tails. The sepals are often hairy or ciliate; the ovate dorsal sepal is three-veined and the variously united, lateral sepals each have two to three veins. The ovate to triangular petals are reduced and inconspicuous. The small, sharply recurved, tongue-shaped, entire lip forms a collar around the short, broad, wingless, footless column.

TEKA

An orthographic variant introduced in *Encycl. (Lamarck)*, **1**: 189 (1783). The correct spelling is *Theka*.

TELIPOGON

Kunth
Nov. Gen. Sp. **1**: 335, *t.* 75 (1815).

Epidendroideæ ◊ **Cymbidieæ** • **Oncidiinæ**
ETYMOLOGY: Greek for end or extremity and beard. Descriptive of the hairy tip of the column.
TYPE SPECIES: *None designated*

One hundred thirty-three delicate, sympodial epiphytes or moss-growing terrestrials are found in damp, cool upper elevation, montane forests (not only damp but with a permanent fog

covering the ground) from Costa Rica to Bolivia with the greatest concentration found in Colombia. These dwarf plants have short to long, vine-like, branching stems, often subtended by overlapping sheaths, each with a few to several, distichous, fleshy to slightly leathery, basal to two ranked, narrow, pleated leaves. The slender, few-flowered inflorescence has extremely fragile but, widely varied colored flowers that are up to several inches across or quite small, each is subtended by bracts. The sepals are quite small; the large petals and broad, entire lip are vividly colored, varying from golden-yellow to almost blue, often with roughened hairs or other projections. The flowers have a short, footless, wingless column that is hairy or has long bristles. This bristled or whiskered column lures the male fly into mounting the flower.

TELOPOGON

An orthographic variant introduced in *Anleit. Kenntn. Gew.*, ed. 2, **2**(1): 291 (1817). The correct spelling is *Telipogon*.

TESTICULI

An orthographic variant introduced in *Commentarii*, 409 (1554). The correct spelling is *Testiculus*.

TESTICULIS

Pliny
Hist. Nat. **XXVI**: 95 (AD 56).

Pre-1753, therefore not validly published in fulfillment of nomenclatural rules; this name is most often referred to *Orchis*.

TESTICULO

An orthographic variant introduced in *Annot.*, 129a, 129b (1561). The correct spelling is *Testiculus*.

TESTICULORUM

An orthographic variant introduced in *Pl. Libri XVI*, 428 (1583). The correct spelling is *Testiculus*.

TESTICULUS

L'Obel
Pl. Stirp. Hist. 89b (1576).

Pre-1753, therefore not validly published in fulfillment of nomenclatural rules; this name is most often referred to *Orchis*.

TETRORCHIS

L'Obel
Icon. Stirp. 186, *f.* 2 (1591).

Pre-1753, therefore not validly published in fulfillment of nomenclatural rules; this name is most often referred to *Spiranthes*.

TETRABACULUM

M.A. Clements & D.L. Jones
Orchadian **13**(11): 490 (2002).
ETYMOLOGY: Greek for having four or fourfold and Latin for rod, staff or walking stick. Refers to the sharply four-angled stems.
TYPE SPECIES: *Tetrabaculum tetragonum*
(A. Cunningham ex Lindley) M.A. Clements & D.L. Jones
(*Dendrobium tetragonum* A. Cunningham ex Lindley)

Recognized as belonging to the genus *Dendrobium*, *Tetrabaculum* was proposed to include four epiphytes found in low elevation, coastal rain forests and along river banks of eastern Australia. These small plants have sharply, four-angled stems with long, initially erect pseudobulbs then arching to hanging, slender stems, each with several, thinly textured but tough, dark green leaves. The few-flowered inflorescence, borne near the tip of the pseudobulb, has spidery, star-shaped, cream, green or bronze flowers with dark margins. The sepals taper, forming long, thin tails; the narrow petals are much shorter in length. The white, trilobed lip has a few red to purple stripes, erect, small side lobes, and the broad midlobe tapers to a point.

TETRAGAMESTUS

Reichenbach *filius*
Bonplandia **2**(2): 21 (1854).
ETYMOLOGY: Greek for fourfold and marriage. In possible reference to the square stigma.
LECTOTYPE: *Tetragamestus aureus*
(Reichenbach f.) Reichenbach f.
(*Scaphyglottis ruberrima* var. *aurea* Reichenbach f.)
indirectly designated by Reichenbach f, *Linnaea*, **41**: 85 (1876).
LECTOTYPE: *Scaphyglottis arundinacea* Regel
invalidly designated by Pfeiffer, *Nomencl. Bot. (Pfeiffer)*, **2**(2): 1373 (1874).

Now recognized as belonging to the genus *Scaphyglottis*, *Tetragamestus* was previously considered to include five epiphytes or lithophytes found in low to mid elevation, scrub ranging from Cuba to Trinidad, Panama to Colombia, Venezuela, the Guianas and northern Brazil. These small plants have erect,

Currently Accepted | Validly Published | Invalidly Published | Published Pre-1753 | Superfluous Usage | Orthographic Variant | Fossil

O r c h i d   G e n e r a   • **386**

cane-like to spindle-shaped stems, subtended by overlapping sheaths that proceed upward, each with two narrow leaves borne at each node. The several, extremely short, solitary-flowered inflorescences have overlapping sheaths with a tiny, yellow-green to pale brown flower, not opening widely, borne in the axils of the leaves. The trilobed lip, joined to the often obscure column foot, has rounded side lobes and a larger, round to shallowly notched midlobe. The flowers have a short, slightly curved column.

TETRAGOCYANIS

Thouars
Hist. Orchid.   Table 1, sub 2k (1822).

Name published without a description. Today this name is most often referred to *Phaius*.

TETRAMAGESTUS

An orthographic variant introduced in *Bot. Centralbl.*, **76**(49): 345 (1898). The correct spelling is *Tetragamestus*.

TETRAMICRA

Lindley
Gen. Sp. Orchid. Pl.   119 (1831).

Epidendroideæ ᵂ Epidendreæ • Laeliinæ

ETYMOLOGY: Greek for fourfold and small. Refers to the four tiny and four large pollinia.

TYPE SPECIES: *Tetramicra rigida* (Willdenow) Lindley
(*Cymbidium rigidum* Willdenow)

This type name is now considered a synonym of *Tetramicra canaliculata* (Aublet) Urban; basionym replaced with *Limodorum canaliculatum* Aublet

Fourteen terrestrials, lithophytes or epiphytes are found in dry to moist, low to mid elevation, hill forests, limestone slopes and rocky crevices from Barbados, northward to Puerto Rico, Hispaniola, Jamaica and Cuba to the southeastern United States (Florida), usually exposed to full sunlight. These stout plants have short stems or rarely, with tiny pseudobulbous, subtended by overlapping, papery sheaths, each with rigid, thick or fleshy, channeled leaves often arranged in small, fan shapes. The tall, wiry, few-flowered inflorescence has showy, well-spaced, mauve to pink, slightly fragrant flowers often suffused redbrown. The rosy-pink, flat, deeply trilobed lip, attached to the column base, has a yellow centerline with radiating white lines. The side lobes are on a short claw and has a broad, entire midlobe. The flowers have an erect, pencil-like, broadly winged column that form a swollen nectary at the base.

TETRAPELTIS

Wallich ex Lindley
Edwards's Bot. Reg.   **18**: sub 1522 (1832), and
Gen. Sp. Orchid. Pl.   212 (1833).

ETYMOLOGY: Greek for fourfold and small shield or buckle. In reference to the four pollinia that are found on a single gland.

TYPE SPECIES: *Tetrapeltis fragrans* Wallich ex Lindley

Now recognized as belonging to the genus *Otochilus*, *Tetrapeltis* was previously considered to include one epiphyte found in mid to upper elevation, montane cloud forests from northern India (Kashmir to Assam), southern China (Yunnan) and Myanmar to Vietnam. Each slender pseudobulb of this plant arises from the tip or near the tip of the previous, wrinkled, dark brown pseudobulb, each with several, pleated leaves. The erect, few-flowered inflorescences are borne between the top leaves in the young shoot. The small, white flower and the lip are sometimes suffused yellow. The trilobed lip has tiny, erect side lobes embracing the column. A spear-shaped midlobe narrows to a claw at the base. There are three, thick ridges with an unusual downward hanging, horn-like appendage located at the tip of the long, erect, wingless column. The above type name is now considered a synonym of *Otochilus porrectus* Lindley.

TETRODON

(Kraenzlin) M.A. Clements & D.L. Jones
Orchadian   **12**(7): 310 (1998).

ETYMOLOGY: Greek for fourfold and tooth. The significance of this name is obscure.

TYPE SPECIES: *Tetrodon oppositifolius*
(Kraenzlin) M.A. Clements & D.L. Jones
(*Eria oppositifolia* Kraenzlin)

Now recognized as belonging to the genus *Dendrobium*, *Tetrodon* was proposed to include two epiphytes found in humid, mid elevation, rain forests of New Caledonia. These miniature plants have short, squat, laterally flattened, orange pseudobulbs, each with usually just two leaves at the tip. The simple or sparsely branched, erect or arching few-flowered inflorescence has yellow-green flowers that open widely. The lateral sepals are united, forming a small pouch in front of the column foot. The immovable, deeply trilobed lip has small, rounded, erect side lobes, and the broad midlobe has a white basal splash. The concave to flat, bright magenta midlobe has three, deeply ridged calli, a scalloped margin and a false spur located at the base.

TEUSCHERIA

Garay
Amer. Orchid Soc. Bull.   **27**(12): 820 (1958).

Epidendroideæ ᵂ Cymbidieæ • Maxillariinæ

ETYMOLOGY: Heinrich Henry Teuscher (1891-1984), a German-born Canadian gardener, horticulturist, dendrologist, landscape architect, curator and originator of the Montréal Botanical Garden.

TYPE SPECIES: *Teuscheria cornucopia* Garay

Seven sympodial epiphytes are found in wet, mid to upper elevation, montane cloud forests from southern Mexico to Panama, Venezuela and Colombia to Ecuador. These plants have small, distant or clustered, pear-shaped or ovoid pseudobulbs, subtended by overlapping, papery sheaths, each with a solitary, narrow, pleated leaf borne at the tip. The erect to hanging, solitary-flowered inflorescence has a large, fleshy, short-lived, white to green-bronze flower suffused pale maroon. The lateral sepals are united to the column foot forming a short chin-like projection. The white, trilobed lip, attached to the tip of the long column foot, is often suffused pink at the margins, and has a short spur. The flowers have a short, fleshy, wingless, green column.

THAENIA

An orthographic variant introduced in *Bot. Centralbl.*, **53**(51): 477 (1899). The correct spelling is *Tainia*.

THAIA

Seidenfaden
Bot. Tidsskr.   **70**(1): 73, *f.* 8 (1975).

Epidendroideæ ᵂ Neottieæ

ETYMOLOGY: Name used for a native member of the predominately ethnic group of Thailand, a people with both Mongoloid and Indonesian characteristics. The Kingdom of Thailand is located in southeastern Asia, between Myanmar and Cambodia.

TYPE SPECIES: *Thaia saprophytica* Seidenfaden

One primitive saprophyte orchid is found in humid, mid elevation, evergreen forests and is confined to a small area of central Thailand and southeastern Myanmar. This erect, leafless plant has simple to rarely branched stems, subtended by enveloping sheaths. The numerous to few-flowered inflorescence bears tiny flowers with similar, pale green sepals that are slightly warty on the outer surfaces and yellow-green on the inner surfaces. The erect dorsal sepal and small, narrow yellow-green petals converge, forming a hood over the slender, curved, erect column that has a wide foot. The lateral sepals form a minute, chin-like protuberance that encloses the base of the lip. The long, blunt, bright lime-green, entire lip, movably attached to the column foot, has a notched tip and a basal, two keel disc, each having a pointed tooth.

THALIA-maravara

Rheede

Hort. Malab. **12**: 9, *t. 4* (1693).
Not *Thalia* Linnaeus (1753) Marantaceæ.

ETYMOLOGY: The Malayalam word for soapy foam or shampoo. When the plant is pressed a juice is formed which is used as a soap by the local people.

TYPE SPECIES: *Thalia-maravara* Rheede

Pre-1753, therefore not validly published in fulfillment of nomenclatural rules; this binomial name is most often referred to *Acampe*. *Thalia* was previously considered to include one epiphyte found in low elevation, hill forests of northern India, Bangladesh, Myanmar, Thailand, Laos and Vietnam. This climbing plant, forming massive clusters, has a tangled mass of cord-like roots and the stems have oblong, recurved leaves arranged in two ranks. The short, comb-like inflorescence has honey fragrant, white to yellow flowers covered with yellow-brown bars and spots. The trilobed lip has triangular side lobes, an ovate midlobe which is quite hairy in the lower half, and a sac-like or cone-shaped, basal spur. The flowers have a small, fleshy, footless column. This name is now usually considered a synonym of *Acampe praemorsa* (Roxburgh) Blatter & McCann.

THECKA

An orthographic variant introduced in *Exot. Fl.*, **2**: sub 138 (1825). The correct spelling is *Theka*.

THECOPUS

Seidenfaden

Opera Bot. **72**: 101 [1983](1984).

Epidendroideæ ▪ Cymbideæ • Eulophiinæ

ETYMOLOGY: Greek for a box or envelope and a foot. Referring to the shape of the column base.

TYPE SPECIES: *Thecopus maingayi*
(Hooker f.) Seidenfaden
(*Thecostele maingayi* Hooker f.)

Two sympodial epiphytes are found in dry, low to mid elevation, deciduous forests and savannas of Thailand, Malaysia, Vietnam and Indonesia (Borneo). These plants have small pseudobulbs, each with a solitary, fleshy leaf. The hanging, few-flowered inflorescence, borne near the base of the pseudobulb, has small bracts. The large, fleshy,

pale green-yellow to green flowers are spotted or streaked dark maroon. The concave dorsal sepal forms a hood over the slender column and has small petals. The white, downward-turned, shortly clawed, trilobed lip has purple markings, is covered with fine hairs, and is joined at the base with an outgrowth from the slender, erect then strongly curved column. The hollow, tubular column foot unites with the lip forming a massive structure.

THECOSTELE

Reichenbach *filius*

Bonplandia **5**(3): 37 (1857).

Epidendroideæ ▪ Cymbideæ • Eulophiinæ

ETYMOLOGY: Greek for receptacle and column or style. Refers to the box-like base of the column.

TYPE SPECIES: *Thecostele zollingeri* Reichenbach f.
This type name is now considered a synonym of *Thecostele alata* (Roxburgh) C.S.P. Parish & Reichenbach f.;
basionym
Cymbidium alatum Roxburgh

One sympodial epiphyte is found in low elevation, hill forests and savanna scrub from Bangladesh, Myanmar to Vietnam and Indonesia to the Philippines. These small plants have clustered, ovoid or compressed, heavily grooved pseudobulbs, each with one to two narrow, thinly leathery leaves; these leaves are usually withered by flowering time. The hanging, slender, branched, few-flowered inflorescence, borne from the pseudobulb base, slowly lengthens as the flowers bloom. The sepals and petals of these showy, insect-like, small, short-lived, slightly fragrant flowers are blotched brick-red and have pale yellow at their base with pale purple tips. The white, trilobed lip is marked with bright magenta, and has small, roundish side lobes. The midlobe has a hairy, basal callus and is joined to the tip of the column foot forming a hollow tube. The flowers have a slender, abruptly bent, almost wingless column.

THEKA-maravara

Rheede

Hort. Malab. **12**: 43, *t. 22* (1693).
Not *Theka* Adanson (1763) Verbenaceæ.

ETYMOLOGY: Refers to the species of the teak, *Tectona grandis*, upon which this species was found. But Rheede's illustration of the tree is most likely that of *Mallotus philippensis*.

TYPE SPECIES: *Theka-maravara* Rheede

Pre-1753, therefore not validly published published in fulfillment of nomenclatural rules; this binomial name is most often referred to *Bulbophyllum*. *Theka* was previously considered to include one epiphyte found in low to mid elevation, hill scrub and montane forests of northeastern India (Assam), Nepal and

Bhutan. This tiny, mat-forming plant has ovoid, grooved, compressed pseudobulbs, each with a solitary, oblong, leathery leaf. The erect, short, few to numerous-flowered inflorescence has large, dull brown-yellow to purple-green flowers with the dorsal sepal hooded over the long column. The creamy-white, trilobed lip has erect, recurved side lobes and an entire, grooved midlobe. This name is now usually considered a synonym of *Bulbophyllum sterile* (Lamarck) Suresh.

THELASIA

An orthographic variant introduced in *J. Bot.* (Hooker), **9**: 139 (1857). The correct spelling is *Thelasis*.

THELASIS

Blume

Bijdr. Fl. Ned. Ind. **8**: 385, *t. 75* (1825).

Epidendroideæ ▪ Podochileæ • Thelasinæ

ETYMOLOGY: Greek for a nipple. Refers to the common belief that epiphytes were parasites and sucked sap from their live hosts.

LECTOTYPE: *Thelasis carinata* Blume

Twenty-two small, but interesting sympodial epiphytes, uncommon lithophytes or terrestrials are found in low to mid elevation, tropical rain and coastal forests, thickets and along river banks from southern China (Yunnan to Hainan), Taiwan, Myanmar to Vietnam Malaysia, Indonesia and northern Australia to the Philippines. These small, fan-shaped plants have stems forming small, ovoid or depressed pseudobulbs, subtended by leaf-like sheaths, each with a solitary, narrow leaf. They may have stems that are not pseudobulbous, each with numerous, laterally flattened leaves arranged in two rows. The long to short, numerous to few-flowered inflorescence has minute, tubular flowers not opening fully, with similar sepals and petals, that are almost white or dark green at their base, becoming yellow-white toward the pointed tips. Only a few flowers are scarcely open at any one time. The concave, entire lip is nearly as long as the sepals and has a short pointed tip. The flowers have an erect, short, footless column.

THELEMITRA

An orthographic variant introduced in *Nat. Pflanzen-Syst.*, 195 (1829). The correct spelling is *Thelymitra*.

Currently Accepted   Validly Published   Invalidly Published   Published Pre-1753   Superfluous Usage   Orthographic Variant   Fossil

Orchid Genera • 388

THELICHITON

An orthographic variant introduced in *Dict. Univ. Hist. Nat.*, **9**: 169 (1847). The correct spelling is *Thelychiton*.

THELIMITRA

An orthographic variant introduced in *Nouv. Dict. Hist. Nat.*, **22**: 130 (1804). The correct spelling is *Thelymitra*.

THELIMYTRA

An orthographic variant introduced in *Elem. Bot. (Duchartre)*, 1127 (1885). The correct spelling is *Thelymitra*.

THELIPOGON

An orthographic variant introduced in *Dict. Sci. Nat.*, **36**: 304 (1825). The correct spelling is *Telipogon*.

THELYCHITON

Endlicher

Prodr. Fl. Norfolk. 32 (1833).

ETYMOLOGY: Greek for female, and dress or covering. An allusion to the column that surrounds the stigma like a dress.

LECTOTYPE: *Thelychiton macropus* Endlicher

Now recognized as belonging to the genus *Dendrobium*, *Thelychiton* was previously considered to include three epiphytes or lithophytes found in low to mid elevation, rain forests from eastern Australia (including Norfolk Island) to Fiji and New Caledonia, usually in very exposed areas. These plants which form small to large clumps, have slender, cylindrical, pseudobulbous stems, each with several, narrow, thinly textured leaves borne near the tip. The numerous to few-flowered inflorescence, borne from any node on the upper half of the cane, has small, fragrant, green-yellow, bright yellow to orange flowers with various red-brown blotches on the outside surfaces. The trilobed lip has small side lobes with a broad midlobe; both are heavily red-veined with a white margin.

THELYMITHRA

An orthographic variant introduced in *Encycl. (Lamarck) Suppl.* 5, 299 (1817). The correct spelling is *Thelymitra*.

THELYMITRA

J.R. Forster & G. Forster

Char. Gen. Pl. 97, *t.* 49 (1775).

Orchidoideæ • Diurideæ • Thelymitrinæ

ETYMOLOGY: Greek for female, and hat or turban. In reference to the prominent hooded column of some of the species.

TYPE SPECIES: *Thelymitra longifolia*
    J.R. Forster & G. Forster

Seventy-eight sympodial terrestrials are found in low to mid elevation, coastal scrub, woodlands, rocky crevices, grasslands and sphagnum swamps of Australia with a few species scattered throughout Indonesia (Timor, Java and Borneo), central New Guinea, New Zealand, New Caledonia and the southern Philippines often forming huge colonies. These plants are known as sun orchids because the flowers expand only when the sun is shining and remain closed on cloudy days during the hot, dry summer. The plants reproduce solely from seed. The slender, erect plants have unbranched stems, each with a solitary, erect, somewhat fleshy leaf that is often prominently ribbed lengthwise. The erect, wiry, solitary to few-flowered inflorescence has flowers whose colors are quite variable even in a single species. The showy, flat-faced flowers are pleasant smelling and vary in color from yellow, pink, purple, brown, white to true blues, a very rare color in orchids. The oblong, entire lip is similar to the other floral segments. The flowers have a footless column with short, sharp appendages and the fused wings surround the column.

THELYPOGON

An orthographic variant introduced in *Syst. Veg. (Sprengel)*, ed. 16, **3**: 682, 742 (1826). The correct spelling is *Telipogon*.

THELYSCHISTA

Garay

Bot. Mus. Leafl. **28**(4): 377 (1980)[1982].

Orchidoideæ • Cranichideæ • Spiranthinæ

ETYMOLOGY: Greek for female and to split or divided. In reference to the stigma having two, separate receptive areas.

TYPE SPECIES: *Thelyschista ghillanyi* (Pabst) Garay
    (*Odontorrhynchus ghillanyi* Pabst)

One sympodial terrestrial is found in low elevation, sandy and rocky woodlands of eastern Brazil (Bahia). This tall plant has unbranched stems, each with a basal rosette of several, pale green leaves. The erect, slender, hairy, numerous-flowered inflorescence has rather large flowers whose floral segments are more or less similar to the stalkless lip. The mid-section of the obscurely trilobed lip is fused to the sides of a short, rather fleshy, stout, club-shaped column. The bases of the lateral sepals are united with the lip, forming a conspicuous spur. The obscurely trilobed lip has a toothed margin. The flowers have a long column with the viscidium wedged between the teeth of the rostellum which is essentially reduced to two pointed teeth enclosing the viscidium; the third median tooth is a dorsal extension of the clinandrium.

THEOCOSTELE

An orthographic variant introduced in *Sander's Orch. Guide*, ed. 4, 424 (1927). The correct spelling is *Thecostele*.

THEODOREA

Barbosa Rodrigues

Gen. Sp. Orchid. **1**: 144, *t.* 480 (1877).
Not *Theodora* Medikus (1786) Fabaceæ, and not *Theodorea* (Cassini) Cassini (1827) Asteraceæ.

ETYMOLOGY: In honor of Theodoro Machado Freire Pereira da Silva (1832-1905), a Brazilian minister of public works in Paraíba who assisted Barbosa Rodrigues with the discovery of new plants.

TYPE SPECIES: *Theodorea gomezoides* Barbosa Rodrigues

Not validly published because of a prior use of the name, this homonym was replaced by *Rodrigueziella*.

THICUANIA

Rafinesque

Fl. Tellur. **4**: 47 (1836)[1837].

ETYMOLOGY: Derived from a local Myanmar vernacular name for this species.

TYPE SPECIES: *Thicuania moschata*
    (Buchanan-Hamilton) Rafinesque
    (*Epidendrum moschatum* Buchanan-Hamilton)

Now recognized as belonging to the genus *Dendrobium*, *Thicuania* was previously considered to include one epiphyte found in mid elevation, open forests from northern India (Kashmir to Assam), Nepal, southern China (Yunnan) and Myanmar to Vietnam often growing in full sunlight. This plant has erect, arching or hanging, slender stems (dark brown with age), each with a few prominently veined, leathery leaves toward the tip. They are arranged in two ranks along the length of the stem which turn dark brown as it aged; the leaves tend to turn purple when exposed to bright sunlight. The hanging, few-flowered inflorescence, borne from leafless stems, has short-lived, heavily textured, creamy to yellow, musky fragrant flowers suffused rose and lilac. The slipper-shaped, shortly clawed, pale yellow, entire lip has large, black blotches located on each side, an inrolled margin, and an outer surface that is covered in short hairs. The flowers have a short column.

THIEBAUDIA

Not *Thiebaudia* M.E.J. Chandler (1954) Fossil.

An orthographic variant introduced in *Nat. Syst. Bot.*, ed. 2, 340 (1836). The correct spelling is *Thiebautia*.

THIEBAUTIA

Colla

Mém. Soc. Linn. Paris **3**: 161, *t. 4* (1825), and *Hortus Ripul.* 139 (1824).

Not *Thiebaudia* M.E.J. Chandler (1954) Fossil.

ETYMOLOGY: Dedicated to Arsenne Thiébaut-de-Berneaud (1777-1850), a French agronomist, botanist, secretary of the Linnaean Society of Paris and author of *Coup d'œil historique*.

TYPE SPECIES: *Thiebautia nervosa* Colla nom. illeg.

Bletia florida (Salisbury) R. Brown
(*Limodorum floridum* Salisbury)

Now recognized as belonging to the genus *Bletia*, *Thiebautia* was previously considered to include one terrestrial found in low elevation, scrub from the southeastern United States (Florida) and Cuba to Jamaica. This erect plant, borne from large, ovoid corms, has short stems, each with two thinly textured, fairly large, prominently veined leaves. The often branched, purple, few-flowered inflorescence has showy, long-lived, pale to deep rose or white flowers. The trilobed lip has erect, veined side lobes; the oblong midlobe has raised, yellow keels and a wavy margin. The flowers have a small, curved to arching, winged column.

THIENARIA

An orthographic variant introduced in *Orchideen (Schlechter)*, ed. 1, 249 (1914). The correct spelling is *Thicuania*.

THILXOCHILL

An orthographic variant introduced in *About Vanilla*, 19. (1900). The correct spelling is *Tlilxóchitl*.

THISBE

Falconer ex **Lindley**

Veg. Kingd., ed 2 183 (1847).

ETYMOLOGY: Roman Mythology. Thisbe was a young woman from Babylon. Thinking that Thisbe had died, her lover Pyramus killed himself, but when Thisbe found her dying lover, she too killed herself. Shakespeare used this old tale to create *Romeo and Juliet*.

TYPE SPECIES: *None designated*

Name published without a description. Today this name is most often referred to *Herminium*.

THORVALDSENIA

Liebmann

Bot. Not. **1844**: 103 (1844).

ETYMOLOGY: In honor of Albert Bertel Thorvaldsen (1770-1844), a Danish neoclassic period sculptor from Copenhagen who studied in Rome. He designed the Lion of Lucerne, a statue carved from solid native stone which is today found in Lucerne, Switzerland.

TYPE SPECIES: *Thorvaldsenia speciosa* Liebmann

Now recognized as belonging to the genus *Chysis*, *Thorvaldsenia* was previously considered to include one epiphyte found in humid, low to mid elevation, semi-deciduous woodlands from southern Mexico to Nicaragua. This hanging plant has long, club-shaped pseudobulbs, subtended by papery sheaths, each with several, broad, arching leaves which are usually shed after one season. The short, arching, few-flowered inflorescence, subtended by large floral bracts, has fragrant, waxy, white flowers suffused yellow at the tips. The yellow, deeply trilobed lip has an inrolled margin and brown-red markings. The flowers have an erect, incurved, broadly winged column. The above type name is now considered a synonym of *Chysis bractescens* Lindley.

THORWALDSENIA

An orthographic variant introduced in *Bot. Zeitung (Berlin)*, **4**: 396 (1846). The correct spelling is *Thorvaldsenia*.

THRICHOPILIA

An orthographic variant introduced in *Ann. Rep. Park Comm. Milwaukee*, 118 (1906). The correct spelling is *Trichopilia*.

THRIOSPERMUM

An orthographic variant introduced in *Bot. Centralbl.*, **70**(19-20): 217 (1897). The correct spelling is *Thrixspermum*.

THRISPERMUM

An orthographic variant introduced in *Orch. Ambon*, 109 (1905). The correct spelling is *Thrixspermum*.

THRIXPERMUM

An orthographic variant introduced in *Dict. Sci. Nat.*, **54**: 320 (1829). The correct spelling is *Thrixspermum*.

THRIXSPERMUM

Loureiro

Fl. Cochinch. **2**: 516, 519 (1790).

Epidendroideæ ◊ Vandeæ • Aeridinæ

ETYMOLOGY: Greek for hair and seed. Descriptive of the plant's hair-like seeds.

TYPE SPECIES: *Thrixspermum centipeda* Loureiro

One hundred forty-four monopodial epiphytes are widespread in low to mid elevation, hill scrub, savannas and montane evergreen to deciduous forests from Sri Lanka and Malaysia to the Philippines, with the center of development in Indonesia. They have vast vegetative and floral variations within this genus. These upright or hanging, small, vigorously ascending plants have long or short, branching stems, or are miniature, twig plants with usually well-spaced, flattened, sometimes fleshy, thick leaves. The solitary or in pairs, flattened or densely spiral, numerous to few-flowered inflorescence has spidery or rounded, white, pale lilac to pale yellow flowers (often turning dark yellow as they age) that are rather large, have a pleasant fragrance and open one by one in succession. The flowers appear either side by side or facing in all directions. A sudden change in temperature will initiate flowering of most species. The sac-like, immobile, white, spotted purple or orange, trilobed lip has a small spur. The flowers have a short, erect, stout, wingless column.

THRYXPERMUM

An orthographic variant introduced in *Orchid Album*, **10**: *t. 436* (1846). The correct spelling is *Thrixspermum*.

THULINIA

P.J. Cribb

Kew Bull. **40**(2): 401 (1985).

Orchidoideæ ◊ Orchideæ • Orchidinæ

ETYMOLOGY: In honor of Mats Thulin (1948-), a Swedish professor of botany at Uppsala University who collected the type species. He is a specialist on African flora, especially those from Somalia.

TYPE SPECIES: *Thulinia alboluotea* P.J. Cribb

One sympodial terrestrial is found in mid elevation, steep grassy slopes on the Nguru Mountain of southeastern Tanzania and known only from the type specimen. This slender plant has slightly hanging to erect, unbranched stems, each with several, narrow, basal leaves. The wiry, few-flowered inflorescence has relatively showy, white flowers with similar sepals and petals. The fan-shaped, bilobed lip is much larger

Currently Accepted   Validly Published   Invalidly Published   Published Pre-1753   Superfluous Usage   Orthographic Variant   Fossil

than are the other segments, it has a yellow, ascending callus, is deeply notched, and has a fused, short, cylindrical spur united for its entire length to the ovary. The flowers have a small, short, erect column.

THUNIA

Reichenbach *filius*

Bot. Zeitung (Berlin)   **10**: 764 (1852).

Epidendroideæ ⚘ Arethuseæ • Coelogyninæ

ETYMOLOGY: In honor of Leo Friedrich Thun-Hohenstein (1811-1888), an Austrian count from Tetschen (located in the present day Czech Republic). He helped Austria become a constitutional monarchy and was an activist for educational causes and religion reform.

TYPE SPECIES: *Thunia alba* (Lindley) Reichenbach f.
(*Phaius albus* Lindley)

Five sympodial epiphytes, lithophytes or terrestrials are found in low to upper elevation, hill to montane forests, rocky scrub and cliff faces of northern India (Kashmir to Sikkim), Nepal, southern China (Xizang to Sichuan), Myanmar to Vietnam, Thailand and Malaysia. These tall, leafy, pale green plants have stout, clustered, erect or spreading, cane-like stems, each with the several, deciduous leaves arranged in two ranks. The short-lived canes shrivel and die after just one season, and the foliage turns from a deep green to golden-yellow before being discarded. The short, drooping, few-flowered inflorescence, borne at the tip of the stem, has large, showy, short-lived, fragrant flowers, superficially resembling those of *Phaius*, they are papery thin and do not open widely. The showy, bright white or purple flowers have lips with fringed ridges of orange-yellow or purple. The bell or trumpet-shaped, entire lip is irregularly notched or frilled and has a short spur. The flowers have a slender, hood-like, club-shaped, footless column that has a flattened tip.

THYLACIS

Gagnepain

Bull. Mus. Natl. Hist. Nat., sér. 2   **4**(5): 599 (1932).

ETYMOLOGY: Greek for small and sac, bag or pouch. In reference to the unusual sac-like lip.

TYPE SPECIES: *None designated*

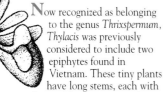

Now recognized as belonging to the genus *Thrixspermum*, *Thylacis* was previously considered to include two epiphytes found in Vietnam. These tiny plants have long stems, each with several, narrow leaves. The erect, wispy, few-flowered inflorescence has small, white or yellow flowers that are borne on a thin stalk. The long, narrow sepals and petals are widespread. The large, trilobed lip, attached to the column base, has erect side lobes and the a thick, sac-like midlobe. The flowers have a short, thick column.

THYLACOGLOSSUM

(Schlechter) Brieger

Orchideen (Schlechter), ed. 3   **3**: 377 (1975).

ETYMOLOGY: Greek for bag or box shaped and tongue. Refers to the shape of the spur.

TYPE SPECIES: *Thylacoglossum hamadryas*
(Schlechter) Brieger
(*Glossorhyncha hamadryas* Schlechter)
This type name is now considered a synonym of
Glomera hamadryas (Schlechter) J.J. Smith;
basionym
Glossorhyncha hamadryas Schlechter

Not validly published, this name is referred to *Glomera*. *Thylacoglossum* was considered to include one epiphyte found in the Solomons, Vanuatu and New Guinea.

THYLACOPHORA

Not *Thylacophora* Ridley (1916) Zingiberaceæ.

An orthographic variant introduced in *Orchids New Guinea*, 546 (1980). The correct spelling is *Thylacoglossum*.

THYLOSTYLIS

An orthographic variant cited in *Handb. Orchid.-Namen*, 702 (2005). The correct spelling is *Tylostylis*.

THYNNINORCHIS

D.L. Jones & M.A. Clements

Orchadian   **13**(10): 457 (2002).

ETYMOLOGY: Named derived from *Thynnine*, a genus of wasps and Greek for orchid. Referring to the specific type of pollinator for this genus.

TYPE SPECIES: *Thynninorchis huntiana*
(F. Mueller) D.L. Jones & M.A. Clements
(*Drakaea huntiana* F. Mueller)

Recognized as belonging to the genus *Arthrochilus*, *Thynninorchis* was proposed to include two saprophytes found in cool, low elevation, open forests and woodlands of southern Australia (Western Australia to New South Wales) and Tasmania. These slender to moderately stout, erect, leafless plants have red or green, unbranched stems, each with several, small, clasping bracts. The few-flowered inflorescence has an insect-like, red-green or green flower, each subtended by a short blunt bract. The narrow segments are of equal length and are reflexed against the ovary. The unusual, entire lip is attached by a movable joint to a narrow projection of the long, rod-like column. The base is divided into two calli, each with a swollen, knob-like, dark colored protuberance. The long, multilayered, barbed callus has numerous long, purple, dark red or green hairs.

THYSANOCHILUS

Falconer

Proc. Linn. Soc. London   **1**: 14 (1839).

ETYMOLOGY: Greek for tassel or fringe and lip. Refers to the hairy lip.

TYPE SPECIES: *None designated*

Name published without a description. Today this name is most often referred to *Eulophia*.

THYSANOGLOSSA

Porto & Brade

Anais Reunião Sul-Amer. Bot.   **3**: 42 (1938)[1940].

Epidendroideæ ⚘ Cymbidieæ • Oncidiinæ

ETYMOLOGY: Greek for tassel or fringe and tongue. Refers to the lace-like margin of the lip.

TYPE SPECIES: *Thysanoglossa jordanensis*
Porto & Brade

Two sympodial epiphytes are found in humid, low elevation, Atlantic rain forests of eastern Brazil (Rio de Janeiro and São Paulo). These tiny, tufted or fan-shaped plants have small, flat leaves. The hanging, few-flowered inflorescence has large, bright yellow, *Oncidium*-like flowers with small, narrow, widespreading sepals and petals. The large, trilobed lip has small, notched or fringed side lobes, and the long midlobe has two rows of green nobs at the base, is deeply bilobed at the tip and has either a notched or entire margin. The flowers have a wingless, strongly V-shaped column.

TICOGLOSSUM

R.L. Rodríguez ex Halbinger

Orquidea (Mexico City), n.s.   **9**(1): 4 (1983).

Epidendroideæ ⚘ Cymbidieæ • Oncidiinæ

ETYMOLOGY: From the local native slang word *tico* (*pequeñitico*) for very small. This affectionate name is applied to a native Costa Rican. And Greek for tongue.

TYPE SPECIES: *Ticoglossum oerstedii*
(Reichenbach f.) R.L. Rodríguez ex Halbinger
(*Odontoglossum oerstedii* Reichenbach f.)

Two sympodial epiphytes are found in mid to upper elevation, montane forests and coffee plantations from Nicaragua and central Costa Rica to western Panama. These small plants have roundish, compressed, blue-green pseudobulbs, subtended by leafy sheaths, each with two pale green, leathery leaves. The erect, few-flowered inflorescence, borne from the axils of the basal bracts, has large, showy, fragrant flowers with a glossy, waxy texture. The long-lived flowers are rosy violet, lilac or ivory white. The shortly clawed, slightly angled and variously shaped, entire lip has a yellow, boat-shaped callus, unmarked or spotted purple with white or red-brown bands in front. The flowers have a short, straight, wingless column.

TILOCHILUS

An orthographic variant introduced in *Hort. Donat.*, 152 (1858). The correct spelling is *Tylochilus*.

TINAEA

Not *Tinaea* Garzia (1845) Gramineæ.

An orthographic variant introduced in *Fl. Dalmat.*, **3**: 354 (1852). The correct spelling is *Tinea*.

TINEA

Bivona-Bernardi

Giorn. Sci. Sicilia **1833**: 149 (1833).

Not *Tinea* Sprengel (1821) Tiliaceæ.

ETYMOLOGY: Dedicated to Vincenzo Tineo (1791-1856), an Italian professor of botany at the University of Palermo, a director of the Palermo Botanical Garden and a writer about the flora of Sicily.

TYPE SPECIES: *Tinea cylindrica* Bivona-Bernardi
This type name is now considered a synonym of *Neotinea maculata* (Desfontaines) Stearn; basionym *Satyrium maculatum* Desfontaines

Not validly published because of a prior use of the name, this homonym was replaced by *Neotinea*.

TINEOA

An orthographic variant cited in *Lex. Gen. Phan.*, 561 (1904). The correct spelling is *Tinea*.

TINIA

An orthographic variant introduced in *Fl. Balearica*, 398 (1921). The correct spelling is *Tinea*.

TIPULARIA

Nuttall

Gen. N. Amer. Pl. (Nuttall) **2**: 195 (1818).

Not *Tipularia* F.F. Chevallier (1822) Myxomycetes.

Epidendroideæ ⚘ Calypsoeæ

ETYMOLOGY: Latin for water spider or crane fly. An allusion to the long, slender spur that resembles a crane or dragonfly.

TYPE SPECIES: *Tipularia discolor* (Pursh) Nuttall (*Orchis discolor* Pursh)

Five sympodial terrestrials are found in shady, mid to upper elevation, montane mixed and deciduous forests of the eastern United States (New York to Florida, Indiana to Texas), Japan, Korea, northern India (Assam) Nepal, Bhutan, Myanmar, southern China (Xizang to Shaanxi) and Taiwan in highly organic, leafy soil. These inconspicuous plants have oblong corms or small pseudobulbs, each with a solitary, dark green leaf, usually produced in the fall after the flowers have withered. The corms or pseudobulbs form a short chain from the previous year's growth. The green leaf has raised purple or pale brown spots, is dark satiny purple on the underside and strongly nerved. The erect, slender, few-flowered inflorescence is produced during the upcoming summer growing season. The small, nodding flowers vary from green-white, lemon yellow, dark green, pale purple to even bronze, and last for only a day. The trilobed lip has small, rounded side lobes, a narrow, spreading midlobe with a wavy margin, and has a long, slender, recurved spur that lies behind the flower and gives it the gangling look of a crane fly. The flowers have a long, slender, straight to slightly curved, wingless, footless column.

TISSOCHILUS

An orthographic variant introduced in *Hort. Donat.*, 219 (1858). The correct spelling is *Tylochilus*.

TITANIA

Endlicher

Prodr. Fl. Norfolk. 31 (1833).

Not *Titania* Berlese (1900) Fungi.

ETYMOLOGY: Medieval Folklore. Named for *Titania*, the mythical queen of the fairies, who was forced into a spell by *Oberon*, the mythical king of the fairies, to love a creature who is half man and half donkey (the story was used as the basis for William Shakespeare's play *A Midsummer Night's Dream*). This genus is closely related to *Oberonia*.

TYPE SPECIES: *Titania miniata* Endlicher

Now recognized as belonging to the genus *Oberonia*, *Titania* was previously considered to include one epiphyte

found in low to upper elevation, hill scrub and montane forests of Thailand, Indonesia, Malaysia and New Caledonia. This plant has long stems, each with compressed overlapping, flattened, sword-shaped leaves. The whip-like, usually arching inflorescence is covered with tiny, orange flowers appearing in irregular whorls. The broadly oblong, green, trilobed lip has small, raised, roundish appendages at the base, and the small to tiny side lobes surround the very short, fleshy column. The above type name is now considered a synonym of *Oberonia titania* Lindley.

TLILTIXÓCHITL

An orthographic variant introduced in *Gen. Hist. Things New Spain*, **12**: 12 (1590). The correct spelling is *Tlilxóchitl*.

TLILTXÓCHITL

An orthographic variant introduced in *Opera (Hernández)*, **2**: 33 (1790). The correct spelling is *Tlilxóchitl*.

TLILXÓCHITE

An orthographic variant introduced in *Pl. Amer.*, 183 (1755). The correct spelling is *Tlilxóchitl*.

TLILXÓCHITL

Cruz

Badianus Manuscript pl. 104 (1552).

Hernández

Hist. Pl. Nueva España 305 (1577), *Rerum Med. Nov. Hisp. Thes.* **1**: 38 (1651), and *Opera (Hernández)* **3**: 219, 302 (1790).

ETYMOLOGY: A local Nahuatl (Aztec) word for black and flower. Referring to the blackish seed capsules of the plant that were used to flavor local drinks.

TYPE SPECIES: *Tlilxóchitl* Cruz and also Hernández

Pre-1753, therefore not validly published in fulfillment of nomenclatural rules; this name is most often referred to *Vanilla*. *Tlilxóchitl* was previously considered to include one epiphyte or semi-epiphyte found in mid elevation, oak-pine forests and woodlands of central Mexico, but is now found growing in many parts of the globe. The plant requires high humidity and shade from the bright sunlight. This climbing vine has thick stems, each with several, smooth, bright green leaves and aerial roots. The several to few-flowered inflorescence has showy, short-lived, pale yellow-green flowers produced in succession. The tubular, narrowly clawed, trilobed lip has a fringed margin and a central

Currently Accepted   Validly Published   Invalidly Published   Published Pre-1753   Superfluous Usage   Orthographic Variant   Fossil

tuft of downward hairs. The flowers have a slender column. The hanging fruit is a black to dark brown capsule that when cured and dried was used by the local natives to flavor drinks, promote sleep, and as a charm to safeguard travelers. The above name is usually now considered a synonym of *Vanilla planifolia* Jackson ex Andrews.

NOTE: The vanilla flavoring obtained from this cultivated plant is widely used today in commerce.

TLILXÓCHITL

de Laet

Besch. West-Ind. **3**: 10 (1630).

Pre-1753, therefore not validly published in fulfillment of nomenclatural rules; this name is most often referred to *Tlilxóchitl* Hernández.

TLIXÓCHIL

An orthographic variant introduced in *Indian Nectar*, 52 (1662). The correct spelling is *Tlilxóchitl*.

TLIXÓCHITL

An orthographic variant introduced in *Med. Pflanzen*, **2**: sub 114 (1888). The correct spelling is *Tlilxóchitl*.

TODAREA

An orthographic variant introduced in *Cat. Descr. Orquid., Estac. Exp. Agron. Santiago, Cuba*, **60**: 198 (1938). The correct spelling is *Todaroa*.

TODAROA

A. Richard & Galeotti

Ann. Sci. Nat., Bot., sér. 3 **3**: 28 (1845).

Not *Todaroa* Parlatore (1843) Apiaceæ.

ETYMOLOGY: Named in honor of Agostino Todaro (1818-1892), a Sicilian botanist, director of the Palermo Botanical Garden and author of numerous books on botany including *Orchideæ Siculæ, sive enumeratio Orchidearum in Sicilia hucusque detectarum*.

TYPE SPECIES: *Todaroa micrantha* A. Richard & Galeotti

Not validly published because of a prior use of the name, this homonym was replaced by *Campylocentrum*.

TOENEOPHYLLUM

An orthographic variant cited in *Pl. Alkaloids*, 163 (1996). The correct spelling is *Taeniophyllum*.

TOLUMNIA

Rafinesque

Fl. Tellur. **2**: 101 (1836)[1837].

Epidendroideæ • Cymbidieæ • Oncidiinæ

ETYMOLOGY: Roman Mythology. Named for a Rutulian nymph (*Tolumnius*) mentioned by Publius Virgilius Maro (70-19 BC), an ancient Roman poet and author of the epic poem *Aeneid*.

TYPE SPECIES: *Tolumnia pulchella* (Hooker) Rafinesque (*Oncidium pulchellum* Hooker)

Thirty-six small, sympodial epiphytes, lithophytes or uncommon terrestrials are distributed in low to upper elevation, oak-pine forests, woodlands, grasslands and mangroves throughout Cuba, Jamaica, Trinidad, the Guianas and the southeastern United States (Florida). These small, tufted, twig plants have short, leafy stems (pseudobulbs reduced or absent), each with overlapping, distichous, flattened, fleshy to leathery, channeled leaves that are three sided and arranged in a loose fan shape. The arching, few-flowered inflorescence has flat, showy flowers (disproportionately large for the size of the plant), ranging from bright yellow, off-white, pink to purple, and sometimes with spotted segments. The sepals are smaller than the large petals with the lateral sepals more or less united and held behind the lip. The large, trilobed or usually four-lobed lip has small side lobes and an entire or notched midlobe with a prominent basal callus. The flowers have a small, erect, footless column with round or pointed, petal-like wings.

NOTE: These species were formerly grouped in *Oncidium* but differ in certain technical details and habit.

TOMOTRIS

Rafinesque

Fl. Tellur. **2**: 89(1836)[1837].

ETYMOLOGY: Greek for cutting or to divide and three. Referring to the shortened lateral branch that bears a flat-topped inflorescence.

LECTOTYPE: *Tomotris flava* (Swartz) Rafinesque (*Serapias flava* Swartz)

This type name is now considered a synonym of *Corymborkis flava* (Swartz) Kuntze; basionym *Serapias flava* Swartz

Now recognized as belonging to the genera *Corymborkis* and *Tropidia*, *Tomotris* was previously considered to include two rarely seen terrestrials of primitive morphology found from southern Mexico to Brazil. These tall, slender, leafy-stemmed plants have a simple to sometimes branched, few to numerous-flowered inflorescences with long, small, tubular, pale green-white to bright yellow flowers.

TOMZANONIA

Nir

Lindleyana **12**(4): 186 (1997).

Epidendroideæ • Epidendreæ • Pleurothallidinæ

ETYMOLOGY: In honor of Thomas Arthur Zanoni (1949-), an American botanist at the New York Botanical Garden, the collections manager in the herbarium, a specialist in Greater Antilles flora and former editor of the journal *Brittonia*.

TYPE SPECIES: *Tomzanonia filicina* (Dod) Nir (*Dilomilis filicina* Dod)

One sympodial epiphyte is found in upper elevation, montane forests of southwestern Haiti (Massif de la Hotte), and then known only from the type collection. This small, delicate plant has erect or somewhat pencil-like, simple or branched stems, subtended by leafy sheaths, each with numerous, distichous, leathery leaves and floral bracts. The solitary-flowered inflorescence has a white flower with similar, narrow, green suffused sepals and petals that have a bright red stripe down the center. The small, oblong, entire lip has a shortly hinged claw that is attached to a short footed, curved column and has a bright red, basal splash.

TONALOXÓCHITL

Hernández

Opera (Hernández) **1**: 239 (1790).

Sahagún

Gen. Hist. Things New Spain **11**: 198 (1590).

ETYMOLOGY: A local Aztec (Nahuatl language) name for spring (calendar) and flower. Referring to its small corms and that the plant blooms during springtime.

TYPE SPECIES: *Tônaloxóchitl sive Txacyxichitl altera* Hernández

Not validly published, this polynomial name is referred to *Bletia*, *Tônaloxóchitl* was considered to include one terrestrial found in mid elevation, montane forests and woodlands of central Mexico (Michoacán). This small plant has subterranean pseudobulbs (corm-like), each with several, narrow, pleated leaves. The erect, few-flowered inflorescence, borne from the side of the corm, has showy, bright orange-red flowers opening successively over a period of time, with similar sepals and petals. The trilobed lip has erect side lobes and the long-clawed midlobe has a notched tip. This name is now usually considered a synonym of *Bletia coccinea* Lexarza.

NOTE: During the time of the Aztecs the little corms of these plants were collected and ground to extract a glue that was used as a waterproof adhesive for the feather mosaics and various weaponry.

TOWNSONIA

Cheeseman

Man. New Zealand Fl. 691 (1906).

ETYMOLOGY: Dedicated to William Lewis Townson (1855-1926), a British-born New Zealand pharmaceutical chemist from Westport, and an amateur flora collector who collected mainly within the local Nelson Mountains for Thomas Cheeseman.

TYPE SPECIES: *Townsonia deflexa* Cheeseman

Now recognized as belonging to the genus *Acianthus*, *Townsonia* was previously considered to include two terrestrials found in low elevation, leaf litter of southern beech or *Nothofagus* forests of New Zealand and Tasmania. These insignificant plants have creeping rhizomes with short, erect, unbranched stems, each with one to two, flat, heart-shaped leaves that have scalloped edges. The long, stout, one- to three-flowered inflorescence has a much smaller leaf at mid-stem. The small, pale green to red flowers have a broad, hood-shaped dorsal sepal; the minute, erect petals are narrow, and the incurved, narrow lateral sepals bend downward. The heart-shaped or roundish, green, entire lip is suffused purple-red, especially on the margins, and often has obscure basal calli reduced to two flat ridges or they are absent. The flowers have a curved, footless column. The above type name is now considered a synonym of *Acianthus viridis* Hooker f.

TRACHELOSIPHON

Schlechter

Beih. Bot. Centralbl. 37(2): 423 (1920).

ETYMOLOGY: Greek for a neck and tube. Referring to the sepals that are united at the base into a tube.

LECTOTYPE: *Trachelosiphon actinosophilum*
(Barbosa Rodrigues) Schlechter
(*Spiranthes actinosophila* Barbosa Rodrigues)

Now recognized as belonging to the genus *Eurystyles*, *Trachelosiphon* was previously considered to include seven epiphytes found in seasonally wet, low to mid elevation, rain forests of Costa Rica to Ecuador, Venezuela and Brazil with a wide range of climate requirements. These erect to hanging plants vary considerably in both shape and size. The basal rosette of thinly textured to fleshy, gray-green leaves have variously notched to hairy margins. The hairy, erect to nodding, few-flowered inflorescence has a tightly bunched, heavily bracted, rosette of small, hairy, white flowers suffused green. The small dorsal sepal and petals converge, forming a hood over the small column. The white-green, narrow to arrow-shaped, entire lip has a covering of fine, white hairs at the tip and has a channeled, warty front lobe.

TRACHOMA

Garay

Bot. Mus. Leafl. 23(4): 207 (1972).

ETYMOLOGY: Greek for roughness. In reference to the short inflorescence that is quite rough because of the remnants of the densely packed bracts.

TYPE SPECIES: *Trachoma rhopalorrhachis*
(Reichenbach f.) Garay
(*Dendrocolla rhopalorrhachis* Reichenbach f.)

Now recognized as belonging to the genus *Tuberolabium*, *Trachoma* was previously considered to include six epiphytes found in low elevation, rain forests and woodlands of Thailand, Indonesia and the Philippines to Taiwan. These small robust plants have short leafy stems, each with several, leathery leaves arranged in a fan shape. The downward-curved, short, thick, multiple-flowered inflorescences continue to elongate over time. The small, fragrant, dull yellow flowers do not open widely, last for a few hours to several days and are produced over several intervals during the blooming season triggered by sudden weather changes. The white, immobile, compressed, trilobed lip is firmly attached to a short, wingless, footless column, and has a cone-shaped spur with a small mouth that is just a narrow slit between the side lobes.

TRACHORCHIS

Bergen

Fl. Francof. 240 (1750).

Pre-1753, therefore not validly published in fulfillment of nomenclatural rules; this name is most often referred to *Orchis*.

TRACHYPETALUM

Szlachetko & Sawicka

Orchidee (Hamburg) 54(1): 88 (2003).

ETYMOLOGY: Greek for rough and petal. Refers to the often hairy petals.

TYPE SPECIES: *Trachypetalum kraenzlinianum*
(Kraenzlin) Szlachetko & Sawicka
(*Habenaria trachypetala* Kraenzlin)

Recognized as belonging to the genus *Habenaria*, *Trachypetalum* was proposed to include five terrestrials found in low to mid elevation, hill forests, savannas, dune scrub, grasslands or marshes from Burundi to Zimbabwe, growing singly or in small groups. These erect plants have tall, unbranched stems, each with narrow, erect to curved leaves proceeding up the stem. The few-flowered inflorescence has rather large, green flowers with a narrow dorsal sepal. The bilobed or entire petals are usually hairy throughout or

only on the upper half. The interior petal lobe is joined with the dorsal sepal forming a wide hood. The deeply trilobed lip has narrow segments and a short, more or less twisted spur that is slightly swollen at the tip. The flowers have a short, massive column. The above type name is now considered a synonym of *Habenaria trachypetala* Kraenzlin.

TRACHYRHACHIS

Szlachetko

Richardiana 7(2): 85 (2007).

ETYMOLOGY: Greek for rough and inflorescence. Refers to the rough texture of the inflorescence.

TYPE SPECIES: *Trachyrhachis barbilabia*
(Schlechter) Szlachetko
(*Bulbophyllum barbilabium* Schlechter)

Recognized as belonging to the genus *Bulbophyllum*, *Trachyrhachis* was proposed to include twelve epiphytes found in humid, mid elevation, thickets and forests of New Guinea and the Solomons. This small plant has tiny, pale green, smooth pseudobulbs each with a solitary, leathery leaf. The branching, numerous-flowered inflorescence, covered with papillae, has small, bell-shaped, white or yellow flowers suffused purple. The above type name is now considered a synonym of *Bulbophyllum bulliferum* J.J. Smith.

TRACHYRHIZUM

(Schlechter) Brieger

Orchideen (Schlechter), ed. 3 1(11-12): 687 (1981).

ETYMOLOGY: Greek for rough and root. In reference to the rough surface of its roots.

TYPE SPECIES: *Trachyrhizum schlechteri*
(Schlechter) Rauschert
(*Dendrobium trachyrhizum* Schlechter)

Now recognized as belonging to the genus *Dendrobium*, *Trachyrhizum* was previously considered to include nine epiphytes found in moist, low to mid elevation, hill scrub and montane forests from New Caledonia and New Guinea to northern Australia (Queensland). These plants have slender, well-spaced pseudobulbous or slightly swollen stems, each with several, thinly textured, narrow leaves arranged in two ranks on the upper half of the stem. The short, few-flowered inflorescence, borne from the upper nodes, will often flower continuously for several years. The small, more or less cup-shaped, waxy, yellow to pink, fragrant flowers have twisted lateral sepals and petals and a recurved dorsal sepal. The hinged, trilobed lip has long, narrow side lobes with purple-brown veins, and the midlobe is usually bilobed at the tip with a spur-like backward-pointing projection. The above type name is now considered a synonym of *Dendrobium angustipetalum* J.J. Smith.

Currently Accepted   Validly Published   Invalidly Published   Published Pre-1753   Superfluous Usage   Orthographic Variant   Fossil

Orchid Genera • 394

TRADESCANTIA

Linnaeus

Sp. Pl. (Linnaeus), ed. 1 **1**: 288 (1753).

ETYMOLOGY: Honoring both John Tradescant, the younger (1608-1662), a British naturalist and head gardener for King Charles I, and his father John Tradescant (c1570-1638), the elder, a Dutch-born British naturalist who was a head gardener for Lord Salisbury, owner of a botanical garden at Lambert. Both were world travellers, collectors and importers of exotic flora.

TYPE SPECIES: *Not Orchidaceæ*

Linnaeus did not include this genus in Orchidaceæ. However, there was one species placed in this genus now recognized as belonging to *Telipogon*. This delicate epiphyte is found in upper elevation, montane cloud forests of Colombia and Venezuela. This plant that has long, creeping stems and a few-flowered inflorescence with large flowers. The sepals are pale green; the petals and broad, entire lip are green-yellow, and lined with brown or purple. The flowers have a short, stout column with a crest of long, erect hairs concealing the anther. This species *Tradescantia nervosa* Linnaeus (*Mant. Pl.*, ed. 2, 223 (1771)) was mistakenly included in the Commelinaceæ (Spiderwort) family, but the name should now be correctly identified as a synonym of *Telipogon nervosus* (Linnaeus) Druce, *Bot. Soc. Exch. Club Brit. Isles*, 650 (1916).

TRAGI

Cordus

Annot. 129b, 130a (1561).

Pre-1753, therefore not validly published in fulfillment of nomenclatural rules; this name is most often referred to *Orchis*.

TRAGORCHIN

An orthographic variant introduced in *Stirp. Hist. Pempt.*, 234 (1616). The correct spelling is *Tragorchis*.

TRAGORCHIOS

An orthographic variant introduced in *Fl. Coron. Herb. Hist.*, 215 (1578). The correct spelling is *Tragorchis*.

TRAGORCHIS

L'Obel

Pl. Stirp. Hist. 90 (1576).

Pre-1753, therefore not validly published in fulfillment of nomenclatural rules; this name is most often referred to *Orchis*.

TRAUNSTEINERA

Reichenbach

Fl. Saxon. 87 (1842), and
Deut. Bot. Herb.-Buch 50 (1841).

Orchidoideæ · Orchideæ · Orchidinæ

ETYMOLOGY: Honoring Joseph Traunsteiner (1798-1850), an Austrian pharmacist, apothecary, amateur botanist from Tyrol and author of *Monographie der Weiden von Tirol and Voralberg*.

TYPE SPECIES: *Traunsteinera globosa*
(Linnaeus) Reichenbach
(*Orchis globosa* Linnaeus)

Two sympodial terrestrials are quite common in mid to upper elevation, montane meadows from Italy to Poland, Switzerland to western Russia (Black Sea), Turkey, Ukraine and Kyrgyzstan in a wide range of habitats. These small plants have two to three, smooth, narrow leaves placed in the middle of the unbranched, erect stem. The densely packed, numerous-flowered inflorescence has a mass of vividly colored, showy flowers tightly packed into a pyramidal ball at first, then lengthening as the flowers fade. The small flowers are usually pale pink-purple to creamy white. The each sepal and petals are extended into a narrow point with a club-shaped tip. The wedged-shaped, trilobed lip has toothed side lobes; the often spotted dark purple midlobe has a thread-like tip and a short to long, narrow spur. The flowers have a small, slightly curved column.

TRAUNSTEINERIA

An orthographic variant cited in *Etym.-Bot.-Handw.-Buch*, ed. 1, 889 (1852). The correct spelling is *Traunsteinera*.

TRECHOPILIA

An orthographic variant introduced in *Floric. Cab. & Florist's Mag.*, **20**(7): 153 (1852). The correct spelling is *Trichopilia*.

TREVORIA

F. Lehmann

Gard. Chron., ser. 3 **21**: 345 (1897).

Epidendroideæ · Cymbidieæ · Stanhopeinæ

ETYMOLOGY: In honor of James John Trevor Lawrence (1831-1913), a British horticulturist, president of the Royal Horticultural Society of London and a famous orchid grower of his time during the Queen Victoria era.

TYPE SPECIES: *Trevoria chloris* F. Lehmann

Six spectacular sympodial epiphytes are found in cool, mid elevation, montane forests from Nicaragua and Costa Rica to Ecuador. These uncommon plants have clustered, cylindrical or ovoid, one-noded pseudobulbs, each with several, pleated, leathery or thinly textured leaves at the tip. The hanging, numerous to few-flowered inflorescence has large, showy, green, green-orange or creamy white flowers with the lateral sepals united at the base to the column foot. The fleshy, white, three part (tripartite) lip, attached to the base of the column, has a base (hypochile) that is unlobed and hood-shaped. The concave midsection (mesochile) has a callus which sometimes has a free tip, and the spear-shaped tip (epichile) has a gradually tapering point. The flowers have a short, fleshy column.

TRIANGIS

Thouars

Hist. Orchid. Table 2, sub 3o, t. 49 (1822).

Name published without a description. Today this name is most often referred to *Angraecum*.

TRIARISTELLA

(Reichenbach *filius*) Brieger

Orchideen (Schlechter), ed. 3 **7**(25-28): 448 (1975).

Name published without a description. Today this name is most often referred to *Trisetella*.

TRIARISTELLA

Brieger ex Luer

Selbyana **2**(2-3): 205 (1978).
Not *Triaristella* Malyavkina (1949) Fossil.

ETYMOLOGY: Latin for three, bristle, a beard of grain and diminutive. Referring to the hair-like tails of the sepals.

TYPE SPECIES: *Triaristella reichenbachii* Brieger ex Luer
(*Masdevallia triaristella* Reichenbach f.)

Not validly published because of a prior use of the name, this homonym was replaced by *Trisetella*.

TRIARISTELLINA

Rauschert

Feddes Repert. **94**(7-8): 469 (1983).

ETYMOLOGY: A derivative of *Triaristella*, a genus of orchids and Latin for not.

TYPE SPECIES: *Triaristellina triaristella*
(Reichenbach f.) Rauschert
(*Masdevallia triaristella* Reichenbach f.)

A superfluous name proposed as a substitute for *Triaristella*.

TRIAS

Lindley

Gen. Sp. Orchid. Pl. 60 (1830), and
Numer. List 54, no. 1977 (1829).

Epidendroideæ ❦ Dendrobiinæ • Currently unplaced

ETYMOLOGY: Greek for triad or three. Descriptive of
the triangular shape of the open flower.

TYPE SPECIES: *None designated*

Thirteen uncommon, seldom seen sympodial epiphytes are found in low to mid elevation, hill and montane evergreen forests of Sri Lanka, India, Myanmar, Thailand to Vietnam and Indonesia (Borneo). These inconspicuous, miniature plants have ovoid to roundish, often compressed pseudobulbs, each with a solitary, oblong leaf. The short, solitary to few-flowered inflorescences, borne from the pseudobulb base, have attractive large, triangular-shaped, brown-green, white, red or yellow flowers. The tiny petals are much smaller than are the sepals, and the lateral sepals are fused to the short column foot. The heavily-textured flower is often densely spotted purple or maroon and not long-lasting. The mobile, often obscurely trilobed lip is hinged to the minute column.

TRIBAUDIA

An orthographic variant introduced in *Hort. Donat.*, 129 (1858). The correct spelling is *Thiebautia*.

TRIBRACHIA

Lindley

Bot. Reg. 10: *t.* 832 (1824).

Not *Tribrachia* A. Mann (1925) Bacillariophyta.

ETYMOLOGY: Greek for of three and Latin for arm-like or branched. Refers to the three sepals.

TYPE SPECIES: *Tribrachia reptans* Lindley

Now recognized as belonging to the genus *Bulbophyllum*, *Tribrachia* was previously considered to include seven epiphytes or lithophytes found in mid to upper elevation, montane moss laden forests of northern India, Nepal, Myanmar to Vietnam and Thailand. These small plants have ovoid pseudobulbs, each with one or rarely two leathery leaves. The drooping, red-brown, numerous-flowered inflorescence has small, yellow flowers packed tightly into a cylindrical arch. The foul smelling flowers are densely spotted or striped purple-brown on the outside surfaces. The dull brown, fuzzy, tongue-shaped, entire lip is folded down the middle or is bent downward and

then outward from the middle and has a blunt tip. The flowers have a tiny column.

TRIBRACHIUM

An orthographic variant introduced in *Gen. Pl. (Bentham & Hooker* f.), 3: 501 (1863). The correct spelling is *Tribrachia*.

TRIBULAGO

Luer

Monogr. Syst. Bot. Missouri Bot. Gard. 95: 265 (2004).

ETYMOLOGY: Latin for a pronged implement used to impede cavalry. Refers to the prickly fruit.

TYPE SPECIES: *Tribulago tribuloides* (Swartz) Luer
(*Epidendrum tribuloides* Swartz)

Recognized as belonging to the genus *Specklinia*, *Tribulago* was proposed to include two epiphytes found in wet, mid elevation, evergreen or deciduous forests from southern Mexico to Panama, Cuba, Hispaniola and Jamaica. These small plants form dense clusters with erect stems, subtended by white, papery sheaths, each with a solitary, narrow, leathery leaf. The short, few-flowered inflorescence, borne from the leaf axils, has tiny, fleshy, brick-red to orange flowers that do not open widely. The outer surfaces are minutely warty and the tips of the sepals are united or fused together. The narrow, entire lip has a fringed margin especially at the tip. The flowers have a minute column with two triangular, tooth-like wings.

NOTE: Each flower can have a small, cocklebur-like appendage at its base; this spiny seed capsule turns a dark blue-green when mature.

TRICERATORHYNCHUS

Summerhayes

Bot. Mus. Leafl. 14: 232 (1951).

Epidendroideæ ❦ Vandeæ • Aerangidinæ

ETYMOLOGY: Greek for three, horn and beak or snout. Descriptive of the rostellum that looks like a three-horned structure.

TYPE SPECIES: *Triceratorhynchus viridiflorus*
Summerhayes

One miniature, monopodial epiphyte is found in humid, mid elevation forests of Rwanda, Burundi and southwestern Uganda to southwestern Kenya. This unremarkable, often easily overlooked plant has short stems, each with several, narrow, obscurely bilobed leaves. The erect, wiry, few-flowered inflorescence, often longer than the leaves, has small bracts and small, green or yellow-green flowers. The concave, obscurely

trilobed lip recurves, and tapers to a sharp tip with an upward curved, thread-like to slender spur. The flowers have a short, wingless, footless column with a distinctive rostellum structure that has three prominent prongs or horns protruding both up and down with a short center prong.

TRICERATORRHYCHUS

An orthographic variant introduced in *Fragm. Florist. Geobot.*, 3(Suppl.): 93 (1995). The correct spelling is *Triceratorhynchus*.

TRICERATOSTRIS

(Szlachetko) Szlachetko & R. González

Fragm. Florist. Geobot. 41(2): 1021 (1996).

ETYMOLOGY: *Triceratops*, a genus of dinosaurs and Latin for stiff. In reference to the rostellum remnant that resembles the bony plate covering the neck of this horned herbivorous dinosaur species.

TYPE SPECIES: *Triceratostris rhombilabia*
(Garay) Szlachetko & R. González
(*Deiregyne rhombilabia* Garay)

Recognized as belonging to the genus *Deiregyne*, *Triceratostris* was proposed to include two terrestrials found in dry, mid elevation, stony clay soils of central Mexico (Jalisco and Morelos). These erect plants have unbranched, stout stems, completely subtended by small sheaths, each with a basal rosette that is usually withered at time of flowering. The erect, twisted, few-flowered inflorescence is concealed by long, papery bracts often exceeding the flower in size. The small, inconspicuous, green-white, broadly opening flowers have green mid-veins, and the dorsal sepal is joined at the backside of the column base. The oblong to diamond-shaped, entire lip has thickened, basal margins and a blunt tip with small, soft protuberances or warts. The flowers have a slender, slightly curved, club-shaped column.

TRICHOCENTRON

An orthographic variant introduced in *Edwards's Bot. Reg.*, 24(Misc.): 94, section no. 178 (1838). The correct spelling is *Trichocentrum*.

| Currently Accepted | Validly Published | Invalidly Published | Published Pre-1753 | Superfluous Usage | Orthographic Variant | Fossil |

O r c h i d   G e n e r a   • **396**

TRICHOCENTRUM

Poeppig & Endlicher

Nov. Gen. Sp. Pl. (Poeppig & Endlicher)
2(1-2): 11, *t. 115* (1836).

Epidendroideæ ᴠ Cymbidieæ • Oncidiinæ

ETYMOLOGY: Greek for hair and a spur. Alluding to the very slender, long, nectarless spur found in some of the species.

TYPE SPECIES: *Trichocentrum pulchrum*
Poeppig & Endlicher

Sixty-nine showy, sympodial epiphytes, lithophytes or terrestrials are found in seasonally dry to wet, low to mid elevation, hill scrub to montane forests ranging from the southeastern United States (Florida), Cuba to Trinidad, southern Mexico to Bolivia, the Guianas, Venezuela, Argentina and Paraguay with the most species found in southern Brazil. These stout to tufted plants have small to minute, compressed, clustered pseudobulbs, subtended by scale-like, sheathing bracts, each with a solitary, small, flat, thick to ridged, fleshy to leathery, deciduous leaf. The erect to hanging, solitary to few-flowered inflorescence, borne from the base of the pseudobulb, has comparatively large, showy, widespreading brown to green flowers suffused with paler hues on the outside. The white or purple, fleshy lip usually far exceeds the other floral segments in dimensions. The fiddle-shaped, entire or obscurely trilobed lip has two yellow, basal keels and a slender or pouch-like, elongate, hollow spur (in some species). The flowers have a short, stout, erect, footless column.

TRICHOCERAS

Not *Trichoceras* Kuetzing (1849) Ceramiaceæ.

An orthographic variant introduced in *Anleit. Kenntn. Gew.*, ed. 2, **2**(1): 291 (1817). The correct spelling is *Trichoceros*.

TRICHOCEROS

Kunth

Nov. Gen. Sp.   **1**: 337, *t. 76* (1815).
Not *Trichoceras* Kuetzing (1849) Ceramiaceæ.

Epidendroideæ ᴠ Cymbidieæ • Oncidiinæ

ETYMOLOGY: Greek for hair and horn. Refers to the short, stiff hairs found on each side of the column.

TYPE SPECIES: *None designated*

Nine showy, sympodial terrestrials or rare epiphytes are found in seasonally dry or wet, mid to upper elevation, montane forests from Venezuela and Colombia to Peru. These stout plants have small to minute, widely-spaced pseudobulbs, almost obscured in the center by distichous, overlapping, gray green, leaf-like sheaths, each with a small, solitary, flat, thick to rigid, fleshy leaf. The erect, solitary to few-flowered inflorescence, only one open at a time, has comparatively, large flowers suffused brown to green with paler hues found on the outside and open in succession with one at a time. The white or purple, fleshy lip usually far exceeds the other floral segments in dimensions. The entire or obscurely trilobed lip, which resembles a female fly, has erect or spreading side lobes, and a large, usually ovate midlobe. The flowers have a short, stout, footless, wingless column.

TRICHOCEROTIS

Kunth ex Schlechter

Repert. Spec. Nov. Regni Veg. Beih.   **8**: 106 (1921).
ETYMOLOGY: Greek for hair and Latin for stiff. Refers to the stiff hairs found on the column.

TYPE SPECIES: *Trichocerotis angustifoliae*
Kunth ex Schlechter

Not validly published, this name is most often referred to *Trichoceros*.

TRICHOCERUS

An orthographic variant introduced in *Cat. Samm. Ausstell.*, 120 (1869). The correct spelling is *Trichoceros*.

TRICHOCHILA

Lindley ex Wittstein

Etym.-Bot.-Handw.-Buch, ed. 1   893 (1852).

Name published without a description. Today this name is most often referred to as a section of *Disa*.

TRICHOCHILUS

Ames

J. Arnold Arbor.   **13**: 142 (1932).
ETYMOLOGY: Greek for hair and a lip. Referring to the shaggy, soft, slender hairs on the midlobe of the lip.

TYPE SPECIES: *Trichochilus neoebudicus* Ames
This type name is now considered a synonym of
Dipodium squamatum (G. Forster) R. Brown;
basionym
Ophrys squamata G. Forster

Now recognized as belonging to the genus *Dipodium*, *Trichochilus* was previously considered to include one terrestrial found only in low elevation, thickets, coastal woodlands and among grasses of Vanuatu, New Caledonia, eastern Australia and Tasmania. This long-stemmed plant has narrow, triangular, conspicuously nerved leaves and an extensive system of long, fleshy roots. The erect, red-brown, few-flowered inflorescence, but varying in color, has small, white, pink to even pale yellow flowers suffused mauve at their tips. The conspicuously trilobed lip has a small spur.

TRICHOGLOTTIS

Blume

Bijdr. Fl. Ned. Ind.   **8**: 359, *t. 8* (1825).

Epidendroideæ ᴠ Vandeæ • Aeridinæ

ETYMOLOGY: Greek for hair and tongue. Probably alluding to the generally hairy lip of the type species.

LECTOTYPE: *Trichoglottis retusa* Blume

Sixty-four monopodial epiphytes occasional lithophytes are scattered in low to mid elevation, hill to montane forests and cliff faces throughout Taiwan, India, Sri Lanka, Myanmar to Vietnam, Malaysia, Indonesia, New Guinea, northeastern Australia (Queensland) and the northwestern Pacific Archipelago with the greatest development occurring in the Philippines. These short or long plants have climbing or hanging stems, each with narrow, distichous, fleshy, usually unequally bilobed leaves arranged in two rows. The several, short, few-flowered inflorescences, borne from different nodes on one stem, have small, highly variable, brown to yellow flowers, faintly fragrant, heavily-waxy or fleshy and long-lived. The immobile, trilobed or obscurely trilobed lip has an erect, hairy, strap-shaped tongue on the back wall just below the base of the wingless, footless, short column. This usually white lip has a large, almost flat, oblong midlobe that is entire or trilobed with blunt or rounded ends, is covered with very fine hairs; has erect, triangular side lobes, and has a distinct, sac-like or strongly concave spur.

TRICHOPELIA

An orthographic variant introduced in *Cat. Pl. Trinidad*, 83 (1870). The correct spelling is *Trichopilia*.

TRICHOPHILA

Not *Trichophila* Oudemans (1889) Coelomycetes.

An orthographic variant introduced in *Icon. Bot. Index*, **1**: 1115 (1855). The correct spelling is *Trichopilia*.

TRICHOPILIA

Lindley

Edwards's Bot. Reg. **22**: *t. 1836* (1836), and
Intr. Nat. Syst. Bot., ed. 2 446 (1836).

Epidendroideæ ⚬ **Cymbidieæ** • **Oncidiinæ**

ETYMOLOGY: Greek for hair and felt, cap or hat.
Refers to the ciliate or fringed margin of the
clinandrium.

TYPE SPECIES: *Trichopilia tortilis* Lindley

Twenty-six small, sympodial
epiphytes but occasionally lithophytes
or terrestrials are found in wet, mid to
upper elevation, montane forests
widespread from Cuba to
Trinidad, Mexico to Bolivia,
the Guianas, Venezuela
and Brazil. Without exception,
these attractive flowers are quite
showy and are commonly called the
corkscrew orchid. These evergreen plants have
small, clustered, highly flattened, ovate
pseudobulbs, often subtended by brown
spotted, papery bracts, each with a solitary,
leathery leaf. The short, drooping, hanging to
arching, few-flowered inflorescence has large,
super fragrant, showy flowers with similar,
narrow, pale green, pink to white sepals and
petals that are sometimes strongly twisted with
or without wavy margins. The short claw of
the pale green to white, tubular-shaped,
obscurely trilobed or trilobed lip, fused to the
base of the column, surrounds the erect,
slender, club-shaped column forming a funnel-
shaped throat.

TRICHOPOLIA

An orthographic variant introduced in *Ann.
Hort. Bot.*, **5**: 182 (1862). The correct spelling
is *Trichopilia*.

TRICHOPYLIA

An orthographic variant introduced in
Gartenflora, **15**: 178 (1866). The correct
spelling is *Trichopilia*.

TRICHORHIZA

G. Don

Hort. Brit. (Sweet), ed. 3 647 (1839).

Name published without a description. Today
this name is most often referred to *Trichorhiza*
Steudel.

TRICHORHIZA

Lindley ex Steudel

Nomencl. Bot. (Steudel), ed. 2 **2**: 702 (1841).

ETYMOLOGY: Greek for hair and root. Referring to
the hairiness of the roots.

TYPE SPECIES: *Trichorhiza teretifolia*
(Gaudichaud-Beaupré) Lindley ex Steudel
(*Luisia teretifolia* Gaudichaud-Beaupré)
This type name is now considered a synonym of
Luisia tristis (G. Forster) Hooker f.;
basionym replaced with
Epidendrum triste G. Forster

Now recognized as
belonging to the genus
Luisia, Trichorhiza was
previously considered
to include one epiphyte
widely distributed in
mid elevation, montane
forests from southern China (Yunnan, Guangxi
and Sichuan), Taiwan, northern India
(Kashmir to Assam), Myanmar to Vietnam,
Malaysia, the Philippines, New Guinea and
northern Australia to the southwestern Pacific
Archipelago. This rigid, stout, noded plant has
erect stems, each with several, fleshy, narrow,
dark green leaves. The erect, few-flowered
inflorescence has small, faintly foul smelling,
waxy, long-lived, yellow to green flowers with
similar sepals and petals. They do not open
widely, all open simultaneously. The purple or
green, thick, entire lip is attached to the base
and sides of the large column.

TRICHORRHIZA

An orthographic variant introduced in *Nat.
Pflanzen-Syst.*, 197 (1829). The correct
spelling is *Trichorhiza*.

TRICHOSALPINX

Luer

Phytologia **54**(5): 393 (1983).

Epidendroideæ ⚬ **Epidendreæ** • **Pleurothallidinæ**

ETYMOLOGY: Greek for hair and trumpet or tube.
Descriptive of the trumpet-shaped sheaths of the
stems that are ringed by small hairs.

TYPE SPECIES: *Trichosalpinx ciliaris* (Lindley) Luer
(*Specklinia ciliaris* Lindley)

One hundred twenty-two sympodial
epiphytes, lithophytes or terrestrials are
found in low to upper elevation, hill
scrub and montane cloud forests from
Cuba to Trinidad, the Guianas,
Venezuela and southern Mexico to
Bolivia and Brazil. These small, tufted
or sprawling, clump-forming plants
have erect, slender stems, subtended
by overlapping, ringed, ribbed,
tubular sheaths with hairy margins, each with
narrow, thick to fleshy, pleated leaves. The
terminal, few-flowered inflorescence has tiny,
purple-red or even yellow-green flowers. The

minute petals are smaller than the sepals
which are sometimes fringed or entire, and the
lateral sepals are free to entirely united. The
often fringed to hairy, entire and oblong or
trilobed lip is attached or hinged to the
distinct column foot. The flowers have a short,
winged, long, slender, hooded column or a
false, swollen column.

TRICHOSIA

Not *Trichosia* A.C. Batista & R. Garnier (1960) Microthyriales.

An orthographic variant introduced in *Tab.
Pl. Jav. Orchid.*, *t. 11* (1825), and *Bijdr. Fl.
Ned. Ind.*, 436 (1825). The correct spelling is
Trichosma.

TRICHOSMA

Lindley

Edwards's Bot. Reg. **28**: *t. 21* (1842).

ETYMOLOGY: Greek for hair. Referring to the fringed
crests on the lip.

TYPE SPECIES: *Trichosma suavis* Lindley nom. illeg.
Eria coronaria (Lindley) Reichenbach f.
(*Coelogyne coronaria* Lindley)

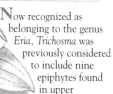

Now recognized as
belonging to the genus
Eria, Trichosma was
previously considered
to include nine
epiphytes found
in upper
elevation, montane forests from northeastern
India (Assam) to Malaysia. These plants have
slender, tufted pseudobulbs with a single node.
The bases are subtended by dry sheaths and
each has two thinly textured, veined leaves.
The few-flowered inflorescence has waxy,
fragrant, white to yellow-green flowers with
deep purple lateral veins. The oblong, trilobed
lip has small, roundish side lobes, and a
golden-yellow midlobe with vague keels down
the center and has a wavy margin.

TRICHOSPERMA

An orthographic variant introduced in *Contr.
Bot. Dept. Nebraska Univ.*, **3**(1): 53 (1902).
The correct spelling is *Thrixspermum*.

TRICHOSPERMUM

Not *Trichospermum* Blume (1825) Tiliaceæ.

An orthographic variant introduced in *Nat.
Pflanzenfam.*, 234 (1897). The correct spelling
is *Thrixspermum*.

TRICHOSTA

An orthographic variant introduced in *Tab.
Pl. Jav. Orchid.*, *t. 11* (1825). The correct
spelling is *Trichotosia*.

Currently Accepted Validly Published Invalidly Published Published Pre-1753 Superfluous Usage Orthographic Variant Fossil

Orchid Genera • **398**

TRICHOSTOSIA

An orthographic variant introduced in *Icon. Pl. Asiat.*, **3**: 331-332, *t. 315* (1851). The correct spelling is *Trichotosia*.

TRICHOTISIA

An orthographic variant introduced in *Enum. Phan. Born.*, 175 (1942). The correct spelling is *Trichotosia*.

TRICHOTOSIA

Blume

Bijdr. Fl. Ned. Ind.   **7**: 342 (1825).

Epidendroideæ ᴥ Podochileæ • Eriinæ

ETYMOLOGY: Greek for hairy and a bow. Referring to the shape of the densely hairy sepals.

LECTOTYPE: *Trichotosia pauciflora* Blume

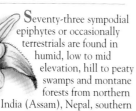

Seventy-three sympodial epiphytes or occasionally terrestrials are found in humid, low to mid elevation, hill to peaty swamps and montane forests from northern India (Assam), Nepal, southern China (Guangxi to Hainan), Myanmar to Vietnam, Malaysia, New Guinea, Indonesia and northern Australia to the southwestern Pacific Archipelago. These plants have long or short, but not fleshy, cane-like, clustered stems, each with distichous, flat, usually hairy to smooth leaves. The majority of the species are usually covered throughout with red-brown or rare white hairs; sometimes these hairs are restricted to the leaf sheaths and inflorescence. The outside surface of the flower is densely covered in long, soft, yellow or red-brown hairs. The often solitary-flowered inflorescence has a small, green-yellow, yellow, cream or pale pink flower, not opening widely, which lasts for a few days. The white, entire or trilobed lip often has a maroon disc with or without keels. The flowers have a short, erect to slightly curved, fleshy column. These species are often included as the section *Cylindrolobus* in *Eria*.

TRICHOTSIA

An orthographic variant introduced in *Enum. Phan. Born.*, 178, 184 (1942). The correct spelling is *Trichotosia*.

TRICOCHILUS

An orthographic variant introduced in *Vasc. Pl. Fam. Gen.*, 436 (1992). The correct spelling is *Trichochilus*.

TRICOPILIA

An orthographic variant introduced in *Kultuur Orchid.*, 130 (1856). The correct spelling is *Trichopilia*.

TRICOPILIA

An orthographic variant introduced in *Fl. World Gard. Guide*, **6**: 89 (1863). The correct spelling is *Trichopilia*.

TRIDACHNE

Liebmann ex Lindley & Paxton

Paxton's Fl. Gard.   **3**: 45 (1852-53).

ETYMOLOGY: Greek for three and colorless. Refers to the color and shape of the flowers.

TYPE SPECIES: *Tridachne virens* Liebmann

Name published without a description. Today this name is most often referred to as a synonym of *Notylia*.

TRIDACTYLE

Schlechter

Orchideen (Schlechter), ed. 1   602 (1914).

Epidendroideæ ᴥ Vandeæ • Aerangidinæ

ETYMOLOGY: Greek for three and a finger. Descriptive of the distinctly trilobed lip.

LECTOTYPE: *Tridactyle bicaudata* (Lindley) Schlechter
(*Angraecum bicaudatum* Lindley)

Forty-three monopodial epiphytes, lithophytes or rare terrestrials are found in shady, moist, low to upper elevation, evergreen woodlands and forests from Liberia to Ethiopia, south to Zimbabwe, Mozambique and South Africa. These small to medium-sized plants have short to long, leafy, woody stems (erect to hanging or slender to climbing), each with a few narrow, distichous leaves unequally bilobed or toothed at the tip. These leaves are usually twisted at their base to lie in one plane. The stems are subtended in remains of old leaf bases and grow in rather untidy clumps. The long or short, numerous to few-flowered inflorescence has small to tiny, ochre brown, yellow, green or rare white, fragrant flowers alternating on the spike, often turning pale orange with age. The long, entire or distinctly trilobed lip has long, heavily fringed side lobes, a narrowly triangular midlobe, and a long to short, often club-shaped spur. The flowers have a short, erect, wingless, footless column.

TRIDELTA

Luer

Monogr. Syst. Bot. Missouri Bot. Gard. **105**: 232, *f. 184* (2006).

ETYMOLOGY: Greek for three and delta-shaped or triangular. Refers to the three initials of Donald Dungan Dod (1912-) who collected this species.

TYPE SPECIES: *Tridelta aurantiaca* (Dod) Luer
(*Cryptophoranthus aurantiacus* Dod)

Recognized as belonging to the genus *Pleurothallis*, *Tridelta* was

proposed to include one epiphyte found in the Dominican Republic (Sierra de Neiba). This small, tufted plant, often forming dense clumps, has stout, erect stems, subtended by thinly textured, tubular sheaths, each with a solitary, thick, leathery leaf that has notched or toothed margins. The solitary-flowered inflorescence has an orange, fleshy flower with a concave dorsal sepal united basally to the lateral sepals which are united into a concave synsepal and have small, oblong petals tucked inside. The thick, oblong, trilobed lip has long, narrow side lobes and the midlobe has a disc channeled between a pair of tall scales and is hinged to the tip of the column foot. The flowers have a slender, curved column. The above type name is now considered a synonym of *Pleurothallis spiloporphyrea* Dod.

TRIDRIS

An orthographic variant introduced in *Hist. Orchid.*, *t. 3* (1822). The correct spelling is *Triodris*.

TRIGOGLOTTIS

An orthographic variant introduced in *Just's Bot. Jahresber.*, **25**(2): 505 (1900). The correct spelling is *Trichoglottis*.

TRIGONANTHE

(Schlechter) Brieger

Orchideen (Schlechter), ed. 3   **7**(25-28): 448 (1975).

ETYMOLOGY: Greek for three, angle and flower. Refers to the three sepal points forming a triangle.

TYPE SPECIES: *None designated*

Not validly published, this name is referred to *Dryadella*. *Trigonanthe* was considered to include eleven epiphytes found in Guatemala, Colombia to Peru and southern Brazil.

TRIGONANTHUS

Korthals ex Hooker *filius*

Fl. Brit. Ind.   **5**: 826 (1890), and
Hooker's Icon. Pl.   **21**: *t. 2100* (1892).

Not *Trigonanthus* Spruce ex Mitten (1865) Cephalziaceæ.

ETYMOLOGY: Greek for three angled and anther.

TYPE SPECIES: *Trigonanthus pendulus*
Korthals ex Hooker f.

This type name is now considered a synonym of *Ceratostylis pendula* Hooker f.

Not validly published, this name is referred to *Ceratostylis*. *Trigonanthus* was considered to include one epiphyte found in Malaysia and Indonesia (Borneo and Sulawesi).

TRIGONIDIUM

Lindley

Edwards's Bot. Reg. **23**: *t. 1923 (1837).*
Not *Trigonidium* Pascher (1932) Oocystaceæ.

Epidendroideæ ᴡ **Cymbidieæ** • **Maxillariinæ**

ETYMOLOGY: Greek for three cornered or angle. An allusion to the triangular form of the floral segments.

TYPE SPECIES: *Trigonidium obtusum* Lindley

Fourteen unusual, sympodial epiphytes, lithophytes or semi-terrestrials are found in wet, low to mid elevation, hill scrub and montane forests ranging from Mexico to Brazil, Peru and Bolivia. These small plants have short, slightly compressed pseudo-bulbs, each with one to two, narrow or wide, leathery, strap-like leaves. The stiff, wiry, solitary-flowered inflorescence, borne from the base of the pseudobulb, has a large, green-yellow to pink-tan flower with mostly tightly curved sepals that are united at the base forming a tube. The sepals, obscuring the tiny petals, have conspicuous, red-brown veins; and the undersides are covered with red-brown hairs. The small, trilobed or obscurely trilobed lip has a prickly or narrow, basal callus, erect side lobes, and a fleshy, recurved midlobe. The flowers have a short, wingless column that is often footless.

TRIGONIUM

An orthographic variant introduced in *Orchids Ecuador*, 100 (1988). The correct spelling is *Trigonidium.*

TRIGONOCHILUM

Königer & Schildhauer

Arcula **1**: 13 (1994).

ETYMOLOGY: Greek for three-angled and lip. Refers to the flowers which have fairly exact triangular lips.

TYPE SPECIES: *Trigonochilum flexuosum*
(Kunth) Königer & Schildhauer
(*Cyrtochilum flexuosum* Kunth)

Now recognized as belonging to the genus *Cyrtochilum, Trigonochilum* was proposed to include twenty-five epiphytes found in mid to upper elevation, montane forests from Colombia and Brazil to Peru. These plants have oblong pseudobulbs, subtended by leaf-bearing sheaths, each with several, narrow leaves borne near the tip. The long or short, simple or frequently branched, zig-zagging, few-flowered inflorescence has inconspicuous, small to large, yellow flowers with tiny sepals and petals. The large, entire or obscurely trilobed lip diverges from the stout column

at a sharp angle and has a distinct callus with several, small lobes. The flowers have a short, wingless, footless column.

TRIODRIS

Thouars

Hist. Orchid.   Table 2, sub 1a (1822).

Name published without a description. Today this name is most often referred to *Disperis.*

TRIOPSIS

An orthographic variant introduced in *J. Hort. Prat. Belgique*, **5**: 256 (1848). The correct spelling is *Eriopsis.*

TRIORCHIS

Fuchs

Hist. Stirp. (Fuchs)   559 (1542).

Pre-1753, therefore not validly published in fulfillment of nomenclatural rules; this name is most often referred to *Serapias.*

TRIORCHIS

Millán

Jac. Pet. Opera   *t. 68, f. 7 (1765).*

Name published without a description. Today this name is most often referred to *Spiranthes.*

TRIORCHOS

Small & Nash

Small's Fl. S.E. U.S.   329, 1329 (1903).

ETYMOLOGY: Greek for three and orchid. Refers to the arrangement of the dorsal sepal and petals.

TYPE SPECIES: *Triorchos ecristatus* (Fernald) Small
(*Cyrtopodium ecristatum* Fernald)
This type name is now considered a synonym of
Eulophia ecristata (Fernald) Ames;
basionym
Cyrtopodium ecristatum Fernald

Now recognized as belonging to the genera *Pteroglossaspis* and *Eulophia, Triorchos* was previously considered to include twelve terrestrials found in dry, low to mid elevation, sandy fields and open pine-oak forests of the southeastern United States (eastern Carolinas and Florida to southern Louisiana) and Cuba. These erect plants have several, long, narrowly ribbed leaves with two that dominate. The plants resemble the tough grasses and seedling palmettos among which they grow. The long, extremely tall, few-flowered inflorescence has several flowers, borne at the tip, with yellow-green to white

floral segments that converge over the velvety deep purple-brown to white, trilobed lip.

TRIOTOSIPHON

Schlechter ex Luer

Monogr. Syst. Bot. Missouri Bot. Gard.
105: 16 (2006).

ETYMOLOGY: Greek for three and hose. Refers to the tube-like shape of the flowers.

TYPE SPECIES: *Triotosiphon bangii* (Schlechter) Luer
(*Masdevallia bangii* Schlechter)

Recognized as belonging to the genus *Masdevallia, Triotosiphon* was proposed to include six epiphytes or lithophytes found in low elevation, hill forests and scrub from Venezuela and southern Ecuador to Bolivia. These minute plants have short stems, subtended by loose, tubular sheaths, each with a solitary, leathery, narrow leaf. The solitary-flowered inflorescence has a pale yellow flower with the united sepals forming a humped, triangular tube that is more or less constricted above the middle with widespreading tips and has small petals. The tiny, entire lip has a rounded tip. The flowers have a tiny, more or less club-shaped column.

TRIPHORA

Nuttall

Gen. N. Amer. Pl. (Nuttall)   **2**: 192 (1818).

Epidendroideæ ᴡ **Triphoreæ**

ETYMOLOGY: Greek for three-fold and bearing or to carry. Probably in reference to the small number of flowers borne on the inflorescence or the three crests on the lip of the type species.

TYPE SPECIES: *Triphora pendula*
(Mühlenberg ex Willdenow) Nuttall nom. illeg.
(*Arethusa pendula* Mühlenberg ex Willdenow)
This type name is now considered a synonym of
LECTOTYPE: *Triphora trianthophora* (Swartz) Rydberg
(*Arethusa trianthophoros* Swartz)

Eighteen inconspicuous, sympodial terrestrials are found in temperate and tropical, low to upper elevation, montane forests, deciduous woodlands and scrub of the eastern United States (Illinois to New Hampshire, eastern Texas to Florida), Mexico, Belize to Venezuela, the Guianas, Cuba to Hispaniola and Brazil to northern Argentina. These miniscule plants, usually only found in small, scattered populations, have several, fragile stems clasped by small, alternating green to green-purple leaves with smooth margins that are often reduced and bract-like. The erect, red, solitary to few-flowered inflorescence has pale pink, rose-magenta to white flowers often marked with white, green or purple. The shortly clawed, trilobed lip has a broad midlobe with

| Currently Accepted | Validly Published | Invalidly Published | Published Pre-1753 | Superfluous Usage | Orthographic Variant | Fossil |

O r c h i d   G e n e r a   • **400**

three, parallel, green crests and a wavy margin. The flowers have a white to pale green, slender, slightly curved, footless column. Flowers open during the night and will last for only a day, but whole colonies will flower en masse.

TRIPHYLLOCYNIS

Thouars
Hist. Orchid.   Table 1, sub 1d, *t. 14* (1822).

Name published without a description. Today this name is most often referred to *Cynorkis*.

TRIPLEURA

Lindley
Edwards's Bot. Reg.   **19**: sub 1618 (1833), and *Numer. List*   247, no. 7391 (1832).
ETYMOLOGY: Greek for threefold and rib. Referring to the three, projecting, keeled sepals.
TYPE SPECIES: *Tripleura pallida* Lindley
This type name is now considered a synonym of *Zeuxine strateumatica* (Linnaeus) Schlechter;
basionym
Orchis strateumatica Linnaeus

Now recognized as belonging to the genus *Zeuxine*, *Tripleura* was previously considered to include three terrestrials found in low elevation, grasslands and scrub from Afghanistan to southern China and Malaysia, southern Africa and southern Saudia Arabia. These species have also been introduced into the United States via imported grass seed. These small, stout, tiny plants have erect, unbranched stems, each with several, narrow, tapering, purple-green leaves. The erect, numerous-flowered, cylindrical inflorescence has minute, white to dull-colored flowers. The dorsal sepal and lateral petals converge, forming a hood over the short column. The tongue-shaped, entire or trilobed lip has a small splash of vivid yellow-green.

TRIPLORHIZA

Ehrhart
Beitr. Naturk. (Ehrhart)   **4**: 149 (1789).
ETYMOLOGY: Latin for three and root.
TYPE SPECIES: *Satyrium albidum* Linnaeus

Not validly published, this name is most often referred to as a synonym of *Pseudorchis*.

TRIPUDIANTHES

(Seidenfaden) Szlachetko & Kras
Richardiana   **7**(2): 94 (2007).
ETYMOLOGY: Latin for rejoicing or enthusiastic and flower. Refers to the beauty of the flowers.
TYPE SPECIES: *Tripudianthes tripudians*
     (C.S.P. Parish & Reichenbach f.) Szlachetko & Kras
     (*Bulbophyllum tripudians* C.S.P. Parish & Reichenbach f.)

Recognized as belonging to the genus *Bulbophyllum*, *Tripudianthes* was proposed to include ten epiphytes found in low elevation, humid forests from southern and northern India (Assam) to Vietnam and Indonesia (Java). These plants have small, cone-shaped pseudo-bulbs, subtended by leaf-sheaths, each with two deciduous leaves. The tall, arching, few-flowered inflorescence, borne from a mature pseudobulb base, has yellow to bronze-colored flowers covered with small, purple spots. The united sepals have the dorsal sepal much smaller than the long, narrow, lateral sepals. The flowers have a small column.

TRISETELLA

Luer
Phytologia   **47**(2): 57 (1980).
Epidendroideæ · **Epidendreæ** · **Pleurothallidinæ**
ETYMOLOGY: Latin for three or thrice, bristle and diminutive. Refers to the hair-like tails of the sepals.
TYPE SPECIES: *Trisetella triaristella*
     (Reichenbach f.) Luer
     (*Masdevallia triaristella* Reichenbach f.)

Twenty-two dwarf, sympodial epiphytes or lithophytes are found in low to upper elevation, hill and montane forests from Costa Rica to Panama, Venezuela to Bolivia and southern Brazil. These tufted plants have short, erect stems, subtended by overlapping sheaths, each with a solitary, long, narrow, thick, leathery leaf. The several, erect, wiry, numerous-flowered inflorescences, borne at the junction of the secondary stem and leaf, have a solitary flower. The large, dull-colored, thinly textured flowers are stained dark maroon. The small, broad dorsal sepal is shallowly fused to the long, lateral sepals, forming a sepaline cup. The long, tail-like segments have yellow or purple tips. The tiny petals are thinly textured. The small, spear or heart-shaped, entire or trilobed lip has backward pointing basal lobes that are hinged at the base of the wedge-shaped column foot which is massive. The flowers have a long, hooded, wingless column.

TRITELANDRA

Rafinesque
Fl. Tellur.   **2**: 85 (1836)[1837].
ETYMOLOGY: Latin for spathe and man or stamen. An allusion to the lip's unusually broad midlobe.
TYPE SPECIES: *Tritelandra fuscata* (Smith) Rafinesque
     (*Epidendrum fuscatum* Smith)

Now recognized as belonging to the genus *Epidendrum*, *Tritelandra* was previously considered to include one epiphyte or occasional lithophyte found in low to mid elevation, cypress swamps and damp montane forests from central Mexico to Peru, Cuba to Trinidad, the southeastern United States (Florida), Venezuela and Brazil. This commonly found plant forms dense colonies. When exposed to bright sunlight, the entire plant becomes red or maroon, but when shaded, the red fades away to green. The plant has tufted, strongly compressed, leafy stems. The few-flowered inflorescence has rigid, long-lasting, yellow-green to red-brown flowers often suffused purple. The trilobed lip, attached to the short column, has short, roundish side lobes, and the oblong midlobe has a centrally keeled disk. The above type name is now considered a synonym of *Epidendrum anceps* Jacquin.

TRITELANDRIA

An orthographic variant introduced in *Orchideen (Schlechter)*, ed. 1, 190 (1914). The correct spelling is *Tritelandra*.

TRIXEUXIS

An orthographic variant introduced in *Orchid. Scelet.*, 15 (1826). The correct spelling is *Trizeuxis*.

TRIXSPERMUM

An orthographic variant introduced in *Scent Orchid.*, 172 (1993). The correct spelling is *Thrixspermum*.

TRIZEUXIS

Lindley
Coll. Bot. (Lindley)   **1**: *t. 2* (1821).
Epidendroideæ · **Cymbidieæ** · **Oncidiinæ**
ETYMOLOGY: Greek for three and yoking or union. Alluding to the sepals that are somewhat united.
TYPE SPECIES: *Trizeuxis falcata* Lindley

One sympodial epiphyte is found in low elevation, forests and groves from Costa Rica to Bolivia, Trinidad and Brazil. This twig-like plant has its leaves arranged in a fan shape, enclosing a small pseudobulb. The long, few-flowered inflorescence has a head-like raceme of minute, bell-shaped, green or pale yellow flowers barely opening because of restrictive fusion of the floral segments. The similar dorsal sepal and petals are united at the base. The fleshy, yellow or orange, trumpet-shaped, obscurely trilobed lip is united to the base of the stout, short, club-shaped, wingless, footless column. This inflorescence has a unique structure with its tightly bundled spirals of buds and flowers.

TROPHIANTHES

An orthographic variant introduced in *Hamburger Garten- Blumenzeitung*, **9**: 77 (1853). The correct spelling is *Trophianthus*.

TROPHIANTHUS

Scheidweiler

Allg. Gartenzeitung   **12**(28): 218 (1844).

ETYMOLOGY: Greek for large or huge and flower. Referring to the well developed, showy flower.

TYPE SPECIES: *Trophianthus zonatus* Scheidweiler

Now recognized as belonging to the genus *Aspasia*, *Trophianthus* was previously considered to include one epiphyte found in low elevation, hill scrub forests of southeastern Brazil. This plant has strongly compressed, pale green pseudobulbs that have a quite narrow base, each with two narrow leaves. The short, solitary to few-flowered inflorescence has green flowers spotted or barred dull brown. The broad, white, trilobed lip has a violet blotch on the midlobe and the side lobes are more or less rounded. The above type name is now considered a synonym of *Aspasia lunata* Lindley.

TROPIANTHUS

An orthographic variant introduced in *Fl. Bras. (Martius)*, **3**(6): 203 (1898). The correct spelling is *Trophianthus*.

TROPIDIA

Lindley

Edwards's Bot. Reg.   **19**: sub 1618 (1833), and *Numer. List*   247, no. 7386 (1831).

Epidendroideæ ⁄ Tropidieæ

ETYMOLOGY: Greek for keel. In reference to the boat-shaped lip of the type species.

TYPE SPECIES: *Tropidia curculigoides* Lindley

Twenty-nine sympodial terrestrials or occasionally saprophytes found in low to mid elevation,

forests scrub and litter. These are distributed in a rather odd range from northern India (Kashmir to Assam), southern China (Xizang to Hainan and Hong Kong), Japan, Taiwan, Myanmar to Vietnam, Indonesia, the Philippines to New Guinea, Fiji and Samoa. There is one species found in the southeastern United States (Florida), the Bahamas, Cuba to Puerto Rico, east central Mexico to Panama, the Galapagos Islands, northern Venezuela and Colombia to Ecuador, with most of the leafless species found in eastern Indonesia (Borneo). These tall, erect plants have often branched, rigid, reed-like stems (often in clusters, erect, rigid, noded, branched or not), each with several to several, broad, tough, grass-like, veined to scale-like leaves. The short, few to numerous-flowered inflorescence, borne from leaf axils near the tip, has small to tiny, green, white or red flowers not opening widely. The lateral sepals enclosing the base of the broad, strongly concave lip. The sepals and petals differ only slightly. The entire or lobed lip is basally sac-like or pouched, often with a short to broad spur or is spurless and is attached to a rather short, fleshy column.

TROPILIS

Rafinesque

Fl. Tellur.   **2**: 95 (1836)[1837].

ETYMOLOGY: Derivation and its meaning are not clear when applied to this name.

TYPE SPECIES: *Tropilis emulum* (R. Brown) Rafinesque (*Dendrobium aemulum* R. Brown)

Now recognized as belonging to the genus *Dendrobium*, *Tropilis* was previously considered to include seventeen epiphytes and occasional lithophytes found in low to mid elevation, hill scrub and open montane forests of Indonesia, New Guinea and Australia. These clump- forming plants have narrow, dark, tightly clustered stems, each with several, dark, shiny, leathery, oblong leaves at the tip. The few-flowered inflorescence has large, fragrant, white to pink flowers often turning darker pink as they age. The white, somewhat diamond-shaped, trilobed lip has small, broad side lobes. The relaxed midlobe has a three-keeled disk and a prominent, wavy, magenta to yellow callus. The above type name is now considered a synonym of *Dendrobium aemulum* R. Brown.

TRUDELIA

Garay

Orchid Digest   **50**(2): 73 (1986).

ETYMOLOGY: Named for Nicolao (Niklaus) Trudel (1942-), a Swiss horticulturist, hybridizer and natural history photographer from the Sonogno region.

TYPE SPECIES: *Trudelia alpina* (Lindley) Garay (*Luisia alpina* Lindley)

Now recognized as belonging to the genus *Vanda*, *Trudelia* was previously considered to include five epiphytes found in humid, mid to upper elevation, montane forests from Nepal, northeastern India to southern China (Yunnan), Thailand and Indonesia (Sumatra). These plants have erect, stout stems, subtended by overlapping leafy bases, each with narrow, leathery to fleshy, strap-shaped leaves. The short, few-flowered inflorescence has small, showy, fleshy, fragrant, waxy, long-lasting, white or green-yellow flowers. The usually spurless, long-clawed, trilobed lip has contrasting maroon or blue-purple stripes or markings, is continuous with the column base. The erect, rounded, creamy side lobes has irregular purple to blue-purple blotching or stripes; the long, narrow midlobe has a widespreading, bilobed or entire tip. The flowers have an erect, short, wingless column.

TRYMENIUM

Lindley

Edwards's Bot. Reg.   **29**: sub 3 (1843).

ETYMOLOGY: Greek for soft and chin.

TYPE SPECIES: *None designated*

Name published without a description. Today this name is most often referred to *Odontoglossum*.

TRYPHIA

Lindley

Gen. Sp. Orchid. Pl.   258, 333 (1835), and *Edwards's Bot. Reg.* **20**: sub 1701, section no. 25 (1835).

Name ICBN rejected vs. *Holothrix* Richard ex Lindley (1835) Orchidaceæ.

ETYMOLOGY: Greek for tenderness or softness. An allusion to the thinly textured leaves.

TYPE SPECIES: *Tryphia secunda* (Thunberg) Lindley (*Orchis secunda* Thunberg)

Although validly published this rejected name is now referred to *Holothrix*, *Tryphia* was considered to include six terrestrials found in the southeastern Cape area of South Africa. These small plants have erect, unbranched stems, each with two thinly textured, oval leaves that lie flat on the ground. The erect, few-flowered inflorescence has tiny, white, cream or yellow-green flowers with green,

Partly Accepted · Validly Published · Invalidly Published · Published Pre-1753 · Superfluous Usage · Orthographic Variant · Fossil narrow to thread-like sepals, a distinctly trilobed lip, and a club-shaped spur.

TSAIORCHIS

T. Tang & F.T. Wang
Bull. Fan Mem. Inst. Biol. Bot.   **7**: 131 (1936).
Orchidoideæ ⸙ Orchideæ • Orchidinæ
ETYMOLOGY: Dedicated to Hse Tao Tsai (1901-1981), a Chinese botanist and collector who worked and collected mainly in Yunnan province of southern China. And Greek for orchid.
TYPE SPECIES: *Tsaiorchis neottianthoides*
T. Tang & F.T. Wang

Two uncommon, sympodial terrestrials are found in mid elevation, river banks and forest slopes of southern China (south-eastern Yunnan and western Guangxi). These small plants have erect, unbranched stems, each with several, oblong, basal leaves. The slender, few-flowered inflorescence has pale purple flowers, all facing one direction along the rachis. The unusual, elongate, trilobed lip has short, rounded side lobes, a short midlobe with a shallow notch, and a short, swollen spur. The oblong, flattened viscidium is enclosed in a chamber formed by lip and column. These species are often included in *Habenaria*.

TSIEROU

An orthographic variant introduced in *Summa Pl.*, **5**: 238 (1791). The correct spelling is *Tsjerou*.

TSJEROU-mau

Rheede
Hort. Malab.   **12**: 11, *t. 5* (1693).
ETYMOLOGY: The meaning of this Malayalam word is unknown.
TYPE SPECIES: *Tsjerou-mau-maravara* Rheede

Pre-1753, therefore not validly published in fulfillment of nomenclatural rules; this trinomial name is most often referred to *Luisia*. *Tsjerou* was previously considered to include one epiphyte found in low elevation, woodlands of southern China, northern India (Kashmir to Assam), Nepal, Myanmar, Thailand to Vietnam, Malaysia, Indonesia (Java), the Philippines, northern Australia and the south-western Pacific Archipelago. This plant is quite variable in all its vegetative parts and has long, slender stems, each with several, pencil-like leaves. The short, few-flowered inflorescence has foul smelling, yellow or green-yellow flowers. The dull purple-brown, thick, trilobed lip has a basal yellow blotch. This name is now usually considered as a synonym of *Luisia tristis* (G. Forster) Hooker f.

TSJEROU-tecka

Rheede
Hort. Malab.   **12**: 45, *t. 23* (1693).
ETYMOLOGY: The meaning of this Malayalam word is unknown. But tecka refers to the tree, *Tectona gandis* on which this orchid was found growing.
TYPE SPECIES: *Tsjerou-tecka-maravara* Rheede

Pre-1753, therefore not validly published in fulfillment of nomenclatural rules; this trinomial name is most often referred to *Bulbophyllum*. *Tsjerou* was previously considered to include one epiphyte found in southwestern India (Karnataka and Kerala). This creeping plant has small, ovate pseudobulbs, each with a solitary, small, oblong, leathery leaf. The short, pink, two-flowered inflorescence has creamy white, purple spotted and veined flowers covered with raised papillose. The large, erect dorsal sepal is boat-shaped; the widespreading, veined petals have entire or notched margins and united, thick lateral sepals. The small, thick, entire lip is tongue-shaped. The flowers have a small, thick, narrowly winged column. This name is usually referred to as a synonym of *Bulbophyllum rheedei* Manilal & Sathish Kumar.

TSOTRIA

An orthographic variant introduced in *Amer. Monthly Mag. & Crit. Rev.*, **2**: 173 (1817). The correct spelling is *Isotria*.

TUBELLA

(Luer) Archila
Revista Guatemal.   **3**(1): 46 (2000).
ETYMOLOGY: Latin for little tube. Referring to the slender sheaths that are characteristic of the species.
TYPE SPECIES: *Tubella acremona* (Luer) Archila
(*Pleurothallis acremona* Luer)
This type name is now considered a synonym of
Trichosalpinx acremona (Luer) Luer;
basionym
Pleurothallis acremona Luer

Now recognized as belonging to a section of *Trichosalpinx*, *Tubella* was previously considered to include seventy-three epiphytes found on the eastern divide of the Andes in moist, cool, mid to upper elevation, montane forests from Colombia to Bolivia. These small to medium-sized, slender, erect plants have often branching stems, each with a few, thick, narrow leaves borne near the tips. The several, few-flowered inflorescences, opening simultaneously, have small, thinly textured, white, pale yellow or pale green flowers. The sepals usually taper forming long tails and the petals are quite tiny. The large, erect entire lip has an irregular or notched margin.

TUBERA

Blume ex d'Orbigny
Dict. Univ. Hist. Nat.   **9**: 170 (1847).

Name published without a description. Today this name is most often referred to as a section of *Aerides*.

TUBEROGASTRIS

Thouars
Hist. Orchid.   Table 1, sub 2i, *t. 31* (1822).

Name published without a description. Today this name is most often referred to *Gastrorchis*.

TUBEROLABIUM

Yamamoto
Bot. Mag. (Tokyo)   **38**: 209 (1924).
Epidendroideæ ⸙ Vandeæ • Aeridinæ
ETYMOLOGY: Latin for bump or swelling and lip. Referring to the relatively large, fleshy lip of the type species.
TYPE SPECIES: *Tuberolabium kotoense* Yamamoto

Twelve monopodial epiphytes are found in low elevation, rain forests from Taiwan to the Philippines, New Guinea and northern Australia to Indonesia (Java and Sumatra). These small plants have short leafy stems, often branching at the base, forming clumps, each with thick, leathery leaves arranged in two rows. The several, arching to hanging, numerous-flowered inflorescences have long-lasting, tiny, white, yellow or green, shallowly cupped, fleshy, fragrant flowers opening simultaneously. They are either lightly or heavily barred red-brown, and are subtended by minute floral bracts. The broad, immobile, conspicuous funnel-shaped, obscurely trilobed lip has contrasting red-purple or brown-purple markings, and has a short spur or is spurless. The flowers have a short, wingless, footless column.

TUBILABIUM

J.J. Smith
Bull. Jard. Bot. Buitenzorg, sér. 3   **9**: 446 (1928).
ETYMOLOGY: Greek for pipe or tube and lip. Alluding to the incurved lip margins that form a tube-like structure.
TYPE SPECIES: *Tubilabium aureum* J.J. Smith

Now recognized as belonging to the genus *Myrmechis*, *Tubilabium* was previously considered to include two terrestrials found in mid to upper elevation, montane cloud forests and limestone rocks of eastern Indonesia (Sulawesi and Maluku). These uncommon, spectacular, erect plants have unbranched, short stems, each with several, beautifully colored leaves that have gold-glittering nerves. They are a part of the Jewel orchid group. The erect, numerous-flowered inflorescence has small, pure white flowers. The curved, narrowly tubular, entire lip is densely covered with hairs at the tip and sac-like at the base. The flowers have a short, curved, wingless, footless column.

TULEXIS

Rafinesque
Fl. Tellur. **4**: 42 (1836)[1837].

ETYMOLOGY: Greek for wart. Descriptive of the warty outer surface appearance of the petals and sepals.

TYPE SPECIES: *Tulexis bicolor* Rafinesque nom. illeg.
Brassavola tuberculata Hooker

Now recognized as belonging to the genus *Brassavola*, *Tulexis* was previously considered to include one epiphyte or lithophyte found in a variety of habitats from cool to hot, in low to mid elevation, hill to montane forests and savannas from Peru, southeastern Brazil and Paraguay to north-eastern Argentina. This plant has clustered, deeply grooved stems, each with several pencil-like, channeled leaves. The short, one- to two-flowered inflorescence has long-lasting, nocturnally fragrant, yellow to yellow-green flowers not usually opening fully. The white, spreading, erect, entire lip, attached to the slightly incurved, club-shaped column base, has a green basal blotch, and tapers to a point with an entire or wavy margin.

TULOTIS

Rafinesque
Herb. Raf. 70 (1833).

ETYMOLOGY: Greek for callus or knob. Referring to the lip that has a callus gland for the nectary.

TYPE SPECIES: *None designated*

Now recognized as belonging to the genus *Platanthera*, *Tulotis* was previously considered to include seventeen terrestrials found in low to mid elevation, open scrub, moist meadows, slopes and swamps of southeastern Canada (Ontario to Nova Scotia), the midwest and northern United States (Missouri to Maine), eastern Russia (Yakutiya to Kuril Islands), north-eastern China (Heilongjiang), Korea and Japan (Hokkaido, Honshu, Sikoku and Kyushu) to Taiwan. These robust plants have several leaves located on the lower third of the erect, unbranched, stout to slender stem. The erect, few-flowered inflorescence has small, yellow-green, widespreading flowers that are somewhat dragonfly-shaped. The dorsal sepal and erect, straight petals converge, forming a hood over the small, stout column. The trilobed lip has small basal side lobes, a narrow midlobe, and a hanging, somewhat curved spur.

NOTE: These species were separated from the genus *Platanthera* because of a small, round projection located at the base of the lip.

TUPISTRA

Ker Gawler
Bot. Mag. **40**: sub 1655 (1814).

ETYMOLOGY: Latin for a mallet or hammer. Refers to the form or shape of the stigma.

TYPE SPECIES: *Not Orchidaceæ*

This genus is not included in the Orchidaceæ family; however, there was one species now recognized as belonging to *Neuwiedia*. This glabrous terrestrial species is found in low elevation, hill scrub from southern China, Thailand, Vietnam, Indonesia (Sumatra and Borneo) to Malaysia. This unattractive plant has erect stems, each with several, stout leaves. The erect, few-flowered inflorescence has densely hairy, pale yellow flowers. The species (*Tupistra singapureana* Wallich ex Baker, J. Linn. Soc., Bot., **14**: 581 (1875)) was originally mistakenly included in the Liliaceæ (lily) family, but the name should now be correctly identified as a synonym of *Neuwiedia zollingeri* (*Neuwiedia singapureana* (Wallich ex Baker) Rolfe *Bull. Misc. Inform. Kew*, 412 (1907)).

TUSSAC

An orthographic variant introduced in *Nouv. Dict. Hist. Nat.*, ed. 2, **30**: 240 (1819). The correct spelling is *Tussaca*.

TUSSACA

Rafinesque
Prec. Decouv. 42 (1814), and
J. Phys. Chim. Hist. Nat. Arts **89**: 261 (1819).
Not *Tussaca* Reichenbach (1824) Gesneriaceæ.

ETYMOLOGY: Dedicated to François Richard de Tussac (1751-1837), a French botanist and author of the four volumes of *Flore des Antilles*.

TYPE SPECIES: *Tussaca reticulata* Rafinesque

A superfluous name proposed as a substitute for *Goodyera*.

TUSSACIA

Not *Tussacia* Willdenow ex J.G. Beer (1856) Bromeliaceæ, not *Tussacia* Willdenow ex J.A. Schultes & J.H. Schultes (1829) Incertæ Sedis, and not *Tussacia* Bentham (1846) Gesneriaceæ.

An orthographic variant introduced in *Observ. Pl.*, 91 (1818). The correct spelling is *Tussaca*.

TUSSAEIA

An orthographic variant introduced in *Fl. Deutschland*, **4**(19): 178 (1855). The correct spelling is *Tussacia*.

TYLEXIS

An orthographic variant cited in *Lex. Gen. Phan.*, 577, 578 (1904). The correct spelling is *Tulexis*.

TYLOCHILUS

Nees
Verh. Vereins Beförd. Gartenbaues Königl. Preuss. Staaten **8**: 194, t. 3 (1832).

ETYMOLOGY: Greek for wart and a lip. Descriptive of the warty condition of the lip.

TYPE SPECIES: *Tylochilus flavus* Nees
This type name is now considered a synonym of *Cyrtopodium andersonii* (Lambert ex Andrews) R. Brown; basionym
Cymbidium andersonii Lambert ex Andrews

Now recognized as belonging to the genus *Cyrtopodium*, *Tylochilus* was previously considered to include one epiphyte found in low elevation, scrub from the southeastern United States (Florida), Cuba, Trinidad, the Guianas, Venezuela and northern Brazil. This large plant has erect, spindle-shaped pseudo-bulbs, subtended by sharp, spiny sheaths, each with several, yellow-green, prominently nerved leaves. The erect, branched, numerous-flowered inflorescence often reaches heights in excess of six feet (1.8 m). The fragrant, waxy, long-lived, yellow flowers are suffused green. The bright yellow, trilobed lip has small, round side lobes, and the short, wide midlobe has a concave base with a small, deep yellow callus. The flowers have a small, short column.

TYLOSTIGMA

Schlechter
Beih. Bot. Centralbl. **34**(2): 297 (1916).
Orchidoideæ ✺ Orchideæ • Orchidinæ

ETYMOLOGY: Greek for wart or knob and stigma or mark. Descriptive of the warty, bilobed stigma.

TYPE SPECIES: *Tylostigma madadascariensis* Schlechter

Eight small, sympodial terrestrials or lithophytes are found in mid to upper elevation, montane marshes and bogs of Madagascar. These dwarf plants have unbranched, erect, slender stems that are bare at the base, each with narrow, fleshy leaves in the middle. The long, smooth, numerous to

Currently Accepted   Validly Published   Invalidly Published   Published Pre-1753   Superfluous Usage   Orthographic Variant   Fossil

Orchid Genera • 404

few-flowered inflorescence has tiny, yellow or green flowers with the sepals and smaller petals slightly converging. The fleshy, pouch-like, entire lip is as long or longer than the petals and has a basal callus that is variously ornate in the front. The flowers have a short, stout, wingless, footless column.

TYLOSTYLIS

Blume
Fl. Javæ   **1**: Praef. vi (1828).
ETYMOLOGY: Greek for major, knob and style or pillar. Refers to the short, fleshy foot of the column.
TYPE SPECIES: *None designated*

A superfluous name proposed as a substitute for *Eria*.

TYLOTIS

An orthographic variant cited in *Lex. Gen. Phan.*, 579 (1904). The correct spelling is *Tulotis*.

TYOLOSTYLIS

An orthographic variant introduced in *Pflanzenr. (Engler)*, **IV50**(IIB21): 15 (1911). The correct spelling is *Tylostylis*.

TYPHIA

An orthographic variant introduced in *Syn. Pl. (D. Dietrich)*, **5**: 146 (1852). The correct spelling is *Tryphia*.

TYSANOGLOSSA

An orthographic variant introduced in *Anais Reunião Sul-Amer. Bot.*, **3**: 42 (1940). The correct spelling is *Thysanoglossa*.

TZACUCÓCHITL

Hernández
Opera (Hernández)   **1**: 238, 239 (1790).
ETYMOLOGY: A Nahuatl (Aztec) word for glue and flower. Describing what the local natives used this plant for.
TYPE SPECIES: *Tzacucóchitl seu florida Tzautli* Hernández

Pre-1753, therefore not validly published in fulfillment of nomenclatural rules; this name is most often referred to *Bletia*. *Tzacucóchitl* was considered to include one terrestrial found in mid elevation, weathered volcanic flows and meadows of central Mexico (Nayarit, Jalisco and Michoacán). This plant has long, subterranean corms, each with two to three, erect, narrow, pleated leaves. The erect, few-flowered inflorescence

has showy, bell-shaped, pink or magenta flowers that scarcely open. The flowers have red-violet sepals and white petals with red tips. The sepals and petals converge, forming a hood over the lip and small column. The trilobed lip is white at the base with red-violet margins on side lobes and midlobe. This name is usually considered a synonym of *Bletia campanulata* Lexarza.

TZACUTLI

Sahagún
Gen. Hist. Things New Spain   197 (1509), and

Lexarza
Nov. Veg. Descr.   **2**: 24 (1825).
ETYMOLOGY: A Nahuatl (Aztec) word for glue.
TYPE SPECIES: *Tzacutli* Sahagún

Pre-1753, therefore not validly published in fulfillment of nomenclatural rules; this name is most often referred to *Prosthechea*. *Tzacutli* was considered to include one epiphyte or occasional lithophyte found in low to upper elevation, pine-oak forests of central Mexico (Michoacán). This plant has long, pear-shaped pseudobulbs, each with two to three, tongue-shaped leaves. The erect, few-flowered inflorescence has wide-spreading, brown flowers with narrow sepals and petals. The white, trilobed lip has small side lobes and a spear-shaped midlobe streaked with purple or yellow. This name is now usually considered a synonym of *Prosthechea pastoris* (Lexarza) Espejo & López-Ferrari.

TZACUXÓCHITL

An orthographic variant introduced in *Nov. Veg. Descr.*, **2**: 13 (1825). The correct spelling is *Tzacucochitl*.

TZAUHTLI

An orthographic variant introduced in *Nov. Veg. Descr.*, **2**: 6, 20 (1825). The correct spelling is *Tzavtli*.

TZAUTLI

An orthographic variant introduced in *Nov. Veg. Descr.*, **2**: 17 (1825). The correct spelling is *Tzavtli*.

TZAUXILOTL

An orthographic variant introduced in *Frama. Mex.*, ed. 3, 64 (1896). The correct spelling is *Tzavtli*.

TZAVÓCHITL

Hernández
Rerum Med. Nov. Hisp. Thes.   **1**: 433 (1651).
ETYMOLOGY: A Nahuatl (Aztec) word for this flower. The original meaning is unclear.
TYPE SPECIES: *Tzavochitl* Hernández

Pre-1753, therefore not validly published in fulfillment of nomenclatural rules; this name is most often referred to *Prosthechea*. *Tzavochitl* was previously considered to include one epiphyte found in mid elevation, dry pine-oak or cool, cloud forests, lava flows and grasslands from central Mexico to Guatemala. This plant has clustered, slightly compressed, cone-shaped pseudobulbs, each with one to three, gray-green, narrow leaves. The erect, few-flowered inflorescence has showy, long-lived, vermilion to scarlet flowers. The yellow or orange, entire lip, joined to the column base, has an oblong callus. The flowers have a slightly club-shaped, winged column. This name is now usually considered a synonym of *Prosthechea vitellina* (Lindley) W.E. Higgins.

TZAVTLI

Hernández
Rerum Med. Nov. Hisp. Thes.   **1**: 283 (1651), and
Opera (Hernández)   **1**: 239 (1790).
ETYMOLOGY: A Nahuatl (Aztec) word for this glue usually obtain from an orchid plant.
TYPE SPECIES: *Tzavtli* or *Tzacutli* Hernández

Pre-1753, therefore not validly published in fulfillment of nomenclatural rules; this name most often referred to *Bletia*. *Tzavtli* was previously considered to include one terrestrial found in mid elevation, pine-oak forests or grassy slopes from central Mexico to Guatemala and Costa Rica. This plant has corm-like pseudobulbs, each with several, pleated, narrow, thinly textured, strongly veined leaves. The erect, few-flowered inflorescence has showy, long-lived, pale rosy pink flowers opening only after the leaves have withered. The trilobed lip has erect, heavily veined side lobes; the midlobe has a raised, basal callus and a wavy margin. This name is now usually considered a synonym of *Bletia reflexa* Lindley.

UCANTHA

An orthographic variant introduced *Dict. Univ. Hist. Nat.*, **9**: 173 (1849). The correct spelling is *Ulantha*.

ULANTHA

Hooker

Bot. Mag. **57**: *t.* 2990, index (1830).

ETYMOLOGY: Greek for crisped or crinkled and flower. In reference to the crisp floral segments.

TYPE SPECIES: *Ulantha grandiflora* Hooker

Now recognized as belonging to the genus *Chloraea*, *Ulantha* was previously considered to include one terrestrial found in the upper Antuco volcano, montane region of southern Chile (Bío-Bío). This erect, extraordinary plant has stout, unbranched stems, each with several, tulip-like, basal leaves. The erect, few-flowered inflorescence has showy, highly textured, white flowers with dull green, boldly netted veins and an unusual fragrance. The oblong, entire lip and the long lateral sepals have wavy margins, and the petals have numerous, elongated papillae at the tips. The flowers have a long, slender, incurved column. The above type name is now considered a synonym of *Chloraea bletioides* Lindley.

ULANTHIA

An orthographic variant introduced in *Fl. Tellur.*, **2**: 60 (1836)[1837]. The correct spelling is *Ulantha*.

ULEIORCHIS

Hoehne

Arq. Bot. Estado São Paulo, n.s. **1**(6): 129, *t. 144* (1944).

Epidendroideæ ⚘ Gastrodieæ

ETYMOLOGY: Commemorating Ernest Heinrich Georg Ule (1854-1915), a German-born Brazilian teacher, botanist and explorer of the Amazon region for rubber plants. He collected the type specimen. And Greek for orchid.

TYPE SPECIES: *Uleiorchis cogniauxiana* Hoehne nom. illeg.
Uleiorchis ulaei (Cogniaux) Handro
(*Wullschlaegelia ulaei* Cogniaux)

Two leafless saprophytes are restricted in low to mid elevation, sheltered leaf litter, moss covered stumps or decaying logs of northeastern Brazil, southern Venezuela, the Guianas and Panama to Peru. These plants have unbranched stems, each with a few thinly textured, scale-like leaves. The smooth, solitary to few-flowered inflorescence has white to pale brown-white, tubular to cup-shaped flowers not opening widely; sometimes may have a bold purple stripe or a faint purple tinge. The sepals and petals are united for most of their length, forming a five-lobed floral tube. The long, narrow, dull yellow, entire lip has a large, brown or sepia, basal patch and has a short, swollen spur that curves upward. The flowers have a long, slender, wingless, footless column.

UNCIFERA

Lindley

J. Proc. Linn. Soc., Bot. **3**: 39 (1858).

Epidendroideæ ⚘ Vandeæ • Aeridinæ

ETYMOLOGY: Latin for a hook and bearing or carrying. Alluding to the pointing downward and backward, hook-like spur on the lip.

TYPE SPECIES: *None designated*

Six relatively insignificant, monopodial epiphytes are found in mid elevation, montane forests from northeastern India, Nepal and Myanmar to Vietnam. These small plants have short to long, erect to hanging stems, each with long, narrow leaves arranged in two rows. The erect, arching or hanging, numerous to few-flowered inflorescence has intricately structured, minute, pale green-yellow or white flowers not opening fully that are best viewed with a magnifying lens. The wide-mouthed, sac-like, trilobed lip has long, projecting side lobes, a tiny, rounded midlobe and a large, angular or curved, blunt, funnel-shaped spur attached to the base of a short, thick, footless column.

UNCIFERIA

Luer

Monogr. Syst. Bot. Missouri Bot. Gard. **95**: 265 (2004).

ETYMOLOGY: Latin for hook and bearing. Referring to the hooked lateral lip lobe tips that are deflexed.

TYPE SPECIES: *Unciferia segoviensis* (Reichenbach f.) Luer
(*Pleurothallis segoviensis* Reichenbach f.)

Recognized as belonging to the genus *Stelis*, *Unciferia* was proposed to include ten epiphytes found in mid elevation, montane forests from Mexico to Panama. These erect plants have secondary stems, each with a solitary, tongue-shaped, leathery leaf. The wiry, few-flowered inflorescence, borne from leaf axils, has slender stalked flowers in various colors, yellow-green blotched brown to dark red-purple. The dorsal sepal is united with the lateral sepals and has slightly rolled under margin. The lateral sepals are united almost to the toothed tip, and the tiny lip has a roundish, two ridged disc. The flowers have a minute column.

UNGUELLA

(Luer) Luer

Monogr. Syst. Bot. Missouri Bot. Gard. **95**: 265 (2004).
Validated: *Monogr. Syst. Bot. Missouri Bot. Gard.* **103**: 310 (2005).

ETYMOLOGY: Greek for a hoof or claw and like. An allusion to the jointed claw of the lip.

TYPE SPECIES: *Unguella lepidota* (L.O. Williams) Luer
(*Pleurothallis lepidota* L.O. Williams)

Recognized as belonging to the genus *Acianthera*, *Unguella* was proposed to include two epiphytes found in low to mid elevation, hill to montane forests and along river banks in Honduras, Costa Rica and northern Panama.

| Currently Accepted | Validly Published | Invalidly Published | Published Pre-1753 | Superfluous Usage | Orthographic Variant | Fossil |

Orchid Genera • **406**

These hanging plants have slender stems, each with a solitary, long, narrow, leathery leaf. The short, numerous to few-flowered inflorescence, borne from the leaf axils, has honey-yellow to pale yellow-green flowers with a slender dorsal sepal, deeply concave united lateral sepals, and small, narrow, entire petals. The trilobed lip has erect, roundish side lobes; the long-clawed midlobe is covered with minute papillose and attached to the tip of the column foot.

UNIVISCIDATUS

An orthographic variant cited in *Orchideen (Schlechter): Liter. Reg. Band I/A, B, and C*, 172, 265 (2003). The correct spelling is *Univiscidiatus*.

UNIVISCIDIATUS

(Kores) Szlachetko
Polish Bot. J. **46**(1): 20 (2001).
ETYMOLOGY: Latin for one, sticky and part or unit. Referring to the solitary viscidium.
TYPE SPECIES: *Univiscidiatus elegans*
(Reichenbach f.) Szlachetko
(*Acianthus elegans* Reichenbach f.)

Now recognized as belonging to the genus *Acianthus*, *Univiscidiatus* was proposed to include fourteen terrestrials endemic to New Caledonia (Île de Pins) with a single species found in eastern Australia. These plants have well-developed, aerial stems, each with a solitary, variably shaped, lobed leaf. The branched, few-flowered inflorescence has small, ascending, pale green, green to green-white flowers suffused red-purple.

UROCHILUS

D.L. Jones & M.A. Clements
Austral. Orchid Res. **4**: 87 (2002).
ETYMOLOGY: Greek for tail-like and lip. Refers to the small tail-like growth found at the base of the lip.
TYPE SPECIES: *Urochilus vittatus*
(Lindley) D.L. Jones & M.A. Clements
(*Pterostylis vittata* Lindley)

Recognized as belonging to the genus *Pterostylis*, *Urochilus* was proposed to include three terrestrials found in low to mid elevation, coastal woodlands and gravelly soil of southwestern Australia. These erect plants have slender, unbranched stems, each with small to almost scale-like, basal leaves, and several, narrow leaves clasping the stem upward. The few-flowered inflorescence has green flowers that are variable in size and color and have bold, red-brown stripes. The prominently ribbed dorsal sepal and transparent petals converge, forming a hood over the column. The oblong, somewhat concave, broadly clawed, bilobed lip has a single hairy or bristly spike arising from the thickened base.

UROPEDILUM

An orthographic variant introduced in *Entwurf Anordn. Orch.*, 95 (1887). The correct spelling is *Uropedium*.

UROPEDIUM

Lindley
Orchid. Linden. 28 (1846).
Name ICBN rejected vs. *Phragmipedium* Rolfe (1896).
ETYMOLOGY: Greek for a tail or foot and slipper or shoe. Refers to the long tail-like shape of the lip.
TYPE SPECIES: *Uropedium lindenii* Lindley

Although validly published this rejected name is now referred to *Phragmipedium*. *Uropedium* was considered to include one epiphyte found in warm to cool, mid to upper elevation, montane forests of Venezuela, Colombia, Ecuador and Peru. This most unusual plant has a short stem concealed in a fan-shaped arrangement of narrow, arching leaves. The erect, hairy, few-flowered inflorescence has large, showy, white to yellow-green flowers graduating to dark green toward the tips and marked with bright green veins. The large, narrow dorsal sepal arches over the lip and has wavy margins. The long, spiraling, twisted, string-like petals are green at the base, graduating to dark maroon tips. The strongly twisted to straight, yellow (at the base graduating to pink or maroon toward the tip), entire lip is strongly incurved. The flowers have a short, thick column.

UROPEDUM

An orthographic variant introduced in *Gart.-Zeitung*, **1**: 341 (1882). The correct spelling is *Uropedium*.

UROSTACHYA

(Lindley) Brieger
Orchideen (Schlechter), ed. 3 **1**(11-12): 716 (1981).
ETYMOLOGY: Greek for a tail and ear of grain or cluster. Refers to the numerous, tiny flowers that are closely arranged like the seeds on an ear of wheat.
TYPE SPECIES: *Urostachya floribunda*
(Lindley) Brieger
(*Eria floribunda* Lindley)

Now recognized as belonging to the genus *Eria*, *Urostachya* was previously considered to include one epiphyte distributed in mid elevation, montane forests from Myanmar to the Philippines. This small plant has narrow, almost stem-like pseudobulbs, each with several, thinly textured leaves. The slender, numerous-flowered inflorescence, covered with short hairs, has small to tiny, white flowers faintly pink-suffused with a bright red splash at the segments' tips. The fan-shaped, trilobed lip has joined side lobes forming a deeply bilobed blade, and the midlobe has a broad, slightly trilobed tip. The flowers have a short, stout, curved, yellow column with a dark purple stigma.

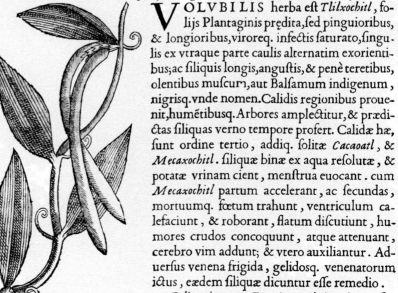

Hernández *Rerum medicarum Novæ Hispaniæ Thesaurus* page 38 (1651).

VAGINARIA

Lindley ex **Wittstein**

Etym.-Bot.-Handw.-Buch, ed. 1   916 (1852).

Not *Vaginaria* Persoon (1805) Cyperaceæ; not
Varginaria S.F. Gray ex Kuntze (1898) Oscillatoriaceæ.

Name published without a description.
This name was published as belonging to
Orchidaceæ which it is not, but the name
should be referred to *Vaginaria* (Cyperaceæ or
Oscillatoriaceæ).

VAINILLA

Salisbury

Parad. Lond.   **2**: sub 82 (1807).

Name published without a description. Today
this name is most often referred to *Vanilla*.

VAINILLAS

Piso

Mant. Aromat.   200 (1658).

Pre-1753, therefore not validly published in
fulfillment of nomenclatural rules; this name is
most often referred to *Vanilla*.

VANDA

W. Jones

Asiat. Res.   **4**: 302 (1795).

Not validly published, this name is most
often referred to *Vanda* R. Brown.

VANDA

W. Jones ex **R. Brown**

Bot. Reg.   **6**: *t.* 506 (1820).

Epidendroideæ 〰 Vandeæ • Aeridinæ

ETYMOLOGY: From a local Sanskrit (ancient parent
language of Hindi and Urdu languages) word for
epiphyte (although the word means mistletoe in
Hindi) and some other plants that have a similar
growth habit. Referring to the species known as
Vanda tessellata found in southern India and Sri
Lanka.

TYPE SPECIES: *Vanda roxburghii* R. Brown
This type name is now considered a synonym of
Vanda tessellata (Roxburgh) Hooker ex G. Don;
basionym
Epidendrum tessellatum Roxburgh

Fifty-seven monopodial
epiphytes or lithophytes
are found in low to
upper elevation, evergreen or
deciduous forests and rocky
cliffs from southern
China (Xizang to
Guangdong), northern India
(Kashmir to Assam), Nepal, southern Japan
(Ryukyu Islands), Sri Lanka, Myanmar to
Vietnam, the Philippines, Indonesia, New
Guinea, the Solomons and northeastern
Australia. These large to tiny plants, often
forming large, scrambling clumps, have semi-
rigid, strap-like to pencil-like, channeled
leaves produced from the stem's tip, with the
lower leaves eventually being shed. Thus, after
a few years, the plants become leggy with a
length of bare stem that has numerous, stout
aerial roots formed along the base of the stem.
The erect, numerous to few-flowered inflorescence, borne from the leaf base, has
comparatively large, showy, fleshy, heavily
textured, fragrant flowers with strong color
variations. They will last from several days to
nearly two months in perfection. The trilobed
lip has a short, oblong to cone-like spur firmly
attached to the short, rather stout, wingless
column that has a short foot or is footless. The
lip has erect side lobes; the often keeled
midlobe is forward pointing, and has cone-like
to oblong, sometimes recurved spur.

VANDAE

An orthographic variant introduced in *Icon.
Pl. Asiat.*, **3**: 352, *t.* 330 (1851). The correct
spelling is *Vanda*.

VANDOPSIS

Pfitzer

Nat. Pflanzenfam.   **2**(6): 210 (1889).

Epidendroideæ 〰 Vandeæ • Aeridinæ

ETYMOLOGY: *Vanda*, a genus of orchids and Greek for
resemblance or likeness. Implying a likeness to *Vanda*.

TYPE SPECIES: *Vandopsis lissochiloides*
(Gaudichaud-Beaupré) Pfitzer
(*Fieldia lissochiloides* Gaudichaud-Beaupré)

Five large, spectacular,
monopodial lithophytes or
terrestrials are found in
low to mid elevation,
hill scrub to evergreen
montane forests and rocky
slopes from southern
China (Yunnan to Guangdong), northern
India (Assam), Nepal, Myanmar to Vietnam,
Malaysia and New Guinea to the Philippines.
These large, robust plants have long, rigid,
sometimes branched, thick stems, each with
several, large, distichous, leathery or fleshy,
narrow or tape-like leaves arranged in two
rows. The plants often form massive clumps.
The long or short, simple or branched,
numerous-flowered inflorescence has large,
showy, widespreading, sweetly fragrant (at
times) flowers that are heavily textured,
extremely long-lived, and densely blotched
with rich colors. The blotches appear as rings
with lighter colored centers. The small,
oblong, red, trilobed lip, attached to the base
of the yellow, short, stout, wingless column,
has erect side lobes. The compressed or flattened midlobe has a few to several, basal calli
and an upcurved tip.

VANILIA

An orthographic variant introduced in
Disionari, **3**: 180 (1815). The correct spelling
is *Vanilla*.

VANILLA

Plumier

Nov. Pl. Amer.   23, *t.* 82 (1703).

Not validly published, this name is most
often referred to *Vanilla* Miller.

Currently Accepted   Validly Published   Invalidly Published   Published Pre-1753   Superfluous Usage   Orthographic Variant   Fossil

O r c h i d   G e n e r a • **408**

VANILLA

Plumier ex **Miller**

Gard. Dict. Abr., ed. 4   [p. 1432] (1754).

Vanilloideæ ⚘ **Vanillineæ**

ETYMOLOGY: Spanish (*vainilla*) for pod, sheath, scabbard or husk and little. In reference to the long, slender, pod-like shaped fruit produced by the plant.

LECTOTYPE: *Vanilla mexicana* (Linnaeus) Miller (*Epidendrum vanilla* Linnaeus)

About one hundred ten, climbing or scrambling, monopodial terrestrials, lithophytes or truly epiphytes are widespread in almost all the tropical areas of the globe. They reach their greatest development in Brazil, with a few species found from the southeastern United States (Florida), the Bahamas to Trinidad, Cuba to Jamaica, the Guianas, Mexico to Paraguay and Africa (Guinea to Zaire) in wet, humid, low to mid elevation, hill scrub and evergreen montane forests, especially in clearings. These are unusual plants with a few species having large, dark green, usually leathery leaves, while other species have viny, essentially leafless stems with the fleshy leaves reduced to scale-like bracts. The short, few to numerous-flowered inflorescence has white, green, green-yellow or creamy colored flowers that for the most part, are large, showy, and fade after only a few hours. The entire to variously lobed lip, fused to the long or short, slender to stout, straight or slightly curved, footless column, forms a funnel-shape, and is often hairy inside. These attractive, fragrant flowers are produced in succession over time, thus, a plant can be in bloom for several weeks or even months.

NOTE: This genus is most noteworthy because its seed capsules contain an alkaloid vanillin that when suitably dried and cured contains the widely used vanilla extract flavoring that is derived for both cooking and as a fragrance ingredient.

VANILLAS

Plukenet

Alm. Bot. Pl.   381, t. 320, f. 4 (1700).

ETYMOLOGY: Spanish for pod and small. Referring to the slender, bean-like seed pod.

TYPE SPECIES: *Vanillas piperis arbori jamaicensis innascens* Plukenet

Pre-1753, therefore not validly published in fulfillment of nomenclatural rules; this polynomial name is most often referred to *Vanilla*. *Vanillas* was previously considered to include one epiphyte found in wet, low elevation, shady thickets and forests of Jamaica, the Guianas, Cuba, Hispaniola and Trinidad. This slender plant has vining, branching stems, each with a solitary, leathery, dark green leaf at each node. The terminal, few-flowered inflorescence has flowers with pale brown, fleshy sepals and almost translucent, pale colored petals. The side lobes of the narrow, golden-yellow, entire lip are

joined to the long, narrow column for most of their length. There are two, white blotches at the base, and several crests in the center which taper to a sharp point. This name is now usually considered a synonym of *Vanilla bicolor* Lindley.

VANILLE

An orthographic variant introduced in *Vera. Surinaemsche Insect., 25, t. 25* (1719). The correct spelling is *Vanilla*.

VANILLIA

Petiver

Gaz.   64, 72 (1704).

Pre-1753, therefore not validly published in fulfillment of nomenclatural rules; this name is most often referred to *Vanilla*.

VANILLO

Merian

Metam. Insect. Surinam.   t. 25 (1682).

Pre-1753, therefore not validly published in fulfillment of nomenclatural rules; this name is most often referred to *Vanilla*.

VANILLOES

Petiver

Musei Pet.   48 (1695).

Pre-1753, therefore not validly published in fulfillment of nomenclatural rules; this name is most often referred to *Vanilla*.

VANILLOPHORA

An orthographic variant introduced in *Fl. Bras. (Martius),* **3**(4): 144 (1893). The correct spelling is *Vanillophorum*.

VANILLOPHORUM

Necker

Elem. Bot. (Necker)   **3**: 134 (1790).

ETYMOLOGY: *Vanilla,* a genus of orchids, and Latin for carrying.

TYPE SPECIES: *None designated*

Not validly published, this name is most often referred to *Vanilla* Miller. Necker originally created the genus *Vanillophorum* but the description he used for the one species was vague. Today it is concluded by various authors that the name might belong with *Vanilla*.

VAPPODES

M.A. Clements & **D.L. Jones**

Orchadian   **13**(11): 492 (2002).

ETYMOLOGY: Latin for moth and like or similar to. Referring to the flat flower's similarity to the broad wingspan of a moth.

TYPE SPECIES: *Vappodes bigibba* (Lindley) M.A. Clements & D.L. Jones (*Dendrobium bigibbum* Lindley)

Recognized as belonging to the genus *Dendrobium*, *Vappodes* was proposed to include eight epiphytes or lithophytes found in low elevation, coastal woodlands growing in small clumps under hot, dry conditions of north-eastern Australia (Queensland) and New Guinea. These small, variable plants have long, cylindrical stems, each with several often purple suffused leaves arranged in two ranks. The one to several, few-flowered inflorescences have spectacular, large, flat-faced, purple, white or lilac flowers. The darker, trilobed lip has rounded side lobes; the pointed midlobe has a white blotched at the base, is notched at the tip, and has a keel with white hairs in the middle. The flowers have a small, short column.

VARGASIELLA

C. Schweinfurth

Bot. Mus. Leafl.   **15**: 150, t. 47 (1952).

Epidendroideæ ⚘ **Cymbidieæ** • **Zygopetalinæ**

ETYMOLOGY: Dedicated to Julio César Vargas Calderón (1907-1960), a Peruvian botanist and professor of botany at the University of Peru in Cusco. And Latin for diminutive.

TYPE SPECIES: *Vargasiella peruviana* C. Schweinfurth

Two uncommon, sympodial terrestrials or epiphytes are found in upper elevation, montane rain forests from southern Venezuela and central Peru (Pasco) to Bolivia (La Paz). These plants have erect, long, slender stems with many joints, each with distichous, thinly textured leaves spaced along the upper portion. The long, straggling, few-flowered inflorescence, borne from the axils of the leaf, has fleshy, white and pink flowers not opening widely. The narrow floral segments form a hood over the short, stout column. The long, narrow, entire lip has a wavy margin, and a fleshy, basal callus.

VARIEPHYLIS

An orthographic variant introduced in *Hist. Orchid., t. 105* (1822). The correct spelling is *Variphylis*.

VARIPHYLIS

Thouars

Hist. Orchid. Table 2, sub 3u, *t. 106* (1822).

Name published without a description. Today this name is most often referred to *Bulbophyllum*.

VASQUEZIELLA

Dodson

Icon. Pl. Trop., ser. 1 **6**: *t. 600* (1982).

Epidendroideæ ⚘ **Cymbidieæ** • **Stanhopeinæ**

ETYMOLOGY: Honoring Roberto Vásquez y Chávez (1942-), a Bolivian botanical illustrator from Jaén and co-author of *Bromeliaceæ of Bolivia* and *Orchids of Bolivia*. And Latin for diminutive.

TYPE SPECIES: *Vasqueziella boliviana* Dodson

One sympodial epiphyte is found in mid elevation, montane forests of Bolivia (Cochabamba). This small plant has large, pear-shaped pseudobulbs, subtended by non-leafy, sheathing bracts, each with several, pleated leaves. The hanging, numerous-flowered inflorescence has yellow to orange-yellow, fleshy, fragrant flowers not opening widely. The trilobed lip has narrow, upcurved, horn-like side lobes and a spreading midlobe. The flowers have a long, slender column that is bent below the tip.

VAUDA

An orthographic variant introduced in *Tijdschr. Natuurl. Gesch. Physiol.*, **6**: 78 (1839). The correct spelling is *Vanda*.

VAUNDA

An orthographic variant introduced in *Veg. World*, 308 (1867). The correct spelling is *Vanda*.

VAYNILLA

Piso

Mant. Aromat. 200 (1658).

Pre-1753, therefore not validly published in fulfillment of nomenclatural rules; this name is most often referred to *Vanilla*.

VENDA

An orthographic variant introduced in *Dict. Sci. Nat.*, **36**: 304 (1825). The correct spelling is *Vanda*.

VENTRICULARIA

Garay

Bot. Mus. Leafl. **23**(4): 210 (1972).

Epidendroideæ ⚘ **Vandeæ** • **Aeridinæ**

ETYMOLOGY: Latin for the belly and Greek for little. Referring to the swollen shape of the spur.

TYPE SPECIES: *Ventricularia tenuicaulis* (Hooker f.) Garay (*Saccolabium tenuicaule* Hooker f.)

Two uncommon, monopodial epiphytes are distributed in low to mid elevation, hill thickets and montane forests of Thailand, Malaysia and Indonesia (Borneo) on limestone cliffs. These small, hanging plants, vegetatively resemble *Trichoglottis*, have slender to stout, slightly zig-sagged stems, each with several, narrow, leathery to fleshy, dark green, unequally bilobed leaves sprinkled with red spots and are arranged in two ranks. The several, short, few-flowered inflorescences, borne at the nodes, have tiny, yellow or pale lemon yellow flowers. The similar sepals and petals have inner surfaces that are sometimes covered with short hairs at the base. The hood-like dorsal sepal appears to cover the short, gently curved column. The white, trilobed lip has erect side lobes; the concave midlobe points upward in front of the column, has a hairy membrane on the back wall, and has a small, squat spur. These species were formerly included in *Gastrochilus*.

VERMEULENIA

Á. Löve & D. Löve

Acta Bot. Neerl. **21**(5): 554 (1972).

ETYMOLOGY: Dedicated to Pieter Vermeulen (1899-1981), a Dutch secondary school teacher, botanist, orchidologist and author of numerous articles on orchids and *Studies on Dactylorchids*.

TYPE SPECIES: *Vermeulenia papilionacea* (Linnaeus) Á. Löve & D. Löve (*Orchis papilionacea* Linnaeus)

Now recognized as belonging to the genus *Anacamptis*, *Vermeulenia* was previously considered to include five terrestrials found in low to mid elevation, open forests, woodlands and nutrient-poor grasslands from France to Greece, Turkey, Cyprus and northern Africa (Morocco to Libya). These highly variable plants have erect, unbranched stems, each with several, narrow leaves in a basal rosette. The numerous to few-flowered inflorescence has large, colorful bracts and pink, purple-violet to brown-pink flowers. The upward, pointing sepals and petals have dark veins. The wide, fan-shaped, trilobed lip is variously covered with blotches and streaks. The long, cone-shaped spur is horizontal at first, then curves downward.

VESICISEPALUM

(J.J. Smith) Garay, Hamer & Siegerist

Nordic J. Bot. **14**(6): 641 (1994).

ETYMOLOGY: Latin for little or eating away and sepal. In reference to the appearance of the flowers with the united sepals forming a bladder-like inflated bag.

TYPE SPECIES: *Vesicisepalum folliculiferum* (J.J. Smith) Garay, Hamer & Siegerist (*Bulbophyllum folliculiferum* J.J. Smith)

Now recognized as belonging to the genus *Bulbophyllum*, *Vesicisepalum* was proposed to include one epiphyte found in Indonesia and New Guinea. This small, hanging plant has snake-like rhizomes. The pseudobulbs are arranged in two rows along the rhizome, each with a solitary, narrow, thinly textured leaf. The short, solitary-flowered inflorescence, borne from the node of the rhizome, has a follicle-like, red-green flower. The lateral sepals (united at the base) form a bladder-like inflated bag, and the dorsal sepal is tiny. The tiny, mobile, ovate, entire lip is strongly curved and channeled. The flowers have a short, stout column.

VESTIGIUM

Luer

Monogr. Syst. Bot. Missouri Bot. Gard. **103**: 309 (2005).

Not *Vestigium* Pirozynski & Shoemaker (1972) Fungi.

ETYMOLOGY: Latin for dressed and surrounded by bracts. Refers to the tiny flowers.

TYPE SPECIES: *Vestigium abortiva* (Luer) Luer (*Pleurothallis abortiva* Luer)

Not validly published because of a prior use of the name, this homonym was replaced by *Pleurothallis*.

VEXILLABIUM

Maekawa

J. Jap. Bot. **11**(7): 457 (1935).

ETYMOLOGY: Latin for a flag or banner and lip. Refers to the T-shaped lip, which protrudes far beyond the sepals, and has the appearance of a banner.

TYPE SPECIES: *Vexillabium nakaianum* Maekawa

Now recognized as belonging to the genus *Kuhlhasseltia*, *Vexillabium* was previously considered to include five uncommon, terrestrials found in upper elevation, montane (rich humus) forests, rocky crevices and along river banks of Japan, southern China (Anhui to Sichuan), Taiwan and the Philippines. These erect, creeping plants have unbranched stems, subtended by sheaths, each with several, small,

Currently Accepted   Validly Published   Invalidly Published   Published Pre-1753   Superfluous Usage   Orthographic Variant   Fossil

variable sized, usually red-green leaves. The slender, few-flowered inflorescence, sparsely covered with a few hairs, has tiny, white flowers that are hairy on the outside. The united (at the middle) sepals form a tube, and the petals converge, forming a hood over the erect, small, stout column. The Y- or T-shaped, entire or trilobed lip has a short, bilobed, sac-like base with two, callose appendages inside and has a small spur.

VEYRETELLA

Szlachetko & Olszewski

Fl. Cameroun   **34**: 100 (1998).

Orchidoideæ ⚬ Cranichideæ • Goodyerinæ

ETYMOLOGY: Dedicated to Yvonne Veyret (1925-). And Latin for diminutive.

TYPE SPECIES: *Veyretella hetaerioides*
(Summerhayes) Szlachetko & Olszewski
(*Habenaria hetaerioides* Summerhayes)

Two terrestrials are found in hot, humid, low elevation, grasslands and woodlands of Gabon. These small plants have short, erect stems, subtended by overlapping sheaths, each with a basal rosette of narrow leaves. The erect, few-flowered inflorescence has large, leaf-like bracts and large to small, white flowers with narrow, veined petals. The large lateral sepals curve backward, and the smaller dorsal sepal is erect. The large, trilobed lip has small, spreading side lobes, a broad, transparent midlobe with a fleshy basal callus, and a long, tapering, thread-like to stout spur. The flowers have a short, stout column.

VEYRETIA

Szlachetko

Fragm. Florist. Geobot.   **3**(Suppl.): 115 (1995).

Orchidoideæ ⚬ Cranichideæ • Spiranthinæ

ETYMOLOGY: Dedicated to Yvonne Veyret (1925-), a French botanist, embryologist and a systematist on orchids who has worked extensively on the flora of Madagascar.

TYPE SPECIES: *Veyretia hassleri* (Cogniaux) Szlachetko
(*Spiranthes hassleri* Cogniaux)

Nine sympodial terrestrials are found in seasonally wet, low to mid elevation, hill scrub, marshes, rocky fields, savannas, prairies and montane rain forests of the Guianas, Trinidad, Venezuela, Colombia, Brazil, Paraguay and northern Argentina (Corrientes and Misiones). These tall, slender, delicate plants have unbranched stems, each with an inconspicuous basal rosette (base subtended by several, red-brown, bladeless sheaths) of grass-like or channeled leaves often withered by flowering time. The slender, numerous to few-flowered inflorescence has small, hairy, tubular, green-yellow or green-white flowers. The lateral sepals are hairy on the outside, and

more or less, ribbon like; the erect dorsal sepal has incurved margins, and the small, smooth petals are slightly notched at their tips. The broad, shortly clawed, obscurely trilobed lip has fine hairs at the base, forms a tunnel-like access to the nectary and has a forked (at the base) spur. The flowers have a long, straight, slender column.

VIEILLARDORCHIS

Kraenzlin

Notul. Syst. (Paris)   **4**: 143 (1928).

ETYMOLOGY: In honor of Eugéne Deplanche Emile Vieillard (1819-1896), a French naval surgeon and botanist who collected flora in New Caledonia and author of *Plantes de la nouvell-Calédonie*. And Greek for orchid.

TYPE SPECIES: *Vieillardorchis le-ratii* Kraenzlin

This type name is now considered a synonym of
Goodyera scripta (Reichenbach f.) Schlechter;
basionym
Rhamphidia scripta Reichenbach f.

Now recognized as belonging to the genus *Goodyera*, *Vieillardorchis* was previously considered to include one terrestrial found in humid, low elevation, woodlands of New Caledonia and then found on only a few occasions. This small plant has erect, unbranched stems, each with several, small leaves midway up the stem. The erect, few-flowered inflorescence has tiny, white flowers.

VIELLARDORCHIS

An orthographic variant introduced in *Acta Bot. Fenn.*, No. 169, **1**: 210 (2000). The correct spelling is *Vieillardorchis*.

VIETORCHIS

Averyanov & Averyanova

Updated Checkl. Orchids Vietnam   92 (2003).

Epidendroideæ ⚬ Nervilieæ

ETYMOLOGY: Honoring Vietnam (a Republic located along the South China Sea in the old French Indochina region). And Greek for orchid.

TYPE SPECIES: *Vietorchis aurea*
Averyanov & Averyanova

One sympodial saprophyte is found in seasonal, low elevation, limestone forests of northern Vietnam. This small, leafless, creeping plant has erect, unbranched, off white stems subtended by several, clasping bracts. The smooth, white, solitary to few-flowered inflorescence has bright yellow flowers with broad lateral sepals and the small petals are finely notched. The unusual trilobed lip has oblong side lobes, a broad, rectangular midlobe with a blunt tip and has basal splashes

and blotches of orange. The flowers have a short column.

VIFCUM

An orthographic variant introduced in *Icon. Pl. Rar. (Jacquin)*, **3**: 17 (1795). The correct spelling is *Viscum*.

VILLANA

An orthographic variant introduced in *Morph. Stud. Orchideenbl.*, 22 (1886). The correct spelling is *Vanilla*.

VILLOSAGASTRIS

An orthographic variant introduced in *Hist. Orchid.*, *t. 32* (1822). The correct spelling is *Villosogastris*.

VILLOSOGASTRIS

Thouars

Hist. Orchid.   Table 1, sub 2j (1822).

Name published without a description. Today this name is most often referred to *Phaius*.

VINELLO

Blome

Present State Majesties Isles Territories Amer.   16 (1687).

Pre-1753, therefore not validly published in fulfillment of nomenclatural rules; this name is most often referred to *Vanilla*.

VISCUM

Plukenet

Alm. Bot. Pl.   390, t. 117, f. 6 (1700).

Pre-1753, therefore not validly published in fulfillment of nomenclatural rules; this name is most often referred to *Brassavola*.

VISCUM

Sloane

Voy. Jamaica   **1**: *ttt. 125, 121, 148* (1707).

ETYMOLOGY: Latin for bird-lime, clammy or the mistletoe. Referring to the type of parasitic evergreen shrubs found in the old world.

TYPE SPECIES: *None designated*

Pre-1753, therefore not validly published in fulfillment of nomenclatural rules. There are at least four species published by Sloane that used the same genus name: *Viscum delphinii flore minus, petalis e viridi albicantibus radice fibrosâ* (251, *t. 125, f. 1*), an epiphyte species widespread from Mexico to Colombia, Aruba, the Guianas and Venezuela. The plant has large, creamy to green-yellow flowers with a white, heart-shaped lip. This name is usually considered as a synonym of *Brassavola nodosa* (Linnaeus) Lindley.

Viscum radice bulbosâ minus, delphinii flore rubro specioso (250, *t. 121, f. 2*), an epiphyte found in Jamaica. The plant has a showy, brilliant crimson to mauve flower that has a roundish, obscurely trilobed, yellow lip with purple veins. This name is considered as a synonym of *Broughtonia sanguinea* (Swartz) R. Brown.

Viscum delphinii flore albo guttato, minus radice fibrosâ (251, *t. 148*), an epiphyte found from Cuba to Puerto Rico. This plant has white or pink flowers marked with red spotting and has a trilobed lip with a kidney-shaped midlobe. This name is now considered as a synonym of *Tolumnia variegata* (Swartz) Braem.

Viscum radice bulbosa majus & elatius, delphinii flore ferrugineo guttato (250, *t. 148, f. 1*), an epiphyte or lithophyte found in Jamaica. This plant has several, yellow-green flowers barred and blotched maroon. The bright yellow, trilobed lip has an oblong, kidney-shaped midlobe. This name is now considered as a synonym of *Oncidium altissimum* (Jacquin) Swartz.

VITEKORCHIS

Romowicz & Szlachetko

Polish Bot. J.   **51**(1): 45 (2006)[2007].

ETYMOLOGY: Named in honor of Ernst Vitek (1953-), an Austrian curator at the Herbarium in Naturhistorishes Museum in Vienna and author of *Euphrasia*. And Greek for orchid.

TYPE SPECIES: *Vitekorchis excavatum* (Lindley) Romowicz & Szlachetko (*Oncidium excavatum* Lindley)

Recognized as belonging to the genus *Oncidium*, *Vitekorchis* was proposed to include twelve terrestrials found in wet, upper elevation, montane

forests, steep slopes and rocky grasslands from Costa Rica to Bolivia, Venezuela and Brazil. These plants have clustered, oblong, slightly compressed pseudobulbs, subtended by leaf-bearing sheaths, each with a solitary, narrow, leathery, pale yellow-green leaf borne at the tip. The stout to slender, erect to arching, branched, few to numerous-flowered inflorescence has small to large, bright canary yellow flowers barred and spotted red-brown; the sepals and petals have wavy margins. The trilobed lip has small, rounded side lobes; the clawed, large midlobe has a basal callus with a number of small, raised protuberances and has a notched tip. The flowers have a short, stout, footless column.

VOLUBILIS

Catesby

Nat. Hist. Carolina, ser. 2   **7**: *t. 7* (1747).

ETYMOLOGY: Latin for turnable or roll. Descriptive of the lip.

TYPE SPECIES: *Volubilis siliquosa plantaginis folio* Catesby

Pre-1753, therefore not validly published in fulfillment of nomenclatural rules; this polynomial name is most often referred to the genus *Vanilla*. *Volubilis* was previously considered to include one epiphyte found in low to mid elevation, hill scrub, woodlands and montane forests from the southeastern United States (Florida), Cuba to Trinidad, Mexico to Nicaragua, Venezuela to the Guianas and Colombia to Brazil. This aerial, climbing plant has occasionally branched, leafy, very slender stems, each with several, leathery leaves. The few-flowered inflorescence has thick, rigid, pale green-yellow flowers with spreading sepals and smaller petals. The white, tubular, obscurely trilobed lip has the rounded side lobes arched over the slender column; the midlobe has a wavy margin and has orange-yellow, basal calli. This name is now usually considered a synonym of *Vanilla mexicana* Miller.

VOLUCREPIS

Thouars

Hist. Orchid.   Table 3, sub 3p, *t. 81* (1822).

Name published without a description. Today this name is most often referred to *Oeonia*.

VONROEMERIA

J.J. Smith

Bull. Dépt. Agric. Indes Néerl.   **39**: 21 (1910).

ETYMOLOGY: In honor of Lucien Sophie Albert Marie von Römer (1873-1965), a Dutch physician and naval medical officer who collected orchids in New Guinea and Java with the 1909 Lorentz Expedition.

TYPE SPECIES: *Vonroemeria tenuis* J.J. Smith

Now recognized as belonging to the genus *Octarrhena*, *Vonroemeria* was previously considered to include one epiphyte found in upper elevation, montane forests of New Guinea and eastern Indonesia (Sulawesi). This erect, simple or branched plant has slender stems, each with several, small, warty, laterally compressed, distichous leaves. The few-flowered inflorescence has small, orange flowers with cup-like sepals and does not open fully. The oblong, entire lip is almost boat-shaped.

VREDAGZENIA

An orthographic variant introduced in *Index Gen. Phan.*, 399 (1888). The correct spelling is *Vrydagzynea*.

VRIESIA

Lindley ex Wittstein

Etym.-Bot.-Handw.-Buch, ed. 1   928 (1852).

Not *Vriesia* Lindley (1843) Bromeliaceæ.

Name published without a description. This name was published as belonging to Orchidaceæ which it is not, but the name should be referred to *Vriesia* (Bromeliaceæ).

VRIJDAGZIJNEA

An orthographic variant introduced in *Orch. Java*, **1**: *f. 59* (1908). The correct spelling is *Vrydagzynea*.

VRYDAGSINIA

An orthographic variant introduced in *Sitzungsber. Königl. Böhm. Ges. Wiss. Prag, Math.-Naturwiss. Cl.*, **31**: 13 (1903). The correct spelling is *Vrydagzynea*.

VRYDAGZENIA

An orthographic variant introduced in *J. Linn. Soc., Bot.*, **18**(110): 344 (1881). The correct spelling is *Vrydagzynea*.

Currently Accepted   Validly Published   Invalidly Published   Published Pre-1753   Superfluous Usage   Orthographic Variant   Fossil

O r c h i d   G e n e r a   • **412**

VRYDAGZINIA

An orthographic variant introduced in *Fl. Brit. Ind.*, **5**: 673 (1890). The correct spelling is *Vrydagzynea*.

VRYDAGZYNEA

Blume

Coll. Orchid. 71, *tt. 17, 19-20* (1858), and *Fl. Javæ Nov. Ser.* 59, *t. 20* (1858).

Orchidoideæ ◊ Cranichideæ • Goodyerinæ

ETYMOLOGY: Commemorating Theodoor Daniel Vrijdag Zijnen (1799-1863), a Dutch scientist, pharmacologist and author who wrote about new medicines of vegetable origin.

LECTOTYPE: *Vrydagzynea albida* (Blume) Blume (*Hetaeria albida* Blume)

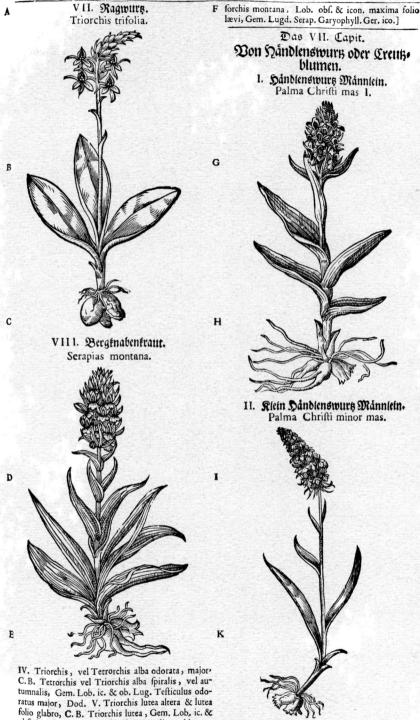

Forty-one sympodial terrestrials, occasional lithophytes or rare epiphytes are widespread in dark, damp, low to mid elevation, montane forest undergrowth from eastern China (Hainan and Hong Kong), Taiwan, northeastern India (Assam), Thailand, Vietnam, Malaysia, Indonesia, the Philippines, to New Guinea, northeastern Australia (Queensland) and the southwestern Pacific Archipelago. The whole plant, including the white to pale green flowers, is quite small. These plants have weak, fleshy stems, each with several, thin-substance, glossy, dark green leaves that often have a wide median, white nerve. The usually short, hairy, numerous to few-flowered inflorescence has small, white to pale green flowers not opening widely. The dorsal sepal forms a hood along with the petals whose tips have a pink tinge. The concave, entire lip has raised edges with a blunt tip and bears two, drumstick-shaped glands inside; the center is distinctly papillose and has a small spur. The flowers have a small, short, erect, footless column.

VRYDASZYNEA

An orthographic variant introduced in *Bot. Centralbl.*, **70**(19-20): 217 (1897). The correct spelling is *Vrydagzynea*.

VULPINUS

L'Obel

Pl. Stirp. Hist. 91 (1576).

Pre-1753, therefore not validly published in fulfillment of nomenclatural rules; this name is most often referred to *Orchis*.

Jacobus Theodorus Tabernaenontanum
Neu vollkommen Kräuter-buch page 1059 (1731).

WAILESA

An orthographic variant introduced in *Concise Fl. Singapore*, **2**: 89 (1989). The correct spelling is *Wailesia*.

WAILESIA

Lindley

J. Hort. Soc. London **4**: 261 (1849).

ETYMOLOGY: Dedicated to George Wailes (1802-1882), an British gentleman farmer, naturalist, botanist, and member of the Literary and Philosophical Society of Newcastle-on-Tyne who cultivated and studied orchids.

TYPE SPECIES: *Wailesia picta* Lindley

Now recognized as belonging to the genus *Dipodium*, *Wailesia* was previously considered to include three monopodial epiphytes, lithophytes or terrestrials found in low to mid elevation, hill scrub and montane forests of Malaysia, Indonesia (Sumatra, Java and Borneo) and the Philippines. These scrambling, climbing plants have long, spiraling stems, each with several, pale green, densely arranged leaves. The plants can reach heights in excess of three feet (90 cm). The stem can take root at any point. The few-flowered inflorescence has large, heavy textured, pale yellow flowers opening widely. On the outer surfaces, the flowers have crimson blotches that vaguely show through the segments. The creamy-white, obscurely trilobed lip can be striped or spotted purple; the side lobes are sickle-shaped, and the midlobe is densely covered with white hairs above. These hairs extend in lines to the base of the lip.

WAIREIA

D.L. Jones, M.A. Clements & Molloy

Orchadian **12**(6): 282 (1997).

ETYMOLOGY: From a local Maori (native New Zealand people) word for water and swampy ground or peat. Referring to the wet peaty habitat of the type species.

TYPE SPECIES: *Waireia stenopetala*
(Hooker f.) D.L. Jones, M.A. Clements & Molloy
(*Thelymitra stenopetala* Hooker f.)

Now recognized as belonging to the genus *Lyperanthus*, *Waireia* was proposed to include one terrestrial found in damp, low to mid elevation, peat bogs of upland, montane meadows of Norfolk, New Zealand, and Stewart, Auckland and Campbell Islands. This slender plant has unbranched stems, each with one to two, flat, stiff, erect leaves. The erect, two to three-flowered, wiry inflorescence has green to yellow-green flowers marked with red streaks or bars. The petals are decurved; the lateral sepals are deeply hooded, and the dorsal sepal surrounds the long, incurved, footless column and base of the entire lip. The above type name is now considered a synonym of *Lyperanthus antarcticus* Hooker f.

WALLNOEFERIA

Szlachetko

Fragm. Florist. Geobot. **39**(2): 517 (1994).

ETYMOLOGY: Honoring Bruno Wallnöfer (1960-), an Austrian botanist, and curator of Phanerogams at the Naturhistorishes Museum in Vienna who collected the type species.

TYPE SPECIES: *Wallnoeferia peruviana* Szlachetko

Now recognized as belonging to the genus *Helonoma*, *Wallnoeferia* was previously considered to include one terrestrial found in shady, mid elevation, moss laden scrub of central Peru (Huanuco and Ucayali). This small, erect plant has several, tiny, thinly textured, basal leaves and has quite hairy rhizomes. The erect, delicate, few-flowered inflorescence has tiny flowers that are a dull brown-white toward either end and barely open. The sepals and petals are fused together for most of their length, forming a long, cylindrical tube. The narrow, entire lip is also fused in the basal portion of the tube

shape and the tip is densely covered with erect, fleshy hairs.

WALNEWA

An orthographic variant introduced in *Gard. Chron.*, ser. 3, **1**: 307 (1891). The correct spelling is *Waluewa*.

WALUEWA

Regel

Trudy Imp. S.-Péterburgsk. Bot. Sada **11**: 309 (1890).

ETYMOLOGY: Honoring Peter Alexandrowitsch Walujew (1807-1890), a Prussian count and statesman who employed Eduard August von Regel (1815-1892) as a director of the Berlin Royal Botanic Garden. Regel also was the author of *Tentamen Floræ Ussuriensis* and numerous other flora books.

TYPE SPECIES: *Waluewa pulchella* Regel

Now recognized as belonging to the genus *Oncidium*, *Waluewa* was previously considered to include one epiphyte found in hot, humid to cool, low elevation, hill forests from southeastern Brazil to Paraguay. This small plant has cone-like, slightly compressed pseudobulbs, each with a solitary, erect, leathery leaf. The erect to hanging, slender, few-flowered inflorescence has green-white bracts. The strongly concave, white to green-yellow flowers are barred pink-purple to red-brown. The obscurely trilobed lip is barred and lined pink-purple and has a purple, basal callus. The above type names is now considered a synonym of *Oncidium waluewa* Rolfe.

NOTE: There has been much debate about the placement of this species which has been placed with both *Leochilus* and *Baptistonia*, but it is currently placed with *Oncidium*.

WARCEWICZELLA

An orthographic variant introduced in *Bot. Zeitung* (Berlin), **10**: 765 (1852). The correct spelling is *Warczewiczella*.

WARCEWITSCHIA

An orthographic variant cited in *Lex. Gen. Phan.*, 591 (1904). The correct spelling is *Warczewiczella*.

Currently Accepted | Validly Published | Invalidly Published | Published Pre-1753 | Superfluous Usage | Orthographic Variant | Fossil

O r c h i d G e n e r a • **414**

WARCZEWICZELLA

Reichenbach *filius*

Bot. Zeitung (Berlin) **10**: 635 (1852).

ETYMOLOGY: Dedicated to Jósef Ritter von Rawiez Warszewicz (1812-1866), a Lithuanian botanist who collected plants in the Americas, and head horticulturist at Kraków Botanic Garden (Poland); he was Reichenbach's assistant for many years. And Latin for diminutive.

LECTOTYPE: *Warczewiczella discolor*
(Lindley) Reichenbach f.
(*Warrea discolor* Lindley)
This type name is now considered a synonym of
Cochleanthes discolor (Lindley) R.E. Schultes & Garay;
basionym
Warrea discolor Lindley

Now recognized as belonging to the genera *Chondrorhyncha* and *Cochleanthes*, *Warczewiczella* was previously considered to include twenty-two epiphytes widespread in low to mid elevation, hill scrub to montane forests from Cuba, Jamaica, Trinidad, Mexico to Panama, Venezuela, Brazil and Colombia to Bolivia. These plants have short stems, each with the leaves arranged in a loose, two-ranked, fan shape that are basally overlapping. The short, solitary-flowered inflorescence bears a showy, spreading to reflexed, green to creamy flower whose thinly textured, erect petals and lip can be either plain or extremely frilly. The entire or obscurely trilobed lip is either concave, kidney-shaped or extended and has an obscure or false spur at the base. The erect side lobes form a tube and enclose the incurved column, and have a thick, ridged callus. The variable, rolled, lateral sepals are often bent backward forming a false spur.

WARCZEWICZIA

An orthographic variant introduced in *Bot. Zeitung (Berlin)*, **10**: 635 (1852). The correct spelling is *Warczewiczella*.

WARCZEWITZIA

Skinner ex Lindley & Paxton

Paxton's Fl. Gard. **1**: 45 (1850).

ETYMOLOGY: Named for Jósef Ritter von Rawiez Warszewicz (1812-1866).

TYPE SPECIES: *None designated*

Name published without a description. Today this name is most often referred to *Catasetum*.

WARMINGIA

Reichenbach *filius*

Otia Bot. Hamburg., fasc. 2   87 (1881).

Name ICBN conserved vs. *Warmingia* Engler (1874) Anacardiaceæ.

Epidendroideæ 〰 Cymbidieæ • Oncidiinæ

ETYMOLOGY: Honoring Johannes Eugene Bülow Warming (1841-1924), a Danish taxonomist, botanist, explorer of South America and the Arctic, collector of the flora of Greenland and Norway, morphologist, anatomist, and plant geographer.

TYPE SPECIES: *Warmingia eugenii* Reichenbach f.

Six miniature epiphytes are found in humid, low to mid elevation, hill to montane forests from Costa Rica to Bolivia, south central Brazil (Minas Gerais, São Paulo, Santa Catarina, Pernambuco and Espírito Santo) and northeastern Argentina (Misiones). These tufted plants have small, short, cone-shaped pseudobulbs, each with a solitary, oblong, prominently mid-veined, fleshy leaf. The long, hanging, numerous-flowered inflorescence, borne near the base of the pseudobulb, has small, translucent, extremely fragile, crisp white flowers with all the narrow segments having notched margins. The spreading trilobed lip has erect, roundish side lobes; the midlobe has a bright yellow basal splash and deep yellow calli. The lobes are continuous with the base of the short, footless and wingless column.

WARREA

Lindley

Edwards's Bot. Reg. **29**(Misc.): 14 (1843).

Epidendroideæ 〰 Cymbidieæ • Zygopetalinæ

ETYMOLOGY: Honoring Frederick Warre (fl. 1820s), a British explorer and collector of orchids and other plants in northeastern Brazil who furnished plants to the Loddiges Nursery in England.

TYPE SPECIES: *Warrea tricolor* Lindley nom. illeg.
Warrea warreana
(Loddiges ex Lindley) C. Schweinfurth
(*Maxillaria warreana* Loddiges ex Lindley)

Four sympodial terrestrials are found in low elevation, hill forests and scrub from southern Mexico to Peru, southeastern Brazil (Espírito Santo to Rio Grande do Sul) and northern Argentina (Misiones). These plants have oblong or ovoid, large or small pseudobulbs with several nodes, subtended by leaf-like sheaths, each topped by several thinly textured, heavily veined leaves. The several to few-flowered inflorescence, borne from the base of the pseudobulb, has large, showy, white to pale yellow, faintly fragrant, long-lasting, heavily textured flowers. The lateral sepals are united at the base forming, a chin-like projection with the column foot. The entire

or obscurely trilobed lip, attached to the column foot, has erect side lobes clasping the rather long, club-shaped, wingless column. The rounded or bilobed midlobe has a large, purple to red, basal callus that is also joined to the column foot.

WARREELLA

Schlechter

Orchideen (Schlechter), ed. 1   424 (1914).

Epidendroideæ 〰 Cymbidieæ • Zygopetalinæ

ETYMOLOGY: *Warrea*, a genus of orchids and Latin for diminutive.

TYPE SPECIES: *Warreella cyanea* (Lindley) Schlechter
(*Warrea cyanea* Lindley)

Two sympodial terrestrials are found in wet, humid, mid to upper elevation, montane cloud forests and scrub of Venezuela and Colombia to Ecuador. These small plants have clustered, smooth, olive-green to yellow-brown, ovoid pseudobulbs, subtended by leaf-like sheaths, each with several, pleated, strongly veined leaves. The erect, numerous to few-flowered inflorescence, borne from axils of leaf sheaths, has rather showy, blue-white or violet flowers opening widely that are suffused pale pink. The white, magenta to bright sea-blue, obscurely trilobed lip either tapers to a point or is blunt and is adorned with several long, fleshy keels. The flowers have a white, long, curved column.

WARREOPSIS

Garay

Orquideologia **8**(1): 51 (1973).

Epidendroideæ 〰 Cymbidieæ • Zygopetalinæ

ETYMOLOGY: *Warrea*, a genus of orchids and Greek for like. Illustrating the similarity to *Warrea*.

TYPE SPECIES: *Warreopsis pardina*
(Reichenbach f.) Garay
(*Zygopetalon pardina* Reichenbach f.)

Four sympodial terrestrials are found in wet, humid, semi-shady, mid to upper elevation, montane cloud forests from Costa Rica to Panama and Venezuela to Ecuador. These plants have fleshy, narrow, compressed pseudobulbs with several nodes, subtended by heavily veined, leafy bases, each with several, narrow, thinly textured leaves. The few-flowered inflorescence has yellow to purple flowers suffused pale pink. The broad, pure white, trilobed lip changes to pale red or pink as the flower fades or ages and has a flat, radiating callus between the side lobes. The lip is united to the column foot at the base of the narrow, wingless column.

WARSCAEA

Szlachetko

Fragm. Florist. Geobot.   **39**(2): 561 (1994).

ETYMOLOGY: In honor of Jósef Ritter von Rawicz Warscewicz (1812-1866), a Lithuanian botanist who collected flora in the Americas and was a director at Poland's Kraków Botanic Garden.

TYPE SPECIES: *Warscaea goodyeroides*
(Schlechter) Szlachetko
(*Spiranthes goodyeroides* Schlechter)

Now recognized as belonging to the genus *Cyclopogon*, *Warscaea* was proposed to include four terrestrials found in mid to upper elevation, montane forests from Bolivia to south-eastern, Brazil, Uruguay, Paraguay and northern Argentina. These erect plants have unbranched stems, subtended by narrow, leaf-like sheaths, each with several, small, basal leaves. The few-flowered inflorescence has small, green or white flowers not opening widely; each flower is subtended by a narrow bract and has a green, ball-like spur that is deeply notched. The trilobed lip has broad side lobes and an arrow-shaped midlobe. The unusual, deeply notched rostellum is broad, short and massive to the point of being obtuse.

WARSCEA

An orthographic variant introduced in *Genus*, **15**(Suppl.): 57, 60 (2003). The correct spelling is *Warscaea*.

WARSCEWICZELLA

An orthographic variant introduced in *Bot. Zeitung (Berlin)*, **10**: 765 (1852). The correct spelling is *Warczewiczella*.

WARSCEWICZIELLA

An orthographic variant introduced in *Gartenflora*, **15**: 342 (1866). The correct spelling is *Warczewiczella*.

WARSCEWICZELLA

An orthographic variant cited in *Cool Orchids*, 159 (1874). The correct spelling is *Warczewiczella*.

WARSCEWICZIA

An orthographic variant introduced in *Beitr. Orchid.-K.*, 23 (1866). The correct spelling is *Warczewitzia*.

WARSCEWIZELLA

An orthographic variant introduced in *Second Cent. Orchid. Pl.*, **2**: *t. 127* (1867). The correct spelling is *Warczewiczella*.

WARSEWITSCHIA

Anonymous

Gard. Chron.   **1849**: 196 (1849).

ETYMOLOGY: Named for Jósef Ritter von Rawiez Warszewicz (1812-1866).

TYPE SPECIES: *None designated*

Not validly published, this name is most often referred to *Cochleanthes*. This unknown plant was to be a new genus and was vaguely described as having drooping inflorescences with yellow and green flowers the size of *Catasetum roseum* (Lindley) Reichenbach f.

WARSZEWICZELLA

An orthographic variant introduced in *Bot. Zeitung (Berlin)*, **10**: 836 (1852). The correct spelling is *Warczewiczella*.

WARSZEWISCZIA

An orthographic variant cited in *Lex. Gen. Phan.*, 591 (1904). The correct spelling is *Warczewiczella*.

WELLIA-theka

Rheede

Hort. Malab.   **12**: 45-48, *t. 24* (1693).

ETYMOLOGY: A local Malayalam word for large and theku refers to the host *Tectona grandis*.

TYPE SPECIES: *Wellia-theka-maravara* Rheede

Pre-1753, therefore not validly published in fulfillment of nomenclatural rules; this trinomial name is most often referred to *Pholidota*. *Wellia* was considered to include one epiphyte or lithophyte found in low to mid elevation, rock faces, cliff edges in hot, mixed montane forests of northeastern India, Bhutan, and Myanmar to Vietnam and New Caledonia. This plant has slender to swollen, wrinkled or sunken pseudobulbs, each with a solitary, oblong to narrow, pleated, prominently veined, dark green leaf. The drooping, zig-zagging, numerous-flowered inflorescence has thinly textured, fragrant, creamy-white flowers. The dorsal sepal and petals converge, forming a hood over the wide, wing-like column. The broadly trilobed lip has erect, roundish side lobes and an irregularly bilobed midlobe. This name is now usually considered a synonym of *Pholidota pallida* Lindley.

WINIKA

M.A. Clements, D.L. Jones & Molloy

Orchadian   **12**(5): 214 (1997).

ETYMOLOGY: The local New Zealand Maori name for this plant. The story goes that the name *Winika* was given to a sacred war canoe of the Tainui people. This orchid plant grew upon the tree whose hollowed out trunk was used to formed this canoe. It was later smashed in 1863 by von Tempsky.

TYPE SPECIES: *Winika cunninghamii*
(Lindley) M.A. Clements, D.L. Jones & Molloy
(*Dendrobium cunninghamii* Lindley)

Now recognized as belonging to the genus *Dendrobium*, *Winika* was proposed to include one epiphyte or lithophyte found in low elevation, rain forests of New Zealand, Chatham and Stewart Islands. This slender plant, often forming dense clumps, has hard, brittle, branching stem-like, yellow-brown pseudobulbs, each with narrow leaves borne on the upper half of the final branches of the stem. The solitary to two-flowered inflorescence, borne from the leaf axils, has small, transparent, pristine white flowers scattered sparsely over the plant but usually in pairs. The trilobed lip has small, erect side lobes with bright purple-red markings, and a broad midlobe with a yellow-green base. The flowers have a curved, purple column.

WOLFIA

Dennstedt

Schlüessel Hortus Malab.   11, 25, 38 (1818).

Not *Wolfia* Schreber (1791) Flacourtiaceæ, and not *Wolfia* Sprengel (1824) Menispermaceæ.

ETYMOLOGY: Named in honor of Nathaniel Matthaeus von Wolf (1724-1784), a German physician, astronomer, botanist and author of *Genera Plantarum* in 1776.

TYPE SPECIES: *Wolfia spectabilis* Dennstedt

Not validly published, this name is referred to *Eulophia*. *Wolfia* was considered to include one terrestrial widespread in low elevation, open or shady grasslands and scrub of India, Sri Lanka, Nepal to Myanmar, southern China (Jiangxi and Yunnan), Thailand, Malaysia, New Guinea to Fiji and Tonga.

WOODFORTIA

Lindley ex B.A. Gomes

Jorn. Sci. Math. Phys. Nat.   **4**(14): 184 (1873).

ETYMOLOGY: Named for Emperor John Alexander Woodford (*fl.* 1790s), a British landowner from Chelsea who was in Brazil.

TYPE SPECIES: *None designated*

Name published without a description. Today this name is most often referred to *Eulophia*.

Currently Accepted   Validly Published   Invalidly Published   Published Pre-1753   Superfluous Usage   Orthographic Variant   Fossil

O r c h i d   G e n e r a   •   **416**

WULLSCHLAEGELIA

Reichenbach *filius*

Bot. Zeitung (Berlin) **21**: 131 (1863).

Epidendroideæ ❦ Calypsoeæ

ETYMOLOGY: Commemorating Heinrich Rudolph Wullschlägel (1805-1864), a Russian-born German (Moravian) missionary, teacher and later a consecrated bishop who collected the flora of Jamaica, Surinam and elsewhere.

TYPE SPECIES: *Wullschlaegelia aphylla*
(Swartz) Reichenbach f.
(*Cranichis aphylla* Swartz)

Three scarce, leafless terrestrials or saprophytes are found in hot, low to mid elevation, grasslands and scrub from eastern Cuba to Trinidad, southern Mexico (Oaxaca) to Peru (Loreto), southern Venezuela (Amazonas), the Guianas, northern (Amazonas to Paraná) and southeastern Brazil, and southern Paraguay (Guairá) to northern Argentina (Misiones). These small to minute, slender, erect plants have several, small scales on the wiry, hairy unbranched stem. The stout, few-flowered inflorescence, covered in minute hairs, has self pollinating, tiny, white flowers not opening widely, that are densely covered in coarse hairs externally. The uppermost, entire lip is located at the base and has a chin-like sac within the chin of the sepals. The tiny anther is found at the back of the erect, short column that is unusual with its curved cavities.

WULLSCHLAEGELLIA

An orthographic variant introduced in *Fragm. Florist. Geobot.*, **3**(Suppl.): 57, 58 (1995). The correct spelling is *Wullschlaegelia*.

TABLEAU DES GENRES FORMES SUR LES PLANTES ORCHIDEES DES ILES AUSTRALES D'AFRIQUE.

Thouars *Histoire Particulière des Plantes Orchidees* table four (1822).

XANTOCHILUM

Burbidge

Cool Orchids   160 (1874).

ETYMOLOGY: Latin for yellow and lip.

TYPE SPECIES: *Xantochilum cordatum* Lindley

Name published without a description. Today this name is most often referred to *Odontoglossum*.

XANTOGLOSSUM

Burbidge

Cool Orchids   160 (1874).

ETYMOLOGY: Latin for yellow and tongue.

TYPE SPECIES: *Xantochilum triumphans* Reichenbach f.

Name published without a description. Today this name is most often referred to *Odontoglossum*.

XARITONIA

Rafinesque

Fl. Tellur.   **4**: 9 (1836)[1837].

ETYMOLOGY: Dedicated to a nymph but there is no nymph known by this name in classical literature. Greek Mythology. Hesiod's (*fl.* 800 B.C.) poem *Theogony* (a codified genealogy of the many myths of the Greek gods) mentions there are some three thousand different nymphs.

TYPE SPECIES: *Xaritonia elegans* Rafinesque nom. illeg.
   Tolumnia guttata (Linnaeus) Nir
   (*Epidendrum guttatum* Linnaeus)

Now recognized as belonging to the genus *Tolumnia*, *Xaritonia* was previously considered to include one epiphyte found in low elevation, thickets and woodlands from Mexico to Guatemala, Jamaica, Trinidad, the Guianas, Venezuela and Colombia. This small, tufted plant has inconspicuous pseudobulbs, each with several, poorly developed, two ranked leaves arranged in a loose fan shape, that have finely serrate edges. The simple or sometimes branched, dark purple, numerous-flowered inflorescence has large, variable, chestnut, red-brown to yellow flowers suffused maroon or yellow. The lateral sepals are united and held behind the lip. The broadly clawed, white or

yellow, four-lobed lip has a prominent basal callus. The flowers have a pronounced column.

XEILYANTHUM

An orthographic variant introduced in *Orchideen (Schlechter)*, ed. 1, 498 (1914). The correct spelling is *Xeilyathum*.

XEILYATHUM

Rafinesque

Fl. Tellur.   **2**: 62 (1836)[1837].

ETYMOLOGY: Greek for lip and flower. Supposedly descriptive of the fiddle-shaped lip, but the source of this derivation is unclear.

TYPE SPECIES: *Xeilyathum altissimum*
   (Jacquin) Rafinesque
   (*Epidendrum altissimum* Jacquin)

Now recognized as belonging to the genus *Oncidium*, *Xeilyathum* was previously considered to include one epiphyte found in damp, low elevation, hill forests of Martinique, Trinidad, Saint Vincent and Jamaica. This plant has clustered, compressed pseudobulbs, subtended by several, overlapping, gray sheaths, usually each with a solitary, tongue-like leaf. The often three foot (90 cm) long, arching, hanging, simple to multibranched, numerous-flowered inflorescence has small, highly variable, waxy, long-lived, yellow to green-yellow flowers with deep brown markings or bars. The deep yellow, kidney-shaped, trilobed lip is minutely lobed at the base. The broadly clawed midlobe has a basal callus that has several teeth. The flowers have a slightly curved, short column with chestnut markings.

XENICOPHYTON

An orthographic variant introduced in *Phylogeny Classif. Orchid Fam.*, 207 (1993). The correct spelling is *Xenikophyton*.

XENIKOPHYTON

Garay

Bot. Mus. Leafl.   **23**(10): 374 (1974).

Epidendroideæ ◊ Vandeæ • Aeridinæ

ETYMOLOGY: Greek for foreign or strange and plant. Referring to the curious mixture and attributes of this genus to *Cleisomeria* and *Sarcophyton*.

TYPE SPECIES: *Xenikophyton smeeanum*
   (Reichenbach f.) Garay
   (*Saccolabium smeeanum* Reichenbach f.)

Two monopodial epiphytes are found in mid elevation, woodlands of southern India (Kerala, Karnataka and Tamil Nadu). These small plants have short, woody stems, each with numerous, overlapping, leathery, bilobed leaves that are arranged in a fan shape and are often purple underneath. The simple to sometimes multibranched, numerous-flowered inflorescence has tiny, yellow to pale blue-purple flowers. The downward hanging, immobile, fleshy, sac-like, entire lip, fused to the short, stout, wingless column, has a very thickly textured tip. The short, swollen spur is without a callus on the backwall.

XENOSIA

Luer

Monogr. Syst. Bot. Missouri Bot. Gard.
95: 265 (2004).

ETYMOLOGY: Latin for strange or unknown. Refers to the unusual morphological characters - a short leaf stem and its trilobed lip.

TYPE SPECIES: *Xenosia xenion* (Luer & R. Escobar) Luer
   (*Pleurothallis xenion* Luer & R. Escobar)

Recognized as belonging to the genus *Pleurothallis*, *Xenosia* was proposed to include two epiphytes found in mid elevation, montane forests of Colombia to Bolivia and northwestern Brazil. These plants have short stems spaced along a creeping rhizome, each with a solitary, long, narrow, thick, leathery leaf. The several, wiry, solitary-flowered inflorescences, borne from the leaf axils, have a rather large, yellow to yellow-orange flower heavily barred chestnut. The large, lateral sepals are united for a short length, then each tapers into long,

| Currently Accepted | Validly Published | Invalidly Published | Published Pre-1753 | Superfluous Usage | Orthographic Variant | Fossil |

Orchid Genera • **418**

tail-like tips. The tiny petals are triangularly shaped. The trilobed lip is centrally fixed at the base of the column foot. The flowers have a small, stout column.

XERORCHIS

Schlechter

Repert. Spec. Nov. Regni Veg. **11**: 44 (1912).

Epidendroideæ ⚘ Xerorchideæ

ETYMOLOGY: Greek for dry and orchid. Referring to the ability of these orchids' habit to withstand long droughts.

TYPE SPECIES: *Xerorchis amazonica* Schlechter

Two uncommon, sympodial terrestrials are found in low elevation, Amazon basin of northern Brazil (Acre, Amazonas and Mato Grosso), Peru (Loreto to Huanuco), Bolivia (La Paz), Colombia, Venezuela (Amazonas and Bolivar) and the Guianas. These erect, slender plants have several, multi-branched, clustered, zig-zagging, brittle stems, subtended by leaf sheaths, each with well-spaced, rigid, narrow, leathery leaves. These orchid species form an usual group because of their eight pollinia, an unusual feature found only among a few of the more advanced orchid genera. The few-flowered inflorescence, borne from the axils of the upper leaves, has small, delicate, pale green flowers. The trilobed lip has erect side lobes lying flat to the very long, slender, footless column. The expanded midlobe has a curly or wavy margin with a callus that has two lateral partitions and one central, longer partition. The flowers have a straight column with a pair of fleshy appendages below the stigma.

XILOBIUM

An orthographic variant introduced in *Orquideas Colomb.*, 171, 172 (1958). The correct spelling is *Xylobium*.

XIPHISUSA

An orthographic variant introduced in *J. Linn. Soc., Bot.*, **18**(110): 298 (1881). The correct spelling is *Xiphizusa*.

XIPHIZUSA

Reichenbach *filius*

Bot. Zeitung (Berlin) **10**: 919 (1852).

ETYMOLOGY: Greek for to dance with open arms. A fanciful allusion to the appearance of the flower.

TYPE SPECIES: *Xiphizusa chloroptera* Reichenbach f.

This type name is now considered a synonym of *Bulbophyllum meridense* Reichenbach f.

Now recognized as belonging to the genus *Bulbophyllum*, *Xiphizusa* was previously considered to include three epiphytes or lithophytes found in low to mid elevation, hill woodlands, montane forests and rocky outcroppings from Colombia to Peru, northwestern Venezuela and Brazil (Rio de Janeiro and Minas Gerais). These small plants have roundish to egg-shaped, clustered pseudobulbs, each with a solitary, leathery to fleshy leaf. The long, few-flowered inflorescence has small, green to yellow-green flowers not opening widely with all turned to one side on the rachis. The tiny, narrow petals, covered with red dots, have hairy margins and are much smaller than are the long, narrow sepals. The narrow, obscurely trilobed lip has small, erect, roundish side lobes and the long, dark maroon spotted midlobe tapers to a point.

XIPHOPHYLLUM

Ehrhart

Beitr. Naturk. (Ehrhart) **4**: 148 (1789).
Not *Xiphophyllum* M.D. Zalessky (1938) Fossil.

ETYMOLOGY: Latin for sword-shaped leaves.

TYPE SPECIES: *Serapias xiphophyllum* Linnaeus

Not validly published, this name is most often referred to as a synonym of *Cephalanthera*.

XIPHOSIUM

Griffith

Calcutta J. Nat. Hist. **5**: 364, t. 25 (1844).

ETYMOLOGY: Greek for sword. Refers to the long, sword-like bracts found along the scape.

TYPE SPECIES: *Xiphosium acuminatum* Griffith

Now recognized as belonging to the genus *Eria*, *Xiphosium* was previously considered to include two epiphytes found in wet, upper elevation, moss laden, montane pine forests of northern India (Assam), Thailand, Vietnam and southeastern China (Hong Kong to Hainan). These plants have masses of cone-shaped to oblong pseudobulbs, each with a solitary, oblong, narrow, leathery leaf. The few-flowered inflorescence, borne at the tip of young pseudobulbs, has several, overlapping, distichous sheaths when young that later

wither. The waxy, green to yellow-green flowers, not opening widely, are suffused red. The dark red, narrow, obscurely trilobed lip is joined with the column foot and tightly curved downward at the tip. The above type name is now considered a synonym of *Eria carinata* Gibson.

XYGOPETALUM

An orthographic variant introduced in *Hist. Br. Guiana.*, **2**: 230 (1855). The correct spelling is *Zygopetalum*.

XYLOBIUM

Lindley

Bot. Reg. **11**: sub 897 (1825).

Epidendroideæ ⚘ Cymbidieæ • Maxillariinæ

ETYMOLOGY: Greek for wood or log and life. Alluding to the epiphyte habit.

TYPE SPECIES: *Xylobium squalens* (Lindley) Lindley
(*Dendrobium squalens* Lindley)

Thirty-two sympodial epiphytes, rare lithophytes or terrestrials are found in wet, low to mid elevation, hill to montane forests of Cuba and southern Mexico to Peru and Bolivia. These tufted plants have ovoid to pear-shaped, almost pencil-like, dark green pseudobulbs, subtended by several, distichous, overlapping, thin, dry bracts, each with one to three, large, often leathery, strongly ribbed or pleated leaves that have veining on the undersides. The solitary to few-flowered inflorescence, borne from the base of a pseudobulb, has small, inconspicuous or showy, faintly fragrant, yellow-white to purple flowers. The entire or obscurely trilobed, pink to creamy-white lip, attached to the column foot, has a white, distinctly warty callus. The flowers have a short, slightly curved column.

YOANIA

Maximowicz

Bull. Acad. Imp. Sci. Saint Pétersbourg, ser. 3
18: 68 (1873).

Epidendroideæ Calypsoeæ

ETYMOLOGY: Named for Wudogawa Yoan (1798-1846), a Japanese botanist, physician, botanical illustrator and the originator of the study of modern Japanese chemistry and botany.

TYPE SPECIES: *Yoania japonica* Maximowicz

Three unattractive, leafless, sympodial saprophytes are found in mid elevation, montane grasslands, meadows and grassy slopes of Japan (Honshu and Kyushu), Taiwan, southeastern China (Fujian), northern India (Assam) and Vietnam. These erect, short plants have stout leafless, unbranched, red-purple stems, subtended by small, scale-like sheaths, each with its leaves reduced to mere scales. The plant is rootless but has stout rhizomes. The relatively few-flowered inflorescence has small, white to pale pink flowers with similar, concave sepals and shorter, wider petals. The slipper-shaped or sac-like, entire lip is joined to the short column foot and has a small, forward pointing spur or is spurless. The flowers have a stout, broad, winged column.

YOLANDA

Hoehne

Arq. Mus. Nac. Rio de Janeiro **22**: 72, *t. 3* (1919).

ETYMOLOGY: Dedicated to Yolanda Kühn née Hoehne (1915-1970), the daughter of Frederico Carlos Hoehne (1882-1959), a Brazilian botanist, author of numerous books on the flora of Brazil and co-author of *Flora Brasilica*.

TYPE SPECIES: *Yolanda restrepioides* Hoehne

Now recognized as belonging to the genus *Brachionidium*, *Yolanda* was previously considered to include three epiphytes or terrestrials found in low to mid elevation, hill scrub to montane forests and deep mosses of southeastern Brazil (São Paulo). These strange, small, creeping plants have leathery, often veined leaves clasping erect, slender stems that are subtended by

overlapping sheaths. The several, long, solitary-flowered inflorescences, borne from the leaf axils, have yellow-green flowers with tiny, thinly textured petals. The lateral sepals are united forming a concave synsepal; both the veined sepals and veined petals sometimes have short to long tails. The small to tiny, thick, entire lip has a central callus with minute hairs. The flowers have a short, thick column.

YONOPSIS

An orthographic variant introduced in *Struct. Orchid.*, *t. 14*, *f. 3* (1883). The correct spelling is *Ionopsis*.

YPSILOPUS

Summerhayes

Kew Bull. **4**: 439 (1949).

Epidendroideæ Vandeæ • Aerangidinæ

ETYMOLOGY: Greek for the letter Y (upsilon) and a foot. Refers to the Y-shaped arms of the stipe associated with the pollen masses.

TYPE SPECIES: *Ypsilopus longifolius*
(Kraenzlin) Summerhayes
(*Mystacidium longifolium* Kraenzlin)

Five uncommon, monopodial epiphytes or occasional lithophytes are found in mid elevation, woodlands and rocky montane slopes from Kenya, Tanzania, Rwanda to Zimbabwe and northeastern South Africa. These small, short-stemmed, hanging plants have leafy bases. The flat to iris-like, narrow, distichous leaves are arranged in two ranks, often in an erect, fan shape. The few-flowered inflorescence, borne from the leaf axils, has elegant, fragrant, white to green, widespreading flowers with the petals slightly shorter and narrower than sepals. The white, diamond-shaped, entire or obscurely trilobed lip tapers to a sharp, green tip and has a long, slender, incurved, green spur that turns pale brown as it ages. Each species is different from one another vegetatively, but all have the same Y-shaped stipe that holds their two pollinia at right angles to the viscidium. The flowers have a short, stout, footless column.

YZTACTEPETZACUXOCHITL

Hernández

Opera (Hernández) **1**: 237. (1790).

ETYMOLOGY: A local Nahuatl (Aztec) word for white, mountain or volcano, ant and flower.

TYPE SPECIES: *Yztactepetzacuxochitl icohueyo*
Hernández

Now recognized as belonging to the genus *Govenia*, *Yztactepetzacuxochitl* was previously considered to include one terrestrial found in mid elevation, highland forests and scrub from central Mexico to Panama. This small, erect plant has subterranean pseudobulbs (corm-like), subtended by leaf sheaths, each with two narrow, thinly textured, pleated, heavily veined leaves. The erect, few-flowered inflorescence, borne from the side of the corm, has showy, pristine white flowers banded pale rose; these flowers open successively over a period of time. The oblong dorsal sepal and elliptical petals converge, forming a hood over the slender, incurved, winged column. The small, erect, entire lip is suffused pink and spotted rusty brown toward the tip. This name is now usually considered a synonym of *Govenia liliacea* (Lexarza) Lindley.

Currently Accepted   Validly Published   Invalidly Published   Published Pre-1753   Superfluous Usage   Orthographic Variant   Fossil

Orchid Genera • 420

ZAHLERIA

Luer

Monogr. Syst. Bot. Missouri Bot. Gard.
105: 17 (2006).

ETYMOLOGY: Named for Alexander Zahlbruckner (1860-1938), an Austrian councilman and mycologist who supplied Fritz Kraenzlin (1847-1934) with many of Reichenbach's herbarium specimens, and author of *Catalogus lichenum universalis*.

TYPE SPECIES: *Zahleria zahlbruckneri* (Kraenzlin) Luer (*Masdevallia zahlbruckneri* Kraenzlin)

Recognized as belonging to the genus *Masdevallia*, *Zahleria* was proposed to include three epiphytes found in deeply shady, low elevation, hill scrub rain forests from Costa Rica to western Ecuador. These densely clustered plants have erect stems, subtended by tubular sheaths, each with a solitary, oblong, erect, leathery leaf. The long to short, solitary-flowered inflorescence, borne low on the ramicaul, has a yellow-green to red-brown flower. The heavily blotched or spotted lateral sepals are united for a short length with each tapering to a short or long tail. The solid colored petals are tiny and the tongue-shaped, entire lip is quite tiny. The flowers have a small, elongate, more or less club-shaped column.

ZEDUBA

An orthographic variant introduced in *Gen. Sp. Orchid. Pl.*, 249 (1830). The correct spelling is *Zoduba*.

ZELENKOA

M.W. Chase & N.H. Williams

Lindleyana **16**(2): 139 (2001).

Epidendroideæ ⋇ **Cymbidieæ • Oncidiinæ**

ETYMOLOGY: Dedicated to Harry Zelenko (1927-), an American graphic designer, illustrator and author of *The Pictorial Encyclopedia of Oncidium*.

TYPE SPECIES: *Zelenkoa onusta* (Lindley) M.W. Chase & N.H. Williams (*Oncidium onustum* Lindley)

One sympodial epiphyte is found in low elevation, coastal forests from Panama to Peru. This small, tough plant is usually found on various desert plants and cacti, in cliff crevices or on tree trunks and it depends on nightly fog for its moisture. This plant has densely crowded clumps of ovoid to oblong, compressed pseudobulbs, each with one to two, narrow to oblong leaves. The long, often branched, numerous-flowered inflorescence has bright yellow flowers all arranged on one side of the rachis. The roundish sepals are much smaller than are the narrow petals. The rounded, deeply trilobed lip has small, spreading side lobes, and the roundish midlobe has a trilobed callus. The flowers have a short column with a pair of crescent-shaped wings.

ZENXINE

An orthographic variant introduced in *Jorn. Sci. Math. Phys. Nat.*, **4**(14): 184 (1873). The correct spelling is *Zeuxine*.

ZETAGYNE

Ridley

J. Nat. Hist. Soc. Siam **4**(3): 118 (1921).

ETYMOLOGY: Greek letter Zeta and woman or female. Alluding to the column that is bent in a somewhat curved shape.

TYPE SPECIES: *Zetagyne albiflora* Ridley

Now recognized as belonging to the genus *Panisea*, *Zetagyne* was previously considered to include one epiphyte found in upper elevation, montane cloud forests of northern Vietnam. This small, congested plant has tiny, wrinkled

pseudobulbs, subtended by thin, dry sheaths when young, each with two narrow, leathery leaves. The solitary to few-flowered inflorescence, borne from a newly developing pseudobulb, has tiny, white flowers which do not open widely. The petals and sepals are similar. The wedge-shaped, trilobed lip has a slightly inrolled margin with two basal keels.

ZEUXINA

Orthography officially rejected vs. *Zeuxine* Lindley (1826).

An orthographic variant introduced in *Coll. Bot.* (*Lindley*), App. [n. 18] (1826). The correct spelling is *Zeuxine*.

ZEUXINA

An orthographic variant cited in *Nomencl. Bot.* (*Steudel*), ed. 2, **2**: 798 (1840). The correct spelling is *Zeuxine*.

ZEUXINE

Lindley

Coll. Bot. (*Lindley*), App. [n. 18] (1826).

Orthography name ICBN conserved vs. *Zeuxina* (Lindley), Roeper, *Linnaea* **2**: 528 (1827).

Orchidoideæ ⋇ **Cranichideæ • Goodyerinæ**

ETYMOLOGY: Greek for union, unite or to yolk in pairs. Referring to the partial union of the column and lip or possibly to the fusion of the pollinia.

TYPE SPECIES: *Zeuxine sulcata* (Roxburgh) Lindley (*Pterygodium sulcata* Roxburgh)

This type name is now considered a synonym of *Zeuxine strateumatica* (Linnaeus) Schlechter; basionym replaced with *Orchis strateumatica* Linnaeus

Seventy-six sympodial terrestrials or sometimes lithophytes have a huge range, extending from cool to warm, low to mid elevation, evergreen forests to grasslands of the Ivory Coast to Uganda, Saudia Arabia to Afghanistan, Pakistan to Sri Lanka, southern China to Malaysia and Indonesia to the southwestern Pacific Archipelago. These small plants have erect or ascending, pencil-like, red to green stems, each a with few to numerous, scattered, sometimes colorful, narrow to broad leaves (sometimes withered by flowering time), often with a prominently colored midvein. The slender, densely packed, numerous to few-flowered inflorescence has tiny, white, green or pale brown flowers, scarcely opening, and nearly hidden by bracts. The concave dorsal sepal and petals converge, forming a hood over the short, winged or wingless, footless column (sepals are hairy or smooth). The often white, trilobed lip is attached for most of its length to the lower margins of the short, winged or wingless, footless column. The semi-roundish hypochile has several, scale-like appendages; the mesochile when present is tubular, and the epichile is entire or bilobed.

ZEUXINELLA

Averyanov & Averyanova
Updated Checkl. Orchids Vietnam 96 (2003).
Orchidoideæ ⚘ Cranichideæ • Goodyerinæ
ETYMOLOGY: *Zeuxine*, a genus of orchids and Latin for diminutive. Refers to a similarity to *Zeuxine*.
TYPE SPECIES: *Zeuxinella vietnamica*
    (Averyanov) Averyanov & Averyanova
    (*Zeuxine vietnamica* Averyanov)

One sympodial terrestrial is found in seasonal, low elevation, limestone forests of northern Vietnam. This erect, small plant has short, unbranched stems, each with several, basal leaves that are a velvety blue-green. The slightly hairy, few-flowered, dark red-brown inflorescence has clasping, hairy, red bracts. The tiny, white flowers do not open widely. The dorsal sepal and petals converge, forming a hood over the short column. The bright yellow, trilobed lip has erect, oblong side lobes, a heart-shaped midlobe, and a swollen, hanging spur.

ZHUKOWSKIA

Szlachetko, R. González & Rutkowski
Adansonia, III **22**(2): 236 (2000).
ETYMOLOGY: Dedicated to Waldemar Zukowski (1935-), a Polish professor of botany at Adam Mickiewicz University in Poznan and author of *Endangered and threatened vascular plants of Western Pomerania and Wielkopolska*.
TYPE SPECIES: *Zhukowskia smithii*
    (Reichenbach f.) Szlachetko, R. González & Rutkowski
    (*Spiranthes smithii* Reichenbach f.)

Now recognized as belonging to the genus *Sarcoglottis*, *Zhukowskia* was proposed to include three terrestrials found in damp, mid elevation, shady forests and woodlands from Honduras to Panama. These small, erect plants have unbranched stems, each with several, silvery striped or mottled green, basal rosettes. The erect, short inflorescence is concealed by overlapping, gray-green sheaths. The numerous to few flowered inflorescence has large, nodding, yellow-brown to green-yellow flowers. The sepals are hairy on the outside; the lateral sepals form a distinct chin-like projection, and the strongly curved petals are united to the dorsal sepal. The strongly bow-shaped, clawed, entire lip has a long, narrow sac-like base with two long, backward pointing teeth. The sac-like based spur is almost completely attached to the ovary. The flowers have a long column. These species were formerly included in *Pelexia*.

ZODUBA

Buchanan-Hamilton ex D.Don
Prodr. Fl. Nepal. 30 (1825).
ETYMOLOGY: The meaning of this word is unclear.
TYPE SPECIES: *Zoduba masuca*
    (D. Don) Buchanan-Hamilton
    (*Bletia masuca* D. Don)
This type name is now considered a synonym of *Calanthe sylvatica* (Thouars) Lindley; basionym replaced with *Centrosis sylvatica* Thouars

Now recognized as belonging to the genus *Calanthe*, *Zoduba* was previously considered to include one terrestrial found in shady, low to mid elevation, hill to evergreen forests ranging from Guinea to Madagascar, southern China to northern India, Indonesia, Japan and Taiwan. This erect, variable plant has tiny, corm-like, noded pseudobulbs, subtended by leaf-like sheaths, each with several, tightly pleated, ribbed, long, dark green leaves that are softly hairy. The erect, densely packed, slightly hairy, numerous-flowered inflorescence has dark violet-purple, pale green to white flowers with widespreading lateral sepals. The wedge-shaped, trilobed lip has a notched tip, and a small, slender spur.

ZODULA

An orthographic variant cited in *Handb. Orchid.-Namen*, 730 (2005). The correct spelling is *Zoduba*.

ZONGORA

An orthographic variant introduced in *Bibliogr. Bot. Handbuch*, 283 (1841). The correct spelling is *Gongora*.

ZOOPHORA

Bernhardi
Syst. Verz.(Bernhardi) 308, 311 (1800).
ETYMOLOGY: Greek for a living being or animal and to bear or carry. The significance of this name as applied here is unknown.
TYPE SPECIES: *None designated*

Now recognized as belonging to the genus *Orchis*, *Zoophora* was previously considered to include two terrestrials found in low to mid elevation, hill thickets and open grasslands mainly from Sweden to Spain, Belgium to Italy, Sardinia, Corsica, and Germany to central Russia (West Siberia to Irkutsk) and Mongolia. These erect plants have unbranched stems, each with several, basal leaves and an erect, densely packed, numerous-flowered inflorescence. The flowers' dorsal sepal and petals converge and curve forming a hood. The lateral sepals are white to pink on the outside with purple veins or spots inside. The trilobed lip has a pale center sprinkled with darker spots and groups of dark colored hairs. Both species are now included as synonyms of *Orchis militaris* Linnaeus.

ZOOTROPHION

Luer
Selbyana **7**(1): 80 (1982).
Epidendroideæ ⚘ Epidendreæ • Pleurothallidinæ
ETYMOLOGY: Greek for animal and menagerie. Refers to the bizarrely shaped flowers.
TYPE SPECIES: *Zootrophion atropurpureum*
    (Lindley) Luer
    (*Specklinia atropurpurea* Lindley)

Twelve sympodial epiphytes are found in low to mid elevation, hill to montane forests on trees, logs and along banks from Cuba to Hispaniola, Jamaica, Nicaragua to Bolivia and Venezuela. These small to large, tufted, clump-forming, creeping to hanging plants have erect stems, subtended by tubular sheaths, each with a solitary, leathery leaf. The several, solitary-flowered inflorescences, borne below the leaf node, have a pale purple flower characterized by the union of the dorsal sepal with sides of the lateral sepals creating a window (synsepal) on either side of the box-like flower. The tiny petals, the trilobed lip that has marginal side lobes near the middle, and even the long, winged column is hidden within this bizarrely shaped flower.

ZOSELORASHYLES

An orthographic variant introduced in *Icon. Pl. Ind. Orient. (Wight)*, **3**: t. 1748, f. 1 (1851). The correct spelling is *Zosterostylis*.

Currently Accepted   Validly Published   Invalidly Published   Published Pre-1753   Superfluous Usage   Orthographic Variant   Fossil

O r c h i d G e n e r a • **422**

ZOSEROSTYLIS

An orthographic variant introduced in *Prakt. Stud. Orchid.*, 321 (1854). The correct spelling is *Zosterostylis*.

ZOSTEROPHYLLANTHOS

Szlachetko & Margońska

Polish Bot. J. **46**(2): 118 (2002).

ETYMOLOGY: Greek for girdle, leaf and flower. Refers to the long leaf stalk.

TYPE SPECIES: *Zosterophyllanthos grandiflorus* (Lindley) Szlachetko & Margońska (*Pleurothallis grandiflora* Lindley)

Recognized as belonging to the genus *Pleurothallis*, *Zosterophyllanthos* was proposed to include fifty-four epiphytes found in cool, moist, mid to upper elevation, montane forests of Venezuela and Colombia to Peru. These small plants usually have heart-shaped leaves, often spreading or curved, that are borne by long stems, which are sometimes lightly compressed near the leaf. The short, one- to two-flowered inflorescence, borne from the leaf axils, has small, yellow-green, yellow to red-brown flowers with a large dorsal sepal. The lateral sepals are united for their whole length and sit behind the small, narrow petals that curve downward. The broad, spoon-shaped, entire lip has rolled margins and sits either flat to the face of the flower or is held outwards. The flowers have a short, stout, footless column.

ZOSTEROSTYLIS

Blume

Bijdr. Fl. Ned. Ind. **8**: 418, *t. 32* (1825).

ETYMOLOGY: Greek for a girdle and column or style. Referring to the margins of the column which are enclosed in a sac formed by the lower portion of the lip.

TYPE SPECIES: *Zosterostylis arachnites* Blume

Now recognized as belonging to the genus *Cryptostylis*, *Zosterostylis* was previously considered to include four terrestrials widely distributed in low to upper elevation, open scrub to montane forests from Thailand to Vietnam, Malaysia, Indonesia to the southwestern Pacific Archipelago. These erect plants have unbranched stems, each with a basal rosette of several, pale green leaves that have a distinct network of darker colored green veins. The erect, few-flowered inflorescence, basally sheathed by large bracts, has spidery, pale green or dull red flowers with similar, narrow sepals and petals. The large, uppermost, purple or orange-red, concave or convex, entire lip has a strongly reflexed margin and is often spotted purple-red.

ZUEXINE

An orthographic variant introduced in *Biol. Mag.*, **13**: 37 (1975). The correct spelling is *Zeuxine*.

ZUXINE

An orthographic variant introduced in *Icon. Pl. Ind. Orient. (Wight)*, **5**(1): 16 (1851). The correct spelling is *Zeuxine*.

ZYGOGLOSSUM

Reinwardt ex Blume

Cat. Gew. Buitenzorg 100 (1823).

Name ICBN rejected vs. *Cirrhopetalum* Lindley (1830) Orchidaceæ.

ETYMOLOGY: Greek for yoke or balance and tongue. An allusion to the lip that may be likened to the beam on a balance.

TYPE SPECIES: *Zygoglossum umbellatum* Reinwardt
This type name is now considered a synonym of *Bulbophyllum pulchrum* (N.E. Brown) J.J. Smith; basionym *Cirrhopetalum pulchrum* N.E. Brown

Although validly published this rejected name is now referred to *Bulbophyllum*, *Zygoglossum* was considered to include one epiphyte widespread in humid, low to mid elevation, evergreen forests from Madagascar, the Seychelles, Thailand, Vietnam and Indonesia to the southwestern Pacific Archipelago. This plant has ovoid pseudobulbs that have a wrinkled appearance, each with a solitary, leathery leaf that is notched at the tip. The wiry, few-flowered inflorescence has a semicircular group of lovely, yellow flowers, all facing outwards. The small, concave, yellow or orange-yellow dorsal sepal is densely spotted and has a bristle-like appendage at the tip. The long, narrow, lateral sepals are united almost to the tips, and the tiny petals have fringed margins with bristle-like extensions at the tip.

ZYGOPETALON

Hooker

Bot. Mag. **54**: *t. 2748* (1827).

ETYMOLOGY: Greek for yoke and petal or sepal. From the thickened callus that lends an appearance of binding the floral segments.

TYPE SPECIES: *Zygopetalon mackaii* Hooker

One epiphyte originally found in southeastern Brazil (Espírito Santo to Santa Catarina) and is often included in the genus *Zygopetalum*.

ZYGOPETALUM

Hooker ex Lindley

Gen. Sp. Orchid. Pl. 187 (1833).

Name and orthographic name conserved vs. *Zygopetalon* (1827) Orchidaceæ.

Epidendroideæ • Cymbidieæ • Zygopetalinæ

ETYMOLOGY: Greek for yoke. From the thickened callus at the base of the lip that lends an appearance of pulling together or yoking of the floral segments.

TYPE SPECIES: *Zygopetalum mackaii* Hooker
This type name is now considered a synonym of *Zygopetalum maculatum* (Kunth) Garay; basionym *Dendrobium maculatum* Kunth

Fourteen sympodial or monopodial terrestrials, rare epiphytes or lithophytes are found in humid, low to mid elevation, hill to montane forests from southeastern Brazil (Minas Gerais, Bahia to Rio Grande do Sul, northern Argentina, Paraguay, Colombia to Bolivia, the Guianas and Venezuela. These plants have short, clustered, stout, ovate to cone-shaped, dark green pseudobulbs, subtended by long-sheathed leaves, each with several, narrow, leathery, pleated leaves. The one to several, arching to erect, inflorescences have large, showy, strongly colored, usually fragrant, waxy flowers often produced in considerable numbers. The rather long-lived, small to large, showy flowers usually have green sepals and petals heavily barred or speckled brown. The lateral sepals are joined to the column foot forming a short, chin-like projection. The spreading, deeply or obscurely trilobed, white lip has irregular, purple or blue streaks, dashes or dots radiating out from the base of the midlobe, and the backside is usually unadorned. The small side lobes are spreading or large and erect. The flowers have an incurved, winged column with a short foot.

ZYGOSEPALON

An orthographic variant cited in *Syn. Bot.*, 104 (1870). The correct spelling is *Zygopetalon*.

ZYGOSEPALUM

Reichenbach *filius*

Ned. Kruidk. Arch. **4**: 330 (1859).

Epidendroideæ ⁄ Cymbidieæ • Zygopetalinæ

ETYMOLOGY: Greek for yoke and Latin for sepal. In reference to the sepals that are united, thus "yoked" together.

TYPE SPECIES: *Zygosepalum rostratum*
(Hooker) Reichenbach f.
(*Zygopetalon rostratum* Hooker)
This type name is now considered a synonym of *Zygosepalum labiosum* (Richard) C. Schweinfurth; basionym replaced with *Epidendrum labiosum* Richard

Eight sympodial epiphytes are found in wet, mid elevation, montane forests from the Guianas, Venezuela, Colombia to Peru and northern Brazil (Amazonas to Amapá). These plants have clustered or scattered, ovoid to oblong pseudobulbs, subtended by overlapping, leafy sheaths, each with several, pleated, narrow leaves. The lateral, erect, solitary to few-flowered inflorescence has large, showy, long-lived, fragrant flowers that are usually white with peachy brown or green highlights. The large, white, flaring, entire or obscurely trilobed lip is distinctly veined with radiating lines and is united with the tip of the column foot forming a short, chin-like projection. The flowers have a curved, club shaped, winged column. These species are closely related to *Galeottia* and *Zygopetalum* but differ in that the petals and lateral sepals do not run downward on the column foot, and the anther has a long, awl-like, fleshy process at the tip.

ZYGOSTATES

Lindley

Edwards's Bot. Reg. **23**: sub 1927 (1837).

Epidendroideæ ⁄ Cymbidieæ • Oncidiinæ

ETYMOLOGY: Greek for yoke and balance or scale. In reference to the well developed appendages at the base of the column that resemble a yoke or scale.

LECTOTYPE: *Zygostates lunata* Lindley

Nineteen sympodial epiphytes are found in high humidity, mid elevation, forests with heavy, nightly dew from Paraguay, Uruguay, northeastern Argentina and Venezuela to Bolivia, with the greatest concentration found in eastern Brazil (Pernambuco to Rio Grande do Sul) usually growing on mossy covered trees. These dwarf, delicate plants have short, erect to hanging stems, each with fans of narrow, fleshy to leathery, dark green leaves. The arching to hanging, numerous to few-flowered inflorescence has close-set, small to minute, white

or yellow, thinly textured flowers suffused green. The sepals and petals have deeply and irregularly serrated or notched margins. The white, cup-shaped, entire lip, continuous with the column base, has two thick, basal calli and an entire or serrated margin. The flowers have a slender, downward curved, wingless column.

Note on taxonomic acceptance

All validly published names are candidates for taxonomic acceptance. The acceptance of names is subject to change within the taxonomic community and can be subjective. The accepted names used in this dictionary follow the taxonomic use in the Orchid Identification Center at Marie Selby Botanical Gardens, Sarasota, Florida USA and may vary from other treatments.

Clusius *Rariorvm plantarvm historia* page 270 (1601).

Currently Accepted | Validly Published | Invalidly Published | Published Pre-1753 | Superfluous Usage | Orthographic Variant | Fossil

Orchid Genera • 424

ORCHID GENERA

E L E V A T I O N S

Upper – Cool

2,000 meters and up
6,560 feet and up
10°C to 19°C • 50°F to 66°F
nightly average temperature

Mid – Warm

1,000 meters to 2,000 meters
3,280 feet to 6,560 feet
20°C to 24°C • 67°F to 75°F
nightly average temperature

Low – Hot

Sea level to 1,000 meters
Sea level to 3,280 feet
25°C to 32°C • 76°F to 90°F
nightly average temperature

CATTLEYA DOWIANA

Samuel Jennings *Orchids: and how to grow them in India and other Tropical climates*   plate 33 (1875).

ORCHID GENERA

TAXONOMISTS

&

ORCHID GENERA

GUIDE TO TAXONOMISTS

The complete literature citation for each genus credited to the author
is provided in the section on **Botanical Descriptions**.

When a person(s) names an orchid genus, his name(s) is affixed
to this new genus name. For example, *Cattleya labiata* Lindley was named in 1821 by John Lindley.
The name enables the reader to readily ascertain who originally described
this genus out of the many thousands of genera published by numerous different authors.

B&P = *Authors of Plant Names* by Richard K. Brummitt & C.E. Powell
Royal Botanic Gardens, Kew, 1992

NOTE: Pre-Linnaean authors do not have standardized abbreviations as used by early authors.

Author(s) Last Name → *Cordus,* Valerius (1514-1544)
  • *Palma, Tragi*

First Name → *Corrêa,* Maevia Noemi (1914-x)
  • *Odontorrhynchus*

Year of Birth-Death
(if known) → *Cretzoiu,* Paul (1909-1946) (Cretz.)
  & Smith, Johann Jacob (1867-1947)
  • *Pristiglottis*

Genus or Genera Names
attributed to this individual
or group of people → *Cribb,* Phillip James (1946-)
  • *Cardiochilos, Holmesia, Margelliantha, Microholmesia,*
  Summerhayesia, Thulinia

Date Unknown
As applied to either birth or death

Abbreviation
B&P standard abbreviation or
past abbreviation for this author

ORCHID GENERA

T A X O N O M I S T S

This list provides only the author's name(s) who have published a new genus name or variant and the standard abbreviations for the author's names. The complete citation for each individual name is provided in the Botanical Descriptions section.

Ackerman, James David (1950-) (Ackerman)
• *Dodsonia*

Albert, Victor Anthony (1958-) (V.A. Albert) &
Chase, Mark Wayne (1951-) (M.W. Chase)
• *Mexipedium*

Ames, Oakes (1874-1950) (Ames)
• *Hintonella, Lankesterella, Lepanthopsis, Nabaluia, Pseudacoridium, Trichochilus*

Ames & Schweinfurth, Charles (1890-1970) (C. Schweinf.)
• *Lindsayella*

Archila-Morales, Fredy Leonel (1973-) (Archila)
• *Pseudolepanthes, Tubella*

Aretius, Benedict (1522-1574)
• *Anckenballen, Braendling*

Ascherson, Paul Friedrich August (1834-1913) (Asch.) &
Graebner, Karl Otto Robert Peter Paul (1871-1933) (Graebn.)
• *Glossadenia*

Averyanov, Leonid Ivanovich (1955-) (Aver.)
• *Evrardiana, Parapteroceras*

Averyanov & Averyanova, Anna Leonite (1981-) (A. Aver.)
• *Hamularia, Vietorchis, Zeuxinella*

Baptista, Dalton Holland (1962-) (D.H. Baptista)
• *Alatiglossum, Carenidium, Rhinocidium*

Barbosa Rodrígues, João (1842-1909) (Barb. Rodr.)
• *Adeneleuterophora, Anathallis, Baptistonia, Calorchis, Capanemia, Centroglossa, Chaetocephala, Cheiropterocephalus, Constantia, Cryptophoranthus, Cyanaeorchis, Cystochilum, Dipteranthus, Geoblasta, Gigliolia, Isabelia, Jansenia, Macroclinium, Orleanesia, Ornithophora, Palmorchis, Parlatorea, Petronia, Platyrhiza, Pleurobotryum, Psilochilus, Regnellia, Reichenbachanthus, Theodorea*

Bauer, Franz Andreas (1758-1840) (F.A. Bauer)
• *Ceratandra*

Bauhin, Casper Gaspard (1560-1624) (C. Bauhin)
• *Camaeorchis, Chamaeorchis, Coagulum, Orchidis*

Bauhin, Jean Johannes (1541-1613) (J. Bauhin)
• *Stateumatica*

Beck, Lewis Caleb (1798-1853) (L.C. Beck)
• *Arietinum*

Beck von Mannagetta und Lerchenau, Günther (1856-1913) (Beck)
• *Arthrochilium, Jonorchis*

Beer, Johann Georg (1803-1873) (Beer)
• *Sarcobodium, Sarcoglossum*

Bennet, Sigamony Stephen Richard (1940-) (Bennet) &
Raizada, Mukat Behari (1907-) (Raizada)
• *Neotainiopsis*

Bentham, George (1800-1884) (Benth.)
• *Campylocentrum, Cryptocentrum, Diacrium, Lanium, Octadesmia, Ornithochilus, Platyclinis, Pleuranthium, Plocostigma*

Bentham & Hooker, Joseph Dalton (1817-1911) (Hook. f.)
• *Astroglossus*

Bergen, Carl August von (1704-1759) (Bergen)
• *Trachorchis*

Bergius, Peter Jones (1730-1790) (P.J. Bergius)
• *Disa*

Bernhardi, Johann Jakob (1774-1850) (Bernh.)
• *Zoophora*

Besler, Basilius (1561-1629) (Besler)
• *Epipactis*

Bivona-Bernardi, Antonio de (1774-1837) (Biv.)
• *Tinea*

Blanco, Mario Alberto (1972-) (M.A. Blanco)
• *Inti, Rhetinantha*

Blanco & Carnevali Ferández-Concha, Germán (1955-) (Carnevali)
• *Maxillariella*

Blaxell, Donald Frederick (1934-) (Blaxell)
• *Goniobulbon, Paracaleana*

Blome, Richard (1635-1705)
• *Vinello*

Blume, Karl Ludwig Ritter von (1796-1862) (Blume)
• *Acanthoglossum, Acanthophippium, Acriopsis, Adenoncos, Adenostylis, Agrostophyllum, Amblyglottis, Amphyglottis, Anecochilus, Anoectochilus, Aphyllorchis, Apista, Aporum, Apostasia, Appendicula, Arachnanthe, Arachnis, Argyrorchis, Arundina, Ascochilus, Calcearia, Callostylis, Ceratium,*

Ceratochilus, Ceratostylis, Cheirostylis, Chelonanthera, Chlorosa, Chrysoglossum, Cistella, Cleisostoma, Cochlia, Collabium, Cordyla, Crepidium, Crinonia, Cryptoglottis, Cylindrolobus, Cyperorchis, Cyrtosia, Cystopus, Cystorchis, Dendrochilum, Dendrocolla, Dendrolirium, Desmotrichum, Dicerostylis, Dichopus, Diglyphosa, Diphyes, Echioglossum, Ephippium, Epicranthes, Epiphanes, Erythrodes, Erythrorchis, Etaeria, Eucosia, Galera, Gastridium, Gastroglottis, Glomera, Grammatophyllum, Grastidium, Gymnochilus, Gyrostachys, Haematorchis, Henicostema, Hetaeria, Hyacinthorchis, Iridorchis, Latouria, Lecanorchis, Leopardanthus, Lepidogyne, Leucorchis, Limatodis, Macrostomium, Mecosa, Microsaccus, Mitopetalum, Mitostigma, Moerenhoutia, Mycaranthes, Myrmechis, Nephelaphyllum, Neuwiedia, Odontochilus, Odontostylis, Omoea, Onychium, Osyricera, Oxystophyllum, Pachychilus, Pachystoma, Pedilonum, Peristylus, Phalaenopsis, Placostigma, Platysma, Plocoglottis, Podochilus, Queteletia, Rhynchanthera, Rhynchostylis, Rophostemon, Roptrostemon, Rynchanthera, Saccochilus, Saccolabium, Sarcostoma, Schoenorchis, Spathoglottis, Stereosandra, Taeniophyllum, Tainia, Thelasis, Trichoglottis, Trichotosia, Tylostylis, Vrydagzynea, Zosterostylis, Zygoglossum

Boehmer, Louis B. (1822-1896) (L.B. Boehm.)
• *Limodorum*

Borkhausen, Moritz Balthasar (1760-1806) (Borkh.)
• *Epipogium*

Bory de St. Vincent, Jean Baptiste Georges Geneviève (1778-1846) (Bory)
• *Angraecum*

Bosser, Jean Marie (1922-) (Bosser) *&*
Cribb, Phillip James (1946-) (P.J. Cribb)
• *Bathiorchis*

Braas, Lothar Alfred (1942-1995) (Braas)
• *Luerella, Rodrigoa*

Braas *&* **Lückel,** Emil (1927-) (Lückel)
• *Darwiniella, Darwiniera*

Brade, Alexander Curt (1881-1971) (Brade)
• *Pygmaeorchis*

Braem, Guido Jozef (1944-) (Braem)
• *Azadehdelia, Chironiella, Gudrunia, Hispaniella, Jamaiciella, Schluckebieria*

Braem, Lückel, Emil (1927-) (Lückel) *&*
Rüssmann, Martin (1940-) (Rüssmann)
• *Braasiella*

Breda, Jacob Gijsbert Samuël van (1788-1867) (Breda)
• *Armodorum, Cionisaccus, Conchoglossum, Hippoglossum, Macrostylis, Macrotis, Odontostylis, Orchipedum, Orthoglottis, Polychilos, Psychechilos, Sestochilos, Styloglossum*

Breda, Kuhl, Heinrich (1796-1821) (Kuhl) *&*
Hasselt, Johan Coenraad van (1797-1823) (Hasselt)
• *Pomatocalpa*

Brieger, Friedrich Gustav (1900-1985) (Brieger)
• *Aeridostachya, Amblyanthus, Australorchis, Bolbidium, Calyptrorchis, Campanulorchis, Conostalix, Cylindrolobus, Cymboglossum, Dendrocoryne, Dichaeastrum, Didymostigma, Dilochiopsis, Dockrillia, Dolichocentrum, Dressleriella, Erectorostellata, Erectorostrata, Eriopexis, Euphlebium, Garayella, Geocalpa, Gunnarorchis, Herpethophytum, Kinetochilus, Latourorchis, Microphytanthe, Minicolumna, Monanthos, Octandrorchis, Pseudelleanthus, Pseudohexadesmia, Pseudoponera, Sessilibulbum, Steliopsis, Thylacoglossum, Trachyrhizum, Triaristella, Trigonanthe, Urostachya*

Brieger *&* **Lückel,** Emil (1927-) (Lückel)
• *Anneliesia, Miltonioides*

Brieger *&* **Senghas,** Karlheinz (1928-2004) (Senghas)
• *Pabstiella*

Britton, Nathaniel Lord (1859-1934) (Britton) *&*
Millspaugh, Charles Frederick (1854-1923) (Millsp.)
• *Nidema*

Brongniart, Adolphe Théodore (1801-1876) (Brongn.)
• *Decaisnea, Guebina, Hexadesmia, Houlletia, Oxyanthera, Sarcadenia*

Brown, Robert (1773-1858) (R. Br.)
• *Aceras, Acianthus, Bartholina, Brassavola, Brassia, Broughtonia, Caladenia, Calanthe, Caleana, Calochilus, Calopogon, Chiloglottis, Corysanthes, Cryptarrhena, Cryptostylis, Cyrtopodium, Cyrtostylis, Dipodium, Epiblema, Eriochilus, Eulophia, Eulophus, Gastrodia, Genoplesium, Glossodia, Gomesa, Goodyera, Gymnadenia, Hexameria, Isochilus, Listera, Lyperanthus, Macradenia, Microtis, Octomeria, Orthoceras, Pleurothallis, Ponthieva, Prasophyllum, Pterostylis, Sarcochilus, Vanda*

Brühl, Paul Johannes (1855-1935) (Brühl)
• *Cleisocentron*

Brunfels, Otto (1488-1534) (Brunfels)
• *Cynosorchis, Perfoliata, Serapias*

Bubani, Pietro (1806-1888) (Bubani)
• *Calliphyllon, Lequeetia, Lonchitis*

Burbidge, Frederick William Thomas (1847-1905) (Burb.)
• *Isantheum, Leucoglossum, Xanthochilum, Xanthoglossum*

Burchell, William John (1781-1863) (Burch.)
• *Orchidea*

Burns-Balogh, Pamela (1949-) (Burns-Bal.)
• *Greenwoodia, Svenkoeltzia*

Burns-Balogh, Greenwood, Edward Warren (1918-2002) (E.W. Greenw.)
& **González-Tamayo,** Robert (1945-) (R. González)
• *Cutsis*

Burns-Balogh, Robinson, Harold Ernest (1932-) (H. Rob.) *&*
Foster, Mercedes Suarez (1942-) (Merc.S. Foster)
• *Synanthes*

Butzin, Friedhelm Reinhold (1936-) (Butzin)
• *Fimbriella*

Caesalpinius, Andrea (1519-1603) (Caesalpinius)
• *Ophrys, Sigillum*

Campacci, Marcos Antonio (1948-) (Campacci)
• *Ampliglossum, Brasilaelia, Brasilidium*

Carlsward, Barbara Sue (1971-) (Carlsward) *&*
Whitten, William Mark (1954-) (Whitten)
• *Scrotella*

Carnevali Ferández-Concha, Germán (1955-) (Carnevali) *&*
Ramírez de Carnevali, Ivón Morillo (1959-) (I. Ramirez)
• *Aracamunia*

Carnevali *&* **Romero-González,** Gustavo Adolfo (1955-) (G.A. Romero)
• *Hylaeorchis*

Carnevali *&* **Singer,** Rodrigo Bustos (1970-) (R.B. Singer)
• *Mapinguari*

Carr, Cedric Errol (1892-1936) (Carr)
• *Ascochilopsis, Neoclemensia*

Carrière, Elie Abel (1818-1896) (Carrière)
• *Cheirorchis*

Castro, Vitorino Paiva (1942-) (V.P. Castro) *&*
  Catharino, Eduardo Luis Martins (1960-) (Cath.)
* *Kleberiella*

Castro *&* Lacerda, Kleber Garcia de (1950-) (K.G. Lacerda)
* *Carria, Carriella*

Catesby, Mark (1682-1749) (Catesby)
* *Volubilis*

Catharino, Eduardo Luis Martins (1960-) (Cath.)
  & **Castro,** Vitorino Paiva (1942-) (V.P. Castro)
* *Neoruschia*

Chabrey, Dominique (1610-1669) (Chabrey)
* *Orchidis*

Chao, Shih-Keng (circa 1233 AD)
* *Lan*

Chase, Mark Wayne (1951-) (M.W. Chase)
* *Goniochilus*

Chase *&* Bennett, David Edward, Jr. (1923-) (D.E. Benn.)
* *Stigmatorthos*

Chase *&* Williams, Norris Hagen (1943-) (N.H. Williams)
* *Zelenkoa*

Cheeseman, Thomas Frederic (1846-1923) (Cheeseman)
* *Townsonia*

Chen, Sing-Chi (1931-) (S.C. Chen)
* *Archineottia, Diplandrorchis, Sinorchis, Tangtsinia*

Chevalier, Auguste Jean Baptiste (1873-1956) (A. Chev.)
* *Nienokuea*

Chien, Sung-Shu (1885-1965) (S.S. Chien)
* *Changnienia*

Chiron, Guy Robert (1944-) (Chiron)
  & **Castro y Neto,** Vitorino Paiva (1942-) (V.P. Castro)
* *Dungsia, Hadrolaelia, Menezesiella, Microcattleya, Microlaelia, Pseudencyclia*

Christenson, Eric Alston (1956-) (Christenson)
* *Brevilongium, Dyakia, Phymatochilum, Taprobanea*

Christenson *&* Jenny, Rudolf (1953-) (Jenny)
* *Archivea*

Clements, Mark Alwin (1949-) (M.A. Clem.)
* *Anisopetala, Davejonesia*

Clements *&* Jones, David Lloyd (1944-) (D.L. Jones)
* *Abaxianthus, Achlydosa, Acianthopsis, Aporopsis, Blepharochilum, Bouletia, Cannaeorchis, Carparomorchis, Cepobaculum, Ceratobium, Chromatotriccum, Dendrobates, Distichorchis, Durabaculum, Eleutheroglossum, Eurycaulis, Exochanthus, Fruticicola, Gastrosiphon, Leioanthum, Maccraithea, Oxyglossellum, Papulipetalum, Sarcocadetia, Serpenticaulis, Tetrabaculum, Tetrodon, Vappodes*

Clements, Jones *&* Molloy, Brian Peter John (1930-) (Molloy)
* *Winika*

Clusius, Carolus (1526-1609) (Clus.)
* *Dentaria, Elleborine, Leimodoron, Lobus, Pseudoleimodoron, Pseudorchis*

Cockerell, Theodore Dru Alison (1866-1948) (Cockerell)
* *Antholithes*

Cogniaux, Célestin-Alfred (1841-1916) (Cogn.)
* *Kochiophyton, Menadenium*

Cohn, Ferdinand Julius (1828-1898) (Cohn)
* *Microthallus*

Colla, Luigi Aloysius (1766-1848) (Colla)
* *Thiebautia*

Corda, August Karl Joseph (1809-1849) (Corda)
* *Rhizonium*

Cordemoy, Eugene Jacob de (1835-1911) (Cordem.)
* *Acrostylia, Bonniera, Camilleugenia, Hemiperis, Lepervenchea, Pectinaria*

Cordus, Valerius (1514-1544) (V. Cordus)
* *Palma, Tragi*

Corrêa, Maevia Noemi (1914-2005) (M.N. Corrêa)
* *Odontorrhynchus*

Cretzoiu, Paul (1909-1946) (Cretz.)
  & **Smith,** Johannes Jacobus (1867-1947) (J.J. Smith)
* *Pristiglottis*

Cribb, Phillip James (1946-) (P.J. Cribb)
* *Cardiochilos, Holmesia, Margelliantha, Microholmesia, Summerhayesia, Thulinia*

Cribb *&* Hermans, Johan (1956-) (Hermans)
* *Paralophia*

Cribb, Hermans *&* Roberts, David Lesford (1974-) (D.L. Roberts)
* *Erasanthe*

Cribb *&* Laan, Frank M. van de (*fl.* 1986s) (Laan)
* *Ossiculum*

Cruz, Martin de la (*fl.* 1500s)
* *Tlilxochitl*

Czerwiakowski, Ignatio Raphaele (1808-1882)
* *Deckeria*

Daléchamps, Jacques (1513-1588) (Daléchamps)
* *Nidus-Avis*

Dalzell, Nicolas Alexander (1817-1878) (Dalzell)
* *Micropera*

Dammer, Carl Lebrecht Udo (1860-1920) (Dammer)
* *Goldschmidtia*

de Laet, Joannes (1593-1649)
* *Tlilxochitl*

Dennstedt, August Wilhelm (1776-1826) (Dennst.)
* *Wolfia*

De Notaris, Giuseppe (Josephus) (1805-1877) (De Not.)
* *Isias*

Descourtilz, Michel Etienne (1775-1836) (Descourt.)
* *Epidendre*

Determann, Ronald Oskar (1957-) (Determann)
* *Degranvillea*

de Vogel, Eduard Ferdinand (1942-) (de Vogel)
* *Entomophobia, Geesinkorchis*

Dietrich, David Nathaniel Friedrich (1799-1888) (D. Dietr.)
* *Spiranthera*

Docha Neto, Americo (1946-) (Docha Neto)
* *Grandiphyllum*

Dockrill, Alick William (1915-) (Dockrill)
• *Papillilabium, Parasarcochilus, Plectorrhiza, Schistotylus*

Dod, Donald Dungan (1912-) (Dod)
• *Quisqueya*

Dodoens, Rembert (1518-1585) (Dodoens)
• *Bifolium, Damasonium, Limodoron, Plantaginis, Pseudoorchis*

Dodson, Calaway Homer (1928-) (Dodson)
• *Benzingia, Dressleria, Embreea, Hirtzia, Raycadenco, Suarezia, Vasqueziella*

Dodson & Carnevali Ferández-Concha, Germán (1955-) (Carnevali)
• *Stictophyllorchis*

Dodson & Chase, Mark Wayne (1951-) (M.W. Chase)
• *Scelochiloides, Scelochilopsis, Stictophyllum*

Dodson & Determann, Ronald Oskar (1957-) (Determann)
• *Caluera*

Dodson & Dressler, Robert Louis (1927-) (Dressler)
• *Cypholoron, Ecuadoria, Psygmorchis*

Dodson & Escobar, Rodrigo Restrepo (1935-) (R. Escobar)
• *Ackermania*

Dodson & Williams, Norris Hagen (1943-) (N.H. Williams)
• *Konanzia*

Don, David (1799-1841) (D. Don)
• *Diplomeris, Gastrochilus, Octomeria, Pinalia, Pleione, Ptilocnema, Zoduba*

Don, George (1798-1856) (G. Don)
• *Cleisomeria, Trichorhiza*

d'Orbigny, Alcide Charles Victor Marie Dessalines (1802-1857) (A.D. Orb.)
• *Blumia, Cuculla, Ensifera, Fornicaria, Pilearia, Pseudovanda, Steleocorys, Tubera*

Dressler, Robert Louis (1927-) (Dressler)
• *Acrorchis, Aetheorhyncha, Daiotyla, Echinorhyncha, Euryblema, Ixyophora, Salpistele, Stenotyla*

Dressler & Dodson, Calaway Homer (1928-) (Dodson)
• *Crossoglossa*

Dressler & Higgins, Wesley Ervin (1949-) (W.E. Higgins)
• *Guarianthe*

Dressler & Pollard, Glenn E. (1901-1976) (G.E. Pollard)
• *Artorima*

Dressler & Williams, Norris Hagen (1943-) (N.H. Williams)
• *Chelyorchis, Cischweinfia*

Dulac, Joseph (1827-1887) (Dulac)
• *Elasmatium, Pollinirhiza*

Dumortier, Barthélemy Charles Joseph, Count (1797-1878) (Dumort.)
• *Coppensia, Gyrostachys, Maelenia, Paliris*

Dusén, Per Karl Hjalmar (1855-1926) (Dusén)
• *Paranaea*

Eaton, Alvah Augustus (1865-1908) (A.A. Eaton)
• *Serapiastrum*

Eaton, Amos (1776-1842) (Eaton)
• *Microstylis*

Ehrhart, Jakob Friedrich (1742-1795) (Ehrh.)
• *Callithronum, Cardiophyllum, Diplorrhiza, Epipogium, Helictonia, Limnas, Limonias, Lonchophyllum, Triplorhiza, Xiphophyllum*

Endlicher, Stephen Friedrich Ladislaus (1804-1849) (Endl.)
• *Cycloptera, Haplochilus, Keranthus, Plexaure, Thelychiton, Titania*

Engler, Heinrich Gustav Adolph (1844-1930) (Engl.)
• *Stachyanthus*

Falconer, Hugh (1808-1865) (Falc.)
• *Cordylestylis, Gamoplexis, Oncidiochilus, Pogochilus, Thysanochilus*

Fawcett, William (1851-1926) (Fawc.)
   & Rendle, Alfred Barton (1865-1938) (Rendle)
• *Harrisella, Neo-Urbania*

Fenzl, Eduard (1801-1879) (Fenzl)
• *Mormolyca*

Finet, Achille Eugéne (1863-1913) (Finet)
• *Ancistrorhynchus, Arethusantha, Dicranotaenia, Hemihabenaria, Monixus, Pelma, Pergamena, Pseudoliparis, Rhaphidorhynchus*

Fischer, Friedrich Ernst L. (1782-1854) (Fisch.) **&**
   Meyer, Carl Anton Andrejewicz (1795-1855) (C.A. Mey.)
• *Seraphyta*

Fitzgerald, Robert Desmond (David) (1830-1892) (Fitzg.)
• *Adelopetalum, Anticheirostylis, Coelandria, Corunastylis, Leptoceras*

Fleischmann, Hans (1875-1928) (H. Fleischm.)
   & Rechinger, Karl (1867-1952) (Rech.)
• *Coralliokyphos*

Focke, Hendrik (Henri) Charles (1802-1856) (H. Focke)
• *Plectrophora*

Foerster, Arnold (1810-1881) (Foerster)
• *Antholiparis, Herminiorchis*

Forster, Johann (John) Reinhold (1729-1798) (J.R. Forst.) **&**
   Forster, Johann Georg Adam (1754-1794) (G. Forst.)
• *Thelymitra*

Fries, Elias Magnus (1794-1878) (Fr.)
• *Lindblomia*

Fuchs, Leonhard (1501-1566) (L. Fuchs)
• *Satyrium, Triorchis*

Gagnebin de la Ferriere, Abraham (1707-1800) (Gagnebin)
• *Corallorhiza, Rhizocorallon*

Gagnepain, François (1866-1952) (Gagnep.)
• *Allochilus, Anaphora, Donacopsis, Epigeneium, Evrardia, Parhabenaria, Schoenomorphus, Semiphajus, Thylacis*

Garay, Leslie Andres (1924-) (Garay)
• *Amesiella, Antillanorchis, Apatostelis, Aspidogyne, Aulosepalum, Brachypeza, Chamelophyton, Chaubardiella, Cotylolabium, Cryptopylos, Cybebus,*

Dichromanthus, Dictyophyllaria, Didymoplexiella, Dithyridanthus,
Dunstervillea, Eparmatostigma, Gularia, Helonoma, Horvatia, Kionophyton,
Kreodanthus, Ligeophila, Loxoma, Megalotus, Mexicoa, Microthelys,
Neoescobaria, Neogardneria, Neowilliamsia, Nothostele, Pabstia, Physogyne,
Physothallis, Platythelys, Polyotidium, Polyradicion, Porrorhachis,
Pseudocranichis, Pseudovanilla, Rhamphorhynchus, Sarcanthopsis, Sarcoglyphis,
Sarcophyton, Seidenfadenia, Skeptrostachys, Stalkya, Stephanothelys,
Stigmatosema, Teuscheria, Thelyschista, Trachoma, Trudelia, Ventricularia,
Warreopsis, Xenikophyton

Garay & Christenson, Eric Alston (1956-) (Christenson)
• *Danhatchia*

Garay & Dunsterville, Galfrid Charles Kenneth (1905-1988) (Dunst.)
• *Epidendropsis, Kalopternix, Otoglossum, Restrepiella*

Garay, Hamer, Fritz (1912-2004) (Hamer) & Siegerist, Emily Steffan (1925-) (Siegerist)
• *Ferruminaria, Mastigion, Rhytionanthos, Synarmosepalum, Vesicisepalum*

Garay & Kennedy, George Clayton (1919-1980) (G.C. Kenn.)
• *Rossioglossum*

Garay & Romero-González, Gustavo Adolfo (1955-) (G.A. Romero)
• *Exalaria*

Garay & Sweet, Herman Royden (1909-1992) (H.R. Sweet)
• *Sedirea*

Gaudichaud-Beaupré, Charles (1789-1854) (Gaudich.)
• *Cadetia, Fieldia, Gabertia, Gersinia, Luisia, Nervilia, Robiquetia*

Geerinck, Daniel (1945-) (Geerinck)
• *Kryptostoma*

George, Alexander Segger (1939-) (A.S. George)
• *Elythranthera, Leporella*

Gerard, John (1545-1612) (J. Gerard)
• *Alisma, Myodes*

Gerlach, Günter (1953-) (G. Gerlach) & Whitten, William Mark (1954-) (Whitten)
• *Brasilocycnis*

Gesner, Conrad von (1516-1565) (Gesner)
• *Calceolus, Chamaestyrax*

Gmelin, Johann Georg (1709-1755) (J.G. Gmel.)
• *Epipogum*

Godefroy-Lebeuf, Alexandre (1852-1903) (God-Leb.)
• *Miltoniopsis*

Goeze, Edmund (1838-1929) (E. Goeze)
• *Phyllostachya*

Gomes, Bernardino António (1769-1823) (Gomes)
• *Polytoma, Woodfortia*

González-Tamayo, Robert (1945-) (R. González)
• *Hagsatera, Nezahualcoyotlia*

González-Tamayo & Szlachetko, Dariusz Lucjan (1961-) (Szlach.)
• *Gracielanthus*

Gopalan, R. (1947-) (Gopalan)
• *Aenhenrya*

Gray, Samuel Frederick (1766-1828) (Gray)
• *Entaticus, Pseudorchis*

Grélet, Louis-Joseph (1870-1945) (Grélet)
• *Rauranita*

Griffith, William (1810-1845) (Griff.)
• *Aclinia, Androgyne, Conchidium, Didymoplexis, Erioidea, Euproboscis, Orchidea, Xiphosium*

Gronovius, Johan Frederik (1686-1762) (Gronov.)
• *Arethusa*

Guéroult, Guillaume (0) (Guéroult)
• *Coillon*

Guettard, Jean Etienne (1715-1786) (Guett.)
• *Neottia*

Guiard, Josiane (1949-) (Guiard)
• *Castroa*

Guillaumin, André (1885-1974) (Guillaumin)
• *Canacorchis, Cephalantheropsis, Podochilopsis*

Guinea López, Emilio (1907-1985) (Guinea)
• *Mariarisqueta*

Haager, Jirí (George) Robert (1943-) (Haager)
• *Christensonia*

Halbinger, Frederico (1925-) (Halb.)
• *Cymbiglossum, Lemboglossum, Mesoglossum, Ticoglossum*

Hallé, Nicolas (1927-) (N. Hallé)
• *Clematepistephium, Tartarinorchis*

Haller, Victor Albrecht von (1708-1777) (Haller)
• *Corallorhiza, Cosmosandalos, Rhizocorallon*

Handel-Mazzetti, (Baron) Heinrich von (1882-1940) (Hand.-Mazz.)
• *Symphyosepalum*

Hartman, Carl Johan (1790-1849) (Hartm.)
• *Androchilus, Coeloglossum*

Harvey, William Henry (1811-1866) (Harv.)
• *Hallackia, Huttonaea*

Hashimoto, Tamotsu (1933-x) (T. Hashim.)
• *Heterozeuxine*

Hasskarl, Justus Carl (1811-1894) (Hassk.)
• *Conchochilus, Nephranthera, Polystylus, Pteroceras, Speiranthes*

Hatusima, Sumihiko (1906-x) (Hatus.)
• *Chrysoglossella*

Hawkes, Alex Drum (1927-1977) (A.D. Hawkes)
• *Flickingeria, Grafia, Helleriella, Hellerorchis, Katherinea, Mendoncella, Paraphalaenopsis*

Hayata, Bunzô (1874-1934) (Hayata)
• *Arisanorchis, Tainiopsis*

Heister, Lorenz (1683-1758) (Heist.)
• *Calceolaria*

Heller, Amos Arthur (1867-1944) (A. Heller)
• *Eburophyton*

Hermann, Paul (1646-1695) (Herm.)
• *Epidendron, Orchidi*

Hernández, Francisco (1514-1578) (F. Hern.)
• *Amazauhtli, Araco, Chichiltic, Coatzonte, Cozticcoatzonte, Tlilxochitl, Tonaloxochitl, Tzacucochitl, Tzavochitl, Tzavtli, Yztactepetzacuxochitl*

Heynhold, Gustav (1800-1860) (Heynh.)
• *Hormidium*

Higgins, Wesley Ervin (1949-) (W.E. Higgins)
• *Microepidendrum, Oestlundia*

Hoehne, Frederico Carlos (1882-1959) (Hoehne)
• *Cogniauxiocharis, Itaculumia, Loefgrenianthus, Marsupiaria, Pseudoeurystyles, Pseudomaxillaria, Rudolfiella, Schlechterella, Uleiorchis, Yolanda*

Hoehne & Schlechter, Friedrich Rudolf (1872-1925) (Schltr.)
• *Phloeophila*

Hoffmannsegg, Johann Centurius von (1766-1849) (Hoffmanns.)
• *Alipsa, Anacheilium, Catachaetum, Gomezia, Gongoras, Leucostachys*

Holttum, Richard Eric (1895-1990) (Holttum)
• *Smitinandia*

Hooker, Joseph Dalton (1817-1911) (Hook. f.)
• *Adenochilus, Adrorhizon, Claderia, Diphylax, Diploprora, Henosis, Lemniscoa, Nematoceras, Trigonanthus*

Hooker, William Jackson (1785-1865) (Hook.)
• *Anisopetalon, Coryanthes, Encyclia, Iantha, Lockhartia, Ornithocephalus, Peristeria, Pholidota, Polystachya, Stanhopea, Ulantha, Zygopetalon*

Hooker & Arnott, George Walker (1799-1868) (Arn.)
• *Pterochilus*

Hopper, Stephen Donald (1951-) (Hopper) & **Brown,** Andrew P. (1951-) (A.P. Br.)
• *Cyanicula, Ericksonella, Praecoxanthus*

Hu, Hsen Hsu (1894-1968) (Hu)
• *Neofinetia*

Hudson, William (1730-1793) (Huds.)
• *Chamaeorchis*

Hultén, Oskar Eric Gunnar (1894-1981) (Hulten)
• *Amerorchis*

Humboldt, Friedrich Wilhelm Heinrich Alexander von (1769-1859) (Humb.) • *Baynilla*

Hunt, Peter Francis (1936-) (P.F. Hunt)
• *Kingidium*

Hunt & Summerhayes, Victor Samuel (1897-1974) (Summerh.)
• *Ephemerantha*

Hunt, Trevor Edgar (1913-) (T.E. Hunt)
• *Peristeranthus*

Irmisch, Johann Friedrich Thilo (1816-1879) (Irmisch)
• *Epipactides*

Jackson, George (1790-1811) (Jacks.)
• *Geodorum*

Jenny, Rudolf (1953-) (Jenny)
• *Braemia, Horichia, Lueckelia, Soterosanthus*

Jones, David Lloyd (1944-) (D.L. Jones)
• *Cooktownia*

Jones & Clements, Mark Alwin (1949-) (M.A. Clem.)
• *Acianthella, Anzybas, Arachnorchis, Bunochilus, Calonema, Chiloterus, Crangonorchis, Demorchis, Drakonorchis, Eremorchis, Glycorchis, Hydrorchis, Hymeneria, Hymenochilus, Kaurorchis, Linguella, Mecopodum, Microtidium, Molloybas, Myrmechila, Nemacianthus, Oncophyllum, Petrorchis, Pharochilum, Pheladenia, Phoringopsis, Pyrorchis, Ranorchis, Rhipidorchis, Speculantha, Spilorchis, Stamnorchis, Stegostyla, Stilbophyllum, Taurantha, Thynninorchis, Urochilus*

Jones, Clements & Molloy, Brian Peter John (1930-) (Molloy)
• *Ichthyostomum, Waireia*

Jones, Henry Gordon (1939-1987) (H.G. Jones)
• *Hoffmannseggella*

Jones, William (1746-1794) (Jones)
• *Vanda*

Joseph, J.E. (1928-2000) (J. Joseph) & **Vajravelu,** E. (1936-) (Vajr.)
• *Proteroceras*

Jussieu, Antoine-Laurent de (1748-1836) (Juss.)
• *Bipinnula, Calogyne, Pogonia*

Kaempfer, Engelbert (1651-1716) (Kaempf.)
• *Angurek, Fu, Katong, Ran, Su*

Karsten, Gustav Karl Wilhelm Hermann (1817-1908) (H. Karst.)
• *Dubois-Reymondia, Duboisia, Talpinaria*

Ker Gawler, John Bellenden (John Gawler) (1764-1842) (Ker Gawl.)
• *Tupistra*

King, George (1840-1909) (King) & **Pantling,** Robert (1856-1910) (Pantl.)
• *Biermannia, Didiciea, Risleya, Ritaia*

Klein, Erick (1931-) (E. Klein) & **Strack,** Dieter (1945-) (Strack)
• *Anteriorchis*

Klotzsch, Johann Friedrich (1805-1860) (Klotzsch)
• *Cyclosia, Leucohyle, Nauenia, Rhynchopera, Scelochilus*

Knowles, George Beauchamp (x-1852) (Knowles) & **Westcott,** Frederic (x-1861) (Westc.)
• *Barkeria, Epithecia, Leochilus, Macrochilus, Nemaconia, Prosthechea*

Koch, Karl Heinrich Emil (1809-1879) (K. Koch)
• *Comperia*

Komarov, Vladimir Leontjevich (1869-1945) (Kom.) & **Nevski,** Sergei Arsenjevic (1908-1938) (Nevski)
• *Holopogon*

Königer, Willibald (1934-) (Königer)
• *Portillia*

Königer & Pongratz, Dieter (1940-) (Pongratz)
• *Stilifolium*

Königer & Schildhauer, Herbert (1963-) (Schildh.)
• *Dasyglossum, Trigonochilum*

Kraenzlin, Friedrich (Fritz) Wilhelm Ludwig (1847-1934) (Kraenzl.)
• *Angraecopsis, Calyptrochilum, Dikylikostigma, Diplocaulobium, Lemurorchis, Lothiania, Neolauchea, Neolehmannia, Neolindleya, Orchidotypus, Pseudoctomeria, Pterostemma, Rodriguesia, Sayeria, Schwartzkopffia, Spitzelii, Viellardorchis*

Kudô, Yûshun (1887-1932) (Kudô)
- *Haraella, Paracalanthe*

Kumar, C. Sathish (1957-) (C.S. Kumar)
- *Seidenfadeniella*

Kumar & Kumar, Pankaj C. Suresh (1953-) (P.C.S. Kumar)
- *Luisiopsis*

Kunth, Karl Sigismund (1788-1850) (Kunth)
- *Altensteinia, Catasetum, Cyrtochilum, Epistephium, Ionopsis, Leptothrium, Odontoglossum, Pachyphyllum, Restrepia, Stenoglossum, Telipogon, Trichoceros*

Kuntze, Carl Ernst Otto (1843-1907) (Kuntze)
- *Hammarbya, Helleborine, Kraenzlinella, Orchiodes, Rodrigueziella, Sanderella, Serapiastrum, Sirhookera*

Kurzweil, Hubert (1958-) & **Linder,** Hans Peter (1954-) (H.P. Linder)
- *Evotella*

Lehmann, Fredrich Carl (1850-1903) (F. Lehm.)
- *Gorgoglossum, Trevoria*

Lehmann & Kraenzlin, Friedrick Wilhelm Ludwig (1847-1934) (Kraenzl.)
- *Otopetalum*

Lemaire, Antoine Charles (1801-1871) (Lem.)
- *Bothriochilus, Cattleyopsis, Lichterveldia*

Lexarza, Juan José Martínez de (1785-1824) (Lex.)
- *Alamania, Arpophyllum, Cuitlauzina, Psittacoglossum, Tzacutli*

Liebmann, Frederik Michael (1813-1856) (Liebm.)
- *Thorvaldsenia*

Linden, Jean Jules (1817-1898) (Linden) & **Reichenbach f.,** Heinrich Gustav (1823-1889) (Rchb. f.)
- *Chrysocycnis, Lueddemannia*

Linder, Hans Peter (1954-) (H.P. Linder)
- *Oligophyton*

Linder & Kurzweil, Hubert (1958-) (Kurzweil)
- *Dracomonticola*

Lindley, John (1799-1865) (Lindl.)
- *Abola, Acacallis, Acampe, Acineta, Acoidium, Acraea, Acrochaene, Acropera, Ada, Aeonia, Aeranthes, Aganisia, Alvisia, Alwisia, Angidium, Ania, Ansellia, Anthogonium, Aopla, Apaturia, Arhynchium, Asarca, Aspasia, Ate, Aviceps, Baskervilla, Batemannia, Bicornella, Bifrenaria, Bilabrella, Bolbidium, Brachionidium, Brachycorythis, Bromheadia, Broughtonia, Brownleea, Bryobium, Bucculina, Burlingtonia, Burnettia, Calota, Camaridium, Camarotis, Cattleya, Centropetalum, Ceratopsis, Cerochilus, Chaenanthe, Cheiradenia, Chiloschista, Chloidia, Chloraea, Chondrorhyncha, Chysis, Cirrhaea, Cirrhaeam, Cirrhopetalum, Cladobium, Cleistes, Clowesia, Cnemidia, Cochlioda, Codonorchis, Coelia, Coeloglossum, Coelogyne, Colax, Collea, Cremastra, Crybe, Cryptopus, Cybele, Cycnoches, Cyrtopera, Cytheris, Decanisnea, Dialissa, Dichaea, Dicrypta, Didactyle, Dienia, Dignathe, Dilochia, Dinema, Diothonea, Diplocentrum, Diplochilus, Doritis, Drakaea, Drymoda, Earina, Empusa, Epiphora, Eria, Eriopsis, Erycina, Eucnemis, Fernandezia, Forficaria, Galeandra, Gastropodium, Georchis, Glossula, Gomphichis, Gomphostylis, Govenia, Grobya, Gunnia, Haemaria, Hartwegia, Helcia, Hemipilia, Hemiscleria, Herorchis, Herpysma, Herschelia, Heterotaxis, Hexisea, Hexopia, Hippopodium, Holothrix, Huntleya, Hylophila, Ione, Ipsea, Lacaena, Laelia, Leptoceras, Leptotes, Lissochilus, Lycaste, Lyraea, Macdonaldia, Macodes, Malachadenia, Megaclinium, Mesoclastes, Metachilum, Microcoelia, Micropera, Miltonia, Monachanthus, Monadenia, Monochilus,*
Monomeria, Monotris, Mormodes, Myanthus, Myoda, Mystacidium, Nanodes, Nasonia, Nelis, Notiophrys, Notylia, Oberonia, Oeceoclades, Oeonia, Ommatodium, Oncodia, Oreorchis, Ornithochilus, Otochilus, Pachites, Panisea, Paphinia, Paxtonia, Pedilea, Pelexia, Penthea, Perularia, Pesomeria, Phreatia, Phymatidium, Physinga, Physosiphon, Physurus, Pilumna, Pinalia, Pinelia, Platystylis, Ponera, Porpax, Prescottia, Promenaea, Pseudocentrum, Pterichis, Quekettia, Repandra, Rhamphidia, Rhizonium, Rhomboda, Saccidium, Sarcanthus, Satyridium, Sauroglossum, Schizodium, Schoenleinia, Schomburgkia, Scopularia, Scuticaria, Sestochilus, Solenidium, Sophronia, Sophronitis, Specklinia, Spiculaea, Stenia, Stenocoryne, Stenoglottis, Stereochilus, Sutrina, Synassa, Tetramicra, Tetrapeltis, Thisbe, Trias, Tribrachia, Trichopilia, Trichosma, Trigonidium, Tripleura, Trizeuxis, Tropidia, Trymenium, Tryphia, Uncifera, Uropedium, Wailesia, Warrea, Xylobium, Zeuxine, Zygopetalum, Zygostates

Lindley & Moore, Thomas (1821-1887) (T. Moore)
- *Anachaste*

Lindley & Paxton, Joseph (1803-1865) (Paxton)
- *Laeliopsis, Ornitharium, Sarcopodium, Tridachne, Warczewitzia*

Lindley & Reichenbach f., Heinrich Gustav (1823-1889) (Rchb. f.)
- *Sertifera*

Link, Johann Heinrich Friedrich (1767-1851) (Link)
- *Calypsodium, Gonogora, Tankervillia*

Linnaeus, Carl von (Linné) (1707-1778) (L.)
- *Alisma, Arethusa, Begonia, Cactus, Cypripedium, Epidendrum, Herminium, Limodorum, Lobelia, Ophrys, Orchis, Pyrola, Satyrium, Serapias, Tradescantia*

Linnaeus, Carl von *filius* (1741-1783) (L. f.)
- *Bipinnula*

Llanos, Antonio (1806-1881) (Llanos)
- *Synptera*

l'Obel, Matthias de (1538-1581) (Lobel)
- *Cullices, Hermaphroditica, Melittias, Ornithophora, Testiculus, Tetrorchis, Tragorchis, Vulpinus*

Loddiges, Conrad. L. (1739-1786) (Lodd.)
- *Ceratochilus*

Loureiro, João de (1717-1791) (Lour.)
- *Aerides, Aristotelea, Callista, Ceraia, Galeola, Phaius, Renanthera, Thrixspermum*

Löve, Áskell (1916-1994) (Á. Löve) & **Löve,** Doris Benta Maira (1918-2000) (D. Löve)
- *Vermeulenia*

Lückel, Emil (1927-) (Lückel) & **Braem,** Guido Jakob (1944-) (Braem)
- *Psychopsiella*

Lückel & Fessel, Hans H. (1929-) (Fessel)
- *Jennyella*

Luer, Carlyle August (1922-) (Luer)
- *Aberrantia, Acinopetala, Alaticaulia, Ancipitia, Andinia, Andreettaea, Antilla, Apoda-Prorepentia, Areldia, Arthrosia, Atopoglossum, Barbrodria, Brachycladium, Buccella, Byrsella, Condylago, Cucumeria, Didactylus, Dondodia, Draconanthes, Dracontia, Dracula, Dresslerella, Dryadella, Effusiella, Elongatia, Empusella, Epibator, Expedicula, Fissia, Frondaria, Gerardoa, Incaea, Jostia, Lindleyalis, Loddigesia, Lomax, Luzama, Madisonia, Megema, Mixis, Muscarella, Niphantha, Ogygia, Ophidion, Orbis, Panmorphia, Petalodon, Proctoria, Pteroon, Regalia, Reichantha, Restrepiopsis, Ronaldella, Rubellia, Sarcinula, Sarracenella, Spectaculum, Spilotantha, Streptoura, Sylphia, Teagueia, Triaristella, Tribulago, Trichosalpinx, Tridelta, Triotosiphon, Trisetella, Unciferia, Unguella, Vestigium, Xenosia, Zahleria, Zootrophion*

Luo, Yi-bo (1964-) (Y.B. Luo) & **Chen,** Sing-Chi (1931-) (S.C. Chen)
- *Hemipiliopsis*

Maekawa, Fumio (1908-1984) (F. Maek.)
• *Chondradenia, Diplolabellum, Eleorchis, Hakoneaste, Kitigorchis, Vexillabium*

Makino, Tomitarô (1862-1957) (Makino)
• *Chondradenia, Cryptorchis, Stigmatodactylus*

Makino & Maekawa, Fumio (1908-1984) (F. Maek.)
• *Chamaegastrodia*

Mansfeld, Rudolf (1901-1960) (Mansf.)
• *Dinklageella, Kegeliella, Sphyrarhynchus*

Margońska, Hanna Bogna (1968-) (Marg.)
• *Platystyliparis, Seidenforchis*

Margońska & Szlachetko, Dariusz Lucjan (1961-) (Szlach.)
• *Alatiliparis, Disticholiparis, Saurolophorkis*

Masamune, Genkei (1899-1993) (Masam.)
• *Nipponorchis*

Massalongo, Abramo Bartolommeo (1824-1860) (A. Massal.)
• *Palaeorchis, Protorchis*

Matsuoka, Jo-an (Gentatsu) (1668-1746)
• *Ran*

Mattioli, Pietro Andrea (1500-1577) (Mattioli)
• *Couillon*

Maximowicz, Carl Johann (1827-1891) (Maxim.)
• *Yoania*

McDonald, Donald (1857-x)
• *Lindheimina*

Mehl, Johannes (1940-) (J. Mehl)
• *Eoorchis*

Merian, Anna Marie Sybilla (1647-1717)
• *Vanillo*

Meyer, Ernest Heinrich Friedrich (1791-1858) (E. Mey.)
• *Leucorchis*

Micheli, Pier (Pietro) Antonio (1679-1737) (P. Micheli)
• *Orchiastrum*

Millán, John (1700-1784) (Millán)
• *Triorchis*

Miller, Philip (1691-1771) (Mill.)
• *Calceolus, Ophris, Vanilla*

Miquel, Frederik Anton Wilhelm (1811-1871) (Miq.)
• *Phaniasia*

Mitchell, John (1711-1768) (Mitch.)
• *Orchidion*

Molloy, Brian Peter John (1930-) (Molloy),
Jones, David Lloyd (1944-) D.L. Jones) &
Clements, Mark Alwin (1949-) (M.A. Clem.)
• *Singularybas*

Moore, Spencer Le Marchant (1850-1931) (S. Moore)
• *Bulbophyllaria*

Morren, Charles François Antoine (1807-1858) (C. Morren)
• *Dossinia, Neippergia*

Morren, Charles Jacques Édouard (1833-1886) (E. Morren)
• *Papiliopsis*

Mueller, Ferdinand Jacob Heinrich von (1825-1896) (F. Muell.)
• *Arthrochilus, Fitzgeraldia, Ledgeria, Niemeyera, Sullivania*

Mytnik, Joanna Ejsmont (1970-) (Mytnik)
• *Potosia, Szlachetkoella*

Mytnik & Szlachetko, Dariusz Lucjan (1961-) (Szlach.)
• *Disperanthoceros, Geerinckia*

Nakai, Takenoshin (1882-1952) (Nakai)
• *Pachyrhizanthe*

Necker, Noel Martin Joseph de (1730-1793) (Neck.)
• *Abrochis, Dactylorrhiza, Eydisanthema, Phaedrosanthus, Vanillophorum*

Nees von Esenbeck, Christian Gottfried Daniel (1776-1858) (Nees)
• *Tylochilus*

Nees von Esenback &
Meyen, Franz Julius Ferdinand (1804-1840) (F. Mey.)
• *Acoridium*

Nelson, Aven (1859-1952) (A. Nelson) &
Macbride, James Francis (1882-1976) (J.F. Macbr.)
• *Amesia*

Nevski, Sergei Arsenjevic (1908-1938) (Nevski)
• *Chusua, Dactylorhiza, Pseudodiphryllum*

Nicholls, William Henry (1885-1951) (Nicholls)
• *Drymoanthus*

Nieuwland, Julius Arthur (1878-1936) (Nieuwl.)
• *Bifolium, Smallia, Triorchis*

Nimmo, Joseph (x-1854) (Nimmo)
• *Synmeria*

Nir, Mark Anthony (1935-) (Nir)
• *Tomzanonia*

Norich, Yvan (*fl.* 1998s) (Norich) & **Tangor,** Albert (*fl.* 1998s) (Tangor)
• *Piscatoria*

Noroña, Francisco (Fernando) (c1748-1787) (Noronha)
• *Flagellaria, Scorpaena*

Nuttall, Thomas (1786-1859) (Nutt.)
• *Aplectrum, Tipularia, Triphora*

O'Byrne, Peter (1955-) (O'Byrne) & **Vermeulen,** Jaap J. (1955-) (J.J. Verm.)
• *Notheria*

Ojeda-Alayon, Isidro (1960-) (Ojeda),
Carnevali Ferández-Concha, Germán (1955-) (Carnevali),
& Romero-González, Gustavo Adolfo (1955-) (G.A. Romero)
• *Nitidobulbon*

O'Neil, Daniel C.
• *Bisonea*

Opiz, Philipp Maximilian (1787-1858) (Opiz)
• *Ortmannia*

Ormerod, Paul (1969-) (Ormerod)
• *Rhinerrhizopsis, Schuitemania*

Ortega, Casimiro Gómez de (1740-1818) (Ortega)
• *Nidus-Avis*

Ortíz Valdivieso, Pedro (1926-) (P. Ortiz)
• *Eloyella, Notyliopsis*

Ospina, Hernandez Mariano (1934-) (Ospina)
• *Colombiana*

Pabst, Guido João Frederico (1914-1980) (Pabst) &
   Braga, Pedro Ivo Soares (1950-) (Braga)
• *Rauhiella*

Pabst & **Garay,** Leslie Andres (1924-) (Garay)
• *Mesadenella*

Parlatore, Filippo (1816-1877) (Parl.)
• *Barlia, Bicchia, Gennaria*

Pedersen, Henrik Aerunlund (1966-) (H.A. Pedersen) &
   Suksathan, Piyakaset (Anne) (1960-) (Suksathan)
• *Sirindhornia*

Perrier de la Bâthie, Joseph Maria Henri Alfred (1873-1958) (H. Perrier)
• *Ambrella, Megalorchis*

Persoon, Christiaan Hendrik (1761-1836) (Pers.)
• *Cynorchis, Diplecthrum, Gyrostachis, Serapias*

Petiver, James (1658-1718) (Petiver)
• *Bontiana, Mecaxochitl, Vanillia, Vanilloes*

Pfitzer, Ernst Hugo Heinrich (1846-1906) (Pfitz.)
• *Acrolophia, Calanthidium, Camelostalix, Cestichis, Chelonistele, Cohniella, Dichaeopsis, Epiphanes. Eulophidium, Eulophiopsis, Gymnostylis, Hologyne, Hygrochilus, Macroclinium, Macroplectrum, Paphiopedilum, Polyrrhiza, Ptychogyne, Ridleya, Scaphosepalum, Sigmatogyne, Vandopsis*

Philippi, Rudolph Amandus (1808-1904) (Phil.)
• *Macrocentrum*

Phukan, Sandhya Jyoti (1950-) (Phukan) &
   Odyuo, Sri Nripemo (1968-) (Odyuo)
• *Penkimia*

Piso, Willem (1611-1678) (Piso)
• *Vainillas, Vaynilla*

Planchon, Jules Émile (1823-1888) (Planch.)
• *Psilanthemum, Rumphia*

Planchon & **Linden,** Jean Jules (1817-1898) (Linden)
• *Schlimmia*

Pliny, the Elder (Gaius Plinius Secundus) (23-79 AD)
• *Cynosorchim, Ophrys, Orchim, Orchis, Satyrii, Satyrion, Satyrios, Serapias, Testiculis*

Plukenet, Leonard (1642-1706) (Pluk.)
• *Orobanche, Vanillas, Viscum*

Plumier, Charles (1646-1704) (Plum.)
• *Convallaria, Helleborine, Ruscus, Vanilla*

Poeppig, Eduard Friedrich (1798-1868) (Poepp.)
• *Gavilea*

Poeppig & **Endlicher,** Stephan Friedrich Ladislaus (1804-1849)(Endl.)
• *Aspegrenia, Comparettia, Cyathoglottis, Diadenium, Encyclia, Evelyna, Myoxanthus, Scaphyglottis, Siagonanthus, Trichocentrum*

Poiteau, Pierre Antoine (1766-1854)
• *Pelexia*

Porta, Giambattista della (1535-1615)
• *Orchidum*

Porto, Paulo Campos (1889-1958) (Porto) &
   Brade, Alexander Curt (1881-1971) (Brade)
• *Duckeella, Eunannos, Pleurothallopsis, Pseudolaelia, Thysanoglossa*

Post, Tom Erik von (1858-1912) (T. Post) &
   Kuntze, Carl Ernst Otto (1843-1907) (Kuntze)
• *Chilyathum, Eudisanthema*

Pradhan, Udai Chandra (1949-) (Pradhan)
• *Kalimpongia*

Prain, David (1857-1944) (Prain)
• *Pantlingia*

Presl, Carl (Karen) Boriwog (Borivoj) (1794-1852) (C. Presl)
• *Acronia, Cyclopogon, Elleanthus, Microchilus, Sarcoglottis, Schismoceras, Stenoptera*

Pridgeon, Alec Melton (1949-) (Pridgeon) &
   Chase, Mark Wayne (1951-) (M.W. Chase)
• *Anthereon, Diodonopsis, Echinella, Echinosepala*

Rafinesque [Schmaltz], Constantine Samuel (1783-1840) (Raf.)
• *Achroanthes, Adipe, Adnula, Anistylis, Anthericlis, Anthogyas, Blephariglotis, Bletiana, Bulbodictis, Caularthron, Cladorhiza, Cochleanthes, Coilostylis, Cordula, Criosanthes, Cuculina, Deppia, Dicrophyla, Didothion, Digomphotis, Dilomilis, Diphryllum, Diplanthera, Diplectraden, Diteilis, Ditulima, Dothilis, Dothilophis, Doxosma, Eltroplectris, Endeisa, Enothrea, Erioxantha, Exeria, Exophya, Froscula, Galearis, Gamaria, Geobina, Gynizodon, Hecabe, Hexalectris, Iebine, Isotria, Jensoa, Jimensia, Larnandra, Lophiaris, Lophoglotis, Lysimnia, Maturna, Meliclis, Menadena, Menadenium, Menephora, Mesicera, Mesoptera, Monustes, Narica, Nemuranthes, Nerissa, Nyctosma, Odonectis, Olgasis, Onkeripus, Ormostema, Orxera, Panstrepis, Pecteilis, Pentulops, Pierardia, Plectrelminthus, Plectrurus, Psychilis, Psychopsis, Sacodon, Sacoila, Stenopolen, Stimegas, Strateuma, Sulpitia, Synadena, Synoplectris, Thicuania, Tolumnia, Tomotris, Tritelandra, Tropilis, Tulexis, Tulotis, Tussaca, Xaritonia, Xeilyathum*

Ramírez, Santiago R. (1977-), **Gravendeel,** Barbara (1968-) (Gravend.),
   Singer, Rodrigo Bustos (1970-), **Marshall,** Charles Richard (1961-)
   & **Pierce,** Naomi Ellen (1954-)
• *Meliorchis*

Rao, A. Nageswara (1954-) (A.N. Rao)
• *India*

Rao & **Mani,** K.J. (Mani)
• *Jejosephia*

Rauschert, Stephen (1931-1986) (Rauschert)
• *Amblyanthe, Cyrtidiorchis, Deiregynopsis, Evrardianthe, Herpetophytum, Herschelianthe, Loxomorchis, Pachystelis, Pinelianthe, Pseudorleanesia, Triaristellina*

Ray, John (1627-1705) (Ray)
• *Andrachnitis, Monorchis*

Redouté, Pierre Joseph (1759-1840) (Redouté)
• *Sabot*

Regel, Edvard August von (1815-1892) (Regel)
- *Waluewa*

Reichenbach, Heinrich Gottlieb Ludwig (1793-1879) (Rchb.)
- *Amalia, Anocheile, Corydandra, Dorycheile, Doryphora, Eckartia, Empusaria, Hypodema, Neottianthe, Pleuroblepharon, Rhynchandra, Streptogyne, Sturmia, Traunsteinera*

Reichenbach *filius,* Heinrich Gustav (1824-1889) (Rchb. f.)
- *Aa, Aerangis, Aeranthus, Barlaea, Bieneria, Bletilla, Bolbophyllaria, Bolbophyllopsis, Bollea, Brachtia, Chaubardia, Chytroglossa, Coeliopsis, Cohnia, Dactylostalix, Dendrophylax, Deroemera, Diplogastra, Ephippianthus, Eriaxis, Esmeralda, Euothonaea, Fregea, Grammangis, Grosourdya, Hofmeistera, Hofmeisterella, Hydranthus, Kefersteinia, Kegelia, Koellensteinia, Listrostachys, Lycomormium, Manniella, Meiracyllium, Mesospinidium, Montolivaea, Myrosmodes, Neodryas, Neogyna, Neotinea, Oerstedella, Oliveriana, Orsidice, Pachystoma, Palmoglossum, Palumbina, Papperitzia, Paradisanthus, Pescatoria, Platycoryne, Pogoniopsis, Polycycnis, Ponerorchis, Porphyrostachys, Preptanthe, Pseudepidendrum, Pseuderiopsis, Pteroglossaspis, Rhopalorrhachis, Rhynchostele, Roeperocharis, Salacistis, Sarcadenia, Saundersia, Scoliochilus, Selenipedium, Sievekingia, Sigmatostalix, Stachyobium, Stanhopeastrum, Stauritis, Stauropsis, Taurostalix, Tetragmestrus, Thecostele, Thunia, Warcewiczella, Warmingia, Wullschlaegelia, Xiphizusa, Zygosepalum*

Reichenbach f. & Warszewicz, Josef von Rawicz (1812-1866) (Warsz.)
- *Crocodeilanthe*

Reinwardt, Casper George Carl (1773-1854) (Reinw.)
- *Hysteria, Schoenorchis*

Renz, Jany (1907-1999) (Renz)
- *Bhutanthera*

Rheede tot Draakestein, Hendrik Adriaan van (1635-1691) (Rheede)
- *Anantaly, Ansjeli, Basaala, Bela, Biti, Ela, Kansjiram, Katou, Kolli, Ponnampou, Thalia, Theka, Tsjerou, Wellia*

Rice, Rod (1963-) (R. Rice)
- *Monanthochilus*

Richard, Achille (1794-1852) (A. Rich.)
- *Aplostellis, Arnottia, Beclardia, Benthamia, Birchea, Carteretia, Centrosia, Gussonea, Hypodematium, Ludisia, Macrolepis, Orthochilus, Platylepis, Rhynchadenia*

Richard, A. & Galeotti, Henri Guillaume (1814-1858) (Gal.)
- *Clinhymenia, Galeoglossum, Galeottia, Ghiesbreghtia, Ocampoa, Orchidofunckia, Todaroa*

Richard, Louis Claude Marie (1754-1821) (Rich.)
- *Anacamptis, Cephalanthera, Chamorchis, Cleistes, Holothrix, Liparis, Loroglossum, Nigritella, Physurus, Platanthera, Proschisia, Spiranthes, Stenorynchus*

Ridley, Henry Nicholas (1855-1956) (Ridl.)
- *Apatales, Aratochilus, Ascochilus, Ascotainia, Elasmium, Forbesina, Glossorhyncha, Leucolena, Orestias, Pelatantheria, Poaephyllum, Porphyroglottis, Radinocion, Renantherella, Saecanthus, Staurochilus, Zetagyne*

Rivinus, Augustus Quirinus (1652-1723) (Riv.)
- *Broccebegens, Nidus*

Rogers, Richard Sanders (1862-1942) (R.S. Rog.)
- *Goadbyella, Petalochilus, Rhizanthella*

Rolfe, Robert Allen (1855-1921) (Rolfe)
- *Adactylus, Amphigena, Ancistrochilus, Anochilus, Binotia, Ceratandropsis, Cymbidiella, Dimorphorchis, Eriodes, Eulophiella, Evota, Giulianettia, Hancockia, Homalopetalum, Hyalosema, Jenmania, Kingiella, Moorea, Myrmecophila, Neobenthamia, Neomoorea, Orthopenthea, Phragmipedium, Podandria, Pseudomacodes, Rusbyella, Serrastylis, Sigmatochilus*

Romero-González, Gustavo Adolfo (1955-) (G.A. Romero) &
Carnevali Ferández-Concha, Germán (1955-) (Carnevali)
- *Guanchezia*

Romowicz, Agnieszka (1960-) (Romowicz) &
Szlachetko, Dariusz Lucjan (1961-) (Szlach.)
- *Aurinocidium, Concocidium, Vitekorchis*

Royen, Pieter van (1923-2002) (P. Royen)
- *Kerigomnia*

Ruiz López, Hipólito (1754-1815) (Ruiz)
- *Orchys*

Ruiz &
Pavón y Jimémez-Villanueva, José Antonio (1754-1844) (Pav.)
- *Anguloa, Bletia, Fernandezia, Gongora, Humboltia, Masdevallia, Maxillaria, Rodriguezia, Sobralia*

Rumphius, Georg Eberhard (1628-1702) (Rumph.)
- *Angraecum, Angrec, Flos, Folium, Herba*

Rupp, Hermann Montague Rucker (1872-1956) (Rupp)
- *Cryptanthemis, Mobilabium, Rhinerrhiza, Rimacola*

Rupp & Hatch, Edwin Daniel (1919-) (Hatch)
- *Aporostylis*

Ruppius, Heinrich Bernhard (1688-1719) (Ruppius)
- *Monorchidis*

Ruschi, Augusto (1915-1986) (Ruschi)
- *Hoehneella, Renata*

Ryan, Angela (1955-) (A. Ryan) &
Oakeley, Henry Francis (1941-) (Oakeley)
- *Ida*

Rydberg, Per Axel (1860-1931) (Rydb.)
- *Denslovia, Galeorchis, Gymnadeniopsis, Limnorchis, Lysiella, Piperia*

Sahagún, Bernardino de (1500-1590) (Sahagún)
- *Mecaxochitl Tonaloxochitl, Tzacutli*

Saldanha, Cecil John (1926-2002) (C.J. Saldanha)
- *Smithsonia*

Salisbury, Richard Anthony (1761-1829) (Salisb.)
- *Aeridium, Amphiglottis, Auliza, Campystes, Calypso, Cathea, Corybas, Criogenes, Cytherea, Diplectrum, Gyas, Ibidium, Lysias, Myodium, Myrobroma, Ornithidium, Otandra, Pachyne, Peramium, Polybactrum, Schizopedium, Strateuma, Vainilla*

Schauer, Johannes Conrad (1813-1848) (Schauer)
- *Centrochilus, Choeradoplectron, Diploconchium, Dissorhynchium, Ptychochilus, Stauroglottis*

Scheidweiler, Michael Joseph Francois (1799-1861) (Scheidw.)
- *Acianthera, Amblostoma, Centranthera, Cryptosanus, Dactylostylis, Scleropteris, Trophianthus*

Schlechtendal, Diederich Franz Leonhard von (1794-1866) (Schltdl.)
- *Neottidium*

Schlechter, Friedrich Richard Rudolf (1872-1925) (Schltr.)
- *Aceratorchis, Acostaea, Aglossorrhyncha, Amesiella, Amitostigma, Amparoa, Androcorys, Anota, Anthosiphon, Ascocentrum, Ascoglossum, Aulostylis, Auxopus, Barbosella, Barombia, Basiphyllaea, Bathiea, Beloglottis, Bolusiella, Brachystele, Brenesia, Buchtienia, Bulleyia, Caloglossum, Calymmanthera, Caucaea, Centrogenium, Centrostigma, Cephalangraecum, Chamaeangis,*

Chamaeanthus, Chilopogon, Chitonanthera, Chitonochilus, Cladobium, Coccineorchis, Codonosiphon, Coilochilus, Costaricaea, Crossangis, Cyphochilus, Cyrtidium, Cyrtoglottis, Cyrtorchis, Dactylorhynchus, Deiregyne, Diaphananthe, Dimerandra, Diplacorchis, Dipterostele, Discyphus, Dithrix, Domingoa, Dryadorchis, Endresiella, Epiblastus, Epilyna, Euanthe, Eurycentrum, Eurychone, Finetia, Fitzgeraldiella, Forsythmajoria, Fractiunguis, Fuertesiella, Funkiella, Galeottiella, Gamosepalum, Gastrorchis, Geissanthera, Genyorchis, Gonatostylis, Gyaladenia, Hapalorchis, Helorchis, Hippeophyllum, Holcoglossum, Huebneria, Hybochilus, Hymenorchis, Imerinaea, Ischnocentrum, Ischnogyne, Jacquiniella, Jumellea, Lemuranthe, Lemurella, Leptocentrum, Lindleyella, Lobogyne, Lyroglossa, Malleola, Megastylis, Mesadenus, Microtatorchis, Microtheca, Mischobulbum, Monophyllorchis, Monosepalum, Neobartlettia, Neobathiea, Neobolusia, Neocogniauxia, Neokoehleria, Neottianthe, Odontostele, Oeoniella, Osmoglossum, Otostylis, Pachyplectron, Pachystele, Papilionanthe, Papuaea, Pedilochilus, Perrieriella, Petalocentrum, Phormangis, Phyllomphax, Physoceras, Pilophyllum, Pittierella, Pityphyllum, Platystele, Podangis, Poicilanthe, Porphyrodesme, Porroglossum, Pseuderia, Pseudogoodyera, Pseudostelis, Pteroglossa, Ramonia, Rhipidoglossum, Rhyncholaelia, Rhynchophreatia, Ridleyella, Rodrigueziopsis, Roezliella, Rolfeella, Saccoglossum, Sarcorhynchus, Sarothrochilus, Schiedeella, Sepalosaccus, Sepalosiphon, Sobennikoffia, Sodiroella, Solenangis, Solenocentrum, Sophronitella, Sphyrastylis, Stellilabium, StevenielIa, Stolzia, Symphyglossum, Systeloglossum, Taenia, Tainiopsis, Tapeinoglossum, Trachelosiphon, Trichocerotis, Tridactyle, Tylostigma, Warreella, Xerorchis

Schlechter & Ames, Oakes (1874-1950) (Ames)
• Philippinaea

Schlechter & Kraenzlin, Wilhelm Ludwig (1847-1934) (Kraenzl.)
• Inobulbon

Schlechter & Porto, Paulo Campos (1889-x) (Porto)
• Leaoa

Schmidt, Franz Wilibald (1764-1796) (F.W. Schmidt)
• Arachnites

Schöffer, Peter (1425-1502)
• Satirion

Schuiteman, André (1960-) (Schuit.)
• Devogelia

Schuiteman & Ormerod, Paul (1969-) (Ormerod)
• Ophioglossella

Schumann, Karl Moritz (1851-1904) (K. Schum.)
• Ctenorchis

Schur, Philipp Johann Ferdinand (1799-1878) (Schur)
• Orchites

Schweinfurth, Charles (1890-1970) (C. Schweinf.)
• Buesiella, Vargasiella

Schweinfurth & Allen, Paul Hamilton (1911-1963) (P.H. Allen)
• Oakes-Amesia

Séguier, Jean Francois (1703-1764) (Ség.)
• Epipactis, Monorchis, Orchiastrum, Pseudorchis

Seidenfaden, Gunnar (1908-2001) (Seidenf.)
• Ascidieria, Cleisostomopsis, Deceptor, Didymoplexiopsis, Lesliea, Thaia, Thecopus

Seidenfaden & Garay, Leslie Andres (1924-) (Garay)
• Rhynchogyna

Senghas, Karlheinz (1928-2004) (Senghas)
• Bidoupia, Briegeria, Ceratocentron, Cribbia, Cydoniorchis, Gunnarella, Hapalochilus, Microterangis, Neobennettia, Pfitzeria, Schunkea, Seegeriella, Solenidiopsis, Strobelia

Senghas & Bockemühl, Leonore (1927-) (Bockemühl)
• Collare-Stuartense

Senghas & Garay, Leslie Andres (1924-) (Garay)
• Sarmenticola

Senghas & Gerlach, Günter (1953-) (G. Gerlach)
• Chondroscaphe

Senghas & Lückel, Emil (1927-) (Lückel)
• Chamaeleorchis

Senghas & Schildhauer, Herbert (1963-) (Schildh.)
• Ascocentropsis

Singer, Rodrigo Bustos (1970-) (R.B. Singer), Koehler, Samatha (1975-) (S. Koehler) & Carnevali Ferández-Concha, Germán (1955-) (Carnevali)
• Brasiliorchis

Sloane, Hans (1660-1753) (Sloane)
• Banillas, Cardamomum, Cereo, Siliqua, Viscum

Small, John Kunkel (1869-1938) (Small)
• Beadlea, Carteria, Epicladium, Fissipes, Habenella, Spathiger

Small & Nash, George Valentine (1864-1921) (Nash)
• Platypus, Triorchos

Smith, James Edward (1759-1828) (Sm.)
• Diuris, Stelis, Sunipia

Smith, Johannes Jacobus (1867-1947) (J.J. Sm.)
• Abdominea, Basigyne, Bogoria, Bracisepalum, Chroniochilus, Cordiglottis, Gynoglottis, Kuhlhasseltia, Lectandra, Mediocalcar, Pennilabium, Saccolabiopsis, Silvorchis, Tubilabium, Vonroemeria

Sonder, Otto Wilhelm (1812-1881) (Sond.)
• Schizochilus

Spach, Édouard (1801-1879) (Spach)
• Diglyphys, Nothium

Spenner, Fridolin Carl Leopold (1798-1841) (Spenn.)
• Distomaea

Sprague, Thomas Archibald (1877-1958) (Sprague)
• Pleuropetalum

Sprengel, Curt Polycarp Joachim (1766-1833) (Spreng.)
• Acrobium, Aerobion, Chamaerepes, Colax, Cybelion, Dipera, Glossaspis, Himantoglossum, Paragnathis, Sieberia, Stenorrhynchos

Stein, Berthold (1847-1899) (Stein)
• Encyclium, Eriura

Steudel, Ernst Gottlieb von (1783-1856) (Steud.)
• Panisea, Physanthera, Trichorhiza

Straus, Adolf Paul Carl (1901-1986) (Straus)
• Orchidacites

Summerhayes, Victor Samuel (1897-1974) (Summerh.)
• Ankylocheilos, Chaseella, Chauliodon, Diceratostele, Distylodon, Eggelingia, Encheiridion, Nephrangis, Rangaeris, Rhaesteria, Taeniorrhiza, Triceratorhynchus, Ypsilopus

Swartz, Olof Peter (1760-1818) (Sw.)
• Centrosis, Corycium, Cranichis, Cymbidium, Dendrobium, Diplodium, Disperis, Lathrisia, Lepanthes, Malaxis, Oncidium, Orchidium, Pterygodium, Satyrium, Stelis

Szlachetko, Dariusz Lucjan (1961-) (Szlach.)
• Acianthopsis, Adamanthus, Afrorchis, Ala, Alinorchis, Appendiculopsis, Arachnaria, Barombiella, Bertauxia, Blumeorchis, Burnsbaloghia,

Caladeniastrum, Calonema, Calonemorchis, Cocleorchis, Coenadenium, Determannia, Diadeniopsis, Fimbrorchis, Fingardia, Garaya, Garayanthus, Gerlachia, Glossochilopsis, Hordeanthos, Imerinorchis, Jejewoodia, Jonesiopsis, Kornasia, Kraenzlinorchis, Kusibabella, Lacroixia, Laricorchis, Lepanthanthe, Lisowskia, Lowiorchis, Medusorchis, Neocribbia, Oberonioides, Ochyrorchis, Oestlundorchis, Oligochaetochilus, Ormerodia, Pentisea, Phlebochilus, Phymatidiopsis, Plantaginorchis, Platantheroides, Platycorynoides, Plumatichilos, Podandriella, Polycycnopsis, Pseudocoeloglossum, Pseudohemipilia, Raciborskanthos, Rhinocerotidium, Sauvetrea, Schidorhynchos, Schlechterorchis, Seidenfia, Senghasia, Senghasiella, Simpliglottis, Stacyella, Tadeastrum, Takulumena, Tamayorkis, Trachyrhachis, Univiscidiatus, Veyretia, Wallnoeferia, Warscaea

Szlachetko & González-Tamayo, Roberto G. (1940-) (R. González)
• Diskyphogyne, Ochyrella, Triceratostris

Szlachetko, Gonzáles-Tamayo & Rutkowski, Piotr (1969-) (Rutk.)
• Pachygenium, Zhukowskia

Szlachetko & Górniak, Marcin (1976-) (Górn.)
• Brassiopsis

Szlachetko, Górniak & Tukallo, Piotr (1977-) (Tuk.)
• Ceratopetalorchis

Szlachetko & Kras-Lapinska, Marta (1969-) (Kras-Lap.)
• Mirandorchis, Monadeniorchis, Tripudianthes

Szlachetko & Margońska, Hanna Bogna (1968-) (Marg.)
• Anettea, Gyalanthos, Jouyella, Lueranthos, Masdevalliantha, Mirandopsis, Mystacorchis, Peltopus, Smithanthe, Spuricianthus, Zosterophyllanthos

Szlachetko & Mytnik, Joanna Ejsmont (1960-) (Mytnik)
• Anettea

Szlachetko, Mytnik & Górniak, Marcin (1960-) (Górn.)
• Andinorchis

Szlachetko, Mytnik, Górniak & Romowicz, Agnieszka (1960-) (Romowicz)
• Irenea, Siederelle

Szlachetko, Mytnik, Górniak & Śmiszek, Magdalena (1960-) (Smiszek)
• Christensonella

Szlachetko, Mytnik & Romowicz, Agnieszka (1960-) (Romowicz)
• Heteranthocidium, Lophiarella

Szlachetko & Olszewski, Tomasz Sebastian (1972-) (Olszewski)
• Halleorchis, Homocolleticon, Pseudoperistylus, Renzorchis, Veyretella

Szlachetko & Rutkowski, Piotr (1969-) (Rutk.)
• Dolabrifolia, Herscheliodisa

Szlachetko & Sawicka, Magdalena (1969-) (Sawicka)
• Macrura, Trachypetalum

Tang, Tsin (Chin/Jin) (1897-1984) (T. Tang) &
Wang, Fa-Tsuan (1899-1985) (F.T. Wang)
• Porolabium, Smithorchis, Tsaiorchis

Thal, Johannes (1542-1583) (Thal)
• Alismatis

Thouars, Louis-Marie Aubert-Aubert Du Petit- (1758-1831) (Thouars)
• Aiolographis, Alismographis, Alismorkis, Altisatis, Amenippis, Amphorkis, Angorkis, Antidris, Aphyllangis, Aplostellis, Arachnabenis, Arachnodendris, Brachistepis, Bulbophyllum, Caestichis, Calcaramphis, Calceangis, Calceolangis, Calographis, Carpangis, Caulangis, Centrosis, Cestichis, Citrabenis, Citrangis, Citrinabenis, Clavophylis, Coespiphylis, Coestichis, Commersis, Commersophylis, Commersorchis, Coniphylis, Corcurborchis,

Corymbis, Corymborkis, Crassangis, Criptangis, Criptophylis, Crypterpis, Cryptophylis, Cucullangis, Cultridendris, Curvangis, Curvophylis, Cyanorkis, Cynorkis, Cynosorchis, Dendrorkis, Densophylis, Dionysis, Distichis, Dolichangis, Dryopria, Dryorkis, Eburnangis, Elangis, Epidorkis, Equitiris, Erporkis, Erythrocynis, Erythrodris, Erythroleptis, Expangis, Filangis, Flabellographis, Flavileptis, Flexuosatis, Fragrangis, Fusidendris, Gastorkis, Gladiangis, Gracilangis, Gracilophylis, Graminisatis, Graphorkis, Gymnerpis, Habenorkis, Hederorkis, Hipporkis, Inermamphis, Iridorkis, Isocynis, Latosatis, Leptorkis, Longiphylis, Macrostepis, Miangis, Minuphylis, Monographis, Myriangis, Nuphylis, Palmangis, Pectangis, Pendiphylis, Phyllorkis, Plicangis, Polydendris, Polystepis, Prismophylis, Purpurabenis, Purpurocynis, Purpuroleptis, Pusiphylis, Ramangis, Rectangis, Rectophylis, Rossatis, Satorkis, Scandederis, Sigillabenis, Spirosatis, Stellorkis, Stichorkis, Striangis, Superbangis, Sylvalismis, Tetragocyanis, Triangis, Triodris, Triphyllocynis, Tuberogastris, Variphylis, Villosogastris, Volucrepis

Thwaites, George Henry Kendrick (1812-1882) (Thwaites)
• Cylindrochilus, Octarrhena

Torrey, John (1796-1873) (Torr.)
• Aplectrum

Tournefort, Joseph Pitton de (1656-1708) (Tourn.)
• Ophris

Trew, Christoph Jakob (1695-1769) (Trew)
• Orchiodes

Tsi, Zhan-Huo (1937-2001) (Z.H. Tsi)
• Nothodoritis

Van den Berg, Cássio (1971-) (Van den Berg) &
Chase, Mark Wayne (1951-) (M.W. Chase)
• Cattleyella

Van den Berg & Gonçalves, César Neubert (1969-) (C.N. Gonçalves)
• Adamantinia

Vermeulen, Pieter (1889-1981) (Verm.)
• Aorchis, Dactylorchis

Wahlenberg, Göran (1780-1851) (Wahlenb.)
• Norna

Wallich, Nathaniel (1786-1854) (Wall.)
• Chrysobaphus, Cryptochilus, Mesodactylis

Wallroth, Karl Friedrich Wilhelm (1792-1857) (Wallr.)
• Conopsidium

Wankow, Iwan Wasiljewitsch (fl. 1928) (Wankow) &
Kraenzlin, Friedrich (Fritz) Wilhelm Ludwig (1847-1934) (Kraenzl.)
• Stevenorchis

Warszewicz, Josef von Rawicz (1812-1866) (Warsz.)
• Anachaste

Wawra von Fernsee, Heinrich (1831-1887) (Wawra)
• Eurystyles

Wight, Robert (1796-1872) (Wight)
• Aggeianthus, Apetalon, Cottonia, Govindooia, Josephia, Lichenora, Oxysepala, Pattonia, Podanthera

Willdenow, Carl Ludwig von (1765-1812) (Willd.)
• Bonatea, Habenaria

Williams, Louis Otto (1908-1991) (L.O. Williams)
- *Cordanthera, Dickasonia, Epidanthus, Macropodanthus, Nageliella, Phragmorchis, Platyglottis*

Williams, Norris Hagen (1943-) (N.H. Williams) *&*
Chase, Mark Wayne (1951-) (M.W. Chase)
- *Cyrtochiloides*

Willis, John Christopher (1868-1958) (Willis)
- *Pinelea*

Withner, Carl Leslie (1918-) (Withner)
- *Euchile*

Withner *&* **Harding,** Patricia A. (1951-) (P.A. Harding)
- *Osmophytum, Panarica, Pollardia*

Wittstein, Georg Christian (1810-1887) (Wittst.)
- *Amphiglottium, Atrichoglottis, Aulizeum, Biaurella, Calodisa, Calonema, Conopsea, Coryphaea, Disella, Eucaladenia, Euceratandra, Eucymbidium, Euepidendrum, Eudisa, Euglossodia, Oregura, Pardoglossa, Phlebidia, Spathium, Stenocarpa, Trichochila, Vaginaria, Vriesia*

Wood, Jeffrey James (1952-) (J.J. Wood)
- *Muluorchis, Neotrachoma*

Wood *&* **Lamb,** Anthony L. (1942-) (A.L. Lamb)
- *Spongiola*

Y

Yamamoto, Yoshimatsu (1893-1947) (Yamam.)
- *Tuberolabium*

Ying, Shao-Shun (1941-) (S.S. Ying)
- *Ascolabium, Collabiopsis*

Z

Zahlbrückner, Alexander (1860-1938) (Zahlbr.)
- *Rolfea*

Zimmermann, Albrecht Wilhelm Philipp (1860-1931) (Zimm.)
- *Parapactis*

Zinn, Johann Gottfried (1727-1759) (Zinn)
- *Epipactis*

Zollinger, Heinrich (1818-1859) (Zoll.) *&*
Moritzi, Alexandre (1806-1850) (Moritzi)
- *Bolborchis*

FASCICULUS OCTAVUS. 183

TABULA CENTESIMA OCTOGESIMA · OCTAVA.

V*Anilla* flore viridi, & albo; fructu nigricante. *Plum. Nov. Gener. pl. Amer. p.* 25. *Geoffr. mat. Med. vol.* 2. *p.* 362.

EPIDENDRUM foliis ovato-oblongis, nervofis, feffilibus, caulinis, cirrhis fpiralibus. *Roy. pr. p.* 13. *Linn. fpec. p.* 952. *no.* 1.

Epidendrum foliis ovato-oblongis, petiolis inferne amplexicaulibus, cirrhis radicatis. *H. Cliff. p.* 430. ubi defcriptio.
Epidendrum fcandens, foliis elliptico-ovatis, nitidiffimis, margine membranaceo cinctis, fubfeffilibus; inferioribus claviculis jugatis, fuperioribus oppofitis. *Brouw. Hift. Jam. p.* 326.
Vanillas piperis arbori Jamaicenfis innafcens. *Plukn. Alm. p.* 381. *Tab.* 320. *Fig.* 4.
Vanillo. Merian. Surin. Tab. 25, S. *Dale Pharmac. p.* 371.
Volubilis filiquofa, plantaginis folio. *Catesb. Carol. app. p.* 7. *Tab.* 7.
Volubilis Americ. capreolata, Plantaginis foliis, filiquis longis, mofchum olentibus. *Moris. Hift. pl. tom.* 3. *p.* 612.
Lobus oblongus, aromaticus. *Cluf. exotic. p.* 72. *Sloan. Cat. pl. Jam. p.* 70. *Hift. Jam. vol.* 1. *p.* 180.
Tlilxochitc. Hernand. Hift. Mexic. p. 38.
β *Angurek Warna*, feu herba fcandens, parafitica; folio arundinaceo, fl. variegato, hexapetalo, papilionem volantem exprimente, probofcide brevi. *Kæmph. amænit. exotic. p.* 867?

Licet hæc planta a variis auctoribus fit commemorata, atque a paucis ipfius fructus, & folia icone expreffa, a nullo tamen, nifi forte a *Catesb.* ipfius flores, totaque forma fimul exhibita, unde eam ab auctore noftro fatis exacte depictam in Tabula oculis exponere volui; defcriptionem vero addere fuperfluum effet, quum exactiffime a *Geoffr. l. c.* (uti apparet ex *Plumierii mff.*) fit defcripta, ubi & aliæ hujus fpecies, quæ potius varietates habendæ, recenfentur, fed inter Auctoris-icones altera minor ejus reperitur fpecies, quæ *Vanilla* flore albo, fructu breviore corallino a *Plum.* in *nov. gen. p.* 25. vocatur; quum vero tantum ipfius flores ac fructus digitum circiter longi, & quafi truncati depicti funt; nec fatis exacte, hinc ulteriori examini in patrio folo eam relinquimus.

Plumier *Nova plantarum americanarum genera*   page 183 (1703).

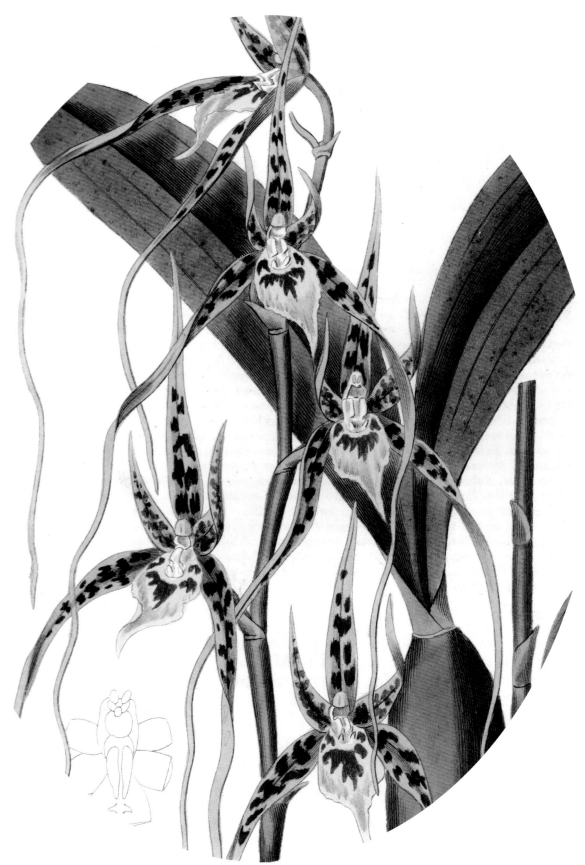

Lindley *Botanical Register* **10**: plate 832 (1824).

ORCHID GENERA

BOOK/PERIODICAL ABBREVIATIONS

ORCHID GENERA

GUIDE TO BOOK/PERIODICAL ABBREVIATIONS

A complete listing of the books and periodicals used with their abbreviations
according to *Botanico Periodicum Huntianum* (BPH) Lawrence et al., 1968,
Botanico Periodicum Huntianum/Supplementum (BPH/S) Bridson and Smith, 1991, and
Botanico-Periodicum-Huntianum 2nd Edition (BPH2) Brudson et al., 2004.

The citation abbreviations used in this dictionary were selected
from standardized abbreviations for publications dealing with plants.
Periodical abbreviations follow *Botanico Periodicum Huntianum* (BPH),
and book abbreviations follow *Taxonomic Literature*, ed. 2 (TL2).
However, where there was uncertainty as to the abbreviation to follow, the International Plant Name Index (IPNI)
was consulted on a case by case basis by the Editorial Committee.

Standardized
abbreviation

Acta Bot. Acad. Sci. Hung - Acta Botanica Academiæ Scientiarum
Hungaricæ, Budapest

Acta Bot. Fenn. - Acta Botanica Fennica - Gynostemia Orchidalium

Acta Bot. Neerl. - Acta botanica neerlandica, Amsterdam

Acta Bot. Mex. - Acta Botanica Mexicana, Pátzcuaro

Acta Helv. Phys.-Math. - Acta Helvetica, Physico-Mathematico-
Anatomico-Botanico-Medica

Full title
of the Reference Book
or Periodical

City
or place of publication

Indianisch Mispel.   Viscum Indicum.

Theodorus *Neu vollkommen Kräuter-buch* page 1379 (1731).

ORCHID GENERA

BOOK/PERIODICAL ABBREVIATIONS

To be consistent in abbreviating titles, we have modified some abbreviations to agree with BPH.

Abh. Königl. Ges. Wiss. Göttingen - Abhandlungen der Königlichen Gesellschaft der Wissenschaften, Göttingen

Acta Bot. Acad. Sci. Hung. - Acta Botanica Academiæ Scientiarum Hungaricæ, Budapest

Acta Bot. Fenn. - Acta Botanica Fennica - Gynostemia Orchidalium

Acta Bot. Mex. - Acta Botanica Mexicana, Pátzcuaro

Acta Bot. Neerl. - Acta botanica neerlandica, Amsterdam

Acta Fauna Fl. Universali, Ser. 2, Bot. - Acta pro fauna et flora universali. Ser. 2: Botanica, Bucharest

Acta Helv. Phys.-Math. - Acta Helvetica, Physico-Mathematico-Anatomico-Botanico-Medica, Basel

Acta Phys.-Med. Acad. Caes. Leop.-Francisc. Nat. Cur. - Acta Physico-Medica Academiæ Caesareæ Leopoldino-Franciscanæ Naturæ Curiosorum Exhibentia Ephemerides sive Observationes Historias et Experimenta, Nuremberg

Acta Phytotax. Sin. - Acta Phytotaxonomica Sinica (Chih wu fen lei hsüeh pao.), Beijing

Acta Soc. Bot. Poloniae - Acta Societatis Botanicorum Poloniae: Publications de la Société Botanique di Pologne, Warsaw

Adansonia - Adansonia Publications Scientifiques du Muséum, Paris

Adnot. Bot. - Adnotationes botanicæ: quas reliquit Olavus Swartz ...: Post mortem auctoris collectæ, examinatæ, in ordinem systematicum redactæ atque notis et præfatione instructæ a J.E. Wikstrom, accedit Biographia Swartzii, auctoribus C. Sprengel et C.A. Agardh, Stockholm

Allg. Bot. Z. Syst. - Allgemeine Botanische Zeitschrift für Systematik, Floristik, Pflanzengeographie etc., Karlsruhe

Allg. Gartenzeitung - Allgemeine Gartenzeitung, Berlin

Alm. Bot. Pl. - Almagesti Botanici Mantissa Plantarum novissimè detectarum ultrà millenarium numerum complectens: cui, tanquam pedi jam stantis columnæ, plus inscribere fas est: cum indice totius operis ad calcem adjecto, London

Am. Exot. - Amoenitarum exoticarum politico-physico-medicarum fasciculi V, quibus continentur variæ relationes, observationes & descriptiones reum Persicarum et ulterioris Asiæ

Amer. Fl. Gard. Directory - American flower-garden directory: containing practical directions for the culture of plants in the flower garden, hot-house, garden-house, rooms, or parlour windows, for every month in the year ... Instructions for erecting a hot-house, green-house, and laying out a flower garden. Also, table of soils most congenial to the plants contained in the work. The whole adapted to either large or small gardens, with instructions for preparing the soil, propagating, planting, pruning, training, and fruiting the grape vine. With descriptions of the best sorts for cultivating in the open air, Philadelphia

Amer. Gard. Cal. - The American Gardener: adapted to the climate and seasons of the United States, Philadelphia

Amer. Midl. Naturalist - American Midland Naturalist; devoted to natural history, primarily that of the prairie states

Amer. Monthly Mag. & Crit. Rev. - American Monthly Magazine and Critical Review, New York City

Amer. Naturalist - American Naturalist; a Popular Illustrated Magazine of Natural History, Boston

Amer. Orchid Soc. Bull. - American Orchid Society Bulletin, Cambridge, West Palm Beach

Anais Reunião Sul-Amer. Bot. - Anais Reunião Sul-America de Botânica, Rio de Janeiro

Anales Jard. Bot. Madrid - Anales del Jardin Botanico de Madrid

Anales Soc. Esp. Hist. Nat. - Anales de la Sociedad Española de Historia Natural, Madrid

Anales Univ. Chile - Anales de la Universidad de Chile, Santiago

Anal. Fam. Pl. - Analyse des Familles de Plantes, Tournay

Anexos Mem. Inst. Butantan, Secç. Bot. - Anexos das Memórias do Instituto de Butantan. Secçaõ de Botânica, São Paulo

Anleit. Kenntn. Gew. - Anleitung zur Kenntniss der Gewächse, Zweite

Ann. Bot. Fenn. - Annales Botanici Fennici (Societas zoologica botanica fennica "Vanamo"), Helsinki

Ann. Bot. Syst. - *Walpers'* Annales Botanices Systematicæ, Leipzig

Ann. erd, Völk. Staat. - Annalen erd, Völker- und Staatenkunde: Unter mitwirkung mehrerer gelehrten verfasst und herausgegeben, Berlin

Ann. Hist. Nat. - Annales d'Histoire Naturelle, Paris

Ann. Hist. Nat. (Scopoli) - Annus IV Historico Naturalis, Leipzig

Ann. Hort. - Annals of Horticulture and Year-Book of Information on Practical Gardening, London

Ann. Hort. Bot. - Annales d'Horticulture et de Botanique ou Flore des Jardins du Royaume des Pays-Bas, Leiden

Ann. Jard. Bot. Buitenzorg - Annales du Jardin Botanique de Buitenzorg

Ann. Mag. Nat. Hist. - Annals and Magazine of Natural History, including Zoology, Botany, and Geology, London

Ann. Missouri Bot. Gard. - Annals of the Missouri Botanical Garden

Ann. Mus. Bot. Lugduno-Batavi - Annales Musei Botanici Lugduno-Batavi, Amsterdam

Annot. - Annotationes in Pedacii Dioscordis Anazarbei de medica materia libros V.: ...: ejusdem Val. Cordi historiæ stirpium lib. IIII: posthumi, nunc primùm in lucem editi, adiectis etiam stirpium iconibus: ...: Sylva, qua rerum fossilium in Germania plurimarum, metallorum, lapidum & stirpium aliquot rariorum notitiam breuissimè persequitur, nunquam hactenus uisa: De artificiosis extractionibus liber: Compositiones medicinales aliquot, non; His accedunt Stocc-Hornii et Nessi in Bernatium Helvetiorum ditione montium, & nascentium in eis stirpium, descriptio Benedicti Aretii ... Item Conradi Gesneri de hortis Germaniae liber recens,: ... Omnia summo studio atque industria Conr. Gesneri collecta, & Praefationibus illustrata, Argentorati

Ann. Rep. Park Comm. Milwaukee - Sixteenth Annual Report on the Park Commissioners of the City of Milwaukee, Milwaukee

Ann. Roy. Bot. Gard. (Calcutta) - Annals of the Royal Botanic Garden

Ann. Sci. Nat. (Paris) - Annales des Sciences Naturelles, Paris

Ann. Sci. Nat., Bot. - Annales des Sciences Naturelles Botanique, Paris

Ann. Soc. Bot. Lyon - Annales de la Société Botanique de Lyon

Ann. Soc. Roy. Agric. Gand - Annales de la Société Royale d'Agriculture et de Botanique de Gand: Journal d'Horticulture et des Sciences Accessoires, Ghent

Ann. Tsukuba Bot. Gard. - Annals of the Tsukuba Botanical Garden, (Tsukuba Jikken Shokubutsuen Kenkyu Hokoku), Ibaraki

Aphor. Bot. - Aphorismi Botanici; Quos, Venia Amplissimi Ordinis Philosophici, Lund

Arch. Bot. (Leipzig) - Archiv für die Botanik (Roemer), Leipzig

Arch. Bot. São Paulo - Archivos de Botanica do São Paulo, São Paulo

Arch. Jard. Bot. Rio de Janeiro - Archivos do Jardim Botânico do Rio de Janeiro

Arch. Pharm. - Archiv der Pharmacie, eine Zeitschrift des Apotheker-Vereins in Norddeutschland, Hannover

Arcula - Arcula: Botanische Abhandlungen (Botanical Treatise), Munich

Argum. Palaeobot. - Argumenta Palaeobotanica, Lehre

Ark. Bot. - Arkiv för Botanik utgivet av Kungliga Svenska Vetenskapsakademien, Stockholm

Arq. Bot. Estado São Paulo - Arquivos de Botânica do Estado de São Paulo

Arq. Inst. Biol. Veg. - Arquivos do Instituto de Biologia Vegetal do Rio de Janeiro

Arq. Mus. Nac. Rio de Janeiro - Arquivos do Museu Nacional do Rio de Janeiro

Arq. Serv. Florest. - Arquivos do Servico Florestal do Rio de Janeiro

Asiat. Res. - Asiatic researches or, transactions of the society, instituted in Bengal, for inquiring into the history and antiquities, the arts, sciences, and literature, of Asia. ... Botanical Observations on Select Indian Plants, London

Atlantic J. - Atlantic Journal & Friend of Knowledge, Philadelphia

Atlas Orchid Poll. - An atlas of orchid pollination: America, Africa, Asia and Australia, Rotterdam

Atti Reale Ist. Veneto Sci. Lett. Arti - Atti del Reale Istituto Veneto di Scienze, Lettere ed Arti, Venice

Atti Soc. Ital. Sci. Nat. - Atti della Societa Italiana di Scienze Naturali, Milan

Australasian Sarcanthinæ - Australasian Sarcanthinæ: a review of the subtribe Sarcanthinæ in Australia and New Zealand, Sydney

Austral. Orch. - Australian Orchids, Sydney

Austral. Orchid Res. - The Australian Orchid Research, Canberra

Austral. Orchid Rev. - The Australian Orchid Review, Sydney

Austral. Syst. Bot. - Australian Systematic Botany, East Melbourne

Austrobaileya - Austrobaileya: A Journal of Plant Systematics, Queensland, Australia

B

Badianus Manuscript - Badianus Manuscript (Codex Barberini, Latin 241)

Bahama Fl. (Britton & Millspaugh) - The Bahama Flora, New York

Beih. Bot. Centralbl. - Beihefte zum Botanischen Centralblatt, Cassel

Beitr. Bot. (Wallroth) - Beiträge zur Botanik: Eine Sammlung monographischer Abhandlungen über besonders schwierige Gewächs-Gattungen der Flora Deutschlands, Leipzig

Beitr. Fl. Vorwelt - Beiträge zur Flora der Vorwelt ... mit sechzig Tafeln Abbilungen, Praha

Beitr. Morph. Biol. Orchid. - Beiträge zur Morphologie und Biologie der Familie der Orchideen, Jena

Beitr. Naturk. (Ehrhart) - Beiträge zur Naturkunde und den damit verwandten Wissenschaften besonders der Botanik, Chemie, Haus- und Landwirthschaft, Arzneigelahrtheit und Apothekerkunst, Hannover

Beitr. Orchid.-K. - Beiträge zu einer Orchideenkunde Central-Amerika's, Hamburg

Beitr. Syst. Pflanzenk. - Beiträge zur Systematischen Pflanzenkunde

Belgique Hort. - La Belgique Horticole; Annales de Botanique et d'Horticulture, Liége

Ber. Arb. Heimische Orch. - Berichte aus Arbeitskreisen Heimische Orchideen, Hanau

Besch. West-Ind. - Beschrijvinghe van West-Indien door Ioannes de Laet. Tweede druck: in ontallijcke plaetsen verbetert, vermeerdert, met eenige nieuwe caerten, beelden van verscheyden dieren ende planten verciert.

Bibliogr. Bot. - Bibliographia botanica. Handbuch der botanischen literatur in systematischer ordnung nebst kurzen biographischen notizen über die botanischen schriftsteller. Zum gebrauche für freunde und lehrer der pflanzenkunde, Berlin

Bijdr. Fl. Ned. Ind. - Bijdragen tot de Flora van Nederlandsch Indië, Synoptische Beschrijving van eenige planten, behoorende tot de familie der Orchideen, op eene, in de jarden 1823-1824 gedanereis over Java, waargenomen en beschreven, Batavia

Biodivers. Res. Conservation - Biodiversity: research and conservation, Poznan

Biogeogr. Madag. - Biogéographie des Plantes de Madagascar, Paris

Biol. Cent.-Amer., Bot. - Biologia Centralia-Americana; or Contributions ot the knowledge of the Fauna and Flora of Mexico and Central America, London

Biol. Mag. - Biological Magazine. [Okinawa Seibutse Gekhai]. Naha, Okinawa

Blumea - Blumea; Tijdschrift voor de Systematiek en de Geografie der Planten, Leiden

Bol. CAOB - Boletim CAOB; Cordenadoria das Associacoes Orquidofilas do Brasil, São Paulo

Bol. Inst. Bot. Univ. Guadalajara - Boletin del Instituto de Botanica, Universidad de Gudalajara, Zapopan

Bol. Inst. Brasil. Sci. - Boletim; Instituto Brasileiro de Sciencias, Rio de Janeiro

Bol. Mus. Nac. Rio de Janeiro - Boletim do Museu Nacional de Rio de Janeiro

Bol. Soc. Brot. - Boletim da Sociedade Broteriana, Coimbra

Bonplandia - Bonplandia; Zeitschrift für die gesammte Botanik. Officielles Organ der K.L.-C. Akademie der Naturforscher. Hannover, London, Paris

Bot. Abstr. - Botanical Abstracts: a monthly serial furnishing abstracts and citations of publications in the international field of botany in its broadest sense, Baltimore

Bot. Beechey Voy. - Botany of Captain Beechey's Voyage; comprising an account of the plants collected by Messrs. Lay and Collie, during the voyage to the Pacific and Bering Strait, performed in H.M.S. Blossom

Bot. Cab. - Botanical Cabinet; Consisting of coloured delineations of Plants from all ountries, with a short account of each, directions for management, London

Bot. Congr. London - Report on the Proceedings of the International Horticultural Exhibition Botanical Congress, London

Bot. Gall., pars prima - Aug. Pyrami de Candolle Botanicon Gallicum, pars prima, seu Synopsis Plantarum in Flora Gallica editio secunda ex herbariis et schedis Candollianis propriisque digestum, Paris

Bot. Gaz. - Botanical Gazette, London

Bot. Jahrb. Syst. - Botanische Jahrbücher für Systematik, Pflanzengeschichte und Pflanzengeopgraphie, Leipzig

Bot. Mag. - Curtis's Botanical Magazine; or, Flower-Garden Displayed in which the most ornamental foreign plants, cultivated in the open ground, the green-house, and the stove, are accurately represented in their natural colours ..., London

Bot. Mag. (Tokyo) - The Botanical Magazine (Shokubutsu-gaku zasshi), Tokyo

Bot. Mitt. Tropen - Botanische Mitteilungen aus den Tropen, Jena

Bot. Mus. Leafl. - Botanical Museum Leaflets of Harvard University, Boston

Bot. North. Middle States - Botany of the Northern and Middle States; or a description of the plants found in the United States, north of Virginia, arranged according to the natural system: with a synopsis of the genera according to the Linnaean system, Albany

Bot. Not. - Botaniska Notiser för år ..., Lund

Bot. Orchids - Botanica's Orchids: Over 1200 species listed, San Diego

Bot. Porto Rico - Britton & Wilson's The Botany of Porto Rico and the Virgin Islands, New York

Bot. Reg. - Botanical Register, consisting of colorured figures of exotic plants, cultivated in British Gardens, with their History and Mode of Treatment, London

Bot. Repos. - H.C. Andrews' Botanical Repository, for New, and Rare Plants; comprising colour'd engravings of new and rare plants only: with botanical descriptions in Latin and English after the Linnean system

Bot. Tidsskr. - Seidenfaden's Botanisk Tidsskrift, Copenhagen

Bot. Zeitung (Berlin) - Botanische Zeitung, Berlin

Bot. Zhurn. (Moscow & Leningrad) - Botanicheskii Zhurnal. Moscow & Leningrad [St. Petersburg]

Bradea - Bradea: boletim do Herbarium Bradeanum, Rid de Janerio

Brittonia - Brittonia; a series of botanical papers, New York City

Bull. Acad. Imp. Sci. Saint-Pétersbourg - Bulletin de l'Académie Impériale des Sciences de Saint-Pétersbourg

Bull. Dépt. Agric. Indes Néerl. - Bulletin de Départment de l'Agriculture aux Indes Néerlandaises, Buitenzorg

Bull. Fan Mem. Inst. Biol. Bot. - Bulletin of the Fan Memorial Institute of Biology - Botany, Beijing

Bull. Fed. Soc. Hort. Belgique - Bulletin de la Federation des Sociétés d'Horticulure de Belgique, Ghent

Bull. Herb. Boissier - Bulletin de l'Herbier Boissier, Geneva

Bull. Inst. Bot. Buitenzorg - Bulletin de l'Institut Botanique de Buitenzorg

Bull. Jard. Bot. Belg. - Bulletin du Jardin Botanique National de Belgique, Brussels

Bull. Jard. Bot. Buitenzorg - Bulletin du Jardin Botanique de Buitenzorg

Bull. Misc. Inform. Kew - Bulletin of Miscellaneous Information, Royal Gardens, Kew

Bull. Mus. Hist. Nat. (Paris) - Bulletin du Muséum d'Histoire N Naturelle, Paris

Bull. Mus. Natl. Hist. Nat. - Bulletin du Muséum National d'Histoire Naturelle, Paris

Bull. Sci. Acad. Imp. Sci. Saint-Pétersbourg - Bulletin Scientifique (publié par l') Académie Imperiale des Sciences de Saint-Pétersbourg, St. Petersburg, Leipzig

Bull. Sci. Nat. Geol. - Bulletin des Sciences Naturelles et de Géologie. Deuxième Section du Bulletin Universei des Sciences et de l'Industrie, Paris

Bull. Soc. Bot. France - Bulletin de la Société Botanique de France, Paris

Bull. Soc. Bot. Deux-Sevres - Bulletin de la Société Botanique des Deux-Sevres, Niort

Bull. Soc. Roy. Bot. Belgique - Bulletins de la Société Royale de Botanique de Belgique, Bruxelles

Bull. Torrey Bot. Club - Bulletin of the Torrey Botanical Club, New York City, Lancaster, PA & Lawrence, KS

Caesiana - Caesiana: Rivista Italiana di Orchidologia, Genoa

Calcutta J. Nat. Hist. - Calcutta Journal of Natural History, and Miscellany of the Arts and Sciences in India, Calcutta

Cat. Descr. Orquid., Estac. Exp. Agron. Santiago, Cuba - Catalogo Descriptivo de las Orquideas Cubanas. Estacion Experimental Agronomica Santiago de las Vegas, Habana

Cat. Geogr. Pl. (Burchell) - Catalogus geographicus plantarum quas in africa australi extratropica itinere annis 1810, 11, 12, 13 & 1815 collegit et descripsit Gulielmus J. Burchell - Unpublished, located at Kew

Cat. Gew. Buitenzorg - Catalogus van eenige der Merkwaardigste Zoo in-als Uit-heemse Gewassen: te vinden in 's lands plantentuin te Buitenzorg, Batavia

Cat. Hort. Bot. Bogor. (Hasskarl) - Catalogus Plantarum in Horto Botanico Bogoriensi cultarum alter, Buitenzorg

Cat. Indian Orchids - Sathish Kumar & Manilal's A Catalog of Indian Orchids, Dehra Dun

Cat. Orch.-Samml. Schiller - G.W. Schiller's Catalog der Orchideen - Sammlung von G.W. Schiller: zu Ovelgönne an der Elbe, Hamburg

Cat. Pl. (Warszewicz) - Catalogus plantarum quæ in C.R. Horto Botanicao Cracoviensi anno 1864; ab erecta C.R. Universitate Studiorum Jagellonica quingentesimo, a fundato vero horto octogesimo educantar

Cat. Pl. Angl. - Catalogus Plantarum Angliæ, et insularum adjacentium tum indigenas, tum in agris passim cultas complectens in quo præter synonyma necessaria, facultates quoque summatim traduntur, unà cum observationibus & experimentis novis medicis & physicis, London

Cat. Pl. Bombay - A Catalogue of the Plants Growing in Bombay and its Vicinity: spontaneous, cultivated or introduced, as far as they have been ascertained, Bombay

Cat. Pl. Cub. - Catalogus Plantarum Cubensium Exhibens Collectionem Wrightianam Aliasque Minores ex insula Cuba Missas, Leipzig

Cat. Pl. Hort. Bot. Bogor. - Catalogus plantarum in Horto botanico Bogoriensi cultarum alter, Bataviae

Cat. Pl. Hort. Gott. - Catalogus plantarum horti academici et agri Gottingensis, Gottingen

Cat. Pl. Horti Paris. - Catalogus Plantanum Horti Regii Parisiensis, Paris

Cat. Pl. Jamaica - Catalogus Plantarum quæ in Insula Jamaica sponte proveniunt, vel vulgo conuntur, cum eqarundem synonymis & locis natalibus: adjectis aliis quibusdam quæ in Insulis Maderæ, Barbados, Nieves & Sancti Christophori nascuntur: Seu Prodromi Historiæ Naturalis Jamaicæ pars prima, London

Cat. Pl. Trinidad - Catalogue of Plants in the Botanical Botanical Gardens, Trinidad, from 1865 to 1870, Port-of-Spain

Cat. Pl. Vasc. Rep. Argentina - Catálogo de las Plantas Vasculares de la República Argentina, St. Louis, Missouri

Cat. Samm. Ausstell. - Catalog sämmtlicher Ausstellungsgegenstände nebst vollständigem Register der Aussteller sowie der ausgestellten Objecte [der] internationale[n] Gartenbau-Ausstellung in Hamburg vom 2. bis 12. September 1869, Hamburg

Cattleyas & Relatives - The cattleyas and their relatives, Portland, Oregon

Cat. Veg. Alger - Catalogue des végétaux cultivés à la pépinière centrale du gouvernement à Alger

Ceiba - Ceiba; a Scientific Journal Issued by the Escuela Agricola Panamericana. Tegucigalpa, Honduras

Char. Gen. Pl. - Characteres Generum Plantarum, quas in itinere ad Insulas Maris Australis, collegerunt, descripserunt, delinearunt, annis 1772-1775, Stuttgart

Chin Chang Lan Pu - Chin Chang Lan Pu

Codex Badianus (Latin 721) - Translated as Badianus Manuscript

Colet. Orquídeas Brasil. - Coletânea de Orquídeas Brasileiras. Taubaté - São Paulo, Brazil

Coll. Bot. (Lindley) - Collectanea Botanica; or, Figures and Botanical Illustrations of Rare and Curious Exotic Plants, London

Coll. Orchid. - Collection des Orchidées les plus remarquables de l'Arichipel Indien et du Japon, Amsterdam

Coloured Ill. Indig. Orchids Taiwan - Coloured illustrations of indigenous plants of Taiwan, Taipei

Commentarii - Commentarii, in libros sex Pedacii Dioscoridis, Anazarbei, de medica materia, Adjectis quam plurimis Plantarum & Animalium imaginibus, eodem authore, Venice

Comment. M.P.A. Matthiole - Commentaires de M.P. André Matthiolus, medecin senois, sur les six livres de Pedacius Dioscoride, Anazarbeen De la matiere medicinale, Lyon

Companion Bot. Mag. - Companion to the Botanical Magazine, London

Comp. Fl. Ital. (Arcangeli) - Compendio della Flora Italiana; ossia, Manuale per la determinzione delle piante che trovansi selvatiche od inselvatichite nell' Italia e nelle isole adiacenti, Torino

Comp. Fl. N. Middle States - Compendium of the Flora of Northern Middle States: containing generic and specific descriptions of all the plants, exclusive of the cryptogamia, hitherto found in the United States, north of the Potomac, New York

Compt. Rend. Hebd. Séances Acad. Sci. - Comptes Rendus Hebdomadaires des Séances de l'Académie des Sciences, Paris

Concise Fl. Singapore - The Concise Floral of Singapore: Monocotyledons, Singapore

Consp. Fl. France - Conspectus de la Flore de France ou catalogue général des espèces, sous-espèces, races, variétés, sous-variétés et formes hybrides contenues dans la Flore de France, Paris

Consp. Regn. Veg. - Conspectus Regni Vegetabilis per gradus naturales evolution. Leipzig

Contr. Biol. Lab. Sci. Soc. China, Bot. Ser. - Contributions from the Biological Laboratory of the Science Society of China, Botanical Series, Nanking

Contr. Bot. Dept. Nebraska Univ. - Contributions from the Botanical Department, Nebraska University, Lincoln

Contr. Fl. Austral. - A Contribution to the Flora of Australia, Sydney

Contr. Fl. Guadeloupe - Contribution à la Flore de la Guadeloupe, Basse-Terre

Contr. Herb. Austral. - Contributions from Herbarium Australiense, East Melbourne

Contr. New South Wales Natl. Herb. - Contributions from the New South Wales National Herbarium, Sydney

Contr. Orchid Fl. Thailand - Contributions to the Orchid Flora of Thailand, Copenhagen

Contr. Univ. Michigan Herb. - Contributions from the University of Michigan Herbarium, Ann Arbor

Contr. U.S. Natl. Herb. - Contributions from the United States National Herbarium, Smithsonian Institution, Washington D.C.

Cool Orchids - Cool orchids, and how to grow them: with a descriptive list of all the best species in cultivation, London

CRC World Dict. Pl. - CRC World dictionary of plant names: common names, scientific names, eponyms, synonyms, etymology, Boca Raton

Cruyde Boeck - Cruÿde Boeck. Nu wederom van nieuws oversien ende verbetert, Antwerpen

Cycl. (Rees) - The Cyclopaedia; or, Universial Dictionary of Arts, Sciences and Literature by Abrahama Rees, London

Dansk Bot. Ark. - Dansk botanisk arkiv udgivet af dansk botanisk forening, Copenhagen

Darwiniana - Darwiniana; Revista del Instituto de Botánica Darwinion, Buenos Aires

Def. Gen. Pl. (ed. 3) - *Ludwig's* Definitiones Generum Plantarum olim in usum auditiorum collectæ nunc auctæ et emendatæ, Leipzig

Defin. Pl. - Definitiones Plantarum in usum auditorum collegit M. Christianus Gottlieb Ludwig, Leipzig

Delessert's Bibliogr. - Delessert's Bibliography, a collection of papers, manuscripts and illustration accumulated by Jean paul Benjamin Delessert but never published and were written and illustrated by various authors

Delic. Gallo-Belg. - Deliciæ Gallo-Belgicæ Silvestres, seu tractatus generalis plantarum gallo-belgicarum ad genera relatarum, Argentorati

Denkschr. Kaiserl. Akad. Wiss., Wien. Math.-Naturwiss. Kl. - Denkschriften der Kaiserlichen Akademie der Wissenschaften, Wien. Mathematisch-Naturwissenschaftliche Klasse, Vienna

De Nov. Fam. Expos. - De Nova Plantarum Families Exposition

De Orchid. Eur. - De Orchideis Europæis Annotationes, Paris

De Pollin. Orchid. - De pollinis Orchidearum genesi ac structura et de Orchideis in artem ac systema redigendis, Leipzig

De Re Bot. Tract. - De re botanica tractatus, in quo, praeter generalem methodum, et historiam plantarum, eae stirpes peculiariter recensentur, quæ in agro Bellunensi, et Fidentino vel sponte crescunt, vel arte excoluntur, Belluno

Descr. Pl. Cap. - Descriptiones Plantarum ex Capite Bonæ Spei, cum differentiis specificis, nominibus trivialibus et synonymis auctorum justis, Secundum systema sexuale, Stockholm

Deut. Bot. Herb.-Buch - Der deutsche Botaniker ... Erster Band. Das Herbarienbuch Repertorium Herbarii, sive Nomenclator generum Plantarum systematicus, synonymicas et alphabeticus, Dresden

Deutsch. Mag. Garten- Blumenk. - Deutsches Magazin für Garten- und Blumenkunde, Stuttgart

Dicc. Nombres Vulg. Pl. - Diccionstio de los diversos nombres vulgares de muchas plantas usuales ó notables del antiguo y nuevo mundo, Madrid

Dic. Etim. Orquid. Brasil - Dicionário etimológico das orquideas do Brasil, São Paulo

Dict. Bot. Prat. - Dictionnaire de Botanique Pratique, Paris

Dict. Class. Hist. Nat. - *Bory de Saint-Vincent's* Dictionnaire Classique d'Histoire Naturelle, Paris

Dict. Class. Sci. Nat. - Dictionnaire Classique des Sciences Naturelles: présentant la définition, l'analyse et l'histoire de tous les être qui composent les trois règnes ... résumant tous les faits présentés par les dictionnaires d'histoire naturelle, augmenté des nombreuses découvertes aquises depuis la publication de ces ouvrages, Bruxelles

Dict. Fl. Pl. - A Dictionary of the Flowering Plants and Ferns, Cambridge

Dict. Gen Names Seed Pl. - Dictionary of Generic Names of Seed Plants, New York City

Dict. Sci. Nat. - *Cuvier's* Dictionnaire des Sciences Naturelles, dans lequel traite méthodiquement des differens êtres de la nature ... suivi d'une biographie des plus célèbres naturalistes ..., Strasbourg & Paris

Dict. Univ. Hist. Nat. - *d'Orbigny's* Dictionnaire universal d'historie naturelle, Paris

Disionari - Disionari piemontèis, italian, latin e fransèis conpòst dal preive Casimiro Zalli, Carmagnola

Diss. Bot. & Zool. - Dissertatio brevis de principiis botanicorum et zoologorum: deque novo stabiliendo ntaurae rerum congruo: cum appendice aliquot generum Plantarum recens conditorum et in Virginia observatorum, Norimbergae

Edinburgh J. Bot. - Edinburgh Journal of Botany, Royal Botanic Garden, Edinburgh

Edinburgh Philos. J. - Edinburgh Philosophical Journal, Edinburgh

Edwards's Bot. Reg. - Edwards's Botanical Register, London

Elem. Bot. (Duchartre) - Elements de Botanique comprenant l'anatomie, l'organgraphie la physiologie des plantes, les familles naturelles et la géographie botanique, Paris

Elem. Bot. (Necker) - Elementa Botanica, genera genuina, species naturales omnium vegetabilium detectorum eorumque characteres diagnosticos ac peculiares exhibentia, secundum systema emologicum seu naturale, evulgata, Paris

Enchir. Bot. (Endlicher) - Enchiridion Botanicum exhibens classes et ordines Plantarum, accedit nomenclator generum ex officinalium vel usualium indicatio, Leipzig

Encycl. (Lamarck) - Encyclopédie méthodique. Botanique, Paris

Encycl. (Lamarck) Suppl. - Encyclopédie méthodique. Botanique ... Supplement, Paris

Encycl. Cult. Orchids - *Hawkes'* Encyclopaedia of Cultivated Orchids, an illustrated descriptive manual, London

Encycl. Pl. - *Loudon's* An encyclopaedia of plants: comprising the description, specific character, culture, history, application in the arts, and every other desirable particular respecting all the plants indigenous, cultivated in, or introduced to Britain, combining all the advantages of a Linnean and Jussieuean species plantarum, an historia plantarum, a grammar of botany, and a dictionary of botany and vegetable culture, London

Ensayo Geobot. Guin. Continent. Espan. - Ensayo geobotánico de la Guinea Continental Española, Madrid

Entwurf Anordn. Orch. - Entwurf einer natürlichen Anordnung der Orchideen, Heidelberg

Enum. (Fabricius) - Enumeratio Methodica plantarum Horti medici Helmstadiensis secundum Linnei et Heisteri systema digesta: stirpium rariorum vel nondum satis extricatarum descriptione subjuncta, Helmstedt

Enum. Hort. Berol. Alt. - Enumeratio Plantarum Horti Regii Berolinensis Altera, Berolini

Enum. Meth. Stirp. Helv. - Enumeratio methodica Stirpium Helvetiæ indigenarum, Göttingae

Enum. Phan. Born. - Enumeratio phanerogamarum bornearum, Formosa

Enum. Philipp. Fl. Pl. - An Enumeration of Philippine Flowering Plants, Manila

Enum. Pl. Hort. - Enumeratio Plantarum Horti Regi et agri Gottingensis aucta et emendata, Göttingen

Enum. Pl. Hort. Bot. Fluminensi - Enumeratio Plantarum in Horto Botanico Fluminensi Cultarum, Rio de Janeiro

Enum. Pl. Jap. - Enumeratio Plantarum in Japonia Sponte Crescentium hucusque rite cognitarum, Paris

Enum. Pl. Mus. Paris - Enumeration des Genres des Plantes Cultives au Muséum d'Histoire Naturelle de Paris, Paris

Enum. Pl. Transsilv. - Enumeratio Plantarum Transsilvaniæ exhibens: Stirpes Phanerogamas sponte crescentes atque frequentius cultas, Cryptogamas vasculares, Characeas, etiam Muscos Hepaticasque, Vindobonae

Enum. Pl. Zeyl. (Thwaites) - Enumeratio Plantarum Zeylaniæ: an enumeration of Ceylon plants, with descriptions of the new and little known genera and species, observations on their habitats, uses, native names, London

Enum. Pl. Vasc. - Enumeratio Plantarum Vascularium in insula inarime sponte provenientium vel oeconomico usu, Napoli

Etim. Orquidófilos - A Etimologia a serviço dos Orquidófilos, São Paulo

Etude Fl. - *Cariot's* Étude des Fleurs: Botanique élémentaire, Descriptive et Usuelle par Ludovic Chirat, Lyon

Etym.-Bot.-Handw.-Buch - Etymologisch-botanisches-Handwörterbuch: enthaltend die genaue Ableitung und Erklärung der Namen sämmtlicher botanischen Gattungen, Untergattungen und ihrer Synonym, Erlangen

Exot. (Clusius) - Exoticorum libri decem: quibus Animalium, Plantarum, Aromatum, alioramque peregrinorum Fructuum Historiæ describuntur

Exot. Fl. - Exotic Flora, containing figures and descriptions of new, rare or otherwise interesting Exotic Plants, Edinburgh & London

Expos. Fam. Nat. - Exposition des Familles Naturelles et de la germination des Plantes, Paris & Strasbourg

Fam. Pl. - Familles des Plantes, Paris

Farma. Mexicana - Nueva Farmacopea Mexicana de la sociedad farmacéutica de la México, Mexico City

Feddes Repert. - Feddes Repertorium: Zeitschrift für Botanische Taxonomie und Geobotanik, Weinheim

Field Guide Orchids - Field guide to Orchids of Britain and Europe, London

Field Guide Orchids Serr. Sao Jose - Field guide to the orchids of the Serra de Sao Jose: Guia de Campo das orquideas da Serra de Sao Jose

First Cat. Gard. Transylv. Univ. - First Catalogues and Circulars of the Botanical Garden of Transylvania University, Lexington, Kentucky

Fl. Alaska Yukon - Flora of Alaska and Yukon. Lund, Gleerup, Sweden

Fl. Analitica Fitogeogr. Estado São Paulo - Flora Analítica e Fitogeográfica do Estado de São Paulo, Sao Paulo

Fl. Angl. (Hudson) - Flora Anglica: exhibens Plantas per Regnum Britanniæ Sponte Crescentes, Distributas Secundum Systema Sexuale: cum Differentiis Specierum, Synonymis Auctorum, Nominibus Incolarum, Solo Locorum, Tempore Florendi, Officinalibus Pharmacopoerum. Editio Altera, Emendata et Aucta, London

Fl. Balearica - Flora Balearica, étude phytogéographique sur les íles Baléares, Montpellier

Fl. Belg. (Dumortier) - Florula belgica, operis majoris prodromus, Tournay

Fl. Belg. Foed. - Flora VII Provinciarum Belgii Foederati Indigena, Haarlem

Fl. Berol. (Schlechtendal) - Flora Berolinensis, Berolini

Fl. Bhutan - Flora of Bhutan: including a record of plants from Sikkim and Darjeeling, Edinburgh

Fl. Boëm. Cent. 1 - Flora Boëmica, inchoata, exhibens plantarum regni Boëmiæ indigenarum species, Centuria 1, Prague

Fl. Bombay - Flora of the Presidency of Bombay, London

Fl. Bor.-Amer. (Hooker) - Flora Boreali Americana, or the botany of the northern parts of British America: compiled principally from the plants collected by Dr. Richardson and Mr. Drummond on the late northern expeditions, under command of Capt. Sir J. Franklin, to which are added those of Mr. Douglas, from North-West of America, and of other naturalists, London

Fl. Brandenburg - Flora der Provinz Brandenburg, der Altmark und des Herzogthurns Magdeburg, Berlin

Fl. Bras. (Hoehne) - Flora Brasilica, São Paulo

Fl. Bras. (Martius) - Flora Brasiliensis; seu enumeratio Plantarum in Brasilia tam sua sponte quam accedente cultura provenientium, quas in itinere ... annis 1817-20 peracto collegit, partim descripsit / alias a Maximiliano Seren, Principe Widensi, Sellovio aliisque advectas addidit, communibus amicorum propriisque studiis secundum methodum naturalem dispositas et illustratas edidit C.F.P. de Martius

Fl. Brit. Ind. - The Flora of British India, London

Fl. Brit. W.I. (Grisebach) - Flora of the British West Indian Islands, London

Fl. Cab. - Floral Cabinet and Magazine of Exotic Botany, London

Fl. Cameroun - Flore du Cameroun, Paris: Museum national d'histoire naturelle - Orchidaceæ

Fl. Cap. (Harvey) - Flora Capensis; being a systematic description of the plants of the Cape Colony, Caffraria & Port Natal, Dublin

Fl. Cochinch. - Flora Cochinchinensis: sistens Plantas in regno Cochinchina nascentes: quibus accdeunt aliæ observatæ in Sinensi imperio, Africa Orientali, Indiæ que locis variis: dispositae secundum Systema Sexuale Linnaeanum, Berolini

Fl. Columb. (H. Karsten) - Florae Columbiae terraumque adjacentium specimina selecta in peregrinatione duodecim annorum observata delineavit et descripsit, Berolini

Fl. Coron. Herb. Hist. - Florum et Coronariarum odoratarumque nonnullarum Herbarum historia, Antverpiae

Fl. Dalmat. - Flora Dalmatica, sive enumeratio Stirpium Vascularium quas hactenus in Dalmatia lectas et sibi observatas, descripsit rariorumque iconibus illustravit, Leipzig

Fl. Deutschland - Flora von Deutschland, Gera-Untermhaus

Fl. Excurs. Aachen - Flora Excursoria des Regierungsbezirkes Aachen, sowie der angrenzenden Gebiete der Belgischen und Holländischen Provinz Limburg Phanerogamen und Gefässkryptogamen: Nebst Uebersicht der geognostischen, der oro- und hydrographis chen Verhältnisse dieses Florengebietes, Aachen

Fl. Francof. - Flora Francofurtana: methodo facili elaborata: accedunt cogitata de studio botanices methodice et quidem proprio marte addiscendae, terminorum technicorum nomenclator, et necessarii indices

Fl. Friburg. - Flora Friburgensis et regionum proxime adjacentium, Fribourg en Brisgau

Fl. Frisica - Flora Frisica, of Naamlijst en Kenmerken der Zigtbaar-Bloeijende Planten van de Provincie Friesland, Leeuwarden

Fl.-Gard. - The flower-garden; or, Breck's book of flowers; in which are described all the various hardy herbaceous perennials, annuals, shrubby plants, and evergreen trees, desirable for ornamental purposes, with directions for their cultivation, Boston

Fl. Germ. Excurs. - Flora Germanica Excursoria, Leipzig

Fl. Hautes-Pyrénées - Flore du Département des Hautes-Pyrénées, Plantes Vasculaires spontanées, Paris

Fl. Iene. - Flora Ienensis Henrici Bernhardi Ruppii ex posthumis auctoris schedis et propriis observationibus aucta et emendata accesserunt plantarum rariorum novæ icones, Ienae

Fl. Ind. Batav. - Flora Indiæ Batavæ, Supplementum Primum. Prodromus Floræ Sumatranæ, Amsterdam

Fl. Ital. (Parlatore) - Flora italiana; ossia, Descrizione delle piante che crescono spontanee o vegetano come tali in Italia e nelle isole ad essa aggaicenti; disposta secondo il metodo naturale, Firenze

Fl. Jamaica (Fawcett & Rendle) - Flora of Jamaica containing descriptions of the flowering plants known from the island, London

Fl. Jap. (Thunberg) - Flora Japonica sistens plantas insularum japonicarum Iaponicarvm secvndvm systema sexvale emendatvm redactas ad XX classes, ordines, genera et species cvm differentiis specificis, synonymis pavcis, descriptionibvs concinnis et XXXIX iconibvs adiectis, Leipzig

Fl. Javæ - *Blume & J.B. Fisher's* Floræ Javæ nec non Insularum Adjcentium, Bruxellis

Fl. Javæ Nov. Ser. - *Blume & J.B. Fisher's* Flora Javæ et Insularum Adjacentium Nova Series, Leiden

Fl. Jen. - *Ruppius'* Flora von Jenensis, sive enumeratio Plantarum tam sponte circa Jenam & in locis vicinis nascentium, quam in hortis obviarum, Jenae

Fl. Lapp. (Linnaeus) - Flora Lapponica exhibens plantas per Lapponiam crescentes, secundum systema sexuale collectas in itinere impensis Soc. reg. litter. et scient, Sveciæ, Amsterdam

Fl. Madagasc. - Flore de Madagascar et des Comores, Tananarive

Fl. Mauritius - Flora of Mauritius and the Seychelles, Lehre

Fl. Miami - Flora of Miami: being descriptions of the seed-plants growing naturally on the Everglade keys and in the adjacent Everglades, southern peninsular Florida, New York

Fl. Ned. Ind. - Flora van Nederlandsch Indië, or alternate title: Flora Indiæ Batavæ, Amsterdam

Fl. New Zealand - Flora of New Zealand, Wellington

Fl. Nieder-Osterreich - Flora von Nieder-Österreich, Eine Aufzählung und Beschreibung der im Erzherzogthume Oesterreich unter der Enns wild wachsenden, oder im Grossen gebauten Gefässpflanzen, nebst einer pflanzengengrafischen Schilderung dieses Landes, Wein

Fl. Nordostdeut. Flachl. - Flora des Nordostdeutschen Flachlandes (ausser Ostpreussen), Berlin

Fl. Nouvelle Caledonie & Depend. - Flore de la Nouvelle-Calédonie et Dépendances, Orchidacées, Paris

Fl. Nov.-Zel. - Flora Novæ-Zelandiæ, London

Flora - Flora; oder, (allgemeine) botanische Zeitung. Regensburg & Jena

Floric. Cab. & Florist's Mag. - Floricultural Cabinet, and Florist's Magazine, London

Florist Hort. J. - Florist and Horticultural Journal, Philadelphia

Flowers - Flowers: Their origin, Shapes, Perfumes, and Colours, London

Fl. Pedem. - Flora Pedemontana, sive enumeratio methodica stirpium indigenarum Pedemontii, Augustae Taurinorum [Turin]

Fl. Peruv. Prodr. - Flora Peruvianæ, et Chilensis Prodromus, sive Novorum generum plantarum peruvianarum, et chilensium descriptiones, et icones: descripciones y láminas de los nuevos géneros de plantas de la flore del Perú y Chile, Madrid

Fl. Prussica - Flora Prussica, sive Plantæ in regno Prussiæ sponte nascentes; Qvarum Catalogum & Nomina Johannes Loeselius ... Olim disseruit, Nunc additis nitidissimis Iconibus Rariorum, partim ab aliis nondum delineatarum plerarumq[ue] Prussiæ propriarum & inqvilinarum Plantarum, Earundemque accuratâ descriptione, nec non Adjectis Synonymiis Veterum Botanicorum, interspersisq[ue] Observationibus Historico-Philologico-Criticis & Medico-Practicis noviter efflorescentes.

Fl. Pyren. (Bubani) - Flora Pyrenaea per ordines naturales gradatim digesta

Fl. Reunion - Flore de l'Île de la Rèunion, (phanérogames, cryptogames, vasculaires, muscinées) avec l'indication des propriétés économiques & industrielles des plantes, Paris

Fl. Saxon. - Flora Saxonica: Die Flora von Sachsen, ein botanisches Excursionsbuch. Nebst Schlüssel zum erleichterten Bestimmen der Gattungen nach Linnee's Sexualsystem und deutschem und lateinischem Register, Dresden & Leipzig

Fl. Serres Jard. Angleterre - Flore des Serres et Jardins de l'Angleterre, reproduction complète des ouvrages périodiques paraissant sous les titres de Botanical magazine et de Botanical register et British flower garden réunis, présentant toutes les plantes récemment introduites en Europe, Bruxelles

Fl. Serres Jard. Eur. - Flore des Serres et des Jardins de l'Europe, Gand

Fl. S.E. U.S. - Flora of Southeastern United States: being descriptions of the seed-plants, ferns and fern-allies growing naturally in North Carolina, South Carolina, Georgia, Florida, Tennessee, Alabama, Mississippi, Arkansas, Louisiana and the Indian territory and in Oklahoma and Texas east of the one-hundredth meridian, New York

Fl. Sibir. (J.G. Gmelin) - Flora Sibirica, sive historia Plantarum Sibiriæ, St. Petersburg

Fl. Suec. (Wahlenberg) - Flora Svecica, enumerans Plantas Sveciæ indigenas cum synopsi classium ordinumque, characteribus generum, differentiis specierum, synonymis citationibusque selectis, locis regionibusque natalibus, descriptionibus habitualibus nomina incolarum et qualitates plantarum illustrantibus, Upsaliæ

Fl. Taiwan - Flora Taiwan, Taipei

Fl. Tellur. - Flora Telluriana, Philadelphia

Fl. Trop. Afr. - *Dyer's* Flora of Tropical Africa, London

Fl. Trop. E. Africa - Flora of Tropical East Africa, Rotterdam

Fl. URSS - *Komarov's* Flora Unionis Rerumpublicarum Sovieticarum Socialisticarum, Leningrad

Fl. Venez. - Flora de Venezuela, Caracas

Fl. Virgin. - Flora Virginica exhibens plantas quas V.J. Clayton in Virginia observavit atque collegit / Easdem methodo sexuali disposuit & minus cognitas descripsit J.F. Gronovius, Lugduni Batavorum

Fl. Vit. - *Seemann's* Flora Vitiensis: a description of the Plants of the ... Fiji Islands, London

Fl. Vit. Nova - Flora Vitiensis Nova: a new flora of Fiji, Lawaii, Hawaii

Fl. World Gard. Guide - The Floral World and Garden Guide, London

Fl. W. Trop. Afr. - *Hutchinson's* Flora of West Tropical Africa: the British west African territories, Liberia, the French and Portuguese territories south of latitude l8 N. to Lake Chad, and Fernando Po, London

Fl. Zhejiang - Flora of Zhejiang: Vol. 7, Typhaceae - Orchidaceae, Hangzhou

Folia Geobot. Phytotax. - Folia Geobotanica et Phytotaxonomica, Praha

Fol. Orchid. - Folia Orchidacea: an enumeration of the known species of orchids, London

Förh. Skand. Naturf. Möte - Förhandlingar vid de Skandinaviske Naturforskeres Möte, Goteborg

Fortsetz. Allg. Teutsch. Gart.-Mag. - Fortsetzung des Allgemeinen Teutschen Garten-Magazins oder gemeinnützige Beiträge für alle Theile des praktischen Gartenwesens, Weimar

Fragm. (Mueller) - Fragmenta Phytographiæ Australiæ, Melbourne

Fragm. Florist. Geobot. - Fragmenta floristica et geobotanica, Crakow

Fragm. Pl. Filip. - Fragmentos de algunas Plantas de Filipinas, no incluidas en la Flora de las Islas, Manila

Fragm. Syn. Pl. - Fragmentum Synopseos Plantarum Phanerogamum ab Auctore Annis 1827 ad 1829 in Chile lectarum, Leipzig

Fundamentals Orchid Biol. - Fundamentals of Orchid Biology, New York

Gartenflora - Gartenflora: Monatschrift für deutsche und schweizerische Garten und Blumenkunde Herausgegeben von E. Regel, Erlangen

Gart.-Zeitung (Berlin) - Garten-Zeitung. Monatsscchrift für Gartner und Garten-Freunde, Berlin

Gaz. - Opera historiam naturalem spectantia; or, Gazophylacium, London

Gazetteer Bombay - Gazetteer of the Bombay Presidency, Bombay

Gen. Coelogyne - The genus Coelogyne: a synopsis, Kota Kinabalu

Gen. Hist. Things New Spain - A General History of the Things of New Spain or Florentine Codex (also known as the Historia General de las Cosas de la Nueva Espa

Gen. N. Amer. Pl. (Nuttall) - The Genera of North American Plants and a catalogue of the species, to the year 1817, Philadelphia

Gen. Orchid. - Genera Orchidacearum, Oxford

Gen. Pl. (Bentham & Hooker f.) - Genera Plantarum ad exemplaria imprimis in Herbariis Kewensibus servata definita, London

Gen. Pl. (Endlicher) - Genera plantarum secundum ordines naturales disposita, Paris

Gen. Pl. (Jussieu) - Genera plantarum secundum ordines naturales disposita, juxta methodum in horto regio Parisiensi exaratum, Paris

Gen. Pl. (Linnaeus) - Genera Plantarum eorumque characteres naturales secundum numerum, figuram, situm, et proportionum omnium fructificationis partium, Holmiae

Gen. Pl. (Sprengel) - Genera Plantarum, Gottingae

Gen. Pl., Suppl. (Endlicher) - Genera plantarum secundum ordines naturales disposita, includes Supplementum, Vienna

Gen. S. Afr. Pl. - The Genera of South African plants, arranged according to the natural system, Cape Town

Gen. Siphon. - Genera Siphonogamarum ad Systema Englerianum, Leipzig

Gen. Sp. Orchid. - Genera et Species Orchidearum Novarum quas Collecit, Descripsit et Iconibus Illustravit, Sebastianopolis

Gen. Sp. Orchid. Asclep. - Genera et Species Orchidearum et Asclepiadearum quas in itinere per insulam Java jussu et auspiciis Guilielmi I, belgarum regis augustissimi, Gandavi
NOTE: See *Fl. Males. Bull.* 10(4): 333. (1991) for current parts, publication dates and genera.

Gen. Sp. Orchid. Pl. - The Genera and Species of Orchidaceous Plants, London

Genus - Genus: International Journal of Invertebrate Taxonomy, Wroclaw

Geogr. Estado Antioquia - Geografía general y compendio histórico del estado de Antioquia en Colombia, Paris

Ges. Naturf. Freunde Berlin Mag. Neuesten Entdeck. Gesammten Naturk. - Gesellschaft Naturforschender Freunde zu Berlin Magazin für die Neuesten Entdeckungen in der Gesammten Naturkunde, Berlin

Giorn. Sci. Sicilia - Giornale di Scienze, Letteratura ed Arti per la Sicilia, Roma

Guide Orchids Sikkim - A Guide to the Orchids of Sikkim: being a guide to the identification of those species of orchids found between the Terai and the northern frontier of independent Sikkim including the Chumbi Valley and British Bhutan, Calcutta

Gard. Bull. Singapore - Gardens' bulletin, Singapore

Gard. Bull. Straits Settlem. - Gardens' bulletin, Straits Settlements

Gard. Chron. - The Gardeners' Chronicle & Agricultural Gazette

Gard. Dict. Abr. - The Gardeners Dictionary, Abridged. London

Gard. Mag. & Reg. Rural Domest. Improv. - Gardener's Magazine and Register of Rural and Domestic Improvement, London

Gartenbeobachter - Gartenbeobachter, Nürnberg

Hamburger Garten-Blumenzeitung - Hamburger Garten- und Blumenzeitung. Eine Zeitschrift für Garten- un Blumenfreunde, für Kunst- und Handelsgärtner, Hamburg

Handb. Bot. (Breslau) - Handbuch der Botanik, Breslau

Handb. Bot. (Spenner) - Handbuch der angewandten Botanik oder Praktische Anleitung zur Kenntniss der medizinisch, technisch und ökonomisch gebräuchlichen Gewächse Teutschlands und der Schweiz, Freiburg

Handb. Fl. Ceylon - *Trimen's* A Handbook to the Flora of Ceylon, Containing Descriptions of all the Species of Flowering Plants Indigenous to the Island, and Notes on Their History, Distribution, and Uses, London

Handb. Gewachsk. - *Mössler's* Handbuch der Gewächskunde, welches, mit Ausnahme der vier und zwanzigsten Klasse des Linneischen Systems, die wilden Gewächse Deutschlands enthält, und von den ausländischen diejenigen, welche dem Arzt und Apotheker, dem Färber, Gärtner, und Landwirth Nutzen bringen, nebst einer kurzen Einleitung in die Gewächskunde und einem erklärende Verzeichnisse der lateinischen Ausdrücke, Altona

Handb. Indian Fl. - Hand-book of the Indian Flora; being a guide to all the flowering plants hitherto described as indigenous to the continent of India, London

Handb. Orchid.-Namen - Handbuch der Orchideen-Namen: Dictionary of orchid names, Stuttgart

Handb. Palaeont., Paleophyt. - Handbuch der Palaeontologie... ii. Abtheilung Paleophytologie, München und Leipzig

Handb. Singapore - Handbook to Singapore, with map, and a plan of the botanical gardens, Singapore

Handb. Skand. Fl. - Handbok i Skandinaviens Flora: innefattande sveriges och norges växter, till och med mossorna, Stockholm

Handb. Syst. Bot. - Handbuch der Systematischen Botanik, Leipzig

Handbuch (Link) - Handbuch zur Erkennung der nutzbarsten und am häufigsten vorkommenden Gewächse, Berlin

Hand-List Herb. Pl. - Hand-List of Herbaceous Plants cultivated in the Royal Botanic Gardens, London

Harvard Pap. Bot. - Harvard Papers in Botany, Cambridge

Heidelberger Jahrb. Lit. - Heidelberger Jahrbücher der Literatur, Heidelberg

Herb. (Brunfels) - Herbarum vivæ eicones ad nature imitationem, summa cum diligentia & artificio effigiatæ, una cum effectibus earundem, in gratiam ueteris illius, & iamam renascentis herbariæ medicinæ, Argentorati

Herb. Amboin. (Rumphius) - Herbarium Amboinense, Plurimas Complectens Arbores, Frutices, Herbas, Plantas Terrestres & Aquaticas, quae in Amboina, et Adjacentibus Reperiuntur Insulis, Adcuratissime Descriptas Juxta Earum Formas, cum Diversis Denominationibus, Cutlura, Usu, ac Virtutibus, Amsterdam

Herbarius - [Herbarius][R]ogatu plurimo[rum] inopu[m] num[m]o[rum] egentiu[m] appotecas refuta[n]tiu[m] occasione illa, q[uia] necessaria ibide[m] ad corp[us] egru[m] specta[n]tia su[n]t cara simplicia et composita -Title from first sentence of book, first character(s) of which are unknown.

Herb. Gen. Hist. Pl. - The herball or Generall historie of plantes, London

Herb. Raf. - Herbarium Rafinesquianum; or Botanical Collections of C.S. Rafinesque, Philadelphia

Hist. Acad. Roy. Sci. Mém. Math. Phys. (Paris) - Histoire de l'académie royale des sciences. Avec les mémoires de mathématique & de physique, Paris

Hist. Br. Guiana - The History of British Guiana, London

Hist. County Berkshire, Mass. - A History of the County of Berkshire, Massachusetts; in two parts, Pittsfield

Hist. Fis. Cuba, Bot. - *Sagra's* Historia Fisica Politica y Natural de la Isla de Cuba, Botany, Paris

Hist. Gen. Pl. - Historia generalis plantarum, in libros XVIII per certas classes artificiose digesta: hæc plusquam mille imaginibus plantarum locupletior superioribus, omnes propemodum quæ ab antiquis scriptoribus, Græcis, Latinis, Arabibus nominantur: necnon eas quæ in Orientis atque Occidentis partibus, ante seculum nostrum incognitis, repertæ fuerunt, tibi exhibit, Lugduni

Hist. Nat. - Historia naturalis or Naturalis Historiæ

Hist. Nat. Veg. (Spach) - Histoire Naturelle des Végétaux: phanérogames, Paris

Hist. Orchid. - Histoire Particulière des Plantes Orchidées recueillies sur les trois iles australes d'Afrique, de France, de Bourdon et de Madagascar, Paris

Hist. Phys. Pl. Europ. - Histoire Physiologique des Plantes d'Europe ou Exposition des Phénomènes qu'elles présentent dands les diverses périodes de leur développement, Paris

Hist. Pl. - Histoire des Plantes. Petites Nouvelles du Jardin Botanique Genève

Hist. Pl. (Bauhin) - Historia plantarum uniuersalis, noua, et absolutissima, cum consensu et dissensu circa eas, Yverdon

Hist. Pl. (Dodoens) - Histoire des plantes, en laquelle est contenue la description entiere des herbes, c'est à dire, leurs especes, forme, noms, temperament, vertus & operations: non seulement de celles qui croissent en ce païs, mais aussi des autres estrangeres qui viennent en usage de medecine, Anvers

Hist. Pl. (Ray) - Historia Plantarum, species hactenus editas aliasque insuper multas noviter inventas et descriptas complectens: in qua agitur primò de plantis in genere, earumque partibus, accidentibus & differentiis: deinde genera omnia tum summa tum subalterna ad species usque infimas, notis suis certis & characteristicis definita, methodo naturæ vestigiis insistente disponuntur: species singulæ accurate describuntur, obscura illustrantur, omissa supplentur, superflua resecantur, synonyma necessaria adjiciuntur: vires denique & usus recepti compendiò traduntur, London

Hist. Pl. Nueva España - Historia de las Plantas de la Nueva España, Valencia

Hist. Pl. Rar. - Historia Plantarum rariorum ob præstantiam denuo edita studio atque opera J. D. Meyeri pictoris. - J. Martyns Beschreibung seltener Pflanzen, Nürnberg

Hist. Settlem. Indian - History of the settlement and Indian wars of Tazewell County, Virginia with a map, statistical tables, and illustrations, Cincinnati, Ohio

Hist. Stirp. (Fuchs) - De Historia Stirpium Commentarii Insignes: adiectis earundem viuis, & ad naturae imitationé artificosè expressis imaginibus / Leonharto Fuchsio medico; hac nostra aetate clarissimo, autore. Accessit ijs, succincta admodum vocum quarundam subobscurarum in hoc opere passim occurrentium explanatio, Basel

Hist. Stirp. Comm. - De Historia Stirpium Commentarii insignes, Lyon

Hist. Stirp. Helv. - Historia Stirpium Indigenarum Helvetiae Inchoata, Bernae

Hooker's Icon. Pl. - *Hooker's* Icones Plantarum; or Figures, with brief Descriptive Characters and Remarks of New or Rare Plants, London

Hooker's J. Bot. Kew Gard. Misc. - *Hooker's* Journal of Botany and Kew Garden Miscellany, London

Hort. Brit. (Loudon) - *Loudon's* Hortus britannicus: a catalogue of all the plants indigenous, cultivated in, or introduced to Britain. Part I. The Linnaean arrangement ... Part II. The Jussieuean arrangement, London

Hort. Brit. (Sweet) - Hortus Britannicus: or, a catalogue of Plants cultivated in the gardens of Great Britain, arranged according to the natural system, with the generic and specific names, English names, accentuation, derivation of generic names ... references to the best figures, the most useful synonymes, the Linnean class and order to which each genus belongs, London

Hort. Cliff. - Hortus Cliffortianus, Amsterdam

Hort. Donat. - *Planchon's* Hortus Donatensis: Catalogue des Plantes Cultivées dans le Serres de S. Ex. le Prince A. Démidoff à San Donato, près Florence, Paris

Hort. Eystet. - Hortus Eystettensis, sive, Diligens et accurata omnium plantarum, florum, stirpium, ex variis orbis terræ partibus, singulari studio collectarum, quæ in celeberrimis viridiariis arcem episcopalem ibidem cingentibus, hoc tempore conspiciuntur delineatio et ad vivum repraesentatio, Nürnberg

Hort. Franc. - L'Horticulteurs Français: Journal des Amateurs et des Intérets Horticoles, Paris

Hort. & J. Rural Art Rural Taste - Horticulturist and Journal of Rural Art and Rural Taste, Philadelphia

Hort. Malab. - Hortus Indicus Malabaricus, continens regni Malabarici apud Indos celeberimi omnis generis Plantas rariores, Latinis, Malabaricis, Arabicis & Bramanum characteribus nominibusque expressas, Amsterdam

Hort. Praticien - L'Horticulteur Praticien, Revue de l'horticulture Française et Étangére, Paris

Hort. Reg. - The Horticultural Register, London

Hort. Spaarn-Berg. - Hortis Spaarn-Bergensis, Enumeratio Stirpium quae, in Villa Spaarn-Berg prope Harlemum, Amsterdam

Hort. Suburb. Calcutt. - Hortus Suburbanus Calcuttensis: A catalogue of the plants which have been cultivated in the Hon. East India Company's botanical garden, Calcutta and in the Serampore Botanical Garden, generally known as Dr. Carey's Garden, Calcutta

Hort. Thenensis - Hortus thenensis: Index des espèces botaniques cultivées dans les collections de m. van den Bossche, ministre résident, à Tirlemont, Bruxelles

Hort. Universel - L'Horticulteur Universel, Journal Général des Jardiniers et Amateurs, Paris

Hortus Kew. - *Aiton's* Hortus Kewensis; or, A catalogue of the plants cultivated in the royal botanic garden at Kew, London

Hortus Ripul. - Hortus Ripulensis, seu enumeratio Plantarum quæ Ripulis coluntur, Turin

Icon. Bogor. - Icones Bogorienses, Leiden

Icon. Bot. Index - Iconum botanicarum index locupletissimus: an alphabetical register of upwards of eighty-six thousand representations of phanerogamic plants and ferns compiled from botanical and horticultural publications of the XVIIIth and XIXth centuries for scientific and practical use, Berlin

Iconogr. Bot. Pl. Crit. - Iconographia Botanica seu Plantæ Criticæ: Icones plantarum rariorum et minus rite cognitarum, indigenarum exoticarumque, iconographia et supplementum, imprimis ad opera Willdenowii, Schkuhrii, Personii, Roemeri et Schultesii, delineatae, et cum commentario succincto editae, Leipzig

Iconogr. Orchid. Europe - Iconographie des Orchidees d'Europe et du Bassin Mediterraneen, Paris

Icon. Orchid. - Icones Orchidacearum, México D.F.

Icon. Orchid. Brasil. - Icones Orchidacearum Brasilienses, São Paulo

Icon. Pl. Asiat. - Icones Plantarum Asiaticarum, Calcutta

Icon. Pl. Fl. Hexapet. (Rivinus) - Icones plantarum quæ sunt flore irregulari hexapetalæ, Leipzig

Icon. Pl. Formosan. - Icones Plantarum Formosanarum nec non et Contributiones ad Floram Formosanam: or, Icones of the plants of Formosa, and materials for a flora of the island, based on a study of the collections of the Botanical survey of the Government of Formosa, Taihoku

Icon. Pl. Formosan. Suppl. - Icones Plantarum Formosanarum nec non et Contributiones ad Floram Formosanam. Supplementa, Taihoku

Icon. Pl. Ind. Orient. (Wight) - Icones Plantarum Indiæ Orientalis or figures of Indian plants, Madras

Icon. Pl. Rar. (Jacquin) - Icones Plantarum rariorum horti caesarei Schoenbrunnensis descriptiones et icones, Vienna

Icon. Pl. Rar. (Link) - Icones Plantarum rariorum Horti Regii Botanici Berolinensis cum descriptionibus et colendi ratione, Berlin

Icon. Pl. Trop. - Icones Plantarum Tropicarum, St. Louis & Sarasota

Icon. Stirp. - Icones stirpium, seu plantarum tam exoticarum, quam

indigenarum, in gratiam rei herbariæ studiosorum in duas partes digestæ, cum septem linguarum indicibus, ad diversarum nationum usum, Antwerp

Identif. Guide Vietnamese Orchids - Identification Guide to Vietnamese Orchids (Opredelitel' orkhidnykh V'etnama), St. Petersburg

Igansai-ranbin - Igansai-ranbin

Ill. Bot. - Illustrierte populäre Botanik, Gemeinfassliche Auleitung zum Studium der Pflanze und des Pflanzenreichs, Leipzig

Ill. Fl. Japan - An Illustrated Flora of Japan with the cultivated and naturalized plants, Tokyo

Ill. Hort. - L'Illustration horticole; journal spécial des serres et des jardins, choix raisonné des plantes les pus intéressantes sous le rapport ornemental, Ghent and Brussels

Ill. Orch. Pl. (Bauer & Lindley) - Illustrations of Orchidaceous Plants with notes and prefatory remarks by John Lindley, London

Ill. Pl. Taiwan - Colored Illustration of Plants of Taiwan

Index Gen. Phan. - Index Generum Phanerogamorum usque ad finem anni 1887 promulgatorum, Bruxellis

Index Kew. - Index Kewensis Plantarum Phanerogamarum; an enumeration of the genera & species of flowering plants from the time of Linnaeus to ..., Oxford

Index Raf. - Index Rafinesquianus; the plant names published by C.S. Rafinesque with reductions, and a consideration of his methods, objectives and attainments, Jamaica Plain

Index Seminum Hort. Bot. Berol. - Index Seminum in Horto Botanico Berolinensi Anno 1854 Collectorum ..., Berlin

Index Seminum Hort. Petrop. - Index Seminum, quæ Hortus Botanicus Imperialis Petropolitanus pro Mutua Commutatione Offert. Accedunt Animadversiones Botanicae Nonnullæ, St. Petersburg

Indian Forester - Indian Forester, Allahabad

Indian Nectar - The Indian nectar, or, A discourse concerning chocolate the nature of cacao-nut and the other ingredients of that composition is examined and stated according to the judgment and experience of the Indian and Spanish writers ... its effects as to its alimental and venereal quality as well as medicinal (especially in hypochondrial melancholy) are fully debated: together with a spagyrical analysis of the cacao-nut, performed by that excellent chymist Monsieur le Febure, chymist to His Majesty, London

Inst. Rei Herb. - *Tournefort's* Institutiones Rei Herbariæ; Corollarium ... in quo Plantæ ... in orientalibus regionibus observatæ recensentur, Paris

Int. J. Pl. Sci. - International Journal of Plant Sciences, Chicago

Intr. Nat. Syst. Bot. - An Introduction to the Natural System of Botany: or, A systematic view of the organisation, natural affinities, and geographical distribution, of the whole vegetable kingdom: together with the uses of the most important species in medicine, the arts, and rural or domestic economy, London

Intr. Orchids - Introduction to Orchids with illustrations and descriptions of 150 South Indian orchids, Trivandrum

Isis (Oken) - Isis von Oken, Jena

Ist. Bot. - Istituzioni Botaniche del dottore Ottaviano Targioni Tozzetti, Firenze

Itin. Pl. Khasyah Mts. - Itinerary Notes of Plants Collected in the Khasyah and Bootan Mountains, Calcutta

Jac. Pet. Opera - *Jacobi Petiveri's* Opera, historiam naturalem spectantia; or Gazophylacium, London

Jahrb. Lit. - Jahrbücher der Literatur, Wien

Jahresber. Naturwiss. Vereins Wuppertal - Jahresbericht des Naturwissenschaftlichen Vereins in Wuppertal, Wuppertal

Jard. Fleur. - Jardin Fleuriste, Journal General des Progres et des Interets Horticoles et Botaniques, Ghent

J. Arnold Arbor. - Journal of the Arnold Arboretum, Cambridge

J. Asiat. Soc. Bengal, Pt. 2, Nat. Hist. - Journal of the Asiatic Society of Bengal - Part 2, Natural History, Calcutta

J. Bombay Nat. Hist. Soc. - The Journal of the Bombay Natural History Society, Bombay

J. Bot. - Journal of Botany, British and Foreign, London

J. Bot. (Desvaux) - Journal de Botanique, Redige par une Société di Botanistes, Paris

J. Bot. (Hooker) - Journal of Botany, (Being a Second Series of the Botanical Miscellany), Containing Figures and Descriptions ..., London NOTE: J. Bot. (Hooker) was published in four different series (titles) from 1830-1857: first was the *Botanical Miscellany* (first series) 1830-1833 (3 volumes); second was the *Journal of Botany* (second series) 1834-1842 (4 volumes); third was the *London Journal of Botany* 1842-48 (7 volumes); and finally *Hooker's Journal of Botany* 1849-1857 (7 volumes); but all these volumes are BPH listed under one title

J. Bot. (Schrader) - Journal für die Botanik, Göttingen

J. Econ. Taxon. Bot. - Journal of Economic and Taxonomic Botany, Jodhpur

J. Educ. Upper Canada - Journal of Education for Upper Canada, Toronto

J. Gener. Litter. - Journal général de la littérature étrangère, ou, Indicateur bibliographique et raisonné des livres nouveaux en tous genres, cartes géographiques, gravures et oueuvres de musique qui paraissent dans les divers pays étrangers a la France, Paris

J. Geobot. - Journal of Geobotany. [Hokuriku no shokubutsu no kai], Kanazawa

J. Hort. Cottage Gard. - The Journal of Horticulture, Cottage Gardener and Country Gentleman; A journal of horticulture, rural and domestic economy, botany and natural history, London

J. Hort. Prat. Belgique - Journal d'Horticulture Pratique de le Belgique, Brussels

J. Hort. Soc. London - Journal of the Horticultural Society of London

J. Indian Bot. Soc. - Journal of the Indian Botanical Society, Madras

J. Jap. Bot. - Journal of Japanese Botany (Shokubutsu Kenkyu Zasshi), Tokyo

J. Linn. Soc., Bot. - Journal of the Linnean Society, Botany, London

J. Nat. Hist. Soc. Siam - Journal of the Natural History Society of Siam, Bangkok

J. Orchideenfr. - Journal für den Orchideenfreund, Göttingen

Jorn. Sci. Math. Phys. Nat. - Jornal de Sciencias Mathematica, Physicas e Naturaes, Lisbon

J. Phys. Chim. Hist. Nat. Arts - Journal de Physique, de Chimie, d'Histoire Naturelle et des Arts, Paris

J. Proc. Linn. Soc., Bot. - Journal of the Proceedings of the Linnean Society, Botany, London

J. Proc. Roy. Soc. New South Wales - Journal of the Proceedings of the Royal Society of New South Wales, Sydney

J. Roy. Hort. Soc. - Journal of the Royal Horticultural Society, London

J. Roy. Soc. Western Australia - Journal of the Royal Society of Western Australia, Perth, W.A.

J. Soc. Centr. Hort. France - Journal de la Société Centrale d'Horticulture de France, Paris

J. Soc. Hort. Seine-et-Oise - Journal de la Société d'Horticulture de Seine-et-oise, Versailles

J. Soc. Trop. Agric. - Journal of the Society of Tropical Agriculture, (Nettai Nogakkai shi), Taihoku

J. Straits Branch Roy. Asiat. Soc. - Journal of the Straits Branch of the Royal Asiatic Society, Singapore

Just's Bot. Jahresber. - *Just's* Botanischer Jahresbericht. Systematisch geordnetes repertorium der botanischen Literatur aller Länder, Berlin

Kew Bull. - Kew Bulletin, Kew, London

Kirkia - Kirkia: The Zimbabwe journal of botany, Hararé

Komarovia - Komarovia, St. Petersburg

Kongl. Svenska Vetensk. Acad. Handl. - Kongl. Svenska Vetenskaps Academiens Handlingar, Stockholm

Kongl. Vetensk. Acad. Nya Handl. - Kongl[iga] Vetenskaps Academiens Nya Handlingar, Stockholm

Kultuur Orchid. - De Kultuur der Orchideën: behelzende inlichtingen betreffende hare inzameling, verzending en kweeking, met eene beschri jvende lijst van ongeveer 550 soorten en verscheidenheden, Te Leyden

Landb. Ind. Archipel - De landbouw in den Indischen Archipel, s'Gravenhage

Land Bolivar - The Land of Bolivar or War, Pace and Adventure in the Republic of Venezuela, London

Lankesteriana - Lankesteriana: la revista cientifica del Jardin Botanico Lankester, Universidad de Costa Rica, Cartago

Lasianthera - Lasianthera: The scientific journal for the orchidaceæ of Papua New Guinea, Boroko

Lex. Gen. Phan. - *Post & Kuntze's* Lexicon Generum Phanerogamarum in de ab anno MDCCXXXVII cum Nomenclatura Legitima Internaionali Simul Scientifica Auctore Tom von Post. Opus Revisum et Auctum ab Otto Kuntze, Uppsala

Lex. Gen. Phan. Prosp. - Lexikon Generum Phanerogamarum in de ab Anno mdccxxxvii ... Prospectus

Liliac. (Redouté) - Les Liliacées, Paris

Lilies, The - The Lilies, Cologne

Lilloa - Lilloa: Instituto Miguel Lillo, Tucumán

Lindenia - Lindenia: Iconographie des Orchidées, Ghent & Brussels

Lindleyana - Lindleyana: Scientific Journal of the American Orchid Society, West Palm Beach/ Delray Beach

Lin. Fl. Manshur. - Lineamenta Floræ Manshuricæ or enumeration of the spontaneous vascular plants hitherto known from Manchuria (northeastern China) together with their synonymy and distribution, Hsinking

Linnaea - Linnaea: Ein Journal für die Botanik in ihrem ganzen Umfange, Berlin

Livre Orchid. - *Kerchove's* Le Livr-e des Orchidées, Gand,

Lloydia - Lloydia: a quarterly journal of biological science, Cincinnati

London J. Bot. - London Journal of Botany, London

Mag. Nat. Hist. & J. Zool. - Magazine of Natural History, and Journal of Zoology, Botany, Mineralogy, Geology, and Meteorology, London

Mag. Zool. Bot. - Magazine of Zoology and Botany, Edinburgh

Malayan Nat. J. - Malayan Nature Journal, Kuala Lumpur

Malay. Penins. - The Malayan peninsula: embracing its history, manners and customs of the inhabitants, politics, natural history, &c. from its earliest records, Madras

Man. Bot. - *Eaton's* Manual of Botany for the Northern and Middle States, Albany

Man. Dict. Fl. Pl. - *Willis'* A Manual and Dictionary of the Flowering Plants and Ferns, Cambridge

Man. Fl. N. States (Britton) - Manual of the Flora of the northern States and Canada, New York

Man. New Zealand Fl. - Manual of the New Zealand Flora, Wellington

Mant. Aromat. - *Gulielmus Piso's* Mantissa Aromatica; sive de Aromatum cardinalibus quatuor, et Plantis aliquot indicis in medicinam receptis, relatio nova, Amsterdam

Mant. Pl. Altera - Mantissa Plantarum Altera. Generum editionis VI & specierum editionis II. Holmiae, Stockholm

Man. Vasc. Pl. Yangtze Valley - Manual of vascular plants of the Lower Yangtze valley, China, Corvallis, Oregon

Maori-Polynesian Comp. Dict. - The Maori-Polynesian Comparative Dictionary, Wellington

Mat. Fl. Malay. Penins. - Materials for a Flora of the Malayan Peninsula, Singapore

Med. Pflanzen - Medizinal-Pflanzen in naturgetreuen abbildungen mit kurz erläuterndem texte. Atlas zur pharmacopoea germanica, austriaca, belgica, danica, helvetica, hungarica, rossica, suecica, neerlandica, British p harmacopoeia, zum Codex medicamentarius, sowie zur Pharmacopoeia of the United States of America, Gera-Untermhaus

Med. Repos. - *Mitchill & Miller's* Medical Repository and Review of American Publications on Medicine, Surgery, and the Auxiliary Branches of Philosophy, New York

Mem. Acad. Ci. Lisboa, Cl. Sci. - Memórias da Academia das Ciencias de Lisboa. Classe de Sciencias Mathematicas, Physicas e Naturaes, Lisbon

Mem. Acad. Real Sci. Lisboa, 2 Cl. Sci. Moraes - Memorias da Academia Real das Sciencias de Lisboa. Segunda Classe de Sciencias Moraes, politicas e bellas lettras, Lisbon

Mém. Acad. Roy. Sci. Belgique - Mémoires de l'Académie Royale des Sciences, Lettres et beaux Arts de Belgique, Bruxelles

Mém. Acad. Sci. Toulouse - Mémoires de l'Académie des Sciences, Inscriptions et Belles-Lettres de Toulouse

Mem. Fac. Sci. Taihoku Imp. Univ. - Memoirs of the Faculty of Science and Agriculture, Taihoku Imperial University

Mém. Herb. Boissier - Mémoires de l'Herbier Boissier suite au Bulletin de l'Herbier Boissier, Genéve

Mém. Mus. Hist. Nat. - Mémoires du Museum d'Histoire Naturelle, Paris

Mem. New York Bot. Gard. - Memoirs of the New York Botanical Garden, Bronx

Mem. Reale Accad. Sci. Torino - Memorie della Reale Accademia delle Scienze di Torino, Turin

Mém. Soc. Hist. Nat. Paris - Mémoires de la Société d'Histoire Naturelle de Paris, Paris

Mém. Soc. Linn. Paris - Mémoires de la Société Linnéenne de Paris, Paris

Mem. Torrey Bot. Club - Memoirs of the Torrey Botanical Club, Bronx

Metam. Insect. Surinam. - Metamorphosis insectorum surinamensium. Ofte verandering der Surinaamsche insecten. Waar in de Surinaamsche årupsen en wormen met alle des zelfs veranderingen na het leven afgebeeld en beschreeven worden, zynde elk geplaast op die gewassen, bloemen en vruchten, daar sy op gevonden zyn; waar in ook de generatie der kikvorschen, wonder baare padden, hagedissen, slangen, spinnen en mieren werden vertoond en beschreeven, alles in America na het leven en levensgroote geschildert en beschreeven, Zutphen

Methodus (Moench) - Methodus Plantas Horti Botanici et Agri Marburgensis, a staminum situ describendi, Marburgi Cattorum

Meth. Pl. (Ray) - Methodus plantarum emendata et aucta. In quâ notæ maxime characteristicæ exhibentur, quibus stirpium genera tum summa, tum infima cognoscuntur & à se mutuo dignoscuntur, non necessariis omissis. Accedit Methodus graminum, juncorum, et cyperorum specialis, London

Mitt. Bad. Landesvereins Naturk. Naturschutz Freiburg - Mitteilungen des Badischen Landesvereins für Naturkunde und Naturschutz e.V. in Freiburg im Breisgau, Freiburg

Monde Pl. - Le Monde des Plantes; Revue Trimestrielle et Internationale de Bibliographie, Toulouse

Monde Pl. Rev. Mens. Bot. - Le Monde des Plantes; revue mensuelle de botanique; organe de l'Académie Internationale de Géographie Botanique, Le Mans

Monogr. Orchid. Bourbon - Monographie des Orchidées des Iles de France et de Bourbon, Paris

Monogr. Syst. Bot. Missouri Bot. Gard. - Monographs in Systematic Botany from the Missouri Botanical Garden, St. Louis

Mont. Bald. - Monte Baldo descritto ... in cui si figurano et descriuono molte rare Piante ... et due commenti dell ... N. Marogna ... sopra l'Amoma de gli antichi / per F. Pona dal Latino tradotti, Venetia

Monthly Rev. - *Griffith's* Monthly Review

Morph. Stud. Orchideenbl. - Morphologische Studien über die Orchideenblüthe, Heidelberg

Muhlenbergia - Muhlenbergia; a Journal of Botany, Lancaster, Pennsylvania

Mus. Bot. - Museum Botanicum Lugduno-Batavum sive stirpium Exoticarum, Novarum vel Minus Cognitarum ex Vivis aut siccis brevis Expositio et Descriptio, Leiden

Musei Pet. - Musei Petiveriani centuria prima [-decima]: rariora Naturæ continens: viz. Animalia, Fossilia, Plantas, ex variis mundi plagis advecta, ordine digesta, et nominibus propriis signata, London

Mus. Zeyl. - Musaeum Zeylanicum, sive catalogus plantarum, in Zeylana sponte nascentium, observatorium & descriptarum, Leiden

Nachtr. Fl. Schutzgeb. Südsee - *Schumann & Lauterbach's* Nachträge zur Flora der deutschen Schutzgebiete in der Südsee, Leipzig

Nat. Arr. Brit. Pl. - A Natural Arrangement of British Plants, According to Their Relation to Each Other, London

Nat. Hist. Carolina - The Natural history of Carolina, Florida and the Bahama Islands, Savannah

Native Ecuadorian Orchids - Native Ecuadorian Orchids, Medellín

Native Orchids Taiwan - Native Orchids Taiwan, Taipei

Nat. Pflanzenfam. - *Engler & Prantl's* Die natürlichen pflanzenfamilien nebst ihren gattungen und wichtigeren arten insbesondere den nutzpflanzen, Leipzig

Nat. Pflanzenfam. Nachtr. - Natürlichen Pflanzenfamilien. Nachträge zum II bis IV Teil, Leipzig

Nat. Pflanzen-Syst. - *Jussieu's & de Candolle's* Natürliche Pflanzen-Systeme, nach ihren Grundsätzen entwickelt und mit den Pflanzen-Familien von Agardh, Batsch und Linné, so wie mit dem Linné'schen Sexual System verglichen, Bonn

Nat. Syst. Bot. - *Lindley's* A Natural System of Botany, London

Nat. Syst. Pl. - Natürliches System des Pflanzenreichs: nach seiner inneren

Organisation, nebst einer vergleichenden Darstellung der wichtigsten aller früheren künstlichen und natürlichen Pflanzensysteme, Berlin

Nature - Nature: a Weekly Illustrated Journal of Science, London

Naturgesch. Pflanzenr. - Naturgeschichte des Pflanzenreichs: grosser Pflanzenatlas mit Text für Schule und Haus, Stuttgart

Ned. Kruidk. Arch. - Nederlandsch Kruidkundig Archief, Verslagen en Mededelingen der Nederlandsche Botanische Vereeniging, Leiden

Neogenyton - Neogenyton, or indication of sixty-six new genera of Plants of North America, Lexington, Kentucky

Neubert's Deutsch. Gart.-Mag. - Dr. Neubert's Deutsches Garten-Magazin, (alternate title) Neue Folge: Illustrierte Monatshefte für die Gesamt-Interessen des Gartenbaues, Stuttgart

Neue Allg. Garten- Blumenzeitung - Neue allgemeine Garten- und Blumenzeitung, eine Zeitschrift für die Garten-und Blumenfreunde, Hamburg

Neue Jahr. Phil. Paedag. - Neue Jahrbücher für Philologie und Paedagogik, Leipzig

Neues Allg. Gart.-Mag. - Neues allgemeines Garten-Magazin: oder gemeinnüssige Beiträge für alle Theile des Deutschen gartenwesens

Nom. Bot. Hort. - *Heynhold's* Nomenclator Botanicus Hortensis, order alphabetische und synonymische Aufzahlung der in den Gasten Europas cultivirlen Gewächse, nebst Angabe ihres Autors, ihres Vaterlandes, ihrer Dauer und Cultur, bearbeitet von Gustav Heynhold nebst einer Vorrede von Dr. Ludwig Reichenbach, Dresden und Leipzig

Nomencl. Bot. (Pfeiffer) - Nomenclator Botanicus: Nominum ad finem anni 1858 publici juris factorum, classes, ordines, tribus, familias, divisiones, genera, subgenera vel sectiones designantium enumeratio alphabetica, Cassellis

Nomencl. Bot. (Steudel) - Nomenclator Botanicus, seu Synonymia Plantarum Universalis, Stuttgart & Tübingen

Nomencl. Fl. Danic. - Nomenclatura Floræ Danicæ Emendata cum Indice Systematico et Alphabetico, Copenhagen

Nordic J. Bot. - Nordic Journal of Botany, Copenhagen

Notes Roy. Bot. Gard. Edinburgh - Notes from the Royal Botanic Gardens, Edinburgh

Notizbl. Bot. Gart. Berlin-Dahlem - Notizblatt des Botanischen Gartens und Museums zu Berlin-Dahlem, Berlin

Not. Maelenia - Notice sur le genre Maelenia de la famille des Orchidées, Bruxelles

Not. Pl. Asiat. - Notulæ ad Plantas Asiaticas, Calcutta

Notul. Syst. (Paris) - Notulæ Systematicæ; Herbier du Muséum de Paris. Phanérogamie, Paris

Nouv. Bull. Sci. Soc. Philom. Paris - Nouveau Bulletin des Sciences, publié par la Société Philomatique de Paris

Nouv. Dict. Hist. Nat. - Nouveau dictionnaire d'histoire naturelle, appliquée aux arts, à l'agriculture, à l'économie rurale et domestique, à la médecine, etc., Paris

Nouv. Mém. Acad. Roy. Sci. Bruxelles - Nouveaux Mémoires de l'Académie Royale des Sciences et Belles-Lettres de Bruxelles

Nova Acta Regiæ Soc. Sci. Upsal. - Nova Acta Regiæ Societatis Scientiarum Upsaliensis, Uppsala

Nov. Actortum Acad. Caes. Leop.-Carol. German. Nat. Cur. - Novorum Actorum Academiæ Caesareæ Leopoldinæ-Carolinæ Germanicae Naturæ Curiosorum, Dresden

Nov. Gen. Sp. - *Kunth's* Nova genera et species plantarum: quas in peregrinatione ad plagam æquinoctialem orbis novi collegerunt descripserunt, partim adumbraverunt, Weinheim

Nov. Gen. Sp. Pl. (Poeppig & Endlicher) - Nova genera ac species plantarum quas in regno Chilensi, Peruviano, et in terra Amazonia collegerunt, Leipzig

Novon - Novon; a journal for botanical nomenclature, St Louis, Missouri

Nov. Pl. Amer. - Nova Plantarum Americanarum genera: (Catalogus Plantarum Americanarum, quarum genera in Institutionibus rei herbariæ jam nota sunt, quasque P.C. Plumier ..., Paris)

Nov. Pl. Gen. - *Micheli's* Nova Plantarum Genera juxta Tournefortii methodum disposita ... Adnotationibus, atque observationibus, præcipue Fungorum, Muscorum, affiniumque Plantarum sationem, ortum & incrementum spectantibus, interdum adjectis, Florentiæ

Nov. Veg. Descr. - Novorum Vegetabilium Descriptiones, Orchidianum opusculum, México

N. Queensland Naturalist - North Queensland Naturalist, Cairns

Numer. List - *Wallich's* Catalog or A Numerical List of Dried Specimens of plant, in the East India Company's Museum, collected under the superintendence of Dr. Wallich of the Company's botanic garden at Calcutta, London

Nuov. Gen. Sp. Monocot. - Nuovi generi e nuovi specie di piante monocotiledoni, Firenze

Nuytsia - Nuytsia; Bulletin of the Western Australian Herbarium, Perth

Oasis (Dora Creek) - Oasis; the Journal. Dora Creek, Australia

Observ. Pl. - Observations sur les Plantes des environs d'Angers, pour servir de supplément à la Flore de maine et Loire, et de suite à l'Histoire naturelle et critique des Plantes de France, Angers & Paris

Oesterr. Bot. Z. - Oesterreichische Botanische Zeitschrift; gemeinütziges Organ für Botanik, Vienna

Omnium Stirp. Sciag. - Omnium stirpium sciagraphia et icones: quibus plantarum et radicum tum in hortis cultarum, tum in urbium fossis & muris, pratis, aruis, montibus, collibus nemoralibus, fluviis, riguis & littoralibus, villis & pagis, spontè provenientium, nomina, figura, natura, natales, synonyma, usus & virtutes, docentur, cum doctissimorum scriptorum circa eas consensu & dissensu, Geneva

Opera (Hernández) - Opera: cum edita, tum inedita, ad autographi fidem et integritatem expressa, impensa et jussu regio, Madrid

Opera Bot. - Opera Botanica a Societate Botanice Ludensi, Copenhagen

Opera Var. - *Linnaeus'* Opera Varia in quibus continentur Fundamenta botanica, Sponsalia plantarum, et Systema naturæ, in quo proponuntur naturae regna tria secundum classes, ordines, genera & species, Lucca

Orchadian - Orchadian: Australasian Native Orchid Society, Sydney

Orch. Ambon - Die Orchideen von Ambon, Batavia [Jakarta]

Orchidaceae (Ames) - Orchidaceae: Illustrations and Studies of the Family Orchidaceae Issuing from the Ames Botanical Laboratory, Boston

Orchid Album - The Orchid Album comprising coloured figures and descriptions of new, rare, and beautiful orchidaceous plants, London

Orchid.-Buch - *Stein's* Orchideenbuch, Berlin

Orchid Conservation - Orchid Conservation, Kota Kinabalu, Sabah

Orchid. Cult. Protect. - Orchidees culture et protection, Levallois-Perret

Orchid. Deutschl. - Die Orchidaceen Deutschlands, Deutsch-Oesterreichs und der Schweiz, Gera-Untermhaus & Berlin

Orchid Digest - Orchid Digest, California

Orchidee (Hamburg) - Die Orchidee; Zeitschrift der Deutschen Orchideen-Gesellschaft, Hamburg-Othmarschen, Hamburg & Hildesheim

Orchideen (Schlechter) - Die Orchideen, ihre Beschreibung, Kultur und Züchtung: handbuch für Orchideenliebhaber, Kultivateure und Botaniker, Berlin

Orchideen (Schlechter): Liter. Reg. Band I/A, B, and C - Die Orchideen: Literaturverzeichnis und register zu Band I/A, B und C, Berlin

Orch. Exot. - Orchidées Exotiques et Leur Culture en Europe, Bruxelles

Orchid. Gen. Sp. - Orchidacearum Genera et Species, Berlin

Orchid Gen. Thailand - Orchid Genera in Thailand, Copenhagen

Orchid. German-Neu-Guinea - The Orchidaceae of German New Guinea: Translation of the German text, Melbourne

Orchid. Icon. Index - Orchidacearum iconum index, Dahlem-Berlin

Orchid J. - Orchid Journal, Coconut Grove, Florida

Orchid. Lex. - An Orchidist's lexicon: with a pronouncing glossary of orchid terms, Portland

Orchid. Linden. - Orchidaceæ Lindenianæ; or, notes upon a collection of orchids formed in Colombia and Cuba, London

Orchid Memories - Orchid Memories: A tribute to Gunnar Seidenfaden, Calicut

Orchid. Mexico Guatemala - Orchidaceae of Mexico and Guatemala, London

Orchid. Nepal - Orchids of Nepal, New Delhi

Orchid. Nilgiris - Orchids of Nilgiris, Howrah

Orchidophile (Argenteuil) - L'Orchidophile; journal des amateurs d'Orchidées, Argenteuil

Orchid. Philipp. - Valmayor's Orchidiana Philippiniana, Manila

Orchid. Philippines - The Orchids of the Philippines, Portland

Orchid Rev. - Orchid Review: An Illustrated Monthly Journal Devoted to Orchidology in all its Branches, London

Orchids - Orchids. A Description of the Species and Varieties Grown at Glen Ridge, A Complete Manual of Orchid Culture, New York

Orchids (West Palm Beach) - Orchids; the magazine of the American Orchid Society, Delray Beach, Florida

Orchids Bolivia - Orchids of Bolivia; Diversity and conservation status, Santa Cruz de la Sierra

Orchids Bombay - The Orchids of Bombay, Delhi

Orchids Borneo - The Orchids of Borneo, Surrey & Kota Kinabalu

Orchids Burma - The Orchids of Burma including the Andaman Islands, Rangoon

Orchid. Scelet. - Orchidearum Sceletos, London

Orchids Cult. Managem. - Orchids, their culture and management: new edition, revised through out and greatly enlarged, contains full descriptions of all species and varieties that are in general cultivation, a list of hybrids and their recorded parentage, and detailed cultural directions, London

Orchids Ecuador - Orquídeas de la costa del Ecuador = Orchids from the coast of Ecuador, Guayaquil

Orchid. Sicul. - Orchideæ Siculæ, sive enumeratio Orchidearum in Sicilia hucusque detectarum, Panormi

Orchids India - Orchids of India, Calcutta

Orchid. Sino-Jap. Prodr. - Orchideologiæ Sino-Japonicæ Prodromus: eine kritische besprechung der Orchideen Ost-Asiens, Dahlem-Berlin

Orchids Java - The Orchids of Java, Richmond, Surrey

Orchids Madagascar - The Orchids of Madagascar, Surrey

Orchids Nepal Himalaya - The Orchids of Nepal Himalaya, Vaduz

Orchids New Guinea - The Orchids of New Guinea, Portland

Orchids S. Ryukyu Islands - Orchids of the Southern Ryukyu Islands, Cambridge

Orchids Sumatra - The Orchids of Sumatra, Richmond, Surrey

Orchids Thailand - Orchids of Thailand: a preliminary list, Bangkok

Orchids Venezuela - Orchids of Venezuela, an Illustrated Field Guide, Cambridge

Orchids Venezuela, ed. 2 - Romero & Carnveail's Orchids of Venezuela, an Illustrated Field Guide, ed. 2, Caracas

Orchid Weekly - Orchid Weekly, Coconut Grove, Florida

Orchis - Orchis: Monatsschrift der Deutschen Gesellschaft für Orchideenkunde, Berlin

Orchis (Ledien & Witt) - Orchis: Mitteilungen des Orhideen-ausshusses des Vereins zur Beförderung des Gartenbaues

Orch. Java - Die Orchideen von Java von J. J. Smith - Band vi der Flora von Buitenzorg, Leiden

Ord. Nat. Pl. - Ordines Naturales Plantarum eorumque characteres et affinitates adjecta generum enumeratione, Gottingae

Orquidea (Mexico City) - Orquidea; organo oficial de la Sociedad Mexicana, "Amigos de las Orquídeas", México City

Orquídea (Rio de Janeiro) - Orquídea, Rio de Janeiro

Orquideas Afic. - Orquideas para aficionados: Culyivos tropicales, Caracas

Orquideas Colomb. - Orquideas Colombianas: Colombian orchids, Bogotá

Orquideologia - Orquideología; revista de la Sociedad Colombiana de Orquideología, Medellín

Orquid. Nov. Estad. Espirito Santo - Orquidaceas Novas do Estado do Espirito Santo, Vitória

Otia Bot. Hamburg. - Otia Botanica Hamburgensia, Hamburg

Palaeontogra. - Palaeontographica Abteilung B, Paläophytologie, Stuttgart

Palmengarten - Der Palmengarten. Frankfurter Monatsschrift für Natur- und Gartenfreunde, Frankfurt am Main

Pansey - A history and description of the different varieties of the pansey, or heartsease, now in cultivation in the British gardens; illustrated with twenty-four coloured figures, of the choicest sorts, London

Parad. Batav. - Paradisus Batavus, contineus plus centum Plantas ... ære incisas & descriptionibus illustratas: Cui accessit Catalogus Plantarum quas pro tomis nondum editis, delineandas euraverat P. Hermannus Parad. Lond. - The Paradisus Londinensis: containing plants cultivated in the vicinity of the Metropolis, London

Parad. Lond. - Paradisus Londinensis: or Coloured Figures of Plants Cultivated in the vicinity of the Metropolis, London

Paxton's Fl. Gard. - Paxton's Flower Garden, London

Paxton's Mag. Bot. - Paxton's Magazine of Botany, and Register of Flowering Plants, London

Pescatorea - Pescatorea; Iconographie des Orchidees, Bruxelles

Pflanze - Die Pflanze: Voträge aus dem Gebiete der Botanik, Breslau

Pflanzenr. (Engler) - Das Pflanzenreich regni vegetabilis conspectus, Leipzig

Phan. Cuming. Philipp. - Cuerpo de Ingenieros de Montes, Comision de la Flora Forestal de Filipinas, Phanerogamæ Cumingianæ Philippinarum ..., Manila

Phylogeny Classif. Orchid Fam. - Phylogeny and classification of the orchid family, Portland

Physiol. Gew. - Physiologie der Gewächse, Bonn

Phytochemistry - Phytochemistry, Oxford

Phytognomonica - Phytognomonica ... octo libris contenta: in quibus nova facillimaque affertur methodus, qua Plantarum, Animalium, Metalloru, rerum deniq. omniu ex prima extimæ faciei inspectione quivis abditas vires assequatur, Neapoli

Phytologia - Phytologia: Designed to expedite botanical publication, Plainfield, New Jersey - Huntsville, Texas

Phytologist - Phytologist: a Popular Botanical Miscellany, London

Pinax - Pinax Theatri botanici Caspari Bauhini sive Index in Theophrasti, Dioscoridis, Plinii et botanicorum qui a seculo scripserunt opera: plantarum circiter sex millium ab ipsis exhibitarum nomina cum earundem synonymiis & differentiis methodice secundùm earum & genera & species proponens: Opus XL. annorum mactenus non editum summoperè expetitum & ad auctores intelligendos plurimùm faciens, Basileae Helvei

Pl. Alkaloids - Plant Alkaloids: A Guide to Their Discovery and Distribution, New York City

Pl. Amer. - Plantarum Americanarum fasciculus primus[-decimus] continens plantas, quas olim Carolus Plumierius botanicorum princeps detexit, eruitque, atque in insulis Antillis ipse depinxit, Amsterdam

Pl. Asiat. Rar. - Plantæ Asiaticæ Rariores; or descriptions and figures of a select number of unpublished East Indian Plants, London

Pl.-Book - *Mabberley's Plant-Book; A Portable Dictionary of the Higher Plants*, Cambridge

Pl. David. - Plantæ Davidianæ ex Sinarum Imperio, Paris

Pl. Effigies - Plantarum eefigies [sic], e Leonartho Fuschio, ac quinque diversis linguis redditæ, Lugduni

Pl. Hartw. - Plantas Hartwegianas imprimis Mexicanas adjectis nonnullis Grahamiania enumerat novasque describit Georgius Bentham, London

Pl. Jav. Rar. (Bennett)- Plantæ Javanicæ Rariores, Descriptæ Iconibus Illustratæ, quas in Insula Java, Annis 1802-1818, Legit et Investigatit Thomas Horsefield, M.D. e Siccis Descriptiones et Characteres Plurimarum Elaboravit Joannes J. Bennett; Observationes Structuram et Affinitates Praesertim Respicientes Passim Adjecit Robertus Brown, London

Pl. Libri XVI - De Plantis Libri XVI, Florentiae

Pl. Ornem. - Les Plantes Ornementales à feuillage panaché et coloré, Gand

Pl. Rar. Horti Upsal. - Plantarum rariorum Horti Upsaliensis fasciculus primus, sistens descriptiones et figuras plantarum minus cognitarum, Stockholm

Pl. Stirp. Hist. - Plantarum, seu, Stirpivm historia, Antuerpiae

Pl. Stirp. Icon. - Plantarum seu Stirpivm icones, Antuerpiae

Pl. Syst. Evol. - Plant Systematics and Evolution, Wein

Pl. Vasc. Gen. (Meisner) - Plantarum Vascularium Genera secundum ordines naturales digesta, eorumque differentiæ et affinitates tabulis diagnosticis expositæ, Leipzig

Pl. Veron. - Plantæ Veronenses, seu Stirpium quæ in agro Veronensi reperiuntur methodica synopsis, Veronæ

Polish Bot. J. - Polish Botanical Journal, Kraków

Polish Bot. Stud. - Polish Botanical Studies, Guidebook Series, Kraków

Prakt. Stud. Orchid. - Praktische Studien an der Familie der Orchideen, nebst Kulturanweisungen und Beschreibung aller schönblühenden tropischen Orchideen, Wien

Prec. Decouv. - Précis des Découvertes et Travaux Somiologiques, Palerme

Present State Majesties Isles Territories Amer. - The Present State of his Majesties Isles and Territories in America, London

Preuss. Pflanzengatt. - Preussens Pflanzengattungen nach Familien geordnet, Königsberg

Prix-Courant Cat. - Linden's Prix-Courant Catalogue; Linden issued sales catalogues (sometimes called prix-courant) from 1846, Bruxelles

Proc. Biol. Soc. Wash. - Proceedings of the Biological Society of Washington

Proc. Indian Natl. Sci. Acad. - Proceedings of the Indian National Science Academy, New Dehli

Proc. Linn. Soc. London - Proceedings of the Linnean Society of London

Proc. Linn. Soc. New South Wales - Proceedings of the Linnean Society of New South Wales, Sydney

Prodr. (Bauhin) - Prodromos Theatri Botanici ... in quo plantæ svpra sexcentæ ab ipso primum descriptæ cum plurimis figuris proponuntur, Basle

Prodr. (Swartz) - Nova Genera Species Plantarum seu Prodromus descriptionum Vegetabilium maximam partem incognitorum quæ sub itinere Indiam Occidentalem annis, Holmiæ

Prodr. Fl. Nepal. - Prodromus Floræ Nepalensis, sive Enumeratio Vegetabilium, quæ in Itinere per Nepaliam Proprie Dictam et Rgiones Conterminas, London

Prodr. Fl. Norfolk. - Prodromus Floræ Norfolkicæ, sive catalogus Stripium quæ in insula Norfolk annis 1804 et 1805 a Ferdinando Bauer collectae et depictae nunc in Museo Caesareo Palatino rerum naturalium Vindobonæ servantur, Vienna

Prodr. Fl. Nov. Holland. - Prodromus Floræ Novæ Hollandiæ et Insulæ van-Diemen, London

Quart. J. Sci. Lit. Arts - Quarterly Journal of Science, Literature and Arts, London

Queensland Naturalist - Queensland Naturalist, Brisbane

Rad. Jugoslav. Akad. Znan. - Rad: Jugoslavenska Akademije Znanosti i Umjetnost, Zagrebu

Rar. Aliq. Stirp. - Rariorum aliquot Stirpium, per Pannoniam, Austriam, & vicians quasdam Prouincias obseruatarum Historia, Antwerp

Rar. Pl. Hist. - Rariorum Plantarum Historia, Antwerp

Rar. Stirp. Hisp. Obs. Hist. - Rariorum aliquot Stirpium per Hispanias observatarum Historia, libris duobus expressa, Antwerp

Recueil Trav. Bot. Neerl. - Recueil des Travaux Botaniques Néerlandais, Nimègue

Refug. Bot. - Refugium Botanicum; or, Figures and Descriptions from Living Specimens of Little Known or New Plants of Botanical Interest, London

Reis. Amur-Land., Bot. - Reisen im Amur-Lande und auf der Insel Sachalin: Botanischer Theil, St. Petersbourg

Reis. Br.-Guiana - Reisen in Britisch-Guiana in den Jahren 1840-1844, Leipzig

Reliq. Haenk. - Reliquiæ Haenkeanæ seu descriptiones et icones platarum, quas in America meridionali et boreali, in insulis Philippinis et Marianis collegit, Amsterdam

Remarques Fl. Polynésie - Remarques sur la Flora de la Polynésie et sur ses rapports avec celle des terres voisines, Paris

Rep. Bot. Gard. Calcutta - Report on the Hon'ble Company's Botanic Gardens, Calcutta

Repert. Spec. Nov. Regni Veg. - Repertorium Specierum Novarum Regni Vegetabilis. Centralblatt für Sammlung und Veröffentlichung von Einzeldiagnosen neuer Pflanzen, Berlin

Repert. Spec. Nov. Regni Veg. Beih. - Repertorium Specierum Novarum Regni Vegetabilis. Centralblatt für Sammlung und Veröffentlichung von Einzeldiagnosen neuer Pflanzen, Beihefte, Berlin

Rep. Geol. Mineral. Bot. Zool. Massachusetts - Report on the Geology, Mineralogy, Botany, and Zoology of Massachusetts, made and published by order of the governmenttf of that state, Amherst

Rep. Geol. Surv. Ohio - Report of the Geological Survey of Ohio, Columbus

Rep. Prog. Zool. Bot. - Reports on the Progress of Zoology and Botany 1841, 1842, Edinburgh

Rep. State Board Geol. Michigan - Report of the State Board of Geological Survey of Michigan, Lansing

Rerum Med. Nov. Hisp. Thes. - Rerum medicarum Novæ Hispaniæ Thesaurus, seu plantarum animalium, mineralium mexicanorum historia, ex Francisci Hernandez Novi Orbis medici primarii relationibus in ipsa Mexicana urbe conscriptis a Nardo Antonio Reccho ... Collecta ac in ordine digesta a Joanne Terentio Lynceo notis illustrata, Rome

Retzia - Retzia; sive Observationes Botanicæ, quas inprimis in Horto Botanico Bogoriensi, Batavia

Rev. Gén. Bot. - *Bonnier's* Revue Générale de Botanique, Paris

Rev. Hort. (Paris) - Revue Horticole: résumé de tout ce qui parait d'intéressant en jardinage ..., Paris

Rev. Hort. Belge Étrangère - Revue de l'Horticulture Belge et Étrangère, Ghent

Revis. Fl. Malay. - A revised flora of Malaya: an illustrated systematic account of the Malayan flora, including commonly cultivated plants, Singapore

Revis. Gen. Pl. - Revisio Generum Plantarum vascularium omnium atque cellularium multarum secundum leges nomenclaturæ internationalis, cum enumeratione Plantarum Exoticarum in itinere mundi collectarum ... mit Erläuterungen, Leipzig

Revis. Handb. Fl. Ceylon - Revised Handbook to the Flora of Ceylon, New Delhi

Revista Guatemal. - Revista Guatemalensis; Publicacion Botánica del Centro Universitario del Norte de la Universidad de San Carlos de Guatemala

Rheedea - Rheedea: Official Journal of Indian Association for Angiosperm Taxonomy, Calicut

Rhodora - Rhodora: Journal of the New England Botanical Club, Boston, Providence & Lancaster

Richardiana - Richardiana: La revue francophone trimestrielle consacrée aux Orchidées et aux Broméliacées, Saint-Genis-Laval

Rumphia - Rumphia sive, Commentationes botanicæ imprimis de plantis Indiæ Orientalis, tum penitus incognitis tum quæ in libris Rheodii Rumphii, Roxburghii, Wallichii aliorum recensentur, Lugduni Batavorum

Russk. Bot. Zhurn. - Russkii Botanicheskii Zhurnal, Journal Russe de Botanique, Moscow & Leningrad

S

Samml. Phys. Aufsätze Böhm. Naturgesch. - Sammlung physikalischer Aufsätze, besonders die Böhmische Naturgeschichte betreffend, von einer Gesellschaft Böhmischer Naturforscher: herausgegeben von J. Mayer, Dresden

Sander's Orch. Guide - Sander's Orchid Guide, Saint Albans

Scent Orchid. - The Scent of Orchids: Olfactory and Chemical Investigations, Boca Raton

Sched. Orchid. - Schedulæ Orchidianæ, Boston

Schlechteriana - Schlechteriana; Zeitschrift für Orchideenkunde. Journal of Orchidology, Lahnau

Schlüssel Hortus Malab. - Schlüssel zum Hortus Indicus Malabaricus: order dreifaches register zu diesem Werke, Weimar

Schriften Ges. Beförd. Gesammten Naturwiss. Marburg - Schriften der Gesellschaft zur Beförderung der Gesammten Naturwissenschaften zu Marburg, Marburg

Sci. Rep. Yokosuka City Mus. - Science Report of the Yokosuka-shi City Museum (Yokosukashi hakubutsu kan kenkyu hokoku), Yokosuka

Sci. Surv. Porto Rico & Virgin Islands - Scientific Survey of Porto Rico and the Virgin Islands, New York

Séance Publique Soc. Argic. - Séance Publique de la Société d'Agriculture, commerce, sciences et arts du départment de la Marne, Chalons

Second Bienn. Oregon State Board Hort. - Second Biennial Report of the Oregon State Board of Horticulture to the Legislative Assembly, Seventeenth Regular Session. Also appendix to the organization and work of the Oregon State Horticultural Society, Portland

Second Cent. Orchid. Pl. - Second Century of Orchidaceous Plants, London

Selbyana - Selbyana: Journal of the Marie Selby Botanical Gardens, Sarasota

Sempervirens - Sempervirens: Geïllustreed Weekblad voor der Tuinbouw in Nederland, Amsterdam

Sert. Mendoc. Alt. - Sertum mendocinum, alterum, Santiago

Sert. Orchid. - Sertum Orchidaceum: a wreath of the most beautiful Orchidaceous Flowers, London

Sin. Fl. Cuzco - Sinopsis de la Flora del Cuzco, Lima

Sitzungsber. Königl. Böhm. Ges. Wiss. Prag, Math.-Naturwiss. Cl. - Sitzungsberichte der Koniglichen Bohmischen Gesellschaft der Wissenschaften. Mathematisch-naturwissenschaftliche Classe, Prague

Sketch Veg. Swan R. - Appendix to the first twenty-three volumes of Edwards's Botanical Register: consisting of a complete alphabetical and systematical index of names, synonyms, and matter, adjusted to the present state of systematical botany; together with A sketch of the vegetation of the Swan River Colony, London

Spec. Inaug. Corallorhiza - Specimen Inagurale de Corallorhiza Quod Jussu et Authoritate Gratiosi Medicorum Ordinis pro Summis in Inclyta Rauracorum Universitate Honoribus et Privilegiis Doctoralibus Legitime Obtinendi(s) Publicæ Defendet Joan. Jacob. Chatelain, Basel

Sp. Pl. (Linnaeus) - Species Plantarum, exhibentes plantas rite cognitas, ad genera relatas, cum differentiis specificis, nominibus trivialibus synonimis selectis, locis naturalibus, secundum systema sexuale digestas, Holmiae

Sp. Pl. (Wildenow) - Species Plantarum, Berlin

S. Sci. Rec. - Southern Science Record, Melbourne

Stat. Account Bengal - A Statistical Account of Bengal, London

Stirp. Hist. Pempt. - Stirpium Historiae Pemptades sex, sive libri XXX, Antwerp

Stirp. Icon. - Stirpium icones et sciagraphia: cum scriptorum circa eas consensu et dissensu, Geneva

Stirp. Rar. Ruth. - Stirpium Rariorum in Imperio Rutheno Sponte Provenientium Icones et Descriptiones Collectae ab Ioanne Ammano, Petropoli

Stocc Hornii et Nessi - Stocc-Hornii et Nessi descriptio in Bernatium Helvetiorum ditione montium, et nascentium in eis stirpium, Argentorati

Struct. Orchid. - Structure des Orchidees, Rio de Janeiro

Stud. Dactylorch. - Studies on Dactylorchis, Utrecht

Stud. Phytologica - Studia Phytologica: (Dissertationes ex Parte Utiles ad Studia Comparativa Vegetationis Mecsekensis): in Honorem Jubilantis A.O. Horvát, Pécs

Summarium - Summarium des Neuesten aus der gesammten Medicin ..., Leipzig

Summa Pl. - Summa Plantarum quae hactenus innotuerunt Methodo Linnaean per Gerera et Species digesta illustrata descripta, Milano

Summa Veg. Scand. (Swartz) - Summa Vegetabilium Scandinaviæ Systematice Coordinatorum, Holmiæ (Stockholm)

Suppl. Pl. - Supplementum Plantarum Systematis Vegetabilium Editionis Decimae Tertiae, Generum Plantarum Editiones Sextae, et Specierum Plantarum Editionis Secundae, Brunsvigae

Svensk Bot. Tidskr. - *J.W. Palmstruh's* Svensk Botanisk Tidskrift Utgifven af Svenska Botaniska Föreningen, Stockholm

Sweet-Scented Fl. - Sweet-Scented Flowers and Fragrant Leaves; interesting associations gathered from many sources, with notes on their history and utility, London

Syll. Pl. Nov. - *Hornschuch's* Sylloge Plantarum Novarum Itemque Minus Cognitarum a Praestantissimis Botanicis adhuc Viventibus Collecta et a Societate Regia Botanica Ratisbonensi Edita, Regensburg

Sylva Hercynia - Sylva Hercynia, sive catalogus plantarum sponte nascentium in montibus & locis pierisque Hercyniae Sylvæ quæ respicit Saxoniam, conscriptus singularl studio, Leipzig

Symb. Antill. - *Urban's* Symbolæ Antillanæ, seu fundamenta floræ Indiæ Occidentalis, Amsterdam

Symb. Sin. - Symbolæ Sinicæ, Botanische Ergebnisse der Expedition der Akademie der Wissenschaften in Wien nach Sudwest-China, Wien

Syn. Bot. - Synonymia Botanica locupletissima generum, sectionum vel subgenerum ad finem anni 1858 promulgatorum: In forma conspectus systematici totius regni vegetabilis schemati Endlicheriano adaptati.- Vollständige Synonymik, Cassellis

Syn. Bot., Suppl. - Synonymia Botanica, Supplement, Cassellis

Syn. Fl. Germ. Helv. - Synopsis Floræ Germanicæ et Helveticæ, exhibens stirpes Phanerogamas rite cognitas, quæ in Germania, Helvetia, Borussia et Istria sponte crescunt, Leipzig

Syn. Meth. Stirp. - Synopsis Methodica Stirpium Britannicarum, in qua Tum Notæ Generum Characteristicæ traduntur, tum Species Singulæ breviter describuntur: Ducentæ quinquaginta plus minus novæ Species partim suis locis inferuntur, partim in Appendice seorsim exhibentur. Cum Indice & Virium Epitome, London

Syn. Mitteleur. Fl. - Synopsis der Mitteleuropaischen Flora, Leipzig

Syn. Pl. (D. Dietrich) - Synopsis plantarum, seu, Enumeratio systematica plantarum plerumque adhuc cognitarum cum differentiis specificis et synonymis selectis ad modum persoonii elaborata, Weimar

Syn. Pl. (Kunth) - Synopsis plantarum, quas in itinere ad plagam æquinoctialem Orbis Novi, collegerunt A. de Humboldt et A. Bonpland, Paris

Syn. Pl. (Persoon) - Synopsis Plantarum seu Enchiridium Botanicum, complectens enumerationem systematicam specierum hucusque cognitarum, Paris

Syst. Nat. - *Linnaeus'* Systema naturae per regna tria naturae: secundum classes, ordines, genera, species, cum characteribus, differentiis, synonymus, locis, Holmiæ

Syst. Pl. Gen. - Systema plantarum generale ex fructificatione cui annectuntur regulæ ejusdem de nominibus plantarum a celeb. Linnaei longe diversæ, Helmstadii

Syst. Veg. (Sprengel) - Systema Vegetabilium, editio decima sexta, Gottingen

Syst. Veg. Fl. Peruv. Chil. - Systema Vegetabilium Floræ Peruvianæ et Chilensis, characteres Prodromi genericos differentiales, specierum omnium differentias, durationem, loca natalia, tempus florendi, nomina vernacula, vires et usus nonnullis illustrationibus interspersis complectens, Madrid

Syst. Verz. (Bernhardi) - Systematisches Verzeichnis der Pflanzen welche in der Gegend um Erfurt gefunden werden, Erfurt

Syst. Verz. (Moritzi et al.) - Systematisches Verzeichniss der von H. Zollinger in den Jahren 1842-44 auf Java gesammelten Pflanzen, nebst einer kurzen Beschreibung der neuen Gattungen und Arten, Solothurn

Tab. Bot. - Tabulæ botanicæ, in quibus classes, sectiones, et genera plantarum in Institutionibus Tournefortianis tradita synoptice exhibentur, in usum praelectionum botanicarum, Matriti

Tab. Pl. Jav. Orchid. - Tabellen en Platen voor de Javaansche Orchideen, Batavia

Taxon - Taxon: Official News Bulletin of the International Society for Plant Taxonomy, Utrecht

Taxon. Vasc. Plants - Taxonomy of vascular plants, New York

Telopea - Telopea, Sydney: New South Wales National Herbarium

Tent. Disp. Pl. German. - Tentamen Dispositionis Plantarum Germaniæ seminiferarum secundum novam methodum a staminum situ & proporkine cum characteribus generum essentialibus, Darmstadt

Tent. Fl. Abyss. - Tentamen Floræ Abyssinicæ seu Enumeratio Plantarum hucusque in plerisque Abyssiniæ, Paris

Tent. Fl. Napal. - Tentamen Floræ Napalensis Illustratæ Consisting of Botanical Descriptions and Lithographic Figures of Select Nipal Plants, Calcutta & Serampore

Tent. Orchidogr. Eur. - Orchideæ in Flora Germanica: additis Orchideis Europae reliquae, reliqui Rossicii imperi, Algerii ergo tentamen Orchidographiae Europaea iconibus, Leipzig

Terry's Mexico - Terry's Mexico: handbook for travellers, London

Thes. Cap. - Thesaurus Capensis: or, illustrations of the South African flora, being figures and brief descriptions of South African plants, selected from the Dublin University Herbarium, Dublin

Thes. Lit. Bot. - Thesaurus Literaturae Botanicae omnium gentium inde a rerum botanicarum initiis ad nostra usque termpora. quindecim millia operum recensens, Leipzig

Tijdschr. Natuurl. Gesch. Physiol. - *Hoeven & de Vriese's* Tijdschrift voor Natuurlijke Geschiedenis en Physiologie, Amsterdam

Tijdschr. Ned. Indië - Tijdschrift voor Nederlandsch-Indië, Jakarta

Tijdschr. Wis - Natuurk. Wetensch. Eerste Kl. Kon. Ned. Inst. Wetensch. - Tijdschrift voor de Wis- en Natuurkundige wetenschappen, Uitgegeven door de Eerste Klasse van het Kon. Ned. Instituut van Wetenschappen, Letteren en Schoone Kunsten, Amsterdam

Timehri - Timehri: being the journal of the Royal Agricultural and Commercial Society of British Guiana, Demerara

Torreya - Torreya, New York City

Trab. 26 Congr. Nac. Bot., Rio de Janeiro - Trabalhos do XXVI Congresso Nacional de Botanica, Rio de Janeiro

Traité Gén. Bot. - Traité Général de Botanique Descriptive et Analytique: 1. partie: abrégé d'organographie, d'anatomie et de physiologie. - 1. partie: iconographie, description et histoire des familles, London

Trans. Amer. Philos. Soc. - Transactions of the American Philosophical Society Held at Philadelphia for Promoting useful Knowledge, Philadelphia

Trans. & Proc. Roy. Soc. South Australia - Transactions and Proceedings of the Royal Society of South Australia, Adelaide

Trans. Hort. Soc. London - Transactions, of the Horticultural Society of London

Trans. Linn. Soc. London - Transactions of the Linnean Society of London

Trans. Linn. Soc. London, Bot. - Transactions of the Linnean Society of London, Botany

Trans. Wisconsin Acad. Sci. - Transactions of the Wisconsin Academy of Sciences, Arts and Letters, Madison

Treas. Bot. - Treasury of Botany; a Popular Dictionary of the Vegetable Kingdom; to which is Incorporated a Glossary of Botanical Terms, London

Trudy Bot. Inst. Akad. Nauk S.S.S.R., ser. 1 Fl. Sist. Vyssh. Rast. - Trudy Botanicheskogo Instituta Akademii Nauk S.S.S.R., ser. 1, Flora i Sistematika Vysshikh Rastenii, Moscow & Lenigrad

Trudy Imp. S.-Peterburgsk. Bot. Sada - Trudy Imperatorskago Saint Peterburgskago Botaniceskago Sada. Acta horti petropolitani, Sankt-Peterburg

Updated Checkl. Orchids Vietnam. - Updated Checklist of the Orchids of Vietnam, Hanoi

Vall. Apl. - Josiae Simleri Vallesiæ et Alpium descriptio, Lugduni Batavorum

Various Contr. Orchids - Various Contrivances by which Orchids are fertilised Insects, New York

Vasc. Pl. Fam. Gen. - Vascular Plant Families and Genera: a listing of the genera of vascular plants of the world according to their families, as recognised in the Kew Herbarium, with an analysis of relationships of the flowering plant families according to eight systems of classification

Vasc. Pl. Syn. Vietnamese Fl. - Vascular plants synopsis of Vietnamese flora = Konspekt sosudistȳkh rastenii florȳ V'etnama, St. Petersburg

Veg. Kingd. - The Vegetable Kingdom or the Structure, Classification and Uses of Plants, Illustrated upon the Natural System with Upwards of Five Hundred Illustrations, London

Veg. World - The Vegetable World; being a history of plants, with their botanical descriptions and peculiar properties, London

Vellosia - Vellosia; Contribuiçoes do Museu Botanico do Amazonas, Rio de Janeiro

Venez. Orchid. Ill. - Venezuelan Orchids Illustrated, London

Vera. Surinaemsche Insect. - Maria Sybilla Meriaen over de voortteeling en wonderbaerlyke veranderingen der Surinaemsche Inseecten, waer in de Surinaemfche Rupsen en Wormen ..., Amsterdam

Verh. Batav. Genootsch. Kunsten - Verhandelingen van het Bataviaasch Genootschap der Kunsten en Wetenschappen, Batavia

Verh. Vereins Beförd. Gartenbaues Königl. Preuss. Staaten - Verhandlungen des Vereins zur Beförderung des Gartenbaues in den Königlich Preussischen Staaten, Berlin

Vers. Neu-Spanien - Versuch aber den politischen Zustand des Königreiche New-Spanien, enthaltend, Tübingen

Verz. Orchid. - Preis-Verzeichniss der Orchideen im Graeflich Hoffmannseggischen Garten zu Dresden füer 1842, Dresden

Vict. Naturalist - Victorian Naturalist; Journal and Magazine of the Field Naturalists' Club of Victoria. Melbourne, Springvale, Victoria

Viti - Viti: an account of a government mission to the Vitian or Fijian Islands, 1860-1861, Cambridge

Voy. Astrolabe - d'Urville's Voyage de découvertes de l'Astrolabe ... Sertum Astrolabianum: description des espèces nouvelles ou peu connues, recueillies par M. Lesson jeune ... Botanique, Paris

Voy. Bonite, Bot. - Vaillant's Voyage Autour du Monde Execute Pendant les Anees 1836 et 1837 sur la Corvette la Bonite, Commandee par M. Vaillant ... Botanique, Paris

Voy. Iles Afrique - Voyages dans les quatres principales Îles des mers d'Afrique, fait par ordre du goverment avec l'histoire de la traversie du Captane Boudin jusqu'au Port Louis de l'Ille Maurice, Paris

Voy. Jamaica - A Voyage to the Islands Madera, Barbados, Nieves, S. Christophers and Jamaica, with the natural history of the Herbs and Trees, Four-footed Beasts, Fishes, Birds, Insects, Reptiles, of the last of those islands, London

Voy. Louisiane - Voyages dans l'intérieur de la Louisiane de la Floride occidentale, et dans les Isles de la Martinioue et de Saint-Domingue, Pendant les Années 1802, 1803, 1804, 1805 et 1806, Paris

Voy. Monde, Phan. - Duperrey's Voyage Autour de Monde, Execute par Ordre du Roi, sur la Corvette de Sa Majeste La Coquille..., Phanerogamie, Paris

Voy. Uranie, Bot. - Freycinet's Voyage autour du Monde entrepris pen dant par ordre du Roi, sous le Ministére et conformément aux instructions de M. le Vicomte Du Bouchage, secrétaire de l'Etat au département de la Marine, exécuté sur les Corvettes de S.M. l'Uranie et la Physicienne, pendant les années 1817, 1818, 1819 et 1820, Botanique, Paris

W. Austral. Naturalist - Western Australian Naturalist, Perth

Westafr. Kautschuk-Exped. - Westafrikanische Kautschuk-Expedition, Kolonial-Wirtschaftliches Komitee, Berlin

Wild Orchids Japan Colour - Wild Orchids of Japan in Colour, Tokyo

Wild Orchids Myanmar - Wild Orchids Myanmar, Tokyo

Willdenowia - Willdenowia: Mitteilungen aus dem Botanischen Garten und Museum Berlin-Dahlem

Wochenschr. Gartnerei Pflanzenk. - Wochenschrift für Gartnerei und Pflanzenkunde, Berlin

Wochenschr. Vereines Beford. Gartenbaues Konigl. Preuss. Staaten - Wochenschrift des Vereines zur Beforderung des Gartenbaues in den Koniglich Preussischen Staaten für Gartneri und Pflanzenkunde, Berlin

Wonders Veg. - The Wonders of Vegetation, New York

World Checkl. Seed Pl. - World Checklist of Seed Plants, Antwerp

Xenia Orchid. - Xenia Orchidacea: Beitraege zur Kenntniss der Orchideen, Leipzig

Zastosowania - Zastosowania metod statystycznych w badaniach naukowych I, Krakow

Jean Jules Linden *Lindenia: iconographie des Orchidées* **9**: plate 382 (1887).

ORCHID GENERA

A C K N O W L E D G M E N T S

 Thanks are due to many experts for their assistance in compiling and conducting the extensive research needed to complete this vast project. Special thanks are due to Victor Strahm Davis, Guido Braem, Ph.D., Eric Christenson, Ph.D., Alva Gosling, Andy Lanier, Kenneth Roberts, and Dariusz Szlachetko, Ph.D. And special thanks to my editors: Bruce Hansen for his patience with my steep learning curve in a new field; Tom Sheehan, Ph.D. and Robert L. Dressler, Ph.D. for taking on an indefinite project; John Atwood, Ph.D. for putting up with my lack of a technical education; Wesley Higgins, Ph.D. for his guidance through the vast maze of data; and for all the encouragement and help that I received from the staff at the Marie Selby Botanical Gardens. Thanks also to the individuals who patiently answered my many e-mails. And last, thanks to the many people who proofread this manuscript and provided many insights and ideas.

The first draft of the manuscript was edited by Bruce Hansen, Ph.D., Robert L. Dressler, Ph.D., Tom Sheehan, Ph.D., John Atwood, Ph.D., Calaway Dodson, Ph.D., and John Beckner. Following external review, an Editorial Board consisting of Wesley Higgins, Ph.D., Ted Kellogg, Ph.D., Mark Leggett, Wesley Rouse, Ph.D., Fred Lowery, Bruce Holst, Joanne Miller, Pep Ruddiman, Fred Bigio, Marty Wolf, Brian Hayden, David Benzing, Ph.D., Mary Jane Fabik, Kay Mannke, Zita Kasza, Harriet Berson, and Stig Dalström edited the manuscript based on reviewer feedback and comparison with original source literature.

This book could not have been produced without the wonderful reference materials embodied in the International Plant Names Index (2008), Harvard University Herbaria, Index Nominum Genericorum, Missouri Botanical Garden's Tropicos, World Checklist of Monocotyledons (2008) Royal Botanic Gardens, Kew as published on the Internet, the University of Florida, the Lee County Florida Library system, and Marie Selby Botanical Gardens Research Libraries where I was given access to their rare books to use as sources for the many illustrations found in this book.

De COATZONTE COXOCHITL, Lyncis flore. seu Lyncea. Cap. VII.

HERBA est *Coatzonte Coxochitl*, folia fundens Iridis, sed long ora, & latiora. caules tenues, virentes, breues, læuesque. flores capitibus serpentum similes, vnde nomen, rubeoque colore, punctis tamen interstincto candido & pallescente, promiscuè. radices verò oblongas, ac præcoci Ficui adhuc virescenti valde similes, striatas, ac contortas. Calidis prouenit, & interdum etiam temperatis regionibus, iuxta rupes, aut arborum truncis adhærescens. licet iam ad hortos, cultaque loca descenderit, viridariaque exornet, in quibus excolitur, deliciarum ac florum gratia. Est enim flos forma spectabilis, Liliacei odoris, & quem quispiam vix posset verbis exprimere, aut penicillo pro dignitate imitari. à Principibusque Indorum ob elegantiam, & miraculum, valde expetitus, & in magno habitus pretio. blandijs, & cultura non eget, sed vnica radice fœcundissimus sit prouentus. Ex hisce flor bus èque alijs quarundam herbarum congenerum, & ex rubro Maizio, parabantur Principibus Indorum Placentæ, quas edebant pro contemperando ventriculi calore. siue is accidisset à Solis æstu, sub cuius radijs contraxissent moras, siue ab alia quauis, interna externavè, caussa. frigida siquidem, humentiq; constat temperie.

Hic elegantissimus flos, & colorum varietate, & macularum aspersione, quemuis in sui admirationem rapere queat. eum Lyncis, exemplo floris Tigridis, & plantam Lynceam duabus præcipuè de causis appellare libuit. Cùm quia versicolorem Lyncis pellem varijs pulchrisq; maculis suis æmulatur, tùm quia Lynceorum Academiæ & Florem hunc, & totum hunc Mexicanarum plantarum nouum & curiosissimum librum, vt lucem aspexerit, debemus, cui auguror, vt quemadmodum pulcherrimus Flos hic Indorum Principibus, ob elegantiam & Naturæ miraculum in delitijs habetur, & ex varia radice fœcundissimus prouenit; ita Lynceorum studia, quæ opulentissimos clausæ Naturæ thesauros recludere, & auidis hominum solertium ingenijs subijcere satagunt, & apud hos & apud Principes bonarum litterarum promotores & patronos gratiam mereantur, cumque pauci adhuc eorum sint numero, radices tamen altas agant, fœcundaq; litterariorum monumentorum sobole suauissimum Musarum odorem longe latèq, spargant, plurimos studiosos sibi deuinciant.pluresq; ad sedulam Naturæ contemplationem sibi socios excitent.

ORCHID GENERA

NOMENCLATURAL RULES

Included here is Section 3. Names of Genera and Subdivisions of Genera - Article 20

Reprinted from International Code of Botanical Nomenclature (Vienna Code).
International Code of Botanical Nomenclature (ICBN) (McNeill & al. *Regnum Veg.* 146. 2006).

Article 20

20.1 - The name of a genus is a noun in the nominative singular, or a word treated as such, and is written with an initial capital letter (see Article 60.2). It may be taken from any source whatever, and may even be composed in an absolutely arbitrary manner, but it must not end in -*virus*.

Example 1: *Rosa, Convolvulus, Hedysarum, Bartramia, Liquidambar, Gloriosa, Impatiens, Rhododendron, Manihot, Ifloga* (an anagram of *Filago*).

20.2 - The name of a genus may not coincide with a Latin technical term in use in morphology at the time of publication unless it was published before 1 January 1912 and accompanied by a specific name published in accordance with the binary system of Linnaeus.

Example 2: "*Radicula*" (Hill, 1756) coincides with the Latin technical term "radicula" (radicle) and was not accompanied by a specific name in accordance with the binary system of Linnaeus. The name *Radicula* is correctly attributed to Moench (1794), who first combined it with specific epithets.

Example 3: *Tuber* F.H. Wigg.: Fr., when published in 1780, was accompanied by a binary specific name (*Tuber gulosorum* F.H. Wigg.) and is therefore validly published, even though it coincides with a Latin technical term.

Example 4: The intended generic names "*Lanceolatus*" (Plumstead, 1952) and "*Lobata*" (Chapman, 1952) coincide with Latin technical terms and are therefore not validly published.

Example 5: *Cleistogenes* Keng (1934) coincides with "cleistogenes", the English plural of a technical term in use at the time of publication. Keng's name is validly published, however, because the technical term is not Latin. Kengia Packer (1960), published as a replacement name for *Cleistogenes*, is illegitimate under Article 52.1.

Example 6: Words such as "*radix*", "*caulis*", "*folium*", "*spina*", etc., cannot now be validly published as generic names.

20.3 - The name of a genus may not consist of two words, unless these words are joined by a hyphen.

Example 7: "*Uva ursi*", as originally published by Miller (1754), consisted of two separate words unconnected by a hyphen, and is therefore not validly published (Article 32.1(c)); the name is correctly attributed to Duhamel (1755) as *Uva-ursi* (hyphenated when published).

Example 8: However, names such as *Quisqualis* L. (formed by combining two words into one when originally published), *Neves-armondia* K. Schum., *Sebastiano-schaueria* Nees, and *Solms-laubachia* Muschl. ex Diels (all hyphenated when originally published) are validly published.

Note 1: The names of intergeneric hybrids are formed according to the provisions of Article H.6.

20.4 - The following are not to be regarded as generic names:

(a): Words not intended as names.

Example 9: The designation "*Anonymos*" was applied by Walter (Fl. Carol.: 2, 4, 9, etc. 1788) to 28 different genera to indicate that they were without names.

Example 10: "*Schaenoides*" and "*Scirpoides*", as used by Rottbøll (Descr. Pl. Rar.: 14, 27. 1772) to indicate unnamed genera resembling *Schoenus* and *Scirpus* which he stated (on p. 7) that he intended to name later, are token words and not generic names. These unnamed genera were later legitimately named *Kyllinga* Rottb. and *Fuirena* Rottb.

(b): Unitary designations of species.

Note 2: Examples such as "*Leptostachys*" and "*Anthopogon*", listed in pre-Tokyo editions of the Code, were from publications now listed in App. VI.

Recommendation 20A

20A.1 - Authors forming generic names should comply with the following advice:

1: To use Latin terminations insofar as possible.

2: To avoid names not readily adaptable to the Latin language.

3: Not to make names which are very long or difficult to pronounce in Latin.

4: Not to make names by combining words from different languages.

5: To indicate, if possible, by the formation or ending of the name the affinities or analogies of the genus.

6: To avoid adjectives used as nouns.

7: Not to use a name similar to or derived from the epithet in the name of one of the species of the genus.

8: Not to dedicate genera to persons quite unconnected with botany or at least with natural science.

9: To give a feminine form to all personal generic names, whether they commemorate a man or a woman.

10: Not to form generic names by combining parts of two existing generic names, because such names are likely to be confused with nothogeneric names (see Article H.6).

Example 1: *Hordelymus* (Jess.) Harz is based on *Hordeum* [unranked] *Hordelymus* Jess. The epithet was formed by combining parts of the generic names *Hordeum* L. and *Elymus* L. (see also Article H.3 Example 2).

Hoehne *Flora Brasilica* **12**: fascicle 6, *t.*56A (1942).

ORCHID GENERA

G L O S S A R Y

Aberrant: Abnormal, unusual or exceptional; a plant or structure that varies from the normal or typical standard for this genus.

Acaulescent: Without a stem or apparently so.

Achlorophyllus: Lacking chlorophyll as do the so-called saprophytic orchids (see *epi-parasite*, *epi-saprophyte*, and the introductory chapter).

Acicular: Needle-like.

Aculeate: Set with prickles.

Acuminate: Ending in a narrow, sharp point.

Acute: Having an apex tapering at less than 90 degrees.

Adnate: United, refers to the union of two unlike parts (sepals with petals, anthers with lip, etc).

Aerial root: A root that grows above ground exposed to the atmosphere; usually originating from a stem. Aerial roots of orchids typically bear conspicuous velamenta (see the introductory chapter).

Allogamy: Sexual reproduction involving eggs and sperm derived from different parents; the consequence of out-crossing

Androceium: The collective male parts of a flower, i.e., the stamens.

Androgynous: Having features of both male and female, not a botanical term.

Angiosperm: A plant that bears true flowers; is a member of Division Magnoliophyta.

Anther: The pollen-bearing part of a stamen.

Anther cap: The removable covering over the orchid pollinia.

Apex: Tip of any structure.

Apical meristem: The masses of embryonic (meristematic) cells located at the tips of growing shoots and roots that extend their lengths and generate lateral appendages such as leaves.

Apiculate: Ending in a short, sharp, flexible point.

Apicule: A short pointed tip at the apex of a leaf or floral segment.

Arcuate: Curved like a bow.

Asexual: Without sex; refers especially to reproduction that does not involve the union of gametes, as in vegetative reproduction.

Asparagales: An Order within the monocot group of flowering plants that consists of about 30 families such as Agaveæ and Iridaceæ in addition to Orchidaceæ.

Asymbiotic: Refers to the germination of orchid seeds free of a fungus, and the cultivation of seedlings in sterile culture.

Atropurpureus: -a, -um, dark purple.

Auricle: A small ear-like appendage or lobe.

Auriculate: Ear-like in appearance.

Autogamy: Sexual reproduction that involves the union of eggs and sperm produced by a single parent, i.e., the consequence of self-pollination.

Autotrophy: To self-feed; a term applied to organisms that use simple inorganic substances and non-chemical energy to manufacture food as do green plants.

Awl-Shaped: Tapering upward from the base to a slender or rigid point.

Axil: The angle formed between a leaf and the stem to which it is attached; where axillary buds occur.

Axillary bud: A bud located in the axil of a leaf; can grow to become a lateral branch such as a ramet in the case of the sympodial orchids.

Barbate: Bearded.

Basal: At or near the base of any structure.

Basionym: A specific or infraspecific name that has priority over other names later given to the same plant by different authors.

Beard: A discrete area equipped with hairs, often found on the lips of flowers.

Bicallosed: Having two hard, waxy projections located on the lip.

Bidentate: Edged with two, tooth-like projections.

Bigeneric: Refers to a hybrid parented by members of two genera, as for *Laeliocattleya* (*Cattleya* x *Laelia*).

Bifid: Having two lobes or divided into two parts.

Bifoliate: Having two leaves; two-leaved.

Binominal: The official, two-parted Latin name for a species. The first word of the binomial identifies the genus and is capitalized; the second word begins in lower case and identifies the specific species within the genus; both names are italicized.

Bisaccate: Having a double sac-like shape.

Bisexual: Having both kinds of sex organs present and functional; usually applies to a flower rather than whole plants.

Bivalvate: Having two variable parts.

Bract: A leaf homolog that is not as normally developed as a foliage leaf; may enfold a bud, an inflorescence, or a stem.

Bulbil: A small bulb or bulb-shaped body, especially one borne upon the stem or leaf, and usually produced for asexual reproduction.

Bulbose: Inflated at the base like a bulb.

Bullate: Being blistered or puckered.

Caespitose: Being tufted.

Calcarate: Spurred.

Calceiform: Slipper-shaped.

Callus: Variously shaped protuberance on the lip of some orchids and there may be more than one; plural is calli.

Calyx: The collective name for the sepals in a flower.

Canaliculate: With a channel or groove, not to be confused with sulcate, which refers to several to numerous grooves.

Capitate (ose): Shaped like a head; collected into a head or dense cluster.

Cataphyll: A scale-like leaf, as on a rhizome or base of a stem (see bract).

Caudate: Having two, long, tail-like appendages.

Caudicle: An extension of a pollinium, formed within the anther; may connect with a stipe or become attached to a pollinator.

Cauline: Belonging to the stem.

Cerro: Spanish for hill.

Chloroplast: A membrane-bound inclusion, many of which reside in a single green cell; chlorophyll and the rest of the apparatus for conducting photosynthesis are located in the chloroplasts.

Ciliate: Fringed with hairs.

Clade: An assemblage of species all of which are derived from a single ancestral lineage. Thus, being monophyletic, the group may qualify for recognition as a taxon, specifically, as a genus, family, or higher rank depending on how closely related its component species.

Classification: As for taxonomy; the ranking and ordering of species into genera, families, and higher taxa according to the Linnaean hierarchy of taxonomy.

Clavate: Shaped like a club.

Claw: The narrow basal section of any flattened structure and that may be a lip, petal or midlobe.

Clinandrium: The anther bed, the portion of the column beneath or surrounding the anther.

Cloud (mist) forest: A mountain forest regularly enveloped by mist and usually characterized by stunted trees and abundant epiphytes.

Cohesion: The joining of like parts, for example petals to form a tubular corolla.

Column: The structure formed by the union of the style and one or more anthers; the central organ of an orchid flower.

Column foot: An extension at the base of the column in some orchids, to which the lip is attached.

Concaved: Curved like the inner surface of a sphere.

Conduplicate: Folded together lengthwise, like the two valves of a pea pod.

Conical: Cone-shaped; widest at the base and tapering to the tip.

Connate: Like parts fused together.

Cordate: Heart-shaped.

Corm: A swollen stem, usually underground and used for storage.

Crassulacean acid metabolism: A process abbreviated CAM; this water-saving mechanism allows many orchids and other plants native to arid habitats to absorb CO_2 at night for reprocessing to sugar by means of photosynthesis the following day.

Corolla: The collective term for all of the petals in a flower.

Corymb: : A type of spreading inflorescence in which each flower stem originates from a different point on the main stem producing a flat-topped flower cluster.

Cucullate: Having the shape of a hood or cowl; hooded.

Cultivar: A horticultural strain or clone that is sufficiently distinct and desirable to be given a special name.

Cuneate: Wedge-shaped as for a leaf base with gradually tapering sides.

Cymbiform: Boat-shaped.

Deciduous: Refers to the clean and synchronized shedding of appendages, especially foliage, at specified times during the year, usually near the beginning of the dry season for the deciduous tropical orchids.

Decurrent: Running down, as when parts of leaves extend down stems below their points of insertion on those stems.

Decurved: Bent down or curved downward.

Deltoid: Refers to an organ, such as the blade of a leaf, with a triangular shape.

Denticulate: Having minutely tooth-like margins that are usually sharp and coarse.

Desiccate: To dry out thoroughly.

Diandrous: Having two anthers.

Digitate: Having finger-like segments.

Dimorphic: Occurring in two forms such as the unisexual flowers of some orchids.

Disc: The center area of an orchid lip, often adorned with callus or keels.

Distichous: Arranged in two ranks or rows on opposite side of an axis, as in leaf arrangement.

Dorsal: Pertaining to the back or the uppermost sepal that is opposite the lip when applied to the orchid flower.

Double citation: The presence of two names at the end of a taxon; the first name, which is in parentheses, identifies the author who named the plant originally. The second name identifies the author of the new name.

Downy: Having a dense cover of soft hairs.

Drought-avoidance: What a plant accomplishes when it sheds its leaves, or in some other way avoids injurious desiccation during prolonged dry weather (dry season).

Drought-deciduous: A condition conducive to drought-avoidance whereby certain plants native to habitats that regularly experience dry seasons avoid desiccation by shedding their foliage.

Drought-tolerance: What a plant accomplishes when it continues to conduct photosynthesis during prolonged dry weather. Xerophytes of this type require substantial capacity to store water and additional structural and physiological adaptations to perform in this manner (see crassulacean acid metabolism and the introductory chapter).

Elongate: Having a long or drawn-out part.

Emarginate: With an indentation, usually at the apex.

Endemic: An adjective applied to a plant only where it occurs naturally. Opposite of exotic and alien plant.

Endodermis: A barrier tissue comprising a single layer of cells located just outside the vascular center (stele) of a root. Passage cells present in this tissue allow nutrients and water to enter the stele prior to loading into the vascular tissues (see the introductory chapter).

Endosperm: A special nutritive tissue formed by the fusion of a sperm and two more haploid nuclei that is present in most seeds at some point during their development. Orchid seeds and those of some species in other plant families lack endosperm (see the introductory chapter).

Entire: Without notches or indentations.

Ephemeral: An adjective applied to an organism, or a part thereof, that has a short life, only a few hours in the case of some orchid flowers.

Epichile: The tip or terminal section of a complex shape, often referred to as the last segment of a lip that is distinctly different from the form of the basal segments.

Epi-parasite: A plant that acts as a parasite on another plant by means of a fungus. Some of the food extracted by the fungus from the roots of the ultimate host is acquired by the epi-paraste; a condition that applies to at least some of the achlorophyllous orchids.

Epiphyte: A plant that grows on another larger plant but does not parasitize that plant.

Epi-saprophyte: A plant that subsists on nutrients derived from dead organic matter, those nutrients first being acquired by a saprophytic fungus. The epi-saprophytic plant, in effect, parasitizes the saprophytic fungus. This condition probably describes the way in which the orchids routinely use fungi to germinate, i.e., how they effect symbiotic germination.

Equitant: Referring to leaves on a shoot that overlap, forming two, tight ranks as is characteristic of the genus Iris.

Erect: Upright or vertical.

ex: Latin preposition meaning from or out of. The connective term used when one publishes a name first used (but is not published) by another person, such as Lindley *ex* Jones.

Exodermis: A barrier tissue consisting of a single-layer of cells located immediately beneath the velamen layer in the roots of most orchids and some members of other families. Only the passage cells present here allow water and nutrients to pass from the velamen into the root core (see the introductory chapter).

Falcate: Sickle-shaped.

Family: In taxonomy – a taxon positioned just above the tribe in the Linnaean system of classification.

Fetid: Disagreeable odor.

Filament: Part of a stamen, the male part of a flower.

Filiform: Thread-like, long slender and round in cross section.

Filius (f.): The Latin word meaning the son of; the standard abbreviation used in botany is "f."

Fimbriate: Having a fringe of long hairs.

Flabellate: Fan-shaped.

Flexuose: Being bent alternately in opposite directions.

Flora: All of the plants native to a given region or country. Also a book containing descriptions of plants from such an area.

Forma (f.): The taxon ranked below variety; the narrowest of the Linnaean taxonomic ranks; members exhibit most of the characteristics of the species, but differ in some conspicuous way such as flower or leaf color, or size of the mature plant. The notation forma is added after the specific binomial and is preceded by an "f."

Fringed: Having a finely dissected border or margin (ciliate).

Fusiform: Spindle-shaped, rounded and tapering from the middle toward each end.

Galeate: Helmet-shaped.

Genera: The plural form of genus.

Genus: A single species or a group of closely related species that collectively constitute the taxon ranked immediately above the species and below tribe in the Linnaean system of classification.

Glabrous: Hairless or smooth.

Glaucous: Covered with a coat of whitish wax.

Globose: Having a round or globe-shape.

Grex: The offspring of multiple crosses involving the same set of parents that assures they display variation reflecting their similar, but not identical, genotypes.

Gynandrium: An organ containing the male and female portions of the orchid flower, also called the column.

Gynostemium: See column.

Hair: A small, often filamentous outgrowth from the surface of a plant that is also known as a trichome.

Hastate: Shaped like an arrowhead, but with the basal lobes pointing outward nearly at right angles.

Hermaphrodite: Describes individual flowers and whole plants equipped with functional male and female organs.

Heteranthous: When an inflorescence emerges from a vegetative shoot that never develops leaves or enlarges to form a pseudobulb.

Heteroblastic: An adjective used to describe a series of organs, often leaves along a shoot, that change form or function through the series.

Heterotype: (adj. holotypic) The single specimen, usually chosen by the author of a newly described species, to represent that new species.

Hispid: Covered with stiff or rough hairs.

Holomycotroph: (often wrongly called saprophyte) A plant deriving its nutrition solely from a mycorrhizal symbiosis, e.g., *Neottia nidus-avis* is a holomycotroph without chlorophyll.

Holotype: The sole specimen chosen by the author or the one specimen designated by the author as the type.

Holotypic: When a species gets a new name, without being included in another taxon (of the same rank). The old name becomes a homotypic synonym of the new name.

Homonym: A scientific name given two or more times to different plants of the same taxonomic rank.

Homotypic: Literally "with the same type." In botanical nomenclature a homotypic synonym comes into being through a nomenclatural act.

Hooded: Describes floral parts that form a hood.

hort: A term used as part of a botanical name to indicate that it is not a properly published binomial but is a name used by gardeners and nurseries. It can stand for three terms: hortus, meaning "garden"; hortorum, meaning "of gardens"; or hortulanorum, meaning "of gardeners." All three are abbreviated hort. and are never capitalized so as to avoid being mistaken for an author's name.

Hybrid: A plant that is the product of a cross between two different strains, subspecies, or species. Hybrids between members of two genera are described as "intergeneric"; continued crossing may result in multigeneric hybrids.

Hyphae: Filament-like structures that comprise the body of a fungus. They consist of elongated individual cells or collections of serially linked cells.

Hypochile: The basal section of complex shape, often referred to as a segment of a lip.

Imbricate: Overlapping, like shingles on a roof.

Incurved: To bend into an inward curve.

Indigenous: Where an organism occurs naturally.

Inflorescence: That part of a shoot system on which the flowers are born.

Internode: The stem segment located between successive nodes.

Isotype: A specimen so designated because it is similar enough to the holotype to replace it for purposes of taxonomy.

Keel: A longitudinal raised ridge or vein.

Labellum or lip: A highly modified petal of a flower, in orchids often brightly colored and shaped to attract pollinators.

Lamellae: Plate-like structures, appearing in multiples; an arrangement of thin, laterally flattened layers.

Lamina: The blade or the expanded part of the leaf or flower.

Lanceolate: Being lance-shaped, i.e., longer than broad and tapering toward the tip.

Lax: Being loose, flexible or drooping.

Leafless: An adjective employed to describe certain species of *Vanilla* and the achlorophyllous orchids. Unlike the so-called shootless orchids, where the entire vegetative shoot is much condensed, only the leaves of the leafless taxa have been affected in this manner.

Lectotype: A specimen selected from the original material used in naming a taxon, when no holotype was designated or if the holotype is missing.

Linear: Long and narrow with more or less parallel edges.

Linguate: Tongue-shaped.

Lithophyte: A plant that typically grows on stones and rocks rather than in soil.

Litteris (litt.): In correspondence.

Lobe (lobed): In any flattened structure, an extension separated or defined by notches or sinuses.

Lobulate: Having irregular, rounded lobes.

Lobule: A subdivision of a lobe.

Magnoliophyta: The taxonomic Division to which all of the flowering plants belong.

Mentum: A chin-like projection formed by the lateral sepals and the extended foot of the column.

Mesochile: The middle or central section of a complex shape, often referred to as the central segment of a lip that has three distinct parts.

Microsperm: The tiny dust-type seed produced by most orchids and certain parasitic plants that belong to several additional families (see the introductory chapter).

Mixotrophy: A mode of plant nutrition under the broader heading mycotrophy whereby the plant manufactures some of its food through photosynthesis and obtains the rest from a root-dwelling fungus.

Mobile: Refers to a labellum that is loosely hinged at its point of attachment to the rest of the flower, therefore easily moveable.

Monadrous: Having one anther.

Monopodial: An adjective used to describe plants characterized by shoots that exhibit open-ended (indeterminate) growth, as displayed, for example, by *Vanda* and related genera.

Multigeneric: An adjective applied to hybrids generated by parents that belong to three or more different genera.

Mutualism: The label applied to relationships between two physically associated but unrelated organisms whereby both partners benefit from the interaction; a type of symbiosis.

Mycoheterotrophy: A mode of plant nutrition under the broader heading mycotropy whereby the plant lacks capacity for photosynthesis, relying instead on a root-dwelling fungus to compensate for that deficiency.

Mycorrhiza: A symbiosis that involves a root and a root-dwelling fungus. The nature of the interaction between the two participants varies with the example. The orchids act as predators, digesting the intruding hyphae of their fungal associates (see the introductory chapter).

Mycotroph: An organism that obtains nutrients from a fungus, e.g., an achlorophyllous orchid.

Naviculate: Boat-shaped.

nec: Latin conjunction; Neither, nor. This notation is placed between the names of two authors indicating that neither individual named the taxon in a valid manner.

Nectary: Gland that produces nectar; among the orchids is often located at the base of the labellum.

Neotype: A preserved specimen selected to serve as the nomenclatural type when the material used for naming the taxon is missing.

Nerve: A small, simple or unbranched vein found on leaves, bracts, and flower parts.

Nocturnal: Refers to some event or action that occurs at night.

Node: The point at which a leaf or bract is attached to a stem.

Nomenclature: The system or process of naming.

Nomen illegitimate: nomen illegitum, an "illegitimate" name that has not been validly published according to the International Rules of Botanical Nomenclature.

non: Latin, Not.

Nudum: Without a description.

Oblong: Describes a broad object that is longer than wide.

Obtuse: Blunt or rounded at the tip.

Orbicular: Round and flat in shape.

Orchidaceæ: The scientific name for the orchid family.

Orthographic: A different spelling of an existing name usually noted as sphalm. (sphalmate: by mistake)

Ovary: That part of the female apparatus (gynoecium) within a flower in which the seeds will develop from the ovules it encloses following their fertilization, i.e., the chamber in the swollen base of a pistil or in a carpel in the case of the more primitive flowering plants.

Ovate: Egg-shaped, two dimensional with the broader end at the base.

Ovoid: Egg-shaped, three dimensional.

Ovule: An unfertilized seed.

Panduriforum: Lute or fiddle-shaped with a rounded base, narrow waist, rounded upper part and long neck.

Panicle: A type of branched inflorescence (see the introductory chapter).

Papillose: Covered with minute, nipple-shaped protuberances.

Passage cell: A cell of the type that mediates nutrient and water transport, and in this case occurs in the exodermis and endodermis of roots (see the introductory chapter).

Pedicle: The stalk of a single flower.

Peduncle: The main or only stalk of an inflorescence.

Peloric: Having an abnormal flower form in which all of the petals resemble the lip, or the lip assumes a petal-like form rather than the usual two petals and a lip.

Pendulous: Hanging downward.

Perianth: The term applied to the sepals and petals of a single flower (see the introductory chapter).

Petal: One member or part of the inner perianth whorl of a flower's corolla.

Petiole: The stem-like structure that attaches the blade of a leaf to the supporting stem.

Phyllotaxis: Describes the pattern of insertion of leaves along a shoot.

Phylogeny: A system depicting the historical relationships among a group of species.

Pilose: Having a soft covering of hairs.

Pistil: The female apparatus that constitutes the gynoecium of most flowers; it consists of a stigma and style and an ovary in which the seeds will develop.

Plicate: Folded or pleated.

Pneumathode: A water-repellent region in the velamen layer of a root that allows gas exchange to continue while that tissue is engorged with moisture (see the introductory chapter).

Pollinarium: A set of pollinia with associated viscidium and stipe.

Pollinium (Pollinia): A hardened, cohesive mass of pollen grains, characteristic of orchids.

Polynomial: Pre-Linnaean name for species that consisted of three or more words or entire phrases.

Protocorm: The early, structurally undifferentiated stage of an orchid seedling prior to the appearance of its first root and shoot (see the introductory chapter).

Pseudobulb: An aerial, thickened stem, usually functioning as a storage organ; leaves may be attached basally, laterally, or terminally (see the introductory chapter).

Pseudocopulation: A type of animal behavior whereby the males of certain species of insects visit the flowers of certain species of orchids because the flowers of these orchids mimic by color, shape, and sometimes odor, the mates of the visiting insects. Attempts by the males to copulate with the mimetic flowers result in pollination.

Psygmoid: Having leaves arranged in a fan-shape, imbricate, equitant, Iris-like.

Pyriform: Pear-shaped.

Raceme: A type of unbranched inflorescence (see the introductory chapter).

Rachis: The central axis of the flower-bearing part of the inflorescence.

Ramet: The lateral, determinant shoots produced in succession by sympodial orchids and other herbs with similarly modular body plans (see the introductory chapter).

Ramical: The leafy stem of some sympodial epiphytes (such as those in Pleurothallidinæ), which are distinguished from the rhizome.

Ranunculaceous: Referring to a buttercup shape.

Recurved: To curve backward or downward or to become curved backward or downward.

Reed-type: A descriptor for sympodial orchids with long lateral stems of uniform thickness bearing many leaves.

Reniform: Kidney-shaped.

Resupinate: Referring to an orchid flower with the lip lowermost.

Retrorse: Pointing backward and downward.

Rhizomatious: An adjective employed to describe sympodial plants whose ramets are connected by elongate, creeping stems (rhizomes).

Rhizome: A creeping stem usually bearing bracts instead of expanded foliage, located underground or at ground level among terrestrial plants.

Rhizosphere: The space immediately surrounding the tip of a growing root. Diverse microbes flourish here owing to the presence of life-sustaining metabolites that have leaked out of the root.

Rhomboid: Diamond-shaped, an equilateral but not a right-angled parallelogram, with the base and tip having acute angles and the sides having obtuse angles.

Rosette: A cluster of radially arrayed leaves separated by short internodes, usually at ground level or born on a much condensed shoot.

Rostellum: A portion of the stigma that separates the fertile stigma from the anther and often supplies some viscid material that aids in attaching the pollen masses to pollinators.

Rostrum: A beak-like extension.

Rosulate: Having leaves born in rosettes.

Rugose: Wrinkled.

Saccate: Sack or bag shaped.

Saprophyte: A term used to describe orchids that lack chlorophyll, i.e., are achlorophyllous (see the introductory chapter and also epi-parasites and epi-saprophytes).

Scandent: Climbing or vining.

Scape: An inflorescence with a leaf- and bract-less peduncle.

Sepal: One of the outer whorl of flower appendages (the calyx) that covers the flower in bud.

Sepaline: Belonging to a sepal.

Septum (Septa): A dividing wall within any structure, e.g., an orchid fruit.

Sessile: Without a stalk, attached directly to a stem without a separate stalk.

Sheath: Any leaf-like structure that envelopes a developing bud and/or an offshoot (ramet).

Shoot: The usually leafy, aerial portion of a plant distinct from its root system.

Shootless: An adjective employed to describe a group of leafless monopodial orchids characterized by extreme reduction of the vegetative plant to a very truncated structure. In the "shootless" orchids, the residual shoot is necessary for flowering and sexual reproduction.

Sinuses: Deep wavy margins.

Spathe: A sheathing bract or pair of bracts that partly encloses an inflorescence.

Species: The taxonomic rank below genus and above subspecies in the Linnaean system of classification; a population or series of populations whose members can interbreed and that are discontinuous in variation from other populations or series of populations representing other species.

Spike: A type of unbranched inflorescence with sessile flowers (see the introductory chapter).

Spiral: Refers to leaves and/or flowers that are arranged in a spiral on the supporting axis, as in spiral phyllotaxis.

Spotted: Having areas of contrasting color on the sepals, petals, or leaves.

Spur: The tubular extension found on the lips of many orchids that usually contains nectar.

Stamen: The male part of a flower.

Stele: The central, vascularized core of a root or a stem that has not yet produced any secondary tissues, or that lacks the vascular cambium necessary to do so (see the introductory chapter).

Stigma: A pollen-receptive structure that is usually represented by a cavity on the outer region of the column in an orchid flower.

Stilidium: A wing-like appendage on the column.

Stipe: A slender stalk that develops from the column surface and attaches the pollinia to a viscidium.

Stipitate: Being stalk or stake shaped.

Stomata: Adjustable pores in the surface of plants whose diameters are controlled by changes in the shapes of the adjacent epidermal cells. Stomata occur only on shoots, and most densely on leaves (see the introductory chapter).

Striped: Having lines of color on sepals, petals, or leaves.

Sub: Indicates under or below.

Subgenus: A taxonomic rank in the Linnaean system of taxonomy between genus and species

Subsessile: Almost stalkless.

Subspecies (ssp.): The rank below species and above variety in the Linnaean system of taxonomy; a subdivision of a species whose members possess certain characteristics that distinguish them from the other subspecies of that species; a subspecies name is added at the end of the binomial and preceded by "ssp."

Subtended: To insert below, as a bract below a flower.

Symbiotic: Two or more different kinds of organisms living in physical association; the nature of their relationship is not specified.

Sympodial: Describes a type of growth habit characterized by orderly, serial, lateral branching, each resulting module (ramet) growing to a certain size before giving rise by axillary bud development to the next module (see the introductory chapter).

Synonym: Any name(s) other than the valid one applied to the same species.

Syntype: Any one of two or more specimens cited by the author when no holotype was designated, or when two or more holotypes were designated.

Systematics: The science of classification based on the phylogenetic relationships of organisms

Taxa (singular = taxon): If valid, a taxonomic unit that includes all of the species derived from a common ancestral lineage making it monophyletic; a taxon can be a subspecies, species, genus, or higher rank. See clade.

Taxonomy: A classification (of plants in its the botanical application).

Tepal(s): A term applied to perianth members (petals and sepals) when they resemble each other.

Terete: Pencil-like, rounded in cross section.

Terminal: At the tip or apex.

Terrestrial: Growing in the ground, as distinct from the epiphytic and lithophytic habits.

Tessellated: Having a chequered or an evenly netted pattern of color.

Texture: Describing the surface quality of flowers or leaves.

Topotype: A specimen collected later from the original type locality of that species.

Transpiration: The loss of water vapor from a shoot, mostly through open stomata while photosynthesis is occurring.

Tribe: A taxonomic rank in the Linnaean hierarchy of classification used to designate a group of closely related genera.

Trichome: A hair-like or bristle-like outgrowth from the shoot surface; they assume many shapes and function. See hair.

Trilobed: Having three lobes.

Trinomial: A Latin name consisting of three words.

Truncate: Ending abruptly as though cut off.

Tuberculate: Forming a tuber-like appendage.

Tuberoid: A thick underground storage organ.

Twisted: Describes plant parts that are spiraling or corkscrew-like in shape.

Type: See holotype, isotype, lectotype.

Umbel: A type of branched inflorescence characterized by flowers borne on pedicles, all of which arise from the same point at the summit of a single axis (simple umbel) or from multiple points at the summits of as many axes (compound umbel). Uncommon in Orchidaceæ.

Unifoliate: Having only one leaf.

Urceolus: Urn or cup-shaped.

Variety (var.): The taxonomic rank below subspecies but above forma in the Linnaean system of classification; in practice, not always distinguished from subspecies. The variety name is added to the specific binomial and preceded by "var."

Vascular cambium: The cylinder of embryonic (meristematic) tissue located in the stems and roots of woody plants that accounts for their woodiness.

Vernacular: Refers to the standard native language of a country or locality.

Vesiculose: Having blisters, small bladders, or air cavities.

Vestigial leaves: Deep green, sometimes flattened roots, sustain these plants in the absence of normally developed foliage, and they represent the bulk of the vegetative body.

Villose: Bearing a covering of long, soft hairs.

Vine: A plant that trails, clings, or twines and requires a mechanical support to grow vertically.

Viscidium: A sticky pad that is attached to the pollinia (by caudicles or the stipe) and removed with the pollinia by a pollinator; derived from the rostellum.

Whorl: Three or more appendages, usually leaves, attached at the same point on a stem or floral axis.

Winged: Describes an organ bearing a flat projection on one or more sides.

Woolly: Covered with long, soft, and sometimes matted hairs.

Xerophyte: A plant adapted to live where drought is a regular feature of its habitat.

Zygomorphic: Bilaterally symmetrical; usually refers to flower shape.

Thomas Moore *Illustrations of Orchidaceous Plants* plate 1 (1857).

ORCHID GENERA

ILLUSTRATIONS

Each page number provides a list of species names used as illustrations for that page.

Letter: *Aerides lawrenceae*

Page 3: *Aa species, Abaxianthus convexa, Abdominea minimiflora, Aberrantia hirtzii*

Page 4: *Acacallis cyanea, Acampe rigida, Acanthoglossum nervosum, Acanthophippium javanicum*

Page 5: *Aceras anthropophorum, Aceratorchis tschiliensis, Achylydosa grandulosa*

Page 6: *Acianthella elegans, Acianthera saurcoephala, Acianthus fornicatus, Acineta superba, Acinopetala attenuata*

Page 7: *Aclinia incurvum, Acoridium glumaceum, Acostaea costaricensis, Acraea multiflora*

Page 8: *Acriopsis liliifolia, Acrochaene punctata, Acrolophia bolusii, Acronia phalangifera, Acropera galeata*

Page 9: *Acrorchis roseola, Ada aurantiaca, Adamanthus dendrobioides, Adamantinia miltonioides*

Page 10: *Adelopetalum bracteatum, Adeneleuterophora graminifolia, Adenochilus nortonii, Adenoncos parviflora, Adipe racemosa*

Page 11: *Adnula petiolaris, Adrorrhizon purpurascens, Aenhenrya agastyamalayana, Aerangis luteoalba*

Page 12: *Aeranthes grandiflora, Aerides quinquevulnerum, Aeridium ordoratum, Aeridostachya robusta, Aerobion calceolus*

Page 13: *Aetheorhyncha andreetae, Aganisia tricolor, Aggeianthus marchantioides, Aglossorrhyncha jabiensis*

Page 14: *Agrostophyllum species, Alamania punicea, Alaticaulia melanoxantha*

Page 15: *Alatiglossum barbatum, Alatiliparis filicornes, Alipsa foliosa, Cephalanthera longifolia*

Page 16: *Allochilus eberhardtii, Altensteinia citrata, Alvisia tenuis, Alwisia minuta*

Page 17: *Amazauhtli, Amblostoma cernuum, Amblyglottis pulchra, Ambrella longituba*

Page 18: *Ameriorchis rotundifolia, Amesia palustris, Amesiella philippinensis, Amitostigma keiskei*

Page 19: *Amparoa beloglossa, Amphigena leptostachya, Amphiglottis elongatum, Amphorkis ridleya, Amphyglottis veratrifolia, Ampliglossum varicosum*

Page 20: *Anacamptis pyramidalis, Anacheilium cochleatum*

Page 21: *Anaphora liparioides, Anathallis barbulata, Ancipitia eumecocaulon, Ancistrochilus thomsonianus, Ancistrorhynchus nactus, Cypripedium calceolus*

Page 22: *Andimia dielsii, Andinorchis heteroclita, Andreettaea ocellus, Androchilus campestris, Androcorys gracile*

Page 23: *Anettea crispum, Angorkis distichum, Angraecopsis falcatum*

Page 24: *Angraecum eburneum, Anguloa cliftonii, Ania penangiana, Anisopetala calicopis*

Page 25: *Anisopetalon careyanum, Anistylis loeselii, Anneliesia candida, Anochilus inversus*

Page 26: *Anoectochilus geniculatus, Anota gigantea, Ansellia africana, Rhynchostylis retusa*

Page 27: *Anteriorchis coriophora, Anthericlis discolor, Anthogonium gracile*

Page 28: *Anthosiphon roseans, Antilla trichophora, Antillanorchis gundlachii, Anzybas unguiculatus, Aopla reinformis*

Page 29: *Aorchis spathulata, Apaturia senile, Apetalon minutum, Aphyllorchis montana*

Page 30: *Apista tenuis, Aplectrum hyemale, Aplostellis species, Aporopsis johnsoniae, Aporostylis bifolia*

Page 31: *Aporum leonis, Apostasia wallichii, Appendicula polystachya, Appendiculopsis stipulata, Aracamunia liesneri*

Page 32: *Arachnanthe flos-aeris,*

Arachnaria armatissima, Arachnis maingayi, Arachnorchis paludosa

Page 33: *Vanilla planifolia, Archineottia gaudissartii, Archivea kewensis, Areldia dressleri, Arethusa bulbosa*

Page 34: *Argyrorchis javanica, Arhynchium labrosum, Arietinum americanum*

Page 35: *Arisanorchis takeoi, Aristotelea spiralis, Armodorum sulingi, Arnottia mauritiana, Arpophyllum giganteum*

Page 36: *Arthrochilum palustre, Arthrochilus irritabilis, Artorima erubescens, Arthrosia purpureoviolacea, Arundina graminifolia*

Page 37: *Asarca glandulifera, Ascidieria longifolia, Ascocentropsis pusilla, Ascocentrum miniatum, Ascochilopsis myosurus, Ascochilus simondii*

Page 38: *Ascoglossum calopterum, Ascolabium pumilum, Ascotainia penangiana, Aspasia epidendroides*

Page 39: *Aspidogyne confusa, Ate virens, Atopoglossum excentrica, Auliza falcata, Aulosepalum hemichrea*

Page 40: *Aulostylis papuana, Aurinocidium pulvinatum, Australorchis monophylla, Aviceps pumila*

Letter: *Bulbophyllum falcatum*

Page 41: *Baptistonia echinata, Barbosella gardneri, Barkeria spectabilis*

Page 42: *Barlaea calcarata, Barlia longibracteata, Barombia gracillima, Barombiella schiebenii, Bartholina burmanniana*

Page 43: *Liparis rheedi, Basiphyllaea hamiltoniana, Baskervillea machupicchuensis, Batemannia colleyi*

Page 44: *Beadlea elata, Beclardia macrostachya, Nervilia bicarinata*

Page 45: *Geodorum densiflorum,*

Beloglottis costaricensis, Benthamia bathieana, Benzingia hirtzii, Bertauxia vaupelliim Bhutanthera albomarginata

Page 46: *Bicchia albida, Bieneria boliviana, Biermannia laciniata*

Page 47: *Bifrenaria aurantiaca, Bilabrella macrostele, Binotia brasiliensis, Bipinnula canisii, Birchea teretifolia*

Page 48: *Rhynchostylis retusa, Blephariglottis albiflora, Blepharochilum purpurascens, Bletia jucunda*

Page 49: *Bletilla striata, Blumeorchis crochetii, Bogoria raciborskii, Bolbidium pachyphyllum*

Page 50: *Bolbophylaria bracteolata, Bolbophyllopsis morphologorum, Bolborchis crociformis, Bollea lawrenceana, Bolusiella maudiae, Bonatea speciosa*

Page 51: *Bonniera corrugata, Bothriochilus bellus, Bouletia finetianum, Braasiella arizajulana*

Page 52: *Brachionidium valerioi, Brachtia andina, Brachycorythis puabescens, Brachypeza hookeriana*

Page 53: *Brachystele bracteosa, Bracisepalum selebicum, Braemia vittata, Orchis ustulata, Brasilaelia crispa, Brasilidium crispum*

Page 54: *Brasiliorchis picta, Brasilocycnis breviloba, Brassavola cuspidata, Brassia lawrenceana*

Page 55: *Brenesia uncinata, Brevilogium globuliferum, Breigeria cernua, Bromheadia palustris, Broughtonia sanguinea*

Page 56: *Brownleea coerulea, Bryobium hyacinthgoides, Buccella nidifica, Bucculina aspera*

Page 57: *Buchtienia ecuadorensis, Buesiella pusilla, Bulbophyllum lobbii, Bulleyia yunnanensis*

Page 58: *Bunochilus smaragdynus, Burlingtonia refracta, Burnettia cuneata, Burnsbaloghia diaphana, Byrsella coriacea*

Colored Plates

 *Thanks*
*are due to the following people and institutions
for the use of their photos and/or illustrations*

Thee Ballmer • Wolfgang H. Bandisch • Cathy Banjorah
Dalton H. Baptista • Dale Borders • Pieter C. Brouwer • Justin Brown
Eric Christenson
Stig Dalström • Danny Delsaert and Van-My Tran • Ed deVogel • Cal Dodson • Robert & Kerry Dressler
Nik Fahmi • Eladio M. Fernandez
Lourens Grobler
Harvard University • Stanley Hendrawidjaja
Wesley Higgins • Alexander Hirtz
History of Science Collections, University of Oklahoma Libraries • Eric Hunt
David Kuehn
Julio A. Larramendi • Carl A. Luer
Roland Jiménez Machorro • Margaret Mee Amazon Trust • Hiroshi Nakayama
Henry F. Oakeley • Peter O'Byrne • Kentaro Osada • Lynn O'Shaughnessy
Olaf Pronk • Franco Pupulin
Reiner Richter • Gustavo A. Romero-González • Royal Botanical Gardens, Kew
André Schuiteman • Gunnar Seidenfaden Trust • Marie Selby Botanical Gardens
Karlheinz Senghas • Peter Smart • Prem Subrahmanyam
Swiss Orchid Foundation at the Herbarium Jany Renz • Dariusz Szlachetko
University of Florida
Jaap J. Vermeulen
William M. Whitten • Bart Wursten

Haeckel *Kunstformen der Natur* plate 74 (1899).

ORCHID GENERA

F E E D B A C K

The Orchid Identification Center at the Marie Selby Botanical Gardens
requests feedback from the readers of this dictionary.
Please contact us if you find errors or omissions in the dictionary.
Additionally, we request to be notified of new orchid generic names that are published
for inclusion in future editions of this dictionary.
Please send your feedback to:

Orchid Identification Center

Marie Selby Botanical Gardens
811 South Palm Avenue
Sarasota, Florida 34236

Telephone: 941-366-5731, ext. 315
Fax: 941-951-1474

sbgpress@selby.org

Submissions need to include:

1. Copy of the publication title page
(showing the book's title, author, and year of publication and volume number if needed).
2. Copy of the page(s) where the new genus or orthographic variant occurred.
3. These can be submitted by mail to the above address or sent as PDF files by e-mail to: sbgpress@selby.org.
4. Please include your name, address, and phone number in case there is need for further inquiries.

Thanks for your help and feedback.

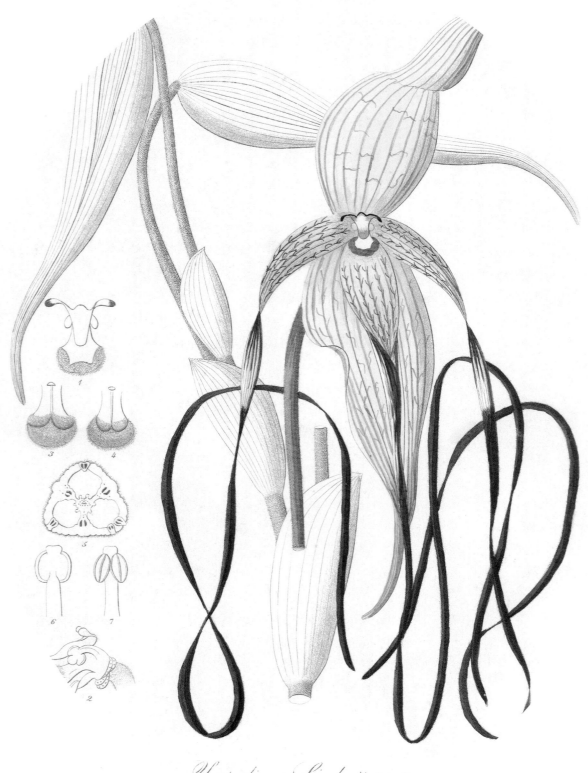

Uropedium Lindenii Lindl.

Reichenbach f. *Xenia Orchidacea* **1**: plate 15 (1858).